WEST ACADEMIC PUBLISHING'S LAW SCHOOL ADVISORY BOARD

SECURED TRANSACTIONS

TEACHING MATERIALS

Fifth Edition

■ ■ ■

James J. White

Robert A. Sullivan Professor Emeritus of Law
University of Michigan Law School

G. Eric Brunstad Jr.

Visiting Lecturer In Law
Yale Law School
Professor (Adjunct) of Law
New York University School of Law and
Partner, Dechert LLP

Heather Hughes

Professor of Law
American University
Washington College of Law

AMERICAN CASEBOOK SERIES®

WEST ACADEMIC PUBLISHING

444 Cedar Street, Suite 700
St. Paul, MN 55101
1-877-888-1330

Printed in the United States of America

ISBN: 978-1-64242-232-0

ACKNOWLEDGMENTS

We wish to thank Brendan Cottington (Yale '13), Noelle Lyle (Yale '12), and Laura Cole (Yale '12) for their research assistance. We also wish to thank Janis Horning for her secretarial support.

FOREWORD

Teaching the rules of Article 9 is only one of the purposes of this book. The student should regard this book and any course in which it is used as an opportunity to examine the economic and commercial reasons for many of the practices that underlie Article 9. This is also an opportunity to learn the nomenclature of secured credit and commercial law. At the end of this course the student should understand the terms "nonrecourse loans," "securitization," "cramdown," and a variety of others that are the everyday fare of commercial lawyers. The student should also have an idea why one might make a recourse as opposed to a nonrecourse loan. Finally, the book introduces the student to some of the forms that are used in secured transactions.

Like the earlier editions, this edition is organized by transactions (Security in Equipment, Security in Inventory, etc.) not by Article 9 events (scope, attachment, perfection). We believe this facilitates learning about the underlying transactions. It also enables the teacher to lead the student into the shallow end of the pool by first dealing with a relatively simple transaction—the security interest in equipment.

In this edition we have revised, updated, and expanded all of the previous chapters; moved the discussion of the history of secured transactions to a new Chapter 9; and moved the chapter on the theory of secured transactions to a new Chapter 10. As in prior editions the book includes significant discussion of bankruptcy law (Chapter 3), focusing on how security interests are treated in business and consumer bankruptcy cases. The course will not substitute for a full-fledged bankruptcy course, but it gives much more than an introduction to bankruptcy.

The book is designed to be used in teaching a basic course on Article 9. One of us (Brunstad) also uses it to teach a seminar on the history and theory secured transactions, as well as an experiential course on negotiating secured transactions.

Have fun.

JAMES J. WHITE
ANN ARBOR, 2020

G. ERIC BRUNSTAD, JR.
NEW HAVEN, 2020

HEATHER HUGHES
WASHINGTON, DC, 2020

SUMMARY OF CONTENTS

TABLE OF CONTENTS

TABLE OF CASES

The principal cases are in bold type.

SECURED TRANSACTIONS
TEACHING MATERIALS

Fifth Edition

CHAPTER 1

INTRODUCTION TO THE STUDY OF SECURED TRANSACTIONS AND SOME THOUGHTS ON HOW TO INTERPRET ARTICLE 9

■ ■ ■

§ 1. INTRODUCTION

This chapter provides some introductory remarks on the study of secured transactions under Article 9. Why study this particular area of the law? Apart from the fact that secured transactions involve literally trillions of dollars' worth of financings, there are at least three reasons. First, much of the doctrinal landscape covered in this book will be vitally useful to those engaged in the practice of commercial law. Among other things, the study of Article 9 offers an excellent opportunity to expand one's commercial law vocabulary, and, along the way, examine a diverse variety of transaction structures. Second, Article 9 is a complex commercial code, and studying its provisions offers the student a good opportunity to work with complex statutory materials. Third, Article 9 is conceptually rich. It encompasses the most complex and diverse collection of property rights concepts within our legal system—the metaphorical equivalent of a vast conceptual zoo. Mastering the relationship between these concepts and how they work together is a good exercise in legal comprehension. In order to begin accessing the logic and complexity of Article 9 in a systematic and productive way, however, it is first useful to introduce and explain a few basic definitional concepts.

Article 9 applies to "a transaction, regardless of its form, that creates a security interest in personal property . . . ."[1] Two ideas are central to the quoted provision, namely the concepts of a "security interest" and "personal property." Focusing first on the phrase "personal property," a reader will likely infer that, by implication, Article 9 does not apply to real property mortgage transactions (for example, financing transactions involving real estate as collateral). That inference is not entirely accurate, but for present purposes a defining aspect of Article 9 is that, as a general matter, it applies to transactions involving items of tangible personal property, such as equipment, inventory, and consumer goods, and a variety of less

[1] UCC § 9–109(a)(1) (2010).

physically tangible assets, including accounts, instruments, and certain causes of action.

In turn, the basic idea of an Article 9 "security interest" is relatively simple: it is an encumbrance (sometimes referred to as a "lien") on personal property designed to secure the performance of an obligation, typically the payment of a debt. For example, suppose an individual (the "debtor") owns a valuable piece of equipment (the "collateral," such as, say, a machine worth $1 million) and wishes to borrow money from a bank (the "creditor"). To induce the bank to make the loan, the debtor may offer to secure his payment obligation by granting the bank a lien on the machine (or, more likely, the bank will require the lien or similar security as a condition of making the loan). In the event the debtor fails to perform his payment obligation, the lien enables the bank to take possession of the machine and, in most instances, sell it, using the proceeds from the sale to satisfy the debtor's obligation in whole or in part (we call a creditor with such lien rights in the debtor's personal property a "secured creditor" or a "secured party").

Note that each of the terms "debtor," "collateral," and "secured party" are defined in Article 9. *See* 9–102(a)(12), 9–102(a)(28), 9–102(a)(73). The term "collateral" is defined to mean "the property subject to a security interest . . . ." The term "secured party" is defined to mean "a person in whose favor a security interest is created or provided for under a security agreement . . . ." Both of these definitions are intuitive. Not so, however, with the definition of "debtor." In plain English, the term "debtor" typically refers to someone who owes a debt. Under Article 9, however, the person who owes the debt secured by the security interest in the collateral is the "obligor." *See* 9–102(a)(59). The term "debtor" is defined to mean the "person having an interest . . . in the collateral whether or not the person is an obligor . . . ." In other words, the debtor is characteristically the person who owns the collateral. In many cases, of course, the debtor will also be an obligor—he will both owe the relevant debt and own the collateral securing its payment. But Article 9 separates these two concepts to accommodate the possibility that the person who owns the collateral in question (the "debtor") may *not* be an "obligor," but nonetheless may have encumbered the collateral in question to secure a debt (or other obligation) owed by another person. *See* 9–102 cmt. 2(a).

Notice several common aspects and implications of the hypothetical transactional structure outlined above. First, the debtor will likely (although not always) retain possession of the machine while repaying the loan; the secured lender will seek to take possession and dispose of the collateral only in the event the debtor fails to perform his obligations to the secured party ("defaults"). We call a security interest of this type "non-possessory" in nature because the transacting parties do not contemplate that the secured creditor will take possession of the collateral prior to the debtor's default. Conversely, a security interest is "possessory" in nature if, prior to default, the secured party does take possession of the collateral.

Second, the structure involves a private contractual agreement between the debtor and the creditor granting the creditor a security interest in the collateral in question (the "security agreement"). Logically, the secured creditor would want its agreement with the debtor to be enforceable against third parties who may also have or acquire interests in the same collateral. Specifically, in the event the debtor defaults, the creditor would want to be able to enforce its lien against the collateral ahead of the claims and interests of these third parties, who might seek to enforce their interests in, or satisfy their claims from, the same property. We call this a question of "priority."

Third, it would be helpful for third parties to have some way of learning of the security arrangement between the debtor and the secured creditor. From the perspective of third parties, enforceable security interests entitled to priority ahead of their claims or interests have the effect of "fencing off" a portion of the debtor's property for the benefit of the secured party. It should come as no surprise, then, that other creditors might want to know about the existence of an enforceable security interest when they evaluate, for example, whether they should extend credit to the debtor. Likewise, a buyer of the collateral would also like to know about the existence of the security interest before it purchases the property. We call this a question of "notice."

Many other considerations come into play in the grant and enforcement of security interests, but these basic matters—possession, priority, and notice—are particularly useful to have in mind at the outset. Similarly useful is some additional consideration of the practical benefits of taking a security interest, in particular how it may assist the secured creditor in obtaining satisfaction of any right to payment the creditor may have. In order to comprehend these benefits, it is useful to contrast "secured" and "unsecured" forms of debt in further detail.

Suppose a debtor wishes to borrow money from a creditor. It is certainly possible for the creditor to lend without taking any collateral as security. Transactions of this type, called "unsecured" transactions, happen all the time. Think of most forms of credit card debt or the typical obligation to pay a doctor's bill. In general, if the debtor defaults and fails to pay the debt to the unsecured creditor, the creditor may sue the debtor in court for the unpaid balance. After obtaining a judgment, the creditor may seek to collect the unpaid amount using whatever legal methods are available in the debtor's jurisdiction (typically by obtaining a writ of execution from a court and enlisting the sheriff or other designated local official to levy execution on the debtor's property). This process has certain disadvantages and risks, however. It can be slow and expensive. Moreover, the creditor may end up with a worthless judgment. For example, the debtor may have dissipated his assets or absconded during the time it takes to obtain the judgment and seek execution.

Alternatively, the creditor might agree to lend on the condition that the debtor assure payment by offering something more than a mere promise of performance—for instance, by granting the creditor an interest in the debtor's property in the form of a lien of some kind. This kind of "secured" debt also arises all the time. Think of most forms of automobile finance lending in which the creditor takes a lien on the vehicle to secure payment of the amount the debtor has borrowed to purchase it. In the event the debtor defaults, the creditor may look more readily to its lien interest in order to satisfy the debt. As an historical matter, this idea first emerged as the "pledge," the simplest form of secured transaction. A pledge occurs when a debtor secures his performance of an obligation by placing one or more items of his property in the possession of the creditor. The obligation is said to be "secured" because the debtor agrees that if he defaults on the obligation the creditor is entitled to keep or dispose of the property in order to satisfy in whole or in part the damage done by the debtor's breach. Although Article 9 does not make use of the term "pledge," the idea behind the pledge—granting the creditor an interest in a particular item of the debtor's property to secure the performance of some obligation—remains conceptually foundational.

The pledge has several advantages. First, because the creditor retains physical possession of the collateral until the debtor fully satisfies his obligation, the creditor may (in most cases) quickly and easily dispose of the collateral in the event of default. The creditor may thus obtain recovery more promptly than is typically possible in an unsecured transaction if the debtor does not voluntarily satisfy the debt. Second, because the creditor has physical possession of the collateral, the creditor can generally rest assured that the collateral will be available to satisfy the debt in the event of the debtor's default.

In addition, consider how the pledge affects or potentially affects the resolution of the questions of possession, priority, and notice. By definition, possession is with the secured creditor. In turn, the secured creditor's possession evinces the creditor's special interest in the collateral to the exclusion of others, and hence with priority over them. (Why else would the creditor rather than the debtor have possession?) Finally, the secured creditor's possession and the debtor's corresponding lack of possession serve as at least a crude form of notice of the creditor's interest—at least enough to make other creditors suspicious if the debtor is less than candid or forthcoming about the state of his assets and financial affairs. (Again, why else would the creditor have possession other than to prevent the debtor from disposing of the asset freely?)

One stunning disadvantage, however, makes the pledge dramatically infeasible in most instances. By handing over possession of a valuable asset to the secured party, the debtor typically loses the ability to make use of the collateral until he satisfies his obligation to the creditor. For example, suppose the debtor owns a valuable piece of farming equipment that he needs to operate his farm. Allowing the creditor to possess the equipment in order to secure a loan would be counterproductive, at least to the extent the farmer wishes to continue his farming operations. Instead, from the debtor's perspective, a superior form of security would be non-possessory: the debtor grants a security interest but keeps possession of the collateral unless and until the debtor defaults. That way the debtor may continue to use the collateral for the duration of the transaction.

To avoid this shortcoming of the pledge (as well as others), creditors and debtors long experimented with a variety of non-possessory security devices. Although non-possessory security interests have taken many forms, they have all sought to strike the same balance between giving the creditor the functional equivalent of a pledge and permitting the debtor to retain possession of—and thus to continue to use—the collateral. Consider, however, that when the debtor retains possession of the collateral, the secured creditor's interest, without more, is often difficult for others to detect. This creates certain "notice" and other problems that legislators, courts, and practitioners have grappled with for centuries in reviewing, designing, and regulating secured transactions. The current procedures of Article 9 represent the culmination of their work.

Historically speaking, the problem of the "secret lien" was one of the most significant "notice" issues affecting non-possessory security interests. Suppose a debtor grants a security interest to a secured creditor by means of a private contract but retains possession of the collateral. Absent some means of supplying notice to third parties, the security interest effectively remains a "secret" between the debtor and the secured creditor. The existence of an enforceable but secret lien poses a substantial risk for at least two groups.

First, potential buyers of the collateral are at risk because they may assume that the debtor with possession of the collateral has the right to sell the property and deliver clear title. If the debtor does not disclose the existence of the security interest, the buyer may pay the debtor and take delivery unaware of the secured creditor's interest. Thereafter, if the debtor neglects to pay the secured creditor, the creditor may come calling to enforce its security interest in the property, now in the hands of the buyer. In that event, the law would be left to sort out a troubling question of priority: which of the two parties—the secured lender or the buyer—is entitled to the property ahead of the other?

Second, other creditors are at risk in evaluating whether to extend credit to the debtor. They may wrongly assume that the debtor with possession of the collateral owns free and clear a valuable asset to which they might look for satisfaction of their claims in the event the debtor fails to perform his obligations to them. If the debtor does not disclose the existence of the security interest, these creditors may extend credit to the debtor unaware of the secured creditor's interest. Once again, if the debtor fails to pay the secured creditor, the secured creditor may attempt to enforce its security interest in the property, leaving the unsecured creditors high and dry.

A variant of this problem occurs when a debtor grants a security interest to two secured parties and the second secured party is unaware of the first security interest. If the debtor neglects to pay the secured parties, they may both seek to satisfy their claims from the same item of collateral. The law would again be left with the troubling task of determining which of the two parties—the first or the second secured creditor—is entitled to the property ahead of the other.

One can imagine a host of different solutions to these problems. To begin with, the law might simply ban non-possessory security interests. Alternatively, the law might allow them but require some form of disclosure of their existence. In turn, the law might resolve conflicting claims to the same collateral based on who received notice and in what way. Roman law recognized security interests and attempted to address the secret lien problem by penalizing the debtor for nondisclosure. Early Germanic law prohibited non-possessory security interests. Following the collapse of the Roman Empire, England initially adopted the Germanic ban. The ban did not endure, however: over time, English debtors and creditors experimented with a variety of non-possessory security devices. Although courts initially refused to enforce many of these devices, some survived judicial scrutiny. Legislative initiatives and the advent of bankruptcy law further complicated the picture. Bankruptcy law was inherently hostile to security devices, which by their very nature defeat bankruptcy law's core equitable concept of equality of distribution among the debtor's creditors. By the nineteenth century, the law recognized numerous security interests, the uses of which varied according to the type of transaction. At the same time, although bankruptcy law came to accept the secured creditor's priority, this recognition was freighted with exceptions. The result was a complicated and confusing body of law and practice. In the United States, this confusion led legislatures to promulgate assorted reforms aimed at rationalizing aspects of the relevant legal landscape. The reforms culminated in Article 9, which streamlined and replaced the miscellaneous state laws governing the taking and enforcement of security interests in personal property.

The history of secured transactions is thus the history of an evolving set of concepts and procedures. In the United States, it is also largely the history of state law. With the significant exception of federal bankruptcy law, federal intervention has been minimal. In general, bankruptcy law currently respects the priority of a secured creditor's security interest, but only if the security interest was taken in accordance with state law. In addition, bankruptcy law may permit the revision of a secured party's security interest and rights under certain conditions. It certainly affects, and in some instances nullifies, the secured party's ability to exercise its rights against its collateral for the duration of the bankruptcy proceeding.

The intersection of Article 9 and current federal bankruptcy law is discussed separately in Chapter 3. The history of secured transactions is treated in greater detail in Chapter 9. In Chapter 2, we begin our study of the details of Article 9 by considering the basic mechanics of how security interests are granted, noticed, prioritized, and enforced in the context of the simplest type of secured loan: equipment financing. Before doing so, however, it is useful first to offer some thoughts on how to go about interpreting the provisions of Article 9, particularly its official commentary, as a comprehensive statutory enactment.

§ 2. THE INTERPRETATION OF ARTICLE NINE

As the reader will soon see in the subsequent chapters, Article 9 is hardly a paragon of clarity. Rather than being written in plain language, it is structured and presented in the manner of a complex commercial loan document and uses language only experienced commercial finance lawyers could even begin to love. Among other oddities, the text makes use of a large number of defined terms that (rather unhelpfully) are not all collected centrally in a single section. Some definitions of terms used commonly in Article 9 are set forth in section 9–102, some in section 1–201, some in individual sections scattered about Articles 1 and 9, and some are set out in the comments, *see, e.g.*, 9–611 cmt. 9 (providing that the term "recognized market" as used in section 9–611 means "one in which the items sold are fungible and prices are not subject to individual negotiation.") In addition, many provisions are opaque and convoluted, if not downright obscure.

With such challenging draftsmanship to manage, how should one go about interpreting the provisions of Article 9? Here a disclaimer is in order. This short discussion is not a substitute for a comprehensive course on legislation, in which the student becomes systematically immersed in such things as the various theories of statutory interpretation, different judicial approaches to interpretive methodology, the canons of construction, and various theories of the legislative process. Instead, the ambition here is much more modest. It aims to provide a taste of several different interpretive approaches relevant to the subject matter, and focuses on one item of particular importance: use of the official commentary to illustrate the meaning of Article 9's provisions.

For centuries, jurists, lawyers, legislators, and academics have tussled over the proper way to interpret statutory text. In general, there are at least three basic approaches in current use: "textualism" (sometimes referred to as "new textualism"); "purposivism" (sometimes referred to as "intentionalism"); and "eclecticism" (sometimes referred to as "pragmatism"). Textualism stresses the importance and primacy of the actual words used in a particular statutory provision, the meaning of which may be illuminated by resort to such aids as the dictionary, common sense, and the canons of construction. If the text is part of a comprehensive code such as Article 9, resort may also be had to other provisions within the same code that shed light on the meaning of the particular text in question—so-called "whole act" considerations. If the words of the text are reasonably clear, inquiry often does not progress much farther than the perceived plain reading. If the words are truly ambiguous, however, good textualists are often willing to consult other potential indicia of the statute's meaning, including such things as the statute's historical origins, its legislative history, its purpose and policy, and the consequences of interpreting the provision one way or the other. On rare occasions, a textualist may feel compelled to ignore what appears to be the plain reading of a statute if, for example, the result is absurd, or the plain meaning is demonstrably at odds with the intention of the drafters. Generally speaking, however, plain meaning controls.

Of course, like beauty, the judgment that a statutory provision is either plain or ambiguous often lies with the beholder, and deciding whether a statute is ambiguous or not may itself be a rather complicated affair. Most statutes embody at least some degree of ambiguity. Running with this observation, purposivism stresses not only the primacy of statutory text, but also consideration of its object and policy. A statute's object and policy may be revealed by such things as its historical origins, its legislative history, and the consequences of interpreting the statute one way or the other. A good purposivist will not impose upon a statute a meaning its words will not reasonably bear. But beyond that, the interpreter has considerable leeway—certainly more than a textualist would often care to endorse.

Eclecticism is more difficult to define. Essentially it is an approach that is neither textualist nor purposivist, but may contain elements of both. In general, it is relatively ad hoc in nature: within reasonable limits, the interpreter uses whatever indicia of meaning are available under the circumstances in whatever proportion seems suitable to the interpreter.

Many jurists are probably best classified as eclectic, though some might not be willing to admit it.

Interpretive philosophy aside, a few additional preliminary points are essential. First, it must be remembered that Article 9 is a species of state law, and thus its interpretation is an exercise in interpreting state, not federal law. As a result, the most relevant rules of construction are not those laid down by the U.S. Supreme Court or its subservient federal tribunals, but by the relevant state courts. Among other things, different state courts have different interpretive traditions. In addition, many states have codified various canons of construction that may be useful (or even mandatory) in the interpretive exercise.

Second, the drafters of Article 9 expected that the official commentary they supplied would not only illuminate the meaning of the official text for practitioners, but would also be used by the courts in interpreting the Code's provisions for the sake of uniformity. Indeed, one of the key goals of the entire Uniform Commercial Code project was to achieve as much uniformity as possible, and certainly the commentary was intended to advance that goal. On the other hand, the commentary may be viewed as akin to a form of legislative history, and under some prevailing interpretative traditions resort to legislative history is not favored. As a result, one may easily imagine how interpretative methodology might advance or interfere with the cause of uniformity by vindicating or disabling one of its most important tools as a resource in the interpretive exercise.

The balance of this chapter is devoted to four subjects. First, it addresses briefly state interpretive traditions. Second, it discusses briefly the use of the canons of construction. Third, it addresses specific perspectives on the use of the official comments. Fourth, it discusses the use of state interpretative methodologies in the federal courts. As it turns out, the relevant traditions and perspectives are themselves far from uniform.

STATE LAW METHODS OF STATUTORY INTERPRETATION

In *The States as Laboratories of Statutory Interpretation: Methodological Consensus and the New Modified Textualism*,[2] Professor Abbe Gluck discusses state efforts to adopt consistent methods and practices of statutory interpretation, at least within their own individual jurisdictions. These efforts generally have two features: legislation directing particular methods, and judicial decisions adopting particular approaches (which may ignore or contradict legislative directives). In particular, she identifies in some states "power struggles" between the courts and the legislatures over "which branch gets to choose" the

---

[2] 119 YALE L.J. 1750 (2010).

framework, leading to questions regarding "the legal status of the methodology itself—whether it is 'law' or something 'less' or 'different.' "[3] This question in turn invites at least two inquiries.

First, there is the question of "methodological *stare decisis*," concerning whether the courts should give "precedential effect to judicial statements about methodology."[4] Gluck observes that methodological *stare decisis* (namely, adherence to a particular method of interpreting statutes across many different cases) "appears to be a common feature of some states' statutory case law."[5] Second, as state legislatures and courts work more consciously to clarify methods of statutory interpretation, the question emerges: who gets to decide what the legal status of methodology is, the legislature or the state's highest court?[6]

In Oregon, for example, the state Supreme Court adopted a particular regime for statutory interpretation in 1993 in *Portland General Electric Co. v. Bureau of Labor and Industries ("PGE")*.[7] *PGE* mandated a three step approach: (1) "the text of the statutory provision itself is the starting point for interpretation," and analysis in the first step may also include contextual inquiry, such as reference to other provisions of the same statute that may shed light on the particular provision in question; (2) "[i]f, but only if, the intent of the legislature is not clear from the text and context inquiry, the court will then move to the second level, which is to consider legislative history"; and (3) if the legislative history does not provide a clear result, "then the court may resort to general maxims of statutory construction to aid in resolving the remaining uncertainty."[8] In 2001, however, the Oregon state legislature enacted a statute purporting to alter the 1993 *PGE* approach by mandating the examination of legislative history as part of the first step. It was not until 2009, in *State v. Gaines*,[9] that the Oregon Supreme Court actually recognized the possibility that the statute might have changed the *PGE* standard, and essentially worked out a compromise: the Court held that "*PGE*'s text-only first step remains the same, but . . . the parties are free to 'proffer' legislative history, and . . . the court will consider it regardless of ambiguity, but only 'where that legislative history appears useful' " although "even clear contradictory evidence of purpose will not trump plain text."[10]

---

[3] *Id.* at 1756–57.

[4] *Id.* at 1754.

[5] *Id.*

[6] *Id.* at 1756–57.

[7] 859 P.2d 1143 (Or. 1993).

[8] *Id.* at 1146.

[9] 206 P.3d 1042 (Or. 2009).

[10] Gluck, *supra* note 2, at 1792.

In both Texas and Connecticut, state legislatures have adopted rules of statutory construction, sparking controversy over whether these rules are binding on the courts within the state. In Texas, for example, a statute provides that courts can consider the purpose of the statute and its legislative history even if the text is unambiguous. Nonetheless, Texas's highest criminal court—the Texas Court of Criminal Appeals—does not look to external sources of a statute's meaning unless the text *is* ambiguous, and the Texas Supreme Court—the state's highest civil court—mostly "include[s] a footnote or sentence" citing the statute "but then still decline[s] to employ extratextual sources absent ambiguity."[11] Given the tension between the statute and its application by the state's highest courts, lower courts in Texas seek "to avoid the conflict by aggressively searching for ambiguity in statutes."[12]

In *State v. Courchesne*,[13] the Connecticut Supreme Court explicitly mandated a "nontextual, eclectic approach in which courts, without the prerequisite of ambiguity," could consider external sources as an aid in statutory interpretation.[14] Within two weeks, however, the Connecticut legislature attempted to overturn this rule by enacting a statute that states "extratextual evidence. . . shall not be considered" if "the meaning of [the statutory] text is plain and does not yield absurd or unworkable results."[15] Nonetheless, in over fifty instances since the passage of the statute, the Connecticut Supreme Court cited *Courchesne* as good law, and will often find the statutory text ambiguous, thus rendering the restriction on extratextual evidence inapplicable.[16]

Finally, Wisconsin and Michigan are examples of states where debate regarding the proper method of statutory interpretation rages within the courts themselves. The Wisconsin Supreme Court adopted a method of statutory interpretation under which the text must be ambiguous before a court can look to external sources, but disputes surround the application of the test. In Michigan, the particular methodology that the Michigan Supreme Court may use in a particular case appears intertwined with politics: the framework that is used appears to vary depending on whether textualists or purposivists control the majority.[17]

As Gluck's analysis reveals, state courts apply a variety of different methods of statutory interpretation that may, or may not, adhere to legislative directives. Because Article 9 is state law, it is easy to imagine how differences in interpretive methodology (particularly between those

11 *Id.* at 1785–90.

12 *Id.* at 1790.

13 816 A.2d 562 (Conn. 2003).

14 Gluck, *supra* note 2, at 1792.

15 Conn. Gen. Stat. Ann. § 1–2z (West 2011).

16 *Id.* at 1792–96.

17 *Id.* at 1799–1811.

that include or exclude resort to the official commentary) could lead to divergent interpretations of the statute, undermining the goal of uniformity. With respect to the official comments accompanying Article 9, any approach that denies consideration of the comments is probably as unhelpful as the comments are illuminating. As we shall see below, courts apply relatively inconsistent approaches in their uses of the commentary. Before getting to the details of that analysis, however, discussion next turns to the canons of construction.

STATE LAW AND THE CANONS OF CONSTRUCTION

What are the canons of construction? For those who have taken a comprehensive course on legislation, terms such as "the *expressio unius* rule" and the "canon of constitutional avoidance" will be familiar. The purpose of this discussion is not to list or review in great detail the substance of the many canons. Rather, the purpose here is simply to identify them loosely and situate them generally in the methodological hierarchy. But first a few introductory remarks are warranted.

The canons are interpretive tools that in some ways work like aphorisms—witty pieces of conventional wisdom that are entirely context bound. For example, you may have heard the expressions "too many cooks spoil the broth," "fools rush in," and "birds of a feather flock together." You may also have heard the expressions "two heads are better than one," "he who hesitates is lost," and "opposites attract." Notice that the second set of aphorisms suggest advice or observations diametrically opposed to the first set. Yet both sets seem true. How can that be? The answer is that the wisdom of each depends entirely on the circumstances. For example, "too many cooks spoil the broth" is apt in describing a disorganized group with individuals working at cross purposes, whereas "two heads are better than one" is apt in describing situations in which multiple persons are able to coordinate their activities in an effective way.

The canons work in a similar fashion. For example, the plain meaning rule applies, except when it doesn't. And it is up to judges to determine when it doesn't, including when a particular statutory text is ambiguous, or application of the plain meaning canon would generate a result that is absurd or demonstrably at odds with the intention of the drafters. Sorting through the circumstances under which the plain meaning rule does not apply is thus a highly contextual exercise. The same applies to all of the other canons.

So how do state courts apply the canons? In particular, do the states have or require the use of some of the canons? Do they have rules governing when courts should resort to legislative history to determine statutory meaning? In his article *Codified Canons and the Common Law of*

Interpretation,[18] Jacob Scott both surveys how state legislatures have codified different canons of statutory construction and assesses "the prevailing interpretive preferences of [state] legislatures across the United States."[19] He concludes that courts (and others) interpreting statutes should not ignore the ways in which legislatures have adopted or rejected the common law canons—particularly the apparent preference that state legislatures have for use of legislative history.

After discussing prevailing interpretive methodologies (textualism, etc.), Scott identifies three basic categories of canons. He explains that, in general, the canons are "a set of background norms and conventions that are widely used by courts when interpreting statutes."[20] He argues that the purpose of utilizing a particular canon is to "legitimize[ ] sources and methods of legal reasoning, all with an eye toward how the legislature would want its intent to be effectuated."[21] Scott's three categories are (1) the "textual canons," (2) the "extrinsic source canons," and (3) the substantive "policy canons," and he addresses the extent to which each have been codified by state legislatures.[22] Because examples of the canons within two of these categories are particularly relevant to the interpretation of Article 9, the discussion here focuses on them.

The textual canons are generally those that embody "linguistic inferences" that purport to "provide guidance about what the legislature likely meant, given its choice of some words and not others."[23] These canons include, among others, the plain meaning rule (namely, advising courts "to follow the plain meaning of language unless the text suggests an absurd result"); the *expressio unius* rule (specifically, the "expression of one thing [in a statute] suggests the exclusion of others"); the *noscitur a sociis* canon (directing that a court should "interpret a general term to be similar to more specific terms in a series"), and the ordinary usage canon (namely, a court should "follow [the] ordinary usage of terms, unless the legislature gives them a specified or technical meaning").[24] Scott finds that "[n]o legislature has expressly codified *expressio unius*, but a few states have implicitly repealed it," while the ordinary usage canon and plain meaning rule are codified in many states.[25]

A second type of textual canon makes use of grammar and syntax to discern statutory meaning. Grammar and syntax canons include "the

---

18 98 GEO. L.J. 341 (2010).

19 *Id.* at 344.

20 *Id.* at 344–46.

21 *Id.* at 346.

22 *Id.* at 352.

23 *Id.* at 353–57.

24 *Id.*

25 *Id.*

punctuation rule" (namely, "interpreters are to presume that legislators intentionally place commas and colons to register their intended meaning"); and the "may/shall" canon (specifically, " 'may' is permissive, while 'shall' is mandatory").[26] The "may/shall" canon has been adopted by many legislatures and repealed by none, while "[t]he codifications related to the punctuation rule are far from straightforward."[27]

A third type of textual canon looks to a statute's context as a method of discerning interpretative meaning. These "textual integrity" canons include the "whole act rule" (specifically, "each statutory provision should be read by reference to [and in light of] the whole act"); and the "inconsistent policy" canon (directing that a court should "avoid interpreting a provision in a way inconsistent with the policy of another provision").[28] Scott reports that the whole act rule "is wildly popular, with thirty states codifying some version of it" and no state "rejecting it," but that "American legislatures have not expressed a view" about the inconsistent policy rule.[29]

The extrinsic source canons are those that guide reference to resources other than the statutory text itself to help illuminate the text's meaning, including a statute's legislative history.[30] While some interpreters believe that extrinsic legislative sources are essentially untrustworthy, where the statutory text is unclear "courts are generally not shy about examining legislative history," and "[e]very state that has addressed extrinsic legislative sources supports their use when the language of the statute is unclear."[31] Examples of these "extrinsic legislative source" canons include the "contemporaneous circumstances" canon (namely, "the circumstances under which a statute was enacted may be considered"); and the "commentary prior to passage" canon (specifically, "official commentary published and available before the enactment or adoption of a statute or rule may be considered").[32]

Scott then analyzes the relationship between the canons of construction (as codified by state legislatures) and prevailing judicial methods of statutory interpretation. He argues that, as a general rule, legislatures "do not forbid consultation of extrinsic sources and values," and in cases of ambiguity, "formally write statutes with their acceptance of external sources as the background."[33] Ultimately, he contends that

---

26 *Id.* at 357–62.

27 *Id.* at 361.

28 *Id.* at 361–71.

29 *Id.* at 364–65.

30 *Id.* at 378–83.

31 *Id.*

32 *Id.*

33 *Id.* at 405–11.

legislatures seek to vindicate "textualism's strengths but not its weaknesses."[34] For example, "they prefer its focus on the written word but not its limited view of what the law is," and, where there is ambiguity, prefer allowing a focus on sources outside the statutory text.[35]

Scott concludes by offering some advice to those who interpret statutes, including a few nuggets relevant to the interpretation of Article 9. He argues that "interpreters [should] evaluate many sources of statutory meaning before settling on the most plausible interpretation."[36] He also contends that, although judges in one state are not bound by the law of foreign jurisdictions, "legislative preferences in this area should not simply be ignored or ruled out of bounds."[37] This supports consideration of uniformity in the interpretative process, which is, after all, a key legislative goal underlying Article 9, and conceivably ought to have its own canon (perhaps the "preference for uniformity of uniform laws" canon).

USE OF THE OFFICIAL COMMENTARY TO ARTICLE 9

In this subsection, we take a look at how courts have actually treated the official comments accompanying Article 9. One preliminary note: although the discussion above has treated the comments as a form of legislative history, that treatment is not precisely accurate. Typically, legislative history consists of committee reports, floor statements by legislators, testimony before legislative bodies, and the like. Obviously, Article 9's official comments are none of those things. Instead, they are a form of legislative history only in the sense that they were intended to explain the statutory text by those responsible for drafting it, as opposed to the commentary and analysis of the actual state legislators responsible for its enactment. Significantly, although all fifty states have enacted Article 9, no state has enacted the comments as an official part of its law. Thus, the comments occupy a somewhat peculiar position.

Nevertheless, and perhaps recognizing the sheer utility of the comments, many courts interpreting the Uniform Commercial Code—both state and federal—rely on them as authoritative without taking a position on whether doing so represents a suspicious use of legislative history. Others, however, profess only to look at the comments when they perceive the text of the Uniform Commercial Code (including Article 9) to be unclear (although one suspects that even strict textualists will at least peek at the comments even if they won't confess to doing so, either to confirm their conclusions or to prompt a revision to avoid embarrassment). This subsection summarizes some of the views of the courts on the subject. Finally, it explores briefly the tensions that may arise when federal courts

34 *Id.*

35 *Id.*

36 *Id.* at 410.

37 *Id.*

interpret Article 9. One federal court in particular—the federal bankruptcy court—routinely interprets the provisions of Article 9. When it does, should it use its own federal method of statutory interpretation, or that of the courts of the particular state whose law it is construing? If one takes the *Erie* doctrine seriously, one might conclude that bankruptcy courts should employ the relevant state court methodology. But what impact might that have on uniformity?

One additional note about method. The decisions cited and summarized below generally refer to Article 9. The analysis, however, might easily be expanded to include other provisions of the Uniform Commercial Code. The reason for this is that each article has official commentary, and the relevant interpretive issues that arise in examining them are essentially the same across the UCC.[38]

Without explicitly stating whether the comments are authoritative, some courts routinely analyze them as an integral part of their method of interpreting Article 9. There are numerous examples of this phenomenon. These include the decisions of two state Supreme Courts in *C&J Vantage Leasing Co. v. Wolfe and Thermal Supply, Inc. v. Big Sky Beef, LLC*,[39] both of which relied on the comments to Article 9 without discussing any particular interpretive philosophy.[40] This practice also occurs frequently in the federal courts.[41]

From a practical perspective, this does not seem particularly troublesome. *Of course* courts will look at the comments. Article 9 is a highly specialized body of law, and its official text is often relatively opaque. The comments are infinitely helpful. From a normative perspective, however, *should* the courts be doing this? Is this consistent with some of the values that are thought to underlie the application of consistent interpretive methodologies—neutrality, consistency, predictability, efficiency, and methodological coherence? What is more important, a coherent judicial philosophy or a coherent, uniformly applied

---

[38] *See, e.g.*, Nat'l Bank of Commerce v. Shelton, 27 So.3d 444, 448 (Miss. Ct. App. 2009) ("While the official comments to the UCC were not adopted by our Legislature, still we look to official comments about uniform laws, when those laws have been adopted all but verbatim by the Legislature, as the most informed source explaining provisions of the original enactment.") (citations and quotation marks omitted); Ticona Polymers, Inc. v. Solutia, Inc., 2008 WL 4162447, at *6 (N.J. Super. Ct. App. Div. Sept. 11, 2008) ("Although the Missouri Legislature did not adopt the official comments to the UCC, the comments have been relied upon to explain the meaning intended by the drafters of article 2 and are useful indicators of the drafters' reasoning.") (citation and quotation marks omitted) (unpublished) (applying Missouri law).

[39] 795 N.W.2d 65 (Iowa 2011) and195 P.3d 1227 (Mont. 2008).

[40] *See also* Karle v. Visser, 118 P.3d 136 (Idaho 2005); Tilghman Hardware, Inc. v. Larrimore, 628 A.2d 215 (Md. 1993); Vt. Indus. Dev. Authority v. Setze, 600 A.2d 302 (Vt.1991).

[41] *See, e.g.*, *In re* Roser, 613 F.3d 1240 (10th Cir. 2010); *In re* Jersey Tractor Trailer Training Inc., 580 F.3d 147 (3d Cir. 2009); *In re* World Auxiliary Power Co., 303 F.3d 1120 (9th Cir. 2002); U.S. Test, Inc. v. NDE Env't Corp., 196 F.3d 1376 (Fed. Cir. 1999); Sony Corp. of Am. v. Bank One, W. Va., Huntington, NA, 85 F.3d 131 (4th Cir. 1996).

commercial code; ideology or getting it right? Of course, one might ask exactly what is meant by "getting it right." Is a coherent judicial philosophy more likely to "get things right" in the long run?

Other courts appear willing to look at the official comments only if the text is unclear—a method generally consistent with textualism. An example is *Interbusiness Bank, N.A. v. First National Bank of Mifflintown*,[42] also involving the construction of Article 9. One of the key issues in the case was whether the collateral listed in the secured creditor's documents had met Article's 9's collateral description requirements, which specify different rules depending on the "type" of collateral at issue. In order to answer this question, the court concluded that it first had to determine what was meant by different collateral "types."[43]

The court explained that judges usually apply a "plain meaning" approach in the interpretation of statutes. Observing, however, that the term "type" could be defined in a number of ways, the court concluded that it needed to look *beyond* the term's mere plain meaning to avoid an undesirable consequence: by potentially defining the phrase too broadly, the court risked eviscerating its intended "restrictive effect."[44] Invoking several canons of construction, the court looked for guidance in other sections of the Code, explaining that "[w]ords draw meaning from those around them, and context sheds light on language otherwise obscured."[45]

The court also supported its analysis by considering the purpose of Article 9. It explained that the inclusion of the particular collateral in question as falling within the scope of the statute was consistent with the relevant purpose of the Code, and rejected an alternative interpretation as inconsistent with that purpose.[46] As a final source of support for its conclusion, the court looked to the comments as evidence of the intent of the Code's drafters, likewise concluding that the intent was to include the collateral in question. In analyzing the comments, the court stated that "[t]his evidence of legislative intent is particularly weighty when the plain meaning of the term provides little interpretive guidance."[47]

Finally, in some cases, courts look to the comments even though the statutory text appears clear and the court has officially indicated that it will examine the comments only if the statutory text is ambiguous.[48] An

---

[42] 318 F. Supp. 2d 230 (M.D. Pa. 2004).

[43] While the Court was analyzing an older version of Article 9, it noted that its result would not likely change under the current version of the statute. *Id.* at 244 n.12.

[44] *Id.* at 241–42.

[45] *Id.* at 242.

[46] *Id.* at 243.

[47] *Id.*

[48] *See, e.g.*, Capitol Nat'l Bank v. Dept. of Treasury, No. 05-000129-MZ, 2008 WL 2745983, at *5, *8 (Mich. Ct. App. July 15, 2008) (unpublished) (stating that the comments can be used when

example is *Davis Forestry Products, Inc. v. DownEast Power Co., LLC.*[49] In *Davis*, two creditors, Davis and DownEast, each claimed certain funds on deposit in the debtor's account at the debtor's bank. DownEast contended that it was entitled to the funds because the deposit account constituted collateral securing a mortgage loan that DownEast held by assignment from another creditor, Prospect. Davis, however, claimed that DownEast and Prospect did not have a valid lien on the deposit account, and, in any event, had never taken the steps necessary to legally "perfect" their security interest (specifically, they had not taken all of the statutory steps necessary to establish the validity of their interest ahead of the claims of attaching creditors like Davis). As a result, Davis argued that *it* was entitled to the funds because it held a judgment against the debtor and a valid lien against the same funds. In order to resolve the dispute, the Court was required to interpret several provisions of Article 9.[50]

The Court first explained that, when interpreting a statute, its "primary purpose" was to "giv[e] effect to the intent of the Legislature," and that, to discern this intent, the Court would "look first to the plain meaning of the statute, and second, *if there is any ambiguity*, to extrinsic sources, such as legislative history."[51] In order to resolve the first issue—whether DownEast had a valid security interest—the Court explained that it needed to determine whether Prospect, DownEast's assignor, held an "enforceable security interest" under section 9–203 of Maine's version of the UCC.[52] Section 9–203 states in relevant part that a

> security interest is enforceable against the debtor and third parties with respect to the collateral only if [certain requirements are satisfied and] . . . [o]ne of the following conditions is met . . . .
>
> (i) The debtor has authenticated a security agreement that provides a description of the collateral . . .;
>
> (ii) . . .
>
> (iii) . . .; or
>
> (iv) The collateral is deposit accounts . . . and the secured party has control . . .[53]

Davis argued that the only way DownEast could have a valid security interest in the debtor's deposit account was if Prospect had complied with subsection (iv) quoted above. In other words, Davis argued that subsection

"the UCC's provisions are ambiguous" but nevertheless looking to the comments for support even without ambiguity).

49 12 A.3d 1180 (Me. 2011).

50 *Id.* at 1183.

51 *Id.* (emphasis supplied) (citation and quotation marks omitted).

52 *Id.* at 1184.

53 *Id.* at 1184 (citing 11 Me. Rev. Stat. § 9–1203).

(iv) was mandatory and exclusive. DownEast contended that it was "merely one alternative listed" and that, by virtue of its written mortgage, Prospect had satisfied subsection (i).[54] Rejecting Davis's argument, the Court explained that "[t]he plain language . . . supports DownEast's interpretation," noting that section 9–203 requires compliance with any one of the four listed methods and that, "[a]s a general rule, the use of a disjunctive ["or"] in a statute indicates alternatives and requires that those alternatives be treated separately."[55]

The Court, however, did not stop with its plain reading of section 9–203. Instead, it went on to analyze the comments accompanying the provision, explaining that they likewise "refer to the four conditions [in the section] as alternative means" of complying with its requirements.[56] Accordingly, it concluded that Prospect had a security interest.

That conclusion, however, did not resolve the controversy. Even though Prospect held a valid security interest, its lien had to be perfected in order to prevail, and the question of perfection is governed by other provisions of Article 9. On this second issue, Davis argued that DownEast had never perfected its interest in the deposit account because DownEast had never taken control of the account as the statute requires.[57] The Court agreed with Davis.[58]

In evaluating whether DownEast had perfected its security interest by taking control, the Court again considered the comments, this time a group of them accompanying multiple sections: 9–610 (governing generally the secured party's right after default to dispose of its collateral); 9–607 (governing the secured party's right to apply the funds in a deposit account that it has perfected by control to the obligation secured by the account); and 9–341 (specifying the depository bank's rights with respect to funds in a deposit account subject to a security interest). Significantly, the Court did so to understand not only the text of Article 9, but also its relevant underlying purpose.[59]

Davis is a good example of the allure of the comments. And if what courts do is more important than what they say, the comments should retain a faithful readership among the judiciary for many years to come.

WHETHER FEDERAL COURTS SHOULD USE STATE OR FEDERAL INTERPRETIVE METHODOLOGIES

In general, when a federal court applies state law, it applies state law as construed by state courts, particularly state Supreme Courts. But what

---

54 *Id.*

55 *Id.* at 1185 (citation and quotation marks omitted).

56 *Id.*

57 *Id.* at 1186–88.

58 *Id.*

59 *Id.* at 1186–88.

about state interpretive methodologies? Are these binding on the federal courts as well? Professor Gluck writes:

> [i]t should be clear—but isn't—whether federal courts interpreting state statutes and state courts interpreting federal statutes are obligated to employ one another's methodology. The answer depends on how 'law-like' methodology is, and, to the extent there is a court-legislature conflict, which branch's chosen methodology, if any, binds the outside world. The *Erie* doctrine looms large here.[60]

So what do federal courts actually do when it comes to the commentary accompanying Article 9? What should they do? Some federal decisions seem to rely on federal principles of statutory interpretation when analyzing the comments.[61] On the other hand, there are numerous examples of federal courts relying explicitly on state methodologies in conducting their analyses.[62] Interestingly, there are also cases in which federal courts seem to apply *both* state and federal principles of statutory construction.[63]

Which approach is more likely to advance uniformity, a consistent federal methodology applicable in all federal courts (assuming that were possible), or federal deference to state methodological preferences? Either way, there is bound to be some disunity. To the extent federal courts adopt a uniform federal method, there will be unity among the federal courts, but disunity between federal and state courts, including federal and state judges sitting within the same state. To the extent federal courts defer to the methodological preferences of the state courts, there will be disunity in

---

[60] Gluck, *supra* note 2, at 1829.

[61] *See, e.g., In re* Peaslee, 547 F.3d 177, 185 (2d Cir. 2008) ("Although the U.C.C. Comments are not 'given binding effect,' they do 'occupy an unusual position as aids to statutory interpretation' and should be regarded as 'an indispensible part of the U.C.C. framework") (citations and quotations omitted) (citing a federal case for support); *In re* Graupner, 537 F.3d 1295, 1301–02 (11th Cir. 2008) (citing federal law regarding interpretation of UCC Comments); McCarthy v. BMW Bank of N. Am., 509 F.3d 528, 530 (C.A.D.C. 2007) ("In interpreting the UCC, this court and other courts have found the Official Comments to the UCC persuasive") (citing federal cases); *In re* Peregrine Ent., Inc., 116 B.R. 194, 198 (C.D. Cal. 1990) (citing federal law for proposition that "although legislative history generally is a poor source of guidance for statutory interpretation, official commentaries are persuasive."); *In re* Trejos, 352 B.R. 249 (Bankr. D. Nev. 2006); *In re* Erwin, 2003 WL 21513158 (Bankr. D. Kan. 2003) (unpublished).

[62] *See, e.g., In re* Pacific/West Comm. Group, Inc., 301 F.3d 1150 (9th Cir. 2002); Williams v. Regency Fin. Corp., 309 F.3d 1045 (8th Cir. 2002); *In re* Clark Contracting Services, Inc., 438 B.R. 913 (W.D. Tex. 2010); *In re* Semcrude, L.P., 407 B.R. 82 (Bankr. D. Del. 2009); *In re* Hayes, 376 B.R. 655 (Bankr. M.D. Tenn. 2007)

[63] *See, e.g., In re* Ford, 574 F.3d 1279, 1289 (10th Cir. 2009) ("Under familiar principles of statutory interpretation, the other items on Comment 3's list shed light on whether negative equity bears the requisite 'close nexus' to the acquisition of a new car") (citing both federal and state cases for support for this proposition); *In re* Buffalo Molded Plastics, Inc., 354 B.R. 731, 742 (Bankr. W.D. Pa. 2006) ("[W]hen interpreting a state statute, the role of the federal courts is to enforce that statute where possible according to its plain terms," but going on to state "in reviewing Pennsylvania statutes there is no need to resort to rules of statutory construction to determine legislative intent when the express language of the statute conveys clear, unambiguous and definite meaning to the words or phrase in question.").

the federal courts. Since states have adopted different interpretive methodologies, federal court methods would change depending upon the preferences of the state whose law they were interpreting. Of course, federal courts are not strangers to this sort of analysis; they routinely apply the different laws of several states. The difference is that the provisions of Article 9 are supposed to be uniform. Perhaps the drafters of the next comprehensive revision of the UCC may include some statutory guidance on the proper interpretive method to be used in construing it provisions, particularly regarding the use of the comments.

CHAPTER 2

SECURITY IN BUSINESS EQUIPMENT

■ ■ ■

§ 1. INTRODUCTION

Chapter 1 introduced some basic concepts and principles useful in comprehending Article 9's regulation of personal property security interests. Chapter 1 also offered some perspectives on how to interpret Article 9 and the role that the official comments play in the interpretive process. This chapter and each of those that follow, through Chapter 8, are dedicated to examining how Article 9 actually works. (Chapter 9 discusses the Anglo-American history of security interests, and the concluding Chapter 10 discusses some theoretical justifications for having a law of personal property security interests.)

Article 9 is divided into seven parts. Part 1 contains some general provisions: the all-important section 9–102, for instance, defines a long list of terms used throughout Article 9. These terms include the names of the different categories of collateral, such as equipment, inventory, accounts, and the like. Note that section 9–102 does not define all the terms used in Article 9. The definition of "security interest," for example, is located not in section 9–102, but rather in section 1–201(b), the general definitional provision of revised Article 1. (Article 1 was revised in 2001.) Part 1 also includes section 9–109, which delineates both the kinds of transactions that Article 9 applies to and those that it excludes.

Part 2 contains a variety of provisions, most notably section 9–203, governing the creation of an enforceable security interest. Part 2 also provides rules addressing the secured party's rights and duties when taking a security interest.

Part 3 addresses priority and perfection. Priority refers to the hierarchical ranking of the various rights different parties have in a particular item of collateral, including those of the secured party, other creditors, and buyers of the debtor's assets. Perfection refers to the steps a secured party must take in order to ensure the full priority of its security interest.

The miscellaneous rules of Part 4 fix the rights of third parties affected by a security interest. These include provisions that render unenforceable certain agreements purporting to restrict the debtor's transfer of rights in certain collateral.

Part 5 comprises rules and procedures for filing a financing statement. Filing a financing statement is by far the most common method of perfecting a security interest, and Article 9 has more rules for filing than for all of the other methods combined. The notable provisions of Part 5 include section 9–502, which specifies the contents of a financing statement, and section 9–516, which governs many other details of the filing process.

The rules of Part 6 specify and regulate the secured party's rights upon the debtor's default. Section 9–601, for example, outlines the secured party's remedies, and section 9–609 describes the secured party's right to take possession of its collateral following default.

Part 7 provides special transition rules. Article 9 was substantially amended in 1999, with an effective date of July 1, 2001. All of the states have enacted the amended version, which features reorganized and renumbered sections and a variety of new rules and procedures. The revision added a special element of transitional complexity to the study of Article 9. Cases decided prior to 2001 typically cite to the provisions of the old statute. Cases decided shortly after 2001 may cite to either the old statute or the revised version, depending on the circumstances. The pre-2001 decisions are frequently still relevant to the study of revised Article 9 because many of the basic rules have changed in only minor ways, if at all. The appendix to this book includes a conversion table translating (roughly) the provisions of old Article 9 to the provisions of revised Article 9. As used hereafter, the term "Article 9" or "revised Article 9" means the current Article 9, effective July 1, 2001 (as amended since then).

If you take a moment to skim through Article 9, you may discern a feature that is particularly relevant to the study of how the statute functions. Some sections contain basic provisions that apply to all, or nearly all, security interests. Section 9–203 is a good example. It specifies the basic requirements that must be met for a security interest to be enforceable. Other sections are more specific in their application, and contain provisions that apply to some kinds of security devices (say, a security interest in equipment) but not others (a security interest in accounts). The insightful reader may deduce a key insight: Article 9 derives much of its complexity from the fact that its rules often vary according to the nature of the collateral in question.

Because Article 9 works in this way (that is, its rules and regulations effectively cluster around collateral types), it makes sense to study it in this way—one type of collateral at a time. It also seems sensible to begin with the simplest kind of security interest and progress to more complicated examples, since a basic knowledge of the former will be transferrable to the latter. In this chapter, we study the most straightforward of all security interests in personal property: a security interest taken by a seller or a financing entity in a debtor's business equipment. The equipment might be construction equipment, automobiles, business machines, or a variety of other personal property, such as office furniture and the like. For purposes of Article 9, the term "equipment" is defined in section 9–102(a)(33). Read it.

Right away, you will notice something odd about section 9–102(a)(33). The provision defines equipment more by what it is not than by what it is: " '[e]quipment' means goods other than inventory, farm products, or consumer goods." (Note that each of the other key terms in this definition—"goods," "inventory," "farm products," and "consumer goods"—are defined elsewhere in section 9–102.) Hence for the purposes of Article 9, there are four basic categories of goods: equipment, inventory, farm products, and consumer goods. Another special category of goods, "fixtures," is a unique type dealt with in Chapter 6. If an item of collateral is properly classified as equipment, it cannot simultaneously be inventory, farm products, or consumer goods. (Although, as we will see, goods may change category: for example, "inventory" in the hands of a retailer may become "consumer goods" in the hands of the retailer's customer.) Thus, equipment is essentially the catchall category left over after inventory, farm products, and consumer goods are subtracted from the general category of goods. If you were a drafter of Article 9, would you have defined equipment in this fashion?

In general, a debtor may obtain financing to acquire equipment in one of two basic ways. On the one hand, the debtor may borrow money from a bank or other financing entity to purchase the equipment from a vendor. In this case, the bank may take a security interest in the equipment to secure the debtor's repayment of the loan. On the other hand, the debtor may buy the equipment from a vendor and agree to pay the vendor over time—in other words, the vendor may sell the equipment to the debtor on credit. In this example, the vendor may take a security interest in the equipment to secure the debtor's payment of the price. Economically, these two transactions are very similar. The only real difference is the identity of the lender extending credit to the debtor to enable the debtor to acquire the equipment. Since both transactions are designed specifically to provide the debtor with the means to purchase specific goods, they are known as "purchase-money" transactions. More broadly, a debtor might also borrow against equipment he already owns, essentially leveraging his existing assets to obtain financing for some purpose.

In general, equipment financings (such as that described in the first example above) are commonly structured as "term loans." The defining characteristic of a term loan is that it is intended to last for a fixed period (say, two years), during which time the debtor typically makes periodic installment payments until the entire debt is paid in full. It is easy to understand why a lender might wish to structure equipment financing in this way. Unlike real estate, equipment typically declines in value ("depreciates") over time. Structured properly, the debtor's installment payments may reduce the debt faster than the equipment depreciates. In this way, the value of the equipment may always remain greater than the amount of the debt outstanding, leaving the secured party at all times fully secured. (In reality, of course, things do not always work out so neatly.)

In the typical equipment loan, the debtor and creditor will sign a written security agreement. This agreement must meet the conditions specified in section 9–203, but those are easy to satisfy, and even a banker or lawyer with a limited understanding of Article 9 can readily draft an adequate security agreement. Perfection of the security interest almost always occurs with the filing of a financing statement that complies with section 9–502 and the other relevant provisions governing perfection in Part 5.

To see what a financing statement looks like, refer to the form in section 9–521. Note how skeletal this document is. It need only identify the debtor, the creditor, and the collateral. Since revised Article 9 eliminated the old requirement of the debtor's signature (*see* 9–502 cmt. 3), the financing statement need not even be signed. And while mistakes in completing this document are possible (especially with regard to the debtor's name), it is designed to be simple and easy to use.

Having lent money to the debtor, having had the debtor sign a security agreement granting a security interest in the equipment, and having filed a financing statement, the secured creditor is now a perfected secured creditor entitled to a priority right in the equipment ahead of the claims and interests of a variety of other persons. These inferior claimants include: (1) lien creditors, who acquire interests in the debtor's equipment through judicial process, attachment, and the like; (2) the trustee in bankruptcy, if the debtor later becomes insolvent and commences a bankruptcy case; (3) later secured creditors; and (4) even good-faith buyers who may have purchased the equipment from the debtor.

In order to understand how all this works, we will first scrutinize the attachment and enforceability requirements of section 9–203, the perfection requirements of sections 9–502, 9–308, and other sections of Part 5, and the kinds of errors one may commit in fulfilling each requirement. We will then consider the legal rights enjoyed by the perfected secured creditor and look at the particular sections that grant priority. In addition, we will examine several practical and economic alternatives to a security interest in business equipment. These include leases as well as agreements that, though styled as "leases," are actually security agreements under section 1–203 of revised Article 1 (section 1–201(37) of old Article 1). We will also consider alternatives to security agreements in general. One example is the "negative pledge clause," a covenant that a debtor makes not to grant security to any other person and that has some of the practical consequences of a security interest. Finally, we will evaluate the secured creditor's rights upon the debtor's default.

§ 2. MAKING AN ENFORCEABLE SECURITY INTEREST

How does a secured party create an enforceable Article 9 security interest? Section 9–203(b) requires only a few steps: (1) value must have been given; (2) the debtor must have rights in the collateral; (3) there must be a "security agreement" (defined in section 9–102(a)(74)); and (4) either the security agreement is one that "describes" the collateral and is "authenticated" by the debtor, or else one of the sets of alternative conditions in section 9–203(b)(3) is satisfied.

Section 9–203 reads in relevant part as follows:

> (a) **[Attachment.]** A security interest attaches to collateral when it becomes enforceable against the debtor with respect to the collateral, unless an agreement expressly postpones the time of attachment.
>
> (b) **[Enforceability.]** Except as otherwise provided in subsections (c) through (i), a security interest is enforceable against the debtor and third parties with respect to the collateral only if:
>
> (1) value has been given;
>
> (2) the debtor has rights in the collateral or the power to transfer rights in the collateral to a secured party; and
>
> (3) one of the following conditions is met:
>
> (A) the debtor has authenticated a security agreement that provides a description of the collateral and, if the security interest covers timber to be cut, a description of the land concerned;
>
> (B) the collateral is not a certificated security and is in the possession of the secured party under Section 9–313 pursuant to the debtor's security agreement;
>
> (C) the collateral is a certificated security in registered form and the security certificate has been delivered to the secured party under Section 8–301 pursuant to the debtor's security agreement; or
>
> (D) the collateral is deposit accounts, electronic chattel paper, investment property, letter-of-credit rights, or electronic documents, and the secured party has control

under Section 7–106, 9–104, 9–105, 9–106, or 9–107 pursuant to the debtor's security agreement.

* * *

(f) **[Proceeds and supporting obligations.]** The attachment of a security interest in collateral gives the secured party the rights to proceeds provided by Section 9–315 and is also attachment of a security interest in a supporting obligation for the collateral.

(g) **[Lien securing right to payment.]** The attachment of a security interest in a right to payment or performance secured by a security interest or other lien on personal or real property is also attachment of a security interest in the security interest, mortgage, or other lien.

Consider how little suffices to bind the debtor under this provision. For example, it is enough for the debtor to write the following on the back of an envelope: "I hereby grant bank a security interest in my cattle. [Signed,] John Jones." If the bank makes a loan and the debtor owns the cattle, the parties have created a valid security interest despite its informality.

The most common way to take a security interest under section 9–203 is by complying with section 9–203(b)(3)(A), which requires a security agreement describing the collateral and authenticated by the debtor. Section 9–102(a)(7) defines the term "authenticate." The most common method of authentication is to sign one's name. Under section 9–102(a)(7)(b), however, one might also authenticate a security agreement electronically by putting the agreement in a "record" of some kind and by adopting a symbol as a means of verifying the debtor's assent.

Note the requirement in section 9–203(b)(3)(A) that the agreement "describe" the collateral. Another provision, section 9–108, provides additional rules on description. Section 9–108 has an organizational structure that recurs throughout Article 9: it begins with a general standard subject to exceptions before proceeding to more focused examples and rules. Specifically, section 9–108(a) states: "[e]xcept as otherwise provided in subsections (c), (d), and (e), a description of personal or real property is sufficient, whether or not it is specific, if it reasonably identifies what is described." What does this mean? Surely this is about as nebulous a standard as one can imagine. Subject to certain exceptions, the description does not have to be "specific" to be valid, but it does have to be "reasonable." What is reasonable?

How about describing the collateral as "all the debtor's assets" or "all the debtor's personal property"? Would that be reasonable? Under section 9–108(c), these so-called "supergeneric" descriptions are forbidden.

What *will* work, then? Here section 9–108(b) comes to the rescue. It states:

> [e]xcept as otherwise provided in subsection (d), a description of collateral reasonably identifies the collateral if it identifies the collateral by: (1) specific listing; (2) category; (3) except as otherwise provided in subsection (e), a type of collateral defined in [the Uniform Commercial Code]; (4) quantity; (5) computational or allocational formula or procedure; or (6) except as otherwise provided in subsection (c), any other method, if the identity of the collateral is objectively determinable.

Of these different examples, which one do you think is the most certain to do the job? Number (3)? This alternative essentially provides that a description of the collateral is reasonable if it makes use of an official UCC collateral type (such as "equipment," "inventory," or "farm products"). Thus, it would suffice for a security agreement to describe the collateral as "all the debtor's equipment," for instance. There is an exception to this rule, however, in section 9–108(e), which requires greater precision in describing certain types of collateral: "a commercial tort claim," "consumer goods," "a security entitlement," "a securities account," and "a commodity account." For example, a sufficiently precise description of consumer goods might read as follows: "the debtor's Maytag washing machine, serial number xyz123." In addition, section 9–108(d) provides special rules for certain investment property-related descriptions.

Few secured creditors would willingly enter into a commercial security arrangement without a written security agreement (or electronic record). Nevertheless, some creditors find themselves unable to produce a signed agreement when trouble comes, often months or years after the agreement was concluded. Others, through inadvertence or incompetence, simply fail to create a written security agreement (or electronic record) that satisfies the requirements of section 9–203. These creditors must then argue that various scraps of paper, some signed by the debtor and some unsigned, together constitute a satisfactory security agreement. The cases that follow furnish examples of this problem.

IN RE TRACY'S FLOWERS AND GIFTS, INC.

United States Bankruptcy Court, W.D. Arkansas, El Dorado Division, 2001.
264 B.R. 1.

MIXON, CHIEF JUDGE:

This adversary proceeding is before the Court upon the complaint of William S. Meeks, the Trustee in this case, to determine the priority, validity, and extent of a lien held by First Bank of South Arkansas ("Bank") in the property of Tracy's Flowers and Gifts, Inc. ("Debtor"). The Trustee alleges that the Bank's lien in the property is unperfected, and, therefore, may be avoided by the Trustee. The issue is whether the Bank has a valid security interest in the property even though the relevant documents do not expressly grant a security interest.

* * *

FACTS

The parties submitted the issue to the Court upon the following stipulated facts in lieu of testimony.

Tracy Lea Passafiume and her mother, Janelle S. Carnes, originally operated the Debtor under the name "Tracy Lea Passafiume or Janelle S. Carnes d/b/a/ Tracy's Flowers and Gifts." The business was later incorporated as a retail florist operation, with Passafiume owning 75% and Carnes owning 25% of the stock. The Debtor was located at 226 California Street, Camden, Arkansas. The incorporated Debtor owned inventory, equipment, and accounts receivable. In November 1999, the Debtor moved its business location to 1226 Country Club Road, Camden, Arkansas.

On September 3, 1999, the Debtor executed a note in favor of the Bank on a form prepared by the United States Small Business Administration ("SBA"). The note evidenced a loan by the Bank to Tracy's Flowers & Gifts, Inc. in the amount of $40,000.00, which was guaranteed by the SBA.

The Debtor executed a financing statement on a U.C.C.–1 Form, which was filed in the office of the Ouachita County Circuit Clerk on September 14, 1999, as filing number 99–788 and in the office of the Arkansas Secretary of State on September 20, 1999, as filing number 1208734. Copies of the financing statements were submitted as Joint Exhibit 2.

Item eight of each financing statement provides space for designating the various types of property to serve as collateral. In Item eight, the following language has been inserted: "This note is secured by all accounts, inventory and equipment now owned or hereafter acquired by Tracy's Flowers and Gifts, Inc. at 226 California in Camden, Arkansas, or wherever located . . . . The loan secured by this lien was made under a United States Small Business Administration (SBA) nationwide program. . . ." (Joint Ex. 2.)

No document titled "Security Agreement" was executed by the Debtor at the time of the making of the loan guaranteed by the SBA. The form filed with the Ouachita County Circuit Clerk was signed by representatives of the Debtor and the Bank. Beneath the Debtor's signature is printed the word "Debtor(s)" and beneath the Bank's signature is the printed term "Secured Party(ies)."

The Debtor filed a voluntary petition for relief under the provisions of chapter 7 of the United States Bankruptcy Code on June 2, 2000, and the Trustee was appointed. The Bank then moved for relief from stay and abandonment, claiming it had a valid first lien in the accounts, inventory and equipment of the Debtor. On August 7, 2000, the Trustee filed an adversary proceeding to avoid the Bank's lien in the personal property as unperfected, alleging that the Bank's security interest did not attach because no security agreement exists expressly granting a security interest.

The Bank's position is that under the composite document rule, the specific language in the financing statement, promissory note, and loan application provides for a security interest in the collateral. The Trustee counters that even if the composite document rule applies in this case, the language in the three documents is insufficient to create a security interest.

LAW

The Bankruptcy Code provides:

> (a) The trustee shall have . . . the rights and powers of, or may avoid any transfer of property of the debtor or any obligation incurred by the debtor that is voidable by—
>
> > (1) a creditor that extends credit to the debtor at the time of the commencement of the case, and that obtains, at such time and with respect to such credit, a judicial lien on all property on which a creditor on a simple contract could have obtained such a judicial lien, whether or not such a creditor exists; [or]
> >
> > (2) a creditor that extends credit to the debtor at the time of the commencement of the case, and obtains, at such time and with respect to such credit, an execution against the debtor that is returned unsatisfied at such time, whether or not such a creditor exists. . .

11 U.S.C. § 544(a)(1) & (2) (1994).

This section of the Bankruptcy Code is referred to as the "strong arm clause," and one of its purposes is to cut off unperfected security interests. 5 Collier on Bankruptcy ¶ 544.03 (Lawrence P. King et al. eds. 15th ed. rev. 2000). Under the strong arm provision, if the Bank's security interest was not perfected on the date the petition was filed, the Trustee's rights in the collateral are superior to the Bank's rights. Ark. Code Ann. § 4–9–301(a) & (b) (Michie Supp. 1999).

Bankruptcy courts determine the nature and extent of property interests based on state law. *Butner v. United States*, 440 U.S. 48, 54, 99 S.Ct. 914, 59 L.Ed.2d 136 (1979) (citing U.S. Const. Art. I, § 8, cl.4); *In re N.S. Garrott & Sons*, 772 F.2d 462, 466 (8th Cir. 1985) (citing 4 Collier on Bankruptcy ¶ 541.02[1] (Lawrence P. King, 15th ed. 1985)). Thus, whether the Bank has a perfected security interest is a matter of state law.

Under Arkansas law, a non-possessory security interest is perfected if: (1) the debtor has rights in the collateral; (2) the debtor signs a security agreement in favor of the secured party which contains a description of the collateral; (3) value is given by the secured party to the debtor; and (4) a valid financing statement is properly recorded. Ark. Code Ann. § 4–9–203(1)(a)–(c) (Michie Supp. 1999); Ark. Code Ann. § 4–9–302(1) (Michie Supp. 1999); *Rice v. Citizens First Bank of Fordyce (In re Cheqnet Systems, Inc.)*, 227 B.R. 166, 168 (Bankr. E.D. Ark. 1998) (citing *In re Hot Shots Burgers & Fries, Inc.*, 169 B.R. 920 (Bankr. E.D. Ark. 1994)).

Under the Arkansas Code, a security agreement is an agreement "which creates or provides for a security interest." Ark. Code Ann. § 4–9–105(1) (Michie Supp. 1999) [9–102(a)(74)]. The term "security interest" means "an interest in personal property or fixtures which secures payment or performance of an obligation." Ark. Code Ann. § 4–1–201(37) (Michie Supp. 1999) [1–201(b)(35)].

The Trustee relies on the definition of "security agreement" to support his argument that the second requirement necessary for a perfected security interest has not been satisfied. He contends that in addition to being signed by the debtor and containing a description of the collateral, an enforceable security agreement under section 4–9–105(1) [9–102(a)(74)] must create or provide for a security interest. The Trustee argues that this requirement is lacking in all documents the Bank offers as potential security agreements.

In support of his contention, the Trustee cites *Gassaway v. Erwin (In re Shelton)*, 472 F.2d 1118 (8th Cir. 1973). In that case, the court held that a buyer and seller of an automobile clearly intended to create a security interest in favor of the seller by executing a bill of sale setting out the terms of payment and by filing an application for title and certificate of title showing the seller as a holder of a first lien and the buyer as owner.

Construing Missouri law on secured transactions with language virtually identical to that in Arkansas, the court held that, regardless of the parties' apparent intent, such documents did not satisfy the U.C.C. requirements for a security agreement. The court further stated that "[a]lthough no precise words are required in the Code, the definitions given indicate that there must be some language in the agreement actually conveying a security interest." *In re Shelton*, 472 F.2d at 1120.

The Trustee also relies on *Gibbs v. King*, 263 Ark. 338, 564 S.W.2d 515 (1978) for the proposition that an enforceable security agreement must evidence language of grant or conveyance in order to create a security interest. The Trustee specifically focuses on the following passage: "Inasmuch as this record is void of any security agreement executed by appellant granting a security interest in the tractor to appellee . . . appellee had no valid security interest in the tractor . . . ." *Gibbs*, 263 Ark. at 342, 564 S.W.2d at 517.

Although the *Gibbs* court states that the grant of a security interest was essential to a document purporting to be a security agreement, the court did not hold that specific or express words of grant or conveyance were necessary. Research reveals no Arkansas case citing *Gibbs* for that proposition. It appears that the Arkansas Supreme Court has not addressed the precise issue of whether specific words of grant are necessary in order to create or provide for a security interest under the Arkansas Code.

The Arkansas Code provisions on secured transactions contemplate two separate documents to achieve perfection, a security agreement to evidence the parties' intent and a financing statement to give notice of the agreement to third parties. State law also permits the security agreement to serve as a financing statement. Ark. Code Ann. § 4–9–402(a) (Michie Supp. 1999). However, it is well settled that a separate document specifically named "security agreement" is not essential to enforce an otherwise valid security interest. *Personal Jet, Inc. v. Callihan*, 624 F.2d 562, 568 (5th Cir. 1980) (letter indicating loan was secured by collateral was enforceable security agreement); *In re Numeric Corp.*, 485 F.2d 1328, 1331 (1st Cir. 1973) (financing statement and directors' resolution together constituted the security agreement); *Nunnemaker Transp. Co. v. United Cal. Bank*, 456 F.2d 28, 31–32 (9th Cir. 1972) (letter agreement served as adequate security agreement).

Although a security agreement can serve as a financing statement, most courts hold that a bare-bones financing statement alone cannot also serve as a security agreement. *In re Shelton*, 472 F.2d at 1120 (a financing statement usually does not meet statutory requirement of a grant of security interest); *General Elec. Credit Corp. v. Bankers Commercial Corp.*, 244 Ark. 984, 429 S.W.2d 60 (1968) (financing statement, standing alone, does not create a security interest).

However, many instances exist in which courts have held that a financing statement also satisfies the definition of a security agreement when further language granting a security interest is added to the document and other statutory requirements are met. *See, e.g., Morey Mach. Co. v. Great Western Indus. Mach. Co.*, 507 F.2d 987, 990 (5th Cir. 1975) (financing statements stamped "Secured Hereby" made provision for a security interest); *Mitchell v. Shepherd Mall State Bank (In re Mitchell)*, 458 F.2d 700, 703–04 (10th Cir. 1972) (when grant of security interest is present, financing statement can serve as a security agreement); *Bossingham v. Bloomington Prod. Credit Ass'n (In re Bossingham)*, 49 B.R. 345, 349 (S.D. Iowa 1985) (standard financing statement could not serve as security agreement in absence of language granting security interest);

Cookeville Prod. Credit Ass'n v. Frazier (In re Frazier), 16 B.R. 674, 679 (Bankr. M.D. Tenn. 1981) (in view of language stating instrument would serve as both financing statement and security agreement and granting a security interest, financing statement was also security agreement). *See, also, In re Wiegert*, 145 B.R. 621, 622 (Bankr. D. Neb. 1991) (sales slip was security agreement); *Komas v. Future Sys., Inc.*, 71 Cal. App. 3d 809, 139 Cal.Rptr. 669, 22 U.C.C. Rep. Serv. 550 (1977) (composite of multiple documents served as security agreement); *In re Bazaar de la Cuisine Int'l., Inc.*, 20 U.C.C. Rep. Serv. 1049 (Bankr. S.D.N.Y. 1976) (promissory note deemed security agreement).

As to the issue of whether specific words of grant or conveyance are required under the U.C.C. definition of "security agreement," two opposing lines of cases have developed. Under the narrow view, termed the "American Card Rule," technical words of conveyance are necessary to create or provide for a security interest. *Mitchell v. Shepherd Mall State Bank (In re Mitchell)*, 458 F.2d 700, 702 (10th Cir. 1972) (enforceable security agreement requires language specifically creating or granting a security interest in the collateral); *Stainer v. Wolfe (In re Carmack)*, 48 B.R. 175, 177 (Bankr. N.D. Okla. 1985) (language stating "note is secured by personal income tax refund" was insufficient to grant a security interest); *Bradley v. K & E Inv. Inc.*, 847 S.W.2d 915, 921–22 (Mo. App. 1993) (floor plan agreement did not create security interest because terms commonly associated with secured transactions were missing); *American Card Co. v. H.M.H. Co.*, 97 R.I. 59, 196 A.2d 150, 152 (1963) (financing statement was not a security agreement because it lacked grant of a security interest). The strict view is apparently the minority view. *Gibson County Farm Bureau Coop. Ass'n v. Greer*, 643 N.E.2d 313, 318 (Ind. 1995) (commenting that "the American Card Rule has been criticized and has, for the most part, been rejected"); James J. White & Robert S. Summers, 4 Uniform Commercial Code § 31–3, n. 37 (West, 4th ed. 1995) (surmising that the strict view is the minority approach and quoting with approval G. Gilmore, 1 Security Interests in Personal Property § 11.4 at 348 (1965)).[1]

The broad view is that the statute is satisfied when a security interest is provided for or stipulated to, regardless of the type of document used or the absence of specific granting language. *Nolden v. Plant Reclamation (In re Amex-Protein Development Corp.)*, 504 F.2d 1056, 1058–59 (9th Cir. 1974) (note stating "this note secured by a security interest in" was sufficient to create a security interest; granting language not necessary); *Markie v. Phillips (In re Phillips)*, 24 B.R. 712, 713–14 (Bankr. E.D. Cal.

[1] Gilmore, one of the drafters of the Uniform Commercial Code, has criticized the American Card case, stating that "[c]ertainly nothing in § 9–203 requires that the 'security agreement' contain a 'granting' clause. The § 9–402 [9–502] financing statement contained all that was necessary to satisfy § 9–203 statute of frauds as well as being sufficient evidence of the parties' intention to create a security interest . . . ." Grant Gilmore, 1 Security Interests in Personal Property § 11.4, 342–348 (1965).

1982) (sales agreement stating "balance is to be represented by a note secured with the stock in trade and merchandise inventory as collateral" was grant of security interest); *Simplot v. Owens*, 119 Idaho 243, 805 P.2d 449, 451 (1990) (no granting language is required to create a security interest); *Komas v. Future Systems*, 71 Cal. App. 3d 809, 139 Cal. Rptr. 669, 22 U.C.C. Rep. Serv. 550 (1977) (no specific form is needed to create security interest; security agreement is enforceable if it leads to the conclusion that parties intended security interest).

Under the broad view, a security agreement is enforceable if its language expresses the intent of the parties to grant a security interest, in contrast to the narrow view focusing on specific granting language regardless of intent. *See, e.g., In re Bollinger Corp.*, 614 F.2d 924, 928 (3d Cir. 1980) (a document signed by the debtor, describing the collateral, and evidencing parties' intent to create security interest is a security agreement); *Maddox v. Federal Deposit Ins. Corp. (In re Maddox)*, 92 B.R. 707, 711 (Bankr. W.D. Tex. 1988) (the composite of several documents evidenced intent to create a security interest); *Evans v. Everett*, 279 N.C. 352, 183 S.E.2d 109, 114 (1971) (financing statement evidencing intent to create security interest met minimal requirements of security agreement).

As previously stated, the Arkansas Supreme Court has not decided the issue of whether language actually conveying a security interest is necessary to create a security interest. However, this Court is of the opinion that the Arkansas Supreme Court would hold the broad view that any language that asserts that specific personal property is encumbered as security for a debt creates or provides for a security interest under section 4–9–105(1) [9–102(a)(74)].

This view is apparently held by courts in the majority of jurisdictions where the definition of "security agreement" is identical to that of section 4–9–105(1) [9–102(a)(74)] of the Arkansas Code. Furthermore, it comports with the goal of Article 9 as originally drafted, which is to provide a simplified structure within which present-day secured financing transactions can be accomplished expeditiously. Finally, this view is supported by a literal reading of the statute, which does not require specific words to create or provide for a security interest.

Applying this reasoning to the instant case, the Court finds that the financing statement executed by the parties and filed with the Ouachita County Circuit Clerk also serves as a valid, enforceable security agreement. The financing statement recites that "This note is secured by" the specified collateral and that "The loan secured by this lien" was made through an SBA program. This additional language is not called for in response to item eight and is not found in a typical, bare-bones financing statement requiring only a recitation of types of collateral covered by the parties' security agreement.

While the first paragraph under item eight does not literally grant a security interest by using those precise words, it does refer to the "note," representing the Debtor's obligation to repay, and it states that the obligation is "secured by" the specified personal property. Read in conjunction with the first paragraph under item eight, the words "The loan secured by this lien" in the second paragraph recognize an interest in personal property to secure payment, a concept synonymous with the term "security interest." As previously stated, the financing statement is signed by the debtor as required by section 203(1)(a) of the Arkansas Code.

Furthermore, the document designates the Debtor as "debtor" and the Bank as "secured party." * * * "Secured Party" means "a lender, seller, or other person in whose favor there is a security interest . . ." Ark. Code Ann. 4–9–105(m) [9–102(a)(73)] (Michie Supp. 1999). These definitions underscore the fact that the parties have entered into an agreement whereby the Bank, as the secured party, has been granted a security interest to secure the obligation owed by the Debtor.

An analysis of the financing statement must include consideration of its terms as defined under secured transactions law. Such a consideration coupled with a focus on the language used to evidence the parties' agreement reveals that the Bank acquired a consensual interest in personal property of the Debtor to secure payment of the loan, in other words, a security interest. The absence of words of grant and the specific term "security interest" does not preclude the creation or provision for a security interest essential to an enforceable security agreement. Nor does it obscure the obvious intent of the parties to create or provide for a security agreement.[2]

In re Shelton, the Eighth Circuit Court of Appeals case that asserted the necessity for language of conveyance of a security interest, can be distinguished on its facts. In that case, the documents consisted of a bill of sale, an application for Missouri car title and the certificate of title. The bill of sale described the automobile, set out the terms of payment and provided that the debtor would insure the automobile. The bill of sale contained no language purporting to establish a security interest. The application for the Missouri car title was signed by the debtor but, rather than establishing a security interest, was an attempt to perfect a security interest, if one existed. The documents signed by the Debtor in *Shelton* do not contain the additional language contained in this case: "This note is secured by all accounts, inventory and equipment . . . The loan secured by this lien was

[2] However, the Court does not condone the Bank's use of a dual purpose financing statement which fails to expressly grant a security interest through a formal security agreement. The Court agrees with the observation of the North Carolina Supreme Court that such a practice "is an example of draftsmanship likely to produce litigation and [is] not to be recommended." *Evans v. Everett*, 279 N.C. 352, 183 S.E.2d 109, 114 (1971).

made under the United States Small Business Administration . . ." (See Joint Ex. 2.)

Furthermore, the credit application submitted and signed by the Debtor in this case recites, "Briefly describe the property to be given as security . . . Property Description: Accounts Receivables Inv. fixtures, etc." (Joint Ex. 3.) This document clarifies what was intended by the additional language of the financing statement. *In re Nickerson & Nickerson, Inc.*, 452 F.2d 56, 57 (8th Cir. 1971) (deficient description of collateral in security agreement can be clarified by financing statement); *In re Cantu*, 238 B.R. 796, 800 (8th Cir. BAP 1999) (creditor's loan documents, considered together, created enforceable security interest), *aff'd*, 221 F.3d 1341 (8th Cir. 2000).

Additionally, in *Shelton* the court did not mention the use of defined terms applicable to secured transactions such as "secured party" and "debtor" that, by definition, evidence the creation or provision of a security interest. Finally, the court in *Shelton* emphasized that, "no precise words are required in the Code," leaving leeway for lower courts to construe more broadly the formal requirements of a security agreement. *See, e.g., United States v. Missouri Farmers Assocs.*, 580 F.Supp. 35, 36 (E.D. Mo. 1984) (holding precise words granting creditor a security interest in debtor's crops were not required to create enforceable security interest), *aff'd per curiam*, 764 F.2d 488 (8th Cir. 1985).

CONCLUSION

Because the financing statement filed in Ouachita County creates or provides for a security interest in the personal property of the Debtor, is signed by the Debtor, and contains a description of the collateral, it is a valid, enforceable security agreement.

The Trustee's complaint to avoid the Bank's lien and for turnover of proceeds from the sale of the collateral is hereby denied.

IT IS SO ORDERED.

NOTE

According to this decision, it is "well-settled" that an enforceable security interest does not require a separate security agreement. So long as it contains the right elements, a financing statement can, as here, fill the role customarily played by a separate security agreement. How would you counsel your client in light of *Tracy's Flowers*? Note that although the decision postdates the 1999 revision of Article 9, the financing statement in question was completed before the 2001 effective date of revised Article 9 and thus complied with the pre-revision rules. How might revised Article 9 affect the outcome? What problems can you foresee? The following case addresses one potential problem under revised Article 9 and suggests that practitioners would be well advised to heed the warning of footnote two in *Tracy's Flowers*.

IN RE SABOL

United States Bankruptcy Court, C.D. Illinois, 2006.
337 B.R. 195.

PERKINS, CHIEF JUDGE:

This adversary proceeding is before the Court, after trial, on the complaint by Charles E. Covey, as Trustee of the Chapter 7 estate ("TRUSTEE"), to determine the validity of a security interest held by Morton Community Bank ("BANK") in several items of sound equipment owned by Michael S. Sabol, one of the Debtors ("DEBTOR"). The matter was taken under advisement by the Court and the parties have submitted briefs. The main issue is whether the Composite Document Rule can rescue the BANK from the absence of a security agreement.

The following facts are not in dispute. On May 25, 2002, the DEBTOR, doing business in the recording industry as Sound Farm Productions, completed an application for a Small Business Administration (SBA) guaranteed loan to expand his business, requesting approval of a loan from the BANK, as Lender, in the principal amount of $58,000. The BANK'S application for the SBA guarantee, comprised of a separate page completed and signed by its loan officers dated June 3, 2002, contains a section entitled "Loan Terms," which includes a subsection for collateral, requesting information as to description, market value and existing liens. Among the assets listed on the application were assets the DEBTOR presently owned and pledged to BankPlus, in addition to two items he intended to acquire using a portion of the proceeds of the loan.

On July 5, 2002, the DEBTOR executed an SBA form promissory note in the principal amount of $58,000 payable to the BANK. In addition to the note, the DEBTOR signed another document, in letter format, which provided:

> In consideration for Morton Community Bank granting a loan to Michael S. Sabol DBA Sound Farm Productions, the undersigned does hereby authorize Morton Community Bank to execute, file and record all financing statements, amendments, termination statements and all other statements authorized by Article 9 of the Illinois Uniform Commercial Code, as to any security interest in the loan or refinancing presently sought by the undersigned, as well as all loans, refinancing or workouts hereafter granted by Morton Community Bank to Michael S. Sabol DBA Sound Farm Productions.

On July 18, 2002, the BANK filed a standard form Uniform Commercial Code (UCC) financing statement, covering inventory, accounts receivable and equipment. The financing statement was not signed by the DEBTOR. No separate document entitled "Security Agreement" was signed by the DEBTOR.

Although he initially dealt with loan officer Will Thomas, the DEBTOR testified that when he went to the BANK to sign the loan documents, a different loan officer handled the closing. He did not recall any discussion about a security agreement or a security interest. The DEBTOR testified that he signed the documents in order to comply with the BANK'S requirements to obtain the loan. The proceeds of the loan were used for operating capital and to purchase additional equipment. The DEBTOR spent less than $20,000 for equipment, which he began to purchase shortly after he received the loan.

The DEBTOR and his wife, Rhonda K. Sabol, filed a joint petition for bankruptcy under Chapter 7 on February 14, 2005. They listed Morton Community Bank as a secured creditor, holding a security interest in "tools" valued at $12,410, with a total claim of $35,792.91. The DEBTOR filed an intent to surrender the "tools" to the BANK. The BANK filed a proof of claim, asserting a secured claim in the amount of $36,967.34.[1] Contending that the BANK'S purported security interest never attached to the equipment, the TRUSTEE filed a report of possible assets, disclosing that he intended to administer the sound equipment as assets of the bankruptcy estate and brought this adversary complaint to determine the validity of the BANK'S lien.

At the trial, the DEBTOR testified concerning the loan transaction. The only other witness was Josh Graber, a representative of the BANK. Although Graber was employed by the BANK at the time the loan was made, he was not involved in the making of the loan to the DEBTOR. He testified that no security agreement was prepared for the loan in question, although the BANK typically used one for secured loans.

The TRUSTEE contends that the BANK does not have a valid purchase money security interest under Article 9 of the UCC, 810 ILCS 5/9–101 *et seq.*, because there is no separate document captioned "Security Agreement" or any language in any other document explicitly granting a security interest.[2] The BANK, relying on the "Composite Document Rule," contends that the loan application, the promissory note, the authorization and the financing statement, taken together, establish an agreement to create a security agreement.

---

1 The TRUSTEE has objected to the BANK'S claim, and as the BANK notes in its response to that objection, the Court's ruling in this proceeding will be determinative of that issue.

2 The TRUSTEE'S suggestion that the revised version of Article 9 should apply here drew no opposition from the BANK. This Court agrees. Although the former Article 9 was in effect at the time the BANK allegedly created its security interest, the financing statement and the bankruptcy petition were filed after revised Article 9 took effect. The majority of courts have held that the revised version should apply under those circumstances. *In re Wiersma*, 283 B.R. 294 (Bankr. D. Idaho 2002); *In re Grabowski*, 277 B.R. 388 (Bankr. S.D. Ill. 2002) (relying on 810 ILCS 5/9–702 (2001), noting that the statute provides that revised Article 9 "applies to a transaction or lien within its scope, even if the transaction or lien was entered into or created before [the statute's] effective date[.]").

ANALYSIS

Generally, state law determines the nature and extent of the property rights in the debtor's assets. *See, e.g., Butner v. U.S.*, 440 U.S. 48, 54, 99 S.Ct. 914, 59 L.Ed.2d 136 (1979). Under Illinois law, which governs the issue of whether the parties have entered into a valid security agreement, a nonpossessory security interest does not attach and is not enforceable unless the debtor has authenticated a security agreement that contains a description of the collateral, value has been given, and the debtor has rights in the collateral.[3] 810 ILCS 5/9–203(b)(3)(A). A "security agreement" is defined as "an agreement that creates or provides for a security interest." 810 ILCS 5/9–102(73) [9–102(a)(74)]. A "security interest" is an interest in personal property or fixtures which secures payment or performance of an obligation. 810 ILCS 5/1–201(37) [1–201(b)(35)]. The requirement of a written security agreement is said to serve two purposes: the first being evidentiary in that it eliminates disputes as to what items are secured and the second in the nature of a statute of frauds, by precluding the enforcement of claims based only on an oral representation. *In re Outboard Marine Corp.*, 300 B.R. 308 (Bankr. N.D. Ill. 2003); *In re Owensboro Canning Co., Inc.*, 82 B.R. 450 (W.D. Ky. 1988); *In re Data Entry Service Corp.*, 81 B.R. 467 (Bankr. N.D. Ill. 1988). No particular words of grant or "magic words" are required to be included in a security agreement to create a security interest. *In re Krause*, 114 B.R. 582, 593 (Bankr. N.D. Ind. 1988). Notwithstanding the lenity of the Composite Document Rule, there must be some language reflecting the debtor's intent to grant a security interest. *In re NTA, LLC*, 380 F.3d 523 (1st Cir. 2004); *In re Zurliene*, 97 B.R. 460 (Bankr. S.D. Ill. 1989). Accordingly, a financing statement which does not contain any grant language by the debtor creating a security interest in the described collateral, but merely identifies the collateral, cannot substitute for a security agreement. *In re Westpfahl*, 171 B.R. 330 (Bankr. C.D. Ill. 1994); *Zurliene, supra.*

Notwithstanding the statutory requirement of a signed or authenticated security agreement that describes the collateral, some courts have adopted a liberal view of what suffices to meet that requirement. Under the "Composite Document Rule," two or more documents in combination may qualify as a security agreement. *In re Numeric Corp.*, 485 F.2d 1328, 1331 (1st Cir. 1973) (separate formal document entitled "security agreement" is not always necessary to satisfy the signed writing requirement of § 9–203). Whether and to what extent the Composite Document Rule applies is a question of state law. *Matter of Bollinger Corp.*, 614 F.2d 924 (3rd Cir. 1980) (Pennsylvania law). The Seventh Circuit Court

[3] The revisions to the UCC that became effective in Illinois on July 1, 2001, changed the § 9–203 requirement from a "signed" security agreement to one that the debtor has "authenticated." This Court is of the view that the change was intended to fast-forward the law into the computer age where electronic signatures or authentication are rapidly becoming the norm. As such, the change is immaterial to the issues resolved in this Opinion.

of Appeals has affirmed a district court's holding that all of the documents constituting a transaction may be considered when analyzing whether an assignment, absolute on its face, was, in fact, intended as a security agreement. *Wambach v. Randall*, 484 F.2d 572 (7th Cir. 1973).

Illinois law governs this dispute. The Illinois Supreme Court has not addressed whether the Composite Document Rule may be used to satisfy the security agreement requirement of UCC § 9–203(b)(3)(A). The only Illinois Appellate Court decision addressing the Rule is *Sears, Roebuck & Co. v. Conry*, 321 Ill.App.3d 997, 255 Ill.Dec. 178, 748 N.E.2d 1248 (Ill. App. 3 Dist. 2001), a case in which a Sears credit card purchase was at issue. After having earlier opened the account by signing a credit card application that contained a security agreement, the customer made credit card purchases and signed sales tickets describing the merchandise and containing language granting Sears a purchase money security interest in the purchased goods.[4] The form of security agreement was periodically updated by Sears by sending the cardholder the new form with no signature required. On the issue of whether Sears proved that it retained a purchase money security interest in the goods listed on the sales receipts, the court held as follows:

> In the instant case, the defendants signed Sears credit card sales receipts incorporating a security agreement by reference and granting Sears a security interest in the items purchased. By analogy with the cases cited above, the signed Sears credit card receipts satisfied the Illinois statutory requirement of a signed security agreement.

Since the sales receipts, by themselves, satisfied the requirements of § 9–203 of a signed writing describing the collateral and granting a security interest therein, *Conry* is not a true composite document case and, in this Court's view, has no application to the issue at bar. It thus appears that no Illinois court has approved or disapproved of the use of the Composite Document Rule.

The pre-UCC era of chattel mortgages, and the technical and sometimes complex requirements associated therewith, fostered common law exceptions in the name of equity and pragmatism.[5] Beginning in 1962,

---

[4] Immediately above the customer's signature on the sales receipts was printed: "Purchased under my Sears account and security agreement, incorporated by reference. I grant Sears a security interest in this merchandise until paid, unless prohibited by law." 321 Ill.App.3d at 999, 255 Ill.Dec. 178, 748 N.E.2d 1248.

[5] Code comment 5 to § 9–203 provides:

> The theory of equitable mortgage, insofar as it has operated to allow creditors to enforce informal security agreements against debtors, may well have developed as a necessary escape from the elaborate requirements of execution, acknowledgment and the like which the nineteenth century chattel mortgage acts vainly relied on as a deterrent to fraud. Since this Article reduces formal requisites to a minimum, the doctrine is no longer necessary or useful. More harm than good would result from allowing creditors to establish a secured

however, the UCC ushered in a new, simplified regime for documenting and perfecting secured transactions. Because the UCC reduces to an absolute minimum the formal requirements for the creation of a security interest, the need for those equitable exceptions no longer exists. In the interests of certainty and maintaining some identifiable standard, it is important to enforce the minimal formal requirements set forth in Article 9 of the UCC. *See, In re Kevin W. Emerick Farms, Inc.*, 201 B.R. 790 (Bankr. C.D.Ill. 1996). Thus, an argument can be made that strict rather than liberal interpretation of the UCC documentation requirements is more consistent with the overall purpose of the UCC to create certainty and reliability in commercial transactions. Other courts have applied the Composite Document Rule narrowly. *See, In re NTA, LLC, supra; In re Zurliene, supra; In re Westpfahl, supra; In re Dean & Jean Fashions, Inc.*, 329 F.Supp. 663 (W.D. Okla. 1971).

The BANK relies upon the DEBTOR'S testimony that he understood that by signing the loan documents that he was granting the BANK a security interest in the equipment that he was going to purchase, as reflected in his treatment of the BANK as a secured creditor in his bankruptcy schedules. The BANK also relies on the itemization of collateral on the loan application, the provision in the note regarding the BANK'S rights in "collateral" and its rights upon default, the debtor's authorization and the description of the collateral in the financing statement. The BANK'S reliance on the listing of collateral under the description of loan terms on its application for the SBA guarantee reveals nothing about the DEBTOR'S intent to grant a security interest. The application consists of two separate portions: one completed by the DEBTOR and one completed by the BANK. The listing of the collateral appears on the BANK'S portion of the document. That page was completed by officers of the BANK and is dated one week after the DEBTOR'S signature on his application for the loan.

The BANK points to the provisions of the note which describe, generically, the BANK'S rights in collateral and upon default. The note defines "Collateral" as "any property taken as security for payment of this Note." Upon default, the note authorizes the BANK to "take possession of any Collateral" and to "sell, lease, or otherwise dispose of any Collateral." The note also provides that the BANK may: "[b]id on or buy the Collateral at its sale;" "preserve or dispose of the Collateral;" "[c]ompromise, release, renew, extend or substitute any of the Collateral;" and "[t]ake any action necessary to protect the Collateral." The note does not identify the collateral. In fact, the note itself contemplates a separate security agreement. Under the heading of general provisions, the note provides that "Borrower must sign all documents necessary at any time to comply with

---

status by parol evidence after they have neglected the simple formality of obtaining a signed writing.

the Loan Documents and to enable Lender to acquire, perfect, or maintain Lender's liens on Collateral."

The DEBTOR'S authorization for the BANK to file a financing statement is equally inefficacious. It authorizes that filing "as to any security interest in the loan . . . presently sought by the [DEBTOR]." *In re Numeric Corp.*, 485 F.2d 1328 (1st Cir. 1973), relied on by the BANK, is distinguishable. In *Numeric*, although the parties had not signed a formal security agreement, the board of directors of the debtor authorized the preparation of a UCC financing statement to cover the creditor's security interest in certain equipment described in a bill of sale.[6] Finding that the directors' resolution established "an agreement in fact" by the parties to create a security interest, the court held that the resolution, taken with the financing statement's itemization of the collateral, constituted a security agreement.

The BANK also relies on its UCC–1 financing statement. The financing statement, as permitted by the Revised UCC, was not signed by the DEBTOR. The financing statement was not filed by the BANK until July 18, 2001, almost two weeks after the loan was closed. No one from the BANK testified that the financing statement was presented to the DEBTOR at the time that he signed the document authorizing its filing. The DEBTOR'S testimony that a security interest was not discussed contradicts any suggestion that the financing statement was presented to the DEBTOR at or prior to the loan closing. This Court will not presume that a financing statement, not shown to be contemporaneous, has any part to play in the Composite Document Rule.

In re Data Entry Service Corp., supra, a case involving an SBA loan, relied on by the BANK, is factually distinguishable. In that case, in addition to the note, the debtor signed a Loan Agreement which listed as collateral, first liens on machinery, equipment, furniture and fixtures, inventory, accounts and general intangibles. Directly above the debtor's signature, at the end of the document, the Agreement provided that the debtor agreed to the conditions imposed. In addition, two financing statements describing the collateral were filed with the Secretary of State, each signed by the debtor. The court determined that the Loan Agreement, by itself or in conjunction with the signed financing statements, was sufficient to create a security interest in favor of the SBA.

---

6 The resolution in *Numeric* provided:

That the Clerk of the corporation prepare standard form, Uniform Commercial Code financing statements on behalf of the corporation as debtor, to Russell Blank, as the secured party, in such manner and form as to cover Russell Blank's security interest in the property of this corporation as set forth in a Bill of Sale dated March 2, 1962, from said Russell Blank to the corporation, and as hereafter acquired, and as evidence of his security interest in the same.

485 F.2d at 1329.

A similar result was reached in *In re Maddox*, 92 B.R. 707 (Bankr. W.D. Tex. 1988), another SBA-guaranteed loan case. As in *Data Entry*, the debtor had signed a loan agreement which identified collateral under "Terms of the Loan" as a "first lien on all equipment, inventory and accounts receivable." The court's decision in *In re Tracy's Flowers and Gifts, Inc.*, 264 B.R. 1 (Bankr. W.D. Ark. 2001), highlights the weakness of the BANK'S position. Recognizing that a "bare bones" financing statement, standing alone, cannot double as a "security agreement," the court held that the following additional language included in the creditor's UCC–1, qualified as a security agreement:

> This note is secured by all accounts, inventory and equipment now owned or hereafter acquired by [the debtor]. . . . The loan secured by this lien was made under [a SBA] nationwide program. . . .

264 B.R. at 2.

Whether considered alone or in combination, this Court finds that there is not sufficient evidence of the DEBTOR'S intent to create a security interest in the documents relied on by the BANK. No language conveying a security interest to the BANK is found in any of the documents. There is no evidence that the DEBTOR read or reviewed, much less agreed to, the "loan terms" contained in the BANK'S application to the SBA. The financing statement, containing the only description of collateral, is not signed by the DEBTOR and, in all likelihood, was never seen by him. What is left? Only boilerplate references in the note to the BANK'S rights in "any collateral" and in the authorization to "any security interest."

Had the BANK'S application for SBA guarantee, which listed the collateral, been signed by the DEBTOR, the minimal requirements of § 9–203 may well have been satisfied. But without a description of the collateral in a signed or authenticated document or in a separate document incorporated by reference into a signed or authenticated document, no security interest can be recognized. This Court is of the view that the Composite Document Rule is most appropriately used, if at all, to allow the debtor's intent to grant a security interest to be demonstrated by reference to the various loan documents where the debtor has signed or authenticated a document containing a description of the collateral that does not contain words of grant. The Rule should not be applied, however, to bypass the necessity of a signed or authenticated writing that describes the collateral, as that is the clearly stated minimum requirement of § 9–203.

Even though the BANK may have intended that there was to be a security interest, the Court does not view the result reached as unduly harsh. The primary purpose of Article 9 of the UCC was to create uniformity and certainty in commercial transactions. The steps required to be taken by secured parties to establish and protect their interests, having been reduced to a minimum, are simple and clearly laid out. *In re Modafferi*, 45 B.R. 370 (S.D.N.Y. 1985). It is not unreasonable to require that they be complied with. *See, In re Swersky*, 1999 WL 135260 (N.D. Tex. 1999) (applying Illinois law).

The TRUSTEE objected to the BANK'S proof of claim filed as secured in the amount of $36,967.34 on the basis that the BANK had no valid security interest. Having now obtained that determination, the objection should be allowed, the BANK should be denied any secured claim, but should be allowed an unsecured claim in the amount stated in its claim.

This Opinion constitutes this Court's findings of fact and conclusions of law in accordance with Federal Rule of Bankruptcy Procedure 7052. A separate Order will be entered.

NOTE

1. Consider again that Article 9 no longer requires the debtor's signature on a financing statement. Why do you think that change was made? For some hints, look at section 9–509 and the accompanying comments.

2. If the financing statement *had* been signed, do you think the *Sabol* decision would have gone the other way?

3. Lawyers can be quite creative when their clients either misplace or neglect to obtain a signed security agreement. Some lawyers have argued that a combination of documents can stand in lieu of a signed security agreement in satisfying the requirements of section 9–203. As suggested in the cases above, such documents may include the minutes of a meeting of the debtor's board of directors, a signed note accompanied by a memorandum indicating that security has been given for the note, and, of course, a financing statement. Since revised Article 9 does not require the financing statement to be signed by the debtor, however, the financing statement alone cannot be an effective security agreement. In some cases the behavior of the parties after the documents were executed, but before default, may provide further evidence that security was intended, particularly when the creditor has filed a financing statement.

What exactly is the nature of section 9–203? Can the parties contract around it? For example, consider a simple hypothetical. A vendor sells an item of equipment to a debtor, and the debtor agrees to pay the vendor by making installment payments for two years. The debtor does not sign a document called a "security agreement." Instead, the vendor inserts a clause in its sales agreement providing that the "vendor hereby retains title to the equipment until debtor finishes paying for it." The vendor also files a financing statement indicating its interest in the equipment. The debtor takes possession of the equipment and makes a few payments, but then files for bankruptcy. Should the vendor's sales agreement and financing statement suffice to constitute a security agreement? Can a vendor purport to retain title as a means of retaining ownership effective against other creditors? Take a look at section 9–

202. In addition, take a look at section 1–201(b)(35) of Article 1. *See also In the Matter of A-1 Paving and Contracting, Inc.*, 116 F.3d 242 (7th Cir. 1997).

Section 9–203 is, in essence, a statute of frauds. Section 1–302(a) of Article 1 provides that the UCC's default rules may be varied by the parties' agreement, subject to certain express exceptions scattered across the UCC. *See, e.g.*, 1–302(b), 9–602. Since these exceptions do not specifically mention section 9–203, does this imply that, under section 1–302(a), the requirements of section 9–203 may be varied by agreement? Would that make any sense? What would be the point of having a statute of frauds requiring written agreements (or their equivalent) if the parties could contract out of it?

In its practical effect, much of Article 9 is a property rights regime whose official requirements—including those of section 9–203—are generally mandatory. Parties to a security agreement are free to contract largely as they like with regard to such things as the circumstances of the debtor's default and the debtor's obligation to maintain the collateral. They are not free, however, to redefine matters that affect the rights of those who are not parties to the security agreement. Such matters include, for example, Article 9's fixed methods of perfection and basic priority structure.

ARTICLE 9 AND DIGITAL COMMERCE

Article 9 includes numerous provisions to facilitate electronic commerce. The Code permits parties to maintain "records" (including both financing statements and security agreements) in either written or electronic form. According to comment 9(a) to section 9–102, a record "need not be permanent or indestructible," but "[t]he information must be stored on paper or in some other medium." The comment lists the following examples of current technologies that would qualify: "magnetic media, optical discs, digital voice messaging systems, electronic mail, audio tapes, and photographic media, as well as paper."

Former Article 9 required the debtor to sign the security agreement; in 1999, Article 9 was revised to substitute "authentication." Under 9–102(a)(7), "authenticate" means "to sign" or "to execute or otherwise adopt a symbol, or encrypt or similarly process a record in whole or in part, with the present intent of the authenticating person to identify the person and adopt or accept a record."

Authentication may be as complex as including a digital rendering of a handwritten signature or as simple as typing one's initials at the end of an email. Clearly "digital signatures" electronically recorded by a dedicated pen on an electronic screen (of the kind now widely used by many merchants) qualify as an authentication. These indicate the intention of the party to be bound and have the virtue of a manual signature. Like a manual signature, these signatures can be examined by a document examiner to determine whether they have the unique qualities associated with a particular person's signature. Other authentications, such as typing one's name at the end of an email, do not have these qualities, yet if they are done with the intention of authenticating, they too are an authentication. For example, a typed name at the end of an email would show that it came from a particular person only by showing that it came from his or her computer and only then if one could show that others could not readily access that computer.

How would one show the "present intent" to "adopt or accept a record"? It probably would be enough to combine the words "John Smith" with a statement such as "I agree to be bound by this security agreement." Typing the words "authorized signature" after the name would also suffice, at least if one can show that the "authorized signature" was done contemporaneously with the typing of the person's name.

How does one put a security agreement into an electronic format in a way that ensures neither party can alter it after it has been authenticated? One possibility is to involve a third party, who retains an electronic copy in its possession. If the debtor and creditor do not wish to use such a service, there are alternatives. A less sophisticated but sufficient method is to use the security tools already provided in most word processing and email software. In most software programs, a party may password protect a file so that a third party may read the file but cannot make any changes. By saving or storing its email containing the document, the recipient can guard against the other party's unauthorized modification. In addition, some programs provide easy-to-use digital signatures and encryption which can secure documents while they are being transported online. While these security methods are far less sophisticated than use of a third party, they may be more than adequate for many secured transactions where the amount at stake does not justify a potentially more expensive three-party procedure.

Another possibility is for the parties to express their transaction using a blockchain-based smart contract: an agreement that is self-executing and self-enforcing, expressed in digital form. In doing so, they could have confidence that neither party can alter the agreement after authentication. This method of transacting is rapidly developing; it may become prevalent for Article 9 secured transactions in some industries. A blockchain is a type of distributed ledger that records transactions. To say that a ledger is "distributed" means that there is no master copy; any participant may maintain a copy of the ledger and all participants know that theirs matches all other copies. Participants can trust that the ledger's content is accurate without reference to a central authority. Distributed ledgers may be public (like the Bitcoin blockchain) or permissioned (like ledgers developed for particular industry groups). Regardless of whether they are public or permissioned, all blockchains contain the same primary components: (i) a ledger, (ii) a computer network, and (iii) consensus, that (iv) cannot be altered by feasible means. The ledger is the database that expands as it incorporates approved transactions. Parties add transactions to the ledger using cryptographic signatures and keys; the transactions are grouped into blocks. Each block contains a cryptographic hash to the previous block, keeping the blocks in order. No one can alter a transaction once approved (by consensus), because the blocks are linked in a sequence that cannot be feasibly altered. There are different types of blockchain-based smart contracts that accomplish different purposes. To enter into secured transactions using this technology, debtors and secured parties would use single smart contracts for trade transactions, executed on a decentralized ledger.

This textbook uses the term "blockchain" to refer to any system comprised of a distributed ledger, a network, and consensus, regardless of whether it is permissioned. (Some commentators contend that the term "blockchain" should refer only to public or permissionless ledgers; others use "blockchain" to mean any distributed ledger.) Blockchain technology has numerous implications for secured transactions, discussed where relevant throughout the book.

PROBLEM 2-1

Your client, First Bank, is trying to reduce its paper records. It would like to store its financing statements and security agreements in electronic format and destroy the hard copies. What risk does First Bank run and what suggestions would you make to ensure that its electronic copies will satisfy the requirements of section 9–203 if litigation occurs?

PROBLEM 2-2

Assume First Bank did not follow your instructions exactly. Instead of getting the debtor to authenticate an electronic record of the written security agreement in each case, it simply scanned several security agreements, transferred the electronic files to diskettes, and then destroyed the hard copies. First Bank is now litigating with a particularly contentious trustee in bankruptcy, who argues that a $20 million loan is unsecured because there is no signed security agreement. Moreover, the trustee in bankruptcy argues that First Bank cannot bring an electronic record into court to prove the presence of a security agreement that was destroyed. She notes correctly that First Bank never obtained the permission of the debtor to record the agreement electronically and to destroy the paper document. The trustee concludes that, since there is no "authentication" as required by section 9–203, First Bank has no security interest and is unperfected. What do you think?

In general, computerized business records are admissible into evidence under essentially the same conditions that apply to the admission of paper records. What First Bank hopes to prove is that its computerized records accurately represent the originals, which have been destroyed. Essentially, the computerized records are copies that are being offered to prove the contents of the originals in satisfaction of the requirements of section 9–203. In order to satisfy the hearsay rule, *see* Fed. R. Evid. 802, First Bank would likely invoke Fed. R. Evid. 803(6), the business records exception. But to do that First Bank would have to satisfy the exception's requirements, including proving reliability. First Bank would also have to authenticate the computerized records. *See* Fed. R. Evid. 901. Under Fed. R. Evid. 1002, original documents are required, unless some exception applies. Under Fed. R. Evid. 1003, duplicates, including computerized copies, are admissible if the conditions stated in the rule apply. *See also* Fed. R. Evid. 1004.

§ 3. PERFECTION

"Perfection" as used in Article 9 is a complex term. Sections 9–308 through 9–316 specify how one perfects in each of the various transactions covered by Article 9. These sections are quite convoluted; read them. To understand how they work, it is helpful to bear in mind three observations. First, there are four general methods of perfection: filing, possession, automatic perfection, and control. Second, the default rule is that a secured party generally perfects by filing a financing statement in the public office designated in section 9–501, unless some other method of perfection is permitted or required. Third, it is best to have a particular type of collateral in mind as you work your way through sections 9–308 through 9–316. For equipment, it turns out that there are only two permissible methods of perfection: filing or possession.

To see how the perfection analysis plays out in the case of equipment, start with section 9–308(a). Here we find the general rule that perfection requires attachment, *see* 9–203, and compliance with all relevant provisions of sections 9–309 through 9–316. Skip to section 9–310(a), which sets forth another general rule: perfection for all security interests occurs by filing, unless another rule specifically directs otherwise. Move next to section 9–313(a), which provides that a security interest in goods may be perfected by possession, and recall that equipment is a type of goods. Move back to section 9–310(b)(6) and observe that filing is unnecessary when a secured party has perfected by possession. These interconnected provisions lead in a roundabout way to a simple point: that filing and possession are permissible alternatives to perfect a security interest in equipment. To confirm that a security interest in equipment cannot be perfected automatically (that is, without possession, filing, or control), refer to section 9–309. To confirm that a security interest in equipment cannot be perfected by control, refer to section 9–314(a). If you were drafting Article 9, would you do it this way? A simpler provision might read as follows: "perfection of a security interest in equipment is accomplished by filing or possession."

What are the benefits of perfection? The perfected secured creditor stands high above the unperfected secured creditor in the priorities pecking order, and even higher above the general unsecured creditor. Perfection also earns the secured party priority over a subsequent lien creditor. (The term "lien creditor" is defined in section 9–102(a)(52).) The lien creditor *par excellence* is the trustee in bankruptcy, who wields rights under section 544(a) of the Bankruptcy Code. *See* 9–102(a)(52)(C). A secured party who perfects prior to bankruptcy usually enjoys a solitary feast, while an unperfected secured party will invariably have to eat from the general creditors' bankruptcy trough, which is often merely sprinkled with crumbs. Just as the mere fact of perfection can determine the priority of claims, so too can the *timing* of perfection, for the date of the secured creditor's perfecting act is commonly the date from which his priority is measured vis-à-vis other perfected secured creditors. *See* 9–322(a). Usually, though not always, a perfected secured creditor takes priority over those who perfect later, yet is subordinate to those who perfect earlier. (One exception is for purchase-money security interests, addressed in Chapter 4.)

As noted, filing a financing statement is by far the most common and important method of perfection. A financing statement is a publicly filed document containing only enough information to notify a reader that the named creditor may claim an interest in the indicated collateral of the debtor. Only rarely is the financing statement also the operative document that creates the security interest between the parties; most often it is a skeletal notice instructing the reader where to hunt for more information.

A much less common method of perfection is possession, which may be used with certain kinds of collateral (for instance, equipment) and *must* be used with certain others (such as money, *see* 9–312(b)(3)). Though undefined in Article 9, "possession" means just that: the creditor must have actual, physical possession of the collateral or its equivalent. *See* 9–313 cmt. 2.

Control is the third method of perfection, permissible for some kinds of intangible collateral (investment property and electronic chattel paper, *see* 9–314(a)) and mandatory for others (such as deposit accounts or letter of credit rights, *see* 9–312(b)(1), (2)). Control is thus to intangibles as possession is to goods.

Finally, as mentioned above, some security interests are automatically perfected at the time of their creation without any additional action by the secured creditor. The most important of this last group are purchase-money security interests in consumer goods. *See* 9–309.

Perfection generally requires some action, such as filing or possession, that would put a diligent searcher on notice of the secured party's claim. In crafting the filing requirements of Article 9, the drafters wished to increase the certainty that a good faith effort by the secured creditor at filing would successfully communicate a sufficient amount of information so that a good faith search by later parties would reveal the presence (if not all the details) of the earlier secured creditor's interest. As we will see, the drafters compromised some of these principles where the cost of providing public notice appeared to outweigh the benefits of that notice. *See, e.g.*, 9–507(c).

Article 9 does not state rules for perfection with respect to all security interests in all types of personalty. Security interests in aircraft, for example, are perfected according to federal law by filing in Oklahoma City. Federal filings may also be required in certain cases for interests in patents, copyrights, and trademarks (addressed in Chapter 5). As to collateral or transactions that are excluded from Article 9 under section 9–109, taking and perfecting a security interest may still be possible under the common law or another state statute.

PERFECTION BY FILING, IN GENERAL

To reiterate, filing is by far the most common method of perfecting a security interest under Article 9. Section 9–310(a) identifies filing as the norm; indeed, it is the only way to perfect a security interest in general intangibles and in most accounts not classified as "proceeds."[1] Filing is a permissible but not exclusive method of perfection for goods, chattel paper, documents, investment property, and—for the first time under revised Article 9—instruments. *See* 9–312(a).

Filing is not universally effective, however. It is an impermissible method of perfection with respect to money, deposit accounts, and letter of credit rights, except when these assets are proceeds. *See* 9–312(b)(1)–(3). Also, a UCC filing is inadequate for goods covered by a certificate of title (for example, many motor vehicles). As to these, filing must be under the applicable certificate-of-title legislation. *See* 9–311(a)(2)–(3). Nor is a UCC filing adequate if federal law calls for a federal filing. *See* 9–311(a)(1).

Again, in most of the security universe, one perfects by filing a financing statement. *See* 9–521. This document is the fig leaf of Article 9; it barely covers the collateral and the parties. It omits almost all the important terms of the parties' agreement. Pre-UCC filing was haphazard and non-uniform: some states had state-wide systems for certain kinds of collateral, while other states required cumbersome "chattel mortgages" be recorded alongside real estate mortgages in local offices. (Pre-Code chattel mortgage laws are discussed in Chapter 9.) The UCC revolutionized the field by promoting the "filing" of a separate, skeletal financing statement document in place of the "recording" of the actual transactional documents executed by the parties. A second major innovation was to move most filings out of local registries and into a single, state-wide registry.

Initially, state-wide filing conflicted with local traditions. As an historical matter, it was generally thought that local creditors should be

---

1 The term "proceeds" is defined in section 9–102(a)(64). We will take up proceeds in greater detail in Chapter 4.

able to walk to the neighborhood courthouse and examine the files there, and that the local recorder of deeds should collect a fee with each filing. Mindful of these notions, the drafters of the 1962 and 1972 versions of the Code proposed three alternative filing systems. They sought to mitigate the concerns of those who preferred to determine a debtor's status from local files, and likewise minimize the political objections of local filing officers, who stood to lose fees to a state-wide system. At the outset, however, the drafters recognized the efficiency of a state-wide filing system: if creditors could search and filers could file in one location, both would avoid the mistake of going to the wrong place.

Under the first of the three alternatives in the 1962 and 1972 versions of the Code, all of which appeared in pre-revision section 9–401, one filed locally only with respect to timber to be cut, oil and gas, and fixtures. All other filings were to be made in a single state-wide office, usually the office of the secretary of state. The second and most widely adopted alternative provided for local filing with respect to timber to be cut, oil and gas, and fixtures, and also required local filing for consumer and farm collateral. The third alternative not only adopted all the local filing requirements of the second alternative, but also required both state-wide and local filing when the debtor's place of business was in only one county in the state. As more state filing systems were computerized, however, it became possible to search by computer and ultimately to file electronically. The walk to the local courthouse began to seem less convenient, and the cost associated with local filing could no longer be justified. Section 9–501 of the 1999 revision thus calls for state-wide filing for all collateral save fixtures, "as-extracted" collateral (oil, gas, and minerals), and timber to be cut.

Of course, the Article 9 filing system is not the only filing system, and section 9–311 recognizes that Article 9's system must bow to federal filing systems that preempt Article 9—for instance, the federal filing system with respect to aircraft. The extent to which federal filing rules preempt the UCC as to patents, copyrights, and trademarks is less clear (this is discussed in greater detail in Chapter 5).

Certificate of title notation rules likewise replace the Article 9 filing provisions in the case of goods covered by certificates of title. Under section 9–311, for example, a secured creditor perfects a security interest in an automobile for which a certificate of title has been issued by complying with the state's certificate of title law, which usually requires notation of the creditor's lien on the automobile's title certificate. This state law exception to an Article 9 filing itself carries an exception: when cars or other goods covered by the certificate of title laws are held as inventory for sale, they are treated like other inventory and so are subject to an Article 9 filing for perfection. *See* 9–311(d). This, of course, only makes sense: a brand new car sitting on the dealer's lot as part of the dealer's inventory waiting to be sold will not yet have a title certificate registered with the local department of motor vehicles, so there would be no certificate on which to note a lien.

Prior to revised Article 9, it was possible to file both locally and at the state capital in certain circumstances when there was a question about the classification of the collateral (whether it was consumer goods subject to a local filing, or equipment calling for a state-wide filing), or when there was uncertainty over the number of counties in which a debtor did business. But many secured creditors did not file in both places, and courts were called upon to determine, for example, whether large broods of laying hens should be classified as inventory (state-wide filing) or farm products (local filing); whether a boat used for Coast Guard volunteer work was equipment as opposed to consumer goods; or whether a computer bought initially for home use became equipment when it was devoted to business use. Section 9–501 sweeps these questions away. Whether the debtor's goods are consumer goods or business equipment, the filing is at the state capital, and searchers use state-wide databases.

Advances in electronic filing, data storage, and searching have revolutionized the states' filing systems. The internet has made state databases available to anyone with a computer connection, and as search software has grown more sophisticated, the filing and search problems discussed below have diminished significantly. Searchers are far more likely to discover a prior filing, and creditors are far less likely to find themselves unperfected, after making a good faith attempt to perfect by filing, because they filed in the wrong place or with the wrong document.

While the filing systems currently in place are quite effective, state legislatures have begun to authorize and consider the use of blockchain-based platforms for UCC filings. These legislative initiatives, in and of themselves, do not create or implement blockchain-based filing systems. They recognize blockchain-based lien registries as legally valid systems for electronic filing, if the state were to use such a platform. Some commentators find the current UCC filing system too slow and error-prone and are calling for innovation. Others find that, given the efficacy of the current UCC filing system, it is not clear as of yet that a blockchain-based system, given its costs, would better serve a state's needs.

That said, some states, such as Delaware, have proposed innovations for UCC filings that could transform certain aspects of secured transactions. Delaware's plan for "smart UCC" filings—UCC filings on a distributed ledger—may do much more than the UCC–1 financing statement as we now know it. These smart UCC filings could (1) automate release or renewal of UCC filings, (2) speed up the searching of UCC records, (3) cut down on mistakes and fraud, and (4) reduce costs. Banks are contemplating the possibility of linking smart UCC filings to programs that can value collateral. The smart filing, then, could automatically call for additional collateral when the value of collateral covered by a UCC financing statement drops below a threshold (loan to value ratio). The UCC filing could become much more than a means of giving public notice of the existence of a lien. It could become a device for secured creditor monitoring and credit risk management. But regardless of its future potential as a transaction-management tool, the UCC financing statement is a method of perfection governed by the rules enacted in Part 5 of Article 9, to which we now turn.

BASICS OF FILING AND THE EFFECTS OF IMPERFECT FILING OR INDEXING

Section 9–502 states the minimum data that must be included in a financing statement for it to be effective. Section 9–516 provides additional requirements and rules concerning the extent of the ineffectiveness of imperfect financing statements. Section 9–520 specifies the duties of the filing office with respect to certain defective financing statements and the legal effects of those statements if they are accepted notwithstanding certain defects. *See also* 9–338.

Subsections 9–502(a) and (b) state what is necessary—if not in all cases sufficient—for a document to qualify as a financing statement:

> (a) **[Sufficiency of financing statement.]** Subject to subsection (b), a financing statement is sufficient only if it:
>
> (1) provides the name of the debtor;
>
> (2) provides the name of the secured party or a representative of the secured party; and
>
> (3) indicates the collateral covered by the financing statement.
>
> (b) **[Real-property-related financing statements.]** Except as otherwise provided in Section 9–501(b), to be sufficient, a financing statement that covers as-extracted collateral or timber to be cut, or which is filed as a fixture filing and covers goods that are or are to become fixtures, must satisfy subsection (a) and also:
>
> (1) indicate that it covers this type of collateral;
>
> (2) indicate that it is to be filed [for record] in the real property records;
>
> (3) provide a description of the real property to which the collateral is related [sufficient to give constructive notice of a mortgage under the law of this State if the description were contained in a record of the mortgage of the real property]; and

(4) if the debtor does not have an interest of record in the real property, provide the name of a record owner.

Under the predecessor to section 9–502 (old section 9–402(1)), a financing statement had to include the debtor's signature and the addresses of the debtor and the secured parties in order to be effective. The drafters of revised Article 9 apparently concluded that the debtor's signature was an unnecessary technicality and that the addresses of the parties were useful but not critical, since a searcher can find the address of any earlier secured creditor and presumably has the address of its debtor. *See* 9–502 cmt. 3. (The requirement for addresses now appears in section 9–516(b), under which, as we will see, their omission has only limited adverse consequences for the secured creditor.) Section 9–502 allows the use of a mortgage as a financing statement in certain real estate transactions. Like the former law, it requires that a financing statement that is to be filed in the real property records contain both a description of the real property and a notice to the filing officer that the statement must be filed in the real property records. Unlike the former law, section 9–502 omits the troublesome requirement of a real estate description covering growing crops: they are now perfected by a plain vanilla financing statement without any mention of real estate.

Other provisions of Article 9 flesh out some of the details of the requirements of section 9–502. To begin with, section 9–503 prescribes the proper way to list the debtor's and secured party's names. Notice that almost all of the provisions of section 9–503 pertain to the debtor's name, while only the last two, subsections (d) and (e), supply a few minor rules about the name of the secured party. Why? The answer is that financing statements are indexed according to the name of the debtor. Thus, it is far more important to get the name of the debtor right than the name of the secured party. *See* 9–503 cmt. 2.

Observe that section 9–503(a)(1) states that a "financing statement sufficiently provides the name of the debtor . . . if the debtor is a registered organization, only if the financing statement provides the name of the debtor indicated on the public record of the debtor's jurisdiction of organization which shows the debtor to have been organized." What does this mean? As defined in section 9–102(a)(71), the term "registered organization" encompasses a variety of entities, such as corporations and limited liability partnerships, for which the government must maintain a public record showing the organization of the entity. Can you think of a more reliable source for a corporation's real name than the official public records attesting to its organization? Probably not. So if the parties neglect the directive of section 9–503(a)(1) and get the debtor's name wrong on the financing statement as a result, who do they have to blame? Only themselves, one might think. But as we shall see, Article 9 is somewhat forgiving even of mistakes involving this critical bit of information.

As amended in 2010, section 9–503 provides two alternatives for determining the correct name of an individual debtor. *See* 9–503 cmt. 2(d). Alternative A requires the use of the debtor's name as it appears on the debtor's driver's license *if* the debtor has been issued such a license. Alternative B permits, but does not require, the use of the debtor's name as it appears on the debtor's driver's license. Complexities regarding how properly to determine the name of an individual debtor when a driver's license is not used are addressed in comment 2(d) to section 9–503.

In general, a botched financing statement that does not comply with the requirements of section 9–502 is ineffective. But just how botched does it have to be? Section 9–506 supplies an answer. In typical Article 9 fashion, the section begins with a standard and then adds a rule to illustrate the standard's application. Section 9–506(a) provides that "[a] financing statement substantially satisfying the requirements of this part is effective, even if it has minor errors or omissions, unless the errors and omissions make the financing statement seriously misleading." What does this mean? How much error is "misleading," and how much misleading error is "serious"? Section 9–506(b) helps by emphasizing the importance of getting the debtor's name right: "[e]xcept as otherwise provided in subsection (c), a financing statement that fails sufficiently to provide the name of the debtor in accordance with Section 9–503(a) is seriously misleading." In other words, failure to comply with the directions set forth in section 9–503(a) is both presumptively "misleading" and sufficiently "serious" to render a financing statement ineffective. But what if the error is not with the debtor's name but rather with the name of the secured party? Section 9–506(b) does not have an answer for this hypothetical, presumably because accuracy is less important for the secured party's name than for the debtor's name. *See* 9–506 cmt. 2. Comment 2 explains:

> Inasmuch as searches are not conducted under the secured party's name, and no filing is needed to continue the perfected status of [a] security interest after it is assigned, an error in the name of the secured party or its representative will not be seriously misleading.

Section 9–506(c) embellishes the "seriously misleading" standard with a fairly clear rule:

> [i]f a search of the records of the filing office under the debtor's correct name, using the filing office's standard search logic, if any, would disclose a financing statement that fails sufficiently to provide the name of the debtor in accordance with Section 9–503(a), the name provided does not make the financing statement seriously misleading.

To illustrate, suppose that "Acme Corp." is the debtor's correct, official name, as set forth in the public records of its state of incorporation.

Suppose, however, the financing statement lists the debtor's name incorrectly as "Acne Corp." Under section 9–506(c), if a searcher looking for "Acme Corp." would pull up "Acne Corp." in the ordinary course of a standard search, then the mistake is not seriously misleading.

What if the debtor changes its name after granting a security interest? For example, suppose the debtor was named "Acme Corp." at the time it granted a security interest in its equipment, and that this name appears (correctly) on the financing statement. Suppose later the debtor changes its name to "Theta Corp." This may be a problem for the secured party, although perhaps not a particularly serious one in the case of equipment collateral. Section 9–507(b) states the general rule that "a financing statement is not rendered ineffective if, after the financing statement is filed, the information provided in the financing statement becomes seriously misleading." In other words, secured creditors can generally rely on the accuracy of the information that appears on the financing statement at the time the financing statement is filed; they need not worry too much about changed circumstances later rendering the information inaccurate.

There is a key exception to this general rule, however, triggered when the debtor changes its name while retaining ownership of the collateral in question (and without changing its location to another state).[2] Here section 9–507(c) kicks in, providing that "[i]f a debtor so changes its name that a filed financing statement becomes seriously misleading under Section 9–506," the secured party essentially has four months to file an amended financing statement with the debtor's new name. If it does not so file, the secured party's security interest will remain perfected with respect to its existing equipment collateral and any equipment covered by its security interest that the debtor acquires within four months after the name change, *i.e.*, so-called "after-acquired collateral" to which the security interest would also attach. (*See* section 9–204 authorizing security interests to attach to collateral existing at the time the debtor initially grants a security interest as well as in after-acquired collateral if so provided in the security agreement.) The security interest will not, however, be perfected as to any new equipment the debtor acquires after four months. In other words, the secured party has a four-month grace period to detect the name change and alter its financing statement accordingly. As a precaution, secured creditors typically include clauses in their security agreements to the effect that the debtor either may not change its name without first notifying the secured party or else must provide prompt notice to the secured party after any name change.

---

[2] We will examine the consequences of the debtor's transfer of ownership of equipment collateral and of a change in the debtor's location in Section 5 of this chapter. What if the debtor changes its name as a result of a merger? That is a special case implicating section 9–508. It will be addressed in Chapter 4, which takes up security interests in inventory.

Doesn't section 9–507 create the potential for a "secret lien"? For example, suppose a debtor, Empire Paving, grants a security interest to First Bank in both its existing tar melting equipment located at its plant and any additional tar melting equipment it acquires in the future. First Bank duly indicates its security interest in a filed financing statement listing "Empire Paving" as the debtor. Six months later, Empire Paving changes its name to "Universal Paving." Under section 9–507, the secured party's financing statement remains effective to perfect its security interest in the debtor's preexisting tar melting equipment even though the debtor has a new name. In addition, any new tar melting equipment the debtor acquires within four months after the name change would be covered. The financing statement would simply be ineffective to perfect First Bank's security interest in any new tar melting equipment the debtor may acquire *after* the four month period, provided First Bank does not file an amended financing statement. But note: if a searcher looks for First Bank's financing statement during the four-month period, she won't find it using the debtor's then-correct name, Universal Paving. The drafters of Article 9 believed it was less important to protect this searcher than to give peace of mind to First Bank. Do you agree? Is this really much of a problem? Consider that a searcher can always ask a debtor if it has recently changed its name and may often be able to check the public records for a name change. Consider also that a subsequent secured party who lends a debtor money to acquire new equipment and takes a purchase-money security interest in the equipment will likely have priority over an existing secured creditor anyway. *See* 9–324(a). (We will address purchase-money security interests in greater detail in Chapter 4.)

Who can file a financing statement? Take a look at sections 9–509 and 9–510. Generally speaking, only someone who is authorized to file a financing statement may do so. Note, however, that by signing a security agreement the debtor automatically authorizes the secured party to file a financing statement covering the collateral described in the agreement. *See* 9–509(b). How long is a financing statement effective? Generally five years, subject to the secured party's ability to extend the duration of the financing statement's effectiveness by filing a continuation statement. *See* 9–515. Note that the time for the secured party to file a continuation statement is during the six months before the expiration of the five-year period. *See* 9–515(d). What if the debtor has satisfied all of his obligations to the secured party and wishes to terminate the financing statement? *See* 9–513. In general, if there are no further obligations owed to the secured party, the secured party must cause a termination statement to be filed.

Notice also that, in addition to requiring the names of the debtor and secured party on a financing statement, section 9–502(a)(3) directs that the financing statement "indicate" the collateral covered by the statement. Recall that section 9–203(b)(3)(A) calls for the debtor to authenticate a security agreement providing a "description" of the collateral in order to demonstrate that the debtor agrees to grant a security interest. Section 9–502(a)(3) does not use the term "describe," however; it uses the term "indicate" instead. Why? Because the standard for "indication" relevant to a financing statement is different from the standard for "description" applicable to a security agreement. Section 9–504 sets forth the former, which is broader and more forgiving than the standard for describing collateral in section 9–108. In particular, section 9–504 permits what section 9–108 forbids: the use of "supergeneric" descriptions such as "all assets of the debtor" or "all personal property of the debtor." Why do you think the drafters made this choice? *See* 9–504 cmt. 2.

Section 9–516(b) contains additional requirements for the financing statement. For example, a financing statement is supposed to provide a "mailing address for the debtor." Section 9–520(a) directs the filing officer to refuse a record that does not meet the additional requirements of section 9–516(b). Yet, if the filing officer mistakenly accepts a financing statement that meets the minimum conditions of section 9–502, but not the additional requirements of section 9–516(b), the filing is effective for most purposes. So we now have two classifications of defective financing statements: defective and *really* defective. Suppose a filing officer mistakenly accepts two defective financing statements, the first defective because it omits the name of the secured party (so failing section 9–502), and the second because it omits the address of the secured creditor (so failing section 9–516(b)(4), but not section 9–502). The first defect renders the security interest unperfected regardless of its acceptance for filing, while the second is perfected notwithstanding the defect owing to the filing office's acceptance of the filing (but would be ineffective if the filing office had refused it).

The additional requirements stated in section 9–516(b) are as follows:

(b) **[Refusal to accept record; filing does not occur.]** Filing does not occur with respect to a record that a filing office refuses to accept because:

(1) the record is not communicated by a method or medium of communication authorized by the filing office;

(2) an amount equal to or greater than the applicable filing fee is not tendered;

(3) the filing office is unable to index the record because:

(A) in the case of an initial financing statement, the record does not provide a name for the debtor;

(B) in the case of an amendment or correction statement, the record:

(i) does not identify the initial financing statement as required by Section 9–512 or 9–518, as applicable; or

(ii) identifies an initial financing statement whose effectiveness has lapsed under Section 9–515;

(C) in the case of an initial financing statement that provides the name of a debtor identified as an individual or an amendment that provides a name of a debtor identified as an individual which was not previously provided in the financing statement to which the record relates, the record does not identify the debtor's surname; or

(D) in the case of a record filed [or recorded] in the filing office described in section 9–501(a)(1), the record does not provide a sufficient description of the real property to which it relates;

(4) in the case of an initial financing statement or an amendment that adds a secured party of record, the record does not provide a name and mailing address for the secured party of record;

(5) in the case of an initial financing statement or an amendment that provides a name of a debtor which was not previously provided in the financing statement to which the amendment relates, the record does not:

(A) provide a mailing address for the debtor;

(B) indicate whether the debtor is an individual or an organization;

(6) in the case of an assignment reflected in an initial financing statement under Section 9–514(a) or an amendment filed under Section 9–514(b), the record does not provide a name and mailing address for the assignee; or

(7) in the case of a continuation statement, the record is not filed within the six-month period prescribed by Section 9–515(d).

If the filing officer rejects the filing for a reason not identified in section 9–516(b), then the attempted filing is effective under section 9–516(d) (provided it meets the requirements of section 9–502(a) and (b)), "except as against a purchaser of the collateral which gives value in reasonable reliance upon the absence of the record from the files." One has to make several rather far-fetched assumptions to raise the issues that are buried in section 9–516(d). First, one must assume the secured creditor presents a financing statement that complies with section 9–502. Second, one must suppose the filing officer refuses the filing on grounds *other than* non-compliance with section 9–516(b). Third, one must imagine either that the filing officer failed to tell the secured creditor that it refused the filing, or that the secured creditor and the filing officer got into an angry standoff. Finally, one must assume that a "purchaser" gives value in reasonable reliance on the absence of the filing. Among those who would qualify as "purchasers" are buyers of the collateral and other secured creditors who might take a security interest in the collateral unaware of the earlier and unrecorded security interest. (Section 1–201 of Article 1 defines "purchaser" to include one who "takes by purchase," and "purchase" to include taking by a security interest.) If each of these improbable events comes to pass, the un-indexed financing statement is valid against non-reliance creditors but not against those who acted in reliance upon the absence of the filed financing statement. Presumably what is most likely to happen is that the filing officer refuses the filing and then mistakenly fails to notify the secured creditor. The debtor then goes bankrupt and the secured creditor in the bankruptcy case has to prove that it attempted to make a filing and that it qualifies for the protection of section 9–520(c).

Suppose the filing office does the opposite—that is, accepts for filing a record it should have refused because of defects of the kind described in section 9–516(b). In this case section 9–520(c) renders the filing effective but opens the possibility that certain subsequent parties would take free of the security interest if they were misled by the statement's inaccuracies. *See* 9–338. Assume a creditor files a financing statement indicating the debtor is an individual when in fact the debtor is a corporation. That financing statement is defective under section 9–516(b)(5)(B). Assume further that a second creditor examines the filing and concludes that there is no filing against its debtor of the same name because its debtor is a corporation, not an individual. In that case sections 9–520(c) and 9–338(1) would together subordinate the earlier secured creditor, who had provided inaccurate information, so long as the later secured creditor could show it had given "value in reasonable reliance upon the incorrect information."

Notwithstanding section 9–520(a)'s instruction to decline financing statements that fail section 9–516(b), filing officers in practice may exercise some discretion. If a filing officer refuses a financing statement because it fails one of the requirements of section 9–516(b), filing does not occur. If, on the other hand, the filing officer accepts the financing statement despite the failure, the secured creditor is properly filed (except against subsequent purchasers, secured parties included, who reasonably rely on the incorrect information) if its financing statement meets the minimum requirements of section 9–502. Filing officers in some states may insist upon compliance with the entirety of section 9–516(b); those in other states may not. Some of section 9–516(b)'s requirements are merely common sense obligations necessary for the proper indexing of an intelligible financing statement. For example, if the "medium of communication" used to transmit an electronic record is incompatible with the electronic communication system of the filing office, presumably filing will be impossible because the filing officer will be unable to extract the communication from the system in a comprehensible form.

Section 9–520 states the limits of the filing officer's discretion:

> (a) **[Mandatory refusal to accept record.]** A filing office shall refuse to accept a record for filing for a reason set forth in Section 9–516(b) and may refuse to accept a record for filing only for a reason set forth in Section 9–516(b).
>
> (b) **[Communication concerning refusal.]** If a filing office refuses to accept a record for filing, it shall communicate to the person that presented the record the fact of and reason for the refusal and the date and time the record would have been filed had the filing office accepted it. The communication must be made at the time and in the manner prescribed by filing-office rule but [, in the case of a filing office described in Section 9–501(a)(2),] in no event more than two business days after the filing office receives the record.
>
> (c) **[When filed financing statement effective.]** A filed financing statement satisfying Section 9–502(a) and (b) is effective, even if the filing office is required to refuse to accept it for filing under subsection (a). However, Section 9–338 applies to a filed financing statement providing information described in Section 9–516(b)(5) which is incorrect at the time the financing statement is filed.
>
> (d) **[Separate application to multiple debtors.]** If a record communicated to a filing office provides information that relates to more than one debtor, this part applies as to each debtor separately.

Although its phrasing is awkward, section 9–520(a) is a legislative direction to the filing officer to refuse filings that fail any of the tests in section 9–516(b). More important, the second official comment to section 9–520(a) gives a stern warning to filing officers, instructing them to keep their fingers out of the pot: "Under this section, the filing office is not expected to make legal judgments and is not permitted to impose additional conditions or requirements." The third official comment to section 9–516 is even more explicit: "Neither this section nor Section 9–520 requires or authorizes the filing office to determine, or even to consider, the accuracy of information provided in a record."

It seems likely that the majority of filing officers will insist upon most of the requirements of section 9–516(b) and that such insistence will improve the quality of the information in the filings and the index. For example, the filing officer may require the mailing addresses of the secured party and the debtor under subsections 9–516(b)(4) and (5)(A). Subsection 9–516(b)(5)(B), meanwhile, allows the filing officer to insist that the statement indicate whether the debtor is an individual or an organization.

To reiterate: (1) if a financing statement fails to meet the conditions of section 9–502, the filing is ineffective, even if it is accepted and indexed; (2) if a financing statement satisfies section 9–502 but not section 9–516(b), and the filing officer refuses it because of its failure, the filing is ineffective; (3) if a financing statement satisfies section 9–502 but not section 9–516(b), and the filing officer accepts it, the filing is effective for most purposes; and (4) if a financing statement satisfies section 9–502 and the filing officer refuses to accept it for a reason other than those stated in section 9–516(b) (for example, the financing statement was submitted by a person wearing a hat), the filing is effective for most purposes.

Revised Article 9 goes well beyond the former law. Among other things, section 9–521 sets forth a uniform financing statement form, devised with input from the filing officers of several states. By encouraging filing parties in all states to use identical documents and by establishing uniform requirements on numbering and indexing in section 9–522, revised Article 9 facilitates uniformity and minimizes the likelihood that a filing will be erroneous or that a proper search will fail to disclose the filed financing statement in question.

PROBLEM 2-3

Your client is lending to Retondo Brothers, an Illinois corporation located in suburban Chicago. How do you perfect an interest in its equipment (drill presses, grinders, and sophisticated machine tools and their operating software)?

Assume the bank officer who filled out the financing statement made a couple of errors in the filing. First, the bank officer used the former, not the current, address for the debtor and omitted the address of the bank entirely. Also, the name of the debtor is not entered in the space for an organization, but rather in the space for an individual, and the bank officer denies proofreading this detail. However, the copy of the statement you retrieved has added after the name of the debtor that it is a sole proprietorship. You are now interested in these issues because the debtor has gone into bankruptcy and the trustee in bankruptcy has claimed that the bank is unperfected. The trustee has pointed out that the financing statement fails to meet several of the requirements of section 9–516. Also, during the course of the bankruptcy, a subsequent secured creditor asserted priority over your client by claiming injury as a result of the financing statement's failure to state the address of the bank and to indicate that the debtor was a corporation.

What do you make of these arguments?

PROBLEM 2-4

Assume you represent Bank One, which proposes to lend $20 million to a large construction company that does business in Wisconsin, Minnesota, and the Dakotas. The construction company is a Delaware corporation. It has an unincorporated joint venture whose principal office is in western North Dakota, where it is constructing a dam. The equipment offered as collateral consists mostly of conventional construction equipment, such as large off-road trucks, bulldozers, hoists, cranes, cement mixers, gravel dispensers, and other more elaborate equipment.

Assume that the parent debtor's name is Bisgard-Larson Construction Co., and that the joint venture is known colloquially as the Williston Dam Co., but in fact has a formal partnership name, Bisgard, Larson and Lempke.

Assume a financing statement filed in North Dakota for the joint venture transposed the individual names in Bisgard, Larson and Lempke so that the joint venture's name read "Lempke-Bisgard, Larson." The filing was accordingly indexed under L, not B. Assume, too, that the excessively cautious banker filed a second financing statement, listing the name of the debtor joint venture as "Williston Dam Co." The joint venture has now gone bankrupt, and the trustee claims that the financing statements are inadequate to perfect the bank's security.

What do you think?

PROBLEM 2-5

In the third year of the loan, assume that Bank One changed its name to Bank of the Universe. Would that render the financing statements invalid?

PROBLEM 2-6

In May 1989, Jeffery Sharp and Thurman Agee, individuals doing business as T & J Logging, approached Krystal Hill about a loan for their business. Hill lent $25,000 to Sharp and Agee in exchange for a note bearing ten percent interest. Simultaneously, Sharp and Agee executed a security agreement granting Hill a security interest in specified collateral. The names appearing on the security agreement and the promissory note were "James Thurman Agee" and "Jeffery Keith Sharp." On June 8, 1989, Hill filed a financing statement under their full names with the Office of the Secretary of State describing the collateral and listing Hill as the secured party.

Three years later, Sharp and Agee borrowed from Fifth Bank and granted it a security interest in the same collateral that secured the note to Hill. The two signatures on the notes to the bank were "Jeff Sharp" and "Thurman Agee" as officers of "T & J Loggers." Fifth Bank filed financing statements under the names "Jeff Sharp," "Thurman Agee," and "T & J Loggers" with the Office of the Secretary of State.

In October 1992, Sharp and Agee defaulted on the loan to Hill, and she repossessed the collateral. When Fifth Bank learned of the repossession, it sent a letter to the Secretary of State's office requesting a list of all financing statements under the names "Jeff Sharp," "Thurman Agee," and "T & J Loggers." The Office of the Secretary of State responded that only Fifth Bank had filed under those names.

Fifth Bank has brought an action seeking a declaratory judgment that Hill's security interest was not perfected by a properly filed financial statement. Fifth Bank has emphasized that the Office of the Secretary of State did not find a copy of Hill's financing statement during its search. As a result, Fifth Bank argues that Hill's financing statement was never properly filed and thus her interest never perfected. In response, Hill has introduced into evidence a copy of her financing statement, properly stamped by the Office of the Secretary of State and filed on June 8, 1989.

Does Fifth Bank win? What is its best argument? *See Hill v. Farmers & Merchants Bank of Waterloo*, 641 So.2d 788 (Ala. 1994).

PROBLEM 2-7

Debtor, Smokee-Linc, Inc., a sausage manufacturer, executed a security interest in its accounts, equipment, and inventory to secure a working capital loan from Centerville National Bank ("CNB"). CNB filed a financing statement, or UCC–1, at the Secretary of State's office. The UCC–1 covered the accounts, equipment, and inventory and listed "Smokee-Linc, Inc." as the debtor.

One month after CNB filed the UCC–1, Debtor filed for a corporate name change as required under the Corporation Code. Debtor changed its name to "Smokey Link, Inc." CNB was not notified of the corporate name change. Six months after CNB filed its UCC–1, Debtor filed for bankruptcy in Chapter 11.

Assume the Secretary of State enters the filed UCC–1s into a central computing system. Whenever a filing search is requested, the computer searches for the debtor's name. Once this name is found, the computer prints out all filings under that name. The computer also prints out the filings under the three names alphabetically prior and subsequent to the spot where the requested name should appear. On the filing date of the petition in bankruptcy, the trustee requested a filing search of "Smokey Link, Inc." and received the following names on the computer printout:

Smoker Heaven, Inc.

Smokers Anonymous, Inc.

Smoker's Nook, Inc.

Smokey Mountain Trails, Ltd.

Smoothee-Cream Ice Creams, Inc.

Smothers, Richard

Smothers, Thomas

The trustee argues that CNB is not perfected because Debtor's new name did not appear among the search results and that the filing is therefore seriously misleading. Is she correct?

NOTE

The International Association of Commercial Administrators ("IACA"), a professional association for government administrators of business organization and secured transaction record systems, has come up with a list of model search logic rules. Under the IACA's model, there is no limit to the number of matches that may be returned in response to any particular search criteria entered into the record system. For example, if the name "John A. Smith" is entered, the system would not artificially limit the results to the first ten individuals with that name. Under the model, no distinction is made between upper and lower case letters. The character "&" (ampersand) is converted into the word "and" anywhere it appears. Punctuation marks and accents are disregarded. All numerals (0 through 9) and letters (A through Z, both upper and lower case) are recognized. Certain ending words and abbreviations are disregarded as "noise," according to the filing office's own list. The word "the" at the beginning of the name of an organization is disregarded. Spaces are disregarded. For the first and middle names of individual debtors, initials are treated as the logical equivalent of all names that begin with the particular initial. Accordingly, "John A. Smith" would return "John Andrew Smith," "John Avery Smith," etc. If the name entered is the last name of an individual without any first or middle name provided, the search will return individual names that consist of only that last name. Non-standard search options may be requested, but are not applied to determine the legal sufficiency of a debtor's name. *See* 9–506(c).

§ 4. PERFECTION IN MULTIPLE STATE TRANSACTIONS

Sections 9–301 through 9–307 deal with choice-of-law issues arising in transactions associated with more than one jurisdiction. Although it is technically correct to regard these sections as full-fledged choice-of-law provisions on perfection and priority, their most significant function is to answer a single question: where to file a financing statement? The adoption of revised Article 9 in the various states has produced a near-unified body of statutory law on how one takes and perfects a security interest, on the rights of the creditor upon default, and on rules of priority.

Things are not so simple with the place of filing, however. When the law of Ohio controls, it will require one to file a financing statement in

Columbus, but when the law of Illinois controls, one must file in Springfield. Because most perfection is accomplished by filing, and because a filing in the wrong place is no filing at all, the choice-of-law rules on place of filing are as important as the choice-of-law rules on other Article 9 questions are unimportant.

PRE-1999 RULES

Section 9–103 of pre-revision Article 9 contained a comprehensive and complicated set of rules about place of perfection. The premise of these rules was that filing with respect to goods should normally be at the goods' location and that filing with respect to intangibles should normally be at the debtor's location. Goods classified as "mobile" were treated like intangibles: filing was to take place at the debtor's location. Under the prior Code, a corporate debtor's location was at its chief place of business, usually the place of the chief executive office. The old section 9–103 also had a separate rule for purchase-money security interests for goods purchased in one state and then shipped to the debtor in another.

Each of these rules had a perfectly understandable, rational basis, and in theory the rules were easy to understand and apply. In practice, however, the pre-1999 rules presented considerable difficulty. First, one needed to ascertain whether the goods were mobile goods or not. If they were mobile, the filing was where the debtor was located; if they were not mobile, the filing was where the goods were located. Second, one needed a rule for goods that were moved from one state to another. Since perfection depended upon the location of the goods in a particular state, a security interest perfected by filing at the original location would necessarily become unperfected at some point after the goods were moved from that state, for the person in the new state would expect to search in the new state. Former section 9–103 provided a four-month "grace period" in which perfection would continue in the new state. If the creditor did not "catch up" with the goods before the end of four months by filing in the new state, its security interest was generally rendered unperfected. Finally, it was not always easy to determine the location of a debtor's "chief place of business." This was particularly true with respect to any company that had businesses in many states. The chief executive officer of such a company might be in one location during one part of the week and in another location during the other part; the remaining members of the executive staff might be in yet a third place. Of all the problems of pre-revision Article 9, those presented by the multi-state rules in former section 9–103 proved to be the easiest to identify and resolve in the 1999 revision.

GENERAL RULE—1999 REVISION

With exceptions we will discuss elsewhere, section 9–301 directs that the law of the debtor's location "governs perfection." Section 9–301(2) excludes possessory security interests from that rule, and section 9–301(3) excludes fixture filings and security interests in timber to be cut, but the general rule applicable to ninety-nine percent of all filings is that one perfects by filing at the debtor's location. This means that the distinctions that formerly had to be recognized between tangible and intangible collateral and between mobile and non-mobile goods are no longer necessary; also unnecessary are the rules about perfection continuing after the debtor moves the collateral from one state to another.

Section 9–307, which addresses the location of the debtor, makes a second important change in the law. Subsection (b) adopts the conventional rules about the location of an individual (the individual's principal residence), of an organization with only one place of business (its place of business), and of an organization with more than one place of business (its chief executive office). But the major change comes in section 9–307(e), which deems corporations and other organizations that qualify as "registered organizations" to be located in the state where they are organized. "Registered organizations" are entities formed under the laws of a U.S. state. Thus, a corporation incorporated under Illinois law is located in Illinois, even if its principal office and all of its business is in California, and a business incorporated in Ohio is located in Ohio, even if ninety percent of its business occurs in states other than Ohio and even if its chief executive office is located in Chicago. This means that for all domestic corporate debtors, along with other entities such as limited liability companies and certain partnerships that qualify as "registered organizations," all the ambiguity about location is gone. The messy factual questions about where the CEO goes to work and whether that location is the chief office are irrelevant.

That the drafters chose to have perfection governed by the law of the debtor's location—in the case of corporate debtors, their place of incorporation—brings a bonus. The movement of a corporation by reincorporation in a new state is far less common than the movement of goods from one state to another. Movement by reincorporation is also, presumably, less frequent than the movement of a chief executive office or other indicia of business affairs. Thus, while the law still needs a provision for change of the debtor's location, the particular indicia of location listed in the current section 9–307 are less likely to change than the former indicia, and the debtor's location is far less likely to change than the location of the goods.

Here the drafters have done us a favor that is hard to exaggerate. Under revised Article 9, it is far easier to determine where to file than under the pre-1999 law. It is also less likely that a security interest, once perfected, will become unperfected because of a change in the location of goods or the like, and the chances are much slimmer that a diligent search will fail to uncover a properly filed financing statement.

To understand the rules we have just described, consider section 9–301, which reads in full:

> Law governing perfection and priority of security interests.
>
> Except as otherwise provided in Sections 9–303 through 9–306 [concerning goods covered by certificates of title, deposit accounts, investment property, and letter-of-credit-rights], the following rules determine the law governing perfection, the effect of perfection or nonperfection, and the priority of a security interest in collateral:
>
> > (1) Except as otherwise provided in this section, while a debtor is located in a jurisdiction, the local law of that jurisdiction governs perfection, the effect of perfection or nonperfection, and the priority of a security interest in collateral.
> >
> > (2) While collateral is located in a jurisdiction, the local law of that jurisdiction governs perfection, the effect of perfection or nonperfection, and the priority of a possessory security interest in that collateral.
> >
> > (3) Except as otherwise provided in paragraph (4), while tangible negotiable documents, goods, instruments, money, or tangible chattel paper is located in a jurisdiction, the local law of that jurisdiction governs:
> >
> > > (A) perfection of a security interest in the goods by filing a fixture filing;
> > >
> > > (B) perfection of a security interest in timber to be cut; and
> > >
> > > (C) the effect of perfection or nonperfection and the priority of a nonpossessory security interest in the collateral.
> >
> > (4) The local law of the jurisdiction in which the wellhead or minehead is located governs perfection, the effect of perfection or nonperfection, and the priority of a security interest in as-extracted collateral.

Having read section 9–301, you might doubt what is said above. Perfection by filing is at the debtor's location, yet subsection (2) seems to adopt the law of the collateral's location and subsection (3)(C) appears to apply the law of the goods' location to the "effect of perfection."

Section 9–301 requires careful, patient reading. First, subsection (2) does choose the law of the collateral's location, but only in the case of a *possessory* security interest—where the secured party perfects by taking possession of the collateral, a rare event. *See* 9–301 cmt. 5(a). Thus, if perfection depends on filing or control or if the security interest attaches automatically, subsection (2) does not apply. Moreover, the universal adoption of revised Article 9 has made subsection (2) largely irrelevant: the sufficient conditions for perfection by possession do not vary significantly from state to state.

But what is the distinction between section 9–301(1), which directs one to the debtor's location, and section 9–301(3)(C), which directs one to the location of the collateral? Compare the phrase in subsection (1), "perfection, the effect of perfection or nonperfection, and the priority . . .," with the phrase in subsection (3), "the effect of perfection or nonperfection and the priority . . . ." The distinction is that subsection (1) includes an element that subsection (3) omits: "perfection." Thus, subsection (1) provides the rule for how one perfects by filing—by looking to the law where the debtor is located. And because subsection (1) only applies "[e]xcept as otherwise provided in this section," and since subsection (3)(C) addresses the "effect of perfection or nonperfection, and the priority of a nonpossessory security interest," subsection (3)(C) provides the rule for determining the effect of perfection and priority—where the collateral is located.

And what is the difference between "the effect of perfection or nonperfection" and the "priority" of a security interest? The term "priority" plainly includes all of the rules in Part 3 of Article 9, such as the rules governing the priority between competing security interests in the same collateral and the priority between a perfected secured party and a buyer of the collateral. *See* 9–301 cmt. 2. In contrast, the meaning of the phrase "the effect of perfection or nonperfection" is less clear. On the surface, it appears to encompass other rights that a secured party enjoys, including a secured party's rights of enforcement under Part 6 of Article 9. *See* 9–301 cmt. 7. But here there is some confusion.

On the one hand, comment 1 to section 9–301 states that "the law applicable to issues such as . . . enforcement is governed by the rules in Section 1–301(a) and (b)." 9–301 cmt. 2. In turn, section 1–301(a) permits the parties to select the law of a particular state or nation so long as the transaction bears a reasonable relation to the selected jurisdiction, and section 1–301(b) provides that, in the absence of such an agreement and "except as provided in subsection (c)," the rules of the UCC govern to the extent provided by general conflict-of-law principles. *See* 1–301 cmt. 3. So the reference to "Section 1–301(a) and (b)" in comment 1 to section 9–301 would appear at first blush to suggest that the law governing a secured party's rights of enforcement is up to the parties' agreement, or, in the absence of an agreement, is left to general choice-of law rules. On the other hand, section 1–301(b) expressly cross-references section 1–301(c), and section 1–301(c) clearly provides that certain specific choice-of-law provisions, including expressly "Sections 9–301 through 9–307," must be followed, and that any contrary agreement is effective only to the extent permitted by those sections. Likewise, comment 1 to section 1–301 clearly explains that any choice-of-law agreement is subject to the "firm rules" stated in section 9–301. *See* 1–301 cmt. 1. Thus reference to section 1–301 simply refers one back to section 9–301. So what is the answer? Does the phrase "the effect of perfection or nonperfection" appearing in section 9–301 include a secured party's enforcement rights, and are those rights determined by the "firm rules" of section 9–301?

Fortunately, there is a fairly straightforward, common-sense response. *Of course* the law governing a secured party's enforcement rights is the law where the collateral is located as set forth in section 9–301. If the collateral is located in New York and New York has particular restrictions on what a secured party may do to enforce its rights against its collateral (*e.g.*, may repossess the collateral only without breaching the peace as provided under section 9–609), it is hard to imagine that a court sitting in New York would permit a secured party to violate those restrictions because the parties inserted into their security agreement a provision that that the law of some other jurisdiction applies (*e.g.*, one that imposed no restrictions on the secured party's ability to repossess its collateral).

To illustrate how section 9–301 operates, assume a court sitting in Ohio is determining the right of a secured creditor against goods located in Ohio. Assume further that the goods belong to a company doing business in Ohio but incorporated in Illinois. Both Ohio and Illinois have adopted revised Article 9. Sections 9–301(1) and 9–307 will direct the court to apply Illinois law in determining whether the secured creditor has filed the proper documents in the proper place—in this case, whether the secured party has filed its financing statement with the Secretary of State in Springfield, Illinois. If the secured creditor has properly filed in Illinois, section 9–301(3)(C) instructs the Ohio court to grant the secured creditor the rights and priority of a perfected secured creditor under Ohio law. If the secured creditor is being challenged by a second creditor or a judicial lien holder in Ohio or by any other claimant, section 9–301(3) directs the court to determine the *priority dispute* by reference to Ohio law. Thanks to the universal adoption of Article 9, the "effect of perfection" in most priority disputes and other cases will be the same under every state's law.

Section 9–301 is hardly a paragon of clarity. If you were drafting this provision, how would you go about setting out the relevant rules?

Consider the following case decided under old Article 9.

KONKEL V. GOLDEN PLAINS CREDIT UNION

Supreme Court of Colorado, 1989.
778 P.2d 660.

VOLLACK, JUSTICE:

Golden Plains Credit Union (Golden Plains) appeals the judgment of the court of appeals in *Golden Plains Credit Union v. Konkel*, 759 P.2d 788 (Colo. App. 1988), holding that the trial court erred in concluding that Golden Plains lost its security interest in a farm combine purchased in Kansas and subsequently moved and sold in Colorado. We affirm in part and reverse in part and remand the case to the court of appeals with directions to remand for further hearings.

I.

Golden Plains is a Kansas credit union. On May 4, 1978, it financed the purchase of two 1978 John Deere combines[1] by Duane Lewis, a farmer[2] and custom cutter.[3] In May 1978, Golden Plains filed a financing statement for the combines with the registrar of deeds in Hamilton County, Kansas, the county in which Lewis resided.

In the latter half of October 1979, Lewis transported the combines from Hamilton County, Kansas, to a farm he had recently purchased in Baca County, Colorado. On February 7, 1980, Lewis sold one of the combines in Colorado to Bud Konkel (Konkel), doing business as Konkel Equipment Company. Konkel made no effort to determine whether a financing statement describing Golden Plains' security interest in the combine was filed, nor did he have actual knowledge of Golden Plains' security interest. Konkel later sold the combine to a Colorado farmer.

In April 1984, Golden Plains filed a complaint in the Baca County District Court against Konkel for conversion of the combine, seeking its return or damages.[4] Golden Plains moved for summary judgment against Konkel on the ground that Golden Plains held a security interest in the combine at the time Konkel bought the combine from Lewis. Konkel moved for summary judgment against Golden Plains on the ground that Golden Plains lost its security interest in the combine in 1980 when it failed to file a second financing statement in Colorado within four months of the date Lewis moved the combine to Baca County.

---

[1] Lewis bought two combines in 1977. He traded them in for two 1978 combines in May 1978.

[2] In his deposition, Lewis stated that he farmed 920 acres of land in Hamilton County, Kansas, in 1978, 600 of which he owned and 320 of which he rented. He also stated that he purchased and maintained an 1120-acre farm in Baca County, Colorado, in 1979.

[3] In his deposition, Lewis stated that he had been a custom cutter of crops since 1970. In 1977, 1978, and 1979, he would cut crops in Oklahoma during the early part of the season, move the operation to Kansas and Nebraska, and finish the season in Colorado. He would then store the combines in Colorado during the winter.

[4] After Golden Plains filed its complaint against Konkel, Konkel filed a third-party complaint against Lewis, alleging false representation at the time of the 1980 purchase.

The trial court granted Konkel's motion for summary judgment. It made no attempt to classify the combine under the Kansas version of the Uniform Commercial Code (UCC or Code). Instead, it held that Golden Plains lost its security interest in the combine four months after Lewis moved the combine to Baca County, Colorado, pursuant to section 84–9–103(1)(d) [9–316(a)] of the law of Kansas.

The court of appeals reversed the judgment of the trial court. It first found that Golden Plains had perfected its security interest in the combine in May 1978 by filing its financing statement in Hamilton County, Kansas. The court of appeals relied on *Sequoia Machinery, Inc. v. Jarrett*, 410 F.2d 1116 (9th Cir. 1969), in concluding the combine was properly classified as "equipment used in farming operations" under section 84–9–401(1)(a) (1983) [9–501] of the law of Kansas because the combine was "specifically designed to be used for farming functions." *Golden Plains Credit Union v. Konkel*, 759 P.2d at 790. The court of appeals noted that the proper place for a creditor to file a financing statement and thereby perfect its security interest in a combine is the office of the registrar of deeds in the county in which the debtor resided, a procedure that was followed in this case.

The court of appeals then concluded that the trial court erred in concluding that Golden Plains lost its security interest in the combine under section 84–9–103(1)(d)(i) [9–316(a)] four months after the combine was "brought into" Colorado. Instead, the court of appeals found that the applicable Kansas statute was section 84–9–103(3) (1983 & 1988 Supp.) [9–301, 9–316(a)], governing "mobile goods." It noted that section 84–9–103(3)(a) and the Code commentary listed "commercial harvesting machinery" as an "excellent example" of mobile goods. It concluded that Golden Plains retained its security interest in the combine under section 84–9–103(3)(e) [9–316(a)(2)] until four months after "a change of the debtor's location to another jurisdiction." The court of appeals remanded the case to the trial court for a factual determination of whether Lewis had "changed his location" within the meaning of section 84–9–103(3)(d) [9–307] when he moved the combine to Colorado in October 1979.

We granted certiorari to determine two issues: first, whether Golden Plains properly perfected its security interest in the combine in May 1978; and second, assuming that Golden Plains had properly perfected its security interest in May 1978, whether Golden Plains lost its security interest in 1980 by failing to file a new financing statement in Colorado within four months of the time the debtor moved the combine to Baca County, Colorado.

II.

A.

Resolution of the first issue requires us to examine the efficacy of the "normal use test" in classifying collateral under the Kansas equivalent of section 9–401(1)(a) [9–501] of the Code. Konkel argues that Golden Plains never perfected its security interest in the combine in May 1978 because Golden Plains did not file its financing statement in the Office of the Kansas Secretary of State. Implicit in this is the argument that the combine is equipment other than "equipment used in farming operations" within the meaning of section 84–9–401(1)(a) [9–501] of the law of Kansas.[5]

* * *

Under Kansas law, the proper place to file a financing statement and thereby perfect a security interest is generally in the office of the secretary of state. Kan. Stat. Ann. § 84–9–401(1)(c) (1983 & 1988 Supp.) [9–501]. The practice of filing with the secretary of state, known as "central filing," however, is subject to a number of exceptions.[6] When the debtor is a resident of the state, the proper place to file a financing statement for collateral properly classified as "equipment used in farming operations," for example, is "in the office of the registrar of deeds in the county of the debtor's residence."[7] The practice of filing in the county of the debtor's residence is known as "local filing." If the combine is properly classified as "equipment used in farming operations," then Golden Plains' local filing was sufficient to perfect its security interest in the combine. If the combine is properly classified as equipment other than equipment used in farming operations, however, then central filing would be required to perfect Golden Plains' security interest in the combine. In order to determine whether the court of appeals erred in concluding that central filing was not required to perfect Golden Plains' security interest, we must first classify the collateral. *In re Reier*, 53 B.R. 395, 396 (Bankr. S.D. Ohio 1985).

In jurisdictions such as Kansas that adopt the second alternative subsection (1) of section 9–401 of the UCC [9–501], the most difficult problem involving equipment not subject to a certificate of title law "is

---

[5] Konkel and Golden Plains agree that the combine is "equipment" within the meaning of section 84–9–109(2) [9–102(a)(33)], which includes goods that are "used or bought for use primarily in business (including farming or a profession) or by a debtor who is a nonprofit organization or a governmental subdivision or agency or if the goods are not included in the definitions of inventory, farm products or consumer goods."

[6] At the time this dispute arose, central filing was not required in Kansas for "equipment used in farming operations," "farm products," "accounts or general intangibles arising from or relating to the sale of farm products by the farmer," "consumer goods," or "crops." Kan. Stat. Ann. 84–9–401(1)(a) (1983), *repealed and reenacted* (1984) (requiring central filing for "equipment used in farming operations," "farm products," and "crops") [9–501]. In such cases the proper place to file a financing statement depended on whether the debtor was a Kansas resident. If the debtor was a Kansas resident, then the proper place to file was "in the office of the registrar of deeds in the county of the debtor's residence." If the debtor was not a Kansas resident, then the proper place to file was "in the office of the registrar of deeds in the county where the goods are kept." *Id.*

[7] Although at the time this dispute arose a security interest in "equipment used in farming operations" could be perfected only by filing locally, the Kansas legislature amended section 84–9–401(1)(a) in 1984 by deleting the phrase "equipment used in farming operations" from the subsection relating to local filing. Ch. 345, sec. 1, § 84–9–401, 1983 Kan. Sess. Laws 1562, 1563. As a result, a security interest in such equipment is now perfected under Kansas law by filing centrally rather than locally. *See* Balloun, *Survey of Kansas Law: Secured Transactions*, 32 U. Kan. L. Rev. 351, 368 (1984).

drawing the line between 'equipment used in farming operations,' which normally requires local filing, and commercial equipment, which normally requires central filing." B. Clark, *The Law of Secured Transactions Under the Uniform Commercial Code* ¶ 8.3[1][a], at 8–8 (1980). The problem arises because the UCC does not define the phrase equipment used in farming operations. *See* 1 P. Coogan, W. Hogan, D. Vogts & J. McDonnell, *Secured Transactions Under the Uniform Commercial Code* § 6.03[2][a], at 6–34 (1989) ("[i]nartful drafting [of the phrase 'equipment used in farming operations'] has unintentionally produced a 'trap for the unwary' ").

As a result of this statutory ambiguity, courts have devised a number of tests to determine whether the collateral is properly classified as equipment used in farming operations. One such test is the "normal use test," which focuses on the inherent qualities of the collateral and the uses to which such collateral would normally be put. The leading case advocating the normal use test is *Sequoia Machinery, Inc. v. Jarrett*, 410 F.2d 1116 (9th Cir. 1969). The normal use test has been adopted by a minority of jurisdictions. *See, e.g., In re Burgess*, 30 B.R. 364, 366 (Bankr. W.D. Okla. 1983).

A second test is the "intended use test," which focuses on the use the debtor intended to make of the collateral as contemplated by the parties at the time of the sale. *See In re Collins*, 3 B.R. 144, 146 (Bankr. D.S.C. 1980). A third test is the "actual use test," which focuses on the use the debtor actually made of the collateral. *See In re Yeager Trucking*, 29 B.R. 131, 134 (Bankr. D. Colo. 1983) ("it is the use by the debtor, not any intended use by the creditor, that is controlling as to classification of the collateral"); *In re Butler*, 3 B.R. 182, 183–84 (Bankr. E.D. Tenn. 1980) ("the purpose for which the goods are bought and used determines the category in which goods should be placed"). Most courts follow either the intended use test or the actual use test. *See generally* T. Crandall, R. Hagedorn, F. Smith, *Debtor-Creditor Law Manual* ¶ 7–06[3][d][i], at 7–87 (1985).

According to Professors White and Summers, the real debate in classifying "equipment used in farming operations" is between the actual use test and the intended use test rather than between those tests and the normal use test:

> How one resolves the intended use versus actual use dispute depends ultimately on whether he values more highly secured creditors' interests or third party creditors' interests. A secured creditor would like to rely upon the debtor's statement about his intended use at the time the loan is made. A careful creditor can procure the debtor's written statement about his intended use and can then file in the proper place according to that use. On the other hand, third party creditors will surely argue for the actual use test.

J. White & R. Summers, *Uniform Commercial Code* § 24–15, at 362 (3d ed. 1988).

Although the normal use test, intended use test, and actual use test each has some logical appeal, the Kansas legislature has demonstrated its preference for the actual use test. The 1983 Kansas commentary to section 84–9–109 (1983 & 1988 Supp.) [9–102][9] states that the key in classifying the collateral "is the use to which the debtor puts the goods, not any inherent quality of the goods themselves." Given this choice by the Kansas legislature, we must conclude that the court of appeals erred in concluding that the normal use test employed in Sequoia Machinery was the proper test to determine whether the combine was "equipment used in farming operations" within the meaning of section 84–9–401(1)(a) [9–102] of the law of Kansas.[10]

While the prudent creditor in close cases such as this should file a financing statement both locally and centrally as insurance against an adverse judicial determination of the proper classification of a particular piece of equipment, *In re Burgess*, 30 B.R. at 366; B. Clark, *The Law of Secured Transactions Under the Uniform Commercial Code*, ¶ 9.5, at 9–21 (1989); J. White & R. Summers, *Uniform Commercial Code* § 24–14, at 359 (3d ed. 1988), the Code does not demand dual filing. Where the financing statement must be filed to perfect a security interest depends on the proper classification of the collateral. The trial court did not classify the combine. On remand, it must decide whether Lewis in May 1978 actually used the combine as "equipment used in farming operations." If the answer to this question is "no," then Golden Plains failed to perfect its security interest and judgment must be entered for Konkel.

B.

If the trial court decides that Lewis' actual use of the combine in May 1978 was as "equipment used in farming operations," however, then the trial court must decide whether Golden Plains' security interest remained in effect after Konkel purchased the combine. Resolution of this issue requires a determination of whether the combine is an "ordinary good"[11] or a mobile good.

---

[9] Section 84–9–109 [9–102] governs the classification of collateral. It creates four such classifications: consumer goods; equipment; farm products; and inventory. As the 1983 Kansas comments to section 84–9–109 [9–102] recognizes: "The classification of goods is important in a number of situations, e.g., to answer questions of priority (84–9–312 [9–322]), in determining the proper place to file a financing statement (84–9–401 [9–501]), and in determining the rights of persons who buy from a debtor goods subject to a security interest (84–9–307 [9–317(b), 9–320])."

[10] We need not decide and therefore express no opinion as to the appropriate test under Colorado law for determining whether a particular piece of machinery is "equipment used in farming operations."

[11] Under section 84–9–103(1)(a) [9–301], what are colloquially known as "ordinary goods" are defined as "goods other than those covered by a certificate of title described in subsection (2), mobile goods described in subsection (3), and mineral described in subsection (5)."

Konkel argues that Golden Plains' security interest lapsed under section 84–9–103(1)(d) [9–316(a)] when Golden Plains failed to file a financing statement in Colorado four months after Lewis brought the combine into Colorado. Golden Plains argues that its security interest remained in effect in February 1980 under section 84–9–103(3)(e) [9–316(a)] because Lewis did not "change" his "location" of Hamilton County, Kansas, when he moved the combine into Baca County, Colorado, in the latter half of October 1979.

Section 84–9–103(1) [9–301, 9–316(a)], the Kansas equivalent of section 9–103(1) of the Code, resolves priority disputes among creditors from different states having an interest in "ordinary goods" moved from one state to another. A security interest in ordinary goods which is properly perfected in one state expires four months after it is brought into the second state "and is thereafter deemed to have been unperfected as against a person who became a purchaser" in the second state. Kan.Stat.Ann. 84–9–103(1)(d)(i) (1983 & 1988 Supp.) [9–316(a), (b)]. This rule, known as the "carry-over perfection rule," gives secured creditors in one state a four-month grace period to relocate the ordinary goods and file a second financing statement. The grace period for ordinary goods begins to run from the time the collateral is brought into the second state. J. White & R. Summers, *Uniform Commercial Code* § 22–21, at 1057 n.28 (1988). Failure to file a second financing statement during the four-month grace period, however, will cause the secured creditor to lose his or her priority and be subordinated to the interest of a purchaser of the ordinary goods during the grace period. *Massey-Ferguson Credit Corp. v. Wells Motor Co.*, 374 So.2d 319, 322 (Ala. 1979); *Rockwell Int'l Credit Corp. v. Valley Bank*, 109 Idaho 406, 408, 707 P.2d 517, 519 (Idaho App. 1985); UCC 9–103 comment 7. As one commentator describes the operation of section 9–103(1)(d) [9–316(a)]:

> When ordinary goods are brought into another state subject to a perfected security interest, there is a carry over into the second state of the perfection obtained in the first state. This carry-over perfection is conditional, being conditioned upon the creditor's taking within the second state the steps required by that state to reperfect the security interest. If such steps are taken in the second state there is a perfection that continues according to the terms of the law of the second state. This perfection relates back to the initial acquisition of perfection in the first state.
>
> If the security interest is not perfected in the second state during the period of the carry-over perfection, it lapses retroactively and relative rights are determined as though such carry-over perfection had never existed.

8 R. Anderson, *Anderson on the Uniform Commercial Code* 9–103:39, at 510 (1985) (footnotes omitted).

In contrast to section 84–9–103(1), section 84–9–103(3) [9–301, 9–316(a)], the Kansas equivalent of section 9–103(3) of the Code, resolves priority disputes among creditors from more than one state having an interest in "mobile goods" moved from one state to another. Mobile goods are defined in section 9–103(3)(a) [9–301] as "goods which are mobile and which are of a type normally used in more than one jurisdiction."[12] A security interest in mobile goods which is properly perfected in one state expires four months after "a change in the debtor's location to another jurisdiction." Kan. Stat. Ann. 84–9–103(3)(e) [9–316(a)]. Under section 84–9–103(3)(d) [9–307], a debtor is deemed to be "located" at his "place of business if he has one, at his chief executive office if he has more than one place of business, otherwise at his residence." Therefore, if the combine is properly characterized as a mobile good and Lewis was deemed to be located in Hamilton County, Kansas, then his transporting of the combine to Colorado in October 1979 would have no effect on his perfected security interest in Kansas and Konkel would take the combine subject to Golden Plains' security interest. If the combine is properly characterized as an ordinary good, however, then Konkel would take free of Golden Plains' security interest.

We agree with the analysis of the court of appeals that the combine is properly characterized under Kansas law as a mobile good. The court of appeals correctly noted that the definition of mobile goods in section 84–9–103(3)(a) expressly included "commercial harvesting machinery and the like." The court of appeals also properly recognized that the 1983 Kansas commentary to section 84–9–103 [9–301] describes precisely the problem presented in this case:

> An excellent example of mobile goods, and one which is set forth expressly in [§ 84–9–103(3)], is commercial harvesting machinery. For example, if the debtor is a custom cutter headquartered in Wichita, [then] Kansas would be the proper place to file the financing statement even though the harvesting machinery goes from Texas to North Dakota during the cutting season.

For these reasons, we conclude that the combine Konkel purchased was a mobile good within the meaning of section 84–9–103(3)(a) [9–301]. Because the combine was properly characterized as a mobile good, the trial court erred in concluding that Golden Plains lost its security interest in the combine solely because Golden Plains failed to reperfect its security interest within four months of bringing the combine into Baca County,

[12] The definition of mobile goods also requires that the goods are not covered by a certificate of title under 9–103(2)(a) and that the goods are either a debtor's equipment or his inventory that he leases to others. UCC § 9–103(3)(a); J. White & R. Summers, *Uniform Commercial Code* ¶ 22–23, at 1063 (1988). Both parties agree that neither of these requirements is at issue.

Colorado. When the collateral was "brought into" the second state is a relevant inquiry for ordinary goods but is an irrelevant inquiry for mobile goods. The relevant inquiry for mobile goods under Kansas law is whether the debtor has "changed his location," *see* Kan. Stat. Ann. § 84–9–103(3)(e) [9–316(a)], which in this case requires a determination of the debtor's place of residence, *see* Kan. Stat. Ann. § 84–9–103(3)(d) [9–307]. The court of appeals correctly noted that this issue was not decided by the trial court. We leave that determination for the trial court on remand.

III.

On remand, the trial court must use the actual use test to determine whether Golden Plains properly perfected its security interest in the combine under Kansas law in May 1978. If it determines that the actual use of the combine was as "equipment used in farm operations," then the trial court must also determine if Lewis had "changed his location" under section 84–9–103(3)(d) [9–307] at the time Konkel purchased the combine.

The judgment of the court of appeals is affirmed with respect to its decision that the combine was a mobile good. The judgment of the court of appeals is reversed with respect to its decision to require application of the "inherent use test." The case is remanded to the court of appeals with directions to remand to the trial court for further hearings.

[some footnotes omitted]

PROBLEM 2-8

How does the *Konkel* case come out if both Kansas and Colorado have revised Article 9 at all relevant times? Most of the issues that troubled the court in *Konkel* are gone. Note particularly that the parties need not concern themselves with the question whether these combines are commercial equipment or farm equipment, nor whether they are mobile goods or only conventional goods. But under revised Article 9, it will remain important to know when and if Lewis ceased to reside in Kansas and commenced to reside in Colorado.

Note the definition of "debtor" in section 9–102(a)(28) as "a person having an interest, other than a security interest or other lien, in the collateral." So long as Lewis owned the combine in question, he was the debtor. Under section 9–316(a)(2), a perfected security interest becomes unperfected four months after a change of the debtor's "location" to a different jurisdiction. So if Lewis changed his "location" from Kansas to Colorado, *see* 9–307, the security interest in the combine would have become unperfected four months after his move, unless Golden Plains perfected it in Colorado.

What about Golden Plains' rights against Konkel? In general, a security interest that has attached to collateral endures notwithstanding the collateral's sale or other disposition. *See* 9–315(a)(1). A filed financing statement likewise generally remains effective notwithstanding the sale or other disposition. *See* 9–507(a). Under section 9–316(a)(3), however, a perfected security interest becomes unperfected one year after the transfer of the collateral to another person who thereby becomes a debtor and who is located in another jurisdiction. When Konkel bought the combine from Lewis he became a debtor. *See* 9–102 cmt. 2(a) ("By including in the definition of 'debtor' all persons with a property interest (other than a security interest in or other lien on collateral), the definition includes transferees of collateral, whether or not the secured party knows of the transfer or the transferee's identity.") One year later, the security interest would have become unperfected unless Golden Plains perfected it in Colorado. If Golden Plains failed to perfect its security interest in Colorado within the one-year period, it would be deemed never to have been perfected as against Konkel as purchaser. *See* 9–316(b). As a result, Konkel would take free of Golden Plains' security interest if Konkel gave value, took delivery, and was unaware of the security interest. *See* 9–317(b).

Could Golden Plains have pursued the farmer who bought the combine from Konkel? Once again, a security interest that attaches to collateral generally endures notwithstanding the collateral's sale or other disposition, *see* 9–315(a)(1), and a filed financing statement likewise generally remains effective, *see* 9–507(a). If Golden Plains perfected its security interest in Colorado within the time required by section 9–316(a), it could assert its security interest against the farmer. If it failed to timely perfect in Colorado, however, then it could not do so if the farmer gave value, took delivery from Konkel, and was unaware of the security interest. *See* 9–317(b).

Golden Plains' potential recourse against the farmer seems a bit unfair, no? The innocent farmer went to a local dealer in farming machinery (Konkel), bought the combine from Konkel's inventory, and took it home blissfully ignorant of Golden Plains' interest. Imagine the farmer's surprise if he were to learn one day that Golden Plains had a valid (and to the farmer entirely secret) security interest in the combine superior to the farmer's ownership interest. Does the law offer the farmer a remedy? Unless disclaimed, Konkel warranted clear title when he sold the combine to the farmer. *See* 2–312. So if Golden Plains swooped down and took the combine from the farmer, the farmer would likely be able to sue Konkel, the dealer, for breach of warranty. But what if Konkel properly disclaimed any such warranty?

If you went to a car dealership and purchased a new car, wouldn't you be surprised to discover that your new car came encumbered with a security interest that the dealer granted to his bank? Before making your purchase, would you have even thought to check the UCC files at the secretary of state's office? Under section 9–320 (discussed in greater detail in Chapter 4), you would typically take free of any such security interest. But can you see why section 9–320 would not protect the farmer who bought from Konkel? Note carefully that section 9–320 applies to "a security interest created by the buyer's seller." The farmer bought from Konkel, and thus Konkel is the farmer's seller, but Konkel did not create the security interest, Lewis did. So section 9–320 does not apply. Does this seem right to you?

PROBLEM 2-9

Assume again the same general facts set out in Problem 2–4 above, namely that you represent Bank One, which proposes to lend $20 million to a large construction company that does business in Wisconsin, Minnesota, and the Dakotas. The construction company is a Delaware corporation with three subsidiaries, of which two are Minnesota corporations and one is a Wisconsin corporation. The construction company also has an unincorporated joint venture whose principal office is in western North Dakota, where the joint venture is constructing a dam. The equipment offered as collateral consists mostly of conventional construction equipment, such as large off-road trucks, bulldozers, hoists, cranes, cement mixers, gravel dispensers, and other more elaborate equipment. In addition, assume that the banker tells you the equipment is worth at least $30 million and is located in various places throughout the four-state area where the debtor does business. It is, of course, possible that during the term of the loan some or much of the equipment will be moved to other places.

What documents must you file, and in which places, in order to perfect Bank One's security interests?

Assume further that the parent debtor's name is Bisgard-Larson Construction Co., that the Wisconsin subsidiary's name is Milwaukee Construction Co., that the two Minnesota subsidiaries are called Minnesota 1 Co. and Minnesota 2 Co., and that the joint venture is known colloquially as the Williston Dam Co., but in fact has a formal partnership name, Bisgard, Larson and Lempke. What should your financing statement or statements say?

NOTE

Here is a good place to pause and reflect for a moment on the durability of a security interest in equipment in the face of changing circumstances. Begin with the concept of attachment. Recall that, under section 9–203(a), a security interest "attaches" when it becomes "enforceable." Under section 9–203(b), a security interest is "enforceable" when (1) value has been given, (2) the debtor has rights in the collateral, and (3) one of the conditions specified in section 9–203(b)(3) has been satisfied—usually that the debtor has authenticated (*e.g.*, signed) a security agreement granting the security interest to the secured party and describing the collateral in accordance with section 9–108. An attached security interest is a form of property right. Under section 1–201(b)(29) it is even treated as a kind of "purchase," and the secured party as a "purchaser" under section 1–201(b)(30). Of course, the secured party does not *actually* purchase the collateral, at least not in the sense of becoming its owner. Absent default and foreclosure (or other disposition), the debtor retains ownership. Nonetheless, once it attaches a security interest is treated as a valid form of property right entitled to protection, including under the Fifth Amendment of the U.S. Constitution.

As a form of property right, it is unsurprising that, once attached, a security interest has a certain persistent durability. After all, under section 9–

201(a), a security interest is supposed to be good against the world—an *in rem* property entitlement. But exactly how durable is it? In general, fairly durable but a number of intervening events may impact the secured party's perfected status, opening the door to third parties potentially defeating the secured party's interest.

The first event is that the debtor may change his name. Here the consequences are relatively modest for the less-than-diligent secured party. If the debtor changes his name to such a degree that it renders a filed financing statement seriously misleading (*i.e.*, a search under the debtor's new name would not pull up the filing), this will not affect the durability of a security interest that has already attached to collateral before the name change. That is because, under section 9–507(c), the previously filed financing statement remains effective to perfect a security interest in collateral the debtor owned before the name change, and is likewise effective to perfect a security interest in collateral that the debtor acquires within four months after the name change (referred to, once again, as "after-acquired collateral"). If the secured party does not reperfect by filing a new financing statement listing the debtor's new name within the four-month period, the only consequence is that the financing statement is ineffective to perfect a security interest in collateral the debtor acquires *after* the four-month period has expired. Here the drafters were willing to sanction a secret lien with only minor adverse consequences to the secured party.

The second is that the debtor may change his location, and here the consequences may be more serious. If the debtor changes his location (*e.g.*, by moving his residence from Kansas to Colorado), this occasions a change in the governing law under section 9–301. Recall that, under sections 9–301(1) and 9–501(a), the correct place to file a financing statement is in the state where the debtor is located as determined in accordance with the rules specified in section 9–307. If the debtor changes his location, the correct place to file under 9–301 becomes the new location, not the old one. Under section 9–316(a)(2), the secured party has four months to reperfect in the new location. If the secured party does so by filing a financing statement in the new location within the four-month period, section 9–316(b) provides that the security interest remains perfected. But if the secured party fails to do so, section 9–316(b) directs that the security interest becomes unperfected and "is deemed never to have been perfected against a purchaser of the collateral for value." This means that, under section 9–317(b) a buyer who acquires the collateral, gives value, and takes delivery without knowledge of the security interest will take the collateral free of the security interest. It also means that a subsequent secured party who perfects a security interest against the same collateral in the new location will also prevail—recall that the taking of a security interest is a form of purchase under section 1–201(b)(29), rendering the secured party a "purchaser" under section 1–201(b)(30). Here the drafters were willing to sacrifice the accuracy of the filing system, but only for four months, and the consequence for failing to detect the debtor's change of location and reperfect in the new jurisdiction are fairly severe.

The third is that the debtor may transfer the collateral to a buyer who is located in a different jurisdiction. Under section 9–315(a)(1), a security interest generally continues in collateral notwithstanding sale or other disposition. In addition, under section 9–507(a), perfection generally follows along for the ride. Thus, when the debtor sells his equipment to a buyer, any perfected security interest generally goes along with it—with the buyer of the equipment then treated as the "debtor" (defined in section 9–102(a)(28) as *anyone* with an interest in the collateral, other than a security interest). But if the buyer is located in another jurisdiction, section 9–316(a)(3) provides that perfection will lapse if the secured party does not file a financing statement against the buyer in the new jurisdiction within one year. And under section 9–316(b), if it lapses the security interest is deemed never to have been perfected as against the buyer. This means that, under section 9–317(b), the buyer will own the collateral free and clear of the security interest if the buyer gave value for the collateral, took delivery, and was unaware of the security interest. Here the drafters were likewise willing to sanction a secret lien for a year, and the consequences to the secured party for failing to reperfect are once again fairly severe: the loss of an effective security interest as against buyers of equipment collateral.

Contrast this last example with what happens if the debtor transfers the collateral to a buyer located in the *same* jurisdiction as the debtor. Once again, sections 9–315(a)(1) and 9–507(a) apply and the perfected security interest will generally continue in the collateral. Does the secured party have an obligation to reperfect against the buyer located in the same jurisdiction? No, although it would probably be wise for the secured party to do so. Here there is no change in the governing law, and the drafters were willing to sanction an indefinite secret lien in equipment collateral. Do you agree with their choice?

Be aware that the rules are somewhat different for different kinds of collateral. In the case of inventory, for example, a special provision, section 9–320, gives certain buyers more protection than buyers of equipment. We will examine this provision in Chapter 4. We will also take up in Chapter 4 the special case of what happens when a debtor merges with another party, giving rise to a creature called a "new debtor" as defined in section 9–102(a)(56).

§ 5. FILING IN INTERNATIONAL TRANSACTIONS

Because revised Article 9 has been adopted everywhere in the U.S., there are very few interesting choice-of-law questions (other than the question of where to file) remaining when the debtor and its assets are located in the U.S. As we have seen, the creditor needs only examine Part 3 of Article 9 to find the place to file. Complications arise when the debtor or the collateral is not located in the U.S.

Under section 9–301, filing is in the jurisdiction of the debtor's location. Under section 9–307(e), the location of a domestic debtor that is a registered organization (such as a corporation) is the state where it is incorporated. Determining the location of the debtor under section 9–307 for companies incorporated outside of the United States is not as straightforward. If a foreign corporation has only one location, Article 9 directs filing at its place of business, not at its place of incorporation. *Compare* 9–307(b)(2) *with* 9–307(e). If the company has multiple locations, Article 9 directs filing at the chief executive office. *See* 9–307(b)(3). If the chief executive office or the sole place of business is abroad, and if the law on filing there is not similar to that of the U.S., section 9–307(c) directs filing in Washington, D.C.

Section 9–307(c) provides a standard for determining when the law of a foreign jurisdiction on filing is not sufficiently similar to that of the U.S. that a filing in Washington, D.C. is required. Section 9–307(c) specifies that the foreign law is not sufficiently similar unless it "generally requires information concerning the existence of a nonpossessory security interest to be made generally available in a filing, recording, or registration system as a condition or result of the security interest's obtaining priority over the rights of a lien creditor with respect to the collateral." This standard is a kind of "equivalence test." The equivalence test set forth in section 9–307(c), however, has proved confusing and difficult to administer. As a practical matter, given the uncertainties surrounding section 9–307(c), secured lenders may choose both to file a UCC–1 financing statement in Washington, D.C., as well as engage local counsel to perfect their security interest in accordance with a foreign jurisdiction's laws. Given the prominence of Article 9 secured transactions in the international project finance industry, and in facilitating foreign direct investment generally, the issue of filing in international transactions is a prominent one in many lawyers' practices.

The issues that arise in applying section 9–307(c) involve the facts that foreign countries: (i) may have filing systems that are limited to certain types of debtors (*i.e.*, many Latin American countries) or secured parties (*i.e.* Taiwan); (ii) may require registration for some types of collateral but not others that would be covered by a domestic UCC–1 financing statement; (iii) may have filing systems that look equivalent on paper, but are incomplete, out-of-date, and poorly administered; and (iv) may have filing systems accessible only through certain local functionaries. In summary, there are some countries for which there are relatively clear answers in applying section 9–307(c). Canada and New Zealand would pass the equivalency test. Germany, Austria, and the Netherlands, with their reliance on unregistered security devices such as conditional sales, fiduciary title, and constructive delivery for nonpossessory security interests, would not. For debtors based in various other countries, it may be difficult to determine with certainty the location of the debtor and governing law for the purposes of Article 9.

Assume a foreign debtor with a chief place of business in Romania. If Romanian filing requirements generally conform to the requirements of section 9–307(c), Article 9 directs filing in Romania. If the Romanian filing system does not conform, then Article 9 directs filing in the District of Columbia. Should a dispute arise in a foreign court, it seems doubtful that a foreign jurisdiction would regard a filing in the District of Columbia as adequate, but that remains to be seen. Also, remember that while under section 9–301(1) the law governing perfection is where the debtor is located, under section 9–301(3) the law governing the effect of perfection or non-perfection and priority of an interest in tangible collateral is the law where the collateral is located.

Consider the following problems:

1. Bank advances a loan to a debtor incorporated in Delaware. Debtor operates outlets in several Canadian provinces, including Saskatchewan. To secure its loan, Bank takes a security interest in the packing equipment used by the debtor in its Saskatchewan operation.

If a priority competition involving this security interest were litigated in the U.S., the law applicable to perfection would be the law of the debtor's location as determined by Article 9, namely Delaware. The Bank would *perfect* by filing in Delaware. *See* 9–301(1), 9–307(e). However, under Article 9, the *priority* of the security interest would be determined by the law of the location of the collateral, Saskatchewan. *See* 9–301(3)(C). If Bank were first to file and Saskatchewan law gave priority to the first perfected, Bank would win any priority dispute.

If the priority competition were litigated in Saskatchewan, the Canadian court would apply Saskatchewan choice of law rules. Under their law, perfection *and* priority are both determined by the law of the location of the collateral. So it would require a Saskatchewan filing for perfection. To protect itself fully, Bank must file in the registries of both Delaware and Saskatchewan.

2. Secured Party 1 ("SP1") takes a security interest in manufacturing equipment owned by a debtor incorporated in Delaware. Debtor does business in several jurisdictions, including Montana, where the equipment is located. Later the equipment is moved to Saskatchewan, and the debtor gives a security interest to Secured Party 2 ("SP2"). SP1 files in Delaware and SP2 files in Saskatchewan.

If the priority competition between SP1 and SP2 were litigated in Montana under Article 9, the place of filing for both security interests would be determined by the location of the debtor, Delaware. However, priority would be determined by the law of the jurisdiction in which the goods are located, Saskatchewan. In this scenario SP1 still wins, since presumably Saskatchewan law (applied by the Montana court) gives priority to the first perfected.

If the same case arose with a debtor incorporated in Saskatchewan and its chief executive office is in Illinois, both a Canadian court and a U.S. court would apply the law of Illinois to the issues of perfection and priority. Understand how this might fool someone who has not read section 9–307 carefully. A filing at the place of incorporation is ineffective under American law, *see* 9–307(b)(3), because the debtor is a foreign corporation. It is also ineffective under Canadian law, which directs a filing at the chief place of business, not at the place of incorporation.

3. Lender loans money to a debtor incorporated in Delaware. Debtor's chief executive office is in Illinois. Debtor operates retail stores in several Canadian provinces, including Saskatchewan. To secure its loan, Secured Party takes a security interest in the delivery vehicles used by the debtor in its Saskatchewan operation. Where should the creditor file, in Delaware, in Illinois, in Saskatchewan, or should it instead get its name on the certificates of title?

Article 9 would determine perfection according to Delaware law. *See* 9–307(e). However, the priority of the security interest would be determined by the law of the location of the collateral, Saskatchewan. *See* 9–301(1), 9–301(3)(c). Since the vehicles would be certificate of title goods in the United States subject to section 9–311, it might appear that Lender should get its name on the certificate of title. But since there are no certificates of title in Saskatchewan, section 9–311 would not apply. So there should be a conventional filing in the Delaware records for these vehicles. If Lender made such a filing, an American court would treat its interests as perfected, and that would give it priority (under Saskatchewan law) over later perfected persons.

If the priority competition occurred in a Saskatchewan court, the relevant choice of law rule would be that applicable to mobile goods. Since the collateral is "goods of a type that are normally used in more than one jurisdiction," and they are held by the debtor as equipment, Saskatchewan law directs a filing at the debtor's principal place of business, Illinois. Accordingly, the law applicable to perfection and priority of the security interest would be the law of the debtor's location, Illinois.

Thus, to protect itself fully, Secured Party must file in the registries of Delaware and Illinois. Note the irony; foreign law directs a filing in an office in Illinois where American law, on its own, would never require a filing.

§ 6. THE LEGAL RIGHTS ACQUIRED BY ATTACHMENT AND THE GREATER LEGAL RIGHTS ACQUIRED BY PERFECTION

Even an unperfected security interest—one that complies with section 9–203, but not with the perfection rules of section 9–308 *et seq.*—gives the secured creditor all the rights it needs vis-à-vis the debtor and unsecured creditors of the debtor. But an unperfected secured creditor will lose to any other secured creditor who perfects—even to one who perfects with knowledge of the preexisting unperfected security interest. Far more important, an unperfected secured creditor will lose to the trustee in bankruptcy, if the debtor goes bankrupt. These conclusions follow from sections 9–201, 9–203, 9–317, and 9–322—read them.

Section 544(a) of the Bankruptcy Code gives the trustee in bankruptcy the rights of a lien creditor under state law on the date the bankruptcy petition is filed. Thus, the trustee (or the debtor in possession in a Chapter

11 case) will enjoy the rights specified in section 9–317 to defeat unperfected security interests. Most of the litigation on perfection occurs in the bankruptcy court to challenge security interests that are not properly perfected. By avoiding a security interest as unperfected, the trustee reduces the secured creditor to an unsecured creditor and forces him to share pro rata with all the other unsecured creditors.

But what are the legal rights of the secured creditor who possesses a security interest that the trustee is unable to avoid? First is the right to repossess and sell the asset, and thus to turn the claim into money. *See* 9–609, 9–610. It is a mistake, however, to assume that repossession is the best course of action for a secured creditor. Here, as elsewhere, the threat of action—the second of the secured creditor's rights—may be more powerful than the action itself. Thus, a threat to deprive the debtor of the collateral—or, where the debtor is insolvent, to deprive other creditors of the collateral—may itself be more productive than actual repossession and sale. Assume, for example, that a particular piece of machinery is critical to the operation of a debtor's business, and that item by itself has a very modest value but is difficult to reproduce. In this case, the threat against the debtor is likely more valuable than the machine itself.

The third right is the specific set of additional benefits that the perfected secured creditor enjoys in bankruptcy. These include the rights to be protected during the bankruptcy, to insist upon the return of the collateral or upon payment in lieu thereof, and to influence the bankruptcy in ways not available to the unsecured creditor. The treatment of secured claims in bankruptcy is taken up in Chapter 3.

THE RIGHTS OF UNPERFECTED SECURED CREDITORS VERSUS THE RIGHTS OF UNSECURED CREDITORS WITH AND WITHOUT JUDICIAL LIENS

Section 9–201 states the basic right of the secured creditor vis-à-vis other creditors. Subsection (a) reads as follows:

> Except as otherwise provided in [the Uniform Commercial Code], a security agreement is effective according to its terms between the parties, against purchasers of the collateral, and against creditors.

Section 9–201 means what it says: the secured creditor, even an unperfected secured creditor, has greater rights in its collateral than any other creditor unless the UCC provides otherwise. In comparison, a creditor without a security interest or a lien has no claim on any specific collateral. Section 9–201 thus gives an unperfected but *secured* creditor rights superior to the rights of the *unsecured* creditor simply because the unsecured creditor essentially has no specific rights in any collateral. But that, of course, is not the end of the story. For example, an unsecured creditor may acquire a judicial lien. What then?

Section 9–317 provides in relevant part as follows:

> (a) **[Conflicting security interests and rights of lien creditors.]** A security interest or agricultural lien is subordinate to the rights of:
>
> > (1) a person entitled to priority under Section 9–322; and
> >
> > (2) except as otherwise provided in subsection (e), a person that becomes a lien creditor before the earlier of the time:
> >
> > > (A) the security interest or agricultural lien is perfected; or
> > >
> > > (B) one of the conditions specified in Section 9–203(b)(3) is met and a financing statement covering the collateral is filed.
>
> (b) **[Buyers that receive delivery.]** Except as otherwise provided in subsection (e), a buyer, other than a secured party, of tangible chattel paper, tangible documents, goods, instruments, or a certificated security takes free of a security interest or agricultural lien if the buyer gives value and receives delivery of the collateral without knowledge of the security interest or agricultural lien and before it is perfected.
>
> (c) **[Lessees that receive delivery.]** Except as otherwise provided in subsection (e), a lessee of goods takes free of a security interest or agricultural lien if the lessee gives value and receives delivery of the collateral without knowledge of the security interest or agricultural lien and before it is perfected.
>
> * * *
>
> (e) **[Purchase-money security interest.]** Except as otherwise provided in Sections 9–320 and 9–321, if a person files a financing statement with respect to a purchase-money security interest before or within 20 days after the debtor receives delivery of the collateral, the security interest takes priority over the rights of a buyer, lessee, or lien creditor which arise between the time the security interest attaches and the time of filing.

Section 9–317(a) subordinates an unperfected secured creditor to a lien creditor and, by negative implication, says that a lien creditor loses to a perfected secured creditor. The most important part of section 9–317 is subsection (a)(2), which renders an unperfected security interest subordinate to the rights of one who "becomes a lien creditor before the earlier of the time: (A) the security interest or agricultural lien is perfected; or (B) one of the conditions specified in Section 9–203(b)(3) is met and a financing statement covering the collateral is filed." Thus, if a bank takes a security interest in the debtor's equipment but fails to file a financing statement (or take possession), and if an unsecured creditor levies against the property and so procures a judicial lien on it, this formerly unsecured creditor—now a "lien creditor"—will defeat the prior unperfected secured creditor. Subsection (e) states an exception to this rule for purchase-money claims: if the holder of a purchase-money security interest files within twenty days "after the debtor receives delivery of the collateral," its security interest takes priority over whatever rights a lien creditor may have attached to the collateral between the time the security interest arose and the time of the filing. (We will address purchase-money security interests in greater detail in Chapter 4.)

Subsections (b) and (c) give priority over unperfected secured creditors to a variety of buyers and lessees. Under Article 9 these parties "take free" of any preexisting unperfected security interests. Although they differ somewhat in their particulars, the rules of the various subsections all require that a party who is to defeat a prior secured creditor must give "value" and, in the case of tangibles, "receive delivery," all "without knowledge of the security interest." *See* 1–202(a)(2) (defining "knowledge" to mean "actual knowledge"), 1–204 (defining "value" to include where a acquires rights "in return for any consideration sufficient to support a simple contract").

In section 9–317 the drafters made several cosmetic and a few minor substantive changes to former section 9–301. For example, they chose the language "takes free" in lieu of "is subordinate to." And the statute now provides that all buyers meeting the qualifications identified in section 9–317(b) take free, not just "buyers in ordinary course of business." *See* 1–201(b)(9) (defining the phrase "buyer in ordinary course of business"). Also, the rule in (a)(2) no longer requires a secured creditor to be perfected before its security interest can trump the rights of a lien creditor; it now suffices that one of the conditions specified in section 9–203(b)(3) is met and the secured creditor files a financing statement before the rights of the lien creditor arise. Thus, if the debtor executes a security agreement and the secured party properly files a financing statement before the rights of the lien creditor arise, the secured creditor will beat the lien creditor even though the secured party's security interest had not yet attached because the debtor did not yet have rights in the collateral or the secured party had not yet given value. (Recall that, under section 9–203, attachment occurs when the security interest is enforceable, and a security interest is not enforceable until value has been given and the debtor acquires rights in the collateral.) This is so even though the secured party was not "perfected" before the rights of the lien creditor arose (perfection requires attachment, *see* 9–308, and, again, attachment does not occur until the necessary requirements of section 9–203 are satisfied), but the secured party's priority remains subject to the limited qualifications set out in section 9–323(b). *See* 9–317 cmt. 4. Thus, section 9–317(a)(2) essentially follows the basic rule always applied in competition among secured creditors: priority dates from the earlier of filing *or* perfection.

It may be useful to understand what is implicit in the drafters' decisions here. In some cases a gap creditor who lends money in the interval between the attachment and perfection of another creditor's security interest can make a plausible claim that he has been injured. Prior to the adoption of revised Article 9, a few states gave gap creditors priority over unperfected secured creditors, even though the gap creditors had no lien. By generally subordinating creditors without liens to unperfected security interests, section 9–201 takes the opposing view, that gap creditors and their ilk are not entitled to protection. This decision means that section 544(b) of the Bankruptcy Code has less significance than it would otherwise have (recall that section 544(b) gives the trustee in bankruptcy the rights of a lien creditor, and thus to the extent the rights of lien creditors are more limited vis-à-vis perfected secured parties under Article 9, they are also more limited in the hands of the trustee).

In general a secured creditor has claims on the collateral superior to those of any unsecured creditor without a lien. A secured but unperfected creditor will usually be subordinate to lien creditors and to all buyers who give value and take delivery without knowledge. Notice the nuanced complexity involved in how Article 9 balances the competing interests of the holders of distinct property rights, particularly secured creditors versus lien creditors. Would you have made the same choices?

BASIC PRIORITIES AMONG CONFLICTING SECURITY INTERESTS: FIRST IN TIME, FIRST IN RIGHT

Section 9–322(a) states the basic priorities among competing secured creditors precisely:

> (a) **[General priority rules.]** Except as otherwise provided in this section, priority among conflicting security interests and agricultural liens in the same collateral is determined according to the following rules:
>
> > (1) Conflicting perfected security interests and agricultural liens rank according to priority in time of filing or perfection. Priority dates from the earlier of the time a filing covering the collateral is first made or the security interest or agricultural lien is first perfected, if there is no period thereafter when there is neither filing nor perfection.
> >
> > (2) A perfected security interest or agricultural lien has priority over a conflicting unperfected security interest or agricultural lien.

(3) The first security interest or agricultural lien to attach or become effective has priority if conflicting security interests and agricultural liens are unperfected.

When section 9–312 (the predecessor to section 9–322) was adopted, it replaced a multitude of unclear and inconsistent state laws. Section 9–322 preserves the certainty that section 9–312 imposed and, like its predecessor, forecloses choice-of-law disputes over priority among secured creditors. First in time, first in right—this general rule runs like a thread through virtually all priority schemes, and section 9–322 is no exception. The Code, however, is uniquely precise. The drafters appreciated the ambiguity inherent in the first-in-time slogan: namely, first to do what? Does the first person to make a loan have priority? Is it, instead, the first to file? Or is it the one who first procures the debtor's signature on a security agreement? Pre-Code law was divided on these questions, particularly in instances where a creditor made repeated advances. (For example, having furnished a line of credit secured by inventory or accounts receivable, the creditor may then have accepted repayments and made extensions of new credit on a daily basis.) Some rules gave the lender priority from the time it filed or performed some other perfecting act; others measured priority only from the time of the advance—that is, the time the loan was actually made. The drafters of section 9–322 and its predecessor chose the former approach and have stated all the rules with precision.

Observe first that subsection (a) is a "pure race" statute as opposed to a "notice-race" statute. That is, whoever wins the "race" to file is superior, even if the winner had "notice" or "knowledge" of an earlier claim. The section nowhere requires the victor to be ignorant of its competitor's claim. Example 1 of comment 4 illustrates both the unimportance of knowledge and the fact that the second to perfect may have priority if first to file. (Section 9–502(d) provides that a financing statement may be filed before a security agreement is made or before a security interest attaches under section 9–203. Under section 9–308(a), meanwhile, attachment is required in order for perfection to occur. Thus, filing may occur before perfection.) One justification for this rule is certainty. As a result of section 9–322, a disappointed secured creditor cannot assert facts, either trumped-up or true, on the basis of which a compassionate court might find sufficient knowledge to subordinate the winner of the race. If the competitor filed or otherwise perfected first, that is the end of it; the competitor wins, even if it was aware of the other party's prior but unperfected claim.

Because the drafters chose to permit perfection by possession and certain other non-filing acts, they could not simply give priority to the first to file. However, they went as far as possible in that direction, and section 9–322(a) is the result: if both competitors perfect by filing, the first to file wins. Since filing is a public act, the timing of which can by proved with accuracy, it is the most certain and satisfactory of the benchmarks for determining priority. And when the drafters wrote "filing," they meant what they wrote, not more and not less. Assume, for example, that an unscrupulous debtor simultaneously negotiates with two creditors. Creditor One files long before it makes a loan; sometime after Creditor One's filing, Creditor Two lends and files. At that point Creditor Two has a perfected security interest under sections 9–203 and 9–310. Creditor One, on the other hand, has no interest at all, for Creditor One has neither made a loan nor agreed to do so and thus has not yet given "value." But suppose Creditor One thereafter receives the debtor's security agreement, lends, and so becomes a perfected secured creditor. Who wins, and why? Although Creditor One was the last to perfect (recall that "perfection" requires "attachment" and that attachment requires the creditor to give "value"), it wins because it filed first. Creditor Two has no meritorious complaint, for Creditor Two could have protected itself by checking the files, where it would have found Creditor One's earlier filing.

The justification for determining priority by order of filing lies in the necessity of protecting the filing system. That is, the filing system depends for its utility on the fact that the first secured party to file can make subsequent advances without each time having to check for subsequent filings as a condition of protection. As to both future advances and after-acquired collateral (*see* 9–204, discussed in greater detail in Chapter 4), a lender's priority generally dates back to the time of filing.

The guiding principle of section 9–322(a) is that the secured party wins if it either files or otherwise perfects before its competitor. If both parties perfect by filing, priority goes to the party who filed first. Likewise, if one or both parties perfect by means other than filing, priority goes to the one who filed or otherwise perfected first. (As we shall see, Article 9 provides an exception to all of this in the case of purchase-money security interests, but that is a matter taken up in Chapter 4.)

PROBLEM 2-10

Debtor One gave a perfected security interest in a large and expensive piece of industrial machinery to Bank One. Debtor One then sold the machine to Debtor Two, whose bill of sale explicitly provided that Debtor Two took subject to Bank One's security interest. Debtor Two later went to Bank Two, represented that he owned the machine free and clear, and procured a $200,000 loan against it. Bank Two checked the files under Debtor Two's name and, finding nothing, perfected its security interest by filing a financing statement. When the scheme was discovered, both Bank One and Bank Two claimed the asset.

Can you identify an argument in favor of Bank One? Who prevails?

§ 7. SUBSTITUTES FOR SECURITY IN BUSINESS EQUIPMENT

Instead of buying equipment and giving the seller or bank a security interest to secure the debt, some businesses lease equipment. The economic characteristics of short-term leases are quite different from those of purchases, but long-term leases—particularly those with concluding options to buy for a small amount of money—are almost identical to purchases, and, as we will see, the law sometimes treats them so. Also, there are particular kinds of leases described in UCC Article 2A as "finance leases." Article 2A explicitly recognizes finance leases as true leases, even though they have some of the financing characteristics of a secured sale. Given these similarities, one might argue that a finance lessor should be required to file a financing statement in order to make its interest a part of the public record. The drafters have not, however, chosen to codify such a requirement.

A quite different substitute for a secured loan is an unsecured purchase or loan documented with a "negative pledge clause." The negative pledge clause is a promise by the debtor not to grant any other person a security interest in the asset purchased or other items of the debtor's property. Should the debtor stay true to his word, the negative pledge clause prevents others from obtaining a security interest that would effectively subordinate the seller's or lender's claim. Of course, a negative pledge clause will not protect against claims of creditors that are asserted involuntarily—for example, as a result of a judgment and a levy on the property. Nor would it protect against the claims of a trustee in bankruptcy. A creditor with a negative pledge clause is treated in bankruptcy as no more than an unsecured creditor.

Secured creditors also commonly put negative pledge clauses in their security agreements in an effort to prevent the debtor from granting additional security interests in the collateral to other creditors—at least without the secured party's consent. Although the debtor's violation of such a negative pledge clause may be a default under the terms of the security agreement, it does not prevent a subsequent security interest from attaching to the collateral. *See* 9–401(b).

Another practice is contractual subordination, whereby one creditor agrees to subordinate its interest or claim to that of another person. Section 1–310 authorizes these agreements. *See also* 9–339. Of course, this kind of protection is only effective as between the parties to the agreement.

Does a right of contractual subordination create a security interest? Section 1–201 defines "security interest" to mean *any* "interest in personal property or fixtures which secures payment or performance of an obligation," a definition broad enough to include *any* distinctive claim to the assets of a debtor that a creditor might assert on default. This definition of security interest, however, cannot be taken entirely at face value. For example, section 9–339 states that nothing in Article 9 prevents a superior creditor from subordinating its interest to another creditor by means of a subordination agreement. It might be argued that when one creditor agrees to subordinate its claim to that of another creditor, the elevated creditor thereby acquires a "security interest." The Permanent Editorial Board for the UCC was worried enough about this possibility that in 1966 it amended the 1962 Official Text, adding section 1–209 (now section 1–310 in revised Article 1), which provides that subordination does not create a security interest.

SECURITY INTEREST OR LEASE?

A fecund source of disputes unresolved by revised Article 9 is the question whether a particular document labeled a "lease" of goods is a true lease—and thus the subject of Article 2A, not Article 9—or whether it is a security agreement that creates a security interest under the terms of section 1–203 of Article 1 (section 1–201(37) of former Article 1). We now address this question.

THE PROBLEM

The rights of a true lessor in personal property do not qualify as an Article 9 security interest. If a levying creditor of the lessee or the lessee's trustee in bankruptcy claims leased goods as against the lessor, Article 9 does not determine the outcome, and the lessor generally prevails under Article 2A. This is so even though no filing or other public record shows the lessor's interest. Although the drafters could have required lessors to file financing statements in order better to apprise third parties dealing with the lessee of the lessor's interests, they opted not to do so. Under section 9–505, a nervous lessor is permitted but not required to file. *See* 9–505 cmt. 2.

If, on the other hand, the transaction is not a true lease but an installment sale, Article 9 governs. In reality, the "lessor" here retains a security interest to secure the obligation of the "lessee" to buy and pay for the goods. Only by complying with section 9–203 will such a "lessor" be entitled to enforce its interest. If it does not file a required financing statement, it will lose to all parties whose interests take priority over an unperfected security interest under Article 9 and other laws. Such parties include, among others, those who have purchased from the "lessee," certain lien creditors of the "lessee," and the trustee of the "lessee" in bankruptcy. Thus, the "lease versus security interest" issue will continue to be one of the most frequently litigated issues under the UCC.

But why do secured creditors persist in claiming to be lessors? There are many reasons. A lessor has different rights than a secured creditor upon the default or bankruptcy of the lessee; under federal, state, and local tax laws; under rules of accounting; and under state usury laws.

The distinction between lessor and secured creditor takes on added importance when the debtor is in bankruptcy. If a true lessee goes into bankruptcy, normally the lessee or trustee must affirm the lease and make full payments, or else reject the lease and return the leased goods. The true lessor's rights to payment or return do not depend upon the filing of a financing statement or any action otherwise to "perfect" the lessor's interest. If, on the other hand, a would-be lessor has filed no financing statement and is found to be a secured seller, it would lose to the trustee in bankruptcy as an unsecured creditor. Even a perfected secured creditor may fare worse than a lessor in a case under Chapter 11 of the Bankruptcy Code, because the debtor may be able to keep the collateral in a "cram down" by paying its fair market value instead of the contracted liability. (More on bankruptcy law in the next chapter.) A lessee, by contrast, would have no such recourse.

The distinction between lessor and secured creditor is important in other contexts as well. Assume a debtor has signed a covenant with a lender in a loan agreement, promising not to borrow additional money without the lender's approval. If "leasing" is not "borrowing," it lies outside the covenant and thus the debtor may lease without the lender's approval. Similarly, a debtor may have signed a security agreement with a secured party, agreeing not to take on additional borrowing obligations. Again, if "leasing" is not "borrowing," then a new lease will not trigger a default under the security agreement. Thus, the parties may choose to classify a transaction in order to exploit or skirt certain preexisting contractual arrangements. Similarly, the lender—either lessor or secured creditor—may characterize a transaction one way for one purpose (to avail itself of Article 9, for example) and another way for another purpose (to take advantage of favorable tax laws). The lessor's lawyer may also try to draft a single document susceptible of multiple interpretations—one, say, that confers the accounting benefits of a lease and the economic rights of a security agreement.

One without experience in commercial law might think it a simple thing to distinguish between a lease and a security agreement. In fact, however, it has been troublesome, and the trouble has not abated in the years since the UCC's enactment. Section 1–203 (former section 1–201(b)(37)) is the road sign that points to Article 9 for true security transactions and to Article 2A or other law for true leases. It has been revised twice since its origin in the 1950s; by far the most significant revision came in 1987, the same year that the lease provision, Article 2A, was drafted and promulgated. Later, in connection with the Article 9 revision, the drafters made cosmetic changes to the opening paragraph of section 1–203 (then section 1–201(b)(37)) that do not bear on the following discussion. Be careful here: the phrase "revised section 1–201(b)(37)" usually refers to the 1987 revision of section 1–201(b)(37), not to section 1–203 of the current revised Article 1.

TRUE LEASES

Consider the purest form of lease and contrast it with the purest form of security agreement. An example of the former would be the lease of a truck for one year. If the truck has a useful life of ten years, the lessor, not the lessee, would stand to gain from appreciation in the truck's value or to lose from its depreciation. The lessor has an "entrepreneurial stake" and a valuable "reversionary" interest in the truck. Compare that to the position of a bank that lends money to a trucker so he can purchase the truck. If the bank takes security in the truck, it has no interest in the truck itself, save, of course, that its value not decline below the amount of the debt outstanding. If the truck proves to be worth twice what was expected, the trucker receives a windfall. Likewise, if the truck is destroyed or declines radically in value, the loss falls on the trucker, provided he is solvent. Thus the trucker, not the bank, has the entrepreneurial stake.

A lease looks more and more like a secured loan—in which the lessee/debtor, not the lessor/creditor, holds the attributes of ownership—when: the lease term gets longer, inching toward the full economic life of the leased commodity; the lessee receives an option to purchase; and the lessee assumes many of the risks of ownership, thereby securing for itself most of the benefits or detriments of ownership. On the other hand, many transactions with financing attributes are true leases under section 1–203. In a 1988 article, Edwin Huddleson, a serious student of personal property leases, suggested that the real issue here is whether the lessor truly possesses a reversionary interest after the agreement is signed. He made the point as follows:

> the central feature of a true lease is the reservation of an economically meaningful interest to the lessor at the end of the lease term. Ordinarily this means two things: (1) at the outset of the lease the parties expect the goods to retain some significant residual value at the end of the lease term; and (2) the lessor retains some entrepreneurial stake (either the possibility of gain or the risk of loss) in the value of the goods at the end of the lease term.[3]

Section 103(1)(j) of Article 2A offers a somewhat less helpful definition of "lease":

> "Lease" means a transfer of the right to possession and use of goods for a term in return for consideration, but a sale, including a sale on approval or a sale or return [*see* 2–326], or retention or

[3] Edwin E. Huddleson, III, *Old Wine in New Bottles: UCC Article 2A—Leases*, 39 ALA. L. REV. 615, 624–25 (1988).

creation of a security interest is not a lease. Unless the context clearly indicates otherwise, the term includes a sublease.

Section 2A–103(1)(j) directs one to section 1–203 (former section 1–201(37)) for answers to the hard questions. As you will see, the drafters of section 1–203 (former section 1–201(37)) failed to focus on the existence of a reversionary interest. Rather than state a bold and explicit definition of "lease" based on reversionary interest, the drafters instead offered a list of factors that either support or preclude an inference of a lease.

Section 1–203 is a complicated provision. Read it carefully. Note that it begins in subsection (a) with a fairly vague standard: "Whether a transaction in the form of a lease creates a lease or a security interest is determined by the facts of each case." Can you think of a more nebulous statement? Probably not. Fortunately, there is more to the section than that.

Subsection (b) of section 1–203 then provides some rules governing when, as a matter of law, a "lease" will be recharacterized as a security arrangement. Note the structure of subsection (b). In order for subsection (b) to apply, the "rent" or other consideration the "lessee" is obligated to pay the "lessor" cannot be subject to termination at will by the "lessee" and at least one of the four other enumerated criteria listed in the subsection must be satisfied. For example, under subsection (b)(1), it must also be true that "the original term of the lease is equal to or greater than the remaining economic life of the goods." Observe what this captures: a transaction styled as a "lease" in which the "lessee" cannot terminate his rental obligation at will and the "lessor" has no meaningful reversionary interest because the debtor's use of the goods for the term of the lease will exhaust the remaining economic life of the goods.

The other examples listed in subsections (b)(2) through (b)(4) are the economic equivalent of what is listed in (b)(1). Namely they cover, in subsection (b)(2), situations in which the "lessee" is obligated to renew the lease for the remaining economic life of the goods or become the owner of the goods; in (b)(3), situations in which the "lessee" has the option to renew the lease for the remaining economic life of the goods for no additional consideration or for only nominal consideration; and in (b)(4), situations in which the "lessee" has the option to become the owner of the goods for no additional consideration or for only nominal consideration. In each of these circumstances, the "lessee" effectively finances the equivalent of ownership of the goods because, once again, the lessee's use and possession will exhaust the value of the goods.

Does subsection (b) capture a typical rent-to-own transaction? In a rent-to-own transaction, the lessee "leases" the goods for a term and, at the end of the term, generally becomes the owner of the goods after having made all the payments required under the lease (*i.e.*, has paid for the goods in full). This kind of transaction would seem to fall within the spirit of subsection (b), but is excluded by the requirement that the rental obligation cannot be terminated at will by the lessee. Under a typical rent-to-own contract, the lessee always has the option of returning the goods to the lessor before the end of the stated lease term, thereby terminating any further rental payment obligation (and thus falling outside the scope of subsection (b)).

Subsection (c) of section 1–203 next provides a list of factors that, by themselves, are insufficient to justify recharacterization of a lease as a security arrangement. These include the criteria stated in subsection (c)(1) that the rent the lessee must pay "is substantially equal to or greater than the fair market value of the goods at the time the lease is entered into . . . ." In other words, it is not enough that the lessee is paying more in rent than it would cost the lessee to purchase the goods. As provided in subsection (c)(4), it is also not enough, by itself, that the "the lessee has an option to renew the lease or to become the owner of the goods." But what if more than one factor is present? Would it be enough if any two of the criteria listed in subsection (c) are satisfied? The section does not say. Nor do the comments that follow it, leaving the matter up to the courts.

Subsection (d) of section 1–203 addresses what constitutes "nominal" consideration. It states rather unhelpfully that "[a]dditional consideration is nominal if it is less than the lessee's reasonably predictable cost of performing under the lease agreement if the option [to renew the lease or purchase the goods] is not exercised." What does this mean? Begin with the idea that, if the lessee has an option to renew the lease or purchase the goods, but does not exercise the option, the lessee typically has to return the goods to the lessor. Return of the goods (together with any fees or charges that the lessee must pay that are associated with the return) is the lessee's cost of performing under the lease if the option is not exercised. If the cost of performance where the option is not exercised is greater than the cost of exercising the option, the cost of exercising the option is nominal.

To see how this plays out, consider hypothetically a situation in which a lessee leases a computer. Assume further that the computer is reasonably predicted to be worth $1000 at the end of the lease term. The lease also states that the lessee has the option to purchase the computer at the end of the lease term for $1, but if the option is not exercise the lessee must return the computer. The consideration involved in exercising the option is nominal because the option price of $1 is obviously less than the reasonably predicted cost to the lessee of returning the goods (*i.e.*, parting with a computer worth $1000).

Subsection (e) of section 1–203 provides some additional rules of construction. It states that, for purposes of section 1–203, the phrases "remaining economic life of the goods" and "reasonably predictable" fair market rent, fair market value, or cost of performing under the lease agreement "must be determined with reference to the facts and circumstances at the time the transaction is entered into." This is intended to put something of a brake on Monday-morning quarterbacking.

Consider the following case construing old section 1–201(37).

DUKE ENERGY ROYAL, LLC V. PILLOWTEX CORP. (IN RE PILLOWTEX, INC.)

Third Circuit Court of Appeals, 2003.
349 F.3d 711.

FUENTES, CIRCUIT JUDGE:

Duke Energy Royal LLC ("Duke") appeals from an order of the District Court denying a motion to compel Pillowtex Corporation ("Pillowtex" or "debtor") to make lease payments owing under the Master Energy Services Agreement ("MESA"), an agreement its predecessor entered into with Pillowtex.[1] The District Court denied Duke's motion on the grounds that the MESA was not a true lease, but rather a secured financing arrangement. The sole issue in this appeal is whether the District Court correctly determined that the MESA entered into between Pillowtex and Duke prior to Pillowtex's bankruptcy filing was a secured financing arrangement rather than a true lease. We affirm because we agree with the District Court that, based on the economic realities of the underlying transaction, the MESA was a secured financing arrangement.

I. *Facts and Procedural Background*

Because the nature of the MESA is at issue, we first turn to its provisions and the transaction underlying the agreement. Pillowtex and Duke entered into the MESA on June 3, 1998. Pursuant to the MESA, Duke agreed to install certain equipment "for the purpose of improving the efficiency of energy consumption or otherwise to reduce the operating costs" incurred by Pillowtex at its facilities. (MESA § 2.5, App. at 299). The MESA covered two different sets of energy services projects, one involving production equipment and the other energy-savings equipment. The production equipment was provided to Pillowtex by Duke pursuant to separate stand-alone agreements, which were recorded as true leases on Pillowtex's books, and which the parties agree constituted true leases. Therefore, only the nature of the parties' arrangements concerning the energy-savings equipment is at issue in this appeal.

The energy-savings equipment included certain lighting fixtures, T8 lamps and electronic ballasts (collectively the "lighting fixtures"), which

---

1 On April 30, 2002, DukeSolutions, Inc., a party to the MESA, transferred its claims against Pillowtex to appellant, Duke Energy Royal LLC ("Duke Royal") pursuant to a Bill of Sale, Assignment and Assumption Agreement. (App. at 251–52). To simplify, we refer to both simply as "Duke."

were installed in nine of Pillowtex's facilities and a new wastewater heat recovery system that included hot water heating equipment (the "wastewater system" and together with the lighting fixtures, the "energy fixtures"), which was installed at Pillowtex's Columbus, Georgia plant. The lighting fixtures were selected, and the wastewater system was constructed, specifically for Pillowtex's facilities. (App. at 336–590).

In order to induce Pillowtex to enter into the energy services projects, Duke offered to originate funding for the production equipment "on a two-to-one basis (*i.e.*, for every $1 million of energy projects Duke would originate $2 million for funding of equipment) with a minimum of $28 million in funding for equipment leasing or financing." (App. at 153). Another incentive Pillowtex had for entering into the agreement was "that the energy projects would be cost neutral to Pillowtex for the term of the agreement; that is, Pillowtex's payments to Duke would be equivalent to Pillowtex's actual savings . . . and Pillowtex would then reap the benefits from the cost savings after the end of the term of the project." (App. at 153). In keeping with this arrangement, Pillowtex accounted for its payments to Duke under the MESA as a utility expense. (App. at 155).

The MESA provided that the cost of acquiring and installing the energy fixtures would be paid by Duke, which incurred total costs of approximately $10.41 million. (MESA § 5, App. at 302; 339). Of this amount, approximately $1.66 million was for material and labor costs for the wastewater system. (App. at 594). Approximately $4.46 million was for labor to install the lighting fixtures and $4.29 million was for material costs for the lighting fixtures, which is to say that the cost of labor to install the fixtures was higher than the cost of the actual materials themselves. (App. at 339, 70). Also, Duke paid approximately $223,000 to dispose of light fixtures and related equipment that it removed from Pillowtex's facilities. (App. at 69–70).

In exchange, Pillowtex was to pay Duke on a monthly basis one-twelfth of Pillowtex's annual energy savings, in an amount the parties agreed to in advance, until the end of the MESA's 8 year term. (MESA § 7.0, App. at 304). In addition, the parties agreed that the simple payback of all of Duke's costs was not to exceed 5 years. (MESA § 4.1(f), App. at 302). "Simple payback" is synonymous with "payback period," an accounting term which refers to "[t]he length of time required to recover a venture's initial cash investment, without accounting for the time value of money." BLACK'S LAW DICTIONARY 1150 (7th ed. 1999). In other words, the payments were structured to ensure that Pillowtex would make predetermined, equal monthly payments and that Duke would recover its costs 3 years prior to the end of the term of the MESA. Although the MESA was for an 8 year term, the parties agree that the useful life of the energy fixtures was 20–25 years. (App. at 74–75).

It is undisputed that Duke and Pillowtex intended to structure the MESA to have the characteristics of a lease and that the parties were trying to create a true lease. Indeed, Pillowtex's counsel conceded during oral argument before the District Court, "I don't disagree that [the MESA] was structured to have those characteristics for tax purposes and, you know, to [the] extent they could, the parties were trying to create a true lease, I would admit that." (App. at 117). The parties intended for the MESA to be structured as a true lease, in large part, because Pillowtex was subject to capital expenditure limitations under its senior credit facility and did not wish to have the energy-savings equipment count as capital expenditures under that facility. Nevertheless, the MESA is not labeled a lease and it does not refer to the parties as lessee and lessor. Also, Duke alleges that the parties were concerned with structuring the MESA's provisions relating to energy-savings equipment in accordance with the requirements of Financial Accounting Standard 13, which sets the standards for financial accounting and reporting for leases. (App. at 164). However, the MESA fails to qualify as a true lease under ¶ 7 of that standard because the present value of the total payments due under the MESA exceeds the value of the original cost of the energy fixtures. (App. at 171).

In keeping with their intent to structure the transaction as a lease, the MESA provides that title to the equipment would remain with Duke. (MESA § 11.0, App. at 308). Also, Pillowtex agreed not to claim ownership of the equipment for income tax purposes, (MESA § 9.13(ii), App. at 307), and Pillowtex was not obligated to purchase the equipment at the end of the term of the MESA. Rather, the MESA provided the following four options to Duke at the conclusion of its term, if Pillowtex was not then in default:

> (i) remove the Equipment installed and replace those [sic] Equipment with equipment comparable to those originally in place, provided that no such replacement shall be required with respect to Production Equipment; or,
>
> (ii) abandon the Equipment in place; or,
>
> (iii) continue this Agreement until the expiration of the term hereof and then extend the term of this Agreement for such additional period(s) and payment terms as the parties may agree upon; or,
>
> (iv) [g]ive the Customer the option of purchasing all (but not less than all) of the Equipment at a mutually agreed upon price.

(MESA § 8.3, App. at 304). If Duke elected to exercise option (i), it was bound to "be responsible for all costs and expenses in removing such Equipment, including costs to repair any damage to [Pillowtex's] Facility caused by such removal." (*Id.*)[2] Despite the existence of the option for Duke to repossess the equipment, Pillowtex's Vice President for Engineering, Michael Abba, testified that in his understanding, there was no chance of that option being exercised:

> It was clearly my understanding that Duke would abandon the Lighting Fixtures and the Wastewater System at the conclusion of the MESA and in fact statements were made to me by Duke sales personnel to that effect. Moreover, because the energy projects were of no economic benefit to Pillowtex until the end of the term when Pillowtex would reap the energy savings going forward, I would not have signed off on the projects if the Lighting Fixtures and Wastewater System were not to be abandoned. I also believe that, based on the prohibitive cost of removing and replacing the Lighting Fixtures and the Wastewater System for Pillowtex, Duke [had] no choice but to abandon the Lighting Fixtures and the Wastewater System at the end of the term of the MESA.

Abba Affidavit at ¶ 6 (App. at 155).

After Duke and Pillowtex executed the MESA, Duke entered into a Master Lease Agreement ("Master Lease") with General Electric Capital Corporation ("GECC"), dated August 2, 1999, pursuant to which GECC agreed to finance the lighting fixtures for four of the nine Pillowtex facilities in which Duke was to install new fixtures pursuant to the MESA. Concurrently with the execution of the Master Lease and the execution of an equipment schedule listing lighting fixtures subject to the Master Lease, Duke and GECC entered into a Collateral Assignment Agreement through which Duke granted GECC a security interest in all of Duke's rights and interests in the MESA, including Duke's right to payment under the MESA, as security for Duke's obligations under the Master Lease. Also, in connection with the Master Lease transaction, Pillowtex executed an Acknowledgment Letter which provides that its interest in the MESA and equipment covered by it "is subject and subordinate to [GECC's] rights under . . . the Master Lease Agreement . . . between GECC and Duke." (App. at 749). Shortly after Duke and GECC entered into the Master Lease, on August 12, 1999, GECC and SouthTrust Bank executed a Master Assignment Agreement, pursuant to which GECC assigned all of its rights and interests in the Master Lease and the Collateral Assignment it had with Duke, as well as the MESA and certain other documents, to SouthTrust. Therefore, with respect to the lighting fixtures, SouthTrust holds the rights and interests under the MESA for the lighting fixtures at

---

[2] In the event of a default by Pillowtex, Duke would have the right to remove the equipment at Pillowtex's expense, without being obligated to replace it, and could terminate the MESA. (MESA § 13.2, App. at 309).

four of Pillowtex's facilities and Duke holds the rights and interests under the MESA for the lighting fixtures at the other five facilities.

On November 14, 2000, Pillowtex and certain of its subsidiaries filed petitions for relief under Chapter 11 of the Bankruptcy Code. Thereafter, Pillowtex stopped making payments due under the MESA. On February 21, 2002, Duke filed a motion under section 365(d)(10) of the Bankruptcy Code to compel Pillowtex to make lease payments on the equipment it had provided to Pillowtex under the MESA. Section 365(d)(10) requires debtors-in-possession, such as Pillowtex, to "timely perform all of the obligations of the debtor . . . first arising from or after 60 days after the order for relief in a case under Chapter 11 . . . under an unexpired lease of personal property . . . until such lease is assumed or rejected . . . ." 11 U.S.C. § 365(d)(10).[3] In response to Duke's motion, Pillowtex filed an objection in which it argued that Duke was not entitled to payment of post-petition monthly obligations, which Pillowtex represented amounted to $1.8 million, because the MESA was not a true lease. After a hearing on the matter, the District Court, sitting in Bankruptcy, denied Duke's motion. Duke timely appealed.

* * *

III. *Analysis*

Whether an agreement is a true lease or a secured financing arrangement under the Bankruptcy Code is a question of state law. *In re Continental Airlines, Inc.*, 932 F.2d 282, 294 (3d Cir. 1991) (citing H.R. Rep. No. 95–595, at 314 (1978), *reprinted in* 1978 U.S.C.C.A.N. 5963, 6271). In this case, the parties agreed that the MESA would be interpreted, performed, and enforced in accordance with the laws of the State of New York. (MESA, Appendix A, § 17.7). Accordingly, we turn to New York law in order to resolve whether the MESA constitutes a secured financing arrangement or a lease. Under New York law, because Pillowtex is seeking to characterize the MESA as a secured financing arrangement rather than a lease, Pillowtex bears the burden of proof on that issue. *In re Owen*, 221 B.R. 56, 60 (Bankr. N.D.N.Y. 1998).

---

[3] Although § 365(d)(10) refers to the obligation of a trustee to make lease payments, its provisions apply to Pillowtex because the Bankruptcy Code provides that debtors-in-possession, such as Pillowtex, are to perform all of the functions and duties of a Chapter 11 trustee. *See* 11 U.S.C. § 1107(a).

In addition to seeking an order compelling Pillowtex to make lease payments, Duke sought an order requiring Pillowtex to provide adequate protection of its interest in the equipment pursuant to 11 U.S.C. § 363(e) or, in the alternative, relief from the automatic stay in order to pursue its state law remedies to recover possession of the equipment. Section 363(e) mandates that adequate protection be provided to entities which have an interest in property used by the trustee or debtor-in-possession and "applies to property that is subject to any unexpired lease of personal property." *See* 11 U.S.C. § 363(e).

Article 2A of the New York Uniform Commercial Code explains that a lease is "a transfer of the right to possession and use of goods for a term in return for consideration, but a sale . . . or retention or creation of a security interest is not a lease." N.Y. U.C.C. § 2-A–103(1)(j) (McKinney 2002). Thus, the definition of a lease expressly excludes security interests. The exclusion of security interests from the definition of a lease requires that we turn to the U.C.C. definition of a security interest.[7]

Section 1–201(37) of the U.C.C. [1–201(b)(35)] provides that a security interest "means an interest in personal property or fixtures which secures payment or performance of an obligation." N.Y. U.C.C. § 1–201(37). After defining the term "security interest," section 1–201(37) [section 1–203 of revised Article 1] sets out a test for determining whether a transaction creates a lease or a security interest. Section 1–201(37) [1–203(a)] begins by noting that whether a transaction creates a lease or a security interest is to be determined on a case-by-case basis. After indicating that courts are to examine the facts of each case in order to characterize a transaction, the statute sets out a bright-line test, sometimes referred to as a per se rule, for determining whether a transaction creates a security interest as a matter of law. Specifically, section 1–201(37) [1–203(b)] provides:

> (a) Whether a transaction creates a lease or security interest is determined by the facts of each case; however, a transaction creates a security interest if the consideration the lessee is to pay the lessor for the right to possession and use of the goods is an obligation for the term of the lease not subject to termination by the lessee, ***and***:
>
> > (i) the original term of the lease is equal to or greater than the remaining economic life of the goods,
> >
> > (ii) the lessee is bound to renew the lease for the remaining economic life of the goods or is bound to become the owner of the goods,
> >
> > (iii) the lessee has an option to renew the lease for the remaining economic life of the goods for no additional consideration or nominal additional consideration upon compliance with the lease agreement, ***or***
> >
> > (iv) the lessee has an option to become the owner of the goods for no additional consideration or nominal additional consideration upon compliance with the lease agreement.

---

[7] *See* U.C.C. § 1–201(37), Official Cmt. ("Lease is defined in Article 2A as a transfer of the right to possession and use of goods for a term, in return for consideration. Section 2A–103(1)(j). The definition continues by stating that the retention or creation of a security interest is not a lease. Thus, the task of sharpening the line between true leases and security interests disguised as leases continues to be a function of this section") [1–203 cmt. 2].

N.Y. U.C.C. § 1–201(37) (emphasis added) [1–203(b)]. Thus, under the two-part test set out in New York's U.C.C., if Pillowtex did not have the right to terminate the MESA prior to the end of its term, and any of the four factors set out in section 1–201(37)(a)(i)–(iv) [1–203(b)(1)–(4)] are met, then the MESA would be considered to create a security interest as a matter of law. *See In re Owen*, 221 B.R. at 60–61. If, on the other hand, it is determined that "the transaction is not a disguised security agreement per se, [we] must then look at the specific facts of the case to determine whether the economics of the transaction suggest such a result." *In re Taylor*, 209 B.R. 482, 484 (Bankr. S.D. Ill. 1997) (citation omitted). *See also In re Murray*, 191 B.R. 309 (Bankr. E.D. Pa. 1996); *In re American Steel Prod.*, 203 B.R. 504, 506–07 (Bankr. S.D. Ga. 1996) (describing the standards for determining whether a disguised security arrangement exists).[8] In this case, the District Court went directly to the economic realities of the transaction memorialized in the MESA. In doing so the Court seems to have implicitly held that the MESA was not a disguised security agreement under the bright-line test of section 1–201(37) [1–203(b)]. We agree.

On appeal, Pillowtex argues that the MESA is a secured financing agreement both under this bright-line test and also based on the economics of the MESA transaction. Specifically, Pillowtex argues that the second and fourth factors set out in the second part of the statutory two-part test are present: (1) that at the end of the MESA's term Pillowtex was bound to become the owner of the energy fixtures and (2) that it was bound to become the owner of the fixtures for no or nominal additional consideration upon compliance with the terms of the MESA. Duke concedes that the first part of the two-part test is satisfied: that the MESA prohibits Pillowtex from terminating its obligation to pay Duke the full cost of the energy fixtures before the termination of the MESA's term. However, Duke maintains that none of the four factors in section 1–201(37)(a)(i)–(iv) [1–203(b)(1)–(4)] are present. These factors are hereafter referred to as "residual value factors" because they relate to whether residual value will remain for the purported lessor, Duke, at the end of the term of the MESA. *See* E. Carolyn Hochstadter Dicker and John P. Campo, *FF & E and the True Lease Question: Article 2A and Accompanying Amendments to UCC Section 1–201(37)*, 7 Am. Bankr. Inst. L. Rev. 517, 552 (1999).

As an initial matter, we note that the first and third residual value factors are not satisfied. The first factor is whether "the original term of the lease is equal to or greater than the remaining economic life of the goods." N.Y. U.C.C. § 1–201(37)(a)(i) [1–203(b)(1)]. Here, the term of the MESA is eight years and Pillowtex concedes that the expected useful life of

[8] Because N.Y. U.C.C. § 1–201(37) is based on the Uniform Commercial Code, decisions from other jurisdictions interpreting this same uniform statute are instructive. *See, e.g.*, *In re Edison Bros. Stores, Inc.*, 207 B.R. 801, 809 n. 7 (Bankr. D. Del. 1997) (applying the reasoning of cases from a variety of jurisdictions to analysis of N.Y. U.C.C. § 1–201(37)); *In re Owen*, 221 B.R. at 61 n. 6.

the equipment is 20–25 years. Thus, the economic life of the equipment exceeds the term of the MESA by a factor of three and the first residual value factor set out in section 1–201(37) [1–203(b)(1)] is not met. The third factor indicative of a security interest is met where "the lessee has an option to renew the lease for the remaining economic life of the goods for no additional consideration or nominal additional consideration upon compliance with the lease agreement." N.Y. U.C.C. § 1–201(37)(a)(iii) [1–203(b)(3)]. This factor is not met because the terms of the MESA do not give Pillowtex the option to renew the lease for the remaining life of the equipment for no or nominal consideration.

As to the second factor, Pillowtex argues that it was bound, if not formally then in a de facto sense, to become the owner of the energy fixtures because the only way that the fixtures would be removed from Pillowtex's facilities is if Duke paid millions of dollars to acquire and install replacements. Along the same lines, Pillowtex argues with respect to the fourth residual value factor that, although the MESA does not expressly give it the option to become the owner of the energy fixtures for no or nominal consideration, in effect it has this option because it can compel Duke to abandon the energy fixtures by refusing to negotiate an extension of the MESA or a purchase of the energy fixtures at the end of the MESA's term.

We agree with Duke that neither the second nor the fourth residual value factors are present here because Pillowtex is not contractually bound to become the owner of the energy fixtures, nor does the MESA provide Pillowtex with the option to become the owner of the energy fixtures for no or nominal consideration. Rather, the existing options as to how to proceed at the end of the term of the MESA were to be exercised only by Duke. Pillowtex provides no authority for the proposition that a de facto arrangement is enough to satisfy the requirements of section 1–201(37)(ii) and (iv) [1–203(b)(2) and (4)]. If anything, the relevant caselaw points us to the opposite conclusion. *See Edison Bros.*, 207 B.R. at 810 ("If the lease agreement *explicitly* provides that the lessee has an option to purchase the leased goods for nominal consideration (e.g., for $1), the agreement is presumed to be a disguised security agreement") (emphasis added). Accordingly, we conclude that none of the four residual value factors set forth in N.Y. U.C.C. § 1–201(37)(a)(i)–(iv) [1–203(b)(1)–(4)] are met.

The parties agree that, where none of the four factors set out in section 1–201(37) [1–203(b)] are present, courts are to consider the economic reality of the transaction in order to determine, based on the particular facts of the case, whether the transaction is more fairly characterized as a lease or a secured financing arrangement. They also agree that the District Court applied the correct standard for evaluating the economic reality of their transaction. As the District Court explained:

> Under relevant case law, courts will look to various factors in evaluating the "economic reality of the transaction . . . in determining whether there has been a sale or a true lease," *Pactel Fin. v. D.C. Marine Serv. Corp.*, 136 Misc.2d 194, 518 N.Y.S.2d 317, 318 (N.Y. Dist. Ct. 1987), including the following: "[a] whether the purchase option is nominal; [b] whether the lessee is required to make aggregate rental payments having a present value equaling or exceeding the original cost of the leased property; and [c] whether the lease term covers the total useful life of the equipment." *In re Edison Bros. Stores, Inc.*, 207 B.R. 801, 809–10 and n. 8, 9, 10 (Bankr. D. Del. 1997). *See also* [N.Y. U.C.C.] § 1–201(37) (McKinney Supp. 1996). "In this regard, courts are required to examine the intent of the parties and the facts and circumstances which existed at the time the transaction was entered into." *In re Edison,* 207 B.R. at 809.

In re Pillowtex, Inc. et al., Nos. 00–4211 to 00–4234, slip op. at 5–6 (Bankr. D. Del. June 4, 2002) ("Dist. Ct. Op.") (footnote omitted). The District Court found that the MESA was substantively better characterized as a security agreement than a true lease because the second *Edison Bros.* factor clearly weighed in Pillowtex's favor, and the first and third factors were largely neutral. We agree with the District Court's conclusion in this regard.

Specifically, with respect to the second factor, Duke concedes that the aggregate rental payments owing by Pillowtex under the MESA had a present value equal to or exceeding the cost of the energy fixtures. The *Edison Bros.* court cogently explained the importance of such a fact in showing the existence of a security agreement:

> The rationale behind this second factor is that if the alleged lessee is obligated to pay the lessor a sum equal to or greater than the full purchase price of the leased goods plus an interest charge over the term of the alleged lease agreement, a sale is likely to have been intended since what the lessor will receive is more than a payment for the use of the leased goods and loss of their value; the lessor will receive a consideration that would amount to a return on its investment.

Edison Bros., 207 B.R. at 814 (*quoted in Owen*, 221 B.R. at 61–62). Applying that logic to this case, Duke has already been well-compensated for the transferral of the lighting fixtures to Pillowtex, undercutting the proposition that the fixtures were merely leased.

Like the District Court, we are unpersuaded by Duke's attempt to rely on the first and third Edison Bros. factors. With respect to the first factor, Duke points out that the MESA provides that it "has the option to . . . give [Pillowtex] the option of purchasing all (but not less than all) of the Equipment at a *mutually agreed price*." App. at 304 (emphasis added).

Based on this provision of the MESA, Duke asserts that "Pillowtex does not have the option to purchase the Equipment unless Duke offers it such option, and even then only if Pillowtex agrees on a satisfactory price with Duke." Duke's Br. at 21. Duke concludes that, therefore, the first economic realities factor weighs in favor of a finding that the MESA is a lease. We agree, however, with Pillowtex's contention that, although the MESA nominally required Pillowtex to bargain for an option price, Pillowtex could essentially ensure a nominal option price by refusing to bargain. This refusal would "effectively compel Duke to abandon the [e]nergy [f]ixtures to avoid the exorbitant expense of acquiring and installing replacements." Pillowtex's Br. at 28. Thus, as an economic reality the option price at the end of the MESA was illusory, nullifying the weight of this factor.

With respect to the third factor, Duke observes that the useful life of the energy fixtures is longer than the term of the MESA, and cites to *Edison Bros.* for the proposition that the long life of the fixtures is indicative of a true lease. In relevant part, the *Edison Bros.* court explained that:

> An essential characteristic of a true lease is that there be something of value to return to the lessor after the term. Where the term of the lease is substantially equal to the life of the lease property such that there will be nothing of value to return at the end of the lease, the transaction is in essence a sale. Conversely, if the lessor expected a remaining useful life after the expiration of the lease term, it can be reasonably inferred that it expected to retain substantial residual value in the leased property at the end of the lease term and that it therefore intended to create a true lease.

207 B.R. at 818 (citations omitted). We agree that under certain circumstances, the fact that transferred goods have a useful life extending beyond the term of the transferring agreement could reveal the transferor's expectation of retaining residual value in those goods. Such an inference would only be proper, however, where the evidence showed a plausible intent by the transferor to repossess the goods.

The economic realities of the particular transaction in this case belie any such intent. Although the useful life of the lighting fixtures is 20–25 years, eclipsing the MESA's 8-year term, it would be unreasonable for Duke to incur the high costs necessary to repossess the fixtures: namely, the costs associated with removing, scrapping, and replacing the fixtures. Also, the uncontroverted evidence in this case establishes that there is little (if any) market value for used lighting fixtures.[9] In short, it would have made no

---

[9] During the course of the hearing held by the District Court on SouthTrust's motion to compel, counsel for Pillowtex called James Klemic to the stand to testify as an "expert in the used

economic sense for Duke to spend large amounts of money to reclaim the fixtures, especially in the face of poor resale prospects. We therefore conclude that the District Court did not err by discounting the significance of the useful life of the lighting fixtures as compared to the length of the MESA when conducting its analysis of the economic realities of the transaction underlying the MESA. On balance, then, applying the three *Edison Bros.* factors to this case leads us to conclude that the MESA was not a true lease.

Beyond reiterating its arguments on the three factors, Duke argues that (1) the mutual subjective intent of the parties was to structure the MESA as a lease; (2) Pillowtex's accounting for the MESA payments as a utility expense is evidence that it did not treat the MESA as a repayment of debt incurred to purchase the energy fixtures; (3) it is of no consequence that the MESA is not labeled a lease; and (4) Duke maintained a meaningful reversionary interest in the fixtures at the end of the MESA's term. None of these arguments is persuasive to us.

First, Duke argues that the District Court erred by failing to analyze the intent of the parties. Duke asserts that the record shows that the parties structured the MESA so that it would qualify as a lease under relevant accounting standards. That way, Pillowtex would not reduce the amount of credit available to it under its senior credit facility. Duke also cites a statement that counsel for Pillowtex made to the District Court, which Duke characterizes as a concession: "I don't disagree that it was structured to have that, those characteristics for tax purposes and, you know, to the extent that they could, the parties were trying to create a lease, I would admit that." App. at 117.

Duke's intent argument fails, however, because the New York U.C.C. no longer looks to the intent of the drafting parties to determine whether a transfer is a lease or a security agreement. Specifically, the 1992 version of § 1–201(37) [1–203] directed courts to determine "[w]hether a lease *is intended* as security" (emphasis added); this language was amended in 1995 to read "[w]hether a transaction *creates* a lease or security interest"

---

building materials market." App. at 85. Klemic detailed for the Court the processes and costs associated with removing and reselling lighting fixtures as follows:

> We would have to carefully remove the lighting fixtures where they would have to be wrapped, brought down wrapped, stored, transferred to a storage place. The cost would probably be, it's speculative, but it would be somewhere maybe $30–$40 a fixture perhaps, ultimately, depending on how long you had to keep them to sell them, if you could find a market. And again, I've been universally told there is no market, with very minor exception [sic].
>
> Q. And that has been your experience as well?
>
> A. That has been my experience for 17 years, and it's been the experience of major wrecking companies that have been in the business much longer than I have.
>
> Q. Have you actually looked at the lighting fixtures in the debtors' plants?
>
> A. Yes.

App. at 89–90.

(emphasis added). In this way, the reference to parties' intent was explicitly omitted. The Official Comment to the amended version confirms the importance of the changed language:

> Prior to this amendment, [s]ection 1–201(37) provided that whether a lease was intended as security (i.e., a security interest disguised as a lease) was to be determined from the facts of each case . . . Reference to the intent of the parties to create a lease or security agreement has led to unfortunate results. In discovering intent, courts have relied upon factors that were thought to be more consistent with sales or loans than leases. Most of these criteria, however, are as applicable to true leases as to security interests . . . Accordingly, amended section 1–201(37) deletes all references to the parties' intent.

U.C.C. § 1–201(37), Official Cmt; *accord In re Murray*, 191 B.R. at 314 (stating that "judicial opinions construing U.C.C. § 1–201(37) and the Official Uniform Commercial Code Comments . . . clearly place the focus of the inquiry under the revised statute on the economics of the transaction rather than on the intent of the parties as had been the emphasis previously").

Duke relies on *Edison Bros.*, 207 B.R. at 809, for the proposition that "[c]ourts are required to examine the intent of the parties and the facts and circumstances which existed at the time the transaction was entered into." *Edison Bros.*, however, explicitly relied on the 1992 version of the statute in looking at intent, and therefore has been superseded by the 1995 version of the U.C.C. Indeed, Judge Walsh, the author of *Edison Bros.*, noted in a later opinion: "I am persuaded by th[e] clear weight of authority that the intent of the parties, no matter how clearly spelled out in the parties' representations within the agreement, can not control the issue of whether the agreement constitutes a true lease or a security agreement." *In re Homeplace Stores*, 228 B.R. 88, 94 (Bankr. D. Del. 1998). Judge Walsh observed that the shift away from intent had been remarked upon by various commentators. *Id.* (citing Richard L. Barnes, *Distinguishing Sales and Leases: A Primer on the Scope and Purpose of UCC Article 2A*, 25 U. Mem. L. Rev. 873, 882 (1995) ("What had been a test of intention has become a test of economic realities; that is, intention has been dropped from section 1–201(37) [1–203] . . . Thus, the parties to a transaction may create a secured transaction under the revised definition even though their every intention was to create a lease")).

Based on the foregoing authority, we are unwilling to characterize the MESA as a lease on the basis that the parties intended it to appear to be one for tax purposes. Duke admonishes the Court in its brief that "[e]quipment leasing between sophisticated commercial entities dealing at arms length for their mutual benefit is an important commercial activity and one that should not be lightly recharacterized." Duke's Br. at 11. This admonition rings hollow in the context of bankruptcy cases, however, because every dollar that is used to pay a purported lessor depletes the pool of assets available to pay other constituencies of the estate. In other words, refusing to defer to the intent of contracting parties in resolving whether their agreement is a lease is particularly appropriate in bankruptcy, as otherwise the costs of the agreement would be externalized to third-party creditors.

Duke's accounting argument is similarly meritless. Duke argues that the District Court erred by attaching significance to the fact that Pillowtex did not account for the energy projects under the MESA as true leases. Duke argues that Pillowtex's accounting for the MESA payments as a utility expense should instead be viewed as evidence that it did not treat the MESA as a repayment of debt incurred to purchase the energy fixtures. We disagree. Pillowtex's accounting for the MESA payments as utility expenses seems to us to be consistent with the parties' agreement that Pillowtex's payments to Duke under the MESA would be equivalent to Pillowtex's actual savings. Moreover, as the District Court noted in its opinion, Pillowtex "entered into separate Production Equipment leases, each of which was recorded as a true lease on Pillowtex's books." Dist. Ct. Op. at 6. We agree with the District Court that it is significant that, while payments for the energy fixtures were treated as utility expenses by Pillowtex, the agreements with respect to manufacturing and production equipment (which are not at issue in this case) were recorded on Pillowtex's books as true leases. This distinction suggests that Pillowtex did not find it appropriate to record its MESA payments as leases, which bolsters our conclusion that they were not in fact true leases.

Next, Duke argues that the District Court erred by taking into consideration that the MESA was not labeled a lease. The District Court merely observed in passing, however, that "[t]he MESA is not labeled a lease," Dist. Ct. Op. at 9, and that there is no indication that the court relied heavily on this observation. Even if it did rely to some extent on this fact, this reliance was harmless since the economic realities independently dictate that the MESA was in fact not a lease. Accordingly, we do not believe that the District Court committed reversible error by mentioning the labeling of the MESA.

Duke goes on to insist that it had a "meaningful residual interest" in the fixtures, such an interest being "the fundamental characteristic distinguishing a lease from a security interest." *E.g.*, *In re Thummel*, 109 B.R. 447, 448 (Bankr. N.D. Okla. 1989). As discussed earlier, however, Duke only has a nominal residual interest, not a *meaningful* one: the combination of the cost of retrieving the fixtures and their poor market value renders the residual interest negligible. Duke claims that we should not "speculate" as to what it might do for economic reasons at the end of the MESA's term, and instead look to the parties' intent at the time of drafting the agreement. As we have mentioned above, however, Duke's argument is backwards: the Court must subordinate the parties' intent to the economic reality that Duke would not have plausibly reclaimed the fixtures at the end of the MESA's term. This is not mere speculation on our part. The uncontroverted evidence shows that removal of the fixtures would be prohibitively expensive, and that the fixtures' value on the market would not make it worth Duke's while to reclaim them. In short, the economic realities analysis not only permits, but *requires* us to examine the state of affairs at the end of the MESA's term.

Finally, Duke asserts that the District Court erred by characterizing the Master Lease between Duke and SouthTrust as a secured financing agreement, as opposed to a lease. The Master Lease applies only to the lighting fixtures that were SouthTrust's collateral and SouthTrust did not elect to appeal the District Court's order. Therefore, the District Court's holding that the Master Lease was a secured financing is not before us on appeal.

IV. CONCLUSION

After carefully considering the arguments discussed above and all other arguments advanced by appellant, we conclude that the District Court correctly determined that the MESA was not a lease and, therefore, that Duke was not entitled to lease payments under 11 U.S.C. § 365(10). We will remand this case to the District Court so that it may determine whether Duke is entitled to adequate protection.

[some footnotes omitted]

PROBLEM 2-11

Assume four leases:

1. United Airlines leases five Airbus A-320s to Delta Airlines for a two-year term with no option to purchase. At the end of the two-year term, the airplanes will be returned to United. This arrangement is a lease covered by Article 2A of the UCC, and it has none of the significant characteristics of a security interest. True?

2. Citicorp agrees to purchase five Airbus A-320s from Delta Airlines for a total price of $300 million and to lease back the airplanes to Delta for a period of 20 years, with no option to purchase. Delta negotiates directly with Airbus for the seat configuration, the galleys, the engines, and the like. This arrangement, too, is a lease governed by Article 2A. Unlike the lease from United, however, the lease from Citigroup is a "finance lease." The upshot is that the lessor, as a quasi-financier, gives more limited warranties to the lessee than a conventional lessor gives. Would the lease from Citigroup be a security agreement if the A-320s had a predicted life of only 20 years?

3. Bank One takes back five nearly new A-320s from American Airlines, which has gone bankrupt, and offers to "lease" them to Delta Airlines for five years, in return for five annual payments of $40 million. In addition, Bank One offers to give Delta the option to buy each airplane for a $100 payment at the end of five years. This transaction is a sale with a security interest attached, even though it is labeled as a lease, no? To confirm your instincts, consider section 1–203. In reality, the repossessing bank has made a time-sale of the airplanes, since it has no expectation of getting them back at the end of the lease period. In the parlance of a first-year property course, the bank has no "reversionary interest."

4. Bank leases five airplanes to Delta Airlines for a total payment of $10 million a year for five years, with an option for Delta to purchase the five airplanes at their fair market value at the end of the five-year term. What do you think? Is the arrangement properly considered a lease or an installment sale?

§ 8. FORECLOSURE

To understand more fully how the secured creditor's rights differ from those of the unsecured creditor, consider the collection rights of a typical secured creditor under Article 9. Upon the debtor's default, the secured creditor has the rights enumerated in section 9–601. In relevant part, this section provides:

> (a) **[Rights of secured party after default.]** After default, a secured party has the rights provided in this part [that is, Part 6 of Article 9] and, except as otherwise provided in Section 9–602 [prohibiting the variability of certain sections], those provided by agreement of the parties. A secured party:
>
> > (1) may reduce a claim to judgment, foreclose, or otherwise enforce the claim, security interest, or agricultural lien by any available judicial procedure; and
> >
> > (2) if the collateral is documents, may proceed either as to the documents or as to the goods they cover.
>
> * * *
>
> (c) **[Rights cumulative; simultaneous exercise.]** The rights under subsection[ ] (a) . . . are cumulative and may be exercised simultaneously.

Notice several features of section 9–601. First, it provides for an election of remedies: the secured party may enforce its rights under the remedial provisions of Part 6 or by other available means, including by commencing an ordinary lawsuit against the debtor for a money judgment or by seeking more immediate relief through a replevin action (as a specialized court proceeding designed for speedy resolution, a replevin action customarily bypasses many of the trappings of a traditional lawsuit). Second, the secured party may proceed with its remedies in any order it chooses. Third, the secured party's rights are triggered upon the debtor's default. As noted previously, Article 9 does not define the term "default," leaving it up to the parties to negotiate the circumstances of the debtor's default and enshrine the agreed-upon terms in their security agreement.

Under Article 9, the rights of the secured creditor upon the debtor's default include a right under section 9–609 to possess all the collateral, and a right to take possession of the collateral by self-help so long as there is no breach of the peace. Section 9–609 states in pertinent part:

> (a) **[Possession; rendering equipment unusable; disposition on debtor's premises.]** After default, a secured party:
>
> (1) may take possession of the collateral; and
>
> (2) without removal, may render equipment unusable and dispose of collateral on a debtor's premises under Section 9–610.
>
> (b) **[Judicial and nonjudicial process.]** A secured party may proceed under subsection (a):
>
> (1) pursuant to judicial process; or
>
> (2) without judicial process, if it proceeds without breach of the peace.
>
> (c) **[Assembly of collateral.]** If so agreed, and in any event after default, a secured party may require the debtor to assemble the collateral and make it available to the secured party at a place to be designated by the secured party which is reasonably convenient to both parties.

Thus, as applied to the facts in Problem 2–9 above, section 9–609 permits Bank One to instruct the debtor, following the debtor's default, to bring all the equipment to the construction lot, where Bank One can retrieve it when Bank One chooses. As a practical matter, of course, the efficacy of the bank's instruction will depend on the debtor's compliance.

If Bank One believes the debtor will resist the request to hand over the collateral (and many equipment lenders have at least a few entertaining anecdotes of debtors who did), Bank One may hire someone to go out on the weekend (or perhaps in the dead of night) and take possession. And Bank One would probably have a right to do so under section 9–609, so long as there is no angry confrontation or breaking and entering at the construction site. As section 9–609(b)(2) makes plain, the relevant standard is whether Bank One's exercise of its self-help remedy would involve a "breach of the peace." There is a colorful body of decisional law construing this term of art, which is undefined in Article 9. *See* 9–609 cmt. 3. Note also that the obligation to proceed without "breach of the peace" is not waivable in the parties' security agreement. *See* 9–609(6). For example, the debtor cannot agree in any enforceable way that the secured party is free to repossess the collateral through violent means. If the debtor refuses to surrender possession, Bank One would typically be entitled to a quick cause of action, such as replevin, that would likely give Bank One possession far sooner than an unsecured creditor could obtain it.

What if someone other than the debtor has possession of the collateral? May the secured party repossess the collateral nonetheless? Typically, yes—so long as the secured creditor has a superior right of possession. For example, suppose the debtor has granted a security interest in an item of equipment to two secured parties. Suppose that the junior secured party has repossessed the collateral before the senior secured party could get its hands on it. Because the senior secured party has a superior right of priority, it generally may take possession of the collateral away from the junior secured party (provided it acts without breaching the peace). *See* 9–609 cmt. 5; 9–610 cmt. 5. If the senior secured party has a right of possession against a junior secured party, it may also sue the junior secured party in conversion if the junior secured party refuses to hand over the collateral. *See* 9–609 cmt. 5.

While Article 9 has been enacted throughout the U.S. with a high degree of uniformity, one issue that states have addressed in a non-uniform way is a secured parties' rights under section 9–609 and so-called "electronic self-help." Electronic self-help is the use of remote starter-interrupters and other recently-developed self-help devices that creditors may use as enforcement mechanisms or to effectuate a constructive or remote repossession. (It is not always clear, under current laws, whether and when remote disablement is a form of repossession.) Consider the prospect of self-driving vehicles. Imagine a vehicle encumbered by a security interest and programmed to drive itself to the bank if its owner defaults. While this example is not yet realized, various modes of remote control of assets have existed for years now, and state legislatures have sought to regulate creditors' uses of these devices to prevent various harms (such as disabling the vehicle while in use). Non-uniform provisions of section 9–609 enacted in Connecticut[4] and in Colorado[5] concern electronic self-help. Numerous other states have enacted legislation apart from Article 9 addressing the issue as well.

Once a secured creditor lawfully repossesses collateral, the creditor is entitled to sell the collateral, provided it gives proper notice, makes "commercially reasonable" efforts under section 9–610(b), and complies with the provisions of sections 9–611 through 9–614. Section 9–610 states in relevant part:

> (a) **[Disposition after default.]** After default, a secured party may sell, lease, license, or otherwise dispose of any or all of the collateral in its present condition or following any commercially reasonable preparation or processing.
>
> (b) **[Commercially reasonable disposition.]** Every aspect of a disposition of collateral, including the method, manner, time, place, and other terms, must be commercially reasonable. If commercially reasonable, a secured party may dispose of collateral by public or private proceedings, by one or more contracts, as a unit or in parcels, and at any time and place and on any terms.
>
> (c) **[Purchase by secured party.]** A secured party may purchase collateral:
>
> > (1) at a public disposition or;
> >
> > (2) at a private disposition only if the collateral is of a kind that is customarily sold on a recognized market or the subject of widely distributed standard price quotations.
>
> * * *

---

[4] *See* CONN. GEN. STAT. § 42a–9–609. Connecticut enacted non-uniform UCC Articles 9 and 2A provisions concerning the use of GPS, remote ignition "kill," and other "electronic self-help" devices by both secured creditors and lessors. Connecticut's section 9–609 prohibits "the use of electronic means to locate the collateral" or to "render equipment unusable" unless (a) "the debtor separately agrees to a term of the security agreement authorizing electronic self-help that requires [advance] notice of exercise" and (b) the secured party gives the debtor at least 15 days' advance written notice of its intent to use electronic self-help. In addition, "electronic self-help may not be used if the secured party has reason to know that its use will result in substantial injury or harm to the public health or safety or grave harm to the public interest substantially affecting third parties not involved in the dispute." *Id.*

[5] *See* COLO. REV. STAT. § 4–9–609. Colorado enacted in section 9–609 non-uniform provisions stating: "In exercising its rights under paragraph (2) of subsection (a) of this section with respect to collateral, a secured party may not disable or render unusable any computer program or other similar device embedded in the collateral if immediate injury to any person or property is a reasonably foreseeable consequence of such action. Any secured party who disables or renders unusable such a computer program or other similar device in such circumstances shall be liable in accordance with applicable rules of law to any person who sustains an injury to person or property as a reasonably foreseeable result of the secured party's action." *Id.* In addition to the foregoing, Colorado enacted a separate non-uniform Article 9 provision specific to electronic self-help and motor vehicles. *See* COLO. REV. STAT. § 4–9–629.

Several features of section 9–610 stand out. First, the secured party's disposition of the collateral must be "commercially reasonable" in all its aspects. Although Article 9 does not define this term per se, it supplies some guidance in section 9–627(b):

> A disposition of collateral is made in a commercially reasonable manner if the disposition is made:
>
> (1) in the usual manner on any recognized market;
>
> (2) at the price current in any recognized market at the time of the disposition; or
>
> (3) otherwise in conformity with reasonable commercial practices among dealers in the type of property that was the subject of the disposition.

As with the term "breach of the peace" used in section 9–609, a large and colorful body of case law fleshes out the meaning of the term "commercially reasonable." *See* 9–610 cmt. 2. The obligation to proceed in a "commercially reasonable" manner also is not waivable. *See* 9–602(7). The standards that may be used to measure the fulfilment of the secured party's duty, however, may be the subject of the parties' agreement, so long as these standards are not "manifestly unreasonable." *See* 9–603.

The term "recognized market," meanwhile, is defined not in the text of Article 9 but in the comments. A "recognized market" is "one in which the items sold are fungible and prices are not subject to individual negotiation." Examples include the New York Stock Exchange. *See* 9–610 cmt. 9; 9–627 cmt. 4.

Second, section 9–610 authorizes both "public" and "private" dispositions. Once again, Article 9 does not define these terms. A "private" disposition would include a secured party selling the collateral to a third party through a privately negotiated contract, perhaps after holding the item out for sale with a broker. In contrast, the quintessential public disposition is an auction at which the public has a meaningful opportunity to engage in competitive bidding. *See* 9–610 cmt. 7.

Third, the secured party may freely purchase the collateral at a *public* disposition. *See* 9–610(c)(1). For example, the secured party may outbid the other bidders if the secured party is unhappy with their bids. It may also use its claim against the debtor as auction currency. This latter practice is known as "credit bidding." For example, suppose the secured party has a claim against the debtor for $100,000.00 secured by a lien on a piece of the debtor's construction equipment worth $120,000.00. Suppose at auction the highest third-party bid for the equipment is $70,000.00. If the secured party wishes to acquire the equipment, it may outbid the third-party and use its $100,000.00 claim as a form of currency, thereby become the successful bidder.

The secured party's ability to purchase the collateral at a *private* disposition is more limited. *See* 9–610(c)(2). As explained in the comments, the secured party's purchase of its collateral at a private sale is essentially the equivalent of a "strict foreclosure." *See* 9–610 cmt. 7. A strict foreclosure occurs when a secured party takes ownership of the collateral in full or partial satisfaction of the debt in lieu of conducting an auction or disposing of the collateral through a private sale. Under Article 9, the process of strict foreclosure is regulated under sections 9–620, 9–621, and 9–622. In general, these provisions call for the debtor's consent to any proposed strict foreclosure, notice to certain third parties, the absence of objection, and certain other requirements. These requirements are not waivable, except as provided in section 9–624(b). *See* 9–602(10), 9–624(b).

In addition, section 9–623 provides for a right of redemption. The term "redemption" means essentially what it implies—the right to get the collateral back under certain conditions by "redeeming" it. In order to redeem collateral, the debtor (or a "secondary obligor" or another non-foreclosing secured party) must tender full payment to the foreclosing secured party plus pay the foreclosing secured party's reasonable fees and expenses. (The term "secondary obligor" is defined in section 9–102(a)(72) to mean an obligor whose liability is "secondary," such as a guarantor of the debtor's indebtedness to the secured party.) In general, a right of redemption may be exercised up until the secured party has disposed of the collateral through a public or private disposition. A right of redemption is not waivable, except as provided in section 9–624(c). *See* 9–602(11), 9–624(c).

Sections 9–611 through 9–614 provide a series of rules governing the provision of notice before the secured party's disposition. Section 9–611 details who is to be given notice (but observe the exception for perishable goods). Section 9–612 regulates the timing of the notice. Section 9–613 specifies the contents of the notice generally, and section 9–614 specifies the contents of the notice in a consumer-goods transaction. Note the reference in the forms appearing in sections 9–613 and 9–614 to an "accounting." This is governed by section 9–210. Section 9–210 permits the debtor to request an accounting of its obligations and likewise requires the secured party to respond. Like many other provisions of Part 6, the requirements of sections 9–611, 9–613, and 9–614 are not waivable, except as provided in section 9–624(a). *See* 9–602(7), 9–624(a). The debtor's right to an accounting is also not waivable. *See* 9–602(2).

Section 9–615 directs how the secured party should apply the proceeds of the disposition. Section 9–615(a) is structured in the form of a classic "waterfall" provision. At the top of the fall, the proceeds are applied first to the secured party's reasonable foreclosure expenses. Next, the proceeds are applied to satisfy the debt owed to the secured party conducting the foreclosure. After that, any leftover proceeds are paid to certain holders of more junior security interests or other liens. If the proceeds of the disposition are greater than what must otherwise be paid under section 9–615(a), the debtor is entitled to the resulting surplus under section 9–615(d)(1). On the other hand, under section 9–615(d)(2), the secured party is entitled to sue the debtor for any deficiency (the difference between the amount due and the amount recovered on the sale if the proceeds of the sale are insufficient to satisfy the secured party's claim), provided that the secured party has recourse to the debtor personally. Some loans are "non-recourse" in nature, meaning that the secured party has agreed to look only to the collateral to satisfy its claim, in which case there would be no deficiency.

The debtor may make several arguments in any deficiency suit. First, he might claim that the notice of the sale was deficient. He might also claim that some element of the sale (timeliness, place, mode of advertising, etc.) was not "commercially reasonable," and thus that the sale cannot be used to establish the deficiency. *See* 9–625, 9–626. What if the secured party disposes of the collateral by transferring it to itself or a "person related to" the secured party? If the amount of proceeds realized through the disposition is significantly below the range of proceeds that would ordinarily be realized by a secured party disposing of collateral in compliance with the requirements of Part 6, then any deficiency must be calculated based on what would ordinarily be realized in a disposition complying with Part 6. *See* 9–615(f), 9–615 cmt. 6. The phrase "person related to" is defined in section 9–102(a)(62) (with respect to individuals) and in section 9–102(a)(63) (with respect to organizations). *See* 9–615 cmt. 7.

The special rules of section 9–615(f) suggest that low-price dispositions are problematic under Article 9. But it should be noted that, in disposing of collateral, the secured party is not under any general obligation to pursue the disposition designed to maximize the value of the collateral. Rather, the secured party is obligated to act in a commercially reasonable manner. Under section 9–627(b)(3), the secured party satisfies this obligation by acting "in conformity with reasonable commercial practices among dealers in the type of property that was the subject of the disposition." So if dealers in the type of property in question would dispose of it by auction, then that is a commercially reasonable practice even though some other disposition might yield a higher price. *See* 9–627 cmt. 2, 9–610 cmt. 10, 9–615 cmt. 5. As explained in the comments, section 9–615(f) is a special case designed to address the specific circumstances of related-party dispositions.

What if, prior to the secured party's disposition of the collateral, the debtor discovers that the secured party is not acting in compliance with Part 6? Under section 9–625(a), a court may order the secured party to comply. What if, notwithstanding the secured party's noncompliance, the disposition has taken place? The debtor may pursue damages occasioned by the secured party's non-compliance. *See* 9–625(b). But what the debtor generally may not do is reassert its rights in the collateral after the collateral has been transferred to a third-person, so long as the transferee has acted in good faith. *See* 9–617(b).

Finally, may a junior secured party conduct a disposition under section 9–610? Yes. *See* 9–610 cmt. 5, 9–615(g). But notice what happens when the junior secured party does so—its disposition does not foreclose the security interest of a more senior secured party. It only discharges the security interest of the secured creditor conducting the disposition, together with any subordinate interests. *See* 9–617(a). The security interest of the more senior, non-foreclosing secured party remains attached. *Caveat emptor*!

The secured creditor also has significant rights if the debtor goes into bankruptcy before repossession. Under section 506 of the Bankruptcy Code, the secured creditor would be recognized as "secured" to the extent of the value of its collateral. And section 361 entitles the secured creditor to "adequate protection" to insulate it from the decline in value of its collateral during the course of the debtor's bankruptcy case. Should a plan of reorganization be proposed in Chapter 11, section 1129 would further protect the rights of the secured creditor, directing that the secured creditor receive an amount, in cash if necessary, equal to the value of its collateral. If, on the other hand, the creditor were not secured, it would have no rights under section 361 and considerably fewer rights under section 1129. The principal right of the unsecured creditor is simply to share pro rata with the other unwashed. (More on bankruptcy law in the next chapter.)

Outside bankruptcy, the unsecured creditor's rights are equally meager. Its remedy is to sue the debtor for the debt that is owed, to recover a judgment, and ultimately, if the debtor has not yet gone into bankruptcy, to realize the judgment by having the sheriff seize and sell the debtor's assets. The lawsuit at the core of this process will not be a quick replevin action. It will be a suit on the debt and resolution may come only at the end of long delays and a long trial, especially if it is brought in a crowded jurisdiction or against a determined debtor that asks for a jury and presents defenses. Pending the outcome of this trial, the debtor will retain possession of the assets and may dissipate them.

PROBLEM 2-12

Assume Bank One (from Problem 2–9 with a security interest in various heavy construction equipment) assembles a team of repossessors who, on a Sunday afternoon, go to the construction site in Williston where the dam is being built. By threatening the security guard, they get him to open the gates. With a caravan of flatbed trucks, the repossessors take away several million dollars' worth of bulldozers, cranes, cement mixers, and other construction equipment. The next day Bank One sends an e-mail to the debtor joint venture, stating it intends to sell, a week from the following Monday, the collateral it has seized. In the meantime, Bank One advertises the material in the local newspaper in Williston and contacts several construction companies in Montana, South Dakota, North Dakota, and Minnesota. On the following Monday, it sells the equipment in a private sale to a Minneapolis construction company. It then commences suit against the joint venture for the difference between the $10 million debt then due and the $2.3 million it recovered in the foreclosure sale. It also commences suit against the parent, which has guaranteed the joint venture's debt.

Assume you are counsel either for the joint venture (which is still outside Chapter 11 and is struggling to stay afloat) or the parent (which is solvent but obviously reluctant to pay a $7.7 million deficiency). What defenses could you raise on behalf of each under Part 6 of Article 9?

PROBLEM 2-13

In 1999, First Bank loaned Northern Construction, Inc., $5 million to finance the purchase of five new cranes to be used in Northern's general operations. Northern granted First Bank a security interest in the cranes, which First Bank perfected.

For a period of three years, Northern's financial condition steadily worsened, although it managed to meet all of its obligations to First Bank. On September 1, 2006, Northern defaulted, leaving an outstanding balance of approximately $2 million. On January 5, 2007, First Bank took possession of the cranes.

1. Assume that First Bank spent $100,000 refurbishing the repossessed cranes and an additional $30,000 storing and maintaining them prior to sale. On April 5, 2007, it sold two of the cranes for $500,000 in cash; in November 2007, it sold the remaining three for $750,000 plus interest to be paid over five years. First Bank would like to recover its deficiency under section 9–615(d). (You may assume that First Bank's behavior has been commercially reasonable and timely, and that it has given all the proper notices.) What can First Bank recover?

2. If First Bank held additional security in the form of a $1 million letter of credit from CitiCorp, how would that affect the outcome? What would First Bank be expected to do?

3. Assume alternatively that First Bank has proposed to take the five cranes in full satisfaction of its debt under section 9–620. What must it do to comply with that section and what are the legal consequences of so proceeding? *See* 9–620, 9–621, 9–622. Incidentally, why would anyone use section 9–620 instead of pursuing a deficiency? *See* 9–620 cmt. 2.

CHAPTER 3

BANKRUPTCY

■ ■ ■

§ 1. INTRODUCTION

Why study bankruptcy law as part of a course on secured transactions? There are at least three reasons. First, most disputes over the priority and enforceability of security interests arise in bankruptcy cases, and after a moment's reflection, it seems inevitable that they would. Default is most likely to occur, and a secured creditor's rights are most likely to count the most, when a debtor is insolvent (that is, unable to pay his debts in full). And bankruptcy law is the law of insolvency *par excellence*. It prescribes a highly regulated process for both the adjustment of an insolvent debtor's liabilities and the disposition of his assets, including those encumbered by security interests. Insolvent debtors frequently file for bankruptcy protection to take advantage of this process, and the bankruptcy court is the setting where most of the drama over a secured party's rights unfolds.

Second, bankruptcy law exists as a federal overlay on the provisions of Article 9. Of course, bankruptcy law is not always directly implicated. It applies only if a bankruptcy case is commenced, and not all insolvent debtors file for bankruptcy. In some cases insolvent debtors surrender their collateral and address their financial difficulties without the intervention of a bankruptcy court. In other cases a secured party will have exercised its rights against its collateral before a bankruptcy case is ever commenced, and that often will be the end of it (at least as far as the secured creditor is concerned). But if a bankruptcy case is filed, bankruptcy law may affect and modify a secured party's rights in numerous ways; this chapter will summarize them.

Third, Article 9 anticipates and incorporates some elements of bankruptcy law, particularly the rights and powers of a bankruptcy trustee. We have seen already how the term "lien creditor" includes a trustee in bankruptcy, and how under Article 9 a lien creditor has priority over a creditor holding an unperfected security interest. This is one way in which Article 9 accommodates bankruptcy law. Another way is in the very concept of perfection itself. As an historical matter, perfection is an invention of bankruptcy law. It was developed as a means of policing the enforceability of security interests in bankruptcy proceedings: only security interests that are properly "perfected" may survive the trustee's scrutiny and the exercise of his avoidance powers—that is, security interests in which the secured party has taken the necessary steps under applicable state law to have priority over other intervening judgment lien creditors and buyers. As we have seen in the case of equipment, this means properly filing a financing statement or taking possession of the collateral.

So how does the bankruptcy process operate? Bankruptcy law is a highly complex creature, and this chapter is not the place for a full-blown examination of all its elaborate details. Instead, the ambition here is a far more modest one: to provide an explanation of the basic features of bankruptcy law, particularly as they affect a secured party's rights under Article 9.

In contrast to the UCC, bankruptcy law is almost exclusively federal law, and the Bankruptcy Code has its own title within the codified statutes of the United States: Title 11. The various sections of Title 11 discussed in this chapter interrelate with and influence the behavior of secured creditors long before bankruptcy is filed. It is sometimes said that the acid test of a security interest is the debtor's filing for bankruptcy. It is a black-letter principle that a fully perfected security interest cannot be invalidated in bankruptcy and will enable the secured creditor both to keep its interest in the asset in which it has security and ultimately to capture the asset's value. There is a gap, however, between the black-letter assertion and the reality of the bankruptcy process. Bankruptcy can prevent—or at the very least delay—a secured creditor's realization on its collateral. In some cases the trustee in bankruptcy can make a plausible challenge to the validity of the security interest, and in many other cases the secured creditor is forced to take part in a lengthy, expensive process to preserve its rights. Since you encountered several bankruptcy cases in the previous chapter, you already have exposure to some of the details of the bankruptcy process, particularly the trustee's "strong arm powers." In each of the last chapter's bankruptcy cases, bankruptcy law loomed ominously and mysteriously over the court's interpretation of Article 9. In short, then, we address bankruptcy here because a student cannot understand the significance or operation of a security interest without also understanding at least some bankruptcy law.

BASIC BANKRUPTCY VOCABULARY

Start with some basic items of bankruptcy vocabulary:

1. *Debtor*: For the purposes of the Bankruptcy Code, the debtor is the person (whether an individual or some other entity) who owes outstanding unpaid debts and is the subject of the bankruptcy proceeding. Note that the definition of "debtor" in the bankruptcy context differs from the Article 9 definition. Under Article 9 the "debtor" is the person who has an interest in the collateral subject to a security interest; the "obligor" is the person who owes the obligation secured by the security interest. Usually, but not

always, the "debtor" and "obligor" are one and the same for the purposes of Article 9.

2. *Bankruptcy Court*: It is perhaps too obvious to state that federal law establishes a bankruptcy court with its own judges, who hear nothing but bankruptcy cases. Unlike the typical state or federal judge, the bankruptcy judges are specialists. Day in and day out, like a cow chewing its cud, they grind away on bankruptcy cases. Obviously they are experts on the meaning and operation of the Bankruptcy Code; less obvious is that they are also experts on the meaning and operation of Article 9, for it is in bankruptcy that security interests are truly tested. Appeals from the bankruptcy courts go usually to local federal district courts. In some districts, certain cases go to bankruptcy appellate panels ("BAPs") made up of bankruptcy judges. Further appeals from the district courts or the BAPs go to the federal courts of appeals and, occasionally, end up in the U.S. Supreme Court (such as the bankruptcy case of the late Anna Nicole Smith, *see Stern v. Marshall*, 564 U.S. 462, 131 S. Ct. 2594 (2011)).

3. *Bankruptcy Case*: A bankruptcy case is commenced by filing a bankruptcy petition with the bankruptcy court. Bankruptcy cases may be either voluntary (commenced by the debtor) or involuntary (commenced by one or more of the debtor's creditors).

4. *Petition Date*: The "petition date" is the date a bankruptcy petition is filed, thus commencing the bankruptcy case.

5. *Pre-Petition and Post-Petition*: The term "pre-petition" refers generally to debts, events, or other matters that arise or occur before the filing of a bankruptcy petition. Conversely, the term "post-petition" refers generally to debts, events, or other matters that arise or occur after the filing of the petition.

6. *Exempt Assets*: Section 522 of the Bankruptcy Code permits an individual debtor to exempt (and therefore keep free of most claims) various assets, such as certain personal and household items. The assets a debtor may exempt from bankruptcy will vary according to whether the debtor elects to take the permitted federal exemptions or those available under applicable state law. Exempt items are subject to certain value caps depending on the relevant category of exemption.

7. *Bankruptcy Estate*: By operation of section 541 of the Bankruptcy Code, a bankruptcy estate is created upon the commencement of every bankruptcy case (except those involving municipalities) and exists to take ownership of the debtor's non-exempt assets. The bankruptcy estate is formed *in custodia legis*—in the custody of the bankruptcy court. After the commencement of a bankruptcy case, the bankruptcy court possesses exclusive *in rem* jurisdiction over the estate.

8. *Automatic Stay*: The commencement of a bankruptcy case triggers the "automatic stay" under section 362 of the Bankruptcy Code. The automatic stay enjoins most debt-collection activity against the debtor and property of the estate, including the foreclosure of a security interest in collateral. Under certain circumstances, the bankruptcy court may "lift," or grant relief from, the automatic stay in order to permit certain debt-collection activity to proceed, such as the foreclosure of a security interest.

9. *Claims and Debts*: Section 101 of the Bankruptcy Code defines the concept of a "claim" very broadly to include virtually any type of right to payment, whether secured or unsecured. Likewise, the term "debt" is defined broadly as any liability on a claim.

10. *Creditor*: Under section 101 the term "creditor" means a person holding a claim that arises before the bankruptcy court enters an order for relief commencing a bankruptcy case. Those who hold claims for debts arising after that are not technically "creditors"; they may, however, be administrative claimants.

11. *Proof of Claim*: Under section 501 a creditor is entitled to file a proof of claim with respect to a pre-petition debt that the debtor owes the creditor. Subject to certain exceptions, only creditors that file proofs of claim are entitled to distributions in bankruptcy. The allowance or disallowance of pre-petition claims is governed by section 502 of the Bankruptcy Code, which lists the grounds for disallowance.

12. *Request for Payment of Administrative Expense*: Claimants holding a right to payment for a post-petition administrative expense may file a request for payment of the post-petition claim. Section 503 of the Bankruptcy Code governs the allowance or disallowance of administrative expense requests.

13. *Holders of Secured and Unsecured Claims*: Under section 506 of the Bankruptcy Code, a person who has a perfected pre-petition security interest in an asset of the debtor (or has a right of set-off against an asset of the debtor) is regarded as a secured creditor, but (with certain exceptions) only to the extent of the value of the collateral. For the purposes of Article 9, we usually refer to anyone with a perfected security interest as a secured creditor, even if the value of the collateral is insignificant. The Bankruptcy Code draws a different line. For example, if a creditor is owed $20 million by a debtor and that debt is secured by collateral with a value of $11 million, the creditor typically would be treated in bankruptcy as though it held two claims: a secured claim for $11 million (equal to the value of the collateral) and an unsecured deficiency claim for $9 million. In a Chapter 11 plan this creditor would usually be a member of two classes entitled to vote its secured claim in one class (of which it would be the only member, in most circumstances) and its unsecured claim in a second class (usually along with many others).

14. *Oversecured Claim*: A secured claim is "oversecured" to the extent that the value of the secured creditor's collateral exceeds the amount of the secured creditor's claim. For example, suppose the secured creditor holds a claim against the debtor for $1 million secured by a lien on collateral worth $1.2 million. The secured creditor is oversecured by $200,000. Under section 506(b) of the Bankruptcy Code, an oversecured creditor is generally entitled to accrue post-petition interest up to the amount of its oversecurity (also known as the "equity cushion").

15. *Equity Cushion*: The term "equity cushion" refers to the positive difference, if any, between the value of a secured creditor's collateral and the amount of its claim. For example, if the secured creditor holds a lien on collateral worth $1.2 million and securing a debt of $1 million, the secured creditor is said to have an equity cushion of $200,000.

16. *Undersecured Claim*: A secured claim is "undersecured" to the extent that the value of the collateral is less than the amount of the debt owed to the secured party. Like unsecured claims in general, undersecured claims are not entitled to accrue post-petition interest in bankruptcy.

17. *Adequate Protection*: Recall that the automatic stay may prevent a secured creditor holding a lien on property of the bankruptcy estate from exercising its rights against its collateral. Under sections 361 and 363 of the Bankruptcy Code, such a secured creditor may be entitled to "adequate protection" to compensate for any diminution in the collateral's value occasioned by the debtor's continued use and control of the collateral during the bankruptcy case. Adequate protection may take the form of periodic payments, additional security, or other treatment to offset the loss in value. If a secured creditor is oversecured, the debtor may argue that the secured creditor is already adequately protected by virtue of its "equity cushion" and therefore entitled to no additional compensation.

18. *Priority Claims*: Under the Bankruptcy Code, certain unsecured claims listed in section 507 are entitled to be paid ahead of other unsecured claims. These "priority claims" include administrative expenses. In general, secured creditors are entitled to be paid from their collateral ahead of priority claims.

19. *Equity Interests*: The term "equity interest" refers to any ownership interest in a debtor, such as stock and similar interests. Under the bankruptcy concept of absolute priority, equity interests are subordinate to debt claims.

20. *Chapter 7*: Chapter 7 is the Bankruptcy Code's basic liquidation procedure. Although the process itself is quite complicated, the basic idea is that the Chapter 7 debtor gives up all his non-exempt assets to the trustee so that the trustee may liquidate the assets and distribute the proceeds pro rata to the debtor's unsecured creditors. In exchange, the debtor receives a discharge of his debts, so long as he has not misbehaved.

21. *Chapter 11*: Chapter 11 is the Bankruptcy Code's general business-reorganization procedure. (Chapter 11 is not limited to corporate business entities, however, and may involve an individual debtor.) The essential idea behind Chapter 11 is to give the debtor the opportunity to salvage its business operations by coming up with a plan of reorganization. In corporate Chapter 11 cases, the debtor's managers typically remain in control of the debtor and its property as the "debtor in possession" ("DIP"). The Chapter 11 process can be enormously complicated, often involving the sale of some or even all of the debtor's assets.

22. *Chapter 13*: Chapter 13 is the Bankruptcy Code's basic wage-earner reorganization procedure. The idea behind Chapter 13 is to give an individual debtor with regular income the opportunity to come up with a plan to retain her assets while she pays off as much of her debts as possible over a period of years. By statutory design, Chapter 13 plans are much simpler than Chapter 11 plans.

23. *Chapter 12*: Chapter 12 is the Bankruptcy Code's basic family farmer reorganization procedure. It is patterned after Chapter 13.

24. *Plan*: In cases under Chapters 11, 12, and 13, the Bankruptcy Code contemplates the filing of a "plan" that provides for, among other things, the disposition of the debtor's assets and the payment of claims to the extent of available funds. By statutory design, plans in Chapter 12 and Chapter 13 cases are far simpler (and less flexible) than Chapter 11 plans.

25. *Disclosure Statement*: Because Chapter 11 plans tend to be highly complicated and technical, the Bankruptcy Code contemplates the preparation of a "disclosure statement." By explaining the terms of a Chapter 11 plan, the disclosure statement helps creditors understand what they are voting on. Disclosure statements are not used in Chapter 12 or Chapter 13 cases, because, among other reasons, creditors are not entitled to vote on the debtor's plan.

26. *Discharge*: The "discharge" in bankruptcy refers to the release of the debtor's unpaid obligations. The type of discharge a debtor may receive depends on the type of bankruptcy case at issue. In general, the effect of a discharge under a particular chapter of the Bankruptcy Code is defined in section 524. Under section 523, some types of debts are non-dischargeable, including alimony and most student-loan obligations.

27. *Trustee*: In bankruptcy there are three kinds of "trustees." The first, called the "United States Trustee," is a federal official who supervises the bankruptcy system and is part of the federal hierarchy within the Department of Justice. In theory, the 1978 Bankruptcy Code separated the judicial functions from the administrative functions in bankruptcy. The former were given to the bankruptcy judge, who before 1978 had also been responsible for many administrative functions, and the latter were given to the U.S. Trustee. According to its mission statement,

> [t]he United States Trustee Program acts in the public interest to promote the efficiency and to protect and preserve the integrity of the bankruptcy system. It works to secure the just, speedy, and economical resolution of bankruptcy cases; monitors the conduct of parties and takes action to ensure compliance with applicable laws and procedures; identifies and investigates bankruptcy fraud and abuse; and oversees administrative functions in bankruptcy cases to promote and defend the integrity of the federal bankruptcy system.

Among its most critical functions, the U.S. Trustee appoints panels from which individual trustees are typically selected for Chapter 7 cases. The U.S. Trustee may also appoint a trustee to supervise a Chapter 11 case, but he usually does not do so. (In Chapter 11 cases the debtor typically continues in possession of, and operates its business in bankruptcy without a trustee; *see* "debtor in possession" below.) The U.S. Trustee is responsible as well for appointing the members of a creditors' committee, which participates in the Chapter 11 reorganization process on behalf of the debtor's general unsecured creditors (and sometimes in Chapter 7 cases also). In Chapter 12 and Chapter 13 cases the U.S. Trustee is authorized to appoint one or more individuals to serve in the role of standing trustee.

A second type of trustee in bankruptcy is the standing Chapter 13 trustee, who supervises and facilitates all the Chapter 13 cases and plans in a particular jurisdiction. When a debtor files for bankruptcy under Chapter 13, she must propose, and a court must approve, a plan under which she promises to devote her disposable income to repaying her claims over a several-year period. Prior to a hearing on confirmation of the plan, someone must determine whether the plan is feasible and whether it conforms to the rules of Chapter 13. This is the responsibility of the standing Chapter 13 trustee, who is thus critical to the operation of the Chapter 13 process. A standing Chapter 12 trustee serves the same function in Chapter 12 cases.

Last, though most important, is the Chapter 7 trustee, who is appointed or elected by creditors in every Chapter 7 case. A private citizen, the Chapter 7 trustee receives a percentage of the assets administered in the case (under section 326 of the Code, up to 25% of the first $5,000; 10% of amounts between $5,000 and $50,000; 5% of amounts from $50,000 up to $1 million; and up to 3% of amounts above $1 million). As the main representative of the debtor's bankruptcy estate, the Chapter 7 trustee is responsible for holding the debtor upside down, shaking him, and retrieving whatever coins fall from his pockets. It is also this trustee's responsibility, where appropriate, either to avoid unperfected security interests under section 544(a) of the Bankruptcy Code, or to set aside those that are preferences under section 547 or are otherwise avoidable. In avoiding a security interest, the trustee is representing the unsecured creditors against a secured creditor. But there is much at stake for the trustee personally, who has a financial incentive to avoid security interests: his contingent fee grows larger as the estate is enhanced by assets that, but for their avoidance, would have gone directly to a secured creditor. The Chapter 7 trustee is a fiduciary, and he is accountable to both the U.S. Trustee and the bankruptcy court.

28. *Debtor in Possession*: The "debtor in possession," sometimes called the "DIP," is the person who runs a company in Chapter 11. The term "debtor in possession" is shorthand for "debtor in possession of property of the bankruptcy estate." In most circumstances the DIP is the manager who ran the debtor company before the bankruptcy petition was filed. In some cases the prior management will be removed and another person installed as the DIP. In rare circumstances a trustee will be appointed to operate a business in Chapter 11, but almost always the DIP operates the business.

A cynic might say that the choice between a DIP and a trustee is the choice between a knave and a fool. By hypothesis, the management that led the debtor into bankruptcy was not able to steer the business well enough to stay out of the ditch, so why should this knave, or group of knaves, stay in charge? One reason is that the alternative may be a fool, a smart lawyer, for example, with no understanding of the particular enterprise and nothing but his intelligence to commend him. Based on experience under the Bankruptcy Act of 1898, the drafters of the Bankruptcy Code thought it better to choose the knaves than the fools. There is, of course, a certain practical logic to this approach. To the extent that bankruptcy law may be used to salvage a viable business, it usually behooves the debtor to file for bankruptcy relief sooner, while there is still a business to save, rather than later, when there might not be. The drafters understood that managers would be extremely reluctant to commence a bankruptcy case if the first consequence is the managers' dismissal. Thus, except in cases of fraud and the like, the pre-petition managers will continue to run the debtor's operations in Chapter 11, at least at the outset of the case.

The DIP in Chapter 11 cases has essentially the same rights and powers as a trustee. As a result, a DIP is authorized to avoid security interests that are not properly perfected and, of course, to make dozens or hundreds of decisions each day with respect to the operation of the business.

29. *Creditors' Committee*: Established in almost all significant Chapter 11 cases, the "creditors' committee" typically consists of creditors holding the largest unsecured claims against the debtor. These creditors are the same as those with the power to vote a Chapter 11 plan up or down under the provisions of section 1129 of the Bankruptcy Code, which prescribes the rules governing confirmation of Chapter 11 plans. Any DIP

who hopes to get out of bankruptcy by an agreed-upon plan of reorganization must listen carefully to the committee's wishes and ultimately negotiate with the committee about the shape of any plan. Sometimes the creditors' committee, rather than the DIP, will bring avoidance actions against a secured party.

30. *Strong-Arm Powers*: The term "strong-arm powers" refers to the powers of a trustee under section 544(a) of the Bankruptcy Code (the so-called "strong-arm clause") to avoid security interests. Section 544(a) operates by vesting in the trustee the applicable non-bankruptcy rights of (a) a creditor holding a judicial lien, (b) a creditor holding an unsatisfied execution on a judgment, and (c) certain purchasers of real property.

31. *Fraudulent Conveyance*: "Fraudulent conveyance" (also known as "fraudulent transfer") refers to a transfer a debtor makes either with the actual intent to delay, hinder, or defraud creditors, or that is constructively fraudulent because it depletes the insolvent (or nearly insolvent) debtor's assets without fair consideration. There are two basic sources of fraudulent conveyance law: (a) various state-law sources, such as the Uniform Fraudulent Transfer Act, and (b) section 548 of the Bankruptcy Code. The trustee in bankruptcy is entitled to avoid fraudulent transfers under applicable state law under section 544(b) of the Bankruptcy Code.

32. *Preference*: "Preference" is another term describing a transfer from a debtor to a creditor. A debtor gives a preference when, prior to the commencement of a bankruptcy case, it transfers to the creditor assets whose value is greater than the fair share that the creditor would receive by pro rata distribution of the estate in bankruptcy. The primary source of preference law is section 547 of the Bankruptcy Code.

33. *Reaffirmation*: Under section 524 of the Bankruptcy Code, consumer debtors may "reaffirm" certain debts, agreeing to be bound again to repay them, so long as the debtor and creditor comply with the requirements stated in the statute. The debtor may reaffirm a debt even though the particular debt may be dischargeable in bankruptcy.

FORMS OF BANKRUPTCY RELIEF

Consider now the various forms of bankruptcy relief outlined briefly above, what they attempt to accomplish, and how they operate. First, understand that the legal issues in a typical Chapter 7 bankruptcy diverge about as far from the legal issues in a Chapter 11 bankruptcy as the issues in an automobile accident case diverge from those in a merger. Each year, the list of Chapter 7 bankruptcies includes hundreds of thousands of relatively straightforward consumer cases. In adjudicating these cases the bankruptcy court is like a giant mill, taking predictable daily input and giving predictable daily output. At the other end of the spectrum are large Chapter 11 cases, which often present many thorny legal issues and idiosyncratic problems for the parties to negotiate and litigate. Chapter 13 proceedings, while similar to Chapter 11 cases in the sense that they involve a plan and a periodic payout under the plan, are in fact more like Chapter 7s, since the issues in question tend to be routine and commonplace.

Individual Chapter 7 cases are the most numerous, with filings in some years exceeding one million, but in recent years (prior to 2020) numbering about half that. These are followed by Chapter 13 proceedings, currently running about 300,000 filings per year (through the end of 2019). Chapter 11 cases are relatively rare, by comparison, numbering in the mere hundreds or thousands per year. In Chapter 13 cases debtors agree to cede their disposable earnings to their creditors for three to five years in exchange for a discharge of their unpaid debts and the retention of their assets. In part to cope with the glut of cases, the Bankruptcy Code was extensively amended in 2005. The new law includes a screening mechanism, known as "means testing," that denies Chapter 7 relief to certain debtors. Means testing permits a bankruptcy court to dismiss a Chapter 7 case when the disposable income of the individual filing for relief exceeds a specified amount. As an alternative to dismissal, these debtors may convert their cases to proceedings under Chapter 13. The 2005 amendments sparked a rush of filings as financially troubled debtors scrambled to take advantage of the old law. Following the economic turmoil of 2008, chapter 7 filings spiked again, rising to over one million in 2010. After 2010, the number declined to about half a million cases filed in 2019. The 2005 amendments did not achieve their goal of decreasing the number of bankruptcy filings, at least in the wake of a general economic downturn. They have, however, dramatically increased the administrative costs associated with consumer bankruptcy.

Understand that many Chapter 7 cases are and will continue to be "no asset" cases. In these cases the debtor gives his unsecured creditors essentially nothing, because, after exempting his personal belongings, the debtor typically has little or nothing to give. The debtor is able to achieve this because the Bankruptcy Code recognizes state-law exemptions in addition to its own set of federal-law exemptions that can sometimes be used. For example, under the federal-law exemptions set out in section 522(d), the debtor can withhold from his unsecured creditors $25,150 in real property, $4,000 in one motor vehicle, and $1,700 in jewelry. (These amounts, set in 2019, are subject to periodic adjustment under section 104 of the Bankruptcy Code.) Particularly galling to some creditors are the generous homestead exemptions permitted by Texas and Florida. In 2005 Congress amended the Bankruptcy Code to restrict these large exemptions, at least for persons who move to Texas or Florida within three years before filing. The debtor's right to exemptions is subject to one general exception: a perfected purchase money security interest can usually override the debtor's exemption entitlement and allow the secured creditor to take the asset (such as a car), which the debtor would otherwise keep from the grasp of his creditors.

A Chapter 7 bankruptcy will often be much kinder to the holder of a perfected security interest in a debtor's asset than to his unsecured brethren. In theory, perfected security interests are respected and protected in bankruptcy. At the end of a Chapter 7 case, a creditor holding a perfected purchase money security interest in a debtor's automobile is not defeated by any exemption. One suspects that a security interest is most useful to the secured creditor during negotiations with the debtor. Two observations suggest as much. On the one hand, the secured creditor typically prefers payment to repossession. On the other hand, by buying and using particular goods, the debtor has already demonstrated an interest in owning them, and he may even have developed an affection for them. Moreover, since these assets are physically located in the debtor's house and operate in a way he understands (and perhaps enjoys), there are likely to be significant transaction costs involved in replacing them. For that reason it is often in the mutual interest of both the debtor and the secured creditor for the debtor to reaffirm a particular debt, even though the debtor might otherwise surrender the collateral and discharge any unsecured deficiency obligation he might owe if the collateral turns out to be less valuable than the amount of the debt it secures.

Under section 524(c) a debtor may reaffirm a debt and, as a result, bind himself to continue to pay his debt in accordance with the reaffirmation agreement even after his discharge. (In order to do this, however, the debtor and creditor will have to follow the procedures set out in the statute.) An appliance store creditor may ask a debtor, "Do you wish to reaffirm or would you rather have us repossess the washing machine?" In doing so, it is initiating a negotiation that may result in a reaffirmation for the benefit of both parties. The debtor is spared the cost and inconvenience of finding a new washing machine, and the creditor gets a larger payment than it probably would get if it had to repossess and resell.

Much, though not all, of the legal action in Chapter 7s involves reaffirmation, the discharge under sections 524 and 727, exceptions to discharge under section 523, and the workings of the exemption law under section 522.

Turn now to Chapter 13 cases and plans, sometimes called "wage-earner plans." Use of Chapter 13 once varied widely among federal districts for reasons that are hard to explain. As noted above, with the retooling of the Bankruptcy Code in 2005, many petitions that were previously filed under Chapter 7 must now be filed under (or converted to) Chapter 13 by virtue of the "means test." Chapter 13 cases hold several advantages for some debtors. Some debtors feel a moral obligation to pay as much of their debts as they can. Chapter 13 allows these debtors to make significant payments over three to five years within the structure established by the chapter. A second benefit is that a debtor in Chapter 13 can generally keep an asset encumbered by a security interest notwithstanding the objection of the secured creditor, provided that the debtor makes the appropriate payments. Moreover, the debtor's payments normally need only equal the "value" of the asset, even though that value may be less than the outstanding debt. Exceptions to this rule include: a mortgage on the debtor's principal residence; a purchase money security interest in his car, securing a debt incurred within 910 days before the petition date; and certain other secured obligations. Thus, for example, a debtor might be permitted to keep his automobile acquired four years before bankruptcy by making payments with a present value of $10,000 for a car worth $10,000 even though the secured outstanding debt is $20,000.

Despite their advantages, Chapter 13 plans are often difficult for the debtor to complete, and the failure rate is high. Unlike Chapter 7 cases, in which the debtor typically receives a discharge shortly after commencing the case, a Chapter 13 debtor does not receive a discharge until she has substantially completed making all the payments under her plan. Many Chapter 13 cases are ultimately converted to Chapter 7 proceedings.

Only a small percentage of all bankruptcies are Chapter 11 cases (reorganizations), but this is where much of the sport is. Corporations file most, but not all, Chapter 11s, many of which wind up as liquidations either in Chapter 7 or through "liquidating" Chapter 11 plans. Some of the corporations will be small, one-horse operations without hope of reorganization. In cases involving such corporations, filing in Chapter 11 is sometimes motivated by the desire of the debtor's managers to remain as the debtor in possession (and to keep earning a salary as such) and to avoid the sharp eye of a Chapter 7 trustee. In small Chapter 11 cases involving assets of less than $200,000, general unsecured creditors typically recover nothing. Upon confirmation of its plan, a corporation reorganizing in Chapter 11 receives a discharge; a corporation liquidating in Chapter 11, however, does not.

In the Chapter 11 proceeding of a sizeable, going-concern business (such as United Airlines, Kmart, GM, Chrysler, Fruit of the Loom, or Owens Corning), the bankruptcy process can be divided into several distinct phases. The first phase generally involves settling the rights and obligations conferred by Chapter 3 of the Bankruptcy Code, including those set forth in section 361 (adequate protection), section 362 (automatic stay), section 363 (use, sale, or lease of property), section 364 (obtaining credit—as remarkable as it may seem, large companies in bankruptcy often borrow large amounts of money), and section 365 (executory contracts and leases, the former being a contract that remains substantially unperformed by both parties at the time the bankruptcy case is commenced, such as a contract for the construction of an airplane that has been neither built nor paid for by the debtor by the date of the petition). In most sizeable Chapter 11 cases, the DIP will propose a "first-day order" for the bankruptcy court's approval. This order will conform to the idiosyncrasies of practice in the court where the bankruptcy is filed, and its terms may have been negotiated, even prior to the bankruptcy filing, with some of the important creditors. Since the first-day order typically allows the DIP to use cash to meet its current expenses, it often gives adequate protection to creditors against losses that might result from the use of that cash. Depending on the case and the court, the first-day order may include many other terms about the payment of fees and the like.

Shortly skirmishes may develop between the DIP and various secured and unsecured creditors. Because of the automatic stay under section 362, secured creditors are generally barred from repossessing their collateral, and unsecured creditors also must refrain from collecting their claims without having the stay lifted. Some secured creditors may ask the court to lift the stay, usually arguing that their collateral is declining in value or will be used up, and thus they will be left in a worse position at the end of the Chapter 11 proceeding. The debtor will often meet these assertions with counter-assertions (for example, that the value of the assets is increasing, not decreasing) and offers of adequate protection under section 361 (such as offers of substitute or additional collateral or periodic payments to slow the decline in value). There may also be skirmishes over section 365, should the debtor choose to reject certain leases or executory contracts (for example, those associated with a retail debtor's least profitable locations, which it intends to shut down).

It is important to understand the essential effect of a Chapter 11 case on even a fully secured creditor. First, section 362 bars repossession and nearly all other acts to collect. Second, the court will refuse to lift the automatic stay if the DIP can make a plausible case for adequate protection under section 361 (a secured creditor has the right to demand adequate protection under section 363(e), and the court is supposed to lift the stay under section 362(d) if adequate protection is required but not forthcoming). The DIP might, for instance, offer terms that purport to compensate the secured creditor for the declining value of the collateral—at least to the satisfaction of the bankruptcy judge. Third, the creditor generally collects no interest on its secured debt unless and to the extent that the value of the collateral exceeds the amount of the debt. Thus, if a secured creditor contemplating a three-year-long Chapter 11 case holds a $30 million loan secured by only $25 million in assets, it can look forward to three years without a meal. Because there is a lot of play in the joints of what constitutes adequate protection, a nervous secured creditor may foresee and fear the possibility that he will receive no interest for the period of the bankruptcy. He may also worry that his collateral will be used up or sold by the DIP (*see* section 363) and replaced with some asset of undetermined value found to be "adequate" by the bankruptcy court. For example, a creditor holding a claim secured by good accounts might be concerned that the bankruptcy judge would substitute a mortgage on a rusty steel plant as adequate protection in return for the DIP's use of the proceeds of those accounts.

A second phase in many Chapter 11 cases involves the DIP's attempt to avoid certain security interests under the strong-arm powers of section 544(a) and under several sections that follow. By granting a trustee the rights of a lien creditor under state law, section 544(a) generally allows the DIP or trustee in bankruptcy to set aside a security interest that is not perfected at the time the bankruptcy petition is filed. A creditor whose security interest has been set aside joins the ranks of unsecured creditors and shares pro rata in the assets of the debtor, which now include the collateral of the formerly secured creditor. In many cases the trustee or DIP can also take back certain payments made on unsecured claims, and in some situations can even avoid security interests perfected within 90 days of the petition date. In rare cases the trustee or DIP can reach back even farther in time on the ground that a particular payment or transfer constituted a fraudulent conveyance, which can be avoided by combining sections 544(b) and state fraudulent-transfer law, or by using section 548, authorizing the avoidance of certain fraudulent conveyances under federal bankruptcy law.

The final phase of the Chapter 11 proceeding is generally the negotiation and approval of the plan of reorganization, so long as the Chapter 11 case has not previously been dismissed or converted to a Chapter 7 proceeding. Plans and their negotiation take many forms. When the debtor and its creditors negotiate a tentative plan before the petition is filed, the bankruptcy is said to be "prepackaged." The various creditors, both secured and unsecured, have given their tentative approval to the plan, and usually the parties expect that the debtor will be in bankruptcy for less than six months.

More often, however, the proposal and negotiation of a plan occur after the petition is filed. The plan may take the form of a sale (as in the case of Enron), wherein the bankruptcy estate sells the principal operating assets of the former company. In other cases the plan may call for the debtor's recapitalization, which would allow the debtor to emerge from bankruptcy as a new company, having retained most, if not all, of its assets. A recapitalization plan may sharply reduce the debtor's pre-petition debt obligations, some of which may be converted into post-confirmation equity interests (namely, stock ownership interests in the newly reorganized company), thereby either cutting off pre-petition equity holders or giving them only a small sliver of the new enterprise. In a negotiated plan, each class of creditors (though not necessarily each creditor) is generally entitled to vote on the plan's terms. If there are sufficient favorable votes, and if the plan meets the other requirements of section 1129 of the Bankruptcy Code, the bankruptcy court may confirm the plan. (Only confirmed plans may become effective.) Although some confirmed Chapter 11 plans may be "cram downs," most are negotiated plans. The term "cram down" refers to a plan that the bankruptcy court approves notwithstanding the contrary vote of at least one class of claims.

Turn now to section 1129(a) and look at the requirements for confirmation of a plan. Note the general rule under section 1129(a)(8) that all classes must vote in favor of the plan. (In the alternative, section 1129(a)(8) requires that the rights of all classes be "unimpaired," which means essentially that the members of the class retain all their rights against the debtor notwithstanding the debtor's bankruptcy filing and discharge.) Note further the key exception to this voting requirement: a plan can be approved over a class's objecting vote if section 1129(b) is satisfied. In other words, section 1129(b), the "cram down" provision, is a substitute for the favorable vote required by section 1129(a)(8). For this course we concern ourselves with section 1129(b)(2)(A), which describes what has to be done in order to impose a plan on a non-agreeing class of secured creditors. While there are several ways to satisfy subsection (A), the central requirement is stated in (A)(i): if the debtor intends to keep the secured party's collateral, the secured creditor must retain its lien and receive "cash payments totaling at least the allowed amount of [its secured claim]." For example, a secured creditor holding a security interest in a $10 million asset securing a $10 million claim must be given rights in the plan of reorganization that are worth $10 million on the date the plan is confirmed. (And this, in turn, generally means that whatever periodic payments the debtor may subsequently make to the secured creditor must include an appropriate rate of interest, which often is not the rate stated in the parties' contract.) Alternatively, under subsection (A)(iii) the secured creditor may be required to take "the indubitable equivalent" of its claim.

What does "indubitable equivalent" mean? In theory it means that, should the secured creditor give up its lien on its original collateral and receive periodic cash payments, the secured creditor must receive treatment that is indisputably the equivalent of retaining its lien and receiving cash payments. For example, instead of the secured creditor retaining its lien on its original, real-estate collateral and receiving cash payments to pay off its secured claim over time, the debtor may propose that the secured creditor be given a replacement lien on other assets and receive payment from the income these assets generate. The question then becomes whether this treatment is the "indubitable equivalent" of the secured creditor's original rights. (A third alternative, set out in subsection (A)(ii), applies to sales of a secured creditor's collateral.)

It is relatively rare for a debtor successfully to cram down a plan on a class of creditors that votes against it. On the other hand, it is equally rare for the DIP and individual secured creditors to negotiate without both parties considering—and doubtless the DIP threatening—a cram down under section 1129(b)(2)(A). Thus, negotiation (often extensive and intense) will take place in the shadow of section 1129, and no lawyer representing a secured creditor or a debtor in Chapter 11 dares ignore it.

Now that you have read the foregoing, beware the reaction of the little boy who received the book about penguins for Christmas, only to protest, "this book tells me more than I wish to know about penguins." Only by knowing something about bankruptcy can one understand the importance of Article 9 and appreciate the practical concerns of a secured creditor.

§ 2. SECTION 506 AND THE DETERMINATION OF SECURED CLAIMS

For the purposes of most commercial transactions, every creditor with a security interest is a secured creditor, even if the collateral is of little or no value. In bankruptcy, however, one is a secured creditor under section 506 of the Bankruptcy Code only "to the extent of the value of such creditor's interest in the estate's interest in such property." This means that the parties must agree on, or the bankruptcy court must determine, the *value* of the collateral claimed by the secured creditor. For example, if the creditor has a $10 million claim secured by a perfected security interest on an asset worth $100,000, the creditor is an unsecured creditor for $9,900,000 and a secured creditor for only $100,000. As we will see, it is sometimes in the creditor's interest to argue that its collateral is declining in value and has a value lower than the amount of its debt (for example, in order to have the automatic stay lifted on the theory that the debtor cannot provide adequate protection), and other times it behooves the creditor to maintain that its collateral has a high value (for example, in order to justify a large payment as part of a confirmed plan).

The following case is a classic example of a debtor's attempt to wash away some of its creditors' claims while emerging from bankruptcy in control of the bankruptcy estate's principal asset. If the property in the case is valued at $300,000, as the debtor proposes, the second mortgagee will be rendered unsecured, freeing the debtor to dispose of the second mortgagee's claim by paying the second mortgagee an unsecured dividend of 20 cents on the dollar. If, on the other hand, the property is valued at $400,000, no plan can be approved over the objection of the secured creditors that does not pay out a present value of $400,000 to the secured creditors. Under a plan that treats the collateral as having a value of $400,000, the second mortgagee will receive a payment of approximately $100,000 for its secured claim and will recover 20 cents on the dollar for the remaining unsecured deficiency.

WINTHROP OLD FARM NURSERIES, INC. V. NEW BEDFORD INSTITUTION FOR SAVINGS

United States Court of Appeals, First Circuit, 1995.
50 F.3d 72.

STAHL, CIRCUIT JUDGE:

Chapter 11 debtor Winthrop Old Farm Nurseries, Inc. ("Winthrop"), appeals the district court order affirming the bankruptcy court's decision that, to determine the status of the claim of undersecured junior mortgagee New Bedford Institution for Savings ("NBIS") pursuant to 11 U.S.C. 506(a), Winthrop's real property (the "Property") should be valued at its fair market value. We affirm.

I. Background

Winthrop operates a retail garden shop and commercial landscaping business on the Property, located at 462 Winthrop Street in Rehoboth, Massachusetts. On February 2, 1993, Winthrop filed a petition for relief under Chapter 11 of the Bankruptcy Code (the "Code"). On July 16, 1993, Winthrop filed its Disclosure Statement and Plan of Reorganization (the "Plan"). The Plan provides that Winthrop will retain all of its assets except for the Property, which is to be transferred to a new entity apparently controlled by Winthrop's principal, which will in turn lease it back to Winthrop. Thus, under the Plan, Winthrop effectively retains control of the Property and its use.

The Property is encumbered by a first mortgage in the amount of $287,000 held by Northeast Savings, F.A., and by tax liens of approximately $20,000. NBIS, the holder of a junior mortgage on the Property, is owed approximately $576,000. The parties stipulated to a liquidation value for the Property of $300,000 and a fair market value of $400,000. Winthrop's Plan would transfer the Property to the new entity free and clear of all liens except for the Northeast Savings mortgage. The Plan would "strip down" the NBIS mortgage to the liquidation value of the Property, leaving NBIS's claim entirely unsecured. The Plan proposes a payout of twenty cents on the dollar over a four-year period to unsecured creditors, whose claims, including NBIS's, total approximately $756,761.

NBIS objected to the Plan, claiming that the Property should be valued at fair market value, not liquidation value. If the Property is valued at fair market value, NBIS would have a secured claim in the amount of approximately $100,000, with the remainder of its claim unsecured.

The bankruptcy court, citing a line of cases holding that fair market or going concern value is the appropriate standard in valuing collateral that a Chapter 11 debtor proposes to retain and use, granted NBIS's motion and valued the Property at $400,000. The district court affirmed, and Winthrop now appeals.

* * *

III. Discussion

Section 506(a) governs the determination of whether any portion of a creditor's claim should be classified as a secured claim:

> (a) An allowed claim of a creditor secured by a lien on property in which the estate has an interest, or that is subject to setoff under section 553 of this title, is a secured claim to the extent of the value of such creditor's interest in the estate's interest in such property, or to the extent of the amount subject to setoff, as the case may be, and is an unsecured claim to the extent that the value of such creditor's interest or the amount so subject to setoff is less than the amount of such allowed claim. *Such value shall be determined in light of the purpose of the valuation and of the proposed disposition or use of such property,* and in conjunction with any hearing on such disposition or use or on a plan affecting such creditor's interest.

11 U.S.C. 506(a) (emphasis added) [editor's note: section 506(a) was amended in 2005]. The statute does not direct courts to choose any particular valuation standard in a given type of case [editor's note: following its amendment in 2005, section 506(a)(2) now provides a valuation standard for certain kinds of personal property collateral in chapter 7 and 13 cases]. As evidenced by the emphasized language in the statute's second sentence, Congress apparently did not intend that courts would use either a liquidation or fair market value standard exclusively, envisioning instead a flexible approach by which courts would choose a standard to fit the circumstances. Relevant legislative history buttresses this notion. The House Report states:

> Subsection (a) of [§ 506] separates an undersecured creditor's claim into two parts—he has a secured claim to the extent of the *value of his collateral*; he has an undersecured claim for the balance of his claim. *"Value" does not necessarily contemplate forced sale or liquidation value of the collateral; nor does it imply a full going concern value. Courts will have to determine value on a case-by-case basis, taking into account the facts of each case and the competing interests in the case.*

H. R. Rep. No. 595, 95th Cong., 1st Sess. 356 (1977), *reprinted in* 1978 U.S.C.C.A.N. 5787, 6312 (emphasis added). The Senate Report's commentary on § 506 offers little insight, but its commentary on § 361—the Code section that provides for adequate protection payments to secured creditors in some circumstances—is further evidence that Congress intended that courts would sometimes value collateral at something greater than its liquidation price:

> Neither is it expected that the courts will construe the term value to mean, in every case, forced sale liquidation value or full going concern value. There is wide latitude between those two extremes although *forced sale liquidation value will be a minimum*. In any particular case, *especially a reorganization case, the determination of which entity should be entitled to the difference between the going concern value and the liquidation value must be based on equitable considerations arising from the facts of the case.*

S. Rep. No. 989, 95th Cong., 2d Sess. 54 (1978), *reprinted in* 1978 U.S.C.C.A.N. 5787, 5840 (emphasis added). Although this commentary is not specifically addressed to § 506(a), it is nevertheless relevant, since a valuation for § 361 purposes necessarily looks to § 506(a) for a determination of the amount of a secured claim.[1] Indeed, since adequate protection payments immediately deplete the estate's assets—even before it is certain that a reorganization plan will be confirmed—one would expect that the valuation standard used to determine whether such payments are justified should be extremely conservative. *See* In re Case, 115 B.R. 666, 670 (9th Cir. BAP 1990) (stating in dictum that in a valuation for adequate protection purposes, "forced liquidation would be assumed and a deduction for selling costs would be logical"). Nevertheless, the Senate language suggests that even in a § 361 context, a court might value collateral at something more than its liquidation value.

We have not previously considered this issue. A number of courts, however, including four Circuit Courts, have adhered to this clear expression of congressional intent and declined to value collateral that a debtor proposes to retain based on a hypothetical foreclosure sale. These courts reason that because the reorganizing debtor proposes to retain and use the collateral, it should not be valued as if it were being liquidated; rather, courts should value the collateral "in light of" the debtor's proposal to retain it and ascribe to it its going-concern or fair market value with no deduction for hypothetical costs of sale.

Other courts, however, have chosen to read § 506(a) as requiring in virtually all cases a valuation of collateral limited to the net amount a secured creditor could recover if it seized or foreclosed on the collateral and disposed of it in accordance with applicable state law. These courts tie their interpretation to the first sentence of § 506(a), reasoning that even if the debtor proposes to retain and make profitable use of the collateral in the reorganized enterprise, the statute commands a valuation of the "creditor's interest" in the property—i.e., of the *lien*—and that value can only reflect

1 *See* United Sav. Ass'n of Tex. v. Timbers of Inwood Forest Assoc., 484 U.S. 365, 371–72, 108 S.Ct. 626, 630–31, 98 L.Ed.2d 740 (1988) (stating that statutory construction is a "holistic endeavor" and defining value of "entity's interest in property" entitled to adequate protection under §§ 361 and 362 in light of meaning of value of "creditor's interest" in property under § 506(a)).

what the creditor would be entitled to recover from the collateral under non-bankruptcy law. Thus, if the collateral is subject to the Uniform Commercial Code, the creditor's interest would reflect what it could recover from a commercially reasonable sale under the U.C.C.; if real estate, then from a foreclosure sale, perhaps with some value added if the creditor has the right and the wherewithal to bid-in, hold and resell the property on the open market. *See, e.g.*, In re Tenney Village Co., 104 B.R. 562, 567 (Bankr. D.N.H. 1989) (valuing property at fair market value because mortgage holder had ability to bid in and obtain fair market value through later private sales); In re Robbins, 119 B.R. 1, 5–6 (Bankr. D. Mass.1990) (recognizing second mortgage holder's bid-in rights but declining to ascribe any value to them where circumstances make it "unreasonable to expect" creditor to exercise them); *see generally* James F. Queenan, Jr., *Standards for Valuation of Security Interests in Chapter 11*, 92 Com. L.J. 18, 60 (1987) (real estate mortgage holder's bid-in rights "should be valued as an inherent part of his property interest").

We are persuaded that the first line of cases correctly interprets the statute. This interpretation gives meaning to both sentences of § 506(a), and enables bankruptcy courts to exercise the flexibility Congress intended. By retaining collateral, a Chapter 11 debtor is ensuring that the very event Winthrop proposes to use to value the property—a foreclosure sale—will not take place. At the same time, the debtor should not be heard to argue that, in valuing the collateral, the court should disregard the very event that, according to the debtor's plan, *will* take place—namely, the debtor's use of the collateral to generate an income stream. In ordinary circumstances the present value of the income stream would be equal to the collateral's fair market value. Under such circumstances, a court remains faithful to the dictates of § 506(a) by valuing the creditor's interest in the collateral in light of the proposed post-bankruptcy reality: no foreclosure sale and economic benefit for the debtor derived from the collateral equal to or greater than its fair market value. Our approach allows the bankruptcy court, using its informed discretion and applying historic principles of equity, to adopt in each case the valuation method that is fairest given the prevailing circumstances.

The interpretation championed by the second line of cases renders the second sentence of § 506(a) virtually meaningless. Moreover, it would allow a reorganizing debtor to reap a windfall by stripping down the lien to liquidation value and quickly selling the collateral at fair market value, thus pocketing equity that would have been completely beyond reach save for the filing of the bankruptcy petition. *Cf.* Butner v. United States, 440 U.S. 48, 55, 99 S.Ct. 914, 918, 59 L.Ed.2d 136 (1979) (bankruptcy law should "prevent a party from receiving a windfall merely by reason of the happenstance of bankruptcy") (quotation omitted). It is true that the debtor's intention to reorganize under Chapter 11 is what gives the collateral its going-concern value. And while it is also true that, absent a reorganization plan, the creditor might not recover the difference—assuming that there is in fact a difference—between the collateral's fair market value and the amount recoverable through its state law rights, we would not characterize this additional recovery as a "windfall" to the creditor, and certainly not one that will spur secured creditors to eschew their state law remedies and seek refuge in the comfortable confines of the bankruptcy courts.

We find that the bankruptcy court correctly interpreted § 506(a) as according it flexibility in choosing among possible standards of valuation, and properly applied the statute to the particular facts of this case. Winthrop proposes in its Plan to retain control of the Property and continue using it in its nursery and landscaping business to generate income. In light of this proposed use, the bankruptcy court committed no error in valuing the Property at its stipulated fair market value.

* * * For the foregoing reasons, the order of the district court is

Affirmed.

[some footnotes omitted]

NOTE

Consider what the debtor in *Winthrop* hoped to accomplish in conjunction with the bedrock bankruptcy concept of absolute priority. The U.S. Supreme Court has famously explained the concept as "the familiar rule that the stockholder's interest in the property [of the debtor] is subordinate to the rights of creditors. First, of secured, and then of unsecured creditors." *Louisville Trust Co. v. Louisville, N.A. & C. Ry. Co.*, 174 U.S. 674, 684 (1899). The absolute priority rule reflects the basic commercial understanding that, although there is no theoretical limit to how much the owners of a business enterprise stand to gain if the business is successful, their interests are subordinate to the claims of creditors if the business fails. Conversely, although the amounts creditors may recover from a business enterprise are limited to the amounts of their claims and therefore they have no upside potential beyond the amount of their claims, they are entitled to payment ahead of the equity interests of the owners. This understanding represents a basic assignment of the relative risks and rewards of lending and equity investment in the event of insolvency.

It will not surprise you, however, that in individual bankruptcy cases equity holders would prefer, and sometimes attempt, to avoid absolute priority in ways that permit them to recover something even though creditors are not paid in full. By definition, if a debtor is insolvent on a balance-sheet basis, there is insufficient value to pay all creditors in full. Accordingly, in order for equity holders to recover something, their recovery must come out of the creditors' hide. In *Winthrop*, the debtor hoped to divert the value of the real estate in question from its secured creditors by using a liquidation value rather than a fair market value for the collateral. Although it may be true that in a foreclosure the real estate would have fetched $300,000, the property was not going to be sold in foreclosure—the debtor was going to keep it. Subsequently, if the debtor ever sold the property (for example, by hiring a broker and offering it for sale in the retail market), the debtor could recover $400,000 (or more) for it. But if the debtor was only obligated to pay its secured creditors $300,000, then the debtor would receive the difference. The concept of absolute priority is codified in section 1129(b) as part of the standard applicable to the treatment of claims in the cram down context (discussed below in Section 9 of this chapter). *See Bank of Am. Nat'l Trust & Sav. Ass'n v. 203 North LaSalle St. P'ship*, 526 U.S. 434 (1999).

PROBLEM 3-1

What is the consequence in the *Winthrop* case of a finding that the collateral is worth $400,000:

1. For the purposes of section 362?
2. For the purposes of sections 1129(a)(7) and 1129(b)?

NOTE

Under the 2005 amendments to section 506, consumer goods subject to a security interest must be valued at "replacement value." Replacement value is "the price a retail merchant would charge." To understand the relevance of this, consider an automobile with a wholesale value of $12,000 and a retail value of $15,000 that secures a loan of $20,000. Section 506(a)(2), as amended, in effect requires that the debtor pay an amount with a present value of $15,000 to keep the car. Note that replacement value (the price a merchant would charge for the goods) is different from foreclosure value (the price a secured creditor would realize at a foreclosure sale such as an auction), and both are different again from wholesale value (the price a merchant would pay for the goods from the manufacturer).

§ 3. SECTION 362 AND THE AUTOMATIC STAY

The automatic stay applies to all creditors, but here we consider only secured creditors. Mostly it means no repossession, no set-off, and no disposition of assets already under the secured creditor's control pending foreclosure while the bankruptcy is pending. Of course, the stay also stops any judicial action to collect.

Over the years Congress has had some second thoughts about the stay and has gradually reduced its reach. In 2005 Congress provided that the stay automatically ends in certain circumstances and that it never arises in other egregious circumstances. *See* 362(c)(3), 362(c)(4), 362(d)(4). In most cases the points of contention between the debtor and the creditor will not concern the stay itself, but rather the creditor's request that the stay be lifted or that the creditor be given "adequate protection" of its security interest.

In practice, quarrels over the stay might come early (when the stay halts the pre-bankruptcy creditor collection activity at the beginning of the case) or later (when the stay is used to ensure that in a Chapter 11 case the DIP remains in possession of business assets during the bankruptcy). During the latter stage, sections 361 through 363 become windows through which the court observes the DIP's use of assets, particularly when creditors seek the return or sale of those assets.

Prior to the 1978 Code, the debtor's ability to modify the rights of secured lenders under Chapter XI was limited and uncertain. The current Chapter 11 and the rest of the 1978 Code changed that by giving the DIP weapons to offset the secured creditors' rights. But what policy is served by putting the secured lender at the mercy of the DIP and the bankruptcy judge? If the creditor loses value through delay alone, does someone else enjoy a comparable offsetting benefit? And if the stay is lifted too readily, how will a reorganization be possible? These questions underlie decisions on lifting the stay.

Section 362(d)(1) orders relief from the stay "for cause, including the lack of adequate protection of an interest in property." (Section 362(d)(2) separately authorizes relief from the stay for cause if the debtor has no equity in the property and the property is not necessary to an effective reorganization.) As noted, in response to a creditor's request for relief from the stay, the debtor is likely to argue that the secured creditor either: (1) is already adequately protected (for example, because the value of the collateral vastly exceeds the secured creditor's claim, the collateral is increasing in value, or the collateral is at least not declining in value), or (2) may be adequately protected in some other way (for example, by receiving additional collateral from the debtor to protect its interest, or by receiving periodic payments from the debtor to compensate for any loss of value). So although the creditor's first choice may be to have the stay lifted in order to foreclose, the creditor's fallback is usually to seek and obtain some form of "adequate protection" under sections 361 and 363(e). Examine these sections. Relief under their provisions for lack of adequate protection runs only to parties holding an "interest in property" that is inadequately safeguarded by the trustee or debtor in possession. An unsecured creditor gets no adequate protection under sections 361 and 363 since it holds no interest in the debtor's property within the meaning of these sections.

The need for adequate protection stems in part from Fifth Amendment prohibitions on taking property without just compensation, but a more important reason is the belief that the secured lender's bargain should be recognized in bankruptcy, except where some more powerful policy overrides. In bankruptcy "giving a secured creditor an absolute right to his bargain may be impossible or severely detrimental . . . , the purpose of [section 362] is to ensure that the secured creditor receives *in value* essentially what he bargains for." Benjamin Weintraub & Alan Resnick,

Puncturing the Equity Cushion—Adequate Protection for Secured Creditors in Reorganization Cases, 14 UCC L.J. 284, 285 (1982) (emphasis added).

Subsection 362(d)(1) requires adequate protection of the value of the creditor's interest in the property. But how is "value" defined? *Winthrop* gives a partial answer. Does it include the value of the lost opportunity to sell promptly and reinvest? Whether section 361's value includes the right to be compensated for this lost opportunity cost was a grand bankruptcy controversy until 1988, when the Supreme Court held in *United Savings Ass'n of Texas v. Timbers of Inwood Forest Associates, Ltd.*, 484 U.S. 365 (1988), that the concept of adequate protection does not include lost opportunity costs.

To understand the issue, assume a creditor holds a mortgage debt of $1 million secured by an asset worth $800,000. Assume further that, under state law, the creditor would have been able to complete its foreclosure and sell the property on January 1, 1987. If the debtor files a petition in bankruptcy in December of 1986 and no plan is confirmed until the end of 1989, the creditor will have been deprived of interest on the value of the collateral ($800,000) for three years in comparison to results under state law. In effect, the creditor has lost the opportunity to reinvest the $800,000 and earn a return on it. Some courts regarded this lost income as part of the value to be protected under sections 361 and 362; others did not.

In *Timbers*, the Supreme Court held that the creditor's lost opportunity cost was not part of the concept of value in section 362(d)(1) and section 361. So the debtor in our hypothetical is required neither to pay interest nor to protect the creditor's right to interest on the $800,000. Only the creditor's right to receive its principal amount of $800,000 is protected.

Section 506(b) grants oversecured creditors (those who hold security interests in collateral worth more than the amount of their claims) the right to accrue post-petition interest up to the amount of the equity cushion (the difference between the value of the collateral and the amount of the oversecured creditor's claim). To illustrate, assume the creditor holds a claim against the debtor in the amount of $1 million and the value of its collateral is $1.2 million. The secured creditor is oversecured because the value of the collateral exceeds the amount of the debt, generating an equity cushion of $200,000. The creditor is thus entitled to accrue up to $200,000 in post-petition interest.

The time of valuation is important because, if the collateral is appreciating or payments are being made, a creditor who is not originally oversecured may become oversecured sometime after filing. Creditors may move for valuation of the collateral anytime after the petition and before confirmation to determine if they are oversecured and thus entitled to recover post-petition interest. Since interest is allowed only if the creditor is oversecured, post-petition interest accrues up to the point at which the debt plus the interest equals the value of the collateral; beyond that point, interest no longer accrues. Often the interest is not paid until confirmation of the debtor's plan. This poses some risk to the creditor, who will be left with a reduced source of recovery should the value of its collateral decline while the debtor tries, and perhaps ultimately fails, to confirm a plan.

Decisions such as *Timbers* show which of a secured creditor's interests are protected. For instance, the creditor has a right to recover the principal amount of its claim up to the value of its collateral, but not a right to lost opportunity costs. Nonetheless, such decisions leave open the issue of how that protection will be provided. Section 361 steps into the breach, stating three ways of providing adequate protection. These three illustrations are not exhaustive, however; indeed, the possibilities are seemingly limitless.

To begin with, adequate protection may be provided by periodic cash payments. This method, outlined in section 361(1), is occasionally used to provide payments that offset the depreciation of the collateral. But cash payments are not the DIP's favored method. Some DIPs will not have sufficient cash to make such payments, and even if cash is available, nearly every debtor wants the discretion to use that cash to operate its business.

The second method, stated in section 361(2), authorizes the DIP to give adequate protection by granting security in other property. This security takes the form of a replacement lien, the value of which is determined by the extent that the stay "results in a decrease in the value of [the creditor's] interest" in the collateral. Although a replacement lien may seem to be a plausible method of giving adequate protection, in practice it too has drawbacks. Many Chapter 11 debtors will have long since granted a security interest in everything of value.

Section 361(3) derives from an opinion of Judge Learned Hand, *In re Murel Holding Corp.,* 75 F.2d 941 (2d Cir. 1935). The subsection provides for adequate protection through any other relief that will result "in the realization by [the creditor] of the indubitable equivalent of [the creditor's] interest" in the collateral. The term "indubitable equivalent" was seldom used in judicial opinions or legislation until the adoption of the 1978 Code, and its meaning continues to be mysterious.

The various provisions on adequate protection have one thing in common: they balance the interests of the bankrupt estate and DIP in continuing to use important property against the financial interest of the secured creditor. A fully secured creditor wants its asset; a DIP wants to use the asset to raise revenue and conduct its business. After *Timbers*, the secured creditor will usually suffer some uncompensated economic loss due to the delay in retaking its collateral. The concept of adequate protection recognizes that the creditor has a valid interest in being adequately, if not completely, protected.

To understand the options actually used by debtors, one needs to make a basic distinction in treatment between an undersecured creditor and an oversecured creditor with an equity cushion. As discussed, an equity cushion exists when the collateral's appraised value exceeds the creditor's claim. If the equity cushion is large enough, the DIP may argue successfully that this alone provides adequate protection. Thus, for the purposes of determining adequate protection, the DIP has an incentive to overvalue the collateral. On the other hand, for the purposes of confirming a plan, the DIP may well want to argue that the collateral has a low value, thereby minimizing the payments it must make to the secured creditor under the plan in order to keep the collateral. Thus, the DIP may find itself in something of a strategic dilemma: having argued at the outset of the case that the collateral has a high value, the DIP may find it uncomfortable to argue later that the value is in fact much lower.

In addition to the hope that the stay will be lifted or that the court will order adequate protection, there are other strategic reasons to ask for adequate protection relief. In particular, if the secured creditor asks for adequate protection and the additional protection granted turns out *not* to be adequate, the secured creditor may be entitled to a backup priority claim under section 507(b).

ORIX CREDIT ALLIANCE, INC. V. DELTA RESOURCES, INC.

United States Court of Appeals, Eleventh Circuit, 1995.
54 F.3d 722.

PER CURIAM:

Delta Resources, Inc., ("Delta") appeals the district court's order requiring payment of postpetition interest as part of the adequate protection it was required to pay as debtor-in-possession to appellee, Orix Credit Alliance Inc. ("Orix"). We reverse.

I. FACTS AND PROCEDURAL BACKGROUND

On November 30, 1992, appellant Delta filed a voluntary petition under Chapter 11 of the Bankruptcy Code, 11 U.S.C. 101 et seq., in the United States Bankruptcy Court for the Northern District of Alabama. On December 29, 1992, appellee Orix, claiming to be an oversecured creditor, moved for relief from the automatic stay, pursuant to 11 U.S.C. § 362, on the ground that, *inter alia*, its perfected security interest in the purchase money equipment was not adequately protected.

At the final hearing before the bankruptcy court the parties agreed that the then-value of the collateral, approximately 13 pieces of heavy equipment, was $643,500. The bankruptcy court concluded that the collateral was slightly depreciating but did not find whether Orix in fact was an oversecured creditor. Instead, the court merely assumed, as Orix had asserted, that Orix was an oversecured creditor.

The bankruptcy court determined that the equipment at issue was necessary to the effective reorganization of the debtor and thus, under 11 U.S.C. § 362(d)(2), Orix could not receive relief from the automatic stay.[2] However, the bankruptcy court did not determine whether the creditor was entitled to post-petition interest reasoning that that issue should be dealt with at the time of confirmation of the debtor's Chapter 11 plan.

The bankruptcy court also determined that Orix's secured interest in its collateral would be adequately protected by periodic cash payments in accordance with 11 U.S.C. § 361(1). The bankruptcy court granted Orix adequate protection in the amount of $9,972.41 per month to cover accruing depreciation of the equipment, but rejected Orix's contention that as an oversecured creditor it was entitled to receive post-petition interest as part of adequate protection. Accordingly, the bankruptcy court denied Orix's motion for relief from stay.

* * *

After Delta failed to pay the first required adequate protection payment, Orix filed a motion to compel payment which the bankruptcy court denied on April 19, 1993.

* * *

On October 19, 1993, the district court entered a "final order" reversing the bankruptcy court. Extending the holding of *United Sav. Ass'n v. Timbers of Inwood Forest Assocs., Ltd.*, 484 U.S. 365, 108 S.Ct. 626, 98 L.Ed.2d 740 (1988), the district court determined that an oversecured creditor is entitled to postpetition interest as part of adequate protection. The district court found that Delta should retroactively pay to Orix monthly adequate protection payments consisting of $9,972.41 for the monthly depreciation of its collateral, as well as an additional amount of $8,292.90 in postpetition interest to maintain its equity cushion. The district court remanded the case to the bankruptcy court directing that Delta pay that amount to Orix retroactive to March 17, 1993, the date of

---

[2] "On request of a party in interest and after notice and a hearing, the court shall grant relief from the stay provided under subsection (a) of this section, such as by terminating, annulling, modifying, or conditioning such stay—

(1) for cause, including the lack of adequate protection of *an interest in property* of such party in interest; or

(2) with respect to a stay of an act against property under subsection (a) of this section, if—

(A) the debtor does not have an equity in such property; *and*

(B) such property is not necessary to an effective reorganization." 11 U.S.C. §§ 362(d)(1) and (2)(A) and (B) (emphasis added).

the bankruptcy court's order from the bench denying relief from stay but ordering adequate protection.

* * *

C. Adequate Protection

The question before us is not whether an oversecured creditor whose collateral is worth more than the amount of its debt in a Chapter 11 bankruptcy case may obtain postpetition interest as part of its claim. Indeed, it seems beyond peradventure that a creditor's right to recover postpetition interest on its oversecured claim pursuant to 11 U.S.C. § 506(b) is virtually "unqualified." *United States v. Ron Pair Enters., Inc.*, 489 U.S. 235, 241, 109 S.Ct. 1026, 1030, 103 L.Ed.2d 290, 298 (1989). *Equitable Life Assurance Soc'y v. Sublett (In re Sublett)*, 895 F.2d 1381 (11th Cir.1990). *Cf. Rake v. Wade*, 508 U.S. 464, 113 S.Ct. 2187, 124 L.Ed.2d 424 (1993) (oversecured claimant entitled to preconfirmation and postconfirmation interest on arrearages in Chapter 13 cases). Rather, the narrow legal issue presented for decision is whether Orix, purportedly an oversecured creditor, was entitled to receive periodic cash payments for accruing post-petition interest as part of adequate protection, pursuant to 11 U.S.C. § 362(d)(1), in order to preserve the value of its equity cushion. Appellant Delta does not dispute that an oversecured creditor is entitled to postpetition interest on its claim, although[ ] Delta does dispute whether Orix was, in fact, an oversecured creditor.

* * *

[W]e conclude that 11 U.S.C. § 506(b), providing for post-petition interest on oversecured claims, read *in pari materia* with 11 U.S.C. § 362(d)(1), concerning conditioning the automatic stay on adequate protection, and 11 U.S.C. § 502, regarding the allowance of claims, requires that the payment of accrued postpetition interest to an oversecured creditor await the completion of reorganization or confirmation of the bankruptcy case. The *ratio decidendi* enunciated by the Supreme Court in *Timbers* that an undersecured creditor is not entitled to receive post-petition interest on its collateral *during the stay* to assure adequate protection under 11 U.S.C. § 362(d)(1) applies equally well to an oversecured creditor. Such an interpretation of the Bankruptcy Code is consistent whether the secured creditor is undersecured or oversecured, otherwise "§ 506(b) would simply have said that the *secured* creditor [whether oversecured or undersecured] is entitled to interest 'on his allowed claim, or on the value of the property securing his allowed claim, whichever is lesser.'" *Timbers*, 484 U.S. at 372–73, 108 S.Ct. at 631, 98 L.Ed.2d at 749 (emphasis added). Accordingly, viewing the allowance of post-petition interest to oversecured creditors as a limited exception only,[8] we hold that an oversecured creditor's interest in property which must be adequately protected encompasses the decline in the value of the collateral only, rather than perpetuating the ratio of the collateral to the debt. The bankruptcy court accomplished that by allowing adequate protection in the amount of accruing depreciation. *See In re Westchase I Assoc.*, 126 B.R. 692 (W.D.N.C. 1991); David G. Epstein et al., *Bankruptcy* § 3–27, at 142–43 (1993).

We think this rule results in the appropriate balance between the conflicting interests of the oversecured creditor on the one hand and the estate, as well as other creditors, secured and unsecured, on the other hand. As one commentator points out:

> [t]here is certainly no reason intrinsic to the phenomenon of credit that entitles over-secured creditors to interest out of their collateral before junior creditors, whether secured [perhaps by the identical collateral] or unsecured, receive any of their principal.

Niall L. O'Toole, *Adequate Protection and Postpetition Interest in Chapter 11 Proceedings*, 56 Am. Bank. L.J. 251, 253 (1982).

Here, even accepting the bankruptcy court's assumption that Orix was an oversecured creditor, although it never made such a factual finding, for the reasons stated above, Orix, as a matter of law, was not entitled to receive periodic payments for accruing post-petition interest as part of adequate protection for any period of time.

The district court's order awarding Orix monthly postpetition interest in the amount of $8,292.90 is REVERSED and this case REMANDED to the district court for further proceedings not inconsistent herewith.

[some footnotes omitted]

NOTE

If the interest that accrued each month were paid at the end of that month pending the outcome of the bankruptcy case, the creditor would remain oversecured, since the amount of accrual would not be added to its debt and would not reduce the equity cushion. By calling for accrual and denying the creditor's claim to periodic payment, the court not only leaves the secured creditor at risk of not receiving the payment, it also effectively changes the amount that will be received by the creditor even if things work as planned.

Consider an example. Assume a creditor is owed $100,000 against collateral worth $110,000. If there were an accrual of $1,000 a month and that amount were added to the principal, the equity cushion of $10,000 would be gone after ten months, and the secured creditor would have no right to interest

8 *See*, Niall L. O'Toole, *Adequate Protection and Postpetition Interest in Chapter 11 Proceedings*, 56 Am. Bank. L.J. 251 (1982).

for periods after the tenth month. If, on the other hand, the $1,000 were paid to the creditor at the end of each month, and if the value of the collateral remained the same, the creditor would continue to collect interest indefinitely because each payment would merely be a payment of current interest and would not have any effect on the equity cushion.

PROBLEM 3-2

In *Orix* the debtor apparently failed to pay even the first payment. This failure resulted in the suit that caused the appeal. If you were the lawyer for Orix, how would you minimize the possibility that your debtor could default and then force you to litigate with him (an expensive proposition by the time you are done appealing to the 11th Circuit)?

PROBLEM 3-3

Assume that at the outset of the bankruptcy case, Orix's debt was $500,000 and the value of the collateral was $643,500. Assume also that the debtor made five monthly payments of $9,972.41 (totaling $49,862.05) before the trustee sold the property.

1. If the property were sold for $700,000, what part would go to Orix?
2. If the property were sold for $500,000, what part would go to Orix?

FINANCIAL SECURITY ASSURANCE INC. V. T-H NEW ORLEANS LIMITED PARTNERSHIP

United States Court of Appeals, Fifth Circuit, 1997.
116 F.3d 790.

PARKER, CIRCUIT JUDGE:

* * * The Appellant, Financial Security Assurance, Inc. ("FSA"), appeals the bankruptcy court's ruling that it was not entitled to post-petition preconfirmation interest from the petition date notwithstanding FSA's overcollateralization at confirmation; [and] the value assigned to the collateral[.]

* * *

FACTS AND PROCEDURAL HISTORY

In June of 1988, T-H NOLP acquired a Days Inn Hotel (the "Hotel") in New Orleans, Louisiana and has operated the Hotel continuously since that date. T-H NOLP is a limited partnership with a corporate general partner, Tollman-Hundley New Orleans Corp., and five individual limited partners. [FSA was a secured creditor holding a mortgage lien on the hotel and also a lien on the income generated from the operations of the Hotel.]

* * *

On February 25, 1991, T-H NOLP filed for bankruptcy under Chapter 11 of the Bankruptcy Code[.] * * * At the time T-H NOLP filed bankruptcy, FSA's allowed claim was $18.424 million.

Subsequent to the bankruptcy filing, FSA filed a motion for adequate protection or segregation of hotel receipts. The bankruptcy court granted FSA's motion, finding that it had a security interest in the Hotel's prepetition and postpetition revenues from its operations, and ordered that the Hotel's business revenues be segregated. The bankruptcy court also entered a cash collateral order (dated May 1, 1992) which provided that T-H NOLP make payments from the Hotel's net revenues in order to reduce its obligation to FSA.

* * *

The bankruptcy court, early in the case, found that the appraised value of the Hotel was $12.2 million; this valuation was based upon an appraisal report as of July 1, 1991 which was commissioned by FSA. FSA's motion for adequate protection was based upon this appraised value. Subsequently, the bankruptcy court held a hearing to determine the fair value of the Hotel and found, after considering the evidence presented by T-H NOLP and FSA, that, as of July 14, 1994, the fair value of the Hotel was $13.7 million. Accordingly, the bankruptcy court found that the value of FSA's security interest in the Hotel was $13.7 million. The bankruptcy court also found that based on the uncontroverted testimony, the fair value of the Hotel would increase over the two year period following confirmation of T-H NOLP's proposed amended plan.

The bankruptcy court also held a hearing on FSA's allowed claim. FSA stipulated for purposes of the confirmation hearing that its allowed claim as of the petition date was $18,424,000. T-H NOLP presented evidence showing that it had made post-petition cash collateral payments of $4,675,945 through the end of September, 1994. Thus, the bankruptcy court, after accounting for the postpetition rent payments (pursuant to the May 1, 1992 cash collateral order) on FSA's claim and not including any potential entitlement to postpetition preconfirmation interest, found that FSA's claim amounted to $13,748,055 as of September 30, 1994.[4]

The bankruptcy court therefore found that because FSA's claim of $13,748,055 [FSA's claim of $18,424,000 less the $4,675,945 in payments FSA received during the case from revenues generated from the operations of the hotel] was greater than the fair value of the Hotel ($13.7 million),

---

[4] The bankruptcy court applied the cash collateral payments against the unsecured portion of FSA's claim, following the bankruptcy court in In re 354 East 66th Street Realty Corp., 177 B.R. 776 (Bankr. E.D.N.Y. 1995). In reaching its decision, the bankruptcy court analyzed the two line[s] of cases that have addressed this issue, i.e., the addition cases and the subtraction cases. See, e.g. In re Union Meeting Partners, 178 B.R. 664 (Bankr. E.D. Pa. 1995). However, we do not answer today the question of whether the bankruptcy court's reduction of the unsecured portion of FSA's claim was proper, as that issue was not raised on appeal.

thus making FSA's claim undersecured, FSA was not entitled to post-petition, preconfirmation interest on its claim under § 506(b) of the Bankruptcy Code until the time when the value of its collateral exceeded the amount of its claim. At that point, FSA would be entitled to interest at the contract rate on its claim to the extent that the value of the collateral exceeds its allowed claim, i.e. the equity cushion, and that any post-petition interest was limited to the equity cushion created by the monthly accrual of net rents generated by the Hotel.

* * *

On March 30, 1995, the bankruptcy court entered an order confirming T-H NOLP's amended Plan under the cramdown provisions of Chapter 11.

* * *

DISCUSSION

* * *

1. FSA's Entitlement to Postpetition Interest

FSA asserts that the value of the Hotel was increasing during the bankruptcy proceedings, and that its claim was decreasing due to the monthly cash collateral payments. Thus, at some point between September 1994 and the March 30, 1995 confirmation order the value of the property became greater than its claim. Therefore, FSA argues that since the collateral's value exceeded its claim on the day the Chapter 11 plan was confirmed or became effective, it was entitled to postpetition interest under § 506(b) to the extent of its contract rate for the entire postpetition period. FSA also argues that it should have been paid the postpetition interest monthly instead of at confirmation. In response, T-H NOLP relies on the bankruptcy court's conclusion, and objects to the allowance of any post-petition preconfirmation interest on FSA's claim until that point in time when the Hotel's value was greater than FSA's claim. T-H NOLP also asserts on cross-appeal that the bankruptcy court erred by requiring it to make postpetition preconfirmation interest payments while FSA appealed the bankruptcy court's order confirming T-H NOLP's Plan.

The parties' arguments raise the following questions for our consideration. First, where a secured creditor is receiving cash collateral payments which reduce the creditor's allowed claim such that at some point in time prior to plan confirmation the creditor may become oversecured, is that creditor entitled to accrue interest under § 506(b)? Second, when, under § 506(b), does interest begin to accrue, and the extent to which a creditor is entitled to postpetition interest?

There is no question that a creditor's entitlement to postpetition interest on its claim is determined under § 506(b) of the Bankruptcy Code. Section 506(b) states in relevant part that "[t]o the extent that an allowed secured claim is secured by property, the value of which . . . is greater than the amount of such claim, there shall be allowed to the holder of such claim interest on such claim . . . ." 11 U.S.C. § 506(b). The United States Supreme Court in *United States v. Ron Pair Enter., Inc.*, 489 U.S. 235, 109 S.Ct. 1026, 103 L.Ed.2d 290 (1989) made clear that under § 506(b) a creditor is unqualifiedly entitled to post-petition interest on its oversecured claim. *Id.* at 241, 109 S.Ct. at 1030; *see In re Pointer*, 952 F.2d 82 (5th Cir. 1992); *In re Sublett*, 895 F.2d 1381 (11th Cir. 1990). However, § 506(b) applies only from the date of filing through the confirmation date. *Rake v. Wade*, 508 U.S. 464, 468, 113 S.Ct. 2187, 2190, 124 L.Ed.2d 424 (1993) (overruled on other grounds by 11 U.S.C. § 1322(e)).

Under § 506(b), the creditor's entitlement to postpetition interest is clearly predicated on the threshold establishment of the two values to be compared, that of the property and the claim. Thus, the first inquiry under § 506(b) is usually a finding of whether the creditor is oversecured and thus entitled to accrue postpetition interest on its claim. In arguing that at some point between the time the petition was filed and confirmation of the Plan, the value of the Hotel became greater than the value of FSA's claim thus entitling FSA to postpetition interest, FSA invites us to consider when valuation should occur for purposes of determining a creditor's entitlement to postpetition interest.

With respect to the first question, the parties in their argument cite this Court to *United Sav. Ass'n of Texas v. Timbers of Inwood Forest Assoc., Ltd. (In re Timbers of Inwood Forest Assoc., Ltd.)*, 793 F.2d 1380 (5th Cir. 1986), *on reh'g*, 808 F.2d 363 (5th Cir. 1987) (en banc court reinstating panel opinion), *aff'd*, 484 U.S. 365, 108 S.Ct. 626, 98 L.Ed.2d 740 (1988). In *Timbers*, an undersecured creditor sought postpetition interest representing lost "opportunity costs" on the amount of its secured claim under § 362(d) of the Bankruptcy Code. This Court declined the creditor's request and held that an undersecured creditor was not entitled to post-petition interest on the value of its collateral as an element of adequate protection. In reaching its ruling, the *Timbers* court examined other Bankruptcy Code provisions that bore "indirectly" on the question considered. In considering § 506(b) and (c), the Court noted that:

> [t]he timing of the payment of accrued interest to an oversecured creditor (at the conclusion of the proceeding) is doubtless based on the fact that it is not possible to compute the amount of § 506(c) recovery (*and, accordingly the net allowed secured claim on which interest is computed*) until the termination of the proceeding.

Timbers, 793 F.2d at 1407 (emphasis added).

Although beneficial, this language does not answer the question we are presented with in the instant case. In addition, the *Timbers* Court was not confronted with the question we are presented today. We note that the creditor in *Timbers* was undersecured at the time of the adequate protection hearing and its appeal to this Court, and the value of the collateral was not increasing and there was no evidence that future appreciation would provide for postpetition interest.[7]

Under § 506, valuations are to be made in light of the purpose of the valuation. *In re Landing Assoc., Ltd.*, 122 B.R. 288 (Bankr. W.D. Tex. 1990). We recognize that the value of a debtor's collateral and the amount of a creditor's claim are among the most important issues between the debtor and the secured claimholder. Valuation issues can arise in various contexts throughout the entire bankruptcy case. *See In re Stanley*, 185 B.R. 417 (Bankr. D. Conn. 1995). Establishing equity, allowing claims, adequate protection, and plan confirmation are only a few examples of when the issue of valuation can be raised. *Id.* at 423. Neither Bankruptcy Code § 506(b) nor the Bankruptcy Rules define or establish the time for determining valuation of collateral for purposes of § 506(b). *In re Fox*, 142 B.R. 206 (Bankr. S.D. Ohio 1992). The legislative history to § 506(b) is also silent on this point. This Court's research has not disclosed any circuit authority which has discussed the question before us today, although we note that the lower courts that have faced this circumstance have selected a single valuation date. *See, e.g., In re Hulen Park Place Ltd.*, 130 B.R. 39, 43 (N.D. Tex. 1991) (determining whether creditor's claim is oversecured must be determined as of the petition date); *In re Landing Assoc., Ltd.*, 122 B.R. 288, 297 (Bankr. W.D. Tex.1990) (measurement date is confirmation date).

We decline to follow such a narrow path. Therefore, we conclude that for purposes of determining whether a creditor is entitled to accrue interest under § 506(b) in the circumstance where the collateral's value is increasing and/or the creditor's allowed claim has been or is being reduced by cash collateral payments, such that at some point in time prior to confirmation of the debtor's plan the creditor may become oversecured, valuation of the collateral and the creditor's claim should be flexible and not limited to a single point in time, such as the petition date or confirmation date. We further hold that, notwithstanding the bankruptcy court's determination of a creditor's secured status as of the petition date (if such a finding is made), the *party* who contends that there is a dispute

---

[7] We also note that *In re Delta Resources, Inc.*, 54 F.3d 722 (11th Cir.), *cert. denied, sub nom. Orix Credit Alliance, Inc. v. Delta Resources, Inc.*, 516 U.S. 980, 116 S.Ct. 488, 133 L.Ed.2d 415 (1995), addressed the narrow issue of whether a purportedly oversecured creditor was entitled to receive periodic cash payments for accruing postpetition interest as part of adequate protection in order to preserve the value of its equity cushion. We are not confronted with this question. In comparing when adequate protection is measured versus interest under § 506(b), the *Delta Resources* court held that a creditor's claim is measured as it existed at the time of the petition date because postpetition interest is limited to the amount by which the claim was oversecured at that time. We agree with this general proposition in the ordinary "underwater" asset case; however, in the context where the collateral is rising and the creditor's claim is decreasing (as in the present case), we find this ruling to be inappropriately narrow.

as to whether a creditor is entitled to interest under § 506(b) must motion the bankruptcy court to make such a determination. The creditor though bears the ultimate burden to prove by a preponderance of evidence its entitlement to postpetition interest, that is, that its claim was oversecured, to what extent, and for what period of time. *In re Grabill Corp.*, 121 B.R. 983, 991–92 (Bankr. N.D. Ill. 1990). This ruling recognizes the discretionary nature of bankruptcy courts as courts of equity. However, bankruptcy courts are not precluded from fashioning remedies to prevent unwarranted multiple redeterminations.

A flexible approach recognizes the fact that a creditor's allowed claim, which is being reduced over time, may become entitled to accrue postpetition interest, and that under the plain language of § 506(b) there is nothing limiting that right. *See United States v. Ron Pair Enter., Inc.*, 489 U.S. 235, 109 S.Ct. 1026, 103 L.Ed.2d 290 (1989) (employing a plain meaning reading of § 506(b)). A flexible approach also recognizes that any increase over the judicially determined valuation during bankruptcy rightly accrues to the benefit of the creditor, and not to the debtor. Moreover, as the bankruptcy court in *In re Addison Properties* noted, the single valuation approach generally balances the bankruptcy process in favor of the debtor. *In re Addison Properties Ltd. Partnership*, 185 B.R. 766, 772 (Bankr. N.D. Ill. 1995). Because of the equitable nature of bankruptcy in seeking a balance between debtors and creditors (debtor's right to a fresh start versus the creditor's right to the value of its claim), we reject the single valuation approach under the particular facts of this case.

Thus, applying this ruling to the instant case, if FSA believed that under § 506(b) it was entitled to accrue post-petition interest on its claim during the period following the confirmation hearing, then absent agreement between the parties as to the point in time when FSA's claim became oversecured, FSA was required to motion the bankruptcy court for a redetermination of its secured status. The bankruptcy court in this case was presented with the unusual fact situation where FSA's claim was being reduced and the Hotel's value was appreciating during the time from the petition date to the confirmation hearing. However, the bankruptcy court found that, for the period from the confirmation hearings to Plan confirmation, FSA's claim went from being undersecured to being oversecured and that this would probably occur in October 1994. Because the bankruptcy court made the factual finding as to when FSA would become oversecured, under the particular facts of this case we cannot say that the bankruptcy court was clearly erroneous in its decision.[9]

We next address the accrual of interest under § 506(b) and the extent to which a creditor is entitled to interest under § 506(b). We find this

---

[9] We note that the bankruptcy court found that FSA "probably" would become oversecured sometime in October 1994. Although we find it to be a close question, we are persuaded that the bankruptcy court's finding is supported by the evidence in this case.

question to be relatively straightforward. The measuring date on which the status of a creditor's collateral and claim are compared is determinative of a creditor's right to accrue interest under § 506(b). Thus, a secured creditor's entitlement to accrue interest under § 506(b) matures at that point in time where the creditor's claim becomes oversecured.[10] However, as *Timbers* dictates, accrued interest under § 506(b) is not paid to an oversecured creditor until the plan's confirmation or its effective date, whichever is later. *United Sav. Ass'n of Texas v. Timbers of Inwood Forest Assoc., Ltd. (In re Timbers of Inwood Forest Assoc., Ltd.)*, 793 F.2d 1380, 1381, 1407 (5th Cir. 1986), *on reh'g*, 808 F.2d 363 (5th Cir. 1987 (en banc court reinstating panel opinion)), *aff'd*, 484 U.S. 365, 108 S.Ct. 626, 98 L.Ed.2d 740 (1988). Thus, to the extent that the bankruptcy court's order does violence to the teachings of *Timbers* by ordering the payment of interest pending confirmation as opposed to ordering interest to accrue, it was error. However, because of the particular facts of this case, we are not inclined to set aside the bankruptcy court's ruling. On the effective date of the Plan's confirmation T-H NOLP would be receiving a credit for the interest paid during this time.

FSA also asserts that it was entitled to the postpetition interest that would have accrued during the entire postpetition preconfirmation period on its claim since the petition date. We disagree. The Supreme Court has made it clear that an oversecured creditor is entitled to postpetition interest on its claim only "to the extent that such interest, when added to the principal amount of the claim, [does not] exceed the value of the collateral." *Timbers*, 484 U.S. at 372, 108 S.Ct. at 631; *see also Landmark Financial Serv. v. Hall*, 918 F.2d 1150, 1155 (4th Cir. 1990) (an oversecured creditor's claim may include interest up to the value of the collateral). Thus, the amount of interest allowed under § 506(b) is limited to that amount of interest which, when added to the amount of FSA's allowed claim, will not exceed the value of its collateral.

Finally, we address FSA's assertion that the bankruptcy court erred in valuing the Hotel at $13.7 million at the confirmation hearing. The Bankruptcy Code does not prescribe any particular method of valuing collateral, but instead leaves valuation questions to judges on a case-by-case basis. *See* House Rep. No 95–595, 95th Cong. 1st Sess. 216, 356 (1977), *reprinted in* 1978 U.S.S.C.A.N. 5963, 6176, 6312. Valuation is a mixed question of law and fact, the factual premises being subject to review on a clearly erroneous standard, and the legal conclusion being subject to de novo review. *In re Clark Pipe & Supply Co., Inc.*, 893 F.2d 693, 697–98 (5th Cir. 1990). Value under § 506 is to be determined in light of the purpose of the valuation and of the proposed disposition or use of the

[10] In the instant case, the parties agreed that FSA could accrue interest under § 506(b) when its claim became oversecured. Thus, the parties [sic] agreement comports with our reading of the law under § 506(b).

property. *Associates Commercial Corp. v. Rash*, 520 U.S. 953, 117 S.Ct. 1879, 1884–85, 138 L.Ed.2d 148 (1997); *In re Sandy Ridge Dev. Corp.*, 881 F.2d 1346 (5th Cir. 1989). In this particular case, valuation was made for the purpose of plan confirmation. We note that FSA's appraisal expert agreed with T-H NOLP's expert regarding the Hotel's value once FSA's appraisal incorporated the overhead allocation charge, which the bankruptcy court found to be a necessary expense. Therefore, based on our review of the record, we concluded that the bankruptcy court did not err in its valuation of the Hotel. We find FSA's remaining arguments to be without merit. * * *

[some footnotes omitted]

NOTE

Assume a creditor holds a claim worth $20 million against a property with a value of $18 million. If the creditor receives periodic payments of rent as adequate protection, would the creditor want those payments to be allocated to the unsecured portion of the debt ($2 million) or to the secured portion ($18 million)? The allocation is irrelevant to determining whether the creditor is oversecured or undersecured, because the entire $20 million loan is treated as a unit for that purpose, and its total value is compared with the value of the collateral. But the creditor might have a different view for the purposes of the plan. If under the plan unsecured creditors are to be paid 10 cents on the dollar and secured creditors get the value of their collateral, then the creditor would like the payments to be allocated toward the unsecured portion of the debt.

§ 4. SECTION 363 AND THE DEBTOR'S USE OF COLLATERAL

Sections 363, 1107, and 1108 of the Bankruptcy Code gives the DIP in a Chapter 11 case the right to continue to run the business the day after the bankruptcy filing in essentially the same way as it did the day before. The DIP may buy and sell goods and services, continue its manufacturing operations, pay salaries, and do most of the other things that businesses do in the ordinary course without a court order and under the protection of the automatic stay.

There are two important limitations. First, subsection 363(b) bars non-ordinary course uses, sales, or leases of property without a hearing; it forestalls unilateral business transactions that are out of the ordinary course, such as sales of equipment and other fixed assets that the debtor would not routinely sell. Second, subsection (c)(2) prohibits the use of "cash collateral" unless there is either an agreement with everyone who has an interest in the cash collateral or an order of the court. Subsection (a) defines cash collateral. In most cases a deposit account held with a creditor bank is cash collateral, so the first order of business in a bankruptcy case (even before the filing) is to negotiate with the bank a cash collateral agreement that can be entered as a court order.

This of course means that a secured creditor's inventory can be sold in the ordinary course, that a secured creditor's equipment can be damaged or otherwise reduced in value by use, and that with the court's approval even non-ordinary course sales of subsidiaries and divisions may be made. So a Chapter 11 proceeding can be treacherous for the secured creditor. Generally the secured creditor must watch out for its own interests by negotiating with the DIP or by asking the court for protection.

PROBLEM 3-4

Kahn Craft, a manufacturer of commemorative plates, is contemplating bankruptcy. It comes to you for advice. Kahn wonders whether section 363(c)(2) will bar use of its bank accounts.

1. Kahn owes Bollinger Bank $2 million, which it had borrowed for operating expenses. Kahn's account at Bollinger Bank has a balance of $500,000. This is cash collateral even if Bollinger is unsecured. Do you see why? Recall that for bankruptcy purposes a right of set-off is treated as a secured claim. Could Kahn avoid the restrictions of subsection 363(c)(2) by moving its account to a bank to whom it does not owe a debt prior to the filing?

2. If Kauper Bank has a security interest in proceeds from the sale of plate inventory, would this be cash collateral even if it were not deposited in an account at a non-creditor bank?

NOTE

Collins & Aikman (C&A) began in 1891 as an upholstery manufacturer dealing in lampshades, among other things. David Stockman, a key Reagan economics adviser, decided that C&A had great potential. He created Heartland Industrial Partners, an investment fund that bought up controlling interests in C&A and in smaller suppliers with the intent to create a giant auto parts supplier. C&A became one of the largest American auto parts suppliers boasting $4 billion in annual sales. By 2005 nine out of ten vehicles assembled in North America had components from C&A. It provided automotive flooring, fabric, instrument panels, and other equipment to the Big Three (Ford, GM, and Chrysler), and also to Toyota, Honda, and Nissan.

In March 2005, the price of C&A stock dropped 23.9% in one day to finish at $1.24. A year prior to that, it was selling at $6; three years prior, it was selling in the $20-dollar range. In May of 2005, the stock was at 78 cents per share and the NYSE sought to suspend and delist the stock. Despite its $4 billion in annual sales, C&A posted a profit only once between 1999 and 2004.

In May of 2005, C&A's board booted Stockman, then the CEO, because of the rapidly approaching financial crisis. C&A hoped that with the help of its customers, the automakers, it could overcome its difficulties and steer clear of bankruptcy. That hope, however, was not realized.

As its financial picture deteriorated, vendors started to extract hostage payments from C&A. They would refuse to deliver a shipment unless the payment for it was made along with an additional payment to be put toward accrued debt. A few days after Stockman's termination, banks were refusing to honor roughly $9 million in checks because the accounts were overdrawn. In a free fall and very cash poor, C&A was forced to file for bankruptcy to obtain new financing.

The most important reason behind the failure of C&A was the company's proclivity to take on losing contracts. At least 35 such contracts were identified in the days following the filing, one of which was losing over $100 million per year. Apparently, Stockman's strategy was to get contracts no matter the price and then figure out how to make them profitable. One way of doing this was to pressure C&A's vendors to deliver at cheaper prices. This was a fool's bargain because some vendors, such as GE Plastics and Exxon, were more powerful than C&A.

JP Morgan Chase (JPMC) stepped in to become the DIP lender (on behalf of itself and a group of other lenders) after C&A filed for bankruptcy. Thereafter the bankruptcy court entered an order allowing post-petition financing in an amount up to $300 million. As is typical, the terms of this order were quite complex. Among other things, C&A already had approximately $700 million in existing secured indebtedness. Of course, one would not expect JPMC to lend additional funds into this troubled situation unless it could do so on a secured basis, and then only if its liens would "prime" (outrank in priority) the liens of the existing secured lenders. The financing order provided for this priming. In exchange, the pre-existing secured lenders were granted various benefits as adequate protection, including certain payments to be made to them during the bankruptcy case.

JPMC brought in new managers, including two who had recently led Enron through its bankruptcy as interim executives. JPMC ended up providing only $125 million of the $300 million that it was supposed to supply. Apparently, JPMC's duty to lend was contingent on the presence of certain collateral. When this collateral was exhausted by the first $125 million in loans, JPMC refused to lend more. C&A ended up burning through $150 million in two months and needed more financing, which no traditional lender was willing to grant.

Realizing their reliance on C&A's continued operation, certain of the automobile manufacturers agreed to lend C&A $82.5 million, to accept price increases of 15% (roughly equal to another $82.5 million), and to pick up $140 million in tooling, launch costs, and capital expenditures that C&A had been obligated to pay. This financing was designed to keep C&A afloat for 90 days. In return, C&A agreed to keep performing the contracts for GM, Ford, and Chrysler. (All three also agreed not to yank the contracts during the three-month period.)

Do not feel too badly about what appears to be C&A's extortion of the Big Three. The automakers used their market power to get low prices. Prior to its bankruptcy, C&A tended to give into every demand of the automakers, granting contracts that were losing propositions for the supplier.

While Chrysler may have been the largest customer of C&A, Ford placed unique reliance on C&A. It was depending entirely on C&A to manage the fabrication of instrument panels, door panels, and most of the interior for the new Ford Fusion, which was set to debut in the fall of 2005. Ford was banking heavily on this new midsize sedan to replace the Taurus, and its contract with C&A was the largest in C&A's history. C&A built an entire plant adjacent to Ford's Fusion plant in Mexico.

PROBLEM 3-5

1. Exercising a right granted to it by the court's financing order, JPMC brought in a new manager to run C&A effectively. What are the implications of his appointment for creditors, employees, and the car manufacturers who relied on C&A?

2. The financing order also contained what is known as a "carve out" provision permitting the payment of certain fees during the course of the bankruptcy case. The effect of this provision was to set aside a pool of funds for the payment of the fees of the debtor's counsel and the counsel for the creditors' committee, as well as bankruptcy court fees and those of any trustee. What is the purpose of this provision and why would JPMC agree to it?

3. JPMC was the "agent" for both the pre- and post-petition secured creditors. (The agent is typically the lead bank in a syndicate of lenders.) As such, it had a conflict of interest, no? How could it manage that conflict? (One law firm advised JPMC as agent for the pre-petition secured creditors, while another advised JPMC as agent for the post-petition secured creditors.)

4. As often happens, the financing order basically foreclosed challenges the DIP could have made to the priority, perfection, and enforceability of the secured creditors' interests. As is also common, the order left open the ability of the creditors' committee to investigate these issues, but it gave the committee only 75 days to meet and challenge the arrangement before it became binding on the creditors. Provisions blessing the DIP lender's behavior and the effectiveness and perfection of its interests are common in first-day orders. Do you see any problems with this practice?

5. The financing order essentially granted a security interest in all of C&A's assets (including any that happened to be unencumbered) for the benefit of its secured lenders. This basically meant that all of the property of C&A became spoken for, since the loan granted by JPMC was probably equal to or greater than the value of any remaining collateral. The unsecured creditors probably were not happy about this because if the reorganization failed, there was likely to be nothing left for them. But what choice did they have?

6. The financing order also lifted the automatic stay to allow JPMC to enforce its rights fully if C&A defaulted. The only defense left to C&A would be to argue that it was not in default. What role would be left for the bankruptcy court, if any, if C&A defaulted?

7. Another provision of the financing order granted adequate protection, directing that the pre-petition agent (JPMC) be paid accrued and unpaid interest on the outstanding pre-petition secured debt. What was the likely source of this payment? The post-petition financing. Thus, wasn't JPMC simply taking part of its own post-petition loan and giving it right back to itself as the pre-petition agent to pay interest on the pre-petition debt? The effect of such an arrangement is often to turn a portion of the pre-petition debt into post-petition debt.

§ 5. AVOIDANCE POWERS IN GENERAL

Chapter 5 of the Bankruptcy Code grants powers to the trustee in bankruptcy commonly and collectively called the "avoidance" powers. In Chapter 11 cases, the DIP exercises the rights and powers of a trustee, and thus has the "avoidance" powers as well. The principal avoidance powers are found in sections 544(a), 544(b), 547, and 548. In general these sections give the trustee the right: (1) to avoid a security interest that has not been properly perfected (section 544(a)); (2) to set aside a security interest that was granted as part of a "fraudulent conveyance," for example, a mortgage on the debtor's house given by the debtor to his brother on the eve of bankruptcy for no consideration (sections 544(b) and 548); and (3) to avoid certain payments made within ninety days of the bankruptcy to a creditor on account of a preexisting debt, which payments have the effect of preferring the recipient over other unpaid creditors (section 547).

Because the sections on avoidance powers were originally drafted in the 19th century when the power of the federal Congress to enact laws affecting private rights was less clear than it is now, they have quaint references to state laws and are generally built on the back of existing state laws. For example, section 544(a) does not say that a trustee may set aside an unperfected security interest. Rather, it says that a trustee "shall have . . . the rights and powers of . . . a creditor that obtains . . . a judicial lien." To comprehend the meaning of this provision, one must understand that a judicial lien effective from the date the bankruptcy petition is filed would be superior, under section 9–317 of Article 9 (and also under almost all other state law), to a security interest that was unperfected at the time of filing. As discussed earlier, section 544(a) is sometimes called the strong-arm clause, and it is used to deal with the crudest failures of the creditor, namely the failure properly to perfect a security interest.

Sections 544(b) and 548 are more obscure. Section 548 allows the trustee under federal law to set aside a fraudulent conveyance that occurs within two years of the bankruptcy petition. Section 544(b) allows the trustee to subrogate itself to the state-law rights of an actual creditor of the debtor, including the creditor's right to bring a fraudulent-transfer action under state law. Typically section 544(b) allows the trustee to reach back farther (often four to six years) than section 548 permits (two years), although the precise period of time depends on the particular state law in question. In some cases the state law may be more generous to the trustee than section 548, and for that reason too the trustee may wish to use section 544(b) and the state law instead of section 548. Classic fraudulent conveyances occur when a person pressed by his creditors transfers his assets to his children or other relatives for no payment. On rare occasions sections 544(b) and 548 can be used in commercial settings.

The other avoidance section that merits careful study is section 547 on preferences. It allows a trustee to recapture payments that have been made to a creditor, usually within ninety days of the bankruptcy filing, and also to upset some security interests that have been granted or perfected within the ninety-day period. In all cases preferences must be payments or other transfers made on account of an antecedent debt. Thus, if one granted a security interest to a creditor who simultaneously advanced a new $10 million loan, it would not be preferential even if it were within the ninety days. If, on the other hand, the $10 million loan had been made a year previously, and if security were then given without any new consideration within the ninety days, that transfer of security would be challengeable as a preference.

Sections 549 through 552 are adjuncts to the more significant avoidance rights of sections 544, 547, and 548. Of these, section 550 is particularly important because it specifies from whom the trustee may recover if the trustee avoids a transfer. In addition, in any action *against* the trustee, section 558 gives to the trustee the defenses that would have been available to the debtor.

§ 6. SECTION 547 AND AVOIDABLE PREFERENCES

We have touched on section 547 of the Bankruptcy Code above. Because preferences offer interesting and intricate intellectual problems, they probably command more law school time than they deserve. But part of a lawyer's fun is to play with such puzzles.

The principal goal of the preference rule is to prevent a debtor from favoring one creditor over others similarly situated through a transaction occurring within a short period (ninety days) prior to bankruptcy. Evidently Congress believed that an insolvent debtor who sees bankruptcy on the horizon should not be free to favor one creditor over another, but should be required to treat all alike. This view is essentially an extension of the fundamental bankruptcy policy of equality of distribution among creditors. Congress also wished to preserve the debtor's value as a going concern by diminishing the creditors' incentive to dismember the debtor. Thus, the classic preference is a simple eve-of-bankruptcy payment of one creditor's claim, unaccompanied by comparable payments to others. Another classic preference is the seizure of an asset by the judicial process of one—and only one—creditor. Such a transfer or seizure might disable the debtor and destroy its going-concern value.

A second common form of a preference is for the debtor to give property to a creditor, not in the form of money, but rather by granting an "after-thought" security interest to secure an earlier loan. The granting of an unavoidable security interest to a creditor for an earlier loan has the same consequence—at least for competing creditors—as the payment of that creditor's debt, does it not?

Still different is a preference given by means of the *perfection* of a previously created security interest within ninety days of the bankruptcy filing. Here we assume a case in which a security agreement was signed and a loan made long before the ninety-day period prior to bankruptcy, but where perfection occurred within the ninety-day period. One might contend that the "transfer" between the creditor and the debtor occurred when the security agreement was executed and a property interest conveyed to the creditor. Thus, the creditor in this situation could argue that it was not an after-thought creditor because it had received the grant of a security interest well before the ninety-day period.

Section 547 condemns this transaction just as much as (though for different reasons than) the one in which both the security transfer and its perfection occur after the loan and within the ninety-day period. True, the creditor here is not an after-thought creditor: after all, he bargained for his transfer at a time when bankruptcy was not imminent. Yet the creditor may be guilty of another kind of crime, that of holding an undisclosed security interest. If the court upholds a security agreement that is executed long before the ninety-day period, but perfected by a public filing for the first time on the eve of bankruptcy, the court makes it easier for the debtor and a conspiring creditor to keep that transfer secret, to mislead other creditors into lending in the belief that the debtor has not granted a security interest, and thus ultimately to distort the distribution in bankruptcy. On this view the preference legislation can be justified as an attack on secret liens. By putting the creditor at risk for ninety days *after* he perfects, the bankruptcy law makes granting the sort of secret lien just outlined riskier than it would otherwise be.

There are variations on these themes. For example, what if a debtor fills a secured creditor's pot with property originally acquired within the ninety-day period? Before 1978 the secured creditor could argue that a transfer of such after-acquired property occurred at the time of perfection and thus outside the preference period, but the 1978 Code nixes that argument. *See* 547(e)(3). So a DIP will be able to avoid some security interests to the extent that they attach to collateral acquired within ninety days of bankruptcy (but not if one of the defenses in section 547(c) applies). A second variation is the preference that results not from an intentionally late filing, but rather from a mistaken one. In this case, although the creditor intends to perfect as soon as it makes the loan, it ends up perfecting later, when, for example, it learns that its first financing statement was not filed in the right place.

Read section 547(b). It provides as follows:

> Except as provided in subsections (c) and (i) of this section, the trustee may . . . avoid any transfer of an interest of the debtor in property—
>
> (1) to or for the benefit of a creditor;
>
> (2) for or on account of an antecedent debt owed by the debtor before such transfer was made;
>
> (3) made while the debtor was insolvent;
>
> (4) made—
>
> (A) on or within 90 days before the date of the filing of the petition; or
>
> (B) between ninety days and one year before the date of the filing of the petition, if such creditor at the time of such transfer was an insider; and
>
> (5) that enables such creditor to receive more than such creditor would receive if—
>
> (A) the case were a case under Chapter 7 of this title;
>
> (B) the transfer had not been made; and
>
> (C) such creditor received payment of such debt to the extent provided by the provisions of this title.

Note that the trustee or DIP must satisfy all five of subsection (b)'s conditions to void a transfer. *See* 547(g). If he fails on one, the transfer is not voidable. Several will seldom be disputed. First, the debtor is presumed to be insolvent within the ninety-day period. *See* 547(f). Thus, the trustee will almost invariably satisfy subsection (b)(3). Second, the transfer will almost always be "to or for the benefit of the creditor," so subsection (b)(1) will rarely be an issue. Third, the same factors that control subsection (b)(2) are likely to control subsection (b)(4), and vice versa. When a security interest is at stake, the time of the transfer will invariably be critical.

For purposes of section 547, the time of transfer is a technical matter governed by section 547(e):

(e)(1) For the purposes of this section—

(A) a transfer of real property other than fixtures, but including the interest of a seller or purchaser under a contract for the sale of real property, is perfected when a bona fide purchaser of such property from the debtor against whom applicable law permits such transfer to be perfected cannot acquire an interest that is superior to the interest of the transferee; and

(B) a transfer of a fixture or property other than real property is perfected when a creditor on a simple contract cannot acquire a judicial lien that is superior to the interest of the transferee.

(2) For the purposes of this section, except as provided in paragraph (3) of this subsection, a transfer is made—

(A) at the time such transfer takes effect between the transferor and the transferee, if such transfer is perfected at, or within 30 days after, such time, except at provided in subsection (c)(3)(B);

(B) at the time such transfer is perfected, if such transfer is perfected after such 30 days; or

(C) immediately before the date of the filing of the petition, if such transfer is not perfected at the later of—

(i) the commencement of the case; or

(ii) 30 days after such transfer takes effect between the transferor and the transferee.

(3) For the purposes of this section, a transfer is not made until the debtor has acquired rights in the property transferred.

Generally, section 547(e) gives a secured creditor a thirty-day grace period in which to perfect. If it perfects within that time, the "transfer" is deemed to have occurred at the earlier of when the security agreement was signed or when the loan was made. Since this relation back renders the transfer simultaneous with the giving of value, the transfer is *not* one for an antecedent debt. Note that the tests for perfection with respect to real estate and personal property are different.

The final condition of section 547(b), subsection (b)(5), is important mainly with respect to payments to secured creditors. The very idea of a preference is that the transfer enables one creditor to get more than it would have gotten had liquidation occurred immediately prior to the transfer. If a creditor has a perfected security interest that gives it a claim to collateral equal to the value of its debt, a transfer would be no more valuable to the creditor than what it would receive upon liquidation under Chapter 7 without the transfer. Upon liquidation the creditor would take no more than 100 cents on the dollar, namely the amount for which its collateral could be sold. If, on the other hand, the creditor should receive a payment prior to liquidation, its claim would be reduced by that amount, and it would be entitled to 100 cents on the remaining debt. The pre-liquidation payment would, moreover, free collateral for other creditors. Thus, a secured creditor with a $100,000 claim and collateral worth $120,000 would receive $100,000 on liquidation. A pre-bankruptcy payment up to $100,000 will neither improve the secured creditor's position nor injure others. Even though the payment comes out of the estate, the estate is not diminished because the payment frees $100,000 of collateral for the other creditors. Hence, the payment does not constitute a preference. *See* 547(b)(5).

After mastering the substantive provisions in section 547(b), turn to the exceptions (or "defenses") in section 547(c). With the 1984 and 2005 amendments to the Bankruptcy Code, the exceptions became so expansive that they may be more important than subsection (b).

Subsection (c)(1) might be looked upon as a loosening of the restraints imposed by subsection (b)(2). Subsection (c)(1) provides that a transfer is not a preference to the extent that it constitutes a "contemporaneous exchange." Note the exchange does not have to be simultaneous; it need only be contemporaneous. For example, subsection (c)(1) would cover the case in which a creditor transfers goods to a debtor, the debtor pays by check, and the check clears a week or ten days later. On a strict reading of section 547(b), the transaction might constitute a voidable preference because the payment made ten days after the creditor's transfer of goods might be regarded as for an antecedent debt under subsection (b)(2). Subsection (c)(1) insulates contemporaneous transfers from the reach of section 547(b), provided that all the requirements of the subsection are satisfied.

Many payments both to secured and unsecured creditors that would otherwise be voidable preferences will now also be saved, this time by subsection (c)(2), which provides that a transfer is not a preference to the extent that it constitutes an ordinary-course transaction. Study the subsection to see which payments within the ninety-day period might not qualify under its terms. Surely it cannot be intended to save all payments. Prior to the 1984 amendments, subsection (c)(2) was much more limited: it applied only to payments made "not later than 45 days after the debt was incurred." Under this version the exception could conceivably apply only to short-term obligations such as trade credit or utility obligations; payments to commercial lenders rarely fit within the forty-five-day rule. Congress removed the forty-five-day limit in 1984, greatly expanding the scope of the ordinary-course defense. Congress further expanded the saving power of the subsection in 2005. Instead of requiring that the transfer be made "in the ordinary course of business" between the parties *and* that the transfer must have been "made according to ordinary business terms," Congress inserted the term "or" between the two requirements. This allows the creditor to protect more transfers by relieving it of the need to prove that the transfer at issue meets both qualifications.

The major justification for the ordinary-course defense is fairly simple. Suppose that in exchange for an unsecured loan from a bank, a debtor has been making monthly payments to the bank like clockwork for years—the same payment in the same amount on the first of each month, just as the debtor's loan agreement with the bank stipulates. Suppose further that the debtor, without any prodding by the bank, continues to make its usual, customary payments within the ninety-day period before it files for bankruptcy. Because there has been no unusual debt collection activity by the bank, the payment would likely qualify for the ordinary-course defense under section 547(c)(2). Suppose, however, that the debtor stops making payments to the bank 180 days before filing. After repeated threats by the bank, the debtor then makes an irregular, lump-sum payment on the eve of bankruptcy. This payment, elicited by unusual debt-collection activity, would probably not qualify under subsection (c)(2).

Subsection (c)(3) protects purchase money interests that might otherwise run afoul of section 547(b), and subsection (c)(4) covers the case in which the creditor receives a preference, but then later makes a loan to the same debtor, thereby supplying "new value."

Subsection (c)(5), though intricate and interesting, is of limited significance. It deals with after-acquired property, and we will return to it in problems 3–9 and 3–10 below.

The following step-by-step analysis is useful in applying section 547:

1. Did the debtor make a "transfer of an interest of the debtor in property?" *See* 101(54), 547(b).

2. When was the transfer made? *See* 547(e). Note that if the transfer was a payment, it was made at the time it took effect between the parties. *See* 547(e)(2)(A). If, however, the transfer was the grant of a security interest, it may have been made later than the time it took effect between the parties. Read section 547(e) carefully.

3. Is the transfer voidable because all five conditions in section 547(b) are satisfied?

4. If the answer is yes, is the transfer saved by any of the five exceptions in section 547(c)?

PROBLEM 3-6

Debtor, a small business, borrowed $200,000 from Creditor 1 on July 1 and $400,000 from Creditor 2 on July 15. The loans were unsecured. Debtor issued Creditor 1 a note payable in six months and issued Creditor 2 a note payable on demand. Debtor filed a bankruptcy petition on December 1.

Can either of the following transfers be avoided under section 547? The DIP asserts that they should be, arguing that both are "unfair" grabs within the ninety-day period.

1. On September 15, Creditor 1 "coerced" Debtor into granting a security interest in certain collateral in consideration of the existing $200,000 debt. Creditor 1 perfected the security interest by filing on September 17. This would constitute a preference. Do you see why?

2. On October 20, Creditor 2 demanded payment of the note. Debtor paid Creditor 2 $175,000 by check on October 25. This too is a preference, is it not?

PROBLEM 3-7

In the ninety days before bankruptcy, Debtor makes payments in four situations. Which of these payments is protected by section 547(c)(2)?

1. Debtor makes payments to various utilities for electricity, phone, and water. These are classic ordinary-course payments, are they not?

2. Debtor makes a $2 million payment on a loan that is amortized at $2 million per month. Assume either (i) that Debtor made payments regularly until six months ago, and that this is the only payment in the last six months (more likely a preference), or (ii) that Debtor has never missed a payment (less likely a preference).

3. Having established a practice of making large payments on a loan at irregular intervals, Debtor makes a $2 million payment. This is the only payment of the year, and Debtor made two payments last year, one in January and one in December. Since there is a practice of irregular payments, this is arguably a tougher case, and it is unclear how it would turn out. What do you think?

4. Debtor makes a $2 million payment. This is the only payment Debtor has ever made on the $10 million line of credit that has been outstanding for six months. This is similar to the last question.

PROBLEM 3-8

Unsecured Creditor comes to Debtor and demands payment of its $5 million claim, on which Debtor is in default. Creditor offers in the alternative to take either security or a letter of credit.

1. Eighty days before bankruptcy, Bank issues a $5 million letter of credit to Creditor with Debtor as applicant. Debtor grants Bank no security. Is there a preference?

2. The letter of credit in question 1 is called by Creditor, and Bank pays Creditor ten days before the bankruptcy. Is there a preference?

3. Debtor gives Bank a perfected security interest (to secure its promise of reimbursement) at the time the letter of credit is written. Is there a preference? Here Bank argues that there is no preference because it gave new value in the form of its new promise. There is new value, but surely there is a preference here somewhere, is there not? Consider the language of section 547, "for the benefit of a creditor," and the language of section 550, which allows recovery either from the one who benefits from the transfer or from the initial transferee.

NOTE

Since there is a presumption that a debtor is insolvent within ninety days prior to bankruptcy, and since the world is full of the walking dead (businesses whose liabilities greatly exceed the value of their assets, but who nevertheless continue to operate), parties seldom litigate the question whether a debtor was insolvent at the time of a transfer. The party challenging the preference will frequently be forced to concede that the debtor was insolvent at the time of the transfer. Occasionally the issue will be litigated, with the parties each presenting expensive expert testimony on the debtor's value. You may be astounded to learn that honest and intelligent valuation "experts" can come to radically different conclusions regarding estimations of a debtor's value, leaving the bankruptcy court to decide who has the more accurate view (sometimes by simply splitting the difference). For an interesting case, see *In re Heilig-Meyers Co.,* 319 B.R. 447 (Bankr. E.D. Va. 2004).

THE SPECIAL CASE OF THE FLOATING LIEN IN BANKRUPTCY—SECTIONS 552 AND 547(c)(5)

Article 9 permits a secured party to create a security interest in existing and after-acquired collateral and in proceeds with a single, written security agreement, and to perfect that security interest by filing a single financing statement. (The taking of a security interest in after-acquired collateral is discussed in greater detail in Chapter 4.) If the financing statement is filed first, the security interest attaches to and is perfected in the after-acquired collateral when the debtor has "rights in the collateral." *See* UCC 9–203(b)(2). Under Article 9, a creditor that creates and perfects a security interest in this way has priority over almost all later creditors. *See* UCC 9–317, 9–322.

An initial problem for the secured creditor with an after-acquired property clause governing a Chapter 11 debtor's assets is posed by section 552(a) of the Bankruptcy Code, which reads as follows:

> Except as provided in subsection (b) of this section, property acquired by the estate or by the debtor after the commencement of the case is

> not subject to any lien resulting from any security agreement entered into by the debtor before the commencement of the case.

By itself section 552(a) effectively blocks the attachment of a security interest to proceeds and after-acquired property gained after the petition date. Yet section 552(b) gives back some of what section 552(a) takes away. Subsection (b) allows the security interest to attach to "proceeds, products, offspring, rents, or profits." Thus, if new inventory is the proceeds of old inventory, and if the secured creditor's claim does not depend exclusively on an after-acquired property clause, the security interest will attach. However, even section 552(b)'s modest concession with respect to proceeds and products is subject to the discretion of the court, which may rule that it does not apply, "based on the equities" of the case.

Property acquired within ninety days before the date of the bankruptcy petition and falling within the grasp of a secured creditor's after-acquired property clause will be claimed by the DIP on the ground that the attachment of a security interest to that property was preferential. Outside of bankruptcy, the time of the financing statement's filing determines priority against other secured creditors (*see* 9–322), and it is clear that the security interest is effective between the debtor and the secured creditor at the time of attachment. In bankruptcy, however, if attachment occurs within ninety days before the petition is filed, section 547(e)(3) treats the time of attachment as the time of transfer. Thus, in bankruptcy at least, the law considers a transfer in after-acquired property to be a transfer for an antecedent debt.

The Seventh Circuit's decision in *Grain Merchants of Indiana, Inc. v. Union Bank & Savings Co.*, 408 F.2d 209 (7th Cir. 1969), decided prior to the Bankruptcy Reform Act of 1978, held that a secured creditor had an unassailable security interest in after-acquired collateral. In *Grain Merchants* the trustee challenged the secured creditor's right to after-acquired accounts that had arisen within the preference period preceding the debtor's bankruptcy filing. (The debtor had sold items to customers during that period, generating the accounts.) The trustee argued that since no transfer of the accounts to the secured party could occur until the transferred assets (the accounts) came into existence, at which time the creditor was not making contemporaneous loan advances, the after-acquired accounts constituted preferential transfers.

The secured creditor's most powerful response in *Grain Merchants* was that the "turnover" of the collateral had neither injured nor misled any other creditor, regardless of whether the collateral constituted inventory, accounts, or something else. The secured creditor also put forward several other arguments. The central textual argument was that the transfer of the accounts as defined in section 60 of the Bankruptcy Act of 1898 (the predecessor to section 547) had occurred at the time the security interest was so far perfected that no lien creditor could have priority over it. Under Article 9, the secured creditor maintained that perfection occurred upon filing of its financing statement, which happened well outside the preference period. The court accepted this argument, leaving critics uncomfortable. Some observers noted that the argument would validate the acquisition of after-acquired property by a creditor that had coerced its debtor into building up its accounts or inventory immediately prior to bankruptcy, thus (arguably) preferring the secured creditor over other creditors. Since the transfer here would be deemed to have occurred when the financing statement was filed (typically long before the preference period), there would be no preference. In response to these concerns, Congress passed section 547(e)(3), which destroys the creditor's textual argument in *Grain Merchants*. On the other hand, Congress added section 547(c)(5), which protects after-acquired property claims involving inventory and accounts in cases where there is no "buildup."

Grain Merchants accepted several other of the creditor's arguments. One is that the accounts themselves should be looked at as a single item transferred at the outset, even though individual accounts come and go. If one regards the accounts as some metaphysical group, not as single accounts (a river rather than its drops of water), then section 547(e)(3) would not necessarily invalidate a transfer. But doesn't section 547(e)(3) reject this conception of accounts? It appears to contemplate the possibility that each item of inventory, each account—commonly recognized as having an individual identity—is to be treated separately for bankruptcy purposes.

A second argument that has some continued vitality is the "substitution of collateral doctrine." Presumably no preference occurs when a secured creditor agrees within the preference period to allow its debtor to substitute one asset as collateral for another. In that case, contemporaneous value is given by the creditor's release of the original collateral in return for acquiring new collateral. The *Grain Merchants* court reasoned as follows:

> as existing accounts receivable were collected by Grain Merchants and deposited to its accounts at the Bank, the funds from previously collected accounts were made available to the debtor, enabling it to continue in business and obtain new accounts receivable. . . . Here the newly arising accounts receivable may be considered as having been taken in exchange for the release of rights in the earlier accounts and for present consideration.

408 F.2d at 217. Nothing in section 547 overtly rejects the substitution theory.

PROBLEM 3-9

On July 1, Seller sold Debtor equipment on credit. Seller created and perfected a security interest in Debtor's "equipment, existing and after-acquired," and Debtor agreed to pay the balance of the contract price on January 2. On September 1, Debtor owed Seller $25,000, and the value of Debtor's equipment was $25,000. On October 1, Debtor sold the equipment to Buyer for $25,000 and used the proceeds to purchase new equipment from another seller. On December 1, the date of bankruptcy, Debtor owed Seller $25,000, and the value of the new equipment was $27,500.

1. The transfer of the security interest in the new equipment is not protected by section 547(c)(5). Do you see why?

2. Do any of the other safe harbor provisions apply?

PROBLEM 3-10

On July 1, Debtor granted Secured Party a written security interest in "inventory, accounts, and proceeds, existing and after-acquired." Secured Party made a first advance of $5 million and agreed to make additional advances over the next twelve months of no more than $95 million "in its sole discretion." A financing statement was filed on July 1.

On September 1, Debtor owed Secured Party $30 million, and the collateral was valued at $25 million. On December 1, the date of bankruptcy, Debtor owed Secured Party $25 million, and the value of the collateral (which had completely turned over) was $23 million.

1. Is the transfer of the inventory (clearly a preference to some extent under section 547(b)) saved by section 547(c)(5)?

2. On October 1, Debtor pays $10 million to Secured Party. Is this a preference? *See* 547(c)(2). If so, and if Secured Party must return the payment, how should this affect the application of section 547(c)(5)?

3. On September 5, Secured Party advances an additional $10 million, so the debt stands at $40 million and the collateral has a value of $25 million. Before the bankruptcy on December 1, the inventory turns over completely; it now totals $35 million. The DIP argues that there is a $35 million preference under section 547(b) and that only $25 million is saved under section 547(c)(5). The Secured Party argues that section 547(c)(5) saves the entire $35 million since the "gap" at the end is no smaller than it was 90 days earlier. Read section 547(c) carefully and think about the implications of the arguments. The DIP should win. Do you see why? Do you see why the new advance on September 5 does not immunize other transfers under section 547(c)(4)?

§ 7. FRAUDULENT CONVEYANCES UNDER SECTIONS 544(b) AND 548

In general, there are two types of fraudulent transfers: (1) those involving actual intent to hinder, delay, or defraud creditors ("actual fraud"), and (2) those involving so-called "constructive fraud." The classic example of actual fraud involves a debtor, hard-pressed by his hounding creditors, who transfers his property to a relative in order to frustrate the creditors' collection efforts. Perhaps the debtor memorialized his intent in a letter to a relative, asking the relative to keep his property safe until his creditors give up in frustration. This kind of fraud is ancient, and fraudulent-transfer laws have long provided a remedy: avoidance of the transfer and recovery of the transferred property for the benefit of the debtor's creditors. (Early fraudulent transfer law is discussed in Chapter

9.) Section 548(a)(1)(A) covers this kind of shenanigan (if it occurred within two years of the petition date), as do the fraudulent-transfer laws of the various states, which have been incorporated into the bankruptcy process under section 544(b) (typically with longer reach-back periods). In order to prove actual fraud, the trustee need not have the debtor's admission. Proof of actual fraud may be shown by circumstantial evidence—the so-called "badges of fraud," namely circumstances courts generally accept as suggesting fraudulent intent. Nonetheless, actual fraud remains difficult to prove in all but the most clear-cut cases, and this theory is not the most commonly used.

The second type (constructive fraud) is more objective in nature. Rather than requiring proof of the debtor's intent, it focuses on whether the debtor made a transfer while "insolvent" (or nearly so) and for less than "reasonably equivalent value." For example, suppose that although a debtor owns a home worth $1 million, he is insolvent because his debts far exceed the value of his assets. Suppose further that, while insolvent, the debtor transfers his home to his sister for $10. The transfer is obviously for less than "reasonably equivalent value," and it may be set aside as constructively fraudulent. The theory behind this approach is that the debtor must be just (to his creditors) before he is generous (to his sister). Section 548(a)(1)(B) allows the trustee to avoid constructively fraudulent transfers that occur within a two-year period before the bankruptcy filing.

The analysis of solvency under section 548(a)(1)(B) is basically the same as that used in section 547 preference cases. Section 548(d)(2)(A) defines value as it pertains to the section's "reasonably equivalent value" requirement. This definition is sparse. For example, it does not tell how to deal with investments and other intangibles that have value to some degree, even if they do not pay off. A gambler is certainly gaining something of value for the money he spends: even if he doesn't win, he gets the chance of winning. The "reasonably equivalent value" test looks at the risk and compares it to the price paid by the debtor. When the risk is higher, the price paid for the chance should be lower. Analyze the following case in this context.

IN RE R.M.L., INC., PREVIOUSLY KNOWN AS INTERSHOE, INC.

United States Court of Appeals, Third Circuit, 1996.
92 F.3d 139.

COWEN, CIRCUIT JUDGE:

We confront in this case a difficult issue arising under 11 U.S.C. § 548(a)(2), the provision of the Bankruptcy Code (the "Code") allowing for avoidance of constructively fraudulent transfers. The principal question we must decide is whether a commitment letter Mellon Bank issued in connection with a contemplated $53-million loan conferred "reasonably equivalent value" on Intershoe (the debtor) in exchange for $515,000 in commitment fees that Intershoe paid to Mellon Bank. This question is complicated by the fact that the loan, which could possibly have saved Intershoe from bankruptcy, ultimately failed to close. We also must decide whether Intershoe was insolvent when it transferred the commitment fees to Mellon Bank.

After finding that Intershoe was insolvent during the relevant period, the bankruptcy court, relying on a "totality of the circumstances" test, concluded that Intershoe had not received "reasonably equivalent value" in exchange for the $515,000 in fees it had paid to Mellon. The court found that the loan commitment was so conditional when issued that it conferred virtually no indirect economic benefit on Intershoe. It therefore ordered Mellon Bank to remit to the bankrupt estate all but $127,538.04 of the commitment fees, an amount representing Mellon Bank's out-of-pocket expenses. The district court summarily affirmed. Because the commitment letter was so conditional that the chances of the loan closing were minimal, we agree that Intershoe did not receive value that was reasonably equivalent to the fees it paid Mellon Bank. Accordingly, we, too, will affirm.

I

At all times relevant to this dispute, Intershoe was a large-scale wholesale distributor of women's shoes. Through 1991, its primary secured lender was Signet Bank. In the spring of 1991, Intershoe was aware that its financing arrangement with Signet would terminate that fall. It therefore sought to recapitalize and refinance its operations. Intershoe wanted to attract a $15 million equity investment; it also wanted to replace Signet as its lender with a bank group that would extend a $53 million loan facility.

In March of 1991, Three Cities Research ("TCR") made an initial, nonbinding proposal to make a $15 million investment in Intershoe and began to conduct due diligence and negotiations toward that end. Hoping that the prospect of an equity infusion would entice potential lenders, Intershoe approached Mellon Bank, Bank of New York ("BNY") and Citicorp to discuss potential refinancing. Each bank made clear that an equity infusion would be a prerequisite to any refinancing. Representatives of Mellon and Intershoe first met in either February or March of 1991.

On June 13, 1991, Mellon issued a proposal letter documenting its interest in extending a $53 million revolving line of credit and a $100 million foreign exchange line of credit. The proposal was contingent upon TCR's injection of $15 million in cash[.] * * *

On August 9, 1991, Mellon Bank issued a second proposal letter that was similar to the first in that it was conditioned upon the injection of new capital funds of at least $15 million. The letter also stated that Intershoe would be required to pay: (1) a facility fee equivalent to ¾ of one percent (.0075) of the committed facility (half upon issuance of the commitment letter, half at closing); (2) a collateral management fee of $10,000; (3) all of Mellon's out-of-pocket expenses, regardless of whether the financing occurred; and (4) a "good faith deposit" of $125,000 to be remitted with written approval of the proposal letter. A fifth provision in the letter was that Mellon would be permitted to spread $28 of the $53 million loan among a group of banks. The loan contemplated by Mellon was known as a highly leveraged transaction ("HLT"), an asset-based loan bearing greater risk than an ordinary loan that requires extraordinary due diligence and monitoring of the borrower's accounts receivable, inventory and business plan.

On August 12, 1991, Intershoe remitted to Mellon the $125,000 "good faith deposit" in accordance with the proposal letter. Because it had reached its borrowing limit with the Signet Group, Intershoe could not borrow additional sums. Between August and October of 1991, Intershoe failed to pay the majority of invoices from its suppliers. While accounts payable increased by $10 million, its debt to the Signet Group decreased by the same amount; Intershoe was using what funds it had to pay down its debt. As a result, the Signet group agreed to extend its loan facility from September 30 to November 29, 1991, which permitted Intershoe to continue its business operations.

In early October of 1991, Mellon Bank requested an additional good faith deposit from Intershoe of $125,000, although there was nothing to document this request. On October 8 or 9, 1991, Intershoe remitted the additional $125,000 to Mellon Bank by wire transfer. On October 31, 1991, Westinghouse, to whom Intershoe had subordinated indebtedness, agreed to restructure Intershoe's indebtedness in order to accommodate the proposed recapitalization.

On November 7, 1991, Mellon issued a formal commitment letter (the "Letter") with terms that tracked the August 9 proposal letter. The Letter referred to the $250,000 in good faith deposits that Mellon had previously received and indicated that the entire amount would be retained even if the loan did not close. These deposits would cover Mellon's expense, time and effort in attempting to consummate the financing. The Letter also required the remittance of an additional $265,000, half of which represented a nonrefundable "facility fee" for Mellon's commitment, with the other half representing a nonrefundable agent's fee for Mellon's syndication of the loan. The Letter also contained several conditions: (1) Intershoe had to produce a draft audited financial statement indicating that it had a net worth of at least $6.5 million; (2) Intershoe was required to repay or retire Westinghouse's debt and stock warrants and retain Westinghouse as a creditor for subordinated debt of at least $5 million; (3) $28 million of the loan commitment had to be participated out to a group of banks; and (4) Intershoe would be required to pay a separate collateral monitoring fee relating to administering the loan after closing. By its terms, the commitment was set to expire on November 29, 1991, the same day that Signet's loan facility was due to expire.

On November 7, 1991, Intershoe accepted Mellon's commitment and remitted the $260,000 fee as contemplated by the Letter. That day Mellon began a "takedown examination" to update Intershoe's financial information through the closing date. Eight days later Mellon received a draft financial statement confirming that Intershoe possessed a positive net worth of $6.5 million dollars. Mellon then scheduled a meeting for November 20, 1991, with Intershoe, the loan participants, TCR (the equity investor) and Peat Marwick to discuss further the financial statements.

On November 17, 1991, however, TCR advised Intershoe that it had decided not to make the $15 million equity investment and confirmed its withdrawal from the proposed refinancing. Intershoe informed Mellon of this development the next day, and the entire deal collapsed. Intershoe's trade creditors continued to extend credit even after the collapse of the Mellon financing.

On November 15, 1991, Peat Marwick issued to Intershoe an audited financial statement for the fiscal year ending August 31, 1991. This statement indicated that as of August 31, Intershoe's liabilities exceeded its assets by four million dollars. In accordance with Generally Accepted Accounting Principles ("GAAP") and Generally Accepted Accounting Standards ("GAAS"), the financial statement took into account events subsequent to the end of the fiscal year (e.g., the collapse of the Mellon financing) as evidence of Intershoe's financial condition. Several questionable items on Intershoe's balance sheet were corrected or adjusted, resulting in an even lower net worth. The financial statement also indicated that Intershoe would have difficulty continuing as a going concern. On December 11, 1991, Intershoe agreed to accept Peat Marwick's suggested changes to its financial statements. Intershoe's financial condition continued to decline, reaching a point where its liabilities exceeded assets by $14 million. Intershoe sought protection under Chapter Eleven of the Code on February 18, 1992.

* * *

III.

As it did in the courts below, Mellon Bank urges reversal on two grounds. First, Mellon Bank asserts that the commitment letter conferred "reasonably equivalent value" on Intershoe, the measure of which is the fair market value of the services it rendered (i.e., the $515,000 in commitment fees Intershoe paid). Second, Mellon Bank claims that based upon Intershoe's own balance sheets *at the time of the disputed transfers*, Intershoe was not insolvent.

A.

Reasonably Equivalent Value

* * *

1.

a.

* * * [W]e turn first to the appropriate method of determining reasonably equivalent value. The concept of reasonably equivalent value unfortunately has not been defined in the Code. As the Supreme Court noted in *BFP v. Resolution Trust Corp.*, "[o]f the three critical terms 'reasonably equivalent value', only the last is defined: 'value' means, for purposes of § 548, 'property, or satisfaction or securing of a . . . debt of the debtor' . . ." (quoting 11 U.S.C. § 548(d)(2)(A)). Thus, "Congress left to the courts the obligation of marking the scope and meaning of [reasonably equivalent value]."

The lack of a more precise definition has led to considerable difficulty. This definitional problem is exacerbated in cases where, as here, the debtor exchanges cash for intangibles, such as services or the opportunity to obtain economic value in the future, the value of which is difficult, if not impossible, to ascertain. Because such intangibles are technically not within § 548(d)(2)(A)'s definition of "value," courts have struggled to develop a workable test for reasonably equivalent value.

In attempting to determine whether Mellon's commitment letter conferred any value on Intershoe, the bankruptcy court purported to apply a totality of the circumstances test. Drawn from other reasonably equivalent value cases, that test takes into account the fair market value of the item received by, or services performed for, the debtor; the existence of an arm's-length relationship between the debtor and the transferee; and the good faith of the transferee. These factors, however, have no bearing on whether any "value" was actually conferred on the debtor. At most, the fair market value and the arm's-length nature of the relationship are relevant to the price the debtor paid. But the price that the debtor paid, in and of itself, reveals nothing about whether the debtor received something of actual "value." A simple example illustrates our point:

> Within one year of filing for bankruptcy, *D* pays a window-washer $1,000 to clean the windows in an office building. The $1,000 constitutes the going rate for such a job, and the window-washer is unaware of *D*'s financial condition.

That the $1,000 *D* paid represents the fair market value of the window-washer's services and that the transaction was at arm's length say absolutely nothing about whether the debtor received "value;" "value" was conferred because *D* obtained a palpable benefit from the service performed—i.e., clean windows.

The bankruptcy court, therefore, conflated two inquiries that should remain separate and distinct: before determining whether the value was "reasonably equivalent" to what the debtor gave up, the court must make an express factual determination as to whether the debtor received any value at all.

* * *

c.

* * * [W]e [have previously held] that "the purpose of the laws [in question] is estate preservation; thus, the question whether the debtor *received* reasonable value must be determined from the standpoint of the creditors." Mellon Bank's assertion in this case that it has conferred value simply because the fees it charged Intershoe represent the fair market value of Mellon Bank's services similarly misses the mark.

* * *

2.

Its application of the totality of the circumstances test notwithstanding, the bankruptcy court announced two conclusions essential to the resolution of the question whether Intershoe had received any value in exchange for the commitment fees it had remitted to Mellon Bank. The court first determined that Mellon Bank's commitment letter did not confer any tangible, indirect benefits on Intershoe. For instance, the court found that Signet's extension of its credit facility beyond the original expiration date and the trade suppliers' decision to extend credit to Intershoe were not the direct result of Mellon Bank's willingness to lend funds to Intershoe. The court then determined that the loan commitment failed to confer any significant *intangible* benefits on Intershoe. Specifically, the court determined that the commitment letter essentially offered only a very slim "chance" of obtaining a substantial economic benefit in the future because it contained numerous conditions that, in all likelihood, could not have been satisfied.

With this latter determination the bankruptcy court implicitly held that money spent on an investment bearing a certain degree of risk *can* generate cognizable value within the meaning of § 548(a)(2) of the Code, even where the investment ultimately fails to generate a positive return. The Committee [of Unsecured Creditors challenging Mellon Bank's fees] disputes this legal conclusion, arguing that money spent on a losing investment fails to confer "value" as a matter of law. If the Committee is correct, then we would be compelled to affirm since it is undisputed that Intershoe exchanged $515,000 in fees for a loan that never closed.

Accordingly, we address this preliminary question before reviewing the propriety of the bankruptcy court's factual findings.

a.

* * * [T]he Committee argues that where the debtor's financial condition either continues to deteriorate or fails to stabilize, money spent on a losing investment cannot confer "value" as a matter of law:

> The touchstone is whether the transaction conferred realizable commercial value on the debtor reasonably equivalent to the realizable commercial value of the assets transferred. Thus, *when the debtor is a going concern and its realizable going concern value after the transaction is equal to or exceeds its going concern value before the transaction, reasonably equivalent value has been received.*

[*Mellon Bank, N.A. v. Metro Communications, Inc.*,]945 F.2d [635,] 647 [(3rd Cir. 1991)] (emphasis added). We disagree. The Committee's argument depends for its validity on the contention that the highlighted sentence is part and parcel of the *Metro Communications, Inc.* court's holding. * * * But we view the highlighted passage as providing an example of how a court can determine that a debtor received *direct* benefits and, thus, "value" from a transaction. Significantly, the court in *Metro Communications, Inc.* went on to discover several *potential*, intangible benefits that, although incapable of precise measurement, conferred value on Metro despite their failure to materialize. That should dispel any suggestion that *Metro Communications, Inc.* stands for the proposition that a debtor must receive a direct, tangible economic benefit in order to receive "value" for purposes of § 548(a)(2) of the Code.

Furthermore, were we literally to apply the highlighted statement from *Metro Communications, Inc.* as the categorical test for value under § 548(a)(2), we would announce a rule for this Circuit that only successful investments can confer value on a debtor. This would permit a court viewing the events with the benefit of hindsight to conclude that any transfer that did not bring in the actual, economic equivalent of what was given up fails to confer reasonably equivalent value as a matter of law. Such an unduly restrictive approach to reasonably equivalent value has been soundly rejected by other courts and with good reason. Presumably the creditors whom § 548 was designed to protect want a debtor to take *some* risks that could generate value and, thus, allow it to meet its obligations without resort to protection under the Bankruptcy Code[.] * * * Accordingly, we hold that money spent on investments that fail to stabilize or improve the debtor's condition (i.e., "losing" investments) can confer value within the meaning of § 548(a)(2) of the Code.

The question, then, is how to determine whether an investment that failed to generate a positive return nevertheless conferred value on the debtor. We think our decision in *Metro Communications, Inc.* answers this question implicitly. We held there that the mere expectation that the fusion of two companies would produce a strong synergy (an expectation that turned out to be inaccurate in hindsight) would suffice to confer "value" so long as the expectation was "*legitimate and reasonable*." Thus, so long as there is some chance that a contemplated investment will generate a positive return at the time of the disputed transfer, we will find that value has been conferred.

We think our analysis appropriately balances a creditor's interest in estate preservation against a debtor's legitimate, pre-bankruptcy efforts to take risks that, if successful, could generate significant value and, possibly, avoid the need for protection under the Code altogether. As we noted above, requiring that all investments yield a positive return in order to find that they conferred value on the debtor would be unduly restrictive. But so, too, would a rule insulating from § 548's coverage investments that, when made, have zero probability of success. The best solution, therefore, is to determine, based on the circumstances that existed at the time the investment was contemplated, whether there was any chance that the investment would generate a positive return. In this way creditors will be protected when an irresponsible debtor invests in a venture that is obviously doomed from the outset.

b.

With these legal principles in mind, our review of the bankruptcy court's conclusion that Intershoe did not receive reasonably equivalent value proceeds in two, discrete steps: first, we determine whether the commitment letter conferred any value on Intershoe; second, we consider the bankruptcy court's finding that whatever value was conferred was not "reasonably equivalent" * * * is clearly erroneous.

Although the bankruptcy court did not announce an explicit finding on the question whether Mellon Bank's commitment letter conferred any value on Intershoe, it is clear that the court implicitly answered that question in the affirmative. The bankruptcy court stated that "all parties should have known there was *a substantial probability that the loan would not close*[.]" Put another way, the court concluded that by November 7, 1991, there was a slight chance that the loan *would* close. This finding is amply supported by the record and, hence, cannot be disturbed on appeal. First, although TCR had not formally committed to participate in the deal, there is no evidence in the record that TCR had made known its intention to withdraw before November 17, 1991. Thus, as of November 7, 1991, when the commitment letter was executed and the disputed fees remitted, there was at least some chance that the most important condition in the letter could be fulfilled. With respect to the other conditions in the letter, which pertained mainly to Intershoe's financial condition, record evidence reveals that, despite Intershoe's deteriorating condition, Mellon was willing to waive or modify many of these conditions. Since we review the transaction at the time the transfer was made, the bankruptcy's court's implicit determination that the letter provided Intershoe with at least *some* chance of receiving a future economic benefit and, therefore, "value" is not clearly erroneous.

We next consider the bankruptcy court's determination that whatever value was conferred by the letter, it was not "reasonably equivalent" to the $390,000 in lending fees Intershoe paid to Mellon Bank. We conclude that in assessing the reasonable equivalence issue, the bankruptcy court appropriately relied on the totality of the circumstances test.

Mellon Bank insists that the court's findings that: (1) the fees Intershoe paid were in line with market rates; (2) Mellon Bank acted in good faith; and (3) for the most part, the parties dealt at arm's length, render clearly erroneous its conclusion that Intershoe did not receive value that was "reasonably equivalent." We disagree. As our discussion of "value" should have made clear, while the chance of receiving an economic benefit is sufficient to constitute "value," the size of the chance is directly correlated with the amount of "value" conferred. Thus, essential to a proper application of the totality of the circumstances test in this case is a comparison between the value that was conferred and fees Intershoe paid.

So understood, the bankruptcy court's conclusion that the chance of receiving value represented by the commitment letter was so small that it was not reasonably equivalent to the $390,000 in fees Intershoe paid in no way conflicts with the court's observation that the commitment fees were in line with market rates. The bankruptcy court concluded that while a debtor reasonably might pay $390,000 in fees for a *real* chance to obtain a $53 million credit facility, the commitment letter at issue *in this case* was so conditional that it provided Intershoe with little chance, if any, to obtain the loan it sought. Accordingly, as long as there is support in the record for the bankruptcy court's conclusion that the commitment letter was highly conditional (and, thus, of little "value"), we must affirm.

That the loan was highly conditional cannot seriously be disputed. The bankruptcy court concluded that "both transfers were made in exchange for a highly conditional loan commitment, and all parties should have known there was a substantial probability that the loan would not close." Significantly, the court found that "TCR had made no commitment to participate in the transaction and Intershoe's deteriorating financial condition was a deterrent to an equity investor." The court further stated that "there was a significant possibility that Intershoe could not meet one or more of the conditions of the commitment letter, including the TCR equity investment." Finally, the court noted that "Intershoe's financial survival was contingent upon the Mellon refinancing and the Mellon refinancing was contingent upon dozens of conditions, the least certain and most important of which was an equity infusion from TCR." Since all of these findings have ample support in the record, the bankruptcy court's conclusion that the commitment letter conferred minimal value—value that was not reasonably equivalent to the fees Intershoe paid—is not clearly erroneous.

We acknowledge that the measurement and comparison called for by *Metro Communications, Inc.* is no easy task. Indeed, we noted in that case that "the ability to borrow money has considerable value in the commercial world. To quantify that value, however, is difficult." Yet we expressed no reservations about the bankruptcy courts' ability to analyze such potential, intangible benefits. We also acknowledge that whether a contemplated investment provided a significant "chance" to receive value more often than not will be bound up in the bankruptcy court's factual determinations and, thus, largely immune from attack on appeal. But this is as it should be; the bankruptcy court, with its unique expertise, is in [a] far better position than either the district courts, sitting as appellate tribunals, or the courts of appeals to make such determinations.

In sum, because Intershoe expended $390,000 in commitment fees for a loan that had little chance of closing, we agree that the Committee met its burden of establishing that Intershoe failed to receive reasonably equivalent value.

B.

Insolvency

Mellon Bank next contends that the Committee failed to establish that Intershoe was "insolvent," *see* 11 U.S.C. § 548(a)(2)(B)(i), on the dates of the disputed transfers. Section 101(32)(A) of the Code defines insolvency as a "financial condition such that the sum of such entity's debts is greater than all of such entity's property, at a fair valuation . . . ." 11 U.S.C. § 101(32)(A). For purposes of § 548, solvency is measured at the time the debtor transferred value, not at some later or earlier time. This is known as the "balance sheet" test: "assets and liabilities are tallied at *fair valuation* to determine whether the corporation's debts exceed its assets." ([E]mphasis added).

Mellon Bank's principal argument is that the bankruptcy court inappropriately relied on an audited, year-end financial statement indicating that Intershoe had a net worth of negative $4 million as of August 31, 1991. That financial statement was prepared several months *after* the disputed transfers were made and, according to Mellon Bank, reflected "substantial adjustments" that were "precipitated by the collapse of the Mellon-TCR transaction . . . ." But for that unexpected collapse, Mellon Bank argues, several alleged "credits" Intershoe was carrying on its books rendered it solvent, at least on paper, at the time it remitted the disputed commitment fees to Mellon Bank. In short, Mellon [B]ank accuses the bankruptcy court of relying on hindsight to conclude that Intershoe was insolvent in October through November of 1991. This argument need not detain us long.

The use of hindsight to evaluate a debtor's financial condition for purposes of the Code's "insolvency" element has been criticized by courts and commentators alike. Hindsight, however, is not what prompted the bankruptcy court to ignore certain alleged "credits" and, thus, conclude that Intershoe was insolvent. On the contrary, and as Mellon Bank acknowledges, at least two alleged "credits," which together totaled $4.3 million,[8] depended for their validity on Intershoe's belief that the loan would close. As we have already discussed, the bankruptcy court found, as a matter of fact, that Intershoe knew or should have known that its deteriorating financial condition would preclude it from meeting one or more of the conditions in the commitment letter[.] * * * This conclusion is fatal to Mellon Bank's position. The bankruptcy court correctly determined that a debtor's creative accounting practices, which have the effect of grossly overstating its financial condition, cannot be the basis of a court's solvency analysis.

Furthermore, if a debtor's treatment of an item as an "asset" depends for its propriety on the occurrence of a contingent event, a court must take into consideration the likelihood of that event occurring from an objective standpoint. Such an analysis is by no means unknown to the law. Far from "hindsight" or "*post-hoc*" analysis, a court looks at the circumstances as they appeared to the debtor and determines whether the debtor's belief that a future event would occur was reasonable. The less reasonable a debtor's belief, the more a court is justified in reducing the assets (or raising liabilities) to reflect the debtor's true financial condition at the time of the alleged transfers.

In this case, moreover, Daniel Coffey, a certified public accountant who served as the Committee's insolvency expert, revealed that in the course of performing an audit, accountants abide by a far more stringent rule. Mr. Coffey testified that "in reality, if an auditor didn't think there was a real 99 percent chance that this loan is going to close, they wouldn't leave [the 'credits'] on the balance sheet. Everybody would say let's sit and wait and see what happens." Since the bankruptcy court found that the probability of the loan closing was essentially zero, a finding we have already determined is amply supported by the record, the court properly discounted (to zero) the $4.3 million Intershoe had carried on its balance sheet as

[8] Those credits include a $3.668-million advance owed to Intershoe by IS International, a subsidiary, and $754,000 in "pre-paid financing fees" in connection with the Mellon Bank/TCR financing. Had the loan closed, Intershoe's subsidiary could have continued to operate as a going concern, which in turn would have enabled it to repay the $3.668-million advance from its parent. Similarly, had the loan closed, Intershoe would have been permitted to expense the financing fees gradually over the life of the loan.

alleged "assets." Thus, by November of 1991, Intershoe's actual assets were $4.3 million lower than its balance sheet had reflected.

* * *

In sum, Intershoe was found to have a net worth of negative $4 million on August 31, 1991, and negative $8 million on November 15, 1991. The bankruptcy court properly refused to consider various items totaling $8.8 million that Intershoe had attempted to portray as assets. Since the transfers at issue here occurred on November 7, 1991, the bankruptcy court's insolvency determination will be affirmed.

[some footnotes and citations omitted]

What happens if a parent corporation essentially uses the assets of its subsidiaries to pay off a debt the subsidiaries do not owe in an effort to avoid inevitable disaster? Is this a fraudulent conveyance? Consider the following case.

IN RE TOUSA, INC.

United States Court of Appeals, Eleventh Circuit, 2012.
680 F.3d 1298.

PRYOR, CIRCUIT JUDGE:

This bankruptcy appeal involves a transfer of liens by subsidiaries of TOUSA, Inc., to secure the payment of a debt owed only by their parent, TOUSA. On July 31, 2007, TOUSA paid a settlement of $421 million to the Senior Transeastern Lenders with loan proceeds from the New Lenders secured primarily by the assets of several subsidiaries of TOUSA. Six months later, TOUSA and the Conveying Subsidiaries filed for bankruptcy. In an adversary proceeding filed by the Committee of Unsecured Creditors of TOUSA, the bankruptcy court avoided the liens as a fraudulent transfer because the Conveying Subsidiaries did not receive reasonably equivalent value; ordered the Transeastern Lenders to disgorge $403 million of the loan proceeds because the transfer of the liens was for the benefit of the Transeastern Lenders; and awarded damages to the Conveying Subsidiaries. The Transeastern Lenders and the New Lenders, as intervenors, appealed. The district court quashed the judgment as to the Transeastern Lenders and stayed the appeal of the New Lenders. This appeal by the Committee of Unsecured Creditors presents two issues: (1) whether the bankruptcy court clearly erred when it found that the Conveying Subsidiaries did not receive reasonably equivalent value in exchange for the liens to secure loans used to pay a debt owed only by TOUSA, 11 U.S.C. § 548; and (2) whether the Transeastern Lenders were entities "for whose benefit" the Conveying Subsidiaries transferred the liens, 11 U.S.C. § 550(a)(1). We hold that [the] bankruptcy court did not clearly err when it found that the Conveying Subsidiaries did not receive reasonably equivalent value for the liens and that the bankruptcy court correctly ruled that the Transeastern Lenders were entities "for whose benefit" the liens were transferred. We reverse the judgment of the district court, affirm the liability findings of the bankruptcy court, and remand for further proceedings consistent with this opinion.

I. BACKGROUND

* * *

A. *Factual Background*

As of 2006, TOUSA, Inc., was the thirteenth largest homebuilding enterprise in the country, with operations in Florida, Texas, the mid-Atlantic states, and the western United States. The company had grown rapidly, chiefly by acquiring independent homebuilders that became subsidiaries of TOUSA. These subsidiaries owned most of the assets of the enterprise and generated virtually all of its revenue.

To finance its growth, TOUSA borrowed a lot. TOUSA issued more than $1 billion of public bonds. That debt was unsecured, but was guaranteed by the Conveying Subsidiaries. TOUSA also borrowed funds under a revolving line of credit agreement administered by Citicorp North America, Inc. The Conveying Subsidiaries and TOUSA were jointly and severally liable for repayment of the revolving loan, which was secured by liens on the assets of the companies. Both the bond debt and revolving loan agreements provided that an adverse judgment for more than $10 million against TOUSA or any of its subsidiaries or a bankruptcy filing by TOUSA or any of its subsidiaries would constitute an event of default, which would permit the bondholders and Citicorp to declare all outstanding amounts of debt due immediately. As of July 31, 2007, TOUSA had approximately $1.061 billion of principal outstanding on its bond debt and $224 million outstanding on its revolving loan.

In June 2005, TOUSA entered a joint venture with Falcone/Ritchie LLC to acquire homebuilding assets owned by Transeastern Properties, Inc., in Florida. TOUSA incurred more debt, this time from the Transeastern Lenders, to fund the Transeastern Joint Venture, but none of the Conveying Subsidiaries became an obligor or guarantor of the Transeastern debt.

The downturn in the housing market soon threatened the Transeastern Joint Venture. By October 4, 2006, the joint venture had defaulted on several obligations. At the end of that month, the Transeastern Lenders alleged defaults and demanded payment from TOUSA. In December 2006, the Transeastern Lenders sued TOUSA, and in January 2007, the Transeastern Lenders alleged that TOUSA was responsible for damages of over $2 billion.

On July 31, 2007, TOUSA executed settlements with its partner in the joint venture and the Transeastern Lenders. The settlements required TOUSA to pay more than $421 million to the Transeastern Lenders. To finance the settlements, TOUSA and some of its subsidiaries incurred new debt. Citicorp North America, Inc. agreed to syndicate two new term loans to TOUSA and the Conveying Subsidiaries: a $200 million loan from the First Lien Lenders, to be secured by first-priority liens on the assets of the Conveying Subsidiaries and TOUSA; and a $300 million loan from the Second Lien Lenders, to be secured by second-priority liens. Both loan agreements with these New Lenders required that the funds be used to pay the $421 million settlement with the Transeastern Lenders. TOUSA also amended its revolving credit agreement with Citicorp.

The transaction was executed in several parts. First, Citicorp transferred $476,418,784.40 to Universal Land Title, Inc., a wholly-owned subsidiary of TOUSA that was not one of the Conveying Subsidiaries. Universal Land Title then sent a wire transfer of $426,383,828.08 to CIT, the administrative agent for the Transeastern Lenders. CIT disbursed the proceeds of that transfer on July 31 and August 1, 2007. The Transeastern Lenders received $421,015,089.15 and the remaining funds were dispersed to third parties to cover professional, advisory, and other fees.

B. Bankruptcy Court Proceedings

Six months later, TOUSA and the Conveying Subsidiaries filed petitions for bankruptcy under Chapter 11. The Committee of Unsecured Creditors of TOUSA, on behalf of the estate of TOUSA, later filed an adversary proceeding against the New Lenders and the Transeastern Lenders to avoid as a fraudulent transfer, *see* 11 U.S.C. § 548(a)(1)(B), the transfer of the liens to the New Lenders and to recover the value of the liens from the Transeastern Lenders, *see* 11 U.S.C. § 550(a)(1). The Committee alleged that the transfer of the liens by the Conveying Subsidiaries to the New Lenders was a fraudulent transfer under section 548(a)(1)(B) because the Conveying Subsidiaries were insolvent when the transfer occurred, were made insolvent by the transfer, had unreasonably small capital, or were unable to pay their debts when due; and the Conveying Subsidiaries did not receive reasonably equivalent value in exchange for their transfer. *See* 11 U.S.C. § 548(a)(1)(B). The Committee demanded that the bankruptcy court avoid the liens and order the Transeastern Lenders, as the entities "for whose benefit" the transfer was made, 11 U.S.C. § 550(a)(1), to disgorge the proceeds of the loans.

The Transeastern Lenders and New Lenders responded that the transfer of the liens was not fraudulent because the Conveying Subsidiaries had received reasonably equivalent value in exchange for their liens. The Transeastern Lenders and New Lenders highlighted numerous purported benefits of the transaction, but the crucial source of alleged value for the Conveying Subsidiaries was the economic benefit of avoiding default and bankruptcy. The Transeastern Lenders and New Lenders contended that the Transeastern Lenders were likely to secure a judgment against TOUSA, which would have constituted an event of default on more than $1 billion of debt that the Conveying Subsidiaries had guaranteed. The default would have likely forced TOUSA and the Conveying Subsidiaries into bankruptcy. The transaction staved off this event and gave TOUSA and the Conveying Subsidiaries an opportunity to continue as an enterprise and possibly become profitable again. The Transeastern Lenders and New Lenders contended that this opportunity was reasonably equivalent in value to the obligations the Conveying Subsidiaries incurred. The Transeastern Lenders and New Lenders also argued that the Conveying Subsidiaries received numerous other benefits, including a higher debt ceiling on the revolving loan, new tax benefits, the elimination of adverse business effects from the Transeastern litigation, and the opportunity to retain access to various centralized services provided by TOUSA such as cash management, purchasing, and payroll administration. The Transeastern Lenders argued alternatively that, if the transfer of liens was fraudulent, they could not be liable as entities for whose benefit the transfer was made because they were subsequent transferees of the loan proceeds from TOUSA, not entities that benefitted immediately from the transfer. *See* 11 U.S.C. § 550(a)(1).

After a 13-day trial, during which the bankruptcy court heard extensive fact and expert testimony and admitted over 1800 exhibits, the bankruptcy court issued its findings of fact and conclusions of law. *See Official Committee of Unsecured Creditors of Tousa, Inc. v. Citicorp North America, Inc. (In re TOUSA, Inc.)*, 422 B.R. 783 (Bankr. S.D. Fla. 2009). The bankruptcy court found that the Conveying Subsidiaries were unable to pay their debts when due, had unreasonably small capital, and were insolvent before and after the transaction; that the Conveying Subsidiaries did not receive value reasonably equivalent to the $403 million of obligations they incurred; and that the Transeastern Lenders were entities for whose benefit the Conveying Subsidiaries granted liens to the New Lenders.

The bankruptcy court credited expert opinion testimony that the Conveying Subsidiaries were insolvent both before and after the transaction of July 31, 2007. Experts in real estate value, public accounting, and insolvency examined the financial records of TOUSA and the Conveying Subsidiaries and concluded that the liabilities of each of the Conveying Subsidiaries exceeded the fair value of their assets before the transaction. The bankruptcy court found that the Conveying Subsidiaries became even more deeply insolvent after incurring additional debt through the transaction. The bankruptcy court also credited expert opinion testimony that, after the transaction, the Conveying Subsidiaries had unreasonably small capital and were unable to pay their debts as they came due.

The bankruptcy court then assessed whether the Conveying Subsidiaries received reasonably equivalent value from the transaction. The bankruptcy court first noted that "value" is defined in section 548 as being "property" or "satisfaction or securing of a present or antecedent debt of the debtor." 11 U.S.C. §§ 548(a)(1)(B)(i), (d)(2)(A). The bankruptcy court determined that "the Conveying Subsidiaries could not receive 'property' unless they obtained some kind of enforceable entitlement to some tangible or intangible article." *In re TOUSA*, 422 B.R. at 868 n.55. Under this definition of "value," the bankruptcy court found that, because the Conveying Subsidiaries did not receive any property, they did not receive reasonably equivalent value.

The bankruptcy court also issued alternative findings in which it assessed the value the Conveying Subsidiaries received under the broadest definition of "value" proposed by the Transeastern Lenders and New Lenders. The bankruptcy court found that, even if all the benefits highlighted by the Transeastern Lenders and New Lenders were legally cognizable, their value "considered . . . as a whole, . . . f[e]ll[ ] well short of 'reasonably equivalent' value." *Id.* at 869. The bankruptcy court determined the value the Conveying Subsidiaries lost in the transaction and compared that value with the value of the benefits they received. The bankruptcy court determined that the tax benefits, property, and services that the Transeastern Lenders and New Lenders proffered did not provide reasonably equivalent value to the Conveying Subsidiaries. The bankruptcy court also found that the transaction could not have provided substantial value predicated on the opportunity to avoid bankruptcy because the filing of bankruptcy became "inevitable." *Id.* at 846. The bankruptcy court credited the expert opinion testimony of an accountant who had calculated that the Conveying Subsidiaries had incurred $403 million of obligations when they granted liens to help secure $500 million of loans from the New Lenders.

The bankruptcy court found that the alleged benefits of the transaction were insubstantial. The Transeastern Lenders and New Lenders alleged that one of the Conveying Subsidiaries received control of property from the Transeastern venture, but the bankruptcy court found that the property was worth only $28 million and was burdened with $32 million in liabilities in accounts payable and customer deposits. The bankruptcy court refused to credit the property as value. The bankruptcy court also rejected the argument of the Transeastern Lenders and New Lenders that the Conveying Subsidiaries received valuable tax benefits from the transaction. The Transeastern Lenders and New Lenders argued that losses on the Transeastern venture could reduce past and future tax liability, but the bankruptcy court found that the Conveying Subsidiaries received no benefits because the benefits would accrue to TOUSA, not the Conveying Subsidiaries, and all of the substantial loss-generating events that ostensibly arose from the transaction would have accrued without the transaction. The Transeastern Lenders and New Lenders argued that the Transeastern litigation had negative effects on the day-to-day business operations of the Conveying Subsidiaries and that the July 31 transaction conferred an indirect benefit on the Conveying Subsidiaries by eliminating those effects, but the bankruptcy court found that those arguments were unsupported by the evidence. The bankruptcy court also found that the purported benefits of continued access to TOUSA corporate services, such as purchasing and payroll administration, were not received by the Conveying Subsidiaries in exchange for their liens because the Conveying Subsidiaries enjoyed all of these benefits before the transaction and continued to enjoy the corporate services even after TOUSA filed for bankruptcy. The bankruptcy court rejected the arguments of the Transeastern Lenders and New Lenders that the Conveying Subsidiaries obtained value because the transaction allowed the Conveying Subsidiaries access to an enhanced revolving credit facility. The Transeastern Lenders and New Lenders asserted that, when TOUSA acquired assets from the Transeastern Joint Venture, the borrowing limit on the revolving loan increased, but the bankruptcy court found that there was no evidence that the Conveying Subsidiaries had any need for a higher borrowing limit on the revolving loan.

The bankruptcy court found that an earlier bankruptcy for TOUSA would not have seriously harmed the Conveying Subsidiaries. Two experts testified that a TOUSA bankruptcy would not necessarily have caused the Conveying Subsidiaries to declare bankruptcy because they held 95 percent of the assets of the TOUSA enterprise, which they could have used to obtain new financing. The bankruptcy court credited this testimony and found that Conveying Subsidiaries would not have been forced into bankruptcy by a TOUSA bankruptcy. The bankruptcy court also found that the Conveying Subsidiaries could have operated as independent entities without the services provided by TOUSA.

The bankruptcy court found that "even assuming that *all* of the TOUSA entities would have spiraled immediately into bankruptcy without the July 31 Transaction, the Transaction was *still* the more harmful option." *Id.* at 847. The bankruptcy court found that bankruptcy for the Conveying Subsidiaries was "inevitable" if TOUSA executed the transaction, *id.* at 846, so the transaction could not have conferred value by giving the Conveying Subsidiaries an opportunity to avoid bankruptcy. The bankruptcy court found that the management and controlling shareholders at TOUSA decided to risk hundreds of millions of dollars of their creditors' money despite the impending disaster the company faced.

* * *

II. DISCUSSION

We divide our discussion into three parts. We first explain that the bankruptcy court did not clearly err when it found that the Conveying Subsidiaries did not receive reasonably equivalent value in exchange for their liens. We then explain that the bankruptcy court did not err when it found that the Transeastern Lenders were entities for whose benefit the liens were transferred. * * *

A. The Bankruptcy Court Did Not Clearly Err When It Found That the Conveying Subsidiaries Did Not Receive Reasonably Equivalent Value in Exchange for the Liens They Transferred to the New Lenders.

The Committee argues that the bankruptcy court did not clearly err when it found that the conveyance of the liens by the Conveying Subsidiaries to the New Lenders was a fraudulent transfer. Section 548(a)(1)(B) of the Bankruptcy Code provides for the avoidance of "any transfer . . . of an interest of the debtor in property, or any obligation . . . incurred by the debtor, that was made or incurred . . . within two years before the date of the filing" of the bankruptcy petition, if the debtor "received less than reasonably equivalent value in exchange for" the transfer or obligation, and the debtor (1) "was insolvent on the date such transfer was made or such obligation was incurred, or became insolvent as a result of such transfer or obligation;" (2) "was engaged in business or a transaction, or was about to engage in business or a transaction, for which any property remaining with the debtor was an unreasonably small capital;" or (3) "intended to incur, or believed that the debtor would incur, debts that would be beyond the debtor's ability to pay as such debts matured." 11 U.S.C. § 548(a)(1)(B). The parties do not dispute, in this appeal, that the Conveying Subsidiaries were either insolvent, had unreasonably small capital, or were unable to pay their debts when the liens were conveyed. Their dispute concerns whether the Conveying Subsidiaries received less than reasonably equivalent value. "The purpose of voiding transfers unsupported by 'reasonably equivalent value' is to protect creditors against the depletion of a bankrupt's estate." *G.E. Credit Corp. v. Murphy (In re Rodriguez)*, 895 F.2d 725, 727 (11th Cir. 1990).

The bankruptcy court endorsed a definition of "value" that the district court rejected as too narrow and potentially "inhibitory of contemporary financing practices," *In re TOUSA*, 444 B.R. at 659, but we need not adopt the definition of either court. We decline to decide whether the possible avoidance of bankruptcy can confer "value" because the bankruptcy court found that, even if all the purported benefits of the transaction were legally cognizable, they did not confer reasonably equivalent value. *See In re TOUSA*, 422 B.R. at 869. Because these findings are not clearly erroneous, they settle this matter.

The bankruptcy court was entitled to find that the benefits of the transaction were not reasonably equivalent in value to what the Conveying Subsidiaries surrendered. "It has long been established that '[w]hether fair consideration has been given for a transfer is 'largely a question of fact, as to which considerable latitude must be allowed to the trier of the facts.' " *Nordberg v. Arab Banking Corp. (In re Chase & Sanborn Corp.)*, 904 F.2d 588, 593 (11th Cir. 1990) (quoting *Mayo v. Pioneer Bank & Trust Co.*, 270 F.2d 823, 829–30 (5th Cir.1959) (Wisdom, J.)). The record supports the finding by the bankruptcy court that, for the Conveying Subsidiaries, the almost certain costs of the transaction of July 31 far outweighed any perceived benefits.

The Transeastern Lenders and New Lenders argue that the transaction of July 31 allowed the Conveying Subsidiaries to escape the "existential threat" of the likely bankruptcy that would ensue and that this chance to avoid bankruptcy was a benefit reasonably equivalent in value to the obligations the Conveying Subsidiaries incurred, but we are unpersuaded that the record compels that finding. "A corporation is not a biological entity for which it can be presumed that any act which extends its existence is beneficial to it." *Bloor v. Dansker (In re Investors Funding Corp. of New York Sec. Litig.*, 523 F. Supp. 533, 541 (S.D.N.Y. 1980). In other words, not every transfer that decreases the odds of bankruptcy for a corporation can be justified. The bankruptcy court considered the potential benefits of the transaction and found that they were nowhere close to its expected costs. In the light of all the evidence, we are not "left with the definite and firm conviction that" the bankruptcy court clearly erred. *In re Int'l Pharmacy & Disc. II, Inc.*, 443 F.3d at 770.

The Transeastern Lenders and New Lenders argue that the record establishes that an adverse judgment in the Transeastern litigation would have caused TOUSA to file for bankruptcy, the revolving financing for the Conveying Subsidiaries to disappear, and the Conveying Subsidiaries to become liable for immediate payment of more than $1.3 billion to the revolving loan lenders and TOUSA bondholders. They contend that the bankruptcy court clearly erred when it found that the Conveying Subsidiaries could have survived a TOUSA bankruptcy. They argue that the bankruptcy court found that the Conveying Subsidiaries were insolvent before the transaction, and they argue that it is unlikely that the insolvent Conveying Subsidiaries could have obtained new financing. They also argue that the absence of standalone financial statements was a "clear obstacle" to new financing. They highlight that one of the experts for the Committee described the intercompany payables and receivables for TOUSA and the Conveying Subsidiaries as a "huge pile of tangled spaghetti." The Transeastern Lenders and New Lenders assert that it would have taken months, if not years, to sort through the mound of records, which proves that the Conveying Subsidiaries had no chance to receive standalone financing.

The bankruptcy court found this evidence to be irrelevant because, "even assuming that *all* of the TOUSA entities would have spiraled immediately into bankruptcy without the July 31 Transaction, the Transaction was still the more harmful option." *In re TOUSA*, 422 B.R. at 847. "[A]t most it delayed the inevitable." *Id.* at 846. The bankruptcy court found that the benefits to the Conveying Subsidiaries were not close to being reasonably equivalent in value to the $403 million of obligations that they incurred. The Transeastern Lenders and New Lenders attack this finding as "hindsight reasoning . . . at its most extreme," but the bankruptcy court based its extensive findings on a thorough review of public knowledge available before July 31, 2007; expert analysis of data available before July 31, 2007; and statements by TOUSA insiders made before July 31, 2007.

The Transeastern Lenders and New Lenders argue that the finding of an "inevitable" bankruptcy is against the weight of the evidence, but the only evidence they cite, in contrast with the thorough findings of the bankruptcy court, are the opinions of a TOUSA advisor that the company would remain viable after the transaction and statements from Tony Mon about a comprehensive strategy to shrink TOUSA after the transaction, shore up its finances, and rebuild the company. The Transeastern Lenders and New Lenders contend that the projections of TOUSA look unreasonable now only because weeks after the transaction, "a tragic global financial crisis of unprecedented proportions" began. They assert that the unexpected downturn was described by Alan Greenspan as "a once in a century credit tsunami" and by Warren Buffett as an "economic Pearl Harbor." The Transeastern Lenders and New Lenders argue that they cannot be held liable for failing to foresee the unforeseeable, that their actions were reasonable, and that the bankruptcy court clearly should have found that the transaction was a reasonable risk for the Conveying Subsidiaries to take.

The record supports a determination that the bankruptcy of TOUSA was far more like a slow-moving category 5 hurricane than an unforeseen tsunami. The bankruptcy court considered the evidence from outside advisors to TOUSA and found much of it suspect or based on faulty premises. The bankruptcy court considered and discounted Mon's deleveraging strategy for TOUSA in the light of the dire predictions he and other insiders made regarding the effects the transaction would have on TOUSA. And the bankruptcy court found that, even though Alan Greenspan and Warren Buffet could not foresee the general economic downturn that began in earnest in August 2007, numerous external observers and insiders at TOUSA recognized that the relevant housing markets for TOUSA had begun their free fall before the July 31 transaction. In contrast with the surprise attack at Pearl Harbor, the warnings about the collapse of TOUSA made that event as foreseeable as the bombing of Nagasaki after President Truman's ultimatum.

The opportunity to avoid bankruptcy does not free a company to pay any price or bear any burden. After all, "there is no reason to treat bankruptcy as a bogeyman, as a fate worse than death." *Olympia Equipment Leasing Co. v. Western Union Telegraph Co.*, 786 F.2d 794, 802 (7th Cir. 1986) (Easterbrook, J., concurring). The bankruptcy court correctly asked, "based on the circumstances that existed at the time the investment was contemplated, whether there was any chance that the investment would generate a positive return." *See Mellon Bank, N.A. v. Official Committee of Unsecured Creditors of R.M.L., Inc. (In re R.M.L., Inc.)*, 92 F.3d 139, 152 (3rd Cir. 1996). And the record supports the negative answer found by the bankruptcy court.

B. The Bankruptcy Court Did Not Err When It Ruled That the Committee Could Recover from the Transeastern Lenders under Section 550(a)(1).

If a transfer is avoided under section 548 or one of several other provisions of the Bankruptcy Code, section 550(a)(1) allows the recovery of the property transferred or its value from the initial transferee or from an "entity for whose benefit such transfer was made." 11 U.S.C. § 550(a)(1). Although the liens of the Conveying Subsidiaries were transferred to secure loans to pay the Transeastern Lenders, the Transeastern Lenders argue that they are not covered by section 550 because they were subsequent transferees, not entities that benefitted from the initial transfer. Their argument is contradicted by the loan agreements, which required that the proceeds of the loans secured by the liens be transferred to the Transeastern Lenders. Under the plain language of section 550(a)(1) and the precedent of our Court, the Transeastern Lenders are entities for whose benefit the Conveying Subsidiaries transferred their liens.

To be sure, we have stated that "the paradigm case of a benefit under § 550(a) is the benefit to a guarantor by the payment of the underlying debt of the debtor." *Reily v. Kapila (In re Int'l Mgmt. Ass'n)*, 399 F.3d 1288, 1292 (11th Cir. 2005). The guarantor receives an immediate benefit when the debtor pays back a creditor, which reduces the liability of the guarantor. Although this relationship may be the paradigmatic case, it is not the only circumstance that can give rise to "for whose benefit" liability.

We have also held that a creditor similarly situated to the Transeastern Lenders can be liable as an entity for whose benefit a transfer was made. In *American Bank of Marin County v. Leasing Service Corp. (In re Air Conditioning, Inc. of Stuart)*, 845 F.2d 293 (11th Cir. 1988), we ruled that section 550(a)(1) allowed the trustee to recover the value of a $20,000 certificate of deposit from the creditor of a company that had transferred a security interest in the certificate of deposit to a bank, which had transferred a $20,000 letter of credit to the creditor. *Id.* at 299. The company in *Air Conditioning* owed its creditor $20,000. *Id.* at 295. When the company began falling behind on payments, the parties worked out a deal to keep the company in business. *Id.* As part of the deal, the company issued a $20,000 promissory note to a bank secured by a $20,000 certificate of deposit. *Id.* The bank, in turn, executed a $20,000 letter of credit to the creditor. *Id.* After the company entered bankruptcy, we ruled that the transfer of the security interest in the certificate of deposit to the bank constituted an avoidable preference under section 547(b) because it was a transfer of property of the debtor to a creditor within 90 days of filing for bankruptcy that provided more value to the creditor than it would have received under chapter 7 of the Bankruptcy Code. *Id.* at 296–97; *see also* 11 U.S.C. 547(b). We then ruled that the bankruptcy trustee could recover the value of the certificate of deposit from the creditor because the company granted the security interest to the bank for the benefit of the creditor. *Id.* at 299. We explained that the text of section 550(a)(1) allows the trustee to recover from a creditor when it was an entity for whose benefit the transfer of the certificate of deposit was made. *Id.*

Our decision in *Air Conditioning* controls this appeal. In *Air Conditioning*, the debtor transferred a lien to a lender who transferred funds to a creditor. The transfer of the lien was avoided and, under section 550(a)(1), the creditor was an entity for whose benefit the transfer was made. In the same way, the Conveying Subsidiaries transferred liens to the New Lenders, who transferred funds to creditors, the Transeastern Lenders. The bankruptcy court avoided the transfer of the liens and, under section 550(a)(1), the Transeastern Lenders were entities for whose benefit the transfer was made.

The Transeastern Lenders attempt to distinguish their appeal from *Air Conditioning* in two ways, but their arguments ignore the material similarities between the preference in that decision and the fraudulent transfer at issue in this appeal. First, the Transeastern Lenders contend that Air Conditioning involved a preference under section 547 instead of a fraudulent transfer under 548, but "[t]he theory under which a transfer has been avoided is irrelevant to the liability of the transferee against whom the trustee seeks to recover [under section 550]." *Danning v. Miller*, 922 F.2d 544, 546 n.2 (9th Cir. 1991). Second, the Transeastern Lenders argue that section 550(a)(1) applied in Air Conditioning because a letter of credit was involved, but the Transeastern Lenders cannot provide a principled basis for limiting section 550(a)(1) to factual scenarios that involve letters of credit.

The Transeastern Lenders also contend that they cannot be liable under section 550(a)(1) because they benefitted from a subsequent transfer of funds from TOUSA, not from the initial transfer of the liens, but the record contradicts their assertion. The new loan agreements required that the loan proceeds be used to pay the Transeastern settlement, and the Transeastern settlement expressly depended on the new loans. When the liens were transferred to the New Lenders, the proceeds of the loans went to the Transeastern Lenders. The Transeastern Lenders assert that the funds passed from the New Lenders to a wholly-owned subsidiary of TOUSA before the funds were paid to the Transeastern Lenders, but the subsidiary that wired the money to the Transeastern Lenders did not have control over the funds. The loan documents required the subsidiary to wire the funds to the Transeastern Lenders immediately. Although the funds technically passed through the TOUSA subsidiary, this formality did not make the Transeastern Lenders subsequent transferees of the funds because TOUSA never had control over the funds. *See Nordberg v. Societe Generale (In re Chase & Sanborn Corp.)*, 848 F.2d 1196, 1199 (11th Cir. 1988) (stating that courts must apply a "very flexible, pragmatic" test that "look[s] beyond the particular transfers in question to the entire circumstance of the transactions" when deciding whether debtors had controlled property later sought by their trustees); *Bonded Fin. Servs.*, 838 F.2d at 893 (holding that a bank was not an initial transferee because it held funds "only for the purpose of fulfilling an instruction to make the funds available to someone else").

The Transeastern Lenders warn that our reading of section 550(a) would drastically expand the potential pool of entities that could be liable for any transaction, but these concerns are unsubstantiated. The Transeastern Lenders offer examples of a parent company taking out a loan secured by its subsidiaries with the specific intent of paying a contractor to build a building for the parent company or paying the dry cleaning bill of the parent company. The Transeastern Lenders caution that the contractor or dry cleaner could be forced to return their payments if the loan securing the money involved a fraudulent transfer, which would impose "extraordinary" duties of due diligence on the part of creditors accepting repayment. But every creditor must exercise some diligence when receiving payment from a struggling debtor. It is far from a drastic obligation to expect some diligence from a creditor when it is being repaid hundreds of millions of dollars by someone other than its debtor.

* * *

III. CONCLUSION

We **REVERSE** the order of the district court, **AFFIRM** the liability findings of the bankruptcy court, and **REMAND** to the district court for further proceedings consistent with this opinion.

REVERSED AND REMANDED.

NOTE

Section 544(b) is used when a trustee wishes to take advantage of applicable state fraudulent-conveyance law. As suggested above, the trustee might use this route (rather than the more direct route under section 548) because the transfer occurred more than two years before the filing, or because the local law is more favorable for other reasons. Local fraudulent-conveyance laws fall under three headings: those of the Uniform Fraudulent Conveyance Act, the later Uniform Fraudulent Transfer Act, or some homegrown variation of English or other law on fraudulent conveyances. Notably, section 548 is patterned after the Uniform Fraudulent Transfer Act.

§ 8. SECTION 365 AND LEASES

The Bankruptcy Code treats leases of goods very differently from security interests. If a transaction is a true lease, section 365 of the Bankruptcy Code gives the debtor essentially two options: (1) assume the lease (with the possibility of assigning it to some third party); or (2) reject the lease. If the debtor assumes the lease, it must honor virtually all of its lease obligations in full, including any and all rental obligations. If the debtor rejects the lease, it must return the goods to the lessor. The debtor cannot use the bankruptcy process to modify the rent or alter the term of the lease: section 365, for example, denies the debtor the power to keep possession of the leased goods simply by paying their current value. Likewise, because a lease can be valid without being "perfected," the opportunity to avoid it in bankruptcy is minimal—unless the trustee can demonstrate that the lease is not, in fact, a true lease, but rather a disguised security interest that the "lessor" neglected to perfect. *See* UCC 1–203 (1–201(37) in pre-revision Article 1).

As indicated above, the treatment of leases in bankruptcy is governed by section 365 of the Code. This section, however, is so unclear, convoluted, and filled with exceptions that it is nearly incomprehensible. Moreover, it mostly treats real-estate leases and executory contracts, subjects ignored in this course. For the purposes of this section, we are concerned only with personal property leases that cannot be construed as security agreements. (To refresh your memory of this distinction, review the materials in Section 6 of Chapter 2.)

To understand how section 365 operates, consider an example. Assume that, prior to bankruptcy, a debtor bought a ship for a purchase price of $40 million, which the debtor was obligated to pay in installments over 20 years, plus interest. Assume further that the debtor has since entered bankruptcy, and that the current market value of the ship is only $30 million. If the debtor had granted a security interest in the ship, the DIP could "strip the lien" and force the unwilling secured creditor to accept $30 million under the reorganization plan. (The remaining $10 million would be treated as an unsecured debt, entitled to a pro rata share of whatever small payment might be made to the unsecured creditors.) On the other hand, if the debtor had signed a lease for the ship, the DIP would have to either give up the ship or pay the $40 million value according to the terms of the lease.

This distinction between a lease and a security agreement is important only if the DIP values the ship at more than its $30 million "market value." If the DIP could buy a new ship on the market for a present value of $30 million, it would be foolish to reaffirm a lease for a ship with a present value of $40 million. There are several reasons, however, why a DIP might reaffirm an apparently uneconomical lease (or bargain to buy the ship for a price higher than $30 million). First, a claim that the ship has a market value of $30 million may be false: just because the ship has a courtroom market value of $30 million does not mean that $30 million is the real market value. Second, the market may not be open to the DIP (who by hypothesis is bankrupt), yet the DIP's current creditors are bound to the DIP by agreement. Thus, if the DIP assumes the lease (or crams down a plan in the case of a security interest), these creditors may be made to stay with the DIP against their will under section 365. Third, there may be other idiosyncratic factors (such as a large potential tax liability that would arise from cancellation of the lease) that tie the DIP to the lease or exclude the DIP from the market. If any of these three circumstances exist, keeping the current lease may be more favorable than entering into a new one in a market that has a lower valuation for the ship.

Why does the Code treat leases and security interests so differently? Although some leases behave economically just like security interests, not all do. Under a true lease, the debtor is not the owner of the goods; rather, the debtor typically has a mere right of use and possession. By contrast, in the case of a secured transaction, the debtor owns the goods subject to a security interest. The debtor's lack of ownership in the leasing context seems to have mattered to the drafters of the Code, which gives the debtor greater flexibility in the treatment of security interests. Does this explanation seem persuasive to you?

§ 9. SECTION 1129 AND THE TREATMENT OF SECURED CREDITORS UNDER PLANS OF REORGANIZATION

It would be beyond unfair in a course on Article 9 to expect a student to learn all the intricate rules of business reorganizations under Chapter 11. So we focus here by surveying the few provisions governing plan confirmation that are most relevant to the treatment of secured claims.

Section 1129 contains the main provisions governing plan confirmation, including the famous cram down provisions. Even though nearly every plan is negotiated and very few plans are crammed down, all plans are influenced by, and put together to conform to, section 1129. With sixteen subsections, section 1129(a) appears daunting. For the purposes of this course, however, it is enough that we focus on three: 1129(a)(7), 1129(a)(8), and 1129(b)(2)(A).

In simple English, section 1129(a)(7) says that a plan cannot be approved unless each holder of a claim (not merely each class) will get a value under the plan no less than what the holder would get if the debtor were liquidated in Chapter 7. In other words, the distribution that any particular creditor would get under Chapter 7 is the floor: approval under section 1129(a)(7) requires that the creditor get *at least* that. Section 1129(a)(7)'s approval criterion is called the "best interest of creditors test."

Now consider section 1129(a)(8). It speaks in terms of a "class" of claims, not individual "holders" within a class. Only if every class has accepted the plan under section 1129(a)(8) can the plan be confirmed, unless the plan alternatively satisfies the cram down provisions of section 1129(b).

How is the plan accepted or rejected? Under section 1126, acceptance requires that voting creditors holding at least two-thirds in amount and more than one-half in number of the allowed claims in a particular class vote to confirm the plan. Under the Code's classification rules (*see* 1122), most secured creditors are put in a class without any other creditors. Accordingly, the negative vote of a single secured creditor can usually prevent the satisfaction of subsection (a)(8). In contrast, a creditor in a class with many others can stop acceptance only if the amount of its claim exceeds one-third of the total of the voting claims in that class.

One way to think about Chapter 11 reorganizations is to conceive of them as grand and extensive negotiations among various creditors (both secured and unsecured), the DIP, shareholders, employees, perhaps even the judge, and some other parties too. This way of thinking transforms section 1129 into a set of rules that mainly constrain what kind of plan will be negotiated. In general, the secured creditors' interests are protected by sections 1129(a)(8) and (b)(2). Section 1129(b)(2) says the plan cannot be crammed down on a secured creditor that votes "no" unless: (1) the secured creditor retains its lien and receives cash payments with a present value equal to the amount of its secured claim; (2) there is a sale of the collateral, the secured creditor is afforded whatever right it may have to "credit bid," and the secured creditor receives the benefit of the sale proceeds; or (3) the plan provides the secured creditor with the "indubitable equivalent" of its rights. (The right to "credit bid" is discussed in the *RadLax* case at the end of this Chapter.) The combination of the rules in sections 1129(a)(8) and (b)(2) gives every secured creditor a fairly strong hand in the often long and complex negotiation of Chapter 11 reorganizations.

As we have seen in the preceding parts of this chapter, the DIP and the unsecured creditors have the ability to inflict many small cuts on the secured creditor during the pendency of an expensive Chapter 11 proceeding. The secured creditor may get no interest, it may be denied adequate protection, and it bears the risk that its collateral will decline in value while the debtor is in Chapter 11. For all of these and other reasons, it appeared in 1978 as though the adoption of the new Bankruptcy Code substantially reduced the secured creditors' relative strength. Experience has proven otherwise. By adopting or merely benefiting from a variety of practices, secured creditors have, if anything, increased their power in many bankruptcies in the years since the adoption of the 1978 Code.

Consider some of the ways secured creditors have strengthened their hands. First, they have resorted to securitizations, the practice of which will be considered in Chapter 5. In a securitization transaction the debtor typically transfers accounts collateral to a third party or "special purchase vehicle." This transfer is designed to put the property beyond the reach of the DIP and the bankruptcy court in any subsequent bankruptcy proceeding, and it is an almost perfect substitute for secured loans on intangibles.

Another possibility is for a secured creditor to transform its purchase money security interest into a lease. Particularly if the asset has substantial value, the secured creditor disguised as a lessor can often get full value in bankruptcy under section 365. If the interest is a security interest, on the other hand, the secured creditor would risk having it challenged or written down.

Other things too have occurred in the forty-plus years since 1978. Judges today are more willing to see some debtors split up and sold off piecemeal early in the bankruptcy process. For example, TWA filed for bankruptcy only to consummate the sale of its planes and gates to American Airlines. Enron's main assets, including its trading operation and its valuable pipelines, were sold within a few months of its filing. These sales have the potential both to capture the going-concern value for the estate and to achieve a rapid and comparatively favorable payoff for creditors.

In addition, rights that belong to the DIP (and that the creditors' committee might use against the secured creditor) have proved to be less threatening than they first appeared. For example, the possibility of cram downs has remained largely just that—a possibility, and one that is uncommon in large Chapter 11s. Another contingency that has proved to be more threat than reality is the possibility under section 364(d) of granting to a new post-petition lender a security interest that would have priority in the same collateral above that of the existing secured creditor.

Moreover, certain Code provisions meant to protect the secured creditor have served their purpose in a way that may have been unexpected at the time the Code was made law. For example, one of the recurring worries of secured creditors is that the adequate protection ordered by a court under section 361 will turn out to be inadequate. A check against that risk is buried in section 507(b). Where adequate protection proves to be inadequate, the recipient of the protection has a right to treat the resulting loss not only as an administrative expense under section 507(a)(2) (provided the adequate-protection order so provides), but also, and better, as an expense that puts the creditor at the head of the section 507(a)(2) line, ahead of the lawyers, accountants, and other post-petition creditors.

Sometime in the 1980s or 1990s, it became apparent to secured creditors that were the principal lenders to companies facing Chapter 11 that it might be in their interest to align themselves with, rather than oppose, the DIP. Assume that Bank is the main secured creditor of a medium-size manufacturing company, and that Bank has lent the company $10 million against assets with a likely value of only $5 million. Bank believes the company can be successfully reorganized, and Bank itself made better off, if Bank becomes the DIP lender, putting in another $5 or $10 million with security. Indeed, if Bank is particularly clever, Bank can take a portion of the new loan to pay off its existing pre-petition loan, thereby transforming partially unsecured pre-petition debt into fully secured post-petition debt (which may, as a hedge, also have priority as an administrative expense entitled to payment ahead of all unsecured creditors).

As the DIP lender, Bank may be able to elicit other benefits from the debtor, which, by hypothesis, is now looking to Bank as one of its few possible saviors. Among other things, Bank might ask the DIP to appoint a chief restructuring officer, who will help the debtor revamp his business, and who, incidentally, might rat on the debtor to Bank if the debtor gets out of line. As a condition to issuing the new DIP loan, Bank might also ask for substantial fees in addition to its normal interest payments. And of course Bank will try to get the DIP to advocate the "rollup" of Bank's preexisting debt, thus transforming Bank's undersecured pre-petition debt into possibly fully secured post-petition debt.

Initially there was doubt about whether courts would permit this transformation, which, in the words of earlier cases, "cross-collateralized" pre-petition debt with post-petition assets. There were also questions about many of the other provisions appearing in the first-day orders submitted in connection with heavily negotiated deals, by which DIP lenders intend to put substantial money into their debtors' pockets. The DIP's motivation in agreeing to these terms is clear: he is turning to the only port in a terrible storm. But how amenable are the judges? The answer is found in the generous venue rules contained in the Bankruptcy Code. Large corporations (such as United Airlines and many others) can establish venue at its place of incorporation, at its place of business, or possibly at the places of incorporation or places of business of subsidiaries or other affiliates going into bankruptcy first. The power of a debtor contemplating bankruptcy to choose among various venues means that the debtor often has the ability to choose the judge. Since many judges like large Chapter 11s, and since both they and the DIP lenders know the venue rules, judges have incentives to make their rules friendly to the DIP and the DIP lender, who make the decisions about where to file.

Of course, the DIP cannot be a complete pushover in its bargain with the DIP lender. Indeed, there are at least two reasons why the DIP managers also must have an eye on the interests of the unsecured creditors. First, the DIP management may hope to ride out the Chapter 11 and continue to operate the reorganized company. Further, the unsecured creditors may comprise a large block of the reorganized company's new stockholders, and they may be able to prevent the approval of a plan with a large enough concentration of votes. If the DIP agrees to a deal that is too favorable to the DIP lender, the unsecured creditors' committee may vote it down or challenge it in court. If the deal deviates too far from the norm, even a lenient court will reject it.

All of these observations imply the existence of a private market for the reorganization and sale of distressed public companies. The major effect of the Bankruptcy Code is that it facilitates this private market, whose participants are the bankruptcy courts, the DIPs, the professional DIP lenders, traders in bankruptcy debt, lawyers and investment bankers specializing in bankruptcy, and bankruptcy managers (professional chief restructuring officers, turn-around experts, and the like). In addition, except for the claim of the DIP lender, who typically participates in the bankruptcy case from beginning to end, both secured and unsecured claims are frequently bought and sold continuously during the course of a large Chapter 11 case, in a vibrant claims-trading submarket.

Thus, it is sensible to think of Chapter 11s that involve public companies as large and unruly markets, where many interrelated deals lead incrementally to a corporate reorganization. To be sure, neither the law nor the courts are irrelevant. On the contrary, private bargains often depend on the courts' power to bind dissenting members of a class, and the parties derive their bargaining power from rights granted by Article 9 and by many provisions of the Bankruptcy Code. Of course, the judge must also approve the plan and, perhaps, even resolve a conflict or two. But make no mistake, a reorganization plan is rarely crammed down: it usually has the agreement of every class. Thanks to the Bankruptcy Code, the parties will have chosen a venue where the court is unlikely to grant an outsider's wish, and where the controlling outcome is one that was negotiated in the private market and reflects the economic power of the parties.

Before looking once more at section 1129, return briefly to section 506 (governing the determination of a creditor's secured status in bankruptcy) and visit section 1122 (governing the classification of claims for the purposes of Chapter 11 plans). Because secured and unsecured creditors are put into different classes, one must determine, for the purposes of section 1129, whether and to what extent a creditor's claim is secured. Recall that a creditor with a perfected and unassailable security interest will nevertheless be undersecured, for the purposes of section 1129, if the creditor's collateral is worth less than the amount of its claim. So a reorganization plan will treat a creditor with a $20 million claim on a piece of equipment worth $5 million as if the creditor were a secured creditor for $5 million and an unsecured creditor for $15 million. *See* 506. (There is an elaborate exception set forth in section 1111, which we will not consider here.)

Under section 1122, only claims that are "substantially similar" can be put together in the same class. In general, no secured creditor's claim is considered to be substantially similar to that of any other secured creditor; therefore, each secured creditor will have its own class. The reason for this is that, by virtue of the secured creditor's particular interest in particular collateral, its claim is thought to have unique aspects that require individual treatment. This is not the case for unsecured claims, and parties often fight over whether a particular unsecured claim should be included in or excluded from a particular unsecured class. The issue may become especially heated when a secured creditor also has a large unsecured deficiency claim. The secured creditor may wish to include such a claim with the other unsecured claims, so that the secured creditor (now voting its unsecured portion) can ensure that no class votes for a plan it dislikes.

Section 1126(c) provides that a class accepts a plan only upon the affirmative vote of "two-thirds in amount" and "more than one-half in number" of the voting claims of the class. So a single holder of 34% of the value of the claims in a class can veto an approval by the others no matter their number or unanimity. Thus, in order to solicit the favorable vote of a friendly class of unsecured creditors, the DIP may propose to exclude a secured creditor's overpowering unsecured claim from that class. The case that follows involves such a proposal.

BOSTON POST ROAD LIMITED PARTNERSHIP V. FEDERAL DEPOSIT INSURANCE CORPORATION

United States Court of Appeals, Second Circuit, 1994.
21 F.3d 477.

POLLACK, SENIOR DISTRICT JUDGE:

Debtor seeks confirmation of a Plan of Reorganization filed under Chapter 11 of the Bankruptcy Code. The Bankruptcy Court denied confirmation, holding that the Plan impermissibly (i) separately classified similar claims solely to create an impaired assenting class; and (ii) classified as "impaired" a class of residential security depositors whose interests were in fact benefited by the Plan. The District Court affirmed the Bankruptcy Court's rulings on both issues. Debtor challenges both holdings.

Background

Plaintiff-Appellant, Boston Post Road Limited Partnership ("BPR"), is a limited partnership formed pursuant to the Connecticut Uniform Limited Partnership Act, Conn. Gen. Stat. §§ 34–9 to –82 (1993), consisting of a single individual general partner, George Boyer, and a single limited partner, George Myers. BPR was formed in 1984 to acquire and manage a residential and office complex located in Waterford, Connecticut. In March of 1988, BPR mortgaged the complex to Connecticut Bank and Trust Company ("the Bank") to secure a loan of approximately $1.6 million. BPR thereafter defaulted on the mortgage payments, and on July 20, 1990, the Bank instituted a mortgage foreclosure action in Connecticut state court. In January 1991, the Bank became insolvent, its assets were seized by the U.S. Comptroller of Currency, and the Federal Deposit Insurance Corporation ("FDIC") became the holder of BPR's mortgage.

The FDIC continued to pursue foreclosure of the mortgaged property and on August 1, 1991, the Connecticut Superior Court entered a judgment of strict foreclosure against BPR and set October 28, 1991 as BPR's last day for redemption. On that date, BPR filed a voluntary *pro se* petition for relief under Chapter 11 of the Bankruptcy Code in the United States Bankruptcy Court for the District of Connecticut, thereby staying foreclosure. Approximately six months later, on March 16, 1992, the FDIC filed its proof of claim in BPR's bankruptcy.

On June 18, 1992, BPR filed its Second Amended Plan of Reorganization (the "Plan") in the Bankruptcy Court. The Plan proposed the following seven classes of creditors:

> Class 1—unsecured claims of residential tenants to security deposits entitled to priority under Section 507(a)(7) of the Bankruptcy Code;

Class 2—secured claims held by creditors with liens and/or security interests on or in the real estate asset of the debtor (i.e., the secured portion of the FDIC's mortgage);

Class 3—secured interests of residential tenants whose security deposits are being held by the Debtor in interest-bearing bank accounts;

Class 4—unsecured claims of trade creditors;

Class 5—unsecured deficiency claims of creditors who have some security for their debt but not enough to cover the full amount owed (i.e., the unsecured portion of the FDIC's mortgage);

Class 6—interests of the limited partner; and

Class 7—interests of the general partner.

In relevant part, the Plan proposed to pay the FDIC's secured claim (Class 2), estimated at $1.445 million, over a fifteen-year term, utilizing negative amortization with a balloon payment at the end of the fifteenth year following confirmation of the Plan; to pay the trade creditors' unsecured claims (Class 4), totaling approximately $5000, over a six-year term without interest; to pay the FDIC's unsecured mortgage deficiency claim (Class 5), estimated at $500,000, without interest following the earlier of a sale of the property or the fifteenth year following Plan confirmation; and to pay the residential security deposit holders (Class 3) a rate of interest on their residential security deposits higher than that statutorily mandated. In essence, the Plan was fashioned to permit a possible "cramdown," under 11 U.S.C. § 1129(b), over the anticipated objections of the FDIC, by far BPR's largest unsecured creditor. Ultimately, Class 1 turned out to be non-existent; Classes 2 and 5 voted to reject the Plan; and Classes 3, 4, 6 and 7 voted to accept the Plan.

On August 12, 1992, the Bankruptcy Court (Robert L. Krechevsky, Chief B.J.) held a hearing on the Plan's confirmation. At the hearing, the FDIC challenged the Plan on several grounds. In particular, it faulted the Plan for (i) segregating the Class 4 unsecured trade debts from the unsecured mortgage deficiency claim of the FDIC solely to gerrymander an impaired class which would approve the Plan; and (ii) classifying as "impaired" the Class 3 residential tenants with security deposits who would receive a higher interest rate on their security deposits than the statutorily mandated rate.

After hearing initial arguments, the Bankruptcy Court requested briefs and thereafter rendered a decision denying confirmation of the Plan on October 2, 1992. In its decision, the Bankruptcy Court held that (i) the FDIC's unsecured claim should have been placed in the same class with other unsecured creditors; and (ii) the residential security deposits were not "impaired" within the meaning of Bankruptcy Code § 1124(1). In light of these two rulings, the Code requirements for Plan confirmation were not satisfied because the Plan failed to obtain an affirmative vote of a legitimately impaired class of non-insider creditors. The District Court affirmed on June 23, 1993, and the Debtor has appealed to this Court.

DISCUSSION

A plan of reorganization under the Bankruptcy Code may be confirmed if either of two voting requirements is met: (i) each class of impaired claims has accepted the Plan, 11 U.S.C. § 1129(a)(8); or (ii) "at least one class of claims that is impaired under the plan has accepted the plan, determined without including any acceptance of the plan by any insider." 11 U.S.C. § 1129(a)(10). The latter makes available a "cramdown" procedure. If the debtor chooses to utilize the cramdown procedure (having failed to secure the vote of all the impaired classes), the plan must meet all of the statutory requirements enumerated in § 1129(b) (essentially that the plan is fair and equitable and does not discriminate unfairly against any impaired claims), in addition to the prerequisites of § 1129(a) which are imposed on every plan.

The voting structure set forth in the Bankruptcy Code for approval of a reorganization plan mandates that claims be placed in classes and that votes be counted on a class basis. Acceptance by a particular class of creditors occurs when "at least two-thirds in amount and more than one-half in number of allowed claims of such class . . . have accepted . . . such plan." 11 U.S.C. § 1126(c).

Cramdown of a plan of reorganization involving claims secured by real property owned by the debtor also often implicates Sections 506(a) and 1111(b) of the Bankruptcy Code. Section 506(a) provides that a claim secured by a lien on property is considered secured up to the value of such property and unsecured for the remainder. In this case, the FDIC's claim, totaling $1,945,000, is secured by the Debtor's sole asset, a residential and office complex. The value of the property, as agreed to by Debtor and the FDIC, is $1,445,000. Thus the FDIC has a secured claim in the amount of $1,445,000 and is entitled to an unsecured deficiency claim for the remaining $500,000. Under Section 1111(b)(2), a secured creditor may elect to have its entire mortgage claim treated as secured notwithstanding Section 506(a), thereby waiving its entitlement to an unsecured deficiency claim and increasing the amount of its secured claim. Here, however, the FDIC did not make such an election and the time to do so has expired.

In a typical single asset real estate case such as this, the mortgagee creditor often objects to the proposed plan, thereby requiring the debtor to seek cramdown of the Plan over the mortgagee creditor's objection. Here the Debtor took two approaches in an attempt to obtain a consenting class of "impaired" creditors. First, Debtor classified the FDIC's unsecured mortgage deficiency claim of $500,000 separately from unsecured trade claims, which total only $5,000. If the deficiency claim were classified together with the other unsecured claims, the FDIC's vote against the Plan would preclude acceptance by that class. This is so because the amount of the FDIC's deficiency claim is one hundred times the amount of all other unsecured claims, making it impossible for Debtor to obtain the affirmative vote of two-thirds in amount of such class as required by Section 1126(c) of the Bankruptcy Code. Debtor's second approach to obtaining a consenting class of "impaired" creditors was to create a purportedly impaired class of residential tenants who placed security deposits with Debtor (Class 3). The Plan provided that holders of such claims would receive interest on their security deposits at a rate of 8% rather than the 5¼% mandated by Connecticut state law. Debtor asserted that this "enhancement" of that class' claims constituted "impairment" within the meaning of Section 1124.

Debtor contended that the approval of each of classes 3 and 4 satisfied the requirement of consent of an impaired class. (The consent of classes 6 and 7, the general and limited partners, could not be counted because these were insider classes.) Both the Bankruptcy Court and the District Court held (i) classifying the FDIC's unsecured mortgage deficiency claim separately from the unsecured claims of trade creditors solely to create an assenting allegedly impaired class was impermissible; and (ii) the class of claims comprising residential tenants with security deposits was not properly classified as impaired, because the value of such claims was enhanced—not impaired—under Debtor's Plan. These rulings precluded Debtor from obtaining acceptance of its Plan by an impaired class of claims, and thereby precluded cramdown. Debtor challenges both holdings on appeal.

A. Separate classification of the several unsecured claims was without a legitimate reason.

Section 1122 of the Bankruptcy Code generally governs classification of claims:

> § 1122. Classification of claims or interests.
>
> (a) Except as provided in subsection (b) of this section, a plan may place a claim or an interest in a particular class only if such claim or interest is substantially similar to the other claims or interests of such class.
>
> (b) A plan may designate a separate class of claims consisting only of every unsecured claim that is less than or reduced to an amount that the court approves as reasonable and necessary for administrative convenience.

11 U.S.C. § 1122 (1993). While the section bars aggregating dissimilar claims in the same class, it does not explicitly address whether similar claims *must* be placed in the same class. This issue of the permissibility of

separate classification of similar types of claims is one that has yet to be addressed by the Second Circuit, and it remains a "hot topic" both among practitioners and in the academic community. *See* Peter E. Meltzer, *Disenfranchising the Dissenting Creditor Through Artificial Classification or Artificial Impairment*, 66 Am. Bankr. L.J. 281 (1992).

In addressing this question, the Bankruptcy and District Courts in the instant action were guided by the holdings of several other circuits, in decisions cited *infra*, that similar claims could not be placed in different classes solely to gerrymander a class that will assent to the plan. *See In re Boston Post Road Ltd. Partnership*, 145 B.R. 745, 748 (Bankr. D. Conn. 1992) ("The courts . . . have uniformly prohibited a debtor from classifying similar claims differently in order to gerrymander an affirmative vote in favor of a reorganization plan."); *In re Boston Post Road Ltd. Partnership*, 154 B.R. 617, 621 (D. Conn. 1993) ("classes may not be manipulated so as to gerrymander the voting process and circumvent the § 1129 requirements"). The other circuits have generally held that separate classification of similar claims is permissible only upon proof of a legitimate reason for separate classification, and that separate classification to gerrymander an affirmative vote is impermissible. *See, e.g., Phoenix Mut. Life Ins. Co. v. Greystone III Joint Venture (In re Greystone III)*, 995 F.2d 1274, 1279 (5th Cir. 1991), *cert. denied*, 506 U.S. 821, 113 S.Ct. 72, 121 L.Ed.2d 37 (1992) ("[T]hou shalt not classify similar claims differently in order to gerrymander an affirmative vote on a reorganization plan.").

Debtor contends that the Second Circuit should decline to follow the leads of the other circuits. It urges that Section 1122 be interpreted to permit far more liberal separate classification of similar claims. Debtor attempts to support its contentions with reference to recent judicial interpretations of Section 1122, legislative intent, and policy considerations.

Debtor first cites two recent opinions by bankruptcy judges holding that separate classification of similar claims is in fact mandated. *See In re D & W Realty Corp.*, 156 B.R. 140, 141 & n. 3 (Bankr. S.D.N.Y. 1993) (holding that "separate classification is not only appropriate, it is in fact mandated by the Bankruptcy Code and Rules," but acknowledging that it "has not found [this opinion] articulated anywhere else"), *rev'd*, 165 B.R. 127 (S.D.N.Y. 1994); *In re SM 104, Ltd.*, 160 B.R. 202, 218–19 (Bankr. S.D. Fla. 1993) (holding that unsecured deficiency claims created by § 1111(b) are not substantially similar to other unsecured claims, while asserting that the "circuit courts and the majority of district and bankruptcy courts have missed the forests for the trees").

Debtor then notes that the wording of Section 1122 does not require that all unsecured claims be classified together, but merely states that only claims that are substantially similar *may* be placed together. Debtor contends that this wording, especially when compared with the less flexible wording of the Bankruptcy Act of 1898, reflects Congress' intent to dispense with the requirement that similar claims be classified together.

Finally, Debtor contends that prohibiting separate classification effectively bars the debtor in single-asset cases from utilizing the cramdown provisions of the Code. In single-asset bankruptcy cases, the creditor-mortgagee usually has an unsecured deficiency claim, which, if placed in the class containing other unsecured claims (usually trade debt), will often overwhelm the class. Consequently, the mortgagee will control the vote of the class and the debtor will be unable to present an impaired class to approve the plan. Debtor suggests that such an outcome creates a "conflict of interest": the mortgage creditor will vote its deficiency claim primarily to protect its interests as a secured creditor, whereas only those creditors who have truly unsecured claims should be the spokespeople of the unsecured class.

Debtor's arguments in support of its suggested interpretation of § 1122 are unavailing. First, the ruling in *In re D & W Realty Corp.*, 156 B.R. 140 (Bankr. S.D.N.Y. 1993) was reversed on appeal. *In re D & W Realty Corp.*, 165 B.R. 127 (S.D.N.Y. 1994). The ruling in *In re SM 104 Ltd.*, 160 B.R. 202 (Bankr. S.D. Fla. 1993), runs counter to the overwhelming weight of judicial authority. All the circuit courts that have heretofore visited the question of when similar claims may be classified separately have held that similar claims may not be separately classified solely to engineer an assenting impaired class:

> [I]f § 1122(a) permits classification of "substantially similar" claims in different classes, such classification may only be undertaken for reasons independent of the debtor's motivation to secure the vote of an impaired, assenting class of claims. *Greystone III*, 995 F.2d 1274, 1279 (5th Cir. 1991), *cert. denied*, 506 U.S. 821, 113 S.Ct. 72, 121 L.Ed.2d 37 (1992);
>
> [A]lthough separate classification of similar claims may not be prohibited, it "may only be undertaken for reasons independent of the debtor's motivation to secure the vote of an impaired, assenting class of claims." *Travelers Ins. Co. v. Bryson Properties, XVIII (In re Bryson Properties, XVIII)*, 961 F.2d 496, 502 (4th Cir.) (quoting *Greystone III*, 995 F.2d at 1279), *cert. denied*, 506 U.S. 866, 113 S.Ct. 191, 121 L.Ed.2d 134 (1992);
>
> [I]f the classifications are designed to manipulate class voting . . . , the plan cannot be confirmed. *Olympia & York Florida Equity Corp. v. Bank of New York (In re Holywell Corp.)*, 913 F.2d 873, 880 (11th Cir. 1990);
>
> The debtor's discretion to place similar claims in different classes is not unlimited, however. Classifications designed to manipulate

> class voting must be carefully scrutinized. There is potential for abuse when the debtor has the power to classify creditors in a manner to assure that at least one class of impaired creditors will vote for the plan, thereby making it eligible for the cram down provisions. *Hanson v. First Bank of South Dakota, N.A.*, 828 F.2d 1310, 1313 (8th Cir. 1987);

> Unless there is some requirement of keeping similar claims together, nothing would stand in the way of a debtor seeking out a few impaired creditors (or even one such creditor) who will vote for the plan and placing them in their own class. *Teamsters Nat'l Freight Industry Negotiating Comm. v. U.S. Truck Co. (In re U.S. Truck Co.)*, 800 F.2d 581, 586 (6th Cir. 1986).

Indeed, some courts have gone even further, holding that a plan must classify all substantially similar claims together, regardless of the debtor's intent. *See Granada Wines, Inc. v. New England Teamsters and Trucking Indus. Pension Fund,* 748 F.2d 42, 46 (1st Cir. 1984).

The preeminent case on the question is *Greystone III*, a case whose facts are quite similar to those in the instant case before the court. In *Greystone III*, the Court of Appeals for the Fifth Circuit observed that although similar claims may be placed in different classes, a wholly permissive reading of the statute would render subsection (b) of § 1122, which specifically allows separate classification of small claims, superfluous. In widely quoted language, the Fifth Circuit concluded:

> [There is] one clear rule that emerges from otherwise muddled case law on § 1122 claims classification: thou shalt not classify similar claims differently in order to gerrymander an affirmative vote on a reorganization plan.

Greystone III, 995 F.2d at 1279.

Furthermore, contrary to Debtor's position, several courts have concluded that an analysis of legislative history in fact sheds little light onto the meaning of Section 1122. *See U.S. Truck*, 800 F.2d at 585–86 (concluding, after careful analysis of the classification sections of the former Bankruptcy Act and legislative history of Section 1122, that "Congress has sent mixed signals on the issue"); *In re Jersey City Medical Center*, 817 F.2d 1055, 1060 (3d Cir. 1987) (noting that "the legislative history behind § 1122 is inconclusive" regarding the significance of the wording of the section). Moreover, a reading of Section 1122 in the context of the rest of the Code suggests that discretionary separate classification of similar claims would undermine the Section 1111(b) election. As explained above, Section 1111(b) of the Bankruptcy Code permits an undersecured creditor to choose whether (i) its claim should be divided into a secured claim equal to the court-determined value of the collateral and an unsecured claim for the deficiency, or (ii) its entire claim should be considered secured. The purpose of the Section 1111(b) election is to allow the undersecured creditor to weigh in its vote with the votes of the other unsecured creditors. Allowing the unsecured trade creditors to constitute their own class would effectively nullify the option that Congress provided to undersecured creditors to vote their deficiency as unsecured debt.

Finally, approving a plan that aims to disenfranchise the overwhelmingly largest creditor through artificial classification is simply inconsistent with the principles underlying the Bankruptcy Code. A key premise of the Code is that creditors holding greater debt should have a comparably greater voice in reorganization. Thus, although Debtor protests that prohibiting it from separating the unsecured claims of the FDIC from those of its trade creditors will effectively bar single asset debtors from utilizing the Code's cramdown provisions, Debtor fails to persuade that a single-asset debtor *should* be able to cramdown a plan that is designed to disadvantage its overwhelmingly largest creditor. Chapter 11 is far better served by allowing those creditors with the largest unsecured claims to have a significant degree of input and participation in the reorganization process, since they stand to gain or lose the most from the reorganization of the debtor. This Court thus holds that separate classification of unsecured claims solely to create an impaired assenting class will not be permitted; the debtor must adduce credible proof of a legitimate reason for separate classification of similar claims.

In the instant case, Debtor was unable and failed to adduce credible proof of any legitimate reason for segregating the FDIC's unsecured claim from the unsecured claims of BPR's trade creditors. Debtor's reasons for why it should have been permitted to separately classify the FDIC's unsecured claim were: (1) the FDIC's and the trade creditors' unsecured claims were created from different circumstances and arise under different Bankruptcy Code sections; and (2) BPR's future viability as a business depends on treating its trade creditors more favorably than the FDIC. Neither is availing. The different origins of the FDIC's unsecured deficiency claim and general unsecured trade claims, claims which enjoy similar rights and privileges within the Bankruptcy Code, do not alone justify separate segregation. *See* Meltzer, *supra* at 299. More importantly, BPR has failed to present any evidence of a legitimate business reason for the separate classification of similarly situated unsecured creditor claimants. The trade creditors in Class 4 were few and consisted of a landscaper, property appraisers, rubbish removers, and accountants. None were essential to BPR's future. Both lower courts accordingly found an absence of a valid justification for the isolation of the FDIC deficiency claim. No evidence to the contrary was adduced.

B. The residential security holders are not a class entitled to vote on the Plan

Debtor classified the residential tenants whose security deposits it was holding as a separate and "impaired" class for the purposes of a cramdown under § 1129(a). In fact those interests were not harmed at all by the Plan, but are better off under the Plan. Under Connecticut law, residential security holders are entitled to interest on their security deposits at a rate of 5¼%. Conn. Gen. Stat. § 47a–21 (1993). Under the proposed Plan, the interest payable on security deposits held by the landlord was increased beyond the statutory rate to 8%.

Debtor urges that the word "impaired" in § 1124 be interpreted merely as "altered" or "changed" and contends that the Class 3 creditors' rights were certainly altered by the Plan. In support of its interpretation of § 1124, Debtor points first to the language of the statute, legislative history, and a recent Ninth Circuit opinion, *In re L & J Anaheim Assoc.*, 995 F.2d 940 (9th Cir. 1993), which allegedly adopted Debtor's interpretation of Section 1124.

This Court need not even reach the issue of whether an "altered" claim may qualify as "impaired." In this case, the Class 3 tenant security depositors could not constitute a voting class of creditors for purposes of effecting cramdown. Any claim for return of tenant security deposits would arise from the lease between the debtor and the tenant. Under the Bankruptcy Code, unexpired leases must be assumed or rejected by the Debtor. 11 U.S.C. § 365. When, as in the instant case, the Debtor does neither, the leases continue in effect and the lessees have no provable claim against the bankruptcy estate. *Greystone III*, 995 F.2d at 1281. The obligations assumed by the debtor under the continued leases constitute post-petition administrative claims. *See* 11 U.S.C. § 503(b)(1)(A). Such administrative claims are defined as priority claims under 11 U.S.C. § 507(a)(1), and must be paid in full in cash pursuant to 11 U.S.C. § 1129(a)(9)(A); their holders are not entitled to vote on a plan of reorganization. As the Fifth Circuit held in *Greystone III*:

> A debtor in Chapter 11 must either assume or reject its leases with third parties. 11 U.S.C. § 365. If the debtor does neither, the leases continue in effect and the lessees have no provable claim against the bankruptcy estate. *See Matter of Whitcomb & Keller Mortgage Co.*, 715 F.2d 375, 378–79 (7th Cir. 1983); *In re Cochise College Park, Inc.*, 703 F.2d 1339, 1352 (9th Cir. 1983). Under the Code, only creditors are entitled to vote on a plan of reorganization. *See* 11 U.S.C. § 1126(c). A party to a lease is considered a "creditor" who is allowed to vote, 11 U.S.C. § 1126(c), only when the party has a claim against the estate that arises from rejection of a lease. *In re Perdido Motel Group, Inc.*, 101 B.R.

> 289, 293–94 (Bankr. N.D. Ala. 1989). If, however, the debtor expressly assumes a lease, the lessee has no "claim" against the debtor under § 1126(a). *See* 11 U.S.C. § 365(g), 502(g). The rights created by assumption of the lease constitute a post-petition administrative claim under section 503(b)(1)(A) of the Code. *LJC Corp. v. Boyle*, 768 F.2d 1489, 1494 n. 6 (D.C. Cir. 1985). The holder of such a claim is not entitled to vote on a plan of reorganization. 11 U.S.C. § 1126(a); *In re Distrigas Corp.*, 66 B.R. 382, 385–86 (Bankr. D. Mass.1986).

Greystone III, 995 F.2d at 1281. *See also In re Cantonwood Assocs. Ltd. Partnership*, 138 B.R. 648, 656 (Bankr. D. Mass. 1992) (where Debtor neither assumes nor rejects leases, tenants' claims are post-petition administrative claims). Thus the Class 3 creditors' approval of the Plan was of no effect because its members were not entitled to vote on the Plan.

CONCLUSION

To summarize: Debtor's Plan of Reorganization was properly denied confirmation for lack of the assent of an impaired non-insider class of creditors. The unsecured trade creditors do not qualify as such a class; they were segregated without any demonstrated legitimate reason from like unsecured creditors, who rejected the Plan and whose claims predominated in amount over those of the trade creditors. Nor do residential security deposit holders qualify as such a class; as holders of administrative claims, they were not entitled to vote on the Plan of Reorganization.

Affirmed.

[footnotes omitted]

Turn again to section 1129. To cram down a secured creditor, the DIP must satisfy section 1129(b)(2)(A), excerpted below. Read the section carefully and consider its meaning and significance.

(A) With respect to a class of secured claims, the plan provides—

(i) (I) that the holders of such claims retain the liens securing such claims, whether the property subject to such liens is retained by the debtor or transferred to another entity, to the extent of the allowed amount of such claims; and

(II) that each holder of a claim of such class receive on account of such claim deferred cash payments totaling at least the allowed amount of such claim, of a value, as of the effective date of the plan, of at least the value of such holder's interest in the estate's interest in such property;

(ii) for the sale, subject to section 363(k) of this title, of any property that is subject to the liens securing such claims, free and clear of such liens, with such liens to attach to the proceeds of such sale, and the treatment of such liens on proceeds under clause (i) or (iii) of this subparagraph; or

(iii) for the realization by such holders of the indubitable equivalent of such claims.

RADLAX GATEWAY HOTEL, LLC V. AMALGAMATED BANK

United States Supreme Court, 2012.
566 U.S. 639.

JUSTICE SCALIA delivered the opinion of the Court.

We consider whether a Chapter 11 bankruptcy plan may be confirmed over the objection of a secured creditor pursuant to 11 U.S.C. § 1129(b)(2)(A) if the plan provides for the sale of collateral free and clear of the creditor's lien, but does not permit the creditor to "credit-bid" at the sale.

I

In 2007, petitioners RadLAX Gateway Hotel, LLC, and RadLAX Gateway Deck, LLC (hereinafter debtors), purchased the Radisson Hotel at Los Angeles International Airport, together with an adjacent lot on which the debtors planned to build a parking structure. To finance the purchase, the renovation of the hotel, and construction of the parking structure, the debtors obtained a $142 million loan from Longview Ultra Construction Loan Investment Fund, for which respondent Amalgamated Bank (hereinafter creditor or Bank) serves as trustee. The lenders obtained a blanket lien on all of the debtors' assets to secure the loan.

Completing the parking structure proved more expensive than anticipated, and within two years the debtors had run out of funds and were forced to halt construction. By August 2009, they owed more than $120 million on the loan, with over $1 million in interest accruing every month and no prospect for obtaining additional funds to complete the project. Both debtors filed voluntary petitions for relief under Chapter 11 of the Bankruptcy Code.

A Chapter 11 bankruptcy is implemented according to a "plan," typically proposed by the debtor, which divides claims against the debtor into separate "classes" and specifies the treatment each class will receive. *See* 11 U.S.C. § 1123. Generally, a bankruptcy court may confirm a Chapter 11 plan only if each class of creditors affected by the plan consents. *See* § 1129(a)(8). Section 1129(b) creates an exception to that general rule, permitting confirmation of nonconsensual plans—commonly known as "cramdown" plans—if "the plan does not discriminate unfairly, and is fair and equitable, with respect to each class of claims or interests that is impaired under, and has not accepted, the plan." Section 1129(b)(2)(A), which we review in further depth below, establishes criteria for determining whether a cramdown plan is "fair and equitable" with respect to secured claims like the Bank's.

In 2010, the RadLAX debtors submitted a Chapter 11 plan to the United States Bankruptcy Court for the Northern District of Illinois. The plan proposed to dissolve the debtors and to sell substantially all of their assets pursuant to procedures set out in a contemporaneously filed "Sale and Bid Procedures Motion." Specifically, the debtors sought to auction their assets to the highest bidder, with the initial bid submitted by a "stalking horse"—a potential purchaser who was willing to make an advance bid of $47.5 million. The sale proceeds would be used to fund the plan, primarily by repaying the Bank. Of course the Bank itself might wish to obtain the property if the alternative would be receiving auction proceeds that fall short of the property's full value. Under the debtors' proposed auction procedures, however, the Bank would not be permitted to bid for the property using the debt it is owed to offset the purchase price, a practice known as "credit-bidding." Instead, the Bank would be forced to bid cash. Correctly anticipating that the Bank would object to this arrangement, the debtors sought to confirm their plan under the cramdown provisions of § 1129(b)(2)(A).

The Bankruptcy Court denied the debtors' Sale and Bid Procedures Motion, concluding that the proposed auction procedures did not comply with § 1129(b)(2)(A)'s requirements for cramdown plans. *In re River Road Hotel Partners, LLC*, Case No. 09 B 30029 (ND Ill., Oct. 5, 2010), App. to Pet. for Cert. 40a. The Bankruptcy Court certified an appeal directly to the United States Court of Appeals for the Seventh Circuit. That court accepted the certification and affirmed, holding that § 1129(b)(2)(A) does not permit debtors to sell an encumbered asset free and clear of a lien without permitting the lienholder to credit-bid. *River Road Hotel Partners, LLC, et al. v. Amalgamated Bank*, 651 F. 3d 642 (2011). We granted certiorari. 565 U.S. ___ (2011).

II

A

A Chapter 11 plan confirmed over the objection of a "class of secured claims" must meet one of three requirements in order to be deemed "fair and equitable" with respect to the nonconsenting creditor's claim. The plan must provide:

> "(i)(I) that the holders of such claims retain the liens securing such claims, whether the property subject to such liens is retained by the debtor or transferred to another entity, to the extent of the allowed amount of such claims; and (II) that each holder of a claim

of such class receive on account of such claim deferred cash payments totaling at least the allowed amount of such claim, of a value, as of the effective date of the plan, of at least the value of such holder's interest in the estate's interest in such property;

"(ii) for the sale, subject to section 363(k) of this title, of any property that is subject to the liens securing such claims, free and clear of such liens, with such liens to attach to the proceeds of such sale, and the treatment of such liens on proceeds under clause (i) or (iii) of this subparagraph; or

"(iii) for the realization by such holders of the indubitable equivalent of such claims." 11 U.S.C. § 1129(b)(2)(A).

Under clause (i), the secured creditor retains its lien on the property and receives deferred cash payments. Under clause (ii), the property is sold free and clear of the lien, "subject to section 363(k)," and the creditor receives a lien on the proceeds of the sale. Section 363(k), in turn, provides that "unless the court for cause orders otherwise the holder of such claim may bid at such sale, and, if the holder of such claim purchases such property, such holder may offset such claim against the purchase price of such property"—*i.e.*, the creditor may credit-bid at the sale, up to the amount of its claim.[2] Finally, under clause (iii), the plan provides the secured creditor with the "indubitable equivalent" of its claim.

The debtors in this case have proposed to sell their property free and clear of the Bank's liens, and to repay the Bank using the sale proceeds—precisely, it would seem, the disposition contemplated by clause (ii). Yet since the debtors' proposed auction procedures do not permit the Bank to credit-bid, the proposed sale cannot satisfy the requirements of clause (ii).[3] Recognizing this problem, the debtors instead seek plan confirmation pursuant to clause (iii), which—unlike clause (ii)—does not expressly foreclose the possibility of a sale without credit-bidding. According to the debtors, their plan can satisfy clause (iii) by ultimately providing the Bank with the "indubitable equivalent" of its secured claim, in the form of cash generated by the auction.

We find the debtors' reading of § 1129(b)(2)(A)—under which clause (iii) permits precisely what clause (ii) proscribes—to be hyperliteral and contrary to common sense. A well established canon of statutory

---

[2] The ability to credit-bid helps to protect a creditor against the risk that its collateral will be sold at a depressed price. It enables the creditor to purchase the collateral for what it considers the fair market price (up to the amount of its security interest) without committing additional cash to protect the loan. That right is particularly important for the Federal Government, which is frequently a secured creditor in bankruptcy and which often lacks appropriations authority to throw good money after bad in a cash-only bankruptcy auction.

[3] Title 11 U.S.C. § 363(k)—and by extension clause (ii)—provides an exception to the credit-bidding requirement if "the court for cause orders otherwise." The Bankruptcy Court found that there was no "cause" to deny credit-bidding in this case, and the debtors have not appealed that disposition.

interpretation succinctly captures the problem: "[I]t is a commonplace of statutory construction that the specific governs the general." *Morales v. Trans World Airlines, Inc.*, 504 U.S. 374, 384 (1992). That is particularly true where, as in § 1129(b)(2)(A), "Congress has enacted a comprehensive scheme and has deliberately targeted specific problems with specific solutions." *Varity Corp. v. Howe*, 516 U.S. 489, 519 (1996) (THOMAS, J., dissenting); *see also HCSC-Laundry v. United States*, 450 U.S. 1, 6 (1981) (per curiam) (the specific governs the general "particularly when the two are interrelated and closely positioned, both in fact being parts of [the same statutory scheme]").

The general/specific canon is perhaps most frequently applied to statutes in which a general permission or prohibition is contradicted by a specific prohibition or permission. To eliminate the contradiction, the specific provision is construed as an exception to the general one. *See, e.g., Morton v. Mancari*, 417 U.S. 535, 550–551 (1974). But the canon has full application as well to statutes such as the one here, in which a general authorization and a more limited, specific authorization exist side-by-side. There the canon avoids not contradiction but the superfluity of a specific provision that is swallowed by the general one, "violat[ing] the cardinal rule that, if possible, effect shall be given to every clause and part of a statute." *D. Ginsberg & Sons, Inc. v. Popkin*, 285 U.S. 204, 208 (1932). The terms of the specific authorization must be complied with. For example, in the last cited case a provision of the Bankruptcy Act prescribed in great detail the procedures governing the arrest and detention of bankrupts about to leave the district in order to avoid examination. The Court held that those prescriptions could not be avoided by relying upon a general provision of the Act authorizing bankruptcy courts to " 'make such orders, issue such process, and enter such judgments in addition to those specifically provided for as may be necessary for the enforcement of the provisions of [the] Act.' " *Id.*, at 206 (quoting Bankruptcy Act of 1898, § 2(15), 30 Stat. 546). The Court said that "[g]eneral language of a statutory provision, although broad enough to include it, will not be held to apply to a matter specifically dealt with in another part of the same enactment." 285 U.S., at 208. We recently quoted that language approvingly in *Bloate v. United States*, 559 U.S. ___, ___ (2010) (*slip op.*, at 10). Or as we said in a much earlier case:

> "It is an old and familiar rule that, where there is, in the same statute, a particular enactment, and also a general one, which, in its most comprehensive sense, would include what is embraced in the former, the particular enactment must be operative, and the general enactment must be taken to affect only such cases within its general language as are not within the provisions of the particular enactment. This rule applies wherever an act contains general provisions and also special ones upon a subject, which,

> standing alone, the general provisions would include." *United States v. Chase*, 135 U.S. 255, 260 (1890) (citations and internal quotation marks omitted).

Here, clause (ii) is a detailed provision that spells out the requirements for selling collateral free of liens, while clause (iii) is a broadly worded provision that says nothing about such a sale. The general/specific canon explains that the "general language" of clause (iii), "although broad enough to include it, will not be held to apply to a matter specifically dealt with" in clause (ii). *D. Ginsberg & Sons, Inc., supra,* at 208.

Of course the general/specific canon is not an absolute rule, but is merely a strong indication of statutory meaning that can be overcome by textual indications that point in the other direction. The debtors point to no such indication here. One can conceive of a statutory scheme in which the specific provision embraced within a general one is not superfluous, because it creates a so-called safe harbor. The debtors effectively contend that that is the case here—clause (iii) ("indubitable equivalent") being the general rule, and clauses (i) and (ii) setting forth procedures that will always, *ipso facto*, establish an "indubitable equivalent," with no need for judicial evaluation. But the structure here would be a surpassingly strange manner of accomplishing that result—which would normally be achieved by setting forth the "indubitable equivalent" rule first (rather than last), and establishing the two safe harbors as provisos to that rule. The structure here suggests, to the contrary, that (i) is the rule for plans under which the creditor's lien remains on the property, (ii) is the rule for plans under which the property is sold free and clear of the creditor's lien, and (iii) is a residual provision covering dispositions under all other plans—for example, one under which the creditor receives the property itself, the "indubitable equivalent" of its secured claim. Thus, debtors may not sell their property free of liens under § 1129(b)(2)(A) without allowing lienholders to credit-bid, as required by clause (ii).

* * *

It is so ordered.

[some footnotes omitted]

PROBLEM 3-11

Assume Bank holds a perfected security interest in twenty items of machinery of the bankrupt Company. The machines are each worth between $10 million and $15 million; Bank's debt is $500 million. Which of the following plans could be approved under section 1129(b) over the objection of Bank?

1. A plan that continues Bank's security in the twenty machines, which will be used by the reorganized Company. As part of the plan, the new

Company will promise to pay Bank $200 million over 10 years, with 10% interest. (It would be relevant whether the prime rate was 7% or 12%. Why?)

2. A plan to sell the machines over a two-month period and remit the proceeds to the Bank. (Assume that such a sale would probably bring $9 to $10 million per machine.)

3. A plan to give the Bank 49% of the stock of the new company. (Assume the DIP's investment bankers will testify that half of the reorganized company will be worth at least $300 million.)

CHAPTER 4

SECURITY IN INVENTORY, FARM PRODUCTS, AND THEIR PROCEEDS

■ ■ ■

§ 1. INTRODUCTION

As we have seen, "inventory" is one of the four main types of goods ("equipment," "inventory," "farm products," and "consumer goods"). It is defined in section 9–102(a)(48) to mean "goods, other than farm products, which: (A) are leased by a person as lessor; (B) are held by a person for sale or lease or to be furnished under a contract of service; (C) are furnished by a person under a contract of service; or (D) consist of raw materials, work in process, or materials used or consumed in a business." The term "farm products," a category like inventory but treated differently in some respects, is defined in section 9–102(a)(34) to mean "goods, other than standing timber, with respect to which the debtor is engaged in a farming operation and which are: . . . crops . . .; livestock . . .; supplies used or produced in a farming operation; or products of crops or livestock in their unmanufactured states." *See also* 9–102(a)(35) (defining "farming operation").

Some things that seem intuitively to be inventory fall neatly within the definition provided in section 9–102(a)(48), such as the merchant's stock in trade that she displays for sale on her shelves; the automobiles a car dealer offers for sale or lease on her showroom floor; and the completed items a manufacturing company holds in its warehouse awaiting sale and shipment to its retail customers. Other things fit clearly but less intuitively: the leather a shoemaker uses to make custom shoes; the stones a mason uses to construct walls; and the fabric a tailor keeps on hand to make custom suits. Still other things straddle the line between inventory and equipment.

Suppose, for example, a debtor manufactures custom precision machinery. For most of the machines it makes, it uses a specialized drill with an expensive, reusable bit that costs $100,000. The debtor uses this bit to make hundreds of machines over the course of several years. Is the bit equipment or inventory? It is almost certainly equipment. In contrast, for one special type of machine the debtor makes, it uses a different drill bit that also costs $100,000 but can be used only once. In other words, the drill bit is consumed entirely in the manufacture of just one machine. Is this second drill bit equipment or inventory? It is probably inventory. *See* 9–102 cmt. 4(a). So, if you are a secured creditor taking a security interest in the debtor's expensive drill bits that it keeps on hand, how would you describe the collateral?

In general, a debtor may obtain financing to acquire inventory in one of several ways. It may buy merchandise on credit from trade suppliers. In addition, it may borrow money from a bank or finance company to pay for its inventory purchases. Inventory financing transactions with banks and finance companies are typically structured as "revolving" lines of credit. Unlike a term loan, a revolving line of credit is available for multiple advances and repayments: the debtor borrows over time what it needs as it needs it (subject to any applicable borrowing limits), and pays down the debt periodically from the proceeds of its inventory sales and other income. The inventory financer will typically want a security interest in both the debtor's inventory and the "proceeds" from the sale of the debtor's inventory.

But what are "proceeds"? Proceeds are whatever the debtor receives on the sale or other disposition of the collateral. *See* 9–102(a)(64). In the case of a car dealer who has granted a security interest in its inventory of cars, the proceeds are the personal checks, cashier's checks, other funds transfers, or the notes and security agreements the car dealer gets back when it sells the cars to buyers. In the case of a department store, the proceeds are likely to be not only cash and checks, but also payment obligations on a credit card issued by the store or a bank that customers use to make purchases. The inventory financer who has extended a revolving line of credit to the debtor to finance the debtor's acquisition of inventory will want a lien on the proceeds from the sale of the inventory because that typically will be the financer's source of repayment.

As the foregoing suggests, taking security in inventory and its proceeds is far more complex than taking security in business equipment. In the first place, inventory typically changes every day a business is open, and money is collected on the sale of inventory all the time. The proceeds of sales will often be paid to the lender to reduce the loan, and the loan will then be increased when the debtor has to buy new inventory. Thus, the security agreement must take into account the fact that there will be "future advances" (new extensions of credit), and that much of the collateral will be "after-acquired" (namely, acquired by the debtor after it initially grants a security interest to the secured lender). *See* 9–204. This kind of claim against the debtor's assets is sometimes called a "floating lien" because it floats on top of a river of inventory and proceeds.

Life is further complicated by the fact that some lenders lend against inventory, and others lend against promises of payment (such as "accounts" and "instruments") the debtor receives from its customers. Indeed, a common form of financing is "accounts receivable" financing, whereby a lender extends a revolving line of credit to the debtor secured by the debtor's "accounts" (*e.g.*, the debtor's rights to payment from customers to whom it has sold goods but have yet to pay for them). Sometimes promises of payment are embodied in notes and other security agreements that are called "chattel paper." (Accounts, instruments, and chattel paper are taken up in greater detail in Chapter 5.) So, there is a potential conflict in many cases between (a) one secured creditor's claim to proceeds collateral (such as accounts) arising from the disposition of the secured creditor's original collateral (such as inventory), and (b) a second secured creditor's claim to the same collateral (the accounts) as its original collateral (because it took a security interest in the accounts directly). To accommodate all of this, the security agreement typically is quite complicated, for it has to cover not only proceeds, the original collateral and the original loan, but also new loans, after-acquired property, and proceeds derived months or years after the initial loan. In addition, the law is quite complicated, for it must supply a set of rules that sort and rank the various interests of the competing parties in the different kinds of property at issue. It is here that one begins truly to appreciate the claim made at the beginning of Chapter 1—that Article 9 encompasses the most complex and diverse collection of property rights concepts within our legal system.

Life is even more complicated by the fact that some persons deliver goods to the debtor to sell on "consignment." What is a consignment? Article 9 has a technical definition that is narrower than the common understanding of the concept. *Compare* 9–102(a)(20) *with* 2–326. In general, however, a consignment is a transaction in which the owner of the goods (the "consignor") delivers them to the debtor (also called the "consignee") so the debtor may sell them to a third party with the understanding that the debtor has no obligation to pay the consignor for the goods unless and until the debtor sells them. *See* 9–102(a)(28) (defining the term "debtor" to include a "consignee"). And if the debtor does not sell the consigned goods within the agreed time, the debtor then returns the goods to the consignor. This is a common structure for transactions in clothing, books, and diamonds. Of course, in the debtor's hands consigned goods may look and behave just like inventory, unless the debtor posts signs or otherwise publicly broadcasts that it is selling the goods of others on consignment. Absent such publicity, doesn't the consignor's interest seem like a secret lien? Article 9 treats consignments in this way, and compels the consignor to file a financing statement (provided the consignment falls within the scope of Article 9). *See* 9–109 cmt. 6. Now we have another potential conflict: that of the secured lender with a security interest in the debtor's inventory, and a consignor with an interest in consigned goods that effectively function as the debtor's inventory.

To render things still more challenging, we must distinguish Article 9 "consignments" from "bailments." What is a bailment? Article 9 does not define the term, but essentially it is a transaction whereby a person delivers possession of an item to the debtor for a particular purpose (for example, delivers a car to a mechanic to repair it) and without authorizing the debtor to sell the item (or do anything else but perform the agreed-upon task, such as make repairs, and then return the item to the person who delivered it to the debtor). In general, a bailment does not give the debtor sufficient rights in the item for a security interest to attach. *See* 9–203 cmt. 6, 9–330 cmt. 10(a)(1). On the other hand, an unperfected consignment does give the debtor sufficient, meaningful rights. *See* 9–319 cmt. 2. We will deal with consignments and bailments in Section 6. *See also* 2–403 (addressing "entrusting").

In this chapter we also address a special form of security interest—a purchase-money security interest. *See* 9–103. The purchase-money security interest might occur, for example, when a second-in-time creditor, usually a seller, offers to finance a new line of merchandise for the merchant debtor. If that secured creditor complies with certain conditions, it can have priority over the earlier perfected secured creditor, despite the fact that it comes much later. *See* 9–324. There are complexities in defining what is purchase-money, understanding the priority rules, and understanding the conditions that have to be satisfied for a secured creditor to hold purchase-money status.

It will not surprise you to know that buyers of inventory typically take free of a secured creditor's interest even if that interest in the inventory is perfected. *See* 9–320. When you last bought something at Macy's, Nordstrom, or some other store, did you inspect the filings at the Secretary of State's office to determine whether there was a perfected security interest that would prevail over your claim of ownership? No. Section 9–320 allows a "buyer in ordinary course of business" to take free of even a perfected security interest in inventory. Note that the definition of "buyer in ordinary course of business" is in Article 1, not Article 9. *See* 1–201(b)(9). Note also that buyers in ordinary course do not include those who buy the debtor's inventory in bulk.

By its terms, section 9–320 does not apply to a person buying farm products from a person engaged in farming operations. So for the purposes of Article 9, when you purchase a bag of apples from the roadside fruit stand of a local grower, they will remain encumbered with the security interest the grower might have granted to her creditor. Of course, it is highly implausible that the creditor would ever appear on your doorstep to repossess the apples just before you consume them. But there are instances in which purchasers of more valuable forms of farm products, such as livestock, might have cause for concern. Federal law steps into the breach here, with a complex set of provisions discussed in Section 8 of this chapter.

SECURED TRANSACTION DOCUMENTATION

Before turning to an in-depth study of the rules governing security interests in inventory and proceeds, purchase money security interests, and consignments, it is important that students of Article 9 have a sense of what a security agreement actually looks like.

In complex secured transactions the parties may negotiate a variety of documents in addition to the security agreement. Logically, the terms of the security agreement focus on the grant of a security interest, the identity of the collateral, the creditor's rights against the collateral upon the debtor's default, and various other provisions concerning the collateral and the parties' respective rights and obligations therewith. In addition to a security agreement, the parties may negotiate a separate "commercial finance agreement" (labelled as such, or alternatively some variation of "loan agreement," "note purchase agreement," or "financing agreement") that focuses more specifically on the terms of the credit arrangement between the parties (*e.g.*, governing the terms of any line of credit supplied by the secured party). The commercial finance agreement may contain all kinds of covenants, such as those governing the relevant interest rate being charged, the repayment terms, and the debtor's (or other obligor's) eligibility to borrow under the line of credit. In addition to a commercial finance agreement, the debtor (or other obligor) will almost certainly be required to execute a note evidencing the indebtedness owed. There may also be guarantees by other parties and perhaps even an intercreditor agreement between the secured party and one or more of the debtor's other creditors. These documents can be quite complex and interact with the security agreement in complex ways.

Lenders making secured loans of significant size often require, as a condition to closing the deal, that counsel for the debtor issue an opinion letter in favor of the secured party and its assignees, attesting to the enforceability and perfection of the security interest the transaction creates. "Opinions practice," as it is known, is central to the lives of transactional lawyers, especially those who work with Article 9. While these letters often contain ample qualifications and exceptions, in essence they require debtor's counsel to take responsibility for establishing that their client's assignment of a security interest will constitute an enforceable interest under section 9–203 and that the interest will be perfected as intended under the relevant Article 9 provisions. While a lender may request an opinion as to priority as well, a prudent attorney for the debtor will not render such an opinion and will expressly limit the opinion's scope to matters of attachment and perfection. Can you speculate as to why? Opinion letters may enhance the value of a transaction, especially if the secured party intends to assign its interest after closing. There is much for new lawyers to learn about rendering "closing opinions" or "third-party opinions," as they are often called. The objective, here, is simply to make students of Article 9 aware of this practice. In negotiating and structuring a secured transaction, attorneys must keep the provisions of Article 9 close at hand, as they may be required to attest to the transaction's compliance with the statute's requirements.

In contrast, in a comparatively simple consumer financing transaction, the documentation is more streamlined. The security agreement may be included as part of a single document called a "consumer finance agreement," "retail installment contract," or some variation thereof. The consumer finance agreement may include within its four corners all the lending and security terms between the parties, including such details as the amount of the relevant debt, the relevant interest rate, the grant of a security interest, a description of the collateral, and the secured party's rights upon the debtor's default. Various other laws may regulate the content and format of the consumer finance agreement. (These are addressed in Chapter 7.)

Consider the following example of a security agreement that an inventory lender might ask its debtor to sign. This agreement refers to both a debtor and a borrower to allow for the possibility of an obligor distinct from the debtor. However, the borrower and the debtor will typically be the same.

Security Agreement

(All Assets)

For value received, DEBTOR, INC. ("Debtor") grants to LENDER, INC, a Michigan banking corporation ("Bank"), a continuing security interest and lien (any pledge, assignment, security interest or other lien arising hereunder is sometimes referred to herein as a "security interest") in the Collateral (as defined below) to secure payment when due, whether by stated maturity, demand, acceleration or otherwise, of all existing and future indebtedness ("Indebtedness") to the Bank of "Borrower" and/or Debtor. Indebtedness includes without limit any and all obligations or liabilities of the Borrower and/or Debtor to the Bank, whether absolute or contingent, direct or indirect, voluntary or involuntary, liquidated or unliquidated, joint or several, known or unknown; any and all obligations or liabilities for which the Borrower and/or Debtor would otherwise be liable to the Bank were it not for the invalidity or unenforceability of them by reason of any bankruptcy, insolvency, or other law, or for any other reason; any and all amendments, modifications, renewals, and/or extensions of any of the above; all costs incurred by Bank in establishing, determining, continuing, or defending the validity or priority of its security interest, or in pursuing its rights and remedies under this Agreement or under any other agreement between Bank and Borrower and/or Debtor or in connection with any proceeding involving Bank as a result of any financial accommodation to Borrower and/or Debtor; and all other costs of collecting Indebtedness, including without limit attorney fees. Debtor agrees to pay Bank all such costs incurred by Bank, immediately upon demand, and until paid all costs shall bear interest at the highest per annum rate applicable to any of the Indebtedness, but not in excess of the maximum rate permitted by law. Any reference in this Agreement to attorney fees shall be deemed a reference to reasonable fees, costs, and expenses of both in-house and outside counsel and paralegals, whether or not a suit or action is instituted, and to court costs if a suit or action is instituted, and whether attorney fees or court costs are incurred at the trial court level, on appeal, in a bankruptcy, administrative, or probate proceeding or otherwise. Debtor further covenants, agrees and represents as follows:

1. Collateral shall mean all of the following property Debtor now or later owns or has an interest in, wherever located:

(a) all Accounts Receivable (for purposes of this Agreement, "Accounts Receivable" consists of all accounts; general intangibles; chattel paper (including without limit electronic chattel paper and tangible chattel paper); contract rights; deposit accounts; documents; instruments; rights to payment evidenced by chattel paper, documents or instruments; health care insurance receivables; commercial tort claims; letters of credit; letter of credit rights; supporting obligations; and rights to payment for money or funds advanced or sold),

(b) all Inventory,

(c) all Equipment and Fixtures,

(d) all Software (for purposes of this Agreement, "Software" consists of all (i) computer programs and supporting information provided in connection with a transaction relating to the program, and (ii) computer programs embedded in goods and any supporting information provided in connection with a transaction relating to the program whether or not the program is associated with the goods in such a manner that it customarily is considered part of the goods, and whether or not, by becoming the owner of the goods, a person acquires a right to use the program in connection with the goods, and whether or not the program is embedded in goods that consist solely of the medium in which the program is embedded),

(e) specific items listed below and/or on attached Schedule A, if any, is/are also included in Collateral:

____

____

(f) all goods, instruments, documents, policies and certificates of insurance, deposits, money, investment property, or other property (except real property which is not a fixture) which are now or later in possession or control of Bank, or as to which Bank now or later controls possession by documents or otherwise, and

(g) all additions, attachments, accessions, parts, replacements, substitutions, renewals, interest, dividends, distributions, rights of any kind (including but not limited to stock splits, stock rights, voting and preferential rights), products, and proceeds of or pertaining to the above including, without limit, cash or other property which were proceeds and are recovered by a bankruptcy trustee or otherwise as a preferential transfer by Debtor.

In the definition of Collateral, a reference to a type of collateral shall not be limited by a separate reference to a more specific or narrower type of that collateral.

2. Warranties, Covenants and Agreements. Debtor warrants, covenants and agrees as follows:

2.1 Debtor shall furnish to Bank, in form and at intervals as Bank may request, any information Bank may reasonably request and allow Bank to examine, inspect, and copy any of Debtor's books and records. Debtor shall, at the request of Bank, mark its records and the Collateral to clearly indicate the security interest of Bank under this Agreement.

2.2 At the time any Collateral becomes, or is represented to be, subject to a security interest in favor of Bank, Debtor shall be deemed to have warranted that (a) Debtor is the lawful owner of the Collateral and has the right and authority to subject it to a security interest granted to Bank; (b) none of the Collateral is subject to any security interest other than that in favor of Bank; (c) there are no financing statements on file, other than in favor of Bank; (d) no person, other than Bank, has possession or control (as defined in the Uniform Commercial Code) of any Collateral of such nature that perfection of a security interest may be accomplished by control; and (e) Debtor acquired its rights in the Collateral in the ordinary course of its business.

2.3 Debtor will keep the Collateral free at all times from all claims, liens, security interests and encumbrances other than those in favor of Bank. Debtor will not, without the prior written consent of Bank, sell, transfer or lease, or permit to be sold, transferred or leased, any or all of the Collateral, except for Inventory in the ordinary course of its business and will not return any Inventory to its supplier. Bank or its representatives may at all reasonable times inspect the Collateral and may enter upon all premises where the Collateral is kept or might be located.

2.4 Debtor will do all acts and will execute or cause to be executed all writings requested by Bank to establish, maintain and continue an exclusive, perfected and first security interest of Bank in the Collateral. Debtor agrees that Bank has no obligation to acquire or perfect any lien on or security interest in any asset(s), whether realty or personalty, to secure payment of the Indebtedness, and Debtor is not relying upon assets in which Bank may have a lien or security interest for payment of the Indebtedness.

2.5 Debtor will pay within the time that they can be paid without interest or penalty all taxes, assessments, and similar charges which at any time are or may become a lien, charge, or encumbrance upon any Collateral, except to the extent contested in good faith and bonded in a manner satisfactory to Bank. If Debtor fails to pay any of these taxes, assessments, or other charges in the time provided above, Bank has the option (but not the obligation) to do so and Debtor agrees to repay all amounts so expended by Bank immediately upon demand, together with interest at the highest lawful default rate which could be charged by Bank on any Indebtedness.

2.6 Debtor will keep the Collateral in good condition and will protect it from loss, damage, or deterioration from any cause. Debtor has and will maintain at all times (a) with respect to the Collateral, insurance under an "all risk" policy against fire and other risks customarily insured against, and (b) public liability insurance and other insurance as may be required by law or reasonably required by Bank, all of which insurance shall be in amount, form, and content, and written by companies as may be satisfactory to Bank, containing a lender's loss payable endorsement acceptable to Bank. Debtor will deliver to Bank immediately upon demand evidence satisfactory to Bank that the required insurance has been procured. If Debtor fails to maintain satisfactory insurance, Bank has the option (but not the obligation) to do so, and Debtor agrees to repay all amounts so expended by Bank immediately upon demand, together with interest at the highest lawful default rate which could be charged by Bank on any Indebtedness.

2.7 On each occasion on which Debtor evidences to Bank the account balances on and the nature and extent of the Accounts Receivable, Debtor shall be deemed to have warranted that except as otherwise indicated (a) each of those Accounts Receivable is valid and enforceable without performance by Debtor of any act; (b) each of those account balances are in fact owing, (c) there are no setoffs, recoupments, credits, contra accounts, counterclaims, or defenses against any of those Accounts Receivable, (d) as to any Accounts Receivable represented by a note, trade acceptance, draft or other instrument or by any chattel paper or document, the same have been endorsed and/or delivered by Debtor to Bank, (e) Debtor has not received with respect to any Account Receivable, any notice of the death of the related account debtor, nor of the dissolution, liquidation, termination of existence, insolvency, business failure, appointment of a receiver for, assignment for the benefit of creditors by, or filing of a petition in bankruptcy by or against, the account debtor, and (f) as to each Account Receivable, except as may be expressly permitted by Bank to the contrary in another document, the account debtor is not an affiliate of Debtor, the United States of America or any department, agency or instrumentality of it, or a citizen or resident of any jurisdiction outside of the United States. Debtor will do all acts and will execute all writings requested by Bank to perform, enforce performance of, and collect all Accounts Receivable. Debtor shall neither make nor permit any modification, compromise or substitution for any Account Receivable without the prior written consent of Bank. Debtor shall, at Bank's request, arrange for verification of Accounts Receivable directly with account debtors or by other methods acceptable to Bank.

2.8 Debtor at all times shall be in strict compliance with all applicable laws, including without limit any laws, ordinances, directives, orders, statutes, or regulations an object of which is to regulate or improve health, safety, or the environment ("Environmental Laws").

2.9 If Bank, acting in its sole discretion, redelivers Collateral to Debtor or Debtor's designee for the purpose of (a) the ultimate sale or exchange thereof; or (b) presentation, collection, renewal, or registration of transfer thereof; or (c) loading, unloading, storing, shipping, transshipping, manufacturing, processing or otherwise dealing with it preliminary to sale or exchange; such redelivery shall be in trust for the benefit of Bank and shall not constitute a release of Bank's security interest in it or in the proceeds or products of it unless Bank specifically so agrees in writing. If Debtor requests any such redelivery, Debtor will deliver with such request a duly executed financing statement in form and substance satisfactory to Bank. Any proceeds of Collateral coming into Debtor's possession as a result of any such redelivery shall be held in trust for Bank and immediately delivered to Bank for application on the Indebtedness. Bank may (in its sole discretion) deliver any or all of the Collateral to Debtor, and such delivery by Bank shall discharge Bank from all liability or responsibility for such Collateral. Bank, at its option, may require delivery of any Collateral to Bank at any time with such endorsements or assignments of the Collateral as Bank may request.

2.10 At any time and without notice, Bank may (a) cause any or all of the Collateral to be transferred to its name or to the name of its nominees; (b) receive or collect by legal proceedings or otherwise all dividends, interest, principal payments, and other sums and all other distributions at any time payable or receivable on account of the Collateral, and hold the same as Collateral, or apply the same to the Indebtedness, the manner and distribution of the application to be in the sole discretion of Bank; (c) enter into any extension, subordination, reorganization, deposit, merger or consolidation agreement or any other agreement relating to or affecting the Collateral, and deposit or surrender control of the Collateral, and accept other property in exchange for the Collateral and hold or apply the property or money so received pursuant to this Agreement; and (d) take such actions in its own name or in Debtor's name as Bank, in its sole discretion, deems necessary or appropriate to establish exclusive control (as defined in the Uniform Commercial Code) over any Collateral of such nature that perfection of Bank's security interest may be accomplished by control.

2.11 Bank may assign any of the Indebtedness and deliver any or all of the Collateral to its assignee, who then shall have with respect to Collateral so delivered all the rights and powers of Bank under this Agreement, and after that Bank shall be fully discharged from all liability and responsibility with respect to Collateral so delivered.

2.12 Debtor delivers this Agreement based solely on Debtor's independent investigation of (or decision not to investigate) the financial condition of Borrower and is not relying on any information furnished by Bank. Debtor assumes full responsibility for obtaining any further information concerning the Borrower's financial condition, the status of the Indebtedness, or any other matter which the undersigned may deem necessary or appropriate now or later. Debtor waives any duty on the part of Bank and agrees that Debtor is not relying upon nor expecting Bank to disclose to Debtor any fact now or later known by Bank, whether relating to the operations or condition of Borrower, the existence, liabilities, or financial condition of any guarantor of the Indebtedness, the occurrence of any default with respect to the Indebtedness, or otherwise, notwithstanding any effect such fact may have upon Debtor's risk or Debtor's rights against Borrower. Debtor knowingly accepts the full range of risk encompassed in this Agreement, which risk includes without limit the possibility that Borrower may incur Indebtedness to Bank after the financial condition of Borrower, or Borrower's ability to pay debts as they mature, has deteriorated.

2.13 Debtor shall defend, indemnify and hold harmless Bank, its employees, agents, shareholders, affiliates, officers, and directors from and against any and all claims, damages, fines, expenses, liabilities, or causes of action of whatever kind, including without limit consultant fees, legal expenses, and attorney fees, suffered by any of them as a direct or indirect result of any actual or asserted violation of any law, including, without limit, Environmental Laws, or of any remediation relating to any property required by any law, including without limit Environmental Laws.

3. Collection of Proceeds.

3.1 Debtor agrees to collect and enforce payment of all Collateral until Bank shall direct Debtor to the contrary. Immediately upon notice to

Debtor by Bank and at all times after that, Debtor agrees to fully and promptly cooperate and assist Bank in the collection and enforcement of all Collateral and to hold in trust for Bank all payments received in connection with Collateral and from the sale, lease, or other disposition of any Collateral, all rights by way of suretyship or guaranty, and all rights in the nature of a lien or security interest which Debtor now or later has regarding Collateral. Immediately upon and after such notice, Debtor agrees to (a) endorse to Bank and immediately deliver to Bank all payments received on Collateral or from the sale, lease, or other disposition of any Collateral or arising from any other rights or interests of Debtor in the Collateral, in the form received by Debtor without commingling with any other funds, and (b) immediately deliver to Bank all property in Debtor's possession or later coming into Debtor's possession through enforcement of Debtor's rights or interests in the Collateral. Debtor irrevocably authorizes Bank or any Bank employee or agent to endorse the name of Debtor upon any checks or other items which are received in payment for any Collateral, and to do any and all things necessary in order to reduce these items to money. Bank shall have no duty as to the collection or protection of Collateral or the proceeds of it, nor as to the preservation of any related rights, beyond the use of reasonable care in the custody and preservation of Collateral in the possession of Bank. Debtor agrees to take all steps necessary to preserve rights against prior parties with respect to the Collateral. Nothing in this Section 3.1 shall be deemed a consent by Bank to any sale, lease, or other disposition of any Collateral.

3.2 Debtor agrees that immediately upon Bank's request (whether or not any Event of Default exists), the Indebtedness shall be on a "remittance basis" as follows: Debtor shall at its sole expense establish and maintain (and Bank, at Bank's option, may establish and maintain at Debtor's expense): (a) a United States Post Office lock box (the "Lock Box"), to which Bank shall have exclusive access and control. Debtor expressly authorizes Bank, from time to time, to remove contents from the Lock Box for disposition in accordance with this Agreement. Debtor agrees to notify all account debtors and other parties obligated to Debtor that all payments made to Debtor (other than payments by electronic funds transfer) shall be remitted, for the credit of Debtor, to the Lock Box, and Debtor shall include a like statement on all invoices; and (b) a non-interest bearing deposit account with Bank which shall be titled as designated by Bank (the "Cash Collateral Account") to which Bank shall have exclusive access and control. Debtor agrees to notify all account debtors and other parties obligated to Debtor that all payments made to Debtor by electronic funds transfer shall be remitted to the Cash Collateral Account, and Debtor, at Bank's request, shall include a like statement on all invoices. Debtor shall execute all documents and authorizations as required by Bank to establish and maintain the Lock Box and the Cash Collateral Account.

3.3 All items or amounts which are remitted to the Lock Box, to the Cash Collateral Account, or otherwise delivered by or for the benefit of Debtor to Bank on account of partial or full payment of, or with respect to, any Collateral shall, at Bank's option, (a) be applied to the payment of the Indebtedness, whether then due or not, in such order or at such time of application as Bank may determine in its sole discretion, or (b) be deposited to the Cash Collateral Account. Debtor agrees that Bank shall not be liable for any loss or damage which Debtor may suffer as a result of Bank's processing of items or its exercise of any other rights or remedies under this Agreement, including without limitation indirect, special or consequential damages, loss of revenues or profits, or any claim, demand or action by any third party arising out of or in connection with the processing of items or the exercise of any other rights or remedies under this Agreement. Debtor agrees to indemnify and hold Bank harmless from and against all such third party claims, demands or actions, and all related expenses or liabilities, including, without limitation, attorney fees.

4. Defaults, Enforcement and Application of Proceeds.

4.1 Upon the occurrence of any of the following events (each an "Event of Default"), Debtor shall be in default under this Agreement:

(a) Any failure to pay the Indebtedness or any other indebtedness when due, or such portion of it as may be due, by acceleration or otherwise; or

(b) Any failure or neglect to comply with, or breach of or default under, any term of this Agreement, or any other agreement or commitment between Borrower, Debtor, or any guarantor of any of the Indebtedness ("Guarantor") and Bank; or

(c) Any warranty, representation, financial statement, or other information made, given or furnished to Bank by or on behalf of Borrower, Debtor, or any Guarantor shall be, or shall prove to have been, false or materially misleading when made, given, or furnished; or

(d) Any loss, theft, substantial damage or destruction to or of any Collateral, or the issuance or filing of any attachment, levy, garnishment or the commencement of any proceeding in connection with any Collateral or of any other judicial process of, upon, or in respect of Borrower, Debtor, any Guarantor, or any Collateral; or

(e) Sale or other disposition by Borrower, Debtor, or any Guarantor of any substantial portion of its assets or property or voluntary suspension of the transaction of business by Borrower, Debtor, or any Guarantor, or death, dissolution, termination of existence, merger, consolidation, insolvency, business failure, or assignment for the benefit of creditors of or by Borrower, Debtor, or any Guarantor; or commencement of any proceedings under any state or federal bankruptcy or insolvency laws or laws for the relief of debtors by or against Borrower, Debtor, or any Guarantor; or the appointment of a receiver, trustee, court appointee, sequestrator, or otherwise, for all or any part of the property of Borrower, Debtor, or any Guarantor; or

(f) Bank deems the margin of Collateral insufficient or itself insecure, in good faith believing that the prospect of payment of the Indebtedness or performance of this Agreement is impaired or shall fear deterioration, removal, or waste of Collateral; or

(g) A default shall occur under any instrument, agreement, or other document evidencing, securing or otherwise relating to any of the Indebtedness.

4.2 Upon the occurrence of any Event of Default, Bank may at its discretion and without prior notice to Debtor declare any or all of the Indebtedness to be immediately due and payable, and shall have and may exercise any one or more of the following rights and remedies:

(a) Exercise all the rights and remedies upon default, in foreclosure and otherwise, available to secured parties under the provisions of the Uniform Commercial Code and other applicable law;

(b) Institute legal proceedings to foreclose upon the lien and security interest granted by this Agreement, to recover judgment for all amounts then due and owing as Indebtedness, and to collect the same out of any Collateral or the proceeds of any sale of it;

(c) Institute legal proceedings for the sale, under the judgment or decree of any court of competent jurisdiction, of any or all Collateral; and/or

(d) Personally or by agents, attorneys, or appointment of a receiver, enter upon any premises where Collateral may then be located, and take possession of all or any of it and/or render it unusable; and without being responsible for loss or damage to such Collateral, hold, operate, sell, lease, or dispose of all or any Collateral at one or more public or private sales, leasings or other disposition, at places and times and on terms and conditions as Bank may deem fit, without any previous demand or advertisement; and except as provided in this Agreement, all notice of sale, lease or other disposition, and advertisement, and other notice or demand, any right or equity of redemption, and any obligation of a prospective purchaser or lessee to inquire as to the power and authority of Bank to sell, lease, or otherwise dispose of the Collateral or as to the application by Bank of the proceeds of sale or otherwise, which would otherwise be required by, or available to Debtor under, applicable law are expressly waived by Debtor to the fullest extent permitted.

At any sale pursuant to this Section 4.2, whether under the power of sale, by virtue of judicial proceedings or otherwise, it shall not be necessary for Bank or a public officer under order of a court to have present physical or constructive possession of Collateral to be sold. The recitals contained in any conveyances and receipts made and given by Bank or the public officer to any purchaser at any sale made pursuant to this Agreement shall, to the extent permitted by applicable law, conclusively establish the truth and accuracy of the matters stated (including, without limit, as to the amounts of the principal of and interest on the Indebtedness, the accrual and nonpayment of it, and advertisement and conduct of the sale); and all prerequisites to the sale shall be presumed to have been satisfied and performed. Upon any sale of any Collateral, the receipt of the officer making the sale under judicial proceedings or of Bank shall be sufficient discharge to the purchaser for the purchase money, and the purchaser shall not be obligated to see to the application of the money. Any sale of any Collateral under this Agreement shall be a perpetual bar against Debtor with respect to that Collateral. At any sale or other disposition of Collateral pursuant to this Section 4.2, Bank disclaims all warranties which would otherwise be given under the Uniform Commercial Code, including without limit a disclaimer of any warranty relating to title, possession, quiet enjoyment or the like, and Bank may communicate these disclaimers to a purchaser at such disposition. This disclaimer of warranties will not render the sale commercially unreasonable.

4.3 Debtor shall at the request of Bank, notify the account debtors or obligors of Bank's security interest in the Collateral and direct payment of it to Bank. Bank may, itself, upon the occurrence of any Event of Default so notify and direct any account debtor or obligor. At the request of Bank, whether or not an Event of Default shall have occurred, Debtor shall immediately take such actions as Bank shall request to establish exclusive control (as defined in the Uniform Commercial Code) by Bank over any Collateral which is of such a nature that perfection of a security interest may be accomplished by control.

4.4 The proceeds of any sale or other disposition of Collateral authorized by this Agreement shall be applied by Bank first upon all expenses authorized by the Uniform Commercial Code and all reasonable attorney fees and legal expenses incurred by Bank; the balance of the proceeds of the sale or other disposition shall be applied in the payment of the Indebtedness, first to interest, then to principal, then to remaining Indebtedness and the surplus, if any, shall be paid over to Debtor or to such other person(s) as may be entitled to it under applicable law. Debtor shall remain liable for any deficiency, which it shall pay to Bank immediately upon demand. Debtor agrees that Bank shall be under no obligation to accept any noncash proceeds in connection with any sale or disposition of Collateral unless failure to do so would be commercially unreasonable. If Bank agrees in its sole discretion to accept noncash proceeds (unless the failure to do so would be commercially unreasonable), Bank may ascribe any commercially reasonable value to such proceeds. Without limiting the foregoing, Bank may apply any discount factor in determining the present value of proceeds to be received in the future or may elect to apply proceeds to be received in the future only as and when such proceeds are actually received in cash by Bank.

4.5 Nothing in this Agreement is intended, nor shall it be construed, to preclude Bank from pursuing any other remedy provided by law for the collection of the Indebtedness or for the recovery of any other sum to which Bank may be entitled for the breach of this Agreement by Debtor. Nothing in this Agreement shall reduce or release in any way any rights or security interests of Bank contained in any existing agreement between Borrower, Debtor, or any Guarantor and Bank.

4.6 No waiver of default or consent to any act by Debtor shall be effective unless in writing and signed by an authorized officer of Bank. No waiver of any default or forbearance on the part of Bank in enforcing any of its rights under this Agreement shall operate as a waiver of any other default or of the same default on a future occasion or of any rights.

4.7 Debtor (a) irrevocably appoints Bank or any agent of Bank (which appointment is coupled with an interest) the true and lawful attorney of Debtor (with full power of substitution) in the name, place and stead of, and at the expense of, Debtor and (b) authorizes Bank or any agent of Bank, in its own name, at Debtor's expense, to do any of the following, as Bank, in its sole discretion, deems appropriate:

(i) to demand, receive, sue for, and give receipts or acquittances for any moneys due or to become due on any Collateral (including without limit to draft against Collateral) and to endorse any item representing any payment on or proceeds of the Collateral;

(ii) to execute and file in the name of and on behalf of Debtor all financing statements or other filings deemed necessary or desirable by Bank to evidence, perfect, or continue the security interests granted in this Agreement; and

(iii) to do and perform any act on behalf of Debtor permitted or required under this Agreement.

4.8 Upon the occurrence of an Event of Default, Debtor also agrees, upon request of Bank, to assemble the Collateral and make it available to Bank at any place designated by Bank which is reasonably convenient to Bank and Debtor.

4.9 The following shall be the basis for any finder of fact's determination of the value of any Collateral which is the subject matter of a disposition giving rise to a calculation of any surplus or deficiency under Section 9–615(f) of the Uniform Commercial Code (as in effect on or after July 1, 2001): (a) the Collateral which is the subject matter of the disposition shall be valued in an "as is" condition as of the date of the disposition, without any assumption or expectation that such Collateral will be repaired or improved in any manner; (b) the valuation shall be based upon an assumption that the transferee of such Collateral desires a resale of the Collateral for cash promptly (but no later than 30 days) following the disposition; (c) all reasonable closing costs customarily borne by the seller in commercial sales transactions relating to property similar to such Collateral shall be deducted including, without limitation, brokerage commissions, tax prorations, attorneys' fees, whether inside or outside counsel is used, and marketing costs; (d) the value of the Collateral which is the subject matter of the disposition shall be further discounted to account for any estimated holding costs associated with maintaining such Collateral pending sale (to the extent not accounted for in (c) above), and other maintenance, operational and ownership expenses; and (e) any expert opinion testimony given or considered in connection with a determination of the value of such Collateral must be given by persons having at least 5 years experience in appraising property similar to the Collateral and who have conducted and prepared a complete written appraisal of such Collateral taking into consideration the factors set forth above. The "value" of any such Collateral shall be a factor in determining the amount of proceeds which would have been realized in a disposition to a transferee other than a secured party, a person related to a secured party or a secondary obligor under Section 9–615(f).

5. Miscellaneous.

5.1 Until Bank is advised in writing by Debtor to the contrary, all notices, requests and demands required under this Agreement or by law shall be given to, or made upon, Debtor at the first address indicated in Section 5.15 below.

5.2 Debtor will give Bank not less than 90 days prior written notice of all contemplated changes in Debtor's name, location, chief executive office, principal place of business, and/or location of any Collateral, but the giving of this notice shall not cure any Event of Default caused by this change.

5.3 Bank assumes no duty of performance or other responsibility under any contracts contained within the Collateral.

5.4 Bank has the right to sell, assign, transfer, negotiate or grant participations or any interest in, any or all of the Indebtedness and any related obligations, including without limit this Agreement. In connection with the above, but without limiting its ability to make other disclosures to the full extent allowable, Bank may disclose all documents and information which Bank now or later has relating to Debtor, the Indebtedness or this Agreement, however obtained. Debtor further agrees that Bank may provide information relating to this Agreement or relating to Debtor to the Bank's parent, affiliates, subsidiaries, and service providers.

5.5 In addition to Bank's other rights, any indebtedness owing from Bank to Debtor can be set off and applied by Bank on any Indebtedness at any time(s) either before or after maturity or demand without notice to anyone. Any such action shall not constitute an acceptance of collateral in discharge of the Indebtedness.

5.6 Debtor waives any right to require the Bank to: (a) proceed against any person or property; (b) give notice of the terms, time, and place of any public or private sale of personal property security held from Borrower or any other person, or otherwise comply with the provisions of Section 9–504 of the Uniform Commercial Code in effect prior to July 1, 2001 or its successor provisions thereafter, including Sections 9–610, 9–611, 9–615, 9–617, 9–618, and 9–624 of the Uniform Commercial Code in effect on or after July 1, 2001; or (c) pursue any other remedy in the Bank's power. Debtor waives notice of acceptance of this Agreement and presentment, demand, protest, notice of protest, dishonor, notice of dishonor, notice of default, notice of intent to accelerate or demand payment of any Indebtedness, any and all other notices to which the undersigned might otherwise be entitled, and diligence in collecting any Indebtedness and agree(s) that the Bank may, once or any number of times, modify the terms of any Indebtedness, compromise, extend, increase, accelerate, renew or forbear to enforce payment of any or all Indebtedness, or permit Borrower to incur additional Indebtedness, all without notice to Debtor and without affecting in any manner the unconditional obligation of Debtor under this Agreement. Debtor unconditionally and irrevocably waives each and every defense and setoff of any nature which, under principles of guaranty or otherwise, would operate to impair or diminish in any way the obligation of Debtor under this Agreement and acknowledges that such waiver is by this reference incorporated into each security agreement, collateral assignment, pledge and/or other document from Debtor now or later securing the Indebtedness and acknowledges that as of the date of this Agreement no such defense or setoff exists.

5.7 Debtor waives any and all rights (whether by subrogation, indemnity, reimbursement, or otherwise) to recover from Borrower any amounts paid or the value of any Collateral given by Debtor pursuant to this Agreement.

5.8 In the event that applicable law shall obligate Bank to give prior notice to Debtor of any action to be taken under this Agreement, Debtor agrees that a written notice given to Debtor at least ten days before the date of the act shall be reasonable notice of the act and, specifically, reasonable notification of the time and place of any public sale or of the time after which any private sale, lease, or other disposition is to be made, unless a shorter notice period is reasonable under the circumstances. A notice shall be deemed to be given under this Agreement when delivered to Debtor or when placed in an envelope addressed to Debtor and deposited, with postage prepaid, in a post office or official depository under the exclusive care and custody of the United States Postal Service or delivered to an overnight courier. The mailing shall be by overnight courier, certified, or first class mail.

5.9 Notwithstanding any prior revocation, termination, surrender, or discharge of this Agreement in whole or in part, the effectiveness of this Agreement shall automatically continue or be reinstated in the event that any payment received or credit given by Bank in respect of the Indebtedness is returned, disgorged, or rescinded under any applicable law, including, without limitation, bankruptcy or insolvency laws, in which case this Agreement shall be enforceable against Debtor as if the returned, disgorged, or rescinded payment or credit had not been received or given by Bank, and whether or not Bank relied upon this payment or credit or changed its position as a consequence of it. In the event of continuation or reinstatement of this Agreement, Debtor agrees upon demand by Bank to execute and deliver to Bank those documents which Bank determines are appropriate to further evidence (in the public records or otherwise) this continuation or reinstatement, although the failure of Debtor to do so shall not affect in any way the reinstatement or continuation.

5.10 This Agreement and all the rights and remedies of Bank under this Agreement shall inure to the benefit of Bank's successors and assigns and to any other holder who derives from Bank title to or an interest in the Indebtedness or any portion of it and shall bind Debtor and the heirs, legal representatives, successors, and assigns of Debtor. Nothing in this Section 5.10 is deemed a consent by Bank to any assignment by Debtor.

5.11 If there is more than one Debtor, all undertakings, warranties, and covenants made by Debtor and all rights, powers, and authorities given to or conferred upon Bank are made or given jointly and severally.

5.12 Except as otherwise provided in this Agreement, all terms in this Agreement have the meanings assigned to them in Article 9 (or, absent definition in Article 9, in any other Article) of the Uniform Commercial Code, as those meanings may be amended, revised or replaced from time to time. "Uniform Commercial Code" means Act No. 174 of the Michigan Public Acts of 1962, as amended, revised or replaced from time to time, including without limit as amended by Act No. 348 of the Michigan Public Acts of 2000. Notwithstanding the foregoing, the parties intend that the terms used herein which are defined in the Uniform Commercial Code have, at all times, the broadest and most inclusive meanings possible. Accordingly, if the Uniform Commercial Code shall in the future be amended or held by a court to define any term used herein more broadly or inclusively than the Uniform Commercial Code in effect on the date of this Agreement, then such term, as used herein, shall be given such broadened meaning. If the Uniform Commercial Code shall in the future be amended or held by a court to define any term used herein more narrowly, or less inclusively, than the Uniform Commercial Code in effect on the date of this Agreement, such amendment or holding shall be disregarded in defining terms used in this Agreement.

5.13 No single or partial exercise, or delay in the exercise, of any right or power under this Agreement, shall preclude other or further exercise of the rights and powers under this Agreement. The unenforceability of any provision of this Agreement shall not affect the enforceability of the remainder of this Agreement. This Agreement constitutes the entire agreement of Debtor and Bank with respect to the subject matter of this Agreement. No amendment or modification of this Agreement shall be effective unless the same shall be in writing and signed by Debtor and an authorized officer of Bank. This Agreement shall be governed by and construed in accordance with the internal laws of the State of Michigan, without regard to conflict of laws principles.

5.14 To the extent that any of the Indebtedness is payable upon demand, nothing contained in this Agreement shall modify the terms and conditions of that Indebtedness nor shall anything contained in this Agreement prevent Bank from making demand, without notice and with or without reason, for immediate payment of any or all of that Indebtedness at any time(s), whether or not an Event of Default has occurred.

5.15 Debtor represents and warrants that Debtor's exact name is the name set forth in this Agreement. Debtor further represents and warrants the following and agrees that Debtor is, and at all times shall be, located in the following place [mark applicable provision]:

— Debtor is an individual, and Debtor is located (as determined pursuant to the Uniform Commercial Code) at Debtor's principal residence which is (street address, state and county or parish): ____.

— Debtor is a registered organization which is organized under the laws of one of the states comprising the United States (e.g. corporation, limited partnership, registered limited liability partnership, or limited liability company), and Debtor is located (as determined pursuant to the Uniform Commercial Code) in the state under the laws of which it was organized, which is (street address, state, and county or parish): ____.

— Debtor is a domestic organization which is not a registered organization under the laws of the United States or any state thereof (e.g. general partnership, joint venture, trust, estate or association), and Debtor is located (as determined pursuant to the Uniform Commercial Code) at its sole place of business or, if it has more than one place of business, at its chief executive office, which is (street address, state, and county or parish): ________________________________.

— Debtor is a registered organization organized under the laws of the United States, and Debtor is located in the state that United States law designates as its location or, if United States law authorizes the Debtor to designate the state for its location, the state designated by Debtor, or if neither of the foregoing are applicable, at the District of Columbia. Debtor is located (as determined pursuant to the Uniform Commercial Code) at (street address, state, and county or parish): ________________________________.

— Debtor is a foreign individual or foreign organization or a branch or agency of a bank that is not organized under the laws of the United States or a state thereof. Debtor is located (as determined pursuant to the Uniform Commercial Code) at: ________________________________.

If Collateral is located at other than the address specified above, such Collateral is located and shall be maintained at

____

STREET ADDRESS

____

CITY, STATE, ZIP CODE, COUNTY

Collateral shall be maintained only at the locations identified in this Section 5.15.

5.16 A carbon, photographic or other reproduction of this Agreement shall be sufficient as a financing statement under the Uniform Commercial Code and may be filed by Bank in any filing office.

5.17 This Agreement shall be terminated only by the filing of a termination statement in accordance with the applicable provisions of the Uniform Commercial Code, but the obligations contained in Section 2.13 of this Agreement shall survive termination.

6. DEBTOR AND BANK ACKNOWLEDGE THAT THE RIGHT TO TRIAL BY JURY IS A CONSTITUTIONAL ONE, BUT THAT IT MAY BE WAIVED. EACH PARTY, AFTER CONSULTING (OR HAVING HAD THE OPPORTUNITY TO CONSULT) WITH COUNSEL OF THEIR CHOICE, KNOWINGLY AND VOLUNTARILY, AND FOR THEIR

MUTUAL BENEFIT, WAIVES ANY RIGHT TO TRIAL BY JURY IN THE EVENT OF LITIGATION REGARDING THE PERFORMANCE OR ENFORCEMENT OF, OR IN ANY WAY RELATED TO, THIS AGREEMENT OR THE INDEBTEDNESS.

7. Special Provisions Applicable to this Agreement. (*None, if left blank)

Debtor: ______________________________

By: ______________________________

Signature of:

Its: ______________________________

By: ______________________________

Signature of:

Its: ______________________________

PROBLEM 4-1

Each provision of the sample security agreement reproduced above has a purpose relevant to the Bank's status as a secured party. For example, the preamble to the agreement includes the all-important "granting" clause conveying a security interest to the Bank, and likewise identifies the obligations secured thereby. Recall the requirement of section 9–203(b)(3)(A) that the debtor must authenticate a "security agreement," and recall further the definition of a "security agreement" in section 9–102(a)(74) to mean "an agreement that creates or provides for a security interest." *See also* 1–201(b)(3) (defining "agreement"), 1–201(b)(35) (defining "security interest"), 9–102(a)(7) (defining "authenticate"). Is the grant language in the sample security agreement sufficient to create or provide for a security interest? Notice that the preamble provides that the security interest secures both existing and future indebtedness. *See* 9–204. Why would the Bank want that? Section 1 of the sample security agreement describes the collateral subject to the Bank's security interest. Recall the requirements of section 9–108. Does the description of the Bank's collateral pass muster under this provision?

Note the various covenants in section 2. Why are these there? Note in particular the debtor's agreement in section 2.3 that the debtor will keep the collateral free from other liens. This is an example of a "negative pledge" clause discussed in Section 6 of Chapter 2. Why would the Bank want to be the sole secured party with respect to its collateral? Note the debtor's covenant in section 2.5 that it will pay its taxes when due. Why would the Bank want to make sure the debtor is not delinquent on its tax obligations? Hint: the debtor's failure to pay its taxes when due may give rise to a tax lien on the debtor's property. Note the debtor's obligation in section 2.6 to keep the collateral insured and to include the Bank as a "loss payee" on the debtor's insurance policy. Why would the Bank want that? Note the debtor's agreement in section 2.10 that "[a]t any time and without notice, Bank may . . . cause any or all of the Collateral to be transferred to its name or to the name of its nominee . . . ." Isn't that a bit aggressive? Consider that the Bank's right under this provision does not require an event of default. Although section 9–609 recognizes the right of a secured party to take possession of collateral, it does so only "[a]fter default . . . ." Why would the debtor agree that the secured party may transfer collateral to its name regardless of whether there has been a default? Is this the same thing as taking possession? In addition, to the extent section 2.10 of the sample security agreement purports to waive any obligation of notice or any of the other requirements of Part 6 of Article 9, is it enforceable? *See* 9–602.

Note the list of rights the Bank gets in section 3. Are these enforceable as literally written, even if the debtor resists? *See* 9–609. Observe the provision toward the end of section 3.2 providing that "Bank shall have no duty as to the collection or protection of Collateral or the proceeds of it, nor as to the preservation of any related rights, beyond the use of reasonable care in the custody and preservation of Collateral in the possession of Bank." *See* 9–207(a).

Section 4 is of particular importance—it defines what constitutes a default by the debtor triggering the Bank's enforcement rights. Recall that under section 9–601 a secured party is entitled to various remedies "[a]fter default . . . ." The circumstances that constitute a "default," however, are not defined in the UCC, which leaves it to the parties' agreement. *See* 9–601 cmt. 3. The events of default listed in section 4 seem rather broad. If you were negotiating this document on behalf of the debtor, would you agree to all of these terms? What leverage might you have to alter them? Notice in particular the terms of section 4.1(a) making it an event of default not only if the debtor fails to pay "the Indebtedness" (defined in the preamble to mean the obligations owed to the Bank), but also "any other indebtedness when due . . . ." This is an example of a "cross-default" provision making it an event of default if the debtor fails to pay when due any indebtedness owed to some third party. Why would the Bank what that? Note the provisions in section 4.2(d), particularly those regarding the Bank's right to dispose of all or any of the collateral as it sees fit combined with a broad waiver by the debtor, including any right to notice or right of redemption. These are in addition to, and somewhat redundant of, the waiver provisions contained in section 2.10. Are these enforceable? *See* 9–602. Contrast the waiver provisions in sections 2.10 and 4.2(d) (stipulating that the debtor waives various rights) with the anti-waiver provision of section 4.6 (purporting to shield the bank from an inference of waiver in certain circumstances—*see Minor v. Chase Auto Finance Corporation* reproduced in Part 6 of Chapter 7). Note the provisions of section 4.4 regarding the Bank's disposition of the sale proceeds of any collateral. *Compare* 9–615. Note also the parties' agreement in section 4.9 regarding the standards to be used in making certain determinations of value for purposes of calculating any surplus or deficiency under section 9–615(f). *See* 9–603, 9–626.

Notice the basket of miscellaneous provisions in section 5. In particular, why is the Bank concerned about any change in the debtor's name or location? *See* 9–316(a)(2), 9–507(c). Observe the broad waiver provisions of section 5.6.

Here the debtor agrees to waive (yet again) any right to require the bank to "give notice of the terms, time, and place of any public or private sale of personal property security . . ." or otherwise comply with a variety of requirements under Article 9. Is this waiver enforceable? *See* 9–602. Note that if it turns out that the Bank is required to give notice in spite of the waiver, the parties agree in section 5.8 to certain notice details. *Compare* 9–611, 9–612, 9–613. Finally, note the jury-trial waiver in section 6. Why would the Bank want this provision?

PROBLEM 4-2

Your client, ClientCo, a Maryland corporation, is entering into a $750 million revolving line of credit with Bank, secured by all of ClientCo's assets, the most important of which are inventory, equipment, and accounts. ClientCo has two subsidiaries, Sub One and Sub Two. Sub One is a Delaware limited liability company and Sub Two is a New York corporation. These subsidiaries hold substantial amounts of inventory and accounts; Bank intends to take security interests in their assets even though the loan agreement will be only with ClientCo. In addition to the security agreements and other related documentation, Bank will require an opinion of debtor's counsel regarding the enforceability and perfection of the security interests this deal creates. Bank's form of security agreement contains a choice-of-law clause electing Maryland law as the governing law for all of its transactions.

1. Assume that you (and the attorneys in your firm) are licensed in Maryland only. Can you render a perfection opinion regarding the security interests assigned by Sub One and Sub Two? Can you render an enforceability opinion regarding the security agreements between Bank and each of these subsidiaries?

2. In view of section 9–203, what information do you need to opine as to the enforceability of Bank's security interests? How do you establish the relevant facts?

3. How many "obligors" are involved in this transaction and how many "debtors"? If the loan agreement with Bank extends only to ClientCo, how will Bank's agreements with Sub One and Sub Two satisfy all of the requirements for enforceability?

4. Recall your study of sections 9–502, 9–516, and related provisions, in Chapter 2. Bank's form of opinion letter requests that you opine that Bank's security interest in ClientCo's assets will be perfected upon the filing of a UCC–1 financing statement in the form of Exhibit A to the opinion. You've been given Exhibit A—a UCC–1 financing statement prepared by a paralegal at Bank that appears complete. How do you take responsibility for the effectiveness of this UCC–1, as completed, to perfect Bank's interest?

§ 2. FUTURE ADVANCES AND PRIORITY IN AFTER-ACQUIRED COLLATERAL

AFTER-ACQUIRED COLLATERAL

Section 9–204(a) states that a security agreement "may create or provide for a security interest in after-acquired collateral." This rule does not extend to commercial tort claims nor, with limitations, to consumer goods, but in general a debtor and creditor may agree that a security interest automatically attaches to after-acquired collateral. The section adopts the principle of a "continuing general lien" or "floating lien," even though the debtor "has liberty to use or dispose of collateral without being required to account for proceeds or substitute new collateral." *See* 9–204 cmt. 2. That the priority in after-acquired collateral relates back to the original time of priority (filing or other method of perfection) is clear from the words of section 9–322(a). The point is made explicitly in comment 5 and example 4 to section 9–322.

FUTURE ADVANCES

Section 9–204(c) also provides that a security interest may secure "future advances." In addition, future advances have earned their own entire section (9–323) in Article 9. The language of subsection (a) of section 9–323 does its best to obscure the general rule of priority as to future advances. It appears to say, on first reading, that priority as to a future advance dates from the time of that advance and not from the time of an earlier filing or perfection. Of course, that is not what subsection (a) *really* says; the drafters state the rule much more clearly in comment 3 as follows:

> Under a proper reading of the first-to-file-or-perfect rule of Section 9–322(a)(1) (and former Section 9–312(5)), it is abundantly clear that the time when an advance is made plays no role in determining priorities among conflicting security interests except when a financing statement was not filed and the advance is the giving of value as the last step for attachment and perfection. Thus, a secured party takes subject to all advances secured by a competing security interest having priority under section 9–322(a)(1).

To understand the general rule, assume the secured creditor takes a security interest and perfects it by filing a financing statement. Assume further that the debtor makes periodic payments and the creditor allows the debtor to make periodic draws on the underlying line of credit. These draws will be "future advances." Under section 9–322, the secured creditor's priority as to each advance will relate back to the time of the original filing. Section 9–323(a) will not apply to these advances because they have been perfected by a prior filing. In rare circumstances, a lien creditor under section 9–323(b), or a buyer of goods under section 9–323(d), might achieve priority over the secured creditor as to some of these future advances.

The real role of section 9–323 is thus to state several intricate, but rather unimportant, *exceptions* to the general rule. In limited cases identified in sections 9–323(b) and (d), lien creditors and buyers will gain priority over certain later advances.

PROBLEM 4-3

Ajax Sisters, a famous private banking concern, wants to file a financing statement covering "inventory existing and after-acquired" of Neiman Marcus to perfect its security interest. You are counsel for Ajax and they ask you the following questions:

1. If we file on January 15 with respect to inventory as above, but neither lend nor make any agreement to lend at the time, and on January 20 a second creditor files and lends on the same inventory, will that lender have priority over us if we lend money on January 30?

2. If in the foregoing example we make a series of non-obligatory advances to Neiman Marcus, will we continue to have priority over the intervening creditor after we have knowledge of its loan, or will we be subordinated to the extent of our subsequent non-obligatory advances?

3. What will be our relative ranking with respect to collateral that is acquired one month, six months, or one year after our financing statement is filed? Do we continue to have the same relative priority?

4. If Neiman Marcus goes into Chapter 11 but continues to do business, as we understand they are entitled to do in Chapter 11, and sell off all old inventory and buy new inventory, will our after-acquired rights continue to accrue? That is, will our security interest continue automatically to attach to new inventory? We have been told that section 552 of the U.S. Bankruptcy Code (look at it) keeps that from happening. How would we protect ourselves before or during bankruptcy from the possibility that our collateral would be sold off and our security interest would not attach to new collateral? Consider not only section 552, but also section 361 on adequate protection and sections 363(c)(1) and (c)(2).

PROBLEM 4-4

Assume that Macy's grants a security interest to Citibank in all of the inventory and proceeds of its New York stores. Citibank lends $10 million initially. Assume the collateral that is subject to a security interest is in the $10–$15 million range. Over time, the debt is reduced to $100,000.

1. On November 30, when the debt to Citibank stands at $100,000, an unsecured creditor gets a judicial lien on all of Macy's inventory in its New York stores, thereby becoming a lien creditor. On December 15, Citibank learns of the judicial lien and asks on that same day whether it can safely advance

another $5 million to Macy's and enjoy priority over the intervening lien creditor. *See* 9–323(b).

2. Macy's sells three-quarters of the inventory in its New York stores to Bloomingdales. Three months after the sale, Citibank advances an additional $5 million to Macy's at a time when some people at Citibank know of the sale. Later, Citibank claims that its security interest attached to the property that was allegedly sold and has priority over the rights of the purchaser. What do you think? *See* 9–323(d). The combination of sections 9–201(a) and 9–315(a)(1) makes clear that a sale does not usually cut off a perfected security interest. *See also* 9–507. But what about the second $5 million advance?

3. Citibank has a perfected security interest in all of Macy's inventory in New York but its loan has been paid down to $100,000. Finance Company has a subordinate perfected security interest in all the inventory to secure a $10 million loan. Bank of America has a $5 million unsecured loan and proposes to buy Citibank's loan and take an assignment of its security interest. If it does that, will it enjoy priority over Finance Company to the extent of its entire $5 million loan? If you have doubts about the outcome, could you arrange the transaction in a different way to ensure success for Bank of America? For example, what if Macy's were to pay off the $5 million unsecured loan by an advance under the Citibank loan? *See* 1–201(b)(20), 1–304; *see also*, 9–310(c), 9–509 cmt. 8, 9–511 cmt. 3, 9–514 cmt. 2.

§ 3. PERFECTION

In general, perfection for inventory and farm products is not significantly different from perfection for business equipment that we considered in Chapter 2. In almost all cases, the creditor will file a financing statement. *See* 9–308, 9–310(a). Perfection by possession is also permitted, but in most cases what would be the point? *See* 9–313. Recall the basic requirements for the financing statement: contents of the statement (*see* 9–502); name of the debtor and secured party (*see* 9–503); indication of the collateral (*see* 9–504); and additional filing requirements (*see* 9–516). As before, filing is in the place of the debtor's location. *See* 9–301(1), 9–307, 9–501.

In the case of farm products, there is an additional filing requirement in certain states for certain purposes. This is discussed in Section 8 below (dealing with certain buyers of farm products).

By now, the steps necessary to perfect a security interest under Article 9 may seem routine to you. From time to time, however, mistakes are made. Consider the following case decided under former Article 9.

LMS HOLDING COMPANY V. CORE-MARK MID-CONTINENT, INC.

United States Court of Appeals, Tenth Circuit, 1995.
50 F.3d 1520.

BALDOCK, CIRCUIT JUDGE:

Coremark and Amcon ("Coremark") appeal the district court's grant of summary judgment in favor of Retail Marketing Company ("RMC"). The district court held that Coremark did not have a perfected security interest in RMC's after-acquired inventory. We exercise jurisdiction pursuant to 28 U.S.C. § 1291 and affirm.

In 1988, MAKO, Inc. (MAKO), a chain of convenience stores, granted Coremark a security interest in its inventory, after-acquired inventory, and inventory proceeds. Coremark perfected its security interest by filing a financing statement naming MAKO as the debtor. MAKO subsequently filed a Chapter 11 bankruptcy petition.

As part of MAKO's reorganization plan, RMC, an unrelated third party entity, agreed to acquire certain assets in MAKO's convenience stores and take over store operations. The acquired assets included specific inventory subject to Coremark's perfected security interest. The plan provided that Coremark would retain its lien in the "assets . . . acquired by RMC pursuant to [the] Plan" and that this lien would "continue in full force and effect in accordance with [its] terms." The bankruptcy court confirmed the MAKO plan in August 1989.

Following confirmation of the MAKO plan, RMC executed a new promissory note and security agreement in order to assume the indebtedness of MAKO. The security agreement granted Coremark a security interest in RMC's inventory, after-acquired inventory, and inventory proceeds. Coremark, however, did not file a new financing statement naming RMC as the debtor to perfect its security interest in RMC's inventory. Thereafter, RMC sold the MAKO inventory in the regular course of business and commingled the proceeds from the sale with other RMC assets. These proceeds are no longer identifiable. RMC replaced the MAKO inventory with after-acquired inventory. On September 21, 1991, RMC filed a Chapter 11 bankruptcy petition.

On November 20, 1991, Coremark filed a proof of claim in the bankruptcy proceeding. Thereafter, on July 29, 1992, RMC commenced this adversary proceeding seeking *inter alia* to avoid Coremark's asserted security interest in its after-acquired inventory pursuant to 11 U.S.C. 544(a)(1). On December 10, 1992, RMC filed a motion for summary judgment arguing that Coremark's security interest in its after-acquired inventory was unperfected because Coremark did not file a financing statement naming RMC as the debtor after RMC acquired the MAKO assets and took over store operations under the MAKO plan.

The bankruptcy court rejected this argument and denied the motion. In so holding, the bankruptcy court relied on Okla.Stat.Ann. tit. 12A, § 9–402(7) [9–507(a)], which provides in pertinent part that "[a] filed financing statement remains effective with respect to collateral transferred by the debtor even though the secured party knows of or consents to the transfer." Under this provision, the bankruptcy court concluded that the term "collateral" encompassed after-acquired property. Thus, the court held that Coremark's financing statement covering the MAKO collateral remained effective and served to perfect its security interest in RMC's after-acquired inventory "without the necessity of refiling a financing statement in [RMC's] name."

RMC appealed to the district court which reversed the bankruptcy court's holding. Specifically, the district court held that under § 9–402(7) [9–507(a)], Coremark's financing statement remained effective only as to the collateral actually transferred by MAKO under the bankruptcy plan. Thus, the district court concluded that Coremark's security interest in RMC's after-acquired inventory was unperfected because Coremark failed to file a new financing statement naming RMC as the debtor. Consequently, the district court granted summary judgment in favor of RMC. This appeal followed.

On appeal, Coremark argues the district court erred in granting summary judgment in favor of RMC. Specifically, Coremark contends that under § 9–402(7) [9–507(a)], the financing statement it filed naming MAKO as the debtor served to perfect its security interest in RMC's after-acquired inventory. We review the district court's grant of summary judgment de novo. *Eaton v. Jarvis Products Corp.*, 965 F.2d 922, 925 (10th Cir.1992). Summary judgment is appropriate when there is no genuine dispute over a material fact and the moving party is entitled to judgment as a matter of law. *Id.*

Pursuant to 11 U.S.C. § 544(a)(1), a debtor-in-possession (RMC in this case) may assert the rights of a hypothetical lien creditor once it files a bankruptcy petition. The rights of a lien creditor are determined by state law. *Woodson v. Utica Square Nat'l Bank of Tulsa (In re McClain)*, 447 F.2d 241, 243–44 (10th Cir.1971). Under Oklahoma law, a lien creditor has priority over an unperfected, secured creditor. Okla.Stat.Ann. tit. 12A, § 9–301(1)(b), (3) [9–317(a)]. Thus, in a bankruptcy proceeding, if the creditor's security interest is not perfected, the creditor " 'stands as [a] general unsecured creditor who must defer to the trustee.' " *Jones v. Small Business Admin. (In re Cohutta Mills, Inc.)*, 108 B.R. 815, 817 (N.D.Ga.1989) (quoting *In re Merts Equipment Co.*, 438 F.Supp. 295, 298 (M.D.Ga.1977)).

Under Oklahoma law, a secured creditor perfects a security interest in part by preparing and filing a financing statement describing the collateral subject to the security interest and naming the debtor. Okla.Stat.Ann. tit. 12A, § 9–302(1) [9–308, 9–310]. Once a financing statement is filed, the security interest becomes perfected, *id.* § 9–303 [9–308], protecting the secured party against conflicting interests in the same collateral. *Id.* § 9–312 [9–322].

Section 9–402 [9–502, 9–512, 9–516, 9–521] covers the formal requisites of the initial filing and subsequent amendment of a financing statement. Subsection (7) addresses a secured party's duty to refile a financing statement in certain enumerated instances:

> A financing statement sufficiently shows the name of the debtor if it gives the individual, partnership or corporate name of the debtor, whether or not it adds other trade names or the names of partners. Where the debtor so changes his name, or in the case of an organization, its name, identity, or corporate structure that a filed financing statement becomes seriously misleading, the filing is not effective to perfect a security interest in collateral acquired by the debtor more than four (4) months after the change, unless a new appropriate financing statement is filed before the expiration of that time. *A filed financing statement remains effective with respect to collateral transferred by the debtor even though the secured party knows of or consents to the transfer.*

Okla.Stat.Ann. tit. 12A, § 9–402(7) [9–503, 9–507] (emphasis added). Under this section, the second sentence addresses a secured creditor's obligation to refile a financing statement in instances where there has been a "change[ ] in the identity or structure of the debtor in which the 'new' debtor is a successor enterprise of the original debtor." *Bluegrass Ford-Mercury, Inc. v. Farmers Nat'l Bank of Cynthiana (In re Bluegrass Ford-Mercury, Inc.)*, 942 F.2d 381, 388 (6th Cir.1991) (citing *Bank of the West v. Commercial Credit Fin. Serv.*, 852 F.2d 1162, 1169 (9th Cir.1988)). In contrast, the third sentence applies only to those instances where there has been a "bona fide transfer[ ] [of collateral] to third parties unrelated to the transferor." *Bank of the West*, 852 F.2d at 1169–70 n. 6.

Applying these principles to the instant case, the parties agree that the only provision applicable to the facts before us is the third sentence of § 9–402(7) [9–507(a)]. Under this provision, the parties agree that Coremark's security interest remained perfected in the collateral actually transferred to RMC under the MAKO plan. The parties disagree, however, as to whether the financing statement naming MAKO as the debtor operated to perfect Coremark's security interest in collateral acquired by RMC *after* the MAKO transfer. Thus, the central issue we must resolve in this appeal is whether under the last sentence of § 9–402(7) [9–507(a)], Coremark's financing statement perfected its security interest in collateral acquired by RMC *after* the MAKO transfer.

Courts which have addressed the scope of § 9–402(7) [9–507(a)] have reached differing conclusions. For example, in *In re Taylorville Eisner Agency*, 445 F.Supp. 665 (S.D.Ill.1977), a bank made a loan to individual debtors secured by fixtures, equipment, inventory, and after-acquired property. In order to perfect its security interest, the bank filed a financing statement naming the individuals as debtors. On the same day as the note and security agreement were signed, the individual debtors transferred the collateral to a corporation they had previously formed and the corporation assumed the bank loan. The bank did not file a new financing statement naming the corporation as the new debtor. After selling the inventory which had been transferred and replacing it with after-acquired inventory, the corporation declared bankruptcy. *Id.* at 666–67.

Relying on the last sentence of § 9–402(7) [9–507(a)], the trustee argued that because the bank had not filed a new financing statement naming the corporation as the new debtor, the bank did not have a perfected security interest in the corporation's after-acquired inventory. The district court disagreed, stating in pertinent part:

> [T]he final sentence speaks of collateral transferred by the debtor, which must mean the property subject to the security interest as defined in UCC § 9–105(1)(c) [9–102]. In this case the security interest covered existing fixtures and equipment as well as acquired inventory and merchandise.
>
> . . .
>
> . . . The third sentence of subsection 7 is clear that the filed statement remains effective with respect to collateral transferred by the debtor regardless of the knowledge or consent of the secured party. *This also means collateral which is after-acquired property.*

Id. at 669 (emphasis added). Consequently, the district court held that the bank did not have to file a new financing statement naming the corporation as the new debtor in order to retain its perfected security interest in after-acquired property. *Id.* at 670.

The Sixth Circuit reached a contrary result in *Bluegrass*, 942 F.2d at 386. In *Bluegrass*, a bank made a loan to Bluegrass-Ford, a car dealership. The bank perfected its security interest by filing a financing statement which covered "all new cars and demonstrators in the inventory of Bluegrass Ford, Inc." The assets of the dealership were subsequently sold to an individual who then transferred the assets to a new, unrelated corporate entity called Bluegrass Ford-Mercury, Inc. The bank did not file a new financing statement naming Bluegrass Ford-Mercury as the new debtor. The new dealership subsequently filed bankruptcy. *Id.* at 383.

On appeal, the bank argued that the financing statement filed in the name of Bluegrass Ford perfected its security interest in the after-acquired inventory of Bluegrass Ford-Mercury. The Sixth Circuit rejected this argument. The court noted that the last sentence of § 9–402(7) [9–507(a)] applies only "to collateral transferred by the debtor." *Id.* at 387. The court then held that this language did not "encompass collateral not yet acquired by the transferee debtor." *Id.* Consequently, the court concluded that the bank's financing statement originally filed in the name of Bluegrass Ford did not perfect its security interest in Bluegrass Ford-Mercury's after-acquired inventory. *Id.* at 388.

In accordance with the Sixth Circuit, other court's [sic] have concluded that pursuant to § 9–402(7) [9–507(a)], after-acquired property cannot constitute collateral transferred by the debtor, *see In re Cohutta Mills*, 108 B.R. at 820 n. 4, and that a creditor perfects a security interest in after-acquired property of the debtor's transferee by filing a new financing statement in the name of the debtor's third party transferee. *See Steinberg v. American Nat'l Bank & Trust Co. of Chicago (In re Meyer-Midway, Inc.)*, 65 B.R. 437, 444 (Bankr.N.D.Ill.1986) ("The Court agrees with the Trustee that the Bank would be obligated to file a revised financing statement to be perfected in new collateral or collateral intended to secure the Bank under the after-acquired property clause."); *Citizens Savings Bank v. Sac City State Bank*, 315 N.W.2d 20, 28 (Iowa 1982) (same); *see also* William M. Burke, *The Duty to Refile Under Section 9–402(7) of the 1999 Article 9*, 35 Bus.Law. 1083, 1089 (1980) ("In order to perfect any security interest in the new property acquired by the transferee, the secured creditor must either file a financing statement signed by the transferee or take possession of the new property.").

We conclude the Sixth Circuit's reasoning is correct. As the court noted, under § 9–402(7) [9–507(a)] a filed financing statement remains effective only as to collateral transferred by the debtor." *Bluegrass*, 942 F.2d at 387. Inventory purchased by the transferee after the transfer cannot constitute property "transferred by the debtor." *See id.; In re Cohutta Mills*, 108 B.R. at 820 n. 4. Thus, a financing statement filed prior to a transfer of collateral in the name of the transferor does not serve to perfect a security interest in the transferee's after-acquired property. *See Bluegrass*, 942 F.2d at 387; *In re Meyer-Midway*, 65 B.R. at 443–44.

Applying this reasoning to the instant case, we conclude the financing statement Coremark filed in the name of MAKO did not perfect its security interest in RMC's after-acquired inventory. Rather, in order to perfect its security interest in RMC's after-acquired property, Coremark should have filed a new financing statement naming RMC as the debtor. Because Coremark failed to do so, its security interest in RMC's after-acquired inventory remained unperfected.

Coremark contends this result would contravene the express provisions of the MAKO bankruptcy plan which provided that Coremark's lien would "continue in full force and effect in accordance with [its] terms." Aplt.App. at 26. Coremark contends this provision of the bankruptcy plan relieved it from the requirement of filing a financing statement in the name of RMC to perfect its security interest in RMC's after-acquired inventory. We disagree.

The plan provided that Coremark's lien would continue as to assets "*to be acquired by RMC pursuant to* [*the*] *Plan*." As noted above, the assets to be acquired consisted of the inventory transferred by MAKO to RMC. Consequently, under the express terms of the plan, Coremark's lien remained perfected only as to property acquired by RMC under the MAKO plan. Thus, contrary to its assertions otherwise, the MAKO plan did not relieve Coremark of the requirement that it file a financing statement naming RMC as the debtor in order to perfect its security interest in RMC's after-acquired inventory.

AFFIRMED.

How does revised Article 9 deal with the problem in the *LMS* case? Start with section 9–201(a). Move next to section 9–315(a). After that, consider sections 9–203(d) & (e), 9–507, and 9–508. Confused?

To unlock the mysteries of these provisions, it is helpful initially to distinguish two things. First, there is the actual inventory the debtor/seller (MAKO) transferred to the buyer (RMC). Second, there is the inventory the buyer (RMC) acquired thereafter on its own—the "after-acquired" inventory.

When RMC acquired the first category of inventory from MAKO, RMC became a "debtor" with respect to this collateral and took the inventory subject to the security interest of MAKO's secured creditor (Coremark). *See* 9–102(a)(28) cmt. 2(a), 9–201(a), 9–315(a). Coremark perfected its security interest against MAKO by filing a financing statement, and this filing remained good to perfect its security interest in the goods that *were actually transferred* from MAKO to RMC. *See* 9–507(a). This is true even though Coremark did not file a new financing statement in RMC's name. In other words, section 9–507(a) condones a secret lien with respect to goods actually transferred.

The second category of collateral—the after-acquired inventory RMC acquired on its own—would be a problem for Coremark. RMC's name is obviously different from MAKO's name, and a searcher using "RMC" would probably not pull up Coremark's financing statement. Thus, the "debtor" (the person with the interest in the collateral—here RMC) has a name different from the name appearing on the filing. Coremark would be unperfected with respect to the "after-acquired" inventory. Could Coremark argue that the change from MAKO to RMC was simply a "name change"? No, because this is not a situation in which MAKO simply changed its name to RMC—the two are unrelated entities. But if Coremark could make this argument, it might get a limited benefit under section 9–507(c).

RMC signed a security agreement with Coremark. Might this make RMC a "new debtor" and thus provide Coremark with some cover? Only if RMC became "bound by" *MAKO*'s security agreement. *See* 9–102(a)(56). This could happen in one of two standard ways: (1) RMC agreed contractually to be bound by *MAKO's* security agreement, or (2) RMC became obligated to honor MAKO's obligations by operation of law (for example, merger law). *See* 9–203(d), 9–508 cmt. 3. If RMC is a "new debtor," Coremark's financing statement naming MAKO would remain effective to perfect its security interest in RMC's after-acquired inventory, but only for a period of four months. *See* 9–508. Coremark would have to file a new financing statement within that four-month period.

Here it is worth noting that, like the definition of "debtor," the definition of "new debtor" under Article 9 is a non-intuitive, technical construct. Although one would ordinarily think of a "debtor" as one who owes a debt, that is not how Article 9 makes use of the term. Under Article 9, the debtor is the entity that has an interest in the collateral subject to a security interest. *See* 9–102(a)(28). In contrast, the entity that owes the relevant debt is the "obligor." *See* 9–102(a)(59). Again, Article 9 draws this distinction because, although the debtor and the obligor will often be the same entity (*e.g.*, an individual who both owes the relevant debt and owns the relevant collateral), they may also be different entities (*e.g.*, a parent corporation that owes the relevant debt, and a subsidiary that owns the relevant collateral subject to the security interest).

As used in Article 9, the phrase "new debtor" is even more arcane—it tracks neither the common meaning of the terms "new" and "debtor," nor adheres exactly to the logic of how Article 9 makes use of the term "debtor." Consistent with how the terms "new" and "debtor" are used in ordinary English, one might well think the phrase "new debtor" refers to someone who has recently become obligated for a debt of some kind. Alternatively, following the logic of how Article 9 makes use of the term "debtor" one might well think the phrase "new debtor" refers to someone who comes to have a "new" interest in the relevant collateral—a transferee of some kind. But as we have seen, a transferee of the collateral, including a buyer, is generally treated as a "debtor" (unless, of course, the transferee takes free of the relevant security interest, in which case the property in question is not "collateral" and the transferee is thus not a "debtor"). *See* 9–102(a)(28). The concept of a "new debtor" is distinctly narrower: under section 9–203(d) it refers only to those transferees who become *bound by* someone else's security agreement. Ordinarily, a transferee of collateral, such as a buyer, does not become bound by a transferor's security agreement simply because the transferee acquires an interest in the relevant collateral. Under section 9–315(a)(1), the general rule is that a transferee ordinarily takes collateral subject to a preexisting security interest (unless the security interest is cut off by section 9–320 or some other provision of law). But taking collateral subject to a security interest is not the same thing as becoming bound by someone else's contractual security agreement. Something more is required for that. Either the transferee must agree contractually to be bound by the security agreement or the transferee must become bound by operation of law, as in the case of a merger. *See* 9–203(d) cmt. 7.

For a twist on the fact pattern of *LMS*, suppose RMC is located in a jurisdiction different from MAKO (for example, suppose MAKO is a Delaware corporation, and RMC is incorporated in New York). *See* 9–307. With respect to the inventory MAKO actually transferred to RMC, Coremark would have one year to file a financing statement in New York (or perfect by possession). *See* 9–316(a)(3) cmt. 2 (explaining the one-year period). In other words, section 9–316 also condones a secret lien, although only for one year.

Now suppose MAKO and RMC actually merged (with RMC being the surviving entity). Suppose further that, as a result of the merger, the inventory that MAKO originally owned was combined with inventory originally owned by RMC, forming one collateral pool owned by RMC as the surviving entity. Suppose further that both MAKO and RMC had their own secured creditors (Coremark as a secured creditor of MAKO, and Citibank as a secured creditor of RMC) each holding perfected security interests in the inventory of their respective original debtors. Do the security interests of the two secured parties continue in the combined assets? Yes. *See* 9–315. But which secured creditor has priority? Each has priority in its respective original collateral. *See* 9–325.

Section 9–325 is somewhat difficult to decipher. It addresses what is known as the "double debtor" problem—situations in which a debtor acquires property subject to a security interest created by a previous debtor and then creates a new security interest on the same property. *See* 9–315 cmt. 2. To understand how the section works, start with the first part of section 9–325(a): "a security interest created by a debtor is subordinate to a security interest in the same collateral created by another person . . . ." The complexity arises because it is not immediately clear which "debtor" the section is referring to. Is it the first debtor who created the first security interest or is it the transferee debtor? It is the latter. Section 9–325(a) comes into play at the point in time in which property that is already encumbered by the first debtor is transferred to a second person (who thereby becomes a "debtor") and a second security interest attaches to the collateral in the hands of the second debtor (*e.g.*, because the second debtor has authenticated his own security agreement with a second secured part). The second security interest is subordinate to the first security interest created by the first debtor, so long as the first one remains perfected. *See* 9–325 cmt. 3.

Suppose finally that both Coremark and Citibank each have after-acquired property clauses in their respective security agreements. Following the merger, RMC is a "new debtor" with respect to Coremark. *See* 9–203(d), 9–508 cmt. 3. Does Coremark's after-acquired property clause have the effect of causing its security interest to attach to RMC's inventory, and, if so, will it remain perfected? Yes, and it will remain perfected for four months (unless Coremark files a new financing statement naming RMC, in which case it will continue). *See* 9–203(e), 9–508. But who has priority in the RMC's inventory that was not transferred from MAKO to RMC, Coremark or Citibank? Citibank, to the extent Coremark relies on the effectiveness of its financing statement in the name of MAKO under section 9–508 to reach RMC's inventory. *See* 9–326. If Coremark files a new financing statement in the name of RMC, the ordinary priority rules of Article 9 would govern any conflict between Coremark's security interest perfected by its new financing statement naming RMC and Citibank's security interest perfected by its financing statement naming RMC. For even more outrageously complicated examples, look at the comments to sections 9–325 and 9–326.

Like section 9–325, section 9–326 requires careful, patient reading. It provides that "a security interest that is created by a new debtor in collateral in which the new debtor has or acquires rights and is perfected solely by a filed financing statement that would be ineffective to perfect the security interest but for application of Section . . . 9–508 is subordinate to a security interest in the same collateral which is perfected other than by such a filed financing statement." What exactly are the drafters saying here? The key to understanding this obscurely worded provision is its reference to section 9–508. As we have seen, section 9–508 extends the perfection of a security interest in property of an original debtor to a new debtor. *See also* 9–203(e). But for section 9–508, the financing statement filed against MAKO would be ineffective to perfect a security interest in collateral owned by RMC that was not transferred to RMC from MAKO. That is so because the financing statement filed against MAKO does not name RMC. And we know that section 9–326 does not apply to collateral that is actually transferred from MAKO to RMC because section 9–326 applies to security interests perfected solely under section 9–508. In turn, section 9–508(c) provides that "[t]his section [9–508] does not apply to collateral as to which a filed financing statement remains effective against the new debtor under Section 9–507(a)," and section 9–507(a) applies to "collateral that is sold . . . and in which a security interest . . . continues . . . ." *See* 9–507 cmt. 3. So section 9–325 governs priority disputes between the security interest of the secured party of the first debtor and the security interest of the secured party of the second debtor with respect to collateral that is actually transferred from the first debtor to the second debtor. Section 9–326 governs priority disputes between, on the one hand, the security interest of the secured party of the first debtor that extends to property of a new debtor under section 9–203(e) and is perfected under section 9–508, and, on the other hand, the security interest of the secured party of the new debtor that extends to the same collateral and is perfected other than under section 9–508 (*e.g.*, by a filed financing statement naming the new debtor).

Sections 9–325 and 9–326 are default provisions governing the treatment of combined asset pools encumbered by competing security interests. In most cases in which there will be multiple secured parties holding liens in a combined asset pool following a merger, the details of the secured parties' respective priorities will be worked out in advance through one or more contractual "subordination agreements." These are permitted under sections 1–310 and 9–339.

One final question: why wasn't RMC a buyer in ordinary course of business who took free of Coremark's security interest under section 9–320? Two reasons. First, Mako's Chapter 11 plan provided that Mako's lien would continue in the collateral, and as a matter of federal law this would override any inconsistent provision of state law. Second, the definition of "buyer in ordinary course" excludes buyers in bulk. *See* 1–201(b)(9). We will discuss section 9–320 and buyers in ordinary course further in Section 6 of this chapter.

PROBLEM 4-5

JPMorgan Chase files a financing statement with respect to Macy's, a Delaware corporation, in Dover. The financing statement identifies Macy's as the debtor and identifies the collateral as "all inventory located in Macy's Manhattan stores." Assume the security agreement gives JPMorgan Chase a right to "all inventory located in Macy's Manhattan stores" and includes after-acquired property.

1. If the inventory is moved to Macy's New Jersey store, is JPMorgan Chase unperfected as to that inventory?

2. What if it is not only moved but also sold to a Macy's subsidiary that has no security agreement with JPMorgan Chase?

3. Suppose Macy's files for bankruptcy under Chapter 11. The DIP suggests JPMorgan Chase is unperfected in any case because its financing statement failed to mention after-acquired property. What do you think? *See* 9–502 cmt. 2.

§ 4. PURCHASE-MONEY SECURITY INTERESTS: SECOND IN TIME, FIRST IN RIGHT

Section 9–324 grants priority to a purchase-money security interest over a prior conflicting security interest even though the purchase-money security interest is later perfected; we sometimes call this "super priority." The purchase-money secured creditor is often the seller of a product who has retained a security interest to secure payment of its purchase price, but a bank or other financing agency can also be a purchase-money secured creditor. For example, suppose the debtor wishes to finance its purchase of some new inventory. Suppose further that the debtor borrows money from a bank for that purpose and then actually uses the borrowed funds to acquire the new inventory from a vendor. If the debtor grants the bank a security interest in the inventory to secure repayment of the funds it borrowed to acquire that very inventory, the bank's security interest will be entitled to purchase-money status (provided certain other requirements are met). And that is perhaps the best way to conceptualize the purchase-money priority: as a special status that inures to the benefit of a secured party who extends credit or lends money to the debtor to enable the debtor to acquire specific goods, and in return takes a security interest in the very goods that the secured party's extension of credit or loan enabled the debtor to obtain.

To see how Article 9 provides for this, take a look at section 9–103. Observe that section 9–103(a) begins with a composite definition of what constitutes a "purchase-money security interest." It begins by defining the concept of "purchase-money collateral" as goods or software that secures a purchase-money obligation with respect to that collateral. It then defines the concept of "purchase-money obligation" as an obligation incurred "as all or part of the price of the collateral or for value given to enable the debtor to acquire rights in or the use of the collateral if the value is in fact so used." It next tells us that a security interest in goods is a purchase-money security interest "to the extent that the goods are purchase-money collateral with respect to that security interest . . . ." Would you have defined the concept in this way? In order to fully grasp the complexity of the concept, take a look at the comments to section 9–103.

The priority of a purchase-money security interest is set out in section 9–324. Section 9–324 specifies different criteria for purchase-money status based on the type of goods at issue. Sections 9–324(b) and (c) govern the priority of purchase-money security interests in inventory. Sections 9–324(d) and (e) govern the priority of purchase-money security interests in livestock. Software purchase-money priority is treated in subsection (f). Purchase-money priority with respect to other goods (*e.g.*, equipment and consumer goods) is treated in section 9–324(a). Each of these subsections elevate the priority of a purchase-money security interest over non-purchase-money security interests, so long as the relevant requirements of section 9–324 are satisfied. The priority of purchase-money secured creditors has long been recognized in real estate transactions and in pre-Code rules for personal property. What is the justification for this special priority?

First, one might argue that a seller of goods (who is going to retain a security interest) should not be obliged to inspect public filings with respect to its buyer in order for the seller to maintain priority in goods which it owns and proposes to sell; yet the Code does not consistently follow any such principle. A purchase-money secured creditor claiming inventory (including a seller) must inspect the files to be sure of priority under section 9–324.

A second possible justification for purchase-money priority is that the debtor needs some protection from an earlier secured creditor who may have filed a financing statement with respect to many of the debtor's assets (including after-acquired), but who is unwilling to advance additional funds. Absent purchase-money priority, an earlier filing with broad after-acquired coverage would give the prior creditor priority over other lenders, leaving the debtor unable to borrow despite the fact that other lenders might be willing to finance new purchases if they could have priority as to the new goods purchased. The possibility of priority for purchase-money lenders gets the debtor out from under the thumb of an original creditor; it may enable the debtor to borrow notwithstanding the reluctance of the original lender.

Finally, some law and economics scholars maintain that purchase-money lenders should be permitted to go to the head of the line because they do not threaten preceding creditors in ways that general creditors might. In an article in the Virginia Law Review (80 Va. L. Rev. 2103 (1994)), Professors Kanda and Levmore make a sophisticated argument on behalf of purchase-money lenders. First, they argue that the justification for a first-in-time rule for secured creditors is to keep the debtor from "altering the risk" to the debtor's advantage and to the creditor's disadvantage after the deal has been struck. For example, a debtor in financial difficulty might choose to engage in risky activity with the knowledge that most of the risk will be borne by his creditors. First-in-time rules inhibit that behavior. Kanda and Levmore hypothesize that creditors who come later in time may have better information than earlier creditors and so know which loans should be made (efficient) and which are too risky (inefficient). They suggest that purchase-money lenders are often better informed than creditors who have made earlier loans and that they will not undermine the position of earlier secured creditors because their claim will be limited to the collateral purchased with their loan. Does this seem plausible to you?

Consider the following case.

ZINK V. VANMIDDLESWORTH

United States District Court, Northern District of New York, 2003.
300 B.R. 394.

MORDUE, DISTRICT JUDGE:

BACKGROUND

Presently before this Court are appeals by Robert and Ruth Zink from a Memorandum Decision and Order signed by Hon. Robert E. Littlefield, Jr., United States Bankruptcy Judge, on August 1, 2002, in two bankruptcy cases, *In re William G. Vanmiddlesworth, Jr.* (Bankr. No. 02–12746), and *In re Frank F. Vanmiddlesworth, Jr.*, (Bankr. No. 02–12747). The Vanmiddlesworths, cotenants of a dairy farm, are proceeding under Chapter 12 of the Bankruptcy Code, which provides for reorganization of family farms and permits debtors to operate their farms during the proceedings.

The Zinks moved in both cases for adequate protection and lifting of the stay under 28 U.S.C. §§ 157(a), (b)(1), (b)(2)(G) and 1334(b), relative to the Zinks' purchase-money security interest in 54 head of cattle sold by the Zinks to the Vanmiddlesworths pursuant to a promissory note and security agreement. Prior to the transaction with the Zinks, Frank Vanmiddlesworth had signed a security agreement covering after-acquired livestock in favor of Marine Midland Bank, the predecessor of HSBC Bank USA ("HSBC"). In the August 1, 2002 order which is now before this Court, Judge Littlefield addressed the interests of both William and Frank Vanmiddlesworth and held that although the Zinks have a purchase-money security interest in the 54 cows, they did not achieve "livestock purchase-money security interest priority" over HSBC, at least not with regard to Frank Vanmiddlesworth's interest. He further held that with respect to both Vanmiddlesworths, the Zinks had not demonstrated their entitlement to an order conditioning the use of the collateral on adequate protection payments or terminating the automatic stay. Accordingly, he denied the motions.

Subsequent to the issuance of Judge Littlefield's August 1, 2002 decision, the Vanmiddlesworths brought an adversary proceeding against the Zinks seeking to avoid their security interest on the ground that it constitutes a preference under 11 U.S.C. § 547(b)(4)(A). The trustee moved to dismiss the Vanmiddlesworths' bankruptcy cases for failure timely to file proposed plans under 11 U.S.C. § 1221. The trustee's dismissal motion was settled, giving the Vanmiddlesworths additional time to file [proposed plans] after the determination of the appeal herein and the adversary proceeding.

* * *

THE ORDER ON APPEAL

In addressing the motions for adequate protection or termination of the automatic stay, Judge Littlefield first found that the Zinks have a purchase-money security interest in the 54 cows. Applying N.Y.U.C.C. § 9–324(d) and (e), he held, however, that the Zinks did not achieve "livestock purchase-money security interest priority" over HSBC with regard to the interest of Frank Vanmiddlesworth. In reaching these conclusions, Judge Littlefield made the following factual findings, based largely on the stipulation of facts filed by the parties and the bankruptcy petitions and schedules filed by the Vanmiddlesworths:

> On or about April 7, 1998, Debtor Frank F. Vanmiddlesworth, Jr. signed a security agreement in favor of Marine Midland Bank ("MMB"). The security agreement states that it includes dairy cattle "now owned or hereafter owned or acquired by Debtor." That same day he also signed a second security agreement in favor of MMB, assigning to it all his accounts, general intangibles and chattel paper. On or about April 13, 1998, MMB filed a UCC–1 financing statement in the St. Lawrence County Clerk's Office. The financing statement states that it covers all cattle, equipment, supplies, accounts, general intangibles and chattel paper "now owned or hereinafter acquired, wherever located."
>
> On or about May 7, 2001, Debtor Frank F. Vanmiddlesworth, Jr. and Debtor William G. Vanmiddlesworth, Jr., his brother, signed a document entitled "Optional Advance Time or Demand Grid Note" ("grid note 1") in favor of HSBC Bank USA ("HSBC")[1] in the amount of $10,000. They signed another grid note on or about August 7, 2001 ("grid note 2"). Grid note 2 was in the amount of $431,000.
>
> On or about November 26, 2001, the Debtors executed a contract to purchase 54 cows from the Zinks. On that same day, they also signed a promissory note and a security agreement in favor of the Zinks. The sales contract places a unit value price of $1,700 on 52 of the cows, $800 for cow with identification # 492 and $600 for cow with identification # 471. The security agreement granted the Zinks a security interest in "54 head of cattle (livestock) including any additions, substitutions or replacements."
>
> The Debtors also signed a financing statement, using the form adopted by the Secretary of State prior to the revision of Article 9 of the New York Uniform Commercial Code

[1] HSBC acquired MMB but the date of the acquisition is not in the record.

("N.Y.U.C.C."). They did not use the new form created in connection with Article 9's revisions which became effective in New York on July 1, 2001.

The language of the Zinks' UCC–1 form mimics the language of their security agreement. Like the security agreement, the Zinks' UCC–1 form does not cover "products of the collateral." The Zinks' UCC–1 form does not list the Debtors' last names first as that form required; it lists them as "William Van Middlesworth, Jr." and "Frank F. Van Middlesworth, Jr." It does not state whether the Debtors are individuals.

The Zinks did not send a notice to HSBC indicating that they intended to acquire a purchase-money security interest in the Debtors' livestock. On December 4, 2001, the Debtors received the 54 cows. Those cows are among the total of 96 head owned by the Debtors according to the parties' stipulation of facts.

On or about December 5, 2001, William F. Reynolds, attorney for the Zinks, mailed their UCC–1 form to the New York State Secretary of State by regular, first class mail; they included a check in the amount of $7.00. On December 6, 2001, at or about 9:00 a.m., the New York State Secretary of State physically received the form. On or about December 7, 2001, the New York State Department of State mailed a letter to Mr. Reynolds, rejecting their filing. The letter includes a section called "Reason(s) for rejection." That section states, in part, "The form submitted is an obsolete form that does not contain sections for all information required under Revised Article 9." It also contains paragraphs which describe how to resubmit corrected documents and how to resubmit a rejected filing.

On or about February 1, 2002, Mr. Reynolds submitted an official form adopted by the New York Secretary of State pursuant to 19 N.Y.C.R.R. Part 143. It included the same description of collateral that the Zinks' rejected form had contained. On or about February 5, 2002, the New York State Department of State sent a letter to Mr. Reynolds, acknowledging the filing of the February financing statement and indicating that the statement had been assigned the following information: "Filing Number: 027424" and "Filing Date: 02/04/2002."

Both Debtors filed Chapter 13 petitions on April 25, 2002. Debtor Frank F. Vanmiddlesworth, Jr.'s original Schedule B states that he owns 42 cows with a value of $42,000. On June 26, 2002, he filed an amended schedule which states he owns 54 cows valued at $42,000 "as tenant in common with brother, William." Frank's Schedule H lists "William G. Vanmiddlesworth, Jr." as the codebtor on the HSBC secured debts he lists on his Schedule D.

Debtor William G. Vanmiddlesworth, Jr.'s Schedule B states that he owns 54 cows valued at $54,000. Although he lists Frank as a codebtor of HSBC on his Schedule H, none of his original schedules lists HSBC as a creditor. The amended Schedule F William filed on June 26, 2002, however, lists HSBC as a general unsecured creditor for a May 7, 2001 loan in the amount of $3,987 and an undated loan in the amount of $399,390. These amounts match those listed on his brother's Schedule D where the "Codebtor" box is checked.

On May 3, 2002, the Debtors filed their Chapter 13 plans. Both plans specifically address the Zinks' financing statement by providing that unless the matter is settled, the Debtors will commence adversary proceedings "to avoid the unperfected lien." The Debtors' cases were converted to Chapter 12 on May 17, 2002, the same day the Zinks filed their motions in each case, seeking a lift stay or adequate protection.

The primary ground the Zinks' attorney cites in the motions is cause under 11 U.S.C. § 362(d)(1) (including lack of adequate protection, default of responsibilities like insurance, accruing interest, late charges and fees and irreparable injury and loss); he also cites 11 U.S.C. § 362(d)(2) in his wherefore clause, but does not allege anything regarding it.

Another stipulated fact worth noting is that for the years 2000 and 2001, the Debtors filed partnership income tax returns. On both of their Statement of Financial Affairs, the Debtors answered Question # 21 (Current Partners, Officers, Directors and Shareholders) by stating that during 2001, "debtor operated as Vanmiddlesworth Farm Partnership." Each of the Debtors listed himself and the other as a 50% interest holder in the partnership.

(Citations to record omitted.)

Judge Littlefield summarizes the parties' arguments as follows:

Despite moving for adequate protection or, in the alternative, relief from the automatic stay, the Zinks conclude both their opening and reply memoranda by asking for adequate protection only. To that end, they assert four issues that the court must resolve. They are:

(1) whether the Zinks have a perfected security interest that is not subject to being set aside as a preference;

(2) the extent of HSBC's security interest in the 54 cows when its security interest in after-acquired cattle attaches only to cattle belonging to Debtor Frank Vanmiddlesworth, Jr.;

(3) if both HSBC and the Zinks have perfected security interests, their relative priority; and

(4) if the Zinks have a perfected security interest, the appropriate adequate protection payment.

Judge Littlefield found that the Zinks have a purchase-money security interest in the 54 cows. Under New York law,

> a perfected purchase-money security interest in livestock that are farm products has priority over a conflicting security interest in the same livestock, and, except as otherwise provided in Section 9–327 [which is not applicable here], a perfected security interest in their identifiable proceeds and identifiable products in their unmanufactured states also has priority, if:
>
> (1) the purchase-money security interest is perfected when the debtor receives possession of the livestock;
>
> (2) the purchase-money secured party sends an authenticated notification to the holder of the conflicting security interest;
>
> (3) the holder of the conflicting security interest receives the notification within six months before the debtor receives possession of the livestock; and
>
> (4) the notification states that the person sending the notification has or expects to acquire a purchase-money security interest in livestock of the debtor and describes the livestock.

N.Y.U.C.C. § 9–324(d). Judge Littlefield construed section 9–324(d) as requiring compliance with subparagraphs (1) through (4) to establish purchase-money security interest priority over a conflicting security interest both in livestock and in their identifiable proceeds and products.

The parties stipulated that the Zinks never notified HSBC of their purchase-money security interest. Thus, Judge Littlefield determined, the Zinks failed to satisfy subparagraphs (2) through (4) of section 9–324(d). Moreover, he determined that subparagraph (1) was not satisfied, even assuming that the Zinks perfected their purchase-money security interest on December 6, 2001[2] (when the Department of State received and rejected their initial UCC–1 form), because the Vanmiddlesworths had already

[2] HSBC argues that, if the Zinks' purchase-money security interest is deemed to have been perfected on February 4, 2002, the date of the second filing, it would be avoidable as a preference because filed within 90 days of the filing of the Vanmiddlesworths' bankruptcy petitions and schedules.

taken possession of the 54 cows on December 4, 2001. Judge Littlefield concluded that, inasmuch as the Zinks failed to satisfy the requirements of 9–324(d)(1)–(4), they failed to create a purchase-money security interest in the 54 cows which would take priority over HSBC's interest arising from the April 7, 1998 security agreement signed by Frank Vanmiddlesworth in favor of HSBC's predecessor.

Judge Littlefield then turned to consider the nature of the interest held by each Vanmiddlesworth. It is undisputed that the two Vanmiddlesworths shared a tenancy in common in the 54 cows. Judge Littlefield observed that one cotenant may encumber or dispose of his interest in the whole without the consent of the other. *See Cary v. Fisher*, 149 A.D.2d 890, 541 N.Y.S.2d 138, 140 (3d Dep't 1989). Moreover, one tenant in common may sever his interest in commonly-held personalty in a replevin and/or conversion action against a cotenant where the personalty is "alike in quality and value and divisible by weight, tale or measure." *Gates v. Bowers*, 169 N.Y. 14, 17, 61 N.E. 993 (1901). In this respect, Judge Littlefield noted that the sales contract and debtors' schedules provide "some evidence" of the value of the 54 cows as of the date the petition was filed and that the evidence was "arguably" sufficient to enable the court to calculate the value of the Zinks' purchase-money security interest in half of them. However, he based his denial of the Zinks' request for adequate protection on another ground, that is, the lack of proof of need for adequate protection.

Section 1205(b) of the Bankruptcy Code provides:

> [W]hen adequate protection is required under section 362, 363, or 364 of this title of an interest of an entity in property, such adequate protection may be provided by—
>
> (1) requiring the trustee to make a cash payment or periodic cash payments to such entity, to the extent that the stay under section 362 of this title, use, sale, or lease under section 363 of this title, or any grant of a lien under section 364 of this title results in a decrease in the value of property securing a claim or of an entity's ownership interest in property;
>
> (2) providing to such entity an additional or replacement lien to the extent that such stay, use, sale, lease, or grant results in a decrease in the value of property securing a claim or of an entity's ownership interest in property;
>
> (3) paying to such entity for the use of farmland the reasonable rent customary in the community where the property is located, based upon the rental value, net income, and earning capacity of the property; or

(4) granting such other relief, other than entitling such entity to compensation allowable under section 503(b)(1) of this title as an administrative expense, as will adequately protect the value of property securing a claim or of such entity's ownership interest in property.

11 U.S.C. § 1205(b). The provision is not mandatory; its purpose is to protect the creditor against decreases in the value of the collateral where necessary. *See In re Bluridg Farms, Inc.*, 93 B.R. 648, 656 (Bankr. S.D. Iowa 1988); *see also In re Anderson*, 137 B.R. 819, 822–23 (Bankr.D.Colo.1992).

Judge Littlefield concluded that the Zinks did not adduce evidence that the security had declined in value since the Vanmiddlesworths filed their bankruptcy petition, nor did they demonstrate their right to adequate protection relief on any other ground. Further, they did not offer evidence in support of lifting the stay on the ground of lack of adequate protection under 11 U.S.C. § 362(d)(2), nor did they brief the issue. Accordingly, in both cases Judge Littlefield denied the motions for adequate protection or to lift the stay.

THE APPEAL

* * *

As Judge Littlefield noted, even assuming that the Zinks had a purchase-money security interest in the 54 cows as of December 6, 2001, it is undisputed that they did not notify HSBC of their interest and that the Vanmiddlesworths had already taken possession of the 54 cows on December 4, 2001. This Court agrees with Judge Littlefield's reading of the requirements of section 9–324 as applying to purchase-money security interests in livestock as well as in their identifiable proceeds. Thus, Judge Littlefield correctly determined that the Zinks failed to satisfy the requirements of subparagraphs (1) through (4) of section 9–324(d), and that, regardless of the date they filed their financing statement relative to their purchase-money security interest, they did not obtain "livestock purchase-money security interest priority" over HSBC with respect to Frank Vanmiddlesworth's interest in the 54 cows.

* * *

CONCLUSION

Upon de novo review of Judge Littlefield's legal conclusions, this Court finds no error.

* * *

IT IS SO ORDERED.

NOTE

As one can see, parties ignore the requirements of section 9–324(d) at their peril, and the foregoing case has several messages for a lawyer. First and foremost is the need to understand how one prepares a proper financing statement and where and how one files it. Second, one needs to know section 9–324 on purchase-money security. Third, the lawyer must know the nature of the legal organism that is the debtor. Some of the behavior of the brothers and some of the documents suggested that they were operating as a partnership and that the partnership was the owner of the cows. Other documents and representations in the case indicate that the brothers individually held the cows.

Before one can hope to create and perfect a valid security interest, one needs to know the proper name and form of the owner of the collateral. Do the brothers have joint ownership? Did they hold certain cows individually or was there a real partnership that held title? Lawyers who deal mostly with large corporations and multi-million dollar businesses typically will not have this problem. Sophisticated people in the company will make it their business to know who is the parent, who is the subsidiary, and who is the owner of the collateral. In an informal business, such as the farming business of Frank and William Vanmiddlesworth, many of these things will be in doubt and the individual parties may not understand the importance of precision in identifying the debtor and in finding its proper name.

So the case is a good lesson. It appears that the lawyer was not sufficiently experienced in the art of preparing and filing financing statements. When completing and filing financing statements, one cannot be too compulsive or systematic. If one's clients do not wish to be bothered with such nit-picking questions, the lawyer must press them and get the answers or later risk the claim that he was guilty of negligence.

The rules contained in section 9–324(b) regarding priority of purchase money security interests in inventory require careful reading and compliance if a purchase money lender expects to prevail over earlier creditors with perfected interests in after-acquired collateral. Consider the following case. It also offers several good lessons for lawyers; it highlights the need for detailed attention to both Article 9 and to the deal documentation their clients will rely on.

IN RE VIC SUPPLY COMPANY, INC.

United States Court of Appeals, Seventh Circuit, 2000.
227 F.3d 928.

POSNER, CIRCUIT JUDGE:

This case involves a dispute between two creditors of the bankrupt Vic Supply Company. Bank One had a security agreement with Vic, covering all of Vic's assets. Falconbridge sold Vic nickel for resale, acquiring a purchase money security interest covering the proceeds of the resale. The bankruptcy court, seconded by the district court, to which Falconbridge had appealed, ruled that Bank One's security interest was prior to Falconbridge's under Article 9 of the Uniform Commercial Code (codified in Illinois as 810 ILCS 5/9). Falconbridge argues that its interest is prior because the security agreement between the bank and Vic was never accepted by the bank. The argument turns on whether a secured lender's failure to sign such an agreement, when the agreement provides that it is effective only when signed by the lender, allows a subsequent secured lender to take priority over the earlier one.

The bank began lending money to Vic in 1980, and that year it filed a U.C.C. financing statement with the Secretary of State of Illinois covering all of Vic's inventory, accounts receivable, and equipment. The statement implied that the parties had or intended soon to make an agreement granting the bank a security interest in these assets, the purpose of filing such a statement being to perfect such an interest. The U.C.C. does not require, for a security interest to be perfected, that the security agreement precede the filing of the financing statement, § 9–402 [9–502(d)], let alone that it be attached to the statement (the statement "indicates merely that the secured party who has filed may have a security interest in the collateral described," § 9–402, official comment 2 [9–502 cmt. 2]; see *In re Varney Wood Products, Inc.*, 458 F.2d 435 (4th Cir. 1972)), although that is often done; and we do not know the agreement's terms.

Ten years later, with the bank continuing to extend credit to Vic, Vic signed another agreement, granting the bank a continuing security interest in all Vic's assets. The agreement expressly covered—what was anyway implicit, § 9–306(2) [9–315(a)(2)]—the proceeds of sales from inventory. A few months earlier the bank had filed with the Illinois Secretary of State a continuation financing statement materially identical to the one filed back in 1980.

Years passed, and Falconbridge, having obtained a purchase money security interest in the nickel that it was selling to Vic, filed a financing statement, just as Bank One had done. This security interest, like Bank One's, automatically extended to the proceeds of Vic's resale of the nickel. When Vic later defaulted, Bank One's security interest, having been recorded before Falconbridge's, would normally have had priority, § 9–312(5)(a) [9–322]; Falconbridge was not entitled to the superpriority that is accorded to a purchase money security interest when the debtor receives cash proceeds in a sale of the collateral, § 9–312(3) [9–324], because the proceeds that Vic received were in the form of accounts receivable rather than cash.

But Bank One had failed to sign the 1990 security agreement, and Falconbridge argues that this failure means that the agreement did not become effective. The agreement provides that "the terms and provisions of this agreement shall not become effective and Bank shall have no duties hereunder unless and until this agreement is accepted by Bank as provided below"—and below is a blank for a signature that was never filled in. Falconbridge reminds us that "a security agreement is effective according to its terms between the parties, against purchasers of the collateral and against creditors." UCC § 9–201. "According to its terms," Falconbridge argues, the agreement never came into effect. Although the agreement authorizes the bank to fill in any blanks in it, the bank had not done that; and according to Falconbridge, it was too late for the bank to do so once Falconbridge perfected its own security interest by filing a UCC financing statement. In short, Falconbridge argues, the bank had no security interest when Falconbridge acquired its own security interest.

Ordinarily, only a party (actual or alleged) to a contract can challenge its validity, *e.g.*, *Williams v. Eggleston*, 170 U.S. 304, 309, 42 L. Ed. 1047, 18 S. Ct. 617 (1898); *IDS Life Insurance Co. v. SunAmerica, Inc.*, 103 F.3d 524, 529 (7th Cir. 1996); *OPE Shipping Ltd. v. Allstate Ins. Co.*, 687 F.2d 639, 643 (2d Cir. 1982); *Tri-Star Pictures, Inc. v. Leisure Time Productions, B.V.*, 749 F. Supp. 1243, 1250 (S.D.N.Y. 1990), and neither party to the security agreement that is at issue in this case—neither Bank One nor Vic—challenges the validity of the agreement. Of course there are illegal contracts that the government, or persons injured by the contract, can challenge, such as a contract in restraint of trade, but there is no suggestion of that here. Obviously the fact that a third party would be better off if a contract were unenforceable does not give him standing to sue to void the contract. A contract that while not unenforceable by either party, or within the class of contracts deemed illegal, might, intentionally or negligently, deceive a third party, who in that event might have a tort remedy. But there is no suggestion that the defect in the bank's security agreement with Vic—the absence of the bank's signature—harmed Falconbridge. So far as appears, Falconbridge was unaware of the defect or of anything else about the agreement. It knew, or at least thought, there was an agreement, because before extending credit to Vic it checked the U.C.C. registry and read the bank's financing statement, which notified Falconbridge that the bank had a security interest, implying, as we said, that it had a security agreement with Vic. Falconbridge even wrote Bank One that it was planning to obtain a purchase money security interest in the nickel it was selling Vic and in any proceeds of resales of the nickel. The bank cannot be accused of having misled Falconbridge. *National Bank v. Haupricht Bros., Inc.*, 55 Ohio App. 3d 249, 564 N.E.2d 101, 114 (Ohio App. 1988) (per curiam); *cf. Elhard v. Prairie Distributors, Inc.*, 366 N.W.2d 465, 468 (N.D. 1985).

So Falconbridge cannot appeal to any general legal or equitable principle that might enable it to challenge the validity of the bank's agreement with Vic. But we must consider the bearing of U.C.C. § 9–

203(1)(a) [9–203(b)], which provides that a security interest is not "enforceable against the debtor or third parties with respect to the collateral" unless (the collateral not being in the creditor's possession or control) "the debtor has signed a security agreement which contains a description of the collateral." Some courts have permitted a subsequent creditor to use this provision to knock out the priority of an earlier creditor without requiring proof that he was actually misled or otherwise prejudiced by any defect in the security agreement. *World Wide Tracers, Inc. v. Metropolitan Protection, Inc.*, 384 N.W.2d 442 (Minn. 1986); *In re Middle Atlantic Stud Welding Co.*, 503 F.2d 1133, 1136 (3d Cir. 1974). This result, which is contrary to the *Haupricht* case cited earlier, strikes us as questionable despite its conformity to the literal language of section 9–203; it gives the later creditor a windfall by enabling him to knock out a priority on the basis of a defect on which he did not rely. No matter. The debtor signed the security agreement in this case and the agreement describes the collateral. The fact that section 9–203 requires the debtor to sign and does not mention signature by the creditor helps to show that the draftsmen did not think that a priority should be lost merely because the creditor's signature was missing.

A complicating factor in some cases, though not in this one, is that a trustee in bankruptcy (or debtor in possession) has the status of a hypothetical lien creditor "without regard to any knowledge of the trustee or of any creditor," 11 U.S.C. § 544(a), entitling him to void a security interest because of defects that need not have misled, or even have been capable of misleading, anyone. *Pearson v. Salina Coffee House, Inc.*, 831 F.2d 1531 (10th Cir. 1987); *In re Sandy Ridge Oil Co.*, 807 F.2d 1332 (7th Cir. 1986); *Sommers v. International Business Machines*, 640 F.2d 686, 688–89 (5th Cir. 1981). The trustee did not assert this right here, probably because the only benefit would have been to another secured creditor, Falconbridge, and the trustee's duty is to maximize the recovery of the unsecured creditors. [Ed. note, *but see* section 551 of the Bankruptcy Code, 11 U.S.C. § 551 (preserving an avoided transfer, including a lien, for the benefit of the bankruptcy estate); H.Rep. No. 95–595, 95th Cong., 1st Sess. 376 (1977) ("The section as a whole prevents junior lienors from improving their position at the expense of the estate when a senior lien is avoided.").]

For completeness we further note that while the provision requiring an adequate description of the collateral is intended in part for the protection of subsequent creditors, *In re Martin Grinding & Machine Works, Inc.*, 793 F.2d 592, 596–97 (7th Cir. 1986); *In re Laminated Veneers Co.*, 471 F.2d 1124, 1125 (2d Cir. 1973), and so may be enforced by them, at least when they can show they were misled by an inadequate description, the provision requiring the debtor's signature is not intended for their protection. It is a statute of frauds provision intended to make it easier for courts to resolve disputes over the meaning of the agreement. 2

James J. White & Robert S. Summers, Uniform Commercial Code § 24–4 at 305 (1988). Falconbridge had no standing to enforce it. See UCC § 2–201, official comment 4; cf. *BDS, Inc. v. Gillis*, 477 A.2d 1121, 1123 (D.C. App. 1984) (per curiam); 2 E. Allan Farnsworth, Farnsworth on Contracts § 6.10, p. 168 (1990).

The real significance of section 9–203 in this case is in helping to explain section 9–201. In providing that a security agreement is effective only according to its terms, the draftsmen meant to state the general rule to which section 9–203 creates an exception. See U.C.C. § 9–201, official comment. An agreement that violates section 9–203 may not be effective according to its terms. But that is not the only function of section 9–201. For the fact that Falconbridge is not permitted to question that the bank had a security interest does not automatically extinguish Falconbridge's security interest. That depends on the relative priority of the contestants' security interests, and this is where section 9–201 could bite in this case: the bank can enforce a security agreement against a subsequent creditor of its debtor, that is, can retain its priority, only insofar as the agreement gives it a security interest. Had the agreement granted the bank a security interest only in inventory by expressly disclaiming any grant of a security interest in proceeds as well, the bank could not claim the proceeds in derogation of Falconbridge's later-perfected security interest in them. But there is nothing like that here. There is no discrepancy between the bank's financing statement and its security interest. Both cover all the assets of Vic, leaving nothing for Falconbridge until the bank's claim has been satisfied.

Although unnecessary to add, the security agreement was valid; that is, Vic would have had no defense against enforcement of the agreement by the bank, or vice versa. For one thing, it is apparent from the wording of the signature requirement and the fact that the bank was authorized to fill in any blank in the agreement that the requirement was intended solely for the bank's protection, and was not intended to confer any right on Vic; it was a defect of which no one could complain. For another thing (but it is actually closely related), after the agreement was not signed the bank lent money to Vic against its inventory nonetheless, and the parties assumed that this credit was pursuant to the terms of the security agreement. Acceptance can be effectuated by performance as well as by a signature. Restatement (Second) of Contracts § 30(2) (1981); 1 Farnsworth, supra, § 3.12, p. 222; see also U.C.C. § 2–206(1)(a); 1 White & Summers, supra, § 1–5, p. 55. And while parties can specify that performance shall not be effective as acceptance, *Golden Dipt Co. v. Systems Engineering & Mfg. Co.*, 465 F.2d 215 (7th Cir. 1972); *In re Newport Plaza Associates, L.P.*, 985 F.2d 640, 645 (1st Cir. 1993); Restatement, supra, § 30, comment a, this would be an implausible interpretation of the acceptance clause that we quoted earlier. It would amount to saying that if the parties had been asked, "if the bank fails to sign the agreement, will the agreement be void even if the parties behave in a way that shows they thought it was in effect?" they would have said "yes." Or that if they had been asked, "does the bank's failure to sign mean that the debtor could repudiate the agreement at any time?" they would have said "no." What they really would have said would have been, "don't be silly; it was just an oversight, of no significance—and anyway the requirement of the bank's signature was for the protection of the bank, not of the debtor."

Falconbridge's argument that the bank's effort to show acceptance by performance violates the parol evidence rule (which both parties call the "parole evidence" rule) is frivolous. The rule bars evidence oral or written concerning negotiations leading up to an integrated contract, not evidence of events subsequent to the writing that is claimed to be the statement of the parties' contract. *Fischer v. First Chicago Capital Markets*, 195 F.3d 279, 282 (7th Cir. 1999); *Williams v. Jader Fuel Co.*, 944 F.2d 1388, 1394 (7th Cir. 1991); 2 Farnsworth, supra, § 7.6 p. 228. Anyway, to repeat a theme of this opinion, the parol evidence rule, like other contract defenses, is intended for the protection of parties or alleged parties to contracts; it is not intended to enable a stranger to break up a contractual relation. *Northern Assurance Co. v. Chicago Mutual Building Ass'n*, 198 Ill. 474, 64 N.E. 979 (Ill. 1902); *Quality Lighting, Inc. v. Benjamin*, 227 Ill. App. 3d 880, 592 N.E.2d 377, 382, 169 Ill. Dec. 890 (Ill. App. 1992); *Rittenhouse v. Tabor Grain Co.*, 203 Ill. App. 3d 639, 561 N.E.2d 264, 271, 148 Ill. Dec. 958 (Ill. App. 1990). So there was acceptance; but if there hadn't been, yet the parties agreed they had a contract, that would be enough to defeat Falconbridge's effort to invalidate a contract on which (or on the defect in which) it did not rely in extending credit to Vic. Affirmed.

WILLIAMS, CIRCUIT JUDGE, concurring:

I agree with my colleagues that Falconbridge cannot challenge the validity of the security agreement between Bank One and Vic Supply. I write separately to voice my concern regarding the majority's further determination that the security agreement is, in any event, valid. While I am sympathetic to the majority's intuition that Bank One and Vic Supply could not have intended the signature provision to mean what it says, I am not persuaded that such an intuition justifies reading the provision out of the agreement.

Under the signature provision, the security agreement becomes effective only if and when Bank One accepts the agreement by filling in the signature blank; something Bank One did not do. The signature provision is not at all ambiguous, nor is there any reason to believe it is merely surplusage. It is a cardinal principal of contract law that since the language of a contract is the best evidence of the parties' intent, every provision of a contract should be given content and effect, and unambiguous contractual language should be given its plain and natural meaning. *See, e.g.*, *Emergency Med. Care, Inc. v. Marion Mem'l Hosp.*, 94 F.3d 1059, 1061 (7th Cir. 1996) (applying Illinois law); *River Forest State Bank & Trust Co. v. Rosemary Joyce Enters. Inc.*, 294 Ill. App. 3d 173, 689 N.E.2d 163, 167, 228 Ill. Dec. 291 (Ill. App. Ct. 1998). It does not matter that in hindsight one or both parties (or a court) might have second thoughts about the wisdom of including a particular term. Our task is to enforce the terms the parties included in their contract.

To my mind, moreover, it is telling that the majority cites not a single case adopting the same pragmatic approach it employs in interpreting the signature provision of the security agreement. No rule of law of which I am aware allows us to disregard the unambiguous terms of a contract in favor of what we believe the parties must have intended. Again, our task is to enforce the terms the parties included in their contract. Accordingly, I cannot join in the majority's conclusion that the security agreement between Bank One and Vic Supply is valid.

NOTE

How can you tell, from the outset of this case, that it involves a security interest in inventory? Notice that Falconbridge expected to have priority over Bank One in the inventory and proceeds of inventory of Vic Supply. Why did it not have the priority it expected—what might have happened that left Falconbridge in the position of having to challenge the enforceability of Bank One's interest all together? The opinion explains that Falconbridge was not entitled to superpriority as a purchase money security interest holder because it was asserting its interest in proceeds of inventory in the form of accounts. Can you find the citation for this rule under current Article 9? If superpriority does not extend to proceeds of an inventory purchase money interest in the form of accounts, why does it extend to proceeds in the form of chattel paper? This issue will become clearer after you study accounts and chattel paper in Chapter 5, but you should be able, at this point, to use the statute to formulate answers to these questions now. Finally, the case is decided on standing, and yet it was extensively litigated and involves ample dicta and a concurring opinion. Why does the court bother to continue its analysis of Bank One's security interest if it is rejecting Falconbridge's argument on standing grounds?

PROBLEM 4-6

The Great Outdoors Company operated five large department stores in Indiana. In 1999, Bank One took a security interest in all of the Great Outdoors' inventory and proceeds and properly perfected that security interest by filing in Indianapolis. In 2001, Hart Schaffner & Marks ("HSM") lent the Great Outdoors $2,000,000 to finance the purchase of HSM clothing. HSM also filed a financing statement in Indianapolis and received a proper security agreement. This security agreement covered all HSM clothing sold to the Great

Outdoors together with accounts receivable arising from the sale of such clothing, all such proceeds and the like. In September 2004, Great Outdoors went bankrupt, and at the time of its bankruptcy, it held $1,200,000 of HSM clothing and $500,000 of credit card receivables arising from the sale of HSM clothing. Who has priority between Bank One and HSM in each of the following cases?

1. If HSM gave no notice of its interest to Bank One.

2. If HSM gave proper notice of its interest to Bank One.

3. Would Bank One's rights vis-à-vis HSM be the same as to the first loan it made (before it knew of HSM) and as to another $1,000,000 advance after it had learned of HSM's security interest either by examining the records again or by being told?

4. Assume Bank One's filing had been made on March 4, 1999. Assume HSM had examined the files and had seen Bank One's filing in 2001. Assume further that Bank One never filed a continuation statement and that the Great Outdoors filed for bankruptcy on April 1, 2004. Is Bank One subordinate to HSM, the DIP, both, or neither?

5. Assume Bank One has a fully perfected security interest securing its $5 million loan. Assume Bank Two has a fully perfected but subordinate security interest also securing a $5 million loan. In order to get Bank Three to make a loan, Bank One agrees to subordinate its security interest to Bank Three's claim. Accordingly, Bank Three makes a $4 million unsecured loan. If, upon liquidation, the inventory and proceeds are sold for $7 million, how is the $7 million divided among Banks One, Two, and Three, and a trustee in bankruptcy?

PROBLEM 4-7

Bank has a security interest in car dealer's inventory of automobiles. Bank has properly perfected its security interest and claims all after-acquired inventory as well as proceeds. Several years ago, dealer purchased assets of a failed Toyota dealer, and your client, Toyota Finance, lent it $2 million to purchase Lexus and Toyota automobiles. Your client went through the proper procedure to notify Bank and to achieve priority over them. The dealer has now gone into bankruptcy, and Bank claims your client is not a purchase-money lender as to approximately $1 million worth of Toyota Camrys. It seems that the Lexus cars, although later acquired, were first sold because they were a hot item, whereas the Camrys remained on the lot for a long period of time. Bank claims that when the Lexus cars were sold, the money received from them under Toyota Finance's accounting procedure went to pay off the earlier acquired Camrys, and thus, there is at best a non-purchase-money security interest in those cars which would be subordinate to Bank's interest. What do you think?

How malleable is the purchase-money priority? Consider the following case decided under former Article 9.

MBANK ALAMO NATIONAL ASSOCIATION V. RAYTHEON COMPANY D/B/A RAYTHEON MEDICAL SYSTEMS

United States Court of Appeals, Fifth Circuit, 1989.
886 F.2d 1449.

REAVLEY, CIRCUIT JUDGE:

MBank Alamo National Association ("MBank") and E.I. DuPont de Nemours Company, Inc. ("DuPont") pressed this conversion action against Raytheon Company ("Raytheon"), claiming that Raytheon collected certain accounts receivable, in which MBank and DuPont had security interests superior to those of Raytheon. Raytheon's defense was that it had a purchase money security interest in the accounts receivable. Concluding that Raytheon had no purchase money security interest in the accounts, the district court held that Raytheon's security interests were subordinate to those of MBank and DuPont, and granted MBank's and DuPont's motions for summary judgment. We affirm.

I. Background

MBank and DuPont entered various security agreements with Howe X-ray ("Howe"). By January 10, 1983, in accordance with these agreements, both DuPont and MBank held perfected liens in Howe's present and future accounts receivable. MBank also held a perfected security interest in Howe's present and after acquired inventory.

Beginning in January 1983, Raytheon, an x-ray equipment manufacturer, entered a series of transactions with Howe who was one of its distributors. Raytheon agreed to ship x-ray equipment to Howe after Howe contracted with one of its customers for the sale, delivery, and installation of certain Raytheon equipment. In exchange, Howe agreed to assign the specific accounts receivable to Raytheon. Subsequent to the assignments, Raytheon filed financing statements in specific accounts receivable of Howe. Between July 1983 and December 1984, Raytheon collected over $850,000.00.

By November 1984, Howe had defaulted on its obligations to MBank and DuPont. MBank and DuPont, pursuant to their security interests, demanded payment from Raytheon from the accounts receivable that it had collected. Raytheon refused, claiming that it had a purchase money security interest ("PMSI") in the accounts receivable and that its interests were therefore superior to those of MBank and DuPont.

In addition to its contention that it had a PMSI in the accounts receivable, Raytheon claimed that even if it did not have a PMSI in those accounts, MBank waived its security interest in the accounts. The district court granted MBank's and DuPont's motions for summary judgment, deciding that Raytheon had no PMSI in the accounts receivable and that Raytheon had not raised an issue of MBank's alleged waiver.

Raytheon appeals the district court's determination that it did not have a PMSI in the accounts receivable. In the alternative, Raytheon contends that if our construction of the PMSI statutory provisions excludes the Raytheon-Howe transaction, the ruling should not apply to this case under the doctrine of nonretroactivity. Raytheon also appeals the district court's finding that Raytheon failed to produce sufficient evidence of waiver to overcome MBank's motion for summary judgment.

II. Analysis

A. *Purchase Money Security Interests*

The rules governing the rights of creditors are set out in Chapter 9 of the Texas Business and Commerce Code (Code), which essentially adopted the provisions of the Uniform Commercial Code—Secured Transactions. *See* Tex.Bus. & Com.Code Ann. § 9.101 et seq. (Vernon 1989). These provisions were enacted "to provide a simple and unified structure within which the immense variety of present-day secured financing transactions can go forward with less cost and with greater certainty." § 9.101, 1972 Official U.C.C. Comment. In keeping with these goals, rules were enacted prioritizing conflicting security interests in the same property.

The general rule provides that the first perfected security interest to be filed has priority and other perfected interests stand in line in the order in which they were filed. *See* § 9.312(e) [9–322]. PMSIs are excepted from the first-to-file rule and take priority over other perfected security interests regardless of the filing sequence. § 9.312(c), (d) [9–324]. The district court found that Raytheon did not fall within the PMSI exception, that MBank had priority as the first to file, under § 9.312(e)(1) [9–322], and that DuPont takes second priority since it filed next.

Raytheon claims the district court erred by not recognizing its priority in the accounts receivable as a PMSI under § 9.312(d) [9–324]. Section 9.312(d) [9–324] provides that "[a] purchase money security interest in collateral other than inventory has priority over a conflicting security interest in the same collateral or its proceeds if the purchase money security interest is perfected at the time the debtor receives possession of the collateral or within 20 days thereafter."

As a threshold matter, Raytheon must establish that it meets the statutory definition of a PMSI. Raytheon contends that it fits the statutory requirements of a PMSI under § 9.107(2) [9–103], which provides:

> A security interest is a "purchase money security interest" to the extent that it is. . . (2) taken by a person who by making advances or incurring an obligation gives value to enable the debtor to acquire rights in or the use of collateral if such value is in fact so used.

To meet these requirements Raytheon must show: (1) that it gave value; (2) that the value given enabled Howe to acquire rights in the accounts receivable; and (3) that the accounts receivable qualify as collateral within the meaning of the statute.

The value requirement is satisfied by any consideration sufficient to support a simple contract. *See Thet Mah and Assoc. v. First Bank of North Dakota*, 336 N.W.2d 134, 138 (N.D.1983); § 1.201(44)(D) (Vernon 1968) [1–204]. Assuming *arguendo* that Raytheon gave value by extending credit to Howe in exchange for Howe's promise to assign the accounts receivable to Raytheon, *see Thet Mah*, 336 N.W.2d at 138, Raytheon has failed to satisfy the other two requirements.

To create a PMSI, the value must be given in a manner that enables the debtor to acquire [an] interest in the collateral. This is accomplished when a debtor uses an extension of credit or loan money to purchase a specific item. *See Ingram v. Ozark Prod. Credit Assoc.*, 468 F.2d 564, 565 (5th Cir.1972); *In re Dillon*, 18 B.R. 252, 254 (Bkrtcy.E.D.Cal.1982) (PMSI lien attaches to item actually purchased); Jackson & Kronman, *Secured Financing and Priorities Among Creditors*, 88 Yale L.J. 1143, 1165 (1979) (PMSI priority limited "to loans that can be traced to identifiable, discrete items of property.").

The collateral at issue here is the accounts receivable. In an attempt to force its interest into the PMSI mold, Raytheon has characterized the transaction as follows: "Raytheon, by agreeing to extend credit on its equipment, enabled Howe X-Ray to enter into subsequent contracts of sale with its customers, thereby acquiring rights in the contract accounts which, upon the specific advance and delivery of equipment, blossomed into a right to the collateral accounts receivable." Raytheon, however, cannot force this transaction to fit. To accept this characterization, we would have to close our eyes to the true nature of the transaction.

Raytheon, in essence, is claiming that it advanced x-ray machines to Howe on credit, which then enabled Howe to purchase accounts receivable from its customers. This, however, does not comport with our view of commercial reality. While, as Raytheon suggests, it may be theoretically possible to create a PMSI in accounts receivable by advancing funds for their purchase, *see Northwestern Nat'l Bank Southwest v. Lectro Systems*, 262 N.W.2d 678, 680 (Minn.1977); Gilmore, *The Purchase Money Priority*, 76 Harv.L.Rev. 1333, 1372 (1963), the same cannot be done by advancing x-ray machines. We view this as a two-step transaction in which Raytheon first advanced machines to Howe for retail sale and, once these machines were sold, Howe then assigned the accounts receivable to Raytheon. Through the credit advance, Howe acquired an interest in the machines, not the accounts receivable. Raytheon's credit advance, therefore, did not enable Howe to acquire an interest in the accounts receivable, as collateral within the meaning of the statute.

Additionally, in its characterization of the transaction, Raytheon is attempting to benefit from the PMSI's preferred status in a manner that was not contemplated by the U.C.C. drafters. PMSIs provide an avenue for heavily burdened debtors to obtain credit for specific goods when creditors who have previously loaned money to the debtor may be unwilling to advance additional funds. Jackson & Kronman, *Secured Financing and Priorities Among Creditors*, 88 Yale L.J. 1143, 1145 & n. 9 (1979). By giving a PMSI holder a priority interest in the specific goods purchased, there is some incentive for a lender to advance funds or credit for the specific transaction. The scope of a PMSI holder's preferred interest, however, is specifically limited by the Code.

Under § 9.312(c) [9–324(b)], a PMSI in inventory is limited to that inventory or to "identifiable cash proceeds received on or before the delivery of the inventory to a buyer . . . ." The drafters noted that general financing of an inventory business is based primarily on accounts resulting from inventory, chattel paper and other proceeds. § 9.312 [9–324], Official U.C.C. Reasons for 1972 Change comment (4). Reasoning that "[a]ccounts financing is more important in the economy than the financing of the kinds of inventory that produce accounts, and [that] the desirable rule is one which makes accounts financing certain as to its legal position," *id.*, they specifically excluded accounts resulting from the sale of inventory from the protections of a PMSI. Thus, financing statements that are filed on a debtor's accounts take precedence over any subsequent claim to accounts as proceeds of a PMSI in inventory. Additionally, to protect lenders who make periodic advances against incoming inventory, the PMSI holder is required to notify other secured parties before it can take priority. § 9.312(c)(2) [9–324(b)]; *see id.*, 1972 Official U.C.C. Comment comment 3 [cmt. 8].

The priority scheme, however, differs in the context of collateral other than inventory. Under § 9.312(d) [9–324(a)], a PMSI in collateral other than inventory entitles the holder to a superior interest in both the collateral and its proceeds regardless of any intervening accounts. The differing entitlement to proceeds is due to differences in the expectations of the parties with respect to the collateral involved.

Collateral other than inventory generally refers to equipment used in the course of business. *See id.*, Official U.C.C. Reasons for 1972 Change comment (4); Gilmore, *The Purchase Money Priority*, 76 Harv.L.Rev. 1333, 1385 (1963). Since, unlike inventory, "it is not ordinarily expected that the collateral will be sold and that proceeds will result, [the drafters found it] appropriate to give the party having a purchase money security interest in the original collateral an equivalent priority in its proceeds." § 9.312 [9–324(a)], Official U.C.C. Reasons for 1972 Change comment (3).

Howe's business primarily involved the sale of inventory, which included the Raytheon x-ray machines. *See* § 9.109(4) [9–102(a)(48)]. The accounts receivable are proceeds resulting from the sale of the machines. MBank and DuPont took security interests in the accounts receivable, in accordance with their expectation that sale of the inventory would generate the accounts. If we were to accept Raytheon's argument that it holds a PMSI in Howe's accounts receivable, we would be giving Raytheon a priority interest in the proceeds of inventory, in direct contravention to the express intent of the drafters. Additionally, Raytheon would have successfully avoided the notice requirements of § 9.312(c)(2) [9–324(b)].

Raytheon argues, however, that the policies underlying PMSIs actually favor recognizing Raytheon's priority interest in Howe's accounts. It points out that Howe could find no other source of financing besides Raytheon and that "MBank and DuPont benefited by the financing arrangements because the extension of [credit] by Raytheon helped Howe X-ray stay in business thereby servicing its debts." Raytheon also contends that if the Code is interpreted to limit the security interests of creditors, such as Raytheon, to a mere promise of repayment and the grant of a PMSI in inventory, a "valuable source of credit" to similarly encumbered debtors would "dry up." This is because the risk of default is too great in the face of prior liens on the debtor's accounts.

The Code itself, however, answers this argument. The drafters were apparently well aware that the failure to extend a PMSI holder's priority status to the resulting accounts would provide less incentive for inventory financers to provide credit. *See* § 9.312 [9–324], 1972 Official U.C.C. Comment comment 8. Yet, they did not extend the protections of a PMSI and merely noted that "[m]any parties financing inventory are quite content to protect their first security interest in the inventory itself, realizing that when inventory is sold, someone else will be financing the accounts and the priority for inventory will not run forward to the accounts." *Id.* The drafter's recognition of the problem and the statutory favoring of accounts financing demonstrate that the drafters were not overly concerned that this source of financing would "dry up."

Additionally, Raytheon had alternative means of securing its right to receive payment. Besides obtaining a PMSI in the inventory by complying with the § 9.312(c)(2) [9–324(b)] notice requirements, it could have entered subordination agreements with MBank and DuPont on the specific accounts resulting from the sale of Raytheon's x-ray machines. It also could have sold the machines to Howe's customers who would have paid Raytheon directly, with Howe receiving a commission on the sale. If Raytheon had followed either of these courses, it would not have subverted the notice and filing requirements of the Code. As this transaction goes beyond that contemplated by the PMSI provisions, we decline "to expand the scope of special protection afforded a purchase money security interest, lest in so doing we defeat the underlying purposes of the Code: to bring predictability to commercial transactions." *Mark Prod. U.S., Inc. v. Interfirst Bank Houston, N.A.*, 737 S.W.2d 389, 393 (Tex.App.-Houston [14th Dist.] 1987).

Since Raytheon did not have a PMSI in Howe's accounts receivable, the first-to-file priority rules govern. *See Ford Motor Credit Co. v. First State Bank of Smithville*, 679 S.W.2d 486, 487 (Tex.1984). As the last to file, Raytheon's interest is subordinate to those of MBank and DuPont.

B. The Doctrine of Nonretroactivity

Having concluded that Raytheon did not have a PMSI, Raytheon now contends that because this case presented a novel question of law, the doctrine of nonretroactivity should apply. Under the doctrine of nonretroactivity a court deciding a question of first impression, in a manner that was not clearly foreshadowed, makes the ruling inapplicable to the parties before it. *See Chevron Oil Co. v. Huson*, 404 U.S. 97, 106, 92 S.Ct. 349, 355, 30 L.Ed.2d 296 (1971). This is no case for nonretroactivity. The holding that Raytheon did not have a PMSI in the accounts receivable is required by the statute and commentary, given the PMSI restrictions and the Code's clear mandate that first-to-file rules establish the priorities in accounts resulting from the sale of inventory. The goal of providing predictability in commercial transactions is furthered by the present application of our holding. Moreover, we find no inequity in applying the rule to Raytheon. Raytheon's credit managers were well aware of the first-to-file rule yet, at no time, attempted to notify MBank or DuPont about its purported interest in the accounts. It did not pursue alternative means of securing payment, but merely claimed a priority right in the absence of any authority to do so.

C. Waiver

Lastly, Raytheon contends that the district court erred in holding that Raytheon failed to produce sufficient evidence that MBank waived its security interest in the accounts to overcome MBank's motion for summary judgment. To support its claim, Raytheon presented evidence that MBank was informed that Howe and Raytheon were engaged in ongoing credit negotiations and that Howe was assigning the accounts receivable to Raytheon. Additionally, while MBank was aware that it was not receiving full payment of Howe's accounts receivable, MBank never requested that the accounts proceeds be segregated or held in trust for the bank.

Waiver is a valid defense to an action to enforce a security interest. *Weisbart & Co. v. First Nat'l Bank of Dalhart, Texas*, 568 F.2d 391, 396 (5th Cir.1978); *Montgomery v. Fuquay-Mouser, Inc.*, 567 S.W.2d 268, 270

(Tex.Civ.App.1978). Under Texas law, "[w]aiver is the intentional relinquishment of a known right or intentional conduct inconsistent with claiming it, with full knowledge of the material facts." *Montgomery*, 567 S.W.2d at 270.

Although Raytheon's evidence suggests that MBank knew about the assignment of the accounts receivable, the assignment alone did not interfere with MBank's rights, because any assignment would be subordinate to MBank's security interest. MBank's rights were not infringed until Raytheon collected the accounts receivable. To raise the issue of whether MBank intended to relinquish its security interest in the accounts receivable, Raytheon would at least have to present evidence that MBank knew Raytheon was collecting the accounts. Raytheon did not do so. The district court properly granted the motions for summary judgment. *See Anderson v. Liberty Lobby, Inc.*, 477 U.S. 242, 248–49, 106 S.Ct. 2505, 2510–11, 91 L.Ed.2d 202 (1986); *Washington v. Armstrong World Indus.*, 839 F.2d 1121, 1122–23 (5th Cir.1988) (per curiam). The judgments for MBank and DuPont are AFFIRMED.

GOLDBERG, CIRCUIT JUDGE, dissenting:

What we confront today is another nettle in the thicket of the Texas Uniform Commercial Code. A thorny question of statutory interpretation that could cause scratch and abrasion if not reconnoitered under the illumination provided by the Texas Supreme Court. After examining the relevant statutes and commentaries, however, I believe that the majority has not construed the code as would the Texas Supreme Court in the face of the same problem. So because the scratch of a thorn may cause infection if not properly treated, I must respectfully DISSENT.

The nettle of this case is whether an account receivable should be considered "collateral" in the words of the purchase money security interest statute so that the purchase money interest has priority over a security interest previously perfected in an identical account. My belief is that accounts receivable are an appropriate form of collateral because they can be used to invigorate marginal businesses. I would thus hold that Raytheon established a purchase money security interest in the specified accounts of Howe [X]-ray.

I. The Facts

Both MBank and DuPont had loaned money to Howe, a dealer in medical equipment including expensive x-ray machines. To guard against the possibility that Howe would default on these loans, MBank, whose loan was made before DuPonts [sic], perfected a security interest in Howe's accounts receivable then existing and subsequently arising and also perfected a similar security interest in Howe's inventory. DuPont's security interest was also perfected in Howe's accounts receivable then existing and subsequently arising but was filed after MBank's interest.

While the MBank/DuPont loans were outstanding, Raytheon entered into a series of transactions with Howe. Each transaction was executed according to a preexisting distribution agreement which allowed Howe to contract with customers for the sale of Raytheon x-ray machines. Under this agreement, Raytheon promised to supply an x-ray machine to Howe in exchange for Howe's promise to assign the account receivable that arose from the sale of the machine to Raytheon. Raytheon gave notice of its security interest in each account by filing a financing statement within the applicable 20 day period after the creation of the account. The structure of this agreement between Howe and Raytheon arose because Howe had begun to experience difficulty in obtaining additional financing and was spiraling down toward bankruptcy, its final fate.

II. Discussion

Before I get involved in the details of Raytheon's purchase money security interest, however, a momentary step back is in order to scan the general landscape of security interests. As a general observation, the usual method for growth in the area of commercial law has been the daring creativity of a company pushing out beyond the boundaries of "normal practice" in response to business exigencies. The history of trust receipts, the factor's liens, and the eventual adoption of Article 9 of the Uniform Commercial Code illustrates this general observation in the area of security interests. *See* G. Gilmore, *Security Interests in Personal Property*, Ch 1–8 (1965).

> "The idea which the draftsmen [of Article 9] started with was that the system of independent security devices [developed in different area of commerce] had served its time; that the formal differences which separated one device from another should be scrapped and replaced with the simple concept of a security interest in personal property; *that all types of personal property*, whether held for use or for sale, should be recognized as available for security." *Id.* at 290 (emphasis added).

Article [9] was thus intended to be a flexible statute that could respond to divergent commercial needs.

The facts of this case present exactly the type of problematic situation which demands a creative solution. Raytheon, as a manufacturer of expensive x-ray equipment, often does not seek out customers itself but instead uses local distributors such as Howe to make sales. But Howe had to borrow money for it to function as a merchant of medical equipment. MBank and DuPont provided this money protecting themselves by with security interests in the collateral Howe had available, Howe's present and future accounts receivable and inventory. This type of security interest in a borrower's intangibles such as accounts receivable is extremely common.

The key to who has priority is to determine who filed the security interest in the collateral first. First in time, first in line goes the rhyme.

The problem with this situation is that a manufacturer will not loan or give a heavily indebted merchant any goods to sell on credit because once the merchant sells the goods, the banker, not the manufacturer, will have priority in the resulting accounts under the first in time first in line principle. Raytheon would thus not advance any x-ray machines to Howe because MBank and DuPont would have priority in any accounts that arose from the sale of the machines. Yet it is these very sales which would enable Howe to make profits to pay off its loans to MBank and DuPont. So how does an indebted merchant, who is unable to pay a manufacturer for goods that the merchant must sell to service the banker's loan, stay in business? Often what occurs is a scenario where the banker's loan is not paid, the merchant goes out of business, and the manufacturer loses an opportunity to distribute its goods on the market.

Article 9 provides a solution: the purchase money security interest. This device, with its root in the Railroad Car Trusts of the Nineteenth Century, has priority over security interests filed earlier because of its specific transaction oriented function. *Id.* at 743–53 (citing *U.S. v. New Orleans R.R.*, 79 U.S. (12 Wall.) 362, 364–65, 20 L.Ed. 434 (1871) (pre *Erie* commercial case giving priority to the later in time party)). The purchase money security interest operates outside the notice principle which favors early interest holders over later ones. Notice is not the driving force behind the purchase money security interest.

It was this purchase money device that allowed Howe an opportunity to continue doing business to the benefit of MBank, DuPont and Raytheon. Howe did not have enough money to purchase a $140,000 x-ray machine for inventory but Raytheon would not advance a machine on credit to Howe. A creative alternative was necessary. Raytheon agreed to advance a machine to Howe in exchange for Howe's enforceable purchase order or account receivable. Raytheon thus used the account as a vehicle to ensure Howe's payment for the machine. It was a creative solution to the meeting of two creditors, a manufacturer of expensive equipment, and a heavily indebted retailer, that allowed commerce to continue to flow.

But for the law to recognize this creativity, it must be determined whether Raytheon has complied with the elements of the Texas purchase money security interest statute. Admittedly this arrangement does not present a paradigmatic purchase money security interest, but I believe that creativity, when in harmony with the statutory requirements, should be encouraged.

A. *The Value Requirement*

Purchase money security interests are defined in section 9.107 [9–103] of the Texas Uniform Commercial Code. Section 9.107 [9–103], states, in pertinent part:

> A security interest is a "purchase money security interest" to the extent that it is . . . (2) taken by a person who by making advances or incurring an obligation gives value to enable the debtor to acquire rights in or the use of collateral if such value is in fact so used.

Under the statute, Raytheon must satisfy three requirements. Raytheon must demonstrate that: (1) it gave value to Howe by making advances or incurring an obligation; (2) its extension of value enabled Howe to acquire rights in the collateral—the account receivable in each particular transaction; and, (3) the Texas U.C.C. recognizes an account receivable as collateral for the purposes of a purchase money security interest.

There is no question that Raytheon extended value. Raytheon gave value when it shipped, according to the purchase order, an x-ray machine that a particular customer had ordered. This interpretation of the value requirement is consistent with the definition of value as set out in section 1.201(44) [1–204] of the Texas Uniform Commercial Code. Section 1.201(44) [1–204] is applicable through the direction of the definitional cross reference of section 9.107 [9–102(c)]. It states in pertinent part, that: "[a] person gives 'value' for rights if he acquires them . . . (D) generally, in return for any consideration sufficient to support a simple contract." Raytheon satisfied section 1.201(44) [1–204] because the advance of the x-ray machine in exchange for a promise from Howe to assign an accounts receivable arising from the sale of that x-ray machine is consideration sufficient to support a contract. Moreover, under section 9.107(2) [1–204] itself, " 'A secured party may give value by committing . . . to supply goods or [by] actually supply[ing] the goods.' " *Thet Mah and Associates Inc. v. First Bank of North Dakota*, 336 N.W.2d 134, 138 (N.D.1983) (citing 1 Bender U.C.C. Service, Secured Transactions, section 4.05(4) p. 304 (1983)).

This advance also satisfied the limitation on the type of value that may be given as defined in comment 2 of section 9.107 [9–103]. Comment 2 states, in pertinent part:

> [t]his section . . . provides that the purchase money party must be one who gives value " 'by making advances or incurring an obligation' ": the quoted language excludes from the purchase money category any security interest taken as security for or in satisfaction of a preexisting claim or antecedent debt.

This antecedent debt limitation is satisfied here because Howe's debt to Raytheon was not preexisting but was instead created by the advance of the machine. Only then was Howe indebted to Raytheon for the machine's value. In turn, the debt was secured by the accounts receivable that Howe assigned to Raytheon pursuant to their agreement.

B. *The Enabling Requirement*

The second element of a purchase money security interest is the requirement that Raytheon give value "to enable" Howe to acquire rights in the particular account receivable. This requirement means that the advance made by Raytheon must have made it possible for Howe X-ray to obtain the collateral. In the present case, the enabling requirement is satisfied because Raytheon's agreement with Howe, which preceded all of the particular transactions, was that Raytheon would advance an x-ray machine to Howe in exchange for an accounts receivable generated by Howe's sale of the machine to a customer. This preexisting agreement, together with the advance of the machine by Raytheon, enabled Howe to make the sale. At the same moment in time, in the twinkling of an eye, the sale created the particular account receivable payable to Howe which Howe then assigned to Raytheon pursuant to their preexisting agreement. "If the loan transaction appears closely allied to the purchase transaction, that should suffice. The evident intent of paragraph (b) [U.C.C. 9–107(b)] [9–103] is to free the purchase-money concept from artificial limitations; rigid adherence to particular formalities and sequences should not be required." G. Gilmore, I Security Interests in Personal Property, 782 (1965).

C. *The Collateral Requirement*

The thorny question in this case centers on whether accounts receivable should be considered collateral for the purpose of a purchase money security interest under Section 9.107(b) [9–103]. To my mind, Raytheon has jumped this hurdle.

Under section 9.105(a)(3) [9–102(a)(12)], which is listed in the definitional cross references of section 9.107, collateral is defined as "the property subject to a security interest and includes accounts and chattel paper which have been sold . . . ." Moreover, under section 9.106 [9–102(a)(2)], which is also listed in the definitional cross references of section 9.107, "[a]ccount means any right to payment for goods sold or leased or for services rendered which is not evidenced by an instrument or chattel paper, whether or not it has been earned by performance." The comment to 9.106 [9–102(a)(2)] states that the section is referring to "ordinary commercial accounts receivable." By reading these two definitional sections in tandem, it is clear that an account receivable can be collateral for the purposes of a purchase money security interest under section 9.107 [9–103].

There is, however, no other authority to our knowledge that expressly states that accounts receivable should be considered collateral for the purpose of a purchase money security interest. The Supreme Court of Minnesota has suggested that a purchase money security interest in accounts could validly arise. *See Northwestern National Bank Southwest v. Lectro Systems*, 262 N.W.2d 678, 680 (Minn.1977) ("This is not a case in which funds were advanced and used for purchase of a receivable."). And, Professor Grant Gilmore, one of the original drafters of Article 9, has stated in his treatise on security interests, that the purchase money concept might apply to intangible property in occasional cases. G. Gilmore, I *Security Interests in Personal Property*, 781 (1965) ("There seems to be no reason, however, why the term 'collateral' should have other than its normal meaning: the purchase-money concept may thus, in an occasional case, apply to intangible property . . . .").

MBank and DuPont have asserted that accounts receivable should not be considered collateral for the purpose of defining a purchase money security interest under Section 9.107(2) [9–103]. Their argument, adopted by the majority, is that because accounts receivable financing has been accorded a special importance by the Texas Uniform Commercial Code, its legal position should not be made less certain by the operation of Sections 9.107(2) [9–103] and 9.312(d) [9–324]. Once a security interest has been created under section 9.107(2) [9–103], section 9.312(d) [9–324] grants it special status. Section 9.312(d) [9–324] states that "a purchase money security interest in collateral other than inventory has priority over a conflicting security interest in the same collateral or its proceeds if the purchase money security interest is perfected at the time the debtor receives possession of the collateral or within 20 days thereafter."

The significance of this special priority granted to purchase money security interests in subsection (2) becomes apparent when compared to the general priority rule in section 9.312(e) [9–322]. Under section 9.312(e)(1) [9–322], conflicting security interests in the same collateral rank according to the time of filing. The first party to file notice of its interest in an account has priority over any subsequently filed interests in the identical account.

Because of the operation of section 9.312(d) [9–324], however, the first party to file notice of a security interest in an account would not necessarily have priority under section 9.312(e)(1) [9–322]. Section 9.312(d) [9–324] would grant priority over any interest filed previously in the same account if purchase money status in the account was first established under section 9.107 [9–103]. The legal position of accounts receivable financing might thus be made less certain if a purchase money security interest could be claimed in accounts receivable under section 9.107(2) [9–103]. Diminished certainty could result in the sense that the first party to file notice of its interest in an account under section 9.312(e) [9–322] would be uncertain as to whether it had priority in the account or whether another party has priority because the latter established purchase money status in the same account under 9.107(2) [9–103].

MBank and DuPont argue that this uncertainty in the legal position of accounts receivable financing should be prohibited because of the special importance accorded to accounts receivable financing under the code. They find this importance in the history of section 9.312(c) [9–324(b)] which prohibits the establishment of purchase money security interests in accounts receivable, derivatively, as proceeds of inventory. The argument points out that this prohibition was created due to the importance of accounts receivable financing in the economy. Based on these premises, the argument concludes that the possibility of a purchase money security interest in accounts receivable under section 9.107(2) [9–103] should also be prohibited. The fallacy of this logic, however, is that it equates the value of accounts receivable as applied to a problem that arose in the area of inventory financing with the values behind the section 9.107 [9–103] purchase money security interest.

The argument thus rests upon MBank and DuPont's interpretation of section 9.312(c) [9–324(b)]. Section 9.312(c) [9–324(b)] provides that "a perfected purchase money security interest in inventory has priority over a conflicting security interest in the same inventory and also has priority in any identifiable cash proceeds received on or before the delivery of inventory to a buyer." This section of the code was changed in 1972 to address the problem of priority conflicts between a claim to accounts receivable derivatively as proceeds of inventory and a claim to the accounts established by the filing of a direct security interest. The conflict arose between inventory financers who claimed priority in the accounts as proceeds of the inventory that they helped the debtor to acquire and lenders who had taken a direct security interest in the accounts as collateral for money loaned to the debtor.

Section 9.312(c) [9–324(b)] offered a solution to this conflict. It states that a prior right to the inventory of a debtor does not confer a prior right to any proceeds that arise from the sale of the inventory except for identifiable cash proceeds. There is no prior right to accounts receivable as proceeds from the sale of the inventory. Under this section, it would not be possible to establish a purchase money security interest in inventory and then claim a purchase money security interest in any of the accounts that arose from the sale of that inventory. This exclusion of accounts receivable as proceeds of inventory under section 9.312(c) [9–324(b)] rests upon the assumption that accounts receivable financing is more important in the economy than the financing of the types of inventory that produce accounts when sold.

MBank and DuPont thus argue that a purchase money security interest in accounts receivable should not be permitted under section

9.107(2) [9–103] because a purchase money security interest in accounts receivable may not be claimed derivatively as proceeds of the sale of inventory under section 9.312(c) [9–324(b)]. However, when this argument is examined in light of the policy interests underpinning section 9.107(2) [9–103], the argument's core assumption, the importance of accounts receivable financing in the economy, dictates precisely the opposite result.

The most important policy justification for a purchase money security interest under section 9.107(2) [9–103] is the protection that it gives to a debtor who is unable to raise additional funds to remain in business. Creditors who have previously loaned money to the debtor and taken a security interest in the debtor's goods may be unwilling to advance additional value or funds. These additional funds, however, could enable a debtor to purchase goods, make sales, and in turn, generate profits. Profits which could not only be used to create more business, but also, to allow the debtor to pay off the creditor's loans. The purchase money security provisions thus enable a leveraged debtor who is able to find a new lender to give that new lender a first claim on the new collateral purchased notwithstanding a prior filing by another creditor.

The arrangement between Raytheon and Howe exemplifies the use of accounts receivable to advance the policy rationale behind the purchase money security interest. It was the use of the accounts receivable by Raytheon as collateral for the x-ray machines that allowed Howe to continue to do business. The additional business that Howe was able to generate with the advance of the x-ray machines, at minimum, gave Howe an additional opportunity to stay in business. This opportunity was a benefit to creditors such as MBank and DuPont whose loans would not be repaid unless Howe had the ability to generate profits. It also demonstrated the importance of accounts receivable financing in another forum, the creation of purchase money security interests.

The use of accounts receivable as collateral in this case benefited MBank and DuPont as creditors because the consequences of an unpaid account were relatively greater to Raytheon. Raytheon, MBank and DuPont would each have been harmed if Howe's customers failed to pay their accounts. If an account receivable were to remain unpaid, Raytheon would lose the entire value of the x-ray machine advanced to Howe. In contrast, it is unlikely that the failure of one account would drive Howe into bankruptcy so that Howe would be unable to repay MBank and DuPont. Yet it is this additional risk taken by Raytheon which allowed Howe a profit that could be used to fund its business to the advantage of MBank and DuPont.

Finally, any obligation imposed on MBank and DuPont to determine whether Howe was using its accounts receivable to collateralize purchase money security transactions is diminished in two respects. First, as stated, it is these very purchase money transactions that allowed Howe an additional opportunity to service its debts to these creditors. Second, MBank and DuPont as creditors had already established relationships with Howe. In future transactions, it would not have been difficult for them to ascertain whether Howe was using any accounts to collateralize purchase money transactions with other creditors and draft the loan contracts accordingly.

D. The Limit of Raytheon's Purchase Money Security Interest

I would, however, posit a serious limit on the extent of Raytheon's purchase money security interest. Under section 9.107 [9–103], a security interest has purchase money character only to the extent of the value given to acquire the collateral. In the present case, the value given by Raytheon was the price of the x-ray machine as measured by the difference in the price Howe charged customers and the price Raytheon charged Howe. This price measures the extent of Raytheon's purchase money security interest in the specific accounts receivable of Howe. I do not mean to imply that the value given to a distributor such as Howe will always be measured by the wholesale price. In some situations, it could be the retail price depending upon what the debtor was meant to gain by the transaction. I would leave these transactional details for the district court.

The difference between the price Raytheon charged Howe and the price Howe charged its customers would thus not be a part of Raytheon's purchase money security interest. There is evidence to the effect that Howe used a portion of this difference, Howe's profit margin, to pay a preexisting debt owing from Howe to Raytheon. This money could not be a part of Raytheon's purchase money security interest because a purchase money security interest may not be used to secure a preexisting debt.

There is also evidence which suggests that Raytheon may have loaned money to Howe to cover Howe's costs of installing the x-ray machine. Any such money would not be a part of Raytheon's purchase money security interest. There should not be any additional opportunities created under the code to give simple loans purchase money character.

To my mind, Raytheon has established a valid purchase money security interest under section 9.107(2) [9–103] of the Texas Uniform Commercial Code. The x-ray machine advanced by Raytheon constituted the value that enabled Howe to acquire accounts receivable, the collateral, for the purposes of section 9.107(2) [9–103]. As such, this case should be reversed and remanded, where the issue of waiver could be examined with a headlight's incandescence and the retroactivity issue appropriately explored. I therefore respectfully DISSENT.

[footnotes omitted]

Analyze the *MBank* case under revised Article 9. Revisit the definition of purchase-money security interests in section 9–103. Does section 9–103 contemplate a purchase-money security interest in accounts? Section 9–103(b) recognizes and provides for a purchase-money security interest in "goods," but "accounts" are not goods. *See* 9–102(a)(2) (defining "account"); 9–102(a)(44) (excluding "accounts" from the definition of "goods"). Move next to section 9–324 governing the priority of a purchase-money security interest. Does section 9–324 contemplate a purchase-money security interest in accounts (other than accounts as proceeds of some other type of collateral)? *See* 9–324 cmt. 2. It does not. Section 9–324 contemplates a purchase-money security interests in various forms of *tangible* collateral (for example, "goods"), but not accounts (other than accounts generated as proceeds from the disposition of collateral subject to a purchase-money security interest). *See* 9–324 cmt. 2 ("A purchase-money security interest can be created only in goods and software.").

So although Raytheon certainly could have taken a purchase-money security interest ("PMSI") in the machines it sold to Howe (namely, it could have taken a PMSI in these machines as Howe's inventory), it could not take a PMSI in Howe's accounts under revised Article 9. But could Raytheon claim that its purchase-money security interest in the inventory extends to any accounts that are proceeds of the inventory under section 9–324? *See* 9–102(a)(64) (defining "proceeds"). No. Although section 9–324(*a*) extends a purchase-money security interest in goods to the identifiable proceeds of the relevant collateral (including accounts generated from the sale of the collateral), it does not apply to inventory or livestock. Section 9–324(*b*) *does* apply to inventory, but does not extend any purchase-money priority to accounts generated as proceeds from the disposition of the inventory. (In contrast, section 9–324(b) extends the priority to chattel paper and instruments generated as proceeds to the extent provided in section 9–330; section 9–330 is discussed in Section 4 of Chapter 5.) *See* 9–324 cmt. 5 (discussing when a purchase-money security interest may extend to proceeds). Security interests in "proceeds" are examined in greater detail in the next section of this chapter.

As the court observes, the real issue in the *MBank* case is the importance of preserving the expectation of accounts financers—here MBank and Dupont—that they will have priority in the debtor's accounts. In the ordinary course, sales of inventory often generate accounts—the debtor's rights to payment from its customers who owe the debtor money for goods the customers have bought from the debtor. By recognizing that a secured party's purchase-money priority in a debtor's inventory does not extend to any accounts generated from the sale of the inventory, Article 9 protects the expectation of accounts financers that they will have priority in a debtor's accounts even over the holder of a purchase-money security interest in the debtor's inventory who claims the accounts as proceeds of its collateral.

Is this unfair? In the usual course, accounts financers such as MBank and Dupont lend the debtor money on the strength of the debtor's accounts. The debtor then typically uses the borrowed funds to purchase more inventory. Thus, in the ordinary course, vendors such as Raytheon will often receive payment for the goods they ship to debtors like Howe from advances from financers such as MBank and Dupont. In *MBank*, of course, these financers had ceased lending because Howe was in default. Howe wanted to stay in business, and to do that it needed to keep selling inventory to its customers. Any new accounts Howe generated, however, would constitute MBank and Dupont's collateral. Should Raytheon have been able to effectively sidestep the priority of MBank and Dupont's security interests?

Finally, the *MBank* case centered on MBank and DuPont's conversion action against Raytheon for money Raytheon received, namely to claw back payments that had already been made to Raytheon. Is such an action maintainable under revised Article 9? Take a look at section 9–332. *See also* 9–315 cmt. 2; 9–331 cmt. 5; 9–607 cmt. 5; 9–609 cmt. 5.

PROBLEM 4-8

How might Raytheon have structured the transaction to protect itself under revised Article 9? What if Raytheon had delivered the x-ray machines directly to Howe's customers and then paid Howe a commission for the sales? In addition, note that, although section 9–324(b) does not extend a secured party's purchase-money priority in inventory to accounts that are proceeds of the inventory, it does extend the purchase-money priority to other forms of proceeds, including chattel paper and instruments to the extent provided in section 9–330 (and so long as the other requirements of section 9–324(b) are satisfied). *See* 9–102(a)(11) (defining "chattel paper"), 9–102(a)(47) (defining "instrument"). Take a look at section 9–330, and also section 9–331. What if Raytheon had insisted that Howe accept only instruments or chattel paper in exchange for the sale of the x-ray machines to its customers? Security interests in accounts, chattel paper, and instruments are examined in Chapter 5, which likewise addresses section 9–330.

§ 5. PROCEEDS, ETC.

PROCEEDS: ATTACHMENT AND DEFINITION

Section 9–203(f) of Article 9 provides automatic attachment of a security interest to the "rights to proceeds provided by section 9–315." This rule, codified for the first time in 1972, presumes that the parties intend the security interest to attach to proceeds of the collateral even where their agreement is silent. To understand the effect of section 9–203, one must understand the meaning of "proceeds" and the reach of section 9–315. Section 9–102(a)(64) defines "proceeds" to include a number of items, including most prominently in subsection (A) "whatever is acquired upon the sale, lease, license, exchange, or other disposition of collateral . . . ." In addition, section 9–102(a)(9) further defines "cash proceeds" to mean "proceeds that are money, checks, deposit accounts, or the like."

With experience under the 1962 and 1972 versions of Article 9, the definition of proceeds has gradually changed and expanded to include more than the excerpt quoted above. For example, section 9–102(a)(64)(E) clearly covers insurance proceeds that are payable on injury to, or destruction of, collateral. Likewise subsection (B) covers distributions such as cash and stock dividends. Both of these provisions reverse court decisions under the former Code. Under the 1972 version, the debtor apparently had to "receive" personal property for that property to be "proceeds." There was no reason for the requirement, and the drafters of the 1999 Code omitted the word "receive." *See* 9–102 cmt. 13.

What if the debtor sells collateral but calls the transaction a "lease"? In that case, the ersatz "lease" is a security agreement taken by the debtor and is chattel paper. According to PEB Commentary No. 9, the chattel paper itself constitutes proceeds. The same commentary states that payments to the debtor under true leases are proceeds. Even a true lease itself could be considered proceeds of, say, inventory. One can argue that a lessor of goods for a limited time does not "dispose" of the collateral. But even though only a portion of the debtor's rights are disposed of (for example, a two-year right to use the item out of a ten-year useful life), one can argue that the lease itself is a disposition and that both the lease and the payments under the lease are proceeds.

There are other transactions that look like sales or dispositions, but are not. What if a cow gives milk or bears a calf? There is, of course, no sale or other disposition of the cow, but the production of the milk or a calf certainly looks like a stock dividend, and stock dividends are now included as proceeds under section 9–102(a)(64)(B). But until the drafters expand the definition, and subsection (B), such natural production and reproduction are not proceeds. Presumably that is the reason why many security interests dealing with animals include the term "product" covering milk, eggs, and young. The term "product" is not defined in Article 9, but is used in section 9–324(d) in the context of specifying the priority of purchase-money security interests in livestock, and is also mentioned in comment 10 to section 9–324(d). The term "product" is used again in a different sense in section 9–336 governing security interests in commingled goods. If you were a drafter of Article 9, wouldn't you want to define this term? How might you do it in a way that captures its use in both sections 9–324(d) and 9–336?

To further test the boundaries of "disposition" under section 9–102(a)(64), assume a debtor has given a security interest in a valuable piece of industrial machinery. Because the debtor wishes to sell the machinery or move it to another location, the debtor proposes that the creditor's security interest be transferred from that machine to another. The other machine becomes subject to the security interest not because it is proceeds of the first, but because of the agreement of the parties. The second machine is not proceeds of the first. The concepts of "exchange," "disposition," and the like used in section 9–102(a)(64) probably contemplate a transfer by the debtor to a third party, not the transfer of a security interest from one asset of the debtor to another. *Compare* 9–336.

What about the "proceeds of proceeds"? Formerly, the definition of proceeds included "proceeds of proceeds." Revised Article 9 has changed this. Consistent with section 9–203(f), which provides for the automatic attachment of a security interest in the proceeds of collateral, the definition of "collateral" in section 9–102(a)(12) now includes "proceeds to which a security interest attaches." *See* 9–102 cmt. 13(c). Thus, "proceeds of proceeds" is now included in the concept of "collateral" rather than the definition of "proceeds."

Under section 9–315(a)(2), a security interest attaches only to "identifiable" proceeds. In most cases, proceeds will be easily identifiable as having come from particular collateral. For example, if a secured creditor had a security interest in an automobile that was sold and if the buyer gave the seller a security interest and a note (namely, "chattel paper"), the security interest would make a specific reference to the automobile and would be directly traceable to that particular piece of collateral.

By far the most common trouble comes when collateral is sold for cash, for a check, or for some other form of payment, and the proceeds of that payment or the payment itself are deposited into a bank account. If there are other funds in that account, one will need some accounting fiction to determine which part of the bank account should be regarded as proceeds and which part as something else. Prior to 1999, the courts allowed creditors to use various tracing methods to identify their collateral in deposit accounts. A common method was the "lowest intermediate balance" test. To see how this test works, assume a secured creditor could prove the debtor had deposited $10,000 of proceeds into its bank account; assume that thereafter the lowest balance in the account was $8,000. In that case, the lowest intermediate balance fiction would treat the remaining $8,000 as identifiable proceeds of the secured creditor. Revised section 9–315(b)(2) blesses this kind of fictional tracing doctrine: commingled proceeds in the form of cash and the like are identifiable "to the extent that the secured party identifies the proceeds by a method of tracing, including application of equitable principles, that is permitted under law other than this article with respect to commingled property of the type involved."

Section 9–315(b)(1) allows a secured creditor to claim commingled *goods* to the extent provided by section 9–336, a provision that deals explicitly with commingled collateral such as grain and the like. Section 9–336 is a fairly complex provision. To understand how it works, it is helpful first to distinguish the concept of "commingled goods" from "accessions." Accessions are defined in section 9–102(a)(1), and include attachments to collateral that do not lose their individual character as goods, such as a snow plow affixed to the front of a dump truck. Accessions are treated specially in section 9–335.

In contrast, under section 9–336(a), commingled goods are defined to mean those that are "physically united with other goods in such a manner that their identity is lost in a product or mass." For example, suppose the debtor (a baker) uses flour and eggs to make cakes that the baker sells to the public. Both the flour and the eggs are part of the debtor's inventory (they are raw materials—*see* 9–102(a)(48)), and each may be encumbered with a security interest in favor of a different secured party (for example, the supplier of the flour may have a security interest in the flour to secure the debtor's obligation to pay for flour deliveries, and the supplier of the eggs may have a security interest in the eggs). When the flour and the eggs are combined to make cakes, their individual identify is lost and they become commingled goods. Are the cakes "proceeds" of the flour and eggs? No. They are instead a "product" of the combination of the flour and the eggs, and the point of section 9–336 is to provide rules governing what happens to the security interests in the flour and the eggs once the collateral is combined. The text of section 9–336 is challenging to follow. Its operation is explained more fully in the accompanying comments—read them.

Section 9–336 has a complicated relationship with section 9–322, the general priority provision, and section 9–324, the purchase-money priority provision. In the hypothetical above, sections 9–336(b) and (c) effectively transform the security interests in the flour and eggs into security interests that attach to the cakes. Section 9–336(f) then states priority rules for these transformed security interests. But what about a secured creditor, say a bank, who takes a security interest in the cakes rather than the flour or the eggs? How would the bank's security interest relate to the security interests of the flour and egg suppliers? The priority between the two suppliers would be governed by section 9–336(f), but the priority between the bank and the two suppliers would be governed by either section 9–322 or 9–324 (depending on whether the bank and the suppliers had purchase-money security interests). *See* 9–336 cmt. 7.

PROCEEDS: PERFECTION

Sections 9–315 (c) and (d) state the rules for perfection of a security interest in proceeds:

> (c) **[Perfection of security interest in proceeds.]** A security interest in proceeds is a perfected security interest if the security interest in the original collateral was perfected.
>
> (d) **[Continuation of perfection.]** A perfected security interest in proceeds becomes unperfected on the 21st day after the security interest attaches to the proceeds unless:
>
> (1) the following conditions are satisfied:
>
> (A) a filed financing statement covers the original collateral;
>
> (B) the proceeds are collateral in which a security interest may be perfected by filing in the office in which the financing statement has been filed; and
>
> (C) the proceeds are not acquired with cash proceeds;
>
> (2) the proceeds are identifiable cash proceeds; or
>
> (3) the security interest in the proceeds is perfected other than under subsection (c) when the security interest attaches to the proceeds or within 20 days thereafter.

For the secured creditor, the reassuring starting point is that the interest in the proceeds is automatically perfected if the security interest "in the original collateral was perfected." Under subsection (d), that perfection continues for 20 days; if the creditor wishes to continue its perfection beyond 20 days, it must either fit within one of the other subsections or take whatever action would be necessary to perfect a security interest in the particular assets constituting the proceeds.

Consider two cases where perfection continues without any act on the part of the secured creditor. First are the cases in section 9–315(d)(1): the creditor has filed a financing statement—as to the original collateral at the same office where one would file with respect to the proceeds if one were perfecting an original security interest in them. There is an additional condition that these proceeds cannot have been purchased with earlier cash proceeds. To see how this provision might work and how pervasive its reach, consider an example. Assume the debtor is a Kentucky corporation and the secured creditor has filed a financing statement at the state capital in Frankfort covering the debtor's inventory. Assume further that the financing statement covers only "debtor's inventory of used automobiles," and the proceeds are chattel paper received on the sale of some of those automobiles. Since one originally perfecting as to the debtor's chattel paper would file a financing statement in the "same office" and since the proceeds have not been acquired with "cash proceeds," the secured creditor is perfected as to the chattel paper without taking any action and despite the fact its financing statement does not list chattel paper. Since almost all filings under the revised Code will be at the place of a corporate debtor's incorporation, the general rule will be that perfection continues as to proceeds without any action by the secured creditor. Presumably the drafters assumed that anyone who searches in the name of the debtor will find the filing as to inventory and will understand that the prior secured creditor likely claims proceeds of the inventory as well.

The second indefinite extension of perfection appears in section 9–315(d)(2) covering "identifiable cash proceeds." Section 9–102(a)(9) defines cash proceeds as "money, checks, deposit accounts, or the like." The good news is that the secured creditor is indefinitely perfected with respect to these identifiable cash proceeds; the bad news is that money, checks, and the like are seldom long in the hands of a troubled debtor. Of course, this section does mean that our secured creditor has a continuously perfected security interest in the debtor's bank account, at least if the secured creditor can "identify" the proceeds portion of that account. (Note, however, that a special provision, section 9–327, governs the priority of competing security interests in deposit accounts.)

Now consider an example involving "proceeds of proceeds" in which the secured creditor it not indefinitely perfected. Assume that the secured creditor has a security interest in the debtor's equipment perfected by filing a financing statement with the correct filing office indicating the collateral as the debtor's equipment. Assume the debtor sells the equipment for $100,000 cash. Next assume that the debtor uses the cash to purchase some inventory. Does the secured creditor have a perfected security interest in the inventory? To the extent it is identifiable, the $100,000 constitutes "cash proceeds," and the secured creditor's security interest would continue in the $100,000 under section 9–315(d)(2). The secured creditor's security interest in the inventory as "proceeds of proceeds," however, would lapse after 20 days, unless the secured creditor perfected its security interest in the inventory either by filing a financing statement indicating the collateral as inventory, or by possession. Section 9–315(d)(1) does not continue the secured party's perfection beyond 20 days because the debtor acquired the inventory using cash proceeds. Section 9–315(d)(2) likewise does not continue perfection because the inventory is not itself cash proceeds. Finally, section 9–315(d)(3) does not continue the perfection because, without a new filing covering the inventory (or the secured party's taking possession), the secured creditor's security interest in the inventory would only be perfected by operation of section 9–315(c) (recall that its original financing statement indicated only the debtor's equipment).

Adding to the current landscape of issues, blockchain-based transactions present new questions surrounding proceeds. For example, cryptocurrencies may yield "forks" of assets or "air drops" of assets. Forks and air drops can both involve sudden distributions of currency to an investor's digital wallet, but forks are likely proceeds under Article 9 and air drops likely are not. A fork is a second branch of a currency using the same basic code. A fork arises when a critical mass of nodes in a network changes parameters and upgrades software, creating a new or separate blockchain from the previously existing one. When a fork occurs, holders of digital currency may be given new tokens in an equivalent amount of their current holdings. If a holder of digital currency assigned a security interest in these assets, this type of distribution surrounding a fork would most likely constitute proceeds under Article 9. In contrast, air drops are distributions of a cryptocurrency to certain investors made to boost recognition or promote a new coin or token. Air drop distributions do not seem to be proceeds of digital currency. The bottom line, at present, is that lenders taking security interests in digital assets should draft their agreements clearly, using collateral descriptions such as, for example, "Bitcoin, but not Bitcoin forks" or "Bitcoin and Bitcoin forks," or "[cryptocurrency] forks, but not air drops," to avoid confusion in this evolving context.

NOTE

It is no surprise to learn that operating businesses that grant security interests in their inventory and intangibles fill their bank (deposit) accounts with the proceeds of those security interests. Under the provisions of section 9–315, creditors who hold perfected security interests in the collateral that produced the money deposited into these accounts will have a perfected security interest in the deposit accounts. *See* 9–102(a)(29) (defining a "deposit account" to mean "a demand, time, savings, passbook, or similar account maintained with a bank"); 9–314 (governing perfection of a security interest in a deposit account through control); 9–104 (defining "control" of a deposit account); 9–327 (governing priority of interests in a deposit account); 9–102(a)(9) (including deposit accounts as an example of "cash proceeds"). Note that a "deposit account" is technically distinct from "money." The term "money" is defined in section 1–201(b)(24) to mean currency and its equivalent (for example, actual dollar bills and coins). Under section 9–312(b)(3), a secured creditor may perfect a security interest in money only by taking possession.

Under section 9–315(a)(1) a security interest in a retailer's inventory of refrigerators and washing machines, or in the retailer's accounts, attaches to the "identifiable proceeds of the collateral." A consumer's check or promise to pay arising from the consumer's purchase of an appliance will be identifiable. As noted, section 9–315(b) endorses the equitable case law methods of tracing proceeds into deposit accounts and thus of making those proceeds still "identifiable" after deposit. The section specifically refers to identification "by a method of tracing, including application of equitable principles, that is permitted under law other than this article . . . ." Comment 3 to section 9–315 refers to the "lowest intermediate balance rule" as a permissible method of tracing. Assume an account with a balance of $1 million; assume an additional $1 million from the sale of collateral is deposited; assume that the balance then goes down to $900,000 and back up to $5 million. The lowest intermediate balance rule tells us that $900,000 of the $5 million in the account is "identifiable" as coming from the $1 million of proceeds that were earlier deposited. Never mind that the rule might be more generous to the secured creditor than you think it should be; that is the rule.

These security interests in deposit proceeds continue to be perfected without any new filing under the terms of section 9–315(d) as identifiable "cash" proceeds. Once again, section 9–102(a)(9) explicitly includes "deposit accounts" as "cash proceeds." Note finally that this method of perfection continues indefinitely, but of course, it will be completely defeated if the account balance goes to zero each night or at any time between the deposit of the proceeds and the time the creditor asserts its claim to the proceeds. So it is common for a secured creditor to have a perfected security interest in its debtor's deposit account.

Under pre-1999 Article 9, one could not take a direct security interest in a deposit account. The only security interest recognized was an interest in proceeds that might have been deposited there. For that reason, the depositary bank (assuming it was not the entity financing the debtor's inventory or intangibles) had to rely on its rights of setoff to challenge a third party who claimed a perfected proceeds interest in a deposit account with the bank. The conventional learning on the priority of setoff is that it is not effective until some act is taken by the bank to do the setoff (for example, putting a hold on the deposit account, reducing the balance in the account, or the like). For those reasons, a depositary bank who lent money to its depositors in reliance on a deposit account was likely to lose to a third-party secured creditor who was lending on other assets whose proceeds were funding the account.

Two parts of Article 9 almost completely reversed the former rules. It is now permissible to take a direct security interest in a deposit account, perfected by control. *See* 9–104, 9–312(b)(1), 9–314. The priority rules with respect to that security interest, stated in section 9–327, elevate the rights of the depositary bank over any creditor who does not have control (the bank invariably has control over deposit accounts maintained at the bank) or for that matter over almost every other secured creditor even in the unusual case in which the depositary bank gets perfection by a proceeds claim. If that were not enough, sections 9–340 and 9–341 appear to give the bank's setoff rights priority over competing security interests even when the setoff is exercised after the perfection of the competing secured creditor. Note that sections 9–340 and 9–341 do not explicitly say there is priority, but that must be the meaning of the language stating that a competing security interest does not "affect the right of recoupment or set-off" and that the depositary bank's rights are not "terminated, suspended or modified" by another's perfected security interest in a deposit account.

Presumably, most depositary banks will be able to claim the benefit of section 9–327 (as one holding a security interest perfected by control), for control will come automatically by having the deposit at the bank, and the attachment will come because the typical deposit account agreement will have a clause that grants the bank a security interest in the deposit account when and if the depositor borrows money from the bank. Deposit accounts are discussed further in Section 7 of Chapter 5.

PROBLEM 4-9

Your client, Buckeye Finance, has a security interest in the inventory of a regional department store. The department store runs tens of thousands of dollars through bank accounts at Bank One each week. Your client is fearful that Bank One might lend money to the store and then "prime" it (come ahead of it) under section 9–327 as to amounts in the deposit accounts or defeat its interest by setoff (under sections 9–340 and 9–341). You may assume that Buckeye has put all the normal provisions in its security agreement that prohibit its debtor from borrowing from Bank One or from any other bank where it deposits money, but it recognizes that a mere promise does not insure priority vis-à-vis a third party.

In view of sections 9–104, 9–327, 9–340, and 9–341, how might you assure Buckeye of priority to its proceeds in the deposit account when bankruptcy or other trouble comes?

PROBLEM 4-10

General Merchandise, a regional department store that does business in New England and is incorporated in Connecticut, sells furniture, hardware, and a variety of other home furnishings. It has granted a security interest in all of its inventory to Bank One. Bank One's security agreement covers not only inventory but proceeds and after-acquired inventory. Its financing statement, filed in Hartford, identifies only inventory as collateral. Consider two alternatives:

1. Bank Two lends $2 million to General Merchandise and takes a security interest in and files a financing statement as to "accounts, chattel paper, and other intangibles."

2. Alternatively, assume that Bank Two takes a purchase-money security interest in a new line of inventory, say Herman Miller furniture. Bank Two complies with the requirements of section 9–324(b) and lends $2 million.

Upon the bankruptcy of General Merchandise, analyze the rights of Bank One and Bank Two in both of the above scenarios if each claims the $700,000 of retail installment sales contracts written for the purchase of individual pieces of furniture (a retail installment sales contract typically is a security agreement granted by the consumer purchaser to the seller, together with a promise to pay, making it "chattel paper"). Assume that $250,000 of these contracts came from the sale of Herman Miller furniture and another $450,000 came from the sale of other goods.

To understand how devilishly complex proceeds claims can be, consider the following problem. Do not overlook the special priority that is granted to security interests in deposit accounts.

PROBLEM 4-11

Assume Bank One takes a security interest in Debtor's "inventory" and perfects its security interest by a proper filing. Assume Bank Two does the same but files after Bank One, and that Finance Company takes and perfects a security interest by filing after both Bank One and Two have filed. Bank One, Bank Two, and Finance Company each lend $10 million.

1. On Debtor's failure, the inventory has a value of only $3 million, but there is a $1 million bank account located at Bank Two. Who gets that account? (Assume the $1 million in the account is proceeds of the collateral subject to the security interest of Bank One, Bank Two, and Finance Company and that the secured creditors have done everything a smart lawyer would advise.)

2. If Debtor does not fail until it has used the $1 million from the bank account to purchase a large piece of equipment for use in its business, who gets that equipment?

§ 6. CONSIGNMENT: AN ALTERNATIVE TO CONVENTIONAL INVENTORY SECURITY

What is a consignment? In a typical "true" consignment (also known rather unhelpfully as a "bailment for the purpose of sale"), an owner of goods ("consignor") puts the goods in the possession of a person ("consignee") with instructions to the consignee to sell the goods to a third party. *See* 9–109 cmt. 6; *see also* 9–102(a)(21) (defining "consignor" as a person "that delivers goods to a consignee in a consignment"), 9–102(a)(19) (defining "consignee" to mean "a merchant to which goods are delivered on consignment"). Although Article 9 has a more precise definition, the basic idea is that a consignment is a transaction in which the consignor delivers goods to the consignee so the consignee can sell them and with the understanding that the consignee does not have to pay the consignor for the goods unless and until the consignee sells them. If the goods are sold, the consignee takes a percentage (say 20%) of the sales price and remits the proceeds to the consignor. If the goods are not sold, the consignor agrees to take the goods back. Consignments are common with certain goods, such as diamonds, certain clothing, and books. A typical consignment has some of the economic characteristics of a loan against inventory, for the consignor's capital enables the consignee to display inventory on its sales floor and to make sales it could not otherwise make.

In general, Article 9 treats a consignor's interest in consigned property as essentially a purchase-money security interest in inventory (so long as the transaction fits the Article 9 definition of a consignment). *See* 1–201(b)(35), 9–103(d). Consistent with this approach, Article 9 labels the consignee a "debtor." 9–102(a)(28) (defining "debtor" to include "consignee"). If the consignor perfects its security interest, the consignor will generally have priority. If it does not, it is treated essentially like a secured creditor with an unperfected security interest in the debtor's inventory. *See* 9–319.

Prior to the 1999 revision, most of the Code law on the rights of consignees and their creditors was found in former section 2–326. In general, that section subordinated the consignor's interest to rights of the creditors of the consignee in any case in which the consignee did business under a different name than the consignor, unless the consignor could prove that the consignee was "generally known to be dealing in goods of another," or the consignor complied with a relevant sign law showing its interest, or filed a financing statement under Article 9. As amended in 1999, section 2–326 recognizes in a more streamlined fashion two kinds of consignments: the "sale on approval" and the "sale or return."

The typical "sale on approval" transaction generally contemplates a two-party structure. The consignee essentially agrees to take the goods on trial. If the consignee decides to keep the goods, the consignee need only pay the agreed purchase price. If the consignee decides not to keep the goods, it returns them to the consignor without further obligation. *See* 2–326 cmt. 1.

The typical "sale or return" transaction generally contemplates a three-party structure. The consignor agrees to deliver the goods to the consignee with the understanding that the consignee has no obligation to pay for the goods unless the consignee resells the goods to a third-party buyer. If the goods are not so resold, the consignee returns the goods to the consignor without further obligation.

Under subsection 2 of section 2–326 goods held on approval are not subject to the claims of the consignee's creditors until the consignee accepts them. In contrast, goods held on sale or return are subject to the claims of the consignee's creditors while in the consignee's possession. In essence, section 2–326 treats consigned goods in a sale or return transaction as the consignee's inventory. Under both transaction forms section 2–326 treats the consignee as a "buyer" and the consignment itself as a type of "sale." *See* 2–326 cmt. 4.

In addition to the relatively arcane provisions of former section 2–326, former Article 9 contemplated transactions where the parties used consignment language, but the deals were truly "secured transactions," not conventional consignments. If, for example, a debtor borrowed money from a creditor, granted a security interest in inventory, and promised to repay the sum whether or not the goods were sold, that transaction would be treated in all respects like a secured transaction even if the parties labeled it a "consignment." The foregoing type of transaction differs significantly from the usual consignment in which the consignee has no obligation to pay if it returns the goods. If a court concluded the transaction was in fact intended as security, then knowledge by the consignee's creditors would not save it from the claim of a trustee or a judicial lien creditor, for it would be treated in all respects like a security interest. This division left some "consignments" entirely within Article 9 but some only partly there, and left the courts in doubt about what parts of Article 9 applied to which transactions.

The current Article 9 and conforming amendments to section 2–326 are substantial improvements. First, section 9–102(a)(20) defines a consignment for Article 9 purposes as follows:

> "Consignment" means a transaction, regardless of its form, in which a person delivers goods to a merchant for the purpose of sale and:
>
> (A) the merchant:
>
> (i) deals in goods of that kind under a name other than the name of the person making delivery;
>
> (ii) is not an auctioneer; and
>
> (iii) is not generally known by its creditors to be substantially engaged in selling the goods of others;
>
> (B) with respect to each delivery, the aggregate value of the goods is $1,000 or more at the time of delivery;
>
> (C) the goods are not consumer goods immediately before delivery; and
>
> (D) the transaction does not create a security interest that secures an obligation.

The definition incorporates most of the conditions of former section 2–326. In a second important definitional change, section 1–201(b)(35) of Article 1 states that any consignment (as that term is defined in section 9–102(a)) is a "security interest." This means that all consignors who are not explicitly excluded by the definition in section 9–102(a)(20) hold security interests that are subject to subordination by lien creditors and others under section 9–317 if their interests are unperfected. *See* 9–319. To protect their interests, consignors will have to perfect them like any other security interest. *See* 9–505(a) (permitting them to do this using the name "consignor"). The combination of section 9–102(a)(20) and section 1–201(b)(35) has moved almost all commercial consignments into Article 9, at least for most purposes. *See also* 9–102(b), 2–104 (defining who is a "merchant").

Certain transactions a layperson would describe as consignments are not consignments as that term is used by Article 9. Thus, a consignment of used clothing or used household furnishings to a consignment store is not a "consignment" under Article 9. So there will still be a subset of transactions regarded as "consignments" to laypersons, but not consignments under section 9–102(a)(20), such as consignments of consumer goods.

What of the other cases excluded from section 9–102(a)(20) by subsection (D), not because they are not sufficiently secured transactions but because they secure "an obligation"? The drafters here have preserved a distinction between a conventional commercial consignment, which in almost all cases is a "security interest," and the unusual commercial consignment which creates a security interest "that secures an obligation." But if all consignments under section 9–102(a)(20) must be perfected and enjoy more or less the same priority as any other security interest, who cares whether a transaction is merely a consignment subject to Article 9 or whether it is a security interest "that secures an obligation"? If it secures an obligation, Article 9 will apply anyway.

Part 6 of Article 9 on foreclosure treats these transactions differently. A consignor whose interest also "secures an obligation" under section 9–102(a)(20)(D) must follow the restrictive rules on repossession, resale, and the like. If, on the other hand, the transaction is a consignment that creates a security interest in the consignor but does not "secure an obligation" (namely, if it is a mine run consignment of diamonds or books with a duty of sale or return but no duty to pay for unsold goods), then the consignor must protect its interest by filing a financing statement and is, for the purposes of perfection and priority, treated like a secured creditor, but is not so treated for the purposes of foreclosure. *See* 9–601(g). The consignor may get its goods back by whatever method is permitted under state law outside of Article 9. One way to think of the two transactions is to say that a classic consignment creates an interest that behaves like a security interest for the first five parts of Article 9 but not for the sixth, whereas a consignment "that secures an obligation" is a security interest for all parts of Article 9.

That leaves a third type of consignment. These transactions—consignments of consumer goods to a consignment store, consignments of items of a value less than $1,000, and consignments to a person generally known by its creditors to be substantially engaged in selling the goods of others or to a consignee who acts in the name of consignor—are not within

Article 9. They are governed by revised section 2–326, which, in its amended form, reads as follows:

> (1) Unless otherwise agreed, if delivered goods may be returned by the buyer even though they conform to the contract, the transaction is:
>
> > (a) a "sale on approval" if the goods are delivered primarily for use, and
> >
> > (b) a "sale or return" if the goods are delivered primarily for resale.
>
> (2) Goods held on approval are not subject to the claims of the buyer's creditors until acceptance; goods held on sale or return are subject to such claims while in the buyer's possession.

The most obvious way to read section 2–326 is to find that subsection (2) subordinates the consignor's claims to the claims of other creditors because of the last clause: "goods held on sale or return are subject to such claims while in the buyer's possession." So the poor starving artist who puts paintings in the hands of fly-by-night consignees loses them to fly-by-night creditors, true? That seems unfair; presumably the drafters cut the small time consignor out of the rules in Article 9 to protect him, not to injure him (for example, because the small time consignor would not think to file a financing statement, and it would be bothersome to comply with all of Article 9's requirements to properly perfect his interest).

A way to avoid the conclusion suggested above is to find that the paintings were not delivered to a "buyer" under the terms of section 2–326(1) and therefore that section does not govern this transaction at all. *See* 2–103(1)(a) (defining "buyer" as "a person who buys or contracts to buy goods"). If, for example, the agreement between the consignor and the consignee was that the consignee was acting merely as the agent of the consignor, the consignee would never get title so the consignee would not be a "buyer," and section 2–326 would not apply. If that is so, one is out in the common law; presumably the common law will protect the right of the starving artist, consignor, or bailor. This argument, however, hardly stands on firm ground. As noted, section 2–326 clearly treats the consignment as a form of sale. Thus, "consignment" includes cases where title might pass through the consignee's hands at the time of the transfer to a third person as well as cases in which the consignee is merely a distributor acting as the consignor's agent (although the latter are not technically a type of "sale on approval" or "sale or return"). *See* 2–326 cmt. 4; *see also* 9–202. In addition, if a consignee were not a buyer and correspondingly had no interest in the goods sufficient for any interest of creditors to arise, there would seem to be little meaning left to the phrase "goods held on sale or return are subject to such claims while in the buyer's possession."

To summarize, if goods are consigned to a merchant in a conventional commercial transaction (where the merchant operates in its own name and not that of the consignor, is not an auctioneer, and is not "generally known by its creditors to be substantially engaged in selling the goods of others"), the transaction is a consignment, and the consignor's interest is a security interest. The consignor must perfect a security interest under Article 9 to protect itself from the consignee's trustee in bankruptcy and from other and later perfected secured creditors. If the transaction falls outside of the definition in section 9–102(a)(20) because the transaction creates a security interest "that secures an obligation," the rules are practically the same. The consignor is still the holder of a security interest who must perfect it under Article 9. The only difference, and probably an insignificant one, is that on default this latter consignor must comply with Part 6 of Article 9. There is little need to distinguish between garden variety commercial consignments under Article 9 and those which are in every respect security agreements because they secure "an obligation." If the transaction is not covered by the definition in section 9–102(a)(2) because it involves consumer goods, etc., then the transaction is either governed by section 2–326 or the common law.

Consider the following case, which involves a clash between a secured lender with a perfected security interest in the debtor's inventory, and a consignor with an unperfected interest in the same inventory.

RAYFIELD INVESTMENT COMPANY V. KREPS

District Court of Appeal of Florida, Fourth District, 2010.
35 So.3d 63.

FARMER, J.:

Opposing creditors clash over security interests in a painting found in the inventory of a failed art gallery. One creditor is its operating capital lender claiming a perfected security interest in all its inventory. The other is a consignor who placed a painting with the gallery for sale but without perfecting his interest in the consigned goods. Concluding that the governing statutes for security interests give the priority to the lender, we reverse the judgment awarding the painting to the consignor.

Lender made a series of loans totaling $300,000 over a three-year period to a New York corporation doing business in Palm Beach under the trade name *Style de Vie*. Apparently its lifestyle did not allow it to pay its lender, for the gallery defaulted on the loan. Lender sued to foreclose its security interest on the gallery's inventory. Lender proved non-payment and that it had perfected its security interest by filing a UCC–1 financing statement in Florida. Lender obtained a judgment and a writ of replevin for the inventory.

Consignor intervened after lender's replevin of the inventory and claimed the painting. The evidence showed that he placed the painting with the gallery after lender's security interest had been perfected.[1] He did not attach any tag or legend to the painting that it was on consignment.[2] Nor did he file a UCC–1 financing statement in Florida giving notice of his prior interest in the painting. Following a trial, the court found consignor's interest superior to lender's perfected interest, reasoning:

> [lender] had actual knowledge that [gallery] sold antiques and other goods on consignment. Specifically . . . [lender] entered into a Profit Participation Agreement with [gallery] which contemplated participation in the profits of the sales of consigned goods. Further . . . [lender] had actual knowledge and contemplated the continuing consignment of goods at [gallery], and contemplated participation in the profits from the sale of consigned goods. [Consignor] has shown by clear and convincing evidence that he has a superior right and title to the painting that is the subject of this law suit.

From the judgment in consignor's favor, lender appeals.

The Florida Uniform Commercial Code (UCC) governs sales and secured transactions. The UCC specifies that the term "security interest" means "an interest in personal property . . . which secures payment or performance of an obligation" and "includes any interest of a consignor. . . ." § 671.201(35), Fla. Stat. (2009) [1–201(b)(35)]. As for consignments, UCC Article 9 further specifies:

> *Consignment* means a transaction, regardless of its form, in which a person delivers goods to a merchant for the purpose of sale and:
>
> 1. The merchant deals in goods of that kind under a name other than the name of the person making delivery; is not an auctioneer; and is not generally known by its creditors to be substantially engaged in selling the goods of others;
>
> 2. With respect to each delivery, the aggregate value of the goods is $1,000 or more at the time of delivery;
>
> 3. The goods are not consumer goods immediately before delivery; and

[1] The painting was by an artist named Cortes. The consignment agreement stated that gallery was free to sell for not less than $42,000.

[2] Florida law requires the consignor of works of art to give notice to the public by:

> affixing to such work of art a sign or tag which states that such work of art is being sold subject to a contract of consignment, or such consignee shall post a clear and conspicuous sign in the consignee's place of business giving notice that some works of art are being sold subject to a contract of consignment.

§ 686.502(2), Fla. Stat. (2009).

4. The transaction does not create a security interest that secures an obligation. [internal subheadings omitted]

§ 679.1021(1)(t), Fla. Stat. (2009) [9–102(a)(20)]. Again the record indisputably shows that consignor did nothing to perfect a prior interest in the painting by filing a UCC–1, by affixing a tag or by having the gallery post a sign that some inventory is on consignment.

At trial consignor presented evidence that lender's principal knew some of the gallery's items were on consignment. The lender's principal complained that the gallery failed to furnish inventories during the three years before the consignment. When he finally received an inventory, it listed several thousand items for sale but there were not more than 60 at the time. According to some records, consignment goods never exceeded 15% of inventory in the few years preceding the store's demise.

While lender knew there were some consignment goods for sale, there is absolutely no record evidence as to whether the gallery was "generally known by its creditors to be substantially engaged in selling the goods of others." § 679.1021(1)(t)1c [9–102(a)(20)]. Consignor presented no evidence as to who or how many creditors the gallery had when he placed his painting there for sale in 2006. Similarly there is no evidence that lender knew this painting was on consignment or of any agreement between the gallery and consignor. So it is clear this case involves a prior perfected security interest in inventory and a subsequent unperfected security interest in a painting placed with the gallery for sale on consignment.

The law does not support the trial judge's decision. The Florida UCC explicitly provides that a perfected security interest in goods takes priority over all subsequently perfected and unperfected security interests in the same goods. § 679.322(1), Fla. Stat. (2009) [9–322]. Florida law also explicitly provides that a consignor's interest in goods placed for sale with a consignee who routinely sells such goods is merely an unperfected security interest subject to the claims of those with prior perfected security interests. *See* §§ 679.319 and 679.322(1)(b), Fla. Stat. (2009) [9–319, 9–322]; *see also* In re Corvette Collection of Boston Inc., 294 B.R. 409, 414 (Bkry.S.D.Fla.2003) (holding that as to consigned goods, presumption is that goods are held by consignee on sale or return basis subject to claims of consignee's creditors).

The consignor in this case could have defeated the priority of secured creditors only by proving that a majority of the gallery's creditors knew that it was substantially engaged in consignment sales. *See e.g.* Corvette Collection, 294 B.R. at 414. But consignor offered no evidence as to who the gallery's creditors were or what they knew about his goods for sale. The cases follow a general rule of thumb that consignees are not considered to be "substantially engaged" in selling the goods of others unless they hold at least 20% of inventory on a consignment basis. *See* In re Valley Media

Inc., 279 B.R. 105, 125 (Bkry.D.Del.2002); *see also* In re Wedlo Holdings Inc., 248 B.R. 336, 342 (Bkry.N.D.Ill.2000) (holding as a matter of law that consignee who obtained only 15% to 20% of its inventory on consignment was not substantially engaged in selling goods of others).

To satisfy the "generally known" requirement, a consignor must show that a majority of the consignee's creditors were aware that the consignee was substantially engaged in selling the goods of others by consignment sales, and the majority is determined by the number of creditors, not by the amount of their claims. *See* Valley Media, 279 B.R. at 126; In re Wicaco Mach. Corp., 49 B.R. 340, 344 (E.D.Pa.1984) (holding that 20% of creditors knowing of consignment relationship does not satisfy general knowledge requirement, notwithstanding that such creditors represented 63% of claims against debtor). Again, here the consignor had no idea who or how many creditors the gallery had. Consignor's case authorities are inapposite, for they involve actual knowledge by the lender of a specific consignment.

This case is factually similar to *Valley Media*. There, some of the debtor's vendors had entered into consignment arrangements with the debtor before the debtor filed for bankruptcy. 279 B.R. 105 at 115. The consigned inventory was commingled with all of the other inventory of the debtor at two warehouse locations. 279 B.R. 105 at 116. No signs were posted at the warehouses, and there were no signs or markings on the consigned inventory indicating that the inventory had been obtained on a consignment basis. 279 B.R. 105 at 116. When the debtor moved the bankruptcy court to sell all of its inventory, the consignment vendors objected, arguing that they owned their consignment inventory by virtue of their consignment arrangements. 279 B.R. 105 at 121–22. The court observed that the consignors could have obtained a prior interest in their consigned goods if they had either (1) filed UCC–1 financing statements identifying their goods as required under UCC Article 9, or (2) proved that the consignee was generally known by its creditors to be substantially engaged in selling the goods of others. 279 B.R. at 123. *See also* In re New York Diamond & Jewelry Exch. Inc., 26 B.R. 32 (Bkry.S.D.Fla.1982) (consignor failed to perfect security interest by filing financing statement and failed to establish that debtor was generally known by its creditors to be substantially engaged in sale of goods of others, had unperfected security interest in diamonds, subject to trustee's right, and since trustee did not have diamond among assets of estate, trustee was entitled to judgment against plaintiff); ITT Commercial Fin. Corp. v. Unlimited Auto. Inc., 166 B.R. 637 (N.D.Ill.1994) (secured creditor of debtor-dealer had priority over consignor of motor vehicle, where consignor did not comply with applicable filing requirements of UCC and secured creditor enjoyed status of perfected secured creditor with claim to inventory of debtor).

What this case presents is the common collision between a legal rule and an opposing claim for individualized justice. Ours is supposed to be a rule of law, not of judges. Some rules of law are meant to be categorical and unavoidable. The law requires, for example, citizenship to vote, driving on the right side of the road, recorded title to real property, timely assertion of civil claims—to mention just a few—all of which cannot be avoided by an individual claim for sympathetic understanding. Some legal rules explicitly allow their application to be varied by individual circumstances, using equitable principles, but the commercial law on secured transactions is not among them.

The rules for acquiring and enforcing security interests were not written to permit individualized justice and equity contrary to their requirements. It would not be much of a uniform code, for example, if legal rules on sales rights and remedies transformed themselves from case to case, or negotiable instruments were not predictably and reliably negotiable, or [ ] priorities of security interests were adjustable depending on whose individual circumstance is more sympathetic. The statutes give us no authority to refuse to enforce priorities under UCC Article 9 on the basis that the painting has been in the family for years, or that the lender knew the gallery did some consignment sales, or that this lender's funding agreement with the gallery allowed it to share to some extent in its profits, or by framing the painting's sale as a bailment instead of a consignment.[3]

The law creating the priority rule afforded consignor effective tools to avoid a prior security interest in gallery's inventory. These tools were simple, not burdensome, and easily satisfied. He needed only to file a UCC–1 under Florida law. Aside from that, he could have required the gallery to affix a tag onto the painting and place a sign alerting prospective buyers of a consignment sale. He did none of these things. Nothing in the record we have been given suggests that lender or gallery did anything to dissuade him from prior consultation with a lawyer to protect his painting by complying with statutes for avoiding prior interests. In the end he failed to offer any evidence that most of gallery's creditors knew that a substantial part of its sales were consignments.

The judgment of the trial court is in error. The perfected security interest of lender has priority over the claim of consignor.

Reversed.

NOTE

The result in *Rayfield* may well strike one as unfair. How often do you think an individual consignor will be cognizant of the filing requirements that Article 9 imposes to fully protect the consignor's interest? One might well have little sympathy for commercial consignors who presumably make it their business to understand the relevant legal requirements. If they are stung,

[3] *See* § 679.1021(1)(t), Fla. Stat. (2009) (*consignment* means any transaction—regardless of its form—in which a person delivers goods to a merchant for purpose of sale).

perhaps one might conclude that they have only themselves to blame. But what of individual consignors? Of course, if the consigned item constituted consumer goods in the hands of the consignor immediately before delivery to the consignee, Article 9 would not apply. *See* 9–102(a)(20)(C). So it may be effectively immaterial that consignors of consumer goods are unlikely to know of the filing requirements imposed under section 9–319. But the relevant priority rule under section 2–326 for a "sale or return" transaction involving consumer goods is essentially the same—goods in the hands of the consignee will be subject to the claims of the consignee's creditors. *See* 2–326(2). Do you think this is fair?

Note how the court observes in *Rayfield* that the lender did nothing to lull the consignor into a false sense of security. Why is this relevant? Suppose the lender had promised the consignor that, if the debtor defaulted, the lender would not consider the consigned painting to be part of its collateral. Can you make an argument that the outcome of the case would be different as a result? Take a look at section 1–103(b). Section 1–103(b) provides that, unless displaced, the principles of law and equity, including principles of estoppel and the like, supplement the provisions of the UCC. Could you make an estoppel or waiver argument? How about a broader argument that, as a matter of equity, the consignor should prevail? Clearly the court in *Rayfield* was not inclined to consider any sort of broad based resort to "individualized justice." Does equity have a role to play here?

§ 7. BAILMENTS AND OSTENSIBLE OWNERSHIP

What is a bailment? In general, a "bailment" is created when one person (the "bailor") gives something (for example, a car) to another (the "bailee") for a particular purpose (say, to fix the car) and that other person (the bailee) is supposed to return it thereafter. This definition is not entirely precise. For example, as an historical matter a "true" consignment of goods was also considered to be a form of bailment (namely, a "bailment for the purpose of sale") and this reference appears in the official comments to the UCC. *See, e.g.*, 9–109 cmt. 6. In addition, in historical terms there were other forms of bailments that did not involve the prospect of the bailee returning the goods (for example, a "bailment for the purpose of delivery").

In its most general sense, the concept of a "bailment" historically included any one of a group of transactions whereby the bailor delivered possession to the bailee for a specific purpose that did not include vesting ownership in the bailee (for example, the bailee was to repair the goods, store and care for them, deliver them to a third party, sell them as the agent for the bailor on commission, or possess them for a term under a lease). *See, e.g.,* 2–326 cmt. 4. In modern parlance, the concept of a bailment has taken on a more limited and distinct meaning that focuses on the bailee's possession in order to repair or otherwise care for the goods on a temporary basis, with the understanding that eventually they will be returned to the true owner. In contrast, a consignment (at least for Article 9 purposes) is created when one person gives something to another to sell and expects return of the item only if it is not sold. Read the following case to get a sense of the complexity involved in drawing a line between consignment and bailment.

AMERICAN BANK & TRUST V. SHAULL

Supreme Court of South Dakota, 2004.
678 N.W.2d 779.

MEIERHENRY, JUSTICE:

* * *

The issues before this Court center on priority of the claims to [various] cows among American, Fin-Ag, Feldman, and AgStar. American claims it has a valid perfected first security interest. Fin-Ag claims it has a valid perfected security interest subject to the perfected first security interest of American. Feldman claims ownership of the collateral giving him priority over American and Fin-Ag. AgStar claims an interest through a security agreement with Feldman. The bifurcated claim and delivery cause of action was tried to the court. The trial court entered a judgment declaring that American has a valid perfected first security interest to the collateral, that Fin-Ag has a valid perfected security interest subject to American's interest, that any ownership claim of Feldman or security interest of AgStar are subordinate and inferior to the perfected security interest of American and Fin-Ag. Feldman and AgStar appeal. We affirm. The issues on appeal are as follows:

I. WHETHER SHAULL HAD SUFFICIENT RIGHTS IN THE COLLATERAL TO SUPPORT THE ATTACHMENT OF AMERICAN'S AND FIN-AG'S SECURITY INTERESTS TO ENTITLE AMERICAN TO IMMEDIATE CLAIM AND DELIVERY.

II. WHETHER AMERICAN AND FIN-AG OR FELDMAN BROTHERS ARE ESTOPPED FROM ASSERTING A SECURITY INTEREST IN THE COLLATERAL.

III. WHETHER THE COWS AND CALVES ARE INVENTORY OR FARM PRODUCTS.

Background and Facts

The core of this case centers on the demise of Nathan Shaull's livestock operations in the spring of 2002. Shaull owned and operated the Livestock Auction in Highmore, South Dakota; he bought and sold cattle through the sale barn and additionally acted as a cattle broker, buying and selling cattle as H.S. Cattle. American had financed Shaull. The financing consisted of a promissory note for [a] $750,000 revolving line of credit dated

September 27, 1999 and a second note for $498,413.50 for "breeding livestock" and refinancing of debt on June 8, 2001. The amount due to American on the revolving line of credit was over $750,000 and the amount due on the livestock loan was $325,461. In conjunction with both loans, Shaull executed a security agreement granting to American a security interest in all livestock owned or later acquired and additionally on the second loan, a security interest in all inventory and farm products, owned or thereafter owned by Shaull. American filed financing statements in the office of the South Dakota Secretary of State (Secretary) which covered the livestock and specifically as to the second transaction covered "all cows and 2001 future offspring, all increase, issue offspring, products and products from the livestock" and included the proceeds from the collateral.

Prior to American's financing, Shaull had financed his operation with Fin-Ag who had filed a financing statement with the Secretary in June of 1997 and July of 1998. When Shaull refinanced with American, Fin-Ag subordinated its security interest in the cows and calves by a Subordination Agreement and Assignment of Security Interest in June of 2001 which was formalized with the filing of [a] UCC–3 with the Secretary. Fin-Ag claims that approximately 4,500 head of cattle which it financed were missing and that Shaull owes Fin-Ag over two million dollars. Fin-Ag last inventoried Shaull's herd in May of 2001, approximately one month before American inspected Shaull's cattle for refinancing.

The Feldman brothers operated a farming and cattle feeding business in Minnesota. Feldman entered into an agreement with Shaull on November 30, 2000 wherein Feldman placed cows with Shaull for feeding and care. Pursuant to the agreement, Feldman purchased 1,536 cows between November 28, 2000 and December 15, 2001 which were placed with Shaull, 915 of which should have been in Shaull's possession at the time American did its refinancing inspection in June of 2001. AgStar had a Security Agreement with Feldman wherein it acquired a security interest in all the livestock owned or later acquired by Feldman. AgStar had not filed a financing statement in South Dakota.

American's Inspection of the Collateral

On June 5, 2001, Shaull took two officers of American to inspect his cattle at three locations around Highmore and Miller, South Dakota. One location was owned by Shaull; the other two were rented. Because of the rough terrain, it was difficult to get an exact count of the herd; however, the group counted about 1,000 cows. Shaull ultimately set the number at 900 for purposes of collateral because he intended to cull some of the herd. Some of the cows were branded, some had ear tags, and some may not have had any identifying tag or brand. Shaull maintained that he owned these cattle. If so, they would have been the same cattle previously financed by Fin-Ag. In Shaull's dealings with Fin-Ag, Fin-Ag had required Shaull to brand or ear tag his cattle with Fin-Ag's identification. American's inspection, although noting that some of the cattle were marked, did not specifically identify the brands or ear tags.

In addition to Shaull's representation to the bank that he owned the cows, American reviewed Shaull's financial statement and last tax return with the depreciation schedule for the cows. American further spoke with Fin-Ag who had financed the herd previously. No other verification of ownership was done by American prior to the loan approval. American knew that Shaull bought and sold cattle through his sale barn; however, it did not know of the agreement Shaull had with Feldman or that Shaull brokered cattle through H.S. Cattle.

Identifying the 910 Cows Remaining

Around the middle of April, 2002, when Shaull's financial troubles became apparent, the South Dakota State Brand Board instigated an investigation of the remaining cows. All of the remaining cows were gathered in an effort to identify them. A total of 910 cows were counted. Of the total, 82 cows had Fin-Ag identifying ear tags; 571 can be traced to cows purchased by Feldman.

Basis of Feldman's Claim to the Remaining Cows Held by the Receiver

Feldman claims that American and Fin-Ag's security interests cannot attach to the cows that he purchased and placed with Shaull under the Bred Cow Agreement. Feldman and AgStar claim that the Agreement established a bailment not requiring them to file a UCC–1 to protect their interests. American argues that had Feldman and AgStar filed financing statements, the bank would have been put on notice of their interest in the collateral.

Whether the Trial Court Erred in Its Findings of Facts or Conclusions of Law

This was a two-day trial to the court. At the end of the evidence, the trial court announced its decision in favor of American and directed counsel for American to propose Findings of Fact and Conclusions of Law for the court's signature. The trial court's Conclusions of Law 7 and 8 form the basis of the decision against Feldman and AgStar:

> 7. By their failure to file UCC–1 financing statements and by allowing Shaull to appear to be the actual owner of the cow herd, Feldman and AgStar are estopped from asserting that Shaull, as the apparent owner, did not have rights in the cow herd.
>
> 8. The cows and calves which are the subject of this action are farm products and not inventory.

* * *

Feldman claims that American and/or Fin-Ag cannot have a superior interest in the collateral because of Feldman's ownership interest which is detailed in the Bred Cow Agreement between Feldman and Shaull. Feldman provided evidence that he had purchased 1,536 cattle from November 28, 2000 to December 15, 2001 to be cared for by Shaull as part of the agreement, 1,407 of which he purchased from Shaull (as H.S. Cattle). Fin-Ag claims that the cows held by the receivership were the same cows that Fin-Ag had previously owned and sold to Feldman and were the same cows Fin-Ag had identified and inventoried on May 22, 2001. Feldman claims that American's own negligence caused its loss and that both American and Fin-Ag should be estopped from claiming a security interest in the collateral. Feldman points to American's failure to ascertain the ownership of the cattle prior to extending credit to Shaull, its lack of any inspection subsequent to loaning Shaull money, and its failure to follow its own internal policy in monitoring the custodial account.

The trial court found that American "had neither actual nor constructive knowledge of any claim of ownership by Feldman or any security interest claimed by AgStar." FF 26. The court further determined that, "[p]rior to making the June, 2001 loan to Shaull, American took all steps reasonably necessary to determine that its perfected security interest would attach to the cow herd." FF 28. * * * A thorough review of the evidence supports the court's findings and conclusions. The bank inspected the cows Shaull claimed were his, reviewed his financial statement and tax return and did a record search for UCC filings. The evidence further indicates that neither American nor others who dealt with Shaull knew of Feldman's ownership of the cows, except for one of Shaull's employees who worked with the cattle. Shaull did not indicate to the landowners from whom he rented the pasture that the cows were owned by someone else and he certainly did not tell American that Feldman owned the cattle.

The trial court further found that 625 of the cows that were inspected by American in June of 2001 were part of a lease purchase agreement between Shaull and Ron Jennings, a farmer near Miller, South Dakota. The court found that the Jennings' "cows were in Shaull's possession, control and apparent ownership at the time American inspected the cow herd in June, 2001 and were represented by Shaull as being owned by him." The Jennings' cows were later sold to Feldman in December of 2001.

The trial court was not clearly erroneous in finding that all the cows inspected by American in June of 2001 were the same cows held by the receiver. In fact, Shaull's employee testified that was the case. The trial court did not base its decision on the actual ownership of the cows and whether a bailment existed but on the apparent ownership of the cows under an estoppel theory.

We have previously stated that control rather than ownership of collateral determines a debtor's rights to collateral. *First Nat. Bank of Omaha v. Pleasant Hollow Farm, Inc.*, 532 N.W.2d 60, 63 (S.D.1995). We said in *Pleasant View Farms, Inc. v. Ness*, 455 N.W.2d 602 (S.D.1990):

> If the owner of collateral allows another to appear as the owner or to dispose of the collateral, such that a third party is led into dealing with the apparent owner as though he were the actual owner, then the owner will be estopped from asserting that the apparent owner did not have rights in the collateral.

Id. at 604 (citing *In re Pubs, Inc.*, 618 F.2d 432 (7th Cir.1980)).

The trial court found that AgStar was aware that Feldman placed cows with Shaull and that a UCC–1 financing statement needed to be filed in South Dakota to protect its interest. As early as 1999, AgStar had requested Feldman to provide Shaull's name, address and social security number, which Feldman did. However, neither AgStar nor Feldman filed a financing statement. The trial court determined that had they done so, American would have been put on notice of their claims prior to making the loan to Shaull in 2001. Although Feldman as the bailor could have filed a financing statement, he was not obligated to under the Uniform Commercial Code. SDCL 57A–9–505.

Finally, Feldman claims that the trial court erroneously determined that the cows were farm products and not inventory. Although Shaull invoked his right to remain silent under the Fifth Amendment rather than answer many of the questions put to him by the attorneys, he did admit that the cows he sold as H.S. Cattle were part of his farming operation, not the sale barn, thus making them farm products and not inventory. The trial court based this finding upon the testimony and evidence presented at trial. Although there may have been evidence to the contrary, "[d]oubts about whether the evidence supports the court's findings of fact are to be resolved in favor of the successful party's 'version of the evidence and of all inferences fairly deducible therefrom which are favorable to the court's action.' " *Maryhouse*, 473 N.W.2d at 474.

The question presented to the trial court was to determine the priority of claims. The question presented to this Court was whether Feldman's ownership of the cows gave Feldman and AgStar priority over American and Fin-Ag. The trial court determined based on the evidence, that Feldman and AgStar were estopped from claiming that Shaull did not have sufficient rights in the cows for a security interest to attach. Based upon the record, we cannot say that the trial court was clearly erroneous. The trial court is affirmed on all issues.

GILBERTSON, CHIEF JUSTICE, and KONENKAMP, JUSTICE, and TRIMBLE, CIRCUIT COURT JUDGE, sitting by Order of the Court, concur.

JOHNS, CIRCUIT JUDGE, dissenting:

This is an appeal from a judgment entered by the circuit court for claim and delivery of a herd of cattle and for declaratory relief determining the rights of the parties to the herd. I would affirm in part, reverse in part, and remand.

At the outset, some further development of the facts is useful to our inquiry in this case. This action was brought by American Bank and Trust (American), a South Dakota state chartered bank, against Nathan and Deborah Shaull, d/b/a Highmore Auction Sales, and Fin-Ag, Inc. (Fin-Ag). The South Dakota Wheat Growers Association intervened as a party plaintiff and AgStar Financial Services, PCA (AgStar) and Feldman Brothers (Feldman) intervened as party defendants.

* * *

Shaull was the owner of Highmore Auction Sales, a sale barn in Highmore, South Dakota. In addition, he conducted a cattle order brokering business under the name of H.S. Cattle and also had a cattle operation in which he ran his own cattle as well as those of Feldman. The genesis of this action was Shaull's refusal to account for several hundred head of cattle missing from the cattle operation and his repeated invocation of his right to remain silent about the cattle.

The trial court held that Nathan Shaull (Shaull) had an interest in the cattle at issue and that the security interests he gave to American and Fin-Ag attached to his interest. The trial court also held that since Feldman and AgStar failed to file UCC–1 financing statements on the cattle and allowed Shaull to appear as the actual owner and to borrow money against them from American, Feldman and AgStar were estopped from claiming any interest in the cattle against American and Fin-Ag.

Feldman and AgStar appeal. * * *

American, Fin-Ag and AgStar each claim a security interest in the 910 cattle that are the subject matter of this action. American and AgStar each claim a first priority interest. Feldman claims an interest subject only to AgStar's security interest. Fin-Ag claims an interest subject only to American's interest.

American's Interest

Shaull obtained financing from American in the form of a revolving line of credit for $750,000 to cover any overdrafts in connection with the sale barn. Subsequently, he obtained an additional $498,413 to refinance a herd of brood cows previously financed by Fin-Ag. To date $750,000 remains due and owing on the line of credit and $325,461 on the refinanced herd.

In connection with the line of credit, Shaull executed a security agreement on September 27, 1999 granting American a security interest in all of his owned or after-acquired livestock. On October 19, 1999, American filed a financing statement in the office of the Secretary of State of South Dakota covering owned or after-acquired livestock.

In connection with the refinancing of the herd, Shaull executed a security agreement on June 8, 2001 granting American a security interest in all inventory and farm products owned or thereafter owned by Shaull. On June 13, 2001, American filed a financing statement in the office of the Secretary of State of South Dakota that covered all cows as well as all offspring, all products from the livestock and all proceeds.

Fin-Ag's Interest

Shaull's relationship with Fin-Ag began with his participation in Fin-Ag's value added program. As part of the program, Fin-Ag placed a herd of cattle with Shaull for care and feeding. Fin-Ag later converted the value added program into two loans to Shaull. Fin-Ag took perfected security interests in the cattle in June 1997 and July 1998.

Sometime in 2001, Shaull approached Fin-Ag about expanding the cattle operation to include feeder cattle. Fin-Ag did not want to loan Shaull any additional money but did agree that, if he refinanced the brood cows with American, he could use the loan proceeds to buy the feeder cattle. Thus, in June 2001, Fin-Ag subordinated its perfected security interest in Shaull's breeder cattle to American.

AgStar's Interest

AgStar's interest is contingent upon Feldman's interest. AgStar is Feldman's lender and holds a security agreement in all livestock owned or later acquired by Feldman.

Feldman's Interest

Feldman's claim is grounded upon its ownership interest in the cattle it placed with Shaull for feeding and care pursuant to a bred cow agreement dated November 30, 2000.

Feldman placed cattle with Shaull on a number of occasions[.] * * *

The bred cow agreement was entered into by the parties on November 30, 2000 and was to cover a period of two years. According to the agreement, Feldman was to place 500 to 1300 bred cows with Shaull. Shaull would be paid by Feldman for the cost of feedlot feed and the cost to rent pasturage which costs were preset in the agreement. Feldman would be paid eleven percent interest on the cost of the cattle and feed. After the first year of the contract, Shaull was to provide bulls to impregnate the herd. Calves were to be sold by November 1, 2001 and November 1, 2002.

The agreement also provided that:

> On or before December 1, 2001 and December 1, 2002, cows will be pregnancy checked, opens will be sold. We have the option on the pregnant cows to either sell them or keep them or add to them until next year.

Finally, the agreement provided that the parties were to split the profits or losses equally on the date of final settlement which was to be on or before December 15, 2002.

With this factual background, the issues presented in this case can be stated as follows: [w]hether the trial court erred when it concluded that Shaull had rights in the cow herd and all calves born from that herd sufficient to allow American and Fin-Ag's security interests to attach to the animals[;] [w]hether the trial court erred when it concluded that Feldman and AgStar were estopped from making any claim that their interests in the animals were first and superior to those of American and Fin-Ag[; and] [w]hether the trial court erred when it concluded the cattle were farm products rather than inventory.

* * *

ANALYSIS

ISSUE ONE

Whether the trial court erred when it concluded that Shaull had rights in the cow herd and all calves born from that herd sufficient to allow American and Fin-Ag's security interests to attach to the animals.

In *Continental Grain Co. v. Brandenburg,* 1998 SD 118, ¶ 16, 587 N.W.2d 196, 200, this Court determined that:

> SDCL 57A–9–203(1) provides three requirements that must be met before a security interest will attach and be enforceable against a debtor or third party:
>
> (a) The collateral is in the possession of the secured party pursuant to agreement, or the debtor has signed a security agreement which contains a description of the collateral . . . ; and
>
> (b) Value has been given; and
>
> (c) *The debtor has rights in the collateral.*

(emphasis original).

At issue here is whether Shaull had rights in the collateral sufficient for American and Fin-Ag's security interests to attach and also the extent of such interests.

Although the phrase "rights in the collateral" is not defined in the Uniform Commercial Code (SDCL ch. 57A),

> [The] language merely states a truism, namely, that the debtor normally can only convey something once it has something, and that something may be less than the full bundle of rights that one may hold in such property. The "rights in the collateral" language is a gateway through which one looks to other law to determine the extent of the debtor's rights, and thus the interest the debtor can grant to a third party by way of a security interest.

4 JAMES J. WHITE & ROBERT S. SUMMERS, UNIFORM COMMERCIAL CODE § 31–6 (4th ed. 1995).

In looking to other law, we have used both legal and equitable concepts to determine the extent of a debtor's rights in collateral. *Continental Grain*, 1998 SD 118 at ¶ 21, 587 N.W.2d at 202; SDCL 57A–1–103. One such concept is the doctrine of estoppel.

> Although it is not always determinative on the issues of attachment and priority, the doctrine of estoppel may defeat competing claims when owners fail to protect themselves and allow others to retain control over collateral. SDCL 57A–1–103 permits legal and equitable concepts to supplement the provisions of the UCC.

Continental Grain, 1998 SD 118 at ¶ 21, 587 N.W.2d at 202. *See also Pleasant View Farms, Inc.*, 455 N.W.2d at 604.

Feldman, AgStar and Amicus argue that the bred cow agreement created a voluntary bailment relationship and, therefore, Shaull obtained no rights in the collateral to which the security interests of American and Fin-Ag could attach. They cite *Rohweder v. Aberdeen Production Credit Ass'n*, 765 F.2d 109, 113 (8th Cir.1985) for the proposition that, if parties intend to create a bailment with the owner retaining complete ownership of the cows and relinquishing only possession, the feeder does not have sufficient rights for attachment of a creditor's lien. On the other hand, American and Fin-Ag cite us to a line of cases holding that a debtor acquires rights in collateral sufficient to estop the owner from claiming ownership against an innocent third party when the owner imbues the debtor with evidence of ownership and control and does not file a UCC–1 financing statement. * * * In *Court of Monies*, 417 N.W.2d 187, 188 (S.D.1987), we quoted with approval the following language from *Brown*, 622 F.Supp. at 1049–1050:

> Even if the plaintiff had established ownership of the cattle, the court is unconvinced that a third party's ownership interest in collateral bears any substantial weight in determining a debtor's "rights in collateral" for the purposes of attachment of a security

> interest. The official comment to § 9–202 states unequivocally that "[t]he rights and duties of parties to a security transaction and of third parties are stated in this Article without reference to the location of 'title' to the collateral." Even if a party retains ownership interest in a piece of collateral, a debtor who retains that collateral is still able to mislead potential creditors by exercising his "rights" of possession and control over the collateral. It is the outward appearance of a *debtor's* rights of ownership and control in the collateral that determines whether attachment of a security interest is effective and not the rights of a party who may have title to the collateral. (emphasis in original). [citation omitted]

The trial court concluded that "Shaull had rights in the cow herd and all calves born from that herd sufficient to allow a security interest to attach to the animals." This conclusion was premised, in part, on the express terms of the bred cow agreement.

I agree with the trial court that, as a matter of law, Shaull did have an interest in the herd under the terms of the bred cow agreement. Reading the document as a whole, as we must, it is clear that, although Feldman was to buy the cows, *both* parties had rights in and to the calves and their proceeds. Feldman was obligated to pay Shaull fifty percent of the net proceeds from the sale of calves or to share equally in any loss resulting from such sale. Net proceeds were arrived at by deducting the fixed costs of feed and pasture per cow paid to Shaull, the variable veterinary costs and the eleven percent interest Feldman was to receive based on what it spent on the cost of the cows and the feedlot and pasture costs. Although some portions of this agreement suggest a bailment, it was much broader in scope. It created a joint venture relationship between the parties because each was to share equally in the profits or losses and because Shaull was obligated to provide the bulls to breed the cows after the first year. This agreement is also distinguishable from a bailment because it provided that Feldman was to receive an eleven percent return on its investment. This gave the agreement the complexion of a creditor/debtor relationship between Feldman and Shaull.

Recognizing that the bred cow agreement expressly gave Shaull an interest in the calves sufficient for attachment of a security interest, the next question is whether Shaull also had a tangential interest in the cows. Since Shaull had an interest in the calf crop, it follows that he also had an equitable interest in each of the pregnant cows, albeit not a legal or ownership interest. However, ownership is not the critical factor as "[o]ur cases demonstrate that *control* over the collateral, rather than record ownership, is the key factor in determining a debtor's rights in collateral." *First Nat'l Bank*, 532 N.W.2d at 63 (emphasis added).

The trial court never did assess the extent of Shaull's interest in the cattle under the agreement since it also held that Feldman and AgStar were estopped from making any claim that their interests in the animals were first and superior to those of American. In light of my proposed disposition on issues two and three, I would remand to the trial court the question of the extent of Shaull's interest under the agreement.

ISSUE TWO

Whether the trial court erred when it concluded that Feldman and AgStar were estopped from making any claim that their interests in the animals were first and superior to those of American and Fin-Ag.

As already stated, a person can acquire rights in collateral by one of two ways[:] by express agreement of the parties or by actions of the owner cloaking a bailee or another with indicia of ownership such that the equitable principle of estoppel by negligence estops the true owner from making a claim. Estoppel by negligence is "[a]n estoppel arising when a negligent person induces someone to believe certain facts, and then the other person reasonably and detrimentally relies on that belief." Black's Law Dictionary 571 (7th ed. 1999). Estoppel by negligence must be distinguished from equitable estoppel which requires an element of deception or gross negligence amounting to constructive fraud. *See Kahler, Inc. v. Weiss,* 539 N.W.2d 86, 91 (S.D.1995). Other than in secured transaction cases, we have recognized the concept of estoppel by negligence in the law of agency concerning the authority of an agent to act for a principal.

American's $498,413.50 loan to Shaull

The trial court found that, by the terms of the bred cow agreement and the actions of the parties, Shaull had actual physical control and possession of the cattle. The court also found that the "cows were in Shaull's possession, control and apparent ownership at the time [American] inspected the cow herd in June 2001 and were represented by Shaull as being owned by him." While Feldman and AgStar dispute the finding of apparent ownership I am satisfied from the record that Feldman cloaked Shaull with sufficient indicia of ownership to mislead an innocent third party into believing that Shaull was the actual owner and was capable of granting a security interest in the cattle. Clearly Shaull had physical possession of the cattle, was responsible for leasing their pasture, decided if and when the cattle were to be moved and decided whether veterinarian work was to be done. Moreover, Shaull's employees cared for the cattle and took their orders from Shaull. Finally, although Feldman would consult periodically with Shaull's hired man, no other person associated with the care or keeping of the cattle in South Dakota had any idea that Feldman had any interest in the cattle.

The trial court found that, on or about June 8, 2001, American made a $498,413.50 loan to Shaull and that Shaull gave American a security interest in the cattle. The court also found that, at the time American took its security interest, it "had neither actual nor constructive knowledge of any claim of ownership by Feldman or any security interest claimed by AgStar" and that it "took all steps reasonably necessary to determine that its perfected security interest would attach to the cow herd." Feldman and AgStar argue that these findings are clearly erroneous. They contend that American failed to take reasonable measures to ensure that Shaull had an interest in the cattle and that it also failed to act reasonably when it did extend credit to Shaull by paying his checking overdrafts.

An element of estoppel by negligence is reasonable reliance on the part of the innocent party. In this case, that requires proof that American acted in a reasonable manner when it took its security interest and extended credit. A creditor "cannot prevail on an estoppel theory without showing facts demonstrating both reliance and lack of knowledge of the true facts or means to discover them." *Estate of Harris v. Harris*, 218 F.3d 1140, 1152–53 (10th Cir.2000).

To verify Shaull's representation in his loan application that he owned the cattle, American took the following steps: its bankers were accompanied by Shaull in conducting a physical inspection of the cattle in their pastures; it obtained Shaull's last income tax return to ensure that the cattle were on a depreciation schedule; it reviewed Shaull's two most recent financial statements; it confirmed with Fin-Ag the existence of the cattle; and, it did a comprehensive lien search, obtaining releases or subordinations of all liens of record. Furthermore, the only evidence before the trial court on the issue of American's efforts to verify Shaull's ownership was from American's witnesses who testified that American followed standard banking practices and procedures in making the loan.

I am satisfied that this record supports the trial court's findings that American took reasonable measures to verify Shaull's ownership claim. Although American could have taken some of the additional measures suggested by AgStar such as an inspection of every animal or requiring Shaull to produce some proof of purchase, it must be remembered that this was a refinancing of an existing herd, not a purchase money financing. American acted as a reasonable lender would have under the same or similar circumstances and, thus, I would affirm that part of the trial court's judgment determining that Feldman and AgStar should be estopped from claiming that their interests in the 910 head of cattle are first and superior to the interest resulting from American's $498,413.50 loan to Shaull.

Fin-Ag's loan

The trial court concluded that Fin-Ag had a perfected security interest in the cattle, subject only to American's interest. I agree with this conclusion to the extent that it recognizes the interest acquired by Fin-Ag through the bred cow agreement and the after-acquired property clause of its 1999 security agreement. I disagree, however, with any conclusion that Feldman and AgStar should be estopped from claiming their share since the bred cow agreement was not entered into by Feldman and Shaull until November 30, 2000. The trial court never entered any findings of fact on this issue and there is simply no evidence in the record that Fin-Ag ever detrimentally relied upon the conduct of Feldman and AgStar in extending credit to Shaull after November 30, 2000. Therefore, I would reverse that part of the trial court's judgment holding that Feldman and AgStar are estopped from claiming their interests are first and superior to that of Fin-Ag.

American's $750,000 loan to Shaull

There remains the question of whether Feldman and AgStar should be estopped from claiming their share in the cattle because of the $750,000 debt due to American on the September 27, 1999 revolving line of credit account. This account was established specifically to cover overdraft checks drawn on Shaull's sale barn account. Of the $750,000, approximately $635,782 was extended over a two day period on April 11 and 12, 2002. Feldman and AgStar contend that it was unreasonable for American to extend this credit. I would not reach this issue since the trial court never addressed whether American detrimentally relied upon the appearance of ownership of the Feldman/Shaull cattle when it extended the credit to the sale barn operation. Thus, I would reverse and remand that part of the trial court's judgment determining that Feldman and AgStar should be estopped from claiming that their interests in the 910 head of cattle are first and superior to the interests resulting from American's $750,000 loan to Shaull. With the remand I would instruct the trial court to consider whether American detrimentally relied upon the appearance of ownership and, if so, to then balance the equities between the parties considering that estoppel is an equitable remedy.

ISSUE THREE

Whether the trial court erred when it concluded the cattle were farm products rather than inventory.

The final issue concerns the trial court's conclusion of law that "[*a*]*ny* sales of cattle from the cow herd from Shaull to Feldman were sales of farm products by a farmer and, as such, the perfected security interests of [American] and Fin-Ag attached to any cattle purchased by Feldman from Shaull." (emphasis added). The result of this conclusion is that American and Fin-Ag would have a one hundred percent interest in any cattle Shaull sold to Feldman by reason of the after-acquired property clauses of the multiple security agreements. The trial court erred in reaching this conclusion.

Shaull wore a number of different hats. He owned and operated a sale barn, he ran a cattle brokerage business, he ran cattle of his own, and he also managed the bred cow operation for Feldman. These were very distinct and different roles.

The issue is whether the cattle Shaull sold to Feldman were inventory of the cattle brokerage business or farm products of Shaull's personal cattle operation. If they were inventory, a buyer in the ordinary course of business would take them free of any security interest. If they were farm products, the buyer would take them subject to any security interest. SDCL 57A–9–320 (a).

> Under the Uniform Commercial Code, goods are classified as consumer goods, equipment, farm products, or inventory. Livestock used or produced in farming operations and in the possession of a debtor engaged in raising, fattening, grazing, or other farming operations are farm products. If goods are farm products they are neither equipment nor inventory. [9–102 cmt. 4(a)].
>
> Goods which are held for sale or lease are classified as inventory. [*Id.*] The Comment to section 9–10[2], UCC, states that the classifications are mutually exclusive and that the principal test to determine whether goods are inventory is whether they are held for immediate or ultimate sale. In borderline cases the principal use to which the property is put should be considered determinative.

First State Bank v. Producers Livestock Marketing, 200 Neb. 12, 261 N.W.2d 854, 858 (1978).

In Finding of Fact #45 the trial court found:

> The cows which are the subject of this action are brood cows and were intended to be held for an extended period of time for calf production. The calves were intended to be raised and ultimately sold. Both the cows and calves are farm products and not inventory.

This finding is a correct statement to the extent that it recognizes that the joint venture bred cow operation of Feldman and Shaull did hold the cattle for breeding purposes and, ergo, they were farm products of that business venture. It does not necessarily support a conclusion that they were farm products of Shaull's personal cattle breeding operation.

In Finding of Fact #49 the trial court found:

> Shaull maintained and cared for the cow herd as a farmer and not as an order buyer. Any purchase of cattle by Feldman from the

> cow herd maintained by Shaull was a purchase of farm products from a farmer and not from a sale barn operator or order buyer.

Again this finding is correct to the extent that it recognizes how the cattle were held by the Feldman/Shaull business venture. It is, however, clearly erroneous in respect to all of the cattle sold by Shaull to Feldman and then cared for by Shaull in that on March 15, 2001, Feldman purchased from H.S. Cattle 370 head of bred cows which H.S. Cattle purchased on that same date from three sources. These cattle were never held by Shaull in his personal cattle operation for breeding purposes. Rather, these cattle were held by Shaull for resale and were clearly inventory.

There were two other sales of cattle from Shaull to Feldman during the life of the bred cow agreement. The first sale was November 28, 2000 when Feldman purchased 122 bred cows from H.S. Cattle. Because the trial court did not trace the ownership history of the 910 head of cattle present at the time of the count, it is impossible to determine, with the exception of the 82 head bearing the Fin-Ag brand or ear tag, which of the 910 head were purchased by Feldman from Shaull and which of them were procured by Feldman from other sources.

As to the 82 Fin-Ag cows the trial court found in Finding of Fact #16:

> Fin-Ag loan officers inspected the cow herd on a regular basis, and noted that the cow numbers were intact on each occasion. The last such inspection was conducted in May 2001.

And in Finding of Fact #51 it found:

> At the time the South Dakota Brand Inspectors conducted a brand inspection in June 2002, approximately 82 cows carrying F/A brands or ear tags were present. Those cows were some of the same cows which had been previously inspected by Fin-Ag and AB&T.

Based on these findings, which are not clearly erroneous, it is apparent that the 82 were part of the cow herd placed with Shaull by Fin-Ag in the mid-1990s under the value added program and later purchased by him from Fin-Ag. These cattle were held by Shaull in his own name for the purposes of breeding and were clearly farm products if and when they were sold to Feldman.

The third sale was December 15, 2001 when Feldman purchased 625 bred cows, known as the Jennings cattle, from H.S. Cattle. Shaull held these cattle for approximately nine months under a lease with an option to purchase and he exercised the option immediately upon Feldman's commitment to buy them. The lease and American and Fin-Ag's security interests in the lease ended on the exercise of the purchase option as those interests would have merged into Shaull's ownership interest. Since Shaull did not own the cattle at the time he conducted his farming operation with them and since these cattle were purchased for immediate resale, they were clearly inventory at the time of their sale to Feldman. Therefore, the trial court erred in concluding as a matter of law that the "Jennings" cattle were farm products of Shaull at the time of their sale to Feldman.

With the exception of the 82 Fin-Ag cows and possibly the balance of the 122 head from the November 28, 2000 sale, the trial court's conclusion of law is not supported by the findings of fact and the record and, thus, I would reverse and remand for further consideration of the 122 November 28, 2000 cattle.

DISPOSITION

I would affirm that part of the trial court's judgment holding that American and Fin-Ag jointly hold a security interest in a portion of the herd because of the bred cow agreement. However, I would remand this issue for the trial court to determine the extent of those interests. I would affirm that part of the trial court's judgment holding that Feldman and AgStar are estopped from claiming any interest in the herd with respect to American's June 8, 2001 loan to Shaull. I would reverse that part of the trial court's judgment determining that Feldman and AgStar should be estopped from claiming their respective ownership and security interests against Fin-Ag. I would reverse and remand that part of the trial court's judgment determining that Feldman and AgStar should be estopped from claiming their respective ownership and security interests against American's September 27, 1999 revolving line of credit account. Finally, I would reverse and remand that part of the trial court's judgment determining that all of the cattle Shaull sold to Feldman were held by Shaull as farm products rather than inventory.

[footnotes omitted]

NOTE

This case shows how hard it can be to differentiate a consignment from a bailment. It also shows the continuing power of the doctrine of ostensible ownership. The UCC has mostly supplanted this common law doctrine, but it continues to affect cases on the border between consignment and bailment.

Ostensible ownership means that the bailor has allowed the bailee to appear to be the owner and therefore has lost his right, as the true owner, to cancel a "purchase" by a third party from the bailee, whether that "purchase" is a security interest or a sale. *See* 1–201(b)(29) (defining "purchase" to include taking by a security interest). The owner allowed third parties to be fooled and must bear the loss, or so the theory goes. This doctrine can take account of trade customs, the way the particular goods were held, normal expectations in the industry, etc. In general, the UCC elects to protect owners when they are bailors and to subordinate them when they are consignors. *But see* 2–403(2).

The doctrine of ostensible ownership has a long history. As one court explained over a century ago, the idea was that "where the owner of property clothes another with indicia of title or allows him to appear as owner thereof . . . , an innocent third party thus led into dealing with such apparent owner . . . will be protected." *First Nat'l Bank v. Kissare*, 22 Okla. 545, 98 P 433, 434 (1908). Where this occurred, the bailee of goods could be deemed to have the power to sell the goods to a third party free and clear of the bailor's interest, or the power to grant a security interest in the goods enforceable against the bailor. Merely entrusting the bailee with possession, however, was not enough. Nor was it sufficient that the bailee generally dealt in goods of the kind. Rather, the bailor was required to have proclaimed the bailee's ownership of the goods in some way, or otherwise approved of (or at least acquiesced in) the bailee's substantial acts of ownership. In addition, the innocent third party (whether a purchaser or secured creditor) must have relied upon these indications of ostensible ownership.

To see the remnants of the doctrine of ostensible ownership, look at sections 2–326, 2–327, 2–403, 9–102(a)(20), and 9–109(a). For a consignment, the goods have to be delivered for "sale." It is pretty clear that the bred cow agreement in the case did not call for "sale" of the goods delivered (the cows—other than the ones that failed to bear calves), but it did call for "sale" of the offspring. Therefore, it could be held that the offspring were subject to an unperfected security interest by Feldman. This would be clearly in line with the spirit of consignment, as Feldman had never been in possession of the offspring; they were brought about by Shaull's acts, and he was given the power to sell them without many, if any, apparent restrictions. However, the cows were never consigned, but were always intended to be returned.

Under section 2–403(2) (which goes beyond the common law), if one entrusts goods to the possession of a merchant who deals in goods of that kind, the merchant then has the power to transfer all rights in the goods to a *buyer in ordinary course of business*. This too does not apply here since one taking a security interest in the goods is a purchaser, but is not a buyer in ordinary course. *See* 1–201(b)(9), (b)(29), (b)(30). Also, these goods probably are not part of Shaull's inventory, as noted by the dissent. He had a few distinct operations, and one of them was breeding, which makes those particular cows farm products. *See* 9–102(a)(34), (a)(35).

The last claim that one can make here would come under section 9–203(b)(2). The Court asserted, and it is probably true, that Shaull did have "rights" in the collateral. However, it is pretty clear that any "rights" he had did not extend far enough to grant a security interest that covers all the ownership rights in the cows. *See* 9–203 cmt. 6; 9–330 cmt. 10(a)(1). For example, he probably did not have power to transfer voidable title, as noted above, and receiving a security interest does not make one a buyer in ordinary course. Therefore, he could not transfer any more than his own rights in the cows to any of his secured creditors.

The Court probably got this one wrong, at least according to the UCC. The Court was clearly influenced by the idea of ostensible ownership, which is found in the UCC only in the rules in sections 2–326, 2–327, 2–403, and the Article 9 provisions on consignment. Despite its lack of codification, the doctrine has power.

This case also shows the weakness of a system of filing. Even if AgStar had filed, they would have filed under Feldman's name. Therefore, when American searched they would not have found the other filing since they would be searching under Shaull's name, not Feldman's. The UCC deals with a similar problem in section 9–325. This section does not quite contemplate our situation, but it deals with a security interest created prior to the transfer of the collateral to another who then creates a second independent security interest in the transferee's name. When this happens, if the first possessor's secured creditor was perfected, the second possessor's secured creditor will lose. However, if the first possessor's secured creditor was not perfected or at any time became unperfected, the second possessor's secured creditor would win.

PROBLEM 4-12

General Motors is having a problem with one of its struggling suppliers. It purchased a large quantity of copper to assist the supplier. The supplier took that copper and put it on its manufacturing floor, commingling it with its own copper. It then manufactured radiator cores out of its copper and General Motors's copper and sold the completed radiators back to General Motors (less a credit for the supplied copper). During manufacturing, it was impossible to tell which copper belonged to the supplier and which to General Motors.

General Motors never filed a financing statement, and the supplier has now gone bankrupt. The supplier's trustee in bankruptcy claims that General Motors' rights to the $1.5 million worth of copper were lost by its failure to file a financing statement. According to the trustee, General Motors has an unsecured claim for $1.5 million against the bankrupt estate. Is there any way out for General Motors? Might it claim successfully that it bailed the copper that it supplied to the debtor?

§ 8. BUYERS OF GOODS

In one way or another, many sections of the Code pose the question whether a buyer takes free of a prior security interest. Suppose, for example, that you are interested in purchasing a new car. In the ordinary course of business, you would likely go to a car dealer, pick out the one you want, pay for it (either by check or through financing), and then drive it away. Suppose the dealer had previously granted to a bank a security interest in the car as part of the dealer's inventory to secure a line of credit, but the dealer neglected to pay the bank and now the bank wants the car. Certainly you would be appalled at the idea that the bank could repossess your car for this reason. As a buyer, you shouldn't have to worry about such things, no? After all, in the debtor's hands, the car was the dealer's inventory, and the whole purpose of inventory is to be sold. Who would buy anything if word got around that every sale came with such potential strings attached, at least anything of significance? *See* 9–320.

But now change the situation. Suppose you own an heirloom watch that you inherited from your great-grandmother. Suppose further you took the watch to a watch dealer for repair, trusting him to return it to you after he fixed it. Assume that he did indeed fix it, but then sold it to another customer who spotted it in his display case, paid for it, and took it home. Where are your sympathies now? You essentially bailed the goods to the merchant for repair, but the merchant was also in the business of selling watches. As between two innocent parties (you and the purchaser), who should bear the loss? *See* 2–403.

Many buyers will take free of a security interest because the secured party has "authorized the disposition free of the security interest." *See* 9–315(a)(1). Thus, the starting point for any analysis about the rights of a buyer vis-à-vis a prior secured creditor is the security agreement itself. The general statutory rule stated in section 9–201 is that the security agreement "is effective . . . against purchasers of the collateral." The rule of that section is confirmed by section 9–315(a)(1), which states that the security interest "continues in collateral notwithstanding sale . . . or other disposition." Likewise, perfection generally follows the security interest. *See* 9–507(a). As we have seen, there are also major exceptions to the general rule favoring the durability (and perfection) of a security interest notwithstanding disposition of the collateral. For example, section 9–317(b) states that a buyer who "gives value and receives delivery of the collateral" without knowledge of a prior security interest "before it is perfected" takes free of the security interest. As examined in Chapter 2, this situation may arise in one of several ways. Perhaps the secured party neglected to perfect its security interest. Or perhaps the debtor transferred the collateral to a person located in a different jurisdiction and the secured party failed to perfect against the transferee within one year. *See* 9–316(a)(3), (b). Section 9–320 goes even further—it allows certain buyers to take free even of some perfected security interests. Consider the following case.

HAVENS STEEL COMPANY V. COMMERCE BANK, N.A. (IN RE HAVENS STEEL COMPANY)

United States Bankruptcy Court, W.D. Missouri, 2004.
317 B.R. 75.

VENTERS, CHIEF JUDGE:

The Debtor, Havens Steel Company, filed the above-captioned adversary proceeding to obtain a declaratory judgment determining the priority of interests in inventory[1] at various locations. Havens named all of the parties claiming an interest in that inventory as defendants. Commerce Bank ("Commerce") claims an interest in all of the inventory pursuant to a security agreement executed by the Debtor in conjunction with a $15 million loan Commerce made to the Debtor. Parsons Odebrecht Joint Venture; The Austin Company/Cypress Media LLC, d/b/a The Kansas City Star; and Polk County, Iowa (collectively "Purchasers") each claim an interest in the inventory purchased or identified for use on construction projects for which they hired the Debtor to design, fabricate, supply, and erect steel structures. * * * Shortly before the trial, though, the parties announced that all of the Purchasers except Austin had settled with Commerce. This left Austin and Commerce to duke it out in a greatly shortened trial.

Commerce and Austin stipulated to all of the facts necessary for our resolution of this matter, so the dispute boils down to a legal issue which, although simply stated, is surprisingly complicated to resolve: When does a lender's security interest in a seller's inventory terminate?

Commerce, the secured lender, contends that a security interest in inventory terminates when title to the inventory is transferred to a buyer, and, in a construction contract (such as the one between Austin and the Debtor), that transfer occurs when the inventory (steel, in this case) is actually incorporated into the final project. Because none of the steel at issue had been incorporated into the final project, but rather was in the Debtor's possession or delivered to Austin's Project site, Commerce claims a superior security interest in all of the steel.

Austin, on the other hand, maintains that title is irrelevant to determining when a lender's security interest in inventory terminates; instead, Austin argues, a lender's security interest in inventory terminates when the seller "identifies" the goods for sale to the purchaser. Since all of the steel at issue had been identified for use on Austin's project (a fact to which the parties stipulated), Austin claims a superior interest in all of the steel. Austin's argument is based on the application of Uniform Commercial Code ("UCC") Revised Article 9–320,[3] which provides that a

---

[1] In order to prevent the Debtor's operations from grinding to a halt as a result of Commerce's claim to all of the Debtor's inventory, the Court entered an order on March 25, 2004, requiring the establishment of a segregated account at Commerce Bank into which purchasers of the Debtor's inventory would have to pay (in some cases, a second time) for any inventory used for their respective projects. The money in the segregated account would then represent, in all respects, the legal equivalent of the inventory, and the parties would have the opportunity to litigate the respective priorities in the inventory (now cash) at a later date. This adversary brings that opportunity to fruition. * * *

[3] Federal courts use the choice of law rules of the state in which the court sits. *Klaxon v. Stentor Electric Mfg. Co.*, 313 U.S. 487, 490–98, 61 S.Ct. 1020, 1021–22, 85 L.Ed. 1477 (1941); *Jump v. Goldenhersh*, 619 F.2d 11, 13 (8th Cir.1980). Missouri Revised Statute § 400.9–301 provides that the law of the state where the collateral is located governs the priority of security interests in that collateral. In this case, some of the inventory at issue was located at the Debtor's

"buyer in the ordinary course" ("BIOC") takes goods free and clear of any security interest in those goods created by the seller, and Austin claims that it was, indeed, a BIOC.

Alternatively, Austin argues that if title is relevant to the termination of a lender's security interest, under the Subcontract between Austin and the Debtor, title to the inventory (goods) passed to Austin no later than upon Austin's payment for those goods, and as of the petition date, Austin had paid for approximately 70% of the inventory at issue.

At trial, the parties offered evidence and lengthy argument in support of their positions. Upon consideration of the evidence and arguments, and review of the relevant law, the Court is now prepared to rule.

I. BACKGROUND

The Debtor is a fully integrated steel construction company providing "design-build" services to contractors and subcontractors. These services include the procurement of raw materials, design, fabrication, and erection of steel structures. On or about March 31, 2003, Defendant Commerce Bank loaned the Debtor $15 million to fund the operation of its business. As of the petition date, March 18, 2004, the Debtor owed Commerce $11,344,579.70 plus interest and fees. This indebtedness was secured by, among other things, the Debtor's inventory, accounts receivable, and all proceeds thereof. The parties have stipulated to the validity of Commerce's security interest.

On February 5, 2003, the Debtor entered into a contract ("Subcontract") with The Austin Company, Cypress Media LLC d/b/a the Kansas City Star, and Oak Street Redevelopment Corp., (collectively "Austin") to furnish, fabricate, and erect steel for the construction of the Kansas City Star newspaper's new printing facility (the "Project"). More specifically, under the Subcontract the Debtor was required to: (1) prepare shop drawings and erection drawings for each piece of steel that would be used on the Project; (2) purchase finished components and the structural steel shapes identified in the shop drawings; (3) transform the structural steel shapes into usable steel for the Project; and (4) erect the finished steel. The parties agree that the services portion of the Subcontract predominates over the goods portion.

As of the petition date, the Project was not finished and a large amount of steel was in various stages of the design-build process: 85,611 pounds of steel, with a value of $20,889.72, was in the Debtor's possession and in the process of being fabricated; 376,424 pounds of fabricated steel, with a value

Ottawa, Kansas facility ("Ottawa Plant") and some at the Project site in Missouri. Accordingly, the UCC as adopted in those states would govern respectively. However, because the provisions of the UCC implicated here do not differ in any material way from the versions adopted in Kansas and Missouri, the Court will cite only to the UCC. Additionally, there is no controlling case law in either state that would affect the Court's interpretation of the UCC provisions at issue.

of $556,908.72, was located at the Ottawa Plant; and 402,305 pounds of fabricated steel, with a value of $154,485.12, was being stored at the Project site. In total, $732,283.56 worth of steel had been identified for the Project but not erected.

The Debtor agreed to complete the work under the Subcontract for a total price of $7,518,390, but because it would be very difficult, if not impossible, for the Debtor to wait until the Project was completed to receive full payment, the Subcontract provided for a procedure according to which the Debtor could apply for partial "progress" payments before completion of the Project. The basic steps of that procedure were as follows:

1. The Subcontract defined the "Work" to be performed by the Debtor as "the construction and services required by the Subcontract Documents, whether completed or partially completed, and includes all labor, materials, equipment and services provided or to be provided by the Subcontractor (the Debtor) to fulfill the Subcontractor's obligations." (Subcontract para. 1.1.6).

2. The Debtor supplied Austin with a "Schedule of Values" which allocated the cost of the Work by sequence to each and every activity included in the Debtor's scope of work. (Subcontract para. 8.1.2)

3. The Debtor submitted an "Application for Payment" based on the Schedule of Values on the first of each month for the "Work" performed in the prior month. (Subcontract para. 8.1.2)

4. Austin paid Applications for Payment approximately 20 days later. (Subcontract para. 8.3.2)

Pursuant to this process, as of the petition date Austin had paid for $447,260.08 of the steel located at the Plant and for $107,813.18 of fabricated steel delivered to the Project site but not erected.

In the course of the hearing, the parties argued that two other provisions of the Subcontract are germane to the Court's inquiry. Austin contends that paragraph 8.2.2, which provides that "the Subcontractor (the Debtor) warrants that title to all Work covered by an Application for Payment will pass to the Owner no later than the time of payment," controls the transfer of title for the inventory paid for by Austin. In response, Commerce argues that because Subcontract paragraph 8.2.1.3 provides that "[s]uch [payment] applications shall not include request for payments of amounts on account of materials and equipment not yet incorporated into the Work," [the Debtor] wasn't entitled to apply for payment on account of steel not yet incorporated into the project, *i.e.*, erected, and, therefore, title did not pass to Austin for any steel not yet erected.

II. DISCUSSION

The starting point for our answer to the question posed above—When does a lender's security interest in a seller's inventory terminate?—is UCC Revised Article 9, and more particularly, UCC §§ 9–201 and 9–315.[4] Section 9–201 provides that a security agreement is effective against purchasers of collateral and § 9–315 provides that "a security interest . . . continues in collateral notwithstanding sale, lease, license, exchange, or other disposition thereof unless the secured party authorized the disposition free of the security interest . . . ." The Official Comments to both §§ 9–201 and 9–315 (also the same in Missouri and Kansas) explain that these code sections contain the general rule that a secured party's interest in collateral continues upon the sale of the collateral unless the secured party consents to the release of its security interest or one of the provisions in Article 9 under which a party takes free and clear of the security interest applies. Both comments list § 9–320 * * *—the code section relied upon by Austin—as an example of such an exception.

However, before moving on to our discussion of whether Commerce consented to the sale of its collateral free of its security interest or whether § 9–320 applies to any of the steel at issue here, it is important to note the effect §§ 9–201 and 9–315 have on Commerce's primary argument that the transfer of title determines when a buyer takes collateral free of a lender's security interest, without regard to the buyer's BIOC status under § 9–320. Under § 9–201 and § 9–315 a buyer (other than a buyer in ordinary course) of goods subject to a security interest takes title to the goods purchased, but that title is subject to the lender's security interest. It seems that Commerce may have lost sight of this fundamental rule of secured transactions in its zeal to fix the point in time when its security interest finally ceded priority to Austin at the last possible moment, *i.e.*, upon the steel's incorporation into the project. It is hard to imagine, though, that Commerce, a major lending institution, does not routinely take the position that a buyer who purchases Commerce's collateral, sold without contractual or statutory authorization, takes title to the collateral *subject to Commerce's continuing security interest.* However, Commerce's argument on this point is directly contrary to that position and the law and will therefore be disregarded.

The proper inquiry is whether Commerce consented to the sale of its collateral free of its security interest or whether Austin qualified as a buyer in ordinary course.

---

4 Commerce's suggestion that UCC Article 9 does not apply to this transaction is wholly without merit. Section 9–109 provides that Article 9 applies to "a transaction, regardless of its form, that creates a security interest in personal property or fixtures by contract." UCC § 9–109. This transaction undeniably fits that description. Moreover, because Article 9 governs the transaction, the termination of the security interest created under Article 9 is also governed by Article 9.

A. Commerce's Consent

The parties did not offer any evidence of Commerce's contemporaneous consent (or lack thereof) to the Debtor's sale of Commerce's collateral, but the security agreement between the Debtor and Commerce submitted as a joint exhibit sets forth the conditions upon which the Debtor has authority to sell Commerce's collateral free and clear of Commerce's security interest. Specifically, it provides that, "while Grantor (the Debtor) is not in default under this Agreement, Grantor may sell Inventory, but only in the ordinary course of its business and only to *buyers in the ordinary course of business*." (Joint Exh. 13 at p. 2; emphasis added). Thus, under this provision Austin would have to show that the Debtor was not in default on the date the Debtor "sold" the inventory to Austin and that Austin qualifies as a buyer in the ordinary course of business. In light of our ruling below regarding Austin's status as a buyer in the ordinary course of business, we do not need to address how the term "sell" applies here, whether the Debtor was in default on the date of the sale, and ultimately, whether Commerce consented to the sale of its collateral; however, we do note that the security agreement, presumably a Commerce form document, belies Commerce's position at trial that § 9–320 does not apply to the Subcontract.

B. Buyer in Ordinary Course of Business

Section 9–320 provides that "a buyer in ordinary course of business takes free of a security interest created by the buyer's seller, even if the security interest is perfected and the buyer knows of its existence." UCC § 9–320. Official Comment 3 to § 9–320 references § 1–201[5] for the definition of buyer in ordinary course of business, which, in turn, provides in pertinent part:

> "Buyer in ordinary course of business" means a person that buys in good faith, without knowledge that the sale violates the rights of another person in the goods, and in the ordinary course from a person . . . in the business of selling goods of that kind. A person buys goods in the ordinary course if the sale to the person comports with the usual or customary practices in the kind of business in which the seller is engaged or with the seller's own usual or customary practices .... Only a buyer that takes possession of the goods or has a right to recover the goods from the seller under Article 2 may be a buyer in ordinary course of business.

UCC § 1–201. Under this definition, we find that Austin qualifies as a BIOC of all of the steel in its possession, and with regard to the steel located at the Ottawa Plant, Austin is a BIOC of the steel for which it had paid.

[5] Section 1–201 was revised when UCC Article 9 was revised, and both became effective in Missouri and Kansas on July 1, 2001.

1. Conduct, Knowledge, and Ordinary Course

Section 1–201's requirement that Austin buys goods "in good faith, without knowledge that the sale violates the rights of another person in the goods, and in the ordinary course from a person . . . in the business of selling goods of that kind," is easily dispatched. Good faith in this context means "honesty in fact in the conduct or transaction concerned," UCC § 1–201, and there has been no allegation or evidence introduced that Austin was dishonest in its conduct in the transactions with the Debtor.[6] The parties stipulated to the existence of the rest of these elements.

2. When Does BIOC Status Attach?

In contrast, because the UCC does not identify the point in a transaction when a buyer attains BIOC status, this element requires considerably more analysis, especially since the Court has not found any dispositive cases from Missouri or Kansas on this issue.

There are at least five potential points at which the ascendancy to the honored role of BIOC can be fixed—upon contracting, upon identification of the goods, upon transfer of title, upon delivery, or upon acceptance of the goods—but only transfer of title and identification have received serious consideration. And, not surprisingly, the parties do not agree on which event controls. To the extent that Commerce recognizes that BIOC status is an issue here, it advocates using title as the watershed, and as mentioned above, Commerce contends that title did not pass until the steel was incorporated into the project. (Austin maintains that it took title to the steel when it paid for the steel.) Austin, on the other hand, argues that a buyer attains BIOC status when goods are identified to a contract, and the parties have stipulated that all of the steel at issue had been identified.

Commerce's position—as well as the position of the cases favoring title as the determining factor—is that a sale must have taken place in order for a purchaser to be a BIOC, and "sale" is defined in UCC Article 2 (§ 2–106) as the passing of title from the seller to the buyer for a price. Therefore, Commerce reasons, a purchaser cannot be a BIOC until it obtains title to goods. The Court declines to adopt this position for four reasons.

First, the Court believes that it misconstrues the statute. The statute does not specifically require that a sale has taken place (interposing "contract for sale" would be equally sensible), and to the extent that § 1–201 implicitly requires a sale, the reference to Article 2's definition of sale

[6] Although Austin bears the burden of proof to establish that it is entitled to protection as a BIOC under § 9–320, including the element of good faith, good faith is difficult to prove in the affirmative. It is similar to proving the negative—we were not dishonest. Accordingly, in the absence of allegations or evidence to the contrary, the Court will infer Austin's good faith in its conduct with the Debtor.

is unwarranted in light of Article 2's express de-emphasis of the importance of title,[9] and perhaps more importantly, the existence of a specific cross-reference to Article 2 in *another part of the statute*. Rules of statutory construction[10] dictate that the cross-reference to Article 2 in one section militates against a reference to Article 2 where it is not mentioned.

Second, identification makes more sense in the context of the statute. One of the requirements of § 1–201 (discussed in greater detail below) is that a BIOC either has possession of the goods or has "the right to recover the goods from the seller under Article 2." The quoted section of the statute is understood to refer to a buyer's remedy to recover goods from an insolvent seller under § 2–502 or a buyer's right to replevin or specific performance under § 2–716. A review of these provisions reveals that identification, rather than title, is key to the buyer's right to recover goods. *See* UCC §§ 2–502, 2–716.

Third, there is an apparent trend in the case law away from transfer of title as the point at which BIOC status is attained. After *Daniel* [*v. Bank of Hayward*, 425 N.W.2d 416 (Wis. 1988)], the case that overruled *Chrysler* [*v. Adamatic, Inc.*, 208 N.W.2d 97 (Wis. 1973)] (the seminal case advocating the use of title), there are apparently no cases holding that BIOC status is attained upon the transfer of title.

Finally, from a policy standpoint we note that using identification rather than passage of title advances Article 9's policy of protecting innocent buyers and places the risk of loss on the secured party who has the ability to protect itself by requiring various inventory controls and reports and who may be in a better position to absorb the loss.

Therefore, the Court concludes that a buyer attains BIOC status at the time goods are identified to a contract, and in this case, the parties stipulated that all of the steel had been identified to the Subcontract.

3. Possession of, or Right to Recover, the Steel

Having determined that Austin had reached the point in the transaction when it could qualify for BIOC status, whether Austin actually attained BIOC status with regard to particular steel turns on the final test set forth in § 1–201, which limits BIOC status to buyers who "take possession of the goods or [have] a right to recover the goods from the seller under Article 2." Because Austin had physical possession of the 402,305 pounds of steel (worth $154,485.12) located at the Project site, no further discussion is necessary; Austin was a BIOC with regard to that steel. Austin was also a BIOC of most of the steel at the Ottawa Plant as of the petition date, but the application of the statute with regard to that steel is not as straightforward.

---

9 *See* UCC § 2–401.

10 *Expressio unius est exlusio alterius* [sic].

At first blush, the statute appears to preclude Austin from being a BIOC of the steel in the Debtor's possession on the petition date because Austin did not have physical possession of that steel and Austin did not have the right to recover it *under Article 2*, inasmuch as the Subcontract was not covered by Article 2.[14] However, upon comparison of the revised § 1–201 to its predecessor statute and a consideration of cases applying the predecessor statute and of the official comment to revised § 1–201, we find that a party that can establish a common law (versus an Article 2-based) "right to recover" may qualify as a BIOC, assuming the other requirements of the statute are met.

The former UCC § 1–201 did not contain the requirement that a BIOC have possession of or the right to recover the good from the seller under Article 2.[15] Nor did the cases applying former § 1–201. Based on a review of the cases applying former § 1–201, the incorporation of the "right to recover" requirement into revised § 1–201 is most likely a function of the fact that BIOC litigation most often arises in the context of a replevin action brought by or against the buyer of goods in which the seller's lender has a security interest, and establishing a right to possession is a fundamental element of a replevin action. *See First Nat. Bank of Steeleville v. ERB Equipment Co., Inc.*, 972 S.W.2d 298, 300 (Mo.Ct.App.1998). In light of the origins of the "right to recover" requirement, the Court does not believe that the embodiment of that requirement into § 1–201 was intended to limit recourse under the statute to only Article 2 buyers. Official Comment 9 to Revised § 1–201 further supports this interpretation, stating:

> The penultimate sentence [of § 1–201(9)] prevents a buyer that does not have the right to possession as against the seller from being a buyer in ordinary course of business. Concerning when a buyer obtains possessory rights, see Sections 2–502 and 2–716. However, the penultimate sentence is not intended to affect a buyer's status as a buyer in ordinary course of business in cases (such as a "drop shipment") involving delivery by the seller to a person buying from the buyer or a donee from the buyer. The

---

14 As mentioned above, the parties stipulated that the services portion of the Subcontract predominated, so the Subcontract would not be governed by Article 2. * * *

15 Former § 1–201 provided: [']"Buyer in ordinary course of business" means a person who in good faith, and without knowledge that the sale to him is in violation of the rights or security interest of a third party in the goods, buys in ordinary course from a person in the business of selling goods of that kind but does not include a pawnbroker. All persons who sell minerals or the like (including oil and gas) at wellhead or minehead shall be deemed to be persons in the business of selling goods of that kind. "Buying" may be for cash, by exchange of other property, or on secured or unsecured credit, and includes receiving goods or documents of title under a pre-existing contract for sale but does not include a transfer in bulk or as security for or in total or partial satisfaction of a money debt.['] *See* Thomas M. Quinn, *Quinn's Uniform Commercial Code Commentary and Law Digest*, 1–28 (1991).

> requirement relates to whether *as against the seller* the buyer or one taking through the buyer has possessory rights.

Official Comment 9, Revised § 1–201 (emphasis in original).

This Comment suggests that the inclusion of the Article 2 "requirement" was for referential value rather than for purposes of restricting the statute to Article 2 contracts. Therefore, the Court believes that a party that establishes its possessory rights over goods *as against the seller*, without reference to Article 2, also qualifies as a BIOC under this portion of the statute. The Court finds that Austin had such a right with respect to the steel located at the Ottawa Plant and which had been identified for the Project.

There are at least two common law causes of action which would give rise to Austin's right to recover. And it is no surprise that these parallel similar rights were granted by Article 2 to purchasers of goods. Under a replevin theory (UCC § 2–716(3)), Austin had a right to recover the goods for which it had paid, and Austin had an equitable right to specific performance (UCC § 2–716(1) and (2)) for delivery of all of the steel in the Debtor's possession, although Austin would have to pay for any steel for which payment was owing.

a. Austin's Right to Recover Under Replevin Theory

To prevail on a replevin claim under Missouri common law, a party must establish that it is entitled to possession of the property, that the defendant has exercised unauthorized control over the property, and that the defendant deprived plaintiff of its right to possession. *First Nat. Bank of Steeleville*, 972 S.W.2d at 300. In the context of the hypothetical posed by § 1–201, and the artificial circumstances in which this issue has arisen, the second two requirements are inapplicable. For in the absence of the Debtor's bankruptcy filing and the Court's order creating the segregated account, Commerce likely would have exercised its right as a secured creditor and taken possession or control of the inventory. The effect of that conduct, which must be implied here, would be that Commerce would have been in possession or control of the steel to the exclusion of Austin. Therefore, all that is required here to establish a right to replevin is Austin's superior possessory right to the steel, *id.*, and the Court finds that Austin has that right because it paid for the steel and, therefore (as discussed below), held title to the steel. *See, e.g., Strothkamp v. St. John's Community Bank, Inc.*, 329 S.W.2d 718, 720 (Mo.1959) (title may establish right to possession, although it is not crucial to a replevin action); *Fawley v. Bailey*, 512 S.W.2d 477, 480 (Mo.Ct.App.1974) (same).

Based on the Stipulation and the evidence submitted by Austin, the Court found (above) that Austin paid for $447,260.08 of the steel located at the Ottawa Plant. The parties did not agree, however, as to the effect of Austin's payment for that steel. As detailed earlier, Austin contends that under the Subcontract title to the steel passed "no later than payment," whereas Commerce argues that title did not pass upon payment, but, rather, title to the steel passed upon incorporation of the steel into the final project. Although the parties spent considerable time debating this point, the Court dispatches it easily.

Under a non-Article 2 contract, title passes at the time agreed upon by the parties, and a contract is the best evidence of the parties' intent. *Miller v. Municipal Electric Lighting & Power Co.*, 133 Mo. 205, 34 S.W. 585 (1896). In this case, the Subcontract provides a clear indication of the parties' intent regarding the passage of title. Paragraph 8.2.1 states: "the Subcontractor (the Debtor) warrants that title to all Work covered by an Application for Payment will pass to the Owner no later than the time of payment."[17] Commerce attempts to muddy the clarity of this provision by pointing to another provision in the Subcontract (paragraph 8.2.1.3) which states that "[payment] applications shall not include request for payments of amounts on account of materials and equipment not yet incorporated into the Work," and then arguing that title did not pass to Austin upon payment because it applied for payment on account of steel not yet "incorporated" into the project, i.e., erected. Aside from questioning Commerce's standing to interpret a contract to which it was not a party, the Court finds Commerce's interpretation strained and illogical.

First, as Austin pointed out in its response to Commerce's pre-trial brief, Commerce misconstrues the Subcontract's use of the word "incorporate" in paragraph 8.2.1.3 and completely ignores the effect of the defined term "Work" as it relates to "incorporate." Commerce argues that "incorporate" must be given its plain, ordinary meaning, and that doing so in the context of paragraph 8.2.1 means that Austin cannot apply for payment for work not physically *incorporated* into the Project. The Court agrees that "incorporate" should be given its plain, ordinary meaning, *i.e.*, to unite or work into something already existent so as to form an indistinguishable whole.[18] But "incorporate" is not modified by "Project", "building", or "structure" as Commerce's interpretation suggests; rather, "incorporate" is linked to and modified by a defined term, "Work", which means "the construction and services required by the Subcontract Documents, *whether completed or partially completed,* and includes all labor, materials, equipment and services provided *or to be provided* by the Subcontractor (the Debtor) to fulfill the Subcontractor's obligations." (Subcontract paragraph 1.1.6; emphasis added). Thus, paragraph 8.2.1 provides unambiguously that [the Debtor] can apply for payment for goods or services performed before that "work" is actually incorporated into the

17 The only possible ambiguity in this provision is the wording that suggests that title may have passed before payment, and no evidence has been introduced to clarify that statement. But that ambiguity does not detract from Austin's argument here, inasmuch as Austin has not argued that title passed earlier.

18 Merriam-Webster's online dictionary, *www.m-w.com*.

Project; in fact, the definition of "Work" specifically contemplates such an application.

Second, the result suggested by Commerce does not follow even if we adopt Commerce's interpretation of the Subcontract. Title would still pass to Austin no later than payment, even if the payment was for goods for which Austin was not yet entitled to apply for payment. In other words, the Debtor's (hypothetical) breach of the contract by prematurely applying for the payment of goods not yet incorporated into the Project does not prevent paragraph 8.2.2 from transferring title of the goods for which payment (rightly or wrongly) was made. Therefore, the Court finds that under the Subcontract between the Debtor and Austin, Austin held title to all of the steel for which payment was made as of the petition date, and thereby had the right to replevin that steel.

b. Austin's Right to Recover Under Specific Performance Theory

Under Missouri law, a plaintiff is entitled to specific performance as a matter of right if there is no adequate remedy at law and the contract is fair and plain. *In re Laclede Gas Co. v. Amoco Oil Co.*, 522 F.2d 33, 38 (8th Cir.1975) (citing *Miller v. Coffeen*, 365 Mo. 204, 280 S.W.2d 100, 102 (1955)). Although specific performance relating to the sale of personal property is less common than for real estate, specific performance is appropriate when the goods are unique or difficult to obtain elsewhere. *Id.* at 39–40; *Boeving v. Vandover*, 240 Mo.App. 117, 218 S.W.2d 175, 178 (1949) (ordering an auto dealer to specifically perform on a contract for the sale of a car at a time when new cars were extremely difficult to obtain).

In this case, specific performance is warranted because there is no adequate remedy at law, inasmuch as the steel at issue had either been custom-ordered or fabricated to Austin's specifications, and the Court finds that the contract was fair and plain, as evidenced by the parties' stipulation to the values of the steel at issue. That some of the steel at the Ottawa Plant may not have been ready for delivery as of the petition date is not a barrier to Austin's recovery here because the values to which the parties stipulated account for the lesser value of the undelivered, partially fabricated, and fabricated steel.

In short, the Court reiterates its findings in this section that § 1–201's requirement that a BIOC have a right to recover the goods under UCC Article 2 encompasses the right to recover goods under non-Article 2 law, and Austin had a right to recover the undelivered steel for which Austin paid under either a common law replevin or specific performance theory.

c. Constructive Possession

Austin also fulfills § 1–201's requirement that Austin "take possession of the goods or [have] a right to recover the goods from the seller under Article 2," because Austin had "constructive possession" of the paid-for, undelivered steel, and the Court interprets "possession" as used in the statute to include "constructive possession."

Constructive possession is a concept, used in a variety of contexts, which recognizes that there are circumstances under which the right or ability to possess an object is strong enough to give rise to the legal effect of "possession" in the absence of actual physical possession. *See, e.g., Vogelsang's Adm'r v. Fisher*, 128 Mo. 386, 31 S.W. 13, 17 (1895) (discussing constructive possession conferred upon delivery of a warehouse receipt); *Emory v. Arnold*, 184 Mo.App. 99, 168 S.W. 320, 321 (1914) (acknowledging that action in replevin will lie against defendant in constructive possession of plaintiff's goods if defendant has control over and ability to deliver those goods). *See also, State v. Chavez*, 128 S.W.3d 569, 574 (Mo.Ct.App.2004) (drawing distinction between "actual possession" of an illegal substance, where the person has the substance on his person or within his easy reach and convenient control, and "constructive possession," where a person has the power and intention at a given time to exercise dominion or control over the substance either directly or through another person or persons) (citations omitted). Accordingly, the Court finds that Austin's possessory rights, arising from Austin's payment for and title to the steel, were sufficiently strong to imbue Austin with constructive possession of the steel, in the context of § 1–201.

The Court's interpretation of "possession," as used in § 1–201, to encompass constructive possession is supported by the fact that the UCC does not define possession and the suggestion in the Official Comment to § 9–313 that "possession" in the code does not require actual possession. Official Comment 3 states that agency principles should be applied to determine whether a party not in actual possession of collateral should be considered to have constructive possession of it, although the comment does not use that specific term. So, for example, a secured creditor may have a perfected security interest in certain collateral, *e.g.*, a certificated security, for which possession is necessary to perfect, if the secured creditor's agent is in possession of the collateral. The Comment goes on to say that a court could find that the debtor may have possession of the collateral (thereby defeating perfection), if the collateral is possessed by a person in control of the debtor, even if that person holds the collateral for the ostensible benefit of the secured creditor. *See also*, J. White & R. Summers, *Handbook of the Law under the Uniform Commercial Code* s 23–10 at 935–936 (2d ed.1980) (discussing perfection by possession under Article 9). Thus, in light of the flexible definition of possession contemplated by the Official Comment, the Court finds it appropriate to apply that term, as it is used in § 1–201, to the situation where a seller of goods retains the goods after full payment for those goods and the transfer of title to the buyer.

Further, the decision to apply constructive possession principles here also advances the apparent goal of § 1–201 (and § 9–320), which is to provide BIOC protection to innocent buyers. *See Chrysler Corp. v. Adamatic*, 59 Wis.2d 219, 208 N.W.2d 97, 107 (1973) ("It seems clear that, if there is a sale and the buyer has obtained title to the goods, his status as a buyer in ordinary course will not be defeated merely because he has not taken possession.") *overruled on different grounds by Daniel v. Bank of Hayward*, 144 Wis.2d 931, 425 N.W.2d 416 (1988).

Thus, the Court finds that with regard to the steel located at the Debtor's Ottawa Plant and for which Austin had paid, Austin had constructive possession of that steel and such possession satisfies § 1–201's requirement that a BIOC have possession of the goods.

CONCLUSION

In sum, for the reasons stated above, the Court finds that Commerce's security interest in the steel identified to the Austin project as of the petition date terminated to the extent Austin qualifies as a buyer in ordinary course of business under UCC § 9–320. The Court further finds that Austin qualifies as a buyer in ordinary course of business with regard to the $154,485.12 worth of steel in Austin's possession and the $384,017.08 worth of steel for which Austin had paid, and which was located at the Debtor's Ottawa Plant. Thus, in total, Austin has an interest superior to Commerce in $538,502.20 of the $732,283.56 of steel at issue. In light of the Court's March 25, 2004, ruling, as incorporated in the May 10, 2004 Final Order, this finding translates to a requirement that Commerce turn over to Austin $538,502.20 of the money Commerce now holds in the segregated account. * * *

[some footnotes omitted]

NOTE

The main issue in *Havens Steel* can be summarized by the question: when does one become a "buyer?" Only a buyer can be a buyer in ordinary course, and only a buyer in ordinary course takes free of prior perfected security interests under section 9–320. In *Chrysler v. Adamatic, Inc.*,[1] an earlier case cited in *Havens Steel*, the Wisconsin Supreme Court concluded that, at least under the facts presented, the purchaser was not a buyer "in the absence of a physical transfer or assignment of the goods."[2] In a later case, *Daniel v. Bank of Hayward*,[3] the same Court could not stomach its *Chrysler* rule as applied to a consumer non-possessor and overruled it. As the court in *Havens Steel* pointed out, "there is an apparent trend in the case law away from transfer of title as the point at which BIOC status is attained." 317 B.R. at 83.

1 208 N.W.2d 97 (1973).

2 *Id.* at 107.

3 425 N.W.2d 416 (1988).

Consider the more general question about when one might become a buyer. A typical sales transaction proceeds in an irregular movement from the making of a sales contract through payment of a portion of the price through possession or disposition by the buyer. Almost always the contract comes first, but possession might come before or after payment and payment might be in installments. The court must determine, as it did in *Havens Steel* and *Daniel* and *Chrysler*, how far one must proceed down this spectrum before the potential buyer becomes truly a buyer as that term is used in the Code. One analogy, that of a holder in due course, might say one does not get these super priority rights that attach to a buyer in ordinary course or to the holder in due course status until one has not only given value but also taken possession. On the other hand, there are buyers, perhaps even more sympathetic than the Daniels, who never expect to take possession and where it would be inappropriate to make that a condition of the status. Assume for example that the goods to be sold are bulk oil or gravel that are expensive to move and that might be resold by the buyer in place without their ever being moved. In those circumstances it is inappropriate to say that the prospective buyer himself must take possession in order to become a "buyer" under the UCC.

PROBLEM 4-13

Daisy Bank and Trust has a security interest in refrigerators, stoves, appliances, and all other hard goods of Marie Louise, Inc., a department store. Assume that the security agreement purports to continue the security interest in the goods even after they have been sold. Now consider the following transactions in goods covered by the perfected security interest.

1. Wilbur buys a washing machine for cash. Wilbur takes free of Daisy's security interest, true or false?

2. Wilbur buys a washing machine on credit and signs a security agreement giving Marie Louise a security interest in the machine. Wilbur takes free of Daisy's security interest, true or false?

3. Wilbur buys a refrigerator on credit from Marie Louise and signs a security agreement. A month later Wilbur sells the refrigerator to his next-door neighbor, Charlotte. Which statements are correct?

   a. Charlotte takes free of the security interests of both Daisy and Marie Louise;

   b. Charlotte takes free of Daisy's security interest because she qualifies under subsection 9–320(a);

   c. Charlotte takes free of Marie Louise's security interest because she qualifies under 9–320(a);

   d. Charlotte does not qualify for the protection of 9–320(a); nevertheless she takes free of both security interests.

FEDERAL LIMITATION ON THE FARMER EXCEPTION TO UCC SECTION 9–320

Section 9–320(a) (derived from former 9–307 of old Article 9) excludes "a person buying farm products from a person engaged in farming operations" from the scope of the provision. Thus, as noted at the outset of this chapter, a person who buys produce at a local farm stand from a grower engaged in farming operations would take the produce subject to the security interest the grower granted to its secured creditor. One might readily imagine a few somewhat comical and farfetched hypotheticals involving repo persons hired by secured creditors to repossess produce just as the purchasers were preparing to eat them. Such hypotheticals, of course, seem unlikely to arise because the stakes are typically so small. But what about large quantities of grain or herds of expensive livestock?

For example, suppose a rancher engaged in the business of breeding and selling cattle sells a thousand cows in the ordinary course of business to a neighboring dairy farmer. Suppose the farmer qualifies as a buyer in ordinary course of business—she buys the cows in good faith, without knowledge that the sale violates the rights of another person in the cows, and purchases the cows from a person (the rancher) engaged in the business of selling goods of that kind. Because the cattle qualify as farm products, the farmer would not take free under section 9–320 of any security interest the rancher granted to his secured creditor. As a result, the rancher's secured creditor would be protected—it may repossess the cows notwithstanding their sale to the farmer if the rancher defaults. But what about the farmer? Why protect the secured creditor in this situation, but not, for example, where a car dealer grants a security interest in its inventory of new and used automobiles?

By 1985 legislation, Congress provided a mechanism that can override the "farm products" exception in current section 9–320 and former section 9–307(1). Enacted within the Food Security Act of 1985, 7 U.S.C. § 1631 (Supp.1985), the statute grants federal protection to purchasers of farm products. In relevant part section 1631(d) states:

> (d) Except as provided in subsection (e) and notwithstanding any other provision of Federal, State, or local law, a buyer who in the ordinary course of business buys a farm product from a seller engaged in farming operations shall take free of a security interest created by the seller, even though the security interest is perfected; and the buyer knows of the existence of such interest.

By itself, this general prohibition against lien enforcement seems relatively straightforward. However, lengthy and complex exceptions may swallow the rule. The most important exceptions to the protection of purchasers of farm products are found in section 1631(e).

The first exception appears in section 1631(e)(1). This exception provides that, notwithstanding section 1631(d) above, a purchaser of farm products will take the goods subject to the security interest created by the farmer/debtor if, within one year before the sale, the buyer receives a form of specialized notice sent by the debtor or secured creditor. The statute specifies the contents of this notice and directs, among other things, that the notice list the names of the debtor and secured party, describe the collateral, and state any payment obligations the secured creditor wishes to impose in exchange for relinquishing its security interest. This scheme contemplates that the farmer/debtor and its secured creditor will have agreed in their security agreement that the debtor will furnish the secured party a list of all prospective buyers of the debtor's farm products, and the debtor agrees not to sell to anyone else without first notifying the secured creditor. *See* 7 U.S.C. § 1631(h)(2). As noted, the notice will state the secured party's payment instructions, such as whether the secured creditor requires payment of the purchase price directly to the creditor. If the purchaser complies, it takes the goods free of the security interest. The statute imposes a fine on the debtor for failure to comply with the requirements of subsection (h)(2) (unless the debtor accounts to the secured creditor for the proceeds of the sale within ten days thereafter). *See* 7 U.S.C. § 1631 (h)(2) & (3). Note that the *purchaser* will receive the protection of 1631(d) notwithstanding the debtor's failure to comply—the purchaser must receive the required notice in order for it to be stuck with the security interest. At first blush, this first exception seems to turn the traditional notice system on its head. No longer can a secured party depend on a centralized filing system for protection; if the secured party desires priority, notice of the security interest must be sent to potential purchasers of farm products from the debtor.

The second exception appears in section 1631(e)(2). This exception provides that the purchaser will not take free of the security interest if (1) the farm products in question were produced in a state that maintains a "central filing system," (2) the buyer has failed to register with the relevant Secretary of State's office prior to the purchase, and (3) the secured party has filed an "effective financing statement or notice" covering the farm products being sold. Note: the central filing system referenced in the federal statute is not the regular UCC filing system for Article 9 financing statements. The Food Security Act mandates a special kind of filing system certified by the U.S. Secretary of Agriculture that requires different and more detailed information than the Article 9 system, requires the Secretary of State's office to maintain and disseminate various lists, and also requires the Secretary of State's office upon request to confirm orally and in writing the existence of an effective financing statement filed against a particular debtor. The federal statute also directs what constitutes an "effective financing statement." *See* 7 U.S.C. § 1631(c)(4). The Department of

Agriculture keeps a list of certified central filing systems. Around twenty states have adopted such a system.

The third exception appears in section 1631(e)(3). This exception provides that the purchaser will not take free of the security interest if (1) the farm products were produced in a state that maintains a central filing system, (2) the buyer receives notice from the Secretary of State's office that specifies that the seller and the farm products in question are covered by an effective financing statement, and (3) the buyer does not secure the release of the security interest from the secured party (such as by paying the purchase price directly to the secured party in exchange for a release). Under the federal statutory scheme, the Secretary of State is supposed to distribute periodically all registered financing information to all registered buyers. Accordingly, if a state adopts a central filing system into its zoo of regulatory animals, an ordinary course purchaser of farm products will lose the general protection of 1631(d) if he is either (1) not registered in the system and the secured party has filed an effective financing statement, or (2) he has received notice of a prior security interest from the Secretary of State. Thus, a state's enactment of a central filing system can return to the farm products exception contained in section 9–320(a).

The basic effect of section 1631 is to shift the burden of informing. The purchaser's burden to seek out information regarding prior security interests is shifted either to the secured party (to make sure all potential purchasers in non-central filing system states are notified) or to the Secretary of State (to notify all registered purchasers in central filing system states).

CHAPTER 5

SECURITY IN RIGHTS TO PAYMENT AND OTHER INTANGIBLES

■ ■ ■

§ 1. INTRODUCTION

Rights to payment (also known as "intangibles") come in at least fourteen different flavors under Article 9: "accounts" (including "health-care-insurance receivables"); "instruments" (including "promissory notes"); "chattel paper" (including "tangible chattel paper" and "electronic chattel paper"); "general intangibles" (including "payment intangibles" and "software"); "deposit accounts"; "letter-of-credit rights"; "commercial tort claims"; and "investment property." The most common of these are accounts, instruments, and chattel paper. We encountered these briefly in the previous chapter. Each of these forms of collateral is defined in section 9–102. If you haven't done so already, turn there and try to figure out how an account is different from chattel paper, and how accounts and chattel paper are different from instruments.

Start with accounts. Section 9–102(a)(2) defines an account as a "right to payment of a monetary obligation, whether or not earned by performance" if the right to payment falls into one of the several categories set forth in the definition. These categories include rights to payment "for property that has been or is to be sold, leased, licensed, assigned, or otherwise disposed of"; "for services rendered or to be rendered"; and "winnings in a lottery." What unites these disparate definitional examples of accounts? For a clue, look further at what is expressly *excluded* from the definition of accounts, namely "(i) rights to payment evidenced by chattel paper or an instrument, (ii) commercial tort claims, (iii) deposit accounts, (iv) investment property, (v) letter-of-credit rights or letters of credit, and (vi) rights to payment for money or funds advanced or sold, other than rights arising out of the use of a credit or charge card . . . ." These excluded items involve distinct transactions or claims, most of which are documented by some form of a *writing*. In contrast, accounts are typically rights to payment that are not evidenced by a writing memorializing the precise debt that is owed.

To illustrate, consider the following hypothetical. Suppose Law Firm and Client have a written retention agreement stating that Client will pay Law Firm for the time it spends working on Client's legal matters. Law Firm does work for Client and sends out a written invoice for services rendered in the amount of $5,000. What is Law Firm's right to payment of the $5,000 amount reflected by this invoice? It is an account because it is a "right to payment . . . for services rendered." 9–102(a)(2). Note that Client has not signed a promissory note or IOU for the $5,000 debt. Client simply owes the debt reflected in the bill. Although Law Firm and Client have a written retention agreement that governs their overall relationship, this written agreement also is not written evidence of the *particular* $5,000 debt; it is simply a memorialization of the parties' overall business relationship. The specific debt (and corresponding right to payment) arises from the Law Firm's provision of legal services. Note that, for purposes of Article 9, Client is what we call an "account debtor"—the party obligated to pay the account. *See* 9–102(a)(3). Note also that a law firm's accounts are usually a valuable asset. Collectively, they reflect all the unpaid invoices the law firm has sent out. Some law firms borrow tens of millions of dollars from banks on the strength of their outstanding accounts.

Now suppose that, when Client receives the $5,000 invoice, it does not pay it right away, but instead sends Law Firm a written note that Client has signed promising to pay Law Firm $5,000 in 30 days (as a practicing lawyer you would probably not be very happy if your client did this instead of just paying the bill). Is the right to payment still an account? No. Because the right to payment is now evidenced by a writing in the form of a signed note, it is an instrument (assuming the other requirements of the definition of "instrument" are satisfied). *See* 9–102(a)(47). Note that the concept of an "instrument" for the purposes of Article 9 includes a "negotiable instrument" governed by Article 3 as well as a "promissory note," and that the obligor on an instrument is not an "account debtor." *See* 9–102 cmt. 5(c), 9–102(a)(3), 9–102(a)(65). Rather, the obligor on an instrument may be the "issuer" of the instrument (if the instrument is a negotiable instrument governed by Article 3), *see* 3–105(c), or some other person, who may be referred to as the "payor," "maker," or the like. *See* 9–102 cmt. 5(h).

Now suppose further that, in addition to sending Law Firm the written note, Client also executes and delivers a security agreement granting Law Firm a lien on Client's equipment to secure Client's payment of the $5,000 debt. As a result, Law Firm now holds two documents: (1) Client's written note promising to pay the $5,000 debt, and (2) Client's security agreement granting a lien on its equipment. Is this collection of documents an instrument? No. Because of the addition of the security agreement, this collection of documents is now "chattel paper." *See* 9–102(a)(11).

In spite of its arcane name, chattel paper is very common. For example, suppose you wish to purchase a car but need financing to make your purchase. Suppose the car you want to buy costs $25,000 and you and the dealer agree that you will pay for the car by making a down payment of $2,000 with the balance of $23,000 to be financed over time. In particular, suppose the sales agreement obligates you to pay the financed amount in equal monthly installments over five years (60 months) with interest at 5%. In addition, the sales agreement grants a security interest in the car to secure your payment obligation. So in addition to supplying the contractual terms governing your purchase of the car, the agreement also supplies the relevant financing terms, including the grant of a security interest. This contract, which may be labelled a "sales agreement" or a "consumer retail installment contract" or the like, is a good example of chattel paper. Note how it evidences not only a right to payment of the monthly installments due but also a security interest in the item being purchased to secure that right to payment.

Every day, legions of buyers sign contracts of this type to finance their purchases of things like automobiles. In the typical case, the car dealer will not actually provide the financing itself. Rather, the dealer intends to assign the contract to a bank or other finance company that has pre-approved the lending arrangement. The dealer is only interested in selling the car; the finance company is interested in financing the purchase, and thereafter the buyer will characteristically make the monthly installment payments directly to the finance company (or its servicer or assignee), not the dealer. Note that a person obligated to make the payments set forth in the chattel paper is also an "account debtor." *See* 9–102(a)(3); *see also* 9–102 cmt. 5(h).

Take a close look at the other definitions in section 9–102 of the other types of intangibles mentioned above (deposit accounts and the like). Notice once again that, like the basic varieties of goods (namely, equipment, inventory, consumer goods, and farm products), each category of intangibles is mutually exclusive. For example, a single right to payment cannot at the same time be both an account and an instrument. But observe how a right to payment can change from an account to an instrument if the account debtor decides to memorialize the debt in a certain kind of writing—for example, the account debtor on an account executes a written note promising to pay the particular debt.

There are at least two reasons to understand the technical definitions of a particular type of intangible. First, the modes of perfection are different for many of them. While most may be perfected by filing a financing statement, that is not true, for example, for deposit accounts or letter-of-credit rights. *See* 9–312(b), 9–314. Likewise, security interests arising from "sales" of promissory notes and payment intangibles are automatically perfected upon attachment of the security interest. *See* 9–309. The difference between a "sale" of a promissory note and payment intangible, as opposed to a security interest in these items, is addressed later in this chapter.

The second reason to understand the technical definitions is to be sure the terms used in the parties' legal documents—such as the security agreement or the financing statement—correctly reflect what the parties intend. A secured creditor that takes a security interest in "instruments" that turn out to be "accounts" is likely to find itself unsecured because the documents do not describe the collateral properly.

In many ways a security interest in rights to payment is the best of all security. By their nature, these rights typically turn into cash and, if collected directly from the account debtor, are self-liquidating. In most cases they bring with them the promises of payment from third parties with whom the creditor has not dealt directly. This multitude of payors means that neither the failure of the debtor itself nor some small fraction of the account debtors will likely degrade significantly the overall value of the collateral.

To understand the basic modes of perfection for intangibles, take a quick walk through the relevant provisions of Part 3 of Article 9. For accounts, begin with section 9–308(a), which provides that perfection occurs if the security interest has attached (*see* 9–203(a)) and the applicable requirements of sections 9–309 through 9–316 are satisfied. Section 9–310(a) states the general rule that filing is required to perfect a security interest, unless some other method is permitted. After going through all of the other provisions in the series, you will see that no other method of perfection is authorized for accounts (unless the accounts are the proceeds of some other kind of collateral, *see* 9–203(f), 9–315). Accordingly, filing is the only permissible means of perfecting a security interest in accounts (other than accounts as proceeds). Would you have drafted Article 9 this way? Why not simply state the following: "A security interest in accounts is perfected only by filing."

Turning to other types of intangibles, take a look at the different ways these may be perfected. For example, section 9–309 allows automatic perfection for a "sale of a payment intangible" and a "sale of a promissory note." Automatic perfection is also permitted for certain assignments of "a health-care-insurance receivable," at least to the "provider of health care goods and services."

Section 9–312(a) states that one may perfect a security interest in "chattel paper . . . instruments, or investment property" by filing. (To permit one to perfect a security interest in instruments by filing is a change from the prior law.) Despite their absence from the list in section 9–312, filing is also a permissible method of perfection for general intangibles and payment intangibles, but not for deposit accounts or letter-of-credit rights. The latter two may be perfected (except where they constitute proceeds) only by control. *See* 9–312(b), 9–314. A security interest in investment property may be perfected either by control or by filing. (We consider investment property in Chapter 8.) *See* 9–314. Finally, possession under section 9–313 is a permissible method of perfection for "instruments, money or tangible chattel paper." *See also* 9–310(b)(6), 9–312(b)(3). (Note that the definition of "money" is not in Article 9; it is in section 1–201(b)(24) of Article 1.)

There are reasons for the various rules that permit, require, or prohibit certain methods of perfection for distinct types of intangible collateral. One may seem obvious to you—it would make little sense to say that one could perfect a security interest in an account by possession because there is nothing tangible to take possession of; in contrast, one can easily take possession of an instrument or tangible chattel paper. As we go through the chapter, be sure to consider why a certain mode of perfection is required for certain assets and prohibited for others. Hint: many of the reasons will be historical and practice-based.

Section 9–102 of the 1972 Code covered not only transactions intended to create conventional security interests but also "any sale of accounts or chattel paper." This provision recognized historical forms of financing that had long been practiced in many industries called "factoring." As discussed in Chapter 9 outlining the history of security devices, the factor was a person who "bought" accounts. Typically, the factor would pay the owner of the account 85, 90, or even 95 cents on the dollar in return for an assignment of 100% of the account. The factor would then make his money by attempting to collect 100 cents on the dollar from the account debtor. The spread (100–85) was the payment for the loan, the equivalent of an interest charge. The classic factor's bargain was "nonrecourse": the buyer of the account agreed to take the full credit risk that the account debtor would not or could not pay and so would have no recourse against the original owner of the account. Thus the factor got both the full upside (100 cents) and the full downside (0 cents). In practice, there are many variations between full recourse (the debtor promises to pay the full amount if the account debtor defaults) and a sale completely without recourse (no claim against the seller/debtor even if all account debtors default).

Modern practice has expanded the factoring business; the new practice is called "securitization." In a typical securitization transaction the debtor sells its accounts to a trustee who in turn sells "shares" or "participations" in the trust to investors. We discuss this in Section 3 below. In Section 4, we discuss the specific case of buyers of chattel paper and the competing priority between such buyers and those who hold security interests in the same collateral. *See* 9–330.

Section 5 turns to the special case of accounts that consist of money earned or to be earned from the provision of goods or services. These include moneys owed to the debtor on yet-to-be-performed construction contracts. As we will see, these kinds of accounts pose unique risks for the secured party, particularly in the form of the competing interest of surety companies who may have assured the debtor's performance of the underlying contract. Section 6 addresses some unique aspects of the collection rights a secured party enjoys with respect to intangible collateral.

In Section 7 we discuss security interests in general intangibles. The category of "general intangibles" is the catchall of intangible rights. It includes copyrights, patents, trademarks, and the rights associated with those forms of property. It likewise includes the equity interests in many limited liability companies and partnerships, and in some contexts emerging digital assets. Everything that is intangible but is not an account, instrument, chattel paper, investment property, etc., is a "general intangible" (unless excluded from the scope of Article 9, *see* 9–109). General intangibles also include such exotic rights such as the right to breed a mare to a particular stud.

As collateral, general intangibles present two significant problems for the secured creditor. First, many general intangibles carry anti-assignment provisions. For example, it is common for software licenses to prohibit their assignment to a third person or use by anyone other than the licensee. As we will see, section 9–408 deals with that issue, but in a complex way that is not likely to be completely satisfactory to the typical secured creditor. The second major problem with taking security interests in general intangibles is that some of the most valuable general intangibles—copyrights, patents, and trademarks—are subject to federal law. The federal law that governs those rights have their own filing provisions and it is often argued (and sometimes held) that a UCC filing is inadequate to perfect a security interest in such collateral. Congress may eventually delegate security filing with respect to general intangibles to the states, but until that happens, a UCC filing may not be adequate to perfect in some instances.

Finally, in Section 8 we discuss security interests in deposit accounts. A security interest in a deposit account is perfected by control. *See* 9–314, 9–104. The priority of competing interests in deposit accounts is governed by section 9–327. *See also* 9–340 to 9–342.

§ 2. PERFECTION AND PRIORITY OF SECURITY INTERESTS IN RIGHTS TO PAYMENT

To test your ability to distinguish among the different forms of intangibles and to understand the legal consequences that flow from those differences, consider the following problem (and as you do, remember to take a look at section 9–109 governing the scope of Article 9):

PROBLEM 5-1

Debtor is a large metropolitan hospital located in Manhattan. On any given day, it will have thousands of patients; some of them are paying out of their own pockets, some of them are members of HMOs who are paying, and some of them are Medicare or Medicaid patients whose fees are paid by state or federal governments. Bank intends to give hospital a $5 million revolving line of credit and to take a security interest in all of its intangibles. Bank currently has a financing statement on file in Albany claiming all "accounts and proceeds." There is some possibility that the hospital could go bankrupt and you think that at least two other creditors have filed as to certain receivables. The receivables consist of the following:

1. Claims against current and former patients who have no insurance.

2. Claims against current and former patients' credit cards who have paid by drawing on their credit cards (hint: *compare* 9–102 cmt. 5(a) *with* 9–102 cmt. 5(d)).

3. Rights to payment from HMOs and private insurers.

4. Rights to payment from Medicare and Medicaid (hint: *see* 9–102 cmt. 5(i)).

5. Rights to rentals arising from transactions in which the hospital pharmacy leases wheelchairs, crutches, and other devices.

6. Rights to payment from sales by the hospital store that sells knee braces, wheelchairs, and various home-health devices. Many of these are sold on 24-month contracts under which the hospital retains a security interest in the item sold and the former patient promises to pay in installments.

7. Right to payment to the hospital from one of its subsidiaries of a million dollar loan the hospital made to the subsidiary two months ago.

8. A seven figure deposit account maintained at Citibank in Manhattan.

9. Right to the rent from a five year real estate lease of a building adjacent to the hospital that is now leased to a large group of doctors (hint: *see* 9–109(d)(11)).

If the hospital fails tomorrow and files a petition in bankruptcy, in which assets will the Bank have a perfected security interest?

SECURITY INTERESTS IN INTANGIBLES AND RELATED ASSETS

Creditors often seek security not only in a debtor's intangibles, but also in related assets. For example, suppose the debtor owns expensive diagnostic machines that it leases out to hospitals under short-term written lease agreements. When the debtor actually leases out the machines, it has two distinct assets: its ownership interest in the machines out on lease, and its right to the payment of rent under the lease agreements. What are these distinct assets? The machines are the debtor's inventory, correct? *See* 9–102(a)(48) (providing that inventory includes goods that are "leased by a person as lessor"). The written leases and the debtor's rights to payment of rentals under them are chattel paper, no? *See* 9–102(a)(11) (providing that chattel paper includes "a lease of specific goods"). How is a security interest in these assets perfected? Can one include the other? Can the parties contract around Article 9's collateral types and perfection methods and come up with their own?

Before it filed for bankruptcy, Leasing Consultants ("Leasing") was engaged in the business of leasing heavy construction equipment to various lessees. Its secured creditor, First National City Bank ("Bank") held a properly perfected security interest in the relevant leases as chattel paper and also held a properly perfected security interest in Leasing's general intangibles. Bank neglected, however, to take a properly perfected security interest in the actual equipment subject to the leases. After Leasing filed for bankruptcy, the trustee sold the equipment to a purchaser and claimed that Bank had no security interest in the proceeds from the sale. Bank argued that it held a perfected security interest in Leasing's "reversionary interest" in the leased equipment as a general intangible (specifically the debtor's right to recover the goods at the end of the lease period).

Bank's argument was clever, but the Court of Appeals for the Second Circuit didn't buy it. The court held that the leased equipment constituted goods, specifically the debtor's inventory. It held further that the debtor's reversionary interest in the goods was an interest in the goods that could not be separated from the goods themselves. In other words, Bank could not avoid its failure to take a properly perfected security interest in the goods by claiming that it held a properly perfected security interest in the debtor's "reversionary interest" as a general intangible. *See In re Leasing Consultants*, 486 F.2d 367 (2d Cir. 1973).

Leasing Consultants illustrates the relatively inflexible boundaries that separate categories of collateral types. A debtor's ownership interest in particular goods consists of a bundle of rights accompanying the goods (including the right to lease the goods), and the sticks in the bundle are not divisible into slices that can be separately labeled "general intangibles." On the other hand, the debtor's *right to payment* arising from its disposition of the goods to a third party, whether by sale or by lease, is a separate item for purposes of Article 9.

Leasing Consultants involved a combination of rights in inventory (the leased property) and chattel paper (the leases of the leased property). What about other combinations of assets? Suppose the debtor makes loans to home owners and, in exchange, takes back promissory notes secured by mortgage liens on the home owners' real property. As a result, for each loan there are two documents: (1) a promissory note from the home owner to the debtor, and (2) a mortgage instrument filed with the local recorder of deeds granting the creditor a lien on the home. For Article 9 purposes, what kind of collateral is this set of rights? You may be tempted to say "chattel paper." Look carefully, however, at the definition of chattel paper in section 9–102(a)(11). Note that chattel paper includes "a record or records that evidence both a monetary obligation and a security interest *in specific goods* . . . ." Is a mortgage lien on real property "a security interest in specific goods"? No. Real estate is not a good; it is realty. The promissory note is an instrument (if the other requirements of section 9–102(a)(47) are satisfied; if not, it is a payment intangible, *see* 9–102(a)(61)). But what about the mortgage lien securing the note? If the debtor grants a security interest in its instruments to a secured creditor, does the secured creditor get the benefit of the mortgage lien as well? Yes. Take a look at section 9–203(g) and comment 9, and section 9–308(e). *See also* 9–604(a) & cmt. 2.

How about the following: suppose the debtor sells an expensive machine to a customer, and the debtor gives the customer one year to pay for it. Suppose further that the customer's brother-in-law guarantees the customer's payment of the purchase price. As a result, the debtor now has two distinct rights: (1) a right to payment from the customer, and (2) a right to payment from the brother-in-law in the form of his guarantee. What are these rights for Article 9 purposes? The right to payment from the customer is an account. What about the guarantee? It is a "supporting obligation." *See* 9–102(a)(78) & cmt. 5(f). If the debtor grants a security interest in the account to its bank, does the bank also have a security interest in the guarantee, or must the bank do something else? Take a look at section 9–203(f) and comment 8. *See also* 9–322(c), 9–618(a).

PROBLEM 5-2

Your client wants not only the stream of payments but also an interest in the underlying equipment of a lessor who leases goods nationwide. Taking possession of the leases and filing at the debtor's (lessor's) place of incorporation will give you a perfected security interest as to the leases and the leased goods. Is that correct? Client would prefer to leave the leases in the debtor's hands. Does it risk its perfection or its priority by doing so?

PROBLEM 5-3

1. Greater Chicago Mortgage Co. makes mortgage loans to individual home owners in the Chicago area and also purchases documents that are variously called "land sale contracts" or "contracts for deed." These are contracts made between a buyer and seller of real estate; they do not include a note, but they can be recorded and when they are will have the same effect as a mortgage under state law. If the debtor executes a mortgage, it will be recorded and the debtor will also sign a note. Greater Chicago wishes to sell some of these interests to your client, Bank. In order to have a first claim not only on the stream of payments but also on the underlying real estate, Bank understands that it need do nothing more than sign a security agreement with Greater Chicago. It understands that it is automatically perfected under section 9–309 as to both the underlying real estate assets and the stream of payments. Is that correct?

2. Would your conclusion in 1 change if your client told you that it proposed to "buy" the receivables on a nonrecourse basis and then to have Greater Chicago execute a separate document called a "Guaranty" under which

Greater Chicago would be obliged to buy back any loan on which the account debtor defaulted?

3. Assume that Greater Chicago has failed and its trustee in bankruptcy has challenged your client on the ground that Bank did not have a valid and perfected security interest in the underlying mortgages and property. The trustee suggests your client was obliged to record an assignment of mortgage or a land sale contract in the real estate records in order to enjoy priority. Secondly, the trustee notes that as to some of the mortgage transactions, Greater Chicago failed to record the mortgage. How will that affect the outcome of the case described above?

PRIORITY OF SECURITY INTERESTS IN INTANGIBLES

In general, the priority of a security interest in an intangible is governed by section 9–322. Might one also have a *purchase money* security interest in an intangible? Generally speaking, no (with exceptions for software and certain intangibles as proceeds of purchase money collateral). Look again at the definition of purchase money collateral in section 9–103(a)(1). Notice that it provides that " 'purchase money collateral' means goods or software." Intangibles are not goods; and software is a specific type of general intangible. *See* 9–102 cmt. 25.

As we saw in Chapter 4, section 9–324 provides a variety of rules governing when the purchase money status of certain collateral carries over to the proceeds of the collateral, including intangibles as proceeds. *See also* 9–315. Under section 9–324(a), a purchase money security interest in equipment extends to the proceeds of the equipment (including accounts, chattel paper, and the like arising from the debtor's disposition of the equipment), except as provided in section 9–327 governing conflicting security interests in deposit accounts. Under section 9–324(b), a security interest in inventory extends to chattel paper or an instrument constituting proceeds of the inventory as provided in section 9–330, subject to certain conditions set forth in the section.

Section 9–330 is a complicated provision. It provides a set of rules governing when a purchaser of chattel paper has priority over the holder of a security interest in the same chattel paper; and, in conjunction with section 9–331, provides a set of rules governing when a purchaser of an instrument takes priority over the holder of a security interest in the same instrument. Section 9–330 is challenging in part because the term "purchaser" is defined in section 1–201 to include a secured party holding a security interest. Section 9–330 is discussed in greater detail in Section 4 of this chapter.

What about a conflict between a secured party holding a perfected security interest in a debtor's accounts and the purchaser of the same accounts? Under section 1–201, a security interest includes the interest of "a buyer of accounts" (and also includes the interest of a "buyer of . . .

chattel paper, a payment intangible, or a promissory note," but not the buyer of an instrument). Accordingly, the buyer of the debtor's accounts is treated as the holder of a security interest. Under section 9–322, the first to file or perfect will generally have priority.

§ 3. SECURITIZATION

Before 1999, rights to payment that arose from a *loan* by a creditor to a debtor were "general intangibles" and not "accounts" under Article 9; "accounts" arose only on the sale of goods or services. Thus, for example, a securitization of $100 million of commercial loans or $200 million of credit card receivables would not have been covered by Article 9 because they would have amounted to the "sale of general intangibles" and not the "sale of accounts or chattel paper." The change in the definition of accounts (to include credit card receivables, *see* 9–102(a)(2)(vii)) and the expansion of Article 9's coverage (to include sales of payment intangibles and promissory notes, *see* 9–109(a)(3)), brings almost all securitizations within Article 9. The new definition of payment intangibles and their inclusion in section 9–109(a)(3) brings the sale of loan participations into Article 9 as well.

To understand how Article 9 might apply to the sale of various intangibles, consider four cases. First, assume that Ally, an automobile finance company, makes 1,000 car loans (complete with perfected security interests in the cars being financed) to 1,000 consumer car buyers, then sells those loans (constituting in this case "chattel paper"—a security agreement and a note) to a trust or other Special Purpose Vehicle ("SPV") that issues shares to investors. Second, assume the original lender is not Ally, but a mortgage company that takes notes secured by real estate mortgages from 1,000 homeowners and transfers its notes and mortgages to a trustee. Third is a credit card company that sells its receivables. Fourth is Citibank who lends $100 million to a debtor and then sells off $90 million of "participations" in its $100 million loan to 9 other banks so that each of the ten banks now owns only $10 million of the loan.

All of these cases are covered by Article 9. The collateral transferred in Ally's case was "chattel paper"; that transferred by the real estate lender was "promissory notes" (a type of "instrument") or "payment intangibles"; the credit card company sold "accounts"; and Citibank transferred "payment intangibles." Although each of these four transactions is covered under Article 9, they do not get identical treatment. Under section 9–309, the banks who bought loan participations and the purchaser of the notes from the mortgage company are automatically perfected without filing or possession. The buyer from Ally, however, will either have to file in Ally's name or take possession of the chattel paper if it wants to be perfected (or obtain control in the case of electronic chattel paper). The buyer of accounts from the credit card company will have to file in the name of the credit card company to perfect its interest. Note here how section 9–318 treats sales of accounts, chattel paper, payment intangibles, or promissory notes that are perfected under Article 9; and correspondingly how it treats sales of accounts and chattel paper that are unperfected. Section 9–318 provides:

> (a) **[Seller retains no interest.]** A debtor that has sold an account, chattel paper, payment intangible, or promissory note does not retain a legal or equitable interest in the collateral sold.
>
> (b) **[Deemed rights of debtor if buyer's security interest unperfected.]** For purposes of determining the rights of creditors of, and purchasers for value of an account or chattel paper from, a debtor that has sold an account or chattel paper, while the buyer's security interest is unperfected, the debtor is deemed to have rights and title to the account or chattel paper identical to those the debtor sold.

One might ask why the sale of anything is ever treated as though it were a secured loan. Part of the reason is that the sale of intangibles that produce payments behave economically like loans against those same assets. If, for example, Ally had $100M of receivables from consumers who had purchased cars, it could either "sell" the receivables to a bank or it could borrow from the bank and grant the bank a security interest in the receivables. The two transactions have almost the same economic consequences for Ally. The sale of loans or other receivables is almost exactly like a "nonrecourse" loan against those assets. A nonrecourse loan is a loan in which the creditor agrees to lend money and to limit its claims for satisfaction of the loan to particular assets of the debtor. For example, by law most purchase money mortgages on residential homes in California are nonrecourse loans. By law the mortgagee can foreclose on the residence and sell it to satisfy its debt if the homeowner defaults, but is prohibited from going after the wages or any other assets of the homeowner. For a time, it was common for banks to make nonrecourse loans against commercial buildings and thus to limit themselves to the right to foreclose and sell the building.

An historical reason why it is easy for commercial lenders to regard securitizations as loans is that securitizations are no more than an exaggerated version of the ancient transaction called "factoring." As early as 1900, it was common for a factor to purchase the accounts receivable of sellers in certain industries. As discussed previously, the factors would pay $.80 or $.95 for $1.00 of accounts receivable and would enjoy the entire upside (if, for example, the factor collected one hundred cents on the dollar from the account debtors) or suffer the entire downside (bear the loss with respect to any account debtor who failed to pay). Factoring, securitization, and every form of nonrecourse lending come in increments; they are not bi-modal. For example, a bank that was willing to purchase an automobile dealer's paper might require the dealer to take back (guarantee) any loan on which there was a default within six months of the transfer. Such limited recourse against the automobile dealer would diminish his incentive to make loans to non-creditworthy debtors and then sell those loans completely free of recourse to the bank.

Whether something is a "sale" as opposed to a "loan" accompanying a security interest is often a function of the amount of recourse involved in the transaction. If there is full recourse, the transaction is a loan with a security interest regardless of what the parties call it. If there is none, it is a sale. Whether one ounce, a quart, or a gallon of recourse is enough to cause the transaction to cross the line from sale to loan with security cannot be predicted with certainty, but it is something that should concern everyone who wishes to be treated as a buyer and not as a lender.

Whether one is a seller or borrower is usually not important for the purposes of Article 9, for whatever the transaction is called, the "creditor" or "buyer" will normally take whatever action is necessary to perfect a security interest under Article 9. However, the distinction between a sale and a loan may be critical for the purposes of bankruptcy law. If there is a sale of a particular asset, the asset is not "property of the estate" under section 541 of the Bankruptcy Code and thus is not subject to interference by the Chapter 11 debtor in possession ("DIP") or by the debtor's trustee in bankruptcy.

The key to securitization (and perhaps the only significant thing about securitization) is that it removes the assets that are securitized beyond the reach of any DIP or trustee of the seller. The critical step in the securitization transaction is to transfer the relevant assets (the seller's accounts, chattel paper, promissory notes, etc.) to a trust or other special purpose vehicle ("SPV"). If structured properly, this SPV will have no creditor other than the investors themselves who purchase shares or interests in the pool of assets (*i.e.*, shares or other interests in the SPV that entitle these investors to distributions from the SPV funded by the proceeds from the assets the SPV has acquired). If the SPV has no other creditors, it cannot fail to pay other obligations and thus cannot itself be put into bankruptcy (at least in theory).

The greater concern is the DIP or trustee of the seller (debtor). As indicated in the discussion of bankruptcy in Chapter 3, the trustee or DIP has a variety of ways under sections 362 and 363 to affect the rights of a secured creditor, even a fully perfected one. The DIP can use the creditor's collateral and can sometimes substitute other collateral as adequate protection, can stop paying interest when the value of the collateral is less than the debt, etc. One way to free the assets (for example, the accounts that Ally is selling) from the reach of Ally's DIP is to insure that there is a "sale" such that the assets are not in the estate of Ally should it go bankrupt. *See* section 541 of the Bankruptcy Code (discussing what constitutes property of the debtor's bankruptcy estate subject to administration in bankruptcy).

If the securitization is properly done so that the credit rating agencies and the investors believe that the assets are beyond the reach of all DIPs and trustees, the rating agencies will give a higher rating to the SPV than they would give to the seller of the receivables who likely has many other creditors. If the rating agencies give a better rating to the SPV than to the original seller, it means that the SPV can borrow at a lower interest rate or, alternatively, that its investors will pay more for the debt the SPV issues than they would pay for the seller's debt. In addition to this benefit, there may be other small ones that are unrelated to the effect on bankruptcy.

THE FUNDAMENTALS OF SECURITIZATION TRANSACTIONS

To grasp how securitizations are structured and what makes them attractive, consider a common example. Suppose a finance company ("Finance") has made 1,000 car loans to consumers to enable them to purchase their vehicles. Finance has taken back 1,000 notes from these consumers reflecting their promises to repay the loans they have taken. The terms of the loans require the consumers to repay their loans in installments over the course of 60 months. Finance has also taken a security interest in the consumers' cars to secure payment of the notes. As a result, Finance now holds a lot of "chattel paper" consisting of the notes and the security interests in the cars.

Finance is in the business of making car loans and would like to make more, but its capital is currently tied up in the 1,000 car loans it has made. Finance has several options to raise cash to make more loans. First, it could hold the chattel paper and collect the payments from the 1,000 consumers until the consumers pay off their loans, using the collections to make new loans as they come in. That would mean, of course, that Finance would have to wait the full 60 months to get all of its money back (assuming the consumers did not prepay their loans prior to maturity).

Second, rather than wait 60 months, Finance could immediately borrow money from a bank or other lender and use the proceeds from this borrowing to make new loans. To get the best rate, Finance could offer its portfolio of chattel paper as collateral. In this way Finance could effectively cash out its portfolio of chattel paper. Of course, in a secured financing transaction Finance would continue to own the chattel paper, and if Finance filed for bankruptcy the chattel paper would become property of Finance's bankruptcy estate. Finance's secured lender holding a security interest in the chattel paper would then be subject to the automatic stay and other features of bankruptcy law discussed previously.

Third, rather than borrow money from a bank or other lender in a secured financing transaction, Finance could sell its portfolio of chattel paper to a buyer through a securitization. Structured properly, a securitization transaction is frequently a cheaper way to raise capital than secured lending because the purchaser ends up owning the assets in question. As a result, the purchaser is far less concerned about the seller's (Finance's) solvency or the consequences of the seller's potential future bankruptcy filing.

Correspondingly, a purchaser in a securitization transaction will typically pay a price for the assets that is more attractive to the seller than alternative financing terms.

Securitizations can be structured in several ways. First, Finance might sell its chattel paper to a grantor trust formed exclusively for the purpose of purchasing the paper. In order to raise the funds necessary to purchase Finance's chattel paper, the trust might issue participation certificates to investors representing undivided fractional interests in the trust. A trustee would be appointed to administer the trust, but neither the trustee nor the trust would typically hold the chattel paper. Instead, the trust would enter into a servicing agreement with Finance or some entity affiliated with Finance to monitor, collect, and enforce (if necessary) the chattel paper. Thus, although the trust would own the chattel paper, Finance or some affiliated entity would service it as a custodian. As the servicer collects the money coming in from the consumers, the servicer would then pay the funds to the investors holding the participation certificates (after deducting its servicing fee).

Second, Finance might sell its chattel paper to a limited purpose finance corporation or business trust in a transaction similar to the one described above. In order to raise the funds necessary to acquire the chattel paper, the finance corporation or business trust might issue debt securities to investors collateralized by the chattel paper. These debt securities are commonly referred to as "collateralized debt obligations" or "CDOs." (Somewhat confusingly, the finance corporations or business trusts that issue them are also commonly referred to as CDOs.) The finance corporation or business trust would be run by a board of directors or a trustee, as the case may be. Once again, there would typically be a servicing agreement with Finance or some entity affiliated with Finance to monitor, collect, and enforce the chattel paper. As the servicer collects the money coming in from the consumers, it would then pay the funds to the investors holding the debt securities of the finance corporation or business trust. The equity interest in the finance corporation or business trust could be retained by Finance as the seller of the chattel paper, or sold off to third-party investors. Together with grantor trusts, limited purpose finance corporations and business trusts used in securitization transactions are all types of SPVs. SPVs are also referred to as "issuers," referring to the participation interests or debt securities they issue to investors to raise the capital necessary to purchase the securitized assets.

The interests of the investors can be structured in many ways. In a "pass-through" structure, payments are made to the investors through the SPV essentially on a pro rata basis. In other words, the money the servicer collects is basically divided among the investors who typically form a single class of interests.

In a "pay-through" structure, the investors are generally divided into different classes, each holding securities with different maturities and payment priorities. For example, the securities might be divided into three classes, also known as "tranches." Tranche A might be entitled to payment ahead of tranches B and C, and tranche B might be entitled to payment ahead of tranche C. As a result, much of the risk of nonpayment would be concentrated in tranche C. Investors purchasing debt securities in tranche C would typically insist on a higher rate of return to compensate for this risk. Conversely, investors purchasing debt securities in tranche A would typically receive a lower rate of return.

The tranches can be divided in other ways as well. One tranche might be entitled to payment from the principal component of the underlying loans. A second tranche might be entitled to payment from the interest component. An interest-only collateralized debt obligation can be quite risky. If the consumers pay off their loans early, there may be little interest collected. Purchasers of interest-only debt securities correspondingly demand a higher rate of return to compensate for this risk.

In order to attract investors to purchase its participation interests or debt securities, the SPV may obtain credit support enhancements to hedge against the poor performance of the underlying chattel paper or other securitized assets. These enhancements may take one of several forms. First, Finance might provide a letter-of-credit from a banking institution to the SPV. If the chattel paper performs poorly, the SPV would be entitled to draw on the letter of credit to cover at least a portion of its loss. Second, Finance might provide a surety bond from a surety company to the same effect. Third, Finance might provide a limited guaranty of the performance of the chattel paper such that, if it performs poorly, Finance or some affiliate would be obligated to make up at least part of the SPV's loss. Fourth, the SPV may have access to special reserve or "spread" accounts to absorb at least part of any loss. Fifth, Finance might "over-collateralize" the SPV with additional chattel paper to cover any shortfall.

The securities that an SPV issues are often rated by independent rating agencies. Typically, the higher priority tranches receive a higher rating. Rating agencies may require credit enhancements to achieve a rating sufficient to attract investors at a reasonable rate.

It is sometimes claimed that securitizations offer numerous benefits to the sellers of financial assets such as Finance. The primary benefit is the opportunity to achieve a lower cost of funds as compared to other methods of obtaining available capital. Other claimed benefits include the seller's ability to: (1) match its assets with its liabilities; (2) achieve off-balance-sheet treatment for the transaction, which may avoid breaching preexisting covenants limiting the seller's ability to borrow funds; and (3) transferring the performance risk of its portfolio to the purchaser. Of course, the first benefit is also achieved in a secured lending transaction where the secured creditor takes a security interest in the precise collateral it values in making the loan. The second benefit is characteristic of any sale and comes at a cost: in exchange for the purchase price, the seller gives up a valuable asset, namely the securitized property. Further, sophisticated commercial agreements often limit not only a debtor's ability to borrow, but also its ability to sell significant assets. Finally, with respect to the third benefit, presumably the purchaser discounts its purchase price based on the perceived riskiness of the portfolio in question. At least in theory, the transfer of risk should be reflected in the purchase price. As suggested above, the real benefit of securitizations is the perceived avoidance of the risk of the seller's bankruptcy.

Securitizations first emerged tentatively in the late 1970s, and exploded in the early 2000s. It is estimated that by 2008 there were approximately $10 trillion in outstanding securitizations in the United States. Securitization transactions declined precipitously with the financial crisis of 2007–2008. In the years following 2008 they became popular yet again as general economic conditions improved.

A key aspect of any properly structured securitization transaction is that the transfer of the assets to the SPV must constitute a "true sale." If the transfer is not a true sale, the seller may be deemed to own the assets in question notwithstanding their erstwhile transfer. Transfers denominated as "sales" may be recharacterized as loans under certain circumstances. *See* 9–109 cmt. 4 (remarking that the question of recharacterization is an issue "left to the courts"). In any recharacterization analysis, the most important consideration is whether and to what extent the SPV has recourse against the seller if the assets in question perform poorly. As indicated previously, if the SPV has full recourse against the seller, it is hard to justify the transaction as a true sale. A limited amount of recourse is generally permissible, but exactly where to draw the line remains unclear.

Other less important factors in any recharacterization analysis may include whether the seller as servicer is scrupulous in managing and segregating the funds it collects on behalf of the SPV; whether the seller has retained any significant economic rights in the assets it has transferred; and whether the transaction would be treated as a financing rather than a sale under generally accepted accounting principles or for tax purposes. Other considerations may also come into play in the analysis, depending on the circumstances. Generally speaking, the more the seller appears to act like the owner of the underlying assets, the less likely it is that the transaction will be treated as a true sale.

States take different approaches to the "true-sale doctrine," as it is known. Some follow common law, factors-based tests that require fact-intensive inquiries and that distinguish among different types of recourse. A handful of states have enacted "asset-backed securities facilitation acts" or "ABS statutes" that deem assignments of assets for purposes of securitization to be sales regardless of economic substance. It is not clear whether these ABS statutes effectively prevent the attachment of a bankruptcy trustee's lien to securitized assets assigned to an SPV in a transaction that would be deemed a loan if subjected to a substantive true-sale analysis. In securitizations in which the originator is a bank subject to the Federal Deposit Insurance Act, FDIC rules, which contain safe-harbor provisions and reference accounting standards, may determine the status of securitized assets. In any event, for lawyers who represent securitization originators, these rules are of frequent concern. Investors in the securities the SPV issues typically require a true-sale opinion letter: a highly qualified analysis through which the attorneys opine that the assignment of assets from their client to the SPV would be treated as a sale if tested in court. The issuance of a true-sale opinion letter, along with bankruptcy non-consolidation and enforceability and perfection opinion letters, can affect the rating that a rating agency will assign to the transaction.

A related aspect of any properly structured securitization transaction is compliance with the requirements of Article 9. Although Finance is selling its chattel paper to the SPV, if the SPV fails to perfect its interest, section 9–318(b) deems Finance to have retained the rights and interests it sold with respect to its creditors and purchasers. Accordingly, if the SPV fails to perfect its interest, and Finance subsequently files for bankruptcy, the SPV would be treated merely as an unsecured creditor with respect to the chattel paper. Section 9–318(b) applies to sales of accounts and chattel paper. Sales of payment intangibles and promissory notes are automatically perfected under section 9–309.

One risk that securitization transactions face is the risk that the seller and the SPV may be "substantively consolidated" in the event the seller commences a bankruptcy proceeding. Substantive consolidation is an equitable bankruptcy procedure that is sometimes used to consolidate legally distinct entities into a single entity for bankruptcy purposes. Generally speaking, substantive consolidation may result if the SPV fails to comply with basic corporate formalities or allows its operations to be so intermingled with those of the seller that it would be impractical or inequitable to treat them as separate entities.

Another risk is that, if the seller files for bankruptcy, the sale to the SPV might be undone as a fraudulent transfer. Generally speaking, this may occur if the assets in question are transferred for less than "reasonably equivalent value" and either the transfer is made while the seller is insolvent or the transfer renders the seller insolvent. Fraudulent transfer risk is generally foreclosed if the sale is made for a price that represents or fairly approximates the fair market value of the assets in question. Fraudulent transfer analysis is addressed in Section 7 of Chapter 3.

PROBLEM 5-4

You have been hired by Mutual Fund who proposes to buy several sets of receivables and wants your opinion about its rights in each of the circumstances. In one case, Merchandise Company, a Midwestern department store, has a subsidiary known as M-Credit that issues credit cards to Merchandise Co.'s customers. Credit card receivables will be assigned to a trust and your client proposes to buy several millions of dollars of receivables from the trust. In the second case, All American Credit Card and Loan Company makes loans in various ways: it has credit card receivables; it makes automobile loans and takes security interests in the automobiles; it makes automobile leases; and it makes unsecured consumer loans. It proposes to assign all of these to a trustee and your client proposes to buy "participations" from the trust. How would the following play out?

1. Representatives of Merchandise Co. and All American claim that the trust's interest is either outside of Article 9 or is automatically perfected under the terms of section 9–309. Moreover, they maintain there is no problem because the trust is "bankruptcy remote," meaning the trust will have no obligations to any creditor except for the obligation it might have to your investor and to others and so could not be forced into bankruptcy. To be particularly safe, they have filed one financing statement in the name of Merchandise Co. and one in the name of All American covering all of debtor's "receivables and their proceeds." Do you think they are adequately perfected? Should your client file in the trust's name?

2. What bankruptcy risk do you see, if any, if either of the trusts, Merchandise Co., its subsidiary or All American goes into bankruptcy?

3. What action is necessary to insure perfection as to the automobiles leased or sold by All American? As to the cars sold, All American normally would have put its name on the Certificates of Title as "Secured Party" and would have signed security agreements from the purchasers. In the case of the leased cars, All American's name appears as the owner on the Certificates of Title. Does the purchaser have to take any further action to protect itself with respect to the underlying collateral? How can one tell whether All American has a perfected security interest in the automobiles?

4. Can different tranches of receivables be set up for different investors with different tastes for risk (for example, some receivables with lower return and risk and others with greater returns but greater risk)? What problems does this pose?

PROBLEM 5-5

It is now 18 months after you were asked for your advice. It turns out that Merchandise Co. was not as solvent as it could have been. It and its subsidiary have gone into Chapter 11 and their bankruptcy cases have been consolidated. The debtor in possession (DIP) has recently proposed to keep several months of payments that are passing through its hands. (After the securitization, the subsidiary continued to service the loans by collecting the payments from the customers.) The DIP's attorney claims the right to keep the payments for a limited period of time "in order to make the bankruptcy estate more liquid." He notes that the bankruptcy estate will give "adequate protection" under section 361 (in the form of a mortgage on some property that is unencumbered). He asserts that section 541 brings these assets into the bankruptcy estate. Moreover, he notes that section 362 keeps your client and the trust from suing Merchandise Co. and its subsidiary. His claim under section 541 depends in part upon UCC section 9–318(b). He argues that this section necessarily means that a seller of a receivable under Article 9 has retained title sufficient to bring it into the bankruptcy estate. He also notes that under the arrangement between the trust and the subsidiary, the trust could return any receivable to the debtor on which there was a default within 6 months of the assignment to the subsidiary. He says this makes the transaction into a "secured loan" (with title to the receivables remaining in the subsidiary) and not a "sale."

What do you think of the DIP's arguments?

Courts occasionally wander into the securitization Garden of Eden. Consider the following case that arose out of LTV Steel's second bankruptcy proceeding and caused horror in the securitization world. Read the case carefully and decide for yourself whether it is a correct interpretation of the law. As indicated above, securitization has grown to become a huge industry (subject to various ups and downs associated with general economic conditions). We suspect, however, that it is merely a by-product of current bankruptcy law.

IN RE LTV STEEL COMPANY, INC.

United States Bankruptcy Court, Northern District of Ohio, 2001.
274 B.R. 278.

BODOH, BANKRUPTCY JUDGE:

This cause is before the Court on the emergency motion of Abbey National Treasury Services PLC ("Abbey National") for modification of an interim order entered by the Court on December 29, 2000. That order permitted LTV Steel Company, Inc., Debtor and Debtor-in-Possession in these jointly administered proceedings ("Debtor"), to use cash assets that are claimed to be cash collateral in which Abbey National has an interest. * * *

Discussion

A. Facts

Debtor is one of the largest manufacturers of wholly-integrated steel products in the United States. Debtor mainly produces flat rolled steel products, hot and cold rolled sheet metal, mechanical and structural tubular products, and bimetallic wire. Debtor currently employs approximately 17,500 people in various capacities, and Debtor is also responsible for providing medical coverage and other benefits to approximately 100,000 retirees and their dependents. Debtor and 48 of its subsidiaries filed voluntary petitions for relief under Chapter 11 of Title 11, United States Code, on December 29, 2000. These cases are jointly administered.

This is not the first occasion on which Debtor has filed for relief under the Bankruptcy Code. Debtor previously filed a voluntary Chapter 11 petition in the Bankruptcy Court for the Southern District of New York on July 17, 1986. Debtor successfully emerged from Chapter 11 on June 28, 1993. Indeed, the current controversy stems from a series of financial transactions that Debtor executed after its previous reorganization. The transactions in question are known as asset-backed securitization or structured financing ("ABS"), and are generally designed to permit a debtor to borrow funds at a reduced cost in exchange for a lender securing the loan with assets that are transferred from the borrower to another entity. By structuring the transactions in this manner, the lender hopes to ensure that its collateral will be excluded from the borrower's bankruptcy estate in the event that the borrower files a bankruptcy petition.

Abbey National is a large financial institution located in the United Kingdom. Debtor and Abbey National entered into an ABS transaction in October 1994. To effectuate this agreement, Debtor created a wholly-owned subsidiary known as LTV Sales Finance Co. ("Sales Finance"). Debtor then entered into an agreement with Sales Finance which purports to sell all of Debtor's right and interest in its accounts receivables ("receivables") to Sales Finance on a continuing basis. Abbey National then agreed to loan Two Hundred Seventy Million Dollars ($270,000,000.00) to Sales Finance in exchange for Sales Finance granting Abbey National a security interest in the receivables. On the date Debtor's petition was filed, Chase Manhattan Bank ("Chase Manhattan") was Abbey National's agent for this credit facility.

In 1998, Debtor entered into another ABS financing arrangement. To that end, Debtor created LTV Steel Products, LLC ("Steel Products"), another wholly-owned subsidiary. Debtor entered into an agreement with Steel Products which purports to sell all of Debtor's right, title and interest in its inventory to Steel Products on a continuing basis. Chase Manhattan and several other banking institutions then agreed to loan Thirty Million Dollars ($30,000,000.00) to Steel Products in exchange for a security interest in Steel Products' inventory. Abbey National is not involved in this ABS facility, and it had no interest in pre-petition inventory allegedly owned by Steel Products.

Neither Sales Finance nor Steel Products is a debtor in this proceeding. Nevertheless, Debtor filed a motion with the Court on

December 29, 2000 seeking an interim order permitting it to use cash collateral. This cash collateral consisted of the receivables and inventory that are ostensibly owned by Sales Finance and Steel Products. Debtors stated to the Court that it would be forced to shut its doors and cease operations if it did not receive authorization to use this cash collateral. A hearing was held on Debtor's cash collateral motion on December 29, 2000 as part of the first day hearings.

Abbey National was not present at the cash collateral hearing. However, the Court notes that Abbey National had actual notice of the hearing, first, in the form of an e-mail sent by a Chase Manhattan employee to Abbey National on December 28, 2000, and second, in the form of a telephone call made from a Chase Manhattan employee to Abbey National on December 29, 2000. Furthermore, it is clear that Debtor had given advance notice of its intention to file for bankruptcy protection to Chase Manhattan, Abbey National's agent, in the week prior to December 29, 2000. Chase Manhattan was present at the December 29, 2000 hearing.

On December 29, 2000, Debtor and Chase Manhattan reached an agreement regarding an interim order permitting Debtor to use the cash collateral. Chase Manhattan did not formally consent to the entry of this order, as it could not secure Abbey National's consent to the form of the order, but Chase Manhattan did negotiate some of the terms of the order and did not raise an objection to its entry by the Court. The Court determined that entry of the interim order was necessary to permit Debtor to continue business operations, that the interests of Abbey National and all other creditors who had an interest in the cash collateral were adequately protected by the order, and that entry of the order was in the best interests of the estate and creditors of the estate. Accordingly, the Court entered the order tendered by Debtor, the relevant provisions of which are summarized below:

1. Recognition that there is a dispute between Debtor and the secured lenders of Sales Finance and Steel Products as to whether the transactions between Debtor and those entities were true sales or disguised financing vehicles;

2. An order requiring the secured lenders to turn over to Debtor the cash proceeds of the inventory and receivables which are to be used to provide working capital for Debtor;

3. Recognition that in the event the Court determines these transactions to be true sales, the secured lenders whose cash collateral was used will be entitled to administrative expense claims against the estate;

4. Adequate protection was provided to the secured lenders in the form of senior liens on the inventory and receivables and

weekly interest payments to the lenders at pre-petition non-default rates.

It is this order that Abbey National seeks to modify. Specifically, Abbey National asks the Court to modify the interim cash collateral order *nunc pro tunc* to include the following provisions:

a. The Debtors shall transfer to Sales Finance all receivables created on or after December 29, 2000 and not previously sold to Sales Finance and that would have been sold to Sales Finance were it not for the occurrence of a Liquidation Event;

b. Steel Products would continue to purchase Inventory from the Inventory Sellers and Sales Finance would continue to purchase Receivables from the Receivables Sellers, each on the same basis and on the same terms as existed prior to the Petition Date;

c. The respective Collection Accounts would be administered by the Collateral Agent in the same manner as was administered prior to the Petition Date. Therefore, notwithstanding the occurrence of any Termination Date, collection on account of the Receivables would not be required to be applied to principal payments or amortization payments (other than any payments required in connection with the maintenance by the borrowers of their respective borrowing bases);

d. Steel Products and the Collateral Agent under the Inventory Facility would continue to automatically release all liens against the Receivables purchased by Sales Finance from Steel Products;

e. All minimum borrowing base and collateral value requirements set forth in the Receivables Facility and the Inventory Facility will continue in full force and effect;

f. In all other respects, the Receivables Facility and the Inventory Facility will continue to operate as required after the occurrence of a Liquidation Event including without limitation, the reimbursement of all expenses of each Receivables Lender and Inventory Lender. (Abbey National's Emergency Motion to Modify Interim Order at 14–16).

Abbey National argues that the interim cash collateral order should be modified because: 1) it did not receive effective notice of the December 29, 2000 hearing and was thus denied due process of law; 2) there is no basis for the Court to determine that the receivables which are Abbey National's collateral are property of Debtor's estate and 3) that even if the receivables are property of Debtor's estate, that Abbey National's interests are not adequately protected because the pre-petition receivables are diminishing at a rapid rate and will soon be depleted. Debtor argues that

Abbey National did receive notice of the December 29 hearing, that Abbey National has failed to state grounds to modify the interim order pursuant to Fed. R. Bankr. P. 9024, and that Abbey National's interests in the receivables are adequately protected.

B. Issue

There are four issues before the Court. These are: 1) the procedural basis for Abbey National's motion; 2) whether the circumstances surrounding the December 29, 2000 hearing deprived Abbey National of its right to due process; 3) whether the interim order should be modified because the cash collateral was not property of Debtor's estate; and 4) whether the interim order failed to adequately protect Abbey National's interest in the collateral.

C. Analysis

1. Procedural Basis for Abbey National's Motion

As a preliminary matter, the Court must address the procedural basis for Abbey National's motion. Abbey National has not cited a single rule of civil or bankruptcy procedure in support of its motion. Debtor contends that because Abbey National's motion seeks to modify a previous order of the Court, it must be construed as a motion for relief from judgment pursuant to Fed. R. Civ. P. 60(b), made applicable to this proceeding pursuant to Fed. R. Bankr. P. 9024. Abbey National has not responded to this contention. Because it is clear that Abbey National is seeking relief from the Court's interim order, we shall treat Abbey National's motion as a motion brought under Rule 60(b).

The decision to grant a motion for relief under Rule 60(b) lies within the Court's discretion. *Miller v. Owsianowski (In re Salem Mortgage Co.)*, 791 F.2d 456, 459 (6th Cir.1986). A Rule 60(b) motion may be granted for the following reasons:

> (1) mistake, inadvertence, surprise, or excusable neglect; (2) newly discovered evidence . . . (3) fraud (whether heretofore denominated intrinsic or extrinsic), misrepresentation, or other misconduct of an adverse party; (4) the judgment is void; (5) the judgment has been satisfied, released, or discharged . . . or (6) any other reason justifying relief from the operation of the judgment. Fed. R. Civ. P. 60(b).

Because Abbey National has not presented its arguments in conformity with Rule 60(b), we shall address Abbey National's arguments in relation to the subsections of Rule 60(b) that appear to coincide with those arguments. We can safely say at the outset that Abbey National has not raised any argument relating to newly discovered evidence or the satisfaction of a judgment and thus we will not consider those elements of Rule 60(b).

2. *Due Process*

* * *

Based upon this analysis, the Court concludes that the circumstances surrounding the hearing of December 29, 2000 provided Abbey National with sufficient due process.

* * *

3. *Whether the Receivables are Property of Debtor's Estate*

Abbey National's next argument is that the receivables which constitute its collateral are not property of Debtor's estate, and thus this Court lacked jurisdiction to enter the interim order. We shall construe this as an argument that the interim order is void pursuant to Rule 60(b)(4).

Section 541(a) of the Bankruptcy Code provides that upon the filing of a bankruptcy petition an estate is created consisting of "all legal or equitable interests of the debtor in property as of the commencement of the case." 11 U.S.C. § 541(a)(1). The estate created by the filing of a Chapter 11 petition is very broad, and property may be included in Debtor's estate even if Debtor does not have a possessory interest in that property. *United States v. Whiting Pools, Inc.*, 462 U.S. 198, 204, 205–06, 103 S.Ct. 2309, 2313–14, 76 L.Ed.2d 515 (1983).

Abbey National contends that the interim order is flawed because, on its face, the transaction between Debtor and Sales Finance is characterized as a true sale. Therefore, Abbey National argues, since Debtor sold its interests in the receivables to Sales Finance, Debtor no longer has an interest in the receivables and they are not property of the estate. However, Abbey National has admitted to the Court, both in its pleadings and in oral argument, that the ultimate issue of whether Debtor actually sold the receivables to Sales Finance is a fact-intensive issue that cannot be resolved without extensive discovery and an evidentiary hearing.

We find Abbey National's argument for "emergency" relief to be not well taken for several reasons. First, Abbey National's position in this regard is circular: we cannot permit Debtor to use cash collateral because it is not property of the estate, but we cannot determine if it is property of the estate until we hold an evidentiary hearing. We fail to see how we can conclude that the receivables are not property of Debtor's estate until an evidentiary hearing on that issue has been held. Because the determination of this issue must await further discovery, we decline to grant Abbey National relief from the interim order.

Furthermore, there seems to be an element of sophistry to suggest that Debtor does not retain at least an *equitable* interest in the property that is subject to the interim order. Debtor's business requires it to purchase, melt, mold and cast various metal products. To suggest that Debtor lacks some ownership interest in products that it creates with its own labor, as well as the proceeds to be derived from that labor, is difficult to accept. Accordingly, the Court concludes that Debtor has at least some equitable interest in the inventory and receivables, and that this interest is property of the Debtor's estate. This equitable interest is sufficient to support the entry of the interim cash collateral order.

Finally, it is readily apparent that granting Abbey National relief from the interim cash collateral order would be highly inequitable. The Court is satisfied that the entry of the interim order was necessary to enable Debtor to keep its doors open and continue to meet its obligations to its employees, retirees, customers and creditors. Allowing Abbey National to modify the order would allow Abbey National to enforce its state law rights as a secured lender to look to the collateral in satisfaction of this debt. This circumstance would put an immediate end to Debtor's business, would put thousands of people out of work, would deprive 100,000 retirees of needed medical benefits, and would have more far reaching economic effects on the geographic areas where Debtor does business. However, maintaining the current status quo permits Debtor to remain in business while it searches for substitute financing, and adequately protects and preserves Abbey National's rights. The equities of this situation highly favor Debtor. As a result, the Court declines to exercise its discretion to modify the interim order pursuant to Rule 60(b)(4).

4. Adequate Protection

The final argument Abbey National has raised in support of its motion is that its interests in the collateral are not adequately protected. Specifically, Abbey National contends that the pre-petition receivables in which Abbey National has an interest are being depleted at a rate of Ten Million Dollars ($10,000,000.00) per day, and that the receivables will be entirely consumed in short order. Additionally, Abbey National asserts that the interim order diminished the value of Abbey National's liens. We shall treat this line of argument as one arising under Rule 60(b)(6).

Abbey National's contentions that its interest is not adequately protected can be boiled down to a simple issue. Prior to the filing of Debtor's petition, the outstanding balance on Abbey National's loan to Sales Finance was approximately Two Hundred Twenty-Four Million Eight Hundred Thousand Dollars ($224,800,000.00). This loan to Sales Finance was secured by the receivables transferred to Sales Finance, and this financing arrangement was rated AAA by Standard & Poors. However, the terms of the interim order have altered the nature of Abbey National's liens. Under the terms of the interim order, Abbey National and the other secured lenders have been granted liens on Debtor's post-petition inventory and receivables. Abbey National's loan is thus now secured by inventory and assets which do not have a AAA rating, and Abbey National must now share its liens with Debtor's other secured lenders.

We find Abbey National's arguments to be not well taken. First, we find Abbey National's contention that its collateral is being consumed at a rate of Ten Million Dollars ($10,000,000.00) per day to be disingenuous. It is true that the pre-petition receivables are being used by Debtor to purchase and manufacture more steel. However, Debtor's use of the pre-petition receivables will inevitably lead to an increase in the value of post-petition receivables and inventory, in which Abbey National has a security interest.

This conclusion is amply supported by the affidavit of John T. Delmore, Debtor's Assistant Controller. Mr. Delmore's affidavit indicates that as of January 15, 2001, there was a sufficient equity cushion in both post-petition inventory and receivables to provide adequate protection to all of Debtor's secured lenders. The amount of the respective equity cushions equaled 39% for the receivables lenders and 179% for the inventory lenders. Furthermore, it appears that Debtor's business will continue to generate additional post-petition receivables and inventory sufficient to protect Abbey National's interest in the near future. Because we find that Abbey National's interest in cash collateral is adequately protected by an equity cushion and by the other terms of the interim order, the Court declines to exercise its discretion to modify the interim order pursuant to Rule 60(b)(6).

Conclusion

For the reasons stated above, the Court concludes that Abbey National's motion seeking to modify the Court's interim order permitting the use of cash collateral on December 29, 2000 is properly characterized as a motion seeking relief from judgment pursuant to Fed. R. Civ. P. 60(b). Furthermore, the Court finds that Abbey National has failed to establish that modification of the interim order is warranted. Accordingly, Abbey National's emergency motion is overruled.

An appropriate order shall enter.

NOTE

Asset-backed securities facilitation acts respond to concerns about the legal foundations of the multi-trillion dollar securitization industry, especially following *In re LTV Steel Company, Inc.* Lawmakers worried that the securitization market would collapse if courts were to find that assets assigned to collateralize securities are not the property of the issuer under the true-sale doctrine. ABS statutes attempt to override this possibility; they sanction an ownership interest in receivables despite the substantive scope of legal rights and obligations of the parties. Delaware's ABS statute, for example, provides that "any property, assets or rights purported to be transferred, in whole or in part, in . . . securitization transactions shall be deemed to no longer be the property, assets or rights of the transferor."[1]

Taking a slightly different approach, Texas has enacted a non-uniform section 9–109(e), which provides that "in the absence of fraud or intentional misrepresentation, the parties' characterization of a transaction as a sale of [accounts, chattel paper, payment intangibles, or promissory notes] shall be conclusive that the transaction is a sale and is not a secured transaction and that title, legal and equitable, has passed to the party characterized as the purchaser of those assets regardless of whether the secured party has any recourse against the debtor, whether the debtor is entitled to any surplus, or any other term of the parties' agreement."[2]

Considering what you learned from *In re LTV Steel,* if you were a state legislator would you support the enactment of an ABS statute? Why or why not? If you support enacting an ABS statute, would you support a free-standing act (like Delaware) or non-uniform provisions of Article 9 (like Texas)? The effect of these statutes is not entirely clear. Can you speculate as to why?

Years before the enactment of ABS statutes, the Tenth Circuit attempted a different formalistic approach to characterizing sales and loans using UCC Article 9. Under section 9–318(b), a purchaser of accounts or chattel paper that fails to perfect its interest is essentially treated as an unsecured creditor with respect to the debtor's other creditors and purchasers. Section 9–318 has an interesting derivation. In 1993, the Court of Appeals for the Tenth Circuit decided *Octagon Gas Systems, Inc. v. Rimmer*, 995 F.2d 948 (10th Cir. 1993). In *Octagon Gas*, the debtor ("Poll") operated a natural gas gathering system. An individual ("Rimmer") purchased something called an "overriding royalty interest" in the funds Poll collected from selling natural gas to third parties. In other words, Rimmer held an interest in Poll's accounts. After Poll filed for bankruptcy, it sold the system, which ultimately ended up in the hands of Octagon Gas Systems, Inc. ("Octagon"). Thereafter, Rimmer asserted his interest in the system, which Octagon disclaimed.

The bankruptcy court concluded that Rimmer's interest survived the sale because he "owned" the interest in question. The Tenth Circuit, however, disagreed in terms that sent shockwaves through the securitization industry. Specifically, the court held that "because, under Article 9, a sale of accounts is treated as if it creates a security interest in the accounts, accounts sold by a debtor prior to filing for bankruptcy remain property of the debtor's bankruptcy estate." In other words, a debtor's sale of an account, prior to filing for bankruptcy, does not necessarily place that account beyond the reach of the bankruptcy trustee.

---

[1] DEL. CODE ANN. tit. 6, §§ 2701A–2703A.

[2] TEX. BUS. & COM. CODE ANN. § 9–109(e) (West 2015).

The decision produced an angry Permanent Editorial Board commentary (PEB 14) almost overnight, and ultimately resulted in the inclusion of section 9–318 in revised Article 9. PEB 14 states as follows:

PEB COMMENTARY NO. 14

SECTION 9–102(1)(b) [Section 9–109 of revised Article 9]

ISSUE

Does the application of Article 9 to the sale of accounts and chattel paper prevent the transfer of ownership of accounts or chattel paper?

DISCUSSION

Section 9–102(1)(b) [section 9–109(a)(3) of revised Article 9] provides, subject to certain exceptions, that Article 9 applies "to any sale of accounts or chattel paper." Comment 2 to 9–102 explains that "a sale of [accounts or chattel paper is] covered by subsection (1)(b) whether intended for security or not . . . . The buyer then is treated as a secured party, and his interest as a security interest." This Commentary examines whether that application means that ownership of receivables may not be transferred or that a buyer's interest in receivables is limited to one of security.

It is a fundamental principle of law that an owner of property may transfer ownership to another person. Were a statute intended to take away that right, it would do so explicitly and such a significant curtailment of rights would be supported by substantial reason. No such reason is expressed or implied in the Code or the Official Comments. Indeed, the sale of receivables long antedates adoption of the Code, and it cannot be supposed that either the drafters of the Code or the legislatures that enacted it intended to work so drastic a change in existing law without clearly saying so. Moreover, a close reading of the text of Article 9 and its Comments, particularly in the context of the pre-Code history, compels the conclusion that Article 9 does not prevent the transfer of ownership.

Article 9 contemplates that sales of receivables may exist, and that the consequences of a sale differ from those of a transfer for security. For example, 9–502(2) [9–608] recognizes a distinction in the consequences under Article 9 between sales of receivables and transactions secured by receivables. It provides that, "[i]f the security agreement secures an indebtedness, the secured party must account to the debtor for any surplus . . . . But, if the underlying transaction was a sale of accounts or chattel paper, the debtor [as seller of the receivables] is entitled to any surplus [from collections of the sold receivables] . . . *only if* the security agreement so provides." (Emphasis added.) Section 9–504(2) [9–615(e)] has virtually identical language. Furthermore, Comment 4 to 9–502 [9–109 cmt. 4], after acknowledging that "there may be a true sale of accounts or chattel paper," clarifies that "[t]he determination whether a particular assignment constitutes a sale or a transfer for security is left to the courts."

Why, then, was Article 9 made "applicable" to the sale of receivables? The introductory Comment and Comment 2 to 9–102 [9–109 cmt. 4] explain that Article 9 applies to both sales and security transfers of receivables to avoid the need to distinguish between such transfers for Article 9 purposes: "[C]ertain sales of accounts and chattel paper are brought within this Article [9] to avoid difficult problems of distinguishing between transactions intended for security and those not so intended." * * *

2. * * *

Commercial financing on the basis of accounts and chattel paper is often so conducted that the distinction between a security transfer and a sale is blurred, and a sale of such property is therefore covered by subsection (1)(b) whether intended for security or not. . . .

The reason for subjecting both sales and secured transactions to Article 9 was to inform third parties of existing interests in a debtor's receivables and to provide protection for all types of assignments of receivables:

> There was an obvious reason for the inclusion of sales: it was necessary to *protect* [transferees] not only [in] straight accounts receivable financing but also [in] arrangements of the factoring type. [Emphasis added.] Article 9 merely follows the pre-Code accounts receivable statutes [covering sales of accounts and chattel paper as well as security transfers].

This is not to say, however, that Article 9 has no impact upon a buyer's ownership rights regarding the purchased receivables. For example, a failure to perfect as required by Article 9 may leave the transferee's ownership of the receivables subject to the claims of third parties, such as the seller's lien creditors or trustee in bankruptcy. This perfection requirement, however, does not by its terms or by implication affect the transfer of ownership as between the seller and buyer.

At least two Circuit Court opinions interpret the Code consistently with this Commentary. In *Major's Furniture Mart v. Castle Credit Corp.* [602 F.2d 538 (3d Cir. 1979)], the Third Circuit considered whether a transfer of a company's receivables should be construed as a sale or a secured loan. By considering that question, the court started from the premise that a transaction that Article 9 calls a security interest could nonetheless be a sale. If the transaction was a sale, the transferee would be entitled to surplus collections of the receivables. If the transaction was only for security, then the transferor would be entitled to the surplus collections. The court followed Comment 4 to 9–502 and looked to non-UCC law to determine whether the transaction was a sale.

In the case of *In re Contractors Equipment Supply Co.* [861 F.2d 241 (9th Cir. 1988)], the Ninth Circuit affirmed a lower court decision by looking to non-UCC law to determine that the transfer of receivables in question was a loan. The court stated that had there been a sale, the transferor would not be entitled to any surplus because "[a] sale entails the passage of title."

In *Octagon Gas Systems, Inc. v. Rimmer*, however, the Tenth Circuit, after stating that a purchased royalty interest in a natural gas system was an account, erroneously stated that "[t]he impact of applying Article 9 to [the buyer's] account is that Article 9's treatment of accounts sold as collateral would place [the buyer's] account within the property of [the seller's] bankruptcy estate." The court reached this determination despite the transfer of the royalty interest purporting to be an outright sale of all the seller's interest. To the extent the court relied on Article 9 in reaching its determination, this Commentary adopts a contrary position.

CONCLUSION

Article 9's application to sales of receivables does not prevent the transfer of ownership. Official Comment 2 to 9–102 [9–318] therefore is amended by adding the following paragraph:

> Neither Section 9–102 nor any other provision of Article 9 is intended to prevent the transfer of ownership of accounts or chattel paper. The determination of whether a particular transfer of accounts or chattel paper constitutes a sale or a transfer for security purposes (such as in connection with a loan) is not governed by Article 9. Article 9 applies both to sales of accounts or chattel paper and loans secured by accounts or chattel paper primarily to incorporate Article 9's perfection rules. The use of terminology such as "security interest" to include the interest of a buyer of accounts or chattel paper, "secured party" to include a buyer of accounts or chattel paper, "debtor" to include a seller of accounts or chattel paper, and "collateral" to include accounts or chattel paper that have been sold is intended solely as a drafting technique to achieve this end and is not relevant to the sale or secured transaction determination. * * *

§ 4. CHATTEL PAPER

An interest in chattel paper may be perfected by filing, by possession (of tangible chattel paper), or by control (of electronic chattel paper). As discussed above, priority of interests is generally first-in-time, first-in-right under section 9–322, unless a creditor enjoys later-in-time priority under section 9–324 as a purchase money security interest holder. Article 9 also deviates from the first-in-time approach to priorities, however, in contexts where secured parties may perfect by possession or control. The statute enables "non-temporal priority," awarding priority to secured parties with interests perfected by control or possession, in advance of those perfected by filing, regardless of timing.

BUYERS OF CHATTEL PAPER AND THE LIKE

Section 9–330 governs the priority rights of most buyers of chattel paper. The classic case that section 9–330 addresses involves a competition between (1) a secured creditor with a floating lien on inventory and a claim to chattel paper arising as proceeds of the inventory, and (2) the interest of a "purchaser" of the same chattel paper. In some cases the inventory lender may have expected the debtor to sell the chattel paper and remit the proceeds from the sale as payment on its secured debt. When the debtor sells the chattel paper but fails to use the proceeds to reduce the inventory loan, the inventory lender and the purchaser of the chattel paper may assert conflicting claims to the same paper. In other cases, the original secured creditor may have lent money against specific items of chattel paper and may therefore assert an even more credible claim against that paper in competition with the purchaser of the paper.

Section 9–330 states rules that allow a buyer of chattel paper to take free of such an earlier claim if the buyer meets a certain set of conditions.

> (a) **[Purchaser's priority: security interest claimed merely as proceeds.]** A purchaser of chattel paper has priority over a security interest in the chattel paper which is claimed merely as proceeds of inventory subject to a security interest if:
>
> > (1) in good faith and in the ordinary course of the purchaser's business, the purchaser gives new value and takes possession of the chattel paper or obtains control of the chattel paper under Section 9–105; and
> >
> > (2) the chattel paper does not indicate that it has been assigned to an identified assignee other than the purchaser.
>
> (b) **[Purchaser's priority: other security interests.]** A purchaser of chattel paper has priority over a security interest in the chattel paper which is claimed other than merely as proceeds of inventory subject to a security interest if the purchaser gives new value and takes possession of the chattel paper or obtains control of the chattel paper under Section 9–105 in good faith, in the ordinary course of the purchaser's business, and without knowledge that the purchase violates the rights of the secured party.

Subsection (a) deals with the case where the original secured creditor claims chattel paper "merely as proceeds"; subsection (b) covers the case where the original secured creditor claims an interest in the paper as something more than just "proceeds." In the latter case, the original secured creditor has loaned money to the debtor somehow in reliance upon the chattel paper. *See* 9–330 cmt. 3. Comment 3 states that the section does not elaborate on the phrase "merely as proceeds"; rather, it directs one to PEB Commentary No. 8: "a lender who agrees to lend up to a specified percentage of the cost of inventory and receivables, has more than a mere proceeds interest in the chattel paper which is a part of the receivables covered by the security agreement." In other words, if the value of the chattel paper was included in the formula to determine the amount of the loan, the Commentary suggests that a person making the loan is asserting a claim greater than a "mere proceeds" claim in the chattel paper and, therefore, is entitled to the greater protection of subsection (b).

Assume an original secured creditor lent principally against inventory. That is, assume its claim to the chattel paper was *merely* a proceeds claim. Under former section 9–308, a buyer took free of the original secured creditor's interest if the buyer gave new value and took possession in the ordinary course of business, even if the buyer knew "the specific paper" was "subject to a security interest." On the other hand, if the claim of the original secured creditor was considered to be something *more than a mere* proceeds claim, the buyer had to act "without knowledge that the specific paper" was "subject to a security interest."

The rules in section 9–330 are similar but different. Under section 9–330(a), the secured creditor beats the buyer of chattel paper if the chattel paper itself "indicate[s] that it has been assigned." Thus, a stamp on chattel paper showing the interest of an assignee-secured creditor will protect the secured creditor even though that creditor has only a proceeds claim. *See* 9–330(f). Unlike former section 9–308, new subsection (a) makes no mention of the knowledge of the buyer. Thus, by subordinating the buyer where there is a legend on the face of the paper, the new law cuts back on the buyer's rights. On the other hand, it expands the buyer's rights by allowing the buyer to take free even if the buyer knows that its purchase may violate the rights of the prior secured creditor. (The only restriction on the buyer's knowledge is the requirement that it act in good faith.)

Subsection 9–330(b) allows a buyer of chattel paper to take free of a prior perfected security interest claimed "other than merely as proceeds" if that buyer meets the usual conditions (new value, possession, ordinary course) and is "without knowledge that the purchase violates the rights of the secured party." The change from the former law (which subordinated the buyer when the buyer had "knowledge that the *specific paper*" was "subject to a security interest") is to conform to what the drafters believed to be the current practice. In comment 6 to section 9–330, the drafters note that it is insufficient to subordinate a purchaser of chattel paper simply because that purchaser has "seen a financing statement covering the chattel paper" (and so knows it is probably subject to a security interest). The comment goes on to state, however, that a purchaser who has seen "a statement in a financing statement to the effect that a purchase . . .would violate the rights of the filed secured party" has the kind of knowledge that would and should subordinate the purchaser. Subsection (f) adds that if "chattel paper . . . indicates that it has been assigned to an identified secured party," this will be conclusive proof of the purchaser's knowledge that its purchase "violates the rights of the secured party." So a legend on the face of the paper protects a secured creditor whether that creditor claims its interest "merely as proceeds" or otherwise. *See also* 9–332 cmt. 4 (contrasting different standards of knowledge under the UCC).

The changes in section 9–330 point in opposite directions. They give safe harbor to the inventory lender who wishes to ensure that no buyer of chattel paper will gain priority. If the inventory lender stamps the chattel paper to show that the paper has been assigned to it, the purchaser's claim is subordinated. *See* 9–330(a) & (f). The changes also expand the rights of a purchaser. First, subsection (b) allows the purchaser to take free of a prior perfected security interest even though the purchaser knows of the existence of a security interest in the particular paper so long as the purchaser does not know that its purchase will "violate" the rights of the prior secured party. Second, subsection (a) omits any reference to the knowledge of the purchaser.

PROBLEM 5-6

Great Bank had a perfected security interest in the inventory and proceeds of a large Arizona mobile home dealership, Raising Arizona ("Raising"). In 2002, Raising sold ten mobile homes on retail installment contracts (security interests with notes) to ten different consumers who took possession of the homes and moved into them in various mobile home parks around Phoenix. Raising then sold all ten of those contracts to Ally, but it did not, as Ally apparently expected, pay the proceeds to Great Bank. Rather, it used the funds to pay other creditors. When Raising went bankrupt, both Ally and Great Bank claimed first rights in the stream of payments that came from the ten purchasers. Ally claims priority over the bank under section 9–330. Great Bank responds with the following arguments, which you have been asked to evaluate:

1. Section 9–330 does not apply in this case because Ally, as it admits, knew of Bank's prior perfected security interest.

2. The rights here are not chattel paper because the dealer never gave the "Certificate of Origin" to Ally (a document the dealer gets from the manufacturer).

3. In one case, no security agreement was signed, and the only document transferred to Ally was a non-negotiable note. As to this transaction, Bank is particularly insistent that section 9–330 does not apply. *See* 9–330(d).

TANGIBLE VERSUS ELECTRONIC CHATTEL PAPER

In the abstract, it is easy to understand the difference between electronic and tangible chattel paper, and correspondingly the appropriate method of perfection that goes with each category (filing or control in the case of electronic chattel paper, filing or possession in the case of the tangible variety). In practice, however, businesses utilize transacting and storage methods that can make this distinction difficult. If a customer signs a printed lease agreement at a car dealer but the dealer then scans the transaction documents and stores them both in physical and digital form, is this chattel paper tangible or electronic? Given the variety of devices for reading, printing, executing, and storing transaction documents, it is prudent to confirm with a debtor exactly how they administer the creation of chattel paper. Only with accurate information in this regard can one determine whether chattel paper is properly classified as electronic or tangible. While electronic chattel paper is prevalent at this point in time, it is crucial not to make assumptions about the chattel paper at issue in any given transaction.

§ 5. ACCOUNTS ARISING FROM MONEY EARNED AND TO BE EARNED BY THE SALE OF GOODS AND THE PERFORMANCE OF SERVICES

There is another universe of "accounts" that is almost completely separate from the conventional business variety described above in the first several sections of this chapter. This is the universe composed of construction contracts, defense production contracts, and the like. Here the buyer of the debtor's goods or services (often a state or local government, or a federal governmental agency, such as the Department of Defense) has an obligation to pay the debtor, which may be a construction company building a road or an airport, or a manufacturing company making aircraft, ammunition, or missiles. Under the 1962 Code, these rights were not "accounts" but were instead "contract rights," as the payments had not yet been earned by performance. Later versions of Article 9 made contract rights a subclass of "accounts."

Notwithstanding that definitional change, it is a mistake to think of the two kinds of accounts as the same. In many ways rights to payment arising under construction and manufacturing contracts are far more precarious than rights to payment consisting of conventional consumer or business accounts. Moreover, the competitors of the secured creditor are likely to be different persons and the threats to the security come from different directions in the two settings.

Note the first significant difference between the two universes. With conventional business accounts, the seller has completed its performance by delivering the goods to the buyer. But where, for example, the loan is made to a debtor construction company doing work for a state or governmental agency, the debtor may not have poured even the first yard of concrete at the time of the loan. Months or even years of work may yet need to be done. Those months and years of work before payment carry with them daily opportunities for the construction company to default, and for the state or governmental agency's assertion of a defense because of that default. Section 9–404(a)(1) instructs that such defenses can normally be asserted (when they arise out of the same contract) by the account debtor not only against the debtor (construction company) but also against the bank that has taken a security interest in the right to payment. For that reason alone, the bank's right in these contract claims is often more precarious than a similar right in a set of payments arising from completed sales.

A second characteristic of the latter universe is that the secured creditor has all or most of its eggs in one basket. If a contractor who has agreed to pave two runways defaults, all payments will stop. In classic accounts, this ending will not typically occur. Even if the debtor has delivered shoddy goods in a number of transactions, the large numbers of accounts may protect the secured creditor, and even a significant number of returns by buyers will not wipe out the security.

A final difficulty relates to bonding companies. With rare exceptions, those who manufacture goods for the federal government, and those who enter into construction contracts for state, local, or federal governmental agencies, must provide bonds to assure their performance and assure payment to those who deal with them on the project (subcontractors and suppliers). Bonding companies are contingent creditors, and when they become actual creditors (upon default of the contractor and payment or performance by the bonding company), they are certain to compete with the bank for any payments owed to the debtor under the broken contract. As the following case will show, these companies typically assert rights outside of Article 9 and their rights are often recognized as superior to a bank's Article 9 rights.

There are two types of bonds protecting different interests. The "payment" bond typically protects the project owner from mechanic's liens and the like by assuring that laborers, subcontractors, and materialmen who contribute work and materials to the job will be paid. The "performance" bond typically assures that the bonding company will hire replacements to complete performance of the bonded contract if the original contractor defaults.

The principal claim of the bonding companies will be subrogation. They will claim this equitable right to money to be paid for performance after default and for money already earned at the time of default that has been held back under the terms of the contract. This latter money is sometimes called a "retainage"; it commonly equals ten to fifteen percent of each payment. That is to say, owners of projects typically make "progress payments" to contractors—payments at various stages of the project as work is completed. The owner, however, will typically pay only 85 to 90 percent of the amounts due as progress payments and will hold back ten to fifteen percent against the possibility that performance has not been done properly and against the possibility that remaining work will not be done properly or at all. Although the bonding companies sometimes take assignments from their debtors of their debtors' rights to payment, usually these companies do not assert claims as assignees or as secured creditors. Frequently a bank or other lender will already have filed a financing statement in the contractor's name before any bond is issued and a later bonding company would be subordinated to that claim in an Article 9 contest. On the other hand, bonding companies frequently win on the equitable battlefield.

To whom are the bonding companies subrogated? (To be "subrogated" to someone is to stand in another's shoes and assert that person's rights.) It depends. To the extent they pay materialmen, subcontractors, and such under their "payment" bond, sureties are subrogated to the rights of those persons. To the extent those persons hold mechanics' liens or other priority claims, they might have priority over everyone else on the job. Obviously a bonding company will also have a right to assert the claims of the defaulted contractor, but—at least as against a secured creditor—those claims would seem to do little or no good because, by hypothesis, the contractor has agreed to make payment to the secured creditor and has granted it security. The bonding company may also be subrogated to the rights of the owner of the particular project (for example, the particular state, local, or federal government involved). If that party would have the right to set off vis-à-vis the bank under section 9–404, then the bonding company would too.

Bonding companies have frequently described themselves as purchase money lenders. They advance money so the project may be completed, so they argue. Without their new money the project would not be completed and—so the argument goes—there would be no asset or security for anyone. Thus, they claim the status of purchase money lenders who routinely enjoy priority over prior creditors. The purchase money analogy goes only so far. The bank often may also claim to be a purchase money lender, for if it had not advanced money, the first mile of concrete would not have been laid, and to the extent the retainage has been earned by the laying of that mile of concrete, the bank will argue it is entitled to the retainage over the rights of the bonding company. Banks are not the only ones the surety can beat. Consider the following case.

AMERICAN STATES INSURANCE CO. V. UNITED STATES

United States District Court, Northern District of Texas, 2005.
324 B.R. 600.

GODBEY, DISTRICT JUDGE:

Before the Court is Appellant American States Insurance Co.'s ("ASIC") appeal from the Bankruptcy Court's Orders of January 13, 2004 and March 8, 2004. Because the Court determines that the Bankruptcy Court failed to give full effect to *Pearlman v. Reliance* and unduly limited a surety's equitable subrogation right under Texas common law, the Court vacates those orders and finds for ASIC.

I. BACKGROUND

On August 28, 2000, Debtor SSEM Corp. ("SSEM") entered into a subcontract with Manhattan Construction Co. ("Manhattan") as general contractor in connection with the City of Dallas Convention Center Expansion and Renovation (the "Project"). ASIC, as surety, issued both performance and payment bonds for the Project on behalf of SSEM and for the benefit of Manhattan. SSEM performed some work on the subcontract and then defaulted.

Pursuant to the subcontract, SSEM was to submit payment applications monthly for work done. The subcontract further provided that Manhattan was not required to pay SSEM in the event of default, and could retain 5% of the amounts earned by SSEM. Apparently pursuant to those two provisions, Manhattan withheld approximately $88,631.73 (the "Withheld Balances"). Following SSEM's default, ASIC as surety paid $430,806.66 to complete SSEM's work on the Project.

On April 11, 2003, SSEM filed a voluntary petition for relief under Chapter 11 of the Bankruptcy Code, which was converted to a Chapter 7 case. One of SSEM's significant creditors was the Internal Revenue Service ("IRS"), which had filed a pre-petition lien against SSEM for unpaid payroll taxes exceeding $500,000. On August 7, 2003, the United States, on behalf of the IRS, filed a motion for relief from automatic stay, claiming that the Withheld Balances were property of the SSEM estate, and that the IRS had a priority claim on the Withheld Balances due to its pre-petition liens. ASIC disagreed with the IRS's motion and filed its own motion for relief from automatic stay on August 12, 2003, arguing that it was entitled to the Withheld Balances under its equitable subrogation rights and that the Withheld Balances were never earned by SSEM and thus never became part of the estate. The Trustee opposed the IRS's motion on the basis that the IRS tax lien may be subordinated to other claims under Section 724 of the Bankruptcy Code.

On January 13, 2004, the Bankruptcy Court entered its thoughtful and scholarly order (the "Order") denying both motions * * *

II. THE NATURE OF SSEM'S INTEREST

* * *

The subcontract was for a face amount of $1,290,000. SSEM was to make applications for payment monthly for work performed during the month. Subject to a variety of conditions, SSEM would eventually receive payment for each application. Payment for each approved application, however, was subject to five percent (5%) retainage. Finally, the subcontract provides: "Notwithstanding any provision of the Subcontract to the contrary, Manhattan is not obligated to make any payment to [SSEM] under the Subcontract if any one or more of the following conditions exists: (a) Subcontractor . . . otherwise is in default under the Subcontract or the Contract Documents."

* * *

[When a debtor commences a bankruptcy case, a bankruptcy estate is formed by operation of law.] Property of the estate includes "all legal or equitable interests of the debtor in property as of the commencement of the case." 11 U.S.C. 541(a)(1). Thus, it would appear that retainage and earned but unpaid balances would become property of SSEM's [bankruptcy] estate absent any intervening factors.

III. *PEARLMAN* SURVIVES THE BANKRUPTCY CODE

The Court now turns to *Pearlman v. Reliance Ins. Co.*, 371 U.S. 132, 83 S.Ct. 232, 9 L.Ed.2d 190 (1962). That case, decided under the Bankruptcy Act, considered whether a surety or trustee had the right to retainage held by the United States as owner, when the contractor failed to pay suppliers and subcontractors and the [surety] had to make those payments. The Court initially noted:

> Property interests in a fund not owned by a bankrupt at the time of adjudication, whether complete or partial, legal or equitable, mortgages, liens, or simple priority of rights, are of course not a part of the bankrupt's property and do not vest in the trustee. The Bankruptcy Act simply does not authorize a trustee to distribute other people's property among a bankrupt's creditors. So here if the surety at the time of adjudication was, as it claimed, either the outright legal or equitable owner of this fund, or had an equitable [lien] or prior right to it, this property interest of the surety never became a part of the bankruptcy estate to be administered, liquidated, and distributed to general creditors of the bankrupt.

Id. at 135–36, 83 S.Ct. 232 (footnote omitted). The Court then proceeded to analyze the equitable subrogation rights of a surety under common law, and concluded:

> We therefore hold in accord with the established legal principles stated above that the Government [owner] had a right to use the retained fund to pay laborers and materialmen; that the laborers and materialmen had a right to be paid out of the fund; that the contractor, had he completed his job and paid his laborers and materialmen, would have become entitled to the fund; and that the surety, having paid the laborers and materialmen, is entitled to the benefit of all these rights to the extent necessary to reimburse it. Consequently, since the surety in this case has paid out more than the amount of the existing fund, it has a right to all of it.

Id. at 141–42. *Pearlman* thus holds that a surety's equitable subrogation rights can prevent retainage from becoming part of the bankruptcy estate, at least under the Bankruptcy Act. The next two questions are whether the Bankruptcy Code changes the result of *Pearlman*, and whether the rights of a surety under Texas law are different from the common law rights that drove the result in *Pearlman.*

* * *

This Court concurs with the clear majority trend and holds that *Pearlman* survives the enactment of the Bankruptcy Code in its entirety * * *

Under *Pearlman*, the label placed on the surety's equitable subrogation interest was not important; the outcome did not turn on whether that interest was characterized as a lien or an ownership interest. *See Pearlman*, 371 U.S. at 136, 83 S.Ct. 232 ("if the surety . . . was . . . *either* the outright legal or equitable owner of this fund, or had an equitable lien or prior right to it, this property interest of the surety never became a part of the bankruptcy estate . . .") (emphasis added). The point was that under common law principles of equitable subrogation, the surety's interest prevented the res from becom[ing] property of the bankruptcy estate. Application of that same principle here leads to the same result: ASIC's interest in the Withheld Balances prevents those balances from becom[ing] part of SSEM's bankruptcy estate. * * *

IV. A SURETY'S EQUITABLE SUBROGATION RIGHT IS NOT A CLAIM

* * *Texas case law regarding the nature of a surety's equitable subrogation interest indicates that it is *not* simply a claim. In *Interfirst Bank Dallas, N.A. v. U.S. Fid. and Guar. Co.*, 774 S.W.2d 391 (Tex.App.-Dallas 1989, writ den.), the court considered whether a surety's subrogation rights were security interests under Article 9 of the UCC. The Court held they were not a lien:

> Although there is some minor difference of opinion on this legal issue, the majority rule clearly appears to be the one which was

> sanctioned by Justice Robert Braucher in his definitive analysis of the subject in *Canter v. Schlager*, 358 Mass. 789, 267 N.E.2d 492 (1971). According to Justice Braucher's analysis, a surety's subrogation rights are not security interests within the purview of Article Nine. This being the case, the promulgation of the UCC and the enactment of its progeny (such as the Texas Business and Commerce Code) do not adversely affect the pre-Code subrogation rights traditionally afforded to sureties. Further, it necessarily follows from Braucher's analysis that a surety's right to equitable subrogation is not adversely affected by the lack of perfection of lien claimants' rights if the surety is obliged to satisfy all lienable claims of laborers and materialmen, whether perfected or not.
>
> The overwhelming and essentially unanimous post-UCC decisions have held that the interest of a surety, such as USF & G, continues to be superior to the claim of a contract assignee, such as Bank. * * *

By the same logic, a surety's equitable subrogation interest is not a claim and takes precedence over mere claim interests.

Other Texas cases have acknowledged that one purpose of retainage is that "[i]t supplies a salvage fund for the contractor's surety in the event it makes good on defaults for which it is bound." *Corpus Christi Bank and Trust v. Smith*, 525 S.W.2d 501, 505 (Tex.1975). *Accord Economy Forms Corp. v. Williams Bros. Constr. Co.*, 754 S.W.2d 451, 457 (Tex.App.-Houston [14th Dist.] 1988, no writ) ("The fact that these funds were retained by the general contractor rather than the property owner does not change the beneficiary or the purpose. . . . (3) the retainage provides salvage funds for its surety if the surety makes good on defaults for which it is bound; . . . .").

* * * [U]nder Texas common law ASIC's equitable subrogation interest is greater than a lien; ASIC has an equitable ownership interest in the "salvage fund" to the extent of its completion costs. Thus, regardless whether or not *Pearlman* alone is sufficient to keep the Withheld Balances out of SSEM's estate, ASIC is still entitled to the Withheld Balances. Because the Withheld Balances never enter SSEM's estate, the IRS's priority is immaterial.

* * *

[footnotes omitted]

§ 6. COLLECTION RIGHTS

The beauty of receivables is that they turn into money even if the secured creditor takes no action. In the case of "notification" lending, where the secured party has notified the account debtors and they are making payment directly to the secured party, it is possible that default by the debtor will be inconsequential as the account debtors will continue to make payments and those payments will go to reduce the recourse or nonrecourse loan that the creditor has made to the debtor. In modern practice notification lending is unusual; in many cases the debtor, as agent of the buyer of the debtor's accounts, will continue to collect payments from the account debtor after it has sold the rights. Even if the debtor is merely the agent for the secured creditor, in practice it will have the power to control the payments and perhaps even to assert the rights suggested in Problem 5–5 above (where the debtor in possession asserted the right to hold the payments for a period of time and to use that money in the bankruptcy estate).

Section 9–607 gives the secured creditor the right to notify the account debtors and to collect payments from them and to go against the account debtors if necessary. It reads in full as follows:

> (a) **[Collection and enforcement generally.]** If so agreed, and in any event after default, a secured party:
>
> > (1) may notify an account debtor or other person obligated on collateral to make payment or otherwise render performance to or for the benefit of the secured party;
> >
> > (2) may take any proceeds to which the secured party is entitled under Section 9–315;
> >
> > (3) may enforce the obligations of an account debtor or other person obligated on collateral and exercise the rights of the debtor with respect to the obligation of the account debtor or other person obligated on collateral to make payment or otherwise render performance to the debtor, and with respect to any property that secures the obligations of the account debtor or other person obligated on the collateral;
> >
> > (4) if it holds a security interest in a deposit account perfected by control under Section 9–104(a)(1), may apply the balance of the deposit account to the obligation secured by the deposit account; and
> >
> > (5) if it holds a security interest in a deposit account perfected by control under Section 9–104(a)(2) or (3), may instruct the bank to pay the balance of the deposit account to or for the benefit of the secured party.
>
> (b) **[Nonjudicial enforcement of mortgage.]** If necessary to enable a secured party to exercise under subsection (a)(3) the right of a debtor to enforce a mortgage nonjudicially, the secured party may record in the office in which a record of the mortgage is recorded:

(1) a copy of the security agreement that creates or provides for a security interest in the obligation secured by the mortgage; and

(2) the secured party's sworn affidavit in recordable form stating that:

(A) a default has occurred with respect to the obligation secured by the mortgage; and

(B) the secured party is entitled to enforce the mortgage nonjudicially.

(c) **[Commercially reasonable collection and enforcement.]** A secured party shall proceed in a commercially reasonable manner if the secured party:

(1) undertakes to collect from or enforce an obligation of an account debtor or other person obligated on collateral; and

(2) is entitled to charge back uncollected collateral or otherwise to full or limited recourse against the debtor or a secondary obligor.

(d) **[Expenses of collection and enforcement.]** A secured party may deduct from the collections made pursuant to subsection (c) reasonable expenses of collection and enforcement, including reasonable attorney's fees and legal expenses incurred by the secured party.

(e) **[Duties to secured party not affected.]** This section does not determine whether an account debtor, bank, or other person obligated on collateral owes a duty to a secured party.

Suppose you are an account debtor who owes $100,000 to Distributor for an expensive machine that you bought. Suppose you are obligated to pay Distributor $10,000 per month until the debt is paid. Suppose further that Distributer has granted a security interest in your account to Bank to secure a line of credit. You have been making your monthly payments to Distributor, but now receive a letter from Bank instructing you to send your payments to a P.O. Box in Akron. Do you comply? If you continue paying Distributor notwithstanding receipt of Bank's letter, is there a risk you may have to pay twice? Can you ask Bank for proof of its interest? Take a look at section 9–406. *See also* 9–209.

PROBLEM 5-7

1. Assume the state of Florida enters into a $20 million contract with Contractor to construct a highway. Contractor grants a security interest in its right to payment to Bank. Ultimately Contractor breaches the contract and the state of Florida refuses to pay under section 9–404. Clearly Bank loses. Would

the outcome be different if the state of Florida refused to pay not because of the breach of the highway construction contract but because it had recently discovered defective performance in an earlier contract and suffered $2 million of damages on that contract which it now proposes to set off against its obligation to pay on the second contract that has been assigned to Bank? To answer that question, what do you need to know under section 9–404(a)(2)?

2. Assume General Motors Corporation owes $100,000 to Missouri Car Dealer for bonuses and other payments on cars that Dealer has sold and that Ally, a finance company that finances consumers' purchases of GM cars, owns Dealer's premises and has leased those premises to Dealer. Dealer is now in bankruptcy and is behind approximately $20,000 on its rent to Ally. The contract between General Motors and Dealer provides that General Motors may set off against the amount Dealer owes to it (General Motors) or to Ally. Bank has taken a security interest from Dealer in the payments owed by General Motors to Dealer. When Dealer defaults and goes into bankruptcy, Bank claims a first right on the $100,000 due from General Motors. General Motors claims the right to set off. What are the best arguments for each? Hint: take a look at section 553 of the Bankruptcy Code.

PROBLEM 5-8

Trust buys $100 million of Debtor's credit card accounts but allows Debtor to continue to collect the receivables. Trust properly perfects by filing. When Debtor (seller) files under Chapter 11, it holds back three months of payments and threatens to hold back even more.

The investors' committee (composed of the largest buyers of these receivables) now threatens to sue the Trustee, the Trust's legal counsel, and the Trust's advisor, Merrill Lynch.

The committee claims:

1. The defendants should have procured promises from Debtor that it would not file for bankruptcy.

2. The defendants should not have allowed Debtor to continue collecting the receivables.

3. Upon the filing under Chapter 11, the defendants should have given the section 9–607 notice at once and started direct collections.

How should the defendants respond?

PROBLEM 5-9

If an assignee or buyer of receivables commences direct collection from account debtors, what duty does it owe to the original debtor? If, for example, the assignee or buyer took $200,000 in settlement of $1 million face amount of accounts, is it liable to the original debtor for making such a generous compromise? (Assume alternatively the assignment was with or without recourse.)

§ 7. SECURITY INTERESTS IN GENERAL INTANGIBLES—INTANGIBLES OTHER THAN RIGHTS TO PAYMENT

The most important general intangibles in which a creditor will take a security interest are (i) copyrights, patents, and trademarks; (ii) membership interests in limited liability companies and partnership interests in partnerships; and (iii) digital assets that do not fall within other Article 9 categories of collateral.

The perfection of security interests in intellectual property is complicated by the presence of federal statutes governing copyrights, patents, and trademarks. These statutes seem to stand above and to displace, to varying degrees, the Article 9 system for the perfection of security interests in general intangibles. As a result, the current state of the law regarding security interests in copyrights, patents, and trademarks is unsettled. In particular, there is uncertainty as to where and how to file, what constitutes notice of a security interest, who has priority, and what collateral is covered by a security interest.

The primary issue surrounding security interests in copyrights, patents, and trademarks is whether such interests must be perfected by a filing in the appropriate state office, in the appropriate federal office, or both. In general, Article 9 governs perfection of all security interests regardless of the form of the transaction or the intent of the parties. Further, under Article 9, a security interest in "general intangibles," including copyrights, patents, and trademarks, must be perfected by filing a financing statement in the appropriate state office. But according to section 9–109(c), Article 9 does not apply "to the extent that . . . a statute, regulation, or treaty of the United States" preempts the Code. *See also* 9–311(a)(1). A prior version of the UCC Official Comments listed the Copyright Act as a prime example of a regulation that preempts the Code's filing requirements. The new commentary is more equivocal. *See* 9–109 cmt. 8.

COPYRIGHTS

The Copyright Act has the most comprehensive scheme for recording of assignments of all the federal intellectual property statutes. Under section 101 of the Copyright Act, a "transfer of copyright ownership" includes "assignment, mortgage, exclusive license, or any other conveyance, alienation, or hypothecation of a copyright." Consider the following case.

IN RE WORLD AUXILIARY POWER COMPANY

United States Court of Appeals for the Ninth Circuit, 2002.
303 F.3d 1120.

KLEINFELD, CIRCUIT JUDGE:

In this case we decide whether federal or state law governs priority of security interests in unregistered copyrights.

FACTS

Basically, this is a bankruptcy contest over unregistered copyrights between a bank that got a security interest in the copyrights from the owners and perfected it under state law, and a company that bought the copyrights from the bankruptcy trustees after the copyright owners went bankrupt. These simple facts are all that matters to the outcome of this case, although the details are complex.

Three affiliated California corporations—World Auxiliary Power, World Aerotechnology, and Air Refrigeration Systems—designed and sold products for modifying airplanes. The FAA must approve modifications of civilian aircraft by issuing "Supplemental Type Certificates." The three companies owned copyrights in the drawings, technical manuals, blueprints, and computer software used to make the modifications. Some of these copyrighted materials were attached to the Supplemental Type Certificates. The companies did not register their copyrights with the United States Copyright Office.

The companies got financing from Silicon Valley Bank, one of the appellees in this case. Two of the companies borrowed the money directly, the third guaranteed the loan. The security agreement, as is common, granted the bank a security interest in a broad array of presently owned and after-acquired collateral. The security agreement covered "all goods and equipment now owned or hereafter acquired," as well as inventory, contract rights, general intangibles, blueprints, drawings, computer programs, accounts receivable, patents, cash, bank deposits, and pretty much anything else the debtor owned or might be "hereafter acquired." The security agreement and financing statement also covered "[a]ll copyright rights, copyright applications, copyright registrations, and like protections in each work of authorship and derivative work thereof, whether published or unpublished, now owned or hereafter acquired."

The bank perfected its security interest in the collateral, including the copyrights, pursuant to California's version of Article 9 of the Uniform Commercial Code,[3] by filing UCC–1 financing statements with the

[3] *See* Cal. Comm.Code §§ 9101 et seq. (1990). Although California adopted the revised Article 9 of the Uniform Commercial Code, effective July 1, 2001, *see id.* §§ 9101 *et seq.* (2002), the revised statute "does not affect an action, case, or proceeding commenced before July 1, 2001," *id.* § 9702(c) (2002). As this litigation was pending on that date, we apply the former Article 9.

California Secretary of State. The bank also took possession of the Supplemental Type Certificates and the attached copyrighted materials. But the copyrights still weren't registered with the United States Copyright Office, and the bank did not record any document showing the transfer of a security interest with the Copyright Office.

Subsequently, the three debtor companies filed simultaneous but separate bankruptcy proceedings. Their copyrights were among their major assets. [The bankruptcy trustees for the three debtors sold the debtors' interests in the copyrights to Aerocon, who also purchased the trustees' rights to avoid Silicon Valley Bank's security interest.]

* * *

Meanwhile, Silicon Valley Bank won relief from the bankruptcy court's automatic stay and, based on its security interest, foreclosed on the copyrights. Then the bank sold the copyrights to Advanced Aerospace * * * which then sold the copyrights to Airweld. [As a result, Airweld and Aerocon held competing interests in the copyrights, with Airweld holding the bank's interest.]

* * *

Aerocon brought an adversary proceeding [in the bankruptcy court to avoid Silicon Valley Bank's security interest, now held by Airweld, and to recover the copyrights or their value. The bankruptcy court granted summary judgment against Aerocon, holding that the bank had a perfected security interest in the copyrights. On appeal, the district court affirmed.] * * * Aerocon appeals from the district court's order.

ANALYSIS

* * *

Copyright and bankruptcy law set the context for this litigation, but the legal issue is priority of security interests. The bankruptcy trustees sold Aerocon their power to avoid any security interest "that is voidable by a creditor that extends credit to the debtor at the time of the commencement of the case, and that obtains, at such time and with respect to such credit, a judicial lien. . . ." Under this "strong-arm" provision, Aerocon has the status of an "ideal creditor" who perfected his lien at the last possible moment before the bankruptcy commenced, and if this hypothetical creditor would take priority over Silicon Valley Bank's lien, then Aerocon may avoid the bank's security interest.

Whether Aerocon's hypothetical lien creditor would take priority turns on whether federal or state law governs the perfection of security interests in unregistered copyrights. The bank did everything necessary to perfect its security interest under state law, so if state law governs, the bank has priority and wins. The bank did nothing, however, to perfect its interest under federal law, so if federal law governs, Aerocon's hypothetical lien creditor arguably has priority, although the parties dispute whether Aerocon might face additional legal hurdles.

We are assisted in deciding this case by two opinions, neither of which controls, but both of which are thoughtful and scholarly. The first is the bankruptcy court's published opinion in this case, *Aerocon Engineering Inc. v. Silicon Valley Bank (In re World Auxiliary Power Co.)*, [244 B.R. 149 (Bankr. N.D. Cal. 1999)] which we affirm largely for the reasons the bankruptcy judge gave. The second is a published district court opinion, *National Peregrine, Inc. v. Capitol Federal Savings & Loan Association (In re Peregrine Entertainment, Ltd.)*, [116 B.R. 194 (C.D. Cal. 1990)] the holdings of which we adopt but, like the bankruptcy court, distinguish and limit.

Our analysis begins with the Copyright Act of 1976[, 17 U.S.C. § 101 *et seq.*]. Under the Act, "copyright protection subsists . . . . in original works of authorship fixed in any tangible medium of expression. . . ." [*Id.* § 102(a).] While an owner must register his copyright as a condition of seeking certain infringement remedies, [*id.* §§ 411(a), 412,] registration is permissive, not mandatory, and is not a condition for copyright protection. [*Id.* § 408(a)]. Likewise, the Copyright Act's provision for recording "transfers of copyright ownership" [*id.* §§ 101, 205(a)] (the Act's term that includes security interests) is permissive, not mandatory: "Any transfer of copyright ownership or other document pertaining to copyright **may** be recorded in the Copyright Office. . ." [*Id.* § 205(a) (emphasis added).] The Copyright Act's use of the word "mortgage" as one definition of a "transfer" is properly read to include security interests under Article 9 of the Uniform Commercial Code.[27]

Under the Copyright Act,

> [a]s between two conflicting transfers, the one executed first prevails if it is recorded, **in the manner required to give constructive notice** . . . within one month after its execution . . . or at any time before recordation . . . of the later transfer. Otherwise the later transfer prevails if recorded first in such manner, and if taken in good faith, for valuable consideration . . . and without notice of the earlier transfer. [17 U.S.C. § 205(d) (emphasis added).]

[27] *See* Grant Gilmore, 1 *Security Interests in Personal Property* § 13.3, at 415 (1965) ("The phrase 'may be mortgaged' in [the Copyright Act of 1909] should be read as equivalent to 'may be transferred for security.' . . . A copyright would not in any case seem to be within the category of intangible property which can be pledged; under Article 9 of the [Uniform Commercial] Code it would be a 'general intangible.' "). *See also In re Cybernetic Services, Inc.*, 252 F.3d 1039, 1056 (9th Cir.2001) ("[T]he Copyright Act, by its terms, governs security interests."); *National Peregrine, Inc.*, 116 B.R. at 199 ("It is clear . . . that an agreement granting a creditor a security interest in a copyright may be recorded in the Copyright Office.").

The phrase "constructive notice" refers to another subsection providing that recording gives constructive notice

> but only if—
>
> (1) the document, or material attached to it, specifically identifies the work to which it pertains so that, after the document is indexed by the Register of Copyrights, it would be revealed by a reasonable search under **the title or registration number** of the work; and
>
> (2) registration has been made for the work. [*Id.* § 205(c) (emphasis added).]

A copyrighted work only gets a "title or registration number" that would be revealed by a search if it's registered. [*See id.* §§ 409, 419(a).] Since an unregistered work doesn't have a title or registration number that would be "revealed by a reasonable search," recording a security interest in an unregistered copyright in the Copyright Office wouldn't give "constructive notice" under the Copyright Act, and, because it wouldn't, it couldn't preserve a creditor's priority. There just isn't any way for a secured creditor to preserve a priority in an unregistered copyright by recording anything in the Copyright Office. And the secured party can't get around this problem by registering the copyright, because the secured party isn't the owner of the copyright, and the Copyright Act states that only "the owner of copyright . . . may obtain registration of the copyright claim. . ." [*Id.* § 408(a).]

Aerocon argues that the Copyright Act's recordation and priority scheme exclusively controls perfection and priority of security interests in copyrights. First, Aerocon argues that state law, here the California U.C.C., by its own terms "steps back" and defers to the federal scheme. Second, whether or not the U.C.C. steps back, Aerocon argues that Congress has preempted the U.C.C. as it applies to copyrights. We address each argument in turn.

A. U.C.C. Step Back Provisions

Article 9 of the Uniform Commercial Code, as adopted in California, provides that unperfected creditors are subordinate to perfected, and as between perfected security interests, the first perfected interest prevails. The bank perfected first under state law by filing a financing statement with the California Secretary of State on existing and after-acquired copyrights. The U.C.C. treats copyrights as "general intangibles." Security interests in general intangibles are properly perfected under the U.C.C. by state filings such as the one made by the bank in this case.

To avoid conflict with the federal law, the U.C.C. has two "step-back provisions," by which state law steps back and out of the way of conflicting federal law. The first, more general "step-back" provision says that Article

9 "does not apply . . . [t]o a security interest subject to any statute of the United States to the extent that such statute governs the rights of parties to and third parties affected by transactions in particular types of property. . . ." [Former section 9–104(a); section 9–109(c) of revised Article 9.] As applied to copyrights, the relevant U.C.C. Official Comment makes it clear that this step-back clause does not exclude all security interests in copyrights from U.C.C. coverage, just those for which the federal Copyright Act "governs the rights" of relevant parties:

> Although the Federal Copyright Act contains provisions permitting the mortgage of a copyright and for the recording of an assignment of a copyright such a statute would not seem to contain sufficient provisions regulating the rights of the parties and third parties to exclude security interests in copyrights from the provisions of this Article. [Comment 1 to former section 9–104(a); *see* comment 8 to section 9–109 of revised Article 9.]

The second step-back provision [former section 9–302(3)(a); section 9–311 of revised Article 9] speaks directly to perfection of security interests. It exempts from U.C.C. filing requirements security interests in property "subject to . . . [a] statute . . . of the United States which provides for a national . . . registration . . . or which specifies a place of filing different from that specified in this division for filing of the security interest." Compliance with such a statute "is equivalent to the filing of a financing statement . . . and a security interest in property subject to the statute . . . can be perfected only by compliance therewith. . . ."

Under the U.C.C.'s two step-back provisions, there can be no question that, when a copyright has been registered, a security interest can be perfected only by recording the transfer in the Copyright Office. As the district court held in *Peregrine,* [116 B.R. at 202–204,] the Copyright Act satisfies the broad U.C.C. step-back provision by creating a priority scheme that "governs the rights of parties to and third parties affected by transactions" in registered copyrights and satisfies the narrow step-back provision by creating a single "national registration" for security interests in registered copyrights. Thus, under these step-back provisions, if a borrower's collateral is a registered copyright, the secured party cannot perfect by filing a financing statement under the U.C.C. in the appropriate state office, or alternatively by recording a transfer in the Copyright Office. For registered copyrights, the only proper place to file is the Copyright Office. We adopt *Peregrine*'s holding to this effect.

However, the question posed by this case is whether the U.C.C. steps back as to unregistered copyrights. We, like the bankruptcy court in this case, conclude that it does not. As we've explained, there's no way for a secured creditor to perfect a security interest in unregistered copyrights by recording in the Copyright Office. The U.C.C.'s broader step-back provision [former section 9–104(a); section 9–109(c) of revised Article 9] says that the U.C.C. doesn't apply to a security interest "to the extent" that a federal statute governs the rights of the parties. The U.C.C. doesn't defer to the Copyright Act under this broad step-back provision because the Copyright Act doesn't provide for the rights of secured parties to unregistered copyrights; it only covers the rights of secured parties in *registered* copyrights. The U.C.C.'s narrow step-back provision [former section 9–302(3)(a); section 9–311 of revised Article 9] says the U.C.C. doesn't apply if a federal statute "provides for a national . . . registration . . . or which specifies a place of filing different from that specified in this division for filing of the security interest." The U.C.C. doesn't defer to the Copyright Act under this narrow step-back provision because the Copyright Act doesn't provide a "national registration": unregistered copyrights don't have to be registered, and because unregistered copyrights don't have a registered name and number, under the Copyright Act there isn't any place to file anything regarding unregistered copyrights that makes any legal difference. So, as a matter of state law, the U.C.C. doesn't step back in deference to federal law, but governs perfection and priority of security interests in unregistered copyrights itself.

B. Federal Preemption

It wouldn't matter that state law doesn't step back, however, if Congress chose to knock state law out of the way by preemption. Federal law preempts state law under three circumstances. The first is "express preemption," where Congress explicitly preempts state law. The second is "field preemption," where Congress implicitly preempts state law by "occupy[ing] the entire field, leaving no room for the operation of state law." The third is "conflict preemption," where we infer preemption because "compliance with both state and federal law would be impossible, or state law stands as an obstacle to the accomplishment and execution of the full purposes and objectives of Congress." We presume that federal law does not preempt "state law in areas traditionally regulated by the States."

Aerocon argues, relying on *Peregrine,* that Congress intended to occupy the field of security interests in copyrights. Aerocon also argues that the U.C.C. actually conflicts with the Copyright Act's text and purpose.

Because Aerocon relies so heavily on *Peregrine* and its progeny, we will briefly review the facts and holding of that case. In *Peregrine,* a bank had secured a loan with the debtor's copyrights in a library of films licensed out for exhibition and related accounts receivable and attempted to perfect its security interest by filing a U.C.C. financing statement. The debtor later filed for bankruptcy and, as debtor-in-possession, sued in the bankruptcy court to avoid the bank's lien on the ground that the bank had failed to perfect its lien by failing to record it with the Copyright Office. The bankruptcy court held for the bank, and the debtor-in-possession appealed to the district court. The district court reversed, holding that "the comprehensive scope of the Copyright Act's recording provisions, along with the unique federal interests they implicate, support the view that federal law preempts state methods of perfecting security interests in copyrights. . . ." The district court reasoned that federal law preempts state law because "the Copyright Act establishes a uniform method for recording security interests in copyrights" and creates a different priority scheme than state law, and because "competing recordation schemes . . . lessen[ ] the utility of each."

Although *Peregrine* did not specify whether the copyrights at issue were registered, it is probably safe to assume that they were, and that the *Peregrine* court did not have a case involving unregistered copyrights, because the collateral at issue was a movie library that got licensed out to exhibitors and, in the ordinary course, copyrights in such films would be registered. Also, as the bankruptcy judge in the case at bar pointed out, *Peregrine*'s "analysis only works if the copyright was registered." The district court in *Peregrine* held that Congress had preempted state law because of "the comprehensive scope of the Copyright Act's recording provisions." As applied to registered copyrights, the Act's recording scheme is comprehensive; it doesn't exclude any registered copyright from its coverage. But as applied to unregistered copyrights, the Act doesn't have comprehensive recording provisions. Likewise, *Peregrine* notes that "[t]o the extent there are competing recordation schemes, this lessens the utility of each." This holds true for registered copyrights. But there aren't two competing filing systems for unregistered copyrights. The Copyright Act doesn't create one. Only the U.C.C. creates a filing system applicable to unregistered copyrights. *Peregrine* reasoned that creditors could get conflicting results under the U.C.C. and the Copyright Act, because each provides a different priority scheme. That's true only for registered copyrights. The Copyright Act wouldn't provide a conflicting answer as to unregistered copyrights because it wouldn't provide any answer at all. *Peregrine*'s holding applies to registered copyrights, and we adopt it, but as the bankruptcy court reasoned in the case at bar, it does not apply to unregistered copyrights.

We accordingly reject two other lower court opinions, *Zenith Productions, Ltd. v. AEG Acquisition Corp.* (*In re AEG Acquisition Corp.*)[, 161 B.R. 50 (9th Cir.BAP 1993), *affirming* 127 B.R. 34 (Bankr.C.D.Cal.1991)] and *In re Avalon Software Inc.*[, 209 B.R. 517 (D.Ariz.1997)] that extended *Peregrine*'s holding to unregistered copyrights. No circuit court has come to that erroneous conclusion. In both cases, the courts held that security interests in unregistered copyrights may not be perfected under the U.C.C.; perfection could be obtained only by registering the copyrights and recording the security interest with the Copyright Office. We reject these opinions because they miss the point made by the bankruptcy judge in this case, and discussed above, that *Peregrine*'s analysis doesn't work if it's applied to security interests in unregistered copyrights. Moreover, such extensions of *Peregrine* to unregistered copyrights would make registration of copyright a necessary prerequisite of perfecting a security interest in a copyright. The implication of requiring registration as a condition of perfection is that Congress intended to make unregistered copyrights practically useless as collateral, an inference the text and purpose of the Copyright Act do not warrant.

In the one instance where the Copyright Act conditions some action concerning a copyright on its registration—the right to sue for infringement—the Act makes that condition explicit. [*See* 17 U.S.C. § 411(a).] Nowhere does the Copyright Act explicitly condition the use of copyrights as collateral on their registration. Second, the Copyright Act contemplates that most copyrights will not be registered. Since copyright is created every time people set pen to paper, or fingers to keyboard, and affix their thoughts in a tangible medium,[*see id.* § 102(a) ("[C]opyright protection subsists . . . in original works of authorship fixed in any tangible medium of expression. . . ."),] writers, artists, computer programmers, and web designers would have to have their hands tied down to keep them from creating unregistered copyrights all day every day. Moreover, the Copyright Act says that copyrights "may" be registered, implying that they don't have to be, and since a fee is charged and time and effort is required, the statute sets up a regime in which most copyrights won't ever be registered.

Though Congress must have contemplated that most copyrights would be unregistered, it only provided for protection of security interests in registered copyrights. There is no reason to infer from Congress's silence as to unregistered copyrights an intent to make such copyrights useless as collateral by preempting state law but not providing any federal priority scheme for unregistered copyrights. That would amount to a presumption in favor of federal preemption, but we are required to presume just the opposite. The only reasonable inference to draw is that Congress chose not to create a federal scheme for security interests in unregistered copyrights, but left the matter to States, which have traditionally governed security interests.

For similar reasons, we reject Aerocon's argument that congressional intent to preempt can be inferred from conflict between the Copyright Act and the U.C.C. There is no conflict between the statutory provisions: the Copyright Act doesn't speak to security interests in unregistered copyrights, the U.C.C. does.

Nor does the application of state law frustrate the objectives of federal copyright law. The basic objective of federal copyright law is to "promote the Progress of Science and useful Arts"[U.S. Constitution, Article 1,

Section 8] by "establishing a marketable right to the use of one's expression" and supplying "the economic incentive to create and disseminate ideas." [*Harper & Row, Publishers v. Nation Enterprises*, 471 U.S. 539, 558 (1985).] Aerocon argues that allowing perfection under state law would frustrate this objective by injecting uncertainty in secured transactions involving copyrights. Aerocon conjures up the image of a double-crossing debtor who, having gotten financing based on unregistered copyrights, registers them, thus triggering federal law, and gets financing from a second creditor, who then records its interest with the Copyright Office and takes priority. We decline to prevent this fraud by drawing the unreasonable inference that Congress intended to render copyrights useless as collateral unless registered.

Prudent creditors will always demand that debtors disclose any copyright registrations and perfect under federal law and will protect themselves against subsequent creditors gaining priority by means of covenants and policing mechanisms. The several *amici* banks and banking association in this case argue that most lenders would lend against unregistered copyrights subject to the remote risk of being "primed" by subsequent creditors; but no lender would lend against unregistered copyrights if they couldn't perfect their security interest. As we read the law, unregistered copyrights have value as collateral, discounted by the remote potential for priming. As Aerocon reads the law, they would have no value at all.

Aerocon's argument also ignores the special problem of copyrights as after-acquired collateral. To use just one example of the multi-industry need to use after-acquired (really after-created) intangible intellectual property as collateral, now that the high-tech boom of the 1990s has passed, and software companies don't attract equity financing like tulips in seventeenth century Holland,[3] these companies will have to borrow more capital. After-acquired software is likely to serve as much of their collateral. Like liens in any other after-acquired collateral, liens in after-acquired software must attach immediately upon the creation of the software to satisfy creditors. Creditors would not tolerate a gap between the software's creation and the registration of the copyright. If software developers had to register copyrights in their software before using it as collateral, the last half hour of the day for a software company would be spent preparing and mailing utterly pointless forms to the Copyright Office to register and record security interests. Our reading of the law "promote[s] the Progress of Science and useful Arts" by preserving the collateral value of unregistered copyrights, which is to say, the vast majority of copyrights. Aerocon's reading of the law—which would force producers engaged in the

---

[3] *See, generally*, Mike Dash, *Tulipomania: The Story of the World's Most Coveted Flower & the Extraordinary Passions It Aroused* (2001).

ongoing creation of copyrightable material to constantly register and update the registrations of their works before obtaining credit—does not.

CONCLUSION

Regarding perfection and priority of security interests in unregistered copyrights, the California U.C.C. has not stepped back in deference to federal law, and federal law has not preempted the U.C.C. Silicon Valley Bank has a perfected security interest in the debtors' unregistered copyrights, and Aerocon, standing in the bankruptcy trustees' shoes, cannot prevail against it.

AFFIRMED.

[some footnotes omitted]

NOTE

The court in *In re Peregrine Entertainment, Ltd.* ruled that the expansive scope of the Copyright Act completely displaced Article 9 for the purposes of perfecting security interests in copyright collateral. The court in *In re World Auxiliary Power Company* limited the holding in *Peregrine*, noting that while the Copyright Act preempts Article 9 for *registered* copyrights, the same is not true for *unregistered* copyrights. For most purposes, a copyright holder enjoys the benefits from the Copyright Act without registering with the Copyright Office; thus, many copyrights are not registered with the Copyright Office. A security interest in unregistered copyrights may be properly perfected under Article 9.

What happens if the secured creditor takes a security interest in the debtor's unregistered copyrights and properly perfects its interest by filing a financing statement with the appropriate secretary of state's office, but the debtor later registers its copyrights? At that point, the secured party would appear to become unperfected, no? What kind of terms might you put in a security agreement to help avoid this problem?

Consider another hypothetical. Suppose Bank takes a security interest in Film Company's registered copyrights and accounts generated from the licensing of films to its customers. Suppose further that Bank neglects to make an appropriate filing with the federal Copyright Office, but properly files a financing statement covering all of Film Company's accounts. Is Bank's security interest in Film Company's accounts also unperfected because of its lapse in neglecting to file in the Copyright Office with respect to the copyrights? The court in *Peregrine* indicated that it would be, stating that the secured creditor's security interests in both the copyrights in question "and the receivables they have generated" were unperfected even though the secured creditor filed a UCC financing statement covering the debtor's accounts. Is this consistent with the analysis in *World Auxiliary*? Does the Copyright Act regulate security interests in accounts? No. Accordingly, *Peregrine* appears to be mistaken on this point. *See Broadcast Music, Inc. v. Hirsch*, 104 F.3d 1163 (9th Cir. 1997).

PATENTS

Section 261 of the Patent Act states that "[a]n assignment, grant or conveyance [of a patent, patent application, or interest therein] shall be void as against any subsequent purchaser . . . unless it is recorded in the Patent and Trademark Office ["PTO"] within three months from its date or prior to the date of such subsequent purchase or mortgage." Apparently, the scope of this provision is limited to transfers that carry full title and ownership rights. A security agreement does not normally transfer title to the creditor. Thus, whenever the debtor retains full ownership rights in the collateral, the security agreement will not qualify as an "assignment, grant or conveyance" for the purposes of section 261. So the federal law does not require a filing with the PTO in order for the creditor to avoid claims made by a later purchaser. Therefore, the perfection of a security interest in a patent and determinations of priority of claims in a patent remain matters of state law under Article 9.

Courts have addressed the rights of a perfected secured creditor with a security interest in a patent as against the trustee in bankruptcy. In the case of *In re Cybernetic Services, Inc.*, 252 F.3d 1039 (9th Cir. 2001), the court held that patent law did not preempt state law governing perfection of security interests in patents. A secured creditor who filed under Article 9 was properly perfected and defeated the trustee. In theory, the perfected secured creditor should receive the same priority as a good faith purchaser or a mortgagee. In practice, the result could be different. In the first case to examine the issue of security interests in patents, the court stated in dicta that a UCC financing statement may not be effective against a good faith purchaser for value or a mortgagee. *In re Transportation Design & Technology, Inc.*, 48 B.R. 635 (Bankr. S.D. Cal. 1985).

TRADEMARKS

Section 1060 of the Lanham Trademark Act provides that "[a]n assignment shall be void against any subsequent purchaser for valuable consideration without notice, unless the prescribed information reporting the assignment is recorded in the [PTO] within 3 months after the date of the assignment or prior to the subsequent purchase." 15 U.S.C. § 1060. The reference to an "assignment" in section 1060 applies only to absolute assignments and not to security interests. Thus, courts have uniformly held that the federal law does not preempt Article 9 for the purposes of perfecting a security interest in trademarks. Consequently, a secured creditor who has filed a financing statement in the applicable state office has properly perfected its interest. A perfected secured creditor will prevail over the trustee in bankruptcy and (probably) a later claimant, even if the later claimant has filed its interest with the PTO. If one accepts that a secured creditor with a perfected interest in a trademark will prevail over a subsequent good faith purchaser, then, a fortiori, the perfected secured creditor will prevail here also. Consider the following case.

TRIMARCHI V. TOGETHER DEVELOPMENT CORP.

United States District Court, D. Massachusetts, 2000.
255 B.R. 606.

GORTON, DISTRICT JUDGE.

Appellants Horace Trimarchi ("Trimarchi") and Personal Dating Services, Inc. ("PDS") appeal the Bankruptcy Court's ruling that Trimarchi does not have a perfected security interest in the "Together" trademark. * * *

I. Background

[Together Development Corp.'s ("TDC's")] business involved selling and servicing various dating services franchises located throughout the United States and Canada. Prior to 1986, Trimarchi owned 25% of the outstanding shares of TDC. In May, 1986, Trimarchi and TDC entered into an agreement pertaining to the repurchase of stock of the corporation ("the Agreement"). In connection with that agreement, TDC executed two separate promissory notes evidencing its obligations to Trimarchi. Both notes were secured by a "Security Agreement/Chattel Mortgage" in TDC's accounts receivable, Trademark, franchise fees and royalties.

In addition to the Security Agreement, TDC assigned to Trimarchi a security interest in TDC's Trademark (Together Dating Service)[,] which is registered under Certificate Number 1,145,365 in the United States Patent Office [ ]along with the goodwill of the business connected with that mark ("the Trademark"). TDC also gave Trimarchi a signed UCC–1 Financing Statement ("UCC–1") governing specifically described collateral, including the "Together" Trademark, Registration No. 1,145,365.

Trimarchi filed the UCC–1 with the United States Patent and Trademark Office ("PTO"), which acknowledged the filing. He did not file the UCC–1 with the Secretary of State of Connecticut, where TDC's principal place of business was then located, or with any other state or town clerk's office.

In November 1997, TDC filed a voluntary petition for reorganization under Chapter 11 of the United States Bankruptcy Code. In 1998, the Bankruptcy Court ordered TDC to sell substantially all of its assets, including the Trademark. Trimarchi objected to the sale of the Trademark, claiming that it was precluded by the earlier "assignment". The Bankruptcy Court overruled the objection and scheduled an evidentiary hearing to adjudicate the validity and perfection of Trimarchi's security interest.

After the hearing, the Bankruptcy Court ruled that Trimarchi's security interest in the Trademark was unperfected because he had failed to file the UCC–1 in the requisite state and local offices. The Bankruptcy Court concluded that Trimarchi was not, therefore, entitled to any lien on the proceeds of the sale of TDC's assets. Trimarchi and PDS appeal the Bankruptcy Court's ruling.

The issue on this appeal is whether the Bankruptcy Court erred, as a matter of law, in holding that a security interest in a trademark may not be perfected solely by the filing of a UCC–1 with the PTO.

II. Discussion

* * *

1. Preemption

It is a well-established principle of law that the Supremacy Clause, U.S. Const., Art. VI, cl. 2, invalidates state laws that "interfere with, or are contrary to," federal law. The United States Supreme Court has held that, under the Supremacy Clause, federal law supersedes state law

> (1) by the federal law's express terms,
>
> (2) where the federal regulation scheme is sufficiently comprehensive to infer that Congress reasonably "left no room" for supplementary state regulation,
>
> (3) where "the federal interest is so dominant that the federal system will be assumed to preclude enforcement of state laws on the same subject", and
>
> (4) where state law actually conflicts with federal law, as when "compliance with both federal and state regulations is a physical impossibility" or when state law "stands as an obstacle to the accomplishment and execution of the full purposes and objectives of Congress".

Hillsborough County, Fla. v. Automated Medical Laboratories, Inc., 471 U.S. 707, 712–713, 105 S.Ct. 2371, 85 L.Ed.2d 714 (1985); *Greenwood Trust Co. v. Com. of Mass.*, 971 F.2d 818, 822–823 (1st Cir.1992).

2. New York Uniform Commercial Code

The Agreement provides that it "shall be interpreted under the Laws of the State of New York . . .", but does not state it shall be "governed" by New York law. Because there is no essential difference among the states on the point at issue, this Court will assume, as did the Bankruptcy Court, that the agreement is governed by New York law in all respects.

New York's Uniform Commercial Code § 9–302(3) [section 9–311] provides in relevant part:

> (3) The filing of a financing statement otherwise required by this Article is not necessary or effective to perfect a security interest in property subject to
>
> > (a) a statute or treaty of the United States which provides for a national or international registration or a national or international certificate of title or which specifies a place of filing different from that specified in this Article for filing of the security interest;
>
> . . .
>
> (4) Compliance with a statute or treaty described in subsection (3) is equivalent to the filing of a financing statement under this Article, and a security interest in property subject to the statute or treaty can be perfected only by compliance therewith except as provided in Section 9–103 on multiple state transactions. Duration and renewal of perfection of a security interest perfected by compliance with the statute or treaty are governed by the provisions of the statute or treaty; in other respects the security interest is subject to this Article.

N.Y. U.C.C. § 9–302(3)–(4) (McKinney 1997).

3. The Lanham Act

The Lanham Act, codified as 15 U.S.C. § 1051 et seq., governs trademarks. Its provision on the transfer of an interest in a trademark states in relevant part:

> A registered mark or a mark for which application to register has been filed shall be assignable with the goodwill of the business in which the mark was used, or with that part of the goodwill of the business connected with the use of and symbolized by the mark. . . . An assignment shall be void as against any subsequent purchaser for a valuable consideration without notice, unless it is recorded in the Patent and Trademark Office within three months after the date thereof or prior to such subsequent purchase.

15 U.S.C. § 1060. The Lanham Act does not define the word "assignment".

* * *

D. Analysis

An analysis of Article 9 of the U.C.C., the Lanham Act, case law and general policy considerations indicates that the Lanham Act does not preempt the U.C.C.'s filing requirements and that the perfection of a security interest in a trademark is governed by Article 9.

1. The U.C.C. Provision

The original 1962 text of § 9–302(3) [9–311] provided that the filing provisions of Article 9 were inapplicable to a security interest in property subject

> to a statute . . . of the United States which provides for a national registration or filing of all security interests in such property [or to certain state statutes].

U.C.C. § 9–302(3) (1962) (amended 1972). The Official Comment to the 1962 Official Text states that this subsection was intended to exempt from U.C.C. filing "transactions as to which an adequate system of filing, state or federal, has been set up outside this Article." U.C.C. § 9–302(3) comment at 8 (1962) [9–311 cmt. 2]. In such cases, "subsection (4) makes clear that when such a system exists perfection of a relevant security interest can be had only through compliance with that system." *Id.*

The comment suggests that a system of national registration of security interests was intended as the prerequisite for federal preemption of Article 9, rather than the mere federal registration of that property. Alice Haemmerli, *Insecurity Interests: Where Intellectual Property and Commercial Law Collide*, 96 COLUM. L.REV. 1645, 1662 (1996). In 1972, § 9–302(3) was amended to its current form, as adopted by New York. The Official Comment to the 1972 Official Text does not mention any change in the meaning of "national registration".

Furthermore, a drafted, proposed revision of the current § 9–302(3) [9–311] supports the view that, even now, it pertains to federal statutes which provide a system for the filing of security interests. A discussion draft submitted by the Council of the American Law Institute (ALI) rewrites the relevant portion to read:

> the filing of a financing statement is not necessary or effective to perfect a security interest in property subject to (1) a statute or treaty of the United States under which the exclusive method of perfecting a security interest is (i) compliance with the requirements of a national or international registration or certificate-of-title system [or] (ii) filing at an office that is different from the office specified in this article for filing a financing statement. . . .

U.C.C. Revised Article 9, § 9–302(c) at 42 (Discussion Draft, 1996), *cited in Haemmerli*, 96 COLUM. L.REV. at 1663. The ALI draft clearly suggests that in order for federal law to preempt the U.C.C., the federal statute itself must provide a method for perfecting a security interest.

2. The Lanham Act

The Lanham Act does not speak of security interests as such nor does it provide for the filing of notification of such interests. Section 1060 requires the recordation of assignments, without providing a definition of the word. The text of that section indicates that an assignee of a trademark must record its assignment if the assignee wants assurance that the assignment is not void as against a subsequent purchaser for value and without notice. 15 U.S.C. § 1060.

In stark contrast are the Federal Aviation Act ("FAA") and the Copyright Act. The FAA provides for recordation of "any conveyance which affects the title to, or any interest in, any civil aircraft. . . ." 49 U.S.C. § 44107 (1994). The Copyright Act specifically addresses the validity of security interests in copyrights. It provides that mortgages and hypothecations are transfers and establishes how they are validly made. It also contains a recordation scheme that requires the recording of copyright transfers at the Copyright Office in order to provide constructive notice of such transfers. 17 U.S.C. § 205 (1994). On the other hand, the Lanham Act contains no such similar provisions relating to mortgages, hypothecations or recordation schemes relating to the perfection of security interests.

Finally, in 1988 the United States Senate passed a bill that, among other things, would have (1) federalized the filing of documents relating to security interests in trademarks and (2) brought the recordation and priority of security interests in trademarks into conformity with the counterpart copyright provisions. S. 1883, 100th Cong. (1988). The portion of the bill related to security interests was not enacted, however, and thus, as one commentator notes, "the U.C.C. continues to control security interests in trademarks". Stuart M. Rilback, *Intellectual Property Licenses; The Impact of Bankruptcy*, 576 PLI/Pat 199, fn. 95 (1999).

3. Case law

Case law addressing the issue at hand consistently supports the proposition that the Lanham Act does not pertain to security interests and that Article 9, therefore, continues to govern the perfection of such interests. *See In re Roman Cleanser Co.*, 43 B.R. 940 (Bankr.E.D.Mich.1984), *aff'd* 802 F.2d 207 (6th Cir.1986) (based solely on interpretation of Lanham Act).

In the *Roman Cleanser* case, a creditor moved to intervene in an adversary proceeding, contending that it had a security interest in trademarks which were sold by the trustee and as to which another creditor claimed ownership. The trustee argued that, in order to perfect a security interest in a federally registered trademark, a creditor must file a conditional assignment with the PTO, and because that creditor failed to do so, its security interest was unperfected.

The court found that the creditor had validly perfected his security interest by his U.C.C. filing. It held that a grant of a security interest could not be characterized as an "assignment" under the Lanham Act because (1) title to the collateral did not pass to the secured creditor and (2) a security interest is an agreement for a future assignment, not a present assignment of the mark or the goodwill associated with the mark. *In re Roman Cleanser*, 43 B.R. at 944. The court noted that

> [t]he terms 'assignment' and 'security interest' are terms of art with distinct and different meanings. If Congress intended to provide a means for recording security interests in trademarks in addition to assignments, it would have been simple to so state.

Id. at 946.

The court pointed out that requiring federal filing of security interests would not further Congress's concern for protecting the public from the deceptive use of trademarks because a secured creditor has no right to use the mark absent debtor default. The court concluded that "since a security interest in a trademark is not equivalent to an assignment, the filing of a security interest is not covered by the Lanham Act" and the manner of perfecting a security interest in trademarks is governed by Article 9 of the U.C.C. *In re Roman Cleanser*, 43 B.R. at 944.

Courts which have subsequently dealt with the same issue have followed the logic and the holding of the *Roman Cleanser* court. *See In re TR-3 Industries*, 41 B.R. 128, 131 (Bankr.C.D.Cal.1984) (the omission by Congress of a registration provision for security interests in trademarks was purposeful and the recordation provision of the Lanham Act does not preempt Article 9); *In re C.C. & Co., Inc.*, 86 B.R. 485, 487 (Bankr.E.D.Va.1988) (Congress did not intend Lanham Act to provide method for perfection of security interest in trade names and lender had properly perfected its security interest in a trade name by filing financing statement under Virginia's U.C.C.); *In re Chattanooga Choo-Choo Co.*, 98 B.R. 792 (Bankr.E.D.Tenn.1989) (Lanham Act provides only for registration of ownership, not notice of security interests, and therefore Article 9 governs perfection of a security interest in a trademark); *In re 199Z, Inc.*, 137 B.R. 778 (Bankr.C.D.Cal.1992) (because Lanham Act refers only to assignments and not to "pledges, mortgages, or hypothecations of trademarks," a PTO filing did not perfect the creditor's security interest in a trademark).

4. Policy Considerations

Finally, in terms of policy, it makes good sense to limit the application of § 9–302 [9–311] to those federal statutes which specifically and systematically provide for the filing of "all security interests" in a given form of property. A federal intellectual property registration or certificate of title, such as a certificate of federal trademark registration, reveals the name of the registrant and identifies the property but does not provide a list of lienholders. If national registration alone, without any federal system for the recordation of security interests, suffices to supplant U.C.C. requirements, the application of § 9–302(3)(a) [9–311(a)(1)] would leave the holder of a security interest with no means of recording or perfecting that interest. Absent a reliable means of verifying the status of their collateral, secured lenders would be more reluctant to extend credit. Such a result would be inconsistent with the stated purpose of Article 9 of providing a "simple and unified structure" for secured transactions. U.C.C. § 9–101 cmt (1962). *See also Haemmerli* at 1662.

ORDER

For the reasons stated in the Memorandum above, the determination of the Bankruptcy Court that: (1) the Lanham Act's registration provision does not preempt U.C.C. filing requirements for the perfection of a security interest in a trademark, and (2) Trimarchi failed to file in accordance with the U.C.C. and therefore did not perfect his security interest in the Trademark, are AFFIRMED.

[footnote omitted]

EQUITY INTERESTS IN LLCS AND PARTNERSHIPS

In most instances, the equity interests in limited liability companies and partnerships are general intangibles. As you will learn in Chapter 8 on investment property, these equity interests may be investment property if the organic documents of the entity elect investment property treatment or if the interests are placed with a "securities intermediary." Unless the members of the LLC or the partners in a partnership take these explicit steps, by default the membership interests or partnership interests are general intangibles.

This category of general intangibles is especially important in certain industries such as real estate development. Real estate developers often create limited liability corporations ("LLCs") or limited partnerships ("LPs") to hold title to projects and then assign security interests in the membership or partnership interests to raise capital. Project entities in other contexts may be LLCs or LPs, the equity of which are general intangibles as well.

DIGITAL ASSETS

If an investor takes a security interest in a smart contract, the contract could be coterminous with virtual coin, or it could be for the assignment of tokenized assets, or it could be an agreement the primary value of which does not lie in cryptocurrency or tokenized assets. Some states are enacting UCC provisions to facilitate markets for digital assets, such as Wyoming, while others are hanging back pending analysis by the American Law

Institute and the Uniform Law Commission regarding whether and how the UCC should evolve to accommodate emerging asset classes.

Cryptocurrencies, for example, are general intangibles, unless their holders take specific steps to make them investment property (that you will learn in Chapter 8). While they may be investment property, cryptocurrencies are not "securities" under the UCC. Also, generally speaking they are not "money" under the UCC. ("Money" is expressly excluded from "general intangibles." *See* 9–102(a)(42).)

Cryptocurrencies are not like securities because they do not represent shares in or the equity of an issuer. (The Securities and Exchange Commission treats some blockchain-created assets as securities for regulatory purposes, but it does not follow from this regulatory choice, of course, that these assets constitute securities under the UCC.) As you will learn in Chapter 8, the UCC definition of securities hinges on the presence of an issuer that issues shares, participations, or interests of the issuer. *See* 8–102(a)(15) (defining "security"), 9–102(b) (incorporating Article 8 definition). Unlike securities issuances, cryptocurrencies do not create contractual claims on a firm's assets in the form of debt or equity. Rather, they are coins issued to entitle investors to services and goods that the issuer is developing. They are more like merchant-issued cash substitutes such as points or miles than they are like securities. While cryptocurrencies do not fit neatly into the UCC definition of securities, they could be securities entitlements—another form of investment property—if they are held as financial assets by a securities intermediary. If cryptocurrencies do not meet the definitional requirements to be investment property, then they fall into the catch-all category of general intangibles.

Cryptocurrencies are general intangibles and not money, in commercial law terms, because they are not, generally, a "medium of exchange currently authorized or adopted by a domestic or foreign government" under UCC section 1–201(b)(24). However, a government may very well adopt a cryptocurrency, making the adopted currency "money" rather than a general intangible. In addition, the UCC definition of money includes "a monetary unit of account established by an intergovernmental organization or by agreement between two or more countries." *See* 1–201(b)(24) (defining "money"). If an intergovernmental organization established a monetary unit that took the form of cryptocurrency, it could be money for commercial law purposes. Current research and fact-specific assessments should precede the closing of any secured transaction involving digital assets as collateral.

RESTRICTIONS ON ASSIGNMENTS

It is common for general intangibles to carry with them anti-assignment provisions prohibiting their assignment to third parties. This is often the case, for example, with software licenses. In general, Article 9 relies on the free assignability of property. In contrast, restrictions on assignment are sometimes validated by applicable state or federal law. In the case of assignments of promissory notes, health-care-insurance receivables, and certain general intangibles, section 9–408 offers a compromise.

Section 9–408 is difficult to decipher, and like many provisions of Article 9 requires diligent, patient reading. Sections 9–408(a) and (c) begin by purporting to render ineffective a variety of anti-assignment restrictions. What sections 9–408(a) and (c) give, however, subsection (d) appears to retract, but not entirely. Under section 9–408(d), what of significance is left for the secured creditor? Hint: think of what happens to the proceeds of the collateral if it is sold.

PROBLEM 5-10

Your client, Software Bank, was pleasantly surprised to hear about *In re World Auxiliary Power* and to find that it could perfect a security interest in an unregistered copyright by filing in the Secretary of State's office where the debtor is located. The bank wonders what happens if the debtor, unbeknownst to the bank, registers its software with the copyright office? Does that registration render the state filing ineffective? It is also concerned about the statement in *Peregrine* that a security interest in accounts and other proceeds that might arise from the use of a copyright (such as payments due on the showing of a movie) might also be subject to a federal filing and thus might not be perfected by filing with the Secretary of State's office. What is your opinion on that? How can your client address those problems?

PROBLEM 5-11

Travelware designs and licenses elaborate computer programs for travel agencies. It has granted a license to TRAVELTOWN, a nationwide travel agency. TRAVELTOWN in turn has made sublicenses with various one-office travel agencies whom it franchises. TRAVELTOWN also uses the software in its own offices located in every state of the U.S. Bank One has taken a security interest in TRAVELTOWN's license and in its rights to payment from its franchisees.

1. Assume that Bank One filed a financing statement in TRAVELTOWN's name and the financing statement indicates only TRAVELTOWN's "goods, including equipment." Bank One claims that it is perfected because software is included in the definition of "goods" in section 9–102. What do you think?

2. Assume alternatively that Bank One takes a security interest in TRAVELTOWN's license and files a financing statement covering "general intangibles" at the state capital. Is it perfected?

3. Assume that Bank One takes a security interest in TRAVELTOWN's accounts owed to it by its franchisees and files a financing statement at the state capital that claims "accounts." Is it perfected?

4. Assume that Travelware claims that the term in its license that prohibits transfers to third parties renders the security interest invalid as to the accounts and license. It relies on section 9–408. What is your response?

5. Assume that Bank One defeats Travelware's claims in number 4. Bank One proposes to "seize" the license and to transfer it to a third party. Travelware again cites section 9–408 and the anti-assignment clause. What now?

PROBLEM 5-12

Bank One wishes to take a security interest in Travelware's software. How does it do it? What if Travelware has never properly recorded its copyright in the federal system? Does that mean Bank One cannot get an effective and perfected security interest?

§ 8. SECURITY INTERESTS IN DEPOSIT ACCOUNTS

In Section 5 of Chapter 4, we considered briefly deposit accounts as proceeds of other collateral. What again is a "deposit account"? Section 9–102(a)(29) defines a "deposit account" to mean "a demand, time, savings, passbook, or similar account maintained with a bank." The term "bank" is defined in section 9–102(a)(8) to mean "an organization that is engaged in the business of banking" including "savings banks, savings and loan associations, credit unions, and trust companies."

What is the relationship between a debtor and the bank where the debtor maintains its deposit account? Essentially, when the debtor deposits funds with the bank, the debtor has a right to payment from the bank for the amount deposited, together with any interest the funds earn while on deposit. Sound familiar? Deposit accounts are simply another example of a right to payment that a debtor may own.

Perfection of a security interest in a deposit account is by control. *See* 9–314, 9–104. Control of a deposit may be obtained in one of three basic ways. First, the parties (debtor, bank where the account is maintained, and secured creditor) may enter into a control agreement that complies with the requirements of section 9–104(a)(2). Second, the secured party may become the owner of the deposit account in question. Third, if the secured creditor is also the bank where the deposit account is maintained, control is automatic. *See also* 9–340, 9–341, 9–342.

The priority of conflicting interests in deposit accounts is governed by section 9–327. Read it. In general, a secured creditor with control beats a secured creditor claiming the funds as proceeds of some other collateral. As between two creditors with control, the first in time generally prevails, unless one of them is the bank where the account is maintained, in which case the bank wins. This is not true, however, if one of the competing secured creditors is the owner of the account. Accordingly, if a secured creditor other than the bank where the account is maintained truly wants to be sure of having priority, how should it perfect its security interest?

Issues arise occasionally about whether certain kinds of accounts maintained at a bank qualify as "deposit accounts." For example, the collateral in question may be a certificate of deposit ("CD"), a digital CD, a 401(k) account, or an individual retirement account ("IRA"). Section 9–102(a)(29) excludes from the scope of "deposit accounts" "investment property or accounts evidenced by an instrument." For collateral classification purposes, the main question is whether CDs, 401(k) accounts, and IRAs are sufficiently similar to demand, time, savings, and passbook accounts to constitute deposit accounts, or instead whether they are investment property or accounts evidenced by an instrument.

If the CD is uncertificated (meaning there is no writing evidencing the bank's obligation to pay), the commentary states that it is a deposit account. *See* 9–102 cmt. 12. On the other hand, a CD evidenced by a writing is not a deposit account if it falls within the definition of an instrument. *See* 3–104(j). In the past, courts have disagreed on the treatment of certificates of deposit, concluding alternatively that they may be deposit accounts, instruments, investment property, or general intangibles.

The commentary states that shares in a money-market mutual fund are investment property. *See* 9–102 cmt. 12. Depending on its specific characteristics, a particular 401(k) account or IRA at a bank may look and behave like an account consisting of shares in a money-market mutual fund, and thus investment property. On the other hand, the account may look and behave like a traditional savings account. Some states prohibit Article 9 security interests in IRAs or 401(k) accounts, and these types of accounts are also subject to federal anti-assignment protection. Moreover, under section 9–109(d)(13), Article 9 does not apply to "an assignment of a deposit account in a consumer transaction," although it does apply to a consumer deposit account used to secure a non-consumer debt.

CHAPTER 6

SECURITY IN FIXTURES

■ ■ ■

§ 1. INTRODUCTION

In general, Article 9 does not deal with real estate security. There are, however, certain exceptions. *See, e.g.*, 9–203(g) (providing that the attachment of a security interest in a right to payment secured by a mortgage lien also constitutes attachment of a security interest in the mortgage lien). And these exceptions include the provisions of Article 9 dealing with "fixtures." *See* 9–102(a)(41) (defining "fixtures"); 9–102(a)(40) (defining a "fixture filing"); 9–301(3)(A) (providing choice of law rules regarding fixture filings); 9–334 (prescribing the priority of security interests in fixtures); 9–501(a)(1)(B) & (a)(2) (designating the office for financing statements filed as fixture filings and financing statements covering fixtures that are not filed as fixture filings); 9–502(b) & (c) (specifying additional requirements for fixture filings); 9–604 (addressing enforcement against fixtures); *see also* 1–201(b)(35) (defining "security interest" to mean "an interest in personal property or fixtures"). Of these, section 9–334 is the most significant. It governs the conflict between personal property interests in fixtures and real property interests in fixtures.

Section 9–102(a)(41) defines fixtures as "goods that have become so related to particular real property that an interest in them arises under real property law." By definition, fixtures are a hybrid classification: they are goods that look like goods in some respects, but are so attached to the land (or to a structure on the land) that they are also considered part of the real estate under local state real property law. One can easily envision the basic tensions this creates. On the one hand, secured lenders may view the goods as personalty, and assume they are covered by their security agreements and financing statements. On the other hand, real property lenders may view the goods as part of the real estate, and assume they are included among the collateral securing their real property mortgage liens. Secured creditors typically perfect by filing a financing statement with the office of the secretary of state. Real estate lenders typically perfect by recording their mortgage documents with the local recorder of real property deeds. So what is the right way to take a security interest in fixtures? It depends, and section 9–334 helps sort this out.

Typical of the priority conflicts we consider here are those that arise when a real estate mortgagee claims not only the relevant real estate itself but also all "appurtenances, fixtures, buildings, equipment" and so on, in a list as long as the mortgagee's lawyer can devise. The general age-old rule of real property law is that such a mortgage lien encumbrance includes not only fixtures attached to the land at the time the lien is recorded, but also those that become attached to the land thereafter as part of any "improvements." After the mortgage lien is placed on the property, the debtor may subsequently purchase a furnace or lathes or some other item of industrial equipment that becomes a fixture on the real property and thus subject to the real estate mortgage under the local real property law of the particular state. At the same time, a secured lender may hold a security interest in the industrial equipment perfected by a financing statement filed with the relevant secretary of state's office *or* in the local land records (or both). *See* 9–501(a)(2) (authorizing the filing of a financing statement in the secretary of state's office for a security interest in fixtures); 9–501(a)(1)(b) (authorizing the filing of a "fixture filing" in the local land records with respect to a security interest in fixtures); 9–501 cmt. 4 ("There are two ways in which a secured party may file a financing statement to perfect a security interest in goods that are or are to become fixtures"—a filing "in the Article 9 records, as with most other goods" or "as a 'fixture filing' " in the local land records).

Also typical of the priority conflicts that section 9–334 addresses are those that arise when a real estate "owner" claims not only the relevant real estate itself but also everything attached to it. *See* 9–334(d) (addressing the "conflicting interest of an encumbrancer or owner of the real property"). Consider that the owner may be different from the debtor. For example, the owner may be a lessor and the debtor a lessee of the real property, or the owner may be a subsequent purchaser of the real estate. The subsequent purchaser who acquires the property may well look to the real estate records to determine if someone else has an interest in any of the fixtures attached, but might not think to look at the Article 9 records. Section 9–334 helps sort out when an owner of the real estate should be required to look before the owner may comfortably assume that its interest will come ahead of some other person (*e.g.*, when the fixtures are readily removable factory or office machines), and when not.

These types of transactions with multiple parties claiming an interest in the same collateral under both Article 9 and local real estate law come in dozens of variants depending on when the interests attach, when they are perfected, the identity of the claimants, and the modes of perfection. Section 9–334 purports to deal with most of the possible conflicts. If the collateral in question is not a fixture, or if the collateral is "ordinary building materials" that have become so intimately associated with the real property that they no longer constitute either personal property or a fixture, other law governs the priority dispute (namely, law other than Article 9). *See* 9–109(d)(11), 9–334(a) ("A security interest does not exist under this article in ordinary building materials incorporated into an improvement on land.").

Accordingly, the secured creditor with a claim to a fixture has a choice: it can either make a filing in the local real estate records (a fixture filing) or do a regular UCC–1 filing in the personal property records at the state capital. As we will see, the former gives the secured creditor protection against certain real estate claimants while the latter gives protection only against lien creditors and certain other claimants where the fixture involved is not considered important to mortgagees and the like. For example, section 9–334(e)(3) grants the secured lender who has done only a personal property filing at the state capital priority over the trustee in bankruptcy (lien creditor) on the theory that a lien creditor is not someone who would rely upon the real estate records. Subsection (e)(2) gives priority to the secured creditor who has only done a personal property filing on certain assets such as factory or office machines on the theory that mortgagees or other purchasers of the real estate do not place any reliance upon such machines when they make loans or buy; thus it is fair and appropriate to grant the secured creditor priority in this case even though the secured creditor does not file in the local real estate records office.

FIXTURES AND FIXTURE FILINGS

Broadly, goods can be classified for the purposes of section 9–334 into three categories: (1) those that remain "pure goods"; (2) those so substantially integrated into real estate as to become real estate themselves, and thus "pure realty"; and (3) those in the gray area that would pass in a deed to the real estate yet remain personal property. Goods within this last classification are fixtures. Comment 3 to section 9–334 presents this as follows:

> this section recognizes three categories of goods: (1) those that retain their chattel character entirely and are not part of the real property; (2) ordinary building materials that have become an integral part of the real property and cannot retain their chattel character for purposes of finance; and (3) an intermediate class that has become real property for certain purposes, but as to which chattel financing may be preserved.

Goods change from pure goods to fixtures when they become sufficiently related to the real estate that they would pass in a deed under the local real estate law. What passes by deed in one state may not pass in another, and what is sufficiently related to a real estate interest in one state might not be sufficiently related in a neighboring state. Thus the general definition of fixtures in section 9–102(a)(41) is no more than a cross reference to local state law. What, then, are the relevant legal principles governing when goods become fixtures? Here, we cannot go much beyond posing the question.

Most courts start from the proposition that the status of goods as fixtures depends upon the intention of the parties. Of course, objective manifestations of intention are the windows through which we view actual intent. One searching for such manifestations might ask: What did the parties say in their agreement? How did they attach the goods to the realty? What is the relationship between the parties? How is the operation of the goods related to the use of the real property? For many courts, intent is most clearly manifested by the firmness with which the goods are affixed to the real estate and the amount of sweat that removal would entail. The *American Law of Property* treatise puts the matter as follows:

> [i]n the United States, whether a given chattel becomes a fixture is said to depend on intention, but whether it is the unilateral intention of the annexor at the time of annexation, or the bilateral intention of the parties to some transaction relating to the chattel or to the land, and whether it is the actual intention, or the manifested intention, or the imputed intention, is not always clear.
>
> Part of the confusion comes from the various meanings ascribed to the term "fixture." Under the modern cases no more precise definition is possible than this: a fixture is a former chattel which, while retaining its separate physical identity, *is so connected with the realty that a disinterested observer would consider it a part thereof.*[1]

This is not the place to inject order into this chaotic and obscure body of law. One must realize only that there is more than one line of authority and the cases must be examined with care to arrive at a reasonable guess about what is and what is not a fixture.

Section 9–102(a)(40) defines "fixture filings" to mean:

> the filing of a financing statement covering goods that are or are to become fixtures and satisfying section 9–502(a) and (b). The term includes the filing of a financing statement covering goods of a transmitting utility which are or are to become fixtures.

The concept of a "fixture filing" was introduced in the 1972 revision of Article 9. The drafters concluded that one should be required to file a fixture filing in the office in which a record of a mortgage for the real property would be filed if one seeks priority over subsequent real estate interests who would typically check in the real estate files and only in those files. *See* 9–501.

As indicated at the outset, comment 4 to section 9–501 explains the two ways in which a secured party may file a financing statement to perfect a security interest in goods that are or are to become fixtures, depending upon the parties against whom protection is sought. To begin with, a secured party may make a non-fixture filing in the Article 9 records, as with goods, in accordance with section 9–501(a)(2). Alternatively, a secured creditor may

---

1 5 AMERICAN LAW OF PROPERTY: A TREATISE ON THE LAW OF PROPERTY IN THE UNITED STATES § 19.1 at 3–4 (A. James Casner ed., 1952) (footnote omitted) (emphasis added).

file a "fixture filing" in the office in which a record of a mortgage on the related real property would be filed. *See* 9–501(a)(1)(B). Given the uncertainty of whether goods are or may become fixtures under applicable real property law, a secured lender may do both: file a financing statement with the office of the secretary of state, and make a fixture filing in the local land records. Comment 3 to section 9–334 recognizes that a secured party may make a fixture filing as a precaution: "[c]ourts should not infer from a fixture filing that the secured party concedes that the goods are or will become fixtures."

In addition to the normal information under section 9–502(a), a financing statement filed as a fixture filing under subsection (b) must include: (1) a showing that it covers goods which are, or are to become, "fixtures"; (2) a recital that the financing statement is to be filed in the real estate records; (3) a description of the real estate; and (4) the name of the record owner if the debtor has no interest of record. Section 9–502(c) states that the recording of a complying mortgage (meaning a mortgage that complies with the requirements of Article 9) is equivalent to a fixture filing.

A final introductory word should be offered about what it means for something to be a fixture for the purposes of Article 9. More specifically, is the concept of a "fixture" a distinct Article 9 category like "equipment" or "account," or is it a status like "purchase money security interest?" This is important because if a fixture is an independent category, a secured party must be certain that, if the collateral category changes for example from "equipment" to a "fixture" and the latter is not considered "proceeds" of the former, the collateral has been described correctly in the parties' security agreement, is properly indicated in the financing statement, and the security interest otherwise remains properly perfected. On the other hand, if the classification is merely a status with consequences limited largely to questions of priority based on where the financing statement is filed (in the land records or in the Secretary of State's office), a secured party should be able to rely on the initial classification, at least for the purposes of retaining some kind perfected status. Although the concept of a fixture is taxonomical, it is more properly viewed as a status rather than a fully independent Article 9 category. As we will see, this has caused some confusion in the courts.

§ 2. PERFECTION AND PRIORITY IN FIXTURES

Suppose a homeowner ("Homeowner") wants to replace her heating system. Homeowner contracts with Heating Co. ("Heating") to supply and install a new furnace and related electrical and duct work in her residence. Homeowner signs a contract with Heating that provides that Homeowner will pay for the work and materials in monthly installments over a two-year period. In order to secure her obligation to make these payments, Homeowner grants Heating a security interest in the new furnace and the related electrical and duct work installed in her dwelling. This new heating system is almost certainly a fixture (assume that it is). How can Heating perfect its security interest?

Heating can perfect in one of three ways. First, to the extent the new heating system is a consumer good and Heating's interest is a purchase-money security interest (which it likely is), Heating is automatically perfected under section 9–309. Second, under section 9–501(a)(2) it could file a regular financing statement with the appropriate secretary of state's office. Third, under section 9–501(a)(1)(B) it could file a financing statement as a fixture filing in the local land records where Homeowner's residence is located. If Heating wants to file its financing statement as a fixture filing, it would have to comply with the additional filing requirements of section 9–502(b).

Any of these methods of perfection would be sufficient to perfect Heating's security interest in the fixtures. The real question becomes: which method gives Heating priority over what kinds of competing interests? If Heating relies on automatic perfection or files a regular financing statement with the secretary of state's office, the priority of its filing as compared to other Article 9 security interests would be governed by the regular priority rules of Article 9, including section 9–322, and Heating would enjoy some of the benefits of section 9–334 (which may or may not be adequate to beat encumbrancers or purchasers of the real estate). *See* 9–334 cmt. 2 ("Priority contests with other Article 9 security interests are governed by the other priority rules of this Article"); 9–309 cmt. 3 ("A fixture filing is required for priority over conflicting interests in fixtures to the extent provided in Section 9–334."). If Heating files a fixture filing in the local land records, the priority of its interest as compared to other persons claiming an interest in the fixtures as part of the real estate (for example, real estate lien holders and purchasers) would be governed by section 9–334. In other words, the main purpose of section 9–334 is to resolve conflicts between the holder of an Article 9 security interest in fixtures and mortgagees and other real property stakeholders in the real estate to which the fixtures are attached.

Suppose Heating assumes that the heating system is not a fixture and files a regular financing statement with the secretary of state's office rather than a fixture filing. Does Heating's assumption control the analysis? Also, what if another state statute apart from Article 9 gives Heating special rights as the holder of a contractor's lien under local real property law? Consider the following case.

IN RE CAMARENO

United States Court of Appeals, Fifth Circuit, 2004.
105 Fed.Appx. 3.

PER CURIAM:

Worry Free Services, Inc., appeals from a bankruptcy court's order granting Camareno's motion to avoid Worry Free's lien, and the district court's subsequent affirmance. Worry Free asserted to the courts below that the air conditioning and heating system ("the system") sold to Camareno and installed in her home was personalty, as opposed to a fixture, making its UCC–1 financing statement filed with Texas's Secretary of State sufficient to qualify Worry Free as a secured creditor. The district court found that the system was a fixture subject to Chapter 53 of the Texas Property Code and that Worry Free's UCC–1 filing was insufficient. Worry Free contends on appeal that the courts below clearly erred in finding the system to be a fixture and in applying Chapter 53 of Texas's Property Code. We disagree and affirm.

* * *

The lower courts did not clearly err by concluding that the system was a fixture. Section 9.313 [section 9–102(a)(40) of revised Article 9] provides that "goods are 'fixtures' when they become so related to particular real estate that an interest in them arises under the real estate law of the state." The Texas Supreme Court explained that,

> [w]hether a chattel attached to permanent improvements has become a part thereof depends on the intention with which the fixture is annexed or put into position, and this intention is to be inferred from the nature of the article affixed, the relation and situation of the party making the annexation and the policy of the law in relation thereto, the structure and mode of the annexation, and the purpose or use for which the annexation is made.
>
> Given that the system was installed in [the debtor's] home, could not easily be removed, and that reasonable buyers and sellers of the system would expect it to be a permanent improvement to the house, we find no clear error in categorizing the system as a fixture.[5]

Given that the system was a fixture incorporated into Camareno's home, Worry Free was required to proceed under Chapter 53 of Texas's Property Code. The Uniform Commercial Code ("UCC") applies, except as otherwise provided, to "a transaction (regardless of its form) which is

---

[5] *See, e.g., Carter v. Straus-Frank Co.*, 297 S.W.2d 195, 197 (Tex.Civ.App.-Texarkana 1956, no writ) (finding an installed air conditioning system to be a fixture).

intended to create a security interest in personal property or fixtures."[6] Section 9.104 [section 9–109 of revised Article 9] describes which transactions are excluded from Article 9's reach, and the relevant exclusion here provides that the chapter does not apply "to a lien given by statute or other rule of law for services or materials." Chapter 53 of the Texas Property Code is one such statute; it governs mechanic's, contractor's, or materialmen's liens, and provides that a person is entitled to a lien if he furnishes materials for construction or repair of a house, building or improvement. [Tex. Prop. Code § 53.021(a)(1)(A).] "Material" is defined as "the material, machinery, fixtures, or tools incorporated into the work." [*Id.* at § 53.001(4)(A).] To claim a lien under Chapter 53, a person "must file an affidavit with the county clerk of the county in which the property is located," and the affidavit must contain specific information. [*Id.* at §§ 53.052(a), 53.054(a)(1)–(7).] Worry Free did not follow these procedures and therefore cannot claim secured status.

Worry Free asserts that its failure to make a fixture filing is not fatal because it has a contractual security interest in the system, and Article 9 states that "this Chapter applies to security interests created by contract." Therefore, Worry Free contends that its contractual security interest is valid despite its lack of any fixture filing under Chapter 53 or Article 9.

This argument ignores the mandate of Article 9 and Chapter 53. In addition to requiring fixture filings to describe the property and be filed in the County Clerk's office of the country where a mortgage of the property would be filed, Article 9 specifically excludes from its coverage liens "given by statute or other rule of law for services or materials." [Section 9–109(d)(2) of revised Article 9.] Here, the lower courts found the system to be a fixture incorporated into Camareno's home; as such, it falls within Chapter 53's coverage and Worry Free was required to follow its mandate. It did not do so, and now has no basis for secured creditor status.

* * *

AFFIRMED.

[some footnotes omitted]

NOTE

In Camareno, Worry Free committed two errors, at least according to the court. First, it misclassified the air conditioning and heating system, which the court concluded was a fixture. Second, it failed to take account of the requirements of other provisions of Texas law (specifically, Chapter 53 of the Texas Property Code) regarding its real property lien rights as a contractor.

---

[6] Tex. Bus. & Com.Code § 9.102(a)(1) [section 9–109(a)(1) of revised Article 9]. The transaction at issue occurred before the new version of the UCC took effect, and the parties agree that the former version applies to this case. All references and citations are to the former Article 9.

The court was undoubtedly correct that the air conditioning and heating system constituted a fixture under Texas law. The Texas decisions it cites clearly support that conclusion. But under Article 9, Worry Free had three options to perfect its contractual security interest: it could have relied on automatic perfection (assuming its interest was a purchase money security interest in consumer goods), it could have filed a regular financing statement, or it could have made a fixture filing (or made both filings). Worry Free did not make a fixture filing; nor did it comply with the provisions of Chapter 53 for creating a valid contractor's lien under Texas real property law. But it *did* file a UCC financing statement. Accordingly, Worry Free was a perfected secured creditor under Article 9 with respect to the system.

As a perfected secured creditor, Worry Free's interest was superior to the interest of a lien creditor under section 9–317(a), including a trustee in bankruptcy. Notice that in *Camareno*, it was the debtor who was seeking to avoid the lien, rather than the trustee. Under section 522(h) of the Bankruptcy Code, a debtor may assert the avoidance powers of a trustee under certain circumstances (namely to avoid a defective security interest in exempt property), and presumably *Camereno* is such a case. But the debtor's avoidance powers under section 522(h) are no greater than the trustee's, and the interest of Worry Free was superior to the interest of the trustee.

The court appears to have thought that the procedures under Chapter 53 for taking a contractor's lien were the exclusive means for establishing an encumbrance on the air conditioning and heating system, and thus the provisions of Article 9 did not apply at all. It is true that Article 9 does not apply to the creation or enforcement of statutory mechanic's liens, contractor's liens, and the like typically available under state real property law to the suppliers of goods and services that improve the real estate. *See* 9–109(d)(2). But Article 9 *does* apply to the creation and enforcement of consensual security interests in fixtures, and Worry Free complied with its requirements.

The court is wrong. Although the provisions of Chapter 53 are available to create a contractor's lien against Texas real estate (including fixtures attached to the real estate), Chapter 53 is a garden variety contractor's lien statute and does not preempt the provisions of Article 9. In other words, Worry Free had four non-exclusive options in this matter, three under Article 9 and one under Chapter 53. Under Article 9 it could have perfected its security interest by relying on automatic perfection, filing a regular financing statement (as it did), or making a fixture filing (or both filings). Alternatively (or in addition), it could have complied with the requirements of Chapter 53 for acquiring a contractor's lien. The different methods would have given Worry Free somewhat different rights (for example, Worry Free's filing of a regular financing statement would not have protected it against a subsequent good faith purchaser of the real estate), but compliance with any one of these options should have been sufficient to beat the trustee (and, by extension, the debtor).

Suppose two debtors ("Debtors") enter into a home improvement contract for the purchase and installation of an energy saving device in their home. Suppose American General Financial Services, Inc. ("American") finances the purchase and installation and takes a purchase money security interest in the device, but neglects to file either a regular financing statement with the appropriate secretary of state's office or a fixture filing. Debtors then file for bankruptcy. American assumed that the device was a consumer good, and therefore that its purchase money security interest was automatically perfected under section 9–309(1). What if the asset was not a consumer good? By failing to file a regular financing statement or a fixture filing, American would be an unperfected secured party entitled to be treated as an unsecured creditor in Debtors' bankruptcy case. *See In re Troutt*, no. 09–40555, 2009 WL 2905923 (Bankr. S.D. Ill. 2009).

COMPETITION BETWEEN UCC FILINGS AND NON-UCC REAL ESTATE INTERESTS

Suppose a debtor ("Debtor") purchases goods that are going to become fixtures and grants a purchase money security interest to the seller ("Seller") to secure payment of the purchase price. Seller files a financing statement covering the goods with the appropriate secretary of state's office, but neglects to make a fixture filing. The goods are then affixed to real estate that Debtor owns. A mortgagee holds a lien on the real estate securing a mortgage debt. Does Seller's perfected security interest have priority over the mortgagee? If Debtor files for bankruptcy, can the trustee avoid Seller's security interest and treat Seller as an unsecured creditor? Consider the following case decided under a former version of Article 9 and a prior version of the Bankruptcy Code.

IN RE FINK

United States Bankruptcy Court, Western District of New York, 1980.
4 B.R. 741.

HAYES, BANKRUPTCY JUDGE:

This is an action by the Trustee to avoid a security interest in a mobile house claimed by defendant, Endicott Trust Company of New York hereinafter referred to as "Endicott" and to preserve that [avoided] lien [for the benefit of the debtor's bankruptcy estate] as to defendant Wemco Corp. hereinafter referred to as "Wemco."

The facts appear to be as follows. The bankrupt, Pauline Fink, purchased a mobile home from Palmer Mobile Homes, Inc. on or about August 20, 1977. She entered into a retail installment contract. The security interest was transferred by assignment to Endicott on or about August 20, 1977. Endicott filed a financing statement which described the collateral as 24x52 1977 Bendix. Thereafter, the mobile home was delivered to Route 415 in the Town of Campbell which the bankrupt was leasing from Wemco. On August 24, 1977, the bankrupt contracted to purchase the real property on which the mobile home was placed from Wemco for $24,000. The realty consisted of about four acres and the only structure, thereon, was a store. The realty was transferred on December 1, 1977 by Wemco to the bankrupt and the bankrupt gave back to Wemco a purchase money mortgage for the full purchase price of $24,000.

The mobile home or modular home, which ever it may be, was delivered by Palmer Mobile Homes, Inc. and was placed on a foundation of concrete footers, concrete blocks and steel and wooden beams running the width and length of the building.

The details of construction follow. A foundation was evacuated. A septic tank was installed. Concrete footers were installed around the edge of the crawl space and at least one pillar of concrete blocks was erected in the center of the crawl space. Concrete blocks were installed and cemented to the footers. After this was done, the house was delivered to the lot in two sections (12′x52′) on steel cradles. The sections with cradles were then placed on the cement blocks. The house sections were bolted together. A roof cap was put on over the place in the roof where the sections were joined together and it was cemented and nailed down. Siding was put on the two ends of the house and nailed over the spot where the joinder of the section occurred to give the appearance of a continuous wall. The septic system was hooked up. Water lines were connected. An electrical line was connected to the store's system and the store's electrical system and capacity were increased. At this point, the top course of cinder blocks were placed in but not cemented to the course immediately below. No tie downs were used in the construction. The house even has an open fireplace, although this hangs on the side of the house. From the pictures in evidence, the house appears to be a normal ranch home without front or back steps.

Additional facts which were developed at the trial follow. Palmer, who installed the mobile home on the foundation, testified that he could remove and transport the home for about $500 by removing the roof cap and the siding and shingles from the end, disconnect water lines, electric septic tank and unbolt the sections of the house and transport it on the cradle of steel beams which support each section.

The officer of Wemco said that the house was constructed in the same fashion as any construction and that the attachment to realty was the same as in any stick built house.

Additionally, when Wemco transferred the property to the bankrupt, Fink, in December, 1977, the attorney for Wemco had the abstract redated. There was nothing on the abstract that gave Wemco any notice of an interest by Endicott in the house. Wemco, when it transferred the property to Mrs. Fink, took back a purchase money mortgage for $24,000.

* * * UCC 9–313 [section 9–334 of revised Article 9] requires a special filing where the item is a fixture. The filing must be in the office where a mortgage on real estate is filed and it must conform to the requirements of UCC 9–402(5) [section 9–502(b) of revised Article 9] which requires that a financing statement filed as a fixture must show that it covers this type of collateral, must recite that it is to be indexed in the real estate records and the financing statement must contain a description of the real estate sufficient for its identification and it must show the name of the record owner.

If the home in question is considered to have ceased to be personalty and become a fixture by annexation to the real property, the filing made by Endicott was improper. The case turns upon whether the home is personalty or a fixture.

UCC 9–313 [section 9–102(a)(41) of revised Article 9] states in part that "(1)(a) 'goods' are fixtures when they become so related to particular real estate that an interest in them arises under real estate law." The official comments which accompany this section say in part, "in cases where mobile homes or prefabricated steel buildings are erected by a person having an ownership interest in the land, the question into which category the buildings fall is one determined by local law." The definition of fixture is not an exact one. A recent law review article on the subject of fixtures under the UCC defines the term as follows:

> A fixture is a former chattel which, because of its annexation to and association with realty, has become part and parcel thereof but which has not lost its separate physical identity. A fixture is neither personalty nor realty within a strict definition of those terms. Rather, it partakes of the characteristics of each, since prior to annexation it is movable and not associated with realty, but after annexation it loses its character as personalty and is deemed realty. Various definitions of fixture have been utilized, all of which emphasize the former chattel aspect and the annexation to realty.[1]

23 N.Y.Jur. *Fixtures* § 2 (1962) says as follows:

> As a general rule, the true criterion of a fixture is based on the united application of three requisites: (1) actual annexation to the real property or something appurtenant thereto; (2) application to the use or purpose to which that part of the realty with which it is connected is appropriated; and (3) the intention of the party making the annexation to make a permanent accession to the freehold . . .

[1] *Trade Fixture—Secured Transactions Under New York's Uniform Commercial Code*, 44 Alb.L.Rev. 165, 165 (1979).

In re Lido Beach Sewage Collection Dist., 40 Misc.2d 384, 243 N.Y.S.2d 223 (County Ct. 1963), said at page 385, 243 N.Y.S.2d at page 225:

> Ordinarily for an article to become a fixture the following requisites must be met: Firstly, there must be annexation to the realty. Secondly, there must be adaptability of the article affixed to the use of the freehold. Thirdly, the intention of the party creating the annexation is to make the article a permanent accession to the freehold.

The two cases which have dealt with mobile homes in the context of UCC 9–313 are *In re Foskett*, 7 UCC Rep.Serv. 267 (W.D.Wisc.1970) and *George v. Commercial Credit Corp.*, 440 F.2d 551 (7th Cir.1971). They seem to follow the New York State tests set forth above. A recent 1979 Vermont Supreme Court case, *Hartford Nat'l Bank & Trust Co. v. Godin*, 398 Atl.2d 286, 26 UCC Rep.Serv. 221 (Vt.Sup.Ct. 1979), also held a mobile home a fixture based on the same three tests set forth above.

Applying these principles to the case at bar, we find that the bankrupt contracted to purchase the mobile home at about the same time she entered into a contract to purchase the realty. She had a crawl space dug. She had footings installed and she had cinder block cemented to the footings to hold the home. The bankrupt installed a septic tank system, ran water and electric into the home. The bankrupt lived in the home.

Looking at the house, in the pictures that were taken of the house, it looks at least to the uninitiated eye like any other ranch house you might see erected in the country. There would be nothing to warn anyone that this was in fact a trailer or a motor vehicle. If it was a trailer, it came certainly in two parts and had to be separated into two parts to be moved along the road. Should someone wish to move the house, they would have to dismantle it, separate it into two parts, remove part of the roofing and remove five to six feet of the center strips of shingles at either end of the home. The house in the manner in which it was annexed to real property certainly meets the test set forth in the cases cited above. Therefore, this court finds that Endicott is an unsecured creditor and that [its] filing should have been under UCC 9–313 rather than under 9–302(1)(d).

With regard to Wemco's interest, it is paramount to the trustee because Wemco had a filed mortgage agreement which is a lien upon the real property.

* * *

NOTE

Because Endicott neglected to make a fixture filing, its interest was inferior to the interest of the real estate encumbrancer Wemco, who held a mortgage lien recorded in the land records. Endicott did, however, file a regular financing statement perfecting its interest. Shouldn't this permit Endicott to defeat the trustee's avoidance action? Not if the property in question was "pure" real estate rather than a fixture (for example, an ordinary home built on a parcel of land). A security interest perfected by filing a regular financing statement is inadequate to establish a lien on pure real estate. (Conversely, an encumbrancer holding a real property lien on pure real estate does not thereby acquire any interest in pure personalty the debtor may own located at the premises, such as furniture, clothing, and the like.) But if the property (the mobile home) constituted a fixture rather than pure real estate, Endicott should prevail against the trustee under the current version of Article 9, right?

Under revised Article 9, Endicott would be a perfected secured party generally entitled to priority over a judgment lien creditor under section 9–317(a), including a bankruptcy trustee. Under section 544 of the Bankruptcy Code, however, a trustee in bankruptcy is also given the powers of a hypothetical holder of a judicial lien *on the debtor's real estate*. Thus, if state law provided that the holder of a judicial lien on real estate beats a secured party holding a security interest in fixtures perfected only by the filing of a regular financing statement, the trustee might avoid the security interest. Section 9–334(e)(3), however, plainly nixes this theory. It provides that "[a] perfected security interest in fixtures has priority over a conflicting interest of an encumbrancer or owner of the real property if . . . the conflicting interest is a lien on the real property obtained by legal or equitable proceedings after the secured interest was perfected *by any method permitted by this article*." As the Commentary explains, "[s]ubsection (e)(3) thus protects a perfected fixture security interest from avoidance by a trustee in bankruptcy under Bankruptcy Code section 544(a), regardless of the method of perfection." 9–334 cmt. 9. Section 9–334(e)(3) derives from former section 9–313(4)(d). So why did the trustee prevail?

Section 544 also gives the trustee the powers of a bona fide *purchaser* of real estate to avoid a security interest. A purchaser of real estate does not acquire its interest by "legal or equitable proceedings"—it acquires its interest by direct transfer—so section 9–334(e)(3) does not apply. The version of section 544 in effect in 1980—when *Fink* was decided—thus appeared to permit the trustee to beat the secured creditor. Section 544, however, was amended in 1984. The amended version gives the trustee the rights of "a bona fide purchaser of real property, *other than fixtures*." The italicized language makes it clear that the trustee cannot use his status as a purchaser to defeat the interest of a secured creditor holding a properly perfected security interest in fixtures. So if Endicott perfected its security interest by filing a regular financing statement with the appropriate secretary of state's office, the trustee should lose under Article 9 because this is a permissible means to perfect a security interest in fixtures.

Might Endicott prevail under some other provision of section 9–334? Under section 9–334(c), the general rule is that a security interest in fixtures is subordinate to the interest of an owner of real estate, including a purchaser, unless one of the exceptions stated in sections 9–334(d) through (h) apply. None of these would appear to help Endicott on the facts of *Fink*, with the possible exception of subsection (e)(4). This subsection creates an exception for certain security interests in manufactured homes perfected by noting the security interest on the certificate of title or other non-UCC registry, but this provision did not appear in former section 9–313. In addition, Endicott filed a financing statement. Accordingly, its interest was subject to avoidance under the law in effect at the time *Fink* was decided.

Section 9–334 is a fairly complex provision. It provides in relevant part as follows:

> (a) **[Security interest in fixtures under this article.]** A security interest under this article may be created in goods that are fixtures or may continue in goods that become fixtures. A security interest does not exist under this article in ordinary building materials incorporated into an improvement on land.
>
> (b) **[Security interest in fixtures under real-property law.]** This article does not prevent creation of an encumbrance upon fixtures under real property law.
>
> (c) **[General rule: subordination of security interest in fixtures.]** In cases not governed by subsections (d) through (h), a security interest in fixtures is subordinate to a conflicting interest of an encumbrancer or owner of the related real property other than the debtor.
>
> (d) **[Fixtures purchase-money priority.]** Except as otherwise provided in subsection (h), a perfected security interest in fixtures has priority over a conflicting interest of an encumbrancer or owner of the real property if the debtor has an interest of record in or is in possession of the real property and:
>
> > (1) the security interest is a purchase-money security interest;
> >
> > (2) the interest of the encumbrancer or owner arises before the goods become fixtures; and
> >
> > (3) the security interest is perfected by a fixture filing before the goods become fixtures or within 20 days thereafter.
>
> (e) **[Priority of security interest in fixtures over interests in real property.]** A perfected security interest in fixtures has priority over a conflicting interest of an encumbrancer or owner of the real property if:
>
> > (1) the debtor has an interest of record in the real property or is in possession of the real property and the security interest:
> >
> > > (A) is perfected by a fixture filing before the interest of the encumbrancer or owner is of record; and
> > >
> > > (B) has priority over any conflicting interest of a predecessor in title of the encumbrancer or owner;

(2) before the goods become fixtures, the security interest is perfected by any method permitted by this article and the fixtures are readily removable:

(A) factory or office machines;

(B) equipment that is not primarily used or leased for use in the operation of the real property; or

(C) replacement of domestic appliances that are consumer goods.

(3) the conflicting interest is a lien on the real property obtained by legal or equitable proceedings after the security interest was perfected by any method permitted by this article; or

(4) the security interest is:

(A) created in a manufactured home in a manufactured-home transaction; and

(B) perfected pursuant to a statute described in Section 9–311(a)(2).

(f) **[Priority based on consent, disclaimer, or right to remove.]** A security interest in fixtures, whether or not perfected, has priority over a conflicting interest of an encumbrancer or owner of the real property if:

(1) the encumbrancer or owner has, in an authenticated record, consented to the security interest or disclaimed an interest in the goods as fixtures; or

(2) the debtor has a right to remove the goods as against the encumbrancer or owner.

(g) **[Continuation of paragraph (f)(2) priority.]** The priority of the security interest under paragraph (f)(2) continues for a reasonable time if the debtor's right to remove the goods as against the encumbrancer or owner terminates.

(h) **[Priority of construction mortgage.]** A mortgage is a construction mortgage to the extent that it secures an obligation incurred for the construction of an improvement on land, including the acquisition cost of the land, if a recorded record of the mortgage so indicates. Except as otherwise provided in subsections (e) and (f), a security interest in fixtures is subordinate to a construction mortgage if a record of the mortgage is recorded before the goods become fixtures and the goods become fixtures before the completion of the construction. A mortgage has this priority to the same extent as a construction mortgage to the extent that it is given to refinance a construction mortgage.

* * *

In order fully to grasp how section 9–334 operates, focus first on section 9–334(c), which states the general rule that fixtures are subordinate to real property encumbrances or ownership interest (other than the interest of the debtor). Sections 9–334(d) through (g) then state exceptions to this general rule. Section 9–334(h) then creates an exception to the exception stated in subsection (d) in the special case of construction mortgages. These provisions are designed to address certain fact patterns where the drafters believed the interest of a creditor holding a security interest in a fixture should have priority.

Section 9–334(d) applies where the debtor acquires a fixture in a purchase-money transaction and the secured creditor holding the purchase money security interest in the fixture makes a fixture filing. That section essentially establishes a purchase-money priority for fixture financers ahead of the conflicting interest of a real estate owner or encumbrancer, provided perfection is accomplished through a fixture filing in the land records and within the time limit set out in subsection (d)(3). *See* 9–334 cmt. 7.

Section 9–334(e) covers several different situations. Subsection (e)(1) applies where the interest of the secured party in a fixture predates the interest of the real estate owner or encumbrancer and the secured party perfects by a fixture filing in the land records. Subsection (e)(1) essentially adopts a first-to-file priority rule in this setting. *See* 9–334 cmt. 6.

Subsection (e)(2) applies to certain kinds of good which, although they may become fixtures under certain circumstances, are not typically regarded as fixtures, but are frequently encumbered with security interests. These include readily removable factory or office machines, such as copiers and computers. *See* 9–334 cmt. 8.

The other two exceptions provided for in section 9–334(e) are subsections (e)(3) covering judicial and equitable liens and (e)(4) covering certain manufactured homes. These are discussed above (manufactured homes transactions are also discussed below in greater detail).

Sections 9–334(f) and (g) create an exception to the general priority rule stated in section 9–334(c) where the particular real estate owner or encumbrancer has consented to or disclaimed an interest in the fixtures. It also creates an exception where the debtor has the right to remove the goods. Suppose, for example, a lessee ("Lessee") executes a lease of real property for a one-year term. Lessee has a lot of expensive computer equipment that it bolts to the floor of the premises. The computer equipment is subject to a security interest in favor of the vendor ("Vendor") who sold the computers to Lessee. Under the terms of the lease and local real estate law, Lessee has the right to remove the computers from the premises. As between Vendor, the owner of the real property, and any real estate encumbrancer, Vendor should prevail regardless of whether it is perfected, no?

Finally, section 9–334(h) creates a limited exception from the purchase-money priority of section 9–334(d) for construction mortgages recorded before the goods become fixtures and where the goods become fixtures prior to the completion of the project. Section 9–334(h) applies both to an original construction mortgage and to a refinancing of the original construction mortgage. *See* 9–334 cmt. 11. Construction lenders typically advance "progress payments" to developers to fund construction, and expect to hold a priority lien on the real estate and all improvements because they typically advance not only the funds necessary to construct the "bricks and mortar," but also the various fixtures that are incorporated into the building, such as the heating and air conditioning systems. This priority first appeared in the 1972 version of Article 9.

Suppose a builder ("Builder") is constructing a new office tower. Suppose a bank ("Bank") is funding construction and records a mortgage document establishing its lien on the real estate and all improvements and fixtures thereon. Bank, however, does not intend to fund Builder's purchase of the tower's heating and air conditioning system. Instead, the seller of the system ("Seller") is willing to finance Builder's acquisition by permitting Builder to pay for the system in installments over a five-year period. Seller intends to take a purchase money security interest in the system and perfect it through a fixture filing. Under section 9–334(h), the installed system would be subject to Bank's previously recorded construction mortgage, and Seller's interest in the system as a fixture would be subordinate to Bank's interest as a real estate encumbrancer. How might Seller obtain a priority interest? It may do so by insisting on Bank's contractual subordination of its interest before proceeding with the transaction. *See* 1–310, 9–339 & cmt. 2.

PROBLEM 6-1

A general practitioner calls you in as a secured transactions expert for your opinion concerning the rights of his client, IR, who sold a complex manufacturing line to a manufacturer of automotive interiors. The line covers several thousand square feet and runs for nearly 300 yards through a large manufacturing complex. Most of it is bolted to the floor and is composed of overhead trams, rails, and attached facilities for spraying and heating. The lawyer is concerned that the "line" may constitute a fixture. He tells you that IR received a $1 million down payment and has an agreement to be paid for the remaining $4 million of the purchase price over five years. IR took a security interest in the line and filed a financing statement with the Secretary of State's office in Lansing. The debtor is a Michigan corporation and is now in financial difficulty. The lawyer has several questions:

1. If the debtor goes into bankruptcy will IR defeat the trustee in bankruptcy despite the fact that it has not done a fixture filing?

2. Will IR defeat Bank who, after IR's interest attached, lent $1 million to the common debtor and took a mortgage on the premises?

3. Is there anything you can recommend that IR do now to improve its chances?

4. If the mortgage proves superior to IR's security interest and the debtor defaults, what can IR do? Can it repossess?

PROBLEM 6-2

Bank holds a properly perfected security interest in debtor's furnace that was installed in an office building in International Falls, Minnesota. Would Bank be within its right to repossess the furnace in the middle of winter? *See* 9–604.

PROBLEM 6-3

Debtor owns several hundred large, liquid fertilizer tanks that it installs on farms throughout Iowa. Several years ago, Bank loaned $1.4 million to finance the purchase of the tanks. It took a security interest in all of the tanks and did a fixture filing in the county where each tank is located. When Bank consulted you last month you told it to file a UCC–1 in Des Moines and it did so.

Last week, Debtor filed under Chapter 11. The lawyer for the DIP has now commenced an adversary proceeding in the bankruptcy court to subordinate Bank's interest. What do you expect the DIP's arguments to be? (One will surely be under section 547 of the Bankruptcy Code, correct?)

MOBILE AND MANUFACTURED HOMES

As discussed above, section 9–334(c) states the general rule that a security interest in fixtures is subordinate to a conflicting interest of an encumbrancer or owner of the related real property (other than the debtor). Section 9–334(e)(4) creates an exception for a security interest in a "manufactured home" involved in a "manufactured home transaction," provided that the security interest is "perfected pursuant to a statute described in Section 9–311(a)(2)." Section 9–311 defers to the perfection methods of various state certificate-of-title statutes covering such things as automobiles, mobile homes, and the like. Under section 9–311(a), the filing of a UCC financing statement is not necessary or effective to perfect a security interest in property subject to these other statutes. Under section 9–311(b), compliance with these other statutes is treated as the equivalent of filing a financing statement if compliance has the effect of giving the secured party priority over a lien creditor. Under section 9–515(b), an initial financing statement filed in connection with a manufactured home transaction is effective for 30 years (rather than the usual 5) if it indicates that it is filed in connection with a manufactured home transaction.

So if a secured party takes a security interest in a "manufactured home" involved in a "manufactured home transaction," and perfects its interest by complying with any applicable certificate of title statute (typically by having its interest noted on the title in the public registry), its interest would be superior to the interest of any real estate owner or encumbrancer even though the manufactured home is affixed to the land and qualifies as a fixture. *See* 9–334 cmt. 10. So what qualifies as a "manufactured home," and what is a "manufactured home transaction"? These terms are defined somewhat unclearly in section 9–102.

Section 9–102(a)(53) defines a "manufactured home" to mean "a structure, transportable in one or more sections" that meets certain size requirements and has a "permanent chassis," or regardless of the size is the subject of a federal filing designated in the statute. The term is borrowed from the Federal Manufactured Housing Act, 42 U.S.C. §§ 5401 *et seq.* Section 9–102(a)(54) defines a "manufactured home transaction" to mean a purchase money secured transaction in a manufactured home (or in which the manufactured home is the primary collateral), other than a manufactured home held as inventory. Do these definitions include trailer-type "mobile homes" of the kind often seen in trailer parks mounted on small foundations and hooked up externally to utility services, or are these definitions intended to focus more on "modular homes" that look more like "stick-built" dwellings similar to the one at issue in *Fink*? The definitions would appear to exclude smaller trailer-type mobile homes, weekend campers, and the like. But what is included? Suppose the "double-wide" does not have a "permanent chassis," but only a temporary one?

There is room for confusion here. Suppose the owner ("Owner") of a mobile home erects a structure on some real estate and afterwards it looks pretty much like a "stick-built" dwelling. Among things, the "permanent chassis" under the structure can no longer be seen. Suppose the vendor of the home ("Vendor") finances Owner's purchase through a purchase-money secured transaction and perfects its interest by having its lien noted on the certificate of title in the local registry. Suppose years later Owner takes out a home equity mortgage loan with a bank ("Bank"), but neglects to mention the still-outstanding financing with Vendor. Before making the loan, Bank searches the land records and finds no record of Vendor's interest. Bank duly records its mortgage in the land records. If Owner defaults, who prevails? If the court concludes that the home is not a fixture, but is instead pure real estate, Vendor is in trouble. If the court concludes that the home is indeed a fixture, Bank is probably out of luck.

The National Conference of Commissioners on Uniform State Laws has promulgated a "Model Manufactured Housing Act." The idea behind the act is to bring uniformity and clarity to the current legal landscape. Most mobile homes are not moved after sited on a parcel of land. Most have a life expectancy comparable to "stick-built" houses. Many are indistinguishable in appearance from a house built from scratch. The proposed model law, if enacted, would permit purchasers of manufactured homes to elect to treat their homes as real estate. One of the benefits of this election would be to permit purchasers to obtain mortgage loan financing, which is often cheaper than "chattel loans" used to finance personal property.

PROBLEM 6-4

In October 2001 debtor bought a mobile home and transported it to a lot south of Phoenix. Bank lent the money to buy the mobile home and had its name put on a Certificate of Title. It appears that Bank has done similar transactions with as many as 100 other residents in the mobile home park. It is now 2007, the mobile homes have all been added on to, their wheels taken off and they appear, from the outside, to be conventional stick-built homes. Friendly Financial, ignorant of the Certificates of Title, has issued home equity loans to 20 to 30 of the owners of the mobile homes in the mobile home park. Friendly has perfected its interest by taking mortgages and recording them.

1. If the mobile home owners default on the loans to Bank, will Bank have priority over Friendly?

2. One of Friendly's lawyers suggested that the mobile homes are no longer just fixtures. She claims they are real estate just like a stick-built house and so not subject to any mode of perfection provided in Article 9. How do you respond?

ENFORCEMENT

Section 9–604(c) details some special provisions governing the enforcement of security interests in fixtures. If a security agreement covers goods that are or become fixtures, section 9–604(b) permits the secured party to proceed with enforcement either under Article 9 or in accordance with enforcement procedures available under local real property law. Section 9–604(c) permits the secured party to remove its fixture collateral from the premises if the secured party holds an interest with priority over all owners and encumbrances of the real estate. Section 9–604(d) requires the secured party to reimburse any encumbrancer or owner of the real property, other than the debtor, for damages done by the removal. *See* 9–604 cmt. 3.

CHAPTER 7

SECURITY IN CONSUMER GOODS

■ ■ ■

§ 1. INTRODUCTION

Most security interests in consumer goods are of the purchase money variety (namely, a security interest taken to secure payment of the purchase price of the goods in question, or to secure repayment of a loan that enables the debtor to acquire the goods). We have seen what a purchase money security interest looks like. Why then a separate chapter devoted largely to purchase money security interests in consumer goods? Because Article 9 supplies a distinct body of rules for this type of transaction, and it likewise intersects uniquely with other consumer laws.

According to sections 9–201 and 9–203, a security agreement need not take any particular form. In business transactions, security agreements are often tens or even hundreds of pages long, and will include multiple attachments and elaborate terms. But in consumer transactions security agreements can be nothing more than a couple of sentences on a sales slip, sometimes enlarged by terms in a credit card agreement, or a few pages setting out not only the terms of the debtor's purchase of an item but also the financing terms within the four corners of a single document labelled as a "retail installment sales contract" or the like. The drafters of Article 9 consciously avoided requiring specific language or formal documents. For example, some retailers take a security interest in the goods that they sell on credit. Their security agreements are typically in a document that is signed (usually digitally) as the consumer takes his purchases and leaves the store.

Most of the case law generated by consumer secured transactions has to do with repossession, resale, and other efforts by the creditor to realize on its collateral and otherwise collect its claim. Commonly such cases will arise when a secured creditor repossesses an automobile and thereafter chooses to sue the debtor for the "deficiency." The deficiency is the difference between the amount owed and the amount realized when the repossessed automobile is sold at auction or privately. (Be assured that there is virtually always a deficiency; in the words of Grant Gilmore, a "surplus" is the "glittering mirage," a deficiency the "grim reality.")

In this introduction to Chapter 7 we summarize the important basic issues relevant to the taking of security interests in consumer goods: the automatic perfection of purchase money security interests in consumer goods, the failure to achieve or maintain purchase money status in certain circumstances, and the proper classification of goods as consumer goods. Other issues addressed in this chapter include perfecting a security interest in collateral subject to various certificate of title statutes, the treatment of consumer car loans under the "hanging paragraph" of section 1325(a)(9) of the Bankruptcy Code, general restrictions that the Federal Trade Commission and other laws place on consumer loans, rules on repossession and resale of consumer collateral, and alternatives to straightforward consumer credit in the form of pawns and rent-to-own contracts.

AUTOMATIC PERFECTION

Should merchants or banks with security interests in consumers' chairs, chainsaws, microwaves, or laptops be required to file like most other secured creditors? They certainly may, *see* 9–310(a), and they may also perfect by taking possession of the collateral, *see* 9–313(a). Under section 9–309, however, perfection of a purchase money security interest in consumer goods is also automatic upon attachment (except for consumer goods covered by a certificate of title statute, such as most automobiles, *see* 9–311(a)). Pre-Code law granted sellers of consumer goods (and those who lent the purchase price of consumer goods) perfected status even without filing. So the Code's "automatic" perfection on the creation of such interests is no departure. In this case, automatic perfection reduces what would otherwise be relatively heavy transaction costs with slight benefits. If creditors had to file with respect to every consumer credit transaction, the filing offices would be bulging at the seams (at least those that still maintain paper records). Further, the benefits to be gained from filing to perfect these security interests are marginal. Because potential creditors have long been aware of automatic perfection of such "conditional sales," they are on guard when a consumer attempts to borrow against consumer goods. Further, most consumer goods cost little and depreciate quickly; creditors, other than purchase money lenders, seldom rely on these goods in making loans, making it unlikely that any subsequent creditor will be misled by the absence of a public filing.

In order to be eligible for automatic perfection, a security interest in consumer goods must be of the purchase money variety. *See* 9–103. This is important for several reasons. We have already seen the sometimes unfortunate fate of a secured creditor with an unperfected security interest. In addition to the usual problems, federal law restricts the ability of lenders to take non-purchase money security interests in consumer goods. The taking of a non-purchase money security interest in certain household goods may be an unfair trade practice under Federal Trade Commission ("FTC") regulations. *See* 16 C.F.R. 444.2(a)(4). Moreover, a consumer debtor who files for bankruptcy may be able to avoid certain non-purchase money security interests in household goods and the like that the debtor claims as exempt under section 522(f)(1)(B) of the Bankruptcy Code, even if the security interests are perfected. Here the case law has revealed two significant lawyer problems under section 9–103. First, what is a purchase money security interest in consumer goods, how is it obtained, and how can it be lost? Second, what exactly are "consumer goods"?

OBTAINING AND MAINTAINING PURCHASE MONEY STATUS

In most circumstances identification of a purchase money security interest is easy. If the seller has retained an interest in goods sold to secure payment of some or all of the price, the seller has a purchase money security interest whether the agreement with the buyer is called a "conditional sales contract," a "bailment lease," or something else. Moreover, a third party (such as a bank or finance company) that lends money to a prospective buyer can, as under prior law, also qualify as a purchase money lender under section 9–103(a)(2). That person must make advances or incur an obligation "to enable the debtor to acquire rights in or the use of the collateral," and the money lent must be "in fact so used." Under this provision, a third party financer has a purchase money security interest only if that party can show that the money the third party lent was "in fact" used to acquire an interest in the collateral in question.

To be automatically perfected, a security interest must *retain* its status as a "purchase money" security interest. Thus it is often in the interest of a trustee in bankruptcy or some other competitor to claim that a security interest that was originally "purchase money" has lost that status or, in some cases, never attained that status. The challenge to purchase money status comes in two forms. First, the challenger might argue that the mixture of a purchase money and non-purchase money security interest in the same security agreement renders the entire security agreement non-purchase money. Second, the challenger might acknowledge the existence of two security interests, one purchase money and one non-purchase money, but argue that the debtor's payments should be allocated first to the purchase money security interest and so reduce that one to the benefit of the trustee (who, by hypothesis, can defeat the non-purchase money unperfected interest but who cannot defeat the purchase money perfected interest). Prior to the 1999 revision of Article 9, case law was equivocal in addressing these challenges, supplying a rich source of divergent precedents. Revised Article 9 provides that a single document can create two security interests in business transactions: one purchase money and one non-purchase money, but section 9–103 declines to take a position on that issue in consumer cases. So, unless a court chooses to apply the business rule by analogy to consumer cases, we are left in the consumer context with the same confusion after the revision that existed before.[1]

There are two common circumstances in which purchase money status is uncertain. The first is the case where the consumer debtor makes several consecutive purchases from one seller. For example, assume the debtor buys a refrigerator in month one, a television in month two, and a stereo in month three. Assume further that the seller finances each of the purchases and takes a security interest in each of the assets purchased. Since the seller has financed all, each would be a purchase money security interest and so be automatically perfected. But life is not so simple. In all likelihood our seller will combine the three items into one security agreement and that security agreement will state that each asset is collateral, not only for its own purchase price but also for the purchase price of the other two items (a concept known as "cross-collateralization"). Now there is a problem. Because the purchase price for the refrigerator was "purchase money" only as to the refrigerator and not as to the television or stereo, to the extent that the television and stereo stand as collateral for the price of the refrigerator, the security is "non-purchase money."

The second circumstance arises when a loan is re-financed or when a debtor makes payments against a loan that is secured by two security interests, one purchase money and one non-purchase money. Assume, for example, the debtor borrows $2,000 from the bank in a purchase money loan to buy a stereo system. Six months later the bank "refinances" the loan; at that time the debtor borrows an additional $1,000. Has the refinancing destroyed the security interest's purchase money status? For consumer cases, section 9–103 declines to give an answer. For business cases, however, section 9–103(f) states that the purchase money status is retained. So in consumer cases section 9–103 leaves a court free to follow its own rule if it has one, to apply the business rule by analogy, or to reason from other cases. *See* 9–103(h) & cmt. 8.

Even if the original security interest in the consumer goods retains its purchase money status, the new loan ($1,000) will not be a purchase money loan and will not be automatically perfected. Now, assume the debtor pays $1,000 against its consolidated debt (leaving a total balance of $2,000). Does this $1,000 payment reduce the loan that is secured by the purchase money security interest, does it extinguish the $1,000 loan that is secured by the non-purchase money security interest, or is it allocated pro rata? This will be important if the secured creditor is depending on the automatic perfection provisions associated with purchase money loans. If the $1,000 payment is allocated on a FIFO (first in, first out) basis to the earliest loan, $1,000 of the loan is now secured by a perfected security interest (purchase

---

[1] Consumer protection provisions have long been a bone of contention in the drafting and revision of the UCC, including Article 9. *See* GRANT GILMORE, SECURITY INTERESTS IN PERSONAL PROPERTY 293–94 (1965).

money) and $1,000 is secured by an unperfected security interest. If, alternatively, the payments are allocated on a LIFO (last in, first out) basis to the last loan, the secured creditor retains a perfected security interest as to its entire remaining $2,000 loan because the payment would have been treated as a payment against the second loan secured by a non-purchase money security interest.

Where there are multiple purchases and later payments, one faces the same allocation problem. If I have paid the price of the item first purchased, do I at least own that? If a court recognizes a "dual status" security agreement, it needs to find an allocation method to determine how a single payment per month by the debtor should be allocated among the various purchase money interests and the non-purchase money interests. Should it be FIFO, LIFO, or some other method? Some courts were offended (*see, e.g., Williams v. Walker-Thomas Furniture Co.*, 350 F.2d 445 (D.C. Cir. 1965)) by allocation schemes that held every piece of collateral subject to the security interest until the last penny was paid; others found a solution to that problem in state law providing an allocation scheme (such as the Uniform Consumer Credit Code adopted in a few states, and other similar state statutes). In any case the creditor needs to provide an allocation scheme in its agreement or find one in the law. Finally, there are cases where the loan was rewritten or "consolidated." In those, too, the courts have disagreed, some finding that the rewriting or consolidation deprived the new loan entirely of the purchase money status; others concluding the opposite.

Other pitfalls await creditors relying on automatic perfection. For example, if the goods are to become fixtures, the filing exemption will not protect the retailer if the security interest is not of the purchase-money variety. *See* 9–334, 9–604. And purchase money status is important not merely for perfection; it is also necessary to preserve a security interest in consumer goods from extinction in bankruptcy under section 522(f) of the Bankruptcy Code (permitting a debtor to avoid certain non-purchase money security interests in certain exempt property).

CONSUMER GOODS: CLASSIFICATION BASED ON USE

The second major question presented by section 9–103 involves the proper classification of the collateral: consumer goods or not? Is a stove designed for home use necessarily a consumer good? Is a $50,000 house trailer a consumer good? According to subsection 9–102(a)(23), " 'consumer goods' means goods that are used or bought for use primarily for personal, family, or household purposes." Section 9–102 does not classify goods according to design or intrinsic nature but according to how their owner uses them. It follows that as use changes, either because the owner finds some new task for the goods, or because an owner sells the goods to another who uses them for a different purpose, the classification of the goods will also change. Of course, borderline cases, such as a physician's car or a farmer's jeep, will arise. When they do, the factfinder must determine whether the debtor used the goods "primarily" for personal, family, or household purposes.

§ 2. PURCHASE MONEY SECURITY INTERESTS IN CONSUMER GOODS; MAINTAINING PURCHASE MONEY STATUS

IN RE MANUEL

United States Court of Appeals, Fifth Circuit, 1975.
507 F.2d 990.

NICHOLS, ASSOCIATE JUDGE:

This case originated in the bankruptcy of James Lucius Manuel. On December 7, 1972, he purchased certain household furniture from appellant Roberts Furniture Co. On February 13, 1973, he purchased a television set, also from appellant. The purchase money security agreement he then signed referred to an unpaid balance of $573.32 from the first purchase, deducted $116.03 for refunds, leaving a prior unpaid balance of $457.29 which was added to the unpaid balance on the TV set, $174.07, making a total balance owed of $631.36. This agreement was never filed for perfection as Georgia law required, nor was perfection obtained by retaining possession. The agreement also failed to indicate the order in which purchases were paid off, and the amounts still due on each item and secured by the paid-up items. The apparent purpose of Roberts Furniture was to ensure that title to nothing passed until title to all passed. The February 13 purchase money agreement provided:

> It is agreed that the contracts, whether one or more, heretofore entered into between Seller and Buyer, having an unpaid balance of $573.32 referred to as "prior balance" shall remain in full force and effect, that Seller's security interest in the goods sold thereunder shall remain perfected, until full payment for said goods has been made, and that the contract evidenced by this instrument shall have no effect on the above mentioned existing contract except to modify the terms of payment thereof.
>
> It is further agreed, however, that for the purposes of the payment of the said prior balance and total of payments on the contract evidenced by this instrument, that Buyer shall make one payment in the amount and for the period set forth below until the total of payments as set forth has been paid. Upon a default in the contract evidenced by this instrument the said existing contract shall also be deemed to be in default. Until all installment payments and all other amounts due hereunder, have been paid, Seller shall retain a

security interest in the Goods and any and all equipment, parts, accessories, attachments, additions and other goods, and all replacements thereof, now or hereafter installed in, affixed to or used in connection with said Goods and, if Buyer sells or otherwise disposes of the Goods in violation of the terms of this agreement, in the proceeds of such sale or disposition. *Goods may secure all present and future liabilities, debts and obligations of whatever nature of BUYER to SELLER or its assigns.* (Emphasis supplied.)

Manuel filed a voluntary bankruptcy petition on May 3, 1973. Roberts Furniture claimed reclamation in bankruptcy on the basis of priority of their "Purchase Money Security Interest." The bankruptcy judge found that except for the TV set Roberts failed to acquire a Purchase Money Security Interest as defined by Georgia Code 109A–9–107; that Roberts failed to perfect the security interest in any other manner provided by the Georgia and Uniform Commercial Codes; and that Section 70(c) of the Bankruptcy Act, 11 U.S.C. 110 [section 544 of the current Bankruptcy Code], and Georgia Code 109A–9–301(3) gave the bankruptcy trustee preference over Roberts' unperfected security interests

The District Judge would have denied reclamation for the TV set also, except that the point was not preserved by cross appeal. Appellee now stipulates, contrary to the impression of the court below, that the combined value of all the involved merchandise is not equal to the debt owed Roberts Furniture Co. Nevertheless, we affirm.

I.

* * *

The issue here is whether Georgia law would allow the arrangement below to be considered a Purchase Money Security Interest, which requires no filing for perfection. Georgia has enacted the Uniform Commercial Code. Georgia Code 109A–9–107 [9–103] defines a Purchase Money Security Interest: [court quotes section 9–107]. Georgia Code 109A–9–302 [9–309] provides the exceptions where filing is not required for perfection. One of the exceptions is:. . .

(d) a purchase money security interest in consumer goods [9–309(1)].

There are other exceptions to the filing requirement, not here relevant. Otherwise, if not perfected by filing, under Georgia Code 109A–9–301 [9–317(a)(2)], the unperfected security interest is subordinate to the rights of "(1)(b) . . . a lien creditor . . .;" which term includes "(3) . . . a trustee in bankruptcy . . . ;" unless all the creditors had actual knowledge of the security interest, which is not contended here.

Roberts Furniture claims the exception for consumer goods. As the judges below noted, citing *Allen v. Lokey*, 307 F.2d 353 (5th Cir. 1962), and *National Silver Co. v. Nicholas*, 205 F.2d 52 (5th Cir. 1953), the burden of proof to establish a security interest is upon the party seeking reclamation, and Roberts has not met that burden. The problem here begins with the fact that the security agreement filed with the court shows about $150 paid on about a $900 total debt, for 7 pieces of furniture and a TV set, with no clues as to what items are paid for and which are not, nor does any rule of first-bought, first-paid for appear.

A plain reading of the statutory requirements would indicate that they require the purchase money security interest to be in the item purchased, and that, as the judges below noted, the purchase money security interest cannot exceed the price of what is purchased in the transaction wherein the security interest is created, if the vendor is to be protected despite the absence of filing. Except as to the TV set, if at all, the interest here is not a "purchase money security interest" because it is not taken or retained by the seller of the collateral solely to secure all or part of *its* (emphasis supplied) price. Roberts attempted to make collateral secure debt other than its own price. The statutory exception does not reach the case.

The judges below drew their conclusion on the statutory language and on authority other than Georgia cases. Appellee has collected and cited to us a number of Georgia cases, which we have examined. We have no doubt that the Georgia courts will henceforward observe the express command of their legislature, but we find it unnecessary to analyze in detail cases which show no more than that they have hitherto done so, with respect to parts of the enactment here involved, other than those to be construed here. The District Judge refers to *In re Simpson*, 4 U.C.C. Rep. 243 (D.C.W.D.Mich.1966). This referee in bankruptcy's opinion is well thought out, and documented with references to the Official Code Comment #2, and to secondary authority. It was a case stronger for the vendor, than the one here, in that the farm machinery item in dispute was sold under the agreement which failed, in the referee's view, to create a purchase money security interest without filing, only because it included a clause making the item security, not only for its own price, but also for future advances. The entire discussion may be regarded as dictum since the referee ends up by holding that the vendor saved its security interest after all by recovering possession before the bankruptcy, without fraud on the creditors. In view of the wide circulation of the referee's opinion by the U.C.C Reporting Service, the absence of contrary case authority, and its inherent reasonableness, we think our District Judge properly gave much weight to it.

The error of the belief below, that the value of the intended collateral exceeded the debt, is not fatal to the conclusion reached, though it does impair some of the reasoning, and prevents us from adopting the opinion below as our own.

We express no view as to whether a valid purchase money security interest was created with respect to the TV set. Nothing we say is to be taken as a holding as to that.

AFFIRMED.

NOTE

Section 9–103 does not overrule *Manuel* in the consumer goods context. Why? Because consumer-goods transactions are largely excluded from the provisions of section 9–103 that resolve many of the same issues in the business loan context. Section 9–103 provides in relevant part as follows:

> (e) **[Application of payment in non-consumer-goods transaction.]** In a transaction other than a consumer-goods transaction, if the extent to which a security interest is a purchase-money security interest depends on the application of a payment to a particular obligation, the payment must be applied:
>
> > (1) in accordance with any reasonable method of application to which the parties agree;
> >
> > (2) in the absence of the parties' agreement to a reasonable method, in accordance with any intention of the obligor manifested at or before the time of payment; or
> >
> > (3) in the absence of an agreement to a reasonable method and a timely manifestation of the obligor's intention, in the following order:
> >
> > > (A) to obligations that are not secured; and
> > >
> > > (B) if more than one obligation is secured, to obligations secured by purchase-money security interests in the order in which those obligations were incurred.
>
> (f) **[No loss of status of purchase-money security interest in non-consumer-goods transaction.]** In a transaction other than a consumer-goods transaction, a purchase-money security interest does not lose its status as such, even if:
>
> > (1) the purchase-money collateral also secures an obligation that is not a purchase-money obligation;
> >
> > (2) collateral that is not purchase-money collateral also secures the purchase-money obligation; or
> >
> > (3) the purchase-money obligation has been renewed, refinanced, consolidated, or restructured.
>
> (g) **[Burden of proof in non-consumer-goods transaction.]** In a transaction other than a consumer-goods transaction, a secured party claiming a purchase-money security interest has the burden of

> establishing the extent to which the security interest is a purchase-money security interest.
>
> (h) **[Non-consumer-goods transactions; no inference.]** The limitation of the rules in subsections (e), (f), and (g) to transactions other than consumer-goods transactions is intended to leave to the court the determination of the proper rules in consumer-goods transactions. The court may not infer from that limitation the nature of the proper rule in consumer-goods transactions and may continue to apply established approaches.

While the drafters of revised Article 9 declined to force the quoted rules on consumers, they did in subsection (h) prohibit the drawing of an adverse inference from the non-consumer rules because of the statutory resolution of a particular issue for non-consumer debtors. That is, one may not infer from a rule limited to non-consumers that the consumer rule must be different (or the same).

Consider the following case, which discusses the "transformation rule," "dual status rule," and payment allocation issues in the context of a security interest in equipment under old Article 9. The case involves farm products, not consumer goods. We put it here because the judge discusses various ways in which one might approach a purchase money security interest that has been refinanced and partially paid off. As noted, such problems have largely been swept away in non-consumer transactions, but remain for security interests in consumer goods.

IN RE MCALLISTER

United States Bankruptcy Court, Northern District Iowa, 2001.
267 B.R. 614.

KILBURG, CHIEF JUDGE:

* * *

Michael and Pamela McAllister (Debtors) bring this action to have the Court determine the priority of two creditor's security interests in an auger, planter, and trailer (hereafter "farm equipment") currently in Debtors' possession. * * *

First Southeast Bank contests the validity of Ag Services' purchase-money security interest and asserts that its prior perfection of its security interest gives it priority status over the farm equipment. Debtors assert that Ag Services has a purchase-money security interest and therefore a superpriority over the Bank's security interest.

The Bank stipulates that Ag Services provided funds for Debtors' purchase of the farm equipment. It contends Ag Services lost its purchase-money security interest due to the contents of its security agreement or, alternatively, that Ag Services' security interest in the farm equipment never attained purchase-money security interest status.

* * *

In May 1985, Debtors executed a security agreement in favor of the Bank, granting it a security interest in all equipment owned and hereafter acquired. The Bank filed a Financing Statement with the Iowa Secretary of State on May 28, 1985. Proper continuances have been filed until present time.

Debtors and Ag Services of America entered into an Agricultural Security Agreement for the production of crops on January 16, 1998. Besides a security interest in the crops, Debtors granted Ag Services a security interest in "All of Debtors' equipment and motorized vehicles and/or trailers, whether or not required to be licensed or registered, whether now owned or hereafter acquired, including but not limited to machinery and tools, together with all accessories, parts, accessions and repairs or hereafter attached or affixed thereto [including] but not limited to items listed below."

Ag Services' security agreement with Debtors contained a future advances clause. The record does not contain evidence as to the amount of principal, the interest rate or the repayment due date for the crop production loan. Ag Services perfected its security interest by filing a financing statement January 23, 1998. It filed a[n] amendment to the original financing statement January 11, 1999, to replace the legal description of the land upon which the crops were produced and to replace the equipment list.

Debtors executed a promissory note with Ag Services raising the principal balance to $112,000 on November 22, 1999. The interest rate was 21.0% with principal balance and accrued interest payable on or before January 15, 2001. The November 22 promissory note contains the clause "The security agreement(s) by which this note is secured include, but are not limited to, security agreements(s), mortgages or deeds of trust dated January 16, 1998."

The parties stipulate that Ag Services advanced funds which enabled Debtors to purchase an auger in November 1999 and a planter and trailer in January 2000. The current value of the auger is $2500. The current value of the planter and trailer is $3500.

On December 14, 2000, Debtors executed a promissory note with Ag Services increasing the principal balance to $119,000. This note is on the same form and contains the same "secured by" clause as the November 22, 1999 note. The note contains an interest rate of 21.0%, with the principal balance and accrued interest payable on or before January 15, 2002.

* * *

This dispute focuses on the conflicting rights of secured creditors First Southeast Bank and Ag Services. Article 9 of the Uniform Commercial

Code, set forth in Iowa Code chapter 554, governs the attachment and perfection of security interests in goods. Iowa Code sec. 554.9203(1) [9–203(b) of revised Article 9] provides that "a security interest is not enforceable against the debtor or third parties with respect to the collateral and does not attach unless: (1) the collateral is in the possession of the secured party pursuant to agreement, or the debtor has signed a security agreement which contains a description of the collateral . . .; (2) value has been given; and (3) the debtor has rights in the collateral." Iowa Code § 554.9203(1) (1999).

A security interest is perfected when it has attached and a financing statement has been filed or the security interest is otherwise perfected. Iowa Code §§ 554.9303(1), 554.9302(1) [section 9–308 of revised Article 9]. "If such steps are taken before the security interest attaches, it is perfected at the time when it attaches." Iowa Code § 554.9303(1) [9–308]. The term "attached" is used to describe the point at which property becomes subject to a security interest. Iowa Code § 554.9303 comment 1 [9–308 cmt. 2].

Where the funds are delivered by the lender for the specific purpose of purchasing equipment that is described in a prior, perfected financing statement between the parties, that security interest is a purchase-money security interest when and to the extent the funds are so used. Iowa Code § 554.9107(b) [section 9–103 of revised Article 9]; section 554.9204 comment 2; *John Deere Co. v. Production Credit Ass'n,* 686 S.W.2d 904, 907 (Tenn.Ct.App.1984). Ag Services' earlier-filed financing statement perfects the subsequent security agreements. *Deutz-Allis Credit Corp. v. Lynch Farms, Inc.,* 387 N.W.2d 593, 595 (Iowa 1986). The filed financing statement gives notice to other creditors that Ag Services may claim a security interest in Debtors' equipment.

Article 9 is a notice filing system. When a conflict exists between secured creditors, the general rule provides that between creditors who perfected their security interests in the same collateral by filing a financing statement, the first in time to file their security interest has priority. Iowa Code § 554.9312(5) [section 9–322 of revised Article 9]. Iowa Code sec. 554.9312 governs the priority of security interests in the same collateral. *Citizens Savs. Bank v. Miller,* 515 N.W.2d 7, 9 (Iowa 1994). In this case both parties have perfected their security interests by filing financing statements. It is undisputed that, unless Ag Services has a purchase-money security interest, the Bank is entitled to priority under this section.

* * *

The paramount exception to the first-to-file rule is the superpriority arising from a purchase-money security interest (PMSI). By definition, a security interest is a "purchase-money security interest" to the extent that it is "taken by a person who by making advances or incurring an obligation gives value to enable the debtor to acquire rights in or the use of collateral if such value is in fact so used." Iowa Code § 554.9107(b) [section 9–103 of revised Article 9]. The Iowa Supreme Court simply describes a PMSI as "a secured loan for the price of new collateral." *Farmers Co-op. Elev. Co v. Union State Bank,* 409 N.W.2d 178, 180 (Iowa 1987).

Debtors claim that Ag Services has a PMSI and, therefore, Iowa Code section 554.9312(4) controls the priority of the conflicting security interests. Section 554.9312(4) [section 9–324 of revised Article 9] provides that a purchase-money security interest in collateral has priority if it was perfected at the time the debtor receives possession of the collateral or within twenty days thereafter. Iowa Code § 544.9107(b). Debtors must establish Ag Services' superpriority status. *In re Relpak Corp.,* 25 B.R. 148, 152–53 (Bankr.E.D.N.Y.1982).

Transformation Rule

Some courts have held that purchase-money security interests are transformed into ordinary security interests under certain circumstances. This doctrine, known as the "Transformation Rule", is applied in cases involving the financing of collateral where the indebtedness has been refinanced, where the security agreement contains after-acquired property and cross-collateralization clauses and where the collateral secures later indebtedness through future advances clauses. *Borg-Warner Acceptance Corp. v. Tascosa Nat'l Bank,* 784 S.W.2d 129, 134 (Tex.Ct.App.1990).

There is a split of authority on whether refinancing through renewal or consolidation causes a purchase-money lender to lose its superpriority status. Some courts apply the transformation rule where a PMSI is automatically "transformed" into a nonpurchase-money security interest when the proceeds of refinancing are used to satisfy the original debt. *In re Matthews,* 724 F.2d 798, 800 (9th Cir.1984) (creditor sacrificed its PMSI when it made the "decision to issue a new loan, and, in its own words, to 'pay net balance due' on the old loan, rather than to extend the payments on the old loan"). This line of cases holds that the resulting lien on the purchased goods no longer qualifies as a PMSI under section 9–107 [9–103] because after refinancing, the collateral secures an antecedent debt rather than a debt for purchase of the collateral or, in the case of a renewal note consolidating debt or advancing new funds, secures more than its purchase price. *In re Short,* 170 B.R. 128, 132–33 (Bankr.S.D.Ill.1994). The refinancing does not "enable" the debtor to acquire rights in the collateral and is therefore a nonpurchase-money security interest. *Matthews,* 724 F.2d at 800; *see also In re Keeton,* 161 B.R. 410, 411 (Bankr.S.D.Ohio 1993).

Other courts hold that the PMSI status is lost if a security interest collateralizes any other debt in addition to the purchase-money debt. *In re Manuel,* 507 F.2d 990 (5th Cir.1975) (seller lost PMSI as to previously purchased items when cross-collateralized and consolidated with loan to purchase TV; court declined to rule whether TV lost its PMSI); *In re*

Norrell, 426 F.Supp. 435 (M.D.Ga.1977) (invalidating the purchase-money aspect of the security agreement even as to merchandise comprising the immediate transaction).

In *Norrell,* the seller used an "add on" clause in an attempt to reserve a security interest in the items purchased plus "any subsequent purchases . . . added to this contract while there is a balance due thereon." *Norrell,* 426 F.Supp. at 436. The court held that the seller did not retain a PMSI because the "loan" to debtor was secured by property other than the collateral for which the funds had been advanced. *Id.* Some courts have determined that the mere inclusion of an after-acquired property or future advances clause in the security agreement transforms a PMSI into an ordinary security interest. *Compare Southtrust Bank v. Borg-Warner Acceptance Corp.,* 760 F.2d 1240, 1243 (11th Cir.1985) (finance company's exercise of the after-acquired property and future advances clauses in its security agreement converted its PMSI into an ordinary security interest leaving unanswered whether mere inclusion of the clauses causes the PMSI to convert into a nonpurchase-money security interest), *and In re Jones,* 5 B.R. 655, 657 (Bankr.M.D.N.C.1980) (presence of a future advances clause in the underlying security agreement was enough to extinguish the PMSI character of the security interest), *with In re Griffin,* 9 B.R. 880, 881 (Bankr.N.D.Ga.1981) (holding that the PMSI status had not been destroyed by the inclusion of future advances clause).

Dual Status

More recent opinions conclude that a security interest may have a "dual status." *In re Leftwich,* 174 B.R. 54, 58 (Bankr.W.D.Va.1994); *Pristas v. Landaus of Plymouth, Inc.,* 742 F.2d 797, 800–01 (3d Cir.1984); *In re Billings,* 838 F.2d 405, 409 (10th Cir.1988). A security interest may be partially purchase-money and partially nonpurchase-money. *E.g., Short,* 170 B.R. at 133. That is, a creditor may retain a PMSI in goods that also secure later purchases to the extent that the PMSI in the original items secures only the unpaid part of their own price. Dual status is premised on the language of Uniform Commercial Code section 9–107 [9–103(b)] which provides that a lien is a PMSI "to the extent" that it is taken to secure the purchase price of collateral. *Id.* Refinancing does not automatically destroy the purchase-money aspect of the lien. *Id.*

Debtors cite *John Deere Co. v. Production Credit Ass'n,* 686 S.W.2d 904 (Tenn.Ct.App.1984), for the proposition that the inclusion of future advances and after-acquired property clauses does not cause a PMSI to lose its superpriority status. In that case John Deere argued that PCA did not have a PMSI because its prior security agreement contained after-acquired and future advance clauses. *Id.* at 905. The court held that PCA held a PMSI up to the amount of the value it gave for the purchase of the combine. *Id.* at 907. It concluded that a lender can be a purchase-money lender irrespective of the terms of its security agreement, to the extent that its PMSI claim is limited to the funds that it can prove were used to purchase the collateral. *Id.*

The Bank does not cite any Iowa cases. It cites the Court to 68A Am.Jur.2d *Secured Transactions* § 847 (1993) as authority for application of the "transformation rule". The American Jurisprudence is not binding authority. It merely notes that "it has been contended" that in some jurisdictions inclusion of future advances and after-acquired property clauses could cause a PMSI to lose its priority or "at least giv[e] it a dual nature, divided between the purchase-money and other portions of the financing." *Id.*

It is the conclusion of this Court that the "dual status" doctrine is properly applied in this case. Application of this doctrine allows the inclusion of after-acquired and future advances clauses. *See In re Hassebroek,* 136 B.R. 527, 530 (Bankr.N.D.Iowa 1991) (determination of whether consolidation causes creditor to lose its PMSI status). "Obligations covered by a security agreement may include future advances or other value whether or not the advances or value are given pursuant to commitment." Iowa Code § 554.9204(3). Section 554.9204 comment 5 reveals that after-acquired property and future advance clauses were meant to be a useful tool in commercial finance and harsh restrictions should not be placed on their use. *In re Estate of Simpson,* 403 N.W.2d 791, 792 (Iowa 1987).

This court's application of the "dual status" doctrine is consistent with recent case law. Courts in this Circuit, like Iowa, apply the "dual status" doctrine. *See In re Hemingson,* 84 B.R. 604, 606 (Bankr.D.Minn.1988); *In re Win-Vent, Inc.,* 217 B.R. 803, 811–12 (Bankr.W.D.Mo.1997), *aff'd,* 217 B.R. 798 (W.D.Mo.1997); *In re Wiegert,* 145 B.R. 621, 623 (Bankr.D.Neb.1991). The new Article 9 revision adopts the dual status doctrine. Revised U.C.C. section 9–103(f) (2001) provides that "[A] purchase-money security interest does not lose its status as such, even if: (1) the purchase-money collateral also secures an obligation that is not a purchase-money obligation; (2) collateral that is not purchase-money collateral also secures the purchase-money obligation; or (3) the purchase-money obligation has been renewed, refinanced, consolidated, or restructured."

Refinancing

Although inclusion of future advances and after-acquired property clauses does not transform a PMSI into a nonpurchase-money security interest, refinancing may cause a creditor to lose its PMSI status. *In re Butler,* No. 86 01651C, 1987 WL 46571, at *1 (Bankr.N.D.Iowa, May 28, 1987). The Bank does not raise this issue. However, the Court feels it appropriate to review the record to determine whether the 1999 and the

2000 promissory notes cause Ag Services to lose its PMSI in the contested equipment.

Refinancing occurs when an existing note is renewed and new credit is extended. *Butler,* 1987 WL 46571 at *2. Common characteristics of refinancing include: (1) an extension in the time of payment, (2) a consolidation of notes, and (3) an extension of new credit with or without additional security. *Id.* at *2. Refinancing a loan can be determined to be (1) a renewal of the original purchase-money obligation, in which case the PMSI survives, or (2) a novation which extinguishes the purchase-money character of the loan. *Short,* 170 B.R. at 134. A novation occurs when the "purpose of the note was to pay off the original note, an antecedent debt." *Eitzen's Estate v. Lauman,* 231 Iowa 1169, 3 N.W.2d 546, 550 (Iowa 1942). Article 9 does not address the effect of refinancing or consolidation on PMSI status. Determining whether Ag Services' third security agreement extinguishes the PMSI on the collateral purchased under the second security agreement depends on a court determination of whether the second and third notes represent a novation. *Butler,* 1987 WL 46571, at *2.

This court has addressed the issue. *Compare In re Averhoff,* 18 B.R. 198 (Bankr.N.D.Iowa 1982) (novation found where each subsequent note advanced new money, increased debtor's payments, provided additional collateral for security, and introduced a new security agreement for each renewal), *with In re Fricke,* No. L91-01056W, slip op. at 5 (Bankr.N.D.Iowa. Oct. 22, 1991) (novation not found even though debt was not perfected until consolidation of three notes), *and Butler,* 1987 WL 46571 (intent to extinguish the original security agreement and substitute the new ones for the antecedent debt was not proven). The primary consideration of whether refinancing constitutes a novation is the "intent" of the parties. *Butler,* 1987 WL 46571, at *3.

Various factors are considered to determine whether the parties intend a novation. They include: (1) whether new money was advanced to the debtors, (2) whether the amount of the monthly payments increased, (3) whether a new security agreement was introduced, and (4) whether additional collateral was provided to secure the creditor's security interest. *Hassebroek,* 136 B.R. at 530. A novation is not presumed. *Id.* The greater the degree of change in the obligation, the more likely a novation will be found. *Short,* 170 B.R. at 134. "Tolerance of 'add-on' debt and collateral provisions, properly applied, carries out the approbation for purchase-money security arrangements and simplifies repeat transactions between the same buyer and [lender]." *Hemingson,* 84 B.R. at 607.

It is the conclusion of this Court that the subsequent promissory notes executed by Ag Services and Debtors were intended as "add on" transactions extending the loan limit. The advances were not made with the intent of paying off the earlier debt. Execution of each subsequent promissory note did not precipitate execution of a new security agreement which was meant to substitute for the prior security agreements. *Butler,* 1987 WL 46571 at *3. The promissory notes, dated November 22, 1999 and December 14, 2000, establish that the prior security agreement was to remain in effect by inclusion of the clause: "The security agreement(s) by which this note is secured include, but are not limited to, security agreements(s), mortgages or deeds of trust dated January 16, 1998."

The promissory notes do not evidence a new beginning but rather a continuance of a prior agreement. The 21.0% interest rate is consistent in both the November of 1999 and December of 2000 agreements. Without evidence to the contrary as to the repayment date for the original loan, the Court concludes that the January 15, 2001 repayment date, set as the repayment date in the November 22, 1999 security agreement and extended one year by the December 14, 2000 security agreement, correlates to the repayment date set in the January 16, 1998 loan. It is clear from the record that the advances had no effect on monthly payments. The phrase: "Said principal and accrued interest to be due and payable in full on or before" indicates repayment in one lump sum.

The Bank has the burden to establish that each subsequent agreement represents a novation. *Butler,* 1987 WL 46571, at *3. This Court concludes that the subsequently executed promissory notes do not extinguish the prior security agreement but rather represent "add ons" to the total amount of principal Debtors could borrow.

* * *

The remaining issue is to determine the extent of Ag Services' PMSI. The difficulty with the dual status rule lies in determining how payments have been allocated and what portion of the debt is purchase-money. *E.g., Hassebroek,* 136 B.R. at 531. If that allocation can be made, the PMSI does not convert to an ordinary security interest. *In re Slay,* 8 B.R. 355, 358 (Bankr.E.D.Tenn.1980). If the security agreement is silent as to how payments are to be allocated, some courts look to state law for a formula while others impose a judicial "first-in first-out" rule, or "FIFO". *Pristas,* 742 F.2d at 801.

Iowa follows the first-in first-out method. *In re Butler,* 1987 WL 46571, at *2 (Bankr.N.D.Iowa, May 28, 1987); *Hassebroek,* 136 B.R. at 531. Other states in the Eighth Circuit also follow the first-in first-out method. *In re Hemingson,* 84 B.R. 604, 606–07 (Bankr.D.Minn.1988); *In re Wiegert,* 145 B.R. 621, 623 (Bankr.D.Neb.1991). The burden is on Debtors to provide evidence that will allow the Court to trace their payments to Ag Services. *Short,* 170 B.R. at 135.

The FIFO method allocates payments first to the unpaid amount of the oldest purchase and then sequentially to the remaining debts in the order in which they were incurred, retaining a valid PMSI in items which have not been paid in full. *Wiegert,* 145 B.R. at 623–22. The purchase price includes the cost of the item and any financing charges and sales taxes attributable to that item. *Short,* 170 B.R. at 136. A general security interest is retained in the paid-in-full collateral. *Id.*

The Bank stipulates that Ag Services provided funds for the three pieces of equipment. This obviates the need for Debtors to provide evidence which demonstrates that they received funds from Ag Services which they in fact used to purchase the farm equipment. However, the record is insufficient to determine what portion of Ag Services' $20,000 claim originally represented purchase-money and what portion of the funds retain PMSI status. Using the FIFO method to allocate payments, it is possible that some of the equipment for which Ag Services originally had a PMSI, has been paid in full. Once the purchase price of a particular item has been fully paid, the security interest in that item becomes a nonpurchase-money security interest. *Short,* 170 B.R. at 136.

* * *

Iowa follows the dual status doctrine for purchase-money security interests. Under Iowa law, the inclusion of after-acquired property and future advances clauses in security agreements, does not "transform" a PMSI into a general security interest. Ag Services' PMSI in the equipment arose from the promissory notes referring back to the January 16, 1998 security agreement for which a financing statement was filed with the Secretary of the State on January 23, 1998.

The record is insufficient for the Court to determine what, if any, equipment has been paid in full and what debts are accounted for in Ag Services' $20,000 claim. An additional hearing is necessary to allow Debtors an opportunity to provide sufficient evidence to allow the Court to make the required calculations. If Debtors are unable to sustain this burden, insufficient payment records could result in a loss of all purchase-money security interests.

* * *

[footnote omitted]

NOTE

Section 9–103(f) of Revised Article 9 (that had not yet become effective in Iowa when the *McAllister* decision was rendered) generally confirms the conclusions that the court reached in non-consumer-goods transactions. What is the appropriate solution to the conundrum that arises in a "dual status" situation where the debtor makes payments that the debtor would like to allocate to the secured debt (and so preserve the unsecured debt that can be written off in bankruptcy) and the creditor would like to allocate the payments to the unsecured debt (and so leave the secured debt on which the creditor will receive a higher payment in bankruptcy)?

PROBLEM 7-1

Debtor purchases a $60,000 mobile home as her residence. She borrows $50,000 from Bank and gives a security interest. By mistake, Bank fails to file a financing statement.

1. Upon Debtor's bankruptcy, Bank claims an automatically perfected security interest. Trustee argues that the automatic perfection provisions do not and should not apply to a commodity with such a large value. Is Bank in trouble?

2. Would Trustee prevail if the mobile home had become a fixture since Bank concedes that it did not do a "fixture filing"?

3. What if one could procure a certificate of title on mobile homes in Arkansas where the transaction takes place, but Debtor never did so? *See* 9–311.

4. What if two months after the sale Debtor moved the mobile home to a construction site where she used it as a construction office?

§ 3. THE SPECIAL CASE OF AUTOMOBILES AND OTHER GOODS COVERED BY CERTIFICATES OF TITLE

The certificate of title laws, which now exist in all states in some form, provide a mode of perfection that was in use in many states at the time the original Code was enacted, and that are entirely separate from Article 9's system of perfection. These certificate of title statutes commonly provide for the maintenance of a central registry listing the ownership of various "title" property, such as automobiles. Liens on the property are generally noted on the title. Section 9–311(a) states that the filing of a financing statement is not necessary or sufficient to perfect a security interest in property subject to a certificate of title statute, and section 9–311(b) provides that satisfying the requirements of such a state statute is equivalent to filing a financing statement for the purposes of Article 9. In addition to this "step-back" provision, sections 9–316(d) and (e) provide rules for changes in the applicable law. More importantly, section 9–303 dictates the law governing perfection and priority of security interests in goods covered by a certificate of title. Section 9–337 provides rules for priority. Although this topic is included in this chapter, one cannot assume that all automobile security interests are granted by consumers. In fact there are many business security interests in trucks or other vehicles that are covered by certificates of title. For example, getting one's name on the certificate of title would be the common way of perfecting a security interest in a trucking company's vehicles. In general the problems of perfection and priority are the same whether the debtor is a consumer or a businessperson.

Note also the exception in section 9–311(d). It provides that while the collateral in question is inventory (such as the cars on a dealer's lot waiting to be sold), section 9–311 does not apply. Accordingly, a secured party holding a security interest in the inventory must perfect its security interest in accordance with the general requirements of Article 9, typically by filing a financing statement. Once the collateral is sold and is no longer inventory, however, section 9–311 does apply.

Why did the drafters of Article 9 leave a separate filing system in place when they proposed Article 9 as a part of the Uniform Commercial Code? They may have thought it impossible to overcome the resistance of automobile manufacturers and automobile lenders who were familiar with the existing system and who might argue persuasively that the certificate of title system need not be fixed since it was not broken.[2] Initial acceptance of the use of the certificate of title as a device for perfection of security interests in vehicles has been carried over in all of the revisions of Article 9.

As states begin to change their written records into digital records, the law with respect to security interests in automobiles will also have to change. Presumably a creditor can "get his name on the certificate" as easily on a digital certificate as on a written one, so there should not be insurmountable problems. But in the transactions between consumer buyers and sellers of cars and between dealers and consumers, it will be risky to rely on a written document that purports to be a true copy of a digital filing. We suspect that it is easier to modify and make an apparently clean counterfeit certificate of title from a digital original than it is from a written original. Under current practice sellers bent on hiding existing security interests in automobiles have typically tricked the motor vehicle department into issuing "clean" certificates by engaging in fraud of various sorts ("I lost my certificate of title, issue a new one.").

PROBLEM 7-2

Assume Bank makes a loan to Debtor and takes a security interest in Debtor's $70,000 truck. The truck, at the time of the loan, is located in and operated from Tennessee. Bank perfects its security interest by getting its name listed as the secured creditor on the Tennessee certificate of title. Consider the rights of Bank vis-à-vis a trustee in bankruptcy or a competing creditor in each of the following cases.

1. Debtor moves to Ohio, establishes his residence there and operates the truck from Cincinnati. He continues to operate the truck under the

---

[2] *See* GRANT GILMORE, SECURITY INTERESTS IN PERSONAL PROPERTY 294 (1965) (discussing the exclusion of motor vehicles covered by certificates of title).

Tennessee certificate of title and 2 years after the move, files bankruptcy. The trustee argues that the failure of the Debtor to get a certificate of title in Ohio and of the creditor to get its name on such certificate subordinated the creditor. Is the trustee correct? *See* 9–303(b), 9–316(d), (e) & cmt 5, 9–337.

2. Now assume that Debtor procured a new certificate of title in Ohio one month after the move to Cincinnati. Either because of Debtor's fraud or because of a mistake in the Ohio Certificate of Title Office, Bank was not listed as a secured creditor on the new certificate. Six months after the move and five months after the clean Ohio certificate had been issued, assume that Debtor sells his truck to a bona fide purchaser or that Debtor files for bankruptcy. In the former case the bona fide purchaser defeats the Tennessee secured creditor, correct? What about the competition between Bank and the trustee in the latter case?

GREEN V. ARCADIA FINANCIAL LTD.

Supreme Court, Erie County, 1997.
174 Misc.2d 411, 663 N.Y.S.2d 944.

MINTZ, JUSTICE:

Plaintiff moves for declaratory judgment and interim relief. Defendant Arcadia cross-moves for summary judgment dismissing the complaint, and defendant Four M Sales (Four M) also seeks dismissal of the complaint. The facts underlying this action are not in dispute.

Antwan Anderson purchased a 1993 Jeep Cherokee from Master Motors of Buffalo on January 4, 1997. Anderson paid $2,500 down and financed the remainder of the purchase price ($18,119.20) through an installment obligation to defendant Arcadia whereby he was to make 72 monthly payments of $424.60 commencing February 4, 1997. Defendant Arcadia secured the installment obligation with a lien which was properly perfected, and such lien was duly noted on Anderson's certificate of title. Anderson made payments in February and March. On February 11, 1997, Anderson submitted a forged release of lien on a piece of stationery which purported to be Arcadia letterhead to the Department of Motor Vehicles. Through the submission of the release of lien, Anderson obtained on March 4, 1997, a new certificate of title without any lien noted thereon. On March 14, 1997, Anderson sold the vehicle to defendant Four M. On April 21, 1997, Four M sold the vehicle to the plaintiff, who financed its acquisition through defendant Pentagon. On June 13, 1997, the vehicle was repossessed by Arcadia's agent. Defendant Arcadia claims that its lien continues despite the filing of the false release of lien, and despite the issuance by the Department of Motor Vehicles of a certificate of title with no liens noted. Plaintiff claims that he acquired the vehicle from Four M without Arcadia's lien.

New York enacted the Uniform Vehicle Certificate of Title Act in 1971 (Vehicle and Traffic Law, 2101 *et seq.*). The Act preempts UCC Article 9 with respect to security interests in automobiles which are created by persons other than dealers; thus, article 9 has no application to this case. Under 2118, a security interest in the automobile is perfected by the filing of an application with the Department of Motor Vehicles. It is undisputed that defendant Arcadia properly perfected its security interest by such a filing. Under section 2121, a security interest is released by the filing of a release of lien which has been executed by the lienholder. Although Anderson filed a release of lien, it is undisputed that such release was not executed by Arcadia. While the certificate of title is prima facie evidence of the information contained thereon (2108[c]), the existence of the certificate of title in question is not dispositive of the issue. Anderson could not and did not convey unencumbered title of the Jeep to Four M. This is not, however, determinative of the issue of whether Four M, as a dealer in used automobiles, could deliver unencumbered title to plaintiff, as a buyer in the ordinary course of business, who is a good-faith purchaser for value.

UCC 2–403(1) provides in part:

> A purchaser of goods acquires all title which his transferor had or had power to transfer except that a purchaser of a limited interest acquires rights only to the extent of the interest purchased. A person with voidable title has power to transfer a good title to a good faith purchased for value.

A purchaser who purchases a vehicle from a thief, or from a dealer who has purchased from a thief does not acquire title under section 2–403. (*See, e.g.*, *Candela v. Port Motors, Inc.*, 208 A.D.2d 486, 617 N.Y.S.2d 49 [2d Dept.1994.]) However, a person who acquires title by fraud has "voidable" title, and can convey good title so long as the goods are transferred to a good-faith purchaser for value before such title is voided. (*See, e.g.*, *Sheridan Suzuki, Inc. v. Caruso Auto Sales, Inc.*, 110 Misc.2d 823, 442 N.Y.S.2d 957 [Sup.Ct.Erie Co.1981.]) A person who acquires a certificate title by fraudulent documents submitted to the Department of Motor Vehicles does not acquire voidable title within the meaning of 2–403. (*Alamo Rent-A-Car, Inc. v. Mendenhall*, 113 Nev. 445, 937 P.2d 69 [1997.]) Such a person has no greater title than he did prior to the acquisition of the documents. For this reason, Arcadia's lien continued in the vehicle after its sale to plaintiff. Had Anderson acquired a properly executed release of lien through fraud or through a dishonored check, his resulting unencumbered title would have been "voidable." However, he did not ever acquire a proper release of lien, and his title, encumbered by the Arcadia lien, remained unchanged by the submission of the forged release of lien. Thus, Anderson conveyed title to Four M subject to Arcadia's lien, and Four M could only convey the same title to plaintiff.

Four M, however, as a dealer in automobiles, warrants unencumbered title under UCC 2–312(3). Since the vehicle sold by Four M to the plaintiff was subject to Arcadia's lien, Four M breached its warranty of title, and plaintiff is entitled to recover his damages due to the existence of this lien from Four M. (*Candela v. Port Motors, supra.*) The measure of damages is the lesser of the outstanding loan balance owed to Arcadia or the amount paid by plaintiff to Four M including the payments under his installment obligation and the outstanding loan balance owed to defendant Pentagon. In the event that the amount paid by plaintiff is greater than the outstanding loan balance owed to Arcadia, Four M is to pay off that loan balance by payment to Arcadia, and the plaintiff will retain the vehicle, and he may maintain his action against Arcadia for the claimed damage to the vehicle during the repossession and retention of the vehicle by Arcadia. In the event that the amount paid by plaintiff is less than the outstanding loan balance owed to Arcadia, Four M is to return to plaintiff any down payment and any payments made by plaintiff to Pentagon on the installment obligation, and Four M is also to pay the outstanding loan balance to Pentagon. In that case, plaintiff is entitled to recover from Arcadia the value of improvements he made to the automobile after its purchase. (*Alamo Rent-A-Car v. Mendenhall*, supra.)

For these reasons, judgment is granted to plaintiff against defendant Four M, and judgment is granted to defendant Arcadia against plaintiff on the issue of the validity of its lien.

TOYOTA MOTOR CREDIT V. C.L. HYMAN AUTO WHOLESALE, INC.

Supreme Court of Virginia, 1998.
256 Va. 243.

LACY, JUSTICE:

In this appeal, we determine whether a lienholder whose lien was omitted from a duplicate certificate of title of an automobile because of the fraud of the owner can enforce that lien against a subsequent bona fide purchaser of the automobile.

The facts are not in dispute. In February 1996, Traci Bowden purchased a Toyota vehicle pursuant to a retail installment contract. The contract was assigned to Toyota Motor Credit Corporation (TMCC) for value. TMCC's security interest was noted on the certificate of title issued by the Virginia Department of Motor Vehicles (DMV). TMCC retained possession of the certificate of title.

In July 1996, Bowden applied for a duplicate certificate of title from DMV, representing that TMCC's lien had been satisfied and released. Bowden's application was accompanied by a letter purportedly from TMCC releasing its lien. This letter was a forgery. Based on these fraudulent representations, DMV issued a duplicate certificate of title showing "no liens" against the vehicle. Bowden then sold the vehicle to C.L. Hyman Auto Wholesale, Inc. (Hyman).

When Bowden fell behind in her payments on the Retail Installment Agreement, TMCC began efforts to bring the account current or to recover the vehicle. Eventually, TMCC discovered Bowden's fraud and that she had sold the vehicle to Hyman. TMCC asked Hyman to return the vehicle. When Hyman refused, TMCC filed a motion for judgment in detinue against Hyman. Following a hearing, the trial court found that Hyman was a *bona fide* purchaser for value without notice of the fraud, was "entitled to rely on the certificate issued by the DMV," and was not subject to TMCC's lien. The trial court dismissed the motion for judgment. We awarded TMCC an appeal.

As the trial court recognized, both parties in this litigation are innocent victims of the fraudulent acts of a third party: "Each has followed the law and done everything which could reasonably be expected in order to protect its interests. . . . However, the case is here, and, like it or not, the loss must fall on one of these two innocent parties." In determining where the loss falls, the trial court concluded that the motor vehicle titling statutes, as interpreted by this Court, require a decision in favor of Hyman. We agree and will affirm the judgment of the trial court.

The motor vehicle titling statutes, Title 42, Chapter 6, were enacted to protect the public by providing for the issuance of certificates of title as evidence of ownership of motor vehicles and to provide potential buyers and creditors with a single place where information about the status of motor vehicles could be found. *Maryland Credit Fin. Corp. v. Franklin Credit Fin. Corp.*, 164 Va. 579, 583, 180 S.E. 408, 409–10 (1935). These statutes, originally enacted in 1924, eliminated any requirement that a lien against a motor vehicle be recorded in the county or city where the purchaser or debtor resides or in any other manner available for recording a security interest in personal property, but imposed the new condition that a security interest in a motor vehicle would not be perfected "as to third parties" unless shown on the certificate of title. Code § 46.2–638; *Bain v. Commonwealth*, 215 Va. 89, 91, 205 S.E.2d 641, 643 (1974).

Code § 46.2–638 specifically provides that a certificate of title showing a security interest "shall be adequate notice to the Commonwealth, creditors, and purchasers that a security interest in the motor vehicle exists." We have recognized that the converse is also true. "[W]hen a certificate of title is issued which fails to show a lien or encumbrance, it is notice to the world that the property is free from any lien or encumbrance, and if transferred to a *bona fide* purchaser the latter would obtain a good title." *Maryland Credit*, 164 Va. at 582–83, 180 S.E. at 409. To hold otherwise would eliminate the ability of potential buyers and lenders to rely on the information contained in certificates of title.

Inevitably, there will be occasions when the information regarding the status of liens contained in a certificate of title will be in error. If the erroneous information is a notation that no liens exist against the vehicle, the interest of the *bona fide* purchaser for value prevails over the interest of the creditor with a security interest in the motor vehicle. *Id.* This rule applies whether the error was the result of an innocent mistake or, as in this case, of fraudulent acts by the owner. A rule which allowed reliance on the absence of lien notations on a certificate of title if such absence resulted from an innocent mistake or clerical error but not if such absence resulted from fraud would negate any ability to rely on the certificate of title. Under such a rule, a potential purchaser or lender would always have to conduct an independent search to determine if, in fact, there are no liens against the vehicle, thus defeating the intent of the General Assembly in creating a single repository for recording liens against motor vehicles. In this case, therefore, Hyman was entitled to rely on the absence of any lien notations on the certificate of title, and TMCC cannot enforce its security interest against Hyman.

TMCC asserts that this conclusion is in conflict with established principles underlying the law relating to title expressed in *First Nat'l Bank of Waynesboro v. Johnson*, 183 Va. 227, 31 S.E.2d 581 (1944), and Code § 8.2–403(1), as well as specific cases decided by this Court in which a lienholder was allowed to enforce its lien against a good faith purchaser for value without notice, *Rudolph v. Farmers' Supply Co.*, 131 Va. 305, 108 S.E. 638 (1921), and *McQuay v. Mount Vernon Bank and Trust Co.*, 200 Va. 776, 108 S.E.2d 251 (1959). Close examination of these cases shows, however, that the conclusion we reach today is not contrary to the authority cited by TMCC.

Longstanding Virginia law provides that one who does not have title to goods cannot transfer title to a buyer, even a *bona fide* purchaser for value without notice. *Johnson*, 183 Va. at 236, 31 S.E.2d at 585. Thus, a thief cannot pass title to stolen goods even to an innocent purchaser who pays for the stolen goods. However, Virginia law has also recognized that a person who purchases goods from one possessing only voidable title can nevertheless receive good title to the goods purchased. *Oberdorfer v. Meyer*, 88 Va. 384, 386, 13 S.E. 756, 756–57 (1891); *Old Dominion Steamship Co. v. Burckhardt*, 72 Va. (31 Gratt.) 664, 668 (1879). These principles have been implicitly recognized in Code § 8.2–403(1). That subsection states, in pertinent part:

> A purchaser of goods acquires all title which his transferor had or had the power to transfer. . . . A person with voidable title has power to transfer a good title to a good faith purchaser for value.

> When goods have been delivered under a transaction of purchase the purchaser has such power even though . . .
>
> (d) the delivery was procured through fraud punishable as larcenous under the criminal law.

Citing the principles embodied in Code § 8.2–403, TMCC argues that Bowden could not pass "greater" title in the automobile than she owned. Since her title was subject to the encumbrance of TMCC's lien, Hyman's title must also be subject to the lien.

TMCC's argument, however, misinterprets the purpose and applicability of Code § 8.2–403. The statute deals with the power of an owner with void or voidable title to pass good title to a *bona fide* purchaser for value. It does not apply to the "rights . . . of lien creditors." Code § 8.2–403(4). In this case, Bowden had a "good" title to the automobile, and she passed a good title to Hyman. She was not a stranger to title, and her title was not made "void" or "voidable" by TMCC's security interest. Code § 8.2–403 and the principle described in *Johnson*, therefore, simply do not apply.

Finally, the two Virginia cases cited by TMCC in which an innocent lienholder has prevailed over a *bona fide* purchaser do not require a different result in this case. Both of these cases involve sales to *bona fide* purchasers for value by motor vehicle dealers and the application of the doctrine of estoppel based on the likelihood that the secured motor vehicle would be put into the stream of commerce. In neither case did the Court consider the impact of the motor vehicle titling statutes or the extent to which potential purchasers are entitled to rely upon a certificate of title which failed to note an existing lien.

Rudolph v. Farmers' Supply Co., as TMCC notes, was decided prior to the enactment of the motor vehicle titling statutes in 1924. *Rudolph*, therefore, did not consider the effect of a certificate of title issued by DMV showing no liens on the motor vehicle, because the General Assembly had not yet authorized its issuance. Consequently, the decision in *Rudolph* is not controlling in this case.

The second Virginia case relied on by TMCC, *McQuay v. Mount Vernon Bank and Trust Co.*, was decided after the enactment of the titling statutes. However, it is not clear whether the *bona fide* purchaser in that case, McQuay, ever saw or received any title certificate from the seller or DMV and he did not assert a defense based on reliance on a certificate of title issued by DMV showing no liens on the vehicle. The ability to rely on a certificate of title issued with no notations of liens, therefore, was not at issue, and thus the holding in *McQuay* does not control the case before us.

For the above reasons, we conclude that the trial court properly held that TMCC was not entitled to enforce its lien against Hyman because Hyman, a *bona fide* purchaser for value without notice of the lien, was entitled to rely on a certificate of title which did not contain a notation of the lien.

AFFIRMED.

[footnote omitted.]

PROBLEM 7-3

The two previous cases boil down to who, as between two innocent parties, should be made to bear the loss when the debtor forges a title. *Green* put the loss on the buyer; *Hyman* put it on the secured creditor. Which court gets it right? Look back to the *Shaull* case in Chapter 4. It deals with some of the same issues in the context of a farming business.

In general, section 2–403(1) provides that a purchaser of goods acquires all the title that his seller had to give "or had power to transfer." The quoted language makes clear that the doctrines of agency, apparent agency, and estoppel apply. So, for example, even though the owner of an item may not have authorized his agent to make the particular transfer in question (for example, because the transfer was made for the wrong price), the transferee still gets good title if the transfer is enforceable under one of these doctrines.

Section 2–403 goes further and provides that "[a] person with voidable title has power to transfer a good title to a good-faith purchaser for value." The term "value" is defined broadly in section 1–204 and is rarely at issue. The concept of "good faith" is defined in section 1–201(b)(20) and its meaning has been the subject of much litigation. Generally, however, a purchaser who pays full value in the ordinary course and without any knowledge of the transferor's shenanigans will be acting in good faith. What is "voidable" title? The UCC does not say exactly. It provides some examples in sections 2–403(1)(a) through (d), including that voidable title is passed where "the delivery was in exchange for a check that is later dishonored" or "the delivery was procured through criminal fraud." These work to protect the subsequent transferees of the wrongdoer who acquired the goods by writing a bad check or as part of some fraudulent scheme. A thief who steals the goods in question, however, does not obtain "voidable" title; the title acquired by an outright thief is "void."

So in the *Green* case, was Anderson a thief? If so, it would appear that he acquired a void title. Accordingly, so the argument goes, he could not pass good title to Four M, and Four M could not pass good title to Green. But not so fast. Anderson was the owner of the vehicle subject to Arcadia's lien; he simply forged a document to get a "clean" title certificate, meaning a certificate of title without Arcadia's lien noted on it. So he did not necessarily "steal" the car; he just faked the document necessary to clean up his title. Accordingly, his title was simply voidable, right? Suppose, for example, Anderson had issued a check to Arcadia for the balance of his loan obligation and Arcadia had sent in a letter to the Virginia Department of Motor Vehicles (where the registry of titles are kept) stating that Anderson had paid off the lien and, accordingly, a clean title certificate could be issued. Suppose later the check bounced. Certainly Arcadia would have been deceived, but doesn't that seem a lot like the example in section 2–403(1)(b)—acquiring title where "the delivery was in exchange for a check that is later dishonored"?

In the *Hyman* case, was Bowden a thief? As in *Green*, Bowden forged a document so she could get clear title to facilitate her sale of the car to Hyman. This would seem to be at least in the nature of a crime. But the court ruled in favor of Hyman as the innocent purchaser, citing section 2–403(4), which provides that the rights of "lien creditors are governed by Article[ ] . . . 9." Was this a correct analysis? The court in *Hyman* observed that Bowden did not acquire title by theft; she was already the owner and thus not a "stranger to title" to her car. Bowden simply forged a document to get a "clear" title document. Accordingly the facts did not fit the paradigm for "voidness," such as where a burglar who is a true "stranger to title" steals a motor vehicle in the dead of night and then sells it to someone else. But what about the court's suggestion that section 2–403 does not apply at all to the rights of lien creditors, but rather these are governed by Article 9? Under section 9–315(a)(1), a security interest typically endures notwithstanding disposition of the collateral. Under section 9–320(a), a buyer in the ordinary course of business takes free of a security interest created in favor of the buyer's seller, but section 9–320 would not apply here to save Hyman: Bowden was not in the business of selling cars. *See* 1–201(b)(9). So under Article 9, wouldn't TMCC's security interest endure? Note that, at least according to the official commentary, Article 9 does not exactly preempt section 2–403. *See* 2–403 cmt 2–3, 9–320 cmt 3. In addition, note that under section 1–201, the term "purchaser" includes one who takes by a "security interest." *See* 1–201(b)(29).

THE "HANGING PARAGRAPH" OF SECTION 1325(a)(9)

When a consumer debtor files under Chapter 13 of the Bankruptcy Code, the debtor must generally make provision in his or her plan for the payment of outstanding car loans secured by a purchase money security interest in his or her automobile. Prior to 2005, consumer debtors had the option under section 506 of the Bankruptcy Code of writing down the secured portion of their purchase money car loans to the value of the automobile. For example, suppose at the time the debtor filed for bankruptcy she owned a car worth $2,000 subject to a purchase money security interest securing an outstanding loan of $3,000. Under section 506, the debtor could treat the secured creditor as the holder of a secured claim in the amount of $2,000, and an unsecured creditor for the balance of $1,000. Although the debtor was required to pay the $2,000 secured portion in full if the debtor wished to keep the car, the debtor was not required in most cases to pay the unsecured deficiency in full. With the 2005 amendments to the Bankruptcy Code, Congress added the so-called "hanging paragraph" to section 1325(a)(9), which reads as follows:

> For purposes of paragraph (5) [governing the treatment of secured claims in a Chapter 13 plan], section 506 shall not apply to a claim

> described in that paragraph if the creditor has a purchase money security interest securing the debt that is the subject of the claim, the debt was incurred within the 910-day period preceding the date of the filing of the petition, and the collateral for that debt consists of a motor vehicle (as defined in section 30102 of title 49) acquired for the personal use of the debtor, or if collateral for that debt consists of any other thing of value, if the debt was incurred during the 1-year period preceding that filing.

The provision is complex. In particular, there has been great confusion over its application in cases in which the debtor has purchased a new car before paying off the debt on an old car and the old debt is rolled over into the new loan secured by the new car. For example, suppose the debtor owns an old car worth $1,000 that secures an outstanding purchase money loan of $5,000. The debtor trades the old car in for a new car that costs $20,000 and finances the new car with a new purchase money loan. The debtor gets a $1,000 credit for the old car and drives away in the new car, which now secures a debt of $24,000 (the purchase price for the new car of $20,000, less the $1,000 trade-in credit, plus the $5,000 old debt). When the debtor files for bankruptcy a year later, does the hanging paragraph require that the entire debt be treated as secured? Is the entire $24,000 indebtedness properly classified as "purchase money"? Consider the following two cases, which reach opposite conclusions on the same question.

IN RE GRAUPNER

United States Court of Appeals, Eleventh Circuit. 2008.
537 F.3d 1295.

VINSON, DISTRICT JUDGE:

This case involves interpretation and application of the so-called "hanging paragraph" in Title 11, United States Code, Section 1325(a)(9), which was added to the Bankruptcy Code ("the Code") by the Bankruptcy Abuse Prevention and Consumer Protection Act of 2005. *See* Pub.L. No. 109–8, 119 Stat. 23 (2005) ("BAPCPA"). Specifically, we are called upon to decide if the anti-bifurcation provision in the hanging paragraph protects against "cramdown" of the negative equity in a trade-in vehicle. This issue has been confronted by a number of bankruptcy and district courts throughout the country (with widely divergent results), but it appears to be of first impression in this or any other circuit.

I. BACKGROUND

The area of bankruptcy law involved in this case is somewhat complex and, as indicated above, rife with terms of art. For better understanding, we will set forth a brief discussion of the statutory background before turning to the facts and history of this particular case.

A. *The Statutory Scheme*

Bankruptcy rehabilitation under Chapter 13 of the Code commonly involves the adjustment of obligations owed to creditors holding liens on the bankruptcy debtor's property. Generally, lien creditors are deemed to hold a secured claim to the extent of the present value of the property that the lien encumbers, while the excess, if any, is treated as a separate and unsecured claim. Section 506(a)(1) of the Code provides in relevant part:

> (a)(1) An allowed claim of a creditor secured by a lien on property . . . is a secured claim to the extent of the value of such creditor's interest in the estate's interest in such property . . . and is an unsecured claim to the extent that the value of such creditor's interest . . . is less than the amount of such allowed claim. Such value shall be determined in light of the purpose of the valuation and of the proposed disposition or use of such property[.]

11 U.S.C. § 506(a)(1). In dealing with the allowed secured claims under section 506(a), the Code provides for one of three possible treatments "with respect to each allowed secured claim:" (1) the creditor can accept the debtor's bankruptcy plan for repayment; (2) the debtor can surrender the property securing the claim to the creditor in lieu of repayment; or (3) the debtor can bifurcate the claim into a reduced secured portion equal to the present value of the collateral and an unsecured portion equal to the excess of the claim, and then receive a "cramdown" of the reduced secured claim upon the creditor. *See generally* 11 U.S.C. § 1325(a)(5). Under the "cramdown" option, as the Supreme Court has recognized, "the debtor is permitted to keep the property over the objection of the creditor; the creditor retains the lien securing the claim, and the debtor is required to provide the creditor with payments, over the life of the plan, that will total the present value of the allowed secured claim, i.e., the present value of the collateral. The value of the allowed secured claim is governed by § 506(a) of the Code." *Associates Commercial Corp. v. Rash*, 520 U.S. 953, 957, 117 S.Ct. 1879, 1882–83, 138 L.Ed.2d 148 (1997) (internal citations omitted). "Cramdown" was a familiar and routine occurrence before BAPCPA was enacted in 2005. As Judge Lundin notes in his treatise:

> Prior to BAPCPA, cramdown of secured claims at confirmation in Chapter 13 cases was uniform and well understood. Oversimplified, under § 506(a) an allowed claim was a secured claim to the extent of the value of the collateral. Undersecured claims were split into secured and unsecured components based on the value of the collateral. With or without consent of the lienholder, a Chapter 13 debtor could confirm a plan that proposed

> to pay the allowed secured claim in full with present value interest and to treat the balance of the debt as an unsecured claim.

Keith M. Lundin, *Chapter 13 Bankruptcy*, at 445–1 (3d ed. 2000 & Supp.2007–1).

However, Congress viewed the pre-2005 use of "cramdown" as abusive, so it amended Section 1325(a) through BAPCPA and added the hanging paragraph, which provides:

> For purposes of paragraph (5), section 506 [cram-down] shall not apply to a claim described in that paragraph if the creditor has a purchase money security interest securing the debt that is the subject of the claim, the debt was incurred within the 910-day [period] preceding the date of the filing of the petition, and the collateral for that debt consists of a motor vehicle (as defined in section 30102 of title 49) acquired for the personal use of the debtor, or if collateral for that debt consists of any other thing of value, if the debt was incurred during the 1-year period preceding that filing.

11 U.S.C. § 1325(a)(*). Although the hanging paragraph has caused significant "confusion and incoherence in the law" and has been rightly criticized for its poor drafting, *In re Long*, 519 F.3d 288, 292 (6th Cir.2008); *see also In re Carver*, 338 B.R. 521, 523 (Bankr.S.D.Ga.2006), its legislative history leaves little doubt that its " 'architects intended only good things for car lenders and other lienholders.' " *See Long, supra*, 519 F.3d at 294 (citations omitted); *see also, e.g., General Motors Acceptance Corp. v. Peaslee*, 373 B.R. 252, 261 (W.D.N.Y.2007) ("To the extent that it is possible to glean any Congressional intent behind the hanging paragraph . . . that intent . . . seems to be to protect creditors from the abuse of 'cramdown.' "); *In re Payne*, 347 B.R. 278, 281 (Bankr.S.D.Ohio 2006) ("[T]hrough the BAPCPA amendments to § 1325(a)(5), Congress was attempting to remedy a perceived abuse by those who buy vehicles on credit on the eve of bankruptcy and then utilize the cramdown provisions of the Bankruptcy Code to pay the secured creditor a lesser amount than its full claim."); *In re Duke*, 345 B.R. 806, 809 (Bankr.W.D.Ky.2006) ("The history [of the hanging paragraph] does indicate that it was meant to discourage bankruptcy abuse. It is interesting to note that the section of BAPCPA that added the hanging paragraph was entitled, 'Section 306-Giving Secured Creditors Fair Treatment in Chapter 13 . . . Restoring the Foundation for Secured Credit.' "). Thus, whatever else may be said about the hanging paragraph, it seems clear that by it "Congress intended to take away the right of debtors to reduce their secured obligations on retained 910 vehicles to the value of the vehicles." *See In re Rodriguez*, 375 B.R. 535, 548 (9th Cir. BAP 2007). To fall within the hanging paragraph and be entitled to this anti-bifurcation protection, four general requirements must be

satisfied: (1) the creditor must have a "purchase money security interest" in the collateral; (2) the debt must have been incurred within 910 days before the filing of the debtor's bankruptcy case; (3) the collateral for the debt must consist of a motor vehicle[2]; and (4) the vehicle must have been acquired for the personal use of the debtor. *See generally* 11 U.S.C. § 1325(a)(*). If these requirements are satisfied, the allowed secured claim is fixed at the amount of the creditor's claim without resort to the "cramdown" provision mandated by section 506(a).

B. Facts and Procedural History

The facts of this case are simple, undisputed, and taken almost verbatim from the district court's order. On June 23, 2005, Stephen Michael Graupner ("Debtor") purchased a 2005 Chevrolet Silverado pick-up truck from a motor vehicle dealer in Georgia. The vehicle was for his personal use and had a "cash price" of $32,919.12. The dealer agreed to finance the sale pursuant to a retail installment contract, with the seller retaining a security interest in the vehicle to secure the unpaid balance of the total sales price.

As part of the transaction, the Debtor traded in a 2002 Chevrolet Silverado pick-up truck. That vehicle had a "negative equity," with the Debtor owing $6,347.50 more on the vehicle than its then-market value. There is nothing in the record of this case to indicate that the trade-in's negative equity was not bona fide and reasonable in amount. The total sales price of the new vehicle included the negative equity, which had the effect of increasing the purchase price. The total amount financed was $36,384.62. The dealer subsequently assigned the retail installment contract to Nuvell Credit Corporation ("Creditor"), which perfected its security interest by having its lien noted on the title to the new vehicle.

Three hundred and one days later, on April 19, 2006, the Debtor filed for Chapter 13 bankruptcy protection. The Creditor filed its secured proof of claim showing an amount due on the contract of $33,670.31. The Debtor retained the vehicle and listed it on his schedules as being valued at $23,375.00. The Debtor proposed a Chapter 13 plan that sought to modify the Creditor's secured claim of $33,670.31 by bifurcating it into secured and unsecured portions based on the retail value of the vehicle. The Creditor objected to the confirmation of the proposed plan, contending that its secured claim could not be modified through "cramdown" because it fell within the hanging paragraph. The parties agreed that the debt for the vehicle was acquired within 910 days of the filing for bankruptcy and that the vehicle was intended for the Debtor's personal use. Consequently, the only question to be decided in the bankruptcy court was whether the

---

[2] The collateral for the debt may consist "of any other thing of value," but in that case, the debt must have been "incurred during the 1-year period preceding that filing." 11 U.S.C. § 1325(a)(*).

Creditor held a "purchase money security interest" in the vehicle. If it did, the debt could not be bifurcated.

Because the term "purchase money security interest" is not defined in the Code, the bankruptcy court began its analysis by stating that the question of "whether a creditor holds a purchase money security interest is a matter of state law." The bankruptcy court referred to Georgia's version of Article 9 of the Uniform Commercial Code ("UCC"), found in the Official Code of Georgia Annotated ("O.C.G.A.") § 11–9–103, which provides:

> (a) *Definitions.* As used in this Code section, the term:
>
> > (1) "Purchase money collateral" means goods or software that secures a purchase money obligation incurred with respect to that collateral.
> >
> > (2) "Purchase money obligation" means an obligation of an obligor incurred as all or part of the price of the collateral or for value given to enable the debtor to acquire rights in or the use of the collateral if the value is in fact so used.
>
> (b) *Purchase money security interest in goods.* A security interest in goods is a purchase money security interest:
>
> > (1) To the extent that the goods are purchase money collateral with respect to that security interest . . .

The bankruptcy court opined that while the definition of "purchase money obligation" in section 11–9–103 appears clear at first glance, it becomes blurred and ambiguous when one attempts to define "price" in subsection (a)(2) because "the extent or reach of the term is uncertain." The bankruptcy court then went on to determine that "price" is more properly understood when viewed in conjunction with a separate, but related, section of the O.C.G.A.: the 1999 amendments to the Georgia Motor Vehicle Sales Finance Act ("MVSFA"), which specifically defines "cash sale price" to include "any amount paid to the buyer . . . to satisfy . . . a lien on or a security interest in a motor vehicle used as a trade-in on the motor vehicle which is the subject of a retail installment transaction under this article." *See* O.C.G.A. § 10–1–31(a)(1). Reading these sections *in pari materia*-which the bankruptcy court determined was proper in light of the ambiguity in section 11–9–103(a)(2) and the relationship between the two statutes-the court held that "the Georgia General Assembly intended, with its 1999 amendment to the MVSFA, to permit negative equity in a trade-in vehicle to be added to the cash sales price of a new vehicle without precluding the financing creditor or its assignee from taking a purchase money security interest in the new vehicle." The Debtor was thus found to have a purchase money security interest in the vehicle pursuant to state law, which precluded bifurcation and "cramdown" under section 506. In affirming this decision, the district court held on appeal:

> [T]he price of the collateral included the negative equity. The trade-in of the vehicle was an integral part of the sales transaction. The value of that trade-in along with its accompanying debt affected the ultimate price that was paid for the new pick-up truck. The negative equity is inextricably intertwined with the sales transaction and the financing of the purchase. This close nexus between the negative equity and this package transaction supports the conclusion that the negative equity must be considered as part of the price of the collateral [footnote omitted]. Accordingly, the Court finds that the Creditor has a purchase money security interest for the full amount of its debt. Thus, § 506 shall not apply to modify the amount of the secured obligation.

The Debtor now appeals.

* * *

III. DISCUSSION

As we noted at the outset of this opinion, the issue presented in this case has been confronted by dozens of lower courts. These decisions generally fall into two broad camps. The first camp holds, as the bankruptcy court held here, that the creditor's purchase money security interest encompasses all components of the new vehicle purchase, including financing of negative equity. *See, e.g., Peaslee, supra*, 373 B.R. at 252; *In re Myers*, 2008 WL 2445214 (Bankr.S.D.Ind. June 13, 2008); *In re Ford*, 387 B.R. 827 (Bankr.D.Kan.2008); *In re Austin*, 381 B.R. 892 (Bankr.D.Utah 2008); *In re Dunlap*, 383 B.R. 113 (Bankr.E.D.Wis.2008); *In re Vinson*, 2008 WL 319678 (Bankr.D.S.C. Jan.25, 2008); *In re Schwalm*, 380 B.R. 630 (Bankr.M.D.Fla.2008); *In re Weiser*, 381 B.R. 263 (Bankr.W.D.Mo.2007); *In re Brei*, 2007 WL 4104884 (Bankr.D.Ariz. Nov.14, 2007); *In re Burt*, 378 B.R. 352 (Bankr.D.Utah 2007); *In re Bradlee*, 2007 Bankr.LEXIS 3863 (Bankr.W.D.La. Oct. 10, 2007); *In re Watson*, 2007 WL 2873434 (Bankr.E.D.Cal. Sept.27, 2007); *In re Wall*, 376 B.R. 769 (Bankr.W.D.N.C.2007); *In re Cohrs*, 373 B.R. 107 (Bankr.E.D.Cal.2007); *In re Petrocci*, 370 B.R. 489 (Bankr.N.D.N.Y.2007).

The second camp holds that certain components of the loan, most notably negative equity in a trade-in vehicle, do not constitute a purchase money security interest. *See, e.g., In re Munzberg*, 388 B.R. 529, 2008 WL 2332267 (Bankr.D.Vt. June 3, 2008); *In re Callicott*, 386 B.R. 232 (Bankr.E.D.Mo.2008); *In re Jernigan*, 2008 WL 922346 (Bankr.E.D.N.C. Mar.31, 2008); *In re Look*, 383 B.R. 210 (Bankr.D.Me.2008); *In re Wear*, 2008 WL 217172 (Bankr.W.D.Wash. Jan. 23, 2008); *In re Johnson*, 380 B.R. 236 (Bankr.D.Or.2007); *In re Tuck*, 2007 WL 4365456 (Bankr.M.D.Ala. Dec. 10, 2007); *In re Lavigne*, 2007 WL 3469454 (Bankr.E.D.Va. Nov.14, 2007); *In re Conyers*, 379 B.R. 576 (Bankr.M.D.N.C.2007); *In re Hayes*, 376

B.R. 655 (Bankr.M.D. Tenn.2007); *In re Pajot*, 371 B.R. 139 (Bankr.E.D.Va.2007); *In re Price*, 363 B.R. 734 (Bankr.E.D.N.C.2007); *In re Hernandez-Simpson*, 369 B.R. 36 (D.Kan.2007); *In re Bray*, 365 B.R. 850 (Bankr.W.D.Tenn.2007); *In re Mitchell*, 379 B.R. 131 (Bankr.M.D. Tenn.2007); *In re Sanders*, 377 B.R. 836 (Bankr.W.D.Tex.2007); *In re Blakeslee*, 377 B.R. 724 (Bankr.M.D. Fla.2007); *In re Acaya*, 369 B.R. 564 (Bankr.N.D.Ca.2007); *In re Vega*, 344 B.R. 616 (Bankr.D.Kan.2006).

The latter group of cases lead to a further inquiry on how to treat "partial" purchase money securities, which has caused still more divergences in the law. Some courts have adopted the "dual-status rule" (which allows the court to treat the purchase-money portion as purchase-money, while the non-purchase-money portion remains non-purchase-money), *see, e.g., Pajot, supra*, 371 B.R. at 139, whereas other courts have adopted the "transformational rule" (which holds that a security interest that is part purchase-money and part non-purchase-money completely loses its purchase-money character and is entirely "transformed" into a non-purchase-money security interest), *see, e.g., Price, supra*, 363 B.R. at 734; *see also Lavigne, supra*, 2007 WL 3469454, at *9 (noting that courts are "divided" on the issue of whether to apply the dual status or transformational rule and collecting cases on both sides). One court has appropriately described the foregoing as a "maddeningly inconsistent body of decisions." *See In re Westfall*, 376 B.R. 210, 213 (Bankr.N.D.Ohio 2007).

The ultimate issue we must decide is whether the Debtor's negative equity in his trade-in vehicle constitutes purchase money. Our Court has defined what is, and what is not, a purchase money security interest, and we apply that definition here:

> A security interest in collateral is "purchase money" to the extent that the item secures a debt for the money required to make the purchase. If an item of collateral secures some other type of debt, e.g., antecedent debt, it is not purchase money.

In re Freeman, 956 F.2d 252, 254–55 (11th Cir.1992). So, the question is whether negative equity on a trade-in vehicle is "debt for the money required to make the purchase" of the new vehicle, or whether it is "antecedent debt." It is, as the split in the decided cases indicates, a close call.

Upon consideration, however, we agree with the bankruptcy court that, when looking to Georgia state law, negative equity is more properly regarded as the former and not the latter. When O.C.G.A. §§ 11–9–103(UCC) and 10–1–31(a)(1) (MVSFA) are read *in pari materia* (which we believe is appropriate for all the reasons stated by the bankruptcy court), it is the only reasonable conclusion to reach. Because this issue was properly considered and analyzed at length by the bankruptcy court, and by certain of the courts in the "first camp" above, we see no reason to duplicate the analysis as the path is by now well-worn. We do add, however, that our decision finds support in the relevant UCC Official Comment and is consistent with legislative intent.

Section 9–103 of the UCC, adopted by O.C.G.A. § 11–9–103, provides that "[a] security interest in goods is a purchase-money security interest . . . to the extent that the goods are purchase-money collateral with respect to that security interest[.]" It then defines "purchase-money collateral" as "goods or software that secures a purchase-money obligation incurred with respect to that collateral." The term "purchase-money obligation" is defined, in turn, as "an obligation of an obligor incurred as all or part of the price of the collateral or for value given to enable the debtor to acquire rights in or the use of the collateral if the value is in fact so used." In sum, therefore, the focus of the definition of a purchase money security interest under the UCC is on the "purchase-money obligation" that is secured by the collateral, and this definition contains two prongs: (i) the price of the collateral; and (ii) value given to enable the debtor to buy the collateral. Official Comment 3 to the UCC explains:

> [T]he definition of "purchase-money obligation," the "price" of collateral or the "value given to enable" includes obligations for expenses incurred in connection with acquiring rights in the collateral, sales taxes, duties, finance charges, interest, freight charges, costs of storage in transit, demurrage, administrative charges, expenses of collection and enforcement, attorney's fees, *and other similar obligations*.[4]

U.C.C. § 9–103, Official Comment 3 (emphasis added). Although the Debtor argues that negative equity is "not equivalent" to the various expenses listed in Comment 3, as the emphasized language indicates, the list is not exhaustive. The expenses identified in Comment 3 are merely examples of additional components of the "price" of the collateral or of "value given" to the debtor, and we see no persuasive reason why traditional transaction costs and the refinancing of reasonable, bona fide negative equity in connection with the purchase of the new vehicle should not qualify as "expenses" within the meaning of the comment. To be sure, as one court has rightly observed, the fact that "attorney's fees" are listed in Comment 3 "belies the notion that 'price' or 'value' is narrowly viewed as only those [traditional] expenses that *must* be paid to drive the car off the lot. Comment 3 expressly 'includes' the broad phrase 'obligations for expenses incurred in connection with acquiring rights in the collateral' "

---

[4] The former Fifth Circuit recognized that UCC Official Comments are " 'by far the most useful aids to interpretation and construction.' " *Weathersby v. Gore*, 556 F.2d 1247, 1256 (5th Cir.1977) (citation omitted) (binding under *Bonner v. Prichard*, 661 F.2d 1206 (11th Cir.1981) (*en banc*)); *accord Westfall, supra*, 376 B.R. at 217–19 (setting forth the history behind UCC Official Comments and observing that although the comments are not " 'given binding effect,' " they do " 'occupy an unusual position as aids to statutory interpretation' " and should be regarded as " 'an indispensable part of the UCC framework' ") (citations omitted).

and, consequently, "the definitions of 'price' and 'value' should be interpreted broadly." *Myers, supra*, 2008 WL 2445214, at *4 (emphasis in original).

Comment 3 further states that a purchase money security interest "requires a close nexus between the acquisition of collateral and the secured obligation." We believe there is such a "close nexus" between the negative equity in the Debtor's trade-in vehicle and the purchase of his new vehicle. The financing was part of the same transaction and may be properly regarded as a "package deal." Payment of the trade-in debt was tantamount to a prerequisite to consummating the sales transaction, and utilizing the negative equity financing was a necessary means to accomplish the purchase of the new vehicle. As the district court held in affirming the bankruptcy court, the negative equity was an "integral part of," and "inextricably intertwined with," the sales transaction. To hold otherwise would not be a fair reading of the UCC.

Nor would it comport with what Congress intended in enacting BAPCPA. In interpreting the hanging paragraph, like any statute, we are guided by the general principle of statutory construction that a statute should be interpreted and applied with an understanding and appreciation of the "purpose it was intended to serve." *United States v. Ballinger*, 395 F.3d 1218, 1237 (11th Cir.2005) (*en banc*). Because the legislature is presumed to act with sensible and reasonable purpose, a statute should, if at all possible, be read " 'so as to avoid an unjust or absurd conclusion.' " *See id.* (*quoting In re Chapman*, 166 U.S. 661, 667, 17 S.Ct. 677, 41 L.Ed. 1154 (1897)). Therefore, in applying the hanging paragraph to the facts of this case, we must keep before us the underlying purpose of, and legislative intent behind, the statute. Here, the hanging paragraph ultimately seeks to require a debtor electing to retain a "910 vehicle" to pay the creditor the full amount of the claim and not (as under pre-BAPCPA law) an amount equal to the present value of the car. *See In re Trejos*, 374 B.R. 210, 220 (9th Cir. BAP 2007) ("[T]he purpose underlying the 'Hanging Paragraph' " is to ensure that debtors " 'repay in a Chapter 13 the amount they actually agreed to pay for a motor vehicle purchased within 910 days of bankruptcy, instead of the true value of the collateral.' ") (citation omitted). The practice in automobile financing over the years has been to extend the repayment period over longer time frames: from three years in the past up to as much as five years, or more, now. One result of such an extended payment period is that having negative equity in a vehicle is common. The hanging paragraph plainly addresses the negative equity that the Debtor may have in a vehicle at the time of filing, and it seems that the intended purpose was, at least in part, to deal with the negative equity practice.

Rolling a trade-in's negative equity into the purchase price of a new vehicle was a common occurrence at the time BAPCPA was enacted in 2005, and it still is to this day. According to estimates cited by the Creditor, and relied on by several courts, negative equity trade-in transactions occurred in from 29 to 38 percent of all new vehicle purchases in past years, and that figure appears to only be on the rise. *See, e.g., Pajot, supra*, 371 B.R. at 153 n. 17 (citing Brian J. O'Connor, *At Trade-In, Many Car Buyers are Left with the Upside-Down Blues*, Detroit News, June 12, 2006 ("Last month nearly 29 percent of U.S. car buyers found themselves 'upside down.' "); and FDIC Supervisory Insights, *The Changing Landscape of Indirect Automobile Lending*, June 23, 2005 ("J.D. Power and Associates estimates that approximately 38 percent of new car buyers have negative equity at trade-in, compared to 25 percent two years ago.")). If Congress did not intend for the hanging paragraph to apply to a trade-in's negative equity, as the Debtor ultimately contends, it would have the effect of excluding a substantial number of lawful auto finance transactions that were industry practice when BAPCPA was enacted (a practice that Congress is presumed to have known about). This would be an absurd result given that it is recognized that the " 'architects [of the hanging paragraph] intended only good things for car lenders and other lienholders.' " *See Long, supra*, 519 F.3d at 294 (citations omitted). It would be particularly absurd because a strong argument can be made that "the primary purpose of the hanging paragraph of Code § 1325(a)(9) is, in fact, precisely to take the unsecured negative equity debt which any Chapter 13 debtor has when his or her less than nine hundred and ten day-old vehicle is not worth the outstanding loan balance, and, by refusing it the Code § 506 treatment, to transform it into secured debt not supported by collateral value, and then require it to be paid in full to the detriment of other unsecured creditors." *Petrocci, supra*, 370 B.R. at 502 (emphasis added) (citation and quotation marks omitted); *accord Dunlap, supra*, 383 B.R. at 118 ("Nothing in BAPCPA declares that negative equity financing bars a secured lender from protection under the hanging paragraph. To the contrary, one of BAPCPA's goals was to afford additional protection for secured creditors and, primarily, for automobile lenders."). A contrary interpretation is not supported by the text of the hanging paragraph or its legislative history.

IV. CONCLUSION

For the foregoing reasons, the order of the district court, in turn affirming the bankruptcy court, is AFFIRMED.

[some footnotes omitted]

IN RE PENROD

United States Court of Appeals, Ninth Circuit, 2010.
611 F.3d 1158.

MILLS, DISTRICT JUDGE:

The question presented in this case is whether a creditor has a purchase money security interest in the "negative equity" of a vehicle traded in at the time of a new vehicle purchase. Because we answer this question in the negative, we affirm the decision of the Bankruptcy Appellate Panel ("BAP").

I. BACKGROUND

In September 2005, Marlene Penrod purchased a 2005 Ford Taurus from a California Ford dealership. According to the figures recited by the BAP, the price of the car, including tax and license, was approximately $25,600. Penrod traded in her 1999 Ford Explorer and paid approximately $1,000 down for her new vehicle. She owed over $13,000 on the Explorer and she received $6,000 in credit for the vehicle. Therefore, there was over $7,000 in "negative equity" on the trade-in vehicle.

The dealership paid off the remaining balance on the Explorer and added the negative equity to the amount financed. Penrod financed approximately $31,700 in order to purchase a vehicle that cost approximately $25,600. According to the contract, Penrod was to pay twenty percent interest on the loan. The dealership subsequently assigned the contract to AmeriCredit Financial Services.

523 days after purchasing the Ford Taurus, Penrod filed for bankruptcy protection under Chapter 13. She still owed $25,675 to AmeriCredit, which included the negative equity from the Ford Explorer. In her Chapter 13 plan, Penrod proposed to bifurcate AmeriCredit's claim into secured and unsecured portions. AmeriCredit objected to the plan, claiming it had a purchase money security interest in the entire amount, including the negative equity.

The bankruptcy court held that AmeriCredit did not have a purchase money security interest in the portion of the loan related to the negative equity charges. However, the bankruptcy court acknowledged that AmeriCredit had a purchase money security interest in the remaining balance. In doing so, the bankruptcy court adopted the dual status rule, which allows part of a loan to have nonpurchase money status, while the remainder is covered by a purchase money security interest.

The bankruptcy court decision was affirmed by the BAP in a published opinion. AmeriCredit challenges the BAP's ruling in this appeal.

* * *

III. DISCUSSION

A.

AmeriCredit has placed great emphasis on the decisions of the other circuit courts of appeal. In total, over some strong dissents, eight circuits have held that a creditor has a purchase money security interest in the negative equity of a debtor's trade-in vehicle. *Nuvell Credit Corp. v. Westfall (In re Westfall)*, 599 F.3d 498 (6th Cir.2010); *In re Howard*, 597 F.3d 852 (7th Cir.2010); *Reiber v. GMAC, LLC (In re Peaslee)*, 585 F.3d 53 (2d Cir.2009) (per curiam) (adopting the response to a certified question of a divided New York Court of Appeals), *In re Peaslee*, 13 N.Y.3d 75, 885 N.Y.S.2d 1, 913 N.E.2d 387 (2009)); *Ford Motor Credit Co. v. Dale (In re Dale)*, 582 F.3d 568 (5th Cir.2009); *Ford Motor Credit Co. v. Mierkowski (In re Mierkowski)*, 580 F.3d 740 (8th Cir.2009); *Ford v. Ford Motor Credit Co. (In re Ford)*, 574 F.3d 1279 (10th Cir.2009); *In re Price*, 562 F.3d 618 (4th Cir.2009); and *Graupner v. Nuvell Credit Corp. (In re Graupner)*, 537 F.3d 1295 (11th Cir.2008).

We decline to adopt the reasoning of our sister circuits. We acknowledge that our decision creates a circuit split, and we do not do this lightly. However, we are persuaded by the well-reasoned decision of Bankruptcy Judge Markell and his colleagues on the BAP.

This appeal involves the application of 11 U.S.C. § 1325(a)(*)—a paragraph added to the Bankruptcy Code by the Bankruptcy Abuse Prevention and Consumer Protection Act of 2005 ("BAPCPA"). The paragraph is commonly called the "hanging paragraph" because it was added to the end of § 1325(a) without a number.

The hanging paragraph prevents the bifurcation of certain claims. Bifurcation occurs when a creditor's claim is split into secured and unsecured claims. The hanging paragraph states:

> For purposes of paragraph (5), section 506 shall not apply to a claim described in that paragraph if the creditor has a purchase money security interest securing the debt that is the subject of the claim, the debt was incurred within the 910-day [sic] preceding the date of the filing of the petition, and the collateral for that debt consists of a motor vehicle (as defined in section 30102 of title 49) acquired for the personal use of the debtor, or if collateral for that debt consists of any other thing of value, if the debt was incurred during the 1-year period preceding that filing.

11 U.S.C. § 1325(a)(*).

The only requirement from the hanging paragraph that is at issue in this case is whether there was a purchase money security interest in the negative equity in the trade-in vehicle.

The term "purchase money security interest" is not defined in the bankruptcy code. In bankruptcy, property interests are usually defined by state law. *See Butner v. United States*, 440 U.S. 48, 54–57, 99 S.Ct. 914, 59 L.Ed.2d 136 (1979). California has adopted the relevant portion of Revised Article 9 of the Uniform Commercial Code ("U.C.C.") and the U.C.C. Official Comment. Purchase money security interest is defined in U.C.C. § 9–103, and in California Commercial Code § 9103.

The code does not provide a precise, encapsulated definition of purchase money security interest, but rather a string of connected definitions. The relevant language provides that "[a] security interest in goods is a purchase money security interest . . . [t]o the extent that the goods are purchase money collateral with respect to that security interest." Cal. Comm.Code § 9103(b). " 'Purchase money collateral' means goods or software that secures a purchase money obligation." Cal. Comm.Code § 9103(a)(1). " 'Purchase money obligation' means an obligation of an obligor incurred as all or part of the price of the collateral or for value given to enable the debtor to acquire rights in or the use of the collateral if the value is in fact so used." Cal. Comm.Code § 9103(a)(2).

In plain English, a purchase money security interest arises when a person buys a good and the seller (if a dealer financed transaction) or lender (if the sale is financed by a loan) retains a security interest in that good for all or part of the price. Purchase money security interests have long been favored at law, and enjoy "super-priority" rights over other types of security interests and liens. *See* Grant Gilmore, *The Purchase Money Priority*, 76 Harv. L.Rev. 1333 (1963).

B.

With all of the foregoing as background, we arrive at the key issue of this appeal—the meaning of "price" for the purposes of the purchase money security interest. The definition is found in the Official Comment.

> As used in subsection (a)(2), the definition of "purchase-money obligation," the "price" of collateral or the "value given to enable" includes obligations for expenses incurred in connection with acquiring rights in the collateral, sales taxes, duties, finance charges, interest, freight charges, costs of storage in transit, demurrage, administrative charges, expenses of collection and enforcement, attorney's fees, and other similar obligations.

U.C.C. § 9–103 cmt. 3.

AmeriCredit argues that the negative equity related to the Ford Taurus Penrod traded in is an "expense[ ] incurred in connection with acquiring rights in the collateral." In doing so, AmeriCredit places more weight on this phrase than it can bear.

The payment of Penrod's remaining debt on her 1999 Ford Explorer cannot easily be characterized as an "expense." It is the payment of an antecedent debt, not an expense incurred in buying the new vehicle. *See In re Peaslee*, 13 N.Y.3d at 83, 885 N.Y.S.2d 1, 913 N.E.2d 387 (Smith, J., dissenting) ("A refinanced loan is not, in accounting terms, properly speaking an 'expense' at all; it is the substitution of a new liability for an old one."). AmeriCredit claims that the transactions are closely connected, and that the requirements of Comment 3 are satisfied as a result. While all things are connected at some level, the question here is whether the negative equity on Penrod's Ford Explorer was sufficiently connected to the purchase of the Ford Taurus to establish a purchase-money security interest. We hold that it is not.

AmeriCredit and some courts have looked to studies indicating that over a third of vehicle purchases in the United States involve negative equity to conclude that they are sufficiently connected. *See, e.g., In re Howard*, 597 F.3d at 857–58. Some circuits have described combining a new vehicle purchase with negative equity as a "package deal." *See In re Graupner*, 537 F.3d at 1302. While the trade-in and new purchase may be performed at the same time, or use one unified document, this does not automatically mean that there is a purchase money security interest. Judge Bye, of the Eighth Circuit, aptly made this point:

> The fact that financing negative equity has become a customary industry practice, and practical reality necessary to many motor vehicle sales transactions, does not alter the fact that negative equity does not fall within Article 9's definition of "price" or "value given." Money or value given to pay off the negative equity in a trade-in vehicle is not, in the strictest sense, given to acquire rights in the secured collateral. Neither does the negative equity represent any part of the price of the vehicle or associated costs arising directly from the sale. The realities of such transactions frequently require the financing of negative equity to facilitate the sale, but the focus should be on price or value given as defined by Article 9, and not what is necessary to entice sellers and lenders into the transaction.

In re Mierkowski, 580 F.3d at 746 (Bye, J., dissenting).

Finally, negative equity cannot fall under the "other similar obligations" category because negative equity is unlike the examples listed in Comment 3. The items in the list are transaction costs related to purchase, and negative equity will "typically be larger, and more readily separable from the purchase transaction itself, than such things as sales tax, duties and finance charges." *In re Peaslee*, 13 N.Y.3d at 83–84, 885 N.Y.S.2d 1, 913 N.E.2d 387 (Smith, J., dissenting); *see also In re Ford*, 574 F.3d at 1289 (Tymkovitch, J., dissenting).

However one structures or describes the transaction, the negative equity is antecedent debt. A seller or lender can obtain a purchase money security interest only for new value, and closely related costs. Old value simply does not fit within that rubric.

C.

AmeriCredit argues that the California Automobile Sales Finance Act ("ASFA") should be used in determining the "price of the collateral." The ASFA includes negative equity charges in the "cash price" of the vehicle. Cal. Civ.Code § 2981(e). AmeriCredit has invoked the in pari materia doctrine to read the ASFA and Article 9 together, to construe the term "price of the collateral."

We disagree. The purpose of the "cash price" definition in the ASFA is to disclose to consumers that they are responsible for negative equity charges. The definition says nothing about whether those charges result in a purchase money security interest. *See In re Ford*, 574 F.3d at 1292–93 (Tymkovitch, J., dissenting). The disclosure provisions of the ASFA were enacted for a different purpose than the "price of the collateral" provision in the U.C.C. Even courts that have ruled in favor of creditors have recognized that laws such as the ASFA are not helpful in determining the "price of the collateral." Writing for the Seventh Circuit, Judge Posner said the following regarding an analogous Illinois law: "[i]t's a consumer-protection statute, intended to require disclosure of the charges that make up the total price that a consumer pays for the car, rather than to prescribe what is and is not included in the purchase money security interest." *In re Howard*, 597 F.3d at 857. Therefore, we ignore the ASFA's "cash price" definition.

D.

AmeriCredit has argued that its position is in harmony with federal bankruptcy law. In its brief, AmeriCredit states that "Section 547(c)(3) of the Bankruptcy Code gives special protection from preference avoidance to 'enabling loans,' which are defined like a purchase-money security interest." However, upon closer examination it appears that AmeriCredit's position runs counter to basic federal bankruptcy principles. Specifically, the statutory language cited by AmeriCredit provides that:

> (c) The trustee may not avoid under this section a transfer—
>
> . . .
>
> (3) that creates a security interest in property acquired by the debtor—
>
> (A) to the extent that such security interest secures new value that was—

> (i) given at or after the security agreement that contains a description of such property as collateral;
>
> (ii) given by or on behalf of the secured party under such agreement;
>
> (iii) given to enable the debtor to acquire such property; and
>
> (iv) in fact used by the debtor to acquire such property; and
>
> (B) that is perfected on or before 30 days after the debtor receives possession of such property[.]

11 U.S.C. § 547(c)(3).

However, new value is defined in the same section as follows:

> "[N]ew value" means money or money's worth in goods, services, or new credit, or release by a transferee of property previously transferred to such transferee in a transaction that is neither void nor voidable by the debtor or the trustee under any applicable law, including proceeds of such property, but does not include an obligation substituted for an existing obligation [.]

11 U.S.C. § 547(a)(2) (emphasis added).

Therefore, AmeriCredit's position is not consistent with the Bankruptcy Code. Under the Bankruptcy Code, security interests are given preferential treatment to the extent that the obligation relates to the receipt of truly new value, not just old obligations that have been repackaged. The negative equity charges related to Penrod's 1999 Ford Explorer would not qualify as new value under 11 U.S.C. § 547(a)(2). Therefore, AmeriCredit's position is not in harmony with federal bankruptcy principles.

E.

Any conclusion in favor of AmeriCredit based upon the phrase "value given to enable the debtor to acquire rights in or the use of collateral" would be erroneous. Many of the courts that have faced this issue have honed in on the "value given to enable" language in describing negative equity. Those courts see "value given to enable" as a good descriptor of how the original car and its loan might be an obstacle to purchasing the new car.

However, there is a difference between "price" and "value given to enable." Both sellers and third party lenders can obtain purchase money security interests. A seller obtains a purchase money security interest through a dealer financed sale, where the merchandise goes out the door upon the credit of the buyer. Payment is to be made to the dealer. A purchase money security interest is only valid for the "price" of the merchandise.

A lender such as a finance company, bank, or credit union obtains a purchase money security interest when it makes funds available to the purchaser to buy the merchandise. The money is provided to the borrower to make the purchase. *See* [Geoffrey M.] *Collins*, [Note, *Negative Equity and Purchase-Money Security Interests Under the Uniform Commercial Code and the BAPCPA*,] 95 Cornell L.Rev. [161] at 186 [2009]. That language is somewhat broader than "price" because the money has to be traced from the lender to the borrower to the seller. *See In re Howard*, 597 F.3d at 855–56 ("The 'value given' part of the definition is intended to make clear that the obligation can be to a finance company . . . rather than to the seller."). Broad language is employed to encompass third party financing, not to expand the scope of purchase money security interests.

In sum, we find that a creditor does not have a purchase money security interest in the "negative equity" of a vehicle traded in during a new vehicle purchase.

IV. CONCLUSION

For the foregoing reasons, the decision of the Bankruptcy Appellate Panel is AFFIRMED and REMANDED to the bankruptcy court for further proceedings regarding how credit should be given for the rebate and down payment.

[footnotes omitted]

Which do you find more persuasive, the reasoning in *Graupner* or *Penrod*?

§ 4. BUYERS OF CONSUMER GOODS, SECTION 9–320(b)

The materials in Chapter 4 illustrate the substantial rights of buyers in ordinary course under section 9–320(a). Recall that, under this section, "a buyer in ordinary course of business, other than a person buying farm products from a person engaged in farming operations, takes free of a [non-possessory] security interest created by the buyer's seller, even if the security interest is perfected and the buyer knows of its existence." On its face, section 9–320(a) might seem to include security interests in consumer goods. After all, the only things expressly excluded from its scope are certain "farm products" and possessory security interests. Surely, if the drafters had intended to exclude consumer goods from the reach of section 9–320(a), they would have followed the drafting convention of noting an express exception either by cross-reference to another provision or by simply excluding "consumer goods" as they did for "farm products." But recall the definition of "buyer in ordinary course" in section 1–201(b)(9).

Among other things, a buyer in ordinary course is one who buys from someone who is in "the business of selling goods of that kind." Is the typical consumer who wants to sell his wide screen TV to his neighbor likely to be someone who is in "the business of selling goods of that kind"? No.

Subsection (b) of section 9–320 governs the sale of consumer goods by one consumer to another and provides that, except for possessory security interests, "a buyer of goods from a person who used or bought the goods for use primarily for personal, family, or household purposes takes free of a security interest, even if perfected, if the buyer buys: (1) without knowledge of the security interest; (2) for value; (3) primarily for the buyer's personal, family, or household purposes; and (4) before the filing of a financing statement covering the goods." Because most security interests in consumer goods are automatically perfected, how often is a buyer of consumer goods likely to be stuck with the security interest of his seller's secured creditor? Not often.

The rights of buyers of consumer goods from consumers under subsection (b) are almost as insubstantial and unimportant as the rights in subsection (a) are substantial and important. Professor Gilmore described the analogous rights in former section 9–307(2) as sales "by amateurs to amateurs." Sometimes the subsection is called the "garage sale" provision. Note that the seller must use the goods primarily for personal, family, or household purposes and the buyer must also purchase the goods primarily for personal, family, or household purposes. That is, if the seller or buyer uses the goods or intends to use them for business purposes, the sale does not qualify for treatment under section 9–320(b). Equally important, the buyer does not take free if the perfection was not automatic (purchase money sale to a consumer) but rather was by the filing of a financing statement. In effect, section 9–320(b) is the appropriate protection for a buyer who could not discover the creditor's security interest even if he tried because, by hypothesis, the creditor has not filed a financing statement and has given the debtor possession of the goods. On the other hand, if the secured creditor perfects by filing, why should Article 9 protect its interests more than it would under section 9–320(a)? Why is protecting the integrity of inventory sales more important than protecting the integrity of garage sales?

PROBLEM 7-4

Daisy Bank and Trust has a security interest in refrigerators, stoves, appliances, and all other hard goods of Marie Louise, Inc., a department store. Assume that the security agreement continues the security interest in the goods even after they have been sold. Now consider the following transactions in goods covered by the perfected security interest.

Wilbur buys a refrigerator on credit from Marie Louise and signs a security agreement. A month later Wilbur sells the refrigerator to his next-door neighbor, Charlotte. Identify the correct statement or statements:

1. Charlotte takes free of the security interests of both Daisy Bank and Marie Louise;

2. Charlotte takes free of Daisy Bank's security interest because she qualifies under section 9–320(a);

3. Charlotte takes free of Marie Louise's security interest because she qualifies under section 9–320(a);

4. Charlotte does not qualify for the protection of section 9–320(a), nevertheless she takes free of both security interests.

§ 5. RESTRICTIONS ON CONSUMER SECURED CREDIT

In re Manuel shows that certain interests thought to be "purchase money" may not be. Under section 522(f) of the Bankruptcy Code, certain non-possessory, non-purchase money security interests in consumer goods can be upset in bankruptcy despite being perfected. The relation between secured creditors and debtors in consumer bankruptcy is discussed in more detail in Chapter 3.

The Federal Trade Commission has adopted restrictions similar to those in the Bankruptcy Code. Here, consider 16 CFR § 444 (cited and quoted after the problem) in answering the following:

PROBLEM 7-5

1. Kimberly Proctor borrowed $2,500 from your client Local Loan Co. which took a non-possessory, non-purchase money security interest in all of Proctor's household goods. Proctor has defaulted on the loan. When Local Loan sued to foreclose on the debt, Proctor's lawyer responded that Local Loan's security interest is in violation of 16 CFR § 444.2(a)(4), and, therefore, the security agreement is void and unenforceable. What do you think?

2. Furniture Co. sells furniture and electronic appliances to a low-income clientele. In separate transactions over a six-month period in 2001, it sold a bedroom suite, two televisions and a radio to Proctor. Furniture Co. retained a security interest in each, and the security agreement contained a cross-collateralization clause. When she defaulted, Furniture Co. sued to recover possession of the goods. Proctor's lawyer has now responded that the obligations are not enforceable because they constitute non-possessory, non-purchase money security interests taken in violation of FTC rule 16 CFR§ 444.2(a)(4). Furniture Co. has asked whether it has a good case. They are fearful because their modus operandi with Proctor is their general way of doing business.

3. Proctor's boyfriend co-signed the note, but has denied that he ever received the notice required under § 444.3. If the court believes him, is he free of liability?

4. A young associate in your firm has argued that the security agreement and guarantee are all enforceable regardless of any FTC violations. She notes that a violation of FTC rules need not void the underlying agreement or give rise to damages to Proctor or her boyfriend. Your associate asserts that the only remedy for an FTC violation is a fine or penalty imposed by the FTC. What do you think?

5. Finally, assume that the applicable state usury laws prohibit Local Loan from making an unsecured loan to Proctor because the resulting interest rate would be too high. Local Loan does not want to take a security interest in Proctor's household goods for fear of violating 16 CFR § 444. An officer at Local Loan has proposed instead to arrange for a consumer's sale to Local Loan of all her household goods and then for a lease of the goods back to the consumer. What do you think?

CODE OF FEDERAL REGULATIONS, TITLE 16—COMMERCIAL PRACTICES, CHAPTER I—FEDERAL TRADE COMMISSION, SUBCHAPTER D—TRADE REGULATION RULES, PART 444—CREDIT PRACTICES

§ 444.1 Definitions.

(a) *Lender.* A person who engages in the business of lending money to consumers within the jurisdiction of the Federal Trade Commission.

(b) *Retail installment seller.* A person who sells goods or services to consumers on a deferred payment basis or pursuant to a lease-purchase arrangement within the jurisdiction of the Federal Trade Commission.

(c) *Person.* An individual, corporation, or other business organization.

(d) *Consumer.* A natural person who seeks or acquires goods, services, or money for personal, family, or household use.

(e) *Obligation.* An agreement between a consumer and a lender or retail installment seller.

(f) *Creditor.* A lender or a retail installment seller.

(g) *Debt.* Money that is due or alleged to be due from one to another.

(h) *Earnings.* Compensation paid or payable to an individual or for his or her account for personal services rendered or to be rendered by him or her, whether denominated as wages, salary, commission, bonus, or otherwise, including periodic payments pursuant to a pension, retirement, or disability program.

(i) *Household goods.* Clothing, furniture, appliances, one radio and one television, linens, china, crockery, kitchenware, and personal effects (including wedding rings) of the consumer and his or her dependents, provided that the following are not included within the scope of the term household goods:

(1) Works of art;

(2) Electronic entertainment equipment (except one television and one radio);

(3) Items acquired as antiques; and

(4) Jewelry (except wedding rings).

(j) *Antique.* Any item over one hundred years of age, including such items that have been repaired or renovated without changing their original form or character.

(k) *Cosigner.* A natural person who renders himself or herself liable for the obligation of another person without compensation. The term shall include any person whose signature is requested as a condition to granting credit to another person, or as a condition for forbearance on collection of another person's obligation that is in default. The term shall not include a spouse whose signature is required on a credit obligation to perfect a security interest pursuant to State law. A person who does not receive goods, services, or money in return for a credit obligation does not receive compensation within the meaning of this definition. A person is a cosigner within the meaning of this definition whether or not he or she is designated as such on a credit obligation.

§ 444.2 Unfair Credit Practices.

(a) In connection with the extension of credit to consumers in or affecting commerce, as commerce is defined in the Federal Trade Commission Act, it is an unfair act or practice within the meaning of Section 5 of that Act for a lender or retail installment seller directly or indirectly to take or receive from a consumer an obligation that:

(1) Constitutes or contains a cognovit or confession of judgment (for purposes other than executory process in the State of Louisiana), warrant of attorney, or other waiver of the right to notice and the opportunity to be heard in the event of suit or process thereon.

(2) Constitutes or contains an executory waiver or a limitation of exemption from attachment, execution, or other process on real or personal property held, owned by, or due to the consumer, unless the waiver applies solely to property subject to a security interest executed in connection with the obligation.

(3) Constitutes or contains an assignment of wages or other earnings unless:

(i) The assignment by its terms is revocable at the will of the debtor, or

(ii) The assignment is a payroll deduction plan or preauthorized payment plan, commencing at the time of the transaction, in which the consumer authorizes a series of wage deductions as a method of making each payment, or

(iii) The assignment applies only to wages or other earnings already earned at the time of the assignment.

(4) Constitutes or contains a nonpossessory security interest in household goods other than a purchase money security interest.

§ 444.3 Unfair or deceptive cosigner practices.

(a) In connection with the extension of credit to consumers in or affecting commerce, as commerce is defined in the Federal Trade Commission Act, it is:

(1) A deceptive act or practice within the meaning of Section 5 of that Act for a lender or retail installment seller, directly or indirectly, to misrepresent the nature or extent of cosigner liability to any person.

(2) An unfair act or practice within the meaning of Section 5 of that Act for a lender or retail installment seller, directly or indirectly, to obligate a cosigner unless the cosigner is informed prior to becoming obligated, which in the case of open end credit shall mean prior to the time that the agreement creating the cosigner's liability for future charges is executed, of the nature of his or her liability as cosigner.

(b) Any lender or retail installment seller who complies with the preventive requirements in paragraph (c) of this section does not violate paragraph (a) of this section.

(c) To prevent these unfair or deceptive acts or practices, a disclosure, consisting of a separate document that shall contain the following statement and no other, shall be given to the cosigner prior to becoming obligated, which in the case of open end credit shall mean prior to the time that the agreement creating the cosigner's liability for future charges is executed:

Notice to Cosigner

You are being asked to guarantee this debt. Think carefully before you do. If the borrower doesn't pay the debt, you will have to. Be sure you can afford to pay if you have to, and that you want to accept this responsibility.

You may have to pay up to the full amount of the debt if the borrower does not pay. You may also have to pay late fees or collection costs, which increase this amount.

The creditor can collect this debt from you without first trying to collect from the borrower. The creditor can use the same collection methods against you that can be used against the borrower, such as suing you, garnishing your wages, etc. If this debt is ever in default, that fact may become a part of *your* credit record.

This notice is not the contract that makes you liable for the debt.

§ 6. FORECLOSURE AGAINST AUTOMOBILES AND OTHER CONSUMER GOODS; CONSUMER PROTECTION IN PART 6 OF ARTICLE 9

In certain ways a creditor's rights against a consumer under Part 6 of Article 9 are more limited than they would be against a business debtor in the same circumstances. For example, section 9–620 has a variety of restrictions on taking collateral in satisfaction of the debt without a sale to a third party. Section 9–625(c)(2) grants a consumer debtor punitive damages equal to 10% of the principal amount plus the full amount of the finance charge in certain circumstances, and section 9–626 does not impose the rebuttable presumption rule on consumers that is imposed on commercial debtors. In addition, the restrictions on waiver found in section 9–602 and on self-help repossession in section 9–609 probably apply more frequently to consumer debtors than to business debtors even though those sections do not state separate rules for consumers. Recall from Chapter 2 that, in some states, cases involving "electronic self-help" or technology-enabled control of assets upon default invoke additional consumer protection provisions.

In fact much of the law under the predecessor of Part 6, in the pre-1999 Code, was made from consumer transactions. A common case would be one in which a debtor granted a security interest in his or her automobile, the debtor defaulted and the creditor repossessed without judicial process. In such circumstances, the interaction between the creditor, or the creditor's agent, and the debtor included a large array of possibilities ranging from an outright fist fight in which the debtor beat up the repossessor or shot him, to cases in which the repossessor pretended to be a policeman and made off with a car or boat. These cases often included disputes about the mode of notice and mode of sale, whether the notice was appropriate, and whether the mode of sale was commercially reasonable. Many of these cases arose out of automobile repossessions.

FORD MOTOR CREDIT V. RYAN

Court of Appeals of Ohio, 2010.
189 Ohio App. 3d 560.

KLATT, JUDGE:

* * *

Ford Motor Credit Company ("Ford"), brought a breach-of-contract action against James and Ryan [&] Ryan, Inc. ("RRI"), in the Franklin County Municipal Court. Ford alleged that James and RRI had failed to pay amounts due under a motor-vehicle lease agreement that James and RRI had entered into when they coleased a 2002 Ford Windstar. James and RRI answered the complaint, and James filed a counterclaim. Because the damages sought in the counterclaim exceeded the municipal court's monetary jurisdiction, the municipal court transferred the case to the common pleas court.

In the common pleas court, Ford sought and received leave to file an amended complaint and a third-party complaint. In the amended complaint, Ford asserted three more breach-of-contract claims against James and RRI. These claims alleged that James and RRI had failed to pay amounts due under (1) a retail installment contract that James and Ryan and Ryan Real Estate Company ("R & R") had entered into when copurchasing a 2004 Mercury Monterey, (2) a retail installment contract that James and R & R had entered into when copurchasing a 2004 Mercury Mountaineer, and (3) a retail installment contract that James and R & R had entered into when copurchasing a 2004 Mercury Mountaineer Premier.

In its third-party complaint, Ford asserted a breach-of-contract claim against James's wife, Carolyn. Ford alleged that Carolyn had failed to pay amounts due under a retail installment contract that she had entered into when she purchased a 2004 Mercury Grand Marquis.

At the time that Ford filed its amended complaint and third-party complaint, it had already repossessed the vehicles at issue in those pleadings. Ford had hired Automobile Recovery Services of Cincinnati, Inc. ("ARS"), to accomplish each of the repossessions. Ford and ARS had a contractual arrangement whereby ARS provided Ford with repossession services. In the contract, ARS agreed to (1) forgo any repossession that would involve a breach of peace and (2) indemnify Ford for all expenses incurred in connection with legal claims that related to ARS's performance of its contractual obligations.

ARS repossessed four of the Ryans' vehicles without incident. However, during the repossession of the Premier, James and the ARS agent engaged in a verbal and physical altercation. James's counterclaim had asserted multiple tort claims against Ford based on the actions of ARS's agent. Therefore, in addition to naming Carolyn, Ford's third-party complaint also named ARS as a third-party defendant. Ford alleged breach-of-contract and indemnity claims against ARS.

In response to Ford's amended and third-party complaints, James and Carolyn each filed an answer and counterclaim. James and Carolyn asserted claims against Ford for (1) conversion, (2) trespass, (3) assault, (4) breach of peace, (5) intentional infliction of emotional distress, (6) invasion of privacy, (7) violation of Section 1983, Title 42, U.S.Code ("Section 1983"), (8) breach of contract, (9) violation of the Fair Debt Collection Practices Act, Section 1692, Title 15, U.S.Code ("FDCPA"), (10) violation of the Ohio Consumer Sales Practices Act, R.C. 1345.01 et seq. ("CSPA"), and (11) violation of the Ohio Retail Installment Sales Act, R.C. 1317.01 et seq. ("RISA"). James alone also asserted a claim for negligence against Ford.

Both James and Carolyn brought a cross-claim against ARS. The cross-claims stated claims for (1) conversion, (2) trespass, (3) assault, (4) breach of peace, (5) intentional infliction of emotional distress, (6) invasion of privacy, (7) violation of Section 1983, (8) violation of the FDCPA, and (9) violation of the RISA.

Additionally, both James and Carolyn named Bob-Boyd Lincoln Mercury, Inc. ("Bob-Boyd") as a third-party defendant. The Ryans had leased or purchased each of the vehicles at issue in the instant case from Bob-Boyd. James and Carolyn asserted claims against Bob-Boyd for (1) breach of contract, (2) violation of the CSPA, and (3) estoppel.

Ford, ARS, and Bob-Boyd moved for summary judgment on all the claims that James and Carolyn had asserted against them. Ford also moved for summary judgment as to its breach-of-contract claim against Carolyn, as well as its four breach-of-contract claims against both James and RRI. In three different judgment entries, the trial court granted all the summary-judgment motions. James and Carolyn separately appealed the three judgments to this court.

* * *

We now turn to the merits of appellants' argument that their claims against ARS for trespass, conversion, assault, and violation of Section 1983 should have survived summary judgment. Appellate review of summary-judgment motions is de novo. *Andersen v. Highland House Co.* (2001), 93 Ohio St.3d 547, 548, 757 N.E.2d 329. " 'When reviewing a trial court's ruling on summary judgment, the court of appeals conducts an independent review of the record and stands in the shoes of the trial court.' " *Abrams v. Worthington,* 169 Ohio App.3d 94, 2006-Ohio-5516, 861 N.E.2d 920, ¶ 11, quoting *Mergenthal v. Star Banc Corp.* (1997), 122 Ohio App.3d 100, 103, 701 N.E.2d 383. Civ.R. 56(C) provides that a trial court must grant summary judgment when the moving party demonstrates that (1) there is no genuine issue of material fact, (2) the moving party is entitled to judgment as a matter of law, and (3) reasonable minds can come to but one conclusion and that conclusion is adverse to the party against whom the motion for summary judgment is made. *Gilbert v. Summit Cty.*, 104 Ohio St.3d 660, 2004-Ohio-7108, 821 N.E.2d 564, ¶ 6.

When seeking summary judgment on the ground that the nonmoving party cannot prove its case, the moving party bears the initial burden of informing the trial court of the basis for the motion and identifying those portions of the record that demonstrate the absence of a genuine issue of material fact on an essential element of the nonmoving party's claims. *Dresher v. Burt* (1996), 75 Ohio St.3d 280, 293, 662 N.E.2d 264. The moving party does not discharge this initial burden under Civ.R. 56 by simply making a conclusory allegation that the nonmoving party has no evidence to prove its case. *Id.* Rather, the moving party must affirmatively demonstrate by affidavit or other evidence allowed by Civ.R. 56(C) that the nonmoving party has no evidence to support its claims. *Id.* If the moving party meets this initial burden, then the nonmoving party has a reciprocal burden outlined in Civ.R. 56(E) to set forth specific facts showing that there is a genuine issue for trial and, if the nonmoving party does not so respond, summary judgment, if appropriate, shall be entered against the nonmoving party. *Id.*

Initially, we note that although ARS sought summary judgment on all appellants' claims, it failed to explain in its motion why the trial court should grant summary judgment on appellants' trespass claims. In fact, the motion does not mention the trespass claims at all, other than listing "trespass" in its recitation of all the claims appellants asserted. Likewise, ARS's brief on appeal contains no argument regarding appellants' trespass claims. Because ARS neither established the absence of a genuine issue of material fact regarding the trespass claims nor presented a legal reason why those claims must fail, we conclude that the trial court erred in granting summary judgment to ARS on appellants' trespass claims.

Appellants next contend that the existence of genuine issues of material fact precluded summary judgment on their conversion claims. " '[C]onversion is the wrongful exercise of dominion over property to the exclusion of the rights of the owner, or withholding it from his possession under a claim inconsistent with his rights.' " *State ex rel. Toma v. Corrigan* (2001), 92 Ohio St.3d 589, 592, 752 N.E.2d 281, quoting *Joyce v. Gen. Motors Corp.* (1990), 49 Ohio St.3d 93, 96, 551 N.E.2d 172. ARS argues that it did not wrongfully take appellants' vehicles because Ford had a contractual right to repossess the vehicles, and Ford hired ARS to exercise its contractual right. Section G of the retail installment contracts states that if the obligor(s) default, Ford "may repossess (take back) the vehicle." In Ohio, this right to repossession is subject to R.C. 1309.609, which provides:

(A) After default, a secured party:

(1) May take possession of the collateral * * *.

(B) A secured party may act under division (A) of this section:

(1) Pursuant to judicial process; or

(2) Without judicial process if it acts without breach of the peace.

R.C. 1309.609 is virtually identical to Section 9–609 of the Uniform Commercial Code ("U.C.C."). The General Assembly incorporated U.C.C. provisions into the Ohio Revised Code "[t]o make uniform the laws among the various jurisdictions." R.C. 1301.02(B)(3). Accordingly, to supplement Ohio law, our analysis of R.C. 1309.609 relies upon precedent from other jurisdictions addressing U.C.C. 9–609 and similar state statutes. Additionally, this court looks to caselaw interpreting former R.C. 1309.46, which preceded R.C. 1309.609 and duplicated former U.C.C. 9–503. 149 Ohio Laws, Part I, 106, 107–108. Like U.C.C. 9–609, former U.C.C. 9–503 also allowed the repossession of collateral upon default if the creditor accomplished the repossession without a breach of the peace. Consequently, precedent from other jurisdictions interpreting former U.C.C. 9–503 and like state statutes also inform our analysis.

R.C. 1309.609 gives a secured party the right to attempt self-help repossession if a debtor defaults. *State v. LeFevre* (May 4, 1995), 10th Dist. No. 94APA09–1376, 1995 WL 258959; *Smith v. John Deere Co.* (1993), 83 Ohio App.3d 398, 408, 614 N.E.2d 1148. However, "[i]f the secured party, or a third party repossessing for the secured party, causes a breach of peace while repossessing the collateral, the repossession will be wrongful, and the debtor may sue the secured party in conversion for return of the collateral or damages." 9 Hawkland, Uniform Commercial Code Series (2001), Section 9–503:3. * * *

Normally, a conversion occurs if a person takes another's vehicle without the owner's permission. *See Toma,* 92 Ohio St.3d at 592, 752 N.E.2d 281. R.C. 1309.609 provides a defense to such a conversion claim because it permits a repossessor to take possession of the vehicle, rendering the repossession lawful. This defense, however, depends on the absence of a breach of the peace. If a breach of the peace occurs, the repossessor cannot rely on R.C. 1309.609 to excuse its actions. *Marcus v. McCollum* (C.A.10, 2004), 394 F.3d 813, 820 ("If a breach of peace occurs, self-help repossession is statutorily precluded"). At the point the peace is breached, the repossessor's exercise of dominion over the vehicle becomes wrongful, exposing the repossessor to liability for conversion.

A breach of peace is:

> [A] violation of public order, a disturbance of the public tranquility, by any act or conduct inciting to violence or tending to provoke or excite others to break the peace, or, as is some times said, it includes any violation of any law enacted to preserve peace and good order. It may consist of an act of violence or an act likely to produce violence.

Morris v. First Natl. Bank & Trust Co. (1970), 21 Ohio St.2d 25, 29, 50 O.O.2d 47, 254 N.E.2d 683, quoting *Akron v. Mingo* (1959), 169 Ohio St. 511, 513, 9 O.O.2d 7, 160 N.E.2d 225. A breach of peace includes " 'all violations of public peace, order or decorum' " and " 'breaking or disturbing the public peace by any riotous, forceful or unlawful proceedings.' " *Makepeace v. Chrysler Motors Corp.* (May 8, 1981), 2d Dist. No. L-80-187, 1981 WL 5572, *quoting Census Fed. Credit Union v. Wann* (Ind.App.1980), 403 N.E.2d 348.

In the case at bar, ARS repossessed three vehicles copurchased by James and R & R, as well as Carolyn's vehicle. Three of the repossessions proceeded uneventfully. On February 7, 2006, ARS towed the Mountaineer from the parking lot of R & R's office building. Although James "saw it go away," he "didn't have any time to respond." ARS took the Monterey that James copurchased from his son's driveway sometime during the night of February 7 and 8, 2006. That same night, ARS took Carolyn's vehicle from the carport of the Ryans' home. Neither James, his wife, nor his son knew that the repossessions had occurred until they awoke the next morning.

Appellants acknowledge that the ARS agents did not threaten, incite, or commit any act of violence when they repossessed the three vehicles on February 7 and 8, 2006. Appellants, however, argue that the ARS agents breached the peace when they entered onto private property to repossess the vehicles.

Generally, no breach of peace occurs merely because the repossessor enters on a person's driveway or carport to retrieve a vehicle. *Geeslin v. Nissan Motor Acceptance Corp.* (June 3, 1998), N.D.Miss. No. Civ. A. 1:97CV186-DA, 1998 WL 433932, *affirmed* (C.A.5, 2000), 228 F.3d 408 (table). * * * Indeed, R.C. 1309.609 gives a repossessor a privilege to enter another's land to effectuate a repossession, so long as the repossessor does not breach the peace. *LeFevre* (because former R.C. 1309.46 gave the secured party the right to take possession of the collateral upon default, the repossessor "had the right to enter [the debtor's] property to repossess the car upon his default if such could be done without a breach of the peace"). * * *

Here, ARS exercised its right under R.C. 1309.609 to enter onto private property to repossess the three vehicles on February 7 and 8, 2006. This trespass, without more, does not constitute a breach of peace. Accordingly, no liability for conversion arose out of the repossessions of the three vehicles.

Appellants, however, argue that ARS did not have the right to enter onto their property because R.C. 1309.609 extends that authority only to the "secured party." Because ARS is not the "secured party," appellants contend that it cannot rely on R.C. 1309.609. We find this argument unavailing. Just because R.C. 1309.609 confers the right of repossession on the "secured party" does not mean that the secured party must personally repossess the collateral. 10 Anderson, Uniform Commercial Code (3d Ed.) 381, Section 9–503:137. The secured party may hire another to make the repossession, and the right of repossession accrues to the hired entity. *Id.* * * * Here Ford, the "secured party," hired ARS to repossess the vehicles, and thus, ARS operated under the auspices of R.C. 1309.609.

Appellants also argue that ARS cannot rely on R.C. 1309.609 to escape liability for conversion because that statute violates the Fourth, Fifth, and Fourteenth Amendments to the United States Constitution and Section 14, Article I of the Ohio Constitution.

Our analysis of the constitutionality of R.C. 1309.609 is guided by the strong presumption of constitutionality that all statutes enjoy. *Kaminski v. Metal & Wire Prods. Co.,* 125 Ohio St.3d 250, 2010-Ohio-1027, 927 N.E.2d 1066, ¶ 58. "Before a court may declare unconstitutional an enactment of the legislative branch, 'it must appear beyond a reasonable doubt that the legislation and constitutional provisions are clearly incompatible.'" *Arbino v. Johnson & Johnson,* 116 Ohio St.3d 468, 2007-Ohio-6948, 880 N.E.2d 420, ¶ 25, *quoting State ex rel. Dickman v. Defenbacher* (1955), 164 Ohio St. 142, 57 O.O. 134, 128 N.E.2d 59, paragraph one of the syllabus.

As an initial matter, we find that the Fifth Amendment is irrelevant to the instant matter. The Due Process Clause of the Fifth Amendment applies to the federal government, not state government. *Dusenbery v. United States* (2002), 534 U.S. 161, 167, 122 S.Ct. 694, 151 L.Ed.2d 597. Appellant, therefore, cannot rely on the Fifth Amendment as a basis for arguing that a state statute is unconstitutional.

The Fourth Amendment, as applied to the states through the Fourteenth Amendment to the United States Constitution and Section 14, Article I of the Ohio Constitution prohibit the government from conducting unreasonable searches and seizures of persons or their property. The Fourteenth Amendment precludes state government from depriving any person of life, liberty, or property without due process of law. Notably, both the Fourth and Fourteenth Amendments provide protection against governmental—not private—action. * * * Enactment of a statute that permits self-help repossession does not amount to the significant state involvement necessary for the Fourth and Fourteenth Amendments to apply. *Winfield v. Soc. Natl. Bank* (C.A.6, 1988), 845 F.2d 328 (table) (finding former R.C. 1309.46, the predecessor to R.C. 1309.609, constitutional). * * * Thus, we conclude that R.C. 1309.609 does not violate the Fourth or Fourteenth Amendments.

Having addressed the repossessions that occurred on February 7 and 8, 2006, we now examine the final repossession to determine if a question of fact exists as to whether ARS breached the peace. Unlike the February 7 and 8, 2006 repossessions, the January 12, 2006 repossession of the Premier occurred over James's objection. On January 12, 2006, at approximately 8:15 a.m., James was dressing when his wife told him that someone with a tow truck was in their carport. James went out to the carport and found an ARS agent hooking the Premier to his tow truck. James told the ARS agent to stop, unhook the Premier, and leave the premises because he was trespassing. James then reached down to unhook the Premier, and the ARS agent grabbed his hands, pushed him, and began screaming at him. According to James, the ARS agent screamed, "I'm going to make your neighbors know about what you're doing[;] you rich bastard, I got you." At that point, James began pushing back and yelling. James eventually backed away, and the ARS agent towed the Premier away.

Based upon this evidence, a reasonable finder of fact could conclude that a breach of the peace occurred. If the finder of fact reached such a conclusion, then it could also find ARS liable for conversion. Accordingly, we conclude that the trial court erred in granting ARS summary judgment on James's claim for conversion of the Premier.

* * * Next, we consider whether the trial court erred in granting ARS summary judgment on appellants' claims that an ARS agent assaulted them during the January 12, 2006 repossession. A plaintiff establishes the tort of assault by showing that the defendant willfully threatened or attempted to harm or offensively touch the plaintiff and that the threat or attempt reasonably placed the plaintiff in fear of such contact. *Stafford v. Columbus Bonding Ctr.,* 177 Ohio App.3d 799, 2008-Ohio-3948, 896 N.E.2d 191, ¶ 15.

Although Carolyn entered the carport briefly during the repossession, she returned to the house after seeing her husband reach down to unhook the Premier. Based on Carolyn's recounting of the events of January 12, 2006, the ARS agent never threatened or attempted to contact her. Consequently, reasonable minds could only conclude that the ARS agent did not assault Carolyn, and thus, the trial court properly granted ARS summary judgment on Carolyn's assault claim.

The situation is different as to James. The ARS agent physically prevented James from unhooking the Premier from the tow truck. James testified that he backed away. He said, "[The ARS agent was] about 30 years younger than I am and about another 150 pounds heavier than I was." In his July 25, 2008 deposition, James stated repeatedly that he had felt threatened by the ARS agent. Despite this evidence, ARS argues that James's actions demonstrated frustration or anger—not fear. We believe that reasonable minds could disagree regarding how to interpret James's actions and whether he reasonably feared that the ARS agent would strike him. We therefore conclude that the trial court erred in granting ARS summary judgment on James's assault claim.

* * * [The court rejected the appellants' claims for violation of section 1983 due to the absence of state action.]

We next turn to the trial court's grant of summary judgment on James's claim against ARS for the conversion of personal property that was in the Premier when ARS repossessed that vehicle on May 9, 2005. To clarify, ARS repossessed the Premier twice—first on May 9, 2005, and after James redeemed the Premier, then again on January 12, 2006. James asserted a claim against ARS for conversion of multiple items of personal property that were in the Premier when ARS repossessed it the first time. This personal property included clothing, prescription eyeglasses, boating paraphernalia, CDs, and cash. After the repossession, James contacted ARS and requested the return of the personal property in the Premier and the vehicle's license plates. ARS returned only the license plates.

Although R.C. 1309.609 permits a repossessor to lawfully take possession of another's vehicle, that permission does not extend to the personal items inside the vehicle. Consequently, even though a lawful repossession leaves the debtor with no claim for conversion of his vehicle, he may assert a conversion claim against the repossessor for any personal property taken with the vehicle and not returned. *Perkins v. City Natl. Bank & Trust Co.* (Mar. 22, 1977), 10th Dist. No. 76AP-730, 1977 WL 200020 (the plaintiff could recover for the conversion of personal items that "the defendant bank had no right, by virtue of the contractual arrangements of the parties on the security agreement, to repossess along with the motor home"). * * *

Here, ARS does not dispute that when it repossessed the Premier in May 2005, the Premier contained personal items that it did not return to James. Accordingly, we conclude that the trial court erred in granting ARS summary judgment on James's claim for conversion of his personal property.

In sum, we conclude that the trial court erred in granting ARS summary judgment on appellants' claims for trespass, James's claim for conversion of the Premier, James's claim for assault, and James's claim for conversion of personal property in the Premier. Consequently, we sustain appellants' second assignments of error to the extent that they challenge those rulings. In all other respects, we overrule appellants' second assignments of error.

* * * [The court rejected the appellants' claims for intentional infliction of emotional distress and punitive damages.]

* * *

By their fifth assignments of error, appellants argue that the trial court erred in granting summary judgment to Ford and Bob-Boyd on appellants' CSPA claims. While we agree with appellants that Carolyn's CSPA claim against Bob-Boyd should have survived summary judgment, we find that the trial court appropriately awarded summary judgment on James's CSPA claims and Carolyn's CSPA claim against Ford.

R.C. 1345.02 and 1345.03 prohibit suppliers from engaging in unfair, deceptive, or unconscionable practices "in connection with a consumer transaction." A "consumer transaction" means "a sale, lease, assignment, award by chance, or other transfer of an item of goods, a service, a franchise, or an intangible, to an individual for purposes that are primarily personal, family, or household." R.C. 1345.01(A). The definition of "consumer transaction" does not include "transactions between persons, defined in sections 4905.03 and 5725.01 of the Revised Code, and their customers." *Id.* The "persons" listed in R.C. 5725.01 include "dealers in intangibles," which R.C. 5725.01(B)(1) defines as follows:

> [E]very person who keeps an office or other place of business in this state and engages at such office or other place in a business that consists primarily of lending money, or discounting, buying, or selling bills of exchange, drafts, acceptances, notes, mortgages, or other evidences of indebtedness.

In the case at bar, Ford claims that appellants cannot sue it for violation of the CSPA because it is a "dealer in intangibles." Ford attached to its motion for summary judgment the affidavit of Randall E. Golliher, a territory sales manager for Ford, in which Golliher testified that Ford maintained an office in Ohio from 2003 through 2006. Golliher also stated that at that office, Ford engaged in a business that primarily consisted of lending money or discounting, buying, or selling bills of exchange, drafts, acceptances, notes, mortgages, or other evidences of indebtedness. Appellants offer no evidence to rebut Golliher's affidavit. Accordingly, as Ford presented uncontradicted evidence that it qualifies as a "dealer in intangibles," appellants' CSPA claims against Ford must fail. *See Reagans v. MountainHigh Coachworks, Inc.,* 117 Ohio St.3d 22, 2008-Ohio-271, 881 N.E.2d 245, ¶ 33 ("As a general matter, transactions between financial institutions and their customers are exempted from the definition of a 'consumer transaction' subject to the Consumer Sales Practices Act"); *Columbus Mtge., Inc. v. Morton,* 10th Dist. No. 06AP-723, 2007-Ohio-3057, 2007 WL 1748142, ¶ 53–59 (affirming the grant of summary judgment on a CSPA claim because the transaction at issue involved a dealer in intangibles).

James, however, argues that Ford has derivative liability for Bob-Boyd's misconduct because the retail installment contracts contain the notice mandated by 16 C.F.R. 433.2, a Federal Trade Commission ("FTC") regulation.[14] Inclusion of the FTC-mandated notice in a consumer credit contract subjects a creditor to the claims the consumer debtor has against the seller of the goods financed by the credit contract. *Reagans,* 117 Ohio St.3d 22, 2008-Ohio-271, 881 N.E.2d 245, at ¶ 22. *See also Milchen v. Bob Morris Pontiac-GMC Truck* (1996), 113 Ohio App.3d 190, 195–197, 680 N.E.2d 698 (although a financial institution could not be directly liable under the CSPA, it could be derivatively liable for the seller's violations of the CSPA due to the inclusion of the FTC-mandated notice). Thus, James argues that he can assert a CSPA claim against Ford despite its being a "dealer in intangibles."

James acknowledges that he raises this argument for the first time before this court. Ordinarily, such a belated assertion of an argument results in its forfeiture. *State ex rel. Ohio Civ. Serv. Emp. Assn.,* 104 Ohio St.3d 122, 2004-Ohio-6363, 818 N.E.2d 688, at ¶ 10. James contends that he did not forfeit this argument because Ford did not attach the page of the retail installment contracts that contained the FTC-mandated notice to its summary-judgment motion. James is mistaken. Ford included that page in the copies of the retail installment contracts reproduced in the appendix to its motion. Thus, we decline to consider James's argument.

Unlike Ford, Bob-Boyd does not claim to be a "dealer in intangibles." Rather, Bob-Boyd argues that summary judgment was warranted on appellants' CSPA claims against it because appellants did not purchase their vehicles for primarily personal, family, or household purposes.

A consumer cannot recover under the CSPA unless he entered into a "consumer transaction," i.e., a purchase made for primarily personal, family, or household purposes. R.C. 1345.01(A); *Giffin v. Crestview Cadillac,* 10th Dist. No. 09AP-278, 2009-Ohio-6569, 2009 WL 4809862, ¶ 21. Purchases of goods for primarily business purposes are not "consumer transactions" and thus cannot support a CSPA claim. *Id.* at ¶ 21. When deciding whether a "consumer transaction" occurred, "courts look to 'the point in time when the parties have entered a binding agreement.' " *Id.* at ¶ 22, quoting *Tomes v. George P. Ballas Leasing, Inc.* (Sept. 30, 1986), 6th Dist. No. L-85-359, 1986 WL 11420. Courts then examine the "objective manifestations" that the purchaser made at that time regarding how he intended to use the purchased item. *Id.* If the purchaser's intentions are unclear, then courts apply the "principal use" test. *Id.* at ¶ 26. The outcome

---

[14] In compliance with 16 C.F.R. 433.2, the notice in the retail installment contracts reads, "NOTICE—ANY HOLDER OF THIS CONSUMER CREDIT CONTRACT IS SUBJECT TO ALL CLAIMS AND DEFENSES WHICH THE DEBTOR COULD ASSERT AGAINST THE SELLER OF GOODS OR SERVICES OBTAINED PURSUANT HERETO OR WITH THE PROCEEDS HEREOF. RECOVERY HEREUNDER BY THE DEBTOR SHALL NOT EXCEED AMOUNTS PAID BY THE DEBTOR HEREUNDER."

of the principal-use test depends on how the owner of the item uses that item after its purchase. *Id.* at ¶ 25. "Factors include 'total time used for business versus total time used for personal activities, evidence of compensation for business use either from an employer or by way of deduction, as well as relative mileage.' " *Id.* at ¶ 25, quoting *Jackson v. Krieger Ford, Inc.* (Mar. 28, 1989), 10th Dist. No. 88AP-1030, 1989 WL 29351.

Here, as to the Premier, James made no objective manifestations regarding how he intended to use the vehicle. Although the retail installment contract contained a section in which the purchaser could indicate the "Use For Which Purchased," that section is blank. As to the Monterey and Mountaineer, James made conflicting objective manifestations regarding his purpose. James checked the "personal" box in the section of the retail installment contracts entitled "Use For Which Purchased." However, James purchased each vehicle jointly with a corporation—R & R. By definition, a corporation purchases goods only for business purposes.

Ford recognized the inconsistency created by the representation that a corporation purchased the vehicles for personal use. Upon review of the retail installment contracts for the purchases of the Monterey and Mountaineer, Ford sent letters to R & R indicating that "[t]he Personal Use box is checked incorrectly" and "[t]he correct use for which [the vehicle was] purchased is Commercial."

Based upon the totality of the evidence, we conclude that the objective manifestations regarding the intended use were either nonexistent or ambiguous. Thus, we turn to the principal-use test to determine whether the vehicles were purchased for personal or business purposes.

After purchase, the vehicles were titled in the name of R & R. Additionally, R & R depreciated the vehicles as business assets on its 2004 federal tax return. That tax return indicates that in 2004, 90 percent of the Monterey's use was for business purposes, 85 percent of the Mountaineer's use was for business purposes, and 95 percent of the Premier's use was for business purposes. Accordingly, we conclude that James purchased the vehicles for primarily business, not personal, use. Because the purchases do not qualify as "consumer transactions," James's CSPA claims against Bob-Boyd must fail.

We reach the opposite conclusion on Carolyn's CSPA claim against Bob-Boyd. Unlike James, Carolyn did not co-purchase her vehicle with a corporation. The only objective manifestation as to Carolyn's purpose is that she checked the "personal" box when designating the purpose for which she purchased the car. Therefore, we conclude that Carolyn engaged in a "consumer transaction," and thus, the trial court erred in granting summary judgment on her CSPA claim against Bob-Boyd.

In sum, we overrule James's fifth assignment of error. We overrule Carolyn's fifth assignment of error to the extent it challenges the trial court's summary-judgment ruling as to Ford, but we sustain that assignment of error to the extent it challenges the trial court's ruling as to Bob-Boyd.

* * *

Given the foregoing, we affirm in part and reverse in part the judgments of the Franklin County Court of Common Pleas, and we remand this case to that court for further proceedings consistent with law and this opinion.

BRYANT AND SANDLER, JJ., concur.

[footnotes omitted.]

WAIVER AND VARIANCE OF RIGHTS IN CONSUMER SECURITY AGREEMENTS

The secured creditor is almost always the drafter of the form security agreement that is signed by the debtor. As one might expect, secured creditors fill these agreements with terms to remedy problems that they have faced in litigation with earlier debtors. Sections 9–602 and 9–603 restrict the power of creditors to favor themselves. The former lists a series of sections whose affect may not be waived or varied by the security agreement:

> **SECTION 9–602. Waiver and variance of rights and duties.**
>
> Except as provided in Section 9–624, to the extent that they give rights to a debtor or obligor and impose duties on a secured party, the debtor or obligor may not waive or vary the rules stated in the following listed sections:
>
> (1) Section 9–207(b)(4)(C), which deals with use and operation of the collateral by the secured party;
>
> (2) Section 9–210, which deals with requests for an accounting and requests concerning a list of collateral and statement of account.
>
> (3) Section 9–607(c), which deals with collection and enforcement of collateral;
>
> (4) Sections 9–608(a) and 9–615(e) to the extent that they deal with application or payment of noncash proceeds of collection, enforcement, or disposition;
>
> (5) Sections 9–608(a) and 9–615(c) and (f) to the extent that they require accounting for or payment of surplus proceeds of collateral;

(6) Section 9–609 to the extent that it imposes upon a secured party that takes possession of collateral without judicial process the duty to do so without breach of the peace;

(7) Sections 9–610(b), 9–611, 9–613, and 9–614, which deal with disposition of collateral;

(8) Section 9–615(h), which deals with calculation of a deficiency or surplus when a disposition is made to the secured party, a person related to the secured party, or a secondary obligor;

(9) Section 9–616, which deals with explanation of the calculation of a surplus or deficiency;

(10) Section 9–620, 9–621, and 9–622, which deal with acceptance of collateral in satisfaction of obligation;

(11) Section 9–623, which deals with redemption of collateral;

(12) Section 9–624, which deals with permissible waivers; and

(13) Sections 9–625 and 9–626, which deal with the secured party's liability for failure to comply with this article.

Section 9–603 states a general standard against which other attempts at restricting a debtor's rights are to be measured:

SECTION 9–603. Agreement on standards concerning rights and duties.

(a) **[Agreed standards.]** The parties may determine by agreement the standards measuring the fulfillment of the rights of a debtor or obligor and the duties of a secured party under a rule stated in Section 9–602 if the standards are not manifestly unreasonable.

(b) **[Agreed standards inapplicable to breach of peace.]** Subsection (a) does not apply to the duty under Section 9–609 to refrain from breaching the peace.

Sections 9–602 and 9–603 should be read in context with section 1–302, setting out the general rule governing variation by agreement of the provisions of the UCC, and section 1–103(b), prescribing the general UCC rule governing the applicability of estoppel, waiver, and related equitable principles. Although section 1–302 generally allows variance by agreement of the provisions of the UCC, it would be a mistake to conclude that a provision of Article 9 may be varied by agreement if not specifically identified in section 9–602 as one that may not be. Consider, for example, section 9–203, governing the requirements for the creation of an enforceable security interest. It is not specifically listed in section 9–602, yet no one would contend seriously that the parties to a security agreement are therefore free to come up with their own criteria of enforceability by virtue of section 1–302. Likewise absent from the anti-variance list in section 9–602 are Article 9's perfection rules. Once again, however, it is not plausible to conclude that the parties to a security agreement may therefore come up with their own methods of perfection. Accordingly, the list of items identified in section 9–602 should not be thought of as exclusive.

PROBLEM 7-6

Section 9–603 has at least two analytical stumbling blocks: distinguishing "standards" from the rule itself and defining "manifestly unreasonable."

1. Is the following a permissible standard? "Mere entrance onto the property of the debtor in an attempt to repossess is not of itself a breach of the peace or the basis for which debtor may recover damages."

Which of the following do you think would be regarded as manifestly unreasonable and therefore not enforceable?

2. A term in the agreement that permits the creditor to bring a police officer along during the act of repossession.

3. A term that blesses the sale of an automobile (for a wholesale price) at a dealer only auction.

4. A term that permits a secured creditor to purchase the automobile at a "private disposition" and use that purchase price as the basis for measuring the deficiency on its purchase. (On this compare section 9–602(7).)

A common provision in a security agreement is a "no waiver" clause that specifies that the creditor's acceptance of late payments once or occasionally does not constitute a waiver of its right to insist upon timely payments thereafter. The following case summarizes the law on this topic and chooses one of the three possible outcomes in applying the law to such clauses.

MINOR V. CHASE AUTO FINANCE CORPORATION

Supreme Court of Arkansas, 2010.
2010 Ark. 246.

SHEFFIELD, JUSTICE.

The Arkansas Court of Appeals certified this case to us pursuant to Arkansas Supreme Court Rule 1–2(b)(1), (4), and (5) (2009), as a case involving an issue of first impression, having a substantial public interest and needing clarification or development of the law. We have been asked to determine whether non-waiver and no-unwritten-modifications clauses in a financing agreement preclude a creditor from waiving future strict compliance with the agreement by accepting late payments. In *Mercedes-*

Benz Credit Corp. v. Morgan, 312 Ark. 225, 850 S.W.2d 297 (1993), this court explicitly reserved ruling on this question until it had been properly raised and argued in an appropriate case. The question is now ripe for our review.

On March 15, 2005, Appellant Mose Minor (Minor) entered into a Simple Interest Motor Vehicle Contract and Security Agreement with Appellee Chase Auto Finance Corporation (Chase) to finance the purchase of a 2003 Toyota Tundra. By the terms of the agreement, Minor was to make sixty-six payments of $456.99 on the fourteenth of each month. The payments would start on April 14, 2003, and end on September 14, 2008. The agreement also included the following relevant provisions:

> G. Default: If you breach any warranty or default in the performance of any promise you make in this contract or any other contract you have with us, including, but not limited to, failing to make any payments when due, or become insolvent, or file any proceeding under the U.S. Bankruptcy Code, . . . we may at our option and without notice or demand (1) declare all unpaid sums immediately due and payable subject to any right of reinstatement as required by law (2) file suit against you for all unpaid sums (3) take immediate possession of the vehicle (4) exercise any other legal or equitable remedy. . . Our remedies are cumulative and taking of any action shall not be a waiver or prohibit us from pursuing any other remedy. You agree that upon your default we shall be entitled to recover from you our reasonable collection costs, including, but not limited to, any attorney's fee. In addition, if we repossess the vehicle, you grant to us and our agents permission to enter upon any premises where the vehicle is located. Any repossession will be performed peacefully. . . .
>
> * * *
>
> J. Other Agreements of Buyer: . . . (2) You agree that if we accept moneys in sums less than those due or make extensions of due dates of payments under this contract, doing so will not be a waiver of any later right to enforce the contract terms as written. . . (12) All of the agreements between us and you are set forth in this contract and no modification of this contract shall be valid unless it is made in writing and signed by you and us. . .
>
> K. Delay in Enforcement: We can delay or waive enforcement of any of our rights under this contract without losing them.

Minor's first payment was late, as were several subsequent payments. At times he failed to make any payment for months. Chase charged a late fee for each late payment, and sent several letters requesting payment and offering to assist Minor with his account. Chase also warned Minor that continued failure to make payments would result in Chase exercising its legal options available under the agreement, including repossession of the vehicle. Minor claims he never received these letters. At one point, Minor fell so far behind in his payments that Chase was on the verge of repossessing the vehicle. However, on October 19, 2004, the parties agreed to a two-month extension of the agreement, such that the final installment would be due on November 14, 2008. The extension agreement indicated that all other terms and conditions of the original contract would remain the same.

On November 2, 2004, Minor filed for chapter 7 bankruptcy in the Eastern District of Arkansas. In his petition, Minor stated that the value of the vehicle was $5000.00. On February 24, 2005, Chase sent Minor a letter acknowledging that Minor's debt to Chase had been discharged in bankruptcy. The letter further stated that Chase still had a valid lien on the vehicle, and if Minor wished to keep the vehicle, he would have to continue to make payments to Chase. Otherwise, Chase would repossess the vehicle. Chase sent a similar letter to Minor on May 22, 2006, and to Minor's bankruptcy attorney on November 16, 2004. Minor claimed he never received any of these letters.

On September 28, 2006, a repossession agent, Joshua Niles of Chamras Asset Recovery Specialists, arrived at Minor's home some time in the afternoon to repossess the vehicle. The repossession agent checked the VIN number of the vehicle and began to hoist it on his truck. There were no fences, gates or garages barring the agent's access to the vehicle. When Minor objected to the repossession, the agent gave him a telephone number for Chase to call to obtain more information. Minor returned to his house to make the phone call, and spoke to a representative of Chase, who told him that Chase was repossessing the car because he was three months behind on his payments. Minor objected to the Chase representative and insisted that he could provide proof of payment in the form of money order receipts. The repossession agent waited outside for several minutes, but when Minor did not return from inside his house, the agent removed Minor's possessions from the vehicle and towed it away. Chase sold the vehicle. The amount of the purchase price was reflected on Minor's account on November 17, 2006.

On January 7, 2008, Minor filed a complaint against Chase in the Johnson County Circuit Court. In the complaint, Minor alleged that, during the course of the contract, the parties had altered the provisions of the contract regarding Chase's right to repossess the vehicle and Chase had waived the right to strictly enforce the repossession clause. Minor further claimed that the repossession agent committed trespass and repossessed the vehicle forcibly, without Minor's permission, and through trickery and deceit, in violation of Arkansas Code Annotated section 4–9–609(b)(2)

(Repl.2001). Also, Minor asserted that he was not in default on his payments, pursuant to the repayment schedule, at the time Chase authorized repossession. Therefore, according to Minor, Chase committed conversion, and breached the Arkansas Deceptive Trade Practices Act, specifically Arkansas Code Annotated section 4–88–107(a)(10) (Supp.2007), and enhanced by Arkansas Code Annotated section 4–88–202 (Repl.2001), because Minor is an elderly person. Minor sought compensatory and punitive damages.

A jury trial was held on February 19, 2009. At the close of Minor's case, Chase moved for a directed verdict. Chase argued that Minor had not asserted sufficient grounds for an award of punitive damages because the act of conversion, alone, does not constitute sufficient grounds for an award of punitive damages, and Minor had not provided any evidence that there had been a breach of the peace. Chase further maintained that, by Minor's own admission when he testified before the circuit court, he was at least three payments past due at the time of the repossession. Therefore, under the terms of the contract, Chase asserted that it had a right to repossess the vehicle peacefully, and Minor's argument that he should have received notice that Chase would require strict compliance with the contract failed because the contract included non-waiver and no-unwritten modification clauses. Chase argued that the case upon which Minor relied, *Mercedes-Benz Credit Corp. v. Morgan,* 312 Ark. 225, 850 S.W.2d 297 (1993), was distinguishable, and instead the holding of *Westlund v. Melson,* 7 Ark.App. 268, 647 S.W.2d 488 (1983), indicated that Chase's acceptance of late payments had not effected a waiver of its right to demand future strict compliance. Finally, Chase asserted that Minor had failed to show that Chase had committed deception or false pretense in order to sustain a claim for a violation of the Arkansas Deceptive Trade Practices Act.

In response, Minor argued that the jury should be allowed to rule on the evidence because there was a question of whether Minor was in default at the time of the repossession, since the evidence indicated Chase had failed to properly credit his account. What is more, Minor maintained, Chase was aware of this error but repossessed the vehicle anyway, against Minor's will, an action that constituted an intentional and willful violation of Minor's rights, warranting an award of punitive damages. Also, according to Minor, his request that the repossession agent stop the repossession constituted a confrontation rising to the level of a breach of the peace. Further, Minor asserted that he had presented sufficient evidence that he had a right to possess the vehicle, and that, by continually accepting late payments, Chase had established a course of dealing that modified the contract and waived Chase's right to repossess the vehicle without notice to Minor that Chase would require strict compliance in the future. Minor cited *Mercedes-Benz Credit Corp. v. Morgan,* 312 Ark. 225, 850 S.W.2d 297 (1993), and *Ford Motor Credit Co. v. Ellison,* 334 Ark. 357,

974 S.W.2d 464 (1998), as support for this position. Finally, Minor argued that Chase had violated the Arkansas Deceptive Trade Practices Act by repossessing the vehicle over Minor's objections and failing to timely acknowledge payments Minor had made.

After hearing these arguments, the circuit court ruled that Minor had presented no evidence that the conduct of Chase or the repossession agent constituted grounds for punitive damages; that by the express terms of the contract Chase's acceptance of late payments did not effect a waiver of its rights in the future; that at the time of repossession, Minor was behind in his payments and in breach of the contract; that Chase had the right under the contract to repossess the vehicle and did not commit conversion; and that there was no evidence to support a claim that Chase had violated the Arkansas Deceptive Trade Practices Act. Therefore, the court granted Chase's motion for a directed verdict on all grounds. On March 27, 2009, the circuit court entered an order reflecting this ruling and dismissed the complaint with prejudice. Minor filed a timely notice of appeal on April 23, 2009.

We have accepted certification of this case from the court of appeals in order to determine the effect of non-waiver and no-unwritten-modification clauses in a contract when a secured creditor has routinely accepted delinquent payments from a debtor. While we have never considered this specific issue, Arkansas courts have held that, when the contract does not contain the provisions at issue before us now, the creditor's previous acceptance of late payments in the past from the debtor waives the creditor's right to demand strict compliance from the debtor in the future. *See, e.g., Ford Motor Credit Co. v. Ellison,* 334 Ark. 357, 974 S.W.2d 464 (1998); *Am. Law Book Co. v. Hurst,* 168 Ark. 28, 268 S.W. 605 (1925). This waiver remains in effect until the creditor notifies the debtor that it will no longer accept late payments, and instead will require strict compliance. *Ellison,* 334 Ark. at 367, 974 S.W.2d at 470. The majority of jurisdictions around the country have adopted this same general rule.

The existence of non-waiver and no-unwritten-modification provisions in the contract changes the situation, however. As previously mentioned, this court in *Mercedes-Benz Credit Corp. v. Morgan,* 312 Ark. 225, 850 S.W.2d 297 (1993), reserved considering the effect of such clauses. In *Morgan,* Morgan purchased a Porsche with an installment contract assigned to Mercedes-Benz Credit Corporation (MBCC). Morgan made many late payments, and about a year into the forty-eight month contract, MBCC decided to exercise its right to repossess the vehicle under the contract. Morgan then brought his account current, and MBCC offered to return the Porsche, but Morgan refused and filed an action for conversion. On appeal, this court considered Morgan's argument that the fact that MBCC had routinely accepted Morgan's late payments constituted a waiver of strict compliance, and, at the very least, MBCC had to provide notice to Morgan before it repossessed the vehicle. This court noted that its prior decisions in *Commercial Credit Co. v. Ragland,* 189 Ark. 349, 72 S.W.2d 226 (1934), and *General Motors Acceptance Corp. v. Hicks,* 189 Ark. 62, 70 S.W.2d 509 (1934), decided before the adoption of the Uniform Commercial Code, required a creditor, who had accepted late payments in the past, to notify a debtor that the practice would no longer be continued before the creditor could take appropriate action to declare a default. The court then quoted a long passage from Steve H. Nickles's *Rethinking Some U.C.C. Article 9 Problems,* 34 Ark. Law Rev. 1, 136–37 (1980–1981), that indicated this rule did not change with the adoption of the Uniform Commercial Code. This court concluded that, given this authority, the jury could have found that MBCC had waived its right to repossession by its course of dealing in accepting late payments, and that MBCC would need to provide Morgan with notice in order to reinstate its right to strict compliance.

However, this court noted that MBCC relied on the holding in *Westlund v. Melson,* 7 Ark.App. 268, 647 S.W.2d 488 (1983), that acceptance of a late payment precludes acceleration of the due date of the note because of the lateness of that payment, but is not a waiver for the right to accelerate when default occurs in a subsequent installment. While this court rejected MBCC's argument because MBCC had brought it up for the first time on appeal, the court did not reject the holding in *Westlund* outright. Further, the court *sua sponte* acknowledged that the contract at issue in the case before it contained non-waiver and no-unwritten-modification clauses, and seemed to imply that if MBCC had addressed these clauses in its argument, the outcome of the case might have been different.

Accordingly, we affirm our previous decisions that when a contract does not contain a non-waiver and a no-unwritten-modification provision and the creditor has established a course of dealing in accepting late payments from the debtor, the creditor waives its right to insist on strict compliance with the contract and must give notice to the debtor that it will no longer accept late payments before it can declare default of the debt. However, we announce today that, if a contract includes non-waiver and no-unwritten-modification clauses, the creditor, in accepting late payments, does not waive its right under the contract to declare default of the debt, and need not give notice that it will enforce that right in the event of future late payments.

In arriving at this conclusion, we adhere to the principle that "a security agreement is effective according to its terms between the parties." Ark.Code Ann. § 4–9–201 (Repl.2001); *Fordyce Bank & Trust Co. v. Bean Timberland, Inc.,* 369 Ark. 90, 97, 251 S.W.3d 267, 273 (2007). We have long held that non-waiver clauses are legal and valid. *See Philmon v. Mid-State Homes, Inc.,* 245 Ark. 680, 684, 434 S.W.2d 84, 87 (1968) (citing

Johnson v. Guar. Bank & Trust Co., 177 Ark. 770, 9 S.W.2d 3 (1928)). Also, section 4–2–209(2) (Repl.2001) of the Arkansas Code declares that no-unwritten-modification provisions are binding.

We acknowledge that there is a difference of opinion amongst the courts in other jurisdictions over the effect of non-waiver and no-unwritten-modification clauses. The United States District Court for the District of Connecticut described this split of authority best:

> There are three schools of thought on the anti-waiver provision and its effect on the general rule. One line of cases has construed the anti-waiver provision as giving the secured party the right to take possession of the collateral without notice upon default. *Virgil Van Bibber, et al v. Norris,* 419 N.E.2d 115 (Ind.1981); *Hale v. Ford Motor Credit Co.,* 374 So.2d 849 (Ala.1979); *Wade v. Ford Motor Credit Co.,* 455 F.Supp. 147 (D.C.E.D.Mo.1978). In contrast, a second line of cases holds that the anti-waiver clause is irrelevant because acceptance of late payments does not constitute a waiver of the secured party's right to demand prompt payments. These jurisdictions have decided that waiver is not the issue to be determined, but rather "the issue is the right of the [debtor] . . . to be notified of a modification of such conduct on part of the [creditor]." *Waters,* 273 So.2d at 100. In reaching a determination of this issue, the courts essentially reverted to the general rule concluding that the debtor has the right to be notified of the secured party's demand of prompt payments. "The basis for imposing this duty on the secured party is that the secured party is estopped from asserting his contract rights because his conduct had induced the justified reliance of the debtor in believing that late payments were acceptable." *Cobb,* 295 N.W.2d at 236.
>
> In *Westinghouse, supra,* the United States Court of Appeals for the Tenth Circuit expressed a third view with respect to the anti-waiver provision. The court concluded that it was possible for the creditor to waive the anti-waiver provision pursuant to basic contract principles as illustrated in Article 2 of the Uniform Commercial Code. *Id.* at 871–74. Arriving at this conclusion, the court reasoned that an Article 9 security agreement may also be a contract for a sale and, therefore, Article 2 principles are applicable. *Id.* at 872 n. 3. The court went on to state that U.C.C. § 2–208 permitted the creditor to waive its right to strictly enforce the contract's terms. *Id.* at 872–73.

Tillquist v. Ford Motor Credit Co., 714 F.Supp. 607, 611 (D.Conn.1989); *see also Smith v. Gen. Fin. Corp. of Ga.,* 243 Ga. 500, 500, 255 S.E.2d 14, 14 (1979) ("[E]vidence of the buyer's repeated, late, irregular payments, which are accepted by the seller, does create a factual dispute as to whether a quasi new agreement was created under Code § 20–116, and a jury question is also raised as to whether the anti-waiver provision in the loan contract was itself waived."); *Battista v. Sav. Bank of Balt.,* 67 Md.App. 257, 270, 507 A.2d 203, 209 (Ct.Spec.App.1986) ("We hold, therefore, that a waiver of a contractual right to prompt payment or a waiver of a contractual right to repossess . . . may be effected by conduct, and the same is true as to the provisions of a non-waiver clause. When such a waiver has occurred, the creditor, before it can insist on future performance in strict compliance with the contract, must give plain and reasonable notice to the debtor that it intends to do so."); *Moe v. John Deere Co.,* 516 N.W.2d 332, 338 (S.D.1994) ("We hold that the repeated acceptance of late payments by a creditor who has the contractual right to repossess the property imposes a duty on the creditor to notify the debtor that strict compliance with the contract terms will be required before the creditor can lawfully repossess the collateral.").

By our holding, we have adopted the reasoning of the first line of cases. We concur with the Supreme Court of Indiana's decision in *Van Bibber v. Norris,* 275 Ind. 555, 419 N.E.2d 115 (1981), that a rule providing that non-waiver clauses could themselves be waived by the acceptance of late payments is "illogical, since the very conduct which the [non-waiver] clause is designed to permit[,] acceptance of late payment[,] is turned around to constitute waiver of the clause permitting the conduct." *Id.* at 563, 419 N.E.2d at 121. We also agree that the approach of jurisdictions that require creditors who have accepted late payments in the past to notify debtors that they expect strict compliance in the future, despite the existence of a non-waiver provision in the contract, is not "sound." *Id.* at 564, 419 N.E.2d at 121. Such a rule, we recognize, "begs the question of validity of the non-waiver clause." *Id.* at 564–65, 419 N.E.2d at 121. Finally, our holding is in line with the Indiana Supreme Court's ruling that it would enforce the provisions of the contract, since the parties had agreed to them, and that it would not require the creditor to give notice, because the non-waiver clause placed the secured party in the same position as one who had never accepted a late payment. *Id.* at 565, 419 N.E.2d at 122; *see also Hale v. Ford Motor Credit Co.,* 374 So.2d 849 (Ala.1979); *Gen. Grocer Co. of Ill. v. Bachar,* 51 Ill.App.3d 907, 365 N.E.2d 1106 (App.Ct.1977); *First Nat'l Bank of Cincinnati v. Cianelli,* 73 Ohio App.3d 781, 598 N.E.2d 789 (Ct.App.1991).

In holding that non-waiver and no-unwritten-modification clauses in a contract preclude waiver of a secured creditor's right to demand strict compliance with the contract in the future, even where the creditor's past acceptance of late payments has established a course of dealing, we address only the question certified to us by the court of appeals. We remand this case to the court of appeals for a determination on the merits.

Certified question answered; remanded to court of appeals.

GUNTER and WILLS, JJ., concur.

GUNTER, J., joins.

[footnote omitted]

NOTE

Creditor argues that its waiver clause actually favors debtors, for, without such a clause, a creditor would be forced: (1) to repossess upon the debtor's first stumble, or (2) forever forfeit its right to enforce the agreement as written. Do you agree?

COMMERCIALLY REASONABLE DISPOSITIONS: THE SIGNIFICANCE OF PRICE

IN RE ESTATE OF SAGMILLER

Supreme Court of North Dakota, 2000.
615 N.W.2d 567.

VANDE WALLE, CHIEF JUSTICE:

Ford Motor Credit Company ("FMCC") appealed from an order denying FMCC's claim against the Estate of Greg Sagmiller. We reverse and remand with directions to enter an order allowing the claim.

In November 1998, Greg Sagmiller bought a 1999 Ford Ranger pickup from Bill Barth Ford/Mercury Motors of Mandan for $19,740.48. FMCC financed the sale in the amount of $18,595.45. Sagmiller died on April 12, 1999. On April 22, 1999, FMCC repossessed the vehicle. It sent a Notice of Repossession and Right to Redeem to Greg Sagmiller's last known address on April 23, 1999. Nineteen days later, on May 12, Ford sold the vehicle at a dealers-only auction, the Minneapolis Auto Auction, for $15,500. After applying the proceeds of the sale to the outstanding balance, FMCC petitioned the Estate to allow its claim and the claim was denied. Ford petitioned the court to allow the claim and asked for a hearing. After the hearing, the district court denied the claim because the pickup was not sold in a commercially reasonable manner.

The district court cites two reasons for concluding FMCC did not meet its burden to demonstrate it acted in a commercially reasonable manner: 1) the manner of sale was a private, dealers-only auction; and 2) the price obtained at the auction. Regarding the manner of sale, the district court said:

> FMCC explained it took all its repossessed vehicles to the auction. It said it could not do otherwise because it did not have a motor vehicle dealer[']s license. This does not explain why it could not have one of its customer dealers sell vehicles on consignment at retail. Presumably a better price could be realized than at a

dealers-only auction when the buyers are motivated to buy at the lowest price possible in order to be able to resell the vehicle for a profit.

Regarding the price obtained for the pickup, the district court said:

Here, the balance owed on the truck at the time of the sale was $18,506.70. FMCC's own internal document says the wholesale value of the truck was $22,150. No evidence of retail value was submitted at trial, but it is reasonable to assume the retail value would exceed the wholesale value. Interestingly, FMCC presented no evidence of value. The truck was sold at auction for $15,500. The evidence viewed most favorably to FMCC is that the auction price and the fair market value of the truck differed by more than $2,000.

I

Section 41–09–50(3), N.D.C.C. [9–610(b)], requires every aspect of a disposition, "including the method, manner, time, place, and terms" to be commercially reasonable. The secured creditor has the burden of proof to show the commercial reasonableness of the disposition of collateral where commercial reasonableness is challenged and the secured party seeks a deficiency judgment. *Am. State Bank of Killdeer v. Hewson,* 411 N.W.2d 57, 61 (N.D.1987). Once the secured party makes a prima facie case indicating the collateral was sold in a commercially reasonable manner, the burden of persuasion, not the burden of proof, shifts to the debtor to elicit specific evidence of commercial unreasonableness. *Id.*

Whether or not a sale of collateral was conducted in a commercially reasonable manner is essentially a factual question. *Id.* at 60. A finding of fact will not be set aside unless it is clearly erroneous. N.D.R.Civ.P. 52(a). A finding of fact is clearly erroneous if it is induced by an erroneous conception of the law, if there is no evidence to support it, or if, although there is some evidence to support it, on the entire record, a reviewing court is left with a definite and firm conviction a mistake has been made. *Kaler v. Kraemer,* 1999 ND 237, ¶ 18, 603 N.W.2d 698.

A primary reason the district court found the sale was not commercially reasonable was the price the automobile garnered at auction. Sagmiller cites, as did the district court, the fact one of FMCC's documents states the wholesale value of the pickup was $22,150. The document was provided to FMCC by the Minneapolis Auto Auction, but there was no testimony as to how this number was calculated. A different FMCC document suggests wholesale value was $16,509.

We have stated before the disparity between price received at auction and the estimated value of the collateral is an important factor, but is not dispositive in determining whether collateral was sold in a commercially reasonable manner. *Hewson,* 411 N.W.2d at 64–65. Section 41–09–53(2), N.D.C.C. [9–627], states:

> The fact that a better price could have been obtained by a sale at a different time or in a different method from that selected by the secured party is not of itself sufficient to establish that the sale was not made in a commercially reasonable manner. If the secured party either sells the collateral in the usual manner in any recognized market therefor or if he sells at the price current in such market at the time of his sale or if he has otherwise sold in conformity with reasonable commercial practices among dealers in the type of property sold he has sold in a commercially reasonable manner.

The price obtained here is not enough to demonstrate the sale was not commercially reasonable. Thus, we turn to the other reason the district court gave for finding the sale to be commercially unreasonable.

Another reason the district court cited in finding the sale commercially unreasonable was the fact the collateral was sold at a dealers-only auction in Minneapolis. A witness from FMCC testified it is FMCC's practice to take all repossessed vehicles to the Minneapolis Auto Auction. Courts in several jurisdictions, under many contexts, have held dealers-only auctions may constitute commercially reasonable sales. * * *

The Estate of Sagmiller criticizes the wholesale disposition of the collateral here because, it argues, the pickup could have garnered a higher price at a retail sale. A dealers-only auction is considered a private sale, *see, e.g., Beard,* 850 S.W.2d at 28–29, and private sales are approved under the Uniform Commercial Code. *See* N.D.C.C. § 41–09–50(3) [9–610(b)] (stating "[d]isposition of the collateral may be by public or private proceedings and may be made by way of one or more contracts").

Moreover, retail dispositions are not necessarily superior to wholesale dispositions. The Kansas Supreme Court stated in discussing the question of wholesale versus retail disposition of goods:

> In many cases, a retail sale of the goods will command a much higher price; however, a retail sale may involve more expenses and usually will take much longer to conclude. This in turn may not be reasonably feasible in view of higher storage expense and higher interest accumulation on the obligation. In some cases, a sale to a dealer on the wholesale market may be the more reasonable approach. Sales to a dealer seem to be suggested under § 9–504 [9–610] and the official comments under that section and also in the official comment to § 9–507(2) which suggests that sale of repossessed collateral through a dealer may be the better method in the long run since the secured party does not usually maintain his own facilities for making such sales. The answer to

> the question whether a sale on the retail or wholesale market is commercially reasonable must generally depend upon the circumstances of each particular case and, therefore, is a question of fact for the factfinder to determine.

Westgate State Bank v. Clark, 231 Kan. 81, 642 P.2d 961, 970 (1982).

Schmitz, 853 P.2d 1180, a case out of Kansas, is particularly persuasive because of its similarity to the case at bar. Schmitz purchased a used automobile for $4,662.40, borrowing the money from Union National Bank of Wichita. He defaulted on the loan and voluntarily surrendered the vehicle to the Bank. The Bank sold the vehicle at a dealers-only auction for $920, minus a $75 sale fee. The Bank sought recovery of the deficiency amount of $2,087.97.

The trial court held the creditor had not sustained its burden of proof to show the sale was commercially reasonable. The Kansas Court of Appeals reversed stating:

> The method utilized to dispose of the collateral in this case was a well-known, regularly scheduled, dealer-only wholesale auction. The trial court's findings that this sale was commercially unreasonable are so broad that they virtually declare any dealers-only wholesale auction to be not commercially reasonable. In deciding this issue, the trial court focused solely on the nature of the auction and the price received for the vehicle. The trial court's decision, if allowed to stand, would mean that a dealer-only wholesale auction could not be commercially reasonable. This is not the law, and the trial court erred in reaching this conclusion.

Id. at 1184.

The district court here stated, "Presumably a better price could be realized than at a dealers-only auction when the buyers are motivated to buy at the lowest price possible in order to be able to resell the vehicle for a profit." With our discussion of retail versus wholesale dispositions in mind, it may not be presumed, without evidence, a retail disposition is superior to a wholesale dealers-only disposition. Furthermore, speculation on whether a different mode of sale may have brought a better price does not support a finding of commercial unreasonableness. *See* N.D.C.C. § 41–09–53(2) [9–627(a)] (stating "[t]he fact that a better price could have been obtained by a sale at a different time or in a different method from that selected by the secured party is not of itself sufficient to establish that the sale was not made in a commercially reasonable manner").

We agree with the *Schmitz* court that such a holding would render dealers-only auctions (and possibly all wholesale auctions) commercially unreasonable per se. Any time collateral is sold at wholesale and there is a deficiency, the debtor can claim the secured creditor should have gotten a better price. This, however, does not demonstrate the collateral was sold in a commercially unreasonable manner. *See* N.D.C.C. § 41–09–53(2). While we do not hold that dealers-only auctions are commercially reasonable per se, neither are they commercially unreasonable per se.

Hewson, a decision of this Court, was cited by Sagmiller's Estate and relied upon by the district court. In October 1984, Hewson purchased a tractor with dozer for the sum of $40,000 borrowed from American State Bank of Killdeer. Hewson defaulted and voluntarily surrendered the tractor with dozer in November 1985. The bank sold the tractor at public auction to the highest bidder for $8,700 and thereafter sought a deficiency for the remaining amount. The district court granted the Bank's motion for summary judgment, concluding the tractor with dozer was sold in a commercially reasonable manner.

This Court reversed and remanded, concluding whether the tractor with dozer was sold in a commercially reasonable manner presented a genuine issue of material fact that precluded summary judgment. We noted the disparity between the price received at the auction and the fair market value of the machinery as stated by the debtor. We also considered Hewson's affidavit, in which he attested:

> Rather than selling the tractor in the normal method and manner of disposing of farm equipment, the tractor was sold along with a bunch of boats and used snowmobiles. Attached to this Affidavit as Exhibit 'B' is a copy of an advertisement of the auction sale. The advertisement shows and reveals that:
>
> 1. The tractor was the only piece of farm equipment offered for sale.
> 2. All of the remaining property was recreational property.
> 3. The sale was held in a cold, unheated building in the middle of winter at 6:30 p.m.
> 4. Much of the property was old.

Id. at 64.

We said the disparity in price, "taken in connection with Hewson's other statements in his affidavit which are supported by the newspaper advertisement, raises an issue of fact which should have been submitted to a jury rather than being decided by the court as a matter of law." *Id.* at 65.

One obvious distinction between this case and *Hewson* is procedural. While in *Hewson,* the trial court determined commercial reasonableness as a matter of law, without a trial, here the district court held an evidentiary hearing and determined commercial reasonableness as the trier-of-fact. Moreover, the facts of this case, determined after evidentiary hearing and not on summary judgment, distinguish it from the alleged facts in *Hewson.*

The disparity between the price received and the claimed fair market value is not as great here as it was in *Hewson*. Secondly, in *Hewson* the creditor allegedly sold the tractor with equipment unlike the tractor, while here the creditor sold the collateral with like equipment, automobiles at the Minneapolis Auto Auction. Unlike *Hewson,* the sale here was targeted to the people who would know the value of the collateral and would have an interest in purchasing it. Finally, in this case there has been no accusation regarding any deficiencies in the specific sale itself, as there was in *Hewson*.

Importantly, the focus in *Hewson* was on all aspects of the sale, not merely on whether the sale was a public or private auction, or whether the price garnered was at or below market value.

We recognize commercial reasonableness is determined on a case-by-case basis and generally depends on the aggregate circumstances of the sale, *see Lindberg v. Williston Indus. Supply Corp.,* 411 N.W.2d 368, 374 (N.D.1987), with the secured creditor having the burden of proof. *Hewson,* 411 N.W.2d at 61. We also recognize deference is to be given to the findings of the trial court. *In re Z.R.,* 1999 ND 214, ¶ 11, 602 N.W.2d 723. Here, however, the district court's narrow rationale relies on an unsupported presumption and, if allowed to stand, would broadly limit a creditor's options. Because the evidence does not support a finding of commercial unreasonableness, we turn to the issue of whether the sale was conducted in a commercially reasonable manner.

II

A creditor is to demonstrate every aspect of a disposition is commercially reasonable, including "the method, manner, time, place and terms." N.D.C.C. § 41–09–50 [9–610(b)]. FMCC could have better targeted its evidence to these specific factors. Nevertheless, the uncontradicted testimony of FMCC's witness is sufficient to demonstrate the collateral was sold in a commercially reasonable manner.

The only witness who testified at the hearing was Aaron Robbins, an account manager for FMCC. Robbins said it was FMCC's practice to bring all of its repossessed cars to auctions. He testified he specifically uses the Minneapolis Auto Auction. Robbins, who said he has provided estimates for the value of "hundreds" of vehicles, testified he thought $15,500 was a reasonable price for the pickup. He also testified the fact the pickup's color was orange would have a negative effect on its value. Robbins said there was an FMCC representative at the auction who had authority to reject an auction price received if she did not think it was equivalent to the pickup's worth. The representative did not object to the price the pickup sold for.

When asked why FMCC did not sell cars at dealerships for retail prices, Robbins said FMCC isn't licensed to sell vehicles themselves. When asked why FMCC did not get licensed, Robbins said, "It wouldn't make a difference even if we did that—even if it was done that way, if you add in the commission costs that are associated with it. Ford Credit would get a higher price just bringing it to an auction—or the Minneapolis auction in our area." Robbins' testimony was challenged on cross-examination:

> Q All right. Thank you. Just one more point Mr. Robbins, you said that one of the reasons that you don't try to sell them on retail and you take them to auction is if you sold them at retail, you'd have to pay commissions and things like that, is that what your testimony was?
>
> A Well Ford Credit isn't licensed to sell them anywhere but at auction.
>
> Q Okay but you could sell them at retail somehow, couldn't you, through consignment or some other arrangement?
>
> A No.
>
> Q You couldn't, huh? Could you get a retail license if you wanted to?
>
> A I suppose. I'm not even sure, I would just be speculating.
>
> Q Okay but I guess what I'm getting at is if you really wanted to sell this at retail or try to sell it at retail, Ford Motor could do that, couldn't it?
>
> A No.
>
> Q You have a dealer network, don't you?
>
> A A dealership might be able to sell their vehicles on their lot for retail but Ford Credit is not a dealership.
>
> Q Yeah, but you work with all the dealers in the State of North Dakota, right?
>
> A I work with them on a business relationship for them to send contracts to Ford Motor Credit, not vehicles.
>
> Q Don't you think one of them would sell it on a-after you repoed it, don't you think one of them would put it on their lot and try to sell it retail for you if you asked them to?
>
> A No.

Robbins' testimony was uncontradicted. While the trial court determines the credibility of witnesses, *Wallwork Lease & Rental Co., Inc. v. Schermerhorn,* 398 N.W.2d 127, 131 (N.D.1986), here the trial court rejected the testimony and relied on an unsupported presumption that a retail sale would bring a better price. That assumption is not warranted by the facts or the law. *See Schmitz,* 853 P.2d at 1186 (concluding based upon the statutes and opinions cited "the mere fact collateral is sold at wholesale and not 'exposed to the retail market' is not in and of itself sufficient to render a sale commercially unreasonable").

The uncontradicted testimony of Robbins is sufficient to sustain FMCC's burden to prove the collateral was sold in a commercially reasonable manner. The evidence not only supports a commercially reasonable sale, but there is little or no evidence to the contrary. The fact the pickup could have brought a higher price at a different sale or on a different day is not sufficient to overcome the evidence of commercial reasonableness. The Estate of Sagmiller has adduced no specific evidence of commercial unreasonableness, short of evidence of the price. *See Hewson,* 411 N.W.2d at 61 (concluding once the secured party makes a prima facie case indicating the collateral was sold in a commercially reasonable manner, the burden of persuasion, not the burden of proof, shifts to the debtor to elicit specific evidence of commercial unreasonableness).

The district court's finding of commercial unreasonableness is clearly erroneous because it was based on a presumption not supported by the law or the facts. We reverse that decision and remand with instructions to enter an order allowing FMCC's claim against the Estate of Sagmiller.

DALE V. SANDSTROM, WILLIAM A. NEUMANN, MARY MUEHLEN MARING, CAROL RONNING KAPSNER, JJ., concur.

[footnotes omitted.]

NOTE

What is a dealer's best argument against an obligation to put repossessed cars for resale in his used car inventory?

PROBLEM 7-7

Assume a peaceful repossession of a pickup truck used as Debtor's personal vehicle. The truck is sold at a wholesale dealer auction for $14,000 at a time when the debt outstanding was $20,000 and the wholesale blue book price was approximately $15,000. Assume the only notice given to Debtor was a phone call given by the bank one week before the sale; the bank officer informed Debtor that the truck would be sold at a private sale seven days later. The bank has sued for a deficiency under section 9–625. Debtor makes the following claims:

1. Where a creditor fails to comply with Part 6, a deficiency is "absolutely barred." Debtor maintains that section 9–626 supports that conclusion.

2. Bank was deficient in giving its notice and conducting its sale. Bank should have sold the truck at retail and, in any case, it should have received at least the wholesale price of $15,000.

Bank responds that its sale price was fair and it need not give notice because a sale at a widely recognized Dealer's Auction is a sale in a recognized market of the kind that obviates the need for notice.

What do you think?

THE REPO MAN

As seen in *Ryan*, when a debtor defaults on his car loan, the job of repossessing the car often falls to an independent collection agent, sometimes known as the "repo man." On average, a simple repossession of a typical car will net a repo man $300. However, a repo man may receive as much as $10,000 for a more difficult repossession of an antique car. In any given year, a typical repo man will earn between $30,000 and $60,000. Like any other job, the level of business depends on the state of the economy. Unlike most work, however, the business of a repo man booms when the rest of the economy busts. Layoffs and recession make the repo man smile.

On any given day, most of a repo man's time is spent tracking down cars and investigating the whereabouts of elusive debtors. Creditors often require a repo man to try to get possession voluntarily from the debtor before they attempt to repossess without his acquiescence. A repo man will attempt to get information from the friends and family of the debtor. Often the best source of information will be an ex-wife, ex-husband, ex-boyfriend, or ex-girlfriend. Using these sources, a veteran repo man will usually find his car in a matter of days.

Once the car is found the real action begins. Many debtors are slow to accept the fact that their car is going to be repossessed. Debtors often confuse a repo man with a car thief. As a result, repossessing a car can be a dangerous business. Given the law and the danger surrounding each repossession, a good repo man has both personal and economic incentive to avoid breaching the peace.

The best repo men find ways of getting the car without sparking a confrontation with the debtor. For example, one repo man in San Jose discovered the power of shame. He noted that many still rich-at-heart dot-com executives (then defaulting on loans in increasing numbers) frequented a particular restaurant. The parking lot was a treasure trove. Even when the car owners noticed their cars being repossessed, most were too embarrassed to make a scene.

Occasionally even a veteran repo man gets caught in a confrontation, sometimes with tragic consequences. In the not too distant past, one repo man was stabbed in the chest with a screwdriver and another was shot and killed execution style. Consider the following account of a repossession gone awry in downtown Philadelphia:

> At 4:00 a.m. Edward Simmons is standing in a dark alley. Rosita Conroy has defaulted on her car loan, and her creditor has hired

> Simmons to repossess her car. Simmons slips down the alley and opens the car door using a duplicate key given to him by the creditor. He starts the car and drives to a nearby gas station where his partner waits with their tow-truck. Unbeknownst to Simmons, however, Jacques Galin witnesses him driving off with the car and follows him to the gas station armed with a loaded gun. When Galin finds the men loading the car, he approaches the car and shoots Simmons through the windshield. Simmons' partner takes cover behind a dumpster while Simmons attempts to return fire. His gun jams. Simmons then slumps in the seat, and the car, still in gear, rolls into Galin. Now pinned against the hood, Galin continues to fire into the car until Simmons' partner returns and shoots Galin in the head. Simmons suffers multiple gunshot wounds to his face, shoulder, chest, abdomen and hand. Miraculously, all involved survive. Simmons later sued Galin over the incident, and the United States District Court for the Eastern District of Pennsylvania ordered Galin to pay the repo man $1.2 million for battery.

See Simmons v. Galin, 2002 WL 109611 (E.D.Pa. Jan. 24, 2002).

Consider also the following case:

CHAPA V. TRACIERS & ASSOCIATES

Texas Court of Appeals, Houston, 2008.
267 S.W.3d 386, 66 UCC Rep.Serv.2d 451.

GUZMAN, JUSTICE:

In this appeal, we must determine whether appellants, the parents of two young children, have legally cognizable claims for mental anguish allegedly sustained when a repossession agent towed their vehicle out of sight before he realized their children were inside. The parents filed suit against the financing company, the repossession company it hired, and the repossession agent who towed the vehicle. They asserted claims for mental anguish and its physical manifestations under (a) section 9.609 of the Business and Commerce Code, (b) the Restatement (Second) of Torts, or (c) negligence law, including the law governing bystander claims. The trial court granted summary judgment for the defendants on the parents' claims. Neither parent witnessed the vehicle being towed from the street, and the repossession agent discovered the children and returned them and the vehicle within minutes. On these facts, we conclude that, as a matter of law, appellants Carlos and Maria Chapa do not have a viable claim for breach of the peace under section 9.609 of the Business and Commerce Code. We further hold that the financing company and its agents are not liable to the Chapas under sections 424 or 427 of the Restatement (Second) of Torts. Moreover, we conclude Maria Chapa's bystander and other negligence claims fail as a matter of law. We therefore affirm the trial court's grant of summary judgment.

I. FACTUAL AND PROCEDURAL BACKGROUND

Ford Motor Credit Corp. ("FMCC") hired Traciers & Associates ("Traciers") to repossess a white 2002 Ford Expedition owned by Marissa Chapa, who was in default on the associated promissory note. Traciers assigned the job to its field manager, Paul Chambers, and gave him an address where the vehicle could be found. FMCC, Traciers, and Chambers were unaware that the address was that of Marissa's brother, Carlos Chapa. Coincidentally, Carlos and his wife Maria Chapa also had purchased a white Ford Expedition financed by FMCC. Their vehicle, however, was a 2003 model, and the Chapas were not in default.

On the night of February 6, 2003, Chambers went to the address and observed a white Ford Expedition. The license number of the vehicle did not match that of the vehicle he was told to repossess, and he did not see the vehicle's vehicle identification number ("VIN"), which was obscured. Chambers returned early the next morning and still could not see the Expedition's VIN. He returned to his own vehicle, which was parked two houses away.

Unseen by Chambers, Maria Chapa left the house and helped her two sons, ages ten and six, into the Expedition for the trip to school. Her mother-in-law's vehicle was parked behind her, so Maria backed her mother-in-law's vehicle into the street, then backed her Expedition out of the driveway and parked on the street. She left the keys to her truck in the ignition with the motor running while she parked her mother-in-law's car back in the driveway and reentered the house to return her mother-in-law's keys.

After Chambers saw Maria park the Expedition on the street and return to the house, it took him only thirty seconds to back his tow truck to the Expedition, hook it to his truck, and drive away. Chambers did not leave his own vehicle to perform this operation, and it is undisputed that he did not know the Chapa children were inside. When Maria emerged from the house, the Expedition, with her children, was gone. Maria began screaming, telephoned 911, and called her husband at work to tell him the children were gone.

Meanwhile, on an adjacent street, Chambers noticed that the Expedition's wheels were turning, indicating to him that the vehicle's engine was running. He stopped the tow truck and heard a sound from the Expedition. Looking inside, he discovered the two Chapa children. After he persuaded one of the boys to unlock the vehicle, Chambers drove the Expedition back to the Chapas' house. He returned the keys to Maria, who was outside her house, crying. By the time emergency personnel and Carlos

Chapa arrived, the children were back home and Chambers had left the scene.

Maria testified that the incident caused her to have an anxiety attack, including chest pain and numbness in her arm. She states she has continued to experience panic attacks and has been diagnosed with an anxiety disorder. In addition, both Carlos and Maria have been diagnosed with post-traumatic stress disorder.

Acting individually and on behalf of their children, Carlos and Maria Chapa sued Traciers, Chambers, and FMCC. Appellees settled the children's claims but contested the individual claims of Carlos and Maria. The trial court granted summary judgment on the parents' claims in favor of Traciers, Chambers, and FMCC, and this appeal ensued.

II. ISSUES PRESENTED

The Chapas present three compound issues for review. In their first issue, they contend that they have legally cognizable causes of action against Traciers and FMCC for the physical and psychological injuries they sustained as a result of the appellees' breach of the duties imposed by (a) section 9.609 of the Texas Business and Commerce Code, (b) the Restatement (Second) of Torts, or (c) the common law governing negligence claims generally. In their second issue, the Chapas argue that, as a bystander, Maria suffered compensable injuries arising from the tort committed against her children. Finally, the Chapas assert in their third issue that the trial court erred in granting summary judgments dismissing their claims.

* * *

IV. ANALYSIS

A. Section 9.609 of the Texas Business and Commerce Code

The Chapas first argue that the trial court erred in granting summary judgment against them on their claim that appellees are liable under section 9.609 of the Business and Commerce Code. This statute provides in pertinent part:

> (a) After default, a secured party:
>
> (1) may take possession of the collateral;
>
> . . .
>
> (b) A secured party may proceed under Subsection (a):
>
> . . .
>
> (2) without judicial process, if it proceeds without breach of the peace.

TEX. BUS. & COM.CODE ANN. § 9.609 (Vernon 2002). The Chapas correctly point out that this statute imposes a duty on secured creditors to take precautions for public safety when repossessing property. *See MBank El Paso, N.A. v. Sanchez*, 836 S.W.2d 151, 153 (Tex.1992) (interpreting predecessor statute). Thus, the creditor who elects to pursue nonjudical repossession assumes the risk that a breach of the peace might occur. *Id.* at 154. A secured creditor "remains liable for breaches of the peace committed by its independent contractor." *Id.* (citing RESTATEMENT (SECOND) OF TORTS, PRECAUTIONS REQUIRED BY STATUTE OR REGULATION, § 424 (1965)). Thus, a creditor cannot escape liability by hiring an independent contractor to repossess secured property.

The Chapas assert that FMCC and Traciers, who employed Chambers as a repossession agent, are liable for any physical or mental injuries sustained by Carlos and Maria as a result of Chambers's breach of the peace. But this argument presupposes that a breach of peace occurred. Although the material facts regarding Chambers's conduct are not in dispute, appellees deny that his conduct constituted a breach of the peace and moved for no-evidence summary judgment on the ground that no such breach occurred. If appellees are correct, then we may affirm summary judgment on the claims asserted under section 9.609 without further analysis. *See* TEX.R.APP. P. 47.1.

In their arguments concerning breach of the peace and its associated liability, the Chapas rely most heavily on authorities addressing breaches of the peace under Texas criminal law and cases from other jurisdictions discussing breaches of the peace under the Uniform Commercial Code. Because a breach of the peace under the criminal code would also constitute a breach of the peace under the Uniform Commercial Code, we address both sources of authority.

1. Breach of the Peace Under Criminal Law

In support of their argument that Chambers breached the peace, the Chapas rely on the following language from Corpus Juris, adopted by the Texas Court of Criminal Appeals in 1936:

> The term 'breach of the peace' is generic, and includes all violations of the public peace or order, or decorum; in other words, it signifies the offense of disturbing the public peace or tranquillity [sic] enjoyed by the citizens of a community; a disturbance of the public tranquillity by any act or conduct inciting to violence or tending to provoke or excite others to break the peace; a disturbance of public order by an act of violence, or by any act likely to produce violence, or which, by causing consternation and alarm disturbs the peace and quiet of the community. By 'peace,' as used in this connection, is meant the tranquillity enjoyed by the citizens of a municipality or a

> community where good order reigns among its members. Breach of the peace is a common-law offense. It has been said that it is not a specific offense, yet it may be, and at times is, recognized as such by statute or otherwise; and only when so regarded will it be considered in this article.
>
> The offense may consist of acts of public turbulence or indecorum in violation of the common peace and quiet, of an invasion of the security and protection which the laws afford to every citizen, or of acts such as tend to excite violent resentment or to provoke or excite others to break the peace. Actual or threatened violence is an essential element of a breach of the peace. Either one is sufficient to constitute the offense. Accordingly, where means which cause disquiet and disorder, and which threaten danger and disaster to the community, are used, it amounts to a breach of the peace, although no actual personal violence is employed. Where the incitement of terror or fear of personal violence is a necessary element, the conduct or language of the wrongdoer must be of a character to induce such a condition in a person of ordinary firmness.

Head v. State, 131 Tex.Crim. 96, 99, 96 S.W.2d 981, 982–83 (1936) (on mot. for reh'g). As further explained in Corpus Juris Secondum, "[t]he acts involved, to constitute a breach of the peace, must also be voluntary, unnecessary, and contrary to ordinary human conduct." 11 C.J.S. *Breach of the Peace* § 4 (1995).

The Chapas argue that Chambers's conduct is of the type that has been found to constitute a breach of peace under Texas criminal law. Without further explanation, the Chapas assert that "[t]he act of taking children from the possession of their mother which leaves her in a hysterical crying state, is clearly a breach of peace."

2. Criminal Breach of the Peace Distinguished

Whether a specific act constitutes a breach of the peace depends on the surrounding facts and circumstances in the particular case. *Miles v. State*, 241 S.W.3d 28, 40 (Tex.Crim.App.2007) (citing *Woods v. State*, 152 Tex.Crim. 338, 341, 213 S.W.2d 685, 687 (1948)). But in each of the cases on which the Chapas rely, the described conduct falls within the proscription adopted in *Head v. State*. Conduct such as driving while intoxicated, or publicly assaulting someone without provocation, with or without a weapon, poses an immediate threat of violent physical injury. Fleeing the scene of an accident or attempting concealment on private property during a manhunt are acts that invade "the security and protection which the laws afford to every citizen." *See id.* The public use of verbally abusive language that is "calculated to disturb" others is an act of "public indecorum" that is intended to disrupt the public peace or tranquility. Finally, all of these acts are "voluntary, unnecessary, and contrary to ordinary human conduct." *See* 11 C.J.S. *Breach of the Peace* § 4 (1995).

In contrast, here the parties do not assert that Chambers behaved violently or threatened physical injury to anyone. *Cf. id.* ("[A]ctual or threatened violence is an essential element of a breach of the peace. . . ."). Further, it is undisputed that Chambers did not know the children were in the vehicle when he moved it; thus, his actions cannot be appropriately characterized as "contrary to ordinary human conduct." *Cf. id.* When Chambers learned of the children's presence, he immediately ceased any attempt to repossess the vehicle and instead drove the children home. He did not communicate by word or gesture with Carlos or Maria Chapa before or during the attempted repossession. *Cf. Coggin v. State*, 123 S.W.3d 82, 92 (Tex.App.-Austin 2003) (suggesting that conduct that would "incite an immediate breach of the peace contemplates a face-to-face encounter").

In sum, the Chapas do not argue that Chambers's words or behavior toward the children or anyone else were intimidating, indecorous, or calculated to have a disturbing effect. *Cf. Heath v. Boyd*, 141 Tex. 569, 573, 175 S.W.2d 214, 216 (1943) (concluding that appellant who did not exhibit a weapon, "yell, shriek, curse, abuse or threaten anybody, or commit any other act denounced as a breach of the peace" by statute did not breach peace). On these facts, we cannot say that Chambers's conduct constitutes a "breach of the peace" as that phrase ordinarily is used in criminal or common law.

3. Breach of the Peace under the Uniform Commercial Code

The Chapas also rely on cases from other jurisdictions specifically addressing breaches of the peace as described in the Uniform Commercial Code concerning repossession of property. They cite *Robinson v. Citicorp National Services, Inc.*, a Missouri case in which Clarence Robinson defaulted on his automobile payments. 921 S.W.2d 52, 53 (Mo.Ct.App.1996). Agents of the financing company's assignee attempted to repossess the car from property owned by Marie Robinson. *Id.* Marie's husband, Odell Robinson, Sr., "told [a repossession agent] to get off the property numerous times to no avail. The alleged trespass and breach of peace ensued, and Odell suffered a heart attack and died." *Id.* (emphasis added). This case stands for the proposition that the duty to avoid a breach of peace is non-delegable, but the conduct constituting a breach of the peace is not described. We can determine only that there was a confrontation on the appellant's property between repossession agents and a person objecting to the repossession. Here, however, Chambers removed the vehicle without confrontation and without trespassing on the Chapas' premises.

The Chapas also point to *Nixon v. Halpin.* 620 So.2d 796 (Fla.Dist.Ct.App.1993). In that case, Halpin, a repossession agent, was seen by the vehicle's owner and mistaken for a car thief. *Id.* at 797. The car's owner summoned his office mate, Nixon, and the two men attempted to detain Halpin. *Id.* While driving away, Halpin struck Nixon. *Id.* The Nixon court concluded that the vehicle owner had a right to object to the attempted repossession. *Id.* at 798. It further held that if the creditor "had not already peaceably removed the vehicle when the owner objected, it's [sic] continuation with the attempt at repossession was no longer 'peaceable and without a breach of the peace.' " *Id.* In this case, however, the repossession agent had "already peaceably removed the vehicle" and did not continue to attempt repossession after he learned of the Chapa children's presence. Thus, the reasoning in Nixon supports the conclusion that Chambers did not breach the peace.

4. UCC Usage Distinguished

Most frequently, the expression "breach of the peace" as used in the Uniform Commercial Code "connotes conduct that incites or is likely to incite immediate public turbulence, or that leads to or is likely to lead to an immediate loss of public order and tranquility." *Johnson v. Grossinger Motorcorp, Inc.*, 324 Ill.App.3d 354, 257 Ill.Dec. 236, 753 N.E.2d 431, 440 (2001); * * *.

Here, there is no evidence that Chambers proceeded with the attempted repossession over an objection communicated to him at, near, or incident to the seizure of the property. To the contrary, Chambers immediately "desisted" repossession efforts and peaceably returned the vehicle and the children when he learned of their presence. Moreover, Chambers actively avoided confrontation. By removing an apparently unoccupied vehicle from a public street when the driver was not present, he reduced the likelihood of violence or other public disturbance.

In sum, the Chapas have not identified and we have not found any case in which the repossession of a vehicle from a public street, without objection or confrontation, has been held to constitute a breach of the peace. *Cf. Wallace v. Chrysler Credit Corp.*, 743 F.Supp. 1228, 1231–33 (W.D.Va.1990) (deputy sheriff did not breach the peace when he repossessed debtor's truck because, even if he violated traffic regulation when he drove away, he did so before debtor had an opportunity to confront him); *Wann*, 403 N.E.2d at 351–52 (no breach of the peace occurred when repossession from parking lot was not verbally or otherwise contested). We therefore conclude that Chambers's conduct did not violate a duty imposed by section 9.609 of the Texas Business and Commerce Code.

B. Restatement (Second) of Torts

The Chapas also contend that appellees violated duties owed to them under two provisions of the Restatement (Second) of Torts. On this record, however, we conclude that neither section applies.

1. Section 424

Section 424 of the Restatement (Second) of Torts provides as follows:

> One who by statute or by administrative regulation is under a duty to provide specified safeguards or precautions for the safety of others is subject to liability to the others for whose protection the duty is imposed for harm caused by the failure of a contractor employed by him to provide such safeguards or precautions.

RESTATEMENT (SECOND) OF TORTS, PRECAUTIONS REQUIRED BY STATUTE OR REGULATION, § 424 (1965). This provision permits a plaintiff to hold an entity vicariously liable for the acts of that entity's independent contractors. The Chapas argue that because section 9.609 of the Business and Commerce Code imposed a duty on Chambers to refrain from breaching the peace, Traciers and FMCC are liable for Chambers's violation of that duty. But because Chambers did not breach the peace, this provision is inapplicable.

2. Section 427

The Chapas additionally assert that Traciers and FMCC also may be liable under section 427 of the Restatement (Second) of Torts. Under this provision, an employer is liable for physical harm caused by an independent contractor's performance of inherently dangerous work:

> One who employs an independent contractor to do work involving a special danger to others which the employer knows or has reason to know to be inherent in or normal to the work, or which he contemplates or has reason to contemplate when making the contract, is subject to liability for physical harm caused to such others by the contractor's failure to take reasonable precautions against such danger.

Lee Lewis Constr., Inc. v. Harrison, 70 S.W.3d 778, 794 n. 36 (quoting RESTATEMENT (SECOND) OF TORTS § 427 (1965)). Such inherently dangerous activities are "those that are dangerous in their normal, nondefective state." *Cent. Ready Mix Concrete Co., Inc. v. Islas*, 228 S.W.3d 649, 652–53 (Tex.2007).

The Chapas reason that nonjudicial repossession is an inherently dangerous activity, and thus, FMCC and Traciers are liable for Chambers's failure to take precautions to prevent their injuries. In support of this argument, the Chapas point to *Sanchez v. MBank of El Paso*, in which the Eighth Court of Appeals, relying on section 427 of the Restatement, held that nonjudicial repossession is inherently dangerous. 792 S.W.2d 530, 531–32 (Tex.App.-El Paso 1990), *aff'd on other grounds*, 836 S.W.2d 151, 152 n. 2 (Tex.1992). In reaching this conclusion, the court reasoned as follows:

> Since there is likelihood that the repossessor will commit a technical trespass by entering upon someone else's property to take possession of the collateral and that the repossession will be done not only without the owner's consent but in many cases against his will, there is a considerable risk that a breach of the peace, assault or worse may occur.

Id. at 532.

Section 427, however, imposes liability only for (a) physical harm (b) caused by the failure to take reasonable precautions against the inherent dangers of the work. As previously discussed, however, no breach of the peace occurred in this case, and there is no allegation of assault. Contrary to the Chapas' characterizations on appeal, FMCC and Traciers did not physically harm them; rather, the Chapas allegedly sustained mental and emotional harm and physical manifestations of anxiety, depression, and post-traumatic stress disorder. These physical manifestations appear to be part of their asserted mental-anguish damages. *See City of Tyler v. Likes*, 962 S.W.2d 489, 496 (Tex.1997) (noting that mental-anguish damages are generally available if the harm arises from bodily injury, intentional or malicious conduct, knowing violation of a statute, breach of a duty arising out of a special relationship, or an injury of such shocking or disturbing nature that mental anguish is highly foreseeable). Moreover, their injuries are not the result of a failure to take reasonable precautions against those risks identified in Sanchez as dangers inherent in nonjudicial repossession.

The claims of Carlos and Maria Chapa do not fall within those described in *Likes*, but instead more closely resemble a common-law claim of negligent infliction of emotional distress. This tort consists of "mental or emotional harm (such as fright or anxiety) that is caused by the negligence of another and that is not directly brought about by a physical injury, but that may manifest itself in physical symptoms." *Consol. Rail Corp. v. Gottshall*, 512 U.S. 532, 544, 114 S.Ct. 2396, 2405, 129 L.Ed.2d 427 (1994). With limited exceptions, claims of negligent infliction of emotional distress are not recognized under Texas law. *Boyles v. Kerr*, 855 S.W.2d 593, 594 (Tex.1993) (op. on mot. for reh'g) ("[T]here is no general duty in Texas not to negligently inflict emotional distress. A claimant may recover mental anguish damages only in connection with defendant's breach of some other legal duty."). And although the Chapas argue that their physical manifestations of emotional distress are distinct physical injuries, the cases on which they rely do not support recovery for such physical manifestations under section 427 and are otherwise distinguishable on the facts.

Because the Chapas' claims consist of negligently inflicted mental anguish and its physical manifestations, we conclude that neither section 427 of the Restatement nor general negligence law supports the Chapas' claims. We therefore overrule the Chapas' first issue.

C. Bystander Claim

A bystander claim falls within an exception to the general rule barring recovery for negligent infliction of emotional distress. *Cavanaugh v. Jones*, 863 S.W.2d 551, 554 (Tex.App.-Austin 1993, writ denied) (bystander theory of recovery is one type of claim of negligent infliction of emotional distress). Under this legal theory, mental-anguish damages are recoverable for the contemporaneous sensory perception of a serious or fatal injury to a close relative. *Boyles*, 855 S.W.2d at 597–98. When the material facts are undisputed, the question of whether a plaintiff is entitled to recover as a bystander is a question of law. *United Servs. Auto. Ass'n v. Keith*, 970 S.W.2d 540, 542 (Tex.1998) (per curiam).

To determine whether a plaintiff has a valid bystander claim, courts consider:

> (1) Whether the plaintiff was located near the scene of the accident as contrasted with one who was a distance away from it.
>
> (2) Whether the shock resulted from a direct emotional impact upon the plaintiff from the sensory and contemporaneous observance of the accident, as contrasted with learning of the accident from others after its occurrence.
>
> (3) Whether the plaintiff and the victim were closely related, as contrasted with an absence of any relationship or the presence of only a distant relationship.

Freeman v. City of Pasadena, 744 S.W.2d 923, 923–24 (Tex.1988) (adopting the "bystander" elements set forth in *Dillon v. Legg*, 68 Cal.2d 728, 69 Cal.Rptr. 72, 441 P.2d 912, 920 (1968)). Here, the material facts are undisputed, but the parties disagree about whether these facts satisfy the second element of the test.

The Chapas argue that Maria, who was out of sight of the Expedition for only about 30 seconds, was a contemporaneous observer of the "accident." They further contend that Chamber's act of removing the vehicle and the children constituted a continuing tort; thus, Maria's observation of their absence renders her a bystander. *See Landreth v. Reed*, 570 S.W.2d 486, 490 (Tex.Civ.App.-Texarkana 1978, no writ) ("[A]ctual observance of the accident is not required if there is otherwise an experiential perception of it, as distinguished from a learning of it from others after its occurrence."). *But see Robinson v. Chiarello*, 806 S.W.2d 304, 310 (Tex.App.-Fort Worth 1991, writ denied) (phrase "contemporaneous perception of the accident" contemplates a sudden and brief event causing injury). But on this record and under existing law, we cannot say that the requirements for bystander recovery have been satisfied.

In applying "bystander" law, Texas courts have implicitly recognized a fundamental distinction between the perception of circumstances that would strike fear into the heart of a close family member, and the relative's first-hand observation that those fears have been realized. *See, e.g., Boyles*, 855 S.W.2d at 597–98 (discussing "the right of bystanders to recover emotional distress damages suffered as a result of witnessing a serious or fatal accident") (emphasis added); *Gen. Motors Corp. v. Grizzle*, 642 S.W.2d 837, 842 (Tex.App.-Waco 1982, writ dism'd) ("A mother may witness a violent collision in which her child is involved, but if the child emerges unharmed, there is no sensory perception and no mental injury."). This distinction was tacitly acknowledged before the Texas Supreme Court adopted the current test for bystander recovery in 1988. For example, in *City of Austin v. Davis*, a father arrived at the hospital where his neurologically impaired son was a patient and discovered that his son was missing. 693 S.W.2d 31, 32 (Tex.App.-Austin 1985, writ ref'd n.r.e.). The patient's father and the hospital staff searched the hospital, grounds, and surrounding areas for three hours before the father discovered his son's body at the base of ten-story airshaft. *Id.* at 32–33. In recognizing the father's right to recover as a bystander, the Third Court of Appeals did not base its decision on the father's discovery that his son was missing, but instead relied on the father's first-hand discovery of his son's death. *Id.* at 34 (explaining that the father "was intensely involved in the search and subsequent discovery of his son. He did not learn of the incident from others, but found his son's body at the bottom of the airshaft."); *see also Freeman*, 744 S.W.2d at 924 (indicating that a contemporaneous observation includes a parent who "experience[s] the shock of unwittingly coming upon the accident scene.").

Such cases illustrate the distinction between the perception of circumstances that would cause a parent intense fear and uncertainty regarding a child's well-being and actually witnessing the realization of such fears first-hand. According to the summary-judgment evidence, Maria was traumatized because the sight of the empty street caused her to think her children had been kidnapped or murdered. But that fear was not realized: these were not the events that caused the children harm. Moreover, Maria was traumatized by that fear as soon as she saw the empty street regardless of whether her children suffered any harm at all. Her distress did not arise from witnessing the children's serious injury or death, but instead, resulted from her lack of information as to their location or condition

Maria Chapa unquestionably experienced fear and shock when she observed an empty street where her vehicle should have been. Although the elements of a bystander claim are applied flexibly and on a case-by-case basis, this case presents an important disjunction between the alleged cause of injury to the primary victim—*i.e.*, the "accident"—and the circumstances observed by the relative. Texas courts have reserved recognition of bystander claims for those cases in which the emotional impact results from a sensory and contemporaneous observance of the accident that caused the close relative's harm. *Keith*, 970 S.W.2d at 542; *cf. Lions Eye Bank v. Perry*, 56 S.W.3d 872, 878 (Tex.App.-Houston [14th Dist.] 2001, pet. denied) (holding family members are not bystanders where they discovered, but did not witness, the removal of decedent's eyes). Here, however, the evidence is undisputed that Maria did not "sense" her children's serious injury or death; to the contrary, she admittedly had no knowledge of what had happened to her vehicle or her children until they were returned. *Cf. Hewitt*, 760 S.W.2d at 334 (holding that parents who "did not contemporaneously perceive the injury to their daughter" are not bystanders). The requirement that a parent bystander's mental anguish "result[ ] from a direct emotional impact upon plaintiff from the sensory and contemporaneous observance of the accident" necessarily excludes circumstances in which the parent saw nothing, heard nothing, does not know what happened to the child, and does not know if the child is injured. Here, Maria seeks to recover not for a terrible injury to her children that she witnessed, but for her fear of not knowing where they were or whether they were seriously injured.

On this record, we conclude that the second requirement of the bystander test has not been satisfied. *Cf. Freeman*, 744 S.W.2d at 923–24 (contrasting contemporaneous observation with "learning of the accident from others after its occurrence."). We therefore overrule the Chapas' second issue.

* * *

V. CONCLUSION

On this record, the Chapas' claims for mental anguish and its physical manifestations do not constitute compensable injuries under existing law addressing section 9.609 of the Texas Business and Commerce Code, sections 424 or 427 of the Restatement (Second) of Torts, or the common-law of negligence, including claims of bystander injury and negligent hiring. We therefore affirm the judgment of the trial court.

[footnotes omitted]

Do you agree?

§ 7. VARIATIONS ON AND ALTERNATIVES TO CONVENTIONAL CONSUMER SECURED CREDIT

Consumers often enter into transactions that have some, but not all, of the characteristics of a conventional Article 9 secured loan. First, there are "pawn" transactions in which the debtor leaves an item of value in the hands of a pawn broker with the understanding that the debtor has a right within a specified time to return and repurchase the item at a specified price, or that the debtor has a right to the return of the item upon the payment of a specified amount together with interest. These transactions are nonrecourse: the debtor is not obliged to return and reclaim the collateral and there is no "default" if the debtor fails to do so. Permissible interest rates vary: although some are quite high (25% per month in Georgia for the first three months, 12.5% thereafter), others are more moderate (3% per month in Minnesota, plus a reasonable fee for storage and services).

Yet one step further removed from Article 9 is the "rent-to-own" contract. In a rent-to-own transaction, a consumer "rents" an item with a right to have title transferred at the end of a rental period that may extend for 52 weeks or, in some cases, 18 months. Sometimes the transfer of title occurs only on the payment of a nominal option price. In other cases, there is no option but simply a right to the conveyance of the property upon completion of a specified number of payments. Like the pawn transaction, the rent-to-own transaction is nonrecourse; the debtor has no obligation to continue paying and may return the goods and cancel the transaction at the end of any payment interval (weekly or monthly). Commonly, the total payments under a rent-to-own contract are two or three times the lessor's cost of the goods in question. Typically this transaction is entered into by working class people who have limited credit and those who have no other credit options.

Is either of these transactions a secured loan?

PROBLEM 7-8

Consider the following provisions from the Minnesota Pawn Broker Statute:

325J.06 Effect of nonredemption.

(a) A pledgor shall have no obligation to redeem pledged goods or make any payment on a pawn transaction. Pledged goods not redeemed within at least 60 days of the date of the pawn transaction, renewal, or extension shall automatically be forfeited to the pawnbroker, and qualified right, title, and interest in and to the goods shall automatically vest in the pawnbroker.

(b) The pawnbroker's right, title, and interest in the pledged goods under paragraph (a) is qualified only by the pledgor's right, while the pledged goods remain in possession of the pawnbroker and not sold to a third party, to redeem the goods by paying the loan plus fees and/or interest accrued up to the date of redemption.

(c) A pawn transaction that involves holding only the title to property is subject to Chapter 168A or 336.

325J.095 Motor vehicle title pawn transactions; special provisions.

(a) In addition to the other requirements of this chapter, a pawnbroker who holds a title to a motor vehicle as part of a pawn transaction shall:

(1) be licensed as a used motor vehicle dealer under section 168.27, and post such license on the pawnshop premises;

(2) verify that there are no liens or encumbrances against the motor vehicle with the Department of Public Safety; and

(3) verify that the pledgor has automobile insurance on the motor vehicle as required by law.

(b) A pawnbroker may not sell a motor vehicle covered by a pawn transaction until 90 days after recovery of the motor vehicle.

How do the quoted sections treat pawn transactions differently from conventional secured loans? Would a pawn broker who failed to do a public sale or give notice be liable for violating 9–625(c)(2) or any other section in Part 6?

Consider the following case:

IN RE SCHWALB

United States Bankruptcy Court, D. Nevada, 2006.
347 B.R. 726.

MARKELL, BANKRUPTCY JUDGE:

I. Introduction

"Then the bird does not belong to any of you?" Spade asked, "but to a General Kemidov?"

"Belong?" the fat man said jovially, "Well, sir, you might say it belonged to the King of Spain, but I don't see how you can honestly grant anybody else clear title to it—except by right of possession." He clucked. "An article of that value that has passed from hand to hand by such means is clearly the property of whoever can get hold of it."

Possession is the central theme in this case. Pioneer Loan & Jewelry, a pawnbroker, possesses two certificates of title that list it as the owner of two motor vehicles. Michelle Schwalb, the debtor, possesses those vehicles. Pioneer claims exclusive ownership, and that Ms. Schwalb has no legal or equitable interest in the vehicles beyond mere possession. Schwalb counters that Pioneer has no interest in the vehicles because she never transferred title or granted any other interest in them to Pioneer.

Pioneer seeks possession of the vehicles, and has asked this court to force Ms. Schwalb to turn them over to it. Ms. Schwalb seeks to keep the vehicles and pay Pioneer nothing under her chapter 13 plan, the confirmation of which is the subject of this opinion.

Both parties' fallback position is that Pioneer's interest is that of a secured creditor, as it is not disputed that Pioneer originally lent money to Ms. Schwalb on the strength of the vehicles as collateral. But this presents a different problem: the documents under which Pioneer lent Ms. Schwalb money provided for an annual interest rate of approximately 120%. As a result, by the time Ms. Schwalb filed her bankruptcy, Pioneer's claim had grown to more than double the original loan. Pioneer thus believes that Ms. Schwalb has insufficient resources to pay this claim over the life of her chapter 13 plan. Ms. Schwalb responds that Pioneer's secured claim is less than Pioneer alleges. She offered evidence that she can afford plan payments at the current plan value. She also asserts, and Pioneer does not dispute, that Pioneer's failure to file a proof of claim prevents Pioneer from asserting any unsecured claim related to its loans.

All of these issues were tried to the court during a confirmation hearing on March 20, 2006. After hearing the testimony, and reviewing all the evidence and the pleadings, the court finds that Pioneer is a secured creditor, and that Ms. Schwalb can fund a chapter 13 plan given the findings regarding value (after offsets for statutory damages). The court will thus require the debtor to file an amended plan consistent with this opinion, and when it is filed, the court will confirm that plan.

II. Relevant Facts

Michelle Schwalb is not a typical chapter 13 debtor. She holds no job, because she can't hold one. Seven years ago she had a brain tumor removed, leaving her unsteady and unable to concentrate for extended periods of time. Social Security disability payments are her only regular income. She is 34 years old, diabetic, has a non-working pituitary gland, and has initial symptoms of Grave's disease. She must take steroids to live. Ms. Schwalb lives with a man who fathered her only child, and they have been together as a family for thirteen or fourteen years. He works outside the home, and pays most of the household expenses.

Ms. Schwalb's chapter 13 plan is being funded entirely from her monthly disability payments, which are currently $580, and from contributions by her father. Her father's current monthly contribution is $640. Ms. Schwalb's father testified at confirmation that he is doing so out of a desire to take care of his daughter and his grandchild. He also testified that, before his daughter filed this chapter 13 case, he regularly contributed between $600 and $800 per month towards her support.

Ms. Schwalb's father gave her the two vehicles at issue, a 1997 Infiniti QX4 Sport Utility Vehicle and a 2002 Cadillac Escalade. Before dealing with Pioneer, Ms. Schwalb had clean title to both vehicles. Then, sometime during 2004, the debtor, her father and her partner decided they needed to contribute funds to a business that Ms. Schwalb's partner ran. They went to Pioneer and obtained two loans totaling $20,000.

The business, however, failed. Ms. Schwalb had no way to repay Pioneer. At this point, Pioneer began to take action to obtain the vehicles. To understand the actions Pioneer took, however, it is necessary to review the transactions by which Ms. Schwalb obtained the $20,000.

Ms. Schwalb and her father initially approached Pioneer in June of 2004. Mr. Schwalb had done business with Pioneer and, at that time, enjoyed some goodwill with it. Ms. Schwalb's Infiniti QX4 Sport Utility Vehicle was offered as collateral, and Pioneer advanced $4,000 against possession of the certificate of title for the vehicle. The parties testified that Ms. Schwalb gave Pioneer her certificate of title after she signed it as seller. The buyer's name was left blank.

When she received the $4,000 in loan proceeds, Ms. Schwalb signed a document referred to by the parties as a pawn ticket. The pawn ticket is a preprinted form used by Pioneer in its pawnbroker business. It is a simple 5-inch-by-8-inch form, with text front and back. Among other things, the front has blanks for describing the property pawned, for the amount of the loan and for the repayment date.

On Ms. Schwalb's pawn ticket, the parties designated the property pawned as an Infiniti QX4 Sport Utility Vehicle, and included its Vehicle Identification Number (VIN). The ticket also contained the loan terms. Ms. Schwalb was to repay the $4,000 in 120 days, plus $1,605 interest. The disclosed annual interest rate was 122.04%. If Ms. Schwalb did not "redeem" the pawn and pay the loan within the 120 days, the pawn ticket indicated that "you shall . . . forfeit all right and interest in the pawned property to the pawnbroker who shall hereby acquire an absolute title to the same." Just before the blank on the pawn ticket in which the parties inserted the description of the Infiniti and its VIN, the pawn ticket indicated, in very small five-point type, "You are giving a security interest in the following property: ". Pioneer did not retain possession of the vehicle. Ms. Schwalb drove off in it with her $4,000. Pioneer put the signed certificate of title in a safe on its premises.

The transaction with the Cadillac was essentially the same, except Pioneer advanced $16,000 against possession of the signed certificate of title, and the interest rate was 121.76%. This transaction occurred on August 19, 2004. In each case, Pioneer's representative testified that the amount Pioneer lent against the certificates of title was within Pioneer's general practice of lending no more than 30% to 40% of the retail value of the vehicle offered as collateral.

Approximately $1,605 in interest on the Infiniti loan was paid on or around November 6, 2004, thus extending the redemption period to March 6, 2005. No interest was ever paid on the Cadillac loan. The final 120-day term expired on the Infiniti loan on March 6, 2005, and on December 17, 2004, for the Cadillac loan.

When Ms. Schwalb did not repay either loan, Pioneer took both certificates of title to the Nevada Department of Motor Vehicles ("DMV") where, sometime in April 2005, Pioneer requested that the DMV reissue the certificates showing Ms. Schwalb as the owner and Pioneer as the "lienholder." The DMV complied. After Pioneer's initial efforts to obtain the vehicles were unsuccessful, Pioneer then presented the newly reissued certificates of title to the DMV, this time requesting that the DMV reissue the certificates of title without any mention of Ms Schwalb, and listing Pioneer as the sole owner. Again the DMV complied. Pioneer then filed a state court lawsuit apparently alleging conversion and seeking recovery of both vehicles. There was testimony that Pioneer consulted with the local police regarding the necessity of changing the certificates of title to facilitate its legal action seeking recovery of the vehicles.

Ms. Schwalb filed her chapter 13 case on August 9, 2005. Pioneer elected not to file a proof of claim, instead opting to claim ownership of the vehicles. Pioneer attempted to obtain relief from stay so that it could obtain the vehicles, but withdrew that motion for procedural reasons.

Ms. Schwalb's plan, filed with her chapter 13 petition, proposes to pay her creditors over 36 months. Her monthly payment is $555 for the first 12 months of her plan, and $709 per month for the remaining 24 months of her plan.

Initially, Ms. Schwalb contends that Pioneer is not a secured creditor, and is barred from participating in her case as an unsecured creditor. Her initial proposal is thus to pay Pioneer nothing under her plan. If Pioneer is found to be a secured creditor despite her objection, she proposes to value the collateral for the secured claims at $16,000 for the Cadillac loan and $4,000 for the Infiniti loan. The plan would then pay these two secured claims in full over the life of the plan, together with 10% simple interest.

III. Pioneer's Property Interests

The parties have focused on the nature of Pioneer's property interest, if any, in the two vehicles. Relying on its pawn ticket and the laws of other states, Pioneer contends that it owns both vehicles, and that Ms. Schwalb has no legal or equitable interest in them. Ms. Schwalb counters that Pioneer is not a pawnbroker with respect to the vehicles since it did not retain possession of them after making the loans. Ms. Schwalb further argues that the language of the pawn ticket is insufficient to create an Article 9 security interest under Nevada's version of the Uniform Commercial Code (UCC).

Pioneer, if forced to yield on its ownership claims, contends that the language in the pawn ticket is sufficient under Nevada's version of Article 9 to create a security interest, and that it has not violated any of Article 9's requirements or restrictions. Ms. Schwalb, however, contends that Pioneer did not comply with significant and mandatory provisions of Article 9, and requests that this court reduce Pioneer's claim.

A. *Pawnbrokers and the Pawning of Goods Generally*

All around the cobbler's bench
The monkey chased the weasel
The monkey thought that all was fun
Pop! Goes the weasel!
A penny for a spool of thread
A penny for a needle
That's the way the money goes
Pop! Goes the weasel!

Under Nevada law, a pawnbroker is a "person engaged, in whole or in part, in the business of loaning money on the security of pledges, deposits or other secured transactions in personal property." NEV. REV. STAT. § 646.010. The parties agree that Pioneer is a licensed pawnbroker under this law. They disagree, however, on the significance of Pioneer's status, and to resolve those differences the court must investigate the history and current status of pawnbrokers, and the impact of pawnbroker status with respect to a nonpossessory vehicle loan.

1. Short History of Pawnbroking

Pawnbrokers engage in transactions in which a debtor pawns goods in return for a short-term loan. Pawnbroking has a significant and positive place in the history of lending. *Italian Banks and Pawnbroking: In Hock,* THE ECONOMIST, May 27, 2006, at 73 (reporting that pawnbroking is a 500-year old business and stating that the bank claiming to be the world's oldest bank, the Monte dei Paschi di Siena, began in the pawn business). According to some accounts, Queen Isabella of Spain pawned her jewels to finance Columbus' trip of discovery. Jarret C. Oeltjen, *Florida*

Pawnbroking: An Industry in Transition, 23 FLA. ST. U.L. REV. 995, 996 (1996). At various times in our history, pawning one's clothes and other possessions was an ordinary and common occurrence.

Pawning one's goods differs from lending against them; in a typical pawn, a debtor deposits goods with the pawnbroker, and receives money in return. If the customer does not "redeem" his pawn within a specified time, tradition has it that the power to sell the goods deposited automatically passes to the pawnbroker. If the pawnbroker's subsequent sale of the goods does not cover the loan, the pawnbroker takes the loss; conversely, if the pawnbroker sells the goods for more than the money lent, custom allows the pawnbroker to keep the surplus. CASKEY, *supra* note 7, at 1. Another way to characterize the transaction is as a nonrecourse loan by the pawnbroker to the customer, with agreed strict foreclosure on the redemption date.

2. Recent History, and the Advent of "Title Pawns"

Despite its venerable history, pawnbroking has lately experienced something of a public relations crisis. Pawnbrokers are regulated in a manner designed to deter personal property theft, and often are found in low-income neighborhoods on the fringe of respectability. Despite efforts to improve this image, "the negative portrait lingers; pawnshops continue to be cast as 'nuisance businesses,' in the company of tattoo shops and massage parlors, and somewhere in rank between liquor stores and houses of prostitution." Oeltjen, *supra,* at 1001.

This negative perception has not been helped by the type of loans present here. As noted in a recent report sponsored in part by the Consumer Federation of America, "car title loans are marketed as small emergency loans, but in reality these loans trap borrowers in a cycle of debt. Car title loans put at high risk an asset that is essential to the well-being of working families—their vehicle." AMANDA QUESTER & JEAN ANN FOX, CAR TITLE LENDING: DRIVING BORROWERS TO FINANCIAL RUIN 2 (2005). As noted by Quester and Fox, some states have passed laws favorable to the title loan industry, *id.* at 10, while others have specifically prohibited pawnbrokers from engaging in "title pawn" transactions, *id* at 11 & n. 101. *See id.* at App. A, pp. 32–34 (collecting state statutes permitting and regulating title loans).

3. Nevada's Regulation of Pawnbrokers and Title Pawn Transactions

Nevada has not directly enacted legislation regarding the relationship between traditional pawnbroking and title lending. As a consequence, Pioneer attempts to support its position with extrapolations of existing state and local regulations, as well as of recent Nevada Attorney General opinions. As will be seen, however, these arguments are unavailing.

a. State

Nevada regulates pawnbrokers through a series of provisions found in Chapter 646 of the Nevada Revised Statutes. NEV. REV. STAT. §§ 646.002 to 646.060. Most of these provisions regulate the business and accounting side of pawnbroking; for example, pawnbrokers are required to keep detailed records of their transactions, *id,* § 646.020, and are required each day to turn over records of the previous day's transactions to law enforcement officials. *Id.* § 646.030.

Of all the sections in Chapter 646, only one, Section 646.050, provides substantive restrictions on the terms of a loan made by pawnbrokers. It requires that pawnbrokers cannot charge more than 10% per month on their loans, and must offer a redemption period of at least 120 days to their customers. *Id.* § 646.050.1. The criminal provisions of the chapter, however, do not refer to this rate regulation; rather, they are concerned with compliance with the recordkeeping provisions. *Id.* § 646.060. This limitation underscores the basic fact that the main purpose of Chapter 646 is not consumer protection, but law enforcement.

Chapter 646 also covers "motor vehicles received in pledge," and permits the storage of such vehicles at a location apart from the pawnbroker's principal place of business. In the late 1990s, when title pawns began to expand in Nevada, the state attorney general was asked to opine on the appropriate classification of such activity. In two opinions cited by counsel, the attorney general found that nonpossessory lending against the strength of a vehicle's title fit within the definition of "pawnbroker" for regulatory purposes because, although it was not the typical possessory lending historically associated with pawnbrokers, it did fit the statutory definition of someone in the business of "loaning money on the security of pledges, deposits or *other secured transactions in personal property.*" NEV. REV. STAT. § 646.010 (emphasis supplied). *See* OP. NEV. ATT'Y GEN. 97–03 (1997); OP. NEV. ATT'Y GEN. 95–20 (1995). *See also* OP. NEV. ATT'Y GEN. 97–13 (1997) (clarifying that opinions were meant to aid in the proper regulations of such lending). The attorney general apparently assumed that such nonpossessory lending was subject to Article 9 of Nevada's version of the UCC, *see, e.g.,* OP. NEV. ATT'Y GEN. 95–20 ("Since pawn transactions authorized by NRS Chapter 646 allow the pawnbroker to engage in 'other secured transactions in personal property. . . .' "), but opined that when practiced with the traditional pledge of personal property, it was within the business of pawnbroking, at least for purposes of exempting pawnbrokers from regulation under the installment lending provisions of Chapter 675 of the Nevada Revised Statutes. *Id.*

b. City

Nevada pawnbrokers are also regulated by municipal governments, and Pioneer was (and is) subject to regulation by the City of Las Vegas. Chapter 6.60 of the Las Vegas Municipal Code in most parts copies and expands on Chapter 646 of the Nevada Revised Statutes. It also requires a pawnbroker to be licensed, and requires a separate license if the person "accepts a motor vehicle as pledged property or in any other matter allows the use of a motor vehicle as collateral or security for a loan." LAS VEGAS MUNICIPAL CODE, §§ 6.6.020 (definition of "auto-pawnbroker"); 6.60.035 (requirement of a separate license for auto-pawnbroker).

The municipal provisions applicable to Pioneer are also primarily related to law enforcement, and not to consumer protection. The municipal code, however, does contain certain disclosure requirements for borrowers, and also makes it unlawful for the pawnbroker to charge or receive more than 10% interest per month.

B. Application of Article 9

Neither the state nor the local regulation specifically refers to the applicability of the primary statute related to personal property collateral—Article 9 of the UCC. Conversely, Nevada has not explicitly excluded pawnbroking from the scope of Article 9. The initial question is thus easily stated: Does Article 9 apply to Pioneer's two transactions with Ms. Schwalb?

1. Does Article 9 Apply to Traditional Pawnbroking Activities?

Pioneer contends (and often assumes without argument) that pawnbroking is excluded from Article 9. That contention is false as a matter of statutory construction. Article 9 is intended to be the primary statute regarding the consensual personal property security. It is a marvel of drafting that consolidates and resolves many issues into one single statute. And it is intentionally broad; as noted in the comments, "all consensual security interests in personal property and fixtures are covered by this Article . . . . When a security interest is created, this Article applies regardless of the form of the transaction or the name that parties have given to it." Cmt. 2 to UCC § 9–109.

To achieve this breadth of coverage, Article 9 looks to substance over form. This is confirmed by its text: Article 9 states that it applies to any "transaction, *regardless of its form,* that creates a security interest in personal property or fixtures by contract." NEV. REV. STAT. § 104.9109.1(a) (emphasis supplied).

Given this broad scope, some states have altered the breadth of Article 9 by either expanding the list of exclusions to Section 9–109 as adopted, or by restricting the effect Article 9 gives to security interests in Section 9–201. *Compare* NEV. REV. STAT. § 104.9109.4(n) (excluding "[a] transfer by a government or governmental unit" from scope of Nevada's Article 9) *and* NEV. REV. STAT. § 104.9201.2 (excluding consumer transactions under Chapters 97 and 97A from Article 9's section validating security agreements) *with* UCC § 9–109(d) (containing no exclusion for governmental transfers) *and* UCC § 9–201(b) (containing generic exclusion for consumer protection laws from Article 9's section validating security agreements generally). *See also* UCC § 9–109(c)(2) (permitting exception for categories of transactions expressly provided by another state statute).

In the area of pawnbroking, however, Nevada has not adopted other states' practice of excluding some or all of pawnbroking's practices from Article 9. *See, e.g.,* CAL. COMM. CODE § 9201(b) (2006) (exempting California's Pawnbroker Law, CAL. FIN. CODE §§ 21000 *et. seq.* from Article 9); 810 ILL. COMP. STAT § 5/9–201(b)(5) (2006) (exempting Illinois' Pawnbroker Regulation Act); N.C. GEN. STAT. 25–9–201(b) (2006) (exempting North Carolina's Pawnbrokers Modernization Act of 1989 (Chapter 91A of North Carolina's General Statutes)).

Given this lack of express exclusion, the court believes that Nevada would join the other states and commentators who have examined the issue, and concluded that pawnbroking is an activity governed by Article 9 of the UCC that neither the parties' contrary language nor an industry's contrary practice can alter. *In re Davis,* 269 B.R. 914 (Bankr.M.D.Ala.2001) (applying Alabama law); *In re Jones,* 206 B.R. 569 (Bankr.M.D.Ala.1997) (applying Alabama law); *Mattheiss v. Title Loan Express* (*In re Mattheiss*), 214 B.R. 20, 28 (Bankr.N.D.Ala.1997) (applying Alabama law); *In re Lopez,* 163 B.R. 189, 191 (Bankr.D.Colo.1994) (despite language of forfeiture in pawn agreement, pawn relationship created a secured transaction capable of being modified in a chapter 13 plan); *Lynn v. Financial Solutions Corp.* (*In re Lynn*), 173 B.R. 894, 900–01 (Bankr.M.D.Tenn.1994) (applying Tennessee law); *Harkness v. EZ Pawn Alabama, Inc.,* 724 So.2d 32 (Ala.Civ.App.1998) (on referral from Alabama Supreme Court); *Reeves v. Foutz & Tanner, Inc.,* 94 N.M. 760, 617 P.2d 149 (1980) (applying Article 9's provisions regarding a surplus following disposition applied to pawn transactions); 4 JAMES J. WHITE & ROBERT S. SUMMERS, UNIFORM COMMERCIAL CODE § 30–1(b), at 4 (5th ed. 2002) ("When a pawnshop takes possession of a debtor's clarinet, the parties are entering into a perfected secured transaction."); 8A LAWRENCE'S ANDERSON ON THE UNIFORM COMMERCIAL CODE § 9–102:152 (3d ed. Lary Lawrence, ed. 2005) ("Pawn transactions are Article 9 secured transactions.") [hereinafter "ANDERSON"].

2. Pioneer's Transactions Are Not Traditional Pawn Transactions

Even if the court held that pawnbroking's practices are impliedly exempt from Article 9, Pioneer would not prevail for the simple reason that the transactions at issue are not those of a traditional pawnbroker. Pawnbrokers are bailees of personal property held as collateral for loans. If the loan is not paid—or, in the argot of pawnbroking, if the pawn is not redeemed—then the pawnbroker sells the goods held, and keeps the proceeds; the debtor is not liable for any deficiency, and the pawnbroker is not accountable for any surplus. *See* Oeltjen, *supra,* at 996–97.

As a result, a true pawn requires a pledge, and a pledge requires delivery of the collateral to the pawnbroker. *See, e.g., Pendleton v. American Title Brokers, Inc.,* 754 F.Supp. 860, 864 (S.D.Ala.1991); *Lynn v. Financial Solutions Corp.* (*In re Lynn*), 173 B.R. 894, 898 (Bankr.M.D.Tenn.1994); *State ex rel McGraw v. Pawn Am.,* 205 W.Va. 431, 433–34, 518 S.E.2d 859, 861–62 (1998). *Cf.* 18 U.S.C. § 921(a)(12) (defining pawnbroker, for purpose of regulating sale of firearms, as "any person whose business or occupation includes the taking or receiving, by way of pledge or pawn, of any firearm or ammunition as security for the payment or repayment of money."); NEB. OP. ATTY. GEN. No. 98027, 1998 Westlaw 344508, at 1 (June 19, 1998) ("[W]e believe that a pawnbroker is required to have actual possession of the automobile in order for the lending arrangement to constitute a pawnbroking transaction under Nebraska law.").

Here, of course, Pioneer did not possess the vehicles (although state law permitted it to do so); at best, it was a bailee of the certificates of title, for whatever good holding on to pieces of officially issued paper did it. As such, the issue as to the exempt status of traditional pawnbroking activities is not directly raised by this case.

Pioneer argues that actual possession was not necessary. Since it had possession of the certificates of title, it has "constructive" possession of the vehicles, and that this constructive possession was sufficient to bring it under the protective reach of pawnbroking status. Nothing in the Nevada statutory scheme authorizes this view, and pre-UCC cases rejected it. *See, e.g., Casey v. Cavaroc,* 96 U.S. 467, 477, 24 L.Ed. 779 (1877) (noting that "possession may be considered as of the very essence of a pledge," and that "constructive delivery cannot be effected without doing what amounts to a transfer of the property," using keys to a warehouse and bills of lading as examples); *Commercial Bank of Jacksonville v. Flowers,* 116 Ga. 219, 42 S.E. 474 (1902) (constructive possession of goods not accomplished by possession of receipt from wharfinger who had actual possession of goods). *See also* Section III.C.1.b, *infra.*

C. Applicability of Article 9 to Pioneer's Loans

As indicated above, Section 9–109 makes Pioneer's transactions with Ms. Schwalb subject to Nevada's version of Article 9. This was not unexpected. Pioneer's form of pawnbroking ticket expressly states that Ms. Schwalb was "giving a security interest" in the two vehicles to Pioneer.

Although more will be said about this language below, it is a clear indication that Pioneer was both aware of the term "security interest," and wanted to use it in the two transactions. And if a "security interest" is involved, the default statute of applicability is Article 9 of the UCC.

Beyond that, however, as the courts and commentators cited above have found, each transaction here fits within the text of Section 9–109—that it be a "transaction . . . that creates a security interest in personal property or fixtures by contract." NEV. REV. STAT. § 104.9109.1(a). This can be seen from an analysis of the components of Section 9–109.

The component most obviously present is a contract—a provision that requires that transaction to be consensual. "Contract," as defined in the UCC is "the total legal obligation that results from the parties' agreement . . ." NEV. REV. STAT. § 104.1201.2(*l*). The UCC defines the term "agreement" as "the bargain of the parties in fact, as found in their language or inferred from other circumstances . . . ." *Id.* § 104.1201.2(c).

Here, Ms. Schwalb and Pioneer had an "agreement"—Pioneer would lend money to her on the security of her two vehicles. That was their bargain in fact. This agreement gave rise to legal obligations—that is, rights that courts would vindicate—some supplied by Nevada's common law of contracts, and others by Nevada's version of Article 9. This consensual agreement combined with the attendant legal consequences form the necessary contract; or, put another way, the transaction was consensual, and breach of it implied various legal consequences.

Was it a contract to create or provide for a security interest? "Security interest" is defined in Article 1 as "an interest in personal property . . . which secures payment or performance of an obligation." NEV. REV. STAT. § 104.1201.2(ii). Here, Ms. Schwalb gave Pioneer an interest in her vehicles as a condition of obtaining the two loans, and Pioneer held onto the title to ensure repayment. When Ms. Schwalb did not repay the loans within the 120-day redemption period, Pioneer's position is that exclusive ownership of the vehicles passed to it. This type of arrangement—in which rights to possession of personal property arise upon failure to repay debt or honor some other obligation—is a classic security interest and fits the definition of "an interest in personal property [that] secure[d] payment . . . of an obligation." NEV. REV. STAT. § 104.9201.2(ii).

As a result, the transactions here were covered by Article 9 of the UCC. This conclusion has serious repercussions for the parties.

1. Attachment Generally

The initial consequence of Article 9's applicability is that the creation and status of Pioneer's interest is governed by a combination of the common law of contract law and the statutory provisions of Article 9. For an Article

9 security interest to be enforceable, it must "attach." NEV. REV. STAT. § 104.9203.

Attachment, in turn, has three requirements: (1) value has to have been given; (2) the debtor must have rights in the collateral; and (3) either (a) the debtor has authenticated a security agreement that provides a description of the collateral, or (b) the secured party possesses the collateral pursuant to a security agreement. NEV. REV. STAT. § 104.9203.2(a)–(c).

Value is present in the form of the loans extended by Pioneer to Ms. Schwalb. NEV. REV.STAT. § 104.1204. Similarly, there is no doubt that, at the time of each transaction, Ms. Schwalb's ownership rights in the vehicles were sufficient "rights in the collateral" for a security interest to attach. *Foothill Capital Corp. v. Clare's Food Market, Inc. (In re Coupon Clearing Service, Inc.)*, 113 F.3d 1091, 1103 (9th Cir.1997) ("Where a debtor has rights to collateral beyond naked possession, a security interest may attach to such rights."), *citing Morton Booth Co. v. Tiara Furniture, Inc.*, 564 P.2d 210, 214 (Okla.1977).

The issue thus boils down to whether the "debtor authenticated a security agreement that provides a description of the collateral," or whether the collateral was "in the possession of the secured party under NRS 104.9313 pursuant to the debtor's security agreement." *Id.* § 104.9203.2(c)(1)–(2).

a. Authenticated Agreement

Ms. Schwalb contends that the pawn ticket is legally insufficient as a security agreement. At trial, she testified that she did not know what she was signing at the time she received each of the two loans. Each pawn ticket used, however, contained the following preprinted language just before a description of the automobile involved as well as its VIN: "You are giving a security interest in the following property:"

Under Article 9, a "security agreement" is "an agreement that creates or provides for a security interest." NEV. REV. STAT. § 104.9102.1(ttt). The pawn ticket was clearly an "agreement" as the UCC uses that term. It contained "the bargain of the parties in fact," as expressed in "their language or [as could be] inferred from other circumstances . . ." *Id.* § 104.1201.2(c). The bargain was simple and standard: Ms. Schwalb borrowed money at interest, and agreed to repay it within 120 days.

Thus, the only question is whether the agreement also included collateral as security for repayment of the loan. Each pawn ticket definitively described the vehicle at issue, by make, model and VIN. The issue is thus whether the words "[y]ou are giving" adequately "create[ ] or provide[ ]" for a security interest in the vehicles. The safest and traditional words to accomplish this task are words of grant or assignment, such as "I hereby grant a security interest in X to secure repayment of my debt to you" or "I assign this property to you to secure what I owe you."

In these phrases, the operative verbs—grant, assign, etc.—are in the present tense and indicate a present act. But the word used by the pawn ticket—"giving"—is not in the present tense but instead is the present participle of the verb "to give." Ms. Schwalb contends that use of the participle "giving" can only be read to refer to Pioneer's description of what Pioneer thought Ms. Schwalb had done or was doing—not as Ms. Schwalb's acknowledgment that she was engaging in a legally significant act. The analogy would be to something like noting that the statement "You are falling" describes an action taken by another rather than separately constituting the act of falling.

But this is a quibble. While a description may not be the act it describes, by signing the pawn ticket Ms. Schwalb acknowledged and adopted the act it described—giving a security interest. Moreover, the statutory verbs are "creates" *or* "provides." Even if the language did not "create" the security interest as Ms. Schwalb contends, it certainly did provide for "giving" one.

The insistence on formal words of grant or transfer is inconsistent with the structure and intent of Article 9. As the Idaho Supreme Court noted with respect to the original version of Article 9:

> Courts have often repeated that no magic words are necessary to create a security interest and that the agreement itself need not even contain the term 'security interest.' This is in keeping with the policy of the code that form should not prevail over substance and that, whenever possible, effect should be given to the parties' intent.

See also Nolden v. Plant Reclamation (*In re Amex-Protein Dev. Corp.*), 504 F.2d 1056, 1059–60 (9th Cir.1974) ("There is no support in legislative history or grammatical logic for the substitution of the word 'grant' for the phrase 'creates or provides for.' ").

The proper policy considerations are well stated by a leading commentator on Article 9: "There is no requirement for words of grant. In fact, such a requirement smacks of the antiquated formalism the drafters were trying to avoid." 1 CLARK & CLARK, *supra,* at ¶ 2.02[1][c], at p. 2–16. *See also* 4 WHITE & SUMMERS, *supra,* at § 31–3 ("the drafters did not intend that specific 'words of grant' be required.").

Ms. Schwalb's further argument that she did not understand the import of the words she subscribed to is also unavailing. Even though they appear in tiny five-point type, the words are discernable as an integral part of the pawn ticket. It has long been the common law rule that signing a document authenticates and adopts the words it contains, even if there was a lack of subjective understanding of the words or their legal effect. In essence, people are presumed to be bound by what they sign. *Campanelli v. Conservas Altamira, S.A.*, 86 Nev. 838, 841, 477 P.2d 870, 872 (1970) ("when a party to a written contract accepts it is (*sic*) a contract he is bound by the stipulations and conditions expressed in it whether he reads them or not. Ignorance through negligence or inexcusable trustfulness will not relieve a party from his contract obligations. He who signs or accepts a written contract, in the absence of fraud or other wrongful act on the part of another contracting party, is conclusively presumed to know its contents and to assent to them . . . ."), *quoting Level Export Corp. v. Wolz, Aiken & Co.*, 305 N.Y. 82, 87, 111 N.E.2d 218, 221 (1953), *quoting Metzger v. Aetna Ins. Co.*, 227 N.Y. 411, 416, 125 N.E. 814, 816 (1920). [The court concluded that Pioneer's security interest attached to the collateral.]

* * *

b. Attachment Based on "Constructive Possession" of the Certificates of Title

Pioneer argues in the alternative that its security interest attached through constructive possession of the vehicles, which was accomplished by possession of the certificates of title. Although at least one court has accepted a form of this argument, *Floyd v. Title Exch. & Pawn of Anniston, Inc.*, 620 So.2d 576 (Ala.1993), it does not square with tradition, commercial practice or Nevada law.

In commercial parlance, a record or writing stands proxy for goods it covers only if it is a "document of title" as defined in Article 1 of the UCC. That definition states:

> "Document of title" means a record:
>
> (1) That in the regular course of business or financing is treated as adequately evidencing that the person in possession or control of the record is entitled to receive, control, hold and dispose of the record and the goods the record covers; and
>
> (2) That purports to be issued by or addressed to a bailee and to cover goods in the bailee's possession which are either identified or are fungible portions of an identified mass. . . .

NEV. REV. STAT. § 104.1201.2(p).

Documents of title, as defined, include warehouse receipts, bills of lading and the like. *Id.* Commercial parties deal with these documents as if they were dealing with the goods themselves; indeed, Article 9 allows perfection of goods covered by a negotiable document to be perfected by possession of that document. NEV. REV. STAT. § 104.9312.3.

But the automobile certificates of title here bear little resemblance to the documents of title described in Article 1. Certificates of title do not serve the commercial purpose of standing proxy for vehicles; they are generally held by the owner or lienholder of the car, not a bailee who controls the goods as its business. This is not particularly surprising. Certificate of title statutes were not designed to facilitate commerce; rather, they are regulatory and anticrime statutes that allow "big-ticket" items such as cars to be tracked by law enforcement authorities. LYNN M. LOPUCKI & ELIZABETH WARREN, SECURED CREDIT: A SYSTEMS APPROACH 406 (6th ed. 2006) ("Certificates of title are part of a complex system that serves a variety of purposes, most unrelated to secured credit. Certificates of title are part of the system by which the police identify the owner of a vehicle that is involved in an accident, lost, stolen, or used in the commission of a crime. Certificates of title are also used to transfer ownership of motor vehicles and to keep track of successive annual registrations and taxation of vehicles.").

Indeed, although Article 9 brings certificates of title into its system, it is only to provide a proxy for the financing statement, not the vehicle. In most states, the only way to perfect an interest in a car or other vehicle is to note the secured party's interest on the certificate of title. Except in rare circumstances, possession of the car will not perfect the already-attached secured party's security interest. NEV. REV. STAT. § 104.9313.2. The upshot of this is that mere possession of the certificate of title is of little legal significance under Article 9; that possession neither creates a security interest nor perfects one otherwise granted in the vehicles. *See, e.g., Lee v. Cox,* 18 U.C.C. Rep. Serv. 807, 21 Fed. R. Serv.2d 828 (M.D.Tenn.1976) (possession of registration certificates for eight Arabian horses did not perfect interest in horses). At best, Pioneer possessed the certificates of title for what they were worth—which is not much, as it turns out; their possession facilitated Pioneer's perfection of its interests as will be seen, but it did not assist Pioneer in divesting Ms. Schwalb of her interests.

Pioneer's interests were thus attached, but that alone is insufficient in this case. While attachment may make the security interest enforceable against the debtor, more is needed when the debtor is a debtor in bankruptcy. What is required in the later case is that the security interest be good against the world. The process by which such validity is obtained is referred to in Article 9 as perfection.

2. Perfection

A security agreement "is effective according to its terms between the parties, against purchasers of the collateral, and against creditors," so long as a contrary result is not specified elsewhere in the UCC. NEV. REV. STAT. § 104.9201.1. Although not immediately obvious, one of the key restrictions on this provision is that, to be effective against lien creditors and purchasers, the security interest must be perfected. *Id.* §§ 104.9317.1;

104.9317.2. The UCC tells us that the default method of perfection is by filing a financing statement. *Id.* § 104.9310.1.

An exception exists for items such as the vehicles involved here. If, as here, the collateral is subject to a certificate of title statute, Article 9 requires compliance with the state certificate of title statute for perfection. *Id.* § 104.9311.1(b). In Nevada, that requires reference to Chapter 482 of the Nevada Revised Statutes, which indicates that perfection occurs when there is "[c]ompliance with the applicable provisions of NEV. REV. STAT. 482.423 to 482.431," NEV. REV. STAT. § 482.432, which includes delivery of information regarding any secured party, and issuance of a certificate of title showing the secured party as a lienholder. *Id.*

Here, the manner in which Ms. Schwalb delivered the certificates of title to Pioneer facilitated perfection. Although the exact date when it occurred is in dispute, Ms. Schwalb testified that at some point she signed the certificates of title in blank, and then gave them to Pioneer. Pioneer held the certificates until default (thus adopting the risky strategy of being secured but unperfected during this time). It then exchanged them at the DMV, initially for certificates showing Pioneer as lienholder, and then ultimately for certificates showing Pioneer as owner.

As a result, when Pioneer initially went to the Department of Motor Vehicles in February of 2004, it became perfected no later than the time when it received the new certificates of title showing it as a lienholder.

3. Enforcement

Perhaps the key difference that attends the application of Article 9 to the transactions at issue lies in how Pioneer may enforce its security interest. Its contract, the pawn ticket, is explicit. It states that:

> In the event of failure to pay the loan with 120 days from date hereof, you shall thereby forfeit all right and title unto such pawned property to the pawnbroker who shall thereby acquire an absolute title to the same.

Before Ms. Schwalb filed her case, Pioneer sought to enforce this clause by first applying to be listed as the owner on the certificates of title, and then by filing a state court action seeking possession of the vehicles.

a. Unenforceable Forfeiture Clause

Pioneer continues to seek enforcement of this forfeiture clause as written. It asserts that both vehicles belong, in all senses of that word, to it and to it alone. This assertion is misguided. Article 9 prohibits the waiver by debtors of certain provisions. In particular, Section 9–602 contains a long list of provisions that "the debtor . . . may not waive or vary." NEV. REV. STAT. § 104.9602. These include the provisions regarding: the obligation to proceed in a commercially reasonable manner, *id.*

§ 104.9602.7, strict foreclosure, *id.* § 104.9602.10, and the debtor's right to redeem the collateral, *id.* § 104.9602.11.

If the parties sign a security agreement containing prohibited waivers, and then seek to enforce them, courts most often remedy violations of Section 9–602 by simply reading the relevant documents as if the offending clause had never been included. They then assess the parties' conduct under the remaining provisions and the default standards set forth in Article 9. *See, e.g., AAR Aircraft & Engine Group, Inc. v. Edwards,* 272 F.3d 468, 472 (7th Cir.2001) (waiver of duty to proceed in commercially reasonable manner unenforceable); *Tropical Jewelers, Inc. v. NationsBank, N.A.,* 781 So.2d 381, 384 (Fla.Dist.Ct.App.2000) (same); *Fleming v. Carroll Pub. Co.,* 581 A.2d 1219, 1223 (D.C.1990) (parties signed document denominated a "lease" that allowed lessor to take leased goods without notice; court finds that Article 9 applies, and that lessor/secured party could not rely on provision dispensing with notice, and held that provision to be unenforceable); *Prescott v. Thompson Tractor Co.,* 495 So.2d 513, 517 (Ala.1986) (predecessor to Section 9–602 precludes waiver by a debtor of the right to notification of the disposition of collateral); *Barber v. LeRoy,* 40 Cal.App.3d 336, 342–43, 115 Cal.Rptr. 272, 277 (1974) (provision allowing secured party to bid at private sale void as against public policy and unenforceable); *C.I.T. Corp. v. Haynes,* 161 Me. 353, 356, 212 A.2d 436, 438 (1965) (waiver of right of redemption in conditional sales contract subject to Article 9 unenforceable as against public policy).

These provisions are of special concern in consumer transactions. As noted in the official comments to Section 9–602:

> our legal system traditionally has looked with suspicion on agreements that limit the debtor's rights and free the secured party of its duties. As stated in former Section 9–501, Comment 4, "no mortgage clause has ever been allowed to clog the equity of redemption." The context of default offers great opportunity for overreaching. The suspicious attitudes of the courts have been grounded in common sense. This section, like former Section 9–501(3), codifies this long-standing and deeply rooted attitude. The specified rights of the debtor and duties of the secured party may not be waived or varied except as stated.

Cmt. 2, UCC § 9–602.

This wariness has been, for the most part, reflected in academic commentary on this subject. *See, e.g.,* Barkley Clark, *Default, Repossession, Foreclosure and Deficiency: A Journey to the Underworld And a Proposed Salvation,* 51 ORE. L. REV. 302, 303 (1972) (noting that a consumer "is as likely to read (let alone understand) [a security agreement] as he is to run windsprints in Red Square"); Michael M. Greenfield, *The Role of Assent in Article 2 and Article 9,* 75 WASH. U.L.Q. 289, 300 (1997) (arguing that a consumer's waiver of a statutory right at the time of contract formation "is highly suspect" and that the "small-print boilerplate" language of the waiver makes a consumer's assent "a fiction").

b. Violations of Part 6 of Nevada's Article 9

If enforced as written, the pawn ticket forfeiture provisions would not only have waived and varied, but they would have effectively obliterated, Ms. Schwalb's right to prohibit Pioneer's strict foreclosure of her interest in the vehicles, as well as her right to redeem the vehicles after default and repossession. NEV. REV. STAT. §§ 104.9602.10; 104.9602.11. But under Section 9–602, these rights may not be waived or varied by private agreement. The result of this clash is that, in accordance with the prevailing law under Article 9 cited above, the pawn tickets will have to be enforced without reference to their forfeiture provisions.

What effect does that erasure have? Initially, it makes Article 9's default standards, rather than the pawn tickets' forfeiture provisions, applicable to Pioneer's action in attempting to dispose of the vehicles. Given the parties prepetition dealings, this legal conclusion has bite, as will be seen later. *See* Section IV.B.2, *infra.* But for the present analysis, it means that Pioneer was obligated to proceed as to the vehicles in the manner required by Part 6 of Article 9. This it did not do. Because violations of Part 6 take on a significant role later in this opinion, it is appropriate to catalog the more egregious of Pioneer's violations.

The cornerstone duty placed on every secured party is the obligation to proceed in a commercially reasonable manner. Article 9 expresses this by requiring that "[e]very aspect of a disposition of collateral, including the method, manner, time, place and other terms, must be commercially reasonable." NEV. REV. STAT. § 104.9610.2.

Although proceeding by judicial action may be commercially reasonable in some case, the manner in which Pioneer proceeded here was not. It sought judicial vindication as the sole owner of the vehicles, a status it claimed through operation of the forfeiture clause in its pawn ticket. Such forfeitures are authorized in some circumstances, and are referred to as "strict foreclosures." *See* NEV. REV. STAT. § 104.9620.

But a secured party's ability to engage in a strict foreclosure with respect to a consumer is heavily circumscribed. In particular, a secured creditor may not strictly foreclose on consumer goods without the consumer's consent, NEV. REV. STAT. § 104.9620.1(a), and may not strictly foreclose on any collateral that it does not possess, *id.* § 104.9620.1(c). Neither of these conditions is present here, thus making Pioneer's attempts to strictly foreclose on the vehicles violations of Part 6 of Nevada's Article 9.

In addition, when Pioneer proceeded in state court as if the vehicles were its sole property, Pioneer violated its duty to give Ms. Schwalb the option to force a public disposition, and deprived her of the opportunity to redeem. NEV. REV. STAT. §§ 104.9602.10; 104.9602.11. Proceeding in this contrary-to-law manner was perforce not commercially reasonable.

There were other violations. Article 9 is explicit that a secured party must notify a debtor before any disposition, NEV. REV.STAT. § 104.9611.2, and is explicit on what that notice must contain. *Id.* § 104.9613.1. But Pioneer could not produce any notice that it sent to Ms. Schwalb, and she could not locate any notice she received from Pioneer. The parties, however, stipulated that Pioneer generally sends a notice to its borrowers on a standard form, and that they had no reason to believe that Pioneer did not send a notice on this standard form to Ms. Schwalb. Pioneer then produced an exemplar of that standard form. While the form appears to contain many of the required disclosures, it does not contain all of the required provisions. In particular, the notice violates NEV. REV. STAT. § 104.9612.1(d), which requires that any notice contain a statement that "the debtor is entitled to an accounting of the unpaid indebtedness and states the charge, if any, for an accounting."

Pioneer omitted this required disclosure, of course, because of Pioneer's belief in the validity of its forfeiture provisions, which did not mention any accounting. Pioneer's erroneous belief, even if in good faith, does not save it; there is no good faith defense to the failure to provide sufficient notice of a proposed disposition. *See, e.g., Kruse v. Voyager Ins. Cos.,* 72 Ohio St.3d 192, 196–97, 648 N.E.2d 814, 817 (Ohio 1995) (failure to send notice to debtor was a violation of Article 9's notice provisions); *Wilmington Trust Co. v. Conner,* 415 A.2d 773, 776 (Del.1980) (failure to give credit for finance charges paid but unearned in notice of disposition was violation of Article 9's notice provisions).

c. *The Irrelevance of Non-Nevada Statutory Law*

Despite this analysis under applicable Nevada law, Pioneer asserts that some states would give full effect to the forfeiture provisions of its pawn ticket, and that these decisions provide a basis for this court to rule similarly. Courts in Alabama, Georgia and Tennessee, for example, have held that upon expiration of the traditional pawnbroker's redemption period, the debtor loses all interest in the car, and the pawnbroker becomes the absolute owner. *See, e.g., Geddes v. Mayhall Enters., LLC (In re Jones),* 304 B.R. 462 (Bankr.N.D.Ala.2003); *Bell v. Instant Car Title Loans (In re Bell),* 279 B.R. 890 (Bankr.N.D.Ga.2002); *Dunlap v. Cash Am. Pawn,* 158 B.R. 724 (M.D.Tenn.1993).

These decisions, however, turn on nonuniform provisions of the applicable states' motor vehicle or pawnbroker laws. In Alabama, for example, the applicable statute provides that "Pledged goods not redeemed within 30 days following the originally fixed maturity date shall be forfeited to the pawnbroker and absolute right, title, and interest in and to the goods shall vest in the pawnbroker." ALA. CODE § 5–19A–6. This section, unlike anything in the Nevada statutes, unambiguously divests debtors of all their property rights when the redemption period expires.

Similarly, the applicable Georgia statute provides that "[p]ledged goods not redeemed within the grace period shall be automatically forfeited to the pawnbroker by operation of this Code section, and any ownership interest of the pledgor or seller shall automatically be extinguished as regards the pledged item." GA. CODE ANN. § 44–14–403(b)(3). This also clearly divests the debtor of any interest at the end of the redemption period.

Finally, the Tennessee pawnbroking statutes state that if the statutory redemption period has run, the statutory notice requirements have been met, and the pawned goods are not redeemed, the debtor forfeits "all right, title and interest of, in and to the pledged goods and the debt becomes satisfied." TENN. CODE ANN. § 45–6–211(e). Again, this non-UCC statute terminates the debtor's interest in the goods pawned.

No Nevada statute, however, has similar provisions. Neither Chapter 646 on pawnbroking nor Chapter 482 on motor vehicles contains any provision that permits or mandates forfeiture if the debtor does not redeem within a stated period of time. In such a vacuum, the only applicable statute that enables Pioneer to divest Ms. Schwalb of her equity of redemption in the vehicles would be Article 9 of the UCC.

D. Summary

Pioneer entered into two transactions with Ms. Schwalb that were and are subject to Article 9 of the UCC. Pioneer believed that each transaction was a pawn of the vehicle, and thus thought that Article 9 did not apply. Both of these beliefs were mistaken. First, the transaction was not a traditional pawn of the vehicles. Throughout her case and this litigation, Ms. Schwalb has retained possession of the vehicles. Thus, the traditional basis of pawnbroking—possession of the collateral by the pawnbroker—is absent.

This absence also has significant consequences for Pioneer with respect to the applicability of Article 9. Although the court expresses no opinion on the applicability of Article 9 to traditional possessory pawns, the nonpossessory financing in this case does come within Article 9. Although Pioneer did not believe that Article 9 applies, the "substance over form" rules of Article 9 render that belief irrelevant.

Applying Article 9 to the parties' agreement—the pawn ticket—shows that some of its key provisions are unenforceable, and that Pioneer violated Article 9 in the manner in which it has proceeded in this matter. The impact of those violations will be explored later, but first the nature and amount of Pioneer's claim in bankruptcy must be established.

IV. Pioneer's Claims In Bankruptcy

A secured party's claim in bankruptcy differs from that claim under most nonbankruptcy law. In bankruptcy, a claim's status as secured turns not only on the contractual or other relations between the parties, but also on the relationship between the value of the collateral and the amount of the debt. Under Section 506(a): (i) a debt is fully secured if the value of the collateral exceeds the amount of the claim; (ii) a debt is unsecured notwithstanding a prepetition contractual grant of security if the collateral is worthless; that is, if its value is zero; and (iii) if the value of the collateral is greater than zero, but less than the amount of the secured party's debt, then the creditor has two claims: a secured claim equal to the collateral's value; and an unsecured claim for the difference between the amount of the claim and the collateral's value.

These standard rules are altered somewhat in this case, given Pioneer's strategy and the basic rules of chapter 13 administration.

A. No Unsecured Claim

As an initial matter, Pioneer concedes that, regardless of the collateral's value, it has no unsecured claim. It reaches this position both as a matter of principle, and as a matter of procedure. As a matter of principle, it argues that, given the forfeiture language in the pawn ticket, it is the owner of the vehicle and thus it is not a creditor. It accordingly contends that it holds no claim, be it secured or unsecured. As a matter of procedure, it followed up this contention by declining to file a proof of claim in this case. Thus, even if its status at the commencement of the case had been that of a partially secured creditor, it would be barred from participating as an unsecured creditor given its failure to file a proof of claim.

B. Secured Claims

Despite its refusal to file a proof of claim, Pioneer may still be treated as a secured creditor if that was its status at the time of bankruptcy filing. This is because of the nature of security. A security interest is an interest in property, and thus under the Fifth Amendment to the United States Constitution no act of Congress—the bankruptcy code or other legislation—can deprive a secured creditor of its property without due process.

In bankruptcy, this bedrock notion is often expressed by stating that a secured claim passes through bankruptcy unaffected absent some affirmative action to set it aside.

Since the court has determined that the pawn ticket's forfeiture provisions are unenforceable, that means that Ms. Schwalb is the owner of the vehicles and that, at best, Pioneer is a secured creditor. But to determine the extent of its secured claim, the court must determine the amount of the claim and the value of the collateral.

1. Allowed Amount of Claim

The initial principal amounts of the loans are easy to calculate. Pioneer lent $4,000 on the Infiniti, and $16,000 on the Cadillac. From that point, as Nevada has no generally applicable usury limits, prepetition interest ran at the rate of 120% on each loan until the filing date. As a consequence, as of filing, Pioneer's accrued interest claim on the Infiniti loan was $3,629.59, and its accrued interest claim on the Cadillac loan was $18,673.98. When added to the original principal amounts, Pioneer's total claim outside of bankruptcy, as of the petition date, was $42,303.57–$7,629.59 on the Infiniti loan, and $34,673.98 on the Cadillac loan.

The amount due on each of the loans exceeds the value of the collateral taken for those loans. As a result, Pioneer's secured claim, at least initially, is capped by the value of the vehicles as of the proposed effective date of the chapter 13 plan. 11 U.S.C. § 506(a).

2. Effect of Pioneer's Violation of Article 9 on Its Allowed Claim

At these levels of secured debt, Pioneer raises significant and serious questions of feasibility under 11 U.S.C. § 1325(a)(6). For example, if a 10% interest rate and a 36-month plan term are used, the monthly payment related to the Infiniti will be $243.72, and the payment related to the Cadillac will be $1,107.64 a month, for a monthly aggregate of $1,351.36. This amount exceeds the disposable income shown on Ms. Schwalb's plan. But, as indicated below, Pioneer's violations of Article 9 work significant reductions in its claim.

a. Statutory Recovery Under NEV. REV. STAT. § 104.9625

Under Article 9, there are significant consequences for failure to follow Article 9's provisions. Section 104.9625.2 provides that "a person is liable for damages in the amount of any loss caused by a failure to comply with this article." Ms. Schwalb offered to prove damages under this section, but did not introduce any evidence on this point.

Notwithstanding this failure of proof, Ms. Schwalb may still have a remedy for Pioneer's failure to comply with the enforcement provisions of Article 9. The record firmly establishes numerous instances of Pioneer's noncompliance with Part 6 of Article 9. *See* Section III.C.3.b, *supra.* When such noncompliance exists, Section 104.9625.3(b) provides as follows:

> If the collateral is consumer goods, a person that was a debtor . . . at the time a secured party failed to comply with this part may

> recover for that failure in any event an amount not less than the credit service charge plus 10 percent of the principal amount of the obligation . . .

As characterized by Barkley and Barbara Clark, leading commentators on Article 9:

> This sanction has been characterized as both a minimum civil penalty and a liquidated damages provision. Its appeal is that it requires no showing of actual loss. . . . This minimum civil penalty, quietly tucked away in a corner of the statute, is probably the most glittering nugget of consumer protection found in all of Article 9.

CLARK & CLARK, *supra,* at ¶ 4.12[4], at pp. 4–335 to 4–336; *see also* 10 ANDERSON, *supra,* at § 9–507:166 ("Even if the consumer debtor cannot prove the actual damages sustained by the noncomplying sale of the collateral, the consumer debtor may recover the statutory minimum damages."); *Davenport v. Chrysler Credit Corp.,* 818 S.W.2d 23 (Tenn.Ct.App.1991).

Does Section 9–625 apply in this case? Initially, it requires the collateral to be consumer goods. Article 9 defines these as goods held or used for "personal, family or household purposes." NEV. REV. STAT. § 104.9201.1(w). Ms. Schwalb testified that she used the vehicles to go to doctors, to run errands and to transport her daughter, and that her partner used them to go to work. This use qualifies as family, if not personal, use.

There is also no doubt that Pioneer, as a secured party, failed to comply with Part 6 of Article 9. *See* Part III.C.3.b *supra.* This noncompliance can form the basis of an award under Section 9–625. *Cf. Kruse v. Voyager Ins. Cos.,* 72 Ohio St.3d 192, 648 N.E.2d 814 (1995) (even if disposition of collateral is commercially reasonable, when collateral is consumer goods, debtor may recover under predecessor of Section 9–625 if secured party fails to provide debtor with reasonable notice of sale of collateral as required by UCC); *Erdmann v. Rants,* 442 N.W.2d 441 (N.D.1989) (award of statutory damages under predecessor of Section 9–625 when secured party failed to give notice, despite fact that sale was made in commercially reasonable manner); *Garza v. Brazos County Fed. Credit Union,* 603 S.W.2d 298 (Tex.Civ.App.1980) (though secured party made small error with respect to notice and debtor proved, noncompliance with notice requirements justified penalty under predecessor to Section 9–625).

Thus, the statutory minimum penalty of NEV. REV. STAT. § 104.9625.3 is applicable. That means that the "credit service charge[s]"—essentially all the paid and accrued interest here—are damages to which Ms. Schwalb is entitled. *See, e.g., Knights of Columbus Credit Union v. Stock,* 814 S.W.2d 427, 432 (Tex.App.1991); *Davenport v. Chrysler Credit Corp.,* 818 S.W.2d 23, 32 & n. 7 (Tenn.Ct.App.1991); 4 WHITE &

SUMMERS, *supra,* at § 34–14(c) ("We interpret that sentence to grant damages equal to the total interest charge (irrespective of the amount that has been paid) in addition to 10% of the original principal amount of the debt, irrespective of how much of the principal has been repaid."). *See also* ZINNECKER, *supra,* at 170–71.

For the two loans, there is $22,303.56 of "credit service charge[s]." These charges consist of accrued but unpaid interest on both loans as of the filing, and $1,600 in interest actually paid on the Infiniti loan. In addition, the statutory damages include 10% of the principal amount of each loan. These amounts would be $400 for the Infiniti and $1,600 for the Cadillac. When added together, the interest and principal components of the statutory damages equals $25,903.56.

This amount is calculated as follows:

Recoverable Item	Infiniti Loan	Cadillac Loan	Total
Unpaid credit service charge	$3,629.59	$18,673.97	$22,303.56
Paid credit service charge	$1,600.00		$1,600.00
10% Principal amount	$400.00	$1,600.00	$2,000.00
Totals:	$5,629.59	$20,273.97	$25,903.56

b. Offset Against Allowed Claim

There are two possible outcomes of the conclusion that Ms. Schwalb is entitled to a statutory remedy under NEV. REV. STAT. § 104.9625.3. The first is that the violation leads to an independent damages claim, which in turn would not affect the allowed amount of Pioneer's claims. Instead, the violation would give rise to the conclusion that Pioneer must pay damages to Ms. Schwalb's chapter 13 estate for distribution to her creditors. The second outcome would be that the amount of the statutory penalty would be applied to reduce Pioneer's allowed claims. In other words, the second method would allow Ms. Schwalb to recoup the amount of the statutory penalty against Pioneer's claim, reducing the amounts she would have to pay to Pioneer under the plan.

Here, recoupment is appropriate. The statutory penalty arises out of the same transactions and occurrences that gave rise to Pioneer's claims for money lent. As a result, an assertion that a penalty is appropriate under Section 9–625(b) would have to be joined as a compulsory counterclaim in any litigation regarding the repayment or collection of Pioneer's loan claims. The consequence of this conclusion is that, inasmuch as "[t]he provisions of a confirmed plan bind the debtor and each creditor," 11 U.S.C.

§ 1327(a), all issues under Section 9–625(b) would have had to have been raised at confirmation. Otherwise Ms. Schwalb would have possibly lost her ability to later raise the issue.

A reduction of Pioneer's claims by the amount of the statutory penalty adjusts and sets the amount owed by Ms. Schwalb. Unless reserved for another time, this reduction should thus be part of the confirmation process, the purpose of which is to adjust the various claims and counterclaims necessary to arrive at the final allowed amount of a creditor's claim. *Cf.* ZINNECKER, *supra,* at 175 (1999) ("To best advance the restoration goal of damage awards, revised § 9–625(d) should be interpreted in a manner that prohibits recovery of actual damages only *to the extent that* (rather than *if*) the deficiency is reduced or eliminated.") (emphasis in original).

* * *

When these damages are recouped against Pioneer's claim, that leaves Pioneer with a claim of $2,000 on the Infiniti loan, and a claim of $14,600 on the Cadillac loan.

3. Determination of Secured Claim—Valuation of Collateral

Are these claims secured? A secured claim in bankruptcy is defined by the value of its collateral. 11 U.S.C. § 506(a). It thus makes sense to begin with the value of the two vehicles in determining whether Pioneer's claims are secured. Valuation of motor vehicles under Section 1325(a)(5)(B) is governed by *Associates Commercial Corp. v. Rash,* 520 U.S. 953, 117 S.Ct. 1879, 138 L.Ed.2d 148 (1997).

Under *Rash,* the relevant valuation analysis under Section 1325(a)(5)(B) is what it would cost to replace the two vehicles. *Rash* defined replacement value as what a willing buyer would pay a willing seller to obtain a car in the same condition as each of the two vehicles at issue here. *Rash,* 520 U.S. at 959 at n. 2, 117 S.Ct. 1879. *See also Mulvania v. IRS (In re Mulvania),* 214 B.R. 1, 9–10 (9th Cir. BAP 1997); *In re Marquez,* 270 B.R. 761, 765–66 (Bankr.D.Ariz.2001). In short, Ms. Schwalb's plan must pay, over time, an amount equal to the present value of the replacement cost of each vehicle.

a. Evidence

Ms. Schwalb initially contends that the value of the collateral should be limited to the amounts lent against each vehicle. She attempts to justify this position by arguing that Pioneer's economic decisions to lend $4,000 against the Infiniti and $16,000 against the Cadillac establish those amounts as the vehicles' value for this proceeding.

The argument is risible. There was no evidence that Pioneer lent 100% of the vehicles' value, and certainly no evidence establishing that these low values were the two vehicles' replacement values. Indeed, the evidence was that Pioneer's normal practice was to lend approximately 30% of the value of vehicles. This would put, at least as of the time of the loans, the range of replacement values at around $13,333 for the Infiniti and $53,333 for the Cadillac.

Of more weight is Ms. Schwalb's own estimation of values at trial of about $6,000 for the Infiniti and $25,000 for the Cadillac. Indeed, on Ms. Schwalb's schedules filed in this case, which speak as of her petition date, she stated under penalty of perjury that, at the time of filing, the Infiniti was worth $6,500, and the Cadillac was worth $30,000.

b. Timing

Each of these estimates has its own strengths and weaknesses, but in the end they present one problem—they value the collateral at different dates. This variance is, unfortunately, reflected by the cases on valuation. Some cases value as of the petition date, *e.g., Chase Manhattan Bank v. Stembridge* (*In re Stembridge*), 394 F.3d 383, 387 (5th Cir.2004); others value the property as of the date of the trial or hearing at which valuation is an issue, *e.g., Winston v. Chrysler Fin. Corp.* (*In re Winston*), 236 B.R. 167, 171 (Bankr.E.D.Pa.1999); still others pick the effective date of the plan, and provide adequate protection under Section 361 to the secured creditor for any gap between filing and the effective date, *e.g., In re Farmer*, 257 B.R. 556, 560–61 (Bankr.D.Mont.2000); *In re Davis*, 215 B.R. 824, 825–26 (Bankr.N.D.Tex.1997). *See also* LUNDIN, *supra,* at § 107.1, at p. 107–1 (3d ed. 2002 & Supp.2004) ("There is little agreement in the reported cases on the date for fixing the value of collateral in chapter 13 cases.").

Fortunately, this court need not decide this issue. In each case, the allowed amount of Pioneer's claim, as set forth above, is less than either valuation. So each claim is fully secured; the claim secured by the Infiniti is an allowed claim for $2,000, and the claim secured by the Cadillac is a secured claim for $14,600.

V. Effect of Debtor's Plan

As indicated above, Ms. Schwalb proposes to "cramdown" Pioneer's claim over 36 months at a 10% rate of interest. She contends that this treatment complies with 11 U.S.C. § 1325(a)(5)(B) in that the stream of payments will return to Pioneer the present value of its claim as of the effective date.

A. Treatment of Secured Claim

Section 1325(a)(5)(B) requires that a chapter 13 plan pay to a secured creditor the present value of its claim; that is the import of requiring the amount to be valued "as of the effective date" of the plan. This is typically done by paying the secured creditor's claim over the life of the plan—in this case 36 months—with a market rate of interest. Here, Ms. Schwalb has proposed 10% interest, and Pioneer has not objected. As a result, the amount of Pioneer's allowed secured claims is known—$2,000 and $14,600—as is the rate at which the payment stream will be discounted—10%. When calculated for debtor's 36-month plan, these factors yield a $63.89 monthly payment for the Infiniti loan, and a $466.39 monthly payment for the Cadillac loan, for a total of $530.28 per month.

B. Feasibility

Pioneer contends that Ms. Schwalb's necessary reliance on her father's donations renders her plan infeasible. Pioneer cites to cases such as *In re Crowder*, 179 B.R. 571 (Bankr.E.D.Ark.1995) and *In re Porter*, 276 B.R. 32, 38 (Bankr.D.Mass.2002) for the proposition that voluntary contributions by relatives are never sufficient to establish Section 1325(a)(6)'s requirement that, to confirm a plan, the court must find that "the debtor will be able to make all payments under the plan . . . ."

Although reliance on donations is heavily disfavored, neither *Crowder* nor *Porter* constitute categorical bars against the use of donations from relatives. In *Crowder,* the court was unconvinced of the stability and long-term willingness of the debtor's father to fund the plan. As Judge Scott stated, "There was no affirmation by [the father] as to any specific amount to be provided or that any specific assistance would continue for the duration of the plan. Indeed, he stated that he was not prepared 'right now' to render assistance other than that currently being provided." 179 B.R. at 574. In *Porter,* the court noted that there was no "evidence of regular contributions having been made in the past." 276 B.R. at 38.

But in the present case, Ms. Schwalb's father testified convincingly that he would pay whatever it took to confirm the plan and make all plan payments, indicating that he would be willing to sign a contract obligating him to make these payments. He has a long and undisputed history of providing for his daughter; indeed, he gave her the vehicles that form the basis of this lawsuit, and he has provided for her necessary well-being for many years.

The sufficiency of Mr. Schwalb's undertaking was under some stress when Pioneer's secured claim appeared to be in excess of $45,000. As reduced, however, there is no serious contention that he is unable to make the necessary payments; indeed, he has been making payments since the case was filed, and this history of commitment, together with his even longer commitment to his daughter's financial well-being, is sufficient to find that all payments under the plan will be made and that Section 1325(a)(6) has been satisfied.

VI. CONCLUSION

Article 9 governs this case. As a result, Pioneer loses on its ownership claims as to the two vehicles. In addition, the application of Article 9 means that all Pioneer has by way of a property interest in the vehicles is a perfected security interest. This application of Article 9, however, also has a second, and similarly adverse, consequence: because of Pioneer's violations of Article 9, Pioneer's claim against Ms. Schwalb will be significantly reduced.

Cramdown of Pioneer's claims, as reduced, is feasible for Ms. Schwalb as assisted by her father. As the ownership issues and the feasibility issues were the only issues seriously contested by the parties, Ms. Schwalb must amend her plan consistent with this opinion, and when so amended the court will confirm it. * * *

RENT-TO-OWN TRANSACTIONS

The following two cases deal with "rent-to-own" contracts. As you will see, the debtors in these cases are arguing that the transactions should be treated as secured loans (namely, that the "rental" company is in fact a purchase money seller of goods and that structuring the contract as a "lease" is merely a façade for what is truly a secured loan). It may not be clear to you why it makes a difference in these cases. Presumably each of these would be an automatically perfected secured loan (as a purchase money security interest in consumer goods), thus the issue cannot be whether the lessor is to be treated as a perfected secured creditor or an unperfected or unsecured creditor.

The fighting issue is usury law. In most states the amount of interest a creditor can charge to an individual debtor is limited by its usury prohibitions. These laws are widely variable and a few states have none at all. In most cases they do not apply to corporate debtors or to business loans. A rent-to-own contract will invariably violate most usury laws, if those laws apply. One needs to do a little gymnastics to produce an "interest rate" on a contract that was never written as a loan. In these cases the debtor will argue that all amounts required or authorized to be paid under the "lease" above the lessor's cost plus a small profit should be treated as interest; this imputed interest will be a large number (often 50 or 100 percent of the price per year) and the contract will thus be in violation of a usury law that might limit interest to 20 or even 30 percent. The following cases are nice illustrations of various courts' approaches to the argument that rent-to-own contracts are loans. Think about how you would represent the lessees (debtors) or the lessors (creditors) in these cases. What policies support the arguments of the lessor (creditor) and what policies support the arguments of the lessee (debtor)?

SILVA V. RENT-A-CENTER, INC.

Supreme Judicial Court of Massachusetts, 2009.
454 Mass. 667.

MARSHALL, C.J.:

From children's musical instruments, dormitory refrigerators, furniture used to stage prospective homes, to seasonal sporting equipment, televisions, and other consumer goods, the modern economy offers consumers diverse opportunities for leasing a variety of products. See Rohner, Leasing Consumer Goods: The Spotlight Shifts to the Uniform Consumer Leases Act, 35 Conn. L. Rev. 647, 649 (2003). A judge of the United States District Court for the District of Massachusetts, considering a "consumer lease agreement" for computer equipment, concluded that "[n]o authorities convincingly 'show how the highest court in the state would decide' " which of two statutory schemes regulate that type of arrangement, and certified the following question to this court pursuant to S.J.C. Rule 1:03, as appearing in 382 Mass. 700 (1981):

> "Is a contract in the form of Exhibit A, entered into within the [Commonwealth] of Massachusetts, subject to the terms of the Massachusetts Consumer Lease Act, [G.L. c. 93, §§ 90] et seq., or the Massachusetts Retail Installment Sales Act, [G.L. c. 255D]?"

On the scant facts in the record before us, we cannot answer the question definitively. Cf. S.J.C. Rule 1:03, § 3(2) (requiring "statement of all facts relevant to the questions certified and showing fully the nature of the controversy in which the questions arose"). Nonetheless, the bare legal issue concerns a significant point of Massachusetts law on which we will offer what guidance is possible on this record. * * *

The certified question concerns a specific contractual form. On these facts, we can and do conclude that the Massachusetts Retail Installment Sales Act (RISA), G.L. c. 255D, does not apply to it. Further, if we assume defendants Rent-A-Center, Inc.; Rent-A-Center East, Inc.; and RentWay, Inc. (collectively, "Rent-A-Center," "RAC," or defendants), regularly are engaged in the business of leasing personal property, G.L. c. 93, § 90, and that the computer equipment was intended "primarily for personal, family, or household purposes," *id.,* factual questions that are not resolved on the record before us, we conclude that the agreement would be subject to the Consumer Lease Act (CLA), G.L. c. 93, §§ 90–92.

1. *Discussion.* The parties stipulated to the following facts: "On or about May 13, 2006, Jaaziel Costa entered into an agreement with Rent-A-Center . . . at its Worcester, Massachusetts store," it was "drafted by RAC," and it "concerned a used Dell laptop computer." The agreement, entitled a "Consumer Lease Agreement," specifies a weekly "rental term," with a total payment of $39.49, consisting of a "rental payment" of $34.99, an "optional liability damage waiver" of $2.62, and tax of $1.88." It provides that, at the

end of the rental term (here weekly), Costa may either (1) continue to rent the property by making another rental payment; or (2) terminate the lease by returning "the rental property and pay[ing] all rental payments and other charges due through the date of return." The agreement further states that RAC is "responsible for maintaining or servicing the property while it is being leased," and that it "retain[s] title to the property at all times and will pay any taxes which might be levied on the property." Under the agreement, Costa is "not obligated to renew this lease and may terminate it at any time without penalty and with no further obligation. To do so, you must return the rental property and pay all rental payments and other charges due through the date of return." The agreement further specifies that Costa may "choose to acquire ownership" by "rent[ing] the property for the [specified] number of weeks" shown in the contract. According to the agreement, "You do not own the property," and "[y]ou will not own the property until you have made the total payment necessary to acquire ownership." In addition, Costa has the "right to exercise an early purchase option. If you wish to purchase the rental property you may do so at any time by the payment of 55% of the remaining Total of Payments calculated at that time." Finally, the agreement specifies that Costa may not "sell, mortgage, pawn, pledge, encumber, hock or dispose of" the property, and that the agreement has been pledged to the lessor's bank as collateral security.

* * *

a. *Retail Instalment* [sic] *Sales Act.* Enacted in 1966, RISA regulates retail installment sales contracts. See Wilkins, The New Massachusetts Retail Installment Sales Act, 51 Mass. L.Q. 205, 207 (1966). The plaintiffs in this case contend that "rent-to-own" agreements, like the agreement executed by Costa, effectively are retail installment agreements subject to RISA that have been mischaracterized by the defendants as leases. The agreement before us, however, does not satisfy the statutory definition. RISA initially defined a "[r]etail installment sale agreement" as follows:

> "[A]n agreement, other than a revolving credit agreement or an agreement reflecting a sale made pursuant thereto, entered into in this commonwealth, involving a *finance charge* and providing for the *sale of goods* or the rendering of services or both *for a specified amount* which the buyer undertakes to pay in more than one payment subsequent to the making of the agreement. A retail installment sale agreement shall not include an agreement which provides (*a*) for the payment of the time sale price in not more than three monthly installments and (*b*) a finance charge not in excess of one dollar and (*c*) no collateral security for the seller." (Emphasis added.)

St.1966, c. 284, § 1. Under that original definition, a bona fide lease terminable at the option of the consumer, such as Costa's agreement, would not qualify as an "installment sale agreement." Among other things, no calculable "finance charge" is involved. A "finance charge" was defined as an amount exceeding the "cash sale price" of the goods and any insurance or "official fees." *Id.* See McCormack, Jr., Consumer Protection, 1968 Ann. Survey Mass. L. 129, 132 (RISA likely inapplicable to "bona fide" leases because such leases do not involve finance charges). The Legislature amended the statute in 1971, amplifying the definition of "retail installment sale agreement" to include agreements nominally in the form of a bailment or lease:

> "[A]n agreement, other than a revolving credit agreement or an agreement reflecting a sale made pursuant thereto, signed by the buyer in this commonwealth, involving a finance charge and providing for the sale of goods or the rendering of services or both for a specified amount which the buyer undertakes to pay in more than one payment subsequent to the making of the agreement, or not involving a finance charge and providing for the sale of goods or the rendering of services or both for a specific amount which the buyer undertakes to pay in five or more installments subsequent to the making of the agreement. *'Retail installment sale agreement' shall also include any contract in the form of a bailment or lease if the bailee or lessee contracts to pay as compensation for use a sum substantially equivalent to or in excess of the value of the goods involved and it is agreed that the bailee or lessee will become, or for no other or for a nominal consideration has the option to become the owner of the goods upon full compliance with his obligations under the contract.* A retail installment sales agreement shall not include an agreement which provides (*a*) for the payment of the deferred payment price in not more than three monthly installments and (*b*) a finance charge not in excess of one dollar and (*c*) no collateral security for the seller." (Emphasis added.)

St.1971, c. 341, § 1. Although the statute has since been amended, the language concerning contracts in the form of a lease or bailment has remained substantively unchanged. See G.L. c. 255D, § 1. The statute thus recognizes that leases may be characterized as installment sales only if specific requirements are satisfied.

Under RISA's definition, Costa's rent-to-own agreement is not an "installment sale agreement." Not only does Costa's agreement not *require* (as opposed to permit) him to pay a "sum substantially equivalent to or in excess of the value of the goods involved," G.L. c. 255D, § 1, but "upon full compliance with his obligations under the contract" for the original term, it does not permit him to become the owner for a "nominal consideration."

Id. Moreover, the agreement does not obligate Costa to pay "a specified amount which the buyer undertakes to pay in more than one payment." G.L. c. 255D, § 1. Costa is obliged to make no payment other than the first weekly payment, and there is no "contract[ ] to pay" a sum substantially equivalent to the value of the item. *Id.* In essence, Costa's contract is a one-week rental contract with multiple options to renew. See *Crumley v. Berry*, 298 Ark. 112, 115, 766 S.W.2d 7 (1989) (in considering whether rent-to-own contract is disguised conditional sale, analysis focuses first on whether there is "obligation to pay the equivalent of the purchase price").

In this case, the absence of any obligation on the part of Costa to pay a sum substantially equivalent to the value of the leased computer is decisive. In *Crumley v. Berry, supra*, for example, the Supreme Court of Arkansas considered whether, under the Arkansas retail installment sale act, a "rent-to-own" contract was a bona fide lease, or a disguised sale. In concluding that the transaction was a lease, the court noted that the lease was "[w]ithout any requirement to pay throughout the contract" and that the lessee had the "corresponding right to terminate the contract at any time." *Id.* at 117, 766 S.W.2d 7. Other jurisdictions, construing similar legislation and similar rent-to-own leases, are in accord. See, e.g., *Givens v. Rent-A-Center, Inc.*, 720 F.Supp. 160 (S.D.Ala.1988); *Hawkes Television, Inc. v. Maine Bur. of Consumer Credit Protection*, 462 A.2d 1167 (Me.1983); *State v. Action TV Rentals, Inc.*, 297 Md. 531, 533, 467 A.2d 1000 (Ct.App. 1983) (rent-to-own contract did not satisfy Maryland's RISA statute because lessee did not make "enforceable promise" to pay an amount at least substantially equivalent to value of goods); *Griffin v. Rent-A-Center, Inc.*, 843 A.2d 393 (Pa.Super.Ct.2004).

It may be that if a consumer exercises his or her right to renew a consumer lease multiple times, the lease payments eventually will exceed the value of the item. But application of a regulatory framework does not depend on the economics of hindsight. We look, instead, to the nature of the contract at the time it was formed, focusing on the parties' contractual rights and obligations at that point. See 4 J.J. White & R.S. Summers, Uniform Commercial Code § 30–3, at 19 (5th ed. 2002) ("Even though certain events or facts that determine the economic consequences of the deal have occurred or exist only at the conclusion of the lease, the agreement is either a lease or a security agreement from the beginning"). In short, because Costa's contract did not require payments totaling an amount substantially equivalent to the value of the leased item, the mere possibility of a nominal purchase option if he undertook multiple renewals of the lease term did not make the transaction an installment sale within the meaning of RISA. See H.J. Alperin & R.F. Chase, Consumer Law § 8.22, at 28–29 (2d ed. 2001) ("It is clear that contracts in the form of a bailment or lease are not credit sales if the consumer has the right to terminate the arrangement at any time without penalty. This excludes [from RISA] rental-purchase or 'rent to own' agreements, under which the consumer ostensibly rents personal property for a minimum one-week or one-month period but has the option of acquiring title to the property by continuing the rental for a specified number of successive periods").

This construction of RISA is consistent with similar language contained in its Federal counterpart, the Federal Truth-in-Lending Act, 15 U.S.C. §§ 1601 et seq (2006). The Truth-in-Lending Act defines a "credit sale" as:

> "[A]ny contract in the form of a bailment or lease if the bailee or lessee contracts to pay as compensation for use a sum substantially equivalent to or in excess of the aggregate value of the property and services involved and it is agreed that the bailee or lessee will become, or for no other or a nominal consideration has the option to become, the owner of the property upon full compliance with his obligations under the contract."

Id. at § 1602(g). Regulation Z, 12 C.F.R. § 226.2(a)(16) (2009), further explains that a credit sale includes certain leases, but not those "terminable without penalty at any time by the consumer." Because Costa's rent-to-own agreement permitted him to terminate it at any time without penalty, it was not a "credit sale" within the meaning of the Federal Truth-in-Lending Act, and it similarly does not involve an "extension of credit" under RISA. See G.L. c. 255D, § 1 (defining "[f]inance charge" as "the cost of credit determined in accordance with the provisions of" G.L. c. 140D); 209 Code Mass. Regs. § 32.02(1) (2002) (defining "[c]redit sale" to exclude a lease "terminable without penalty at any time by the consumer"); H.J. Alperin & R.F. Chase, Consumer Law, *supra* at § 13.10. In similar regard, in a 1996 letter ruling, the Massachusetts division of banks stated that for a lease to be considered a retail installment sale agreement, it must "*require* payments substantially equivalent to or in excess of the value of the goods." LR 96–034 (Mar. 28, 1996) (entities entering into retail installment sales agreements with consumers exempt from licensing requirements of G.L. c. 255D). Under the agreement at issue, Costa was obliged to pay a "weekly" rental in advance of the rental term, but he neither incurred a debt, nor possessed a right to defer payment. RISA simply is not applicable.

Whether an agreement involves an extension of credit also is a significant factor in determining whether a retail installment sale contract constitutes a secured transaction. Where the lessor retains title to the goods, and not a bare security interest to secure performance of a credit obligation, and the lessee may terminate the agreement at will, the retail installment sales act is inapplicable. See 209 Code Mass. Regs. § 32.02 (defining "[c]redit" and "[s]ecurity interest"). As two commentators have noted:

> "A 'lease' terminable at the will of the lessee cannot be a security agreement. That is true even if the apparent lease term continues for the entire economic life or if there is a purchase option for nominal consideration at the end of the term. A prime example of this is the 'rent-to-own' agreement where a retailer leases a television or microwave to a consumer. The lease term is usually short—two weeks or one month—and the lease is renewed automatically unless the consumer returns the goods. The consumer may purchase the goods either by continuing payments for a certain period (such as 52 weeks) or by paying fair market value (usually computed on a sliding scale, such as 60% of all remaining payments). . . . A sale and security agreement cannot be found when the consumer has no obligation to pay the purchase price."

4 J.J. White & R.S. Summers, Uniform Commercial Code, *supra* at § 30–3, at 33–34. Federal bankruptcy courts repeatedly have rejected attempts to classify rent-to-own contracts either as secured transactions or installment sales, concluding that such transactions do not create security interests under the Uniform Commercial Code. See, e.g., *In re Parker*, 363 B.R. 769 (Bankr.D.S.C.2006); *In re Johnson*, 203 B.R. 498 (Bankr.S.D.Ga.1996). In sum, a transaction structured as a lease, terminable at the will of the lessee without penalty, is not equivalent to an installment sale contract.

b. *Consumer Lease Act.* Having concluded that RISA does not apply to Costa's rent-to-own agreement, we next consider whether CLA does. That statute defines a "[c]onsumer lease" as:

> "[A] contract in the form of a lease or bailment for the use of personal property by a natural person for a period of time of four months or less, and for a total contractual obligation not exceeding twenty-five thousand dollars, primarily for personal, family, or household purposes, whether or not the lessee has the option to purchase or otherwise become the owner of the property at the expiration of the lease, except that such term shall not include any of the following: . . . (5) a lease or agreement which constitutes a retail installment transaction as defined in section one of chapter two hundred and fifty-five D; . . . (7) any lease or rental of an item of personal property that is leased or rented for fewer than seven consecutive days, including all renewals and extensions of the lease or rental agreement."

G.L. c. 93, § 90. When the CLA legislation was introduced in 1986, few States had enacted legislation having specific application to the rent-to-own industry. See Ga.Code Ann. § 10–1–680 (2009); Mich. Comp. Laws Ann. § 445.951 (West 2002); S.C.Code Ann. § 37–2–701 (West 2002); Tex. Bus. & Com.Code Ann. § 35.71(f) (since repealed). The language of the

Massachusetts legislation clearly followed the model of the Federal Consumer Leasing Act of 1976, 15 U.S.C. §§ 1667–1667f (2006) (concerning personal property leases of more than four months). For example, it uses the phrase "consumer lease" contained in the Federal statute, rather than "rental-purchase," "lease-purchase," or "rent-to-own," terms that appear in later statutory enactments. * * * The CLA defines "[c]onsumer lease" to apply to leases "for a period of time of four months or less," precisely the period left unregulated by the Federal CLA. Compare G.L. c. 93, § 90, with 15 U.S.C. § 1667 (applying consumer leases "for a period of time exceeding four months").

It is possible that each of the elements of a "consumer lease," as that term is defined in the CLA, is present in the Costa contract, although the undisputed facts do not permit a definitive determination. The computer equipment may be "personal property"; the stated rental period is one week; and the contractual obligation does not exceed $25,000. On the record before us, however, we cannot determine whether the computer equipment was rented "primarily for personal, family, or household purposes."

Assuming those requirements are satisfied, we conclude that the "weekly" rental term of Costa's contract brings it within the regulatory scope of the CLA. The CLA requires that a lease term be for a period of four months or less. While a consumer may choose to renew an agreement for successive terms aggregating more than four months, that eventual choice does not preclude application of the CLA. The language of the statute indicates that the Legislature required consideration of such renewals and extension only in determining whether the statute applies to very short-term contracts—those for fewer than seven days—but not to the determination whether the maximum four-month period is exceeded. Compare G.L. c. 93, § 90(7) (CLA applies to leases or rentals of seven days or more "including all renewals and extensions of the lease or rental agreement"), with G.L. c. 93, § 90 (providing generally that CLA covers leases of four months or more, without mention of renewals or extensions). See H.J. Alperin & R.F. Chase, Consumer Law, *supra* at § 13:10, at 256 n. 8. The regulations promulgated by the Attorney General, 940 Code Mass. Regs. § 6.11 (1993) (lease and rent-to-own transactions), support this construction. Those regulations characterize rent-to-own transactions as leases "for any minimum period of less than four months" as subject to the CLA, and consider them differently from installment sales. * * *

The Federal Reserve Board (board) has analyzed the definition of "consumer lease" in the cognate Federal CLA, 15 U.S.C. § 1667(1), and its conclusions concerning calculation of a lease term are consistent with ours. The Federal statute begins where the Massachusetts statute ends: it applies only to consumer leases having a term of more than four months, see 12 C.F.R. § 213.2(e)(1) (2009) (Regulation M), while the Massachusetts statute applies to those with a term of four months or less. The board's official staff commentary to Regulation M states that a three-month lease, extended on a month-to-month basis, is not covered by the Federal CLA, because the Federal act applies only to leases with a term of "*more* than four months" (emphasis added). 12 C.F.R. § 213.2 Supp. I comment 2(e)–2 (2009). The commentary concludes that the federally required four-month minimum term is ascertained by looking at the initial term, without regard to successive renewals. *Id.* See H.J. Alperin & R.F. Chase, Consumer Law, *supra* at § 13.10 ("Federal requirement that the lease be for more than four months means that the initial term of the lease must be more than four months"). In other words, the Federal CLA does not apply to week-to-week, or month-to-month, agreements, even though such consumers have the right (but not the obligation) to extend such agreements to four months or more. See *In re Hanley*, 135 B.R. 311 (Bankr.C.D.Ill.1990); *Lemay v. Stroman's, Inc.*, 510 F.Supp. 921 (E.D.Ark.1981).

c. *Other jurisdictions.* Forty-seven States, including Massachusetts as well as Guam, Puerto Rico, and the District of Columbia, have enacted rent-to-own legislation. Only New Jersey, Wisconsin, and North Carolina have not. * * * Two of those three States, Wisconsin and New Jersey, have construed their retail installment sales statutes to apply to rent-to-own transactions. Because the Massachusetts CLA applies directly to such transactions, and mindful that "general statutory language must yield to that which is more specific," *Risk Mgt. Found. of the Harvard Med. Insts., Inc. v. Commissioner of Ins.*, 407 Mass. 498, 505, 554 N.E.2d 843 (1990), we conclude that the reasoning of the Wisconsin and New Jersey courts lend little assistance in interpreting our different statutory scheme, and only briefly address it.

The Wisconsin Consumer Act, Wis. Stat. § 421.301(9) (West 2005 & Supp.2008), contains a definition of "[c]redit sale" broader than the Massachusetts definition, because it considers the amounts a consumer actually "pays," rather than what he or she is obligated to pay. Wisconsin defines a "[c]redit sale" to include any "lease . . . if . . . the lessee *pays* or agrees to pay as compensation for use a sum substantially equivalent to or in excess of the aggregate value of the goods." Applying this definition, the United States District Court for the Eastern District of Wisconsin held that, by "expand[ing]" the definition of "credit sale," the Legislature intended the statute to apply to "two situations: where there is obligation and where the customer has made payments equal to the item's value." *Burney v. Thorn Americas, Inc., supra.* The Wisconsin statute, unlike the Massachusetts CLA, defines "[c]redit sale" to include transactions in which the consumer "*has made* payments" equal to the item's value, regardless whether the agreement imposed any obligation to do so. *Id.* at 767–769. The Massachusetts definition of "retail installment sale" has no comparable definition.

New Jersey, like Wisconsin, has no specific rent-to-own statute. The Supreme Court of New Jersey concluded, however, that rent-to-own transactions, while "not a perfect fit with the words" of the New Jersey Retail Installment Sales Act, are nonetheless subject to its requirements. *Perez v. Rent-A-Center, Inc.,* 186 N.J. 188, 208, 892 A. 2d 1255 (2006). The New Jersey statute defines "retail installment contract" as follows:

> "This term includes a security agreement, chattel mortgage, conditional sales contract, or other *similar instrument* in any contract for the bailment or leasing of goods by which the bailee or lessee agrees to pay as compensation a sum substantially equivalent to or in excess of the value of the goods, and by which it is agreed that the bailee or lessee is bound to become, or has the option of becoming, the owner of such goods upon full compliance with the terms of such retail installment contract" (emphasis added).

N.J. Stat. Ann. 17:16C–1(b) (West 2000). The court concluded that, "[b]y including conditional sales, chattel mortgages, security interests, leases, and similar instruments within RISA's protective ambit, the Legislature signaled that it intended to sweep into the Act as many cognate agreements as possible, even those that did not strictly fall within a denominated category." *Perez v. Rent-A-Center, Inc., supra* at 209, 892 A. 2d 1255. The Supreme Court of New Jersey made it clear that the *Perez* decision changed the law in New Jersey, making that decision prospective in application, except for the remand proceedings. *Perez v. Rent-A-Center, Inc.,* 188 N.J. 215, 902 A.2d 1232 (2006). The Massachusetts RISA statute does not include the words "or other similar instrument," and moreover, the Massachusetts CLA facially applies to such instruments. We decline to read into the RISA statute words or policy considerations that are not present.

2. *Conclusion.* The certified question concerns a specific rent-to-own agreement, executed by Jaaziel Costa. For the reasons stated, we answer the certified question by responding that a rent-to-own contract in the form of "Exhibit A" to the order of certification, entered into within the Commonwealth, is not subject to the Retail Instalment Sales Act, G.L. c. 255D. It may be subject to the terms of the Massachusetts Consumer Lease Act, G.L. c. 93, §§ 90–92, depending on the answers to unresolved factual questions outlined *supra.*

The Reporter of Decisions is to furnish attested copies of this opinion to the clerk of this court. The clerk, in turn, will transmit one copy under the seal of this court to the clerk of the United States District Court, District of Massachusetts, in answer to the questions certified, and will also transmit a copy to each party.

So ordered.

IRELAND, J. (concurring).

I write separately because, although I concur with the court's conclusion that the Retail Installment Sales Act, G.L. c. 255D, does not apply to the type of rent-to-own agreement at issue here and that, if the agreements involve renting items for personal, family, or household use, the Consumer Lease Act, G.L. c. 93, §§ 90–92(CLA), does apply, 454 Mass. at 669–670, 912 N.E.2d at 947–48, I want to emphasize that the CLA does not offer any type of protection for those consumers who ultimately purchase the merchandise they rent.

According to a study done by two researchers at the University of Massachusetts at Dartmouth and cited by the defendants, of those consumers who sign contracts to rent merchandise, such as the ones at issue here, over thirty-eight per cent result in an actual purchase either by renting for the term of the agreement or through an early purchase. Anderson, Rent-to-Own Agreements: Purchases or Rentals?, 20 J. Applied Bus. Res. 13, 15 (2004). Although this means that a majority of rental agreements are terminated before purchase, the study also found that agreements ending with the customer in possession of merchandise had eight times the duration time of those that ended in the return of merchandise, and that the median percentage of the total contract time that elapsed before an early purchase occurred was eighty-one per cent. *Id.* at 20. The interest rate paid by this not insignificant number of customers who ultimately purchase the rented merchandise is extremely high. For example, one of the named plaintiffs in this putative class action, Jaaziel Costa, falls near the median of total contract time that elapsed before purchase that was found by the University of Massachusetts study. Costa exercised an early purchase option after approximately sixty-four weeks of an eighty-two week contract (i.e., approximately seventy-eight per cent of his contract time). He ended up paying slightly less than one hundred per cent interest for a computer that was used when he first rented it.[2]

I am aware, as the defendants argue, that many rent-to-own customers use this type of agreement because they cannot get credit elsewhere. However, because of the way the agreements are structured, it is clear that those consumers who ultimately purchase the merchandise fall outside the CLA's statutory protection and can be subject to terms that the United States Department of Defense, as part of a 2006 report to Congress, called "predatory lending practices." See Report on Predatory Lending Practices Directed at Members of the Armed Forces and Their

---

[2] At the time Costa signed his agreement the purchase price of the used computer was listed as $1,434.59. The price he paid as an early purchaser was $2,718.34. The purchase price of an item that is listed in a rent-to-own agreement "most often is unrelated to fair market value. Consequently, the 'total cost to own' may be double the 'cash price' of the goods but effectively four times the true market value of the goods acquired." Drysdale, The Two-Tiered Consumer Financial Services Marketplace: The Fringe Banking System and Its Challenge to Current Thinking About the Role of Usury Laws in Today's Society, 51 S.C. L.Rev. 589, 615–616 & n. 148 (2000).

Dependents 19–20 (Aug. 9, 2006). I am hopeful that the Legislature will consider whether, as a matter of public policy, a balance might be struck between allowing businesses that provide these rent-to-own services to make a profit and offering protection to those customers who end up purchasing rented merchandise at extremely high interest rates.

[some footnotes omitted.]

MILLER V. COLORTYME, INC.

Supreme Court of Minnesota, 1994.
518 N.W.2d 544.

TOMLJANOVICH, JUSTICE:

We are asked to decide whether "rent-to-own" transactions (also known as "rental-purchase" transactions) are consumer credit sales under the Consumer Credit Sales Act, Minn. Stat. §§ 325G.15 and 325G.16 (1992), and if they are consumer credit sales, whether they are subject to the interest rate limitations of the general usury statute, Minn. Stat. § 334.01 (1992). The court of appeals held that rent-to-own agreements entered into by respondents are not consumer credit sales and are not usurious. We reverse and remand.

Respondent D.E.F. Investments, Inc. and its subsidiaries operate several rent-to-own dealerships in Minnesota. They do business under the trade name "Renter's Choice Home Furnishings." DEF uses standard form contracts to lease new and used furniture, televisions, appliances, and various other consumer goods to customers. Under these contracts, which are similar to others used in the rent-to-own industry, customers elect to rent items for a weekly or monthly rental term. At the end of each term, customers have a unilateral option to renew the agreement for another term. If a customer renews an agreement for a specified number of terms, the customer obtains title and ownership of the item rented for no additional consideration. Full payment of the rental fee must be made before or at the beginning of each term. In order to acquire ownership of an item, consumers ordinarily must pay a total price far in excess of fair market value. DEF does not offer consumer items for immediate sale.

Appellants Delilah Miller and Craig Stenzel both have entered into rent-to-own contracts with DEF over a period of several years. For example, on December 18, 1990, Miller entered into a rent-to-own transaction with DEF for a used washer and dryer, the stated cash price of which was $800.75. Under the contract, Miller could acquire ownership of the washer and dryer by making 16 monthly payments of $84.40, for a total of $1,350.40, or by making 69 weekly payments of $21.10, for a total of $1,455.90. As a further example, on October 17, 1990 Stenzel entered into a rent-to-own transaction with DEF for a 19" color television, the stated cash price of which was $470. Under the contract, Stenzel could acquire ownership of the television by making 18 monthly payments of $47.70, for a total of $858.60, or by making 78 weekly payments of $12.75, for a total of $994.50. Some of the contracts Miller and Stenzel have entered into have resulted in completed purchases; others have not.

On April 7, 1992 appellants Stenzel and Miller filed a class action lawsuit against DEF seeking monetary damages as well as declaratory and injunctive relief. In the relevant counts of appellants' complaint, appellants allege that DEF has violated various consumer protection statutes by failing to treat rent-to-own transactions as credit sales under the Consumer Credit Sales Act, and that DEF has engaged in usury in violation of Minn. Stat. § 334.01. On August 3, 1992, appellants moved for partial summary judgment, asking for a declaratory judgment that respondents' contracts constitute credit sales. On August 5, 1992, DEF moved for partial summary judgment, seeking dismissal of appellants' usury claim.

On November 30, 1992, the district court filed an order which granted appellants' motion for summary judgment and declared contracts entered by "Class One" to be "consumer credit sales for all purposes within the meaning of Minn. Stat. § 325G.15 and 325G.16." The court also denied DEF's motion for summary judgment and instead granted summary judgment for appellants on their usury claim, reserving the measure of damages for the fact finder.

After granting discretionary review, the court of appeals issued an opinion on August 3, 1993, reversing the district court. *Miller v. Colortyme, Inc.*, 504 N.W.2d 258 (Minn. App. 1993). The court of appeals held: (1) DEF's rent-to-own agreements are not "consumer credit sales" for all purposes within the meaning of Minn. Stat. §§ 325G.15 and 325G.16, and (2) DEF's agreements are not usurious under Minn. Stat. § 334.01. While not reaching the issue, the court of appeals further suggested that the Rental Purchase Agreements Act (RPAA), Minn. Stat. §§ 325F.84–.98, is in substantial conflict with the Consumer Credit Sales Act (CCSA), Minn. Stat. §§ 325G.15 and 325G.16, and that the provisions of the RPAA are controlling. This appeal followed.

I.

We consider first whether the CCSA defines rent-to-own agreements as consumer credit sales, thereby departing from the common law distinction between leases and sales in order to provide the same protections to consumers who engage in rent-to-own transactions as to consumers who engage in traditional credit sales. At common law a rent-to-own transaction is regarded as a lease and not a sale because a buyer is not bound to pay the total purchase price and can terminate a transaction at any time by returning the property. *See* Samuel Williston, *The Law Governing Sales of Goods at Common Law and Under the Uniform*

Sales Act, § 336 (1948). Prior to enactment of the CCSA this court followed the common law distinction. *Hughes v. Becker*, 260 Minn. 83, 87, 108 N.W.2d 781, 783 (1961).

The CCSA was originally enacted in 1971. In 1981 the legislature amended Minn. Stat. § 325G.15, subd. 5 of the CCSA to define certain terminable leases as a "sale of goods." Act of March 27, 1981, ch. 10, § 1, 1981 Minn. Laws 18–19. Under the amended version of Minn. Stat. § 325G.15, subd. 5, the term "sale of goods" includes:

> a contract in the form of a terminable bailment or lease of goods if: (a) the bailee or lessee has the option to renew the contract by making the payments specified in the contract; (b) the contract obligates the bailor or lessor to transfer ownership of the property to the bailee or lessee for no other or a nominal consideration upon full compliance by the bailee or lessee with the bailee's or lessee's obligations under the contract including any obligation incurred by reason of the exercise of an option by the bailee or lessee to renew the contract; and (c) the payments contracted for by the bailee or lessee, including those payments pursuant to the exercise of an option by the bailee or lessee to renew the contract, are substantially equivalent to or in excess of the aggregate value of the property and services involved.

It is undisputed that DEF's contracts satisfy each of the above criteria and therefore constitute a "sale of goods" within the meaning of Minn. Stat. § 325G.15, subd. 5. First, under DEF's contracts the lessee has the option to renew the contract by making advance rental payments at the beginning of each rental term. Second, the contracts obligate DEF to transfer ownership to the consumer if the consumer renews the agreement for a specified number of payments. Third, the total payments necessary to acquire ownership exceed the value of the property and services provided by respondents.

Given that rent-to-own contracts are "sales of goods" within the meaning of Minn. Stat. § 325G.15, subd. 5, the question is whether they are protected "consumer credit sales" within the meaning of Minn. Stat. § 325G.15, subd. 2. Under Minn. Stat. § 325G.15, subd. 2, a "consumer credit sale" is defined as:

> [A] sale of goods or services in which (a) credit is granted by a seller who regularly engages as a seller in credit transactions of the same kind; (b) the buyer is a natural person; and (c) the goods or services are purchased primarily for a personal, family or household purpose, and not for commercial, agricultural, or business purpose.

The court of appeals concluded that DEF's rent-to-own transactions are not protected "consumer credit sales." It reasoned that DEF does not grant credit to customers because customers prepay for use of leased goods with no further obligation. *Miller v. Colortyme*, 504 N.W.2d at 260.

We believe rent-to-own transactions are "consumer credit sales" within the meaning of Minn. Stat. § 325G.15, subd. 2. The object of all interpretation and construction of laws is to ascertain and effectuate the intention of the legislature. By defining certain terminable leases as "sales" within the CCSA, the legislature has made clear its intent to subject these terminable leases to the same consumer protection laws as ordinary credit sales. There is no conceivable reason why the legislature would amend Minn. Stat. § 325G.15, subd. 5 to define certain terminable leases as sales if it did not intend such leases to be protected "consumer credit sales" within the meaning of Minn. Stat. § 325G.15, subd. 2. The interpretation of the CCSA adopted by the court of appeals renders meaningless the language in Minn. Stat. § 325G.15, subd. 5 defining certain terminable leases as sales.

DEF argues that a seller cannot be deemed to have extended "credit" in the absence of a buyer who has incurred debt. The word "credit" can have different meanings in different statutes and we do not believe it is appropriate to apply a narrow definition of credit in this context. The manifest purpose of the Consumer Credit Sales Act is consumer protection. As a remedial statute, it is entitled to a liberal construction to promote, not frustrate, its objectives. *Governmental Research Bureau v. Borgen*, 224 Minn. 313, 28 N.W.2d 760 (1947). The legislature has specifically defined the transactions at issue as sales, despite their terminable nature. Sales are ordinarily regarded as "credit sales" where a buyer acquires possession but is allowed to defer full payment. *See* Black's Law Dictionary 369–70 (6th Ed. 1990). Accordingly, we hold that rent-to-own transactions are credit sales within the meaning of Minn. Stat. § 325G.15, subd. 2 because buyers of goods are not required to make full payment upon acquiring possession but are allowed to pay for goods sold over time.[2]

II.

Minn. Stat. § 325G.16, subd. 4 provides that "any lease or bailment of goods which constitutes a consumer credit sale shall be deemed to be a sale for all purposes." Because rent-to-own agreements are consumer credit sales for all purposes, they are subject to the same consumer protection laws as ordinary credit sales, including the general usury statute, Minn. Stat. § 334.01.[3] We must decide whether the district court erred in holding

---

[2] By defining rent-to-own transactions as "sales," the legislature recognized that the economic reality of these transactions is like that of ordinary credit sales, despite their terminable nature. As the consumer of a rent-to-own product continues making weekly or monthly payments under the contract, the pressure to keep making payments and to exercise the purchase option grows until it becomes the only feasible rational choice, given the alternative of completely forfeiting all past payments and returning the goods.

[3] The usury statute provides, in relevant part:

> The interest for any legal indebtedness shall be at the rate of $6 upon $100 for a year, unless a different rate is contracted for in writing. No person shall directly or indirectly take or receive in money, goods, or things in action, or in any other way, any greater sum,

that respondents' contracts are usurious as a matter of law and granting summary judgment for appellants.[4]

We have held that four elements must be proven to establish a violation of the usury law:

(1) a loan of money or forbearance of debt,

(2) an agreement between the parties that the principal shall be repayable absolutely,

(3) the exaction of a greater amount of interest or profit than is allowed by law, and

(4) the presence of an intention to evade the law at the inception of the transaction.

Citizen's Nat'l Bank of Willmar v. Taylor, 368 N.W.2d 913, 918 (Minn. 1985).[5]

DEF argues that its rent-to-own contracts are not usurious because they do not involve a forbearance of debt and do not impose an absolute obligation to repay a principal amount. In usury law, the term "forbearance" signifies the "contractual obligation of a lender or creditor to refrain, during a given period of time, from requiring the borrower or debtor to pay a loan or debt then due and payable." *Rathbun v. W. T. Grant Co.*, 300 Minn. 223, 233, 219 N.W.2d 641, 648 (1974). We agree with DEF that rent-to-own consumers technically do not incur any debt because they pay in advance for each rental period and are never obligated to renew an agreement. We also agree with DEF that a rent-to-own consumer technically has no absolute obligation to repay a principal amount. We disagree, however, that the first two common law elements of usury can be applied here to defeat appellants' usury claim where the legislature has defined rent-to-own transactions as "consumer credit sales" for all purposes.

The purpose of the usury law is to protect consumers by limiting the amount of interest which can be charged on a credit sale or loan. The first two common law elements of usury serve merely to clarify what transactions are subject to interest rate limitations. By defining

---

or any greater value, for the loan or forbearance of money, goods, or things in action, than $8 on $100 for one year.

4 There are several statutory exceptions to the general usury statute applying to specific types of credit transactions, but none of these exceptions are applicable to the rent-to-own agreements at issue. The rent-to-own contracts at issue also are not exempt from the usury statute under the judicially created time-price doctrine. This doctrine may apply where a seller fixes one price for cash and another price for credit. Respondents do not offer consumer items for immediate sale.

5 Minn. Stat. § 334.011, subd.2 (1992) provides that if a greater rate of interest than that allowed is charged then the entire interest due on that note, bill or other evidence of debt is forfeited. In addition, if the greater rate of interest has been paid, the person who paid it may recover in a civil action an amount equal to twice the amount of interest paid.

rent-to-own transactions in the CCSA as "consumer credit sales" for all purposes, the legislature has established that consumers who enter into rent-to-own transactions are to benefit from the same protections as consumers who purchase goods through ordinary installment sales, even though rent-to-own consumers do not actually incur any debt and do not have any obligation to repay a principal amount. Consequently, the first two common law elements of usury are met by operation of statute.

The legislature's decision to treat rent-to-own transactions as credit sales recognizes that although these transactions purport to be short-term leases, they operate in substance much like ordinary installment sales. Consumers who purchase goods though rent-to-own agreements may not incur debt, but they still implicitly pay interest in return for the ability to pay for goods over time. Moreover, rent-to-own customers may not have an absolute obligation to repay a principal amount, but their situation is analogous to that of ordinary buyers on credit in that they must either forfeit possession of a good or continue paying for it. * * *

In addressing the scope of the usury statute, we look through the form to the substance of a transaction. *Rathbun*, 300 Minn. at 235, 219 N.W.2d at 649. "There is no shift or device on the part of the lender to evade the [usury] law under or behind which the law will not look to ascertain the real nature and object of the transaction." *Adjustment Service Bureau, Inc. v. Buelow*, 196 Minn. 563, 567, 265 N.W. 659, 661 (1936).

Having determined that the first two elements of the common law usury test are met by operation of statute, we turn to whether the district court was correct in determining that respondents intentionally charged an excessive amount of interest. Under Minn. Stat. § 334.01, the interest for any legal indebtedness generally shall be no greater than six percent.[7] DEF acknowledges the large disparity between the cost of purchasing goods through its rent-to-own agreements and the value of the goods sold, but alleges that there is a factual issue with respect to whether it charged excessive interest, because the total value of goods and services (e.g., free delivery and maintenance) provided by DEF is disputed. We disagree. While there is some question as to the total value of services provided by DEF, DEF offered virtually no evidence to the district court as to the value of such services. Based on the record, we agree with the district court that no reasonable fact finder could conclude that the difference between the total payments required under the contracts and the value of the goods and services extended amounts to as little as six percent of the total payments. The district court properly concluded that DEF charged an excessive amount of interest as a matter of law.

[7] Section 334.01 permits an interest rate of eight percent if the rate is contracted for in writing.

DEF also argues that it did not have the requisite intent necessary to satisfy a usury claim because it acted in good faith and did not intend to violate the law. To be guilty of violating the usury law, a lender need only intend to charge a rate that is in fact usurious. It matters not whether the lender knows he is violating the usury law. *Citizen's Nat'l Bank of Willmar v. Taylor*, 368 N.W.2d at 919. DEF does not claim that it intended to collect less money than is stated on the contracts, and therefore, as a matter of law DEF had the requisite intent.

Because no genuine issue of material fact exists as to whether DEF intentionally charged an excessive rate of interest, the district court properly granted summary judgment for appellants on their usury claim.

III.

We finally consider DEF's argument that the Rental Purchase Agreement Act, Minn. Stat. §§ 325F.84–.98, has repealed the Consumer Credit Sales Act. The RPAA was enacted in 1990 and provides a number of protections to rent-to-own consumers. Among these, the RPAA provides for specified disclosures in the rent-to-own agreement, in advertising, and on in-store merchandise tags (sections 325F.86–.88); imposes restrictions and protections in the event of default (section 325F.89); provides for reinstatement rights to consumers (section 325F.90); limits delivery charges, security deposits and collection fees (section 325F.91); authorizes the commissioner of commerce to adopt rules governing cash price limits (section 325.91); prohibits identified abusive debt collection practices (section 325F.92); and provides for enforcement through both the Attorney General and a private right of action (section 325F.97).

The RPAA on its face does not purport to set up an exclusive system regulating rent-to-own contracts. Section 325F.85 of the RPAA specifically addresses the relationship between the RPAA and the CCSA, and provides:

> If the consumer protection provisions of sections 325F.84 to 325F.97 conflict with sections 325G.15 and 325G.16, sections 325F.84 to 325F.97 apply to a rental-purchase agreement and supersede sections 325G.15 and 325G.16.

Moreover, section 325F.97, subd. 2 of the RPAA provides that the remedies under the RPAA "are cumulative and shall not be construed as restricting any remedy that is otherwise available."

The RPAA's legislative history further indicates that the RPAA was not intended to repeal the CCSA. As originally proposed, the RPAA would have explicitly excluded applicability of the CCSA. Amendments, however, were subsequently adopted which deleted the provisions repealing the CCSA and which substituted the present language of section 325F.85.

* * *

We conclude that the RPAA does not repeal the CCSA; rather the remedies in the two statutes are cumulative. We reverse and remand to the district court for further proceedings.

[some footnotes omitted.]

PROBLEM 7-9

After the *Silva* case, Rent-A-Center asked you to represent them before a Massachusetts state legislative committee that is considering legislation which would make all rent-to-own contracts into security agreements and so (in their current form) in violation of the state's usury law. What arguments would you make?

CHAPTER 8

SECURITY IN STOCKS, BONDS, AND OTHER INVESTMENT PROPERTY

■ ■ ■

§ 1. INTRODUCTION

It is commonplace to borrow against stocks and bonds. Customers borrow from their brokers; brokers borrow from their banks. It is important to have an inexpensive and certain mode of creating a valid security interest in these types of investment property. Notwithstanding the importance of establishing a certain method, changes in the substantive practices of issuing and holding stocks and other securities have resulted in many changes in the way the UCC addressed this issue in the past several decades.

While rules regarding the creation and perfection of security interests in most forms of property are solely the realm of Article 9, important rules and definitions concerning stocks and bonds are also contained in Article 8: Investment Securities. Article 8 has been the subject of two major revisions, one in 1977 and the other in 1994.

Prior to the 1977 amendments, the classic security interest in stocks and bonds was created under Article 9 by the debtor giving the creditor possession of the certificates. This satisfied both the creation and perfection aspects of the security interest. The 1977 amendments, however, changed the law by excluding "certificated securities" from the scope of Article 9 and placing attachment, perfection, and enforceability of security interests in these securities within the scope of Article 8. Article 8 then defined the steps to create a valid security interest through a dizzying set of cross references.

Why was Article 8 modified in this way in 1977? The answer is a bit complex. In a sense, documentation of shares of stock have gone through one full cycle from being completely intangible, to having tangible form, and then back to intangibility. Historically, a shareholder's interest in a corporation was evidenced only by his name on the books of the corporation as the owner of a specific number of shares. Later on it became useful to have certificates that evidenced those shares, and the certificates could be passed back and forth among shareholders, creditors (as pledgees), and others. The certificates were treated as representing the ownership of the shares in the same way as a certificate of title represents ownership of a car or a note represents ownership of the right to payment on account of a debt.

As transactions multiplied and much of the transmission of data became electronic, people began to realize that certificates sometimes inhibited the effective transfer of rights and imposed significant costs on the trading system. In response, they experimented with ways to reduce the inefficiencies and costs of having tangible certificates. Among other things, it became common for a brokerage house customer to permit the brokerage house to keep all of the certificates representing the customer's shares of stock in the broker's name and for the customer to hold no certificates. This enabled the customer to direct the broker over the phone to make trades without having to go to the safety deposit box, get out the certificates, and assign them to the broker in each case. Because one may be able to protect computer memory better than certificates, theft losses may be minimized by keeping only electronic or written records of stock ownership and doing away with physical certificates. Accordingly, at the investor level the actual ownership of stock became more intangible.

This development presents the following question: how can one perfect a security interest in a share of stock that is not represented by a certificate or is represented by a certificate held in the name of a trustee or custodian? If it is merely represented by the shareholder's name on the books of a corporation, presumably the right is something like a general intangible, not an instrument as a certificated security would be. If it were a general intangible, perfection would call for a filing, yet those in the securities industry historically are not accustomed to searching UCC files, and thus such a method might seem inappropriate or at least disfavored.

With these concerns in mind, the 1977 Article 8 amendments created a system in which perfection was effected through the concept of "transfer." The acts necessary to effect "transfer" were complicated, and the nature of these acts depended upon whether there was a certificate outstanding, or whether or not the certificate was held by a financial intermediary. These changes did not deal effectively with the development of commercial practices. For example, the 1977 amendments assumed that changes in ownership would continue to be reflected through transfer of physical certificates or the registration on the books of the issuers, yet that is not how changes in ownership are actually reflected in the modern securities holding system.

Today, most of the outstanding shares of publicly traded companies are held by The Depository Trust Company ("DTC") as part of an elaborate system of financial intermediaries. DTC is a limited purpose trust organized to act as a depository of securities for the benefit of its participants, which include hundreds of broker-dealers and banks. DTC holds the actual securities in the name of its nominee (Cede & Co.) noted on the books and records of these publicly traded companies, and the participants (broker-dealers and banks) have accounts at DTC. Transfers can be accomplished by making adjustments to the participants' accounts at DTC. In turn, when an investor "purchases" a security through a brokerage firm, most firms maintain the investor's securities in "street name," meaning the name of the brokerage firm or its nominee. The investor is listed on the broker's records as the "beneficial owner" and receives account statements reflecting the investor's interest.

To make the securities transfer process even more efficient, adjustments to the participants' accounts at DTC are not made on a trade-by-trade basis, but rather at the end of the day on a "net" basis. Suppose, for example, that during the course of a particular day Smith Brokerage ("Smith") engages in several transactions with Jones Brokerage ("Jones") buying and selling between them various shares of XYZ Corp. for their customers. Suppose that, at the beginning of the day, Smith has 1,000 shares of XYZ Corp. in its DTC account, and Jones has 2,000 shares. At 10:30 am, Jones transfers 100 shares to Smith; at 11:00 am Smith transfers 500 shares to Jones; and at 1:00 pm Jones transfers 100 shares to Smith. At the end of the day, the net difference is that Jones is up 300 shares and Smith is down 200 shares. Their accounts can be adjusted accordingly in a single "netting" transaction at the end of the day. In the United States, this clearing and netting function is not performed by DTC, but by a separate corporate affiliate, the National Securities Clearance Corporation ("NSCC"). At the end of the day, NSCC computes the net "receive" and "deliver" obligations between the participants and instructs DTC to make the corresponding adjustments to their accounts.

Before DTC was formed, brokers physically exchanged certificates, employing armies of messengers and other staff to handle this form of trading. In the late 1960s, trading volumes skyrocketed, causing a transactional crisis that overwhelmed many firms. This led to the formation of DTC in 1973. Although it was once thought that inefficiencies in the certificated securities transfer system would lead to the eventual practice of issuing only uncertificated securities, this did not happen and instead we have the system of intermediaries described above. For the most part, only mutual funds issue uncertificated stocks.

Because of the various inadequacies of the 1977 amendments, Article 8 was again amended in 1994. The 1994 amendments primarily introduced greater flexibility to allow proper response and accommodation of changing securities industry practices. The amendments also included significant changes in the rules concerning security interests in investment property. The revision essentially returned to the pre-1977 structure, in which the rules on security interests are set out in Article 9, rather than Article 8. Moreover, the changes simplified substantially the creation and perfection of security interests in securities and other investment property, whether held directly or indirectly.

These new rules were included in pre-1999 Article 9 in a single provision, section 9–115, covering investment property. With the 1999 revisions, these rules were relocated to appropriate sections of Article 9. For example, attachment is defined within section 9–203 and priority within section 9–328. In addition, important rules and definitions are found in Article 8. The relevant rules are discussed below. For a fairly detailed discussion of the evolution of the treatment of investment property under Article 8, see Article 8, Prefatory Note.

§ 2. RULES UNDER ARTICLE 9

Attachment of a security interest is addressed in section 9–203 and essentially follows the same basic provisions of attachment for any other type of collateral, with one minor and expected addition. Under section 9–203(h), the attachment of a security interest in a "securities account" is also an attachment of a security interest in the "security entitlements" carried in the securities account. Given how securities are actually held and transferred, it is easy to see why this provision exists. The interest of most investors, for example, is a beneficial interest in the securities they have purchased, but do not actually hold. The securities reflected in an account are typically held by financial intermediaries. Note also the provisions of section 9–203(b)(3)(C) & (D). *See also* 9–206.

Article 9 provides alternative means of perfection for investment property and continues to recognize the general historic practice of perfection through possession of certificates. Section 9–313 permits perfection by "delivery" of a certificated security. *See* 9–313(a). Where the debtor has a certificate registered to him, giving possession to the creditor is "delivery." *See* 8–301. Of course, perfection by actual delivery of the certificates is not common.

Article 9 also provides that security interests in stocks and other investment property may be perfected by "control." The idea of control as a means of perfection first came to Article 9 via the 1994 revision to Article 8. With the 1999 revision to Article 9, the concept of control has been expanded beyond investment property to other forms of intangible interests, such as deposit accounts. Control is to intangibles as possession is to tangibles. Although many intangibles cannot be "possessed," some may be put under the "control" of a secured creditor to the exclusion of others, and this will put third parties on notice. Control in its various forms is defined in sections 9–104 (deposit accounts), 9–105 (electronic chattel paper), 9–106 (investment property), and 9–107 (letter-of-credit rights). For investment property, section 9–106 directs one to Article 8, particularly section 8–106, which in turn refers to sections 8–102, 8–301, and 8–508. Note that, although section 8–106 refers to a "purchaser" having control if certain steps are taken, under sections 1–201(a)(29) & (30), a purchaser includes a person who takes by a security interest.

Another significant change that accompanied the 1994 revision of Article 8 is that a security interest in stocks and other investment property may now also be perfected through filing. *See* 9–312(a). Under the priority rules set forth in section 9–328, however, a security interest perfected by filing is inferior to one perfected through delivery or control.

SOME DEFINITIONAL CLARIFICATION

We all recognize a bond or a share of stock, but "investment property" must be more than that, true? Section 9–102(a)(49) gives the following definition of investment property, which is only moderately helpful: "a security, whether certificated or uncertificated, security entitlement, securities account, commodity contract, or commodity account."

The idea of a "security entitlement" is itself somewhat mysterious. As a rough but helpful explanation, most "securities" are stocks and bonds. Typically, "security entitlements" are rights that the customer has against his or her broker as represented by the statement the stockbroker provides the customer monthly or quarterly. *See* 8–102(a)(15), 8–102(a)(17), 8–102(a)(9). Also, "investment property" is explicitly removed from Article 9's definitions of "general intangible" and "instrument." *See* 9–102(a)(42), (47).

The case that follows, where the creditor depends on possession of stock certificates to perfect, shows some of the difficulties in the use of possession as a mode of perfection. You should understand that this case is a throwback to an earlier time, for today few debtors will have possession of certificates that represent their ownership interests.

ROTHROCK V. TURNER

United States District Court,D. Maine, 2010.
2010 WL 2267226, 72 UCC2d 103.

WOODCOOK, JR., CHIEF DISTRICT JUDGE:

* * *

I. STATEMENT OF FACTS

In 2002, CrossHill Georgetown Capital LLP (CrossHill) loaned Parco Merged Media Corp. (Debtor or Parco) $600,000. CrossHill's loan was secured by a pledge of the Debtor's interest, *inter alia,* in 175,000 shares of stock in MultiSpectral Solution, Inc. (MSSI). In 2004, Mr. Rothrock purchased CrossHill's interest in the $600,000 loan to the Debtor, and he obtained possession of the Debtor's MSSI stock certificate as part of the collateral. Mr. Rothrock retained possession of the stock certificate until mid-March 2008.

In early 2008, the Debtor received notice that holders who tendered their MSSI stock would receive a cash payout as part of a merger involving MSSI. In mid-March 2008, Scott Cohen contacted Mr. Rothrock and offered to submit the MSSI stock certificate to J.P. Morgan as part of the MSSI merger and stock redemption. At this time, Mr. Cohen was treasurer of the Debtor and Mr. Rothrock the chairman of its board of directors. Mr. Rothrock accepted the offer with the understanding that Mr. Cohen would act as his personal agent, not as an agent for the Debtor. The two men also agreed that the proceeds from the merger would be sent to a KeyBank account set up for that purpose. In March 2008, Mr. Rothrock physically delivered the stock certificate to Mr. Cohen.

On May 12, 2008, Mr. Cohen mailed the MSSI stock certificate to J.P. Morgan. The stock certificate identified Parco as the holder of the stock certificate and Mr. Cohen signed the transmittal form in his capacity as 'Treasurer, Parco Merged Media Corp.' *Letter of Transmittal* Attach B., 09-ap-2015, at 5 (Docket # 16). The transmittal form directed J.P. Morgan to submit the money to Parco, 'the Holder listed on Box A,' at the KeyBank account. *Id.* at 4. Nothing in the transmittal form communicated to J.P. Morgan that Mr. Rothrock had an interest in the MSSI stock certificate or that the funds were to be submitted to him.

On May 19, 2008, a petition for involuntary bankruptcy was filed against the Debtor. On May 21, 2008, a business bank account called 'Escrow Account for CrossHill Loan' was set up at KeyBank to which Mr. Rothrock had sole signatory power. By check dated May 19, 2008, $295,470.26 in funds were paid to the Debtor care of KeyBank, and on May 23, 2008, this first installment of the merger proceeds was deposited in the KeyBank account. On May 28, Mr. Rothrock caused $295,170.26 to be wired from the KeyBank account to another account that he owned personally, leaving $300 in the Debtor's KeyBank account. On July 16, 2008, an order for relief was entered against the Debtor and John C. Turner was appointed as Trustee to oversee the Debtor's estate.

On August 27, 2008, J.P. Morgan sent a second installment of funds, totaling $48,376.26 to the Debtor at KeyBank, and on September 5, 2008, $43,236.43 of these funds was deposited into the KeyBank account. The other $5,139.83 was withdrawn. On September 9, 2008, Mr. Rothrock transferred $43,236.46 by wire into his personal account.

On March 24, 2009, the Trustee initiated an adversary proceeding against Mr. Rothrock in federal bankruptcy court. *Compl.,* 09-ap-2015 (Docket # 1). * * *

On June 19, 2009, the Trustee moved for partial summary judgment. *Mot. for Partial Summ. J.,* 09-ap-2015 (Docket # 15). The Trustee claimed that as a matter of law the transfer constituted an unauthorized post-petition transaction and a willful violation of an automatic stay and sought judgment for the $338,408.72 that was removed plus interest. * * *

On December 22, 2009, the bankruptcy court issued an oral order granting summary judgment on the unauthorized post-petition transfer claim but denying summary judgment on the willful violation of an automatic stay claim. *Oral Order,* 09-ap-2015 (Docket # 46); *Tr. of Oral Order* (Docket # 11). The bankruptcy court held that because the Debtor remained the registered holder of the MSSI stock and the transmittal form did not indicate that proceeds were to be paid to Mr. Rothrock, J.P. Morgan 'possessed the stock certificate as agent [ ] of Parco thereby terminating Rothrock's perfection.' *Tr. of Oral Order* at 9. On December 29, 2009, the bankruptcy court issued a written order pursuant to its oral order and entered judgment against Mr. Rothrock for $338,408.72. *Order on Mot. for Partial Summ. J.* * * *

II. DISCUSSION

* * *

B. The Parties' Positions

1. Mr. Rothrock

Mr. Rothrock contends that he never lost his perfected security interest because J.P. Morgan was instructed to transfer the stock proceeds to him via the KeyBank account or, in the alternative, that his lack of perfection is due to fraud and 'equity demands that a constructive trust be imposed on both on the Stock Certificate and its proceeds for Rothrock's benefit.' *Appellant Brief* at 22. Mr. Rothrock argues that 'the ownership of the KeyBank Account is clearly a relevant, disputed material fact' to whether he retained a perfected security interest. *Reply Brief* at 2. Because 11 M.R.S.A. § 9–1313(8)(b) provides that possession by a third party does not defeat the secured party's perfection if the third party is instructed '[t]o redeliver the collateral to the secured party,' Mr. Rothrock frames the question as 'to who that Account belonged to-Rothrock or Parco.' *Appellant Brief* at 28. Mr. Rothrock concludes that if 'the KeyBank Account was set up on Rothrock's behalf in his capacity as a secured creditor of Parco, ... JPMorgan was instructed to return the collateral (cash) to the secured creditor (via the KeyBank Account) and § 9–1313(8)(b)' provisions are met. *Reply Brief* at 4.

* * *

2. The Trustee

The Trustee responds that any perfected security interest that Mr. Rothrock might have had in the MSSI stock certificate was cut off when it was sent to J.P. Morgan. Although acknowledging the existence of exceptions by which a secured creditor does not relinquish possession by delivery to a third party, the Trustee contends that the conditions are not met: 'Here, no instructions were given to JPMorgan which would satisfy the provisions of section 9–1313(8).' *Id.* at 15.

* * *

C. Whether Mr. Rothrock Had a Perfected Interest

The Court concludes that Mr. Rothrock lost his perfected interest when the Debtor came into possession of the stock certificate. 'A security interest in a certificated security in registered form is perfected by delivery.' 11 M.R.S.A. § 9–1313(5). Section 8–1301 of the same chapter specifies that delivery occurs when 'the purchaser acquires possession of the security certificate.' Section 9–1313(5) further provides that this perfection is lost when 'the debtor obtains possession of the security certificate.' 11 M.R.S.A. § 9–1313(5); *see also* 11 M.R.S.A. § 9–1313, cmmt. 3 (stating that a debtor 'cannot qualify as an agent for the secured party for purposes of the secured party's taking possession'). Here, Mr. Rothrock held a perfected interest for the period of time he possessed the stock certificate and for the period of time Mr. Cohen possessed the stock certificate on his behalf. However, at the point that Mr. Cohen possessed and submitted the stock certificate on behalf of the Debtor, Mr. Rothrock lost his perfected interest. This point occurred at the latest on May 12, 2008, when Mr. Cohen endorsed the stock certificate as Treasurer of Parco and transmitted the certificate to J.P. Morgan with instructions to deposit the proceeds into a Parco account. In accordance with § 9–1313(5), Mr. Rothrock's security interest was extinguished when Parco 'obtain[ed] possession of the security certificate.'

Mr. Rothrock frames the question as whether the stock certificate was delivered first to Mr. Cohen and then to J.P. Morgan on his behalf. This argument is unavailing. There are two exceptions for when a secured party may retain possession despite delivery to a third party:

> A secured party having possession of collateral does not relinquish possession by delivering the collateral to a person other than the debtor . . . if the person was instructed before the delivery or is instructed contemporaneously with the delivery:
>
> (a) To hold possession of the collateral for the secured party's benefit; or
>
> (b) To redeliver the collateral to the secured party.

11 M.R.S.A. § 9–1313(8). Mr. Rothrock contends that the deliveries to Mr. Cohen and J.P. Morgan fit within these exceptions: his explicit delivery instructions to Mr. Cohen to possess the stock certificate on his behalf qualifies under § 9–1313(8)(a) and the instructions to J.P. Morgan to deliver the proceeds to the KeyBank account amounted to instructions to redeliver the collateral to him and qualifies under § 9–1313(8)(b).[7]

---

[7] Even though possession by the Debtor resolves the issue, the Court goes further because Mr. Rothrock has so energetically pressed his argument that the § 9–1313(8)(b) exception applies. For the § 9–1313(8)(b) [exception] to apply, the third party must have been 'instructed' about the relevant information at or before delivery of the collateral. Here, no instructions were given to J.P. Morgan to transfer the money to Mr. Rothrock; the transmittal form clearly indicates that the merger proceeds were to be transmitted to the Debtor via the KeyBank account. * * *

Whether Mr. Rothrock actually owned the KeyBank account does not address the focus under § 9–1313(8)(b); namely, the instructions given either before or contemporaneously with the transfer. The transmittal form instructs J.P. Morgan to deliver the proceeds to the Holder, identified earlier as Parco, at the KeyBank account. *Letter of Transmittal* Attach B at 4. The only means by which the proceeds could have been transferred to a nonholder—Box C, 'Special Issuance and Payment Instructions'—was left blank. *Id.*

Mr. Rothrock's argument misses a critical step: Mr. Cohen took possession as treasurer of the Debtor when he signed the stock certificate as treasurer and transmitted it to J.P. Morgan on the Debtor's behalf, defeating Mr. Rothrock's interest in two ways. First, Mr. Rothrock lost perfection under § 9–1313(5) when the Debtor took possession. Second, when Mr. Cohen took possession of the stock certificate on behalf of the Debtor, the exception under § 9–1313(8) no longer applied. Even if Mr. Cohen initially received the stock as an agent of Mr. Rothrock, when he signed the certificate and delivered the shares to J.P. Morgan[,] Mr. Cohen was acting as an agent for the Debtor. It is true that Mr. Cohen's dual positions as personal agent and Parco treasurer obfuscate the transaction, but once Mr. Cohen changed hats and endorsed and mailed the certificate as the Parco treasurer, the transfer to Parco was complete and Mr. Rothrock's security interest in the stock thereby expired.

* * *

III. CONCLUSION

The Court AFFIRMS the Bankruptcy Court's Order on Partial Motion for Summary Judgment, 09-ap-2015 (Docket # 47) and DENIES Mr. Rothrock's appeal (Docket # 1).

SO ORDERED

[some footnotes omitted]

NOTE

In *Rothrock*, the original creditor, CrossHill, apparently had possession of the certificates and was therefore perfected. It is unclear whether Rothrock ever had possession, but the court assumes that he did for the purposes of the motion. If Crosshill had done a proper filing, Rothrock would also have been perfected. Do you see why?

Now assume that the stock was "certificated" but that the certificates were held by the Depository Trust Company and that Parco (the debtor) held an interest in the shares in its account at Merrill Lynch. If CrossHill had done nothing to perfect its interest, what would you advise Rothrock to do in order to protect himself from the claims of other creditors or a trustee in bankruptcy?

If physical certificates representing the shares had to be issued to Rothrock to facilitate the merger, how would you protect him from gaps that might occur in his perfection because he might not have "possession" continuously?

PROBLEM 8-1

A stock certificate covering 1 million shares of IBM common stock was issued to and is registered in the name of The Depository Trust Company ("DTC") and is located in DTC's vault in New York City. DTC's books show that it is holding 100,000 of these shares for Salomon Smith Barney and the remaining 900,000 shares for other banks and brokers who are DTC participants. Salomon's records show it is holding 20,000 shares for M Manufacturing ("M") and 80,000 shares for other customers.

On March 1, 2003, M borrowed $100,000 from Lender to acquire equipment. At that time, M signed a written security agreement describing the collateral as "20,000 shares of IBM stock in my account with Salomon Smith Barney."

1. On March 3, Lender sent a copy of the signed security agreement to Salomon. On June 1, Flattened acquired a judicial lien on the stock. Between Lender and Flattened, who has the superior claim?

2. On March 3, Lender filed a financing statement covering "all securities accounts and securities now owned or hereafter acquired by M Manufacturing." Flattened acquired a judicial lien on June 1. Between Lender and Flattened, who has the superior claim?

3. Assume the facts are the same as in 2 above, except that on June 20, M Manufacturing borrowed $5,000 from Salomon Smith Barney under the "margin loan" provisions of their account agreement, identical to the one reproduced below. What are the priorities of Salomon, Lender, and Flattened in the IBM shares?

4. Assume the facts are the same as in 3 above, except that on July 1, Lender presented to Salomon, and Salomon executed, a control agreement identical to the one reproduced below. As of August 1, what are the priorities among Salomon, Lender, and Flattened in the IBM shares?

Consider the following control agreement.

Account Control Agreement Retail Customer

ABC Bank, having an address at _______ ("Creditor"); John Borrower, residing at _______ ("Debtor"); and Broker-Dealer, having an address at _______ hereby agree as follows:[1]

---

[1] The arrangement reflected in this agreement is totally voluntary. A securities intermediary is prohibited from entering into a "control agreement" without the consent of the entitlement holder. Conversely, the securities intermediary is not required to enter into such an agreement even though the entitlement holder so directs. *See* 8–106(g).

Preamble:

1. Broker has established a securities account number _______ in the name of _______ (the "Account").[2]

2. Debtor has granted Creditor a security interest in the Account pursuant to agreement.[3]

3. Creditor, Debtor and Broker are entering into this Agreement to provide for the control of the Account and to perfect the security interest of Creditor in the Account.

Terms:

Section 1. The Account. Broker hereby represents and warrants to Creditor and Debtor that (a) the Account has been established in the name of Debtor as recited above,[4] and (b) except for the claims and interest of Creditor and Debtor in the Account (subject to any claim in favor of Broker permitted under Section 2), Broker does not know of any claim to or interest in the Account. All parties agree that all property held by Broker in the Account will be treated as financial assets under Article 8 of the Uniform Commercial Code of the State of _______.

Section 2. Priority of Lien. Broker hereby acknowledges the security interest granted to Creditor by Debtor. Broker hereby confirms that the Account is a cash account and that it will not advance any margin or other credit to Debtor therein, either directly by executing purchase orders in excess of any credit balance or money market mutual funds held in the Account, executing sell orders on securities not held in the Account or by allowing him to trade in instruments such as options and commodities contracts that create similar obligations, nor hypothecate any securities carried in the Account.[5] Broker hereby [waives and releases/subordinates] all liens, encumbrances, claims and rights of setoff it may have against the Account or any financial asset carried in the Account or any free credit balance in the Account and agrees that, except for payment of its customary fees and commission pursuant to its agreement with Customer and except for payment for financial assets purchased for the Account, it will not assert any such lien, encumbrance, claim or right against the Account or any

[2] The establishment of the account might not be evidenced by a written agreement. If it is, the law chosen to govern that agreement will be relevant. *See* Section 8 of this agreement.

[3] The security agreement need not be written. *See* 9–203(b)(3). The broker is not required to be a party to the security agreement.

[4] If less than all the assets held or to be held in the account are to be subject to the secured party's security interest, a schedule should be provided. In addition, the secured party should keep in mind that any financial assets which are registered in the name of Debtor, payable to his order, or specially endorsed to him, which have not been endorsed to Broker or in blank, will not be considered part of the securities account (and the secured party should seek representations or conduct appropriate diligence to determine whether this is an issue). *See* 8–501(d).

[5] This is not a necessary element for Creditor's security interest; it goes to the issue whether, as a business matter, the Creditor will allow there to be a lien in favor of Broker. *But see* note 7, *infra*.

financial asset carried in the Account or any credit balance in the Account.[6] Broker will not agree with any third party that Broker will comply with entitlement orders concerning the Account originated by such third party without the prior written consent of Creditor and Debtor.[7]

Section 3. Control. Broker will comply with entitlement orders[8] originated by Creditor concerning the Account without further consent by Debtor. Except as otherwise provided in Section 2 above and 4 below, Broker shall also comply with entitlement orders concerning the Account originated by Debtor[9] or his authorized representatives, until such time as Creditor delivers a written notice to Broker that Creditor is thereby exercising exclusive control over the Account.[10] Such notice may be referred to herein as the "Notice of Exclusive Control."[11] After Broker receives the Notice of Exclusive Control and has had reasonable opportunity to comply, it will cease complying with entitlement orders [or other directions] concerning the Account originated by Debtor or its representatives.[12]

Section 4. No Withdrawals. Notwithstanding the provisions of Section 3 above, Broker shall neither accept nor comply with any entitlement order from Debtor [withdrawing/making a free delivery of] any financial assets from the Account nor deliver any such financial assets to Debtor nor pay any free credit balance or other amount owing from Broker to Debtor with respect to the Account without the specific prior written consent of Creditor.[13]

Section 5. Statements, Confirmations and Notices of Adverse Claims. Broker will send copies of all statements and confirmations concerning the Account to each Debtor and Creditor at the address set forth

---

6 Without this waiver, Broker will have priority over Creditor. *See* 9–328(3).

7 This provision is essential in order to ensure the securities intermediary does not comply with a later request by the entitlement holder that it enter into a control agreement with another lender. In such an event, the secured parties would have priority according to the temporal rule of section 9–328(2).

8 "Entitlement order" is defined in section 8–102(a)(8) to mean "a notification communicated to a securities intermediary directing transfer or redemption of a financial asset to which the entitlement holder has a security entitlement." This can be defined in the agreement, or the requirements for an effective communication can be spelled out.

9 Creditor might wish to limit the nature of the trading or investment permitted by Debtor, but this is likely to be perceived by Broker as unduly burdensome from an operational or monitoring perspective. Accordingly, any such limitations are probably best left to the underlying security agreement.

10 Trading rights do not affect perfection or priority but may affect credit decisions as a practical matter. *See* 8–106(d)(2) and comments, 9–328, 9–314.

11 Debtor and Creditor should provide in the relevant security agreement for the circumstances under which Creditor is entitled to send such a notice, which may be before or after default.

12 *See* 8–115 (affording a securities intermediary a reasonable opportunity to act on an injunction, restraining order or other legal process before incurring liability to adverse claimants).

13 The use of the term "withdrawal" appears to be understood in the market to refer to "free deliveries" or other instructions by a customer to deliver securities to a named recipient, as opposed to "trading" in an account, which is accomplished by the broker executing a trade with a third party. Prohibiting "withdrawals" by Debtor is a business issue. It is not necessary in order for Creditor to achieve control as a legal matter.

in the heading of the Agreement. Upon receipt of written notice of any lien, encumbrance or adverse claim against the Account or in any financial asset carried therein, Broker will make reasonable efforts to notify Creditor and Debtor thereof.

Section 6. Limited Responsibility of Broker. Except for permitting a withdrawal or payment in violation of Section 4 above or advancing margin or other credit to Debtor in violation of Section 2 above, Broker shall have no responsibility or liability to Creditor for making trades of financial assets held in the Account at the direction of Debtor, or his authorized representatives, or complying with entitlement orders concerning the Account from Debtor, or his authorized representatives, which are received by Broker before Broker receives a Notice of Exclusive Control and has had reasonable opportunity to act on it. Broker shall have no responsibility or liability to Debtor for complying with a Notice of Exclusive Control or complying with entitlement orders concerning the Account originated by Creditor. Broker shall have no responsibility or liability to Creditor with respect to the value of the Account or any asset held therein. Broker shall have no duty to investigate or make any determination as to whether a default exists under any agreement between Debtor and Creditor and shall comply with a Notice of Exclusive Control even if it believes that no such default exists. This Agreement does not create any obligation or duty of Broker other than those expressly set forth herein.

Section 7. Indemnification of Broker. Debtor and Creditor hereby agree to indemnify[14] and hold harmless Broker, its directors, officers, agents and employees against any and all claims, causes of action, liabilities, lawsuits, demands and damages, including without limitation, any and all court costs and reasonable attorney's fees, in any way related to or arising out of or in connection with this Agreement or any action taken or not taken pursuant hereto, except to the extent caused by Broker's breach of its obligations hereunder.[15]

Section 8. Customer Agreement. In the event of a conflict between this Agreement and any other agreement between Broker and Debtor, the terms of this Agreement will prevail. Regardless of any provision in any such agreement relating to the law governing the Account, the parties hereto agree the establishment and maintenance of the Account, and all interest, duties and obligations with respect thereto, shall be governed by the law of the State of _______.[16]

Section 9. Termination. The rights and powers granted herein to Creditor have been granted in order to perfect its security interest in the Account, are powers coupled with an interest and will neither be affected

---

14 A creditor's willingness to indemnify the intermediary may be a subject for negotiation. Such indemnities, although apparently not uncommon, are by no means universal.

15 Consideration should be given to the appropriate standard for Broker's loss of indemnification for ordinary negligence, gross negligence, etc.

16 This is necessary in order to establish the "securities intermediary's jurisdiction" under section 8–110(b).

by the death or bankruptcy of Debtor nor by the lapse of time. [Unless earlier terminated by Broker pursuant to this section,] the obligations of Broker under Sections 2, 3, 4 and 5 above shall continue in effect until Creditor has notified Broker in writing that this Agreement is to be terminated. Upon receipt of such notice the obligations of Broker under Sections 2, 3, 4 and 5 above with respect to the operation and maintenance of the Account after the receipt of such notice shall terminate, Creditor shall have no further right to originate entitlement orders concerning the Account and any previous Notice of Exclusive Control delivered by Creditor shall be deemed to be of no further force and effect. [Broker reserves the right, unilaterally, to terminate this Agreement, such termination to be effective [X] business days' after written notice thereof is given to Debtor and Creditor.[17]]

Section 10. This Agreement. This Agreement, any schedules or exhibits hereto and the instruction and notices required or permitted to be executed and delivered hereunder set forth the entire agreement of the parties with respect to the subject matter hereof.

Section 11. Amendments. No amendment, modification or (except as otherwise specified in Section 9 above) termination of this Agreement, nor any assignment of any rights hereunder, shall be binding on any party hereto unless it is in writing and is signed by each of the parties hereto, and any attempt to so amend, modify, terminate or assign except pursuant to such a writing shall be null and void.[18] No waiver of any rights hereunder shall be binding on any party hereto unless such waiver is in writing and signed by the party against whom enforcement is sought.

* * *

Section 15. Counterparts. This Agreement may be executed in any number of counterparts, all of which shall constitute one and the same instrument, and any party hereto may execute this Agreement by signing and delivering one or more counterparts.

Section 16. Choice of Law. This Agreement shall be governed by and construed in accordance with the law of the State of _______.

---

[17] The Agreement must give Broker some ability to cease acting in connection with the Account. On the other hand, simply permitting Broker to terminate the control arrangement while the Account is still in operation, would pose too great a practical risk to Creditor, unless Creditor is free (under its agreement with Debtor) to move all the financial assets to its own account or Broker's unilateral right to terminate the control agreement is conditioned upon Creditor's completion of arrangements to move the financial assets to another securities intermediary with which it has entered into a satisfactory control arrangement. The parties will need to negotiate the terms and conditions of any Broker-initiated termination.

[18] Consideration should be given to the possibility of permitting assignment of Creditor's rights in connection with an assignment of the secured obligations and how best to accommodate such an arrangement. One way would be to permit Creditor's rights under this agreement to be assigned to any assignee of the underlying security interest. This would presumably require some sort of documented evidence of the assignment satisfactory to Broker. Debtor's consent would need to cover such an arrangement, so as not to run afoul of Article 8's prohibition on intermediaries entering into control agreements without their entitlement holders' consent. *See* 8–106(g).

ABC Bank
By: __________

Debtor:
By: __________

Investment Securities Corp.
By: __________

To see the terms a stockbroker might require for a loan against investment property, read the following Margin Agreement.

Sample Margin Account Agreement

In consideration of your accepting and carrying one or more accounts for the undersigned, the undersigned hereby consents and agrees that:

Applicable Rules and Regulations

1. All transactions shall be subject to the constitution, rules, regulations, customs and usages of the exchange or market and its clearinghouse, if any, on which such transactions are executed by you (Broker) or your agents, including your subsidiaries and affiliates.

Definition

2. For purposes of this agreement, "securities and other property" shall include, but not be limited to, money, securities, financial instruments and commodities of every kind and nature and all contracts and options relating thereto, whether for present or future delivery.

Collateral Requirements and Credit Charges for the Margin Account Service

3. The undersigned will maintain such securities and other property in the accounts of the undersigned for collateral purposes as you shall require from time to time; and the monthly debit balance of such accounts shall be charged, in accordance with your usual custom, with interest at a rate permitted by the laws of the State of New York. It is understood that the interest charge made to the undersigned's account at the close of a charge period will, unless paid, be added to the opening balance for the next charge period and that interest will be charged upon such opening balance, including all interest so added.

Security Interest

4. All securities and other property now or hereafter held, carried or maintained by you or by any of your affiliates in your possession or control, or in the possession or control of any such affiliate, for any purpose, in or for any account of the undersigned now or hereafter opened, including any account in which the undersigned may have an interest, shall be subject to a lien for the discharge of all indebtedness and other obligations of the undersigned to you, and are to be held by you as security for the payment of any liability or indebtedness of the undersigned to you in any of said accounts. You shall have the right to transfer securities and other property

so held by you from or to any other of the accounts of the undersigned whenever in your judgment you consider such a transfer necessary for your protection. In enforcing your lien, you shall have the discretion to determine which securities and property are to be sold and which contracts are to be closed.

Representations as to Beneficial Ownership and Control

5. The undersigned represents that, with respect to securities against which credit is or may be extended to you: (a) the undersigned is not the beneficial owner of more than three percent (3%) of the number of outstanding shares of any class of equity securities, and (b) does not control, is not controlled by, and is not under common control with, the issuer of any such securities. In the event that any of the foregoing representations are inaccurate or become inaccurate, the undersigned will promptly so advise you in writing.

Calls for Additional Collateral—Liquidation Rights

6. (a) You shall have the right to require additional collateral:

(1) in accordance with your general policies for the margin service maintenance requirements, as such may be modified, amended or supplemented from time to time; or

(2) if in your discretion you consider it necessary for your protection at an earlier or later point in time than called for by said general policies; or

(3) in the event that a petition in bankruptcy or for appointment of a receiver is filed by or against the undersigned; or

(4) if an attachment is levied against the accounts of the undersigned; or

(5) in the event of the death of the undersigned.

(b) If the undersigned does not provide you with additional collateral as you may require in accordance with (a)(1) or (2), or should an event described in (a)(3), (4) or (5) occur (whether or not you elect to require additional collateral), you shall have the right:

(1) to sell any and all securities and other property in the accounts of the undersigned with you or with any of your affiliates, whether carried individually or jointly with others;

(2) to buy any or all securities and other property which may be short in such accounts; and

(3) to cancel any open orders and to close and or terminate all outstanding contracts.

You may exercise any or all of your rights under (b)(1), (2), or (3) without further demand for additional collateral, or notice of sale or purchase, or other notice or advertisement. Any such sales or purchases may be made at your discretion on any exchange or other market where such business is usually transacted, or at public auction or private sale; and you may be the purchaser for your own account. It is understood that your giving of any prior demand or call or prior notice of the time and place of such sale or purchase shall not be considered a waiver of your right to sell or purchase but without any such demand, call or notice as herein provided.

Payment of Indebtedness Upon Demand

7. The undersigned shall at all times be liable for the payment upon demand of any debit balance or other obligations owing in any of the accounts of the undersigned with you, and the undersigned shall be liable to you for any deficiency remaining in any such accounts in the event of the liquidation thereof, in whole or in part, by you or by the undersigned; and the undersigned shall make payment of such obligations and indebtedness upon demand.

* * *

Pledge of Securities and Other Property

9. All securities and other property now or hereafter held, carried or maintained by you in your possession or control in any of the accounts of the undersigned may be pledged and repledged by you from time to time, without notice to the undersigned, either separately or in common with other such securities and other property, for any amount due in the accounts of the undersigned, or for any greater amount, and you may do so without retaining in your possession or under your control for delivery a like amount of similar securities or other property.

Lending Agreement

10. In return for the extension or maintenance of any credit by you, the undersigned acknowledges and agrees that the securities in the undersigned's account, together with all attendant rights of ownership, may be lent to you or lent out to others to the extent not prohibited by applicable laws, rules and regulations. In connection with such securities loans, and in connection with securities loans made to me to facilitate short sales, you may receive and retain certain benefits to which the undersigned will not be entitled. The undersigned understands that, in certain circumstances, such loans could limit the undersigned's ability to exercise voting rights, in whole or part, with respect to the securities lent.

Presumption of Receipt of Communications

11. Communications may be sent to the undersigned at the address of the undersigned or at such address as the undersigned may hereafter give you in writing. All communications so sent, whether by mail, telegraph, messenger or otherwise, shall be deemed given to the undersigned personally, whether actually received or not.

* * *

Agreement to Arbitrate Controversies

13. Arbitration is final and binding on the parties.

- The parties are waiving their right to seek remedies in court, including the right to a jury trial.
- Prearbitration discovery is generally more limited than and different from court proceedings.
- The arbitrators' award is not required to include factual findings or legal reasoning and any party's right to appeal or seek modification of rulings by the arbitrators is strictly limited.
- The panel of arbitrators will typically include a minority of arbitrators who were or are affiliated with the securities industry.

The undersigned agrees that all controversies which may arise between us, including, but not limited to, those involving any transaction or the construction, performance or breach of this or any other agreement between us, whether entered into prior, on or subsequent to the date hereof, shall be determined by arbitration. Any arbitration under this agreement shall be conducted only before the New York Stock Exchange, Inc., the American Stock Exchange, Inc. or arbitration facility provided by any other exchange of which you are a member, the National Association of Securities Dealers, Inc. or the Municipal Securities Rulemaking Board, and in accordance with its arbitration rules then in force. The undersigned may elect in the first instance whether arbitration shall be conducted before the New York Stock Exchange, Inc., the American Stock Exchange, Inc. or arbitration facility provided by any other exchange of which you are a member, the National Association of Securities Dealers, Inc. or the Municipal Securities Rulemaking Board, but if the undersigned fails to make such election, by registered letter or telegram addressed to you at the office where the undersigned maintains the account, before the expiration of five days after receipt of a written request from you to make such an election, then you may make such election. Judgment upon the award of arbitrators may be entered in any court, state or federal, having jurisdiction.

No person shall bring a putative or certified class action to arbitration, nor seek to enforce any predispute arbitration agreement against any person who has initiated in court a putative class action, or who is a member or a putative class who has not opted out of the class with respect to any claims encompassed by the putative class action until: (i) the class certification is denied; (ii) the class is decertified; or (iii) the customer is excluded from the class by the court. Such forbearance to enforce an agreement to arbitrate shall not constitute a waiver of any rights under this agreement except to the extent stated herein.

Joint and Several Liability

14. If the undersigned shall consist of more than one person, their obligations under this agreement shall be joint and several.

* * *

Extraordinary Events

16. You shall not be liable for loss caused directly or indirectly by government restrictions, exchange or market rulings, suspension of trading, war, strikes or other conditions beyond your control.

The Laws of the State of New York Govern

17. This agreement and its enforcement shall be governed by the laws of the State of New York; and shall cover individually and collectively all accounts which the undersigned may open or reopen with you; shall inure to the benefit of your successors, whether by merger, consolidation or otherwise, and assigns, and you may transfer the accounts of the undersigned to your successors and assigns; and this agreement shall be binding upon the heirs, executors, administrators, successors and assigns of the undersigned.

Amendments

18. The undersigned agrees that you shall have the right to amend this Agreement, by modifying or rescinding any of its provisions or by adding any new provision. Any such amendment shall be effective as of a date to be established by you, which shall not be earlier than 30 days after you send notification of any such amendment to the undersigned.

* * *

BY SIGNING THIS AGREEMENT, THE UNDERSIGNED ACKNOWLEDGES: (1) THAT, IN ACCORDANCE WITH PARAGRAPH 13, THE UNDERSIGNED IS AGREEING IN ADVANCE TO ARBITRATE ANY CONTROVERSIES THAT MAY ARISE WITH YOU; (2) THAT, PURSUANT TO PARAGRAPH 10 ABOVE, CERTAIN OF THE UNDERSIGNED'S SECURITIES MAY BE LOANED TO YOU OR LOANED OUT TO OTHERS; AND (3) RECEIPT OF A COPY OF THIS AGREEMENT.

Signature ________________________________ Date _________

Title ________

Signature ________________________________ Date _________

(Second party if joint account; Co-Trustee)

Title __________

(For special accounts, example: Co-Trustee)

Account No.: __________

§ 3. WHAT IS INVESTMENT PROPERTY?

Whether a specific intangible interest is "investment property" is important for several reasons. First (and probably most important) is the description in the security agreement and any financing statement. If the documents describe the collateral as "general intangibles" and it turns out to be investment property, the creditor is unperfected and, possibly, unsecured. Second, even if the loan documents are broad enough to capture both general intangibles and investment property, the creditor will not enjoy the super priority that comes with "control," for "control," as defined in Article 9, is not possible with respect to general intangibles. Finally, the modes of perfection differ between investment property and general intangibles in other respects; possession of a share certificate or a written debt document would perfect an interest if the collateral were investment property, but possession of a document describing the rights of a holder of a general intangible will not perfect a security interest in the general intangible.

When the attachment and perfection of an interest in investment property was omitted from Article 9 and covered by Article 8, the critical definitions—to determine coverage—were those addressed in the case that follows. What is now called investment property had to be a "security" and, as the *Turley* case below shows, had to be "of a type commonly dealt with on securities exchanges or markets or commonly recognized in any area in which it is issued or dealt in as a medium for investment . . . ." Limited partnership rights and other property rights lurking on the fringe of "investments," as we know them, gave lawyers fits. If one recognized the problem, he could often protect against an adverse outcome by complying with both Articles 8 and 9 as though the rights were alternatively securities or some form of Article 9 collateral.

In 1999 the drafters greatly minimized these problems by defining investment property broadly in section 9–102(a)(49) to include not only a "security" but also security entitlements and several other things. Section 8–102(a)(17) defined these entitlements to include "the rights and property interest of an entitlement holder with respect to a financial asset . . . ." Section 8–102(a)(9)(iii) included almost any property held in a securities account "if the securities intermediary has expressly agreed . . . that the property is to be treated as a financial asset under this Article."

These rules enable "investment property" classification for digital assets that would otherwise be general intangibles—a fact of great importance to the rapidly expanding market for virtual currencies. As mentioned in Chapter 5, generally speaking, virtual currencies are not "securities" under Article 8 because they do not represent shares of or interests in an issuer. To derive value from these assets, virtual currency holders have to incur costs and risks associated with converting virtual currency to government-issued currency. Conversion costs, potential tax consequences, and value fluctuations drive holders of virtual currency to seek alternative means of realizing the value of their holdings. Secured lending can accomplish this purpose. As such, in recent years over a half dozen new lending platforms have emerged, designed for the express purpose of giving holders of cryptocurrency access to cash for their holdings without having to convert them to government-issued tender. These secured lenders may file a financing statement to perfect an interest in cryptocurrency as a general intangible. But they also may utilize the rules stated above to achieve investment property status, creating the possibility of perfection by control and its corresponding priority.

In order to be a financial asset, Article 8 requires that the asset be held by a "securities intermediary," that it be held in a "securities account," and the securities intermediary and the client agree that the property will be treated as a "financial asset" for purposes of Article 8. A securities intermediary, as defined in section 8–102(a)(14), is "(i) a clearing corporation; or (ii) a person, including a bank or broker, that in the ordinary course of its business maintains securities accounts for others and is acting in that capacity." A "securities account," as defined in section 8–501(a), is "an account to which a financial asset is or may be credited in accordance with an agreement under which the person maintaining the account undertakes to treat the person for whom the account is maintained as entitled to exercise the rights that comprise the financial asset." State lawmakers are already contemplating statutory provisions expressly reiterating that virtual currency can be designated a "financial asset" by agreement. Virtual currency exchanges, wallets, and the like can organize themselves in a way that satisfies Article 8's financial asset definitional requirements to make this currency "investment property" for Article 9 purposes. They can design their relationships with their clients to be "securities accounts" and they can agree to treat the virtual currency as a "financial asset" under Article 8. Some already have done so.

Under the relatively flexible approach of the current definitional provisions, a properly drawn agreement with Merrill Lynch could even make the breeding rights to a stud horse into investment property if they were "held in the account at Merrill." Rights such as the person's right to be a Championship Auto Racing Teams ("CART") participant or the like would clearly fit. There is no excuse to have the argument that we see in *Turley*; whatever the CART right is, it is investment property if it is held in a brokerage account under the proper terms.

IN RE TURLEY

United States Court of Appeals, Ninth Circuit, 1999.
172 F.3d 671.

RYMER, CIRCUIT JUDGE:

Thomas C. Thompson Sports ("Thompson Sports") appeals from a district court order that affirmed summary judgment in favor of Farmers and Merchants Bank of Long Beach ("Bank"). Both the district court and the bankruptcy court held that the Bank has a prior perfected security interest in certain interpleaded funds. * * * We reverse and remand to the bankruptcy court for the entry of judgment in favor of Thompson Sports.

I.

The resolution of this priority dispute turns on the characterization of certain proceeds. Both the Bank and Thompson Sports lay claim to funds interpleaded by Championship Auto Racing Teams ("CART") after the termination of its association with the debtor, Norman Turley. Thompson Sports holds a perfected security interest in the debtor's general intangibles and argues that it has priority to the interpleaded funds because they represent proceeds from a general intangible—a franchise agreement between the debtor and CART. The Bank, on the other hand, asserts that it is entitled to the funds because the proceeds stem not from a franchise agreement, but from the redemption of the debtor's CART share certificate, which the debtor pledged to the bank.

CART organizes "Indy Car" auto racing events. The debtor raced Indy cars as a member of CART. To race in CART events, one must be a "franchise member." These memberships are subject to strict requirements. Applicants for the one-season franchise memberships must commit to participate in all "Indy Car World Series" events and make a detailed disclosure of the racing team's ownership, the history of the applicant's principals, and the racing team's financial and operational structure. CART's Board of Directors reviews applicants for suitability to participate competitively in the Indy Car World Series. Franchise memberships are not transferable, each race team is restricted to two memberships, and the membership may only be renewed if the member exhibits "bona fide participation in all racing events" and is "otherwise eligible."

In addition to the restrictive franchise membership provisions, CART's by-laws also contain stringent limitations on stock ownership. Once accepted as a franchise member, applicants must purchase one share of CART stock. If a franchise membership terminates, the member must return the stock certificate in exchange for the share value as determined by the Board, as well as a Board determined franchise value. Shareholders cannot "sell, transfer, encumber or otherwise dispose of any share" without first delivering a "written offer to sell to the corporation." According to the by-laws, that offer must include "the resignation of such shareholder's

Franchise Membership in the corporation." And the prospective purchaser "must be another shareholder of the corporation." Confronted with the proposed sale, CART may either redeem the share or allow the transaction to proceed.

Soon after Turley arranged for financing arrangements from both the Bank and Thompson Sports, Turley filed for Chapter 11 bankruptcy protection. After the petition, CART's Board voted to redeem Turley's share of stock for $220,000. Additionally, Turley was entitled to a $29,394 end-of-the-year payment from CART based on his participation in CART-sanctioned races in 1993. Given the competing claims to the funds, CART filed a complaint in interpleader. On cross-motions for summary judgment, the bankruptcy court entered summary judgment in favor of the Bank.

The district court affirmed. *See Thomas C. Thompson Sports, Inc. v. Farmers and Merchants Bank*, 213 B.R. 857 (C.D.Cal.1997). The court held that Turley's share certificate in CART is a "certificated security" under Article 8 of the Uniform Commercial Code ("UCC"). *See id.* at 861. By gaining possession of the share certificate, the bank perfected its security interest in the share and its proceeds. *See id.* at 861–62. According to the district court, the interpleaded funds were proceeds attributable to Turley's share in CART, and the Bank is therefore entitled to the funds. *See id.* at 860–62.

II.

* * *

III.

The pivotal issue in this appeal is whether Turley's share certificate is a "certificated security" under Article 8 of the UCC. If it is, the Bank, which has possession of the certificate, holds a perfected security interest in all funds attributable to the share. *See* Cal. Com.Code § 8321(1) (1993). If it is not, the Bank cannot assert a perfected security interest pursuant to Article 8; this dispute would be governed by Article 9.

A.

Under Michigan law, a "certificated security" is "a share, participation, or other interest in property of or an enterprise of the issuer or an obligation of the issuer" that is:

> (i) represented by an instrument issued in bearer or registered form;
>
> (ii) of a type commonly dealt in on securities exchanges or markets or commonly recognized in any area in which it is issued or dealt in as a medium for investment; and

> (iii) either one of a class or series or by its terms divisible into a class or series of shares, participations, interests, or obligations.

Mich. Comp. Laws Ann. § 440.8102(a) (1993). As the UCC comments explain, the language of subsection (ii) "is intended to cover such interests as the stock of closely-held corporations which, although not in fact dealt in on exchanges or markets, is 'of a type' that is." *Id.* § 440.8102 note (1998) (Official Reasons for 1977 Change).

Whether Turley's CART share is a certificated security therefore turns on whether it is "of a type" that is generally traded in markets and exchanges. The Bank argues that a CART share is nothing more than a share in a close corporation and that the CART transfer restrictions, being typical for such corporations, do not remove the share from Article 8 purview. *But see Motobecane Am., Ltd. v. Patrick Petroleum Co.*, 600 F.Supp. 1419 (E.D.Mich.1985) (holding under Michigan law that a certificate representing an interest in a limited partnership was not an Article 8 security because of transfer restrictions), *aff'd on other grounds*, 791 F.2d 1248 (6th Cir.1986). Thus, according to the Bank, there is nothing special about a CART share and Article 8 applies.

We disagree. As a franchise member, Turley was required to purchase one share of CART stock. Upon termination of his franchise membership, CART's by-laws compelled him to return the share certificate. In order to renew his one-season franchise membership, and thus retain his CART share, the by-laws required Turley to participate in the season's racing events and remain "otherwise eligible." With these requirements, the CART share is definitively *not* "of a type commonly dealt in on securities exchanges or markets or commonly recognized . . . as a medium for investment." *Cf. Morton v. Santa Anna Nat'l Bank (In re Bonnema)*, 219 B.R. 951, 955 (Bankr.N.D.Tex.1998) (noting that the "of a type" test is meant to ensure "that the Article 8 rules do not apply to interests or obligations in circumstances so unconnected with the securities markets that parties are unlikely to have thought of the possibility that Article 8 might apply").

Our conclusion is bolstered by *Giuffre Organization, Ltd. v. Euromotorsport Racing, Inc.*, 141 F.3d 1216 (7th Cir.1998), where the Seventh Circuit, examining facts nearly identical to those here, held that a CART share is not a certificated security under the pre-1994 amendments version of the UCC. As the court explained, a CART share is no ordinary stock certificate:

> CART is not your everyday close corporation—nor are its shares simple investment vehicles. Once shares of ordinary corporate stock have been paid for, the investors have no rights other than to vote for directors (and to receive dividends if any should be declared) . . . . CART certificates are different. They entail not only a right but also an obligation to participate in races.

Id. at 1218. Security instruments that are "commonly dealt in" do not carry with them such affirmative obligations.

B.

Given that Turley's share in CART is not a certificated security, we turn to the question of what *was* Turley's interest in CART, and does the certificate matter.

Since it is not an Article 8 certificated security, Turley's interest is "caught by the 'general intangible' net in Article 9." 4 James J. White & Robert S. Summers, UNIFORM COMMERCIAL CODE § 31–12, at 161 (4th ed.1995); *see also Bonnema*, 219 B.R. at 955 (holding that the certificated capital retains "must fall into the catch-all category of 'general intangibles' "); Cal. Com.Code § 9106 (1993). As a security interest in a general intangible may only be perfected by filing, Cal. Com.Code § 9302 (1993), possession of the share certificate is without consequence. The Bank can have nothing more than an unperfected security interest in Turley's CART share. *See Giuffre*, 141 F.3d at 1219 (stating that only an Article 9 financing statement could perfect a security interest in a CART share).

The interpleaded funds were proceeds attributable to Turley's interest in CART. That interest is a general intangible and Thompson Sports' perfected security interest in Turley's general intangibles trumps any interest the Bank may have in the proceeds. Judgment must be entered for Thompson Sports. Thompson Sports shall be entitled to postjudgment interest from the date of the entry of judgment in accordance with this opinion.

REVERSED AND REMANDED.

[footnotes omitted]

PROBLEM 8-2

Having learned its lesson in the foregoing case, Bank files a financing statement covering general intangibles including Debtor's "CART rights." Later Bank Two takes a security interest in a variety of Debtor's intangibles including its CART rights. Bank Two requires Debtor to put its CART rights into a securities account opened for that purpose at Bank Two's brokerage subsidiary. The brokerage subsidiary then executes a "control" agreement with Bank Two. When trouble comes, Bank Two claims priority under section 9–328. Among other things, Bank Two claims that Bank's financing statement is now entirely ineffective because the collateral is no longer "general intangibles;" it has become "investment property." Consider sections 8–102, 9–102, and 9–507(b).

Who wins?

What if Bank could prove that Bank Two knew of Bank's security interest before it took its security interest?

§ 4. GOVERNMENT SECURITIES

Since U.S. government securities are considered securities under Article 8, they are governed by the UCC in the same manner as any other publicly held debt security, except insofar as the UCC is preempted by applicable federal law.

Treasury securities are no longer issued in certificated form; they can be held only through the book-entry systems established by the Treasury and the Federal Reserve Banks. The treasury offers a book-entry system, known as "Treasury Direct," that enables individual investors to have their positions recorded directly on the books of a Federal Reserve Bank (in a manner somewhat similar to the uncertificated system contemplated by the 1977 version of Article 8). The Treasury Direct system is governed by treasury regulations and is not designed for active trading. Active trading is done at the broker-dealer level.

The majority of Treasury securities are held not through the Treasury Direct system but through a multi-level indirect holding system. The Federal Reserve Banks maintain records of the holdings of member banks of the Federal Reserve System, and those banks in turn maintain records showing what they are holding for their customers, including government securities dealers, institutional investors, or smaller banks that may in turn act as custodians for individual investors. Under the Treasury regulations, parties who may be securities intermediaries range from Federal Reserve Banks to brokers that maintain security accounts for others in the ordinary course of business. *See* 31 C.F.R. § 357.2. Within this multi-tiered system, the upper tiers are composed of a Federal Reserve Bank, acting as an agent of the Treasury, and "Participants," which are other persons, typically banks, that have direct account relationships with a Federal Reserve Bank. A typical chain of ownership might be as follows:

Treasury
|
Federal Reserve Bank
|
Participant
|
Broker-Dealer
|
Individual Holder/Investor

Regulations of the Treasury, *see* 61 Fed. Reg. 43,626 (1996), have substantially adopted Article 8 as the rules on perfection and priority of security interests in treasury securities. For states that had not adopted revised Article 8, federal law preempted the preexisting state law and applied revised Article 8. All states, however, have now adopted revised Article 8. (Because provisions on perfection via filing and automatic perfection of interests granted to a securities intermediary—provisions that would otherwise exist under revised Articles 8 and 9—do not apply, this preemption is not complete.)

31 C.F.R. § 357.12

> (a) [A] Participant's Security Entitlement [is] created [when] a Federal Reserve Bank indicates by book entry that a Book-entry Security has been credited to a Participant's Securities Account.

31 C.F.R. § 357.11

> (a) [T]he law * * * of a Securities Intermediary's jurisdiction govern[s] * * *
>
> > (5) The perfection, effect of perfection or non-perfection and priority of a security interest in a Security Entitlement (except as otherwise provided in paragraph (c) of this section).
>
> * * *
>
> (c) [T]he law * * * of the jurisdiction in which the Person creating a security interest is located governs whether and how the security interest may be perfected automatically or by filing a financing statement.
>
> * * *
>
> (e) [If the jurisdiction specified (as the Securities Intermediary's jurisdiction) is a State that has not adopted Revised Article 8, then] the law for the matters specified in paragraph (a) of this section shall be the law of that State as though Revised Article 8 had been adopted by that State.

PROBLEM 8-3

Borrower requests a loan of $100,000 to purchase an experimental airplane. He states he has $100,000 in U.S. government treasury securities that he can offer as collateral on the loan and will sign a security agreement to that effect. The treasury securities are held for Borrower by his broker.

What steps do you as the bank need to do to perfect this security interest?

PROBLEM 8-4

1. Bank of America acts as the depositary for $1 million worth of treasury securities that belong to its depositor Janis & Co. The bank wishes to lend $1 million to Janis & Co. What must it do to perfect its security interest?

2. If the treasury securities are held at Bank of America, but Janis & Co. wishes to borrow from Wells Fargo, can Wells Fargo perfect by filing in the name of Janis & Co.?

3. Assume that the transaction in number 2 above will take the form of a "repo" transaction (*see* Section 5 below). If you were counsel for Wells Fargo, how would you suggest that they structure the repo transaction? (You might consider the fact that if Janis & Co. fails to make the repurchase, Wells Fargo would like to dispose of the securities on the open market on the day of Janis & Co.'s default.)

§ 5. REPOS: SALES OR SECURED TRANSACTIONS?

Courts have had considerable difficulty classifying certain transactions commonly known as repurchase agreements or "repos." Under these transactions a seller (debtor) commonly sells a security to a buyer (secured creditor) and promises to repurchase the security within a specified period of time (think conditional bill of sale). If the seller does not make the repurchase, the buyer typically has the right to sell the security on the market to satisfy the liability (if the buyer has not sold them sooner, which it may have the right to do). Normally, the repurchase price will be slightly higher than the sales price; the difference may be regarded as the lender's interest charge for the loan that is made.

For example, suppose a debtor wants to borrow $100,000 and owns 100 shares of publicly traded ABC Corp. worth $150,000. The debtor might borrow the $100,000 from a bank and grant the bank a security interest in the shares to secure repayment of the loan. Alternatively, the debtor might "sell" the shares to a broker in a repo transaction. As typically structured, the debtor in the repo transaction would transfer the $150,000 worth of shares to the broker in exchange for the $100,000 purchase price. The "margin" between the initial value of the shares, here $150,000, and the amount of the purchase price, here $100,000, is known as the "haircut." The parties would also agree that at a stated "buy back" time in the future (say, one year), the debtor would be obligated to repurchase the shares from the broker for, say, $105,000. As the buyer of the shares, the broker would typically have the right to sell them at any time; its obligation would be simply to sell back equivalent shares to the debtor at the conclusion of the transaction. If the broker thinks the value of the shares is likely to fall prior to having to sell them back to the debtor, it may sell them in the market hoping to purchase equivalent shares at a later date at a reduced price (say

$120,000) thus increasing its profit (the broker bought 100 shares for $100,000 from the debtor, sold them on day 1 for $150,000, purchased an equivalent 100 shares later in the market for $120,000, and then sold the equivalent shares back to the debtor for $105,000, netting $35,000). Of course, if the broker sold the 100 shares on day 1 and their value only increased thereafter, the broker would face a loss when it came time to replace them in the market so it could sell them back to the debtor.

Under the terms of a typical repo agreement, the broker would usually have the right to protect itself against losses by insisting periodically that the debtor post additional collateral in the event the market value of the shares declined. For example, suppose the value of the shares was $150,000 on day 1, but declined dramatically to $80,000 on day 2. The broker would typically have the right to require the debtor to post additional collateral in the form of cash or additional securities to cover the broker's "margin." If the debtor failed to do so, the broker would have the right to close out the repo, liquidate any shares it was holding, and assert a claim for its loss arising from the debtor's breach. Suppose at the end of the repo period the debtor fails to repurchase the shares as agreed. This would also be a breach and, once again, the buyer would be entitled to close out the repo and assert a claim for its loss (if any) arising from the debtor's breach. Note that repos are thus characteristically recourse in nature—the purchaser typically retains the right to go after the debtor in the event of a deficiency. In theory, there should not often be any deficiency because of the broker's ability to monitor the market price of the shares, demand additional collateral, and close out the repo quickly if the debtor defaults. In the real world, however, things do not always turn out so neatly. We include a sample copy of a relatively simple repo agreement at the end of this section, as well as copy of a more complicated sample document used in international repo transactions.

These kinds of transactions are arguably outright sales of a security. If so, the rules on personal property security in Article 9 and elsewhere have little or nothing to say about them. Some courts, however, have held that these are secured loans under which the seller is transferring a security interest to the buyer for a loan that will be liquidated by the seller's "repurchase."

How are these transactions to be treated if they are secured transactions and not outright sales? Unless the proper documents are signed and the proper actions are taken, a trustee in bankruptcy or debtor in possession in the bankruptcy of the seller may assert rights against the buyer and the buyer may be regarded as an unperfected secured creditor. That is a particularly troublesome possibility in the modern market where government securities are not certificated and therefore are not subject to perfection by possession. Also, the "buyer" (creditor) will not want to be constrained by Part 6 of Article 9 if the "seller" (debtor) defaults and the buyer needs to unload the securities in a falling market (for example, Part 6's notice requirements, and the like).

Consider the following case.

IN RE AMERICAN HOME MORTGAGE HOLDINGS, INC.

United States Bankruptcy Court, D. Delaware, 2008.
388 B.R. 69.

SONTCHI, BANKRUPTCY JUDGE:

INTRODUCTION

Before the Court is a motion to dismiss the bulk of the complaint filed by American Home Mortgage Investment Corp. ["AHMIC"] against Lehman Brothers Inc. and Lehman Commercial Paper Inc. The complaint contains five counts, including five requests for declaratory judgment contained in the fifth count. The first three requests for declaratory judgment center on whether the "safe harbor" protections of section[s] 559 and 555 of the Bankruptcy Code apply to the transaction in question. The Court finds that the transaction in question is a "repurchase agreement" under the statute and the safe harbor provisions of sections 559 and 555 of the Bankruptcy Code are applicable.

Consequently, the Court further finds that the relevant defendant did not violate the automatic stay imposed by section 362(a) of the Bankruptcy Code when it exercised its rights under an *ipso facto* clause. Furthermore, the Court finds that the relevant defendant was not constrained by Article 9 of the Uniform Commercial Code when it exercised its rights under the *ipso facto* clause. Thus, the Court will dismiss four of the five requests for declaratory judgment contained in the fifth count.

Finally, the Court will dismiss Counts I through IV of the complaint. For the reasons set forth below, each of these counts fails to state a claim upon which relief can be granted.

* * *

STATEMENT OF FACTS

* * *

The facts relevant to this dispute center on a structured finance transaction involving AHMIC, Lehman Brothers Inc. ("Lehman Brothers") and Lehman Commercial Paper Inc.

AHMIC was engaged in the business of originating residential mortgage loans. To fund its business of originating loans, AHMIC sold mortgage loans to special-purpose entities ("SPE's"). The SPE's issued commercial paper and subordinated debt to raise funds to purchase the mortgage loans from AHMIC. One such SPE, Broadhollow Funding LLC

("Broadhollow"), issued commercial paper in the form of secured liquidity notes and subordinated notes. Both the commercial paper and the subordinated notes were secured by liens on the mortgage loans it purchased from AHMIC. Relevant to this dispute are the subordinated notes known as Series 2004-A Notes and Series 2005-A Notes. Standard & Poor's rated the Subordinated Notes "BBB," and Moody's rated the Subordinated Notes "Baa2."

In June, 2005, AHMIC purchased the Series 2005-A Notes from Lehman in the aggregate principal face amount of $53,125,000. In July, 2007, AHMIC purchased the Series 2004-A Notes in the aggregate principal face amount of $31,000,000. Lehman agreed to finance both note purchases under the parties' pre-existing master repurchase agreement ("MRA").

Later, in July, 2007, AHMIC and Lehman entered into a transaction under the MRA (the "Subordinated Notes Transaction"). Under the Subordinated Notes Transaction, AHMIC sold the Series 2004-A Notes and Series 2005-A Notes (collectively "Subordinated Notes" or "Notes") to Lehman pursuant to the MRA. Under the terms of the MRA, AHMIC was the "Seller" of the Subordinated Notes and one or more entities comprising or affiliated with Lehman was the "Buyer" of the Notes.

After the initial sale of the Subordinated Notes, the MRA entitled Lehman to make margin calls when the market value of the Notes, as determined by a "generally recognized source," fell below a certain amount. If Lehman made a margin call, AHMIC was required to transfer to Lehman cash or additional securities, so that the value of the cash or additional securities or both combined with the aggregate value of the Subordinated Notes equaled or exceeded the aggregate Buyer's Margin Amount.

Throughout July 2007, Lehman asserted that the market value of the Notes had dropped to 91 percent of their market value. Then on July, 23, 2007, Lehman made a margin call. While AHMIC disagreed with Lehman's characterization of the Notes' value, it satisfied this margin call.

On July 26, 2007, Lehman asserted that the value of the Subordinated Notes had fallen to 80 percent of their face value and that this drop entitled Lehman to make a second margin call. AHMIC did not satisfy this margin call.

On August 1, 2007, Lehman sent notice ("Pre-Petition Default Notice") to AHMIC stating that its failure to pay the latest margin constituted an event of default and that Lehman reserved all of its rights under the MRA. AHMIC and its affiliated debtors and debtors in possession sought protection under chapter 11 on August 6, 2007. Subsequently, on August 27, Lehman issued the Post-Petition Foreclosure Notice in which it notified AHMIC that "it had terminated the MRA and that it either had foreclosed or intended to foreclose on the [Subordinated Notes] in lieu of selling them to a third party." In addition, Lehman notified AHMIC that the market value of the Notes was 68.25 percent of face value. After these events, "Lehman held itself out to third parties, including the Indenture Trustee with respect to the Subordinated Notes, as the owner of the [Notes.]"

LEGAL DISCUSSION

* * *

II. The Master Repurchase Agreement in this Case is a "Repurchase Agreement" Under the Statute, and the "Safe Harbor" Provisions of Sections 555 and 559 of the Bankruptcy Code are Applicable.

a. Background

In *Bevill, Bresler & Schulman Asset Mgmt. Corp. v. Spencer S & L Ass'n,* the Third Circuit succinctly described the nature of the agreement before the Court:

> A standard repurchase agreement, commonly called a "repo," consists of a two-part transaction. The first part is the transfer of specified securities by one party, the dealer, to another party, the purchaser, in exchange for cash. The second part consists of a contemporaneous agreement by the dealer to repurchase the securities at the original price, plus an agreed upon additional amount on a specified future date. A "reverse repo" is the identical transaction viewed from the perspective of the dealer who purchases securities with an agreement to resell.

[878 F.2d 742, 743 (3d Cir. 1989).]

As this Court recently discussed in *Calyon N.Y. Branch v. Am. Home Mortg. Corp.*, [379 B.R. 503, 512 (Bankr. D. Del. 2008),] the market for repurchase agreements is a critical component of, not only the U.S. financial market, but global financial markets as well. To protect the liquidity of repurchase agreements, the Bankruptcy Code provides special protections to non-debtor counterparties. Without these special protections, or safe harbors as they are known, the bankruptcy of a counterparty to a repurchase agreement would impair the liquidity of the repurchase agreement and possibly lead to the bankruptcy of the non-debtor counterparties.

One such special protection applies to *ipso facto* clauses. *Ipso facto* clauses are found in many contracts and allow one party to terminate the contract because the other party files for bankruptcy. The Bankruptcy Code generally prohibits non-debtor counterparties from enforcing an *ipso facto* clause. Section 559 of the Bankruptcy Code provides an exception to this general rule and allows a non-debtor counterparty to a "repurchase agreement" (as defined by section 101(47) of the Bankruptcy Code) to exercise its contractual right under an *ipso facto* clause to liquidate, terminate or accelerate the repurchase agreement. Section 555 provides a similar protection for the non-debtor counterparty to a "securities contract" (as defined by section 741 of the Bankruptcy Code). Thus, if the provisions of either section 559 or 555 are satisfied, enforcement of the non-debtor counterparty's rights under an *ipso facto* clause is not prohibited by section 365(e) or section 362(a) of the Bankruptcy Code.

The MRA contains such an *ipso facto* clause. Specifically, the MRA provides that upon an "Event of Default," the nondefaulting party may:

> [I]mmediately sell, in a recognized market (or otherwise in a commercially reasonable manner) at such price or prices as the nondefaulting party may reasonably deem satisfactory, any or all Purchased Securities subject to such Transactions and apply the proceeds thereof to the aggregate unpaid Repurchase Prices and any other amounts owing by the defaulting party hereunder, or . . . elect . . . to give the defaulting party credit for such Purchased Securities in an amount equal to the price therefor on such date, obtained from a generally recognized source . . . against the aggregate unpaid Repurchase Prices and any other amounts owing by the defaulting party hereunder . . .

Under the MRA an "Event of Default" includes an "Act of Insolvency," which is defined by the MRA to include, "[t]he commencement by such party as debtor of any case or proceeding under any bankruptcy . . . law . . ." Therefore, on August 6, 2007, when AHMIC filed for bankruptcy, an Event of Default occurred under the MRA. Simultaneously, the appropriate Lehman counterparty to the Subordinated Notes Transaction ("Lehman Counterparty") became entitled to exercise it [sic] rights under the MRA's *ipso facto* clause.

[The court determined that the MRA was a repurchase agreement and that sections 559 and 555 of the Bankruptcy Code applied. Accordingly, Lehman did not violate the automatic stay when it terminated the MRA and foreclosed on the notes.]

* * *

III. Applicability of Article 9 to the MRA

In the Plaintiff's fourth request for declaratory relief the Plaintiff seeks a declaration that:

> (i) Lehman's foreclosure and/or liquidation of the AHMIC-Owned Notes, is governed by Article 9 of the N.Y.U.C.C., § 901, *et seq.*, and, at all times Lehman was required to act in a commercially reasonable manner and (ii) any damages AHMIC incurred as a consequence of Lehman's failure to comply with

> those standards and Article 9 shall be determined in accordance with section 562 of the Bankruptcy Code . . .

Article 9 of the Uniform Commercial Code has a definitive scope, and, in order for the Subordinated Notes Transaction to be governed by Article 9, it must fall somewhere within that scope. The Plaintiff represents that the MRA creates a security interest in the Subordinated Notes. Alternatively, if the MRA is found to be a purchase and sale agreement, the Plaintiff argues that Article 9 applies, nonetheless, because the Subordinated Notes qualify as both "promissory notes" and "payment intangibles" and Article 9 applies to the sale of "promissory notes" or "payments intangibles."

a. The Intent of the Parties to the MRA is Relevant to this Court's Consideration of Whether Article 9 of the Uniform Commercial Code Applies to the MRA

Article 9 applies to a transaction "regardless of its form, that creates a security interest in personal property or fixtures by contract . . ." The Plaintiff argues that the Section 6 of the MRA creates a security interest in Purchased Securities, i.e., the Subordinated Notes. Section 6 of the MRA, entitled "Security Interest," provides:

> Although the parties intend that all Transactions hereunder be sales and purchases and not loans, in the event any such Transactions are deemed to be loans, Seller shall be deemed to have pledged to Buyer as security for the performance by Seller of its obligations under each such Transaction, and shall be deemed to have granted to Buyer a security interest in, all of the Purchased Securities with respect to all Transactions hereunder and all Income thereon and other proceeds thereof.

While it appears from an initial reading of this section that the parties to the MRA did not intend to create a security interest in the Subordinated Notes, the Plaintiff represents that this section creates a security interest in the Notes nonetheless.

The Plaintiff first argues, quite simply, that, under the MRA, AHMIC granted Lehman a security interest in Purchased Securities. To support this, the Plaintiff emphasizes that Article 9 applies to a transaction, "**regardless of its form, that creates a security interest in personal property or fixtures by contract.**" The Plaintiff reads the phrase "regardless of its form" to allow this Court to ignore the stated intent of the parties and focus on the portion of Section 6 of the MRA, which provides for a security interest.

To further support this argument, the Plaintiff contrasts Former Section 9–102(1) with its replacement, Revised Section 9–109(a)(1). As discussed above, Revised Section 9–109(a)(1) provides that Article 9 applies to "a transaction, regardless of its form, that creates a security interest in personal property or fixtures by contract . . ." Former Section 9–102(1) provided that Article 9 applies "to any transaction (regardless of its form) which is intended to create a security interest in personal property or fixtures including goods, documents, instruments, general intangibles, chattel paper or accounts . . ." The Plaintiff interprets the deletion of the phrase "which is intended to create a security interest" as evidence that intent is no longer relevant to a court's consideration of whether a transaction creates a security interest. Thus, the Plaintiff concludes, this Court may ignore the parties stated intent in Section 6 of the MRA.

The Plaintiff is correct that Revised Section 9–109(a)(1) replaced Former Section 9–102(1). Furthermore, the Plaintiff is correct that Former Section 9–102(1) provided that Article 9 applies "to any transaction (regardless of its form) which is intended to create a security interest . . ." and that Revised Section 9–109(a)(1) now states that Article 9 applies to "a transaction, regardless of its form, that creates a security interest in personal property or fixtures by contract . . ." However, the Court disagrees that this change eliminated the intent requirement from Former Section 9–102(1). Official Comment 2 to N.Y. U.C.C. § 9–109 expressly states that "Subsection (a)(1) derives from former Section 9–102(1) and (2). These subsections have been combined and shortened. **No change in meaning is intended.**" Thus, while the drafters deleted from the phrase "intended to create a security interest" in order to shorten the section, they did not intend to change the meaning of Former Section 9–102(1). Moreover, the Plaintiff's reading of the Revised Section 9–109(a)(1) conflicts with the principal of New York law that the intention of the contracting parties controls the interpretation of their contract.

The Plaintiff also provides a second, related argument. The Plaintiff argues that Article 9 still applies to the MRA even if Section 6 of the MRA creates a security interest that is contingent upon a court deeming a Transaction to be a loan. To support this, the Plaintiff reads Section 9–109(a)(1) to include such a "contingent" security interest because the section states Article 9 applies to "a transaction, regardless of its form, that creates a security interest." As discussed below, the Court finds that the MRA is a purchase and sale agreement and not a loan. Therefore, this "contingent" security interests does not arise in this case, and Article 9 does not apply. Furthermore, the MRA cannot be simultaneously a purchase and sale agreement and an agreement which creates a security interest. Therefore, the simple existence of a "contingent" security interest, whether or not the contingency ever occurs, also does not give rise to Article 9 applicability.

b. The MRA Provides for the Purchase and Sale of Securities such as the Subordinated Notes Rather than a Security Interest in the Securities

As stated above, under New York law, the intention of contracting parties controls a court's interpretation of their contract. Therefore, "[w]hen interpreting a contract, the court should arrive at a construction which will give fair meaning to all of the language employed by the parties to reach a practical interpretation of the expressions of the parties so that their reasonable expectations will be realized." Courts have applied this rule when interpreting repurchase agreements. Furthermore, if a contract is clear, a court will not look beyond the four corners of the document for evidence of meaning. As the relevant terms of the MRA are clear and unambiguous, their meaning is an issue of law, which the Court may considered in the context of a motion to dismiss.

Turning to the four corners of the MRA, the Court notes that the parties expressed their intent, and that intent was "that all Transactions hereunder be sales and purchases and not loans." However, the MRA further states that "in the event any such Transactions are deemed to be loans, Seller shall be deemed . . . to have granted to Buyer a security interest in all of the Purchased Securities with respect to all Transactions hereunder and all Income thereon and other proceeds thereof." Therefore, if the Court determines that the Subordinated Notes Transaction is a loan, then, and only then, will the Buyer be deemed to have granted the Seller a security interest in the Subordinated Notes.

It is clear, however, from the unambiguous terms of the MRA that the Subordinated Notes Transaction is a sale and purchase agreements and not a loan. First, the MRA denominated the parties "Buyer" and "Seller" rather than lender and borrow or secured creditor and debtor. The terms of the MRA provide that the Seller agrees to transfer to the Buyer securities or other assets against the transfer of funds by the Buyer. The MRA defines these securities or other assets as "Purchased Securities." The date on which the Purchased Securities are transferred by the Seller to the Buyer is defined by the MRA as the "Purchase Date." Also, the price at which the Purchased Securities are transferred by Seller to the Buyer is defined as the "Purchase Price." Furthermore, the "Repurchase Price" is the price at which Purchased Securities are to be transferred from Buyer to Seller. The date on which the Seller is to repurchase the Purchased Securities from the Buyer is defined by the MRA as "Repurchase Date." Furthermore, the Trading Confirmations state that "Lehman Brothers Inc., as principal we bought from you [i.e., AHMIC] . . ." Considering both the stated intent of the parties and the operative provisions of the MRA, the Court concludes that the MRA is a purchase and sale agreement.

Nevertheless, because Article 9 applies to certain purchase and sale agreements, Article 9 may still apply to the MRA. Specifically, Article 9 applies to the sale of accounts, chattel paper, payment intangibles, and promissory notes, as the terms are defined by Article 9. The Plaintiff argues that the Subordinated Notes qualify as both "promissory notes" and "payment intangibles."

However, while Article 9 does apply to purchases and sales of "promissory notes" and "payment intangibles," *the Article 9 commercial reasonableness standard that the Plaintiff seeks to impose on the Defendants is limited in that context.* Specifically, 9–610 outlines the standards applicable to post-default collateral dispositions, including commercial reasonableness. Section 9–601(g), provides, however, that "this part imposes no duties upon a secured party that is a consignor or is a buyer of accounts, chattel paper, payment intangibles, or promissory notes." Official Comment 9 to N.Y. U.C.C. § 9–601 further provides that:

> Subsection (g) provides that, except as provided in Section 9–607(c), the duties imposed on secured parties do not apply to buyers of accounts, chattel paper, payment intangibles, or promissory notes. Although denominated "secured parties," these buyers own the entire interest in the property sold and so may enforce their rights without regard to the seller ("debtor") or the seller's creditors. Likewise, a true consignor may enforce its ownership interest under other law without regard to the duties that this Part imposes on secured parties.

As the MRA is a purchase and sale agreement, the commercial reasonableness standard of Article 9 does not apply whether or not the Subordinated Notes are "promissory notes" or "payment intangibles." Therefore, Lehman Brothers' foreclosure and/or liquidation of the Subordinated Notes is not governed by Article 9. Accordingly, the Court will dismiss the Plaintiff's fourth request for declaratory judgment.

IV. Count I Alleging Breach of Contract is Dismissed

In the Complaint, the Plaintiff alleges that Lehman's conduct, both pre-petition and post-petition, breached the MRA. Specifically, the Plaintiff argues that Lehman wrongly triggered the July 26, 2007 margin call by "misrepresenting the existence of, or overstating the Margin Deficit and . . . ascribing an overly depressed Market Value to the Subordinated Notes." Furthermore, the Plaintiff alleges "[t]o the extent Lehman maintains that . . . it is a 'generally recognized source' as a market maker with respect to the Subordinated Notes, Lehman failed to . . . act in good faith, without conflicts of interest, and in a commercially reasonable manner in calculating Market Value." Also, the Plaintiff alleges that "Lehman was not entitled to issue either the Pre-Petition Default Notice or the Post-Petition Foreclosure Notice, because (a) AHMIC . . . complied with its obligations under the MRA and (b) and Event of Default . . . had not occurred." Finally, the Plaintiff alleges that Lehman "has not complied with or approached the applicable standards of commercial reasonableness." The Plaintiff argues that Lehman's actions damaged them in an amount "not less than $84,125,000, less amounts advanced by Lehman, plus costs and attorneys fees."

Under New York law, to state a claim for breach of contract AHMIC must allege: "(1) the existence of a contract; (2) due performance of the contract by the plaintiff; (3) breach of contract by the defendant; and (4) damages resulting from the breach." As the Court has decided that an "Event of Default" occurred under the MRA when AHMIC filed its bankruptcy petition in August, 2007, Lehman Brothers properly exercised its right to foreclosure or liquidate the Subordinated Notes post-petition. Therefore, Lehman Brothers' actions post-petition did not breach the MRA. Accordingly, the Plaintiff cannot prove the Defendants breached the MRA post-petition and the portion of Count I asserting a post-petition breach of contract will be dismissed.

Since Lehman Brothers' post-petition actions were not a breach of the MRA, the Plaintiff must show how the alleged pre-petition breaches damaged it in order to support its breach of contract claim. However, it is not clear from the Complaint how the pre-petition breaches damaged the Plaintiff differently from the alleged post-petition breaches. Accordingly, the Plaintiff must specify with more particularity how it was damaged by the alleged pre-petition breaches. Since the Plaintiffs' pre-petition breach of contract claim satisfies three of the four required elements, if the Plaintiff had pled the damages element with more particularity it may have survived the Defendants' Motion to Dismiss. Thus, the Court will dismiss *without prejudice* the portion of Count I asserting a pre-petition breach of contract to allow the Plaintiff an opportunity to plead with more specificity its claim of damages.

* * *

CONCLUSION

For the foregoing reasons the Motion to Dismiss is granted. * * *

[footnotes omitted]

NOTE

Should it matter how the parties draft their repurchase agreement? Suppose the debtor enters into a repurchase agreement with Alpha Broker ("Alpha") that states explicitly that the transaction involves a purchase and sale of securities, the parties intend the transfer to be a sale, and the buyer has the right to resell the purchased securities at any time. In addition, suppose the debtor enters into a repurchase agreement with Beta Broker ("Beta") that provides in substance the same thing, but states that the debtor is deemed to grant the purchaser a security interest in the investment property sold to the buyer. Is the former more assuredly a repo than the latter? Should the court refuse to allow extrinsic evidence to determine the parties' intent with respect to the Alpha repo, but allow it with respect to the Beta repo? *See Granite Partners, L.P. v. Bear, Stearns & Co. Inc.*, 17 F. Supp. 2d 275 (S.D.N.Y. 1998).

Assume Ally has an automobile purchaser sign a document called "claim rights" that specify that Ally has a right to possession of the automobile upon default, but that the document is not to be regarded as a security agreement and the transaction should not be subject to Article 9, but treated as a sales transaction. Would a court honor those assertions? The answer is no; substance governs form as a rule in Article 9 and the courts are not hesitant to honor substance over form in many settings. How do you distinguish that case from the one above where, to come to its conclusion, the court relies upon a party's own assertion about whether Article 9 would or would not govern?

PROBLEM 8-5

Bank of Illinois ("Bank"), a good client of yours located in Western Illinois, calls to get advice about repo transactions that it plans to enter into with a local customer. Bank visualizes several ways in which these transactions will be done. In all cases, the customer will be putting up U.S. securities and the transactions will be established in three different ways. First, in some of the cases the treasury securities will be held at Bank One in Chicago. Second, in certain other cases there will be treasury securities held in the customer's various brokerage accounts around the country, some of which will be unidentified and unknown to Bank. Third, in some cases customer is willing to place the federal securities in Bank's name at Bank.

1. What documents should Bank have the customer execute and what filings or other acts should the Bank undertake in order to insure that it has first priority and the capacity to satisfy its debt upon the customer's default?

2. It is now three years later. Bank and customer entered into the transactions described above and customer has defaulted. Bank now has liquidated the securities held in its name, has asked customer to transfer the securities held at different places around the country, and has asked Bank One in Chicago to transfer to Bank the securities held there. The debtor's trustee in bankruptcy has challenged all of these actions. First, he claims that any attempt to get possession of or to sell securities in the possession of Bank One will violate the automatic stay. Second, he claims that Bank is not perfected as to the securities held at Bank One nor to those held at different locations around the country. Bank tells you that it did file a financing statement in the customer's name. What are Bank's rights vis-à-vis the trustee in this case?

3. As to the treasury bills held at Bank One, Bank One claims priority. Unbeknownst to Bank and after it had lent money to the common debtor and filed a financing statement, Bank One made a loan and took a security agreement from debtor. You are fearful that Bank will lose to Bank One. How could it avoid such a loss in the future?

PROBLEM 8-6

Assume Bank has entered into a repo agreement (like the one below) with Debtor. Bank has control of the treasury bills it has purchased and its contract with the Seller permits it to sell the bills upon the Seller's default without notice and without advertising them. Is there anything in Part 6 of Article 9 that would contradict or interfere with the Bank's right to sell according to the terms in its agreement with the Debtor?

Master Repurchase Agreement
September 1996 Version

Dated as of __________

Between __________
and __________

1. Applicability

From time to time the parties hereto may enter into transactions in which one party ("Seller") agrees to transfer to the other ("Buyer") securities or other assets ("Securities") against the transfer of funds by Buyer, with a simultaneous agreement by Buyer to transfer to Seller such Securities at a date certain or on demand, against the transfer of funds by Seller. Each such transaction shall be referred to herein as a "Transaction" and, unless otherwise agreed in writing, shall be governed by this Agreement, including any supplemental terms or conditions contained in Annex I hereto and in any other annexes identified herein or therein as applicable hereunder.

* * *

3. Initiation; Confirmation; Termination

(a) An agreement to enter into a Transaction may be made orally or in writing at the initiation of either Buyer or Seller. On the Purchase Date for the Transaction, the Purchased Securities shall be transferred to Buyer or its agent against the transfer of the Purchase Price to an account of Seller.

(b) Upon agreeing to enter into a Transaction hereunder, Buyer or Seller (or both), as shall be agreed, shall promptly deliver to the other party a written confirmation of each Transaction (a "Confirmation"). The Confirmation shall describe the Purchased Securities (including CUSIP number, if any), identify Buyer and Seller and set forth (i) the Purchase Date, (ii) the Purchase Price, (iii) the Repurchase Date, unless the Transaction is to be terminable on demand, (iv) the Pricing Rate or Repurchase Price applicable to the Transaction, and (v) any additional terms or conditions of the Transaction not inconsistent with this Agreement. The Confirmation, together with this Agreement, shall constitute conclusive evidence of the terms agreed between Buyer and Seller with respect to the Transaction to which the Confirmation relates, unless with respect to the Confirmation specific objection is made promptly after receipt thereof. In the event of any conflict between the terms of such Confirmation and this Agreement, this Agreement shall prevail.

(c) In the case of Transactions terminable upon demand, such demand shall be made by Buyer or Seller, no later than such time as is customary in accordance with market practice, by telephone or otherwise on or prior to the business day on which such termination will be effective. On the date specified in such demand, or on the date fixed for termination in the case of Transactions having a fixed term, termination of the Transaction will be effected by transfer to Seller or its agent of the Purchased Securities and any Income in respect thereof received by Buyer (and not previously credited or transferred to, or applied to the obligations of, Seller pursuant to Paragraph 5 hereof) against the transfer of the Repurchase Price to an account of Buyer.

* * *

6. Security Interest

Although the parties intend that all Transactions hereunder be sales and purchases and not loans, in the event any such Transactions are deemed to be loans, Seller shall be deemed to have pledged to Buyer as security for the performance by Seller of its obligations under each such Transaction, and shall be deemed to have granted to Buyer a security interest in, all of the Purchased Securities with respect to all Transactions hereunder and all Income thereon and other proceeds thereof.

7. Payment and Transfer

Unless otherwise mutually agreed, all transfers of funds hereunder shall be in immediately available funds. All Securities transferred by one party hereto to the other party (i) shall be in suitable form for transfer or shall be accompanied by duly executed instruments of transfer or assignment in blank and such other documentation as the party receiving possession may reasonably request, (ii) shall be transferred on the book-entry system of a Federal Reserve Bank, or (iii) shall be transferred by any other method mutually acceptable to Seller and Buyer.

8. Segregation of Purchased Securities

To the extent required by applicable law, all Purchased Securities in the possession of Seller shall be segregated from other securities in its possession and shall be identified as subject to this Agreement. Segregation may be accomplished by appropriate identification on the books and records of the holder, including a financial or securities intermediary or a clearing corporation. All of Seller's interest in the Purchased Securities shall pass to Buyer on the Purchase Date and, unless otherwise agreed by Buyer and Seller, nothing in this Agreement shall preclude Buyer from engaging in repurchase transactions with the Purchased Securities or otherwise selling, transferring, pledging or hypothecating the Purchased Securities, but no such transaction shall relieve Buyer of its obligations to transfer Purchased Securities to Seller pursuant to Paragraph 3, 4 or 11 hereof, or of Buyer's obligation to credit or pay Income to, or apply Income to the obligations of, Seller pursuant to Paragraph 5 hereof.

Required Disclosure for Transactions in Which the Seller Retains Custody of the Purchased Securities

Seller is not permitted to substitute other securities for those subject to this Agreement and therefore must keep Buyer's securities segregated at all times, unless in this Agreement Buyer grants Seller the right to substitute other securities. If Buyer grants the right to substitute, this means that Buyer's securities will likely be commingled with Seller's own securities during the trading day. Buyer is advised that, during any trading day that Buyer's securities are commingled with Seller's securities, they [will]* [may]** be subject to liens granted by Seller to [its clearing bank]* [third parties]** and may be used by Seller for deliveries on other securities transactions. Whenever the securities are commingled, Seller's ability to resegregate substitute securities for Buyer will be subject to Seller's ability to satisfy [the clearing]* [any]** lien or to obtain substitute securities.

* Language to be used under 17 C.F.R. § 403.5(e) if Seller is a government securities broker or Dealer other than a financial institution.

** Language to be used under 17 C.F.R. § 403.5(d) if Seller is a financial institution.

Would the use of the agreement set out above have helped Bank in Problem 8-5?

Global Master Repurchase Agreement
2011 version

Dated as of ______________

Between:

____ **("Party A")**

and

____ **("Party B")**

1. Applicability

(a) From time to time the parties hereto may enter into transactions in which one party, acting through a Designated Office, ("Seller") agrees to sell to the other, acting through a Designated Office, ("Buyer") securities or other financial instruments ("Securities") (subject to paragraph 1(c), other than equities and Net Paying Securities) against the payment of the purchase price by Buyer to Seller, with a simultaneous agreement by Buyer to sell to Seller Securities equivalent to such Securities at a date certain or on demand against the payment of the repurchase price by Seller to Buyer.

(b) Each such transaction (which may be a repurchase transaction ("Repurchase Transaction") or a buy and sell back transaction ("Buy/Sell Back Transaction")) shall be referred to herein as a "Transaction" and shall be governed by this Agreement, including any supplemental terms or conditions contained in Annex I [form of Annex I omitted] and any annex specified in Annex I, unless otherwise agreed in writing.

(c) If this Agreement may be applied to—

(i) Buy/Sell Back Transactions, this shall be specified in Annex I hereto, and the provisions of the Buy/Sell Back Annex shall apply to such Buy/Sell Back Transactions.

(ii) Net Paying Securities, this shall be specified in Annex I hereto and the provisions of Annex I, paragraph 1(b) shall apply to Transactions involving Net Paying Securities.

2. Definitions

(a) "Act of Insolvency" shall occur with respect to any party hereto upon—

(i) its making a general assignment for the benefit of, or entering into a reorganization, arrangement, or composition with, creditors; or

(ii) a secured party taking possession of, or carrying out other enforcement measures in relation to, all or substantially all assets of such party, provided the relevant process is not dismissed, discharged, stayed or restrained within 15 days; or

(iii) its becoming insolvent or becoming unable to pay its debts as they become due or failing or admitting in writing its inability generally to pay its debts as they become due; or

(iv) its seeking, consenting to or acquiescing in the appointment of any trustee, administrator, receiver or liquidator or analogous officer of it or any material part of its property; or

(v) the presentation or filing of a petition in respect of it (other than by the other party to this Agreement in respect of any obligation under this Agreement) in any court or before any agency or the commencement of any proceeding by any Competent Authority alleging or for the bankruptcy, winding-up or insolvency of such party (or any analogous proceeding) or seeking any reorganization, arrangement, composition, re-adjustment, administration, liquidation, dissolution or similar relief under any present or future statute, law or regulation, such petition not having been stayed or dismissed within 15 days of its filing (except in the case of a petition presented by a Competent Authority or for winding-up or any analogous proceeding, in respect of which no such 15 day period shall apply); or

(vi) the appointment of a receiver, administrator, liquidator, conservator, custodian or trustee or analogous officer of such party or over all or any material part of such party's property; or

(vii) the convening of any meeting of its creditors for the purpose of considering a voluntary arrangement as referred to in section 3 of the Insolvency Act 1986 (or any analogous proceeding);

(b) "Agency Transaction", the meaning specified in paragraph 1 of the Agency Annex to this Agreement as published by ICMA;

(c) "Applicable Rate", in relation to any sum in any currency:

(i) for the purposes of paragraph 10, the rate selected in a commercially reasonable manner by the non-Defaulting Party;

(ii) for any other purpose, the rate agreed by the parties acting in a commercially reasonable manner;

(d) "Appropriate Market", the meaning specified in paragraph 10;

(e) "Base Currency", the currency indicated in Annex I;

(f) "Business Day" means—

(i) in relation to the settlement of a Transaction or delivery of Securities under this Agreement through a settlement system, a day on which that settlement system is open for business;

(ii) in relation to the settlement of a Transaction or delivery of Securities under this Agreement otherwise than through a settlement system, a day on which banks are open for business in the place where the relevant Securities are to be delivered and, if different, the place in which the relevant payment is to be made; and

(iii) in relation to the payment of any amount under this Agreement not falling within (i) or (ii) above, a day other than a Saturday or a Sunday on which banks are open for business in the principal financial center of the country of which the currency in which the payment is denominated is the official currency and, if different, in the place where any account designated by the parties for the making or receipt of the payment is situated (or, in the case of a payment in euro, a day on which TARGET2 operates).

(g) "Cash Equivalent Amount" has the meaning given in paragraph 4(h);

(h) "Cash Margin", a cash sum paid or to be paid to Buyer or Seller in accordance with paragraph 4;

(i) "Competent Authority", a regulator, supervisor or any similar official with primary insolvency, rehabilitative or regulatory jurisdiction over a party in the jurisdiction of its incorporation or establishment or the jurisdiction of its head office;

(j) "Confirmation", the meaning specified in paragraph 3(b);

(k) "Contractual Currency", the meaning specified in paragraph 7(a);

(*l*) "Defaulting Party", the meaning specified in paragraph 10;

(m) "Default Market Value", the meaning specified in paragraph 10;

(n) "Default Notice", a written notice served by the non-Defaulting Party on the Defaulting Party under paragraph 10(b) designating a day as an Early Termination Date;

(*o*) "Deliverable Securities", the meaning specified in paragraph 10;

(p) "Designated Office", a branch or office which is specified as such in Annex I or such other branch or office as may be agreed in writing by the parties;

(q) "Distribution(s)", the meaning specified in sub-paragraph (y) below;

(r) "Early Termination Date", the date designated as such in a Default Notice or as otherwise determined in accordance with paragraph 10(b);

(s) "Electronic Messaging System", an electronic system for communication capable of reproducing communication in hard copy form, including email;

(t) "Equivalent Margin Securities", Securities equivalent to Securities previously transferred as Margin Securities;

(u) "Equivalent Securities", with respect to a Transaction, Securities equivalent to Purchased Securities under that Transaction. If and to the extent that such Purchased Securities have been redeemed, the expression shall mean a sum of money equivalent to the proceeds of the redemption (other than Distributions);

(v) Securities are "equivalent to" other Securities for the purposes of this Agreement if they are: (i) of the same issuer; (ii) part of the same issue; and (iii) of an identical type, nominal value, description and (except where otherwise stated) amount as those other Securities, provided that—

(A) Securities will be equivalent to other Securities notwithstanding that those Securities have been redenominated into euro or that the nominal value of those Securities has changed in connection with such redenomination; and

(B) where Securities have been converted, subdivided or consolidated or have become the subject of a takeover or the holders of Securities have become entitled to receive or acquire other Securities or other property or the Securities have become subject to any similar event other than a Distribution, the expression "equivalent to" shall mean Securities equivalent to (as defined in the provisions of this definition preceding the proviso) the original Securities together with or replaced by a sum of money or Securities or other property equivalent to (as so defined) that receivable by holders of such original Securities resulting from such event;

(w) "Event of Default", the meaning specified in paragraph 10;

(x) "Forward Transaction", the meaning specified in paragraph 2(c)(i) of Annex I;

(y) "Income", with respect to any Security at any time, all interest, dividends or other distributions thereon, including distributions which are a payment or repayment of principal in respect of the relevant securities ("Distribution(s)");

(z) "Income Payment Date", with respect to any Securities, the date on which Income is paid in respect of such Securities or, in the case of registered Securities, the date by reference to which particular registered holders are identified as being entitled to payment of Income;

(aa) "Margin Percentage", with respect to any Margin Securities or Equivalent Margin Securities, the percentage, if any, agreed by the parties acting in a commercially reasonable manner;

(bb) "Margin Ratio", with respect to a Transaction, the Market Value of the Purchased Securities at the time when the Transaction was entered into divided by the Purchase Price (and so that, where a Transaction relates to Securities of different descriptions and the Purchase Price is apportioned by the parties among Purchased Securities of each such description, a separate Margin Ratio shall apply in respect of Securities of each such description), or such other proportion as the parties may agree with respect to that Transaction;

(cc) "Margin Securities", in relation to a Margin Transfer, Securities of the type and value (having applied Margin Percentage, if any) reasonably acceptable to the party calling for such Margin Transfer;

(dd) "Margin Transfer", any, or any combination of, the payment or repayment of Cash Margin and the transfer of Margin Securities or Equivalent Margin Securities;

(ee) "Market Value", with respect to any Securities as of any time on any date, the price for such Securities (after having applied the Margin Percentage, if any, in the case of Margin Securities) at such time on such date obtained from a generally recognized source agreed by the parties or as otherwise agreed by the parties (and where different prices are obtained for different delivery dates, the price so obtainable for the earliest available such delivery date) having regard to market practice for valuing Securities of the type in question plus the aggregate amount of Income which, as at such date, has accrued but not yet been paid in respect of the Securities to the extent not included in such price as of such date, and for these purposes any sum in a currency other than the Contractual Currency for the Transaction in question shall be converted into such Contractual Currency at the Spot Rate prevailing at the time of the determination;

(ff) "Net Exposure", the meaning specified in paragraph 4(c);

(gg) the "Net Margin" provided to a party at any time, the excess (if any) at that time of (i) the sum of the amount of Cash Margin paid to that party (including accrued interest on such Cash Margin which has not been paid to the other party) and the Market Value of Margin Securities transferred to that party under paragraph 4(a) (excluding any Cash Margin which has been repaid to the other party and any Margin Securities in respect of which Equivalent Margin Securities have been transferred or a Cash Equivalent Amount has been paid to the other party) over (ii) the sum of the amount of Cash Margin paid to the other party (including accrued interest on such Cash Margin which has not been paid by the other party) and the Market Value of Margin Securities transferred to the other party under paragraph 4(a) (excluding any Cash Margin which has been repaid by the other party and any Margin Securities in respect of which Equivalent Margin Securities have been transferred or a Cash Equivalent Amount has been paid by the other party) and for this purpose any amounts not denominated in the Base Currency shall be converted into the Base Currency at the Spot Rate prevailing at the time of the determination;

(hh) "Net Paying Securities", Securities which are of a kind such that, were they to be the subject of a Transaction to which paragraph 5 applies, any payment made by Buyer under paragraph 5 would be one in respect of which either Buyer would or might be required to make a withholding or deduction for or on account of taxes or duties or Seller might be required to make or account for a payment for or on account of taxes or duties (in each case other than tax on overall net income) by reference to such payment;

(ii) "Net Value", the meaning specified in paragraph 10;

(jj) "New Purchased Securities", the meaning specified in paragraph 8(a);

(kk) "Price Differential", with respect to any Transaction as of any date, the aggregate amount obtained by daily application of the Pricing Rate for such Transaction to the Purchase Price for such Transaction (on a 360 day, 365 day or other day basis in accordance with the applicable market convention, unless otherwise agreed between the parties for the Transaction) for the actual number of days during the period commencing on (and including) the Purchase Date for such Transaction and ending on (but excluding) the date of calculation or, if earlier, the Repurchase Date;

(*ll*) "Pricing Rate", with respect to any Transaction, the per annum percentage rate for calculation of the Price Differential agreed to by Buyer and Seller in relation to that Transaction;

(mm) "Purchase Date", with respect to any Transaction, the date on which Purchased Securities are to be sold by Seller to Buyer in relation to that Transaction;

(nn) "Purchase Price", on the Purchase Date, the price at which Purchased Securities are sold or are to be sold by Seller to Buyer;

(*oo*) "Purchased Securities", with respect to any Transaction, the Securities sold or to be sold by Seller to Buyer under that Transaction, and any New Purchased Securities transferred by Seller to Buyer under paragraph 8 in respect of that Transaction;

(pp) "Receivable Securities", the meaning specified in paragraph 10;

(qq) "Repurchase Date", with respect to any Transaction, the date on which Buyer is to sell Equivalent Securities to Seller in relation to that Transaction;

(rr) "Repurchase Price", with respect to any Transaction and as of any date, the sum of the Purchase Price and the Price Differential as of such date;

(ss) "Spot Rate", where an amount in one currency is to be converted into a second currency on any date, unless the parties otherwise agree

(i) for the purposes of paragraph 10, the spot rate of exchange obtained by reference to a pricing source or quoted by a bank, in each case specified by the non-Defaulting Party, in the London inter-bank market for the purchase of the second currency with the first currency at such dates and times determined by the non-Defaulting Party; and

(ii) for any other purpose, the latest available spot rate of exchange obtained by reference to a pricing source or quoted by a bank, in each case agreed by the parties (or in the absence of such agreement, specified by Buyer), in the London inter-bank market for the purchase of the second currency with the first currency on the day on which the calculation is to be made or, if that day is not a day on which banks are open for business in London, the spot rate of exchange quoted at close of business in London on the immediately preceding day in London on which such a quotation was available;

(tt) "TARGET2", the Second Generation Trans-European Automated Real-time Gross Settlement Express Transfer System, or any other system that replaces it;

(uu) "Term", with respect to any Transaction, the interval of time commencing with the Purchase Date and ending with the Repurchase Date;

(vv) "Termination", with respect to any Transaction, refers to the requirement with respect to such Transaction for Buyer to sell Equivalent Securities against payment by Seller of the Repurchase Price in accordance with paragraph 3(f), and reference to a Transaction having a "fixed term" or being "terminable upon demand" shall be construed accordingly;

(ww) "Transaction Costs", the meaning specified in paragraph 10;

(xx) "Transaction Exposure", with respect to any Transaction at any time during the period from the Purchase Date to the Repurchase Date (or, if later, the date on which Equivalent Securities are delivered to Seller or the Transaction is terminated under paragraph 10(h) or 10(i)) the amount "E" determined in accordance with (A) or (B) below as specified in Annex I (or as agreed by the parties with respect to particular transactions):

(A) the result of formula E = (R x MR) – MV, where:

R = the Repurchase Price at such time

MR = the applicable Margin Ratio

MV = the Market Value of Equivalent Securities at such time

and so that where the Transaction relates to Securities of more than one description or to which different Margin Ratios apply, E shall be determined by multiplying the Repurchase Price attributable to Equivalent Securities of each such description by the applicable Margin Ratio and aggregating the results and for this purpose the Repurchase Price shall be attributed to Equivalent Securities of each such description in the same proportions as those in which the Purchase Price was apportioned among the Purchased Securities.

If E is greater than zero, Buyer has a Transaction Exposure equal to E and if E is less than zero, Seller has a Transaction Exposure equal to the absolute value of E; provided that E shall not be greater than the amount of the Repurchase Price on the date of the determination; or

(A) the result of the formula E = R – V, where:

R = the Repurchase Price at such time

V = the Adjusted Value of Equivalent Securities at such time or, where a Transaction relates to Securities of more than one description or to which different haircuts apply, the sum of the Adjusted Values of the Securities of each such description.

For this purpose the "Adjusted Value" of any Securities is their value determined on the basis of the formula, (MV(1 – H)), where:

MV = the Market Value of Equivalent Securities at such time

H = the "haircut" for the relevant Securities, if any, as agreed by the parties from time to time, being a discount from the Market Value of the Securities.

If E is greater than zero, Buyer has a Transaction Exposure equal to E and if E is less than zero, Seller has a Transaction Exposure equal to the absolute value of E; and

(yy) except in paragraphs 14(b)(i) and 18, references in this Agreement to "written" communications and communications "in writing" include communications made through any Electronic Messaging System agreed between the parties.

3. Initiation; Confirmation; Termination

(a) A Transaction may be entered into orally or in writing at the initiation of either Buyer or Seller.

(b) Upon agreeing to enter into a Transaction hereunder Buyer or Seller (or both), as shall have been agreed, shall promptly deliver to the other party written confirmation of such Transaction (a "Confirmation").

The Confirmation shall describe the Purchased Securities (including CUSIP or ISIN or other identifying number or numbers, if any), identify Buyer and Seller and set forth—

(i) the Purchase Date;

(ii) the Purchase Price;

(iii) the Repurchase Date, unless the Transaction is to be terminable on demand (in which case the Confirmation shall state that it is terminable on demand);

(iv) the Pricing Rate applicable to the Transaction;

(v) in respect of each party the details of the bank account(s) to which payments to be made hereunder are to be credited;

(vi) where the Buy/Sell Back Annex applies, whether the Transaction is a Repurchase Transaction or a Buy/Sell Back Transaction;

(vii) where the Agency Annex applies, whether the Transaction is an Agency Transaction and, if so, the identity of the party which is acting as agent and the name, code or identifier of the Principal; and

(viii) any additional terms or conditions of the Transaction;

and may be in the form of Annex II [sample form omitted] or may be in any other form to which the parties agree.

The Confirmation relating to a Transaction shall, together with this Agreement, constitute prima facie evidence of the terms agreed between Buyer and Seller for that Transaction, unless objection is made with respect to the Confirmation promptly after receipt thereof. In the event of any conflict between the terms of such Confirmation and this Agreement, the Confirmation shall prevail in respect of that Transaction and those terms only.

(c) On the Purchase Date for a Transaction, Seller shall transfer the Purchased Securities to Buyer or its agent against the payment of the Purchase Price by Buyer in accordance with paragraph 6(c).

(d) Termination of a Transaction will be effected, in the case of on demand Transactions, on the date specified for Termination in such demand, and, in the case of fixed term Transactions, on the date fixed for Termination.

(e) In the case of on demand Transactions, demand for Termination shall be made by Buyer or Seller, by telephone or otherwise, and shall provide for Termination to occur after not less than the minimum period as is customarily required for the settlement or delivery of money or Equivalent Securities of the relevant kind.

(f) On the Repurchase Date, Buyer shall transfer to Seller or its agent Equivalent Securities against the payment of the Repurchase Price by Seller (less any amount then payable and unpaid by Buyer to Seller pursuant to paragraph 5).

4. Margin Maintenance

(a) If at any time either party has a Net Exposure in respect of the other party it may by notice to the other party require the other party to make a Margin Transfer to it of an aggregate amount or value at least equal to that Net Exposure.

(b) A notice under sub-paragraph (a) above may be given orally or in writing.

(c) For the purposes of this Agreement a party has a Net Exposure in respect of the other party if the aggregate of all the first party's Transaction Exposures plus any amount payable to the first party under paragraph 5 but unpaid less the amount of any Net Margin provided to the first party exceeds the aggregate of all the other party's Transaction Exposures plus any amount payable to the other party under paragraph 5 but unpaid less the amount of any Net Margin provided to the other party; and the amount of the Net Exposure is the amount of the excess. For this purpose any amounts not denominated in the Base Currency shall be converted into the Base Currency at the Spot Rate prevailing at the relevant time.

(d) To the extent that a party calling for a Margin Transfer has previously paid Cash Margin which has not been repaid or delivered Margin Securities in respect of which Equivalent Margin Securities have not been delivered to it or a Cash Equivalent Amount has not been paid, that party shall be entitled to require that such Margin Transfer be satisfied first by the repayment of such Cash Margin or the delivery of Equivalent Margin Securities but, subject to this, the composition of a Margin Transfer shall be at the option of the party making such Margin Transfer.

(e) Any Cash Margin transferred shall be in the Base Currency or such other currency as the parties may agree.

(f) A payment of Cash Margin shall give rise to a debt owing from the party receiving such payment to the party making such payment.

Such debt shall bear interest at such rate, payable at such times, as may be specified in Annex I in respect of the relevant currency or otherwise agreed between the parties, and shall be repayable subject to the terms of this Agreement.

(g) Where Seller or Buyer becomes obliged under sub-paragraph (a) above to make a Margin Transfer, it shall transfer Cash Margin or Margin Securities or Equivalent Margin Securities within the minimum period specified in Annex I or, if no period is there specified, such minimum period as is customarily required for the settlement or delivery of money, Margin Securities or Equivalent Margin Securities of the relevant kind.

(h) Where a party (the "Transferor") becomes obliged to transfer Equivalent Margin Securities and, having made all reasonable efforts to do so, is, for any reason relating to the Securities or the clearing system through which the Securities are to be transferred, unable to transfer Equivalent Margin Securities then

(i) the Transferor shall immediately pay to the other party Cash Margin at least equal to the Market Value of such Equivalent Margin Securities (and, unless the parties otherwise agree, such Cash Margin shall not bear interest in accordance with paragraph 4(f)); and

(ii) if the failure is continuing for two Business Days or more the other party may by notice to the Transferor require the Transferor to pay an amount (the "Cash Equivalent Amount") equal to the Default Market Value of the Equivalent Margin Securities determined by the other party in accordance with paragraph 10(f) which shall apply on the basis that references to the non-Defaulting Party were to the other party and references to the Early Termination Date were to the date on which notice under this paragraph is effective.

(i) The parties may agree that, with respect to any Transaction, the provisions of subparagraphs (a) to (h) above shall not apply but instead that margin may be provided separately in respect of that Transaction in which case—

(i) that Transaction shall not be taken into account when calculating whether either party has a Net Exposure;

(ii) margin shall be provided in respect of that Transaction in such manner as the parties may agree; and

(iii) margin provided in respect of that Transaction shall not be taken into account for the purposes of sub-paragraphs (a) to (h) above.

(j) The parties may agree that any Net Exposure which may arise shall be eliminated not by Margin Transfers under the preceding provisions of this paragraph but by the repricing of Transactions under sub-paragraph (k) below, the adjustment of Transactions under sub-paragraph (I) below or a combination of both these methods.

(k) Where the parties agree that a Transaction is to be repriced under this sub-paragraph, such repricing shall be effected as follows—

(i) the Repurchase Date under the relevant Transaction (the "Original Transaction") shall be deemed to occur on the date on which the repricing is to be effected (the "Repricing Date");

(ii) (the parties shall be deemed to have entered into a new Transaction (the "Repriced Transaction") on the terms set out in (iii) to (vi) below;

(iii) the Purchased Securities under the Repriced Transaction shall be Securities equivalent to the Purchased Securities under the Original Transaction;

(iv) the Purchase Date under the Repriced Transaction shall be the Repricing Date;

(v) the Purchase Price under the Repriced Transaction shall be such amount as shall, when multiplied by the Margin Ratio applicable to the Original Transaction, be equal to the Market Value of such Securities on the Repricing Date;

(vi) the Repurchase Date, the Pricing Rate, the Margin Ratio and, subject as aforesaid, the other terms of the Repriced Transaction shall be identical to those of the Original Transaction;

(vii) the obligations of the parties with respect to the delivery of the Purchased Securities and the payment of the Purchase Price under the Repriced Transaction shall be set off against their obligations with respect to the delivery of Equivalent Securities and payment of the Repurchase Price under the Original Transaction and accordingly only a net cash sum shall be paid by one party to the other. Such net cash sum shall be paid within the minimum period specified in sub-paragraph (g) above.

(*l*) The adjustment of a Transaction (the "Original Transaction") under this sub-paragraph shall be effected by the parties agreeing that on the date on which the adjustment is to be made (the "Adjustment Date") the Original Transaction shall be terminated and they shall enter into a new Transaction (the "Replacement Transaction") in accordance with the following provisions—

(i) the Original Transaction shall be terminated on the Adjustment Date on such terms as the parties shall agree on or before the Adjustment Date;

(ii) the Purchased Securities under the Replacement Transaction shall be such Securities as the parties shall agree on or before the Adjustment Date (being Securities the aggregate Market Value of which at the Adjustment Date is substantially equal to the Repurchase Price under the Original Transaction at the Adjustment Date multiplied by the Margin Ratio applicable to the Original Transaction);

(iii) the Purchase Date under the Replacement Transaction shall be the Adjustment Date;

(iv) the other terms of the Replacement Transaction shall be such as the parties shall agree on or before the Adjustment Date; and

(v) the obligations of the parties with respect to payment and delivery of Securities on the Adjustment Date under the Original Transaction and the Replacement Transaction shall be settled in accordance with paragraph 6 within the minimum period specified in sub-paragraph (g) above.

5. Income Payments

Unless otherwise agreed—

(a) where: (i) the Term of a particular Transaction extends over an Income Payment Date in respect of any Securities subject to that Transaction; or (ii) an Income Payment Date in respect of any such Securities occurs after the Repurchase Date but before Equivalent Securities have been delivered to Seller or, if earlier, the occurrence of an Early Termination Date or the termination of the Transaction under paragraph 10(i) then Buyer shall on the date such Income is paid by the issuer transfer to or credit to the account of Seller an amount equal to (and in the same currency as) the amount paid by the issuer;

(b) where Margin Securities are transferred from one party ("the first party") to the other party ("the second party") and an Income Payment Date in respect of such Securities occurs before Equivalent Margin Securities are transferred or a Cash Equivalent Amount is paid by the second party to the first party, the second party shall on the date such Income is paid by the issuer transfer to or credit to the account of the first party an amount equal to (and in the same currency as) the amount paid by the issuer;

and for the avoidance of doubt references in this paragraph to the amount of any Income paid by the issuer of any Securities shall be to an amount paid without any withholding or deduction for or on account of taxes or duties notwithstanding that a payment of such Income made in certain circumstances may be subject to such a withholding or deduction.

6. Payment and Transfer

(a) Unless otherwise agreed, all money paid hereunder shall be in immediately available freely convertible funds of the relevant currency. All Securities to be transferred hereunder (i) shall be in suitable form for transfer and shall be accompanied by duly executed instruments of transfer or assignment in blank (where required for transfer) and such other documentation as the transferee may reasonably request, or (ii) shall be transferred through any agreed book entry or other securities clearance system or (iii) shall be transferred by any other method mutually acceptable to Seller and Buyer.

(b) Unless otherwise agreed, all money payable by one party to the other in respect of any Transaction shall be paid free and clear of, and without withholding or deduction for, any taxes or duties of whatsoever nature imposed, levied, collected, withheld or assessed by any authority having power to tax, unless the withholding or deduction of such taxes or duties is required by law. In that event, unless otherwise agreed, the paying party shall pay such additional amounts as will result in the net amounts receivable by the other party (after taking account of such withholding or deduction) being equal to such amounts as would have been received by it had no such taxes or duties been required to be withheld or deducted.

(c) Unless otherwise agreed in writing between the parties, under each Transaction transfer of Purchased Securities by Seller and payment of Purchase Price by Buyer against the transfer of such Purchased Securities shall be made simultaneously and transfer of Equivalent Securities by Buyer and payment of Repurchase Price payable by Seller against the transfer of such Equivalent Securities shall be made simultaneously.

(d) Subject to and without prejudice to the provisions of sub-paragraph 6(c), either party may from time to time in accordance with market practice and in recognition of the practical difficulties in arranging simultaneous delivery of Securities and money waive in relation to any Transaction its rights under this Agreement to receive simultaneous transfer and/or payment provided that transfer and/or payment shall, notwithstanding such waiver, be made on the same day and provided also that no such waiver in respect of one Transaction shall affect or bind it in respect of any other Transaction.

(e) The parties shall execute and deliver all necessary documents and take all necessary steps to procure that all right, title and interest in any Purchased Securities, any Equivalent Securities, any Margin Securities and any Equivalent Margin Securities shall pass to the party to which transfer is being made upon transfer of the same in accordance with this Agreement, free from all liens (other than a lien granted to the operator of the clearance system through which the Securities are transferred), claims, charges and encumbrances.

(f) Notwithstanding the use of expressions such as "Repurchase Date", "Repurchase Price", "margin", "Net Margin", "Margin Ratio" and "substitution", which are used to reflect terminology used in the market for transactions of the kind provided for in this Agreement, all right, title and interest in and to Securities and money transferred or paid under this Agreement shall pass to the transferee upon transfer or payment, the obligation of the party receiving Purchased Securities or Margin Securities being an obligation to transfer Equivalent Securities or Equivalent Margin Securities.

(g) Time shall be of the essence in this Agreement.

(h) Subject to paragraph 10, all amounts in the same currency payable by each party to the other under any Transaction or otherwise under this Agreement on the same date shall be combined in a single calculation of a net sum payable by one party to the other and the obligation to pay that sum shall be the only obligation of either party in respect of those amounts.

(i) Subject to paragraph 10, all Securities of the same issue, denomination, currency and series, transferable by each party to the other under any Transaction or hereunder on the same date shall be combined in a single calculation of a net quantity of Securities transferable by one party to the other and the obligation to transfer the net quantity of Securities shall be the only obligation of either party in respect of the Securities so transferable and receivable.

(j) If the parties have specified in Annex I that this paragraph 6(j) shall apply, each obligation of a party under this Agreement (the "first party") (other than an obligation arising under paragraph 10) is subject to the condition precedent that none of the events specified in paragraph 10(a) (Events of Default) shall have occurred and be continuing with respect to the other party.

7. Contractual Currency

(a) All the payments made in respect of the Purchase Price or the Repurchase Price of any Transaction shall be made in the currency of the Purchase Price (the "Contractual Currency") save as provided in paragraph 10(d)(ii). Notwithstanding the foregoing, the payee of any money may, at its option, accept tender thereof in any other currency, provided, however, that, to the extent permitted by applicable law, the obligation of the payer to pay such money will be discharged only to the extent of the amount of the Contractual Currency that such payee may, consistent with normal banking procedures, purchase with such other currency (after deduction of any premium and costs of exchange) for delivery within the customary delivery period for spot transactions in respect of the relevant currency.

(b) If for any reason the amount in the Contractual Currency received by a party, including amounts received after conversion of any recovery under any judgment or order expressed in a currency other than the Contractual Currency, falls short of the amount in the Contractual Currency due and payable, the party required to make the payment will, as a separate and independent obligation, to the extent permitted by applicable law, immediately transfer such additional amount in the Contractual Currency as may be necessary to compensate for the shortfall.

(c) If for any reason the amount in the Contractual Currency received by a party exceeds the amount of the Contractual Currency due and payable, the party receiving the transfer will refund promptly the amount of such excess.

8. Substitution

(a) A Transaction may at any time between the Purchase Date and Repurchase Date, if Seller so requests and Buyer so agrees, be varied by the transfer by Buyer to Seller of Securities equivalent to the Purchased Securities, or to such of the Purchased Securities as shall be agreed, in exchange for the transfer by Seller to Buyer of other Securities of such amount and description as shall be agreed ("New Purchased Securities") (being Securities having a Market Value at the date of the variation at least equal to the Market Value of the Equivalent Securities transferred to Seller).

(b) Any variation under sub-paragraph (a) above shall be effected, subject to paragraph 6(d), by the simultaneous transfer of the Equivalent Securities and New Purchased Securities concerned.

(c) A Transaction which is varied under sub-paragraph (a) above shall thereafter continue in effect as though the Purchased Securities under that Transaction consisted of or included the New Purchased Securities instead of the Securities in respect of which Equivalent Securities have been transferred to Seller.

(d) Where either party has transferred Margin Securities to the other party it may at any time before Equivalent Margin Securities are transferred to it under paragraph 4 request the other party to transfer Equivalent Margin Securities to it in exchange for the transfer to the other party of new Margin Securities having a Market Value at the time at which the exchange is agreed at least equal to that of such Equivalent Margin Securities. If the other party agrees to the request, the exchange shall be effected, subject to paragraph 6(d), by the simultaneous transfer of the Equivalent Margin Securities and new Margin Securities concerned. Where either or both of such transfers is or are effected through a settlement system in circumstances which under the rules and procedures of that settlement system give rise to a payment by or for the account of one party to or for the account of the other party, the parties shall cause such payment or payments to be made outside that settlement system, for value the same day as the payments made through that settlement system, as shall ensure that the exchange of Equivalent Margin Securities and new Margin Securities effected under this sub-paragraph does not give rise to any net payment of cash by either party to the other.

9. Representations

Each party represents and warrants to the other that—

(a) it is duly authorized to execute and deliver this Agreement, to enter into the Transactions contemplated hereunder and to perform its obligations hereunder and thereunder and has taken all necessary action to authorize such execution, delivery and performance;

(b) it will engage in this Agreement and the Transactions contemplated hereunder (other than Agency Transactions) as principal;

(c) the person signing this Agreement on its behalf is, and any person representing it in entering into a Transaction will be, duly authorized to do so on its behalf;

(d) it has obtained all authorizations of any governmental or regulatory body required in connection with this Agreement and the Transactions contemplated hereunder and such authorizations are in full force and effect;

(e) the execution, delivery and performance of this Agreement and the Transactions contemplated hereunder will not violate any law, ordinance, charter, by-law or rule applicable to it or any agreement by which it is bound or by which any of its assets are affected;

(f) it has satisfied itself and will continue to satisfy itself as to the tax implications of the Transactions contemplated hereunder;

(g) in connection with this Agreement and each Transaction—

(i) unless there is a written agreement with the other party to the contrary, it is not relying on any advice (whether written or oral) of the other party, other than the representations expressly set out in this Agreement;

(ii) it has made and will make its own decisions regarding the entering into of any Transaction based upon its own judgment and upon advice from such professional advisers as it has deemed it necessary to consult;

(iii) it understands the terms, conditions and risks of each Transaction and is willing to assume (financially and otherwise) those risks; and

(h) at the time of transfer to the other party of any Securities it will have the full and unqualified right to make such transfer and that upon such transfer of Securities the other party will receive all right, title and interest in and to those Securities free of any lien (other than a lien granted to the operator of the clearance system through which the Securities are transferred), claim, charge or encumbrance.

On the date on which any Transaction is entered into pursuant hereto, and on each day on which Securities, Equivalent Securities, Margin Securities or Equivalent Margin Securities are to be transferred under any Transaction, Buyer and Seller shall each be deemed to repeat all the foregoing representations. For the avoidance of doubt and notwithstanding any arrangements which Seller or Buyer may have with any third party, each party will be liable as a principal for its obligations under this Agreement and each Transaction.

10. Events of Default

(a) If any of the following events (each an "Event of Default") occurs in relation to either party (the "Defaulting Party", the other party being the "non-Defaulting Party") whether acting as Seller or Buyer—

(i) Buyer fails to pay the Purchase Price upon the applicable Purchase Date or Seller fails to pay the Repurchase Price upon the applicable Repurchase Date; or

(ii) if the parties have specified in Annex I that this sub-paragraph shall apply, Seller fails to deliver Purchased Securities on the Purchase Date or Buyer fails to deliver Equivalent Securities on the Repurchase Date, in either case within the standard settlement time for delivery of the Securities concerned; or

(iii) Seller or Buyer fails to pay when due any sum payable under sub-paragraph (h) or (i) below; or

(iv) Seller or Buyer fails to:

(A) make a Margin Transfer within the minimum period in accordance with paragraph 4(g) or, in the case of an obligation to deliver Equivalent Margin Securities, either to deliver the relevant Equivalent Margin Securities or to pay Cash Margin in accordance with paragraph 4(h)(i) or to pay the Cash Equivalent Amount in accordance with paragraph 4(h)(ii);

(B) where paragraph 4(i) applies, to provide margin in accordance with that paragraph; or

(C) to pay any amount or to transfer any Securities in accordance with paragraphs 4(k) or (I); or

(v) Seller or Buyer fails to comply with paragraph 5; or

(vi) an Act of Insolvency occurs with respect to Seller or Buyer; or

(vii) any representations made by Seller or Buyer are incorrect or untrue in any material respect when made or repeated or deemed to have been made or repeated; or

(viii) Seller or Buyer admits to the other that it is unable to, or intends not to, perform any of its obligations hereunder or in respect of any Transaction; or

(ix) Seller or Buyer being declared in default or being suspended or expelled from membership of or participation in, any securities exchange or suspended or prohibited from dealing in securities by any Competent Authority, in each case on the grounds that it has failed to meet any requirements relating to financial resources or credit rating; or

(x) Seller or Buyer fails to perform any other of its obligations hereunder and does not remedy such failure within 30 days after notice is given by the non-Defaulting Party requiring it to do so,

then sub-paragraphs (b) to (g) below shall apply.

(b) If at any time an Event of Default has occurred and is continuing the non-Defaulting. Party may, by not more than 20 days' notice to the Defaulting Party specifying the relevant Event of Default, designate a day not earlier than the day such notice is effective as an Early Termination Date in respect of all outstanding Transactions. If, however, "Automatic Early Termination" is specified in Annex I with respect to the Defaulting Party, then an Early Termination Date in respect of all outstanding Transactions will occur at the time immediately preceding the occurrence with respect to the Defaulting Party of an Act of Insolvency which is the presentation of a petition for winding-up or any analogous proceeding or the appointment of a liquidator or analogous officer of the Defaulting Party.

(c) If an Early Termination Date occurs, the Repurchase Date for each Transaction hereunder shall be deemed to occur on the Early Termination Date and, subject to the following provisions, all Cash Margin (including interest accrued) shall be repayable and Equivalent Margin Securities shall be deliverable and Cash Equivalent Amounts shall be payable, in each case on the Early Termination Date (and so that, where this sub-paragraph applies, performance of the respective obligations of the parties with respect to the delivery of Securities, the payment of the Repurchase Prices for any Equivalent Securities, the repayment of any Cash Margin and the payment of Cash Equivalent Amounts shall be effected only in accordance with the provisions of sub-paragraph (d) below).

(d)

(i) The Default Market Values of the Equivalent Securities and any Equivalent Margin Securities to be transferred, the amount of any Cash Margin (including the amount of interest accrued) to be transferred and the Repurchase Prices and Cash Equivalent Amounts to be paid by each party shall be established by the non-Defaulting Party for all Transactions as at the Early Termination Date;

(ii) on the basis of the sums so established, an account shall be taken (as at the Early Termination Date) of what is due from each party to the other under this Agreement (on the basis that each party's claim against the other in respect of the transfer to it of Equivalent Securities or Equivalent Margin Securities under this Agreement equals the Default Market Value therefor and including amounts payable under paragraphs 10(g) and 12) and the sums due from one party shall be set off against the sums due from the other and only the balance of the account shall be payable (by the party having the claim valued at the lower amount pursuant to the foregoing). For the purposes of this calculation, all sums not denominated in the Base Currency shall be converted into the Base Currency at the Spot Rate; and

(iii) as soon as reasonably practicable after effecting the calculation above, the non-Defaulting Party shall provide to the Defaulting Party a statement showing in reasonable detail such calculations and specifying the balance payable by one party to the other and such balance shall be due and payable on the Business Day following the date of such statement provided that, to the extent permitted by applicable law, interest shall accrue on such amount on a 360 day, 365 day or other day basis in accordance with the applicable market convention (or as otherwise agreed by the parties), for the actual number of days during the period from and including the Early Termination Date to, but excluding, the date of payment.

(e) For the purposes of this Agreement, the "Default Market Value" of any Equivalent Securities or Equivalent Margin Securities shall be determined by the non-Defaulting Party on or as soon as reasonably practicable after the Early Termination Date in accordance with sub-paragraph (f) below, and for this purpose—

(i) the "Appropriate Market" means, in relation to Securities of any description, the market which is the most appropriate market for Securities of that description, as determined by the non-Defaulting Party;

(ii) "Deliverable Securities" means Equivalent Securities or Equivalent Margin Securities to be delivered by the Defaulting Party;

(iii) "Net Value" means at any time, in relation to any Deliverable Securities or Receivable Securities, the amount which, in the reasonable opinion of the non-Defaulting Party, represents their fair market value, having regard to such pricing sources (including trading prices) and methods (which may include, without limitation, available prices for Securities with similar maturities, terms and credit characteristics as the relevant Equivalent Securities or Equivalent Margin Securities) as the non-Defaulting Party considers appropriate, less, in the case of Receivable Securities, or plus, in the case of Deliverable Securities, all Transaction Costs which would be incurred or reasonably anticipated in connection with the purchase or sale of such Securities;

(iv) "Receivable Securities" means Equivalent Securities or Equivalent Margin Securities to be delivered to the Defaulting Party; and

(v) "Transaction Costs" in relation to any transaction contemplated in paragraph 10(e) or (f) means the reasonable costs, commissions, fees and expenses (including any mark-up or mark-down or premium paid for guaranteed delivery) incurred or reasonably anticipated in connection with the purchase of Deliverable Securities or sale of Receivable Securities, calculated on the assumption that the aggregate thereof is the least that could reasonably be expected to be paid in order to carry out the transaction.

(f) If—

(i) on or about the Early Termination Date the non-Defaulting Party has sold, in the case of Receivable Securities, or purchased, in the case of Deliverable Securities, Securities which form part of the same issue and are of an identical type and description as those Equivalent Securities or Equivalent Margin Securities (regardless as to whether or not such sales or purchases have settled), the non-Defaulting Party may elect to treat as the Default Market Value—

(A) in the case of Receivable Securities, the net proceeds of such sale after deducting all reasonable costs, commissions, fees and expenses incurred in connection therewith (provided that, where the Securities sold are not identical in amount to the Equivalent Securities or Equivalent Margin Securities, the non-Defaulting Party may, acting in good faith, either (x) elect to treat such net proceeds of sale divided by the amount of Securities sold and multiplied by the amount of the Equivalent Securities or Equivalent Margin Securities as the Default Market Value or (y) elect to treat such net proceeds of sale of the Equivalent Securities or Equivalent Margin Securities actually sold as the Default Market Value of that proportion of the Equivalent Securities or Equivalent Margin Securities, and, in the case of (y), the Default Market Value of the balance of the Equivalent Securities or Equivalent Margin Securities shall be determined separately in accordance with the provisions of this paragraph 10(f)); or

(B) in the case of Deliverable Securities, the aggregate cost of such purchase, including all reasonable costs, commissions, fees and expenses incurred in connection therewith (provided that, where the Securities purchased are not identical in amount to the Equivalent Securities or Equivalent Margin Securities, the non-Defaulting Party may, acting in good faith, either (x) elect to treat such aggregate cost divided by the amount of Securities sold and multiplied by the amount of the Equivalent Securities or Equivalent Margin Securities as the Default Market Value or (y) elect to treat the aggregate cost of purchasing the Equivalent Securities or Equivalent Margin Securities actually purchased as the Default Market Value of that proportion of the Equivalent Securities or Equivalent Margin Securities, and, in the case of (y), the Default Market Value of the balance of the Equivalent Securities or Equivalent Margin Securities shall be determined separately in accordance with the provisions of this paragraph 10(f));

(ii) on or about the Early Termination Date the non-Defaulting Party has received, in the case of Deliverable Securities, offer quotations or, in the case of Receivable Securities, bid quotations in respect of Securities of the relevant description from two or more market makers or regular dealers in the Appropriate Market in a commercially reasonable size, using pricing methodology which is customary for the relevant type of security (as determined by the non-Defaulting Party) the non-Defaulting Party may elect to treat as the Default Market Value of such Securities—

(A) the price quoted (or where a price is quoted by two or more market makers, the arithmetic mean of such prices) by each of them for, in the case of Deliverable Securities, the sale by the relevant market maker or dealer of such Securities or, in the case of Receivable Securities, the purchase by the relevant market maker or dealer of such Securities provided that such price or prices quoted may be adjusted in a commercially reasonable manner by the non-Defaulting Party (x) to reflect accrued but unpaid coupons not reflected in the price or prices quoted in respect of such securities and (y) in respect of any Pool Factor Affected Security, to reflect the realizable value of such Security, taking into consideration the Pool Factor Distortion (and for this purpose, "Pool Factor Affected Security" means a security other than an equity security in respect of which the decimal value of the outstanding principal divided by the original principal balance of such

Security is less than one (as indicated by any pool factor applicable to such security), such circumstance a "Pool Factor Distortion");

(B) after deducting, in the case of Receivable Securities, or adding, in the case of Deliverable Securities the Transaction Costs which would be incurred or reasonably anticipated in connection with such a transaction; or

(iii) if, acting in good faith the non-Defaulting Party either—

(A) has endeavored but been unable to sell or purchase Securities in accordance with sub-paragraph (i) above or to obtain quotations in accordance with sub-paragraph (ii) above (or both); or

(B) has determined that it would not be commercially reasonable to sell or purchase Securities at the prices bid or offered or to obtain such quotations, or that it would not be commercially reasonable to use any quotations which it has obtained under sub-paragraph (ii) above, the non-Defaulting Party may determine the Net Value of the relevant Equivalent Securities or Equivalent Margin Securities (which shall be specified) and may treat such Net Value as the Default Market Value of the relevant Equivalent Securities or Equivalent Margin Securities.

(g) The Defaulting Party shall be liable to the non-Defaulting Party for the amount of all reasonable and legal and other professional expenses incurred by the non-Defaulting Party in connection with or as a consequence of an Event of Default, together with interest thereon at the Applicable Rate or, in the case of an expense attributable to a particular Transaction, the Pricing Rate for the relevant Transaction if that Pricing Rate is greater than the Applicable Rate.

(h) If Seller fails to deliver Purchased Securities to Buyer on the applicable Purchase Date Buyer may—

(i) if it has paid the Purchase Price to Seller, require Seller immediately to repay the sum so paid;

(ii) if Buyer has a Transaction Exposure to Seller in respect of the relevant Transaction, require Seller from time to time to pay Cash Margin at least equal to such Transaction Exposure;

(iii) at any time while such failure continues, terminate the Transaction by giving written notice to Seller. On such termination the obligations of Seller and Buyer with respect to delivery of Purchased Securities and Equivalent Securities shall terminate and Seller shall pay to Buyer an amount equal to the excess of the Repurchase Price at the date of Termination over the Purchase Price.

(i) If Buyer fails to deliver some or all Equivalent Securities to Seller on the applicable Repurchase Date Seller may—

(i) if it has paid the Repurchase Price to Buyer, require Buyer immediately to repay the sum so paid;

(ii) if Seller has a Transaction Exposure to Buyer in respect of the relevant Transaction, require Buyer from time to time to pay Cash Margin at least equal to such Transaction Exposure;

(iii) at any time while such failure continues, by written notice to Buyer declare that that Transaction or part of that Transaction corresponding to the Equivalent Securities that have not been delivered (but only that Transaction or part of Transaction) shall be terminated immediately in accordance with sub-paragraph (c) above (disregarding for this purpose references in that sub-paragraph to transfer of Cash Margin, delivery of Equivalent Margin Securities and payment of Cash Equivalent Amount and as if references to the Repurchase Date were to the date on which notice was given under this sub-paragraph).

(j) The provisions of this Agreement constitute a complete statement of the remedies available to each party in respect of any Event of Default.

(k) Subject to paragraph 10(1), neither party may claim any sum by way of consequential loss or damage in the event of a failure by the other party to perform any of its obligations under this Agreement.

(*l*)

(i) Subject to sub-paragraph (ii) below, if as a result of a Transaction terminating before its agreed Repurchase Date or a Forward Transaction terminating before its Purchase Date under paragraphs 10(b), 10(h)(iii) or 10(i)(iii), the non-Defaulting Party, in the case of paragraph 10(b), Buyer, in the case of paragraph 10(h)(iii), or Seller, in the case of paragraph 10(i)(iii), (in each case the "first party") incurs any loss or expense in entering into replacement transactions or in otherwise hedging its exposure arising in connection with a Transaction so terminating, the other party shall be required to pay to the first party the amount determined by the first party in good faith and without double counting to be equal to the loss or expense incurred in connection with such replacement transactions or hedging (including all fees, costs and other expenses) less the amount of any profit or gain made by that party in connection with such replacement transactions or hedging; provided that if that calculation results in a negative number, an amount equal to that number shall be payable by the first party to the other party.

(ii) If the first party reasonably decides, instead of entering into such replacement transactions, to replace or unwind any hedging transactions which the first party entered into in connection with the Transaction so terminating, or to enter into any replacement hedging transactions, the other party shall be required to pay to the first party the amount determined by the first party in good faith to be equal to the loss or expense incurred in connection with entering into such replacement or unwinding (including all fees, costs and other expenses) less the amount of any profit or gain made by that party in connection with such replacement or unwinding; provided that if that calculation results in a negative number, an amount equal to that number shall be payable by the first party to the other party.

(m) Each party shall immediately notify the other if an Event of Default, or an event which, upon the service of a notice or the lapse of time, or both, would be an Event of Default, occurs in relation to it.

(n) Any amount payable to one party (the Payee) by the other party (the Payer) under paragraph 10(d) may, at the option of the non-Defaulting Party, be reduced by its set off against any amount payable (whether at such time or in the future or upon the occurrence of a contingency) by the Payee to the Payer (irrespective of the currency, place of payment or booking office of the obligation) under any other agreement between the Payee and the Payer or instrument or undertaking issued or executed by one party to, or in favor of, the other party. If an obligation is unascertained, the non-Defaulting Party may in good faith estimate that obligation and set off in respect of the estimate, subject to accounting to the other party when the obligation is ascertained. Nothing in this paragraph shall be effective to create a charge or other security interest. This paragraph shall be without prejudice and in addition to any right of set off, combination of accounts, lien or other right to which any party is at any time otherwise entitled (whether by operation of law, contract or otherwise).

11. Tax Event

* * *

12. Interest

To the extent permitted by applicable law, if any sum of money payable hereunder or under any Transaction is not paid when due, interest shall accrue on the unpaid sum as a separate debt at the greater of the Pricing Rate for the Transaction to which such sum relates (where such sum is referable to a Transaction) and Applicable Rate on a 360 day basis or 365 day basis in accordance with the applicable market convention (or as otherwise agreed by the parties), for the actual number of days during the period from and including the date on which payment was due to, but excluding, the date of payment.

13. Single Agreement

Each party acknowledges that, and has entered into this Agreement and will enter into each Transaction hereunder in consideration of and in reliance upon the fact that all Transactions hereunder constitute a single business and contractual relationship and are made in consideration of each other. Accordingly, each party agrees (i) to perform all of its obligations in respect of each Transaction hereunder, and that a default in the performance of any such obligations shall constitute a default by it in respect of all Transactions hereunder, and (ii) that payments, deliveries and other transfers made by either of them in respect of any Transaction shall be deemed to have been made in consideration of payments, deliveries and other transfers in respect of any other Transactions hereunder.

14. Notices and Other Communications

(a) Any notice or other communication to be given under this Agreement—

(i) shall be in the English language, and except where expressly otherwise provided in this Agreement, shall be in writing;

(ii) may be given in any manner described in sub-paragraphs (b) and (c) below;

(iii) shall be sent to the party to whom it is to be given at the address or number, or in accordance with the electronic messaging details, set out in Annex I.

(b) Subject to sub-paragraph (c) below, any such notice or other communication shall be effective—

(i) if in writing and delivered in person or by courier, on the date when it is delivered;

(ii) if sent by facsimile transmission, on the date when the transmission is received by a responsible employee of the recipient in legible form (it being agreed that the burden of proving receipt will be on the sender and will not be met by a transmission report generated by the sender's facsimile machine);

(iii) if sent by certified or registered mail (airmail, if overseas) or the equivalent (return receipt requested), on the date that mail is delivered or its delivery is attempted; or

(iv) if sent by Electronic Messaging System, on the date that electronic message is received;

except that any notice or communication which is received, or delivery of which is attempted, after close of business on the date of receipt or attempted delivery or on a day which is not a day on which commercial banks are open for business in the place where that notice or other communication is to be given shall be treated as given at the opening of business on the next following day which is such a day.

(a) If—

(i) there occurs in relation to either party an Event of Default; and

(ii) the non-Defaulting Party, having made all practicable efforts to do so, including having attempted to use at least two of the methods specified in sub-paragraph (b)(ii), (iii) or (iv) above, has been unable to serve a Default Notice by one of the methods specified in those sub-paragraphs (or such of those methods as are normally used by the non-Defaulting Party when communicating with the Defaulting Party),

the non-Defaulting Party may sign a written notice (a "Special Default Notice") which—

(A) specifies the relevant event referred to in paragraph 10(a) which has occurred in relation to the Defaulting Party;

(B) specifies the Early Termination Date designated in the Default Notice;

(C) states that the non-Defaulting Party, having made all practicable efforts to do so, including having attempted to use at least two of the methods specified in sub-paragraph (b)(ii), (iii) or (iv) above, has been unable to serve a Default Notice by one of the methods specified in those sub-paragraphs (or such of those methods as are normally used by the non-Defaulting Party when communicating with the Defaulting Party); and

(D) specifies the date on which, and the time at which, the Special Default Notice is signed by the non-Defaulting Party.

On the signature of a Special Default Notice the Early Termination Date shall occur as designated in the Default Notice. A Special Default Notice shall be given to the Defaulting Party as soon as practicable after it is signed.

(b) Either party may by notice to the other change the address or facsimile number or Electronic Messaging System details at which notices or other communications are to be given to it.

15. Entire Agreement; Severability

* * *

16. Non-assignability; Termination

(a) Subject to sub-paragraph (b) below, neither party may assign, charge or otherwise deal with (including without limitation any dealing with any interest in or the creation of any interest in) its rights or obligations under this Agreement or under any Transaction without the prior written consent of the other party. Subject to the foregoing, this Agreement and any Transactions shall be binding upon and shall inure to the benefit of the parties and their respective successors and assigns.

(b) Sub-paragraph (a) above shall not preclude a party from assigning, charging or otherwise dealing with all or any part of its interest in any sum payable to it under paragraph 10(c) or (g) above.

(c) Either party may terminate this Agreement by giving written notice to the other, except that this Agreement shall, notwithstanding such notice, remain applicable to any Transactions then outstanding.

(d) All remedies hereunder shall survive Termination in respect of the relevant Transaction and termination of this Agreement.

(e) The participation of any additional member State of the European Union in economic and monetary union after 1 January 1999 shall not have the effect of altering any term of the Agreement or any Transaction, nor give a party the right unilaterally to alter or terminate the Agreement or any Transaction.

17. Governing Law

* * *

18. No Waivers, etc.

No express or implied waiver of any Event of Default by either party shall constitute a waiver of any other Event of Default and no exercise of any remedy hereunder by any party shall constitute a waiver of its right to exercise any other remedy hereunder. No modification or waiver of any provision of this Agreement and no consent by any party to a departure herefrom shall be effective unless and until such modification, waiver or consent shall be in writing and duly executed by both of the parties hereto. Without limitation on any of the foregoing, the failure to give a notice pursuant to paragraph 4(a) hereof will not constitute a waiver of any right to do so at a later date.

19. Waiver of Immunity

* * *

20. Recording

The parties agree that each may electronically record all telephone conversations between them.

21. Third Party Rights

* * *

[Name of Party]	[Name of Party]
By: ____________________	By: ____________________
Title: __________________	Title: __________________
Date: __________________	Date: __________________

CHAPTER 9

THE HISTORY OF SECURED TRANSACTIONS

■ ■ ■

§ 1. INTRODUCTION

This chapter traces the Anglo-American history of the law of personal property security devices. Why study the history of security interests as part of a course on Article 9 of the Uniform Commercial Code? There are at least three reasons. First, Article 9 is the product of many centuries of fragmented experimentation. Its provisions draw together many disparate historical practices and, in the process, balance a variety of competing considerations.[1] In order fully to understand the subject and the choices that the current law reflects, it is useful to have some sense of the subject's historical development. Second, it is difficult for many students (at least at first) to grasp the "forest" of Article 9 from its numerous individual "trees." Some sense of the history is both grounding and conceptually organizing. Third, the history is particularly rich, not only in terms of how the subject matter evolved from relatively humble origins to encompass a proliferation of forms, but also as an example of persistent ingenuity and innovation. In order to gain some purchase on this history, however, it is useful at the outset to revisit a few basic concepts introduced in Chapter 1.

First, we have the defining idea that a security interest is taken in personal property, as opposed to realty.[2] As we have seen, that is not entirely accurate. For example, as elaborated in Chapter 6, Article 9 also applies to fixtures—a hybrid concept. But the general idea remains characteristically true: a security interest under Article 9 applies to various kinds of transactions involving discretely categorized items of tangible personal property, such as equipment, inventory, and consumer goods, and a variety of less physically tangible personalty, including accounts, instruments, and certain causes of action.

Second, we have the idea of a "security interest" itself. A security interest is an encumbrance (sometimes referred to as a "lien") on personal

---

1 In creating Article 9, the drafters drew extensively on historical analysis. *See* Walter D. Malcolm, *The Uniform Commercial Code As Enacted in Massachusetts*, 13 BUS. LAW 490, 491 (1958) ("[C]ommercial law as far back as that of Rome was considered . . . .").

2 *See* UCC § 9–109(a)(1) (2010) (Article 9 also applies to "a transaction, regardless of its form, that creates a security interest in personal property . . . .").

property designed to secure the performance of an obligation, typically the payment of a debt. The preceding chapters examine in detail different kinds of security interests taken in various types of collateral.

Third, by far the most common kind of security interest is the "non-possessory" kind. A security interest is non-possessory if the debtor is to retain possession of the collateral for the duration of the transaction, with the secured party taking possession only in the event the debtor fails to perform his obligations (*i.e.*, the debtor "defaults"). In contrast, a possessory security interest—where the secured party has possession of the collateral prior to default—is relatively rare. Historically, however, there have been times when the opposite has been true.

Fourth, the structure of a secured transaction under Article 9 characteristically involves a private contractual agreement between the debtor and the particular creditor taking a security interest in the collateral in question, yet is also binding in many ways on third parties. A variety of rules govern the rights of the secured party in the collateral as against third parties who may also have or acquire interests in the same collateral. The ability of the secured party to have its claim satisfied from the collateral ahead of the rights or interests of others is what we call a right of "priority." As the preceding chapters explain, priority under Article 9 is a somewhat complicated affair, with a variety of rules that turn on the circumstances. These rules have complex historical antecedents.

Fifth, we have the idea that, in order for a secured creditor to enjoy enforceable rights ahead of the rights and interests of others, there should be some way for third parties to learn of the security interest and, accordingly, that a particular secured party has "fenced off" certain of the debtor's property for its benefit. In this way, for example, third parties may take the existence of a security interest in particular collateral into account when deciding whether to extend credit to the debtor or buy the collateral. As we have seen, we call this a matter of "notice." Over time, the law has experimented with a variety of different notice requirements, with varying consequences for noncompliance.

As the examination of security interests undertaking in the previous chapters illustrates, many other considerations come into play in their creation and enforcement. Nonetheless the basic concepts of possession, priority, and notice are particularly central to the operation of Article 9. Centuries elapsed while the law, in fits and starts, struggled to settle on a set of fixed procedures for the taking and enforcement of security interests, and considerations of possession, priority, and notice were central to that development.

Also central to the development of the law of secured transactions was a vast amount of frequently ingenious tinkering. Anglo-American creditors and debtors have long experimented with a variety of ways to grant a creditor an enforceable right to obtain satisfaction of an obligation from specific items of the debtor's property ahead of the claims and interests of others. Although different in their particulars, these methods have all sought to structure in a hierarchical way the competing interests of creditors, debtors, and third parties. Secured transactions arose because they have certain advantages (at least for the secured lender). To identify these advantages it is again helpful to recall from Chapter 1 the discussion of the contrasting nature of "secured" and "unsecured" forms of indebtedness.

A lender who extends credit to the debtor in exchange for the debtor's obligation to pay the resulting debt, but who does not take a lien on any of the debtor's property to secure payment of the debt, is a classic "unsecured" creditor. If the debtor defaults, the creditor may sue the debtor, obtain a judgment, and then pursue collection in accordance with whatever enforcement rights are available in the relevant jurisdiction (typically through a court's issuance of a writ of execution to be enforced by a local official).

In contrast, a lender who extends credit to the debtor in exchange for the debtor's obligation to pay the resulting debt, and does take a lien on particular items of the debtor's property to secure payment of the debt, is a classic "secured" creditor. In the event the debtor defaults, the creditor may look more readily to its lien interest in its collateral in order to satisfy the debt. As an historical matter, this idea first emerged as the "pledge," the simplest form of secured transaction. A pledge occurs when a debtor secures his performance of an obligation by placing one or more items of his property in the possession of the creditor.

At outlined in Chapter 1, the pledge has certain advantages, at least for the secured creditor. First, because the creditor retains physical possession of the collateral until the debtor fully satisfies his obligation, the creditor may (in most cases) quickly and easily dispose of the collateral in the event of default. The creditor may thus obtain recovery more promptly than is typically possible in an unsecured transaction. Second, because the creditor has physical possession of the collateral, the creditor can generally rest assured that the collateral will be available to satisfy the debt in the event of the debtor's default.

On the other hand, the pledge also has certain distinct disadvantages. By handing over possession of a valuable asset to the secured party, the debtor typically loses the ability to make use of the collateral unless and until he satisfies his obligation to the creditor. From the debtor's perspective, a superior form of security will often be non-possessory: the debtor grants a security interest but keeps possession of the collateral unless and until he defaults.

To avoid the shortcomings of the pledge, creditors and debtors long experimented with a variety of non-possessory security devices. Although non-possessory security interests have taken many forms, they have all sought to strike the same balance between giving the creditor the functional equivalent of a pledge and permitting the debtor to retain possession of—and thus to continue to use—the collateral. Along the way, debtors, creditors, legislators, and courts have experimented with a variety of ways to address the questions of priority, notice, and enforcement that non-possessory security interests entail, including how best to deal with the problem of secret liens—those that are difficult for third parties to detect if the debtor fails to disclose them. The current procedures of Article 9 represent a comprehensive response to these and other questions derived from a long history of experience with the benefits and shortcomings of a variety of different approaches. Consideration of the relevant history helps reveal not only how we got to the current provisions of Article 9, but also illuminates much of the conceptual foundations of the current law in a way that offers a deeper understanding of its many uses and meaning.

§ 2. THE EARLY USE OF POSSESSORY AND NON-POSSESSORY SECURITY DEVICES

Throughout most of recorded history, numerous cultures have devised various forms of secured transactions. The simplest type of possessory secured transaction, the pledge, has deep roots and is likely the oldest security device.[3] The pledge appears to have been available in China as early as 3,000 years ago.[4]

Early Roman law recognized a form of pledge called the "pignus."[5] The pignus permitted the debtor to hand over possession of an item of his property to a creditor as security for the debtor's satisfaction of an obligation to the creditor.[6] The creditor and debtor would agree to a deadline for performance of the debtor's obligation. If the debtor failed to satisfy his obligation by the agreed date, Roman law provided the creditor several enforcement options.[7] First, the creditor could sell the item and satisfy the debt from the sale proceeds, allowing the debtor any excess beyond the amount necessary to satisfy the debt.[8] Alternatively, by

---

[3] *See* GRANT GILMORE, SECURITY INTERESTS IN PERSONAL PROPERTY 86 (1965); Malcolm, *supra* note 1, at 503.

[4] Jarret C. Oeltjen, *Pawnbroking on Parade*, 37 BUFF. L. REV. 751, 758 (1988).

[5] George Lee Flint, Jr., *Secured Transactions History: The Fraudulent Myth*, 29 N.M. L. REV. 363, 369 (1999). Prior to the pignus, Roman law permitted the transfer of hostages to the creditor to secure an obligation. In the event the debtor failed to perform, the creditor could keep the hostages as slaves in satisfaction of the debt. *See id.* at 365.

[6] *Id.*

[7] *Id.*

[8] *Id.*

bringing an action of "impetratio dominii," the creditor could sue to keep the item itself in satisfaction of the debt.[9] The early history of possessory security interests under Roman law is thus fairly straightforward. In contrast, the early history of non-possessory secured transactions is far more complicated.

In his classic treatise on security interests in personal property, Professor Gilmore—one of the drafters of Article 9—suggested that, prior to the nineteenth century, "the only security devices which were known in our legal system were the mortgage of real property and the pledge of chattels."[10] Gilmore argued that "[s]ecurity interests in personal property which remained in the borrower's possession during the loan period were unknown," and that a "transfer of an interest in personal property without delivery of possession was looked on as being in essence a fraudulent conveyance, invalid against creditors and purchasers."[11] Professor Flint has challenged Gilmore's interpretation, contending that the historical roots of non-possessory security devices under English law extend much deeper, back at least to the seventeenth century.[12] Flint has also traced the use of non-possessory security devices under Roman law.

NON-POSSESSORY SECURITY UNDER ROMAN LAW: THE HYPOTHECA

As Flint explains, Roman law recognized a non-possessory security device known as the "hypotheca." Under this device, the debtor granted the creditor an interest (or "charge") against certain items of the debtor's personal property, originally a tenant's goods or crops, but later other types of personal property as well.[13] The debtor created the interest without delivering possession to the creditor.[14] If the debtor defaulted, the creditor was permitted to claim possession of the property by suing either the debtor (in an action "interdictum salvianum") or a third party in possession of the property (in an action "quasi serviana").[15]

Because the debtor retained possession of the pledged collateral, there was always the risk that he might grant different security interests in the same item to multiple creditors.[16] To address this potential secret lien problem, Roman law required the debtor to notify subsequent secured creditors of both the existence and value of any prior charges he had placed on the collateral; if he failed to do so, he could be subject to civil or criminal

---

9 *Id.*

10 GILMORE, *supra* note 3, at 24.

11 *Id.*

12 *See* Flint, *supra* note 5, at 366.

13 *Id.* at 369.

14 *Id.*

15 *Id.*

16 *Id.*

liability for fraud.[17] Although Roman law had no official recording system to give public notice of security interests, hypothecas made before a public notary or three witnesses were given priority over those that were not.[18] Further, as between two notarized hypothecas, the earlier one was generally given higher priority.[19] Despite the advantages of this early system for breaking ties between multiple secured creditors with interests in the same property, and likewise for penalizing fraudulent debtors who over-encumbered their assets without disclosure, it was yet imperfect. In the absence of an official public notice system, a creditor with a non-possessory security interest in the property of an unscrupulous Roman debtor ran the risk that the property had already been encumbered by a notarized agreement with another creditor holding a superior priority.

Roman law applied in England until the collapse of the Western Roman Empire. Thereafter, Germanic law took hold across much of the northern realms of continental Western Europe. Although early Germanic law incorporated some aspects of Roman law, it banned the hypotheca and other non-possessory security devices for personal property as a species of fraud. Instead, early Germanic law recognized only possessory pledges: a creditor had to have possession of the collateral for the security interest to be valid. The Norman Conquest in 1066 is thought to have brought this aspect of Germanic law to England.

EARLY ENGLISH LAW: THE GAGE, BILLS OF SALE, CHATTEL MORTGAGES, AND DEEDS OF TRUST

Consistent with Germanic practice, early English law recognized a form of pledge called the "gage." Early on, English courts would enforce a gage only if the debtor had already delivered possession of the collateral to the creditor.[20] Moreover, since the courts had sole authority to order the seizure of a debtor's property to satisfy a debt,[21] a creditor who agreed to a gage without delivery would have only limited options in the event of the debtor's default.[22] If the creditor seized the debtor's property without a court's writ, the debtor had the right to sue for recovery of the seized property.[23] As a result, the gage without delivery was effectively a nullity, and by default the gage with delivery became the standard method of obtaining a security interest in a debtor's personal property in England during the Middle Ages.[24] Like possessory security interests generally,

---

17 *Id.*

18 *Id.*

19 *Id.*

20 *Id.* at 369–70.

21 *Id.* at 368.

22 *See id.* at 369.

23 *See id.* at 370.

24 *Id.*

however, the gage with delivery had the distinct disadvantage of depriving the debtor of the use of a valuable asset until the debtor satisfied his secured obligation.

It was not until the fifteenth century that English law first began to recognize certain forms of non-possessory secured transactions as legitimate alternatives to the gage with delivery.[25] Although the details of these transactions differed significantly, they tended to adhere to a common basic structure. In these transactions the debtor would nominally transfer title to the collateral to the creditor (or the creditor's agent or trustee) in exchange for a sum of money. The debtor would not, however, deliver possession of the property at the time of transfer. The premise was that the creditor would take possession in the future only if the debtor in turn failed to pay the creditor a sum of money stipulated in the parties' agreement. In other words, the creditor's payment of money to the debtor in exchange for the transfer of title was actually a disguised loan, and the real point of using this form was to evade the ban on non-possessory security devices.

In the simplest form of these early non-possessory security devices, the parties would enter into a "sales" agreement either orally or in writing.[26] The agreement provided that the debtor would "sell" the collateral to the creditor but retain possession unless he failed to "repurchase" the collateral by a specified date.[27] The basic idea was that if the debtor defaulted in paying the creditor, the creditor could bring an action in detinue to obtain the property that he had "bought" but never received from the debtor. Originally, English common law did not permit the "purchaser" to use detinue in this way because the creditor had never acquired physical possession of the goods and therefore could not claim wrongful interference with his rightful possession.[28] By 1442, however, English courts began to construe the sales agreement as granting a right of possession sufficient to permit the creditor to obtain the goods through detinue.[29]

Another form of early non-possessory security device involved the use of a written instrument of transfer in the form of a sealed deed. At the time of execution and delivery of the deed, the debtor would transfer title to, but not possession of, the property to the creditor.[30] As with the kind of sales agreement discussed above, the idea behind the deed of transfer was that the debtor would "sell" the collateral to the creditor but retain possession barring default. By paying the amount stipulated in the deed, the debtor

---

25 *Id.*

26 *Id.* at 370–71.

27 *See id.* at 370.

28 *See id.*

29 *Id.* at 370–71.

30 *See id.* at 371.

would divest the creditor of title to the property in question. In other words, the debtor would void the transfer by making his payment. Like sales agreements unaccompanied by transfer of possession, a deed of transfer without delivery was originally inadequate to support an action in detinue.[31] By 1465, however, English courts were willing to recognize the deed of transfer as granting an enforceable right of possession.[32]

As these types of instruments became enforceable, they evolved into at least three main forms, each with its own particular features and characteristic practices: the conditional bill of sale, the chattel mortgage, and the deed of trust.[33] Under the chattel mortgage, the debtor transferred legal title to the collateral but retained "equitable title."[34] This gave the debtor two options: (1) he could keep the property if he paid the creditor in accordance with the terms of the mortgage, or (2) within a reasonable period after default, he could "redeem" the property in a court of equity if he paid the creditor the full amount due.[35] In contrast, the conditional bill of sale granted the creditor complete title to the property (subject to the debtor's right to divest the creditor of title by timely payment of the debt) and did not afford the debtor a right of redemption.[36] As a result, with a conditional bill of sale the debtor had only one performance option: the right to repurchase the collateral by satisfying the conditions set forth in the bill.[37] Another difference between the chattel mortgage and the conditional bill of sale related to the parties' risk of loss—that is, who was responsible for bearing the loss if the goods were destroyed or damaged during the course of the transaction. Under a chattel mortgage, the risk of loss remained with the debtor, whereas the risk of loss was transferred to the creditor under a conditional bill of sale.[38] The deed of trust was similar to the chattel mortgage, except that it vested title to the property in a third party trustee rather than the creditor.[39] All three of these forms of transaction were regarded as types of "sales," and the priority of the creditor's interest in the collateral generally ran from the date of sale.[40]

Once again, however, as with the Roman hypotheca, these devices presented the problem of the secret lien: third parties would not have any particular reason to know about the creditor's interest, both because of its private nature and because the debtor retained possession of the collateral.

---

31 *Id.*

32 *Id.*

33 *Id.*

34 *Id.*

35 *See id.*

36 *Id.*

37 *Id.*

38 *Id.*

39 *Id.*

40 *Id.*

In addition, there was a further weakness from the debtor's perspective. If the value of the collateral greatly exceeded the debt, the defaulting debtor could end up forfeiting the entire value of the collateral by failing to satisfy a relatively trivial claim.[41] The debtor's possession of the collateral also created a potential collection problem for the secured creditor, who had to go to court to enforce his right to the collateral if the debtor did not give it up voluntarily after default.

PLEDGES, COLLUSIVE JUDGMENTS, AND EARLY STATUTORY ALTERNATIVES

The necessity of going to court to obtain possession after default, among other shortcomings, discouraged the use of conditional bills of sale, chattel mortgages, and deeds of trust under early English practice.[42] Instead, secured creditors of the period generally made use of two other collateralized collection devices: the pledge and the "collusive judgment."[43] The pledge (essentially the gage with delivery) was attractive in part because English law at the time (until the mid-1500s) banned the collection of interest on loans.[44] By obtaining possession of the pledged property and using it for his own benefit, the creditor could circumvent the prohibition on interest: revenue from the creditor's use of the debtor's property was not considered "interest" and thus did not fall within the scope of the ban.[45] For example, suppose the debtor owned a flock of sheep. If the creditor made a loan to the debtor, the creditor could not directly charge interest on the loan. If the creditor took the sheep as collateral to secure repayment under a pledge arrangement, however, the creditor could shear the sheep, sell the wool, and keep the proceeds. Of course, from the debtor's perspective, the pledge remained undesirable to the extent it deprived him of the use of a valuable asset for the duration of the transaction. In addition, the pledge was inefficient to the extent the creditor lacked the debtor's skill in generating revenue from the asset in question.[46] Following the Protestant Reformation, Parliament passed legislation eliminating the interest ban,[47] and in doing so also eliminated one of the incentives motivating the use of the pledge as a security device.[48]

---

[41] *See* GILMORE, *supra* note 3, at 49.

[42] *See* Flint, *supra* note 5, at 372.

[43] *Id.*

[44] *Id.* The prohibition banning the collection of interest under early English law was based on Catholic teaching and biblical proscription. *See Luke* 6:35 (King James) ("[L]end, hoping for nothing again . . . ."). A similar prohibition appears in the Islamic Qur'an. *See Qur'an* 2:279. That prohibition has given rise to a variety of transactional practices in Islamic countries designed to fall outside the ban.

[45] *See* Flint, *supra* note 5, at 373.

[46] *See id.*

[47] Temporarily between 1545 and 1552, and then permanently in 1571. *Id.*

[48] *See id.*

Like the pledge, the basic transactional structure of the collusive judgment was also straightforward. In exchange for the creditor's loan, the debtor would agree to the entry of a judgment against him for the amount of the debt and likewise to the issuance of a writ of execution against his personal property.[49] The creditor would agree not to execute the judgment unless and until the debtor failed to perform in accordance with the parties' arrangement. In this way, the debtor was permitted to retain possession of the collateral for the duration of the transaction,[50] and his performance would satisfy the judgment. If the debtor defaulted, however, the creditor would have the writ enforced, leaving the dirty work of collection to the local sheriff.

Initially, the priority of the collusive judgment ran from the date of the initial issuance of the writ of execution.[51] As a result, the collusive judgment granted the creditor priority over subsequent interests in the debtor's property. The collusive judgment was particularly attractive in comparison to the conditional bill of sale, chattel mortgage, and deed of trust because it enabled the creditor more quickly to acquire the collateral following the debtor's default (assuming the debtor had not absconded with it).[52] With a collusive judgment, the creditor had no need to bring a suit in detinue after default because the creditor already had a judgment and writ of execution ready to go in the event the debtor failed to perform. Thus the creditor avoided many of the risks associated with commencing and pursuing a lawsuit, including (1) the potential difficulty of getting the debtor into court, (2) the debtor's potential assertion of the defense of "wager of law,"[53] (3) the trouble of securing the appearance of witnesses, and (4) in some instances, the creditor's inability to pursue an action on account of a misplaced or marred deed under seal (if, for example, the transaction involved a deed of transfer).[54]

At first, these features of the collusive judgment spurred its use and development, and subsequent legislation both expanded its application and added additional enforcement mechanisms. For example, the Second Statute of Westminster, enacted in 1285, permitted collusive judgments to be levied against land in addition to personal property.[55] Moreover, the

---

49 *See id.*

50 *Id.*

51 *Id.* at 374. It is important to note, however, that the collusive judgment extended only to property owned at the time the judgment was entered. So called "after-acquired property" was not covered by the collusive judgment.

52 Flint, *supra* note 5, at 373.

53 The defense of wager of law was a procedure whereby witnesses (frequently paid) swore that the debtor told the truth when he said he did not owe the debt. The religious fear of lying under oath was thought to mitigate the risk of perjury. *See id.* n.73.

54 Flint, *supra* note 5, at 373.

55 *Id.* at 374–375. Other judgments were not afforded this power. *Id.* at 375.

Statute of Merchants in 1285 authorized the imprisonment of the defaulting debtor.[56]

Parliament also experimented with statutory alternatives to the collusive judgment. The Statute of Acton Burnell in 1283 and the Statute of Staples in 1353 permitted creditors to enroll mercantile debts in the records of various towns in addition to the courts.[57] In 1362 Parliament enlarged the scope of these mechanisms beyond mercantile transactions to encompass all debts.[58] Following this expansion, the collusive judgment and statutory enrollment mechanisms were widely used for various commercial and non-commercial transactions.[59]

One problem with the collusive judgment, of course, was that it was effectively a secret lien, and thus posed certain risks to other creditors and the purchasers of personal property. Suppose, for example, a debtor wanted to sell his goods to a buyer but had already entered into a collusive judgment covering the goods with a creditor. If the buyer were to purchase the goods and take delivery, he would risk having to surrender them to the creditor if the debtor defaulted on his payment obligation to his creditor. The more popular collusive judgments became, the more risk buyers collectively assumed when they made their purchases.

THE STATUTE OF FRAUDS AND EARLY FRAUDULENT TRANSFER LEGISLATION

In 1677 Parliament responded by enacting the Statute of Frauds, which altered the priority of the collusive judgment.[60] Whereas previously the priority of the collusive judgment had run from the date the creditor obtained a writ of execution, under the new statute the priority date was when the creditor actually delivered the writ to the sheriff for levy against the debtor's goods after default.[61] As a result, a purchaser who bought the debtor's goods before the creditor delivered the writ to the sheriff would have priority. Though disadvantageous to the holders of collusive judgments, this aspect of the Statute of Frauds protected the interests of good faith purchasers, including creditors with interests in the debtor's property under conditional bills of sale, chattel mortgages, and deeds of trust, which, as noted above, were treated as types of sales.[62] The statutory change created an obvious incentive to use these "sales" devices rather than the collusive judgment. All other things being equal, a secured creditor will take advantage of the transactional device that affords him the greatest

---

56 *Id.* at 375.

57 *Id.* at 374–75.

58 *Id.* at 376.

59 *Id.*

60 *Id.*

61 *Id.*

62 *See id.*

priority. Even as the Statute of Frauds made these sales devices more attractive, however, various features of the legal landscape nevertheless operated to diminish their appeal. Among these features were prior statutes designed to remedy certain species of fraud, as well as statutes designed to regulate proceedings in bankruptcy.[63]

As an historical matter, just as creditors were creative in developing and using a variety of "sales" devices to assist in collecting from the property of defaulting debtors, insolvent debtors were likewise clever in pursuing various "sales" techniques to avoid their creditors' legitimate collection efforts. For example, insolvent debtors in the fourteenth and fifteenth centuries sometimes thwarted collection by transferring all of their property to relatives or friends through a variety of fictitious "sales" before their creditors could take action.[64] To avoid imprisonment for not paying their debts, some of these debtors also took refuge in one of the many sanctuaries immune from the authority of the courts. There they might live off the income of the property they had just transferred until their frustrated creditors accepted partial payment to settle their claims.[65] Parliament responded in 1377 by enacting legislation that voided "sales" of this kind where, following transfer, the debtor fled to a sanctuary.[66] Debtors circumvented Parliament's prohibition, however, by giving their property to their relatives or friends for safekeeping without then running away to a sanctuary.[67] In 1488 Parliament responded again: transfers of property made for the benefit of the transferor were void as against third parties prejudiced by the transfer, regardless of whether the transfers were collusive.[68] In 1571 the English Fraudulent Conveyance Statute also broadly voided all assignments of property made with the intent to defraud or delay creditors.[69]

During the seventeenth and early eighteenth centuries, judges had to reconcile the broad language of these enactments (which, as noted, were designed to prevent certain kinds of fraud by debtors) with the realities of popular commercial security devices, as various disgruntled parties (unpaid unsecured creditors, for example) attempted to use the statutes to void otherwise legitimate non-possessory secured transactions. For example, in *Stone v. Grubham*, Edward Coke refused to apply the Fraudulent Conveyance Statute to void a contingent sale,[70] establishing what eventually became known as the "absolute-conditional" test limiting

---

63 *See id.* at 380.

64 *Id.*

65 *Id.*

66 *Id.*

67 *Id.*

68 *Id.*

69 *Id.*

70 (1615) 80 Eng. Rep. 1079 (K.B.) 1080; 2 Bulstrode. 225.

the use of the statute to undo secured transactions.[71] Coke reasoned as follows: if the transaction was an absolute sale from the seller (debtor) to a purchaser without any further conditions to be satisfied, but the seller (debtor) nevertheless retained possession of the property, the transaction would be declared a fraudulent conveyance and therefore unenforceable against injured third parties.[72] On the other hand, if the transaction was a conditional sale requiring further action by one of the parties (such as the seller's payment of a stipulated sum to the purchaser to reacquire title to the asset), and the seller maintained possession only in accordance with the conditions imposed, the transaction would be declared a true sale and therefore enforceable.[73] In other words, Coke limited the reach of the Fraudulent Conveyance Statute to preserve the viability of the conditional bill of sale.[74]

Without citing to it, Coke essentially followed the earlier reasoning of the decision of the Court of Star Chamber in *Twyne's Case*. There a creditor sought a judgment to enforce a debt against the debtor's assets.[75] Twyne was another creditor of the same debtor.[76] Twyne and the debtor had negotiated an absolute deed of gift to Twyne of all the debtor's goods in return for cancellation of the debtor's indebtedness to Twyne.[77] Under their arrangement, however, Twyne permitted the debtor to retain possession of his sheep,[78] which represented the majority of the debtor's assets.[79] The debtor sold some of the sheep, sheared some, and marked them with his mark,[80] suggesting to the world that he still owned them notwithstanding the deed of gift. When the sheriff tried to seize the sheep to satisfy the debtor's obligation to the first creditor, Twyne (through his agents) resisted the sheriff by force, claiming he actually owned the sheep.[81] The court concluded that Twyne's deed of gift constituted a fraudulent conveyance because, among other things, the debtor retained possession of the sheep even though the deed of gift imposed no conditions qualifying Twyne's

---

71 Flint, *supra* note 5, at 381.

72 *Stone*, 80 Eng. Rep. at 1080; 2 Bulstrode. at 226.

73 *Id.*

74 The absolute-conditional rule limited the role of the jury by permitting the court to determine whether the transaction was fraudulent on the basis of the transaction documents as a question of law, rather than leave the issue of fraud in the jury's hands. Flint, *supra* note 5, at 382–83. So long as the transaction documents accurately described the arrangement between the creditor and the debtor, the court would uphold its validity against third parties if the transaction satisfied the test. *Id.* at 383.

75 (1601) 76 Eng. Rep. 809 (Star Ch.) 811; 3 Co. Rep. 80b, 80b.

76 *Id.* at 810–11; 3 Co. Rep. at 80b.

77 *Id.* at 811; 3 Co. Rep. at 80b.

78 *Id.*

79 Flint, *supra* note 5, at 382.

80 *Twyne's Case*, 76 Eng. Rep. at 811; 3 Co. Rep. at 80b.

81 *Id.* at 811–12; 3 Co. Rep. at 80b.

ostensible ownership.[82] In other words, Twyne was convicted of criminal fraud essentially because the transaction documents did not evidence the actual arrangement between the parties.[83] The court explained that those seeking to undertake a transaction of this kind must make it "in a public manner, and before the neighbours, and not in private, for secrecy is a mark of fraud."[84]

Both *Stone* and *Twyne's Case* were decided before the enactment of the 1677 Statute of Frauds. As noted above, this statute altered the priority of the collusive judgment. It also rendered void all sales of goods above a certain value (ten pounds sterling) unless evidenced by actual delivery, delivery in part, earnest money given, or written documentation.[85] Just as disgruntled parties (such as unpaid creditors) had previously attempted to use the Fraudulent Conveyance Statute to challenge the validity of various non-possessory security devices (such as the conditional bill of sale), they also tried to challenge these devices under the 1677 statute. Once again, the courts had to reconcile the broad language of a statutory enactment with the realities of popular commercial practices. In a series of cases, the courts replaced Coke's absolute-conditional test with a "rebuttable presumption rule."[86] According to this rule, a conveyance was presumed to be fraudulent whenever the debtor retained possession of the collateral.[87] The creditor was permitted to rebut the presumption, however, by demonstrating to the jury that the parties intended a legitimate non-possessory secured transaction.[88] In at least two cases applying this standard, the King's Bench upheld the particular non-possessory secured transactions at issue.[89]

EARLY BANKRUPTCY LEGISLATION

Disgruntled parties also challenged the validity of various non-possessory security interests under several early bankruptcy statutes, this time with greater success. Parliament passed a succession of bankruptcy laws in 1543, 1571, 1604, and 1624, each prescribing procedures for the aggregation and ratable distribution of a bankrupt debtor's property.[90] Equality of distribution was a key premise of these procedures: each

---

[82] Flint, *supra* note 5, at 382.

[83] *See Twyne's Case*, 76 Eng. Rep. at 813; 3 Co. Rep. at 81a. Notably, because the transaction documents did not evidence the terms of the parties' actual arrangement, Twyne was not afforded the benefit of an exception to the fraudulent conveyance law for transfers made for valuable consideration and in good faith. Flint, *supra* note 5, at 382.

[84] *Twyne's Case*, 76 Eng. Rep. at 814; 3 Co. Rep. at 81a.

[85] Flint, *supra* note 5, at 384. English decisions subsequently approved the use of symbolic delivery, such as the delivery of a key that would unlock a warehouse where the goods were located. *Id.*

[86] *Id.*

[87] *Id.* at 386.

[88] *Id.*

[89] *Id.* at 386–87.

[90] *Id.* at 388.

creditor would receive a ratable share from the debtor's property based on the amount of his claim. The bankruptcy concept of equality of distribution stood in obvious tension with the core idea behind the non-possessory security interest, namely that the secured creditor holds a preferred interest in his collateral ahead of the claims of others. Far from ensuring equality of distribution, the secured creditor's interest (if enforceable) entitles him to payment from the collateral even if that means there is nothing left over for anyone else.

Under these early English bankruptcy statutes, a creditor could commence a bankruptcy proceeding against a merchant debtor if the debtor committed one or more "acts of bankruptcy," including flight to a sanctuary (to avoid imprisonment for debt), keeping to one's house (to avoid service of process), and, with the Act of 1604, making a fraudulent conveyance of land or goods.[91] The 1604 bankruptcy statute defined the concept of a fraudulent conveyance broadly to include the debtor's making of any "fraudulent [grant], or Conveyance . . . where[by] his . . . Creditors . . . shall, or may be defeated, or delayed for the [recovery] of their [just] and true Debts."[92] The question arose whether the grant of a non-possessory security interest constituted an act of bankruptcy within the meaning of this provision on the theory that it had the effect of defeating the ability of other creditors to recover on their claims. In applying the provision, English courts created what became known as the "modified per se fraud rule."[93] Under this rule, the grant of a non-possessory security interest was fraudulent if the creditor's motive for entering into the transaction was to defeat equality of distribution in bankruptcy.[94] In *Worseley v. Demattos*, the King's Bench determined that the requisite intent to defeat equality of distribution would be inferred if (1) the transaction took place close in time to a more traditional act of bankruptcy (for example, flight to a sanctuary), and (2) the transaction encumbered most or all of the debtor's assets.[95] Having found these requirements satisfied in the case at bar, the court voided the transfer.[96]

It is significant that, in applying the 1604 bankruptcy statute, the court did not rely on the absolute-conditional test developed under the fraudulent conveyance laws. Rather, it crafted a rule tailored to the

---

[91] *Id.*

[92] *Id.* at 392.

[93] *See id.* at 392–93.

[94] *Id.* at 393.

[95] *Id.* As to the first requirement, see (1758) 96 Eng. Rep. 1160 (K.B.) 1167; 2 Keny. 218, 235 (asserting that there was no presumption of fraud where certain suspect transactions took place long before the traditional act of bankruptcy). As to the second requirement, see *id.* at 1165; 2 Keny. at 231 ("There is a great difference between conveyances of all, and of part only[.] [T]he latter may be public, fair and honest . . . . [B]ut a conveyance of all must either be either fraudulent . . . or an immediate bankruptcy must ensue.").

[96] *See id.* at 1168; 2 Keny. at 238.

bankruptcy process. Note also the rule's relatively limited application: bankruptcy proceedings at the time applied solely to merchant debtors, and the rule focused on only those transactions occurring near in time to traditional acts of bankruptcy and involving the bulk of the debtor's assets. Once again, the court construed a statute in a relatively narrow fashion to avoid broadly invalidating popular security devices.

The 1624 bankruptcy statute posed a more serious threat to the validity of non-possessory security interests. First, it denied priority to unexecuted collusive judgments, requiring creditors holding them to share ratably with other creditors.[97] Second, the statute's "reputed ownership" clause granted the commissioners in bankruptcy (that is, the officials charged with collecting the bankrupt debtor's assets, liquidating them, and distributing the proceeds to creditors) the power to sell property in the debtor's possession notwithstanding any secured creditor's non-possessory security interest.[98] At first, the Chancery (one of several major English courts of the time, along with King's Bench, Common Pleas, and Exchequer) employed the absolute-conditional rule, borrowed from the Fraudulent Conveyance Statute, in applying this provision.[99] In several early decisions the Chancery voided a non-possessory security interest in absolute form but not one in conditional form.[100] In 1749, however, the Chancery developed and applied a new rule in *Ryall v. Rolle*[101]: the so-called "per se fraud rule," which voided all secured transactions challenged under the reputed ownership clause where the debtor remained in possession of the collateral.[102]

The facts of *Ryall* were colorful. A merchant made multiple conveyances of his dwelling house, tavern, and equipment while remaining in possession of the same.[103] In essence, the merchant hocked the same collateral multiple times to different parties, creating a dilemma now referred to as the "producer problem" (after the popular movie and play *The Producers*, in which the main characters sell far more than 100 percent of the proceeds of their venture to multiple investors). The court invalidated the conveyances as repugnant to the Act of 1624.[104] Following *Ryall*, virtually all non-possessory security interests could be voided in

---

97 Flint, *supra* note 5, at 389.

98 *See* Bankruptcy Act, 1624, 21 Jac. 1, c. 19, § 10.

99 Flint, *supra* note 5, at 389.

100 *Id.* at 389–90.

101 (1749) 26 Eng. Rep. 107 (Ch.); 1 Atk. 165.

102 Flint, *supra* note 5, at 390.

103 *Ryall*, 26 Eng. Rep. at 107; 1 Atk. at 165.

104 *Id.* at 120; 1 Atk. at 185.

bankruptcy under the statutory provision. In 1784, the King's Bench adopted essentially the same approach as the Chancery.[105]

From the eleventh through the eighteenth centuries, English law struggled to recognize, regulate, and ultimately repudiate in mercantile bankruptcy cases various non-possessory security devices. Although creditors came to prefer the collusive judgment, the 1677 Statute of Frauds effectively destroyed its priority. Further, the 1624 bankruptcy statute rendered unexecuted collusive judgments virtually unenforceable in bankruptcy. Security devices such as conditional bills of sale, chattel mortgages, and deeds of trust had their own difficulties, including the secret lien problem and the tension between enforcing the devices and the fundamental bankruptcy policy of equality of distribution. Another difficulty with these "sales" devices—one the collusive judgment had resolved—was that creditors lacked a speedy method of executing against the collateral following the debtor's default.

Following the American Revolution, the northern states adopted some but not all of the English laws and judge-made doctrines relevant to the recognition, regulation, and repudiation of non-possessory secured transactions. For example, some northern states recognized and applied the English Statute of Frauds and the English fraudulent conveyance laws (together with some version of the absolute-conditional test or the rebuttable presumption rule[106]), but not the English bankruptcy statutes.[107] Due to a lack of reported opinions, the extent to which the southern states adopted the English laws immediately following independence remains uncertain.[108] What is clear is that American jurisprudence played host to many of the tensions and struggles that existed in English practice. Although state legislatures eventually addressed these issues, the path to resolution was anything but smooth.

§ 3. POSSESSORY AND NON-POSSESSORY SECURED TRANSACTIONS IN NINETEENTH CENTURY AMERICA

As in England, debtors and creditors in the United States during the nineteenth century continued to use the common law pledge, with the same advantages and disadvantages identified previously, as a possessory form of security device. It continued to be the simplest and least formal of the methods of granting security. In most commercial transactions the pledge would involve a written agreement identifying the collateral and specifying

---

105 *See* Flint, *supra* note 5, at 391; *see also* Bryson v. Wylie, (1784) 126 Eng. Rep. 791 (K.B.) 791–92; 1 Bos. & Pul. 84, n.

106 Flint, *supra* note 5, at 402.

107 *Id.* at 397–404; *see, e.g.,* Griswold v. Sheldon, 4 N.Y. 581, 587 (1851).

108 *See* Flint, *supra* note 5, at 398.

the creditor's rights (typically at the insistence and for the benefit of the creditor). In general, though, a written agreement was not required, and judges could use parol evidence (such as witness testimony) to ascertain whether the parties intended a pledge, to identify the collateral, and to explain other details of the parties' undertaking. The only necessary legal requirements were the existence of an agreement to create a pledge (written or oral), the giving of value (such as a loan from the creditor to the debtor in exchange for the security), and the condition that the property in question was capable of being pledged to the creditor or his agent (a debtor could not, for example, pledge his mother-in-law to secure payment of a debt). Of course, the hallmark of the pledge remained the understanding that the secured party was to take possession of the collateral, at least at some point, and generally keep possession for the duration of the transaction, until the debtor either satisfied his obligation or defaulted.[109]

From the late eighteenth century through much of the nineteenth century, American creditors and debtors also used a variety of non-possessory security devices, and these generally evolved with changing commercial contexts into a proliferation of distinct forms and practices. That said, two general sets of forms predominated. The first included different types of conditional transfers, such as the conditional bill of sale recognized in English common law. Early on, courts generally upheld these forms of transfer, even though they were essentially private in nature and often did not afford public notice to alert third parties of their existence. Courts required, however, that the conditional transfers pass muster under the prevailing fraudulent transfer standards noted above (such as the absolute-conditional test) and other legal requirements enacted or recognized from time to time.[110]

The second method that emerged in the early 1800s and eventually subsumed and eclipsed many of the older common law methods was the statutory "chattel mortgage."[111] Over time, many states passed chattel mortgage acts recognizing the validity of security devices in which the debtor ("mortgagor") retained possession of the relevant collateral (the "chattels," such as goods and other tangible personal property), *provided that* the creditor ("chattel mortgagee") filed the relevant security document ("mortgage") in accordance with some specified public filing system.[112] The key innovation of these acts was the institution of a system of public notice

---

[109] GILMORE, *supra* note 3, at 22–23; *see also* Casey v. Cavaroc, 96 U.S. 467 (1877) (pledge invalid where the pledgor was in possession).

[110] *See* GILMORE, *supra* note 3, at 26.

[111] *See id.* at 49–51 (discussing the demise of the conditional bill of sale as a security device—outside the realm of consumer finance, at least—in the wake of the enactment of chattel mortgage statutes).

[112] *See* Flint, *supra* note 5, at 363. The English Bill of Sale Act, passed in 1854, was the English version of a chattel mortgage statute. *Id.* at 396.

to address the secret lien problem. The chattel mortgage acts gave their filing requirements teeth by generally voiding security devices that were improperly filed or not filed at all.[113] The typical chattel mortgage statute prescribed that any mortgage or conveyance unaccompanied by an immediate and actual transfer of possession would be void against third parties, such as purchasers and other creditors, unless, for example, "the mortgage or a true copy thereof is filed as directed" by the act.[114] By their terms, these enactments generally did not apply to possessory pledge arrangements, which, as noted, were characteristically accompanied by an actual transfer of possession to the secured party.

THE CHATTEL MORTGAGE ACTS

In theory, the various chattel mortgage acts permitted "[a]nyone [to] give a chattel mortgage on any of his property . . . to anyone to secure any sort of obligation."[115] In reality, these acts prohibited security interests in certain types of personal property, imposed onerous filing formalities, overlapped and clashed with other forms of security devices, and, in the hands of a frequently hostile judiciary, supplied plenty of opportunity for "mortgage murder"—the unceremonious voiding of a security interest "with any weapon that comes to hand."[116]

To begin with, the chattel mortgage came to overlap with the pledge in complex ways. For example, although a pledge by definition involved the secured party's possession of the collateral, a chattel mortgage might also involve possession by the secured party, albeit atypically.[117] This overlap had the effect of blurring the relevant distinctions between the forms: if the secured party had possession of the collateral, was it a pledge or was it a chattel mortgage? It was important to maintain distinctions between these types of transactions because the parties' obligations, rights, and remedies would often vary according to the particular form used.[118] Courts were often left to sort out this problem, frequently through the use of such nebulous standards as " 'the intent of the parties,' out of which courts are so apt to evoke what they most want."[119]

The chattel mortgage acts also clashed in complex ways with the common law conditional sale security device. Recall that, under English common law, a debtor who owned an item of property could effect a non-

---

113 *See* GILMORE, *supra* note 3, at 51.

114 N.Y. Lien Law § 230 (repealed in 1964 by Article 9 of the UCC); GILMORE, *supra* note 3, at 26.

115 *Id.* at 52.

116 *Id.* at 52–53, 55.

117 *See id.* at 5.

118 *Id.* at 6; *see also id.* at 51.

119 *Id.* at 9 (quoting *In re* German Publication Society, 289 F. 509 (S.D.N.Y. 1922) (Hand, J.)).

possessory secured transaction by nominally "selling" the property to his creditor, retaining possession, and contracting for the right to "buy back" the item in accordance with the parties' agreement. In the United States, courts came to recharacterize these fictional "sales" as chattel mortgages, with the consequence that they would be void unless the creditor complied with the filing requirements of the local chattel mortgage statute.[120] So much, then, for the secured lender who claimed to be a "buyer" of the collateral under a conditional bill of sale and neglected to comply with the filing requirements of the relevant chattel mortgage law. But what of a vendor who actually sold and delivered an item of personal property to the debtor but wished to retain a security interest in the item until the debtor paid for it? These "true sales" came to be treated somewhat differently.

VENDOR TITLE RETENTION PRACTICES AND THE CONDITIONAL SALES ACTS

Vendors often sell goods to debtors on credit. For example, a typical sales agreement may provide that, following shipment of the goods, the debtor has 30, 45, 60, or 90 days to pay—and sometimes even longer. But what if the debtor fails to pay? In general, the common law of sales gave the unpaid vendor only limited recourse against the item sold in the event the debtor failed to pony up the purchase price: typically, the vendor was required to sue the debtor as an unsecured creditor.[121] To get around this, vendors long experimented with creative means to obtain repossession of their merchandise, including prominently the idea that, notwithstanding delivery, the vendor had "retained title" to the goods until the debtor finished paying for them.[122] In other words, even if the debtor were to possess the goods, the vendor would claim that transfer of ownership (title) to the debtor was conditioned on the debtor's payment of the purchase price.

To effectuate this title-retention theory, vendors would often include in their sales contracts a clause to the effect that "the seller hereby retains title to the merchandise until the buyer has paid for the merchandise in full."[123] Of course, the vendor's retention of title amounted to a classic secret lien: how would the debtor's other creditors know of the vendor's interest? To address the secret lien problem posed by this popular method of vendor financing, most states enacted some form of conditional sales statute with public notice filing requirements distinct from those specified

---

120 *See* GILMORE, *supra* note 3, at 51.

121 *Id.* at 63; *see also id.* at 65 ("[S]ales law has treated [the unpaid vendor] as an unsecured creditor except for . . . slight concessions . . . .").

122 *See id.* at 64.

123 *See, e.g., In re* American Steel Supply Syndicate, 256 F. 876, 877 (E.D. Mich. 1919) ("Title to the within described property shall remain in you until the purchase price or any judgment therefor has been paid in full . . . .")

under the state's chattel mortgage statute.[124] As a result, many states had a public recording system for chattel mortgages and a separate public recording system for true conditional sales—that is, those in which a vendor sold an item of personal property to the debtor while reserving a security interest in the item until the debtor finished paying for it.[125] Note the trap for the unfortunate secured party who filed with the sales recording office thinking he had a legitimate conditional sales contract when in fact, since the creditor was not a vendor, he held a chattel mortgage. When recharacterized as a chattel mortgage, the security interest could be voided for improper filing: that is, the secured party should have filed in the chattel mortgage recording office, not the sales recording office. Note also the inefficiency of multiple filing systems with separate and distinct recording functions and criteria.

ALTERNATIVE SALES FINANCING STRUCTURES: ERSATZ CONSIGNMENTS AND LEASES, BAILMENT-LEASES, AND EQUIPMENT TRUSTS

In order to secure payment of the purchase price, vendors tried other strategies in addition to "retaining title." First, vendors sometimes attempted to retain ownership of the goods notwithstanding delivery by claiming the sale was a "consignment" and the debtor a "consignee."[126] A second strategy for retaining ownership was to style the sale as a "lease." The vendor adopting this approach would characterize the purchase price as "rent" and label the seller "lessor" and the buyer "lessee."[127] Courts often saw through both the consignment and lease ruses, however, and neither ultimately proved successful, although some states (such as Pennsylvania) long recognized the so-called "bailment-lease" as a legitimate "title-retention" security device.[128]

Under the paradigmatic "true consignment" of personal property, the debtor takes delivery of the goods without any obligation to pay for them unless and until the debtor sells them to a third party.[129] In other words, if the debtor is unable to sell the goods, he is free to return them to the consignor without any further obligation. For the duration of the consignment transaction, the consignor remains the owner of the goods, and it is this feature of consignments that vendors (and their lawyers) found attractive as a vehicle for repossessing the goods should the debtor fail to pay for them. But calling a transaction a consignment does not a consignment make. Regardless of the name chosen by the parties, a

---

124 GILMORE, *supra* note 3, at 68.

125 *Id.*

126 *See id.* at 73–75.

127 *See id.* at 75–81.

128 *Id.* at 77.

129 *Id.* at 73.

transaction is not a consignment when the debtor is obligated to pay for the goods no matter what the debtor does with them (as in the typical "true sale").[130] Thus, courts routinely recharacterized these ersatz consignments as conditional sales and scrutinized them for compliance with applicable conditional sales laws, including any filing requirements.

Under the paradigmatic "true lease" of personal property, the lessee takes delivery and, as a general matter, makes use of the goods with two corresponding obligations: to pay rent for the duration of the lessee's possession and to return possession to the lessor at the end of the lease term. In other words, although the lessee may have an option to purchase the leased items, he has no obligation to do so. For the duration of the lease transaction, then, the lessor remains the owner with an owner's interest in, and rights to, the leased goods. For this reason, the lease thus held the same attraction to vendors as the consignment. But once again, as with consignments, what matters is the substance of the transaction, not how the parties style it. Where the lessee is obligated to pay for the goods and acquires essentially all the rights and obligations of ownership (as in the typical true sale), the transaction is obviously not a lease regardless of how the parties dress it up to look like one. Thus, courts scrutinized purported "lease" transactions where the "lessee" effectively bought the collateral by making installment payments in the form of "rent," and often recharacterized these transactions as conditional sales subject to any applicable filing requirements.[131]

As suggested above, certain types of transactions that were obviously not "true leases" were nonetheless accepted as such in some jurisdictions. One example is the "bailment-lease" mentioned previously. Another example is a family of transactions involving specialized equipment (such as telephones) over which the manufacturer exercised absolute or near monopoly control.[132] A third example is the so-called "Philadelphia plan" equipment trust, which was developed as a means of financing railroad equipment and bus lines.[133]

ADDITIONAL LIMITATIONS ON CHATTEL MORTGAGES: INTANGIBLE COLLATERAL AND AFTER-ACQUIRED PROPERTY

Other problems with the chattel mortgage procedures also emerged. To begin with, notwithstanding that many chattel mortgage statutes applied expressly to security interests in "all personal property," courts

---

[130] *Id.* at 75.

[131] *Id.* at 76.

[132] *Id.* at 78–79.

[133] *Id.* at 79. Under this trust arrangement, a manufacturer of, say, railroad cars would sell the cars to a trust established for the purpose of owning the equipment. The trust was essentially a financing vehicle: it would raise money from investors to pay for the equipment, and its trustee would then "lease" the equipment to the debtor railroad. Special legislation frequently governed equipment trust arrangements. *Id.*

generally construed them as applicable only to security interests in "tangible" goods.[134] Security interests in so-called "intangibles" (such as negotiable instruments) were left to the law of pledge.[135] Similarly, security interests in so-called "pure intangibles" (or "choses in action," such as a debtor's right to bring a lawsuit against a third party) were left to the law of assignment.[136] Security interests in monies to become due under as yet unperformed construction contracts were also, as a species of "contract rights," left to the law of assignment.[137] Note the proliferation of distinct bodies of law dealing with security devices in different kinds of collateral: chattel mortgage statutes for many security arrangements, conditional sales statutes for vendors' title retention contracts, common law equipment trust leases for certain kinds of equipment, and various common law procedures for certain kinds of intangible collateral.

Further, although by their terms the typical chattel mortgage acts applied to all personal property, some important categories of *tangible* goods were also effectively excluded from their scope. For example, courts during the nineteenth century accepted the idea that a debtor could grant a non-possessory security interest in collateral the debtor owned at the time the parties entered into their security arrangement. Such collateral might comprise, for instance, a debtor's existing flock of sheep. But what about so-called "after-acquired collateral," property the debtor acquires in the future? This type of collateral might include additional sheep the debtor adds to the flock after granting the security interest. As the century progressed, after-acquired collateral became increasingly important, particularly in the form of "inventory" collateral, such as a factory operator's unsold stock of manufactured goods or a merchant's "stock in trade" (the goods a merchant displayed on his shelves or kept in his warehouse for sale to customers). After the Industrial Revolution, these goods became increasingly significant commercial assets capable of being offered as security to obtain financing—think of a steel mill's stockpile of finished steel beams, a car manufacturer's inventory of unsold automobiles, or an appliance manufacturer's inventory of unsold washing machines.[138] Courts, however, were not uniformly accommodating in applying the chattel mortgage acts to validate security interests in after-acquired collateral, at least not in ways conducive to efficient commercial financing.

Unlike a debtor's fixed equipment, such as machinery that might be bolted to the factory floor and used for decades, inventory is typically ever-changing. As old inventory is sold, new inventory is manufactured or acquired to replace it, yielding a constant "stream" of goods in the debtor's

---

134 *Id.* at 55.

135 *Id.*

136 *Id.* at 55–56.

137 *See id.* at 250.

138 *See id.* at 25.

hands. As a result, a security interest in a debtor's existing inventory would often be as ephemeral as the goods themselves, bound to disappear as soon as the goods are bought by the debtor's customers. Hence, when a creditor and debtor enter into an ongoing lending relationship secured by the debtor's inventory, the creditor typically wishes to obtain a security interest in the ongoing stream of collateral, not simply the goods in the debtor's possession on the day the parties sign their security agreement. This kind of security interest is known as a "floating lien." Recall, however, that the collusive judgment extended to goods in the debtor's possession when the judgment was entered, but not to goods the debtor acquired thereafter.[139] Should the same rule apply to contractual security devices involving inventory?

In the early case of *Mitchell v. Winslow*,[140] a merchant debtor mortgaged his stock in trade (inventory) to a secured creditor with a security agreement that included an after-acquired property clause.[141] Justice Story, riding circuit, upheld the clause, concluding that the secured creditor's mortgage covered goods the merchant acquired after the initial grant of the mortgage, at least as against a subsequent trustee in bankruptcy who claimed the debtor's after-acquired inventory to be free of the secured creditor's lien and thus available for ratable distribution among all creditors.[142] In subsequent decisions, however, state courts elected not to follow Story's approach.[143] In *Jones v. Richardson*,[144] for example, the Massachusetts Supreme Judicial Court concluded that a security interest in after-acquired property was unenforceable against third parties unless the creditor took steps to "ratify" it, such as by taking possession of the inventory to secure the debtor's obligation or by filing a supplemental mortgage after the debtor acquired new collateral.[145] In *Moody v. Wright*,[146] the Massachusetts court reaffirmed its position in *Jones*[147] and explicitly repudiated Story's approach in *Mitchell*.[148] The New York Court of Appeals also rejected Story's approach, albeit for different reasons.[149]

---

139 *See supra* note 51.

140 17 F. Cas. 527 (D. Me. 1843). In England, the House of Lords subsequently adopted the approach Story took in *Mitchell*. *See* Holroyd v. Marshall, (1862) 11 Eng. Rep. 999 (H.L.) 1007; 10 H.L.C. 191, 211–12.

141 *See Mitchell*, 17 Fed. Cas. at 527.

142 *Id.* at 531.

143 GILMORE, *supra* note 3, at 30–33.

144 51 Mass. (10 Met.) 481 (1845).

145 *Id.* at 488, 493–94; GILMORE, *supra* note 3, at 31.

146 54 Mass. (13 Met.) 17 (1847).

147 *Id.* at 29.

148 *Id.* at 31–32; GILMORE, *supra* note 3, at 31.

149 Griswold v. Sheldon, 4 N.Y. 581, 588, 590 (1851); *see* GILMORE, *supra* note 3, at 32.

Following these decisions and others like them, if a secured party wished to take a security interest in a debtor's after-acquired inventory, he was required either to take possession of the inventory as the debtor acquired it or continually file supplemental mortgages covering the additional collateral. Understandably, both requirements were quite bothersome, so debtors and creditors devised inventive ways around them. Several of these strategies are discussed below.

A similar though less significant problem arose in connection with a debtor's after-acquired equipment—for example, machinery the debtor purchased after the grant of the original security interest. At the most basic level, what distinguishes equipment from inventory is that a debtor does not generally sell his equipment to customers, but rather keeps it in order to conduct his business. A debtor may replace his equipment periodically, however, selling old items and acquiring new ones. When this occurs, does the secured party's security interest attach to the after-acquired equipment? Under the approach taken in *Jones* and *Moody*, it did not unless the secured creditor "ratified" the security interest after the debtor acquired the new equipment. Although inconvenient, the ratification requirement was less bothersome in the context of equipment financing (as compared to inventory financing) on account of differences in the types of lending associated with these different forms of collateral.

In the area of equipment financing, one way around the ratification problem was to treat the equipment as real property, if at all possible. The ancient real property rule is that a real estate mortgage properly encompasses subsequent improvements, or "accessions," to the land.[150] A real estate mortgage also typically includes personal property that becomes sufficiently attached to the land to constitute a "fixture."[151] Thus, for example, if the after-acquired equipment was a large machine bolted to the factory floor, a secured lender might classify it as an "accession" or a "fixture" and thereby claim it as collateral under real property law.[152] Lenders who took a security interest in this way, under the guise of a "real property mortgage," often styled themselves as "bondholders."[153] This artifice would not work, of course, when the equipment in question (a typewriter sitting on a desk, for instance) could not be characterized as either an accession or a fixture.

Another way around the ratification problem was simply to ignore the ratification rule in certain contexts by judicial fiat. This strategy proved successful, for example, in railroad financing, an important area of secured lending during the 1800s. When lenders made loans to facilitate the construction of a particular road, they would typically take a mortgage lien

150 *See* GILMORE, *supra* note 3, at 54.

151 *Id.*

152 *Id.* at 34–35.

153 GILMORE, *supra* note 3, at 38.

on all the debtor company's assets, including its equipment, to secure payment. At the time of the initial financing, however, much of this equipment—rolling stock and other items—often had yet to be acquired. Did the lender's mortgage lien attach to this after-acquired personal property? In *Pennock v. Coe*,[154] the U.S. Supreme Court concluded that it did, at least at the federal level. The Court justified its ruling, in part, by noting the importance of the financing of railroads "and other similar great and important enterprises of the day."[155] Courts and legislatures subsequently expanded the rule of *Pennock* to include public utility corporations.[156] Note here the growing proliferation of disparate rules, which varied not by collateral type, but rather according to the characteristics of the debtor.

JUDICIAL LIMITATIONS ON THE USE OF SECURITY DEVICES IN INVENTORY

Over time, opposition to security interests in inventory came to be identified with concerns over "fraud," and courts responded to these concerns by developing rules similar to the absolute-conditional test and the rebuttable presumption rule discussed above. Whereas courts generally acquiesced to non-possessory security interests in equipment (at least equipment the debtor owned at the time of the grant of the security interest), they appeared troubled that a secured party might take a non-possessory security interest in inventory, which, by its nature, the debtor intends to sell to third parties. In the courts' eyes, this arrangement seemed to vest the debtor with too much authority over the collateral (that is, possession plus the power to sell), and the secured party with too little. In other words, the non-possessory security interest in inventory seemed to stray too far from the fundamental paradigm of the pledge, from which the concept of a security interest originally derived: under the pledge, the debtor has neither possession of the collateral nor the power to sell it until he has satisfied his obligation to the secured creditor; with a non-possessory security interest in inventory, the debtor typically has both.[157]

There were, of course, cases of actual fraud involving security interests. For example, suppose a financially failing debtor owned a valuable asset, such as a piece of equipment worth $10,000. Suppose further that, although the debtor did not owe a debt to his father, he nevertheless granted his father a security interest in the equipment, thus giving his father a right to the collateral ahead of the claims of the debtor's

---

154 64 U.S. (23 How.) 117 (1860).

155 *Id.* at 130.

156 GILMORE, *supra* note 3, at 36.

157 *See, e.g.*, *Robinson v. Elliott*, 89 U.S. 513, 523–24 (1874) ("It is not difficult to see that the mere retention and use of personal property until default is altogether a different thing from the retention of possession accompanied with a power to dispose of it for the benefit of the mortgagor alone. . . . [T]he latter is inconsistent with the nature and character of a mortgage . . . .").

unpaid creditors. If the debtor defaulted on his debts to his unpaid creditors, the creditors might obtain judgments against him and seek to collect by levying against the equipment. Because the debtor granted his father a security interest in the equipment, however, the father could conveniently "claim" the right to the equipment ahead of the debtor's unpaid creditors. But since the debtor was never indebted to his father, it is easy to see how this sham intra-family "secured transaction" was simply the debtor's attempt to shelter assets from the reach of his creditors.

To differentiate frauds of this kind from legitimate security arrangements, courts friendly to the idea of a non-possessory lien on inventory developed and applied a "fraud in fact" standard. Under this standard, the court would instruct the jury that there is nothing inherently wrong with a creditor taking a security interest in collateral such as inventory, so long as the debtor and creditor act in good faith.[158] Evidence of good faith might include that the debtor owed the secured creditor a legitimate debt. Other courts hostile to the idea of a non-possessory lien on inventory, however, developed and applied a "fraud in law" test. Under this test, the court would instruct the jury that the security interest was conclusively fraudulent if the debtor retained possession of the collateral and the collateral was inventory the debtor intended to sell to third parties in the ordinary course of his business.[159] Note the challenges that these standards created for a secured creditor holding a lien on inventory. Under the fraud in fact standard, the validity of the lien was a jury question. Under the fraud in law test, the lien would simply be void.

Approaches like the fraud in law test and the ratification rule effectively undermined the utility of security interests in inventory. Of course, debtors and creditors did not respond by simply folding up their tents and decamping from the secured inventory financing arena. Instead, they developed a variety of clever devices in an effort to circumvent the courts' restrictions.

INNOVATIONS: TRUST RECEIPTS, FACTOR'S LIENS, AND FIELD WAREHOUSING

One particularly ingenious invention was the "trust receipt," which involved three parties: the debtor, a seller of goods, and the debtor's bank. In order to induce the seller to ship inventory, the debtor arranged for his bank to issue a letter of credit to the seller. The letter of credit authorized the seller to obtain payment for the goods directly from the bank by delivering to the bank a "draft" and a "bill of lading" covering the particular goods. (A draft is a document drawing on the letter of credit; a bill of lading is a document issued by a carrier, such as a railroad or ship line, acknowledging receipt of the goods for delivery.) Upon delivery of the two

158 GILMORE, *supra* note 3, at 42.

159 *Id.* at 41–42.

documents, the bank paid the seller and took possession of the bill of lading. The bank then released the goods to the debtor "in trust" for the benefit of the bank. When the debtor sold the goods, he was required to pay the bank the amount the bank paid the seller under the letter of credit. The bank thereby obtained repayment of the money it advanced and, pending payment, held an "ownership" interest in both the goods and the proceeds from the sale of the goods.[160] In this way, the parties to a trust receipt transaction sought to avoid both the limitations and filing requirements of the chattel mortgage acts.[161]

Boiled down to its essence, the bank's "ownership" interest in the goods under the trust receipt was a disguised security device accompanying a loan. It was also, effectively, a secret lien. The trust receipt was thus not universally accepted, and of the various courts that rejected it, several recharacterized the bank's interest as either a chattel mortgage or conditional sale that was void for failure to comply with the relevant chattel mortgage or conditional sales act.[162] Similarly, if a court applying the fraud in law test construed the transaction as a chattel mortgage in inventory, it would invalidate the bank's security interest under the test.[163]

The trust receipt originated as a way to finance imports. Over time, however, it migrated to domestic transactions, including so-called "floor planning" arrangements that lenders used to finance, for example, a car dealer's acquisitions of automobiles to fill his showroom floor.[164] As with the import trust receipt, many courts found this domestic variant to be nothing more than a disguised, unfiled inventory chattel mortgage or conditional sale, with the same consequences.[165]

Another invention was the "factor's lien," which arose largely out of practices in the textile industry. The term "factor" originally referred to a consignee of goods—that is, an agent who took possession of his principal's textile goods in order to sell them but had no obligation to pay for the goods unless and until he actually sold them to a third party. Over time, the term came to encompass two distinct commercial parties: the "selling factor" and the "financing factor."[166]

The selling factor was a consignee who made loans to the debtor and obtained repayment by selling the goods the debtor had consigned to him. Since the selling factor took possession of the debtor's inventory, he had a form of possessory security interest—termed a "factor's lien"—in the

---

[160] For an overview of this process, see *id.* at 87–88.

[161] *See id.* at 88.

[162] *See id.* at 94–95.

[163] *See id.* at 95.

[164] *See id.* at 95–96.

[165] *Id.* at 98.

[166] *See id.* at 128–31.

goods.[167] Over time, the selling factor disappeared, supplanted by the financing factor.

Although the typical financing factor also made loans to the debtor, he did not take possession of the debtor's inventory. Instead, the debtor retained possession in order to sell the goods to customers, and the financing factor generally took a non-possessory lien on the inventory to secure repayment. The financing factor also took an assignment of the debtor's "accounts receivable" or "accounts," which represented the debtor's right to collect from customers the money they owed the debtor for goods the customers purchased on credit from the debtor. The financing factor agreed to this assignment structure on a "nonrecourse" basis: in other words, the factor agreed to look exclusively to the inventory and accounts for payment and would not seek to recover from the debtor personally if there was a shortfall. Moreover, since the debtor typically "notified" his customers to make payment directly to the factor, this type of financing arrangement was known as "notification lending."[168]

The non-possessory nature of the financing factor's lien on the debtor's inventory proved unpalatable to some courts, which held these liens invalid.[169] Further, the financing factor's assignment of the debtor's accounts was potentially problematic under the fraud in law rule if the debtor continued to exercise "dominion and control" over the accounts after their assignment. In *Benedict v. Ratner*, the U.S. Supreme Court extended New York's fraud in law rule to cover the assignment of accounts.[170] Because the debtor in *Benedict* had failed to notify its customers to pay the factor directly, the debtor remained free to collect the accounts—and it did just that.[171] Thus, the factor's interest was essentially both a non-possessory security interest and a classic secret lien. The Court stated that "[u]nder the law of New York a transfer of property . . . which reserves to the transferor the right to dispose of the same, or to apply the proceeds thereof, for his own uses is, as to creditors, fraudulent in law and void."[172]

Another late-nineteenth century inventory financing invention was the practice of "field warehousing." The idea behind this transactional structure was to provide the secured lender with a pledge-like security interest in the debtor's inventory, thereby—at least in theory—enabling the lender to avoid the pitfalls of the non-possessory chattel mortgage in

---

167 *Id.* at 130.

168 *See id.* at 130–32. The factor typically took an assignment of the accounts on a "discounted" basis. For example, suppose the debtor had an account for $100. In other words, a customer owed the debtor $100 for goods the customer had purchased from the debtor. The factor might advance the debtor $95 on the account. If the customer paid the full $100, the factor made $5. If the customer failed to pay, or paid only in part, the factor took the loss.

169 GILMORE, *supra* note 3, at 131 n.6.

170 268 U.S. 353 (1925).

171 *Id.* at 360.

172 *Id.*

inventory. The basic structure involved three parties: the debtor, the debtor's bank, and a warehousing company. In the typical warehousing arrangement, the debtor placed its inventory in a storage facility it leased from the warehousing company. In turn, the warehousing company posted signs designating the facility as a warehousing establishment. The warehousing company also issued receipts to the bank for the goods held at the facility. The bank then made loans to the debtor in an amount up to some agreed percentage (say, 70 percent) of the value of the warehoused inventory represented by the receipts. Because the bank held the receipts and thus controlled the inventory, it likewise controlled when and under what conditions the warehouseman would release the inventory to the debtor. Typically, the bank authorized release of the debtor's goods so long as (1) the debtor delivered new inventory to replenish what the bank released, (2) the value of the remaining inventory was sufficient to cover the bank's outstanding loans under the parties' agreed loan-to-value formula, or (3) the debtor paid down enough of its debt to the bank that the goods were no longer needed as collateral. If the debtor defaulted, the bank could sell the goods in the warehouse to satisfy the debtor's indebtedness.[173]

This arrangement was particularly well-suited to manufacturers of seasonal goods, such as canneries. A particular cannery might accumulate virtually all of its inventory (for example, a stock of canned fish) by one point in the year and sell it gradually during the remainder. The cannery might borrow against its stock using a field warehousing arrangement, paying off the loan as it sold the canned goods over time. Field warehousing was not limited to seasonal goods, however, and came to be used by many different kinds of businesses.[174]

Field warehousing had its limitations. For one thing, the debtor was required to absorb the expense of using a commercial warehousing company to keep its goods. As suggested above, the theoretical legitimacy of the arrangement turned on the bank's constructive possession of the goods through its agent, the third-party warehousing company. Suppose, however, the debtor claimed to be his own warehouseman in order to avoid the expense. In other words, suppose the debtor himself issued "receipts" to the secured party for the inventory in his possession and agreed to hold the goods for the secured party's benefit. In *Geilfuss v. Corrigan*,[175] the Wisconsin Supreme Court rejected exactly this idea, establishing the principle that a debtor could not serve as his own warehousing agent.[176]

---

173 For a discussion of the mechanics of field warehousing, see GILMORE, *supra* note 3, at 146–54.

174 *Id.* at 149.

175 95 Wis. 651 (1897).

176 *See id.* at 669.

The chief beneficiary of this approach was, of course, the various field warehousing companies that, for decades, did a thriving business.[177]

Note the pattern of innovation and regulation that emerged during the course of the nineteenth century and the way this pattern parallels earlier developments in English law. Throughout the 1800s, debtors and creditors in America established a variety of security devices, inventing new ones to address deficiencies in the old. In turn, disgruntled parties (typically unpaid creditors) sought to avoid these new devices, while courts alternately accepted and rejected them. State legislatures intervened sporadically with statutory provisions, such as the various chattel mortgage statutes and conditional sales acts, which validated certain kinds of secured transactions under certain conditions. Courts responded to these acts with myriad qualifications and sometimes with decisions hostile to security interests, particularly those (for example, security interests in inventory) that strayed too far from the paradigmatic example of the pledge. To skirt the adverse effects of these decisions, debtors and creditors again created new devices. Once more, disgruntled parties challenged them, and courts responded by invalidating some of the new creations. All in all, as security devices proliferated and mutated, "the law of personal property security transactions came to resemble the obscure wood in which Dante once discovered the gates of hell."[178]

Adding to the complexity, Congress enacted four distinct bankruptcy acts during the nineteenth century: the short-lived statutes of 1800, 1841, and 1867, and the permanent Bankruptcy Act of 1898. As it had in earlier periods, bankruptcy law in the 1800s threatened many contemporaneous security devices. Much of the more interesting bankruptcy litigation, however, occurred during the early part of the twentieth century, and it is to the developments of that era that our story now turns.

§ 4. SECURITY DEVICES IN TWENTIETH CENTURY AMERICA: THE UNIFORM ACTS, THE NON-UNIFORM STATUTES, AND THE PROMULGATION AND ADOPTION OF ARTICLE 9

At the end of the nineteenth century, the law of secured transactions was not particularly stable. Different states had markedly different practices and procedures. The various chattel mortgage acts were far from uniform, covered only certain kinds of security interests, and overlapped in complex ways with the various conditional sales acts. Courts in several jurisdictions remained hostile to security interests in inventory, accounts, and (absent ratification) after-acquired collateral. The validity of devices like the trust receipt, factor's lien, and field warehousing arrangements

---

177 GILMORE, *supra* note 3, at 161.

178 *Id.* at 27.

remained uncertain, at least absent compliance with cumbersome protocols. Yet as commerce expanded, the demand for reliable security structures increased. Something had to change, and what changed was the law. More particularly, what changed was the rise of experimentation with innovative commercial statutes intended to lend greater coherence and stability to the area. This occurred within the shadow of a broader movement toward the codification of state law.

In the mid-nineteenth century, David Dudley Field, a politically connected attorney, began advocating the codification of the common law of New York. Field was a follower of Jeremy Bentham, an Englishman who sought unsuccessfully to codify the English common law following France's successful codification efforts in 1804. In 1848, Field and others drafted a Code of Civil Procedure for New York, which the state legislature adopted. The Field Code was later revised and enlarged in 1851. It simplified and clarified a variety of common law procedures and reformed the pleading process. The Field Code served as a model for similar codes across the country, and by 1897 thirty-one states and territories had codes of procedure that mirrored its provisions.

In 1892, the National Conference of Commissioners on Uniform State Laws ("NCCUSL") was created to draft and propose model uniform laws for the various state legislatures to enact.[179] Over time, the Conference proposed various uniform acts regulating a variety of commercial transactions, including the Uniform Negotiable Instruments Law in 1896, the Uniform Sales Act in 1906, the Uniform Conditional Sales Act in 1918, and the Uniform Trust Receipts Act in 1933.[180] Some of these uniform acts were adopted in every state; others were adopted in a majority of them. Efforts to create a uniform chattel mortgage act, however, were not successful.[181] In addition to the uniform acts, states also experimented with statutes that validated and regulated a variety of security devices on a non-uniform basis.

THE UNIFORM TRUST RECEIPTS ACT

Recall the popular "trust receipt" device used to finance imports of inventory and so-called "floor planning arrangements" (such as a car dealer's acquisition of automobiles to fill his showroom floor). Once again, the basic idea behind this device was that the bank "owned" the inventory that it entrusted to the debtor, notwithstanding the debtor's possession of the merchandise. As noted, courts sometimes recharacterized the trust receipt transaction as a disguised chattel mortgage, with the consequence

---

179 Peter Winship, *The National Conference of Commissioners on Uniform State Laws and the International Unification of Private Law*, 13 U. PA. J. INT'L BUS. L. 227, 227 (1992).

180 William A. Schnader, *A Short History of the Preparation and Enactment of the Uniform Commercial Code*, 22 U. MIAMI L. REV. 1, 2 (1967).

181 GILMORE, *supra* note 3, at 99.

that it would be invalid if the bank failed to file the proper chattel mortgage documents with the proper recording office, or if the court found the lender's interest to be invalid under the fraud in law standard. In response, a few states (beginning with Ohio) experimented with measures to regulate the device.[182] In the 1920s, the NCCUSL was persuaded to draft the Uniform Trust Receipts Act ("UTRA"), generating (according to Gilmore) "one of the world's most difficult statutes" owing to its cumbersome provisions and convoluted structure.[183]

As promulgated in 1933, the UTRA validated security devices taken by lenders (as opposed to sellers) in newly-acquired inventory as part of a transaction in which the lender's loan enabled the debtor to purchase the particular inventory in question (known as a "purchase money" transaction, so called because the lender supplied the money that the debtor actually used to purchase the collateral, as opposed to a transaction in which the creditor took a lien on collateral the debtor already owned).[184] The Act's chief innovation was to eliminate the common law requirement that the bank had to have taken "title" to the goods before the goods could be entrusted to the debtor.[185] Instead, under the UTRA the debtor could acquire the goods directly from the manufacturer. Another innovation was the UTRA's public notice filing procedure, addressing the problem of the secret lien.[186] A further innovation was the form of this filing requirement. Unlike many of the state chattel mortgage acts, the UTRA did not require the parties to file a copy of the relevant transaction documents or a lengthy description of the transaction or the relevant collateral. Instead, the UTRA required the filing of a much shorter, summary statement describing the nature of the transaction—a truncated procedure known as "notice filing."[187] The popularity of the UTRA caused several states to broaden its applicability to include security interests in inventory generally, not simply purchase money transactions—a move the Uniform Law Commissioners opposed because it introduced non-uniformity among the states that had adopted the UTRA.[188]

THE NON-UNIFORM FACTOR'S LIEN ACTS

Recall also the popular common law "factor's lien" device pursuant to which a financing factor would take a lien on the debtor's inventory and an assignment of the debtor's accounts in exchange for funds paid to the

[182] *Id.* at 98–99 n.12.

[183] *Id.* at 98.

[184] *Id.* at 100–02. The UTRA also applied to certain transactions involving documents and instruments. *Id.* at 109–14, 115–19.

[185] GILMORE, *supra* note 3, at 102.

[186] The filing requirement applied to inventory and documents, but not to instruments. *Id.* at 116.

[187] *Id.* at 468.

[188] *Id.* at 119.

debtor, and agree to look exclusively to the inventory and accounts to recover any amounts the factor had paid. In addition, recall the legal uncertainty surrounding this arrangement, particularly where the debtor exercised "dominion and control" over the inventory and accounts. In 1911, New York enacted the first of a series of Factor's Acts validating and regulating this kind of transaction.[189] The New York Act validated a financing factor's non-possessory lien on the debtor's inventory, provided the factor posted a sign on the debtor's premises identifying himself as the debtor's factor and also filed a lien notice in the town where the merchandise was located and in the town where the debtor had his principal place of business.[190] As originally drafted, the Act also validated the financing factor's lien on the debtor's accounts under the theory that they were "proceeds" of the debtor's inventory (namely what the debtor realized from the sale of his inventory to his customers). The Act required, however, that the customer who owed the money to the debtor (referred to as the "account debtor") had to be notified of the assignment of the account and be instructed to pay the factor directly.[191] As amended in 1931, the Act validated assignments of accounts regardless of whether the factor also took a lien on the debtor's inventory.[192] The Act was designed specifically to overrule *Benedict v. Ratner* in the factoring context (recall that *Benedict* extended New York's fraud in law test to security interests in accounts). In addition, the Act was not construed as preemptive: it merely supplemented the common law of assignment, which continued to apply to factoring transactions as an alternative to the statutory procedure.[193]

The NCCUSL never promulgated a uniform Factor's Act. Instead, following New York's lead, a number of states enacted different versions of the Act on a non-uniform basis.[194] Some adopted New York's original signage requirement, while others did not. Some required public notice filing as a mandatory measure. Some covered all kinds of inventory, while others applied only to inventory of certain types. Like the UTRA, these Acts usually permitted good faith purchasers of the debtor's inventory to take

---

189 *Id.* at 133.

190 *Id.* The signage requirement was deleted in 1954. *Id.* at 134.

191 *Id.* at 135.

192 *Id. See Bloch v. Mill Factors Corp.*, 119 F.2d 536, 538 (2d Cir. 1941).

193 GILMORE, *supra* note 3, at 136. The factor's lien remained distinct from the trust receipt in many important respects. Among other things, under the UTRA the relevant financing had to be used to acquire the collateral in question. Under the Factor's Act, however, the factor's advances could be used for any number of purposes, including the debtor's working capital needs. *Id.* at 137. The UTRA required the handling of the collateral on a unit-by-unit basis (with receipts issued for the items). In contrast, the Factor's Act essentially permitted a "floating lien" on the debtor's inventory and accounts (accordingly, cumbersome individual assignments of each account did not have to be made). After 1931, the Factor's Act validated assignments of accounts regardless of whether the factor also took a lien on the debtor's inventory. In contrast, the UTRA authorized an interest in accounts generated from the sale of the lender's inventory collateral only as proceeds of the inventory. *Id.* at 140.

194 *Id.* at 139.

the merchandise free and clear of the factor's lien, leaving the factor to look only to the proceeds of the sale for payment.[195]

THE NON-UNIFORM ACCOUNTS RECEIVABLE STATUTES

Roughly parallel with the enactment of the various Factor's Acts, states also experimented with a separate group of so-called Accounts Receivable Statutes. The primary impetus behind these statutes was the U.S. Supreme Court's decision in *Corn Exchange National Bank and Trust Co. v. Klauder*,[196] which applied federal bankruptcy law to defeat "non-notification" security interests in accounts. In *Klauder*, a bank entered into a non-notification accounts financing arrangement with the debtor—meaning that the debtor continued to collect and use the proceeds from the accounts notwithstanding their assignment to the bank. Under Pennsylvania law, the bank's security interest in the accounts was inferior to the interest of another assignee of the same accounts who first notified the debtor's customers of the assignment. This was because Pennsylvania law provided that, where two parties claimed to have an assignment of the same account, the first to notify the account debtor had the superior interest. Under federal bankruptcy law at the time, this meant that the bank's interest in the accounts was not "perfected" because the bank had not taken all the steps necessary to ensure the priority of its interest under state law as against other parties who also claimed an interest. As a result, the bank's security interest in the debtor's accounts was set aside and the bank was treated as an unsecured creditor.

Prior to *Klauder*, only one state (Ohio) had enacted a statute that validated generally the assignment of accounts.[197] Within a short time after *Klauder*, however, almost all of the states enacted them.[198] The Accounts Receivable Statutes were generally of two types. The first group validated the assignment of the debtor's accounts without requiring notification to account debtors or the need for a public notice filing.[199] In other words, this group effectively permitted the lender's security interest to exist as a secret lien. The apparent reasoning behind this approach was that the compelled public disclosure of the debtor's "hocking" of his accounts would be embarrassing to the businessman and reflect negatively on his credit standing. As Gilmore remarked, however, "[t]he argument that secrecy is the best policy must be among the strangest that has ever seriously been put forward."[200]

---

195 *Id.* at 143.

196 318 U.S. 434 (1943).

197 GILMORE, *supra* note 3, at 271.

198 *Id.* at 271–72.

199 *Id.* at 274.

200 *Id.* at 275.

The second (and much larger) group of Accounts Receivable Statutes validated the assignment of accounts without notification to account debtors, but required a public notice filing with the appropriate recording office.[201] As a general matter, both groups of statutes applied not only to security interests in the debtor's accounts (for example, assignments of the accounts for purposes of security only), but also to true sales of the debtor's accounts (such as true "factoring" arrangements where the factor agreed to look only to the accounts and had no recourse against the debtor in the event the accounts were uncollectible).[202] Collateral types other than accounts, however, were generally excluded from the scope of these statutes.[203]

JUDICIAL LIMITATIONS ON FIELD WAREHOUSING

Finally, recall the popular field warehousing transaction. Again, the idea behind this transactional structure was to provide the lender with the equivalent of possession of the debtor's inventory through the medium of the warehouseman acting on the lender's behalf. In a series of cases, the U.S. Supreme Court exposed the weaknesses of this form of security device, also in connection with the application of federal bankruptcy law.

In the first case, *Union Trust Co. v. Wilson*,[204] the warehouse company leased space in the basement of the debtor's place of business, and the lender held the receipts for the inventory in the warehouse. When the debtor needed inventory, the debtor would pay down its loan to the lender and the lender would issue the necessary receipts to the debtor permitting the debtor to obtain a certain quantity of goods from the warehouse. Under applicable state law (Illinois), it was permissible for a debtor to establish a warehouse on his own premises. The question was whether this arrangement constituted a legitimate pledge of the debtor's inventory. Under applicable bankruptcy law, the bankruptcy trustee could set aside fraudulent or otherwise defective conveyances and treat the lender as an unsecured creditor. In *Wilson*, the Court held that the particular arrangement in the case was legal, and therefore good against the trustee. As a result, the lender was entitled to its collateral notwithstanding the debtor's bankruptcy.

In the second case, *Security Warehousing Co. v. Hand*,[205] the Court reached essentially the opposite conclusion on roughly similar facts. There the Court stated that the warehousing arrangement constituted a "mere device or subterfuge to enable the bankrupt to . . . raise money upon secret liens on property in the [bankrupt's] possession," and that "[s]uch a scheme

---

[201] *Id.*

[202] *Id.*

[203] *Id.* at 276–77.

[204] 198 U.S. 530 (1905).

[205] 206 U.S. 415 (1907).

. . . was a fraud in fact."[206] Following *Hand*, the legitimacy of any particular warehousing arrangement was thought to turn on the warehouseman's degree of control over the inventory in question.[207] The precise degree, however, was never clearly worked out. Interestingly, *Hand* did not spark the same flurry of legislative activity that *Klauder* did nearly a half-century later on the question of the validity of security interests in a debtor's accounts.

THE PROMULGATION AND ENACTMENT OF ARTICLE 9

As the foregoing illustrates, by the 1940s the law of secured transactions consisted of a legal landscape littered with the debris of disparate uniform and non-uniform legislation, various common law devices existing side-by-side with statutory ones, an overlay of federal bankruptcy law, a multiplicity of diverse filing requirements for certain types of collateral, and general uncertainty over the validity of certain security interests. Further, several of the uniform acts were outdated and out of touch with commercial practices of the day.[208] As Gilmore colorfully explained, "[h]orse law and haystack law are uneasily tolerated in the complex business of mass production and national distribution."[209] Additionally, there were uncomfortable inconsistencies between the several uniform acts.[210] As a result, around 1940 the Commercial Act Section of the NCCUSL began to think seriously about revising and bringing up to date the various promulgated uniform commercial statutes.[211] But as members of the conference came to conclude, merely updating the existing piecemeal uniform statutes was not a truly adequate response.

As one drafter of the Uniform Commercial Code later explained, in the 1940s "chattel security law was like the condition described in the second verse of Genesis, 'without form and void and darkness lay over the face of the deep.' "[212] Another noted that "[i]n the field of secured transactions, the number, type and variety of acts dealing with [various security devices],

---

[206] *Id.* at 426.

[207] GILMORE, *supra* note 3, at 167.

[208] Malcolm, *supra* note 1, at 490; Schnader, *supra* note 180, at 2.

[209] Grant Gilmore, *On the Difficulties of Codifying Commercial Law*, 57 YALE L.J. 1341, 1341 (1948).

[210] Schnader, *supra* note 180, at 2.

[211] Soia Mentschikoff, *Symposium—Origins and Evolution: Drafters Reflect Upon the Uniform Commercial Code: Reflections of a Drafter: Soia Mentschikoff*, 43 OHIO ST. L. J. 535, 537 (1982).

[212] Homer Kripke, *Symposium—Origins and Evolution: Drafters Reflect Upon the Uniform Commercial Code: Reflections of a Drafter: Homer Kripke*, 43 OHIO ST. L. J. 535, 577 (1982). When charged by the Massachusetts legislature to report on how the Uniform Commercial Code would change the then-present law of Massachusetts, Peter Coogan explained that it took him and a number of able associates "one hell of a long time to find out what the old law was." Peter Coogan, *Symposium—Origins and Evolution: Drafters Reflect Upon the Uniform Commercial Code: Reflections of a Drafter: Peter Coogan*, 43 OHIO ST. L. J. 535, 546 (1982).

and particularly the recording requirements of these various acts, constitute[d] little less than a maze of confusion and much of th[at] confusion ha[d] little rhyme or reason other than historical accident."[213] Recognizing this, William Schnader, then President of the Conference, proposed in 1940 the preparation of a single comprehensive uniform commercial code as an alternative to fixing the various uniform acts.[214] Professor Karl Llewellyn—who ultimately became the Chief Reporter of the Uniform Commercial Code project—agreed.[215] The Conference subsequently collaborated with the American Law Institute on a joint undertaking to draft the Code.[216]

Llewellyn insisted at the outset that the provisions of the Code be drafted with a primary focus on what actually takes place in the commercial world instead of the law as it appeared in the relevant statutes and cases.[217] As one of the drafters later explained, however, Llewellyn's functional approach was at least partially abandoned to ensure that the final product was salable to the profession at large and reasonably capable of being enacted by the legislatures of the various states.[218] In addition, in order to produce a Code that states would enact, various interest groups had to be accommodated, including those concerned with farming operations,[219] insurance companies, and railroads.[220] After six years of preparation and revision, the Uniform Commercial Code was finally promulgated in September of 1951, including Article 9 governing security interests in personal property.[221] As another drafter later explained, however, "[t]he only article that was not completed to anybody's satisfaction on the reportorial group by 1952, when the first vote by the states took place, was Article 9."[222]

At the time of promulgation, most of the participants in the drafting process thought Article 9 needed more work, but Schnader and Llewellyn refused to wait and instead presented the entire Code to Pennsylvania in

---

213 Malcolm, *supra* note 1, at 491.

214 Schnader, *supra* note 180, at 1.

215 Mentschikoff, *supra* note 211, at 537; Schnader, *supra* note 180, at 4.

216 Schnader, *supra* note 180, at 3.

217 Mentschikoff, *supra* note 211, at 542; Schnader, *supra* note 180, at 4.

218 Allison Dunham, Symposium—*Origins and Evolution: Drafters Reflect Upon the Uniform Commercial Code: Reflections of a Drafter: Allison Dunham*, 43 OHIO ST. L. J. 535, 569 (1982).

219 Dunham explained in an early mock Commercial Code that the drafters "wanted to add a very simple two-section statute on farm loans. Section 1 is, it shall be a crime not to loan money to farmers; Section 2, it shall be a crime to collect it if you do." *Id.* at 570.

220 Fairfax Leary, *Symposium—Origins and Evolution: Drafters Reflect Upon the Uniform Commercial Code: Reflections of a Drafter: Fairfax Leary*, 43 OHIO ST. L. J. 535, 557–58 (1982). Many of the special exemptions were rolled back or eliminated in subsequent revisions to the Code.

221 Schnader, *supra* note 180, at 5.

222 Mentschikoff, *supra* note 211, at 544.

1952 for passage.[223] In particular, Homer Kripke, a principal drafter of Article 9, advocated shelving the Code, or at least Article 9, for five years so that it could be refined before enactment.[224] In retrospect, however, all came to agree that Schnader and Llewellyn's decision to press forward was politically astute and likely saved the entire project.[225] As one of the drafters later explained, "[i]t was impossible to kill the Code once it had been enacted by Pennsylvania."[226]

Following Pennsylvania's lead, other states began considering and enacting the Code.[227] Pennsylvania had adopted it wholesale without revision, debate, or detailed study.[228] Massachusetts followed, but only after making a limited number of non-uniform amendments.[229] The Massachusetts version was then promulgated as the new uniform statute, and Pennsylvania subsequently adopted the Massachusetts version.[230] This pattern of states making amendments throughout the enactment process led to further changes to the uniform text.[231]

By the 1960s, each state had adopted some version of the Code, but complete uniformity was still out of reach.[232] Because uniformity had always been a central goal, a Permanent Editorial Board was created to review and comment on state amendments to the Code. In light of the many changes, the Board ultimately decided to review and reconsider the original text of Article 9, and established a Review Committee.[233] In 1972, the official text of Article 9 was extensively amended. By 1990, every state had enacted the 1972 version. Subsequent developments led to the formation of a Study Committee to consider the need for further revisions to Article 9. The Study Committee's review led to the creation of a revised Article 9 in 1998. This revised Article 9 has been universally adopted and is currently in effect. Since 1998, the official text of the statute has been amended numerous times, including significantly in 2010.

---

223 *Id.*

224 Kripke, *supra* note 212, at 581.

225 *Id.*; Mentschikoff, *supra* note 211, at 544.

226 Mentschikoff, *supra* note 211, at 544. After its enactment in Pennsylvania, the drafters "discovered no great bugs in its operations." Homer Kripke, *A Reflective Pause Between UCC Past and UCC Future*, 43 OHIO ST. L.J. 603, 603 (1982).

227 Schnader, *supra* note 180, at 8.

228 Coogan, *supra* note 212, at 546.

229 *Id.*

230 *Id.*

231 Schnader, *supra* note 180, at 9–10.

232 Indeed, almost half of the 775 non-uniform amendments as of 1967 were to Article 9 on secured transactions. *Id.* at 10.

233 Kripke, *supra* note 212, at 582. Kripke, Gilmore, and Coogan had freely criticized Article 9, but were told to hold their criticisms until after the Code was successfully enacted. In exchange, they were promised that review and revision would follow. *Id.*

THE CHARACTERISTICS OF ARTICLE 9

A major goal of Article 9 was to consolidate the disparate common law and statutory security devices into a number of recognized forms (for example, a security interest in equipment, inventory, or accounts), and lend some coherence and consistency to the area. It streamlined and simplified the notice filing process for many types of collateral, and sought to elevate substance over form. It currently applies to "a transaction, regardless of its form, that creates a security interest in personal property or fixtures by contract."[234] Similarly, it provides that its provisions apply "regardless of the form of the transaction or the name that parties have given to it."[235] Further, where parties have elected to use certain non-standardized security devices (such as a conditional bill of sale pursuant to which the seller purports to retain title), the Code effectively converts the non-standardized device into one of its recognized forms, and demands satisfaction of the Code's basic requirements in order for the device to be fully effective.

Like the common law before it, Article 9 displays a general distaste for secret liens. Gone, however, is the common law's discomfort with non-possessory security devices. Drawing on centuries of experience, the Code strikes a certain balance between the interests of secured parties, debtors, third party buyers of the debtor's property, and the debtor's other creditors. It also exists in an uneasy harmony with federal bankruptcy law. As discussed above, a primary bankruptcy policy (honored in the breach) is the policy of equality of distribution among an insolvent debtor's creditors. In contrast, the basic idea of a security interest is to prefer the secured creditor over others in any distribution of the value of the secured party's collateral. It is easy to see how this will often result in a secured party receiving more than anyone else in the bankruptcy context. Is this justified? The last chapter in this book is dedicated to exploring this and similar questions in the context of reviewing some of the theoretical underpinnings of the law of secured transactions.

In spite of its popular acclaim and ultimate universal acceptance, Article 9 has (as noted) been continuously and extensively revised since its original promulgation in 1952. As originally drafted, it undertook to regulate the taking, enforcement, and priority of security interests through a body of relatively generalized standards. In its current, heavily revised form, Article 9 is much more of a rigid and rule-oriented statute. What it gains in terms of detail it sacrifices in terms of simplicity—the current Article 9 is much lengthier and more complicated than the original, and many of its provisions are difficult to read (to say the least). Questions

---

234 UCC § 9–109(a)(1) (2010).

235 UCC § 9–109 cmt. 2 (2010).

regarding the reading and interpretation of the Code are addressed in Chapter 1.

Finally, Article 9 is a hybrid in the sense that it essentially treats the creation of a security interest as fundamentally a matter of contract, yet regulates the device largely in the manner of a property right. It further leaves the vindication of certain rights of the secured party to the law of tort. These overlapping characteristics underscore the extent to which Article 9 implicates the interests not only of particular debtors and their secured creditors, but also the interests of third parties affected by the secured creditor's taking of a lien.

The main purpose of the forgoing discussion of the historical evolution of personal property security devices leading up to the enactment of Article 9 has been to examine some of the complexity of the law of secured transactions through the lens of history, and, in the process, offer a conceptual sense of the whole subject matter and some of its fundamental concerns (for example, how the law has treated a variety of possessory and non-possessory security devices, has defeated or incorporated innovation, has dealt with the secret lien problem, has treated the interests of unsecured creditors and buyers of the debtor's property, and has sought to regularize the taking of security interests). In the process of mastering the current Code, the student must inevitably encounter a rich commercial vocabulary and diverse transactional structures. Many (but by no means all) of the relevant concepts and structures have been examined here, albeit from an historical perspective. Understanding something about the origins of these concepts and structures is revealing. For as much as things have changed, much has remained the same, illuminating some enduring truths about the subject matter and its place in the larger context of commercial law and practice as a whole.

CHAPTER 10

THE THEORY OF SECURED TRANSACTIONS

■ ■ ■

§ 1. INTRODUCTION TO THE THEORY OF ARTICLE 9

This chapter addresses the theory of secured transactions. Why discuss theory in a course book on Article 9? There are at least three good reasons. To begin with, theory tackles the hard foundational questions, such as why have a law of security interests in the first place, and why should the law take one form over another? The effort involved in attempting to answer such questions is frequently illuminating and at a minimum forms a good habit of mind. In addition, theory is another conceptually organizing tool that can be used to gain some general perspective on the subject matter. Finally, for those who are interested in theory (admittedly not everyone), the following offers a structured introduction to how a variety of scholars have addressed a number of puzzling questions in their efforts to understand the normative underpinnings of the law of personal property security devices.

Why have a law of secured transactions in the first place? Moreover, if having a law of personal property security devices is a good thing, what should its rules and regulations look like? As Chapter 9 on the history of security interests reveals, security devices have been no stranger to controversy. Given all the fuss, some foundational explanation for the subject's basic utility seems in order.

We can begin with a criticism. From an equitable perspective (for example, the general bankruptcy perspective of equality of distribution among all of an insolvent debtor's creditors), security interests seem at least somewhat unfair.[1] By the simple expedient of executing a contract that vests the secured creditor with a security interest in certain items of the debtor's personal property (and otherwise complying with all applicable legal requirements necessary to render a security interest legally enforceable), the secured creditor effectively fences off these items for its own benefit at the expense of the claims of other creditors if the debtor is later unable to pay everyone in full (namely, becomes insolvent). But if all

---

1 *See* Vern Countryman, *Code Security Interests in Bankruptcy*, 75 COM. L.J. 269 (1970) (criticizing the secured creditor's priority in bankruptcy).

the secured creditor is doing in conjunction with taking a security interest is lending the debtor money, or selling the debtor an item of personal property on credit (which is essentially the same thing), this does not seem much different from what any of the debtor's other creditors are doing. So what justifies privileging the secured party's claim at the potential expense of the claims of others who are similarly situated?

Professor Grant Gilmore offered the explanation of the secured creditor as a type of "policeman" engaged in overseeing the debtor's affairs. In rendering this analogy, he clearly had in mind the paradigm of the secured creditor as an effective and conscientious monitor who understands and supervises the debtor's activities—a sort of benign "big brother." In Gilmore's eyes, the virtuous secured creditor (especially one holding a security interest in the debtor's accounts to secure a working line of credit) knows "from day to day the state of his debtor's business health."[2] In particular, the attentive secured creditor "would recognize—or at all events be in a position to recognize—the symptoms of the last fatal plunge toward bankruptcy,"[3] during which time the debtor "typically succeeds in piling up a large amount of unsecured debt" under circumstances in which "[a]ll but the most demanding creditors are put off, the bills and invoices go unpaid, [and] new sources of credit are explored and exploited."[4] Eventually, "as the debts pile up, sales and receivables fall off" until "the day of reckoning can no longer be staved off" and "the disaster is total."[5] Prior to the advent of this "total disaster," the virtuous secured creditor "might be expected, in his own self-interest, to intervene: if there still seemed to be hope, he might undertake a salvage operation in cooperation with other creditors; if all hope had vanished, he would call his loan, which, in the usual case, would bring the debtor's operation to a halt."[6] The secured creditor has an incentive to do this, so the theory goes, to prevent the debtor from dissipating its assets, which are the secured creditor's collateral.

So how precisely does this role benefit anyone other than the secured creditor who may receive full payment while others receive nothing? In Gilmore's view, the secured creditor's "self-interest in this context [runs] parallel with the interest of his debtor's other creditors."[7] He explained that "[i]t is reasonable to assume in many cases shaky enterprises were preserved as a result of a timely intervention and that in many others the final disastrous ballooning of the unsecured debt just before bankruptcy

[2] GRANT GILMORE, SECURITY INTERESTS IN PERSONAL PROPERTY 261 (1965).

[3] *Id.*

[4] *Id.* at 259.

[5] *Id.* at 259–60.

[6] *Id.* at 261.

[7] *Id.*

was prevented by the [secured party's] cutting off the source of essential working capital."[8]

Of course, all of this turns on the virtuous secured creditor acting as an effective and diligent monitor. If the secured creditor is lax, and the debtor is given unsupervised free reign with its assets, Gilmore hypothesized that perhaps there would be good reason to penalize the secured party in the event of the debtor's financial ruin, even possibly to the extent of voiding the security interest: "ways should be found," he argued, "to penalize a lender who, after allowing his borrower to pile up an intolerable weight of debt, then claims all the assets of the insolvent estate, leaving nothing to satisfy other claims."[9] Likewise, "[b]orrowers should not be encouraged or allowed to hypothecate all that they may ever own in the indefinite future in favor of a creditor who is willing to make a risky loan now."[10]

In Gilmore's analysis, there is therefore the strong assertion that a secured creditor essentially earns its preferred position by acting as a provident lender and watchman for the benefit of the debtor's creditors as a community of interests. Conversely, the secured lender abuses his trust (and perhaps warrants sanction) by lending improvidently and sleeping at the switch. On the surface, this vision seems marvelously intriguing. But is it real? Do secured lenders really serve this heroic function and, if so, do they serve it effectively or efficiently? Are their interests truly aligned with those of unsecured creditors? And, ultimately, does the existence of security interests help make us all better off?

Gilmore essentially denied that the last question was capable of absolute empirical proof one way or the other. He observed in an analogous context that "[t]he social or economic utility of permitting [the] transfer [of] rights is believed to outweigh the utility of [forbidding] the transfer" and that whether "one utility outweighs the other lies beyond demonstration and proof."[11] He continued that, "[a]lthough there is no special virtue in being on the winning side, it is perhaps more true in the law than it is in theology . . . that what is and what ought to be are the same," at least in the sense that "[c]ourts [and, by extension legislatures] reflect social and economic pressures as a mirror reflects objects that are placed before it."[12]

Gilmore viewed the growth and regularization of security devices as essentially part of the logical expansion of credit generally: "[t]he financing institutions which were the source of credit naturally desired security for

---

8 *Id.*

9 *Id.* at 249. *See also* Grant Gilmore, *The Good Faith Purchase Idea and the Uniform Commercial Code: Confessions of a Repentant Draftsman*, 15 GA. L. REV. 605, 626–27 (1981).

10 Gilmore, *supra* note 2, at 248–49.

11 *Id.* at 212–13.

12 *Id.* at 213.

the loans which they were invited, even compelled, to make."[13] He was also very much in favor of a comprehensive codification of the subject, criticizing in blunt fashion the "typically muddle-headed process of thinking known as the genius of the common law."[14] For Gilmore, a statutory regime such as Article 9 delivers in a coherent way what secured lenders and debtors "naturally" desire—a streamlined process that makes the taking of security interests relatively simple and easy. But does that make security devices normatively desirable when the "natural" interests of other creditors are also taken into account, namely to have their own claims paid?

Note here a particularly distinct feature of the history of security devices. The law has always had relatively little difficulty with *possessory* security interests; it is *non*-possessory ones that have caused the most trouble, particularly non-possessory liens on collateral over which the debtor has relatively unfettered control. Why? One potentially differentiating characteristic is the relative risks and responsibilities the creditor undertakes in the contrasting contexts of possessory and non-possessory security devices. For example, suppose the collateral is a flock of sheep. If the creditor has possession, the creditor would typically also have the responsibility for feeding the sheep and otherwise ensuring the animals come to no harm.[15] In other words, the creditor with possession has not only the appearance of ownership but also many of its burdens.

In contrast, where the secured creditor does not have possession and the debtor is free to dispose of the collateral (as in the case of inventory, which, historically, gave the courts difficulty), not only does the creditor lack any appearance of ownership, the creditor also has virtually none of its burdens. Moreover, where the debtor has possession, the debtor typically maintains and makes use of the collateral with the assistance and contributions of other creditors (for example, the utility company that supplies the debtor with power to run the debtor's place of business, the employees who supply the debtor with their labor, and the like)—most of whom are typically unsecured. In this sense, where the secured creditor claims a superior interest in its collateral, yet bears no responsibility for maintaining or making productive use of it, the secured creditor appears to be able to both "have its cake and eat it, too." Even assuming, as Gilmore suggests, that the secured creditor performs some kind of useful policing function with regard to the debtor's affairs, is the secured creditor's priority justified in the case of non-possessory security devices? Are there countervailing downsides?

---

[13] *Id.* at 25.

[14] *Id.* at 202.

[15] *Id.* at 1128 (discussing the history of a pledgee's duties with respect to collateral in his possession, observing that "the lender in possession . . . owes duties of preservation and care with respect to the property temporarily entrusted to him").

Another possible explanation for the utility of security devices is that the secured creditor essentially pays for its priority either (1) by extending credit to the debtor that otherwise would not be available in the absence of security, or (2) by extending credit more cheaply. Secured loans are typically less risky than unsecured loans (owing to the existence of collateral earmarked for the particular creditor), and secured creditors often charge less interest than would be charged if the loan were unsecured. But that is not always the case. In addition, one might doubt the overall utility of the secured creditor's interest discount. In the aggregate and all other things being equal, won't unsecured creditors simply charge more interest to compensate for the additional risk they must shoulder owing to the fact that a secured creditor has fenced off some or all of the debtor's assets for the secured creditor's benefit, leaving them more exposed in the event the debtor becomes insolvent? When the transaction costs of security devices are taken into account, perhaps these devices actually result in a net overall loss.[16]

Yet another possible explanation is that it might be particularly important to protect certain types of lenders over others. For example, banks lend the savings of their depositors, and permitting banks to lend on a secured basis has the indirect effect of protecting the depositors (and the taxpayers, who may have to foot the bill for the insurance that comes with bank deposits). But in reality the taking of security interests is not limited to banks or other specially designated categories of lenders.

Another possibility is that perhaps security interests are useful because they entice the more timid and cautious creditors to part with their capital—an incentive unnecessary for the bold speculators of the world. Certainly it is in some sense useful to encourage the "mattress stuffers" to part with their greenbacks. But the taking of security interests is also not limited to these types.

Alternatively, perhaps security devices are useful to help protect the interests of those who are poor loss spreaders. Creditors who extend credit frequently to a diverse group of debtors are characteristically better able to spread any losses they may sustain as a result of some of their debtors' failure to pay. Among other reasons, they may be able to charge interest to the many as a form of insurance against the default of the few. In contrast, a creditor who does not have this opportunity, such as the typical unpaid employee or tort victim, is more likely to have his economic eggs concentrated in the basket of a single debtor. In the real world, however, the unpaid employee and the tort victim (who are poor loss spreaders) are actually the least likely to be secured (although they may be covered by insurance or protected, at least in part, by special laws).

---

[16] *See, e.g.*, Alan Schwartz, *Security Interests and Bankruptcy Priorities: A Review of Current Theories*, 10 J. LEGAL STUD. 1, 7–8 (1981).

Perhaps security interests may be justified by a simple first-in-time/fair notice rationale: the creditors who get them are the ones who ask for and receive them first, leaving subsequent creditors unsecured. So long as there is a system of public notice in place, subsequent creditors can decide whether to take the risk of extending further credit to the debtor, and have only themselves to blame if they do so (or fail to check the public records). But what about creditors who lend involuntarily, such as tort victims or the tax collector who have no opportunity to check the public records before the debtor incurs obligations to them? Further, the simple first-in-time/fair notice rationale seems rather to beg the question why bother having a system of security interests in the first place.

Finally, perhaps security interests are useful to protect the interests of creditors who are poor monitors for some reason (for example, those who have a limited ability to supervise the debtor's operations, perhaps owing to a lack of expertise). In theory, these creditors might take collateral to compensate.[17] But this notion runs contrary to Gilmore's account and would produce the odd result, in at least some circumstances, of privileging the claims of the incompetent.

Wrestling with such conundrums, scholars have taken a variety of approaches in an effort to explain the fundamental utility of security devices. Out of necessity, the discussion that follows offers simply a survey of some of the relevant literature, but we hope it will serve as an invitation to further inquiry for those who find the topic of interest. Specifically, this chapter canvasses the relatively pragmatic approaches taken by Professors Homer Kripke and Ronald Mann,[18] as well as the more abstractly theoretical approaches and critiques offered by Professors James White, Alan Schwartz, Thomas Jackson, Lucian Bebchuk, Jesse Fried, and Steven Schwarcz.[19] These works mark some of the boundaries of the debate over the desirability and efficiency of security interests in personal property under Article 9, together with the priority afforded secured claims under the current Bankruptcy Code. The Chapter concludes with a discussion of security interests as a form of asset partitioning, and addresses the potential impact of emerging technologies on the future of security devices. Hopefully this overview will help set a tone of critical inquiry that the

---

[17] *See* Thomas H. Jackson & Anthony T. Kronman, *Secured Financing and Priorities Among Creditors*, 88 YALE L.J. 1143, 1161 (1979).

[18] *See* Ronald J. Mann, *Explaining the Pattern of Secured Credit,* 110 HARV. L. REV. 625 (1997); Homer Kripke, *Law and Economics: Measuring the Economic Efficiency of Commercial Law in a Vacuum of Fact*, 133 U. PA. L. REV. 929 (1985).

[19] *See Bankruptcy*, Steven L. Schwarcz, *The Easy Case for the Priority of Secured Claims in* 47 DUKE L.J. 425 (1997); Lucian Arye Bebchuk & Jesse M. Fried, *The Uneasy Case for the Priority of Secured Claims in Bankruptcy*, 105 YALE L.J. 857 (1996); Thomas H. Jackson & Alan Schwartz, *Vacuum of Fact or Vacuous Theory: A Reply to Professor Kripke*, 133 U. PA. L. REV. 987 (1985); Alan Schwartz, *The Continuing Puzzle of Secured Debt*, 37 VAND. L. REV. 1051 (1984); James J. White, *Efficiency Justifications for Personal Property Security*, 37 VAND. L. REV. 473 (1984).

student may carry forward in thinking more deeply about the structure, details, and normative value of Article 9.

§ 2. THE LOGIC AND EFFICIENCY OF SECURED TRANSACTIONS

HOMER KRIPKE: A PRAGMATIC, HISTORICAL APPROACH

Homer Kripke, a professor emeritus of law at New York University and the University of San Diego at the time of his death in 1995, worked on the development of the Uniform Commercial Code (including Article 9) and was a member of its Permanent Editorial Board. In response to a series of articles applying abstract economic analysis to investigate the utility of security interests,[20] Kripke offered a contrasting historical and practical account of the rise and desirability of security devices. In *Law and Economics, Measuring the Economic Efficiency of Commercial Law in a Vacuum of Fact,*[21] Kripke began with the point that most security interests are of the purchase money variety (namely, a security interest taken in an item of personal property to secure the debtor's payment of the price for the item). He then traced the logic behind the purchase money security interest to a transactional principle underlying the law of sales: unless otherwise agreed, the seller's duty to deliver the goods is conditioned on the buyer's duty to pay for them (and vice versa). *See* UCC 2–511(1), 2–507(1). He next contended that "[w]hen credit entered the picture, it was historically an easy step to the concept that, despite physical surrender of the goods, the seller retained title until paid."[22] In other words, Kripke traced the logic behind the purchase money security interest to the logic of the vendor's conditional bill of sale: "one who contributes new assets to the debtor is entitled to be paid for them and should not be required to give up a hold on the assets until paid."[23]

By extension, a bank or other financial institution that loans money to the buyer to enable the buyer to purchase specific goods should also receive purchase money treatment as essentially a substitute for the seller. In Kripke's view, "in purchase money situations the secured party has *added to the assets* of the debtor, and . . . since the purchase money priority requires the secured creditor's funds to be traced into new assets, the secured creditor and the debtor have taken nothing away from the unsecured creditors."[24] Indeed, by increasing the debtor's resources, Kripke

---

20 *See, e.g.*, Schwartz, *supra* note 16; Jackson & Kronman, *supra* note 17.

21 Kripke, *supra* note 18, at 931.

22 *Id.* at 934–35.

23 *Id.* at 936.

24 *Id.* (emphasis in original).

argued that "everyone, including the unsecured creditors, may be better off."[25]

From an historical perspective, Kripke explained that, as the Industrial Revolution gained momentum, advances in manufacturing gave rise to the widespread availability of relatively expensive durable goods (for example, automobiles, appliances, and the like), and a corresponding need for purchasers to pay for them over time:

> [a] decision to purchase such goods involves a commitment to purchase several years of satisfactions in advance. For example, purchase of an automobile may be compared to the purchase of a bus ticket good for five years, or the purchase of a washing machine may be likened to contracting for a person's laundry service for five years. There would be relatively few instances in which a buyer could afford to buy this long-lasting package of satisfactions at once. The installment payment contract is a device for permitting the user to pay for the satisfactions more closely to when they are realized.[26]

Kripke argued, however, that most consumer debtors were relatively bad credit risks:

> [i]n the case of consumer credit, the consumer is seldom a good balance-sheet risk. Her principal assets are household goods, which would be almost worthless on an execution sale and in many states are exempt from execution sale except in purchase money situations. The consumer's principal other 'asset' is her job. One can check on the existence and duration of the job by telephone, but this gives no assurance that the job will continue. The lender places additional reliance on the salvage value of the goods sold subject to the security interest.[27]

Of course, one way to compensate for the risk of the purchaser's default would be for the seller (or lender who financed the purchaser's acquisition of the goods) to charge a relatively high rate of interest. Kripke maintained, however, that doing so encounters at least three problems.

First, it increases the transaction costs for the buyer, making the purchase much more expensive, often prohibitively so: "[t]here are limits to the amount of interest that a debtor can pay before a loan arrangement becomes impractical both for financial reasons and for legal reasons such as usury laws."[28] Second, it is costly to set a rate that appropriately compensates the lender for the risk of default associated with any

---

25 *Id.* at 940.

26 *Id.* at 941.

27 *Id.* at 947.

28 *Id.* at 954–55.

particular debtor because of the amount of information and analysis required in the underwriting process: "passing credit in the absence of security would be a time-consuming and expensive job."[29] Third, in the absence of security, the time it would take to underwrite the extension of credit would delay the transaction: "[o]ur enormous manufacturing system for equipment and consumer goods depends on a distribution system that permits rapid sales on credit at the point of distribution without extended delays involved in the passing of credit and incidental legal matters."[30]

By using cheap and certain forms of security devices (for example, a lien on the item to secure the purchaser's obligation to pay for it), the seller could more easily make a rapid credit decision, reduce the parties' transaction costs, and charge a lower rate of interest:

> [t]he lender's risk is reduced by the taking of security. If the loan is properly structured with a down payment adequate to overcome the depreciation that occurs when a new object becomes used and to keep ahead of future wear and tear, the risks to the seller or lender on most items of durable goods will be relatively small, given the resale value that can be realized readily on repossession. This reduced risk is taken into account in determining whether to make the loan and in establishing the amount of the down payment, the length of the period of credit, and the extent of the credit investigation.[31]

In conjunction with the rise of secured consumer debt financing of the kind described above, small businesses also found themselves in need of financing to facilitate their acquisitions of inventory (for example, the goods they sold to consumers on installment payment plans). According to Kripke, secured lending (or its economic equivalent) also facilitated this financing. For example, suppose an automobile dealer sold a car to a consumer under a five-year installment plan with the seller retaining a security interest in the car to secure the customer's payments under the plan. Under this arrangement, the customer typically would not finish paying for the car for five years. In order to purchase new inventory to replace the car he had sold, the dealer usually needed a way to convert the consumer's five-year installment contract into immediate dollars, and for this he basically had two options: (1) sell the customer's installment contract to a factor at a discount for cash (say, 95% of the face amount of the contract), or (2) borrow funds from a bank or finance company using the customer's installment contract as collateral.[32] Of course, under either scenario, what made the installment contract attractive to the financing entity (either to purchase or to lend against) was the fact that it was

---

[29] *Id.* at 947.

[30] *Id.* at 946.

[31] *Id.*

[32] *Id.* at 944.

secured by a lien on the automobile (such that, if the customer defaulted, the car could be repossessed and sold to cover the unpaid debt).

For large businesses, secured lending also facilitated an expansion of the distribution of goods. Kripke observed that, as a general rule, "[a] manufacturing company should appropriately borrow not more than thirty-five to fifty percent of its capitalization."[33] Accepted leverage ratios, however, were much higher for certain kinds of assets, particularly accounts: "[b]y segregating the [accounts] into a separate subsidiary, thus giving lenders the first claim to them, manufacturers can obtain vastly greater sums."[34] Once again, according to Kripke, secured lending supported the growth of the durable goods distribution system by making more capital available to fuel its expansion.

All of this, of course, depended on the willingness of those with capital in the marketplace to invest it in the ways described above.[35] Financial capital, Kripke argued, will go where it will: "it need not necessarily be engaged in loans to finance the distribution of goods" but rather "can be invested in the securities or commodities markets, used to develop real estate, or used to engage in any other business activity."[36] Kripke contended that, where capital is used "in financing the distribution of goods, lenders can largely dictate the terms to which both debtors (manufactures or dealers) and suppliers, who are the bulk of unsecured creditors, have to agree."[37] And, he claimed, the terms the lenders often demanded included the provision of security.

Like Gilmore, Kripke argued that all of this actually worked to the advantage of unsecured creditors (or at least some of them). True enough, "[a]n unsecured supplier will on occasion appear to have been harmed when its debtor becomes insolvent and a financial lender has security in the inventory or receivables that originated with the supplier."[38] At the same time, "in perhaps hundreds of cases that have not ended in insolvency, the supplier may for years have been receiving payments much faster than the debtor would have been able to provide had there not been a financial lender ready to supply secured credit."[39] He concluded that "[t]he problem is not all or none; it is not a zero-sum game."[40] Rather, unsecured creditors often benefit from the arrangement overall because the funds that secured lenders provide are often used to pay their unsecured invoices.

---

33 *Id.* at 945.

34 *Id.*

35 *Id.* at 944.

36 *Id.*

37 *Id.*

38 *Id.* at 960–61.

39 *Id.* at 961.

40 *Id.*

Similarly, Kripke argued that security devices facilitate monitoring. He claimed that secured lenders monitor more than unsecured creditors because they have a vested property interest in the debtor's assets, and, hence, a special reason to monitor: "[t]he secured creditor has sufficient rights in the collateral to act promptly and curtail losses" whereas "[t]he unsecured creditor lacks any comparable rights."[41] Hence, "[m]onitoring by unsecured creditors scarcely exists outside of reviewing financial statements and including restrictive covenants" and that "[e]ven these covenants are of diminishing importance and frequently are not used in transactions with small businesses."[42]

Kripke acknowledged that the use of security devices was not necessarily an essential feature of every financing transaction in the durable goods distribution system. To begin with, debtors with exceptionally good credit often do not borrow on a secured basis because they can obtain credit at the same (or lower) rate of interest without having to offer collateral.[43] In addition, "[w]hen the market no longer finds security necessary and can accept the proposition that an increased interest rate is an adequate substitute, the market may abandon security."[44] He observed that this has happened in the case of "goods formerly bought on secured credit [that are now] bought with merchant or bank credit cards."[45] He concluded that "where the collateral value is slight, practice confirms . . . that increased interest rates and accelerated payments can be a substitute for security," although "[s]imilar change is noticeably absent . . . in other areas of secured financing" particularly where "the individual exposure is large and the collateral of substantial value . . . ."[46]

According to Kripke, Article 9 represents an enormous improvement over the transactional practices of previous eras because it codified and simplified the field, eliminated legal risk and uncertainty, and reduced the parties' transaction costs—in other words, it made the taking of security interests cheaper and more reliable, and, hence, more attractive. This in turn encouraged banks to engage in asset-based financing, which had the further effect of reducing overall borrowing charges due to the banks' ability to raise capital at a lower cost than other financing entities (for example, banks accept deposits from their customers on which they pay relatively little interest, and thus have a competitive advantage in lending

---

[41] *Id.* at 968.

[42] *Id.* at 967–68.

[43] *Id.* at 969–70.

[44] *Id.* at 972.

[45] *Id.* at 972–73.

[46] *Id.* at 973.

these deposits to borrowers). In this way, Kripke claimed, Article 9 had the further effect of benefiting both debtors and unsecured creditors.[47]

Like Gilmore's account, Kripke's approach to the basic theory of Article 9 is largely historical and pragmatic. He argued that, in explaining the phenomenon of security devices, "[t]here is preeminently a need for the old goal of legal realism: to get beyond appellate opinions into trial records and beyond those records into life itself."[48] Logic alone, he asserted, could not have deduced the realities and practices of the secured financial markets. What is needed, he claimed, is a thorough knowledge of commercial experience, and a careful and critical observer to explain what is actually happening in the real world.

Kripke's account is like Gilmore's in other respects. Recall that Gilmore contended that it was probably impossible to prove one way or the other whether the existence of security devices makes society better off. Gilmore was largely content to observe that security interests have existed in one form or another for a very long time and appear to serve a useful policing function. Kripke takes this a bit further, arguing both that security interests facilitated a great deal of lending that otherwise would not have been available on a relatively cheap basis, and that these devices had the overall effect of supporting the development of a robust distribution system for durable goods. His account, however, is not all encompassing or comprehensive. For example, although he argues that the system of secured financing often benefits those who supply goods to the debtor on an unsecured basis, what about other kinds of unsecured creditors (such as tort victims) who do not get the same benefit? Also, what of security interests that are not of the purchase money variety? For example, suppose an unsecured creditor takes a security interest in various items of the debtor's personal property not to secure a new infusion of capital, but rather to secure an old debt the debtor is having trouble paying? These and other questions remain.

THOMAS JACKSON AND ALAN SCHWARTZ: A RESPONSE TO KRIPKE

In order to drill down further into the utility of security devices and the theoretical underpinnings of the law regulating them, it is useful at this juncture to further refine the analysis by dividing the inquiry more precisely into four distinct questions, two of which are descriptive ("positive") in nature, and two normative. The two positive questions are (1) why do we have a law of security interests, and (2) how does it operate? The answer to the first question is largely historical, and is the subject of Chapter 9 of this book. The answer to the second question involves a detailed consideration of the nuts and bolts of Article 9 in the context of prevailing commercial practices, and is treated in Chapters 2 through 8.

---

47 *Id.* at 975.

48 *Id.* at 984.

Note that Gilmore's and Kripke's analyses responded largely (but not exclusively) to these first two questions.

The two normative questions are (3) why *should* we have a law of security devices that permits a secured creditor to effectively fence off particular items of the debtor's personal property on a priority basis, and (4) assuming that such a law is desirable, what form *should* it take? As noted, Gilmore's response to the third question was that security interests are desirable because they enable the secured party to perform an important policing function that benefits secured and unsecured creditors alike. Kripke added that security devices are also desirable because they facilitated the development of a fully robust durable goods distribution system that, implicitly, would not have arisen otherwise (or at least not as robustly). In particular, the existence of security interests has facilitated lending that otherwise would not have occurred, either because it would not have been available or, if available, would have been more expensive.

With respect to the fourth question (what the law ought to look like), both Gilmore and Kripke spent a considerable amount of their professional careers crafting the provisions of Article 9 to facilitate the widespread use of security devices. Presumably they did so because they believed that having a law that permits the taking of security interests is a valuable thing. But should we accept their faith? What if they were wrong and it turns out that we would have been better off banning security interests? And how might we verify or refute their theories?

One farfetched but revealing way to test the utility of security devices would be to set up two distinct societies equal in every way, except that one permitted security interests to be taken and the other did not. After controlling for all other variables, we might observe over time which society performed better by reference to some set of noncontroversial criteria (if such exist). We might then have a clear answer to the normative question whether we should have a law that permits the use of security devices. Assuming that the answer to that question is yes, we might then proceed to the next consideration: how best to arrange such a law? To answer that question, we might repeat our experiment by again dividing society into two equal halves, the first operating with one type of law permitting certain kinds of security devices in certain ways, and the other operating with a different mix of provisions (for example, different kinds of possessory versus non-possessory security devices, public notice versus no public notice, and the like). We might then repeat this experiment over and over with different combinations of provisions, comparing the results until we arrive at just the right blend of regulations that best enhances the performance of society in the most efficient way.

Of course, in the real world we do not have the luxury of undertaking this kind of social tinkering. So we must rely on other forms of analysis. One form is economic theory.

In their article *Vacuum of Fact or Vacuous Theory: A Reply to Professor Kripke*,[49] Jackson and Schwartz identify an economic approach that some scholars have used prominently in their investigations of the utility of security interests: the Modigliani & Miller irrelevance proposition. Developed as a tool to evaluate claims about optimal capital structures for firms, the proposition postulates that "if capital markets are perfect, information is perfect, all actors have homogeneous expectations, bankruptcy costs are zero, and no taxes exist, a firm cannot increase its value by altering its capital structure."[50] Jackson and Schwartz observe that "[a] change in the mix of a firm's debt, from unsecured debt to secured, is an alteration in its capital structure."[51] Applying the Modigliani & Miller theorem, they conclude that, "[s]ince such a change cannot increase the firm's value and since it is costly for firms to offer security, the irrelevance proposition predicts that no secured debt will be issued."[52]

In reality, of course, secured debt is common. So to help understand what explains the phenomenon of secured debt, scholars "relax the strong assumptions that Modigliani & Miller made to see whether the new models thereby obtained predict security, or they add additional factors—moral hazard, risk aversion, and the like—to see whether models so derived can explain the observed data [namely, that security interests are taken]."[53] Jackson and Schwartz argue that "the Modigliani & Miller irrelevance proposition is valuable not because its assumptions reflect the real world—they do not—but because the proposition orders the scholar's inquiry: *which* assumption, when relaxed, could explain how firms can increase their value by issuing different kinds of ownership forms—a differentiated ownership structure—instead of issuing claims that all have the same level of priority?"[54]

Conceding that security devices reduce a *secured creditor's* risk (and correspondingly lowers the interest rate a secured creditor typically charges), Jackson and Schwartz frame the relevant question as "whether security reduces the secured creditor's risk *more* than it increases the risk of unsecured creditors."[55] They argue that this is the right question

---

49 Jackson & Schwartz, *supra* note 19.

50 *Id.* at 987.

51 *Id.*

52 *Id.*

53 *Id.* at 987–88.

54 *Id.* at 991 (emphasis in original).

55 *Id.* at 993 (emphasis in original). They argue similarly that the question "posed by the Modigliani & Miller irrelevance proposition is whether security [interests] . . . should be prohibited even though particular creditors might desire them, because they are detrimental to all creditors

because, under the irrelevance proposition, unless security reduces the secured creditor's risk more than it increases the unsecured creditors' risk, "the existence of secured credit is at best a wash and, because of the unavoidable costs it introduces (such as filing and search costs), inefficient in the aggregate."[56] In contrast, Kripke (and Gilmore) contended that the costs and benefits to secured and unsecured creditors are not a wash because the taking of security interests actually works to the advantage of unsecured creditors. Jackson and Schwartz counter that the effect is indeed a wash, under Modigliani & Miller's assumptions, because "the consequent lower interest rate the secured creditor charges will be offset exactly by the higher interest rates of the debtor's other creditors, who will adjust to the presence of security."[57]

In reality, do the interest rates that unsecured creditors charge offset "exactly" the secured creditor's lower rate? Kripke argued that, in the real world, interest rates are often set at least somewhat independently of risk, and unsecured creditors do not in fact raise their rates to offset the lower rate charged by the secured creditor. For example, in the case of trade suppliers, "[t]heir credit extension starts with a sale, and the seller who needs to extend trade credit in order to make a sale cannot lightly turn away buyers who will not or cannot pay interest rates high enough to compensate for credit risk."[58] In other words, in order to make a sale, trade creditors may often be willing to accept less of a return than financial lenders would.

Jackson and Schwartz acknowledge that "lenders sometimes will not raise rates in response to increases in debtor demand, even when usury statutes permit the higher rates." They offer several possible explanations for this phenomenon, including that doing so might actually increase their risk. Because the borrower must pay more in interest, it becomes less profitable, decreasing its "return on successful projects."[59] This reduced profitability creates a "moral hazard" incentive for the borrower to invest in higher-risk, higher-reward projects to compensate. But Kripke made use of the same argument, also contending that when a secured creditor charges a lower rate of interest, that reduced rate makes the debtor a relatively *less* risky prospect in general. Under the moral hazard hypothesis, unsecured creditors would only be shooting themselves in their collective foot by raising their rates to offset the lower rate charged by the secured creditor, particularly where (if Kripke and Gilmore are correct) they actually benefit from the secured creditor's monitoring and the

---

taken as a group." *Id.* at 997. They further contend that another way to frame the inquiry is "whether secured borrowing can increase a debtor's net wealth *over what it would have been* with an unsecured loan." *Id.* at 994 (emphasis in original).

[56] *Id.*

[57] *Id.* at 995.

[58] Kripke, *supra* note 18, at 931.

[59] Jackson & Schwartz, *supra* note 19, at 999.

additional capital the secured creditor brings to the table that might otherwise be unavailable.

In the real world, many unsecured creditors do not formally charge different interest rates based on whether the debtor has issued secured debt to some other creditor. In the case of firms, employees extend credit to the debtor by performing services before receiving their salaries or wages. They do not typically charge different rates based on whether the debtor has granted a security interest to some other creditor. Utility companies similarly extend credit to the debtor by delivering power first and then sending the bill later, and likewise do not typically vary their rates based on whether some other creditor has taken a security interest in the debtor's personal property. Tort victims extend credit to the debtor in the sense of suffering damages before receiving compensation, and likewise do not receive different levels of compensation depending on whether the debtor has issued secured debt. The tax collector extends credit to the debtor by accepting payment after the debtor incurs its relevant tax obligation, and also does not typically vary its rates based on whether the debtor has granted a security interest to some other party.

In the case of individuals, a similar pattern exists. Doctors and hospitals extend credit to the debtor by performing services before receiving payment, and do not charge different rates based on whether the debtor has granted a security interest to his bank or some other entity. Similarly, many credit card companies, educational institutions to whom the debtor owes tuition payments, utilities, and myriad other types of unsecured creditors do not vary their rates based on whether the individual debtor has issued secured debt to some other party.

On the other hand, these unsecured creditors all sustain and absorb losses to the extent their recoveries against debtors are reduced because secured creditors have priority. Conceivably their "prices" take these losses into account, and the question perhaps becomes whether the cost to them exceeds the benefits security devices confer. Kripke (and Gilmore) thought the benefits outweigh the costs. Among other things, Kripke argued that the presence of secured lending actually *increases* the chances that the unsecured creditors will be paid by increasing the debtor's liquidity. Jackson and Schwartz are not so sure.

It is worth noting that Jackson and Schwartz's use of the Modigliani & Miller irrelevance proposition focuses on whether security interests have the effect of increasing the value of *the firm*—a perspective that is unsurprising given that the theorem was developed in that context. Kripke, on the other hand, had a different perspective: whether security interests help facilitate the distribution of durable goods for the benefit of society as a whole, and whether they are good for both secured and unsecured creditors alike.

From Kripke's perspective, the fact that a security device increases, decreases, or maintains a firm's value does not mean that the law of secured transactions is necessarily efficient or inefficient—firm value is not necessarily a proxy for efficiency in a broader sense. For example, society might logically accept overall reduced firm values occasioned by capital structures that include secured debt if these are outweighed by the benefits of a more robust durable goods distribution system. In the context of evaluating the overall efficiency of security devices the ultimate issue "is whether the social gain exceeds the social cost,"[60] and Kripke contended that the ideas of "social gain" and "social cost" extend beyond the consideration of the impact of security devices on firm values alone.

Recall that Kripke argued that security interests are particularly useful because they make investments in the durable goods distribution system more attractive as compared to other potential uses of the same capital. Specifically, he contended that, absent security devices, borrowing in the durable goods market would often not be available *at all* because capital would be directed to other purposes. He also argued that (1) the transactional costs of security interests are relatively trivial because they are cheap to take, and (2) the negative impact on unsecured creditors (namely, their inability to collect as much on their claims in the event of the debtor's insolvency) is outweighed by the lower cost of secured lending that debtors enjoy, as well as other benefits to at least some of a debtor's unsecured creditors (for example, if financial creditors refrained from making secured capital investments in retailers, unsecured manufacturers and other trade creditors would likely have fewer customers buying their goods). Of course, Kripke never *proved* that using security interests to attract capital to the durable goods distribution system was better than allowing capital to flow to other uses. He simply believed that this was so, and presented arguments in support of his view.

Note also the clash of methodologies between Kripke's approach and that of Jackson and Schwartz. Kripke based his analysis (at least in part) on his long familiarity with commercial law and the intricacies of its inner workings. In addition, Kripke drew on such sources as first-hand accounts by various players in the secured lending market on prevailing practices, procedures, and attitudes. In contrast, Jackson and Schwartz criticize investigative methods such as interviews with actors in the field on the theory that self-reports are not used by "serious scholars . . . when other data are available."[61] Moreover, in response to Kripke's assertion that use of the Modigliani & Miller irrelevance proposition is misleading in this context because it was developed in a different setting for a different purpose (namely, to evaluate claims about optimal firm capital structures), Jackson and Schwartz argue in favor of the relative universality of the

---

[60] Schwartz, *supra* note 19, at 1060 n.15.

[61] Jackson & Schwartz, *supra* note 19, at 989.

theorem and insist that analysis of the utility of security devices *is* properly a question of the utility of different forms of capital structures. They reject as a "prescription for ignorance" the activity of "staring at the facts until a hypothesis emerges," and claim that doing so is "both unwise and impossible to implement."[62] What do you think? In particular, how would you go about addressing normative questions regarding a complex social phenomenon like the law of secured financing?

JAMES WHITE: ANOTHER TAKE ON THE EFFICIENCY OF SECURED FINANCING

In *Efficiency Justifications for Personal Property Security*,[63] James White digs deeper into the efficiency debate, posing the following question: "[i]s society better off because bankruptcy law, Article 9 of the Uniform Commercial Code, and common law rules have made the taking and perfection of security simple, inexpensive, and efficacious?"[64] His answer is "yes."

White begins by offering another perspective on why unsecured creditors are unlikely to charge higher rates in response to a debtor's issuance of secured debt: the secured lender doesn't actually take anything away from unsecured creditors because if the debtor becomes unable to pay all his debts in full and enters bankruptcy, the unsecured creditors typically wouldn't get anything anyway even if the secured creditor did not exist. He states: "the unsecured creditor will be indifferent to the presence of secured claims on the debtor's assets, for in bankruptcy he will receive nothing . . . in any event."[65]

For example, White points to a typical bankruptcy proceeding under the liquidation provisions of Chapter 7 of the Bankruptcy Code. When a debtor commences a Chapter 7 proceeding, a "bankruptcy estate" is created to take ownership of the debtor's property. The basic idea of a Chapter 7 case is that, in exchange for a discharge of most preexisting debts, the insolvent debtor surrenders his property to a trustee so that the trustee can liquidate the property as part of the bankruptcy estate and distribute the proceeds to creditors. As a general rule, secured creditors are entitled in bankruptcy to have the value of their collateral applied first to satisfy their claims ahead of the claims of others. Accordingly, secured creditors tend to fare much better than unsecured creditors in Chapter 7 proceedings in terms of receiving payment on their claims. But it does not follow, White argues, that unsecured creditors would get much benefit if bankruptcy did not recognize the secured creditor's priority. That is because under the Bankruptcy Code's exemption provisions debtors are typically entitled to

---

62 *Id.* at 991.

63 White, *supra* note 19.

64 *Id.* at 475.

65 *Id.* at 487.

fence off a variety of items of personal property from the reach of unsecured creditors.

For example, suppose a creditor takes a security interest in an individual debtor's automobile to secure a loan the creditor made to enable the debtor to acquire the vehicle in the first place (namely, a purchase money loan). If the debtor files for bankruptcy, the secured creditor is generally entitled to the value of the car ahead of the claims of other creditors. Suppose, however, that no creditor has a lien on the debtor's car. In general, unless the car is worth more than the debtor's vehicle exemption entitlement, the debtor will be able to exempt the car from the unsecured creditors' reach. In the case of the typical consumer debtor (who is not wealthy and whose assets often have a value that is less than the probable exemptions), the unsecured creditor will not care whether secured claims on the debtor's assets exist because he will receive nothing from the estate in any case.[66]

White applies a similar analysis to the bankruptcy proceedings of insolvent firms under either Chapter 7 or Chapter 11. In general, Chapter 11 is designed to provide an insolvent business with an opportunity to reorganize, either by selling its assets as a going concern or by attempting to rehabilitate itself without a sale. Many Chapter 11 cases fail and convert to Chapter 7 liquidation proceedings. According to White, the problem here for unsecured creditors is not the availability of exemptions because, unlike insolvent individuals, bankrupt firms are not entitled to any. Rather, the problem is that the rational unpaid unsecured creditor "correctly fears that any assets available will be dissipated in a fruitless attempt to operate the business," leaving nothing for unsecured creditors in any event.[67] Accordingly, the unsecured creditor of a firm is likewise indifferent to the presence of security.

White next argues that it is easy to overestimate the transaction costs of granting security interests, which include the expense of preparing and filing a notice of the secured party's lien, searching the recording files, negotiating and drafting a security agreement, and so forth. He contends that, although such costs exist, they are typically trivial:

> any creditor, secured or not, who lends a large sum to a closely held corporation, will demand a detailed loan agreement. The creditor will make an investigation of the income and assets of the debtor. Adding a five dollar filing fee and a few standardized clauses to the agreement to make it a security agreement would be a trivial addition to the cost in such a case.[68]

---

66 *Id.* at 482–87.

67 *Id.* at 489.

68 *Id.* at 490.

It follows that, if the transaction costs of taking a security interest are typically trivial, and unsecured creditors do not adjust their charges upward to offset the secured lender's typically lower interest rate, "the traditional arguments about the efficiency of security are easier to sustain and the challenge becomes more tenuous."[69]

White also considers the potential benefits of security devices in terms of the incentives they create to facilitate lending, particularly lending by relatively risk-averse financial institutions such as banks (or, more precisely, the risk-averse lending officers who work at banks and garner little personal advantage by making successful risky loans, but face the risk of substantial personal penalties by making unsuccessful ones). He identifies the relevant risks as those "to the specific employee [who decides to make the loan] that he will suffer demotion or loss of his job and the risk to [his employer] that it will suffer adverse consequences with agencies such as the Comptroller of the Currency, the Federal Reserve, or the FDIC upon inspection if any such risky loans go bad."[70]

White also notes that, between different creditors with different risk aversions, it is probably efficient to give security to the most risk-averse creditor simply because by doing so a debtor can reduce his aggregate interest cost. For example, "if risk-averse creditor A would demand fifteen percent unsecured, while risk-neutral creditor B would make the same loan at twelve percent, but each would lend secured at seven percent, then giving security to A will reduce the total interest cost to the debtor."[71] Like Kripke, White concludes that, because there are larger benefits to secured lending, it is inadequate to evaluate the efficiency of security devices simply by computing and netting the interest costs that secured and unsecured creditors charge. Rather, because the relevant cost/benefit analysis is considerably more complex, proper judgments about the efficiency of security interests are also bound to be more complicated.[72]

Finally, White also considers what would likely happen if security interests in personal property were banned. He argues that, given the desirability of taking security, such a prohibition would simply prompt the use of less efficient substitutes, such as leasing and factoring transactions tailored to approximate security devices. Among other reasons,

> [b]anks and many other creditors are notoriously traditional and unreceptive to change. Creditors who are accustomed to having security in certain circumstances and to pursuing that security in times of difficulty would not readily accept an economist's suggestion that it would be more efficient in the long run for them

69 *Id.* at 481.

70 *Id.* at 492.

71 *Id.* at 491.

72 *Id.* at 493–94.

> simply to raise their interest rates and lend unsecured to the same debtor. They are practical people who know the consequences of their past behavior and are skeptical of theoretical departures from it. . . . [Another] reason why the secured creditor likely would turn to a security alternative as opposed to totally unsecured credit is that that is what his lawyers would tell him to do. A typical lawyer . . . would search for alternatives that conform as closely as possible to past practice. The most clever of the lawyers might even devise something that looks like a lease or other nonsecurity arrangement but performs like a security agreement. Indeed, the cases offer ample evidence of this form of innovative behavior.[73]

For those who have read Chapter 9 on the history of security devices, this will undoubtedly ring true. White also predicts that these substitutes would be much more cumbersome and costly.[74] For all of these reasons, White concludes that the taking of security interests under the current law is probably efficient and therefore justified.[75]

ALAN SCHWARTZ: A RESPONSE TO WHITE

In his article *The Continuing Puzzle of Secured Debt*,[76] Alan Schwartz takes aim at White's analysis. Again invoking the Modigliani & Miller irrelevance proposition, he begins with the now familiar observation that

> under certain assumptions there is only one task [for corporate managers] to perform—to choose appropriate projects [and not bother electing "optimal capital structures"]. A corporation, Modigliani and Miller proved, could not increase its value by altering its capital structure; firm value is solely a function of the size and risk of the firm's income stream. Consequently, the . . . hypothesis concludes that no optimal capital structure exists; any particular structure is as good as any other.[77]

Schwartz acknowledges that the assumptions underlying the Modigliani & Miller theorem are unrealistic, but contends that, even when these are "relaxed," he discovers no justification for existing patterns of secured lending. Hence, in his words, the "continuing puzzle of secured debt."[78]

In response to White's argument that unsecured creditors are indifferent to the presence of security devices because of the effect of bankruptcy law, Schwartz contends that this explanation is implausible

---

73 *Id.* at 503.

74 *Id.* at 503–08.

75 *Id.* at 508.

76 Schwartz, *supra* note 19.

77 *Id.* at 1052–53.

78 *Id.* at 1051–54.

because existing patterns of secured debt predate the current bankruptcy regime (which came into effect in 1979).[79] He states that "[a]n initial difficulty with the argument that secured creditors attach assets unavailable to other creditors is that the pattern of secured lending seems not to have changed materially in the last two decades although many of the legal changes on which White relies have been adopted recently."[80] But virtually all of the elements of the current bankruptcy law that White discusses existed under the former Bankruptcy Act of 1898, albeit it in somewhat different form, and the relevant differences between the current and former law may not be particularly material.

Schwartz also contends that White's hypothesis cannot be true because, if it were, creditors would insist on security to prevent the debtor from holding free assets in bankruptcy, and, because it is cheaper, debtors "always would borrow on a secured basis until they ran out of free assets."[81] Schwartz observes, however, that "[n]either consumers nor firms consistently act in this way, so the facts disconfirm White's theory."[82]

In reality, of course, some firms do "lien up" all of their assets (as do some individuals). In its most common form, the practice is known as granting a fully secured "blanket" lien. It is equally true that firms with exceptionally strong credit ratings never borrow on a secured basis because they can borrow unsecured at the same or lower rate (and so can some individuals). Not surprisingly, many firms (and individuals) occupy a space somewhere between these two extremes—they are able to obtain cheap unsecured credit for some kinds of transactions (for example, obtaining power from the local utility), while for other transactions it is cheaper for them to borrow on a secured basis (for example, to purchase a very expensive durable good such as an automobile and the like). The most relevant variables appear to be the riskiness of the debtor, the risk averseness of the particular creditor extending credit, the particular creditor's lending objectives, and whether it is worthwhile in the context of the particular transaction for the creditor to take a security interest.

To understand why this is so (particularly the last point), it is useful to note that most debtors never enter bankruptcy. They pay their debts as they come due, and the value of any security interest they might grant is never tested. For creditors with relatively little at stake (either because the amount at stake is small, the costs of default are sufficiently spread and hedged, or other factors), it is often just not worth it to even think about taking a security interest to cover the possibility that the debtor may file for bankruptcy. In other words, granting a security interest is of no value to the debtor because the creditor is agnostic about security. On the other

---

79 *Id.* at 1061.

80 *Id.*

81 *Id.*

82 *Id.* at 1062.

hand, where it actually does offer value to the debtor (because the creditor is not agnostic), security is commonly taken—but only up to the point at which it actually provides value to the debtor. Because rational debtors only borrow what they need, and many creditors are willing to lend on an unsecured basis notwithstanding the fact that they may receive nothing if the debtor files for bankruptcy, only the riskiest are likely to run out of free assets.

In the case of individuals, there is another reason why some secured creditors do not take liens on all of the debtor's assets: section 522 of the Bankruptcy Code permits the debtor to avoid a variety of liens that impair the debtor's exemptions (a notable exception being purchase money security interests). For example, if the debtor has already paid for an item of personal property that he may claim as exempt, creditors generally cannot take a security interest in that item that will survive the debtor's bankruptcy filing. In addition, doing so may also be a violation of Federal Trade Commission regulations (discussed in Section 6 of Chapter 7).

Schwartz questions White's theory that security interests are useful because they incentivize risk averse lending officers to extend credit. Schwartz observes that, when the interests of a firm's senior managers are properly aligned with the interests of shareholders (for example, they are given stock options, warrants, and the like), senior managers "whose goal is to maximize [the shareholders' return] thus have incentives to cause [more junior] lending officers to act as if they were risk neutral, even though security exists."[83] Senior managers can do this by rewarding loan officers "more highly for successful performance" such as by making more loans than they would if left to their own cautious devices, and punishing them "less severely for unsuccessful performance that is not the result of their own incompetence."[84] Schwartz contends that, because these methods exist, security interests are not necessary to address the problem of risk averseness among the loan officers.

As White points out, however, many lending firms are answerable not only to their shareholders, but also to regulators who may want these firms to behave conservatively. Presumably a senior executive who may be called out on the carpet by an administrative agency has an incentive to instruct his subordinates to behave in ways that avoid that embarrassment, not to mention other administrative sanctions including fines, increased regulatory oversight, lending restrictions, and, at the extreme, loss of the lending institution's charter.

In addition, unless junior loan officers have the same incentives as senior managers (for example, they are given the same stock options, warrants, and the like), there will always be some misalignment between

83 *Id.* at 1063.

84 *Id.* at 1063–64.

senior and junior managers because they are rewarded in different ways. As Schwartz suggests, one cure would be to eliminate the asymmetry, but that would be expensive for the firm. Because security interests are inexpensive to take, they may be a cheaper substitute.

Schwartz further challenges White's account with the observation that banks may "hold a lower portion of their debt secured than finance companies do,"[85] inviting the question: if banks are so risk averse, why do they engage in so much unsecured lending in comparison to finance companies? It is possible to imagine explanations for this difference having to do with the nature of the lending businesses of these institutions. To begin with, a lender might be highly risk averse, yet still lend largely on an unsecured basis (for example, it may be an arm of a private investment bank that caters exclusively to wealthy clients who are all good credit risks). Conversely, a lender might be relatively agnostic about risk if left to its own devices, but in reality lend only on a secured basis (for example, the lender may be a captive finance entity affiliated with a manufacturer that lends to high-risk consumers). Many consumer finance companies fall into this second category. Their primary incentive is not to make money on the loans they extend *per se*. Rather, it is to support the sales of their manufacturing affiliates (or other businesses they have partnered with). They typically extend cheap credit to facilitate this goal. Understandably, it is often secured.

Note the relatively profound difference between the analytical approaches of White and Schwartz. In evaluating the efficiency of security devices, White appears content to rely on what he believes are plausible arguments grounded in observations about real world practices. In contrast, Schwartz prefers abstract economic reasoning premised on admittedly unrealistic assumptions that produce conclusions that can then be tested against reality. When White makes a claim, he asserts it as an argument, inviting the reader to evaluate its merits. When Schwartz makes a claim, he asserts it as a form of proof—something he has "shown" to be true (based on various assumptions). White talks like a lawyer. Schwartz talks like an economist.

Recall that Gilmore claimed, ultimately, that the utility of security devices is incapable of absolute empirical demonstration. In other words, we will always have our doubts. White echoes this sentiment, suggesting that the sheer volume of macro and microeconomic variables make an elaborate proof impossible. What do you think?

---

85 *Id.* at 1065–66.

§ 3. QUESTIONING THE PRIORITY OF SECURED CLAIMS IN BANKRUPTCY

BEBCHUK AND FRIED: A CRITIQUE OF FULL PRIORITY AND A PROPOSAL FOR PARTIAL PRIORITY

Security devices provide secured parties with a number of benefits. Chief among these is the comfort that if the debtor ever becomes insolvent and unable to pay all debts in full, the secured creditor may recover at least the value of its collateral (assuming the secured creditor can get its hands on that value). Thus, the time when a security interest is arguable the most worthwhile to the secured party is when the debtor goes bust. After all, if the debtor is solvent and remains so, the secured creditor could always sue the debtor and recover its claim in full by obtaining a judgment and executing on it. Indeed, in many instances the debtor's solvency will be more valuable than a security interest. Solvent debtors typically pay their debts; the secured creditor may be paid in full even if the value of its collateral is less than the value of its claim; and the secured creditor won't necessarily lose out if there is something technically wrong with its security interest.

Of course, an insolvent debtor is typically (although not always) a candidate for a bankruptcy case. And historically, U.S. bankruptcy law has long recognized the rule that, as a general matter, a secured creditor is entitled to the value of its collateral ahead of the claims of the bankrupt debtor's unsecured creditors, assuming that the secured creditor was diligent in properly taking and perfecting its security interest. As noted, however, the secured creditor's ability in bankruptcy to obtain the value of its collateral ahead of the claims of others stands in conflict with the fundamental bankruptcy policy of equality of distribution. In essence, recognizing the secured party's security interest in bankruptcy has the effect of subordinating the claims of others to the secured party's claim, at least to the extent of the value of the collateral encumbered by the secured creditor's lien.

To the extent security interests serve a useful purpose, this is probably a good idea. After all, who would want a security interest if, right when the secured creditor typically needs it the most (namely, when the debtor becomes insolvent and files for bankruptcy), it becomes essentially useless because the law disregards it? But what if security interests do not really serve a particularly useful purpose, or they serve a useful purpose only some of the time? Perhaps we might change the longstanding bankruptcy rule to deny the full priority of security interests, or recognize them only in those setting where they are understood to be efficient.

In their article, *The Uneasy Case for the Priority of Secured Claims in Bankruptcy*,[86] Lucian Bebchuk and Jesse Fried argue that security interests are inefficient at least some of the time, and that an appropriate cure may be to afford them partial priority in bankruptcy. They begin with the observation that "two parties [A and B] will have an incentive to transfer value from the nonconsenting party [C] even if doing so reduces the total value that is available to all three parties" so long as the relationship is beneficial to A and B.[87] In other words, A and B will be happy to impose on C an "externality" in the form of the cost of any inefficiency their security agreement generates.

They next observe that at least some of a debtor's unsecured creditors (those that are "nonadjusting" in nature) essentially occupy the position of C when the debtor, A, grants a security interest to one creditor, B, to secure B's claim against A. Nonadjusting creditors are those who either cannot, or rationally will not, increase the rates they charge the debtor in response to being subordinated to a secured creditor's claim. They include tort victims, the tax collector, small creditors whose individual claims are too small to justify the expense of extensive underwriting or monitoring, and certain creditors who extend credit to the debtor before the debtor grants a security interest to some other creditor.

Bebchuk and Fried argue that, in a perfect world in which "the claims of all creditors other than Bank [the secured party] perfectly reflect all elements of the agreement between Bank and Firm [the debtor]," and "all of the other creditors are contractual creditors that are perfectly informed about all aspects of the contract between Bank and Firm and are able to take this information into account in shaping their contracts with . . . Firm," the debtor's granting of a security interest to one creditor "could not impose a negative externality on these other creditors."[88] They posit as a result that, in such a perfect world, the debtor and secured party "would never adopt an inefficient security interest in order to divert value from other creditors" because "[t]hese creditors would simply respond by raising their interest rates to recover the value diverted, leaving Bank and Firm to bear the net efficiency costs associated with the inefficient security interest." In other words, in their perfect world, unsecured creditor C would be perfectly adjusting in the sense of being able to re-impose on A or B the costs that C suffers as a result of A and B's inefficient contractual arrangement, thereby giving A and B an incentive to avoid that cost. Bebchuk and Fried then canvass the relevant costs and benefits of security interests, concluding that, in a perfect world in which unsecured creditors were all perfectly adjusting, A and B would "find it in their interest to

---

86 Bebchuk & Fried, *supra* note 19.

87 *Id.* at 870.

88 *Id.* at 881.

choose the socially optimal arrangement" and, "[t]hus, according full priority to secured claims in bankruptcy could not give rise to any inefficiencies."[89]

Of course, we do not live in a perfect world, and Bebchuk and Fried offer a hypothetical in which they claim to show that, in a world that includes nonadjusting creditors, the debtor and secured creditor may well enter into an inefficient contractual security arrangement. Specifically, they argue that their hypothetical example illustrates how "the use of a security interest providing Bank with full priority in some of Firm's assets will transfer value from these [nonadjusting] creditors" and "[c]onsequently, Firm and Bank will have an incentive to encumber assets with a security interest, even if this results in a loss of social value."[90]

The example they give, however, is unusual. To begin with, we are told to assume that Firm has two nonadjusting creditors (tort claimants) who are owed $500,000 each. Firm has three assets collectively worth $450,000 that could be used either to satisfy in part the nonadjusting creditors' $1 million in claims, or to secure a new $1 million loan from Bank. Firm elects to proceed with a loan from Bank. We are to assume further that, after Firm obtains the loan from Bank, another adjusting creditor will extend $1 million in credit to Firm. In sum, we are told that, if Bank is unsecured, Firm will have a total of $3 million in debt against $450,000 in assets: "Bank and the adjusting creditor would be owed $1 million each, and the two nonadjusting creditors would be owed $500,000 each by Firm, for a total of $3 million in liabilities."[91] As a result, "[t]he payout rate for unsecured claims would thus be ($450,000/$3 million), or 15 cents on the dollar," and Bank, with no security interest, "would thus lose $850,000 in the event of bankruptcy."[92]

Note several oddities about this hypothetical. First, Firm is insolvent from the outset. Its liabilities to the nonadjusting creditors alone ($500,000 plus $500,000) exceed the presumed value of its assets ($450,000). Second, even though Bank and the adjusting creditor will extend $1 million apiece in additional credit to Firm, this collective $2 million does not appear thereafter on Firm's balance sheet—Firm's assets are $450,000 if all of the creditors remain unsecured. Firm's liabilities to the new creditors, however, *do* appear on its balance sheet—we are told that there is $3 million in aggregate claims. Presumably, then, Firm has squandered instantly the $2 million extended by Bank and the adjusting creditor without reducing any of its debt. In addition, even though Firm is insolvent,

---

[89] *Id.* at 882.

[90] *Id.* at 895.

[91] *Id.* at 892 n.126.

[92] *Id.*

we are told to assume that "the probability that Firm will fail by the end of the year is 5%."[93]

Of course, in the real world no bank would ever lend into such a situation, and the decision to secure Bank's hypothetical loan would never be entertained because no rational bank would lend $1 million to an insolvent debtor secured by a lien on assets worth no more than $450,000. Moreover, because Firm is grossly insolvent under the facts presented, the actual probability of its failure is more likely to be around 100%.

The hypothetical continues. Recall that Firm has three assets worth $450,000 if all creditors remain unsecured. "Suppose that if Firm encumbers the first asset—which is expected to have a value of $400,000 in the event of bankruptcy—the amount of bankruptcy assets available to the creditors as a group would increase from $450,000 to $660,000."[94] In other words, the act of securing the first asset is presumed to have the effect of increasing the value of Firm's assets by $210,000. The hypothetical assumes that this increase in value is partially offset by $9,500 in transaction costs.

In addition, "[s]uppose that, once Firm has encumbered the first asset, the effect of encumbering the second asset—which is expected to have a value of $200,000 in bankruptcy—would be to increase the amount of assets available in the event of bankruptcy to $720,000."[95] In other words, the mere act of securing the second asset has the effect of increasing the value of Firm's assets by another $60,000. The hypothetical then assumes this is offset in part by an additional $2,000 in transaction costs.

Finally, "suppose that, once Firm has encumbered the first two assets, encumbering the third asset—which is expected to have a value of $120,000 in bankruptcy—would have no effect on the total value of assets available to creditors in the event of bankruptcy."[96] In other words, Bank's lien on the third asset does not increase the value of Firm's assets any further, which value remains stable, leaving the total value of all three assets at $720,000 ($400,000 for asset one, plus $200,000 for asset two, plus $120,000 for asset three). The transaction costs associated with encumbering the third asset are $1,000. It is further assumed that, with each item of collateral Bank is given, it will charge a lower rate of interest, and the adjusting creditor will charge a higher rate (although not enough to offset Bank's reduction).

Note several features of these additional assumptions. First, they assume that the mere taking of a security interest achieves a value enhancement with respect to the first two assets, but not the third.

---

[93] *Id.* at 891.

[94] *Id.*

[95] *Id.*

[96] *Id.* at 892.

Elsewhere in their article, Bebchuk and Fried identify several benefits to having security interests, including (1) preventing the debtor from squandering assets on inefficient projects or transferring assets to shareholders, (2) reducing collection costs upon default, (3) increasing the secured creditor's ability to monitor effectively, and (4) reducing incentives for other creditors to "rush for assets when a borrower begins suffering financial difficulties."[97] Presumably these explain the enhancement effect of Bank's lien with respect to the first two assets. Presumably, however, the enhancement effect diminishes with each successive asset until it disappears altogether in the case of the third item of collateral. Second, the enhancements are insufficient to render Firm solvent.

Once again, no bank would lend into such a situation because no bank would extend $1 million in credit to an insolvent debtor even on a secured basis where the assets are worth no more than $720,000. This is so even assuming Bank's lien had the effect of increasing the aggregate value of the assets as stipulated.

Nonetheless Bebchuk and Fried postulate that this example illustrates how Firm is better off by "inefficiently pledging the third asset."[98] Recall that granting Bank a lien on the third asset will not increase the asset's value, although Firm obtains a benefit in the form of a reduction in the Bank's interest rate (offset only in part by an increase in the interest rate of the adjusting creditor). Of course, granting the lien renders the third asset unavailable to satisfy the claims of the nonadjusting creditors without any corresponding benefit to them. Bebchuk and Fried postulate that Firm will do this because "nonadjusting creditors will not raise their interest rates to take into account the effect of encumbering that asset on them."[99] This is inefficient, they claim, because Firm and Bank "adopt a security interest that gives the two parties a larger slice of the pie [namely, Firm gets a lower interest rate and Bank gets collateral] even though the security interest at the same time reduces the

---

[97] *Id.* at 876. Bebchuk and Fried contend further that these benefits may be offset by various burdens, including the relevant transactions costs associated with taking security, monitoring costs, and by preventing the debtor in some cases from engaging in more worthwhile projects. *Id.* at 877–78. They maintain that many efficiency benefits and costs that come about as a result of security interests have nothing to do with the bankruptcy priority accorded secured claims over unsecured claims; they are "priority independent." One possible priority-independent efficiency benefit arising from the use of a security interests is a reduction in borrower misbehavior. A firm's misbehavior may include overinvestment (choosing a risky project that makes creditors worse off by more than it makes shareholders better off) or asset dilution (shareholders taking assets out of a firm so that they are beyond the creditors' reach if the firm fails), both of which are inefficient and can be curbed by the use of security interests. The ability to curb such behavior arises in connection with the secured party's "repossessory right" (allowing the secured creditor to seize the collateral more quickly than an unsecured creditor can) and the state-law "priority right" (granting priority in the collateral that usually stays attached even if the collateral is sold or encumbered by third parties). *Id.* at 872–76.

[98] *Id.* at 893.

[99] *Id.*

size of the total pie [because of the transaction costs involved in taking the security]."[100] In other words, they claim that Firm and Bank are happy to lien up the third asset in Bank's favor even though doing so costs money and does not enhance Firm's value because the nonadjusting creditors bear the downside.

Notice perhaps the most interesting feature of Bebchuk and Fried's ingenious hypothetical: it is set up as a zero sum game that makes Bank's lien look more like an asset grab (its loan provides no benefit to anyone and its lien helps only itself). Even though under the hypothetical's terms the granting of security may enhance the value of Firm's assets, Firm's value is never enough at any point to satisfy all claims—Firm is always insolvent. As a result, Bebchuk and Fried can focus on dividing the value of Bank's security interest and how Bank captures more and more of that value with each successive lien and with presumably overall diminishing returns. But recall Kripke's claim that, in the real world, the granting of security is not a zero sum game. For example, Kripke argued that preexisting unsecured creditors are typically better off when a secured creditor appears on the scene, not only because of the secured creditor's enhanced ability to monitor and prevent debtor misbehavior (which presumably enhances the debtor's value overall), but also because the secured creditor's loan increases the debtor's liquidity by infusing capital into the debtor's balance sheet (which presumably lowers the debtor's risk of failure) and provides a source of payment for other claims. By assuming (implausibly) that this is not the case in their hypothetical, Bebchuk and Fried control away the effects of these additional enhancements (for example, Firm's chances of failing are held constant at a rate of 5% regardless of whether Bank is secured or unsecured, and Firm is presumed to have squandered Bank's loan without reducing the amount of any other claims, including those of the nonadjusting creditors).

Bebchuck and Fried's scenario raises some questions. In looking at the impact of security devices on nonadjusting creditors, shouldn't we take into account both the nonadjusting creditors' risk of nonpayment in the event of Firm's failure and the likelihood they will be paid as a result of Bank's loan prior to Firm's failure? Surely many are the nonadjusting tort creditors who have breathed a collective sigh of relief when the debtor borrowed money on a secured basis to pay their claims. Also, what about all the debtors who do not become insolvent? Shouldn't the analysis take into account the positive effects (if any) of security interests in cases in which everyone is paid in full? On the one hand, if security devices generate

---

[100] *Id.* at 896. Interestingly, Bebchuk and Fried postulate that the transaction costs involved in taking the security interest in the third asset ($1,000) are less than benefit of Bank's interest rate reduction as a result of having a lien on the third asset ($4,000) even taking into account the adjusting creditor's corresponding increase in its rate of interest ($2,500). Apparently the net $500 in savings is not thought to increase the total size of the pie, perhaps because it is consumed by Firm's shareholders. *Id.* at 893.

positive effects for solvent debtors (for example, more capital is available to them than otherwise would be the case), and these positive effects outweigh the pain suffered by some of the unsecured creditors of the relatively few debtors who become insolvent, on the whole aren't we still better off? On the other hand, perhaps that is simply all the more reason to seek ways to channel the benefits of some of the positive effects of security interests to unsecured creditors who are in fact harmed in the insolvency context. But why do that at the expense of the secured creditor's full priority, a reduction of which would presumably make security interests less attractive and perhaps diminish their positive effects in all the cases where default and nonpayment do not occur?

To help illustrate these points, we might modify Bebchuk and Fried's hypothetical to make it more realistic and see where that takes us. Like Bebchuk and Fried, suppose Firm has two nonadjusting tort creditors, each with claims of $500,000 against Firm, for a total of $1 million. Suppose further that these claims are covered 80% by Firm's insurance, so Firm's liability is only $200,000 (the insurer is responsible for $800,000). Next, suppose Firm is in the business of selling mattresses and has assets worth $1 million (say, $1 million in inventory and accounts), so Firm is clearly solvent (its assets exceed its liabilities). Firm wants to expand its business and approaches Bank for a $1 million line of credit to lease and build out some new locations and buy some additional inventory for its new stores. Bank is willing to make the loan, but wants a security interest in all of Firm's inventory and accounts. In addition, if Bank is willing to make the loan, a manufacturer of mattresses ("Manufacturer") is willing to extend $1 million in short-term credit to Firm so Firm can acquire new mattresses (for example, Firm receives shipments and has 90 days in which to pay for them). Manufacturer is particularly happy to do this because in the ordinary course Firm will use advances from Bank's line of credit to pay Manufacturer's invoices. There is a small risk that Firm's shareholders will abscond with some or all of Firm's capital, but this risk is lessened by Bank's monitoring and the presence of its security interest (and perhaps a guaranty by the equity holders). Suppose that *before* the financing with Bank and Manufacturer is put in place, there was a 10% chance that Firm would be unsuccessful and go bankrupt within a year, in which case its remaining assets (say, $10,000) would be less than its liabilities (say, $500,000 because, just prior to bankruptcy, Firm will accumulate $300,000 in unsecured debt in the form of unpaid invoices from trade creditors that Firm historically had paid on a current basis). Suppose further that *after* the financing with Bank and Manufacturer is put in place, there is a 5% chance that Firm will be unsuccessful and go bankrupt within a year, in which case its assets (say, $500,000 at the time of insolvency) will be less than its liabilities ($2.5 million).

Under these facts, the nonadjusting tort creditors are not likely to be harmed by Bank's security interest. In fact, they are probably benefited by it—Firm's shareholders are less likely to abscond with Firm's capital, and Firm is more likely to continue in business and pay the portion of their claims not covered by insurance. Manufacturer is likewise not harmed. It now has a new customer with the wherewithal to buy lots of mattresses. Bank is not harmed. Under these facts, "harm" may materialize *only* if Firm becomes insolvent at some point, leaving creditors unpaid (a 5% risk). According to Gilmore, however, if Bank is a virtuous monitor, Bank's diligence will prevent even greater harm in the event of insolvency by keeping Firm from ballooning its unsecured debt on the eve of its bankruptcy filing (here by $300,000). Bank may also step in and help direct a reorganization if Firm is salvageable.

It is certainly true that, in the event of a debtor's insolvency, secured creditors may fare better than unpaid tort creditors. This is not so, however, in our modified hypothetical because Firm's position at the point of insolvency is assumed to have deteriorated to such a degree that the tort creditors actually come out better than other creditors on a percentage basis: the 80% of their claims covered by insurance will yield a greater percentage recovery to them than Bank will obtain after liquidating Firm's inventory and accounts. That is because the stipulated value of Bank's collateral is $500,000, only half of Bank's $1 million claim. Manufacturer might end up with some unpaid invoices, but presumably builds this contingency into its pricing structure. Because the chances of Firm's insolvency within a year are assumed to be 5%, Bank's secured lending has the effect of facilitating Firm's 95% chance of prospering. Why is this inefficient? Alternatively, why is it unfair?

On the one hand, if Firm does not borrow from Bank on a secured basis, the nonadjusting tort creditors holding $200,000 in claims not covered by insurance face a 90% chance of being paid in full, and a 10% chance of recovering only a pro rata share of their claims from whatever assets are available to pay creditors in the event of Firm's insolvency and failure (here $10,000 to be split among $500,000 in aggregate unsecured claims). On the other hand, if Firm borrows from Bank on a secured basis, the nonadjusting tort creditors face a 95% chance of being paid in full and a 5% chance of recovering nothing (because Bank's lien has priority on all the remaining assets worth $500,000). Because of the difference between the probability of Firm's failure based on whether Firm obtains financing from Bank (10% versus 5%), the tort creditors are better off with Bank's financing under this set of circumstances. Following Gilmore and Kripke, granting the lien to Bank is efficient because it (1) supported an extension of credit that otherwise would not have occurred, thereby enhancing Firm's prospects for success, and (2) supplied a number of benefits to unsecured creditors generally, including the tort creditors. Following White, granting the lien is further efficient because (1) security interests are cheap to take, and (2) even if Firm had not granted a lien on its assets to Bank to secure its line of credit, the tort claimants never would have seen much recovery anyway because it is likely that Firm would have frittered away the value of its assets in a fruitless attempt to survive. Do Bebchuk and Fried convincingly dispel these arguments?

In addition to claiming that the secured creditor's entitlement to full priority encourages inefficient security interests at the expense of nonadjusting creditors, Bebchuk and Fried also identify other efficiency concerns associated with granting a security interest full priority in bankruptcy: (1) increased use of security interests that are efficient, but less efficient than contractual covenants; (2) distorted investment and precautionary decisions; and (3) suboptimal enforcement efforts. In essence, they claim that, to the extent a security interest giving a secured creditor full priority reduces its risk of loss, a secured creditor actually has less incentive to control the borrower's behavior, to engage in enforcement activities, or to adopt even highly efficient covenants—a story contrary to Gilmore's account.[101]

Bebchuk and Fried observe that, through the use of contractual covenants in its lending agreement, a creditor can insist that the debtor refrain from a variety of misbehaviors, including transferring assets to shareholders (so-called "asset dilution"). They contend that covenants may provide some of the same benefits as security devices, which also deter asset dilution. All else being equal, one would expect the parties to use covenants or security devices (or some combination of the two) to the extent doing so would be more beneficial under the circumstances. Bebchuk and Fried argue, however, that under certain conditions debtors have an incentive to grant security interests even though covenants would be more efficient.

To illustrate, they posit that "Bank and Firm will choose either a set of covenants or a security interest (but not both) to reduce Firm's ability to engage in inefficient asset dilution after the transaction."[102] They then assume that, in their hypothetical, covenants would be more effective than a security interest in preventing Firm's misbehavior (for example, transferring assets to shareholders), and thus more effective in preserving Firm's value. In spite of this value enhancing effect, however, they argue that Firm and Bank would elect the security interest over the covenants because, although the covenants make everyone better off by increasing Firm's value more, the security interest makes Bank individually better off. This is so because Bank captures the full benefit of its security interest, but must share the benefits of the covenants if no security interest is taken.

---

[101] *Id.* at 895–903.

[102] *Id.* at 897.

Recall Kripke's argument, however, that it is the security interest and the special rights that go along with it that give the secured creditor a particularly strong set of teeth, and correspondingly that it is the secured party's bite that really keeps the debtor in line for everyone's benefit. Are covenants likely to be more effective than security interests in deterring debtor misbehavior? Even assuming they may be in some instances, why is the decision whether to use covenants or a security interest necessarily an either/or proposition? Lenders who take security interests in any sizeable transaction almost always use covenants in their security agreements, including prominently covenants that define the circumstances of the debtor's default because, under Article 9, a default of some kind is what triggers the secured party's right to enforce its security interest. Article 9 does not define the circumstances of default, instead leaving this up to the parties to negotiate. Presumably, if the effect of a set of covenants would enhance Firm's value more than would a security interest, Bank would insist on both covenants *and* a security interest so that (1) Firm would be worth more, and (2) Bank would capture the benefit of this increased value with its lien.

In response, Bebchuk and Fried pose another hypothetical: what if the use of covenants preventing Firm's misbehavior would not add any value to Bank in addition to its security interest, but would be of value to other creditors? For example, suppose Bank is owed $1 million and the value of its collateral in bankruptcy is expected to be $1.2 million (in other words, Bank is "oversecured" because the value of its collateral exceeds the amount of its claim). In addition, Firm has a nonadjusting creditor owed $1 million and an adjusting creditor owed $1 million. The use of covenants in addition to the security interest would not add any value to Bank (its claim is already oversecured), but would be of benefit to the other creditors because it would reduce Firm's chances of failing. Bebchuk and Fried argue that, because the use of covenants is costly to Firm, Bank and Firm have an incentive not to use them even though doing so would be efficient.

Perhaps. But is this plausible? If covenants would enhance Firm's value in addition to Bank's security interest, wouldn't Bank want them even though Bank expected to be oversecured? After all, at the time it lends, how sure can Bank be that it will end up oversecured a year later if Firm defaults? If Bank is unsure, it will want as many value enhancing covenants as it can get. This also raises a larger point: Bebchuk and Fried's analysis assumes a certain precision of predictive ability on the part of Firm and its creditors. Is this realistic?

In any event, if covenants really would enhance Firm's value, wouldn't the adjusting creditor insist on them if Bank declined to do so? Perhaps it would. But perhaps it wouldn't if, for example, the adjusting creditor did not care enough or had an alternative way to protect itself (it preferred to charge a higher rate), leaving the nonadjusting creditor to bear the loss.

But then we have to take into account various legal remedies that may be available to the nonadjusting creditor, including fraudulent transfer laws that force misbehaving shareholders to return assets they misappropriate from insolvent firms. After all, isn't that one of the purposes of such laws, to protect the innocent who cannot protect themselves contractually?

In addition to their effects on the use of covenants, Bebchuk and Fried argue that affording security interests full priority in bankruptcy has the effect of distorting the debtor's investment decisions. To illustrate, "[c]onsider the case in which Firm must decide, prior to contracting with Bank, whether to take certain precautions that will make its products safer and thereby reduce the number of future tort claims against Firm."[103] If Bank does not take a security interest, Bank is presumed to charge a rate of interest that will reflect whether Firm's behavior is likely to generate more or less tort claims. In this way, Bank's interest charge creates an incentive for Firm to take precautions and avoid the tort claims (in order to reduce its borrowing costs). If Bank takes a security interest, however, "[u]nder the rule of full priority . . . [Bank's security interest] more or less protects the value of Bank's loan from being diluted by tort claims."[104] As a result, "Firm will have less incentive to invest in these precautions."[105]

But even assuming this to be true, is this really a security interest question or a question of insurance? It seems unlikely that Firm will forego obtaining insurance simply because it has granted Bank a security interest—Bank's loan and lien will not protect Firm from the potentially devastating impact of tort liabilities. Insurers, however, are adjusting creditors. They adjust their premiums to account for Firm's incentives to engage in risky behavior. And although Firm may tend to underinsure (namely, carry less insurance than it may need), this has the advantage of keeping some of Firm's skin in the game: it cannot put off all the risk of its activities and corresponding tort liability onto its insurer.

Finally, Bebchuk and Fried contend that affording security interests full priority in bankruptcy has the effect of creating an incentive for suboptimal enforcement by the secured party. They argue that the secured creditor's diminished incentive arises "to the extent that it is protected from risk of loss by a security interest giving the creditor's claim full priority in bankruptcy—just as it will have less of an incentive to adopt even highly efficient covenants."[106] They acknowledge that, "by virtue of its sophistication, resources, and leverage, the bank will be able to exert a significant amount of influence over the borrower" and occupies "a unique

---

103 *Id.* at 898.

104 *Id.* at 899.

105 *Id.*

106 *Id.* at 902.

position to control a borrower's behavior."[107] Nonetheless, "to the extent that the bank is insulated by a security interest from the effects of the borrower's misbehavior, the bank will have less incentive to control the borrower's behavior."[108] But is this realistic?

Assume, for example, that Bank has a security interest in Firm's inventory and accounts worth $1 million. Suppose Firm is in a declining state. What would happen to Bank's security interest if Bank simply sat back and allowed things to deteriorate for a year? As Firm sold its inventory and collected its accounts, Firm would use the proceeds to pay its expenses, including most likely the claims of other creditors. Eventually, when Firm failed, there would be essentially no inventory or accounts left to satisfy Bank's claim. Could Bank recover the spent funds from the other creditors Firm paid with the cash proceeds from Bank's collateral? Almost certainly not. In this respect, Article 9 does not take kindly to secured creditors who sleep on their rights while the debtor fritters away their collateral consisting of inventory, accounts, and their proceeds. *See* 9–332.

So how do secured creditors prevent this? By monitoring their debtors and taking action when things begin to go awry. In this regard they are assisted not only by the security interests they take, but also by their covenants. These covenants typically include such things as cross-default provisions and negative pledge agreements, the first making it a default if the debtor breaches an obligation to another creditor, and the second prohibiting the debtor from encumbering its assets for the benefit of others.

For the secured creditor, the chief benefit of the cross-default is that it enables the secured creditor to stay at least even with the debtor's other creditors in terms of being able to exercise its rights. The secured creditor never wants to be in a position where it is stymied from exercising its rights because the debtor has not defaulted on its obligations to the secured creditor but has defaulted on its obligations to other creditors, who are busy exercising their rights against the debtor. A side benefit of the cross-default is that it creates an incentive for the debtor to keep its other obligations current.

The chief benefit of the negative pledge is that it compels the debtor to seek the secured creditor's approval before incurring secured debt with another creditor. The debtor's need to obtain additional secured financing is often an early warning sign that the debtor is in financial hot water. At the very least, by compelling the debtor to request approval before issuing additional secured debt, the existing secured lender has the opportunity to evaluate the debtor's circumstances and perhaps take action if the debtor appears to be headed toward bankruptcy.

---

[107] *Id.* at 903.

[108] *Id.*

Bebchuk and Fried have a different take on the negative pledge covenant. They contend that the widespread use of negative pledge clauses in *unsecured* loan documents indicates that "security interests are often inefficient," otherwise these clauses would not be used.[109] But might not unsecured creditors view negative pledge covenants also as a type of early warning device?

As a potential solution to the efficiency problems they articulate, Bebchuk and Fried offer two partial priority concepts to replace the current full priority principle: the "adjustable priority rule" and the "fixed-fraction priority rule."[110] The adjustable partial priority rule is like the full priority rule, except that each nonadjusting creditor's bankruptcy share would be calculated by treating the secured claims to which it could not adjust as unsecured claims. A secured claim thus could not subordinate the claims of any creditors that could not adjust to it, which would transfer some bankruptcy value from secured creditors to nonadjusting unsecured creditors. The fixed-fraction priority rule, presented as an alternative, would treat a fixed fraction of every secured claim as an unsecured claim, such that all secured creditors would be at least partially unsecured.[111] Bebchuk and Fried argue that the adoption of a partial priority rule should not be left to private ordering—borrowers should not be able to opt out of the rule. This is necessary, they argue, because it is unlikely a firm would choose the partial-priority rule over full priority even if it were efficient.[112] What do you think?

STEVEN SCHWARCZ: A RESPONSE TO BEBCHUK AND FRIED

Once again, should security interests be denied full priority in bankruptcy? In his article, *The Easy Case for the Priority of Secured Claims in Bankruptcy*,[113] Steven Schwarcz takes on Bebchuk and Fried's partial priority proposal.

Schwarcz's main point is that it is essential to place the use of security devices in proper context. The most important form of secured debt, he argues, is new money secured credit (namely, where a lender offers new money in exchange for collateral). He contends that debtors are, and ought to be, generally reluctant to borrow on a secured basis for three reasons. First, borrowing on a secured basis entails a loss of control over the encumbered property, and in this respect "secured credit is similar in certain economic consequences to the sale of an asset for a fair market price."[114] Of course, a debtor who grants a security interest in a particular

---

109 *Id.* at 923.

110 *Id.* at 866, 895–903 (efficiency costs of full priority), 905–11 (alternative rules).

111 *Id.* at 866.

112 *Id.* at 930.

113 Schwarcz, *supra* note 19.

114 *Id.* at 432.

item of collateral does not *actually* sell the asset to the secured party, but the point is that, after granting the lien, the debtor does not enjoy the same freedom he had previously with the asset because he has given up significant rights in it.

Second, like Gilmore and Kripke, Schwarcz points out that borrowing on a secured basis entails reputational costs—it signals that the debtor is not sufficiently credit worthy to borrow on an unsecured basis, or at least as cheaply as on a secured basis. Third, granting a security interest generates opportunity costs. Among other things, the debtor loses the ability to encumber the same collateral later if he needs additional credit and can only obtain it on a secured basis. Further, whereas most unsecured lenders will underwrite a loan by focusing on the debtor's cash flows, secured lenders are more apt to underwrite a loan by focusing on the liquidation value of the collateral, which is typically a less generous form of credit review for the debtor (at least for viable and growing businesses because cash flow analysis typically takes into account anticipated future income).[115] In other words, borrowing on a secured basis narrows the debtor's options.

A rational borrower, Schwarcz posits, would prefer to keep his financial powder dry. Accordingly, he will only borrow on a secured basis if he has to.[116] Schwarcz gives a name to the value of the debtor's ability to keep his options open: he calls this value THETA. Schwarcz defines THETA as "equal to the sum of the opportunity cost of having those assets available to pledge as collateral if the debtor faces a liquidity crisis, the reputational cost of encumbering the assets, and the opportunity cost of obtaining financing on a cash flow (as opposed to liquidation) basis."[117] The existence of THETA, he contends, explains why debtors most often finance on an unsecured basis, even when the interest rate for available secured credit is lower.[118] Schwarcz also asserts that the existence of THETA helps explain why Bebchuk and Fried are wrong: "debtors are unlikely to be economically motivated to use secured credit to take away value from unsecured creditors."[119]

According to Schwarcz, it follows from all of this that, when a debtor does borrow on a secured basis, the debtor most likely needs the credit for liquidity reasons (meaning that the debtor does not have enough cash to keep his operations going smoothly). And enhancing the debtor's liquidity is generally good for the debtor's other creditors because it tends to lessen the risk that the debtor will fail and file for bankruptcy.[120] In support of

---

115 *Id.* at 446–47.

116 *Id.* at 431, 446–47.

117 *Id.* at 431.

118 *Id.*

119 *Id.* at 446–48.

120 *Id.* at 430.

his argument, Schwarcz analyzes a number of troubled debtors who obtained secured financing that increased their liquidity. Among other things, Schwarcz observes that, in response to new financing, trade creditors tended to extend credit on terms more favorable to the debtor, suggesting at a minimum that these creditors "are willing to presume that liquidity provided by secured credit will enable companies to succeed, at least in the short run."[121]

Schwarcz concludes that rational unsecured creditors actually *want* their debtors to have access to secured credit if they need it because the enhanced liquidity that this financing provides means that the debtor is more likely to avoid bankruptcy and pay unsecured claims. Although some unsecured creditors may lose out if the debtor eventually fails, Schwarcz argues that security interests are nonetheless efficient because they tend to benefit unsecured creditors as a whole.

What of Bebchuk and Fried's point about negative pledges? Recall that Bebchuk and Fried argued that unsecured lenders typically include negative pledge clauses in their loan documents prohibiting their debtors from issuing secured debt, suggesting that unsecured creditors believe granting security is generally inefficient. Schwarcz responds in several ways. First, he asserts that "negative pledge covenants are found primarily in bank and insurance company loan agreements; they are almost never imposed by trade creditors."[122] As a result, "the very unsecured creditors that Bebchuk and Fried say are hurt by secured credit do not impose negative pledge covenants."[123]

Second, "negative pledge covenants are commonly directed at restricting the securing of antecedent debt, and much less frequently restrict new money liens."[124] In addition, "[e]ven negative pledge covenants that on their face restrict all secured credit typically have 'baskets' that permit up to a specified amount of new money liens."[125] Schwarcz argues that "[t]his practice suggests, under Bebchuk and Fried's logic, that new money liens indeed may be efficient."[126]

Third, he notes that creditors with negative pledge covenants frequently waive the restriction on security interests in exchange for an "equal and ratable" provision of security:

> [e]ven if negative pledge covenants flatly restricted all secured debt, that would not prove that unsecured creditors regard

---

121 *Id.* at 470. Schwarcz also supported his argument with analysis of stock values following extensions of secured financing and quantitative evaluation.

122 *Id.* at 450.

123 *Id.*

124 *Id.* at 450–51.

125 *Id.* at 451.

126 *Id.*

security interests as undesirable. Such restrictive covenants would give unsecured creditors the power to block future security interests, but those creditors later could choose to waive the covenants. Based on my experience, unsecured creditors frequently choose to waive negative pledge covenants in exchange for a quid pro quo, such as becoming equally and ratably secured. Negative pledge covenants thereby allow unsecured creditors to get their cake (by affording the debtor the liquidity arising from secured credit) and eat it too (by becoming equally and ratably secured).[127]

Fourth, Schwarcz bolsters this point with the observation that "debtors generally do *not* agree to negative pledge covenants when they issue debt to public investors (or in other circumstances where it may be difficult to obtain waivers)."[128] Instead, "these debtors typically agree to covenants that prohibit the debtor from securing debt without equally and ratably securing the beneficiaries of the covenants."[129]

Fifth, Schwarcz argues that the most common benefit of negative pledge clauses is that they serve as a kind of early warning device: "[m]ore sophisticated creditors view a debtor's grant of collateral as an early warning that the debtor is experiencing financial problems and is using collateral as a bargaining chip to restructure some of its loans with third parties."[130] Sophisticated creditors then "use negative pledge covenants to force the debtor to the negotiating table while the debtor is still viable."[131] Schwarcz concludes that this "explains why even fully secured lenders almost always impose negative pledge covenants on their debtors."[132]

What about monitoring? Recall that Gilmore and Kripke thought that security interests provide the secured creditor with an appropriate incentive to monitor the debtor's financial condition for the benefit of all concerned. Schwarcz, however, is not so sanguine. The problem, he contends, is that secured creditors have incentives to pull the trigger at the first sight of trouble, potentially leaving unsecured creditors high and dry:

> [g]eneral monitoring by a secured creditor does not necessarily protect unsecured creditors; indeed, it may prejudice them. Monitoring usually means that the secured creditor will impose covenants on the debtor. Breach of those covenants will trigger default under the loan agreement, permitting the secured creditor to accelerate the maturity of its debt. Acceleration of debt may in

---

127 *Id.*

128 *Id.* (emphasis in original).

129 *Id.* at 451–52

130 *Id.* at 452.

131 *Id.*

132 *Id.*

turn prejudice unsecured creditors, because it allows the secured creditor to be repaid as soon as the debtor becomes troubled, leaving unsecured creditors unpaid if the debtor becomes insolvent.[133]

Recall Schwarcz's hypothesis that debtors use secured borrowing only when they have to. If that is correct, secured creditors, as the lenders of last resort, can be expected to have a certain amount of leverage that, in the aggregate, they can use to negotiate a relatively tight set of loan covenants—covenants that may more readily trip up the debtor. What is the secured creditor's worse nightmare? It is not that the debtor becomes insolvent. After all, that is why the secured creditor has collateral. Rather, the secured creditor's worse nightmare is that, on the road to insolvency, the debtor will dissipate his assets, leaving the secured party essentially unsecured.

How do debtors dissipate a secured creditor's collateral? They do it typically by using the collateral to pay other creditors' claims. In the case of real estate, the debtor's ability to dissipate the secured party's collateral is relatively limited—real estate is not easy to cart away and generally cannot be sold free and clear of the secured party's lien without the secured party's consent (although certainly real property improvements can be allowed to deteriorate). In the case of inventory and accounts, however, dissipation is relatively simple: the debtor merely sells the inventory, collects the accounts, and uses the cash to meet payroll and other necessary expenses until there is no more inventory to sell or accounts to collect.

One way to avoid this nightmare is for the secured creditor to move quickly at the first sign of trouble, seize and liquidate its collateral, apply the proceeds to pay (or at least reduce) the amount of its claim, and move on. At the time of the debtor's default, if the secured creditor's collateral is sufficient to cover its claim, the secured creditor may have little to gain, and perhaps everything to lose, by delay. The problem, however, is that this may give rise to improvident liquidations that occasion an avoidable loss of value. For example, perhaps the debtor's trouble is simply a short-term storm that it might weather with a bit of patient forbearance. In addition, the secured creditor's liquidation of its collateral may well bring the debtor's business to a grinding halt, destroying any "going concern" value. In general, businesses are more valuable as operating entities than as dead hulks sold for scrap. So what keeps the secured creditor from jumping to liquidation at the first drop of the debtor's financial hat?

Schwarcz points to an answer—bankruptcy law, particularly three of its key features that affect secured claims: "(i) the automatic stay against enforcement of collateral remedies; (ii) the risk that a secured creditor's collateral will be replaced [in bankruptcy] by substitute collateral that the

---

133 *Id.* at 438–39.

secured lender may value less; and (iii) a secured lender's inability under fraudulent conveyance law to secure its debt by collateral of excessive value coupled with the fact that an oversecured lender is not always legally entitled to its full collateral cushion."[134] Schwarcz contends that the existence of the automatic stay, and the debtor's ability to invoke it unilaterally, provides the secured creditor with "a significant interest in . . . the continued viability of the borrower."[135]

The other features of bankruptcy law that Schwarcz identifies (risk of collateral replacement and fraudulent conveyance law) have a similar effect. Collectively, they provide the secured creditor with an incentive to forego improvident liquidations because bankruptcy law affords the debtor a way to fight back if the secured lender is too aggressive, or so the theory goes. The point is that bankruptcy law arguably helps the secured creditor remain "virtuous" in the sense Gilmore envisioned by giving the secured party an incentive to act more like a senior partner in the debtor's business, rather than as a completely independent actor out for its own gain. Once again, the idea is that a security interest vests a form of ownership interest in the secured creditor, granting the secured creditor both a unique power over its collateral and a unique responsibility to use it wisely.

Schwarcz, however, labels the features of bankruptcy law outlined above "imperfections."[136] Why? The answer lies in his account of "non-recourse debt" financing and, in his view, its superior utility.

Non-recourse debt financing includes a family of transactions that fall loosely into two categories. The first closely resembles the kinds of secured loans we have seen so far: the debtor borrows from a creditor and in exchange grants the creditor a lien on one or more of the debtor's assets (typically real estate) to secure repayment of the loan. The unique feature of the transaction that makes it "non-recourse" is that the creditor agrees to look only to its collateral for repayment of the debt and not to the debtor personally. For example, suppose the debtor owes the creditor $1 million secured by a lien on the debtor's building. After the debtor defaults, suppose the creditor forecloses, but the building realizes only $750,000 at a foreclosure sale, leaving a deficiency of $250,000. In a typical recourse transaction, the secured creditor could assert a claim for the deficiency as an unsecured obligation. In a non-recourse transaction, however, the secured creditor cannot do this—it agreed to look only to the value of its collateral for payment.

The second kind of non-recourse transaction is a securitization arrangement. In the typical securitization, the purchaser buys the assets in question (say, the debtor's accounts) on a non-recourse basis, meaning

134 *Id.* at 456.

135 *Id.* (quotation marks and citations omitted).

136 *Id.*

that the purchaser agrees to look only to the accounts to realize the value it paid. If the accounts perform poorly and the purchaser suffers a loss, too bad. (Securitizations are addressed in Section 3 of Chapter 5.)

Why securitize? Recall Schwarcz's theory that debtors avoid borrowing on a secured basis because they do not like to give up the kind of control over their assets that secured borrowing entails—they do not like to forego THETA. Securitizations would seem to entail even more of a loss of THETA, yet securitizations are common. Why? And doesn't the existence of securitizations undermine Schwarcz's theory of the utility of security interests if securitizations, though common, are yet even more costly in terms of THETA than secured borrowing?

Schwarcz argues that the existence of securitizations are not inconsistent with his theory for three reasons. First, he argues that they typically involve only "a specific portion of the debtor's assets, such as a pool of financial assets."[137] Thus, "[t]he debtor therefore has all of its remaining assets to pledge as collateral if it later needs liquidity."[138] The same thing, however, could be said about a security interest limited to a portion of the debtor's assets.

Second, Schwarcz contends that, in contrast to the "reputational cost of encumbering the debtor's assets," the hit to the debtor's reputation "is low, perhaps non-existent, for non-recourse financing, which is widely recognized by the financial community as an attractive way for healthy companies to raise funds" and has the added feature of denying the purchaser "access to any of the debtor's other assets."[139] But that is true only because the purchaser acquires complete title to the assets it wants and isn't interested in the debtor's other property. More important, from a reputational perspective why is selling off an asset rationally less damaging than borrowing against it?

Third, recall Schwarcz's theory that secured borrowing is usually less desirable to the debtor than unsecured financing because unsecured financing is typically underwritten on the basis of the debtor's cash flow (including anticipated cash flow), which often yields a more generous valuation for the debtor, as opposed to underwriting on the basis of the liquidation value of the particular collateral in question. Of course, those who purchase assets in a securitization transaction are essentially looking to the "liquidation value" of the assets in making their purchase. The debtor's ability to generate a profit from its overall operations is not taken into account. Therefore, in a securitization transaction, the debtor loses the opportunity to have his overall performance considered as a featured part of the underwriting process—just as he would in obtaining a secured loan.

---

137 *Id.* at 463.

138 *Id.*

139 *Id.*

Schwarcz argues, however, that the opportunity cost to the debtor of financing in this way (as compared to unsecured borrowing) "is low because of the nature of the assets that qualify for non-recourse financing in the first place: A creditor financing non-recourse debt cannot look to the debtor for cash flow; it therefore only finances assets that generate cash flow."[140] But isn't it true that all "assets" generate cash flow, the only question being how the flow is extracted from them? If the debtor is essentially selling his cash flow, won't this impair his ability to borrow in the future if he needs to, either on a secured or unsecured basis?

In reality, although secured creditors may focus on the liquidation value of their collateral in underwriting their loans, they are hardly indifferent to cash flow—they prefer to be paid without having to foreclose, and only the most intrepid lend to debtors whose cash flow prospects are more than temporarily negative. If this is so, under Schwarcz's theory, isn't a debtor actually better off from a loan underwriting perspective by granting a security interest in his property rather than selling it off? When a secured creditor lends against collateral on a recourse basis taking into account the debtor's overall performance, isn't that likely to make the debtor better off as compared to a securitization transaction in which the debtor's overall performance is irrelevant?

The key lies in Schwarcz's observation that "[a] properly structured non-recourse financing may enable the debtor to access low cost capital market funds."[141] In other words, it is often cheaper for the debtor to securitize than borrow on a secured basis. Why? Because securitizations avoid the costs of bankruptcy, particularly its "imperfections." The theory is that, once the debtor sells its accounts or other assets in a securitization transaction, they are no longer the debtor's property. If the debtor later files for bankruptcy, these assets do not become part of the debtor's bankruptcy estate, and the automatic stay and other features of bankruptcy law do not affect them. In the vernacular, the securitized assets have been rendered "bankruptcy remote," and the owner may do whatever it wants with them, the debtor be damned.

But what about Gilmore's concept of the virtuous monitor? The purchaser of the debtor's assets is not a "partner" with the debtor in the sense of having any shared ownership interest. Likewise, the purchaser has little or no incentive to monitor the debtor's financial affairs—it is largely indifferent to the debtor's subsequent success or failure. In essence, the purchaser of the debtor's property has already foreclosed. Because securitizations cash out the lender from the beginning, don't they deprive the drama of a key actor?

---

[140] *Id.* at 463–64.

[141] *Id.* at 464.

And is securitization actually cheaper than secured lending? Consider the following. A secured lender will typically lend against a fraction of the value of its collateral. For example, a secured lender may be willing to lend no more than 75% of the value of the debtor's eligible pool of accounts (*e.g.*, current accounts as to which the account debtors are good credit risks). Suppose a debtor has $1 million in eligible accounts. Under this formula, the secured lender would be willing to lend no more than $750,000. Suppose further that the secured lender agreed to lend at an annual rate of 5%. At this rate, the debtor's interest cost for one year would be $37,500. In contrast, in a securitization transaction the debtor could sell the entire $1 million in accounts (recall that, according to Schwarcz, this is one of the key virtues of such transactions—the debtor's ability to raise more funds immediately by selling the collateral as opposed to borrowing against it). Suppose the buyer agreed to a 4.5% discount, meaning that the buyer would purchase the $1 million in accounts for $995,500. The debtor's "interest" cost for this transaction would be $45,000. True enough, in a securitization transaction the debtor would have $245,500 more in immediate cash to run its business. But in the case of the secured loan, the debtor would collect the full $1 million, albeit over time (assuming the accounts were all good). If the debtor does not have an urgent need for more funds than the bank is willing to lend, why is the $45,000 cost of the securitization transaction better than the $37,500 cost of the secured loan?

Relatedly, isn't a securitization a form of overleverage? There is a reason why banks do not typically lend against 100% of collateral value for things like accounts. In a securitization transaction, however, that is exactly what is happening. Collectively, doesn't this tend to increase overall systemic risk? What do you think?

These and other puzzling questions aside, Schwarcz maintains nonetheless that security interests are generally efficient. At the outset, he takes a helpful look at what the concept of "efficiency" means in the context of evaluating the utility of security devices. As Schwarcz describes it, when scholars use the term "efficiency" they typically mean one of two things: Pareto efficiency or Kaldor-Hicks efficiency. He explains that "Pareto efficiency" would exist if "the secured credit would make the secured creditor and, possibly, the debtor better off but no unsecured creditors worse off."[142] According to Schwarcz, when Bebchuk and Fried use the term "efficiency" they mean Pareto efficiency.

In contrast, "Kaldor-Hicks" efficiency would exist if "the harm to unsecured creditors (minus any benefit to them) does not exceed the benefit to the debtor and the secured creditor."[143] Because the conditions for Pareto efficiency rarely exist in the real world, most scholars conducting efficiency

---

[142] *Id.* at 480.

[143] *Id.* at 480–81.

analysis use the Kaldor-Hicks definition. Schwarcz, however, rejects this approach because "one remains uneasy . . . by the apparent unfairness of justifying secured credit by comparing whether the gain to the secured creditor and debtor exceeds the detriment to unsecured creditors."[144] Instead, he proposes a different concept: "class Pareto efficiency," explaining that "[a] transaction is class Pareto efficient if it is Pareto efficient when each class of persons affected by the class of transactions is viewed as a single collective person."[145] Under this formulation, "class Pareto efficiency exists whenever the overall gains to each affected class exceed the losses to such class even if some members of the class lose value."[146]

Applying his concept, Schwarcz contends that "[n]ew money secured credit appears to be class Pareto efficient because such credit would make the classes of secured creditors and debtors better off, without making unsecured creditors, as a class, worse off."[147] This is so because of the enhancing effects of liquidity that secured financing provides: "[u]nsecured creditors as a class are better off under a rule of full priority because the availability of secured credit increases debtor liquidity and therefore increases the expected value of unsecured claims."[148]

Schwarcz also addresses Bebchuk and Fried's concern that affording secured debt full priority in bankruptcy increases shareholders' incentives to take insufficient precautions and participate in risky activities by noting that fraudulent conveyance law already prevents debtors from engaging in the worst abuses. Moreover, a debtor may have contractual obligations (and directors may have fiduciary duties) that protect creditors quite apart from the existence of secured claims. In addition, although Bebchuck and Fried argue in favor of a partial priority rule on the theory that it may encourage more desirable general monitoring, Schwarcz argues that general monitoring of the debtor's financial condition is not particularly useful. Instead, Schwarcz prefers a more surgical approach: limited monitoring, which entails only supervision of the debtor's use of the proceeds of the secured party's loan to make sure they are used to enhance liquidity, and not diverted to some improper purpose.[149] What do you think?

§ 4. A "BOTTOM-UP" VIEW OF SECURED CREDIT

Culling selectively from the discussion so far, here is one story we might tell about the utility of security interests. To begin with, they clearly

---

144 *Id.* at 481.

145 *Id.*

146 *Id.* at 481–82.

147 *Id.* at 482.

148 *Id.* at 482–83.

149 *Id.* at 439.

reduce the secured creditor's risk. Accordingly, secured credit is often cheaper than unsecured debt. Nonetheless, debtors prefer to borrow on an unsecured basis if they can because unsecured borrowing gives them greater control over their assets and preserves their future borrowing options. Although debtors prefer unsecured borrowing for these reasons, they might be enticed into a securitization transaction because securitizations may be even cheaper than secured financing and/or provide greater liquidity.

In general, secured financing is desirable because it facilitates the distribution of goods and works to the advantage of the debtor's creditors as a group. In particular, it works to the advantage of unsecured creditors because it provides essentially a safety net of liquidity that the debtor may tap in times of need, which tends to increase the likelihood that the debtor will be able to pay unsecured claims. Secured financing also provides the secured lender with an incentive to monitor the use and condition of its collateral, and perhaps the debtor's overall financial performance. Sophisticated monitors may help prevent troubled debtors from getting into even more trouble, and may compel a restructuring of the debtor's business or financial affairs before there is nothing left to restructure. In contrast, securitizations tend to erode the benefits of monitoring to the extent they eliminate the monitor.

Security devices provide secured creditors with an incentive to be relatively aggressive in taking action against their debtors at the first signs of financial difficulty. This may lead to improvident liquidations. Bankruptcy law counteracts this incentive by offering a means to stay the secured creditor's hand, at least temporarily. Secured creditors understand this, and thus have an incentive to participate in working out the debtor's financial troubles rather than jumping to liquidate. Securitizations tend to erode this benefit because purchasers of the debtor's financial assets likely have little or no incentive to participate in any restructuring effort because they have no skin in the game.

The creditors most likely to suffer from the full priority treatment of secured claims in bankruptcy are the debtor's so-called nonadjusting creditors, such as tort claimants. Tort claimants, however, often have the protection of insurance, even though in at least some instances this may not be enough to cover their claims in full. Securitizations may make nonadjusting creditors worse off in bankruptcy because securitizations may increase the likelihood that, if the debtor becomes insolvent, the debtor will have fewer assets available to attempt a successful reorganization.

Certainly this is a lovely story. But does it reflect reality? Among other things, how do debtors and creditors actually evaluate whether to engage in secured debt financing?

RONALD MANN: A VIEW FROM THE MARKETPLACE

Ronald Mann addresses this last question in his article *Explaining the Pattern of Secured Credit*.[150] Eschewing the kinds of "top down" academic evaluations reviewed earlier in this chapter, he interviewed borrowers and lenders and, based on what he learned and other empirical studies, developed a "bottom up" theory to help explain prevailing patterns of secured financing. Mann asserts that previous academic efforts to explain why secured lending is or is not efficient have been unsuccessful, primarily because of the methodology scholars have been using. In his words, most scholars begin their analyses

> with reductionist factual assumptions and then appl[y] abstract economic tools to build a theoretical superstructure upon those assumptions. Only at the end of the process, if at all, have these scholars made any serious effort to compare their theories about the efficiency justifications for secured credit with the actual pattern of secured credit. At that point, when the theory already has been developed, the consideration of empirical evidence almost inevitably becomes a cursory afterthought instead of an integral part of the analysis.[151]

In contrast, Mann begins with investigation of what motivates borrowers to choose to issue secured versus unsecured debt. Further, he observes that the evidence suggests that "one-factor" perspectives are likely to be misguided. In reality, multiple, interrelated considerations motivate borrowers and lenders as they decide how to fashion their transactions.[152] The framework that Mann develops from all of this assumes that a borrower will grant collateral to secure a loan only if he believes "the net benefits of the most favorable secured transaction will be greater than or equal to the net benefits of the most favorable unsecured transaction."[153] In addition, the picture he paints of prevailing practices is a fairly complex one (with many features that by now will seem familiar to the reader).

Mann observes that there are indeed advantages to secured lending that can lower the lender's anticipated costs, which will indirectly lower the borrower's costs because the borrower won't need to pay the lender as much to induce the lender to make the loan. In particular, Mann argues that secured credit is particularly valuable to the secured creditor, and impacts the cost of the loan, because it (1) "focus[es] the lender's oversight on a particular asset," (2) "increase[es] the net value of covenants that

---

150 Mann, *supra* note 18.

151 *Id.* at 628–29 (footnote omitted).

152 *Id.* at 632–33.

153 *Id.* at 635.

constrain the borrower's behavior," and (3) "increase[es] the practical leverage that the lender can use to constrain the borrower's behavior."[154] On the first point, when the lender's attention is focused on a particular asset, this may result in less expensive monitoring because, for example, monitoring activities may become routinized.

On the second point, secured lenders often include clauses in their loan documents designed to assist them with monitoring by requiring the debtor to supply various reports, including those that account for the collateral and its condition, and by allowing the lender to conduct inspections. Other covenants include those prohibiting the sale of the debtor's business or certain of his assets without the lender's consent, and imposing an obligation to keep the collateral in good condition, to maintain insurance, and to pay taxes. Of course, these covenants often entail significant administrative costs because debtors have to spend time and money complying with them, and lenders likewise have to spend time and money superintending them.

On the third point, a secured loan typically increases the lender's ability to coerce payment by encumbering collateral, granting priority, and enhancing the lender's remedial rights. If the debtor defaults, the lender may exercise various self-help remedies rather than rely exclusively on commencing a lawsuit to collect the debt. This generally enables the lender to charge less for its loan, decreasing the aggregate costs involved. In addition, secured credit may "enhance the lender's ability to limit subsequent borrowings, increase the borrower's incentive to attempt to repay the loan voluntarily, and facilitate restraints on the borrower's incentive to engage in risky conduct."[155]

In addition to the matters described above, secured credit transactions also typically entail a variety of routine transactional closing costs. These include information gathering costs (for the borrower: identifying and analyzing competing financing products; for the lender: investigating the merits of the transaction, such as the value of the collateral); documentation costs (formalizing the terms of the transaction and reducing it to written loan documents); and filing fees (including the costs of researching what to file and where to file it). Information costs are significant, but documentation and filing costs are minimal and do not play a significant role in decision making.[156]

Mann observes that the lender's goal of maximizing the probability of repayment is at odds with the debtor's goal of maximizing the value of his equity or the total value of the enterprise, which can hinder value-

---

154 *Id.* at 650.

155 *Id.* at 640–41.

156 *Id.* at 659–63.

increasing business decisions. These costs reduce the net benefit of the secured party's restrictive covenants.[157] In some cases, the lender's leverage enables it to enjoy influence over the debtor's daily decision making, sometimes to the debtor's detriment.[158]

Mann observes that the fact that borrowers and lenders both spend significant amounts of time and money complying with covenants suggests that the general benefits of covenants outweigh their costs. The cost/benefit analysis, however, is not entirely rosy. Secured lenders tend to take a conservative approach when it comes to the debtor's use of their collateral because they bear at least some of the risk that the debtor's use of the assets in novel ways may decrease their value. As a result, secured lenders have an incentive to deter even value-increasing transactions that they view as risky or that they cannot evaluate effectively. Mann asserts that most commentators do not appreciate the negative side of the secured creditor's leverage: it creates the probability that the lender will block many profitable uses of the borrower's assets, which increases the aggregate costs of secured transactions. It is largely for this reason, he contends, that borrowers view secured transactions as more costly and less desirable than unsecured forms of financing.[159] Unsurprisingly, Mann reports that his research is consistent with Kripke's observation that "firms that can avoid giving secured debt do so,"[160] and that in order to avoid the burdens of issuing secured debt, borrowers usually are willing to swallow a significant increase in the interest rates they must pay for their credit.

Long-term creditors often find security to be particularly attractive because it is often hard for them to foresee whether a company will maintain its financial health far into the future, particularly given such variables as changing competitive pressures, new technologies, and changing consumer demands. In general, as the term of a loan increases, the lender's perceived risk of nonpayment also typically increases, making collateral more attractive.[161] In addition, for long-term secured loans that involve durable assets likely to retain their value over time, the relevant transaction costs tend to be lower, at least as a percentage of the loan.

Mann questions the general perception that trade creditors tend not to take security interests in the goods they sell. Mann observes that, on the basis of his interviews, a significant, increasing portion of trade creditors do retain security interests. The important question, according to Mann, is why some trade creditors retain security interests while others do not. Mann offers two considerations: (1) the extent to which the particular trade creditor uses security as a pricing tool, and (2) whether debtors purchase

[157] *Id.* at 654–55.

[158] *Id.* at 650–55.

[159] *Id.* at 663–67.

[160] *Id.* at 658 & n.128 (quoting Kripke, *supra* note 18, at 969).

[161] *Id.* at 674–77.

goods from among a small or large number of suppliers. Some trade creditors build their risk of nonpayment into their pricing structures. Others require security as a tool to reduce the probability that their debtors will default on their obligations to pay for the goods they purchase. In general, a manufacturer is more likely to retain security in those industries where debtors purchase goods from only a small number of suppliers, whereas a manufacturer is less likely to retain security from debtors who deal with a large number.[162]

In closing, Mann advises caution in drawing too many broad conclusions about the utility of security interests owing to the "richness of the real pattern" of secured debt financing, and encourages scholars to "not only acknowledge, but embrace, the variety of the circumstances in which parties make lending decisions."[163] He urges policymakers to "pause before proceeding with reforms predicated on the absence of any legitimate justification for secured credit in commercial borrowing."[164] Mann's "bottom-up" orientation is reminiscent of Kripke's pragmatism. In this sense, we have now come full circle.

§ 5. THE PERSISTENCE OF SECURITY INTERESTS

The preceding discussion of theories of secured transactions, justifications for the priority of secured claims, and secured transactions in the marketplace presumes the continuing existence of the security interest as a recognizable and distinct form of assignment or device. But in some prominent contemporary markets, and in the face of emerging technologies, it can be increasingly difficult to distinguish security interests from entities. These two methods of asset partitioning seem to converge in markets for covered bonds, captive insurance, and mutual funds, for example. In addition, blockchain-based smart contracts for trade transactions can partition assets in ways that mimic both security interests and entities. What is the essence of a security interest?

Asset partitioning, generally speaking, is the practice of dividing assets into pools that can be assigned to different creditors. Henry Hansmann and Reinier Kraakman elucidated this practice in their article, *The Essential Role of Organizational Law*, in 2000.[165] Entity law, they contend, enables legal actors to do things that they cannot accomplish with contract law alone. In a business entity, business assets are shielded from the claims of the shareholders' creditors. Hansmann and Kraakman find

---

162 *Id.* at 677–81.

163 *Id.* at 682.

164 *Id.* at 683.

165 Henry Hansmann & Reinier Kraakman, *The Essential Role of Organizational Law*, 110 YALE L. J. 387, 393–97 (2000).

that "the partitioning off of a separate set of assets in which creditors of the firm itself have a prior security interest"[166] is the essential contribution of entity law, the feature that distinguishes it from contract, property, and agency laws. While scholars may debate whether asset partitioning is the only or most essential function of entity law, Hansmann and Kraakman's description of asset partitioning as a central function of entity law continues to inform scholarly understandings of business entities.

Scholars treat security interests as a form of asset partitioning. Richard Squire contends that asset partitioning should be understood as falling into two basic categories: symmetrical and asymmetrical. He describes asset partitioning as "the nonconsensual subordination of creditor claims to particular assets."[167] Security interests are a form of asymmetrical asset partitioning: they give prior claims to some creditors but not others, "advantaging select creditors by according them both a prior claim to one asset pool and a pro rata claim to remaining debtor assets."[168]

Security interests and entities both reduce information costs by giving designated creditors prior claims to certain assets. In some market contexts, they appear to converge entirely, prompting scholars to formulate new theories of the distinction between security interests and entities. For example, Ofer Eldar and Andrew Verstein posit that "[s]ecurity interests and entities coexist in the world and in particular structures because they offer different and irreplaceable priority schemes for creditors."[169] Security interests create fixed priority in assets, in the sense that it is not possible for an administrator to pledge the assets to change the existing priorities. Business entities create floating priority, in the sense that an administrator of the assets may pledge the same assets to other creditors. Business entities are advantageous when creditors want managers to have discretion. Security interests are advantageous when creditors prefer a fixed scheme that lessens the need for monitoring, they argue. They contend that these two forms of asset partitioning are distinct and cannot be interchanged: only security interests can create fixed priority and only entities can effectively allow floating priority over an asset pool.

This theory of security interests makes sense. But scholars have begun to question whether the distinction between security interests and entities will persist in blockchain-based markets. Blockchain-based smart contracts for trade transactions, because they are self-executing and

---

[166] *Id.* at 393.

[167] Richard Squire, *The Case for Symmetry in Creditors' Rights*, 118 YALE L. J. 806 (2009) at 808.

[168] *Id.* at 808–09.

[169] Ofer Eldar & Andrew Verstein, *The Enduring Distinction between Business Entities and Security Interests*, 92 S. CAL. L. REV. 213 (2019) at 224–25.

automatically capture assets to satisfy obligations, are a novel method of asset partitioning.

Eldar and Verstein raise the question of whether security interests will persist. They note that "blockchain technology might substitute for security interests because it can create fixed priorities to specific assets that bind third parties."[170] "How," they ask, "might blockchain and the collapse of the contract/property divide affect the distinction between entities and security interests?"[171] They contend that their theory of the distinction between entities and security interests will hold up in the context of blockchain-based market activity:

> [t]he property-like function in blockchain will still come in floating and fixed priority variants. Parties will stipulate whether they want a given creditor's claim on a pool to be utterly certain or to be subject to demotion in order to accommodate later creditors. This choice is the essential choice between security interests and entity, and parties will tailor their blockchain commitments in ways that reflect that fundamental choice. . . . [W]e speculate that the species of entity and security interest will survive long after the genus of property has dissolved.[172]

Ultimately, it remains to be seen how the security interest—and secured transactions law—will evolve in markets of the future. Article 9 has so far proven a highly adaptable statute with the capacity to accommodate changing contexts. What do you think may happen?

ADDITIONAL RESOURCES

Barry E. Adler, An Equity-Agency Solution to the Bankruptcy-Priority Puzzle, 22 J. LEGAL STUD. 73 (1993);

Richard L. Barnes, The Efficiency Justification for Secured Transactions: Foxes with Soxes and Other Fanciful Stuff, 42 KAN. L. REV. 13 (1993);

James W. Bowers, Groping and Coping in the Shadow of Murphy's Law: Bankruptcy Theory and the Elementary Economics of Failure, 88 MICH. L. REV. 2097 (1990);

F.H. Buckley, The Bankruptcy Priority Puzzle, 72 VA. L. REV. 1393 (1986);

David Gray Carlson, On the Efficiency of Secured Lending, 80 VA. L. REV. 2179 (1994);

Ofer Eldar & Andrew Verstein, The Enduring Distinction between Business Entities and Security Interests, 92 S. CAL. L. REV. 213, 268–69 (2019);

---

170 *Id.* at 268 (citing Richard Holden and Anup Malani).

171 *Id.* (citing Holden and Malani).

172 *Id.* at 269.

Steven L. Harris & Charles H. Mooney, Jr., A Property-Based Theory of Security Interests: Taking Debtors' Choices Seriously, 80 VA. L. REV. 2021 (1994);

Heather Hughes, Blockchain and the Future of Secured Transactions Law, 3 STAN. J. OF BLOCKCHAIN LAW & POL'Y 21 (2020);

Thomas H. Jackson & Anthony T. Kronman, Secured Financing and Priorities Among Creditors, 88 YALE L.J. 1143 (1979);

Alex M. Johnson, Jr., Adding Another Piece to the Financing Puzzle: The Role of Real Property Secured Debt, 24 LOY. L.A. L. REV. 335 (1991);

Hideki Kanda & Saul Levmore, Explaining Creditor Priorities, 80 VA. L. REV. 2103 (1994);

John D. Leeth & Jonathan A. Scott, The Incidence of Secured Debt: Evidence from the Small Business Community, 24 J. FIN. & QUANTITATIVE ANALYSIS 379 (1989);

Saul Levmore, Monitors and Freeriders in Commercial and Corporate Settings, 92 YALE L.J. 49 (1982);

Lynn M. LoPucki, The Death of Liability, 106 YALE L.J. 1 (1996);

Lynn M. LoPucki, The Unsecured Creditor's Bargain, 80 VA. L. REV. 1887 (1994);

Lynn M. LoPucki, Virtual Judgment Proofing: A Rejoinder, 107 YALE L.J. 1413 (1998);

Lois R. Lupica, Asset Securitization: The Unsecured Creditor's Perspective, 76 TEX. L. REV. 595 (1998);

Randal C. Picker, Security Interests, Misbehavior, and Common Pools, 59 U. CHI. L. REV. 645 (1992);

Alan Schwartz, A Theory of Loan Priorities, 18 J. LEGAL STUD. 209 (1989);

Alan Schwartz, Security Interests and Bankruptcy Priorities: A Review of Current Theories, 10 J. LEGAL STUD. 1 (1981);

Alan Schwartz, Taking the Analysis of Security Seriously, 80 VA. L. REV. 2073 (1994);

Robert E. Scott, A Relational Theory of Secured Financing, 86 COLUM. L. REV. 901 (1986);

Robert E. Scott, The Truth About Secured Financing, 82 CORNELL L. REV. 1436 (1997);

Paul M. Shupack, Solving the Puzzle of Secured Transactions, 41 RUTGERS L. REV. 1067 (1989);

Clifford W. Smith, Jr. & Jerold B. Warner, Bankruptcy, Secured Debt, and Optimal Capital Structure: Comment, 34 J. FIN. 247 (1979);

Richard Squire, The Case for Symmetry in Creditors' Rights, 118 YALE L. J. 806 (2009);

Rene M. Stulz & Herb Johnson, An Analysis of Secured Debt, 14 J. FIN. ECON. 501 (1985);

George G. Triantis, Secured Debt Under Conditions of Imperfect Information, 21 J. LEGAL STUD. 225 (1992);

Elizabeth Warren, Making Policy with Imperfect Information: The Article 9 Full Priority Debates, 82 CORNELL L. REV. 101 (1997);

Lawrence A. Weiss, Bankruptcy Resolution: Direct Costs and Violation of Priority of Claims, 27 J. FIN. ECON. 285 (1990);

James J. White, Corporate Judgment Proofing: A Response to Lynn LoPucki's The Death of Liability, 107 YALE L.J. 1363 (1998);

James J. White, The Recent Erosion of the Secured Creditor's Rights Through Cases, Rules and Statutory Changes in Bankruptcy Law, 53 MISS. L.J. 389 (1983);

James J. White, Work and Play in Revising Article 9, 80 VA. L. REV. 2089 (1994).

APPENDIX

TABLE OF DISPOSITION OF SECTIONS IN FORMER ARTICLE 9 AND OTHER CODE SECTIONS

■ ■ ■

Old Article 9	New Article 9
9–101	9–101
9–102	9–109
9–103(1)(a), (b); (c) omitted	9–301
9–103(1)(d)	9–316
9–103(2)(a), (b); (c) omitted	9–303, 9–316
9–103(2)(d)	9–337
9–103(3)(a), (b); (c) omitted	9–301
9–103(3)(d)	9–307
9–103(3)(e)	9–316
9–103(4)	9–301
9–103(5)	9–301
9–103(6)	9–304, 9–305, 9–306
9–104	9–109
9–105	9–102
9–106	9–102
9–107	9–103
9–108	Omitted as no longer needed
9–109	9–102
9–110	9–108
9–111	Deleted as unnecessary
9–112	Omitted—see 9–102(a)(28)
9–113	9–110
9–114	Omitted—see 9–103 and 9–324
9–115(1)	9–102, 9–106
9–115(2)	9–203, 9–308
9–115(3)	9–108
9–115(4)	9–309, 9–312, 9–314
9–115(5)	9–327, 9–328, 9–329
9–115(6)	9–203, 9–313
9–115(e)	9–106
9–116	9–206, 9–309

9–402(4)	9–512
9–402(5), (6)	9–502
9–402(7)	9–503(a)(4), 9–507
9–402(8)	9–506
9–403(1)	9–516(a)
9–403(2)	9–515
9–403(3)	9–515, 9–522
9–403(4)	9–519
9–403(5)	9–525
9–403(6)	9–515
9–403(7)	9–519
9–404	9–513
9–405	9–514, 9–519
9–406	9–512
9–407	9–523
9–408	9–505
9–501(1), (2)	9–601
9–501(3)	9–602, 9–603
9–501(4)	9–604
9–501(5)	9–601
9–502	9–607, 9–608
9–503	9–609
9–504(1)	9–610, 9–615
9–504(2)	9–615
9–504(3)	9–610, 9–611, 9–624
9–504(4)	9–617
9–504(5)	9–618
9–505	9–620, 9–621, 9–624
9–506	9–623, 9–624
9–507	9–625, 9–627

Other Code Sections	**New Article 9**
2–326(3)	9–102
2A–303(3)	9–407
2A–307(2)(b) and (c)	9–317
2A–307(3)	9–321
2A–307(4)	9–323

TABLE INDICATING SOURCES OR DERIVATIONS OF NEW ARTICLE 9 SECTIONS AND CONFORMING AMENDMENTS

New Article 9 Sections (**Note:** many sections contain some new coverage)	Primary Old Article 9 and Other Code Sections
9–101	9–101
9–102	9–105, 9–106, 9–109, 9–301(3), 9–306 (1), 9–115, 2–326(3)
9–103	9–107
9–104 (New)	Derived from 8–106
9–105 (New)	Derived from 8–106
9–106	8–106 and 9–115(e)
9–107 (New)	Derived from 8–106
9–108	9–110, 9–115(3)
9–109	9–102, 9–104
9–110	9–113
9–201	9–201, 9–203(4)
9–202	9–202
9–203	9–203, 9–115(2), (6)
9–204	9–204
9–205	9–205
9–206	9–116
9–207	9–207
9–208 (New)	
9–209 (New)	
9–210	9–208
9–301	9–103(1)(a), (b), 9–103(3)(a), (b), 9–103(4) 9–103(5) substantially modified
9–302 (New)	
9–303	9–103(2)(a), (b), substantially revised
9–304 (New)	Derived from 8–110(e) and former 9–103(6)
9–305	9–103(6)
9–306 (New)	Derived in part from 8–110(e) and 9–305 and former 9–103(6)
9–307	9–103(3)(d), as substantially revised
9–308	9–303, 9–115(2)
9–309	9–302(1), 9–115(4)(c), (d), 9–116
9–310	9–302(1), (2)
9–311	9–302(3), (4)
9–312	9–115(4) and 9–304, with additions and some changes
9–313	9–305, 9–115(6)
9–314 (New in part)	9–115(4) and derived from 8–106
9–315	9–306
9–316	9–103(1)(d), (2)(b), (3)(e), as modified
9–317	9–301, 2A–307(2)

9–318 (New)	
9–319 (New)	
9–320	9–307
9–321	2A–103(1)(*o*), 2A–307(3)
9–322	9–312(5), (6)
9–323	9–312(7), 9–301(4), 9–307(3), 2A–307(4)
9–324	9–312(3), (4)
9–325 (New)	But see 9–402(7)
9–326 (New)	But see 9–402(7)
9–327	Derived from 9–115(5)
9–328	9–115(5)
9–329(New)	Loosely modeled after former 9–115(5). See also 5–114 and 5–118
9–330	9–308
9–331	9–309
9–332 (New)	But see Comment 2(c) to 9–306
9–333	9–310
9–334	9–313
9–335 (New)	Section replaces former 9–314
9–336 (New)	Section replaces former 9–315
9–337	Derived from 9–103(2)(d)
9–338 (New)	
9–339	9–316
9–340 (New)	
9–341 (New)	
9–342 (New)	Derived from 8–106(g)
9–401	9–311
9–402	9–317
9–403	9–206
9–404	9–318(1)
9–405	9–318(2)
9–406	9–318(3), (4)
9–407	2A–303
9–408 (New)	
9–409 (New)	See also 5–114
9–501	Derived from former 9–401
9–502	9–402(1), (5), (6)
9–503 (New)	Subsection (a)(4),(b) and (c) derive from former 9–402(7); otherwise, new
9–504	9–402(1)
9–505	9–408
9–506	9–402(8)
9–507	9–402(7)
9–508 (New)	But see 9–402(7)
9–509 (New)	

9–510 (New)	
9–511 (New)	
9–512	9–402(4)
9–513	9–404
9–514	9–405
9–515	9–403(2), (3), (6)
9–516 (Basically New)	Subsection (a) is former 9–403(1); the remainder is new
9–517 (New)	
9–518 (New)	
9–519	9–403(4), (7); 9–405(2)
9–520 (New)	
9–521 (New)	
9–522	9–403(3), revised substantially
9–523	9–407; subsections (d) and (e) are new
9–524 (New)	Derived from 4–109
9–525	Various sections of former Part 4
9–526 (New)	Subsection (b) derives in part from the Uniform Consumer Credit Code (1974)
9–527 (New)	Derived in part from the Uniform Consumer Credit Code (1974)
9–601	9–501(1), (2), (5)
9–602	9–501(3)
9–603	9–501(3)
9–604	9–501(4), 9–313(8)
9–605 (New)	
9–606 (New)	
9–607	9–502, subsections (b), (d), and (e) are new
9–608	Subsection (a) is new. Subsection (b) derives from former 9–502(2)
9–609	9–503
9–610	9–504(1), (3)
9–611	9–504(3)
9–612 (New)	
9–613 (New)	
9–614 (New)	
9–615	9–504(1), (2)
9–616 (New)	
9–617	9–504(4)
9–618	9–504(5)
9–619 (New)	
9–620	9–505
9–621	9–505
9–622 (New)	
9–623	9–506
9–624	9–504(3), 9–505,9–506
9–625	9–507

9–626 (New)	
9–627	9–507(2)
9–628 (New)	
9–701	No comparable provision in Article 9 (See Article 10)
9–702	No comparable provision in Article 9 (See Article 10)
9–703	No comparable provision in Article 9 (See Article 10)
9–704	No comparable provision in Article 9 (See Article 10)
9–705	No comparable provision in Article 9 (See Article 10)
9–706	No comparable provision in Article 9 (See Article 10)
9–707	No comparable provision in Article 9 (See Article 10)
9–708	No comparable provision in Article 9 (See Article 10)
9–709	No comparable provision in Article 9 (See Article 10)

Conforming Amendments to Other Code Sections and Comments

1–105(2)	4–210
1–201(9), (32), (37)	5–118 (New)
2–103(3)	Article 6 (unless repealed)
2–210; New subsection (3) added	7–503
2–312; Comment	8–102 Comment
2–326(3)	8–103(f)
2–502 (1) and (2)	8–106 and Comment
2–716(3)	8–110
2A–103(3)	8–301(3)
2A–303	8–302(a)
2A–307	8–502 Comment
2A–309	8–510